the subject is marketing

second canadian edition

Charles W. Lamb, Jr.
Texas Christian University

Joseph F. Hair, Jr.
Louisiana State University

Carl McDaniel
University of Texas at Arlington

A.J. Faria
University of Windsor

Australia Canada Mexico Singapore Spain United Kingdom United States

The Subject Is Marketing.
Second Canadian Edition

by Charles W. Lamb, Jr.,
Joseph F. Hair, Jr., Carl McDaniel, and
A.J. Faria

Editorial Director and Publisher:
Evelyn Veitch

Acquisitions Editor:
Gary Bennett

Senior Project Editor:
Elke Price

Managing Production Editor:
Susan Calvert

Production Coordinator:
Hedy Sellers

Copy Editor/Proofreader:
Matthew Kudelka

Creative Director:
Angela Cluer

Interior Design:
Michael H. Stratton

Cover Design:
Peter Papayanakis

Senior Composition Analyst:
Alicja Jamorski

Indexer:
Andrew Little

Printer:
Transcontinental Printing Inc.

Printed and bound in Canada
1 2 3 4 05 04 03 02

For more information contact Nelson, 1120 Birchmount Road, Scarborough, Ontario, M1K 5G4. Or you can visit our Internet site at http://www.nelson.com

National Library of Canada Cataloguing in Publication Data

Main entry under title:
The subject is marketing
2nd Canadian ed.

Previously published as:
Marketing/Charles W. Lamb, Jr ...
[et al.]. Canadian 3rd ed.

Includes bibliographical references and index.

ISBN 0-17-616955-5

1. Marketing. 2. Marketing-Management. I. Lamb, Charles W. II. Marketing.

HF5415.M29325 2002 658.8
C2001-904029-6

To my wife Barbara,
my daughter and son-in-law, Lara and Dave,
my son Bob,
and my grandchildren C.J. and Beth.

A.J. Faria

CONTENTS

 NEL

PREFACE

Today's marketers face a marketplace that has become more competitive, specialized, global, and Internet-reliant. To succeed in today's changing environment, successful marketing requires—now more than ever—a balance between creativity and knowledge. *The Subject Is Marketing,* Second Canadian Edition, is a vital source for new and essential marketing knowledge. Students can learn it all with this current, comprehensive, and highly readable text. Instructors can have it all with a complete, innovative package of supplements. The subject is marketing—the experience is real.

Customer-Driven Innovations for the Second Canadian Edition

The guiding principle of the text is that of building relationships. We discuss relationship marketing beginning as early as Chapter 1, and we believe in it completely. As authors, we are seeking to build long-term relationships with our customers (both professors and students) that will result in trust and confidence in our product.

We feel a strong sense of responsibility to provide professors and students with the most exciting and up-to-date text possible, and the most useful supplement package. To this end, we have listened to our readers' desires and comments and incorporated their feedback into *The Subject Is Marketing,* Second Canadian Edition.

All-New Internet Activities and Real-Time Examples

Each chapter provides a number of Internet activities, which are available both in the text and through the book's Website. These activities are tied to the organizations mentioned in the text. For example, while students are reading about how Jones Soda is seeking to extend its brand and develop a community, they can also explore what Jones's competitors are doing. Because each activity calls for student production, professors can use these mini-exercises as extra homework or as quizzing opportunities. We have provided background information for students, guidelines to faculty for grading, and opportunities for each exercise to be developed further.

Students will find valuable on-line resources and will learn to analyze current Internet marketing strategies. Links to all the URLs in the book are located on the text's Internet site at **www.lamb.nelson.com**. If a URL listed in the book becomes obsolete, it will be replaced with a new one that still fits the particular context of the activity.

New Marketing Miscues Cases

To help your students recognize some of the obstacles that can arise when a marketing plan is being created and executed, we have added Marketing Miscues cases to the end of each part. These cases illustrate what happens when successful companies' marketing efforts fall short. Students can learn from the challenges faced by companies such as Eatons and General Motors.

Classic Value-Added Features Have Been Updated and Enhanced

Internet Coverage The hottest technology feature of this new edition is the all-new Internet chapter, which goes beyond the Internet's impact on marketing strategy and the marketing mix and discusses the impact that e-commerce is having on finance, strategy, business relationships, and internal business functions. Chapter 19, "Internet Marketing," is available on the Lamb Website as well as on the Student CD-ROM. This chapter takes you straight to the centre of the e-action with information on how the Internet is affecting marketing strategy, and how to conduct marketing research on-line, and with in-depth discussions of the privacy issues surrounding e-commerce. We also provide links to companies that are setting the pace in Web marketing, as well as many tools and resources for on-line marketers. Also, Internet coverage is integrated throughout the text in special "Internet Connections" feature boxes.

All-New End-of-Chapter Video Cases End-of-chapter video cases have been created for the Second Canadian Edition of *The Subject Is Marketing.* Each video is enhanced by text materials at the end of the appropriate chapters. The featured companies are ones both you and your students will recognize: Burton Snowboards, the Toronto Blue Jays, and many more. Previewing, viewing, and follow-up activities are included to help you present the content through the video and make the marketing experience real for your students.

Small Business and Entrepreneurship Are Emphasized in Every Chapter
Many students will either work for a small business or strike out on their own to form one. For this reason, most of the chapters include a feature box titled "Entrepreneurial Insights"; also, an "Application for Small Business" appears at the end of each chapter. The "Entrepreneurial Insights" boxes apply general marketing concepts to the world of small business. The "Applications" are minicases designed to illustrate how small businesses can create strategies and tactics using the material in the chapter. Anyone with an entrepreneurial flair will enjoy these features.

Global Marketing Concepts Throughout the Text

Most businesses today compete not only locally and nationally but also globally. Companies that never gave a thought to exporting now find themselves facing competition from abroad. Thinking "globally" should be part of every manager's tactical and strategic planning. We have integrated many global examples into the text.

Global marketing is fully integrated throughout the text, and in the cases and videos as well. Our "Global Perspectives" boxes, which appear in most chapters, provide expanded global examples and concepts. Each box concludes with thought-provoking questions, which have been prepared carefully to stimulate class discussion. For example, the box in Chapter 5 describes how Whirlpool embarked on a joint venture with a Chinese company that was making inferior products. Students are asked to evaluate the soundness of Whirlpool's decision.

Focus on Ethics

In this edition we continue to emphasize ethics. To underline their importance to decision making, we have placed a section, "Corporate Social Responsibility," in Chapter 3. Also, the "Ethics in Marketing" boxes, found in most chapters, have been revised and end with questions focusing on ethical decision making. Questions and cases designed to highlight ethical issues, such as the Ben & Jerry's case at the end of Chapter 3, give students a sense of the complexity of ethics issues; these cases encourage them to look at issues from all sides.

One-to-One Marketing Coverage Marketing is literally a moving target. That's why we've added a chapter devoted entirely to one-to-one marketing. This chapter considers the challenges involved in building lasting relationships with customers and prospects through database technology. Extra coverage is provided in the "One-to-One Connection" boxes, which provide real-life examples of one-to-one marketing in action. Each of these boxes concludes with questions to stimulate class discussion.

Value-Driven Pedagogy Puts Instructors in the Know

Our pedagogy has been developed in response to what professors have told us delivers value to them and their students. They told us it is important for us to provide current examples, so we have included all-new opening vignettes, new examples throughout the text, and new boxed materials in every chapter. They told us it is important to provide cases that are relevant to their students, so we have replaced all of the video cases with new, current ones; some of these are tied to the CBC's *Venture* and *Undercurrents* programs. They said that many of their students were planning careers in small business, so we have provided many new small business examples, "Entrepreneurial Insights," and small business exercises. Finally, professors told us that the Integrated Learning System helped them organize their lectures and helped their students study more effectively, so we have retained that important feature.

Fully Integrated Learning System

The text and the major supplements have been organized around the learning objectives that appear at the beginning of each chapter. This provides professors and students with an easy-to-use integrated learning system. A numbered icon like the one shown in this margin identifies each chapter objective; this icon appears next to the related materials throughout the text, the Instructor's Manual, the Test Bank, and the Study Guide. In other words, every learning objective provides a link between the text, the Study Guide, the Instructor's Manual, and the Test Bank.

1
Define the term marketing

This integrated system delivers value for students as they prepare for exams. The learning objective icons identify all the materials in the text and Study Guide that relate to each specific learning objective. Students can easily check their grasp of each objective by reading the text sections, reviewing the corresponding summary sections, answering the Study Guide questions for that objective, and returning to the appropriate text sections for further review if they have difficulty with any of the questions. Students can quickly identify all materials relating to an objective simply by looking for the learning objective icon.

Text Pedagogy That Adds Value, Excites Students, and Reinforces Learning

Pedagogical features are intended to reinforce learning, but they need not be boring. We have created teaching tools within the text that will excite the students' interest as well as teach them.

- *Opening Vignettes, Revisited at Chapter Conclusions*: Each chapter begins with a new, current, real-world story about a marketing decision or situation facing a company. A special section before the chapter summary called "Looking Back" answers the teaser questions posed in the opening vignette and helps illustrate how the chapter material relates to the real world of marketing.
- *Key Terms*: Key terms appear in **boldface** in the text, with definitions in the margins, making it easy for students to check their understanding of key definitions. A complete alphabetical list of key terms appears at the end of each chapter as a study checklist, with page citations for easy reference.
- *Chapter Summaries*: Each chapter ends with a summary that distills the main points of the chapter. Chapter summaries are organized around the learning objectives so that students can use them as a quick check on their achievement of learning goals.
- *Discussion and Writing Questions*: To help students improve their writing skills, we have included writing exercises with the discussion questions at the end of each chapter. The writing questions are designed to ensure that students can accomplish writing assignments in a short time and that grading time is minimized.
- *Application for Small Business*: These short scenarios prompt students to apply marketing concepts to small business settings. Each scenario ends with provocative questions to aid student analysis.
- *Critical Thinking Cases:* Our society has an enormous capacity for generating data; our ability to use those data to make good decisions has lagged behind. In the hope of better preparing the next generation of business leaders, many educators are beginning to place greater emphasis on developing critical thinking skills. The challenging, comprehensive cases at the end of each of the five major parts are all new for this edition. Critical Thinking Cases feature nationally known companies such as Staples and The Gap.

- *Video Cases*: All chapters conclude with a new video case. These twenty video segments add a visual dimension to case analysis by demonstrating the marketing concepts presented in the chapter. Nine of the cases are tied to CBC video segments from the popular *Venture* series and *Undercurrents.*

www.lamb.nelson.com

The students' components of this rich resource were developed by and in consultation with marketing instructors who appreciate the value of additional real-world marketing applications and self-test opportunities for students. The activities and exercises available at this site are designed to complement the text's opening vignettes and its coverage of Internet marketing. The site also provides a comprehensive set of review questions, including true/false and multiple choice questions, as well as essay items to help students test their knowledge, and more!

The instructor's site includes "Great Ideas in Teaching Marketing" (a PowerPoint presentation available in viewable and printable formats), the Instructor's Manual, and a sample Test Bank and Study Guide chapter.

More Innovative Student Applications

- Study Guide (ISBN 0-17-616956-3): All questions in the Study Guide are keyed to the learning objectives in the text by numbered icons. Study Guide questions were designed to be similar in type and level of difficulty to the Test Bank questions. This means that review using the Study Guide will help students improve their test scores. Every chapter opens with a pretest to help students assess their level of understanding before beginning to review. Other review tools in the chapter include chapter outlines with definitions of key terms, a synopsis of key points under the learning objectives, and vocabulary practice.
- A CD-ROM is packaged free with every copy of *The Subject Is Marketing*, Second Canadian Edition. This CD was developed as a non-Web-based resource for students. It provides reference materials for use in projects and for review or research; it also provides sources for additional topics of interest. Other valuable resources include marketing career information, further review questions, Chapter 19 on Internet Marketing, and more.

More Innovative Instructor's Supplements

All the components of our comprehensive support package have been developed to help professors prepare lectures and tests as quickly and easily as possible. We provide a wealth of information and activities beyond the text to supplement lectures, as well as teaching aids in a variety of formats to fit different teaching styles.

Instructor's Resource CD–ROM

Managing classroom resources is now easier than ever. The new Instructor's Resource CD–ROM (ISBN 0-17-616962-8) contains all key instructor supplements—Instructor's Manual, Test Bank, and PowerPoint.

A Value-Based Instructor's Manual: The Core of Our Integrated Learning System

Each chapter of the Instructor's Manual (ISBN 0-17-616961-X) begins with the learning objectives and a summary of the key points covered by each objective. The Integrated Learning System then comes together in the detailed outlines of each chapter. Each outline is integrated with the textbook and with other supplements through the learning objectives, and refers professors to the support materials at appropriate points in the lecture. These support materials include exhibits, additional activities, boxed materials, additional examples not included in the text, and discussion questions. These outlines will help professors organize lectures, choose support materials, bring in outside examples not mentioned in the book, and take full advantage of text discussion.

Besides complete solutions to text questions and cases, the manual provides ethical scenarios, summaries of current articles, and class activities. Also included are teaching notes for the video program.Our manual is a complete learning system: truly "one-stop shopping" for everything professors need.

Comprehensive Test Bank and Windows Testing Software

Our enhanced Test Bank (ISBN 0-17-616959-8), like the other supplements, is organized around the learning objectives. The computerized testing software contains all the questions from the printed Test Bank and enables instructors to edit, add, delete, or randomly mix questions for customized tests (ISBN 0-17-616958-X).

A correlation table at the beginning of each Test Bank chapter classifies each question according to Bloom's taxonomy as well as question type, complexity, and learning objective covered. Using this table, you can create exams with the appropriate mix of question types and levels of difficulty. You can prepare tests that cover all learning objectives or that emphasize those objectives you feel are most important. The Test Bank is one of the most comprehensive on the market, with over 2,500 true/false, multiple-choice, and essay questions.

Complete Video Coverage and Instructor's Manual

This video package (ISBN 0-17-616957-1) will add visual impact and current, real-world examples to your lectures. The package includes twenty Video Cases; nine of these are tied to video segments from CBC's *Venture* and *Undercurrents* programs.

Other Outstanding Supplements

- ***PowerPoint Slides®*** (ISBN 0-17-616960-1): More than 400 full-colour images are provided with *The Subject Is Marketing,* Second Canadian Edition. Most of these are creatively prepared visuals that do not repeat the text. Only images that highlight concepts central to the chapter are from the textbook. All you need is Windows to run the PowerPoint viewer and an LCD panel for classroom display.
- **New! *Instructor's Handbook*** (ISBN 0-324-06868-9): This helpful booklet was designed specifically for instructors preparing to teach their first course in principles of marketing. It provides helpful hints on developing a course outline, lecturing, testing, giving feedback, and assigning projects.
- **New Edition! *Great Ideas for Teaching Marketing*** (ISBN 0-324-06864-6): Edited by Lamb, Hair, and McDaniel, *Great Ideas for Teaching Marketing* is a collection of suggestions for improving marketing education by enhancing teaching excellence. The publication includes teaching tips and ideas submitted by marketing educators from Canada and across the United States.

Acknowledgments

There are many individuals to whom I owe gratitude for their help in making *The Subject Is Marketing,* Second Canadian Edition, a reality. In particular, I would like to thank the team at Thomson Nelson, including Evelyn Veitch, Gary Bennett, Susan Calvert, Matthew Kudelka, Vicki Gould, Rebecca Hull, and especially Elke Price. This project could not have been realized without Elke's outstanding commitment and expertise.

This book has benefited tremendously from the work of five outstanding colleagues. Special thanks go to Adam Ahmad of York University, Jana Comeau of the University of New Brunswick, Judith Nash of the Southern Alberta Institute of Technology, Beth Pett of Niagara College, and Shelley Rinehart of the University of New Brunswick for their valuable contributions to specific chapters. Adam Ahmad and Shelley Rinehart also took the time to write many of the boxed features that enhance the text. Also, I wish to thank Selia Karsten of Seneca College and Pat Browne of Kwantlen College for their creative contribution of the *Workouts in Marketing Study Guide* and the Web activities.

Finally, I am indebted to the reviewers who took the time to comment on the Table of Contents and to review the manuscript of the Second Canadian Edition. I would like to extend my gratitude to the following reviewers:

Neil Beattie
Sheridan College

Brad Berry
Mohawk College

Baiba Butkus
Lambton College

Wayne Carlson
Southern Alberta Institute of Technology

Gord Fullerton
Saint Mary's University

Shannon Goodspeed
Mount Royal College

Rob Jakes
Saskatchewan Institute of Applied Science and Technology

Kerry Jarvis
Seneca College

Marianne Marando
George Brown College

Keith Penhall
Red River College

Richard Simon
Kwantlen College

Rod Smith
Cambrian College

Carolyn Sterenberg
Mount Royal College

Rae Verity
Southern Alberta Institute of Technology

1 GETTING STARTED

CHAPTER

1

LEARNING OBJECTIVES

After studying this chapter, you should be able to

1 Define the term marketing

2 Describe four marketing management philosophies

3 Discuss the differences between sales and market orientations

4 Describe the marketing process

5 Describe several reasons for studying marketing

AN OVERVIEW OF MARKETING

To avoid being surprised by shifts in customer behaviour, companies must understand their customers as well as they understand themselves. This understanding goes far beyond reviewing customer satisfaction surveys. It means appreciating customers' unstated and unmet needs and knowing their businesses or lifestyles in ways that extend beyond their use of current products and services.

Levis Strauss & Co. is a case in point. Levi Strauss succeeded originally by satisfying customer needs. To solve the problem that pockets and other areas of strain were constantly ripping on the work pants of customers, it developed the idea of using metal rivets to strengthen the pants. That is why May 20, 1873, the day that Levi Strauss and Jacob Davis received patent #139,121, is considered to be the birthday of blue jeans. These riveted blue jeans were assigned the number 501 by the company and are still known by that number today.

Levi Strauss has continued to innovate to serve its customer's needs. Examples: The company developed Koveralls, a one-piece playsuit for children, in 1913 and quickly made them a national bestseller. Lady Levi's entered the casual clothing line in 1954 with its "Lighter Blues" and "Denim Family." In 1964 Levi's introduced the first wrinkle-free products, STA-PREST slacks. In 1969 Levi's led the fashion parade by introducing bell bottoms. In the 1970s it introduced corduroy and polyester products. In the 1980s it opened the first Original Levi's Stores and introduced Dockers Khakis. In the 1990s it introduced Slates dress pants.

How does Levi's stay attuned to the pulse of the market? Certainly it undertakes market research surveys, as will be discussed later in the book. But it does more than that. Levi's employees have been known to attend rock concerts to view what teenagers are wearing and to ask questions. In this way, Levi's employees learn not only to see what teenagers are wearing but also how they are personally customizing their jeans. According to one Levi's manager, "The kids love to talk about where they shop, what they like, and what they hate. This is where it all begins, this is how we learn, by watching consumers in their natural habitat.[1]

Describe Levi's philosophy of business and how this philosophy translates into sales and profits. These issues are explored in detail in this opening chapter.

Levi Strauss

How does Levi Strauss use its Website to connect with its market? What indications do you have that this is a youth-oriented company?

www.levi.com

on line

What Is Marketing?

1
Define the term marketing

marketing
The process of planning and executing the conception, pricing, promotion, and distribution of ideas, goods, and services to create exchanges that satisfy individual and organizational goals.

What does the term marketing mean to you? Many people think it means the same as personal selling. Others think marketing is the same as advertising and promotion. Still others believe that marketing has something to do with making products available in stores, arranging displays, and maintaining inventories of products for future sales. Actually, marketing includes all of these activities and more.

Marketing has two facets. First, it is a philosophy, an attitude, a perspective, or a management orientation that stresses customer satisfaction. Second, marketing is a set of activities used to implement this philosophy. The definition of marketing adopted for this text encompasses both perspectives: "**Marketing** is the process of planning and executing the conception, pricing, promotion, and distribution of ideas, goods, and services to create exchanges that satisfy individual and organizational goals."[2]

The Concept of Exchange

exchange
The idea that people give up something to receive something they would rather have.

Exchange is the key term in the definition of marketing. The concept of **exchange** is quite simple. It means that people give up something to receive something they would rather have. Normally we think of money as the medium of exchange. We "give up" money to "get" the goods and services we want. Exchange does not require money, however. Two people can barter or trade items such as hockey cards or books.

Five conditions must be satisfied for any kind of exchange to take place:

- There must be at least two parties.
- Each party must have something the other party values.
- Each party must be able to communicate with the other party and deliver the goods or services sought by the other trading party.
- Each party must be free to accept or reject the other's offer.
- Each party must want to deal with the other party.[3]

Exchange will not necessarily take place even where all these conditions exist. All are, however, necessary for exchange to be possible. Say you place an advertisement in your local newspaper stating that your used automobile is for sale at a certain price. Several people may call you to ask about the car, some may test-drive it, and one or more may even make you an offer. But until you reach an agreement with a buyer and actually sell the car, an exchange has not taken place. Notice that marketing can occur even where an exchange does not. In the example just discussed, you have engaged in marketing even if no one buys your used automobile.

Marketing Management Philosophies

2
Describe four marketing management philosophies

Four competing philosophies strongly influence an organization's marketing activities. These philosophies are commonly referred to as the production, sales, market, and societal marketing orientations.

Production Orientation

A **production orientation** is a philosophy that focuses on the internal capabilities of the firm rather than on the desires and needs of the marketplace. A production orientation means that management assesses its resources and asks these questions: "What can we do best?" "What can our engineers design?" "What is easy to produce, given our equipment?" In the case of a service organization, managers ask, "What services are most convenient for our firm to offer?" and "Where do our talents lie?" Some have referred to this orientation as a *Field of Dreams* orientation, in reference to the movie line, "If you build it, they will come."

production orientation
A philosophy that focuses on the internal capabilities of the firm rather than on the desires and needs of the marketplace.

There is nothing wrong with assessing a firm's capabilities; in fact, such assessments are major considerations in strategic marketing planning (see Chapter 2). A production orientation falls short because it does not consider whether the goods and services the firm produces most efficiently also meet the needs of the marketplace. PPG Industries provides an interesting example. From the 1980s into the 1990s, researchers at PPG spent considerable time, effort, and money developing a bluish windshield that would let in filtered sunlight but block out the heat. PPG scientists were convinced that this new product would be significantly better than existing windshields. However, when the new windshield was introduced in 1991, the car makers didn't buy it. They didn't like the colour or the price. "We developed a great mousetrap, but there were no mice," reported Gary Weber, vice-president for science and technology.[4]

Chrysler's implementation of the marketing concept has resulted in the wildly successful PT Cruiser automobile. Order lists are so long that the company expanded production to plants in Austria and Mexico to keep up with demand.

A production orientation does not necessarily doom a company to failure, especially not in the short run. Sometimes what a firm can produce best is exactly what the market wants. The R&D department of 3M's commercial tape division developed and patented the adhesive component of Post-it™ Notes a year before a commercial application was identified for it. In other situations—when competition is weak or demand exceeds supply—a production-oriented firm can survive and even prosper. More often, the firms that succeed in competitive markets are those which understand clearly that they must first determine what customers want and then produce it, instead of focusing on what management thinks the firm should produce and then hoping the customer will buy it.

Sales Orientation

A **sales orientation** is based on the idea that people will buy more goods and services if aggressive sales techniques are used, and that high sales result in high profits. Sales to the final buyer are emphasized, and intermediaries are encouraged to push manufacturers' products aggressively. For sales-oriented firms, marketing means selling things and collecting money.

sales orientation
The idea that people will buy more goods and services if aggressive sales techniques are used, and that high sales result in high profits.

The basic problem with the sales orientation, as with the production orientation, is that it doesn't try to understand the needs or wants of the marketplace. Sales-oriented companies often find that no matter how good their salespeople are, they cannot convince people to buy goods or services they don't need or want.

Market Orientation

The **marketing concept** is a simple and intuitively appealing philosophy. It states that organizations have a right to exist to the extent they satisfy the needs and wants of their customers while meeting their own long-term goals. There is an implicit understanding here that a sale does not depend on an aggressive sales

marketing concept
The idea that organizations have a right to exist to the extent they satisfy the needs and wants of their customers while meeting their own objectives.

Sears Roebuck/Wal-Mart/Nike

Based on the organization of its Web page, how would you describe Sears's marketing orientation? Compare the Sears site to Wal-Mart's site. How do these competitors stack up against each other? Look at the Nike site. Does Nike seem to be more customer oriented than Sears or Wal-mart?

www.sears.com; www.wal-mart.com; www.nike.ca

on line

force, but rather on a customer's decision to purchase a product. What a business *thinks it is producing* is not of primary importance. Rather, what customers *think they are buying*—the perceived value—is what defines a business. The marketing concept includes the following:

- Focusing on customer wants and needs so that the organization can distinguish its product(s) from those of competitors.
- Integrating all of the organization's activities, including production, to satisfy these wants.
- Achieving the organization's long-term goals by satisfying customer wants and needs legally and responsibly.

The marketing concept recognizes that there is no reason why a customer should buy one organization's offerings unless the organization is in some way better at serving the customer's wants and needs than are competing organizations.[5]

Firms that adopt and implement the marketing concept are said to be market oriented. A **market orientation** requires top-management leadership, a customer focus, competitor intelligence, and interfunctional coordination to meet customer wants and needs and to deliver superior value. It also entails establishing and maintaining mutually rewarding relationships with customers.

market orientation
The philosophy that assumes that a sale does not depend on an aggressive sales force but rather on a customer's decision to purchase a product.

Today, companies of all types are adopting a market orientation. Marriott International's CEO logs an average of 250 000 kilometers every year visiting the company's hotels, inspecting them, and talking to employees at all levels in the organization. According to Bill Marriott, "I want our associates to know that there really is a guy named Marriott who cares about them ... I also want to show our team in the field that I value their work enough to take time to check it."[6] Wal-Mart has become the leading discount retailer in the world by focusing on what its customers want: everyday low prices, items always in stock, and cashiers always available. While Wal-Mart was growing rapidly in the 1980s and 1990s, other retailers such as Eatons and Kmart were losing business to newer specialty stores, superstores, and discounters. Eatons was purchased by Sears Roebuck, while Kmart sold all its Canadian stores to Wal-Mart.

Understanding your competitive arena and competitors' strengths and weaknesses is a critical component of a market orientation. This includes assessing what existing or potential competitors might be intending to do tomorrow as well as what they are doing today.[7] Western Union failed to define its competitive arena as telecommunications, and concentrated instead on telegraph services, and was eventually outflanked by fax technology. Had Western Union been a market-oriented company, its management might have better understood the changes taking place, seen the competitive threat, and developed strategies to counter the threat.[8]

A societal orientation, as seen in this Toyota ad, seeks to preserve or enhance society's long-term best interest. Toyota's Prius, a hybrid car, relies on gasoline, but its electric motor assists by supplying extra power when needed. The Prius delivers performance and addresses the environmental issues of automobile emissions.

Market-oriented companies get all business functions working together to deliver customer value. Rubbermaid has developed "cross-functional entrepreneurial teams" to overcome the difficulty of getting people from different functional areas to work together in developing new houseware products. These teams are empowered to make decisions and are responsible for results.

Societal Orientation

A market-oriented organization may decide not to deliver the benefits sought by customers if these benefits might not be good for individuals or society. The **soci-**

ethics in marketing

Healthy Versus Healthy Looking

Sun care products represent a $400 million industry. The trend throughout most of the 1990s was toward higher sun protection factor (SPF) sunscreens because of consumer concerns about skin cancer, wrinkles, premature aging, and other negative outcomes associated with sun exposure. That seems to be changing now.

Apparently, teenagers are ignoring the warnings about the sun's potential to harm them. A survey conducted by *Seventeen* found that 17 percent of teenagers said they never use a sunscreen. Two-thirds didn't know what an SPF label is. Spring breakers travelling to sunny beaches have been reported using baby oil, Crisco, and even motor oil to enhance the tanning effects of the sun's rays.

How has the suntan industry responded? Coppertone has introduced a new low ultraviolet ray (UV) protection product called Coppertone Gold. Banana Boat has followed with Tan Express. Hawaiian Tropic has launched an oil called Total Exposure.

The new low-SPF products now represent 15 to 20 percent of industry sales. "The extreme segment of suncare is growing and it's going to grow more because of the new products," said Jack Surette, Hawaiian Tropic's vice-president for marketing.[9]

Industry executives defend the new lines, saying they're just giving consumers a choice. What do you think?

etal orientation takes it as a basic assumption that an organization exists not only to satisfy customer wants and needs and to meet organizational objectives but also to preserve or enhance individuals' and society's long-term best interests. Marketing products and containers that are lower in toxicity, are more durable, contain reusable materials, or are recyclable is consistent with a societal orientation. Two battery companies, Duracell and Eveready, have reduced the levels of mercury in their batteries and will eventually market mercury-free products. Turtle Wax car wash products and detergents are biodegradable and can be "digested" by waste treatment plants. Also, the company's containers are made of recyclable plastic, and its spray products do not use propellants that damage the earth's ozone layer. This chapter's "Ethics in Marketing" box illustrates a potential conflict between a market orientation and a societal orientation.

societal orientation
The idea that an organization exists not only to satisfy customer wants and needs and to meet organizational objectives but also to preserve or enhance individuals' and society's long-term best interests.

Differences Between Sales and Market Orientations

3
Discuss the differences between sales and market orientations

The differences between sales and market orientations are substantial. Exhibit 1.1 compares the two orientations in terms of five characteristics: the organization's focus, the firm's business, those to whom the product is directed, the firm's main goal, and the tools the organization uses to achieve its goals.

The Organization's Focus

In sales-oriented firms, personnel tend to be "inward looking"—that is, they tend to focus on selling what the organization makes rather than on making what the market wants. Many of the historic sources of competitive advantage—technology, innovation, economies of scale—allowed companies to prosper by focusing their efforts internally. Today, many successful firms derive their competitive advantage from an external, market-oriented focus. A market orientation has helped companies such as Bombardier, Dell Computer, and Hewlett-Packard outperform their competitors.[10] Today, key issues in developing competitive advantage include creating customer value, maintaining customer satisfaction, and building long-term relationships.

Customer Value **Customer value** is the ratio of benefits to the sacrifice necessary to obtain those benefits. As this chapter's "Global Perspectives" box illustrates, the customer determines the value of both the benefits and the sacrifices.

customer value
The ratio of benefits to the sacrifice necessary to obtain those benefits.

exhibit 1.1 | Differences Between Sales and Market Orientations

	What is the organization's focus?	What business are you in?	To whom is the product directed?	What is your main goal?	How do you seek to achieve your goal?
Sales orientation	Inward, on the organization's needs	Selling goods and services	Everybody	Profit through maximum sales volume	Mainly through intensive promotion
Market orientation	Outward, on the wants and preferences of customers	Satisfying customer wants and needs and delivering superior value	Specific groups of people	Profit through customer satisfaction	Through coordinated marketing and interfunctional activities

To penetrate the fiercely competitive luxury car market, Lexus adopted a customer-driven approach, with particular emphasis on service. Lexus stresses product quality and holds itself to a standard of zero defects in manufacturing. The service quality goal is to treat each customer as one would treat a guest in one's home, to pursue the perfect person-to-person relationship, and to strive to improve continually. All of this has enabled Lexus to establish a clear quality image and capture a significant share of the luxury car market.

Customer value is not simply a matter of high quality. A high-quality product that is available only at a high price will not be perceived as good value; nor will a bare-bones, low-quality product selling for a low price. Customers value goods and services of the quality they expect and that are sold at prices they are willing to pay. Value can be used to sell a $60,000 Nissan Infiniti Q45 or a $3.99 package of President's Choice Chocolate Chip Cookies.

Marketers interested in customer value do the following:

- *Offer products that perform:* This is the bare minimum requirement. Consumers have lost patience with shoddy merchandise.

global perspectives

The Customer, Not the Seller, Defines Value

Unlike some Canadian industries that have had trouble breaking into the Russian market, Canadian construction companies have been quite successful. For the new rich in eastern Russia, one of the toniest addresses is on a street named Toronto. The suburb's builder has named his streets in honour of Canada.

All across Russia, Canadian housing companies are making big inroads in the construction industry. From Moscow to Siberia, over 2,000 homes have been built by Canadian companies—a significant number in a country where most people live in grimy apartment blocks. And sales could grow rapidly. These same Canadian companies have set as their target to build 10,000 new homes in the years ahead.

Russians are accustomed to Soviet building methods, which are very slow—a new home can take several years to build. The Canadian-built homes take only a few months, and the houses are better insulated and more energy efficient. Sergei Topkishev, head of Moscow's city construction department, said that Canadians have become the leading foreign builders of detached houses in Russia.

A Yellowknife company, Ferguson Simek Clark, has built more than 1,000 housing units in Russia and earned more than $100 million in revenue. The company specializes in Arctic housing construction, an essential technique in Siberia and the Russian far north. "Just the word Canada has a certain magic for Russians," says Stefan Simek, the company president."[11] Russia has become the biggest foreign market for Mr. Simek's company.

Explain how Canadian construction companies are creating customer value in Russia.

www on line

Volvo

How does Volvo use its Website to maintain customer relations? Do you think Volvo has a sales or a market orientation? What evidence do you have to support your conclusion?

www.volvocars.com

- *Give consumers more than they expect:* Soon after Toyota launched Lexus, the company had to order a recall. The weekend before the recall, dealers telephoned all Lexus owners personally to make arrangements to pick up their cars and to offer replacement vehicles.
- *Avoid unrealistic pricing:* Consumers couldn't understand why Kellogg's cereals commanded a premium over other brands, so the company's market share fell 5 percent.
- *Give the buyer facts:* Today's sophisticated consumer wants informative advertising and knowledgeable salespeople.
- *Offer organizationwide commitment in service and after-sales support:* People fly Calgary-based WestJet Airlines because the airline offers superior value. Passengers do not always get assigned seats or meals when they use the airline; but its service is reliable and friendly and costs less than that of Canada's major airlines. All WestJet employees are involved in the effort to satisfy customers. Pilots tend to the boarding gate when their help is needed, and ticket agents help move luggage.

To the acknowledged Canadian attribute
of modest reserve we now add pure brilliance.
A new source of light has entered the world. The only diamonds certified direct from EKATI™, Canada's Diamond Mine. They can melt a heart from across a room. They define purity. Brilliance. Cut and polished with an artistry and precision that intensifies their rarity, they await your close attention at select jewellers across this country. Find them at www.ekati.ca.

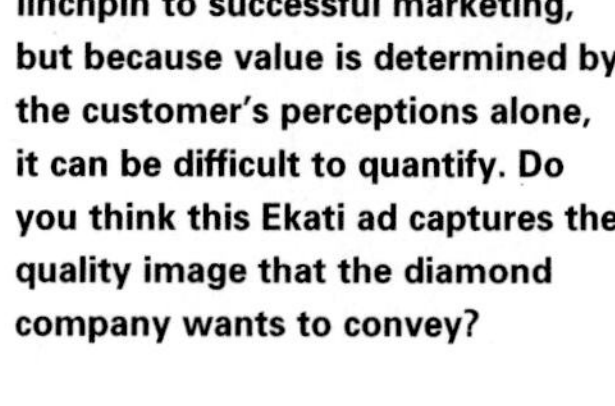

Creating customer value is the linchpin to successful marketing, but because value is determined by the customer's perceptions alone, it can be difficult to quantify. Do you think this Ekati ad captures the quality image that the diamond company wants to convey?

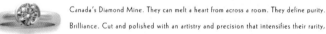

customer satisfaction The feeling that a product has met or exceeded the customer's expectations.

Customer Satisfaction **Customer satisfaction** refers to the feeling among customers that a product has met or exceeded expectations. Keeping current customers satisfied is just as important as attracting new ones—and much less expensive. Firms that have a reputation for delivering high levels of customer satisfaction do things differently from their competitors. Top management is obsessed with customer satisfaction, and employees throughout the organization understand the link between their jobs and satisfied customers. The organization's culture is to focus on delighting customers rather than on selling products.

Staples, the office supply retailer, offers great prices on its papers, pens, fax machines, and other office supplies, but its main strategy is to grow by providing customers with the best solutions to their problems. Their approach is to emulate customer-intimate companies like Home Depot and FedEx. These companies do not pursue one-time transactions: they cultivate relationships.

This is frequent flying.
Receive 5,000 Aeroplan® Bonus Miles.

Diners Club International® enRoute
3612 345678 0009
AIR CANADA
Aeroplan
More Card for your business. More Aeroplan miles for you.
The Diners Club®/enRoute® Card combines all the benefits of a premium card specially designed for your needs as a frequent business traveller with the rewards you really want– Air Canada Aeroplan® miles! So start rewarding yourself with **5,000 Aeroplan Bonus Miles** when you become a Cardmember!* And keep on rewarding yourself with **one Aeroplan mile for every dollar you charge to your Card.**† You'll be on your way to earning more free flights†† faster on Air Canada and its partner airlines. Call 1 800 363.3333 to apply today.
*Available to first-time applicants only upon approval of the application and receipt of the annual fee. †Aeroplan miles are earned on all purchases less credits. Cash advances, fees, late charges, interest and payments do not qualify for Aeroplan miles. ††Taxes, landing and departure fees may be applicable to Aeroplan reward travel. Diners Club, Diners Club International, Reg. TMs of Diners Club International Ltd., enRoute, Aeroplan, Reg. TMs of Air Canada. Citibank Canada is an authorized user of the marks.

Frequent flyer programs encourage customers to become loyal to specific airlines and their partners, and then reward them for that loyalty.

Disney

Disney training stretches beyond the bounds of its own organizational structures. Visit the Disney Website and click on "Disney Difference." What are the main themes of these programs? View a sample agenda to find out. What does this tell you about Disney's business philosophy?

www.disney.com/DisneyWorld/DisneyInstitute/ProfessionalPrograms

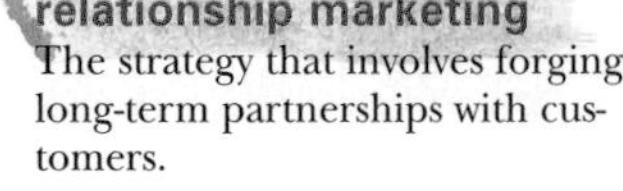

Building Relationships **Relationship marketing** is a strategy that involves forging long-term partnerships with customers. Companies build relationships with customers by offering value and providing customer satisfaction. Companies benefit from repeat sales and from referrals that lead to increases in sales, market share, and profits. Costs fall because serving existing customers is less expensive than attracting new ones. Keeping a customer costs about one-quarter what it costs to attract a new customer. Also, the probability of retaining a customer is over 60 percent, whereas the probability of landing a new customer is less than 30 percent.[12]

relationship marketing
The strategy that involves forging long-term partnerships with customers.

The Internet is an effective tool for generating relationships with customers because it can be used for interacting with customers. On the Internet, companies can use e-mail for fast customer service, discussion groups for building a sense of community, and database tracking of buying habits for customizing products.[13]

Furthermore, customers benefit from stable relationships with suppliers. Business buyers have found that partnerships with their suppliers are essential to producing high-quality products while cutting costs.[14] Customers remain loyal to firms that provide them greater value and satisfaction than they expect from competing firms. This value and satisfaction can come in a variety of forms, ranging from financial benefits, to a sense of well-being or confidence in a supplier, to structural bonds.[15]

Frequent flyer programs are an example of offering customers financial incentives in exchange for their continuing patronage. After flying a certain distance or flying a specified number of times, the participant earns a free flight or some other award such as free lodging. Frequent flyer programs encourage customers to become loyal to specific airlines, and then reward them for that loyalty.

A sense of well-being results when a customer establishes an ongoing relationship with a provider such as a physician, a bank, a hairdresser, or an accountant. The social bonding between provider and customer involves personalization and customization of the relationship. Firms can enhance these bonds by referring to customers by name and by providing continuity of service through the same representative.

The FedEx Powership program, which installs computer terminals in the offices of its customers, is an example of structural bonding. FedEx Powership comprises a series of automated shipping, tracking, and invoicing systems that save customers time and money while solidifying their loyalty to FedEx. The systems are scaled to customers' use. Customers receive a free microcomputer terminal with fully functional software, modem, bar-code scanner, and report printer. FedEx Powership rates packages with the correct freight charges, combines package weights by destination to provide volume discounts for shipments, and prints address labels from the customer's own database. Users can automatically prepare their own invoices, analyze their shipping expenses, and track their packages through the FedEx® system.[16]

Most successful relationship marketing strategies depend on teamwork, customer-oriented personnel, effective training programs, and employees with the authority to make decisions and solve problems. This chapter's "Entrepreneurial Insights" box offers several

on line

Britannica

Go to Britannica's Web page. What evidence do you see that Britannica has redefined its core business? What do you think its business definition currently is? How has it met the challenge of CD-ROM technology?

www.britannica.com

entrepreneurial insights

David versus Goliath

The scenario is familiar, and much lamented this past quarter-century: the big, heartless Wal-Mart or Home Depot megastore moves in, offering everything under the sun and trampling local mom-and-pop shops in the process. How can mom-and-pop retailers save their stores? A recent study produced the following seven tips:

1. Work with other local retailers to offer a complete merchandise selection. Often, consumers complain that they can't find everything they need on "Main Street," so they have to travel to shop.
2. Build strong customer relationships. Local retailers should think back to the days when sales clerks knew the name of every customer who walked in the door, and try to build those kinds of personal bonds. Large, impersonal stores cannot provide this benefit.
3. Get involved with local events and government. Local retailers should identify strongly and overtly with the communities they serve. This can include sponsoring local sports teams, holding breakfasts with industry and government leaders, and helping local schools raise funds.
4. Update merchandise more often. When local retailers improve their selection, they can convince consumers the best products can be found close to home. They can even charge higher prices because consumers will be willing to pay them for the convenience.
5. Train your salespeople so they understand their importance in delivering customer satisfaction.
6. Conduct formal customer research. Distribute customer satisfaction cards in stores with questions about service, merchandise selection, and store appearance. This can help small retailers spot problems before they drive customers away.
7. Don't be afraid to send customers away. Use the *Miracle on 34th Street* approach if your business does not carry an item requested by a customer. Suggesting another local store will build trust and keep customers shopping at the local stores.[17]

relationship tips for small, local firms to use when competing with large national or international marketers.

Customer-Oriented Personnel Before an organization can build relationships with customers, its employees' attitudes and actions must be customer oriented. An employee may be the only contact a particular customer has with the firm. In that customer's eyes, the employee *is* the firm. Any person, department, or division that is not customer oriented weakens the positive image of the entire organization. A potential customer who is greeted rudely may well assume that the employee's attitude reflects that of the entire firm.

The Role of Training Leading marketers recognize the role of employee training in customer service and relationship building. All new employees at Disneyland and Walt Disney World, favourite vacation spots for Canadians, must attend Disney University, a special training program for Disney employees. First they must pass Traditions 1, a day-long course focusing on the Disney philosophy and operational procedures. Then they go on to specialized training. Similarly, McDonald's has Hamburger University. There is an extra payoff for companies such as Disney and McDonald's that train their employees to be customer oriented. Employees who make their customers happy are more likely to derive satisfaction from their jobs. When workers are satisfied with their jobs, they are more likely to hold on to them. The point is that customer-oriented training results in better customer service and greater employee retention.

empowerment
Delegation of authority to solve customers' problems quickly—usually by the first person the customer notifies regarding a problem.

Empowerment Many marketing-oriented firms are giving employees more authority to solve customer problems on the spot. The term used to describe this delegation of authority is **empowerment**. Fedex's customer service representatives are trained and empowered to resolve customer problems. Although the average

FedEx transaction costs only $16, customer service reps are empowered to spend up to $100 to resolve a customer problem.

Kindred Industries of Midland, Ontario, is the largest manufacturer of stainless steel sinks in Canada. Kindred prides itself on high product quality and a high level of customer service. To make sure its customers remain satisfied, Kindred provides each of its sales representatives wide authority to please customers. If a customer—whether a plumber, a building contractor, or a retail store—has a problem with a product, the sales representative has the authority to approve an immediate replacement at the highest-speed transportation, whatever the cost. Kindred sales reps have been known to drive hundreds of kilometres to provide missing parts as quickly as possible to customers.

Empowerment gives customers the feeling that their concerns are being addressed; it also gives employees the feeling that their expertise matters. The result is greater satisfaction for both customers and employees.

Teamwork Many organizations that are noted for delivering superior customer value and providing high levels of customer satisfaction assign employees to teams and teach them team-building skills. **Teamwork** is about people collaborating to accomplish common objectives. Job performance, company performance, product value, and customer satisfaction all improve when people in the same department or work group begin supporting and assisting one another and emphasizing cooperation instead of competition. Performance is also enhanced when people in different areas of responsibility such as production and sales, or sales and service, practise teamwork.

teamwork
The collaborative efforts of people to accomplish common objectives.

The Firm's Business

As Exhibit 1.1 illustrates, a sales-oriented firm defines its business (or mission) in terms of goods and services, whereas a market-oriented firm defines its business in terms of the benefits its customers seek. People who spend their money, time, and energy expect to receive benefits, not just goods and services. This has enormous implications.

Because of the limited way it defines its business, a sales-oriented firm often misses opportunities to serve customers whose wants can be met only through a wide range of product offerings. In 1990 Encyclopaedia Britannica earned more than $40 million after taxes. Just four years later, after three consecutive years of losses, the sales force had collapsed. How did this respected company sink so low? Britannica managers saw that competitors were beginning to use CD-ROMs to store huge masses of information, but chose to ignore the new computer technology.[18] It's not hard to see why parents would rather give their children an encyclopedia on a CD instead of a printed one. The CD versions are either given away or sold by other publishers for under $400. A full set of the Encyclopaedia Britannica costs a minimum of $1,500, weighs 53 kg, and takes nearly a metre and a half of shelf space.[19] Had Britannica defined its business as providing information instead of publishing books, it might not have suffered such a precipitous fall.

Answering the question "What is this firm's business?" in terms of the benefits customers seek, instead of goods and services, has at least three important advantages:

- It ensures that the firm continues to focus on customers and avoids becoming preoccupied with goods, services, or its own internal needs.
- It encourages innovation and creativity by reminding people that there are many ways to satisfy customer wants.
- It stimulates awareness of changes in customer desires and preferences; as a result of this, product offerings are more likely to remain relevant.

A market-oriented organization recognizes that customer groups and their wants and tastes vary, so it creates products and services to address these differences. Tostitos offers its salsa products in a variety of strengths and flavours that meet different customers' needs and that also meet individual customers' changing tastes.

Market orientation—the idea of focusing on customer wants—does not mean that customers will always receive everything they want. It is not possible to profitably manufacture and market automobile tires that will last for 100 000 kilometres and sell for $25. Furthermore, customers' preferences must be mediated by sound professional judgment as to how to deliver the benefits sought. As one adage suggests, "People don't know what they want—they only want what they know." Consumers have a limited set of experiences. They are unlikely to request anything beyond those experiences because they are not aware of the benefits they may gain from other potential offerings. Before the automobile, people knew they wanted quicker, more convenient transportation, but they could not express their need for a car.

Those to Whom the Product Is Directed

A sales-oriented organization targets its products at "everybody" or "the average customer." A market-oriented organization aims at specific groups of people (see Exhibit 1.1). The problem with developing products directed at the average user is that few average users actually exist. Most populations are characterized by diversity. An average is simply a midpoint in some set of characteristics. Because most potential customers are not "average," they are not likely to be attracted to an average product marketed to the average customer. Consider the market for shampoo. There are shampoos for oily hair, dry hair, and dandruff. Some shampoos remove grey, or colour hair. Special shampoos are marketed for infants and elderly people. There is even shampoo for people with average or normal hair—whatever that is—but this is a fairly small part of the total market for shampoo.

A market-oriented organization recognizes that customer groups vary, and so do their wants. It may therefore need to develop different goods, services, and promotional appeals. A market-oriented organization carefully analyzes the market and divides it into groups of people who are fairly similar in terms of selected characteristics. Then it develops marketing programs that will bring about mutually satisfying exchanges with one or more of those groups. Paying attention to the customer isn't exactly a new concept. Back in the 1920s, General Motors helped write the book on customer satisfaction by designing cars for every lifestyle and pocketbook. This was a breakthrough for an industry that had been driven largely by production needs ever since Henry Ford promised any colour as long as it was black.

The Firm's Primary Goal

As Exhibit 1.1 illustrates, a sales-oriented organization seeks to achieve profitability through sales volume and tries to convince potential customers to buy, even if the seller knows that the customer and the product are mismatched. For sales-oriented organizations, it is more important to make a sale than to develop a long-term relationship with a customer. In contrast, the ultimate goal of most market-oriented organizations is to make a profit by creating customer value, providing customer satisfaction, and building long-term relationships.

Tools the Organization Uses to Achieve Its Goals

Sales-oriented organizations seek to generate sales volume through intensive promotional activities—mainly personal selling and advertising. In contrast, market-oriented organizations recognize that promotion decisions are only one of the four basic marketing mix decisions that have to be made. The four: *product* decisions, *place* (or distribution) decisions, *promotion* decisions, and *pricing* decisions. A market-oriented organization recognizes that each of these four components is important. Furthermore, market-oriented organizations recognize that marketing is not just a responsibility of the marketing department. Interfunctional coordination means that skills and resources throughout the organization are needed to deliver superior customer service and value.[20]

The Marketing Process

4 Describe the marketing process

Marketing managers are responsible for the many different activities that together represent the marketing process. These include:

- Understanding the organization's mission and the role marketing plays in achieving that mission.
- Setting marketing objectives.
- Gathering, analyzing, and interpreting information about the organization's situation, including its strengths and weaknesses, and any opportunities and threats in the business environment. (SWOT)
- Developing a marketing strategy by deciding exactly which wants and whose wants the organization will try to satisfy (target market strategy), and by developing appropriate marketing activities (the marketing mix) to satisfy the desires of selected target markets. The marketing mix combines product, distribution, promotion, and pricing strategies in a way that creates exchanges that satisfy individual and organizational goals.
- Implementing the marketing strategy.
- Designing performance measures.
- Periodically evaluating marketing efforts, and making changes if needed.

These activities and their relationships constitute the foundation on which the rest of this book is based.

Why Study Marketing?

5 Describe several reasons for studying marketing

Now that you understand the meaning of the term marketing, and why it is important to adopt a marketing orientation, and how organizations implement this philosophy, you may be asking, "What's in it for me?" or "Why should I study marketing?" These are important questions, whether you are majoring in marketing, or in a business field other than marketing, or in a nonbusiness field. There are several important reasons to study marketing. It plays an important role

Stop the downpour.
Spay or neuter your pet.

Not-for-profit organizations also perform marketing activities and so provide career opportunities in marketing.

in society; it is important to businesses; it offers outstanding career opportunities; and it affects your life every day.

Marketing Plays an Important Role in Society

According to Statistics Canada, Canada's population passed 31 million in 2001. Think about how many transactions it takes each day to feed, clothe, and shelter a population of this size. And the country functions quite well, partly because Canada's economic system is well developed and efficiently distributes the output of farms and factories. A typical family consumes 2.5 tons of food a year. Marketing makes food available when we want it, in desired quantities, at accessible locations, and in sanitary and convenient packages and forms.

Marketing Is Important to Businesses

The fundamental objectives of most businesses are survival, profits, and growth. Marketing contributes directly to all of these. Marketing includes the following activities, which are vital to business organizations: assessing the wants and satisfactions of present and potential customers, designing and managing product offerings, determining prices and pricing policies, developing distribution strategies, and communicating with present and potential customers.

All businesspeople, whatever their specialization or area of responsibility, need to be familiar with the terminology and fundamentals of accounting, finance, management, and marketing. People in all business areas need to be able to communicate with specialists in other areas. Furthermore, marketing is not just a job done by people in a marketing department: it is part of the job for *everyone* in the organization. As David Packard of Hewlett-Packard put it: "Marketing is too important to be left to the marketing department."[21] In sum, a basic understanding of marketing is important to all businesspeople.

Marketing Offers Outstanding Career Opportunities

Between one-quarter and one-third of the entire workforce conducts marketing activities. Marketing offers great career opportunities in areas such as professional selling, marketing research, advertising, retail buying, distribution management, product management, product development, and wholesaling. Marketing career opportunities also exist in a variety of nonbusiness organizations, including hospitals, museums, universities, the armed forces, and various government and social service agencies.

As the world marketplace becomes more challenging, Canadian companies of all sizes are going to have to become better marketers. A recent survey of 160 companies by the search firm Korn Ferry International found that the fastest route up the corporate ladder is through marketing.[22]

Marketing Affects Your Life Every Day

Marketing powerfully affects your everyday life. You participate in the marketing process as a consumer of goods and services. Around half of every dollar you spend pays for marketing costs, such as marketing research, product development, packaging, transportation, storage, advertising, and sales expenses. By developing a better understanding of marketing, you will become a better-informed consumer. You will better understand the buying process and be able to negotiate more effectively with sellers. Moreover, you will be better prepared to demand satisfaction when the goods and services you buy do not meet the standards promised by the manufacturer or the marketer.

Looking Ahead

This book is divided into twenty chapters, which are organized into five major parts. The chapters are written from the marketing manager's perspective. Each chapter begins with a brief list of learning objectives followed by a vignette about a marketing situation faced by a firm or industry.

One-to-one marketing is given special treatment in Chapter 18 and is discussed repeatedly throughout the chapters. Examples of one-to-one marketing are highlighted with icons and special boxes.

Examples of global marketing are found in most chapters and will help you understand that marketing takes place all over the world, between buyers and sellers in different countries.

The profound impact of the Internet on marketing is discussed in depth in Chapter 19 and in boxed features throughout the text titled "Internet Connections."

Marketing ethics is another topic selected for special treatment. Each chapter includes a highlighted story about a firm or an industry that has faced ethical dilemmas or has engaged in practices that some consider unethical.

In this increasingly competitive environment, delivering superior customer value is a key to marketing success. Examples of creating or delivering superior customer value are integrated throughout the text and are highlighted in special service spotlights.

Entrepreneurial insights are highlighted with special boxes. This material illustrates how entrepreneurs and small businesses can use the principles and concepts discussed in the book.

End-of-chapter materials include a final comment on the chapter opening vignette ("Looking Back"), a summary of the major topics examined, a list of key terms introduced in the chapter, and discussion and writing questions. Specific Internet and team activities are provided in the writing and discussion questions. Video cases with discussion questions conclude each chapter. All these features are intended to help you develop a more thorough understanding of marketing and enjoy the learning process.

The remaining chapters in Part I introduce you to the activities involved in developing a marketing plan and the environment in which marketing decisions are made. Part II covers consumer decision making and buyer behaviour; business-to-business marketing; the concepts of positioning, market segmentation, and targeting; and the nature and uses of marketing research, decision support systems, and competitive intelligence. Parts III and IV examine the elements of the marketing mix: product, distribution, promotion, and pricing decisions, and one-to-one marketing, as well as Internet marketing. Part V brings everything we've covered back together into an integrated marketing strategy discussion.

LOOKING BACK

Look back at the story at the beginning of this chapter about Levi Strauss. You should now find the questions at the end of the story to be simple and straightforward. The company is clearly market oriented. Its informal research focuses on identifying customer wants and converting this information into want-satisfying new products before competitors identify emerging trends.

If Levi Strauss can create more customer value than its competitors, customers will be satisfied with its products and remain loyal. As noted in the chapter, there is no reason why customers should buy one organization's offerings unless they in some way serve wants and needs better than those offered by competing organizations. Loyal customers who repeat-purchase increase sales and profits for the seller.

Summary

1 **Define the term marketing.** The ultimate goal of all marketing activity is to facilitate mutually satisfying exchanges between parties. The activities of marketing include the conception, pricing, promotion, and distribution of ideas, goods, and services.

2 **Describe four marketing management philosophies.** The role of marketing and the character of marketing activities are strongly influenced by the organization's philosophy and orientation. A production-oriented organization focuses on the internal capabilities of the firm rather than on the desires and needs of the marketplace. A sales orientation is based on two beliefs: that people will buy more products if aggressive sales techniques are used, and that high sales volumes produce high profits. A market-oriented organization focuses on satisfying customer wants and needs while meeting organizational objectives. A societal market orientation goes beyond a market orientation to include the preservation or enhancement of individuals' and society's long-term best interests.

3 **Discuss the differences between sales and market orientations.** First, sales-oriented firms focus on their own needs; market-oriented firms focus on customers' needs and preferences. Second, sales-oriented companies consider themselves to be deliverers of goods and services, whereas market-oriented companies view themselves as satisfiers of customers. Third, sales-oriented firms direct their products to everyone; market-oriented firms aim at specific segments of the population. Fourth, although the primary goal of both types of firms is profit, sales-oriented businesses pursue maximum sales volume through intensive promotion, whereas market-oriented businesses pursue customer satisfaction through coordinated activities.

4 **Describe the marketing process.** The marketing process includes understanding the organization's mission and the role that marketing plays in fulfilling that mission, setting marketing objectives, scanning the environment, developing a marketing strategy by selecting a target market strategy, developing and implementing a marketing mix, implementing the strategy, designing performance measures, and evaluating marketing efforts and making changes if needed. The marketing mix combines product, distribution (place), promotion, and pricing strategies in a way that creates exchanges that are satisfying to individual and organizational objectives.

5 **Describe several reasons for studying marketing.** First, marketing affects the allocation of goods and services; this in turn influences a nation's economy and standard of living. Second, an understanding of marketing is crucial to understanding most businesses. Third, career opportunities in marketing are diverse, profitable, and expected to increase significantly during the coming decade. Fourth, understanding marketing makes consumers more informed.

Do You Know These Terms?

customer satisfaction 10
customer value 7
empowerment 12
exchange 4
market orientation 6
marketing 4
marketing concept 5
production orientation 5
relationship marketing 11
sales orientation 5
societal orientation 7
teamwork 13

Discussion and Writing Questions

1. Your company president has decided to restructure the firm and become more market oriented. She is going to announce the changes at an upcoming meeting. She has asked you to prepare a short speech outlining the general reasons for the new company orientation.
2. Donald E. Petersen, former chairman of the board of Ford Motor Company, remarked, "If we aren't customer driven, our cars won't be either." Explain how this statement reflects the marketing concept.
3. A friend of yours agrees with the adage, "People don't know what they want—they only want what they know." Write your friend a letter expressing the extent to which you think marketers shape consumer wants.

4. Your local supermarket's slogan is "It's your store." However, when you asked one of the stock people to help you find a bag of chips, he told you it was not his job and that you should look a little harder. On your way out, you noticed a sign with an address for complaints. Draft a letter explaining why the supermarket's slogan will never be credible unless their employees carry it out.
5. Give an example of a company that might be successfully following a production orientation. Why might a firm in this industry be successful following such an orientation?
6. Write a letter to a friend or family member explaining why you think a course in marketing will help you in your career in some field other than marketing.
7. Form a small group of three or four members. Suppose you and your colleagues all work for an up-and-coming gourmet coffee company that has several stores, most of them in large cities across Canada. Your team has been assigned the task of assessing whether the company should begin marketing on the Internet.

   Each member has been assigned to visit three or four Internet sites for ideas. Some possibilities are

   Toys 'R' Us **www.toysrus.com**
   Wal-Mart **www.wal-mart.com**
   Godiva chocolates **www.godiva.com**
   Levi Strauss **www.levi.com**

   Use your imagination and look up others. As you can see, many companies are easy to find, as long as you can spell their names. Typically, you would use the following: **www.companyname.com.**

   Has Internet marketing helped the companies whose sites you visited? If so, how? What factors should your company consider before committing to Internet activity? Prepare a three- to five-minute presentation to give to your class.
8. What is the AMA? What does it do? How do its services benefit marketers across North America? **www.ama.org**
9. What is an ExciteSeeing Tour? What kind of business tours does this site offer? **tours.excite.com**

Application for Small Business

Lisa King enjoyed working as a camp counsellor during the summer. She started around the time she entered high school and continued through university. She even took a job at a camp the summer after graduating from university. She rationalized that this "internship," developing the camp yearbook, would help prepare her for a job in advertising.

As the summer passed, Lisa spent more time thinking about "what she was going to do when she grew up," as she liked to put it. Her thoughts always seemed to return to camping.

Lisa finally decided that she would like to open a small retail store specializing in camping supplies. The more she thought about it, the better she liked the idea.

She finally got up enough nerve to call her father, Tom, to discuss the idea. Tom's first response was, "Have you prepared a written plan?"

Lisa remembered preparing a marketing plan in her first class in marketing at Kwantlen University College. She asked her father to FedEx the text to her.

With financial backing from her father, Lisa and her sister Jill opened Santorini Camping Supply the following autumn. They picked the name Santorini because it was their favourite place in the Greek Isles and, as Jill put it, "We just like the name."

On the first day the store was open, a customer asked Lisa if Santorini's guaranteed the products it sold. Lisa proudly replied, "Every product that is purchased from Santorini Camping Supply has a lifetime guarantee. If at any time you are not satisfied with one of our products, you can return it to the store for a full refund or exchange."

Questions

1. What marketing management philosophy is Santorini's expressing? Why have you reached this conclusion?
2. Do you think a lifetime guarantee for this kind of product is too generous? Explain.
3. Do you think this policy will contribute to success or to bankruptcy?
4. Suggest other customer service policies that might be appropriate for Santorini's Camping Supply.

VIDEO CASE

Lord of the Boards

Burton Snowboards, the industry leader, is the brainchild of Jake Burton, an avid rider. Jake's recipe for success is simple: "We always focused on the sport and everything else took care of itself." Burton practically invented the sport in 1977 when he first made crude snowboards in a small workshop. By 1978 he had hit on a successful formula (horizontally laminated wood) and made 300 boards with an $88 price tag. The next decade saw Jake spending time and money lobbying ski areas to open their slopes to snowboarders. Now they are free to ride just about everywhere. Competitors noted that while they were pegging snowboarding as a regional sport, Jake was keeping his eye on the big picture. He always had a vision. Campaigning tirelessly for snowboarding at resorts led to the establishing of many snowboarding competitions. By the mid-1990s many sporting magazines were calling snowboarding the fastest-growing sport. Finally, the ultimate—snowboarding made its debut in the 1998 Winter Olympics in Nagano, Japan.

Jake didn't let the Olympics go to his head. He kept his company on a clear course: product development, R&D, and lots of riding. The company provides free private lessons for newbies (new riders), so excuses for not riding are hard to find. The sport draws mainly the under-thirty crowd: 88 percent are ages twelve to twenty-four and 83 percent are male. The Newbie snowboarding guide (available on the Burton Website) gives the basics, starting with the idea that equipment and clothing can make or break the ride. First comes the choice of ride (Freestyle, Freeride, or Carving), then three riding options. Next is the choice of board; these are produced in different lengths with different graphics. Boots and bindings are picked next, followed by clothing with the right fit. An on-snow demonstration is considered a must, so Burton posts its travel schedule on the Internet and offers free, local demonstrations and a chance to try on boots, bindings, and the whole setup on the snow. Burton also suggests taking a lesson for maximum fun and safety.

Staying close to the customer is a company hallmark. Burton Snowboards builds on a group of people to get feedback to improve both the company and the sport. Talking to pro riders, sales reps, designers, testers, and Internet users helps the company find out what the riders want. When the company needs new ideas for graphics, designers fly all over the world, sit face to face, and look at what has been developed. The idea is to provide snowboard equipment to all people.

To do this, Burton keeps on adding to its product line. Snowboarding performance may be gender-blind, but fit is not. That is why Burton manufactures gender-specific clothing and boots that are completely different for men and women in fit but are matched in performance. Years of refining the cut of women's clothing have yielded a line of fully featured gear that really works for snowboarding. Women are the fastest-growing segment of riders, and though there are no specific women's boards or bindings, Burton works with their team riders to create board dimensions, flexes, and bindings that work well for smaller, lighter riders. Burton plans to offer functional gear for women, men, and riders of all sizes, abilities, and styles. And as more and more kids between six and fourteen get into riding, Burton is stepping up and delivering products that meet the demands of these mini-snowboarders. Sometimes kids ride first and the parents follow suit. In the process, snowboarding becomes a family passion.

The Burton strategy has paid off. Annual sales figures are now well over $150 million, and the company has 500 employees around the world. As the sport of snowboarding matures, many people in the snowboarding community are using the sport to make valuable social contributions that enrich lives. In 1994, Jake Burton started the Chill Program to share snowboarding with poor and at-risk kids. While it is true that heavy industry competition is out there, innovation and love of the sport still make Jake Burton Lord of the Boards.

Questions

1. Describe the exchange process at Burton.
2. How has Jake Burton's entrepreneurial philosophy made his company successful?
3. Does Burton use a sales orientation or a market orientation? Explain.
4. How does Burton Snowboards achieve customer satisfaction?

Suggested Readings

Reade Bailey, "Jake Burton, King of the Hill," *Ski*, February 1998, pp. 60–7.

Eric Blehm, "The Day of the Locusts," *GQ*, December 1997, pp. 186–7.

1998 Press Kit.

CHAPTER

2

LEARNING OBJECTIVES

After studying this chapter, you should be able to

1. Understand the importance of strategic marketing, and know a basic outline for a marketing plan
2. Develop an appropriate business mission statement
3. Describe the criteria for stating good marketing objectives
4. Explain the components of a situation analysis
5. Identify strategic alternatives, and describe tools used to help select alternatives
6. Discuss target market strategies
7. Describe the elements of the marketing mix
8. Explain why implementation, evaluation, and control of the marketing plan are necessary

THE STRATEGY BEHIND MARKETING

Some executives entertain lavishly with their company's money. If Clive Beddoe tried to, he'd probably get lynched. Clive Beddoe is president and CEO of WestJet Airlines of Calgary. Consider what happened when he threw a barbecue for senior and middle managers at his fishing lodge on the Bow River. When Beddoe returned to his office the following Monday, a WestJet maintenance worker stormed in and demanded to know why the boss was wasting company money on hamburgers and beer for top managers. Mr. Beddoe quickly explained that he had paid for the party out of his own pocket.[1]

The maintenance worker was upset because WestJet has a generous profit-sharing plan. He thought that company money had been wasted on a party.

This simple story tells a lot about WestJet's corporate strategy and culture: from top to bottom there is an intense desire to maximize profits. The airline's employees are not just workers: most of them own shares in the company, and all of them get a share of the profits.

Since it was founded in 1996, WestJet has consistently ranked among the most profitable airlines in North America. In five years the no-frills air carrier has grown to over $400 million in revenue. WestJet's share price has soared by 240 percent since its initial offering in 1999. And for every dollar an employee invests in the company, WestJet matches it. No wonder nearly 90 percent of WestJet employees own stock in the company.[2]

WestJet's marketing plan is modelled after that of Southwest Airlines, the most consistently profitable airline ever. The key elements in the company plan are to run a low-cost airline, to fly short-haul on carefully selected routes, and to offer very low fares. WestJet does not provide seating for different classes, does not provide meals or drinks, and does not have a frequent flier program. The target market for WestJet is people who want to get from point A to point B for the lowest fare possible. Though this is the core of the plan, Beddoe insists that WestJet has succeeded mainly because of its corporate culture.

In contrast to most other businesses, WestJet is managed from the bottom. It offers its employees a great deal of latitude to perform their jobs with little supervision. For example, flight attendants are simply instructed

WestJet

Does the WestJet site give you a feel for the company's corporate strategy and culture? Are you surprised by how the site is organized? Explain.

www.westjet.com

on line

to serve customers in a cheerful manner—the rest is up to them. This approach has resulted in very high productivity. WestJet operates with around 59 people per aircraft; the average for the industry is 140.

On August 2, 2001, WestJet announced its eighteenth consecutive profitable quarter. The same quarter, Air Canada, with twenty times more revenue than WestJet, announced a quarterly loss of $108 million. Industry analysts say that corporate culture is the reason for the difference. When WestJet CEO Clive Beddoe flies on his own airline, he sticks around once the plane lands to help the cabin crew tidy up.[3]

WestJet's profit-sharing plan is also important. If its profit margin is 10 percent, employees share 10 percent of those profits; if its profit margin is 15 percent, employees share 15 percent of those profits, and so on. Last year, WestJet employees shared $8 million in profits and received cheques averaging over $9,000. With this type of incentive, you can see why the maintenance worker did not like the idea of company money being spent on a barbecue. This attitude results in all company employees being careful about all company costs, and all employees pitching in wherever they are needed.

Will WestJet's strategy continue to work as the company grows? Marketing planning is discussed briefly in this chapter, to help you better understand what activities are essential for a new company like WestJet. Strategic marketing planning is discussed in more depth in the final chapter.

The Nature of Strategic Planning

1
Understand the importance of strategic marketing, and know a basic outline for a marketing plan

Strategic planning is the managerial process of creating and maintaining a fit between the organization's objectives and resources and evolving market opportunities. The goal of strategic planning is long-run profitability and growth.

Strategic marketing management addresses two questions: What is the organization's main activity at a particular time? And how will it reach its goals? Here are some examples of strategic decisions:

- Persil laundry soap tablets, introduced by Unilever, promise no measuring, scooping, or pouring. Although a strategic failure in Canada, the tablets have a broad appeal to busy, younger Europeans, who already use tablets in their dishwashers.[4]
- Quaker Oats' $1.7 billion purchase of Snapple (a strategic success for tiny Triarc Company) has been called "the decade's worst acquisition" after marketing bungles caused heavy losses for the beverage.[5]
- Compaq Computer's decision to charge customers for phone technical support to defray the high costs of phone support and encourage customers to read documentation was a strategic failure. Customer rebellion forced

strategic planning
The managerial process of creating and maintaining a fit between the organization's objectives and resources and evolving market opportunities.

Sabian Ltd.

Examine Sabian Ltd.'s Website. What do its recent news releases tell you about current directions the company is taking in its marketing program? Look at the background of the new company president. What does this suggest about new directions for the company?

www.sabian.com

WWW on line

Compaq to rethink this policy.[6] However, Compaq's focus on the inexpensive home computer market segment has been a strategic success.

- Crystal Pepsi, a clear soda, was pulled off the market despite an expensive and extensive market introduction. Consumers clearly did not care for the taste, despite several reformulations.
- The introduction of luxury sports utility vehicles by Lexus, Lincoln, and Mercedes-Benz has been a strategic success. Profit margins are high, and demand is outstripping supply. Even latecomer Cadillac has been successful.[7]

Strategic planning is critical to business success. Dial rolled out its home dry cleaning kit, Custom Cleaner, after the warm reception for Procter & Gamble's Dryel product.

All these decisions have affected or will affect each organization's future direction, its allocation of resources, and ultimately its financial success. In contrast, an operating decision, such as changing the package design for Post's cornflakes or altering the sweetness of a Kraft salad dressing, probably won't have a big impact on the company's long-run profitability.

How do companies go about strategic marketing planning? How do employees know how to implement the long-term goals of the firm? The answer is a marketing plan.

What Is a Marketing Plan?

Planning is the process of anticipating future events and determining strategies to achieve organizational objectives. **Marketing planning** involves designing activities relating to marketing objectives and the changing marketing environment. Marketing planning is the basis for all marketing strategies and decisions. Issues such as product lines, distribution channels, marketing communications, and pricing are all delineated in the marketing plan. The **marketing plan** is a written document that acts as a guidebook of marketing activities for the marketing manager. This chapter's "Entrepreneurial Insights" box helps illustrate the importance of both marketing and planning.

planning
The process of anticipating future events and determining strategies to achieve organizational objectives.

marketing planning
Designing activities relating to marketing objectives and the changing marketing environment.

marketing plan
A written document that acts as a guidebook of marketing activities for the marketing manager.

Why Write a Marketing Plan?

By specifying objectives and defining the actions required to attain them, a marketing plan provides the basis for comparing actual and expected performance. Marketing can be one of the most expensive and complicated business components; it is also one of the most important business activities. The written marketing plan provides clearly stated activities that help employees understand and work toward common goals.

Marketing Plan Elements

Marketing plans can be presented in many different ways. Most businesses need a written marketing plan because such plans are typically broad and complex. Details about tasks and activity assignments may be lost if they are communicated orally. However marketing plans are presented, they all have certain elements in common. All plans define the company's business mission and objectives, per-

entrepreneurial insights

World Famous Cymbals from Meductic, New Brunswick

It's early afternoon and Robert Zildjian, looking very tired, sits down at a table in Grant's Restaurant, next to the Esso station in Meductic, New Brunswick. He has just flown back from Paris, where the European Percussive Arts Society honoured him by entering him in its Hall of Fame.

Sabian was founded twenty years ago when Robert Zildjian left the family business, Avedis Zildjian Co., over a dispute with his brother. Avedis Zildjian of Norwell, Massachusetts, can trace its history back to 1623 in Constantinople. It is the world's largest maker of cymbals for drummers and musicians. Avedis Zildjian sells over $50 million in cymbals every year. Sabian is fast catching up, with sales now in excess of $25 million according to *The Music Trades* magazine. Among its customers are Phil Collins, and Tyler Stewart of Barenaked Ladies.[8]

When Zildjian left the family business, as part of the settlement he was given a large sum of money and a small branch plant in Meductic, the smallest incorporated village in New Brunswick. Avedis Zildjian had purchased the Meductic property in 1968 to make cymbals for the Canadian market, the largest market for the company outside the United States. A big problem for Zildjian was that he would not be allowed to use his famous family name for his new business.

Marketing a new line of cymbals was not easy. Music dealers were not very interested in handling a third line of cymbals. Most of them were already carrying the well-known brands from Zildjian and Paiste AG of Switzerland. Sabian responded by introducing low-priced, prepackaged cymbals for students (the target market). It not only picked up a substantial share of the market, but also increased the size of the market by selling to customers who once had found professional-quality cymbals out of their price range.

Having gained a foothold in the market, Sabian was able to upgrade its products. Thus, it was able to take a significant piece of the professional market as well with its high-quality, hand-crafted bronze cymbals. Today, Sabian claims to have 65 percent of the Canadian market and 37 percent of the American market. To accomodate this growth, it has invested $2.5 million at the Meductic site and expanded its production facilities to 55,000 square feet.[9]

On the shop floor, cymbals are being made much as they were centuries ago. For top-of-the-line professional products, the company's smiths pound the cymbals into shape using hammers and anvils. After that, cymbal testers pass judgment on the results. If the testers aren't satisfied, the cymbals are tossed into a scrap barrel. If the cymbals pass, they get to carry the Sabian name. The low-priced cymbals are hammered out by machine but are still quality-tested before they are allowed to carry the Sabian name.

Marketing at Sabian is handled by Zildjian's two sons and his son-in-law. Bill, the oldest son, handles marketing directly to professionals, international artists, and their managers; Andy, the youngest son, handles distribution to music outlets across North America; John, the son-in-law, handles special products and distribution outside North America.

What do you think of Sabian's marketing efforts? Does it have a marketing plan? How would you describe that plan? What changes to its marketing plan may be necessary as the company grows? If you're not sure, read the remainder of this chapter and then come back to these questions.

form a situation analysis, delineate a target market, and establish components of the marketing mix. Exhibit 2.1 shows these elements. Often, other elements are included in the plan, such as budgets, implementation timetables, necessary marketing research efforts, and elements of advanced strategic planning. Exhibit 2.2 offers an example of a thumbnail marketing plan.

Developing the Marketing Plan

Note that the overall structure of the marketing plan (Exhibit 2.1) should not be viewed as a series of sequential planning steps. Many elements of the marketing plan are decided on simultaneously, in conjunction with one another. Similarly, the summary sample marketing plan (Exhibit 2.2) does not begin to suggest the intricacy and detail of a full marketing plan. It is also important to realize that

exhibit 2.1

The Marketing Process

every marketing plan varies with the organization and its mission, objectives, targets, and marketing mix components. Consider how the marketing plan in Exhibit 2.2 would differ if only cellular communication connectivity services (i.e., not the physical products) were being offered. Also, how would the plan differ if the target market consisted of *Fortune* 500 firms with large sales forces instead of executives?

Exhibit 2.6 provides an expanded set of questions to guide the formulation of a marketing plan. However, this outline should not be regarded as the *only* correct format for a marketing plan. Many organizations have developed their own distinctive formats and terminologies for creating marketing plans. Every marketing plan should be unique to the firm for which it was created. Remember that although the format and order of presentation should be flexible, the same types of questions and topic areas should be covered in any marketing plan. As you can see from Exhibit 2.6, creating a complete marketing plan is neither simple nor quick.

exhibit 2.2

Sample Summary Marketing Plan

Business mission	Ultracel is in the business of providing advanced communications technology and communications convenience to mobile users.
Marketing objective	To achieve 20 percent, in dollar volume, of the wireless telephone market by year end, 2003.
Situation analysis	
Strengths	Well-funded organization, highly skilled workforce with low turnover, excellent relationships with suppliers, unique product features, and sustainable competitive advantage of patented colour screen.
Weaknesses	Company name not well known, small firm with no manufacturing cost advantages, no long-term contracts with distributors, inexperience in the wireless communications market.
Opportunities	Explosive growth of wireless phone users, worldwide acceptance of cellular technology, newly available digital networks.
Threats	Heavy competition from Motorola, Sony, Sanyo, and Nokia; technology is incompatible with current analog systems; not everyone can afford the systems; potential governmental regulation.
Target market selection	Young, mobile executives in North America and Europe, with incomes over $200,000 per year; frequent travellers; computer-dependent individuals.
Marketing mix	
Product	Personal digital telephone. Brand name: Ultracel-2000. Features: simultaneous voice/data communication, Internet access, operation within buildings, linkups to data subscription and e-mail services, computer data storage, colour screen, light weight, 72-hour battery, 3-year unlimited warranty on parts and labour, 24 hour technical support, leather or titanium carrying case.
Place	Available through electronics retailers, upscale computer retailers, or via mail order company direct; products transported via airplane and temperature-controlled motor carrier.
Promotion	Fifty manufacturer's representatives for selling force, with 25 percent commissions; advertising in print media, cable television, and outdoor billboards; sales promotion in the form of introductory product rebates, technology trade shows; public relations efforts to news media and sponsorship of world championship sporting events.
Price	Retail price of $500 (compared to Nokia at $999, Motorola at $750, and Sony at $300); assuming mild price sensitivity and future price wars.
Implementation	First quarter: Complete marketing research on price, design promotional campaign, sign contracts with manufacturer's reps. Second quarter: Public relations campaign, product introduction at trade shows, rollout of advertising. Third quarter: Test market international markets.

The Gillette Company

Gillette is a leader in a number of product categories, including some products that may surprise you. Evaluate Gillette's mission statement as it is posted on its Website. Based on what you learn about Gillette from its mission statement, how well do you think this mission focuses on its markets? Explain.

www.gillette.com

on line

Define the Business Mission

2

Develop an appropriate business mission statement

The foundation of any marketing plan is the answer to this question: "What business are we in and where are we going?" The answer is the firm's **mission statement**. The mission statement is based on a careful analysis of benefits sought by present and potential customers and analysis of existing and anticipated environmental conditions. The firm's long-term vision, embodied in the mission statement, establishes boundaries for all later decisions, objectives, and strategies. PepsiCo's mission statement is shown in Exhibit 2.3.

mission statement
The firm's long-term vision, based on a careful analysis of benefits sought by present and potential customers and analysis of existing and anticipated environmental conditions.

A mission statement should focus on the market or markets the organization is attempting to serve rather than on the good or service offered. Otherwise, a new technology may quickly make the good or service obsolete and the mission statement irrelevant to company functions. Business mission statements that are stated too narrowly suffer from marketing myopia. **Marketing myopia** means that the business is defined in terms of goods and services rather than in terms of the benefits that customers seek.[10] In this context, myopia means narrow, short-term thinking. Frito-Lay defines its mission as being in the snack food business rather than in the corn chip business.

marketing myopia
When business is defined in terms of goods and services rather than in terms of the benefits that customers seek.

exhibit 2.3

PepsiCo's Mission Statement

"PepsiCo's overall mission is to increase the value of our shareholders' investment. We do this through sales growth, cost controls and wise investment of resources. We believe our commercial success depends upon offering quality and value to our consumers and customers; providing products that are safe, wholesome, economically efficient and environmentally sound; and providing a fair return to our investors while adhering to the highest standards of integrity."

Source: Courtesy PepsiCo., Inc., 1998.

Sometimes business missions are stated too broadly. "To provide products of superior quality and value that improve the lives of the world's consumers" is probably too broad a mission statement for any firm except Procter & Gamble (**www.pg.com**). Care must be taken when stating what business a firm is in. The mission of Saturn Corporation, a subsidiary of General Motors, is "to design, manufacture, and market vehicles to compete on a global scale."[11] When the business mission is stated correctly in terms of the benefits that customers seek, the foundation for the marketing plan is set.

Set Marketing Plan Objectives

3

Describe the criteria for stating good marketing objectives

Before the details of a marketing plan can be developed, goals and objectives for the plan must be stated. Without objectives, there is no basis for measuring the success of marketing plan activities. Exxon's return to shareholders over the past five years has been 135 percent. Sounds great, doesn't it? But without previously stated objectives, there is no way to know. Actually, Exxon's goal was to be on par with British Petroleum, which returned over 330 percent to shareholders in the same period, so it did not meet its objectives.[12]

Gillette's strategy to invest $300 million to bring Venus to market is a clear indicator of the critical importance of female shaving products to the company.

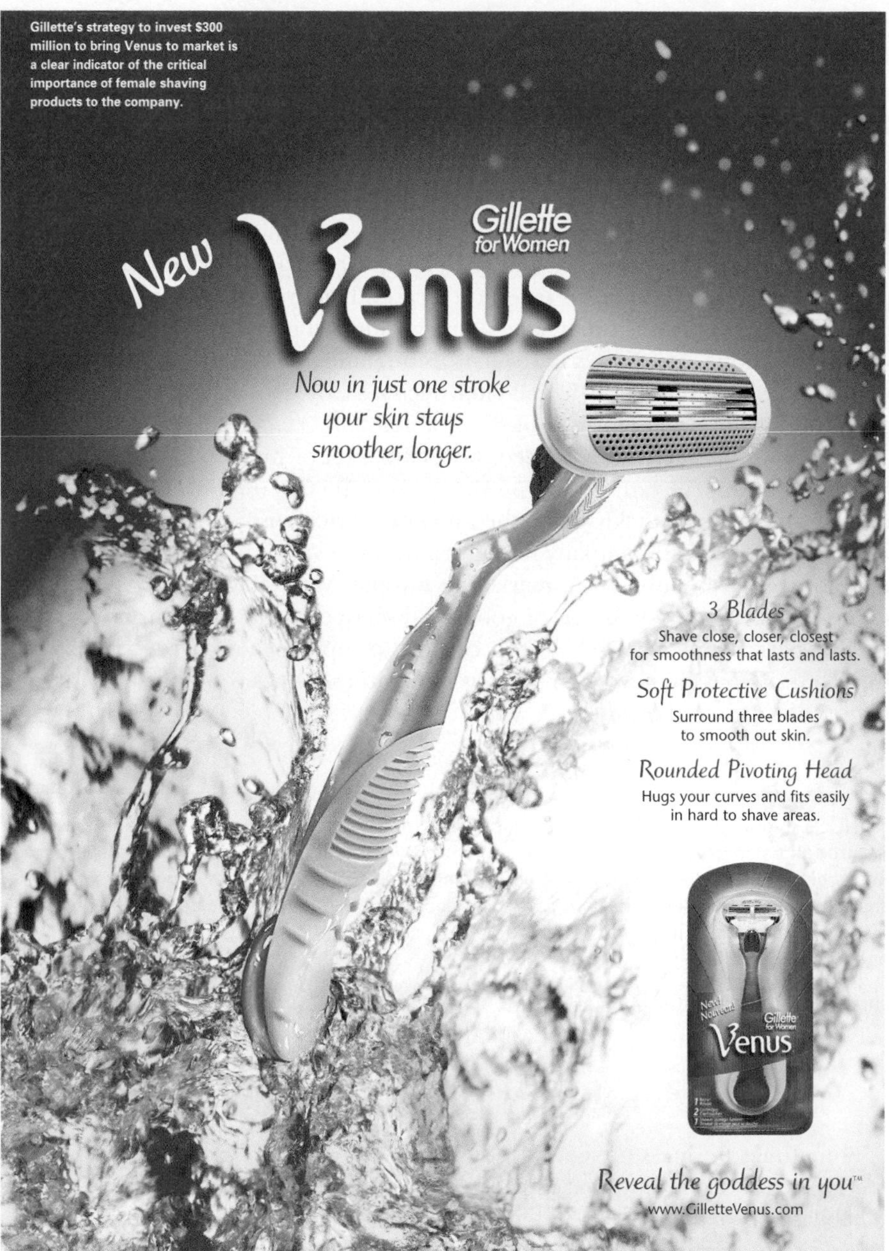

marketing objective
A statement of what is to be accomplished through marketing activities.

A **marketing objective** is a statement of what is to be accomplished through marketing activities. To be useful, stated objectives should meet several criteria. First, they should be realistic, measurable, and time specific. It is tempting to state that the objective is "to be the best marketer of ferret food." However, "best" for one firm may be sales of 1 million pounds of ferret food per year, whereas to another firm, "best" may simply mean dominant market share. Also, by when should the goal be met? A more realistic objective would be, "To achieve 10 percent dollar market share in the specialty pet food market within twelve months of product introduction."

Second, marketing objectives must be consistent with the organization's priorities. Objectives flow down from the business mission statement to the rest of the marketing plan. Exhibit 2.4 shows some well-stated and poorly stated objectives. Notice how well they do or do not meet the above criteria.

Carefully specified objectives serve several functions. First, they communicate marketing management philosophies and provide direction for lower-level marketing managers so that marketing efforts are integrated and pointed in a consistent direction. Objectives also serve as motivators by creating something for employees to strive for. Additionally, the process of writing specific objectives forces executives to clarify their thinking. Finally, objectives form a basis for control; the effectiveness of a plan can be gauged in light of the stated goals.

Conduct a Situation Analysis

4

Explain the components of a situation analysis

Before specific marketing activities can be defined, marketers must understand the current and potential environment for their company's products or services. A situation analysis is sometimes referred to as a **SWOT analysis**; that is, the firm identifies its internal strengths (S) and weaknesses (W) and also examines external opportunities (O) and threats (T).

SWOT analysis
Identifying internal strengths (S) and weaknesses (W) and also examining external opportunities (O) and threats (T).

When examining internal strengths and weaknesses, the marketing manager should focus on organizational resources such as production costs, marketing skills, financial resources, company or brand image, employee capabilities, and available technology. A potential weakness for Algoma Steel is that it is the smallest of Canada's major steel companies; this means it lacks economies of scale. Other weaknesses include high rates for labour and high management turnover. A potential strength is the low operating costs of its newest mill in Sault Ste. Marie, Ontario, which incorporates the latest technology in the industry.

environmental scanning
The collection and interpretation of information about forces, events, and relationships in the external environment that may affect the future of the organization or the implementation of the marketing plan.

When examining external opportunities and threats, marketing managers must analyze many aspects of the marketing environment. This process is called environmental scanning. **Environmental scanning** involves collecting and interpreting information about forces, events, and relationships in the external environment that may affect the future of the organization or the implementation of

exhibit 2.4

Examples of Marketing Objectives

Poorly stated objectives	Well-stated objectives
Our objective is to be a leader in the industry in terms of new product development.	Our objective is to spend 12 percent of sales revenue between 2002 and 2005 on research and development in an effort to introduce at least five new products in 2005.
Our objective is to maximize profits.	Our objective is to achieve a 10 percent return on investment during 2003, with a payback on new investments of no longer than four years.
Our objective is to better serve customers.	Our objective is to obtain customer satisfaction ratings of at least 90 percent on the 2003 annual customer satisfaction survey, and to retain at least 85 percent of our 2002 customers as repeat purchasers in 2003.
Our objective is to be the best that we can be.	Our objective is to increase market share from 30 percent to 40 percent in 2003 by increasing promotional expenditures by 14 percent.

Procter & Gamble

Explore P&G's Website and identify how it uses each of the four strategic alternatives. Does one seem to predominate? Which one? Explain.

www.pg.com

on line

strategic window
The limited period during which there is an optimum fit between the key requirements of a market and the particular competencies of a firm.

5
Identify strategic alternatives, and describe tools used to help select alternatives

market penetration
A marketing strategy that tries to increase market share among existing customers.

market development
Attracting new customers to existing products

its marketing plan. Environmental scanning helps identify market opportunities and threats and provides guidelines for the design of marketing strategies. These six environmental forces are studied most often: social, demographic, economic, technological, political and legal, and competitive. These forces are examined in detail in Chapter 3.

Strategic Windows

One technique for identifying opportunities is to seek strategic windows. A **strategic window** is that limited period during which there is an optimum fit between the key requirements of a market and the particular competencies of a firm. In 1994, Netscape recognized the need for user-friendly Web-browser software that could take advantage of the Internet's exploding popularity. By 1996, Netscape had succeeded in gaining around 90 percent of this market, mainly because it was able to introduce its product before Microsoft did.[13] Netscape knew that Microsoft's Internet Explorer would undermine its market share, but it could afford to lose some because it had started with such a large portion of the market.

Strategic Alternatives

To discover a marketing opportunity or strategic window, management must know where or how to look. One method for developing alternatives is to apply the strategic opportunity matrix (see Exhibit 2.5), which matches products with markets. Firms can explore these four options:

For many U.S. retailers, including Old Navy and Williams-Sonoma, market development means the Canadian market. What challenges does Krispy Kreme Doughnuts face?

- *Market penetration:* A firm using the **market penetration** alternative is trying to increase market share among existing customers. If Kraft General Foods were to start a major campaign for Maxwell House coffee, with aggressive advertising and cents-off coupons to existing customers, it would be following a penetration strategy. McDonald's sold the most Happy Meals in its history with a promotion that included Ty's Teeny Beanie Babies.
- *Market development:* **Market development** involves attracting new customers to existing products. When new uses are found for old products, this stimulates additional sales among existing customers; it also brings in new buyers. McDonald's has opened restaurants in Russia, China, and Italy and is eagerly expanding into Eastern Europe. Coca-Cola and Pepsi are enjoying faster growth in their new foreign markets than at home. An example of international market development is provided in this chapter's "Global Perspectives" box. In the non-profit area, colleges and universities are increasingly emphasizing continuing education and executive development—another example of a market development strategy.
- *Product development:* A **product development** strategy involves creating new products for present markets. As sales growth slumped from an average of 8 percent a year between 1990 and 1998, to 1 percent in 1999, Procter & Gamble decided that new products were the best way to boost sales in Canada. So in early 2000 it launched four new products. One was a spray to eliminate household odours, a second was a product to clean and freshen "dry clean only" clothes, a third was a moplike cleaning device for dry surfaces, and the last was a line of Oil of Olay cosmetics. P&G was forecasting new sales of $150 million for these new products in 2000.[14]

IBM

How would you characterize IBM's overall strategy based on the splash page of its Website?

www.ibm.com

on line

- *Diversification:* **Diversification** involves increasing sales by introducing new products into new markets. LTV Corporation, a steel producer, diversified into the monorail business. Sony practised a diversification strategy when it acquired Columbia Pictures; motion pictures are not a new product for the marketplace, but they are for Sony. Coca-Cola manufactures and markets water-treatment and water-conditioning equipment—a very challenging task for a soft-drink company.

product development
A strategy of creating new products for existing markets.

diversification
A strategy of increasing sales by introducing new products into new markets.

Selecting a Strategic Alternative

Which alternative should be pursued depends on the company's overall philosophy and culture. There are two basic philosophies of profit: some companies seek them immediately, while others first seek to increase their market share and *then* pursue profits. In the long run, market share and profitability are compatible goals. Many companies have long followed this credo: build market share, and profits will surely follow. Michelin, the tire producer, consistently sacrifices short-term profits to achieve market share. But attitudes may be changing. Since becoming CEO of IBM (**www.ibm.com**), Lou Gerstner has stressed profitability and stock valuation over market share, quality, and customer service. A highly desirable alternative for one firm may be completely unattractive for another.

A number of tools exist that can help managers choose from among strategic alternatives. Typically, these tools are in matrix form. Two of these matrices—portfolio, and market attractiveness/company strength—are described in detail in Chapter 20. Here we are only introducing the topic of marketing planning.

Julz Chavez is wagering that the Internet is the best strategy for her company to effectively & reach tech-savvy young girls. GetRealGirl.com is seen as both a marketing tool for her Get Real Doll and a product with the potential for deriving revenue from sponsorships and sales rather than banner advertising.

Differential Advantage

To have a successful marketing plan, an organization must seek a differential advantage over the competition. A **differential advantage** is those unique aspects of a firm that cause target consumers to patronize it rather than the competition. Sometimes a differential advantage rests solely in the firm's image. IBM has differential advantages in its reputation and in its ability to provide entire systems solutions. Differential advantages may be found in any element of the marketing mix. Superior product quality gives Hewlett-Packard a competitive edge

exhibit 2.5

Strategic Opportunity Matrix

	Present product	New product
Present market	Market penetration: McDonald's sells more Happy Meals with the Ty Beanie Baby promotion.	Product development: McDonald's introduces pizzas, soups, and sandwiches.
New market	Market development: McDonald's opens restaurants in China.	Diversification: McDonald's purchases Motown records.

global perspectives

Thumbs Down for Coke in India

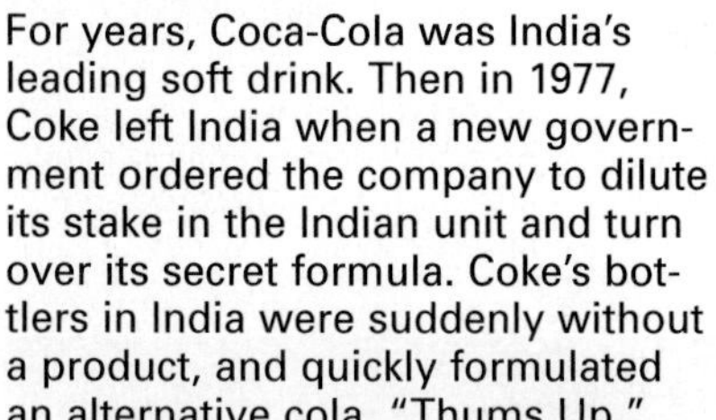

For years, Coca-Cola was India's leading soft drink. Then in 1977, Coke left India when a new government ordered the company to dilute its stake in the Indian unit and turn over its secret formula. Coke's bottlers in India were suddenly without a product, and quickly formulated an alternative cola, "Thums Up."

In 1993 the Indian government liberalized the economy and began encouraging foreign investors. At that point Coke returned. Coke decided that the easiest way to gain a commanding lead in the Indian marketplace was to purchase Thums Up, along with other soft drinks such as Limca, a cloudy lemon drink. Coke's plan was simple: take out its biggest competitor and gain access to the more than fifty bottlers that distributed Thums Up throughout India. The rest, Coke thought, would be easy—after all, India already knew Coke well, and consumers were surely ready to welcome back their old favourite.

Wrong. Much had changed in the sixteen years between 1977 and 1993. A new generation had grown up without Coca-Cola and so was not crying out for its return. In the meantime, Pepsi had beaten Coke back into the Indian market and was turning the new generation into the "Pepsi generation." Pepsi had already made quick strides in the Indian market by staffing its operations with Indians and signing up cricket stars idolized by millions of Indians as endorsers.

To make matters worse, Coke battled with its Indian bottlers, who became less cooperative. Coke also shunned the Indian press, which splashed bottlers' complaints across their pages. Furthermore, Coke did not want to push Thums Up, instead wanting to focus on "the real thing." Consumers and bottlers loyal to the popular Thums Up brand believed that Coke was trying to kill the brand, and this caused further problems.

In 1997, Donald Short became the CEO of Coca-Cola's Indian subsidiary. He saw that Thums Up was outselling Coke by a four-to-one margin in some Indian markets. Noting this, he requested that Coke's head office reprint his Bombay business cards to read CEO of Thums Up rather than CEO of the Coca-Cola Company. Short is hiring Indian professionals and pushing Coke brands heavily with tie-ins to cricket and the movies. He is also improving relations with bottlers, and hopes to double the number of sales outlets to 1 million. At the same time, he has no qualms about giving Thums Up top billing and the highest level of expenditures, because the brand remains the company's biggest seller and is the fastest-growing brand in India.

Coke would like to target a sales growth rate of 20 percent in India rather than the disappointing 5 percent actually being achieved. Pepsi still outsells the Coca-Cola brand, but Coke is ahead of Pepsi in sales if Thums Up is included. In the longer term, Coke may find it hard to push both Coca-Cola and Thums Up. In no other country does Coke heavily promote two sugar colas, but Short plans to export Thums Up out of India.[15]

Should Coke pursue the growth option of exporting Thums Up into international markets where Coke already competes?

differential advantage
One or more aspects of an organization that cause companies to target customers to patronize that firm rather than competitors.

over other makers of laser printers. Wal-Mart has an advantage over Zellers by having a very low-cost and efficient distribution system, but Zellers has better store locations. Intel has produced superior advertisements that have made the Intel Pentium computer chip a household term. Suave hair care products compete on the basis of low price.

The two basic sources of differential advantage are superior skills and superior resources. *Superior skills* are the unique capabilities that distinguish a firm's managers and workers from those of competing firms. Microsoft benefits from the vision and technical expertise of CEO Bill Gates. DuPont technicians have created a new production process that gives the company 20 percent cost savings. Sears hopes the reopened Eatons stores will prosper through superior customer service; to that end, it has carefully screened and intensely trained its new sales staff.

Superior resources are a more tangible form of differential advantage. Popular brand names such as Coke, Nike, and Calvin Klein have immeasurable value. Sony has large, high-tech manufacturing facilities that cannot be copied easily. Fort Howard Paper's differential advantage lies in its cost-saving manufacturing process. Kindred Industries of Midland, Ontario, is so efficient at making and distributing stainless steel sinks that its various brands control over 70 percent of the Canadian market.

sustainable competitive advantage
A differential advantage that cannot be copied by the competition.

Limited Express

What can you learn about Limited Express's target market from its Website? What do you think is the strategy behind the cultural information presented in the "Street Seen" section of the fashion-world girls' page?

www.express.style.com

on line

It is vital to be able to sustain a differential advantage. A **sustainable competitive advantage** is one that cannot be copied by the competition. Nike recently introduced the Nike Tour Precision golf ball. At over $60 a dozen, these balls cost three times as much as regular golf balls, yet they are flying off the shelves. The Nike ball has a patented three-layer construction with a titanium core that improves handling and increases distance. The patent offers a sustainable competitive advantage over Titleist, the #1 competitor. Adding to the Nike Tour Precision advantage is that the ball is used and endorsed by Tiger Woods, the leading player in the sport, and one of the longest hitters in the game.

Datril was introduced into the pain reliever market and was touted as being exactly like Tylenol, only cheaper. Tylenol responded by lowering its prices, thus destroying Datril's differential advantage, along with its ability to remain on the market. In this situation, low price was not a sustainable competitive advantage. Without a differential advantage, target customers don't perceive any reason to patronize an organization instead of its competitors.

Nike's patented ball with a three-layer construction offers a sustainable competitive advantage over that of its main competitor, Titleist. Can you provide some examples of products with a sustainable or differential advantage?

Describe the Marketing Strategy

Marketing strategy involves the activities of selecting and describing one or more target markets and developing and maintaining a marketing mix that will produce mutually satisfying exchanges with target markets.

Target Market Strategy

A market segment is a group of individuals or organizations that share one or more characteristics and that may therefore have similar product needs. Parents of newborn babies need products such as formula, diapers, and special foods. The target market strategy identifies the market segment or segments on which to focus. This process begins with a market opportunity analysis, or MOA. **Market opportunity analysis** is about describing and estimating the size and sales potential of market segments that are of interest to the firm; it also involves assessing key competitors in these market segments. After the firm describes the market segments, it may target one or more of them.

6

Discuss target market strategies

marketing strategy
The activities of selecting and describing one or more target markets and developing and maintaining a marketing mix that will produce mutually satisfying exchanges with target markets.

market opportunity analysis
Describing and estimating the size and sales potential of market segments that are of interest to the firm, and assessing key competitors in these market segments.

There are three general strategies for selecting target markets. A firm can appeal to the entire market with one marketing mix, or it can concentrate on one segment, or it can appeal to multiple market segments using multiple marketing mixes. The characteristics, advantages, and disadvantages of each strategic option, and the different ways of segmenting markets, are described in Chapter 6. Target markets could be smokers who are concerned about white teeth (the target of Topol toothpaste), people concerned about sugar and calories in their soft drinks (Diet Pepsi), or university students needing inexpensive about-town transportation (the Yamaha Razz scooter).

The Marketing Mix

The term **marketing mix** refers to a unique blend of product, distribution, promotion, and pricing strategies designed to produce mutually satisfying exchanges with a target market. Distribution is sometimes referred to as *place*. Thus, there are **four Ps** to the marketing mix: product, place, promotion, and price. The marketing manager can control each individual component of the marketing mix,

7

Describe the elements of the marketing mix

marketing mix
A unique blend of product, distribution, promotion, and pricing strategies designed to produce mutually satisfying exchanges with a target market.

four Ps
Product, place, promotion, and price, which together make up the marketing mix.

but the strategies for all four must be blended if optimal results are to be achieved. Any marketing mix is only as good as its weakest component. The first pump toothpastes were distributed over cosmetic counters, and they failed. Not until pump toothpastes were distributed the same way as tube toothpastes did they succeed. The best promotion and the lowest price cannot save a poor product. Similarly, an excellent product with poor distribution, pricing, or promotion will probably fail.

Successful marketing mixes are carefully designed to satisfy target markets. At first glance, McDonald's and Wendy's seem to have roughly identical marketing mixes, in that both are in the fast food hamburger business. However, McDonald's has been most successful targeting parents with young children for lunchtime meals, whereas Wendy's targets the adult crowd for lunches and dinner. McDonald's has playgrounds, Ronald McDonald the clown, and children's Happy Meals. Wendy's has salad bars, carpeted restaurants, and no playgrounds.

Variations in marketing mixes do not happen by chance. Astute marketing managers devise marketing strategies to gain advantages over competitors and best serve the needs and wants of a particular target market segment. By manipulating elements of the marketing mix, marketing managers can fine tune the customer offering and achieve competitive success.

Product Strategies Typically, the marketing mix starts with the product "P." The heart of the marketing mix is the product offering and product strategy. It is hard to design a distribution strategy, decide on a promotion campaign, or set a price without knowing the product to be marketed.

The product includes not only the physical item but also its package, warranty, after-sale service, brand name, company image, value, and many other factors. A Godiva chocolate has many product elements: the chocolate itself, a fancy gold wrapper, a customer satisfaction guarantee, and the prestige of the Godiva brand name (**www.godiva.com**). We buy things not only for what they do (benefits) but also for what they mean to us (status, quality, or reputation).

Products can be tangible goods such as computers, ideas like those offered by a consultant, or services such as medical care. Product decisions are covered in Chapters 9 and 10; services marketing is discussed in depth in Chapter 11.

A Godiva chocolate has many product elements: the chocolate itself, a fancy gold wrapper, a customer satisfaction guarantee, and a prestigious brand name.

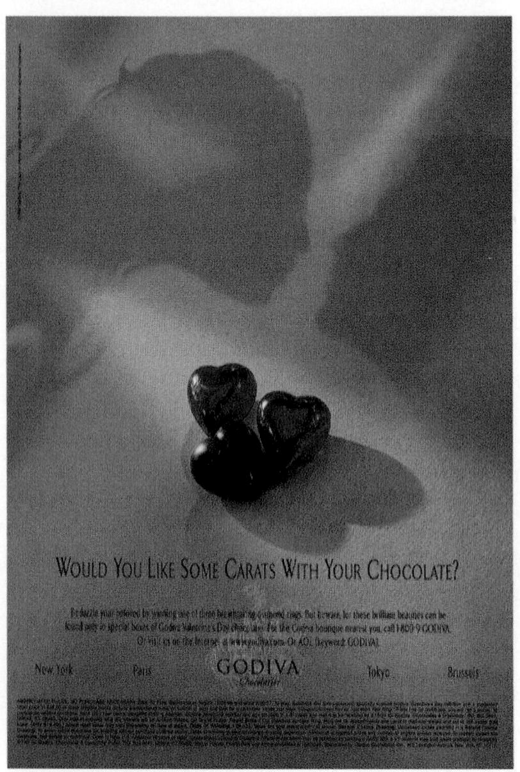

WOULD YOU LIKE SOME CARATS WITH YOUR CHOCOLATE?
New York
Paris
GODIVA
Tokyo
Brussels

Distribution (place) Strategies Distribution strategies are concerned with making products available when and where customers want them. Would you rather buy a kiwi fruit at the twenty-four-hour grocery store within walking distance or fly to New Zealand to pick your own? One part of this place "P" is physical distribution, which involves all the business activities associated with storing and transporting raw materials or finished products. The goal of distribution is to make sure products arrive in usable condition at designated places when needed. Distribution strategies are covered in Chapters 12 and 13.

Promotion Strategies Promotion includes personal selling, advertising, sales promotion, and public relations. Promotion's role in the marketing mix is to bring about mutually satisfying exchanges with target markets by informing, educating, persuading, and reminding customers of the benefits of an organization or a product. A good promotion strategy—for example, using the Dilbert character in a national promotion strategy for Office Depot—can dramatically increase sales. However, good promotion strategies do not guarantee success. Despite a massive promotional campaign, the movie *Godzilla* had disappointing box-office returns. Each element of the promotion "P" is coordinated and managed with the others to create a promotional blend or mix. These integrated marketing communications activities are described in Chapters 16 and 17.

Pricing Strategies Price is what a buyer must give up to obtain a product. It is often the most flexible of the four marketing mix elements—the quickest element to change. Marketers can raise or lower prices more often and more easily than they can change other marketing mix variables. Price is an important competitive weapon and very important to the organization, because price multiplied by the number of units sold equals total revenue for the firm. Pricing decisions are covered in Chapter 15.

Following Up the Marketing Plan

8

Explain why implementation, evaluation, and control of the marketing plan are necessary

Implementation

Implementation is the process that turns marketing plans into action assignments and ensures that these assignments are executed in a way that accomplishes the plans' objectives. Implementation activities may involve detailed job assignments, activity descriptions, timelines, budgets, and plenty of communication. Although implementation is essentially "doing what you said you were going to do," many organizations repeatedly experience failures in strategy implementation. Brilliant marketing plans are doomed to fail if they are not properly implemented.

implementation
The process that turns marketing plans into action assignments and ensures that these assignments are executed in a way that accomplishes the plans' objectives.

Evaluation and Control

After a marketing plan is implemented, it should be evaluated. **Evaluation** entails gauging the extent to which marketing objectives have been achieved during the specified time period. There are four common reasons why marketing managers fail to achieve their goals: unrealistic marketing objectives, inappropriate marketing strategies, poor implementation, and changes in the environment after the objective was specified and the strategy was implemented.

evaluation
Gauging the extent to which the marketing objectives have been achieved during the specified period.

Once a plan is chosen and implemented, its effectiveness must be monitored. **Control** provides the mechanisms for evaluating marketing results in light of the plan's goals and for correcting actions that do not help the organization reach those goals within budget guidelines.

control
Provides the mechanisms for evaluating marketing results in light of the plan's goals and for correcting actions that do not help the organization reach those goals within budget guidelines.

Perhaps the broadest control device available to marketing managers is the marketing audit. A **marketing audit** is a thorough, systematic, periodic evaluation of the goals, strategies, structure, and performance of the marketing organization. A marketing audit helps management allocate marketing resources efficiently. The details of a marketing audit will be presented in Chapter 20.

marketing audit
A thorough, systematic, periodic evaluation of the goals, strategies, structure, and performance of the marketing organization.

The main purpose of the marketing audit is to develop a full profile of the organization's marketing effort and to provide a basis for developing and revising the marketing plan. That said, it is also an excellent way to improve communications and raise the level of marketing consciousness within the organization. Furthermore, it is a useful vehicle for selling the philosophy and techniques of strategic marketing to other members of the organization.

exhibit 2.6 Marketing Plan Outline

I. Business Mission

- What is the mission of the firm? What business is it in? How well is its mission understood throughout the organization? Five years from now, what business does it wish to be in?
- Does the firm define its business in terms of the benefits its customers want rather than in terms of goods and services?

II. Objectives

- Is the firm's mission statement able to be translated into operational terms regarding the firm's objectives?
- What are the stated objectives of the organization? Are they formally written down? Do they lead logically to clearly stated marketing objectives? Are objectives based on sales, profits, or customers?
- Are the organization's marketing objectives stated in hierarchical order? Are they specific so that progress toward achievement can be measured? Are the objectives reasonable in light of the organization's resources? Are the objectives ambiguous? Do the objectives specify a time frame?
- Is the firm's main goal to maximize customer satisfaction or to get as many customers as possible?

III. Situation Analysis (SWOT Analysis)

- Is there a strategic window that must be taken into account?
- Have one or more differential advantages been identified in the SWOT analysis?
- Are these advantages sustainable against the competition?

A. Internal Strengths and Weaknesses

- What is the history of the firm, including sales, profits, and organizational philosophies?
- What is the nature of the firm and its current situation?
- What resources does the firm have (financial, human, time, experience, assets, skills)?
- What policies inhibit the achievement of the firm's objectives with respect to organization, resource allocation, operations, hiring, training, and so on?

B. External Opportunities and Threats

- Social: What major social and lifestyle trends will have an impact on the firm? What action has the firm been taking in response to these trends?
- Demographic: What impact will forecasted trends in the size, age, profile, and distribution of population have on the firm? How will the changing nature of the family, the increase in the proportion of women in the workforce, and changes in the ethnic composition of the population affect the firm? What action has the firm taken in response to these developments and trends? Has the firm re-evaluated its traditional products and expanded the range of specialized offerings to respond to these changes?
- Economic: What major trends in taxation and income sources will have an impact on the firm? What action has the firm taken in response to these trends?
- Political, Legal, and Financial: What laws are now being proposed at international, federal, provincial, and local levels that could affect marketing strategy and tactics? What recent changes in regulations and court decisions affect the firm? What political changes at each government level are taking place? What action has the firm taken in response to these legal and political changes?
- Competition: Which organizations are competing with the firm directly by offering a similar product? Which organizations are competing with the firm indirectly by securing its prime prospects' time, money, energy, or commitment? What new competitive trends seem likely to emerge? How effective is the competition? What benefits do competitors offer that the firm does not? Is it appropriate for the firm to compete?
- Technological: What major technological changes are occurring that affect the firm?
- Ecological: What is the outlook for the cost and availability of natural resources and energy needed by the firm? Are the firm's products, services, and operations environmentally friendly?

IV. Marketing Strategy

A. Target Market Strategy

- Are the members of each market homogeneous or heterogeneous with respect to geographic, sociodemographic, and behavioural characteristics?
- What are the size, growth rate, and national and regional trends in each of the organization's market segments?
- Is the size of each market segment sufficiently large or important to warrant a unique marketing mix?
- Are market segments measurable and accessible to distribution and communication efforts?
- Which are the high- or low-opportunity segments?
- What are the evolving needs and satisfactions being sought by target markets?
- What benefits does the organization offer to each segment? How do these benefits compare with benefits offered by competitors?
- Is the firm positioning itself with a unique product? Is the product needed?
- How much of the firm's business is repeat versus new business? What percentage of the public can be classified as nonusers, light users, or heavy users?
- How do current target markets rate the firm and its competitors with respect to reputation, quality, and price? What is the firm's image with the specific market segments it seeks to serve?
- Does the firm try to direct its products only to specific groups of people or to everybody?
- Who buys the firm's products? How does a potential customer find out about the organization? When and how does a person become a customer?

(continued...)

- What are the major objections given by potential customers as to why they do not buy the firm's products?
- How do customers find out about and decide to purchase the product? When and where?
- Should the firm seek to expand, contract, or change the emphasis of its selected target markets? If so, in which target markets, and how vigorously?
- Could the firm more usefully withdraw from some areas in which there are alternative suppliers and use its resources to serve new, unserved customer groups?
- What publics other than target markets (financial, media, government, citizen, local, general, and internal) represent opportunities or problems for the firm?

B. Marketing Mix

- Does the firm seek to achieve its goal chiefly though coordinated use of marketing activities (product, distribution, promotion, and pricing) or only though intensive promotion?
- Are the objectives and roles of each element of the marketing mix clearly specified?

1. Product

- What are the major product/service offerings of the firm? Do they complement one another, or is there unnecessary duplication?
- What are the features and benefits of each product offering?
- Where is the firm and each major product in its life cycle?
- What are the pressures among various target markets to increase or decrease the range and quality of products?
- What are the major weaknesses in each product area? What are the major complaints? What goes wrong most often?
- Is the product name easy to pronounce? Spell? Recall? Is it descriptive, and does it communicate the benefits the product offers? Does the name distinguish the firm or product from all others?
- What warranties are offered with the product? Are there other ways to guarantee customer satisfaction?
- Does the product offer good customer value?
- How is customer service handled? How is service quality assessed?

2. Place/Distribution

- Should the firm try to deliver its offerings directly to customers, or can it better deliver selected offerings by involving other organizations? What channel(s) should be used in distributing product offerings?
- What physical distribution facilities should be used? Where should they be located? What should be their major characteristics?
- Are members of the target market willing and able to travel some distance to buy the product?
- How good is access to facilities? Can access be improved? Which facilities need priority attention in these areas?
- How are facility locations chosen? Is the site accessible to the target markets? Is it visible to the target markets?
- What is the location and atmosphere of retail establishments? Do these retailers satisfy customers?
- When are products made available to users (season of year, day of week, time of day)? Are these times most appropriate?

3. Promotion

- How does a typical customer find out about the firm's products?
- Does the message the firm delivers gain the attention of the intended target audience? Does it address the wants and needs of the target market, and does it suggest benefits or a means for satisfying these wants? Is the message appropriately positioned?
- Does the promotion effort effectively inform, persuade, educate, and remind customers about the firm's products?
- Does the firm establish budgets and measure effectiveness of promotional efforts?

a. Advertising

- Which media are currently being used? Has the firm chosen the type of media that will best reach its target markets?
- Are the types of media used the most cost-effective, and do they contribute positively to the firm's image?
- Are the dates and times the ads will appear the most appropriate? Has the firm prepared several versions of its advertisements?
- Does the organization use an outside advertising agency? What functions does the ad agency perform for the organization?
- What system is used to handle consumer inquiries resulting from advertising and promotions? What follow-up is done?

b. Public Relations

- Is there a well-conceived public relations and publicity program? Does the program include the ability to respond to bad publicity?
- How is public relations normally handled by the firm? By whom? Have those responsible nurtured working relationships with media outlets?
- Is the firm using all available public relations avenues? Is an effort made to understand each of the publicity outlets' needs and to provide each with story types that will appeal to its audience in readily usable forms?
- What does the annual report say about the firm and its products? Who is being effectively reached by this vehicle? Does the benefit of publication justify the cost?

(continued...)

c. Personal Selling
- How much of a typical salesperson's time is spent soliciting new customers as compared to serving existing customers?
- How is it determined which prospect will be called on, and by whom? How is the frequency of contacts determined?
- How is the sales force compensated? Are there incentives for encouraging more business?
- How is the sales force organized and managed?
- Has the sales force prepared an approach tailored to each prospect?
- Has the firm matched sales personnel with the target market characteristics?
- Is there appropriate follow-up to the initial personal selling effort? Are customers made to feel appreciated?
- Can database or direct marketing be used to replace or supplement the sales force?

d. Sales Promotion
- What is the specific purpose of each sales promotion activity? Why is it offered? What does it try to achieve?
- What categories of sales promotion are being used? Is sales promotion directed to the trade, the final consumer, or both?
- Is the effort directed at all the firm's key publics or restricted to only potential customers?

4. Price
- What levels of pricing and specific prices should be used?
- What mechanisms does the firm have to ensure that the prices charged are acceptable to customers?
- How price sensitive are customers?
- If a price change is put into effect, how will the number of customers change? Will total revenue increase or decrease?
- Which method is used for establishing a price: going rate, demand-oriented, or cost-based?
- What discounts are offered, and with what rationale?
- Has the firm considered the psychological dimensions of price?
- Have price increases kept pace with cost increases, inflation, or competitive levels?
- How are price promotions used?
- Do interested prospects have opportunities to sample products at an introductory price?
- What methods of payment are accepted? Is it in the firm's best interest to use these various payment methods?

V. Implementation, Evaluation, and Control
- Is the marketing organization structured appropriately to implement the marketing plan?
- What specific activities must take place? Who is responsible for these activities?
- What is the implementation timetable?
- What other marketing research is necessary?
- What will the financial impact be of this plan on a one-year projected income statement? How does projected income compare with expected revenue if the plan is not implemented?
- What are the performance standards?
- What monitoring procedures (audits) will take place, and when?
- Does it seem as if the firm is trying to do too much or not enough?
- Are the core marketing strategies for achieving objectives sound? Are the objectives being met, and are the objectives appropriate?
- Are enough resources (or too many resources) budgeted to accomplish the marketing objectives?

LOOKING BACK

Look back at the story about WestJet Airlines's birth. You can now see that WestJet had to embark on a great deal of strategic marketing planning to prepare the takeoff of a new airline. Also, you can see that planning is a continuous process; WestJet may need to modify its marketing strategies as it continues to grow and move into new markets. In fact, WestJet's share price has slipped, even though the airline continues to turn a profit. In addition, other startup airlines are beginning to adopt some of WestJet's strategies.

Note that WestJet's marketing plan copied that of SouthWest Airlines, one of the most continuously profitable airlines in the American marketplace. Other startup airlines have tried to copy SouthWest but have failed. What is different about WestJet? Could it be its dedication to employee empowerment from the top of the organization down?

You should now be able to identify many elements of WestJet's marketing plan: its likely mission statement, its measurable marketing objective, components of its situation analysis, and so on. Also, you should be able to identify its target market and describe its basic marketing mix elements. As well, the vignette highlights aspects of implementation, evaluation, and control.

Summary

1 Understand the importance of strategic marketing, and know a basic outline for a marketing plan. Strategic marketing planning is the basis for all marketing strategies and decisions. The marketing plan is a written document that acts as a guidebook of marketing activities for the marketing manager. By specifying objectives and defining the actions required to attain them, a marketing plan provides the basis on which actual and expected performance can be compared.

Although there is no set formula for a marketing plan, and no single correct outline, basic factors that should be covered include stating the business mission, setting objectives, performing a situation analysis of internal and external environmental forces, selecting target market(s), delineating a marketing mix (product, place, promotion, and price), and establishing ways to implement, evaluate, and control the plan.

2 Develop an appropriate business mission statement. The mission statement is based on a careful analysis of benefits sought by present and potential customers and analysis of existing and anticipated environmental conditions. The firm's long-term vision, embodied in its mission statement, establishes boundaries for all later decisions, objectives, and strategies. A mission statement should focus on the market or markets the organization is attempting to serve rather than on the good or service offered.

3 Describe the criteria for stating good marketing objectives. Objectives should be realistic, measurable, and time specific. Objectives must also be consistent with the priorities of the organization.

4 Explain the components of a situation analysis. In the situation (or SWOT) analysis, the firm should identify its internal strengths (S) and weaknesses (W), and also examine external opportunities (O) and threats (T). When examining external opportunities and threats, marketing managers must analyze aspects of the marketing environment in a process called environmental scanning. The six most often studied macroenvironmental forces are social, demographic, economic, technological, political and legal, and competitive. During the situation analysis, the marketer should try to identify any strategic windows. Also, it is crucial that the marketer identify a differential advantage and establish that it is a sustainable competitive advantage.

5 Identify strategic alternatives, and describe tools used to help select alternatives. The strategic opportunity matrix can be used to help management develop strategic alternatives. The four options are market penetration, product development, market development, and diversification.

6 Discuss target market strategies. The target market strategy identifies which market segment or segments to focus on. This process begins with a market opportunity analysis, or MOA, which describes and estimates the size and sales potential of market segments that are of interest to the firm. In addition, an assessment of key competitors in these market segments is performed. After the market segments are described, one or more may be targeted by the firm. There are three strategies for selecting target markets: appealing to the entire market with one marketing mix, concentrating on one segment, or appealing to multiple market segments using multiple marketing mixes.

7 Describe the elements of the marketing mix. The marketing mix (or four Ps) is a blend of product, distribution (place), promotion, and pricing strategies designed to produce mutually satisfying exchanges with a target market. The starting point of the marketing mix is the product offering. Products can be tangible goods, ideas, or services. Distribution strategies are concerned with making

Do You Know These Terms?

control 37
differential advantage 34
diversification 33
environmental scanning 31
evaluation 37
four Ps 36
implementation 37
market development 32
market opportunity analysis 35
market penetration 32
marketing audit 37
marketing mix 36
marketing myopia 29
marketing objective 30
marketing plan 25
marketing planning 25
marketing strategy 35
mission statement 29
planning 25
product development 33
strategic planning 24
strategic window 32
sustainable competitive advantage 34
SWOT analysis 31

products available when and where customers want them. Promotion includes personal selling, advertising, sales promotion, and public relations. Price is what a buyer must give up to obtain a product and is often the easiest to change of the four marketing mix elements.

8 **Explain why implementation, evaluation, and control of the marketing plan are necessary.** Before a marketing plan can work, it must be implemented; that is, people must perform the actions in the plan. The plan should also be evaluated to see if it has achieved its objectives. On its own, poor implementation can cause a plan to fail. Control provides the mechanisms for evaluating marketing results in light of the plan's goals and for correcting actions that do not help the organization reach those goals within budget guidelines.

Discussion and Writing Questions

1. Your cousins want to start their own business, and they are in a hurry. They have decided not to write a marketing plan because they have already gotten funding from your uncle and do not need a formal proposal and because writing such a document would take too long. Explain why it is important for them to write a plan anyway.
2. How can a new company best define its business mission statement? Can you find examples of good and bad mission statements on the Internet? How could you improve the poor mission statements?
3. The new marketing manager has stated that the marketing objective of the firm is to do the best job of satisfying the needs and wants of the customer. Explain that although this objective is admirable, it does not meet the criteria for good objectives. What are these criteria? What is a specific example of a better objective?
4. Break into small groups and discuss examples (at least two per person) of the last few products you have purchased. What were the specific strategies used to achieve a differential advantage? Is that differential advantage sustainable against the competition?
5. Perform a mini–situation analysis by stating one strength, one weakness, one opportunity, and one threat to your choice of consumer products companies (Question 4). What are the strategic growth options available for this company, based on your evaluation?
6. You are given the task of deciding the marketing strategy for a transportation service. How do the elements of the marketing mix change when the target market is corporate international business travellers? When it is low-income workers without personal transportation? When it is companies with urgent documents or perishable materials to get to customers?
7. Create a marketing plan to increase enrolment in your school. Write down each step and describe the controls on the plan's implementation.

Application for Small Business

Yucca, also known as cassava or manioc, is a plant with a starchy root that is a staple for farmers in the Amazon and other tropical areas. The processed root is also widely used as animal feed. In its raw form, yucca is poisonous (a natural source of cyanide).[16] Despite its bland taste and toxic potential, Gerald Ritthaler is determined to turn the lowly yucca into an upscale "natural" snack in the form of the beloved chip. He has bought land in Venezuela, purchased an abandoned government yucca flour mill, and imported chip-making equipment. His new company, Ritz Foods, packages the yucca chips in a glossy-black 200 gram bag that retails for $3.79. Ritthaler has already obtained a vending machine contract and is now trying to get into stores via food distributors. The unusual chips have received an enthusiastic response from one small chain of specialty food stores, where they are selling well.[17] However, there's already competition. Dana Alexander, Inc., is producing a fancy, multicolour root mix called Terra Chips, which is 10 percent yucca (and also happens to come in glossy black bags).[18] Also, Frito-Lay is marketing fat-free chips and toying with the idea of "alternative roots." Ritthaler is undeterred, citing the immense size of the potato chip market.

Questions

1. What is an appropriate mission statement for Ritz Foods?
2. What is a specific objective you would suggest it achieve?
3. What are the strengths, weaknesses, opportunities, and threats in this situation?
4. What strategic growth options can Ritz Foods pursue?
5. What should the target market be? Explain.
6. What are the elements of your marketing mix? Describe a brief strategy for each of the four Ps.

VIDEO CASE

Comedian Mark Lundholm: Marketing Recovery

Been there. Done that. That's what gives stand-up comic Mark Lundholm the edge. His comic routines tell about his experience as an alcoholic, drug addict, drug dealer, tax evader, cheque forger, and prison inmate. He makes audiences laugh and cry with his personal memories about living in a cardboard box and pointing a loaded gun to his mouth to commit suicide. As for his days of living on the streets, Lundholm says, "There's a pecking order on the street that is unbelievable. How big you are, how long you've been there, and who you know—those things are the important things. Who you know is more important than who you are on the street."

So why would anybody pay to hear what Lundholm calls "comedy for the chemically challenged"? Addiction to drugs or alcohol is so widespread today that despite positive efforts like the Just Say No program, both types of abuse are rising. When Lundholm performs at prisons, treatment centres, and recovery meetings such as Alcoholics Anonymous (AA), audience members can truly identify with Lundholm's stories, and so can their friends and families. The population affected by substance abuse cuts across race, age, gender, and social and economic levels.

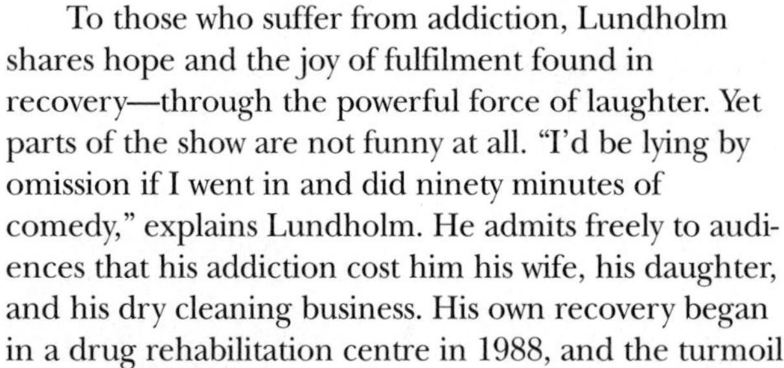

To those who suffer from addiction, Lundholm shares hope and the joy of fulfilment found in recovery—through the powerful force of laughter. Yet parts of the show are not funny at all. "I'd be lying by omission if I went in and did ninety minutes of comedy," explains Lundholm. He admits freely to audiences that his addiction cost him his wife, his daughter, and his dry cleaning business. His own recovery began in a drug rehabilitation centre in 1988, and the turmoil of his own life serves as material for his three comic shows: "An Evening of 12-Step Humour," "The Insanity Remains," and "I'm Not Judgin', I'm Just Sayin'." Whenever his "close to the bone originality" hits too close to home, Lundholm replies, "I'm not judging, I'm just saying." This catch phrase drew so many laughs that it became the name of a show.

But people in recovery are not the only ones who laugh at Lundholm's routines. He plays the comedy club circuit as well, and appeals to "normies," as he calls nonalcoholics. Although the routines revolve around the 12-step program of AA, they embrace enough of life's highs and lows that even "normies" are entertained. Every joke, every story is punctuated with animation—hands waving, feet flying, face contorted into a hundred deviations. Lundholm hits on the trials and tribulations of growing up with parents of the 1950s: "Mark, back away from that TV, you're going to ruin your eyes." Jokes aim at all types of relationships, roles, and human peculiarities.

Now, Lundholm performs at established comedy clubs like Comedy Central, Zanies, and Funny-Bone, but he began his career by opening shows for the well-known Russian comic, Yakov Smirnoff. Lundholm's booking agent and personal manager, Jimmy Goings, sells the one-man show directly to comedy venues and also provides entertainment consulting and production services to organizations conducting events. A Website, videocassettes, tapes, T-shirts, and a book also promote Lundholm as a comedian.

In general, an entertainer's fees grow as name recognition grows, and Lundholm is no exception. As he continues to travel and play the nightclub circuit, higher fees can be negotiated, but he still donates his time to reach people in recovery. Performing forty-six weeks a year nationally and internationally, Lundholm usually includes recovery venues such as the Betty Ford Center, hospitals, halfway houses, and prisons. When performing at a comedy club, he will speak at no charge at a high school in the area about the dangers of drug abuse. Lundholm takes his timely message to teenagers who can really benefit from it.

And this volunteer work has paid off. Solid public relations and much good will have come from this commitment to recovery. The press regularly covers both his nightclub act and his performances at rehabilitation centres and schools. Good public relations and good material have helped Lundholm build his reputation as a comedian and distinguish himself from the multitude of very funny stand-up comics in the entertainment world. That's how Mark Lundholm markets recovery.

Questions

1. What is Lundholm's mission?
2. What is Lundholm's differential advantage?
3. Who is the target market segment? What is the benefit received?
4. Describe Lundholm's marketing mix.

CHAPTER

3

LEARNING OBJECTIVES

After studying this chapter, you should be able to

1 Discuss the external environment of marketing, and explain how it affects a firm

2 Describe the social factors that affect marketing

3 Explain the importance to marketing managers of current demographic trends

4 Explain the importance to marketing managers of multiculturalism and growing ethnic markets

5 Identify consumer and marketer reactions to the state of the economy

6 Identify the impact of technology on a firm

7 Discuss the political and legal environment of marketing

8 Explain the basics of foreign and domestic competition

9 Discuss corporate social responsibility

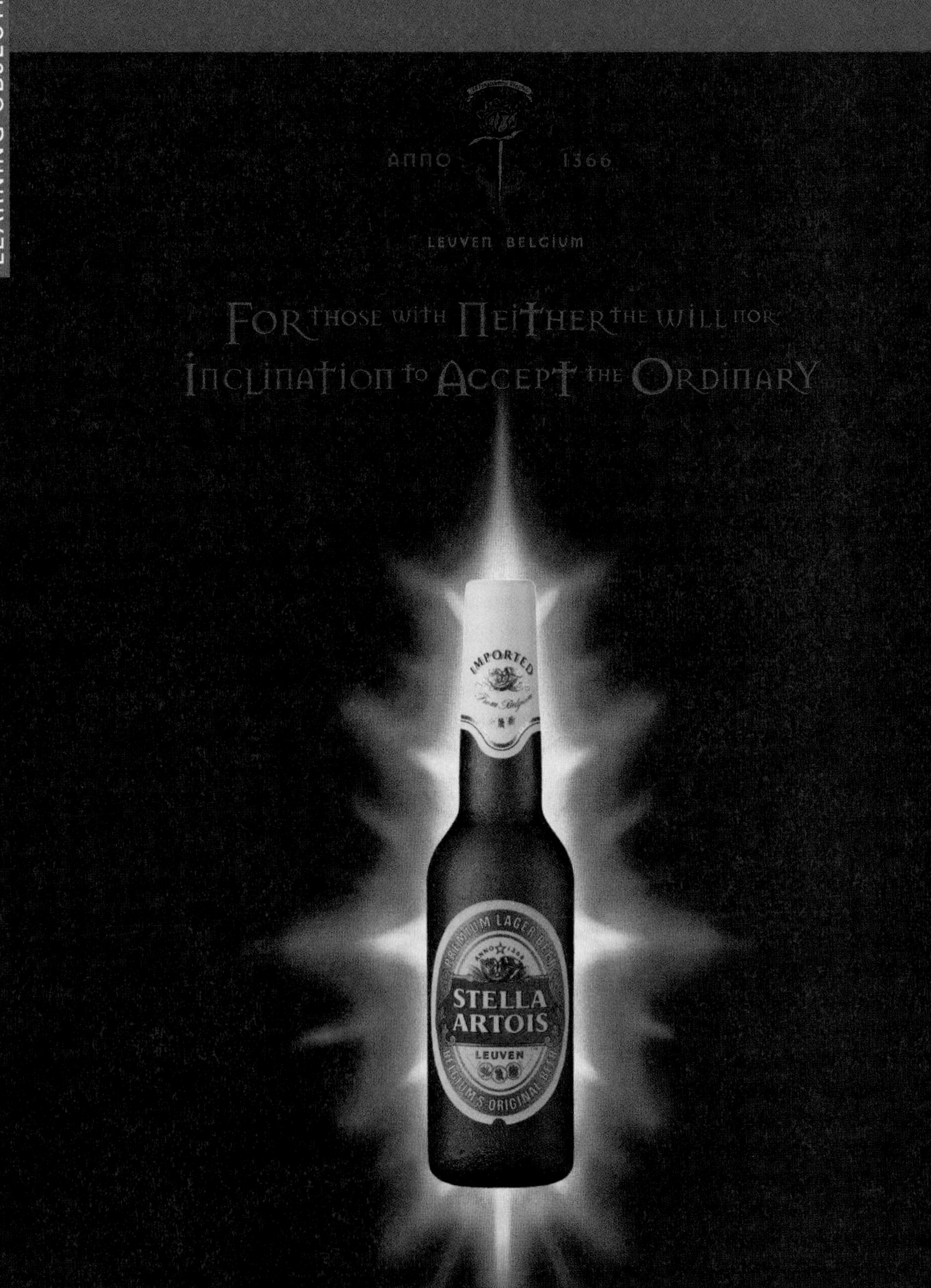

THE MARKETING ENVIRONMENT

When Fred Jaques took over as president of Labatt Brewing Co., he introduced the new slogan of its parent company, Interbrew, the Belgium-based, second-largest brewing group in the world: "World's local brewer."[1]

Labatt Blue is still the company's biggest-selling brand. However, the strongest growth in the Canadian beer market—10 percent a year—is in imported beers, which are sold at premium prices. So Jaques is focusing some of Labatt's marketing efforts on this growing segment. Sales of one of Labatt's imports, Stella Artois from Belgium, have grown by over 500 percent in the past three years. Other Labatt total import volume, which includes brands such as Boddingtons, Leffe, and Belle-Vue Kriek have been growing 33 percent a year compared to 10 percent for all imports. Furthermore, Jaques has been pushing his brewery's products in the United States, where Labatt is an import. Labatt sales have been growing 20 percent a year in the United States, even though the total beer market there actually declined by 1 percent in 2000.[2]

Geoffrey Wilson, a food industry consultant with Toronto's Geoffrey Wilson & Associates, believes that given the flat market for beer, concentrating on a small number of premium beers is a good marketing strategy. "People are willing to pay a premium price for a premium product," he says.[3]

Instead of spending heavily on extensive advertising, Jaques is trying to build import sales steadily through a "soft launch." Highly selective marketing is being used because imported beers appeal to a very selective market. Labatt is promoting imported beers through upscale bars by talking with owners and bartenders. The trick, he says, is to use "point-of-sale knowledge. The key is communicating history, tradition and pride, quality and high standards, authenticity."[4]

For many of the imports the target group is nineteen to thirty-five year olds. This is only one of many segments in the Canadian marketplace. Young people with money to spend are looking for products that create an image.

The changing marketplace poses both threats and opportunities for companies. Age is only one of a number of demographic factors in the external environment that can affect a firm. How does the external environment affect a company's marketing mix? What other uncontrollable factors in the external environment can affect companies like Labatt?

Labatt Brewing Co.

How does Labatt use its Website to build brand identity? What clues do you see on the site that Labatt appeals to a number of select target markets? Take the Labatt tour on its Website. What can you learn on this tour about Labatt products and target markets?

www.Labatt.com

WWW on line

The External Marketing Environment

1

Discuss the external environment of marketing, and explain how it affects a firm

target market
A defined group most likely to buy a firm's product.

As you learned in Chapters 1 and 2, managers create a marketing mix by uniquely combining product, distribution, promotion, and price strategies. The marketing mix, which is under the firm's control, is designed to appeal to a specific group of potential buyers. A **target market** is a defined group that managers feel is most likely to buy the firm's product.

Over time, managers must alter the marketing mix because of changes in the environment in which consumers live, work, and make purchasing decisions. Also, as markets mature, some new consumers become part of the target market and others drop out. Those who remain may develop different tastes, needs, incomes, lifestyles, and buying habits than the original target consumers.

Managers can control the marketing mix, but they cannot control the elements in the external environment that are constantly molding and reshaping the target market. Exhibit 3.1 indicates the controllable and uncontrollable variables that affect the target market, whether that market consists of consumers or business purchasers. The uncontrollable elements are constantly evolving and generating changes in the target market. In contrast, managers have the power to shape and reshape the marketing mix, depicted on the left side of the exhibit, to influence the target market.

Understanding the External Environment

Unless marketing managers understand the external environment, the firm will not be able to plan intelligently for the future. So many organizations assemble a team of specialists to continuously collect and evaluate environmental information—a process known as environmental scanning. The point of gathering environmental data is to identify future market opportunities and threats.

exhibit 3.1

Effect of Uncontrollable Factors in the External Environment on the Marketing Mix

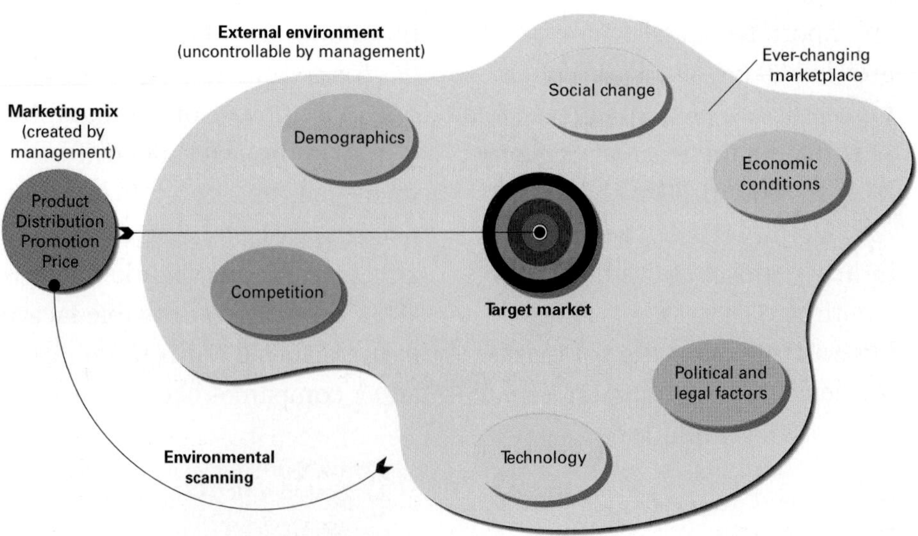

For example, as technology continues to blur the lines between personal computers, television, and CD players, companies like Sony may find themselves competing against companies like Hewlett-Packard. Research shows that children would like to find more games bundled with computer software, whereas adults are more likely to want various word-processing and business-related software. Is this information an opportunity or a threat to HP's marketing managers?

Environmental Management

No one business is large or powerful enough to create major change in the external environment. This is why marketing managers are fundamentally adapters rather than agents of change. Despite the huge size of General Motors and Ford, these companies have not been able to stop the Japanese from capturing a bigger and bigger share of the Canadian automobile market. In the external environment, competition is not something that can be controlled.

Firms are not always completely at the mercy of the external environment. Sometimes a firm can influence external events. Extensive lobbying by Japanese and European auto assemblers ended the thirty-year-old Auto Pact. The Auto Pact allowed its signatories (i.e., the big American car makers) to import cars into Canada duty free as long as they built one car in Canada for each car they imported. Companies that weren't part of the Auto Pact—which included Japanese and European car makers—had to pay a 6.1 percent import duty on all cars they brought into Canada from outside North America. Japanese and European auto assemblers lobbied the Canadian government and the World Trade Organization to repeal the Auto Pact, which they eventually did, in February 2001. A company that attempts to shape its external environment is engaging in **environmental management**.

environmental management
When a company implements strategies that attempt to shape the external environment within which it operates.

The factors in the external environment that are important to marketing managers can be classified as follows: social, demographic, economic, technological, political and legal, and competitive.

Social Factors

2
Describe the social factors that affect marketing

Social change is perhaps the most difficult external variable for marketing managers to forecast, influence, or integrate into marketing plans. Social factors include our attitudes, values, and lifestyles. Social factors influence the products people buy, the prices they will pay for products, the effectiveness of specific promotions, and how, where, and when people expect to purchase products.

Marketing-Oriented Values of Today

Changes are taking place in Canadian culture. These involve shifts in values, views, and ways of life. More and more consumers, often referred to as *cultural creatives*, are interested in new kinds of products and services. Cultural creatives are good at synthesizing information into a "big picture." Their style is to scan an information source efficiently, seize on something they are interested in, and explore that topic in depth.

Another view is that of traditionalism. Traditionalism often takes the form of country folks rebelling against big-city lifestyles. Traditionalists believe in the "good old days"—that is, in the nostalgic image of small towns and strong churches.

Today's shoppers are also environmentalists. In fact, most of today's consumers regard themselves as environmentalists. According to many published studies, most consumers are willing to pay more for products packaged with recyclable or biodegradable materials. Many marketers predict that it will soon be very difficult to sell a product that isn't environmentally friendly.

As we move beyond 2000, fewer consumers are saying that expensive cars, designer clothes, pleasure trips, and "gold" credit cards are necessary to a happy life. Consumers today are placing greater value on nonmaterial accomplishments, such as having control of their lives and being able to take a day off when they want.[5] Dual-career families have a **poverty of time**, with few hours to do anything but work and commute to work, handle family situations, do housework, shop, sleep, and eat.

poverty of time
Lack of time to do anything but work, commute to work, handle family situations, do housework, shop, sleep, and eat.

There is a sense that the daily slack of earlier eras—the weekday golf foursome, the bridge games and vegetable gardens, the long lunches, the chats across the fence, and those moments of pure, uncontrollable laughter—is disappearing. Work is now consuming a huge portion of our time. Also, in the age of the "virtual office" (working at home with a computer and modem), many professionals are finding it more and more difficult to separate work from leisure, or measure the time they spend on either.

The Growth of Component Lifestyles

Many of today's consumers are piecing together component lifestyles. A lifestyle is a mode of living; it is the way people decide to live their lives. **Component lifestyles** involve individuals choosing products and services that do not conform to traditional lifestyles but rather meet their own diverse needs and interests.

component lifestyles
When individuals choose goods and services that do not conform to traditional lifestyles but rather meet their own diverse needs and interests.

In the past, a person's profession—for instance, banker—defined his or her lifestyle. Today a person can be a banker and also a gourmet, fitness enthusiast, dedicated single parent, and Internet guru. Each of these lifestyles is associated with different goods and services and represents a target audience. For the gourmet, marketers offer cooking utensils, wines, and exotic foods through magazines such as *Bon Appetit* and *Gourmet.* The fitness enthusiast buys Adidas equipment and special jogging outfits and reads *Runner* magazine. Component lifestyles increase the complexity of consumers' buying habits. The banker may own a BMW but change the oil herself. He may buy fast food for lunch but French wine for dinner. She may own sophisticated camera equipment and a low-priced home stereo. He may shop for socks at Zellers or Wal-Mart and buy his suits at Harry Rosen's.

All of this means that blending products for a single target market can sometimes result in failure. To the bright young founders of WebTV, it looked like a home run: hook televisions up to the Internet and tap into the vast market of couch potatoes curious about this new phenomenon called the World Wide Web. After burning through an estimated $50 million to advertise the new service, WebTV and its partners Sony and Philips Electronics counted a disappointing number of subscribers.

The problem, WebTV now acknowledges, was the wrong marketing message. Couch potatoes want to be better entertained; computer users are content to explore the Internet using small PC screens. A revamped campaign now emphasizes entertainment over education.[6]

The Changing Role of Families and Working Women

Component lifestyles have evolved because consumers can choose from a growing number of goods and services, and also because most have the money to exercise more options. Rising purchasing power is the result of the increasing number of dual-income families. Over half of all women between eighteen and sixty-five are now in the workforce, and this proportion will continue to grow. Probably, the phenomenon of working women has affected marketing more than any other social change.

As women's earnings grow, so does their expertise, experience, and authority. Women of working age are not the same group that businesses targeted thirty years ago. They expect different things in life—from their jobs, from their spouses, and from the products and services they buy.

Current Demographic Data

Detailed demographic data on the Canadian population are available from Statistics Canada. StatsCan's data are based on the most recent census and provide population projections through 2026. Information on age, education, ethic origin, language, and many other variables is available by province and for Canada's main cities. At last count, British Columbia's population of 3,689,755 included 76,430 Aboriginal people. What other population demographics can you find on Statistics Canada's Website?

www.statcan.ca

WWW on line

The automotive industry is beginning to realize how much power women have in vehicle purchase decisions. Women are the principal buyers for over 40 percent of all cars and trucks sold. Saturn's advertising tries not only to attract women as customers, but also to woo them into the business. In an industry in which very few women work in sales, 16 percent of Saturn's sales staff are women (the industry average is 7 percent). Not coincidentally, Saturn claims that women buy 64 percent of its cars.[7]

More working women has meant more dual-career families. Dual-career families tend to have higher household incomes; they also tend to have less time for family activities (poverty of time). Within these families, purchasing roles are changing (i.e., more men are buying the groceries, more women are getting the lawnmower serviced), and so are purchasing patterns. This is creating new opportunities for marketers. For example, small businesses that cater to dual-career households are opening every day, and offering specialized goods and services. Ice cream and yogurt parlours, cafés, and sports footwear shops are proliferating. With more women than ever working full time, there is a special demand for new household services, such as those offered by on-line retailer grocerygateway.com.

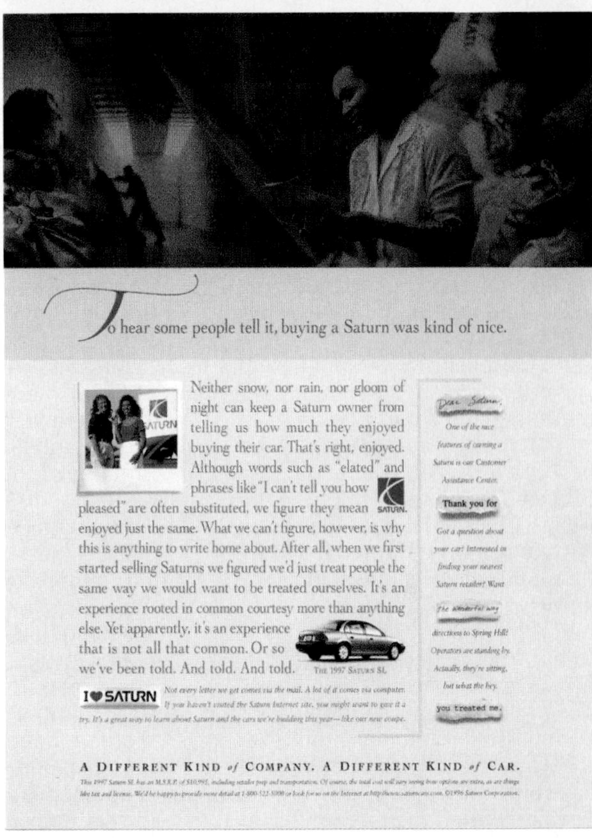

Saturn's advertising is designed to attract women not only as buyers but also as sales employees. Women comprise 16 percent of Saturn's sales staff, and 64 percent of Saturn's cars are purchased by women.

Demographic Factors

Demographic factors—another uncontrollable variable in the external environment—are also extremely important to marketing managers. **Demography** is the study of people's vital statistics, such as their age, ethnicity, and location. Demographics are significant because the basis for any market is people. Demographic characteristics are strongly related to consumers' buying behaviour and are good predictors of how the target market will respond to a specific marketing mix. This section describes some marketing trends related to age and location. We begin by taking a closer look at key age groups.

3

Explain the importance to marketing managers of current demographic trends

demography
The study of people's vital statistics, such as their age, ethnicity, and location.

Generation Y: Born to Shop

Today there are around 7.9 million Canadians under nineteen. These are the people of "Generation Y." Generation Y is smaller than the baby boom generation, but its members are plentiful enough to put their own footprint on society.

Generation Y has had an immense impact on marketing. Companies that sell toys, videos, software, and clothing to kids and teenagers have boomed in recent years. Nine of the ten best-selling videos of all time are animated films from Walt Disney Company. Club Med, the French vacation company, now earns half its revenues from family resorts. Generation Y was born into a world so different from the one their parents entered that they could be on different planets. The changes in families, the workforce, technology, and demographics in recent decades will no doubt affect their attitudes, but in unpredictable ways. Among those changes:

ethics in marketing

Imperial Tobacco Tries Stealth Marketing

It's called *The Art of Simple Living* and looks like most any other glossy women's magazine. Actress Jamie Lee Curtis is on the cover, and it contains ads for perfumes and moisturizers, and it has articles on fashion and cooking. But you won't find this magazine in retail store displays.

The reason you won't find *The Art of Simple Living* on magazine racks is that it's part of a new stealth marketing strategy by the tobacco industry. The magazine is financed by Imperial Tobacco, the maker of Player's, Du Maurier, and Matinee cigarette brands, and it's being target mailed to female smokers across Canada.

What makes this magazine different from general circulation magazines is the number of one and two page ads focusing on Imperial's sponsorship of fashion, sports, and the arts. The ads include Imperial's cigarette names (e.g., the Matinee Fashion Foundation, Team Player's, and du Maurier Arts), as well as cigarette package colours and graphics.

Tobacco advertising has been heavily restricted by federal legislation; in response, cigarette companies are finding new ways to reach consumers. Magazines are not Imperial's only new marketing tool. Imperial has opened a smoking lounge in downtown Toronto with televisions, newspapers, reclining chairs, and free refreshments. Imperial is also employing people in Toronto and Vancouver to walk the streets and light people's cigarettes. The goal of both exercises is to sign people up to Imperial's database. Those who give their name and address get a chance to win $5,000.

Imperial is using these addresses, and the addresses it has acquired in other ways, to target mail its magazines (Imperial also has a men's magazine called *Real Edge*). Anti-smoking activists claim that the magazines, smoking lounges, and contests are ways to keep people smoking and to get former smokers to begin again.

In Canada the tobacco industry spends over $100 million annually on marketing. With this much money available, tobacco companies will continue to find innovative ways to get around legislation limiting tobacco advertising. "I think they will stretch it as much as they can get away with," says David Sweanor, a lawyer for the Non-Smokers' Rights Association. "They're dealing with an incredibly lucrative product where they have to constantly reassure the user that it's okay to use it."[8]

What do you think of "stealth marketing" activities such as those being conducted by Imperial Tobbacco? These companies are especially targeting women. Is this appropriate? Is there anything wrong with it? As long as the product is legal, should marketers be able to target whomever they want in any legal manner?

- Nearly 60 percent of children under six have mothers who work outside the home—the highest number since data have been reported.
- Nearly 60 percent of households with children seven and under have personal computers, according to IDC/LINK Resources, a market research firm.
- More than 13 percent of elementary school students nationwide are visible minorities, compared with 6 percent in 1971.
- Nearly one in six births are to foreign-born mothers.
- More and more births are to unmarried women. With nearly one in three marriages ending in divorce, a significant number of this generation will spend at least part of their childhood in a single-parent home.[9]

Generation Y is also driving the educational software industry, which has grown to a $600 million business from practically nothing in 1990. Titles like Baby-ROM from Byron Preiss Multimedia are designed to help infants as young as six months learn to identify numbers, shapes, colours, and body parts.

Apparel manufacturers from Ralph Lauren to The Gap are targeting the Generation Y crowd, which prefers jeans, sports jerseys, and baseball caps to dress-up clothes. Car makers are courting their parents with minivans and sport utility vehicles, many with built-in child seats. Hotels and cruise lines are offering kids' programs. Some malls, furniture stores, and even supermarkets are providing on-site babysitting. Restaurants are setting out crayons, installing changing tables in rest rooms, and offering more take-out services, all to serve families with children.

Although smaller in numbers than the baby boom generation, Generation Y has already had a significant impact on how companies market to families and to children and teens. Changes in demographics, technology, and the workforce are posing particular challenges as marketers attempt to identify the needs and wants of this group.

Generation X: Savvy and Cynical

Today over 4.6 million consumers are between nineteen and twenty-nine. They have been labelled **Generation X**. As the first generation of latchkey children, they are the product of dual-career households or (roughly half the time) divorced or separated parents. Generation X began entering the workforce in the era of downsizing and downturn, so its members are likelier than the previous generation to be unemployed or underemployed and living at home with Mom and Dad. Nearly 1 million are full-time college or university students, and another 1.5 million are married and not living at home.[10] Having been bombarded by multiple media since their cradle days, they're savvy and cynical consumers.

Generation X
People who are currently between the ages of nineteen and twenty-nine years.

The members of Generation X don't mind indulging themselves. Among the young women of Generation X, 38 percent go to the movies in a given month, compared with 19 percent of women in their thirties and forties. The members of Generation X spend a larger-than-average share of their money on restaurant meals, alcoholic beverages, clothing, and electronic items such as TV sets and stereos. One survey found that members of Generation X aspire to a home of their own (87 percent), a lot of money (42 percent), a swimming pool (42 percent), and a vacation home (41 percent).[11] They are more materialistic than past generations but also have less hope of achieving their goals.

This combination of high aspirations and low expectations makes Generation X a challenge for marketers. "This is a generation that hates to be marketed to," says Scott Kauffman, vice-president of broadcast and news media at *Entertainment Weekly*.[12]

For decades, Ford marketed its light-duty pickups by showing their roughness and toughness. Its ads featured trucks climbing rugged mountains or four-wheeling through mud. But Ford quickly realized that this was not going to work with Generation Xers.

Ford chose to lead with a new product. The company created a new version of its popular Ranger pickup, giving it flares on the fenders, jazzy graphics, and a youthful new name: Splash. The promotion campaign tried to infuse the vehicle with personality by associating it with adventurous sports. One ad featured a young surfer shooting the curl in the bed of a Splash parked in the middle of a wheatfield. There was minimal copy—just a new logo, and one line listing five features.[13]

Baby Boomers: A Mass Market

Between 1946 and 1964, nearly 8 million babies were born in Canada and almost 78 million in the United States. This created a huge market. The oldest **baby**

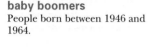

WWW on line

Arts and Entertainment Television Network

As its name indicates, A&E is a specialized television channel that broadcasts shows in arts and entertainment only. But it has even further customized its programming. How? What audience(s) do you think it is targeting? Visiting its satellite pages may help you answer.

www.aande.com; www.biography.com; www.mysteries.com; www.historychannel.com; www.historytravel.com

baby boomers
People born between 1946 and 1964.

boomers are now over fifty, but they cling to their youth. One study found that baby boomers see themselves as continuing to be very active after they turn fifty. They won't even think of themselves as senior citizens until after they turn sixty (39 percent) or seventy (42 percent).[14]

This group cherishes convenience. As a result, boomers are fuelling a growing demand for home delivery of items such as large appliances, furniture, and groceries. The spreading culture of convenience explains the tremendous appeal of many other goods and services as well, from prepared take-out foods to VCRs and cell phones.

Baby boomers' parents raised their children to think for and of themselves. Studies of childrearing practices show that parents of the 1950s and 1960s consistently ranked "to think for themselves" as the number-one trait they wanted to instil in their children. On top of this, postwar affluence allowed parents to indulge their children as never before. They invested in their children's skills by sending them to college and university in greater numbers than ever before. They also encouraged their children to succeed in a job market that rewarded competitive drive more than cooperative spirit, and individual skills more than teamwork.

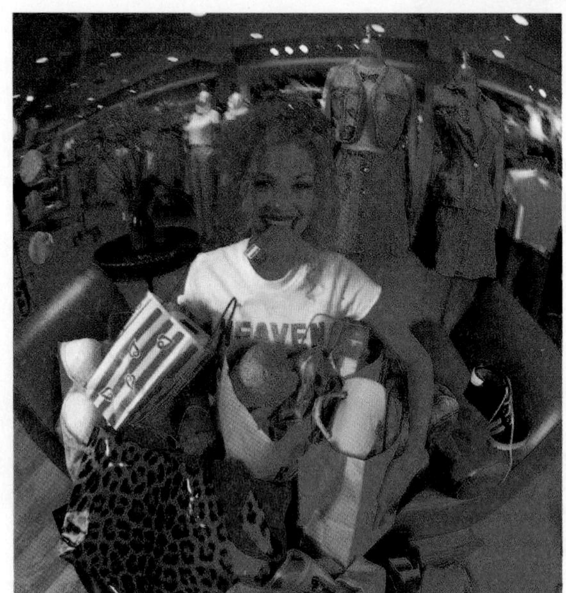

Generation Xers are savvy and cynical consumers who are more materialistic but less hopeful than previous generations. This combination of high aspirations and low expectations makes Generation X a challenge for marketers.

The sheer size of this generation encouraged businesses to promote to the emerging individuality of baby boomers. Over two decades ago, even before the oldest boomers started earning their own living, astute businesspeople saw the profits they could make by giving millions of young people what they want. Businesses offered individualistic baby boomers a growing array of customized products and services—houses, cars, furniture, appliances, clothes, vacations, jobs, leisure time, and even beliefs.

The importance of individualism among baby boomers led to a **personalized economy**. A personalized economy delivers goods and services at a good value on demand. Successful businesses in a personalized economy give customers what they want when they want it. To do this, they must know their customers extremely well. The intimacy between producer and consumer is precisely what makes an economy personalized.

personalized economy
Delivering goods and services at a good value on demand.

In the personalized economy, successful products share three characteristics:

- *Customization:* Products are custom designed and marketed to ever-smaller target markets. Today there are hundreds of cable TV channels from which to choose. In 1950 the average grocery store carried around 4,000 items; today that number is closer to 16,000, as manufacturers target increasingly specific needs.
- *Immediacy:* Successful businesses deliver products and services at the convenience of the consumer rather than the producer. The immediacy of the personalized economy explains the growing number of twenty-four-hour supermarkets and the booming business in one-hour film processing, walk-in medical clinics, and thirty-minute pizzas.
- *Value:* Businesses must price competitively or create innovative products that can command premium prices. But even the most innovative products quickly become commodities in the fast-paced personalized economy. Apple's once-

Grand Circle Travel

Maupintour

How does Grand Circle Travel dispel the stereotypes about seniors on its Web page? Compare it to Maupintour's site. Given that both companies target seniors, which company does this more effectively? Why do you think this is so?

www.gct.com; www.maupintour.com

on line

innovative Macintosh computers must now compete against less expensive machines that offer similar functions.

As the age of today's average consumer moves toward forty, average consumption patterns are also changing. People in their early forties tend to focus on their families and their finances. As this group grows in number, its members will buy more furniture from manufacturers like Lazy Boy and Drexel-Heritage and will do more shopping from home. The demand for family counsellors and wellness programs should also increase. Also, discount investment brokers like Charles Schwab and mutual funds like Fidelity and Dreyfus should profit. Middle-aged consumers buy more reading materials than any other age group, so the market for books and magazines should remain strong throughout the early 2000s. People who buy magazines at newsstands tend to be younger, so newsstand sales may falter even while subscription sales take off.

Right now, baby boomers are concerned about their children and their jobs. These worries will fade as the kids move out of the house and boomers retire. But some things will never change. Baby boomers may always be a little selfish about their leisure time. They may always be a little careless about how they spend their money. They will probably remain suspicious of the status quo. And they will always love rock'n'roll.

Older Consumers: Not Just Grandparents

As mentioned earlier, the oldest baby boomers have already crossed the fifty-plus threshold that many demographers use to define the "mature market." Today's mature consumers are wealthier, healthier, and better educated than those of earlier generations.[15] Although they make up less than 29 percent of the population, fifty-plus consumers buy half of all domestic cars, half of all silverware, and nearly half of all home remodelling.[16] Smart marketers are already targeting this growing segment. By 2020 over one-third of the population will be fifty or older.

Many marketers have yet to tap the full potential of the huge and lucrative seniors market because of enduring misconceptions about mature adults, all based on stereotypes. Here are a few:

- *Stereotype*: Older consumers are sick or ailing. *Fact:* A full 85 percent of mature citizens report themselves to be in good or excellent health. Over two-thirds of the elderly have no chronic health problems.[17] People like Mick Jagger are over fifty-five. These people are fit and healthy.
- *Stereotype*: Older consumers are sedentary. *Fact:* Of all travel dollars spent, 80 percent are spent by people over fifty.
- *Stereotype*: Older consumers have a poor retention rate. *Fact:* Senior citizens are readers and are much less influenced by TV than are younger consumers.[18] Not only do they retain what they read, but they are willing to read far more copy than younger people are.
- *Stereotype*: Older consumers are interested only in price and are intolerant of change. *Fact:* Although senior citizens are as interested in price as anyone else, they are more interested in value. A generation that has survived the better part of a century characterized by more technological change than any other in history can hardly be considered resistant to change.[19]

But acceptance of change doesn't mean a lack of brand loyalty. With cars, the most critical factor determining loyalty is age. The oldest consumers (sixty-five and up) are twice as loyal as the youngest consumers to "their" make of car.[20]

Marketers who want to actively pursue the mature market must understand it. Aging consumers create some obvious opportunities. Easy Dressing brand clothes feature Velcro-fastened clothing for women with arthritis or other ailments, who may have difficulty with zippers or buttons. Sales from the first Easy Dressing catalogue were three times higher than expected.[21] Chapters/Indigo, the bookstore chain, offers books with easy-to-read print and games with larger pieces. Trivia buffs more familiar with Mitch Miller than The Tragically Hip can play Parker Brothers' "The Vintage Years" edition of Trivial Pursuit. This game, aimed at the fifty-plus crowd, poses questions covering the era from Charles Lindbergh to Maurice Richard. Consider these other examples of savvy marketers targeting the mature market:

- To compensate for reduced grip strength associated with advancing age, Procter & Gamble is offering its Tide laundry detergent with snap-on lids rather than the usual perforated flap.
- Wheaton Medical Technologies is marketing a pill bottle with a tiny, battery-operated clock that registers the time the container was last opened.
- F.A.O. Schwarz realizes that grandparents purchase 25 percent of all toys (about $819 per year, spent on their grandkids) and has added a Grandma's Shop to its two largest stores, complete with older-adult salespeople.
- Mattel invited readers of *Modern Maturity* to join its Grandparents Club. For a $10 fee, readers could receive a book of discount coupons; meanwhile, Mattel acquired an invaluable mailing list of potential customers.[22]

Canadians on the Move

Over 16 percent of Canadians move each year.[23] This trend has implications for marketers. A large influx of new people into an area creates many new marketing opportunities for all types of businesses.

Remember, the primary basis of all consumer marketing is people. Conversely, significant out-migration from a city or town may force many of its businesses to move or close down. The cities with the greatest population growth in the 1990s were Blainville, Quebec (30.5 percent), Kelowna, B.C. (28.9 percent), Richmond Hill, Ontario (26.9 percent), and Port Coquitlam, B.C. (26.9 percent).[24] Canada's most populous metropolitan areas are Toronto (4,232,905), Montreal (3,287,645), and Vancouver (1,813,935).[25]

Canada experiences both immigration from other countries and migration within its borders. In the past decade, Ontario, Quebec, British Columbia, and Alberta have attracted the most immigrants. British Columbia and Ontario have attracted the most migrants from other provinces. Quebec and Saskatchewan were net losers when it came to interprovincial migration.[26]

Growing Ethnic Markets

4

Explain the importance to marketing managers of multiculturalism and growing ethnic markets

Canada is undergoing a demographic transition: it is becoming a multicultural society. According to the 1996 census, three in ten Canadians are not of French or British descent. Over the next decade, Canada's population will become even more diverse. Over two-thirds of immigrants to Canada are now classified as "visible minorities." The largest groups of visible minorities now coming to Canada are from China, Southeast Asia, Hong Kong, India, and Africa.[27]

Ethnic and Cultural Diversity

Multiculturalism refers to the roughly equal representation of all major ethnic groups in an given area, such as a city, a country, or a census tract. The trend in Canada is toward greater multiculturalism.

multiculturalism
When all major ethnic groups in an area—such as a city, country, or census tract—are roughly equally represented.

The greatest degree of multiculturalism is found in major metropolitan areas such as Vancouver, Toronto, Montreal, Edmonton, and Calgary. In the 1996 census, nearly 20 percent of the people in these cities listed neither English nor French as their first language. In recognition of this, a number of companies are now including visible minorities in their advertising. Cantel and American Express are advertising in languages other than French and English.

Toronto, Montreal, and Vancouver account for only a little over 30 percent of Canada's population but are home to nearly 70 percent of Canada's visible minorities. The Toronto area alone is home to nearly 1.4 million visible minorities: Chinese account for 25 percent of them, South Asians for 24.7 percent, and Blacks for 20.5 percent. Toronto is also home to substantial numbers of Filipinos, Arabs, Latin Americans, Southeast Asians, Koreans, and Japanese.[28] Exhibit 3.2 shows a sample of the visible minority populations in ten CMAs.

Demographic shifts will be even more pronounced in the future. The marketer's task in a diverse society is more challenging because of differences in educational levels and in the demand for goods and services. What's more, ethnic markets are not homogeneous: there is no single Indian market or Southeast Asian market any more than there is one French market. Instead, there are many niches within ethnic markets that require micromarketing strategies. African Eye, which offers women's designer fashions, blends African and Western influences and offers dresses priced from $50 to $600. The Vancouver Grizzlies basketball team regularly targeted Vancouver's Asian market in its advertising (unsuccessfully, it seems—the franchise has been sold and moved to an American city).[29]

A useful strategy for multicultural marketing is to seek common interests, motivations, or needs across ethnic groups. This is sometimes called **stitching niches**, and involves combining ethnic, age, income, and lifestyle markets, on some common basis, to form a large market. The result may be a cross-cultural product, such as an egg roll flavoured like a frozen pizza. Or it may be a product that serves several ethnic markets simultaneously. Ringling Brothers and Barnum and Bailey Circus showcases acts that appeal to many ethnic groups. It has broad-

stitching niches
A strategy for multicultural marketing that combines ethnic, age, income, and lifestyle markets, on some common basis, to form a large market.

exhibit 3.2
Visible Minority Populations in Canadian Cities

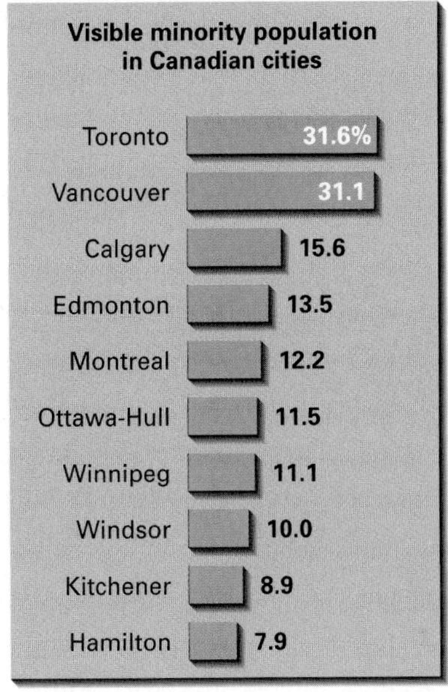

Source: Statistics Canada, Cat. No. 94F0012, Dimensions Series Package No. 9, 1996 Census. Reprinted with permission.

ened its appeal to the Asian-Canadian market by adding the "Mysterious Oriental Art of Hair Hanging."[30]

Economic Factors

5
Identify consumer and marketer reactions to the state of the economy

In addition to social and demographic factors, marketing managers must understand and react to the economic environment. The three economic areas of greatest concern to most marketers are the distribution of consumer incomes, inflation, and recession.

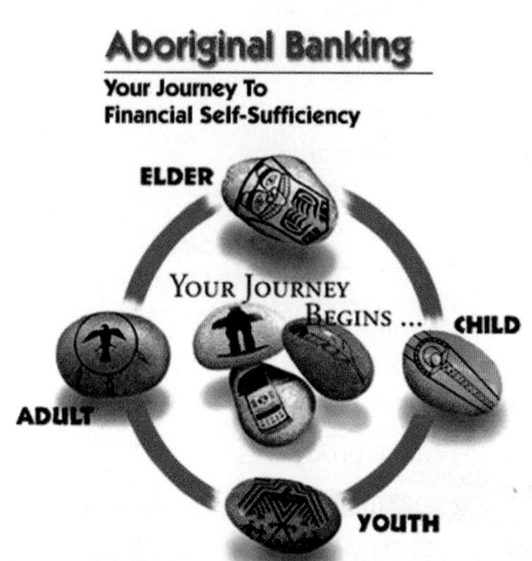

Aboriginal Banking
Your Journey To Financial Self-Sufficiency
ELDER
YOUR JOURNEY BEGINS ...
CHILD
ADULT
YOUTH
2002 National Aboriginal Achievement Awards - The Awards Ceremony will take place in Winnipeg, Manitoba on Sunday, March 10, 2002 at the Manitob Centennial Concert Hall.
Welcome to CIBC's Aboriginal Banking site, dedicated to meeting the financial and non-financial service needs of all Aboriginal people in Canada - First Nations, Inuit and Métis people, male and female, old and young, urban, rural and remote. We have chosen the Medicine Wheel, shared by many Aboriginal people, as the symbol of our holistic and integrated approach to help us achieve balance and harmony in our relationship with Aboriginal people. The site focuses on important financial management information, ideas, tools and solutions created to assist you on your journey to self-sufficiency.

Multicultural marketing is being used more than ever before in Canada. The CIBC targets Aboriginal people with its Website, which is dedicated to meeting the financial and non-financial service needs of Aboriginals.

Rising Incomes

As disposable (or after-tax) incomes rise, more families and individuals can afford the "good life." Fortunately, Canadian incomes have been rising. After adjusting for inflation, median incomes in Canada rose by nearly 3 percent between 1991 and 2001.[31]

Today approximately 55 percent of Canadian households earn a "middle-class" income, which is generally considered to be between $30,000 (well above poverty) and $75,000 (short of wealth). The average household income in Canada has grown to nearly $62,000. The percentage of households earning above $75,000 is now 13 percent.[32] One result is that Canadians are buying more goods and services than ever before. For example, in raising a child to age seventeen, a middle-class family will spend over $125,000. This new level of affluence is not limited to professionals or to individuals in specific age or education brackets. It cuts across all household types, well beyond what businesses traditionally consider to be markets for high-priced goods and services. This rising affluence stems mainly from the increasing number of dual-income families.

Incomes do vary across the country. Average incomes are $10,000 higher in Ontario than in Newfoundland. Average incomes are highest in Ontario, British Columbia, and Alberta, and lowest in Prince Edward Island, Newfoundland, and New Brunswick.[33]

During the 2000s, many marketing managers will be focusing on families with incomes over $45,000, because this group will have the most discretionary income. Discretionary income is the money remaining after paying taxes and buying necessities. Some marketers will be concentrating their efforts on higher-quality, higher-priced goods and services. Lexus automobiles and Breitling watches are examples of such goods.

Inflation

inflation
A general rise in prices without a corresponding increase in wages, which results in decreased purchasing power.

Inflation is a general rise in prices without a corresponding increase in wages; it results in decreased purchasing power. Fortunately, inflation in Canada has been considerably reduced since the double-digit inflation rates of the late 1970s and early 1980s. The late 1990s have been marked by an inflation rate under 4 percent. By early 2001, the inflation rate had dropped to 2.5 percent.[34] The low rate of inflation is due to the tremendous productivity of the high-tech sector of the economy and the stability of the price of services. The other good news is that the Canadian economy grew at an annual rate of 3.1 percent between 1996 and 1999.[35] This may not seem high, but it is twice the rate of Europe and Japan.[36] Such economic conditions benefit marketers, because real wages, and thus purchasing power, go up when inflation stays down. A significant increase in inflation almost always depresses real wages and the ability to buy more goods and services.

In times of low inflation, businesses seeking to increase their profit margins can do so only by increasing their efficiency. If they significantly increase prices, no one will purchase their goods or services.

In more inflationary times, marketers use a number of pricing strategies to cope. But in general, marketers must be aware that inflation causes consumers to either strengthen or diminish their brand loyalty. Inflation pressures consumers to make more economical purchases. However, most consumers try hard to maintain their standard of living.

In devising marketing strategies to cope with inflation, managers must realize that despite what happens to the seller's cost, the buyer is not going to pay more for a product than the subjective value he or she places on it. No matter how compelling the justification might be for a 10 percent price increase, marketers must always examine its impact on demand. Many marketers try to hold prices level as long as is practical.

Recession

A **recession** is a period of economic activity when income, production, and employment tend to fall, and the demand for goods and services is thereby reduced. The problems of inflation and recession go hand in hand, yet recession requires different marketing strategies:

recession
A period of economic activity when income, production, and employment tend to fall, and the demand for goods and services is thereby reduced.

- *Improve existing products and introduce new ones*: The goal is to reduce production hours, waste, and the cost of materials. Recessions increase the demand for goods and services that are economical and efficient, offer value, help organizations streamline practices and procedures, and improve customer service.
- *Maintain and expand customer services*: In a recession, many organizations postpone purchases of new equipment and materials. Sales of replacement parts and other services may become an important source of income.
- *Emphasize top-of-the-line products and promote product value*: Customers with less to spend will seek durability, satisfaction, demonstrated quality, and capacity to save time and money. High-priced, high-value items consistently fare well during recessions.

Technological and Resource Factors

6
Identify the impact of technology on a firm

Sometimes new technology is an effective weapon against inflation and recession. New machines that reduce production costs can be among a firm's most valuable assets. The power of a personal computer's microchip doubles around every eighteen months. The Pentium Pro, introduced in 1995, contained 5.3 million transistors and performed 300 million instructions per second (MIPS). The 886 chip, introduced in 2000, has 15 million transistors and performs 1,000 MIPS. Think of what the power of a chip will be ten years from now! Our ability to maintain and build wealth depends in large part on the speed and effectiveness with which we invent and adopt machines that boost productivity. Coal mining is typically thought of as unskilled, backbreaking labour. But visit a typical coal mine and you will find workers with push-button controls who walk along massive machines that shear metre-long slices from the mine walls. Laptop computers help miners track equipment breakdowns and water quality.

Many companies have difficulty translating the results of R&D into goods and services. The Japanese are masters at making this transformation. VCRs, flat-panel displays, and CD players are all based on North American research that wasn't exploited at home. Canadian and American companies excel at **basic research** (or pure research), which attempts to expand the frontiers of knowledge but is not aimed at specific, pragmatic problems. Basic research aims to confirm an existing theory or to learn more about a concept or phenomenon. For example, basic research might focus on high-energy physics. **Applied research** tries to develop new or improved products. This is where North American companies sometimes fall short, although most Canadian and American companies do conduct applied research. Motorola is using applied research to create Iridium, a constellation of sixty-six satellites that will offer telephone service anywhere on the globe.[37] Some car assemblers are now incorporating night vision technology and satellite-based navigation systems into their vehicles.

basic research
Pure research that aims to confirm an existing theory or to learn more about a concept or phenomenon.

applied research
Attempts to develop new or improved products.

How R&D is managed is just as important as where it is done and how much is spent on it. Canadian companies tend to be obsessed with short-term profits (one to three year time lines) and minimal risk taking. The result is an obsession with making slight variations to existing products—which admittedly are often very profitable—instead of achieving true innovations. Developing new products such as Honey Nut Cheerios and Diet Cherry Coke is probably not the path to world economic leadership.

Companies must also learn how to innovate, and large R&D budgets aren't the sole answer. One of the biggest R&D spenders is General Motors, which by most standards is not a leading innovator. Corning has relatively low R&D budgets but is arguably one of the five most innovative companies in the world. The difference is in management and corporate culture.

Again, we might take a cue from the Japanese. In Japan, teams composed of engineers, scientists, marketers, and manufacturers work simultaneously at three levels of innovation. At the lowest level they seek small improvements in existing products. At the middle level they try for significant jumps, such as Sony's move

The Internet has created new challenges and great opportunities for marketing managers in nearly all industries. Amazon.com has leveraged the technology of the Internet and created the most successful Web-based retail operation to date. (© 2001 Amazon.com, Inc. All Rights Reserved.)

from the cassette recorder to the Walkman. The third level focuses on true innovation—that is, on entirely new products. The idea is to produce three new products to replace each current product. One of the three may then become the new market leader and produce the innovator's profit.

Innovations and new products can create vast new challenges for marketing managers. One of the greatest opportunities of the past ten years has related to the tremendous growth of the Internet. In 1996 advertising spending on the Web was just $267 million; by 2000 it was approaching $2 billion.[38] Furthermore, many retailers are finding the Web an excellent way to build direct sales. The most successful Web retail operation to date has been Amazon.com (**www.amazon.com**). Selling through the Web is especially appropriate in Canada. According to an Ipsos-Reid survey, Canada and Sweden are the world's heaviest Internet users. Seventy-three percent of Canadians used the Web in 2000.[39]

The Internet has helped marketers operate more efficiently through better communications. The use of e-mail has exploded in the past several years. E-mail enables companies like Ford, Nestlé, and Bombardier to communicate quickly with employees in far-flung operations around the world. Because e-mail is so convenient, many of us are using it for personal as well as business purposes. A recent survey by Gartner, a market research firm, found that Canadians are spending nearly an hour a day at work managing e-mail; at least one-third of that time is being wasted on unimportant messages.[40]

Political and Legal Factors

7 Discuss the political and legal environment of marketing

Business needs government regulation to protect consumers, innovators of new technology, one business from another, and the interests of society in general. In turn, government needs business, because the marketplace generates taxes that support public efforts to educate young people, provide universal health care, and so on. Also, the private sector serves as a counterweight to government.

All aspects of the marketing mix are subject to laws and restrictions. Marketing managers or their legal assistants must understand these and conform to them; if they don't, the consequences to the firm can be severe. Sometimes just sensing trends and taking corrective action can render government regulation unnecessary. The tobacco industry didn't do this; as a result, it is facing tougher and tougher restrictions on its promotional activities.

The challenge here is not simply to keep the marketing department out of trouble, but to help it implement creative new programs. It is all too easy for a marketing manager, or sometimes a lawyer, to say no to a marketing innovation that actually involves little risk. An overly cautious lawyer could hold up sales of a desirable new product by warning that the package design could prompt a copyright infringement suit. It is important to understand thoroughly the laws established to regulate the business environment.

Federal Legislation

In Canada, the Combines Investigation Commission was established in 1888 to protect small businesses that were suffering as a result of collusive practices by larger businesses. In 1923 the Combines Investigation Act was passed to prevent anticompetitive conduct among businesses. Until 1975, this was the most important act affecting the legal environment of business.

Dissatisfaction with the Combines Investigation Act led to the passage in 1975 of Bill C-2, known as the Competition Act. At first, this act was administered by the Bureau of Competition Policy, which was part of Consumer and Corporate

The Competition Bureau

As a marketing manager, how could you use the Competition Bureau's Website for help designing a new marketing campaign?

strategis.ic.gc.ca

Affairs Canada. It was updated in 1986 and is now administered by the Competition Bureau of Industry Canada.

Criminal offences under the Competition Act include the following: price fixing, bid rigging, price maintenance (i.e., manufacturers requiring retailers to charge a specific price), price discrimination, predatory pricing, misleading advertising, refusal to deal, and deceptive practices (such as bait-and-switch selling, certain forms of pyramid selling, and double-ticketing). Noncriminal matters dealt with by the act include mergers, exclusive dealing, consignment selling, and tied selling.

Competition Bureau
The federal department charged with administering most marketplace laws.

Most of the consumer and business protection legislation in Canada—the Competition Act, the Consumer Packaging and Labelling Act, the Textile Labelling Act, the Precious Metals Marking Act, and so on—is enforced by the **Competition Bureau** of Industry Canada. This bureau has several agencies (e.g., the Fair Business Practices Branch) and is responsible for enforcing the laws covering bankruptcy, trade practices, competition, credit, labelling and packaging, copyrights, hazardous products, patents, pensions, precious metals, trademarks, and food inspection. Its Website **strategis.ic.gc.ca** lists its full range of responsibilities.

Provincial Laws

For national companies, provincial legislation often poses difficulties because laws vary from province to province. Quebec's Bill 101 requires that French be the primary (and sometimes exclusive) language in all promotional and advertising activities in that province. Also, advertisers in Quebec are forbidden to target children directly. There are many provincial laws regulating pricing, business start-ups, door-to-door selling, and sales of alcoholic beverages. As well, there are provincial laws that apply to certain types of businesses (e.g., travel agents, car dealers, realtors) and to certain types of business activities (e.g., billboard and direct mail advertising). Marketing managers must be aware of any legislation that directly affects their businesses.

Self-Regulation

self-regulation
Programs voluntarily adopted by business groups to regulate the activities of their members.

Some business groups make efforts to police themselves. This is referred to as **self-regulation**. The Canadian Code of Advertising Standards was established by Canada's biggest advertising agencies to monitor honesty and fairness in advertising. The Canadian Broadcasting Association, whose members include Canada's major television and radio stations, has developed its own code of ethics. The Canadian Direct Marketing Association, whose members do over 80 percent of telemarketing in Canada, has established guidelines for its members with regard to protecting consumers' privacy and right to not be contacted. Businesses that belong to the Better Business Bureau voluntarily agree to maintain fair business practices.

NAFTA

North American Free Trade Agreement (NAFTA)
An agreement among Canada, the United States, and Mexico that created the world's largest free trade zone.

Canada has had a free trade agreement with its largest trading partner, the United States, since 1988. The **North American Free Trade Agreement (NAFTA)** created the world's largest free trade zone by bringing Mexico into the free trade agreement. Canada, the United States, and Mexico combined have a population of over 370 million and an economy approaching $10 trillion.

NAFTA has brought about new business opportunities for Canadian companies by lowering the trade barriers between the NAFTA countries. The opening of

The Canadian Direct Marketing Association

Examine the Code of Ethics and Business Practices posted on the Canadian Marketing Association's Website. Look at that organization's list of member companies. Do you feel that all member companies are adhering to the CMA's Code of Ethics and Business Practices?

www.cdma.org

on line

Mexico's borders means expanded markets for exporting companies. NAFTA also means, however, that Canadian businesses must become more efficient, as Mexico has lower wage rates than Canada and less restrictive environmental regulations. Efforts are underway to expand NAFTA to include the countries of Central and South America; this would create a Western Hemisphere Free Trade Zone.

Competitive Factors

8

Explain the basics of foreign and domestic competition

The competitive environment encompasses the number of competitors a firm must face, the relative size of those competitors, and the degree of interdependence within the industry. Management has little control over the competitive environment confronting a firm. Even in a highly competitive environment, however, innovative firms can survive and prosper.

Competition for Market Share

As population growth slows, costs rise, and resources become scarcer, firms are having to work harder to maintain their profits and market share, regardless of competitive conditions. Consider the salty snacks market. Recently, Anheuser-Busch, the largest brewer in the world and marketer of such well-known brands as Budweiser, announced that it was selling its Eagle snacks business because it couldn't compete against Frito-Lay. One consultant noted: "Frito's is a fortress—I would tell anyone trying to get into the salty snack business not to impinge on Frito's territory or you'll get crushed."[41] Eagle is only the latest example. Borden sold off many of its regional snack companies as part of a huge restructuring. Industry executives say dozens of regional companies have collapsed in the past year or two under Frito-Lay's weight.

Frito-Lay is feeding much of its growth with new products. The company's approach has been two-pronged: it is expanding its core line of Fritos, Doritos, Rold Gold Pretzels, and Lays potato chips, and at the same time branching into new, "better for you" products like Baked Lays, Baked Tostitos, and Rold Gold Fat Free Pretzels. Its cheesier Doritos have turned the previously sleepy chip into a billion-dollar brand, and spicier flavours have made Lays the No. 1 potato chip.

Frito-Lay also defeats the competition with its distribution.Over its forty-year history, the company has built a network of 42 plants, 15,000 delivery people, and more than 900 tractor trailers into a retail delivery powerhouse. The company was one of the first to provide its drivers with handheld computers to transmit sales data back to headquarters. Frito-Lay is working on another overhaul of its distribution operation to better serve its expanding base of retail customers—customers that include drugstores, discount giants, grocery stores, and convenience marts.

Frito-Lay continues to maintain its market share in an increasingly competitive market by steadily rolling out new products.

Global Competition

Both Kraft General Foods and Procter & Gamble are savvy international competitors. Each conducts business in over 100 different nations. Many foreign competitors consider Canada a ripe target market, so Canadian marketing managers can no longer worry exclusively about domestic competitors. In automobiles, textiles, watches, TV sets, steel, and many other areas, foreign competition has been strong.

entrepreneurial insights

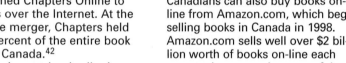

How Do Small Bookstores Compete with a Near Monopoly?

In May 2001 the Competition Tribunal of the Competition Bureau of Industry Canada (see this chapter's Political and Legal Factors section) approved a merger between Chapters and Indigo Books & Music. The resulting company will operate over 300 bookstores, including nearly 90 superstores, and will control nearly two out of every three book sales in this country.

Chapters itself grew out of a 1995 merger between Coles Book Stores and Smithbooks, familiar bookstores to all Canadians. Within a few years, Chapters had built more than 70 superstores, formed a wholesale operation called Pegasus, and launched Chapters Online to sell books over the Internet. At the time of the merger, Chapters held over 40 percent of the entire book market in Canada.[42]

As the largest bookseller in Canada, Chapters was able to command many advantages. Book publishers often gave Chapters preference when shipping hot-selling books that were in short supply because Chapters was such a large customer. When Chapters set up its wholesale division, Pegasus, Chapters demanded from book publishers, and got, discounts of 50 percent on book list prices instead of the usual 45 or 46 percent.[43]

With the merger of Chapters and Indigo, the resulting company will be even larger. In addition to the merged company controlling two out of every three book sales in Canada, Canadians can also buy books on-line from Amazon.com, which began selling books in Canada in 1998. Amazon.com sells well over $2 billion worth of books on-line each year, and commands many of the normal advantages of large size. Amazon.com has recently started selling books at deep discounts.

Though Chapters/Indigo and Amazon.com dominate booksales in Canada, this country still has over 4,000 small, independent bookstores.[44] Many small bookstores, however, are feeling the heat of this competition. Lichtman's, the largest independent Canadian bookseller, with nine stores, has gone bankrupt. How can these small bookstores compete against the giants? Will they be able to survive? As the owner of a small, independent bookstore, what would you do to compete against the giants? Visit the Website of ABE Books (www.ABEbooks.com) to see what its strategy is. Does it take even greater entrepreneurial talents to survive when your competitors are industry giants?

global perspectives

The French Government Steps into the Coke Versus Pepsi Turf Wars

The French government rejected Coca-Cola's proposed $880 million purchase of Orangina from Pernod Ricard on antitrust grounds. This is one indication that Coke is coming under greater scrutiny as rival PepsiCo draws attention to Coke's world domination of the soft drink business.

When Coke reached its agreement to buy Orangina, Pepsi cried foul; it relies on Orangina to distribute Pepsi products in cafes, hotels, and other "on-premise" locations. Pepsi also argued that Coke's purchase of Orangina would give its archrival a near monopoly in France, where Coke already controls around 50 percent of the French market for carbonated soft drinks.

Despite those complaints, Coke officials and industry analysts seemed confident that the French government would approve the deal, although only after Coke agreed to certain conditions to satisfy competition and labour concerns. Coke addressed the latter concern by signing an accord with Orangina employees that guaranteed jobs and salaries as well as a thirty-five-hour work week.

But the government decided that the French antitrust authorities' recommendation "substantiated the serious risks" that competition might be impeded in the on-premise market. "Intensive discussion with the Coca-Cola Co. did not result in sufficient commitments to prevent the risks" to competition, the French government said.

Pepsi refused to speculate as to whether it would make an offer for Orangina. "We're obviously pleased" by the government's decision, the spokesperson said. "This sends an important signal that France has solid and well-defined rules regarding open competition and is prepared to enforce those rules."[45]

Should the French government have involved itself in the Coke versus Pepsi battle for market share? If you were Pepsi management, what factors should you consider before making an offer to buy Orangina? Should Pepsi market Orangina, which is a lightly carbonated drink containing orange juice and pulp, in Canada?

Wm. Wrigley & Jr. Company
Apple Computer Inc.
Ben & Jerry's

How are these companies publicizing their community involvement via the Web? Describe the community activities of each. Does community involvement enhance a company's image?

www.wrigley.com; www.apple.com; www.benjerry.com

on line

At one time, many foreign firms came into Canada concentrating on price; nowadays, the emphasis is on product quality. Nestlé, Sony, Rolls Royce, and Sandoz are noted for quality, not cheap prices.

In this age of globalization, companies often battle one another in international markets just as intensively as in the domestic market, using very different marketing strategies. For an excellent example, check out this chapter's "Global Perspectives" box.

Corporate Social Responsibility

9
Discuss corporate social responsibility

Corporate social responsibility is business's concern for society's welfare. This concern is demonstrated by managers who consider both the long-range best interests of the company and the company's relationship to the society within which it operates.

corporate social responsibility
Business's concern for society's welfare.

One theorist suggests that corporate social responsibility has four components: economic, legal, ethical, and philanthropic.[46] The **pyramid of corporate social responsibility**, shown in Exhibit 3.3, portrays economic performance as the foundation for the other three responsibilities. At the same time that it pursues profits (economic responsibility), business is expected to obey the law (legal responsibility); to do what is right, just, and fair (ethical responsibility); and to be a good corporate citizen (philanthropic responsibility). These four distinct components constitute the whole. If the company doesn't make a profit, the other three responsibilities are moot.

pyramid of corporate social responsibility
A model which suggests that a company's social responsibility is composed of its economic, legal, ethical, and philanthropic responsibilities, and that its economic performance supports the entire structure.

Many companies are already working to make the world a better place. Examples:

- Burger King has donated millions of dollars to assist victims of natural disasters around the world.[47]
- Talisman Energy, a Calgary-based oil company, has developed a code of conduct to govern its activities with regard to how people and the environment are treated (see **www.talisman-energy.com**).[48]
- Ben & Jerry's, the premium ice cream maker, sent seven workers to live with Canada's Cree people to see how they have been displaced by a new hydroelectric power complex.[49]
- Jantzen, the world's leading swimsuit manufacturer, makes direct grants through its clean water campaign to organizations that preserve and clean up beaches and waterways.[50]
- Each year, Apple Computer donates almost $10 million in computer equipment and advice to schools.
- G.D. Searle has begun a program in which its representatives regularly call hypertension (high blood pressure) patients, reminding them to take their medicine.
- Ricoh, a Japanese office equipment maker, has developed a reverse copier that strips away toner and allows copy paper to be used again.

Multinational companies have important social responsibilities. Often a corporation can be a dynamic force for social change in host countries. Multinational

on line

New Balance

Nike

Revisit the New Balance and Nike Web pages. How are these companies using the Internet to advance a social cause? What can you tell about these companies' markets based on the causes they promote and support?

www.newbalance.com; www.nike.ca

corporations played a major role in breaking down apartheid in South Africa, through the economic pressure they exerted on the South African government. Over 300 apartheid laws had been compiled over the years, based purely on the pigmentation of people's skin. Among other things, these laws banned mixed marriages, segregated schools, and forced blacks to live in the most arid regions of South Africa. To protest apartheid, many multinational corporations closed their South African operations altogether. Other companies refused to trade with South Africa. These actions seriously impeded South Africa's economy, and by the early 1990s the government had begun making major social reforms. After apartheid officially ended, many of the companies that had participated in the boycott resumed their operations in South Africa.

exhibit 3.3

Pyramid of Corporate Social Responsibility

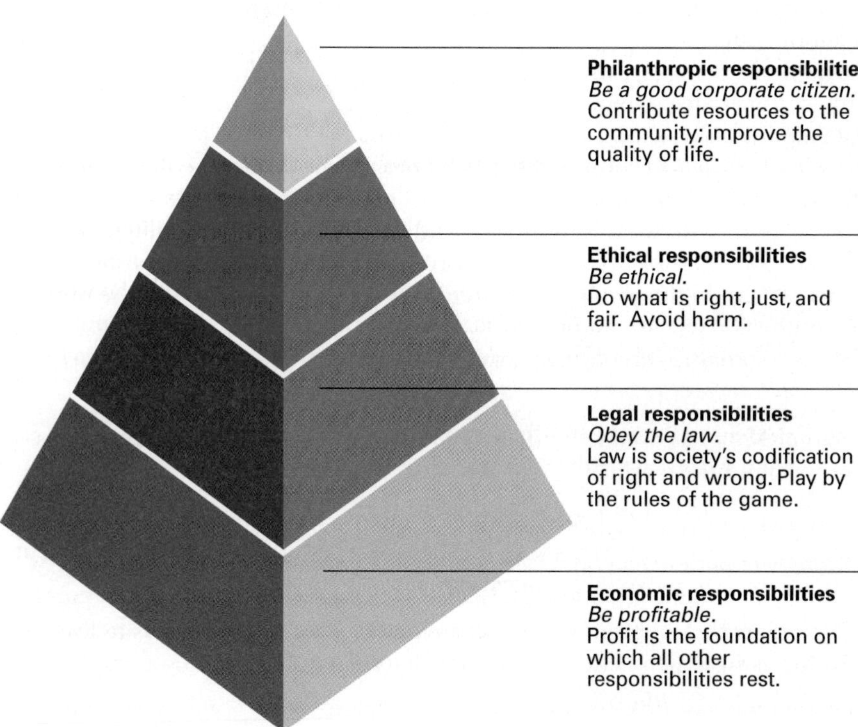
Philanthropic responsibilities
Be a good corporate citizen.
Contribute resources to the community; improve the quality of life.
Ethical responsibilities
Be ethical.
Do what is right, just, and fair. Avoid harm.
Legal responsibilities
Obey the law.
Law is society's codification of right and wrong. Play by the rules of the game.
Economic responsibilities
Be profitable.
Profit is the foundation on which all other responsibilities rest.

Source: Adapted from Archie B. Carroll, "The Pyramid of Corporate Social Responsibility: Toward the Moral Management of Organizational Stakeholders," *Business Horizons*, July–August 1991, pp. 39–48.

LOOKING BACK

Looking back at the story on Labatt Brewing and the import beer market, you should now understand that the external environment affects all firms and their marketing mixes. The opening vignette illustrated how a changing environment and demographic factors can present marketing opportunities. Labatt saw an opportunity in a segment of the otherwise slow-growing beer market and a demographic market target that it could appeal to. Other uncontrollable variables in the Labatt environment could affect the company adversely. Changing cultural and fitness values for middle-aged consumers could reduce consumption of Labatt products. New import competition could cut into Labatt import product sales. A general economic turndown could substantially decrease demand for all Labatt products.

Summary

1 Discuss the external environment of marketing, and explain how it affects a firm. The external marketing environment consists of social, demographic, economic, technological, political and legal, and competitive variables. Marketers generally cannot control the elements of the external environment. Instead, they must understand how the external environment is changing and the impact of change on the target market. Marketing managers can then create a marketing mix to effectively meet the needs of target customers.

2 Describe the social factors that affect marketing. In the external environment, social factors are perhaps the most difficult for marketers to anticipate. Several major social trends are currently shaping marketing strategies. First, people of all ages have a broader range of interests, defying traditional consumer profiles. Second, changing gender roles are bringing more women into the workforce and increasing the number of men who shop. Third, the greater number of dual-career families has led to a poverty of time, creating a demand for time-saving goods and services.

3 Explain the importance to marketing managers of current demographic trends. Today, several basic demographic patterns are influencing marketing mixes. Because the population is growing more slowly, marketers can no longer rely on profits from generally expanding markets. Marketers are also faced with increasingly experienced consumers among the younger generations, many of whom are "turned off" by traditional marketing mixes. And because the population is also growing older, marketers are offering more products that appeal to middle-aged and elderly markets.

4 Explain the importance to marketing managers of multiculturalism and growing ethnic markets. Multiculturalism refers to the condition where all major ethnic groups in a geographic area are roughly equally represented. Growing multiculturalism makes the marketer's task more challenging. Niches within ethnic markets may require micromarketing strategies. An alternative to a niche strategy involves maintaining a core brand identity while straddling different languages, cultures, ages, and incomes with different promotional campaigns. A third strategy is to seek common interests, motivations, or needs across ethnic groups.

5 Identify consumer and marketer reactions to the state of the economy. Marketers are currently targeting the increasing number of consumers with higher discretionary incomes by offering higher-quality, higher-priced goods and services. During times of inflation, marketers generally attempt to maintain level pricing in order to avoid losing customer brand loyalty. During times of recession, many marketers maintain or reduce prices to counter the effects of decreased demand; they also concentrate on increasing production efficiency and improving customer service.

6 Identify the impact of technology on a firm. In today's marketing environment, monitoring new technology is essential to keeping up with competitors. For example, in technologically advanced countries like Canada, many companies are losing business to Japanese competitors, who are prospering by concentrating their efforts on developing marketable applications for the latest technological innovations. In Canada, many R&D expenditures go into developing refinements of existing products. Companies must learn to foster and encourage innovation. Without innovation, Canadian companies won't be able to compete in global markets.

7 Discuss the political and legal environment of marketing. All marketing activities are subject to provincial and federal laws and the rulings of regulatory agencies. Marketers are responsible for remaining aware of and abiding by such regulations. The Competition Act is the major piece of legislation affecting the marketing activities of Canadian companies. The Competition Bureau of Industry Canada is the federal agency most involved in regulating marketing activities.

8 Explain the basics of foreign and domestic competition. The competitive environment encompasses the number of competitors a firm must face, the relative size of the competitors, and the degree of interdependence within the industry. Declining population growth, rising costs, and shortages of resources have heightened domestic competition. Yet with an effective marketing mix, small firms are still able to compete with the giants. Meanwhile, dwindling international barriers are bringing in more foreign competitors and offering expanding opportunities for Canadian companies abroad.

9 Discuss corporate social responsibility. Responsibility in business refers to a firm's concern for how its decisions affect society. There are several arguments in support of social responsibility. First, many consumers feel that business should take responsibility for the social costs of economic growth. Second, firms act in their own best interest when they help improve the environment within which they operate. Third, firms can avoid restrictive government regulation by responding willingly to societal concerns. Finally, because firms have the resources to solve social problems, they are morally obligated to do so.

Some critics make several arguments against corporate social responsibility. First, the free enterprise system has no way to decide which social programs should have priority. Second, firms involved in social programs do not generate the profits needed to support the business's activities and earn a fair return for stockholders.

In spite of the arguments against corporate social responsibility, most businesspeople believe they should do more than pursue only profits. Although a company must consider its economic needs first, it must also operate within the law, do what is ethical and fair, and be a good corporate citizen.

Do You Know These Terms?

applied research 60
baby boomers 54
basic research 60
Competition Bureau 62
component lifestyles 50
corporate social responsibility 65
demography 51
environmental management 49
Generation X 53
inflation 58
multiculturalism 57
North American Free Trade Agreement (NAFTA) 62
personalized economy 54
poverty of time 50
pyramid of corporate social responsibility 65
recession 59
self-regulation 62
stitching niches 57
target market 48

Discussion and Writing Questions

1. What is the purpose of environmental scanning? Give an example.
2. Every country has a set of core values and beliefs. These values may vary somewhat from region to region of the nation. Identify five core values for your area of the country. Clip magazine advertisements that reflect these values, and bring them to class.

3. Baby boomers in Canada are aging. Describe how this might affect the marketing mix for the following:
   a. Club Med
   b. MacDonald's
   c. Whirlpool Corporation
   d. Air Canada
   e. Zellers
4. You have been asked to address a local business group on the subject of the growing singles market. Prepare an outline for your talk.
5. Periods of inflation require firms to alter their marketing mixes. A recent economic forecast expects inflation to be almost 10 percent during the next eighteen months. Your company manufactures hand tools for the home gardener. Write a memo to the company president explaining how the firm may have to alter its marketing mix.
6. Give three examples of technology benefiting marketers. Also, give several examples of firms being hurt by not keeping up with technological change.
7. Form six teams. Each team is responsible for one of the uncontrollable elements in the marketing environment. Your boss, the company president, has asked each team to provide a one-year and a five-year forecast of the major trends the firm will face. The firm is in the telecommunications equipment industry. It has no plans to become a telecommunications service provider like Bell Canada. Each team should use the library, the Internet, and other data sources to make its forecasts. Each team member should examine at least one data source. The team should then pool its data and prepare its recommendation. A spokesperson for each team should present the findings to the class.
8. You are a member of the Competition Tribunal of the Competition Bureau of Industry Canada. You are asked to write a three-page report on the proposed merger of Chapters and Indigo. Do so.
9. What's the latest news at **www.ipo.org**? How can marketers benefit from such information?
10. What social responsibility concerns could be raised about **www.netcasino.com**? For which issues does the Website seem to exhibit social responsibility?

Application for Small Business

Eight years ago Betty Beal earned a bachelor's degree in business administration with a major in marketing. She has been very successful as a sales representative for a major pharmaceutical firm. As part of its social responsibility program, Betty's company urges all of its employees to contribute to the communities in which they live. Betty decided to volunteer at the Judy Freemont Shelter for Battered Women. Judy founded the shelter two years ago. It has served as a safe haven for almost sixty women and many children. Other than a small grant from the city, the only other significant source of funds is donated clothes, which are sold in the shelter's second-hand clothing shop.

Betty noticed very quickly that there was no organized way to obtain donated clothing. She quickly put her marketing skills to work and set up a phone bank to solicit clothes and a collection route to pick them up. Clothing donations quadrupled in two months.

Betty observed two things that disturbed her greatly. First, Judy would sort through all the donated items as they came in from the route truck and take anything she wanted. Betty had seen Judy take two dresses, several sweaters, and a number of blouses. Second, as revenue grew from the second-hand shop sales, Betty couldn't see that additional monies were being spent on food, clients, or the shelter itself. Yet Judy kept insisting that the operation was just breaking even.

Questions

1. Should Betty report Judy to the police, confront Judy, say nothing but continue to work at the shelter, or simply quit?
2. There is no doubt that the shelter is providing a useful social service to many needy women. If word gets out to the general public about the alleged irregularities, the shelter may be forced to close. Should this influence Betty's course of action?
3. What would you do?

VIDEO CASE

Ben & Jerry's: "We Do Good by Doing Good."

Ben & Jerry's tries to make the world a sweeter place. The gourmet ice cream manufacturer makes premium ice cream with catchy names like Cherry Garcia—after the Grateful Dead icon—and uses only top-quality ingredients. We're all in this together, say the company founders, so let's find innovative ways to show concern for people—locally, nationally, and around the world. This philosophy is called "caring capitalism." How does it work?

The concept of linked prosperity goes beyond writing a cheque for charity. Ben & Jerry's actually links itself to others who also wish to improve the quality of life for themselves and others. There are many ways to forge alliances. One way is the PartnerShop, a Ben & Jerry franchise owned and operated by a nonprofit organization. For example, a PartnerShop called Youth Scoops provides employment and training for youths at risk.

Another way to tie business to values is to buy products from "socially aligned" suppliers—those in agreement with Ben & Jerry's social outlook. The brownies in the Chocolate Fudge Brownie Frozen Yogurt are made by Greyston Bakery, a nonprofit social service network that trains homeless and low-income people for self-sufficiency. Coffee extract is made with beans from Aztec Harvests, a farming company owned by Mexican cooperatives. As part of the minority supplier program, Ben & Jerry's encourages its pecan processor to use a farm co-op dedicated to employing minorities. About one-third of Ben & Jerry purchases reflect this social mission.

Caring for our planet is yet another part of the Ben & Jerry's business philosophy. The company is serious about using and producing environment-friendly products even if it means paying top dollar. The only milk and cream that go into the ice cream come from St. Alban's, a co-op of family farmers. These dairies do not use rBGH, a growth hormone believed to be bad for cows and bad for the future of small-scale dairy farms. In fact, Ben & Jerry's has started a food fight. The company is challenging laws against national rBGH labelling so that consumers will be able to make informed choices when buying dairy products.

Another bold step was the elimination of bleach in packaging. The industry standard container was tested and found to be environmentally poor, so the company invested hundreds of staff hours to analyze chlorine-free packaging sources. Most of the technical problems are now solved, and new packaging material is on the way. One dimension of Ben & Jerry's social mission is to create models for change. The company hopes that its use of unbleached paper will stimulate similar demand by others.

Still, everything at Ben & Jerry's is not peachy. The decision to discontinue purchases of organic fruit and cancel the organic ice cream line caused quite a stir in-house. The high prices paid to dairy farmers were also paid to organic fruit farmers. Once again, the idea was not to create a fully organic line, but rather to support organic farming and create a model to stimulate demand for organic products. It was hoped that these initiatives would develop into fully organic products down the line. But organic ingredients proved to be too expensive, and the demand for them too weak. Market research showed that organic ingredient costs exceeded consumers' price expectations. And suppliers could only produce 29 percent of Ben & Jerry's total fruit needs. So the project was shelved, though not without some soul searching. Were social mission values being sacrificed for short-term economic considerations? Was Ben & Jerry's selling out?

Maybe yes, maybe no. After all, growing competition and consumer concerns about eating too much fat have caused financial struggles in recent years. Returns to shareholders have been improving and sales are increasing, yet share prices are still lower than in 1992. The company stakes its identity on the belief that the social mission enhances the economic mission. Yet some feel that's a bit idealistic. Perhaps Ben & Jerry's should ask, "Are we really doing good by doing good?"

Questions

1. What does "values-led" mean in tough, competitive times? How can Ben & Jerry's lead with its social mission if there is always an economic argument that can be made to act otherwise?
2. Do you think it's in the shareholders' best interests to select minority and disadvantaged suppliers?
3. Given Ben & Jerry's stance on environmental issues, do you feel the company has a social responsibility (i.e., to do what is right, just, and fair and avoid harm) to use organic fruit and produce an organic ice cream despite the high cost? (See Exhibit 3.3.)
4. What do you think Ben & Jerry's should do to remain competitive?

Suggested Readings

Ben & Jerry's 2000 Annual Report.

Laura Johannes, "Ben & Jerry's to End Long Relationship with Dreyer's after Takeover Attempt," *The Wall Street Journal*, September 1, 1998, p. A3.

marketing miscues

Burger King's International Whopper

International market development is not new to McDonald's and Burger King. These two fast food pioneers compete head to head both nationally and internationally. McDonald's (number one in market share) has continued to stay one step ahead of Burger King (number two in market share). Unfortunately for Burger King, the company's international marketing strategy made a "whopper" of a mistake in 1999 when it opened its doors in Ma'ale Adunim, the largest Israeli settlement in the West Bank.

The area, seized by the Israelis in the late 1960s, is at the centre of the Middle East conflict. Opening a restaurant in the West Bank was allegedly tantamount to Burger King joining with the Israelis in illegal occupation. As a result, angry Arab and Muslim groups throughout the world threatened a worldwide boycott of Burger King.

Burger King began opening restaurants in Israel in 1993. By 2000 it had forty-six fast food outlets and an Israeli-based supply network. The company also had eighty-four Burger King restaurants in Arab countries.

Country	Number of restaurants
Kuwait	31
Oman	4
Qatar	3
Saudi Arabia	40
United Arab Emirates	6

Burger King Corporation has over 10,500 outlets in fifty-five countries. Slightly over 90 percent of these fast food restaurants are owned and operated by independent franchisees. With its largest customer base in North America, Burger King has begun seeking growth opportunities in Europe, the Middle East, and Africa. A critical mass of customers is clustered in the European markets of Germany, the United Kingdom, and Spain. In 1999 these markets accounted for around 60 percent of Burger King's European sales of $1.3 billion.

One of Burger King's franchisees was blamed for the company's problems in the Middle East. Rikamor Ltd., an independent franchisee in Israel, opened a Burger King food court counter in a new shopping mall in Ma'ale Adumim in early 1999. Ma'ale Adumim is considered to be one of the fastest-growing Jewish settlements in the West Bank. Palestinians consider such Jewish settlements a key obstacle to peace in the West Bank and Gaza Strip.

In August 1999, Burger King cancelled Rikamor's right to operate the site as a Burger King restaurant (which does not mean that the restaurant has to close down, just that the restaurant cannot carry the Burger King name). The company said that Rikamor had told Burger King that the food court counter would be in Israel. According to Burger King, the company saw no reason to think otherwise, since the two parties had agreed that Rikamor could not open a Burger King in the West Bank until there was a peace accord.

Burger King's international mistake was not so easily resolved, however. Upon cancellation of the use of the Burger King name at the West Bank food counter, Jewish settlers and leaders began calling for an international boycott of all Burger King outlets. Their concern—why should the Arabs and Muslims dictate where they eat?

Bibliography

www.burgerking.com

"International: A Whopper of a Mistake," *Economist,* 4 September 1999, p. 47.

"Jewish Settlers Call for Boycott of Burger King," Xinhua News Agency, 27 August 1999, item number 0827265.

Dana Budeiri, "Burger King is Now a Mideast Battlefield," *Boston Globe,* 10 August 1999, p. A15.

Carol Casper, "Rapid Change," *Restaurant Business,* 15 February 2000, pp. 62–9.

--- "Uncommon Market," *Restaurant Business,* 15 February 2000, pp. 55–8.

Questions

1. What important external factors should Burger King (or any multinational corporation) monitor before extending permission to a franchisee to use the company name?
2. What strategies should Burger King implement in attempting to salvage its brand name in the Middle Eastern market and to maintain its international market share?
3. How much control should Burger King have over its franchisees to ensure that another Rikamor situation does not develop?

Critical Thinking

Beyond Starbucks: Extending a Brand Name

Starbucks Corporation was facing a major issue: that of ubiquity versus equity. Should the company focus on growing the business (ubiquity) or on growing the brand (equity)? Could the company manage its various growth directions while keeping employees passionate about the brand? With the opening of restaurants, the purchase of a tea company, and the publishing of a cultural literary magazine, was Starbucks at risk of losing sight of its company objective: "to establish Starbucks as the most recognized and respected brand in the world"?

The Company

Starbucks began its rapid ascent into consumers' lives with the opening of its first Starbucks Coffee retail shop in 1971. A mere thirty years later, there are around 2,500 Starbucks locations in thirteen countries. Fuelling this rapid growth, Starbucks Coffee International (a wholly owned subsidiary of Starbucks Corporation) opened its first overseas location in Japan in 1996 through a joint venture with Sazaby, a Japanese retailer and restaurateur. Beyond its Canadian and American outlets, Starbucks has opened stores in Singapore, the Philippines, Taiwan, Thailand, the United Kingdom, New Zealand, Malaysia, China, Kuwait, South Korea, and Lebanon.

Led by Chairman Howard Schultz (who started with Starbucks in 1982 as director of retail operations and marketing), Starbucks thrives on building a rewarding relationship with its customers. The Starbucks brand is delivered by 37,000 employees to over 10 million customers each week, primarily through company-operated retail stores, where the average daily sale is $3.60. The company went public in 1992. Its success is exemplified by its 1999 revenues of $1.7 billion and 1999 profits of over $100 million.

Market Segmentation

Coffee consumption follows a very obvious age segmentation. The typical coffee consumer is over thirty-five; more than three-quarters of the over-thirty-five crowd drink coffee on a regular basis. In comparison, only around one-third of the under-thirty-five group drink coffee regularly. Canada is a particularly large coffee market; Canadians drink 30 percent more coffee per capita than Americans.

Coffee is considered to be a morning and/or after-meal drink. This regimen of coffee drinking flows logically with a benefit segmentation approach to the coffee market. In such instances, the benefit received is tied closely to the caffeine found in coffee. Thus, the market can be segmented by whether consumers drink coffee to "wake up" or for the taste. As a means to "wake up," coffee consumption becomes a habit; consumers become accustomed to holding a coffee cup in their hands every morning—to get them going.

Starbucks Retail

The Starbucks brand name has long been associated with its freshly brewed, rich-tasting coffees. This high-quality coffee is sold primarily through company-operated retail stores. In an attempt to get its coffee to consumers in various formats, Starbucks introduced a mail-order catalogue in 1988. In 1990 the company's specialty sales group began aligning with airline companies to offer Starbucks coffee during flights. In the mid-1990s, starbucs joined forces with Chapters and Barnes & Noble, an American store, and began operating coffee bars within the larger retail establishments. As of 2000, Starbucks' coffee sales in Canada were $129 million. Second Cup Ltd. of Toronto had 2000 sales of $159 million.

Recognizing that many consumers drink coffee for the taste (not just for the caffeine "kick"), Starbucks in the mid- to late 1990s began serving low-fat, creamy, iced coffee beverages in its retail shops. On the heels of this successful product, the company partnered with Pepsi-Cola to begin selling a bottled version of the drink in supermarkets and convenience stores.

Non-Coffee Brand Extensions

In the late 1990s, Starbucks began expanding into non-coffee beverages by acquiring Tazo, a premium tea company. Also, the company opened Café Starbucks, a full-service restaurant.

Capitalizing on the company's brand name and an extremely popular in-house music program, Starbucks began selling compact discs in 1995. These CDs featured such offerings as Chicago blues, rhythm and blues, jazz, and opera. In 1998 the company began offering a Starbucks/Doonesbury line of products (with proceeds directed toward literary nonprofit organizations). Maintaining this connection with the literary world, Starbucks, in partnership with Time Inc., launched Joe, a cultural literary magazine, in 1999.

In 1998, Starbucks launched its company Website, **www.starbucks.com.** It was at this time that Shultz was confronted with the perils of rapid growth and concerns that the company was moving beyond its core competency.

Starbucks on the Net

By late 1999, Starbucks had invested around $4 million on its entry into the Internet world. Starbucks had plans to expand into such product offerings as kitchenware, home furnishings, and gourmet food. The company's grand scheme involved Starbucks becoming a lifestyle portal on the Net.

However, investors were not sold on the idea that Starbucks could extend its brand name so far beyond coffee and related products. The company's share price fell 28 percent in one day, amidst rumours of delayed store openings, lower than expected sales at existing stores, and disappointing supermarket sales of coffee-flavoured drink products.

Was Schultz losing his way by not focusing on the company's core business? Was he attempting to grow the company at the expense of the brand? Should Schultz back away from the Internet expansion?

Bibliography

www.starbucks.com

"Interview with Howard Schultz: Sharing Success," *Executive Excellence,* November 1999, pp. 16–17.

David A. Kaplan, "Trouble Brewing," *Newsweek,* 19 July 1999, pp. 40–1.

Louise Lee, "Now, Starbucks Uses Its Bean," *Business Week,* 15 February 2000, pp. 92–7.

Terry Lefton, "Schultz' Caffeinated Crusade," *Brandweek,* 5 July 1999, pp. 20–5.

David Wellman, "Premium Youth," *Supermarket Business,* 15 November 1999, pp. 48–9.

Questions

1. What is the core business at Starbucks? How did the company build on this core business?
2. What is the risk associated with moving beyond a company's core business?
3. Should Schultz back away from the Internet business? If so, how can he grow the company? If not, how can he extend the Starbucks brand into unrelated offerings while maintaining the company's core business?

DIRECTION

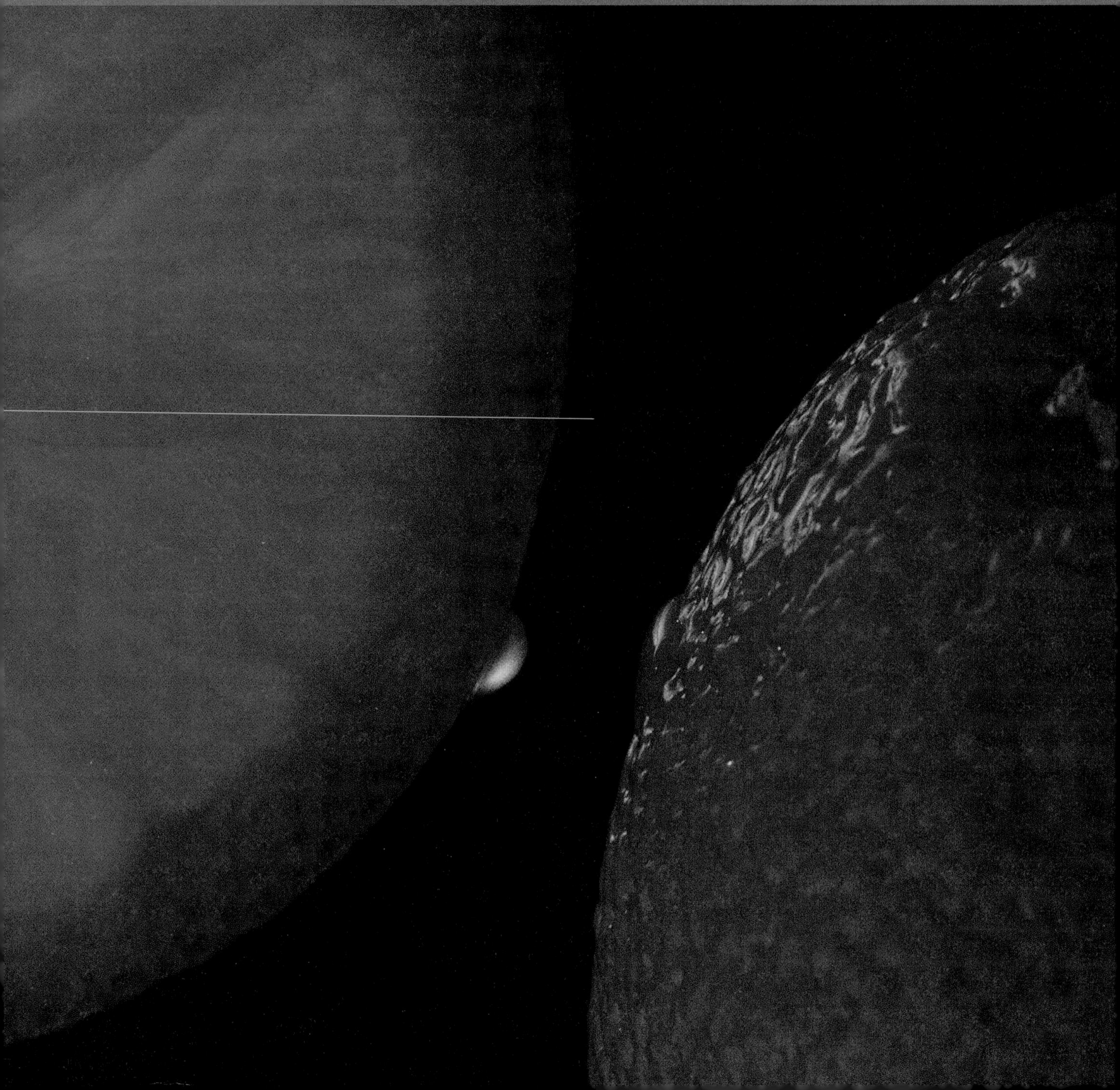

CHAPTER

4

LEARNING OBJECTIVES

After studying this chapter, you should be able to

1 Explain why marketing managers should understand consumer behaviour

2 Analyze the components of the consumer decision-making process

3 Explain the consumer's postpurchase evaluation process

4 Identify the types of consumer buying decisions, and discuss the significance of consumer involvement

5 Identify and understand the *cultural* factors that affect consumer buying decisions

6 Identify and understand the *social* factors that affect consumer buying decisions

7 Identify and understand the *individual* factors that affect consumer buying decisions

8 Identify and understand the *psychological* factors that affect consumer buying decisions

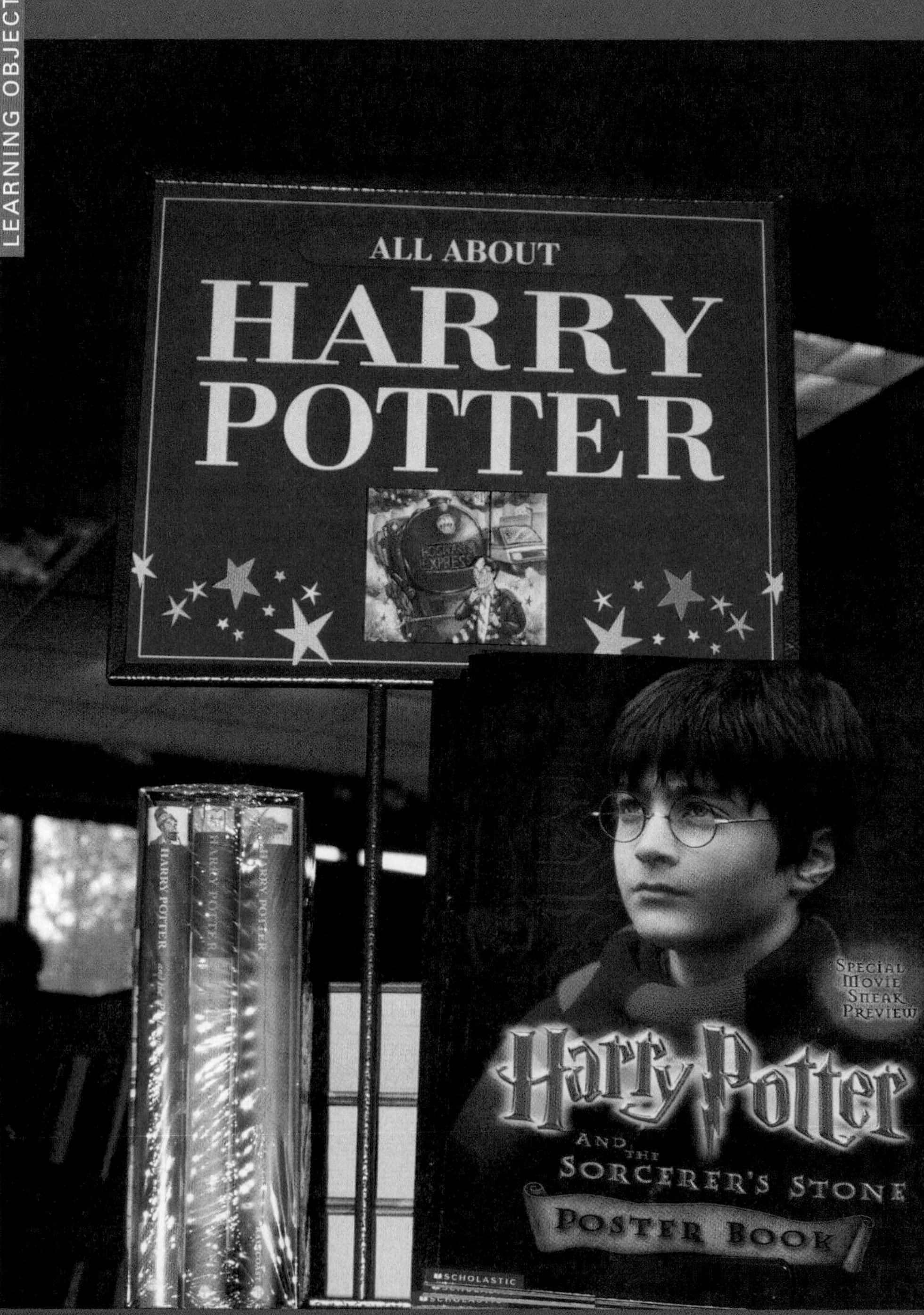

CONSUMER DECISION MAKING

The Harry Potter series, chronicling the adventures of Harry and his classmates at the Hogwarts School of Witchcraft and Wizardry in Britain, was launched in 1997 with *Harry Potter and the Philosopher's Stone.* When the orphaned Harry receives an invitation to a seven-year program of study at Hogwarts, he learns that his parents had been wizards. To reach the secret castle school, which is concealed from ordinary Muggles such as his despicable Aunt Petunia and Uncle Vernon, Harry is instructed to catch the Hogwarts Express in London at King's Cross Platform 9¾. Along with his fellow first-year Gryffindor housemates, Ron Weasely and Hermione Granger, Harry learns how to cast spells, make potions, and ride a broomstick. He also becomes a star Quidditch player and begins to learn more about his parents' death at the hands of the evil wizard Lord Voldemort.

The complicated story and the intriguing cast of characters and young heroes were the ingredients for success.[1] First published in Britain by Bloomsbury, Rowling's series became known to North American audiences by word of mouth spreading quietly across the Atlantic. Even before the series was picked up by Scholastic and Raincoast, friends and relatives travelling in the United Kingdom were bringing the books home in their suitcases and lending them around. Even children who usually disliked reading were eager to read about Harry's life at Hogwarts. Parents and educators alike were delighted by this interest in reading—in fact, Rowling has been credited with "single-handedly teaching a generation of children the joys of reading in an electronic age of short attention spans."[2]

The July 2000 arrival of the fourth book in the series, *Harry Potter and the Goblet of Fire,* became a media event. Because of advance Internet book orders, Rowling's latest was a bestseller even before its official July 8 release date. Fans lined up at bookstores hours before they opened, and even though more than 6 million books were printed, most bookstores ran out of copies within twenty-four hours.

The amusing subtleties, attention to detail, and sheer

Harry Potter

Visit one of the Harry Potter fan sites. What market segments can you identify?

www.harrypotter.warnerbros.com

on line

innovation of Rowling's fictional world appeal to adults as well. The series can be understood at many levels and is becoming darker in mood and ever more complex. On learning that adult readers were enjoying the Potter series, Bloomsbury began reissuing the novels with restrained paperback covers geared toward the adult market.[3]

Despite their British setting, the Potter books have become a global phenomenon. More than 100 million copies of the Harry Potter novels have been sold, in forty-two languages.[4] Three more Potter books are expected to follow, and Pottermania shows no signs of letting up. The November 16, 2001, release of a Warner Bros. movie based on the first book, *Harry Potter and the Order of the Philosopher's Stone,* earned an amazing $90.3 million its first weekend.

In the meantime, those hungry for more Harry can indulge in two of his Hogwarts textbooks, complete with scribbled margin notes and games of tic-tac-toe. Although written by Rowling, *Fantastic Beasts & Where to Find Them* and *Quidditch Through the Ages* are credited to Hogwarts authors Newt Scamander and Kennilworthy Whisp. Potter fans can also purchase a wide variety of licensed merchandise. A quick browse through a guide to Harry Potter collectibles reveals dozens of products within the means of younger consumers, including bookmarks, Collector Stones, and temporary tattoos.[5] Higher-end merchandise, such as the Hogwarts-style bedroom furniture sold by FAO Schwarz, requires an indulgent parent.[6]

Thanks to the Internet, devoted Harry Potter fans have formed a kind of consumption subculture that goes far beyond reading the books and purchasing the merchandise. Websites, both official and unofficial, allow consumers to play Harry Potter trivia, send messages by Owl Post, write and post stories, enter contests, play games, and participate in discussion groups. Afficionados can even attend an on-line Hogwarts School at the Warner Bros. Site![7]

VIA Rail

Visit the VIA Rail home page and note the different ways that VIA presents information and marketing ideas to business travellers, vacationers, students, and families. How do their promotional approaches reflect the values and interests of these different groups?

www.viarail.ca

on line

The Importance of Understanding Consumer Behaviour

1

Explain why marketing managers should understand consumer behaviour

Consumers' product and service preferences are constantly changing. To address this constant state of flux and to create a proper marketing mix for a well-defined market, marketing managers must have a thorough understanding of consumer behaviour. **Consumer behaviour** is about how consumers make purchase decisions and how they use and dispose of the goods and services they purchase. The study of consumer behaviour also includes the analysis of factors that influence purchase decisions and product use.

Understanding how consumers make purchase decisions can help marketing managers in several ways. For example, if a manager knows through research that fuel efficiency is the most important attribute for a certain target market, the manufacturer can (a) redesign the product to meet that criterion, or (b), if it cannot change the design in the short run, use promotion in an effort to change consumers' decision-making criteria. For example, a car maker could advertise a model's maintenance-free features and sporty European style and downplay its fuel efficiency.

consumer behaviour
The processes a consumer follows in making purchase decisions and in using and disposing of purchased goods or services; also includes factors that influence purchase decisions and how products are used.

The Consumer Decision-Making Process

2

Analyze the components of the consumer decision-making process

When buying products, consumers generally follow the **consumer decision-making process** shown in Exhibit 4.1: (1) need recognition, (2) information search, (3) evaluation of alternatives, (4) purchase, and (5) postpurchase behaviour. These five steps represent a general process that begins with the consumer recognizing a product or service need and ends with an evaluation of the purchase. These steps represent a guideline for us to consider how consumers make decisions. Note well that this guideline does not assume that all consumers follow all the steps of the process, or follow them in the order given. In fact, the consumer may end the process at any time; he or she may not even make a purchase. At the end of the chapter, in the section on types of consumer buying decisions, we offer explanations as to why people vary in their progression through these steps. Next, we describe each step in the process in greater detail.

consumer decision-making process
The step-by-step process followed by consumers when buying goods or services.

Need Recognition

The first stage in the consumer decision-making process is need recognition. **Need recognition** occurs when consumers are faced with an imbalance between actual and desired states. For example, do you often feel thirsty after strenuous exercise? Has a television commercial for a new sports car ever made you wish you could buy it? Need recognition is triggered when a consumer is exposed to either an internal or an external **stimulus**. Hunger and thirst are *internal stimuli*; the colour of an automobile, the design of a package, a brand name mentioned by a friend, an advertisement on television, and a cologne worn by a stranger are all considered *external stimuli*.

need recognition
The result of an imbalance between actual and desired states.

stimulus
Any unit of input affecting one or more of the five senses: sight, smell, taste, touch, hearing.

A marketing manager's objective is to get consumers to recognize an imbalance between their present state and their preferred state. Advertising and sales promotion often succeed in this. Marketers survey buyer preferences to learn what consumers want and need, and then tailor their products and services accordingly. Customer relationship marketing (CRM) helps marketers embrace one-to-one relationships with customers. Direct marketing agencies such as the Carlson Marketing Group of Montreal and Toronto help companies understand

exhibit 4.1

Consumer Decision-Making Process

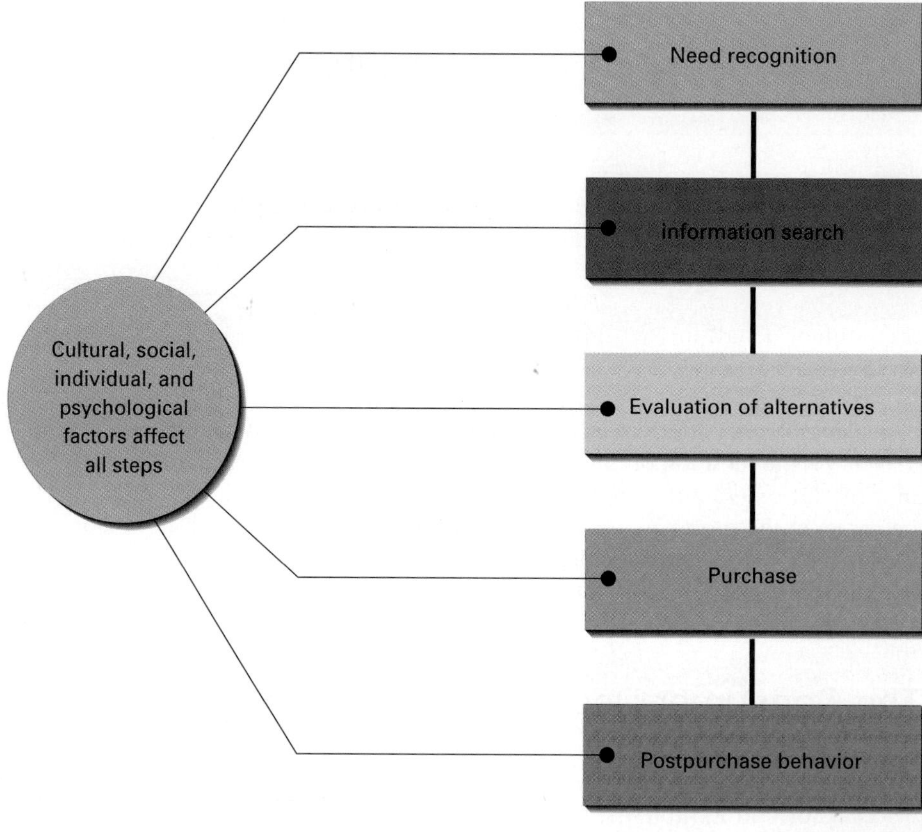

their customers' wants and needs. Says Robert Clarkson, vice-president and general manager of Carlson, "Our particular niche is customer contact, finely gearing individual needs with the appropriate company response. That's why we believe in taking small steps and focusing on the needs of specific groups. Then you learn your customer values and when those values change, because they *do* change."[8]

want
Recognition of an unfulfilled need and a product that will satisfy it.

Marketing managers can create consumers' wants. A **want** exists when someone has an unfulfilled need and has determined that a particular good or service will satisfy it. Young children often want toys, video games, and baseball equipment to meet their innate need to play and learn new skills. Teenagers often want compact discs, fashionable sneakers, and wide-leg jeans so as to fulfil their need to belong. A want can be for a specific product, or it can be for a certain attribute or feature of that product. For instance, adults may want ready-to-eat meals, drive-through dry cleaning services, and catalogue shopping to fulfil their need for convenience. Older consumers may want goods and services that offer convenience, comfort, and security.

Consumers recognize unfulfilled wants in various ways. The two most common: a current product isn't performing properly; *or*, the consumer is about to run out of something generally kept on hand. A third common one is when the consumer becomes aware of a product that seems superior in its features to the one currently used. Such wants are usually created by advertising and by other promotional activities. For example, a young teenager may develop a strong desire for a PlayStation 2 after seeing it displayed in a store and hearing that they sold out everywhere.

Marketers selling their products in global markets must be careful to observe the needs and wants of consumers in different regions. Procter & Gamble hit on an unrecognized need of Japanese consumers when it introduced a highly concentrated liquid dishwashing soap. To determine what Japanese consumers wanted, P&G sent out researchers to study Japanese dishwashing rituals. They discovered that Japanese homemakers felt frustrated that they had to use a lot of soap to get the cleaning power to clean greasy dishes; as a result, they squirted out more detergent than necessary. With its simple pitch, "A little bit of Joy cleans better, yet is easier on the hands," P&G's product flew off Japanese store shelves. Roots Canada sells its shoe and clothing lines in the United States, Canada, Korea, and Taiwan.

internet connections

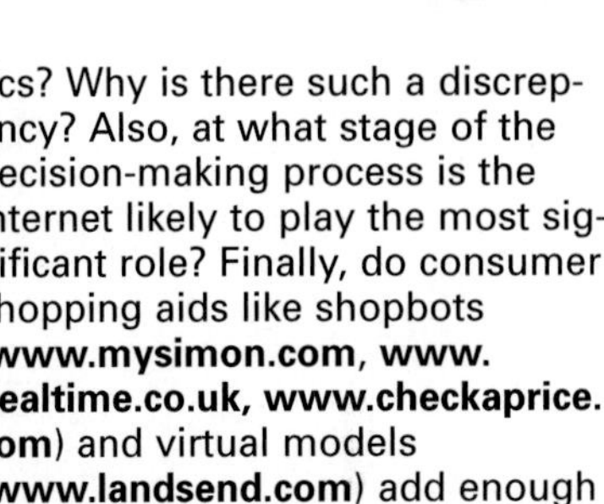

Helping Consumers Navigate the Clutter of the Net

When was the last time you visited Amazon.com, or **www.chapters.indigo.ca**? Did you buy anything, or did you just take a look at what was available? According to CommerceNet, roughly 60 percent of the on-line population are browsers and use the Internet as a shopping aid; far fewer are willing to actually purchase in an on-line environment. Consumers who hesitate to make transactions on line most often cite privacy and security concerns. However, given the Internet's complexity and the consumer decision-making process, other factors are probably involved as well.

Consider the breadth of information available on the Net. Then consider the number of on-line alternatives available to the consumer compared to the number of brick-and-mortar suppliers. Clearly, consumers are faced with an extremely complex task. With on-line shopping there are far more data to sift through, far more alternatives to consider, and far more criteria to evaluate. There is also more risk involved in the actual decision. Some companies are using technology to develop aids to help consumers in the search/evaluation process. Others are improving their Website designs to make them more intuitive and user-friendly as well as easier to navigate. However, the number of Canadian consumers purchasing on-line is still lower than what the connectivity rates would suggest.

How do on-line search statistics compare to on-line purchase statistics? Why is there such a discrepancy? Also, at what stage of the decision-making process is the Internet likely to play the most significant role? Finally, do consumer shopping aids like shopbots (**www.mysimon.com, www.dealtime.co.uk, www.checkaprice.com**) and virtual models (**www.landsend.com**) add enough value to draw consumers on-line and encourage them to complete purchase transactions? What other decision-making aids could on-line retailers offer that would simplify the decision-making process for consumers?

Source: Shelley M. Rinehart, University of New Brunswick, Saint John.

Information Search

After recognizing a need or want, consumers search for information about the various alternatives available to satisfy it. An information search can be carried out internally or externally, or both. **Internal information search** is the process of recalling information stored in the memory. This stored information relates mainly to past experience with a product. Perhaps while shopping you encounter a brand of cake mix that you tried some time ago. By searching your memory, you can probably remember whether it tasted good, pleased guests, and was easy to prepare.

internal information search
The process of recalling past information stored in the memory.

In contrast, an **external information search** involves seeking information in the outside environment. There are two basic types of external information sources: nonmarketing-controlled and marketing-controlled. A **nonmarketing-controlled information source** is not associated with marketers promoting a product. A friend might recommend a ski trip to Sunshine ski resort in Banff because she went skiing there and enjoyed it. Nonmarketing-controlled information sources include personal experience (trying or observing a new product), personal sources (family, friends, acquaintances, co-workers), and public sources such as the Internet, Better Business Bureaux, and consumer magazines. For instance, consumers rely heavily on the advice of doctors and pharmacists when buying over-the-counter (OTC) medications. A recent survey of how consumers choose medicines found that more than half started using an OTC drug because a pharmacist recommended it.[9]

external information search
The process of seeking information in the outside environment.

nonmarketing-controlled information source
A product information source that is not associated with advertising or promotion.

marketing-controlled information source
A product information source that originates with marketers promoting the product.

A **marketing-controlled information source** is biased toward a specific product because it originates with the marketers promoting that product. Marketing-controlled information sources include mass media advertising (radio, newspaper, television, and magazine advertising), sales promotions (contests, displays, premiums, and so on), salespeople, and product packages and labels. In the same survey on consumers and medicines, 56 percent of those interviewed said they were strongly influenced by the information on the label when deciding whether to purchase an OTC medication for the first time.[10] Yet many consumers are wary about the information they receive from marketing-controlled sources, and are convinced that most marketing campaigns stress the attributes of products and don't mention their faults. These sentiments tend to be stronger among better-educated and higher-income consumers. Only 13 percent of consumers interviewed in the medicine study said they were strongly influenced by advertising when deciding whether to purchase OTC medications.[11]

The breadth of an external search depends on the consumer's perceived risk, knowledge, prior experience, and level of interest in the good or service. Generally, as the perceived risk of the purchase increases, the consumer enlarges the search and considers more alternative brands. Assume you want to buy a new car. The decision is a relatively risky one, mainly because of cost, so you are motivated to search for information about models, options, fuel efficiency, durability, and passenger capacity. You may also decide to gather information about more models, because the time expended in finding the data is less than the cost of buying the wrong car. In contrast, you are less likely to expend great effort in searching for the right kind of bath soap. If you make the wrong selection, the cost is minimal; besides, you'll be buying soap again fairly soon and will be able to choose another kind then. A study on the effects of perceived risk found that people who perceive higher risk with a mail-order purchase expend more effort in external information search than do those who perceive lower levels of risk; they also consult a greater number of information sources.[12]

A consumer's knowledge about the product or service also affects the extent of the external information search. A consumer who is knowledgeable and well informed about a potential purchase is less likely to search for additional information. Also, the more knowledgeable the consumer is, the more efficiently he or she will conduct the search process—in other words, the less time he or she will take. Another closely related factor is that some consumers are more confident than others in their decision-making ability. A confident consumer has plenty of stored information about the product as well as a feeling of certainty that the right decision will be made. People who lack this confidence will continue searching for information even after they already know a great deal about the product. Consumers who have bought a certain product before will perceive less risk than those who have not, so they will spend less time searching and limit the number of products they consider.

Nonmarketing-controlled information is often a key resource for consumers facing even the smallest of buying decisions. Consumers Union is a highly recognized ratings organization that performs extensive tests on a wide variety of consumer goods and services and publishes the results in *Consumer Reports®*.

A third factor influencing the external information search is experience with the product. Consumers who have had positive prior experiences with a given product are more likely to limit their search to the product that offered them those experiences. Honda cars tend to need few repairs; consequently, Honda customers tend to be highly satisfied and to own more than one Honda.

Finally, the extent of the search undertaken is also related to the amount of interest a consumer has in a product. A consumer who is more interested in a product will spend more time searching for information and alternatives. Suppose you are a dedicated runner who reads jogging and fitness magazines and catalogues. In searching for a new pair of running shoes, you may enjoy reading about the new brands available, and consequently spend more time and effort than other buyers would in deciding on the right shoe.

The consumer's information search typically yields a group of brands, sometimes called the buyer's **evoked set** (or **consideration set**). These are the consumer's preferred alternatives. The buyer further evaluates the alternatives in this set and then makes a choice. Consumers do not consider all the brands available in a product category. There are dozens of brands of shampoo and close to two hundred makes of cars available in North America, yet most consumers seriously contemplate only about four shampoos and no more than five automobiles when faced with a purchase decision.

evoked set (consideration set)
A group of brands, resulting from an information search, from which a buyer can choose.

Evaluation of Alternatives and Purchase

After getting information and constructing an evoked set of alternative products, the consumer is ready to make a decision. A consumer will use the information stored in memory and obtained from outside sources to develop a set of criteria. These standards help the consumer evaluate and compare alternatives. One way to begin narrowing the number of choices in the evoked set is to pick a product attribute and then exclude all products in the set that don't have that attribute. For instance, assume that John is thinking about buying a new notebook computer to replace his current desktop machine. He is interested in one with a large colour plasma display, DVD capacity, and a processor speed of at least 600 megahertz, so he excludes all notebooks without these features.

Another way to narrow the number of choices is to use cutoffs, or minimum or maximum levels of an attribute that an alternative must have to be considered. Suppose John still must choose from a wide array of notebook computers that have plasma screens, DVD drives, and 600-plus processor speeds. He then names another product attribute: price. Given the amount of money he has set aside for a new computer, John decides he cannot spend more than $2,000. So he excludes all notebook computers priced above $2,000. A final way to narrow the choices is to rank the attributes under consideration in order of importance and then evaluate the products based on how well they perform on the most important attributes. To reach a final decision, John would pick the most important attributes, such as processor speed and plasma display, weigh the merits of each, and then evaluate alternative notebook computers according to those criteria.

As new brands are added to an evoked set, the consumer's evaluation of the existing brands in that set tends to change. As a result, certain brands in the original set may become more desirable. Suppose John sees two notebook computers priced at $2,199 and $2,999. At the time, he may judge the $2,999 notebook computer to be too expensive and decide not to purchase it. However, if he then adds to his list of alternatives another notebook computer that is priced at $3,499, he may view the $2,999 one as less expensive and decide to purchase it.

A marketing manager's goal is to determine which attributes have the strongest influence on a consumer's choice. A single attribute, such as price, may not adequately explain how consumers form their evoked set.[13] Several factors in tandem may affect a consumer's evaluation of products. Moreover, attributes thought by the marketer to be important may not be very important to the consumer. Much to the surprise of car dealers, one study found that automobile warranty coverage was the least important factor in a consumer's purchase of a car.[14]

A brand name can have a significant impact on a consumer's ultimate choice. Roots Canada has expanded its product line, using its well-respected name, into several product areas. When Roots first started it sold only shoes; its full line now includes complete apparel lines, leather goods, fragrances, children's clothing, vitamins, eyeware, and more. In 2001 Roots got into the airline business with the launch of Roots Air, an upscale airline aimed at business travellers. RootsAir got plenty of media attention but failed rather quickly due to lack of passengers. Perhaps the company extended its brand name a little too far. Sears has leveraged its well-known brand name to expand its service business. Most consumers are ill-prepared when the dishwasher overflows or the refrigerator gives out, and frantically look for repair alternatives. Many turn to trusted sources, such as Sears, which markets itself as a logical alternative for harried consumers. In its advertising it portrays itself as a reliable retail chain. Brands, by providing consumers with certain sets of promises, are in essence simplifying the consumer decision-making process; consumers don't have to rethink their options every time they need something.[15]

So the consumer evaluates the alternatives and decides which product to buy, or not to buy a product at all. If he or she decides to make a purchase, the next step in the process is to evaluate the product after the purchase.

Postpurchase Behaviour

3
Explain the consumer's postpurchase evaluation process

Consumers expect certain outcomes from a purchase. How well these expectations are met determines whether the consumer is satisfied or dissatisfied. Say Rita buys a used car with somewhat low expectations for the car's actual performance. Surprisingly, the car turns out to be one of the best cars she ever owned. Her satisfaction is high, because her low expectations have been exceeded. Say Jeet buys a brand-new car and expects it to perform especially well. The car turns out to be a lemon, and he is very dissatisfied because his high expectations have not been met. Price often creates high expectations. One study found that higher monthly cable TV bills were associated with greater expectations for cable service. Over time, cable subscribers tended to drop the premium-priced cable channels because their high expectations were not met.[16]

In any postpurchase evaluation, the consumer will want to reduce any lingering doubts that the decision was sound. When people notice an inconsistency between their values or opinions and their behaviour, they tend to experience an inner tension called **cognitive dissonance**. Suppose a consumer spends half his monthly salary on a new, high-tech stereo system. If he stops to think about how much he has spent, he will probably feel dissonance. Dissonance arises because the consumer knows the purchased product has some disadvantages as well as some advantages. In the case of the stereo, the disadvantage of cost battles the advantage of technological superiority.

cognitive dissonance
The inner tension a consumer experiences after recognizing an inconsistency between behaviour and values or opinions.

Consumers try to reduce dissonance by justifying their decisions. They may seek new information that reinforces positive ideas about the purchase, avoid information that might suggest the decision was poor, or revoke the original decision by returning the product. People who have just bought a new car often read more advertisements for the newly purchased car than for other cars in order to reduce dissonance. People sometimes deliberately seek contrary information in order to refute it and thereby reduce dissonance. Dissatisfied customers sometimes rely on word of mouth to reduce cognitive dissonance, by letting friends and family know they are displeased.

Marketing managers can help reduce dissonance by communicating effectively with purchasers. A customer service manager might slip a note inside the package congratulating the buyer on her wise decision. Postpurchase letters sent by manufacturers and dissonance-reducing statements in instruction booklets can help customers feel at ease with their purchase. Advertising that displays a product's superiority over competing brands can help relieve the possible dissonance of someone who has already bought the product. Guarantees can do the same thing. Sears Canada offers a complete satisfaction guarantee: if a product purchased through Sears does not work out, for any reason, the company provides a prompt, no-hassle refund or exchange. Infiniti car dealers recently offered refunds to new car buyers within three days of their purchase if they decided they were dissatisfied. The same dealers also offered a price protection plan: if prices went down on a new Infiniti, anyone who paid more than the lower price in the previous thirty days was entitled to a refund of the difference.[17]

Types of Consumer Buying Decisions and Consumer Involvement

Identify the types of consumer buying decisions, and discuss the significance of consumer involvement

All consumer buying decisions generally fall along a continuum of three broad categories: routine response behaviour, limited decision making, and extensive decision making (see Exhibit 4.2). Purchases of goods and services in each of these three categories can best be described in terms of five factors: level of consumer involvement, length of time to make a decision, cost of the good or service, degree of information search, and number of alternatives considered. Level of consumer involvement is perhaps the most significant of these five. **Involvement** is the amount of time and effort a buyer invests in the search, evaluation, and decision processes of consumer behaviour.

involvement
The amount of time and effort a buyer invests in the search, evaluation, and decision processes of consumer behaviour.

exhibit 4.2

Continuum of Consumer Buying Decisions

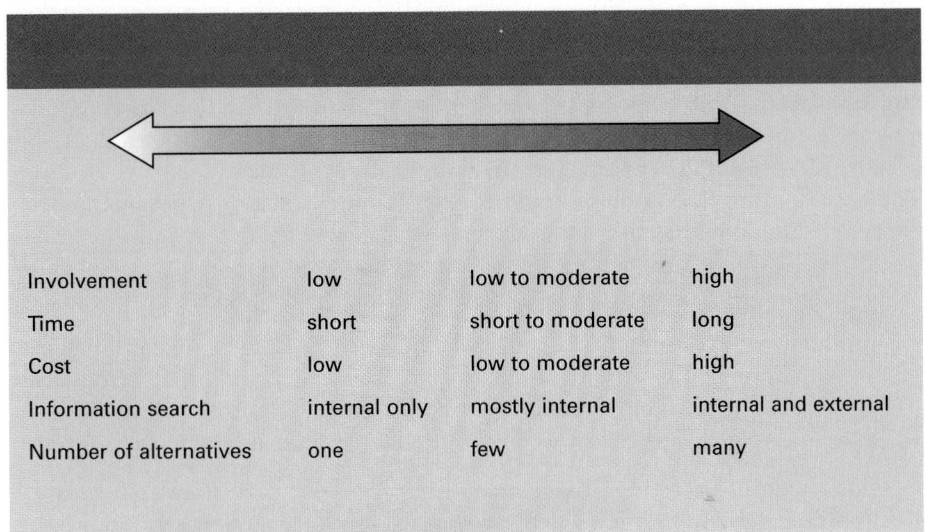

Involvement	low	low to moderate	high
Time	short	short to moderate	long
Cost	low	low to moderate	high
Information search	internal only	mostly internal	internal and external
Number of alternatives	one	few	many

Frequently purchased, low-cost goods and services are generally associated with **routine response behaviour**. These goods and services can also be called low-involvement products, because consumers spend little time on search and decision before purchasing them. Usually, buyers are familiar with several different brands in the product category but stick with one brand. Consumers engaged in routine response behaviour normally don't experience need recognition until they are exposed to advertising or see the product displayed on a store shelf. Consumers buy first and evaluate later, whereas the reverse is true for extensive decision making. A parent will not stand at the cereal shelf in the grocery store for twenty minutes thinking about which brand of cereal to buy for the children. Instead, he or she will walk by the shelf, find the family's usual brand, and place it in the cart.

routine response behaviour
The type of decision making exhibited by consumers buying frequently purchased, low-cost goods and services; requires little search and decision time.

limited decision making The type of decision making that requires a moderate amount of time for gathering information and deliberating about an unfamiliar brand in a familiar product category.

Limited decision making typically occurs when a consumer has previous product experience but is unfamiliar with the current brands available. It is also associated with lower levels of involvement—albeit higher than for routine decisions—in that consumers do expend moderate effort in searching for information and considering various alternatives. Suppose the children's usual brand of cereal, Kellogg's Corn Flakes, is unavailable at the grocery store. The parent is completely out of cereal at home and must now select another brand. Before making a final selection, he or she may pull from the shelf several brands similar to Kellogg's Corn Flakes, such as Corn Chex and Cheerios, to compare their nutritional value and calories and to decide whether the children will like the new cereal.

extensive decision making The most complex type of consumer decision making, used when buying an unfamiliar, expensive product or an infrequently bought item; requires use of several criteria for evaluating options and much time for seeking information.

Consumers practise **extensive decision making** when buying an expensive, unfamiliar product or an infrequently bought item. This is the most complex type of buying decision and is associated with high involvement on the part of the consumer. The process resembles the model outlined in Exhibit 4.1. The consumer wants to make the right decision and so wants to know as much as possible about the product category and available brands. Usually, people experience cognitive dissonance only when buying high-involvement products. Buyers apply several criteria when evaluating their options, and spend much time seeking information. Purchasing a home or a car involves extensive decision making.

The type of decision making that consumers use to purchase a product does not necessarily remain constant. If a routinely purchased product no longer satisfies, consumers may practise limited or extensive decision making before switching to another brand. And people who use extensive decision making for their first purchase may then switch to limited or routine decision making for future purchases. A first-year student may undertake an extensive evaluation of computer options at many different locations before buying a computer for college or university. That student will consider retail stores such as Future Shop and on-line services such as eBay and Dell, as well as various brand-name computers and knock-offs.

Factors Determining the Level of Consumer Involvement

The level of involvement in a purchase depends on five factors: previous experience, interest, perceived risk, situation, and social visibility.

- *Previous experience.* When consumers have had previous experience with a good or service, the level of involvement typically decreases. After repeated product trials, consumers learn to make quick choices. Because consumers are familiar with the product and know whether it will satisfy their needs, they become less involved in the purchase. For example, consumers with pollen allergies typically buy the sinus medicine that has relieved their symptoms in the past.

- *Interest.* Involvement is directly related to the consumer's interest, be it in cars, music, movies, bicycling, or electronics. Naturally, areas of interest vary from one individual to another. Most people have little interest in nursing homes; but a person with elderly parents in poor health may well be highly interested.

- *Perceived risk of negative consequences.* As the perceived risk in purchasing a product increases, so does the consumer's level of involvement. The types of risks that concern consumers include financial risk, social risk, and psychological risk. *Financial* risk is the risk of losing wealth or purchasing power. High risk is associated with high-priced purchases, so consumers tend to become extremely involved in these. It follows that price and involvement are usually directly related: as price increases, so does the level of involvement. Someone who is thinking of buying a home will usually spend a great deal of time and effort finding the right one. Consumers take *social* risks when they buy products that can affect people's opinion of them (e.g., an old, beat-up car or unstylish clothes). Buyers face *psychological* risk when they believe that making the wrong decision could cause them concern or anxiety. Should a working parent hire a babysitter or enrol the child in a daycare centre?

- *Situation.* Sometimes the circumstances of a purchase temporarily transform a low-involvement decision into a high-involvement one. High involvement comes into play when the consumer perceives risk in a specific situation. Perhaps an individual routinely buys low-priced wines. However, when the boss visits, he may well make a high-involvement decision and buy a costlier and more prestigious wine.
- *Social visibility.* Involvement also increases with a product's social visibility. Products often on social display include clothing—especially designer labels—jewellery, cars, and furniture. All these items make a statement about the purchaser and for that reason carry a social risk.

Marketing Implications of Involvement

Marketing strategy varies with the level of involvement associated with the product. For high-involvement product purchases, marketing managers develop extensive and informative promotions for the target market. A good ad gives consumers the information they need for making the purchase decision; it also specifies the benefits and unique advantages of owning the product. Manufacturers of high-tech computers and peripheral equipment such as scanners, printers, and modems run lengthy ads offering detailed technical information about performance, resolution, and speed. Germany's Daimler-Benz AG, maker of Mercedes-Benz automobiles, is developing Virtual Vehicle, which uses virtual-reality technology to let customers test different combinations of colours, fabrics, and hubcaps. A touch screen hung from the ceiling allows customers to walk around a computer-generated image of a car, changing colour, fabric, hubcaps, and headlights with a click. Customers can even alter the speaker configuration and hear the result immediately in Dolby stereo sound.[18]

With low-involvement product purchases, consumers may not recognize their wants until they are actually in the store. So in-store promotion is an important tool for promoting these products. Here, marketing managers focus on package design, the goal being an eye-catching product that is easily recognized on the shelf. Products that take this approach include Campbell's soups, Tide detergent, Velveeta cheese, and Heinz ketchup. In-store displays also stimulate sales of low-involvement products. A good display explains the product's purpose and prompts recognition of a want. Displays of health and beauty aid items in supermarkets have been known to increase sales many times above normal. Coupons, cents-off deals, and two-for-one offers also promote low-involvement items quite effectively.

Marketing managers can also increase sales of low-involvement products by linking those products to higher-involvement issues. Many food products are no longer simply nutritious—they are also low in fat or cholesterol. Packaged foods are often low-involvement items; with these, referring to health issues can raise the involvement level. Oatmeal has been around for hundreds of years. To take advantage of today's interest in healthier foods, Quaker Oats used health appeals in its advertising—specifically, the claim that soluble fiber from oatmeal, as part of a low-fat, low-

Do you think that the television show *Popstars,* which created the pop group Sugar Jones, has created an aspirational reference group for young women? Read the Entrepreneurial Insights feature to find out.

Roots Canada

What does this Website and the products it features tell you about the values of Roots customers? What wants and needs are satisfied by Roots products?

www.roots.ca

on line

cholesterol diet, may reduce the risk of heart disease. Quaker's advertising of that claim—which included the slogan, "Oh, what those oats can do"—helped reverse a slump in oatmeal sales.[19]

Factors Influencing Consumer Buying Decisions

5

Identify and understand the *cultural* factors that affect consumer buying decisions

Consumers don't make their decisions in a vacuum. On the contrary, the process is strongly influenced by underlying cultural, social, individual, and psychological factors, which have an effect from the time a consumer perceives a stimulus through postpurchase behaviour. Cultural factors, which include culture and values, subculture, and social class, exert the broadest influence over consumer decision making. Social factors include the social interactions between the consumer and influential groups such as reference groups, opinion leaders, and family members. Individual factors, which include gender, age, personality, self-concept, lifestyle, and stage in the family life cycle, are unique to each individual and do much to determine which products and services consumers want. Psychological factors—perception, motivation, learning, beliiefs, attitudes, and so on—determine how the consumer perceives and interacts with his or her environment, and thus the ultimate decisions made. Exhibit 4.3 summarizes all these influences.

Cultural factors exert the broadest and deepest influence over a person's behaviour as a consumer. Marketers must understand how a consumer's culture

entrepreneurial insights

Reality TV and Teenage Aspirations

The new millennium is driving consumer behaviour in all sorts of interesting ways. One trend of the first years of this new century is reality TV. American offerings such as the blockbuster *Survivor* have been the catalyst for many new reality TV programs.

Canwest Global TV's hit show *Popstars* provided a number of things that satisfied the needs and wants of its audience, which was predominantly teenage girls. The show was reality TV, with aspiring pop stars auditioning to become famous performers.

"We took five people out of obscurity and made them popstars," says Global TV producer Michael Geddes.[20] The eight-week series chronicled the countrywide search for candidates to attend a training "boot camp" in Toronto. After intensive training, five popstars were selected to form an all-female singing group. All the steps in their selection, training, and preparation were filmed and shown on prime-time TV.

The five young women had been selected from among 4,000 auditions. They were Julie Crochetiere from Quebec, Mirella Dell'Aquila from Quebec, Andrea Henry from Ontario, Sahara MacDonald from British Columbia, and Maiko Watson from Manitoba. Ultimately they became the pop group Sugar Jones, and their first single, "Days Like That," quickly reached the charts.

Reality TV interests viewers because it makes them believe, "This could happen to *me*." The individuals on the screen are ordinary people, not polished and primped actors. Young women can realize their dream of becoming famous or knowing someone famous by watching the entire process, from anonymity to fame, unfold on their TV screens once a week. Barbie Dolls encourage imaginary adventures for young girls; in the same way, *Popstars* allows young women to watch their aspirational reference group for an hour every week.

More Canadian shows like *Popstars* are in the works. *Popstars 2* airs in January 2002, and will result in a five-member band that includes both males and females. Global is also developing *Search for a Supermodel*, which will follow young models to New York, where they will compete for modelling contracts.

Candid Camera was the reality TV of the 1960s; in the new millennium, shows like *Popstars* are dominating the screens.

exhibit 4.3

Factors That Affect the Consumer Decision-Making Process

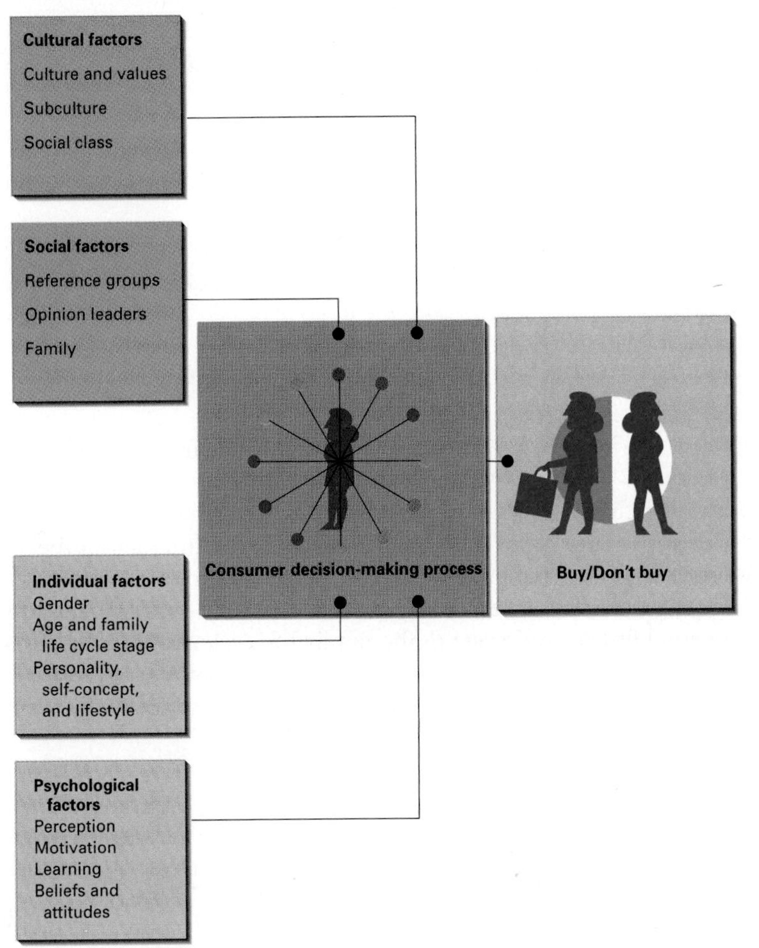

and its accompanying values, as well as his or her subculture and social class, influence buying behaviour.

Culture and Values

culture
A set of values, norms, attitudes, and other meaningful symbols that shape human behaviour; also, the artifacts—or products—of that behaviour as they are transmitted from one generation to the next.

Culture is the essential character of a society; it is what distinguishes any given society from all others. Every culture has its own specific cultural mix—its own values, language, myths, customs, rituals, laws, and so on. All of these shape the behaviour of the culture, as well as the artifacts—that is, the products—of that behaviour as they are transmitted from one generation to the next. Exhibit 4.4 lists some defining components of North American culture. Culture is *pervasive.* Cultural values and influences are the ocean in which individuals swim, and most people are completely unaware of them. What people eat, how they dress, what they think and feel, and what language they speak are all dimensions of culture. Culture encompasses all the things that consumers do without conscious choice because their culture's values, customs, and rituals are ingrained in their daily habits.

Culture is *functional.* Human interaction creates values and prescribes acceptable behaviour for each culture. By establishing common expectations, culture gives order to society. Sometimes these expectations are encoded as laws—for example, drivers in our culture must stop at a red light. Other times these expectations are taken for granted—for example, hospitals are open twenty-four hours a day, whereas bank lobbies are open only during banker's hours.

exhibit 4.4

Components of North American Culture

Component	Example
Values	Success through hard work. Emphasis on personal freedom.
Myths	Santa Claus delivers presents to good boys and girls on Christmas Eve. The tooth fairy leaves money in return for baby teeth.
Customs	Bathing daily. Shaking hands when greeting new people. Standard gratuity of 15 percent at restaurants.
Rituals	Thanksgiving Day dinner. Standing for the "Oh Canada" before baseball games. Going to church on Sundays.
Laws	Child labour laws. Laws preventing unfair competition (Canada's Competition Act).
Material artifacts	Diamond engagement rings. Beanie Babies.

Source: Adapted from *Consumer Behaviour* by William D. Wells and David Prensky. Copyright © 1996 by John Wiley & Sons, Inc. This material was used by permission of John Wiley & Sons, Inc.

Culture is *learned.* Consumers are not born knowing the values and norms of their society. Instead, they must learn what is acceptable from family and friends. Children learn the values that will govern their behaviour from parents, teachers, and peers. As members of our society, they learn to shake hands when they greet someone, to drive on the right-hand side of the road, and to eat pizza and drink Coca-Cola.

Culture is *dynamic.* It adapts to changing needs and an evolving environment. The rapid growth of technology at the end of the twentieth century has accelerated the rate of cultural change. Television has changed entertainment patterns and family communication, and has also heightened public awareness of political and other news events. Automation has increased the amount of leisure time we have, and in some ways has changed the traditional work ethic. Cultural norms will continue to evolve because of our need for social patterns that solve problems.

value
An enduring belief that a specific mode of conduct is personally or socially preferable to another mode of conduct.

The most defining element of a culture is its **values**—the enduring beliefs shared by a society, the shared ethos that a particular mode of conduct is personally or socially preferable to other modes of conduct. People's value systems have a profound effect on their consumer behaviour. Consumers with similar value systems tend to react alike to prices and other marketing-related inducements. Values also correspond to consumption patterns. People who want to protect the environment try to buy only products that don't harm it. Values can also influence consumers' TV viewing habits and the magazines they read. For instance, people who strongly object to violence avoid crime shows, and those who oppose pornography do not buy *Hustler.* North Americans' core values—that is, those values that are considered central to the North American way of life—are presented in Exhibit 4.5.

The personal values of target consumers have important implications for marketing managers. When marketers understand the core values that underlie the attitudes that shape the buying patterns of North American consumers, and how these values have been molded by experience, they can target their message more effectively. For example, the personal value systems of matures, baby boomers, and baby busters are quite different. The key to understanding *matures*—that is, everyone born before 1945—is recognizing how deeply their lives were affected by the Great Depression and the Second World War. These two immense challenges shaped an entire generation, instilling it with discipline, self-denial, financial and social conservatism, and a sense of obligation. *Boomers*, those individuals nurtured in the bountiful postwar years 1945 to 1964, feel themselves entitled to the wealth and opportunity that seemed endless in their youth. *Baby busters*, or Generation X as they are often referred to, are very accepting of diversity and individuality. They are also very entrepreneurial, and ready to tackle life's challenges for themselves rather than as part of a crowd.[21]

exhibit 4.5

North American Core Values

Core Values	
Success	North Americans admire hard work, entrepreneurship, achievement, and success. Those who achieve success in North American society are rewarded with money, status, and prestige. Bill Gates, once a nerdy computer buff, built Microsoft into an international giant. Gates is now one of the richest people in the world.
Materialism	North Americans value owning tangible goods. Our society encourages consumption, ownership, and possession. North Americans judge others by their material possessions—for example, the type of car they own, where they live, and the type of clothes they wear.
Freedom	North American culture was founded on the principles of religious and political freedom. The American Constitution and Canadian Charter of Rights and Freedoms protect individual rights.
Progress	Technological progress and advances in medicine, science, and the quality of products and services are important to North Americans. Each year more than 25,000 new or improved consumer products are introduced on America's supermarket shelves.[22]
Youth	North Americans are obsessed with youth and spend a great deal of time on products and procedures that make them feel and look younger. We spend millions each year on health and beauty aids, health clubs, and healthy foods. The media and advertisers encourage the quest for youth by using young, attractive, slim models, such as those in Calvin Klein ads.
Capitalism	North Americans believe in a free enterprise system characterized by competition and the opportunity to achieve monetary success. Capitalism creates choices, quality, and value. Laws prohibit market monopolies and regulate free trade. North Americans encourage small business success: Apple Computer, Wal-Mart, and McDonald's all started as small enterprises with a better idea that toppled the competition.

Source: Adapted from *Consumer Behaviour* by William D. Wells and David Prensky. Copyright © 1996 by John Wiley & Sons, Inc. This material was used by permission of John Wiley & Sons, Inc.

Oprah Winfrey

What kind of role does spirituality play in Oprah Winfrey's show and in her other ventures? Visit her Web page and find out.

www.oprah.com

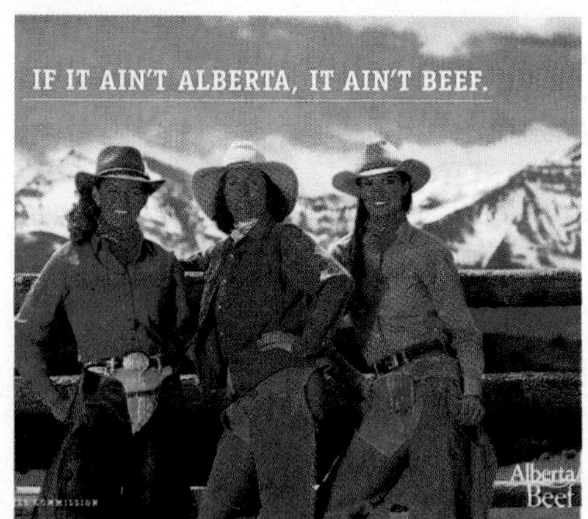

IF IT AIN'T ALBERTA, IT AIN'T BEEF.
Alberta Beef

Which values and beliefs is this ad appealing to? Are they distinctly Canadian values and beliefs?

Canadian researcher Suzanne Peters of Canadian Policy Research Networks found that Canadians believe in self-reliance, in compassion in terms of collective responsibility, and in equal access to education and health care. Other Canadian values include democracy, freedom, equality, and fiscal responsibility.

Values represent what is most important in people's lives. So marketers watch carefully for shifts in consumers' values over time. Millions of North Americans have acquired a passion for spirituality, as evidenced by the soaring sales of books with religious or spiritual themes and by the popularity of CBS's *Touched by an Angel*.[23]

Understanding Culture Differences

Underlying core values vary across cultures. Thus, Asians tend to place a high value on social harmony, whereas North Americans place greater emphasis on individual rights and responsibilities. In a survey of Asian and North American business executives, Asian businesspeople placed hard work, honesty, and respect for learning among their top values. In contrast, honesty and accountability were not among American business executives' top-rated values. They ranked freedom of expression as highly important—a value that did not even make the grade with Asian executives.[24]

Unless it understands a culture, a firm has little chance of selling products in it. Products have their own cultural values and rules, which influence how they are perceived and used. It follows that a culture must be understood before the behaviour of individuals in that culture can be understood.[25] For example, colours often have different meanings in global markets than they do at home. In China, white is the colour of mourning and brides wear red; in Canada and the United States, black is for mourning and brides wear white. Pepsi had a dominant market share in Southeast Asia until it changed the colour of its coolers and vending equipment from deep regal-blue to light ice-blue. In that part of the world, light-blue is associated with death and mourning. Whirlpool Corporation did not consider the huge cultural differences between European countries when it first entered the European market. Clothes washers sold in northern countries such as Denmark must spin-dry clothes much better than in southern Italy, where consumers often line-dry clothes in warmer weather. Whirlpool has since learned its lesson and redesigned more than half the products it sells in Europe.[26]

Language is another important aspect of culture that global marketers must deal with. They must take care when translating product names, slogans, and promotional messages into foreign languages so as not to convey the wrong message. Consider the following examples of blunders made by marketers when delivering their message to Spanish-speaking consumers:

- General Motors discovered too late that Nova—the name of an economy car—literally means "doesn't go" in Spanish.
- Coors encouraged its English-speaking customers to "Turn it loose," but the phrase in Spanish means "suffer from diarrhea."
- When Frank Perdue said, "It takes a tough man to make a tender chicken," Spanish speakers heard, "It takes a sexually stimulated man to make a chicken affectionate."

Canadian advertisers generally prepare completely separate advertisements for use in French- and English-speaking areas of Canada. Ideas presented in English can be meaningless in French, and some French puns and sayings could not be understood by English-speaking Canadians.

As more companies expand their operations globally, the need to understand the cultures of foreign countries becomes more important. Marketers should become familiar with the culture and adapt to it. What's all the rage in Calgary could be a bust in Bombay (or Trois-Rivières) if marketers are not sensitive to the nuances of the local culture. The "Global Perspectives" box talks about the differences in how cultures around the world view and use time.

Subculture

A culture can be divided into subcultures on the basis of demographic characteristics, geographic regions, national and ethnic background, and political and religious beliefs. A **subculture** is a homogeneous group of people who share elements of the overall culture as well as cultural elements unique to their own group. Within subcultures, people's attitudes, values, and purchase decisions are even

subculture
A homogeneous group of people who share elements of the overall culture as well as unique elements of their own group.

global perspectives

The Pace of Life and Use of Time Around the World

How consumers view and use time varies greatly across cultures. These measures relate to the deeply rooted values that are shared within each culture.

Several researchers have studied the tempo of life in other cultures, as well as how people spend their time. Robert Levine, a professor of psychology at California State University, Fresno, has been studying the tempo of life in various cultures for over a decade. John Robinson, a sociology professor at the University of Maryland, College Park, has been involved in the Americans' Use of Time Project since its beginnings in 1965. Here is what these two researchers have learned regarding how Canadians, Americans, and other cultures view and use time.

From his research, Levine developed three measures of the pace of life: 1. walking speed—the speed at which pedestrians in downtown areas walk a distance of sixty feet; 2. work speed—how quickly postal clerks complete a standard request to purchase a stamp; and 3. the accuracy of public clocks. To measure the pace of life in different countries around the world, researchers collected data from at least one large city in each of thirty-one nations.

Japan and Western European countries scored fastest overall, with Switzerland achieving the distinction of first place. Bank clocks in Switzerland were off by an average of only nineteen seconds. Following Switzerland were Ireland, Germany, Japan, Italy, England, Sweden, Austria, and the Netherlands. Canada scored eleventh on walking speed but twenty-first on postal times and twenty-second on clock accuracy, for an overall rank of seventeenth place, one behind the United States.

There were few surprises at the slow end of the list: the eight slowest countries were all nonindustrialized countries in Africa, Asia, the Middle East, and Latin America. In countries such as Brazil, Indonesia, and Mexico—all of which fell to the bottom of the pace-of-life scale—slowness seeps into the fabric of daily life. Brazilians expect a casual approach to time and seem to have abandoned any semblance of fidelity to the clock. When asked how long they would wait for a late arrival to show up at a nephew's birthday party, Brazilians said they would hold on for an average of 129 minutes—over two hours! Few Brazilians wear watches, and the watches they do wear are often inaccurate.

How people spend their time also varies from culture to culture. Time-use specialists often refer to France, Germany, and other Western European countries as "eating and sleeping cultures" because Europeans spend much more time than Americans or Asians on these two activities. Europeans also work fewer hours per week and enjoy more vacation time—up to six weeks mandatory vacation in some European countries. In Sweden, vacation time goes as high as eight weeks per year. In contrast, people in Japan and North America spend more time working and take fewer vacations than their European counterparts.

All cultures have something to learn from others' conceptions of time. Consumers who don't fully understand a culture's context are likely to misinterpret people's motives in that culture. When that happens, the inevitable result is conflict. Marketers who use sales personnel to sell in other countries must consider the pace of life and the use of time of each culture. For instance, marketers from a relatively fast-paced culture like Canada can blunder badly when selling in Mexico, where the pace is far slower.

One of the hardest aspects of time for people of fast cultures to assimilate is the move from "clock time" to "event time." Clock time uses the hour on the clock to schedule activities; event time allows activities to transpire according to their own spontaneous schedules. A move from clock time to event time requires a complete shift of consciousness and the suspension of industrialized society's golden rule: "Time is money." People in the Middle East resist fixed schedules, viewing them as rude and insulting. Canadians, Americans, Japanese, and Europeans are strongly tied to clock time in their daily life.[27]

Identifying subcultures can be a difficult task for a marketing manager. If they can be identified, marketers can design products and services to meet the needs and wants of these specific market segments. The French-language version of *Reader's Digest* serves its particular subculture.

more similar than they are within the broader culture. Subcultural differences may result in considerable variation within a culture regarding what, how, when, and where people buy goods and services.

Canadian society is rich in traditions and complex in interesting ways. Around 14 percent of Canadians are francophone. There are many native people and Ukrainians in the prairie provinces. There are large Asian and Italian communities in Toronto, Vancouver, and Montreal. According to Statistics Canada, this country's top eight ethnic origins are Canadian, English, French, Scottish, Irish, German, Italian, and Aboriginal.

Other subcultures are geographically dispersed. A recent study identified Harley-Davidson owners as a distinct subculture.[28] Computer hackers, military families, and university professors are found throughout the country; yet each of these groups has its own set of identifiable attitudes and values that distinguishes it from the larger culture.

Social Class

social class
A group of people in a society who are considered nearly equal in status or community esteem, who regularly socialize among themselves both formally and informally, and who share behavioural norms.

Canada, like other societies, has a social class system. A **social class** is a group of people who are considered nearly equal in status or community esteem, who regularly socialize among themselves both formally and informally, and who share behavioural norms.

A number of techniques have been used to measure social class, and a number of approaches have been taken to defining it. One view of contemporary status structure is shown in Exhibit 4.6.

As Exhibit 4.6 shows, the upper and upper middle classes constitute a small segment of North Americans. Obviously, they are more affluent. They are also more likely than other classes to contribute to society through volunteer work, active participation in civic affairs, and so on. In terms of consumer buying patterns, they are more likely to be home owners and to purchase new cars and trucks. They are also less likely to smoke. The very rich flex their financial muscle by spending more on vacation homes, vacations and cruises, and housekeeping and gardening services. The most affluent consumers are more likely to attend art auctions and galleries, dance performances, opera, the theatre, museums, concerts, and sporting events.[29]

exhibit 4.6

Social Class

Upper classes		
Capitalist class	1%	People whose investment decisions shape the national economy; income mostly from earned or inherited assets; university connections
Upper middle class	14%	Upper-level managers, professionals, owners of medium-sized businesses; university educated; family income nearly twice national average
Middle classes		
Middle class	33%	Middle-level white collar, top-level blue collar; education past high school typical; income somewhat above national average
Working class	32%	Middle-level blue collar, lower-level white collar; income slightly below national average
Lower classes		
Working poor	11–12%	Low-paid service workers and operatives; some high school education; below mainstream in living standard but above poverty line
Underclass	8–9%	People who are not regularly employed and who depend mainly on the welfare system for sustenance; little schooling; living standard below poverty line

Source: Adapted from Richard P. Coleman, "The Continuing Significance of Social Class to Marketing," *Journal of Consumer Research*, December 1983, p. 267; Dennis Gilbert and Joseph A. Kahl, *The American Class Structure: A Synthesis* (Homewood, IL: Dorsey Press, 1982): ch. 11.

Most Canadians today define themselves as middle class, whatever their actual income or educational attainment. This is probably because working class Canadians tend to aspire to the middle class lifestyle, and because some of those who do achieve affluence aspire "downward" to respectable middle class status as a matter of principle.[30] Middle class consumers consider it important to attain their goals and achieve status and prestige. People in the middle class inhabit the gap between the haves and the have-nots. They aspire to the lifestyle of the more affluent but are constrained by economic realities and by the cautious attitudes they share with the working class.

The working class is a distinct subset of the middle class. Interest in organized labour is one of the more signal attributes of this group. Working class people are more likely to rate job security as the most important reason for taking a job.[31] They depend heavily on their relatives and communities for economic and emotional support. Emphasis on family ties is one sign of this group's intensely local view of the world. They like to watch the local news; middle class audiences much prefer to watch national and world coverage. Working class people are also more likely to vacation closer to home.

Lifestyle distinctions *between* social classes are greater than *within* a given class. The most significant separation is the one between the middle and lower classes. This is where the major shift in lifestyles appears. Members of the lower class typically fall at or below the poverty level in terms of income. This social class has the highest unemployment rate; many individuals and families in this class are subsidized through the welfare system. Many are illiterate or at least have little formal education. Lower class consumers have poorer diets than more affluent consumers and typically purchase very different types of foods when they shop.

Social class is typically measured in terms of occupation, income, education, wealth, and other variables. For instance, upper class consumers are more likely to be executives or self-employed professionals with incomes over $70,000 and at least an undergraduate degree.[32] Working class and middle class consumers are more likely to be service or blue collar workers, to have incomes below $70,000, and to have attained only a high school education. Educational attainment seems to be the most reliable indicator of a person's social and economic status. Those with university degrees or graduate degrees are more likely to fall into the upper classes; those with some university but no degree fall closest to traditional concepts of the middle class.

Marketers are interested in social class in large part because class indicates which medium should be used for advertising. Suppose an insurance company is seeking to sell its policies to middle class families. It might advertise during the local evening news, because middle class families tend to watch more television than other classes do. If the company wants to sell more policies to upscale individuals, it might place print ads in business publication such as *The Globe and Mail* and *The National Post,* which are read by more educated and affluent people.

6
Identify and understand the *social* factors that affect consumer buying decisions

Social Influences on Consumer Buying Decisions

In making purchasing decisions, most consumers are likely to seek out others' opinions to reduce their uncertainty, especially as the perceived risk of the decision increases. Consumers also seek out others' opinions for guidance on new products or services, or products with image-related attributes, or when information on attributes is lacking or uninformative.[33] More specifically, consumers interact socially with reference groups, opinion leaders, and family members to obtain product information and decision approval.

reference group
A group in society that influences an individual's purchasing behaviour.

direct reference groups
Face-to face membership groups that touch peoples lives directly.

primary membership groups
Reference groups with which people interact regularly on an informal, face-to-face basis, such as family, friends, and fellow employees.

secondary membership groups
Reference groups with which people associate less consistently and more formally than with primary membership groups, such as clubs, professional groups, and religious groups.

aspirational reference groups
Groups that an individual wants t join.

norm
A value or attitude deemed acceptable by a group.

nonaspirational reference groups
Groups with which an individual does not want to associate.

Reference Groups

All the formal and informal groups that influence the buying behaviour of an individual are that person's **reference groups**. Consumers may purchase products or brands in order to identify with or become members of a group. They learn by observing how members of their reference groups consume; then they use the same criteria to make their own consumer decisions.

Reference groups can be categorized very broadly as either direct or indirect (see Exhibit 4.7). **Direct reference groups** are the face-to-face membership groups that touch people's lives directly. They can be primary or secondary. **Primary membership groups** include all the groups with which people interact regularly on an informal, face-to-face basis, such as family, friends, and co-workers. People associate with **secondary membership groups** less consistently and more formally. These groups include clubs, professional groups, and religious groups.

Consumers also are influenced by many indirect, nonmembership reference groups they do not belong to. **Aspirational reference groups** are the groups a person wants to join. To join an aspirational group, a person must at least conform to the norms of that group. (**Norms** are the values and attitudes deemed acceptable by the group.) Thus, a person who wants to be elected to public office may begin to dress more conservatively, as other politicians do. He or she may go to many of the restaurants and social engagements that city and business leaders attend and try to play a role that is acceptable to voters and other influential people. Similarly, a teenager may dye her hair and experiment with body piercing and tattoos; a student in the final year of college or university will likely get a more conservative haircut as she begins her career search.

Nonaspirational reference groups, or dissociative groups, influence our behaviour when we try to maintain distance from them. A consumer may avoid buying some types of clothing, going to certain restaurants or stores, or even buying a home in a certain neighbourhood in order to avoid being associated with a particular group.

exhibit 4.7

Types of Reference Groups

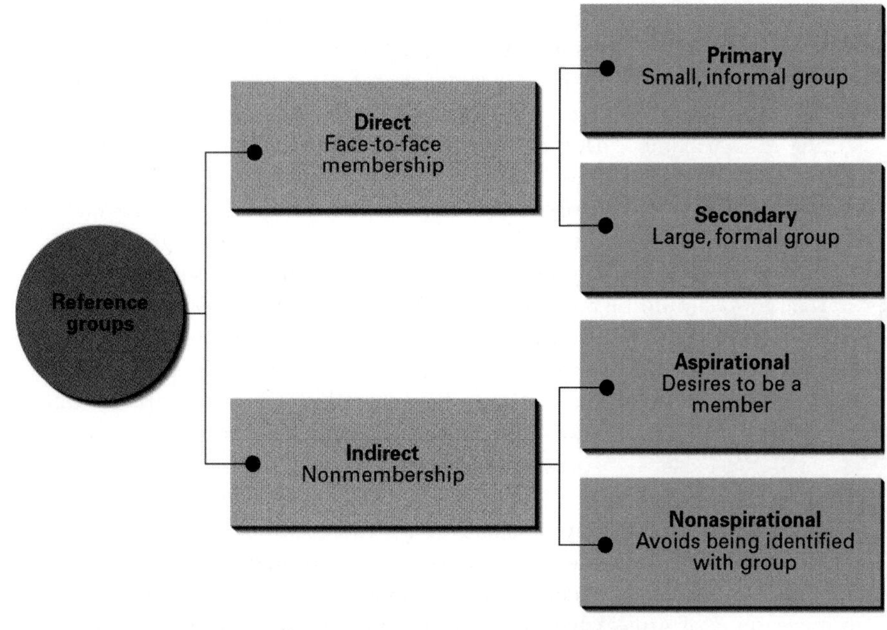

The activities, values, and goals of reference groups directly influence consumer behaviour. For marketers, reference groups have three important implications: they serve as information sources and influence perceptions; they affect an individual's aspiration levels; and their norms either constrain or stimulate consumer behaviour. Many Canadians seek the advice of family and friends when shopping for doctors, lawyers, or auto mechanics. Individuals also are likely to seek others' advice when selecting a restaurant for a special occasion or deciding which movie to see.[34]

Companies in Japan have long relied on the nation's high school girls to test products. Fads that catch on among teenage girls often become big trends throughout the country among Japanese consumers in general. Food manufacturers often recruit Tokyo schoolgirls to sample potato chip recipes and chocolate bars. TV networks survey high school girls to fine tune story lines. CanWest Global Television created its television show *Popstars* to attract teenage girls, whose reference groups include pop stars.

Opinion Leaders

Reference groups often include individuals known as group leaders, or opinion leaders. These are people who influence others. Obviously, it is important for marketing managers to persuade these people to purchase their goods and services. Many products and services that are integral to our lives today got their initial boost from these people. VCRs and sport utility vehicles were embraced by opinion leaders well ahead of the general public.

opinion leader
An individual who influences the opinions of others.

Opinion leaders often try new products and services first, out of pure curiosity. Typically they are activists in their communities, on the job, and in the marketplace. Opinion leaders tend to be self-indulgent, which makes them more likely to explore unproven but intriguing products and services. This combination of curiosity, activism, and self-indulgence makes opinion leaders trendsetters in the consumer marketplace.[35]

Opinion leadership is a casual, face-to-face phenomenon and is usually inconspicuous, so locating opinion leaders can be a challenge. This is why marketers often try to create opinion leaders. They may use high school cheerleaders to model new fall fashions, or civic leaders to promote insurance, new cars, and

Modrobes started by selling its jeans to students in college and university cafeterias, as it had designed its products for them. Was the company's early success a result of understanding reference groups and opinion leadership?

other merchandise. Revatex, the makers of JNCO wide-leg jeans, gives free clothes to trendsetters among teens in the hope that they will influence others to purchase their brand. Big-name DJs in the rave scene are outfitted by JNCO; so are members of hip, alternative bands favoured by the teen crowd. Modrobes founder Steve Debus started selling his pants by travelling to colleges and universities across Canada and making sales in cafeterias. Later his company progressed to concerts and other events where their market could be found.

On a national level, companies sometimes use movie stars, sports figures, and other celebrities to promote products, hoping they are appropriate opinion leaders. Tiger Woods is the most sought-after spokesperson in the world, followed by Michael Jordan. In Canada, Wayne Gretzky is a much sought-after spokesperson for corporations and charities.

The effectiveness of a celebrity endorsement depends largely on how credible and attractive the spokesperson is and on how familiar people are with him or her. Endorsements are most likely to succeed when an association between the spokesperson and the product can be reasonably established. Comedian Bill Cosby failed as an endorser for financial products but succeeded with products such as Kodak cameras and Jell-O desserts. Consumers could not mentally link Bill Cosby with serious investment decisions but could associate him with leisure activities and everyday consumption. Also, when selecting a celebrity endorser, marketers must consider the broader meanings associated with the endorser. The endorser may have certain desirable attributes but other attributes that are inappropriate.

B.C.-born Michael J. Fox has been an effective spokesperson for the Parkinson's Disease Foundation. Canadian Hockey superstar Wayne Gretzky came under fire when he was both volunteer spokesperson for osteoarthritis and a paid endorser for Johnson & Johnson's Tylenol, a product used in the treatment of arthritis.

Family

The family is the most important social institution for many consumers. Families strongly influence values, attitudes, self-concept—and buying behaviour. A family that strongly values good health will have a grocery list distinctly different from that of a family which views every dinner as a gourmet event. Moreover, the family is responsible for the **socialization process** and for passing down cultural values and norms to children. Children learn by observing their parents' consumption patterns, which means they tend to shop in a similar pattern.

socialization process
How cultural values and norms are passed down to children.

Decision-making roles among family members tend to vary significantly with the type of item purchased. Family members assume a variety of roles in the purchase process. *Initiators* are the ones who suggest, initiate, or plant the seed for the purchase process. The initiator can be any member of the family. Sister might initiate the product search by asking for a new bicycle as a birthday present. *Influencers* are those members of the family whose opinions are valued. In our example, Mom might function as a price-range watchdog, an influencer whose main role is to veto or approve price ranges. Brother may give his opinion on certain makes of bicycles. The *decision maker* is the member of the family who actually makes the decision to buy or not to buy. Dad or Mom is likely to choose the final brand and model of bicycle to buy after seeking further information from Sister about cosmetic features such as colour and after imposing additional criteria, such as durability and safety. The *purchaser* (probably Dad or Mom) is the one

exhibit 4.8

Relationships Among Purchasers and Consumers in the Family

Consumer	Purchase Decision Maker: Parent(s) only	Child/children only	Some or all family members
Parent(s)	Golf clubs Cosmetics Wine	Mother's Day card	Christmas gifts Minivan
Child/children	Diapers Breakfast cereal	Candy Small toys	Bicycle
Some family members	Videos Long-distance phone service	Children's movies	Computers Sports events
All family members	Clothing Life insurance	Fast-food restaurant	Swim club membership Vacations

Source: From "Tapping the Three Kids' Market" by James U. McNeal, *American Demographics*, April 1998. © 1998 PRIMEDIA Intertec, Stamford, CT.

who actually exchanges money for the product. Finally, the *consumer* is the actual user—Sister, in the case of the bicycle.

Marketers should consider family purchase situations along with the distribution of consumer and decision maker roles among family members. *Ordinary* marketing views the individual as both decision maker and consumer. *Family* marketing adds several other possibilities: Sometimes more than one family member or all family members are involved in the decision; sometimes only children are involved in the decision; sometimes more than one consumer is involved; and sometimes the decision maker and the consumer are different people. Exhibit 4.8 indicates the various possible patterns of family purchasing relationships.

Today's children often greatly influence the purchase decisions of their parents. In many families, both parents work and are short on time and so encourage the children to participate. Also, children in single-parent households become more involved in family decision making at an earlier age than children in two-parent households. Children are especially influential in decisions about food. Children often help decide where the family goes for fast food, and many influence the choice of full-service restaurant. Kids also have input into the kinds of food the family eats at home, and they often influence even the specific brands their parents buy. Finally, children influence purchase decisions for toys, clothes, vacations, recreation, and automobiles, even though they are usually not the actual purchasers of these items.

Individual Influences on Consumer Buying Decisions

7
Identify and understand the *individual* factors that affect consumer buying decisions

A person's buying decisions are also influenced by personal characteristics that are unique to each individual, such as gender; age and life cycle stage; and personality, self-concept, and lifestyle. Individual characteristics are generally stable over one's lifetime. Most people do not change their gender, and the act of changing personality or lifestyle requires a complete reorientation of one's life. In the case of age and life cycle stage, these changes occur gradually over time.

Gender

Physiological differences between men and women result in different needs, such as for health and beauty products. Just as important are the distinct cultural, social, and economic roles played by men and women and the effects these have on decision making. Women look for different features when purchasing a car than do men. Women in North America do most of the childrearing—shuttling the children to and from school, arranging play dates and sports, and so on—so they often look for vehicles that are large enough and versatile enough for these daily activities. As a result, minivan manufacturers have implemented strategies to accommodate female drivers, such as resizing door handles and controls for women's smaller hands and repositioning seats and pedals.

Men and women also shop differently. Studies show that men and women share similar motivations in terms of where to shop—that is, they seek reasonable prices, good-quality merchandise, and a friendly, low-pressure environment—but they don't necessarily feel the same about shopping in general. Most women enjoy shopping; their male counterparts claim to dislike the experience and shop only out of necessity. Furthermore, men desire simple shopping experiences, stores with less variety, and convenience. Stores that are easy to shop in, that are near home or the office, and that have knowledgeable personnel appeal more to men than to women.[36]

Age and Family Life Cycle Stage

Age and the stages in the family life cycle can have a significant impact on consumer behaviour. How old a consumer is generally indicates which products he or she may be interested in purchasing. Consumer tastes in food, clothing, cars, furniture, and recreation are often age related; for example, among girls there is a dramatic change in fashion choices between the ages of seven and sixteen.

Related to a person's age is his or her place in the family life cycle. As Chapter 6 explains in more detail, the *family life cycle* is an orderly series of stages through which consumers' attitudes and behaviours evolve as they grow older, gain experience, and encounter changes in income and status. Marketers often define their target markets in terms of the family life cycle—"young singles," "young married with children," "middle-aged married without children," and so on. For instance, young singles spend more than average on alcoholic beverages, education, and entertainment. New parents typically increase their spending on health care, clothing, housing, and food and decrease their spending on alcohol, education, and transportation. Households with older children spend more on food, entertainment, personal care products, and education, as well as on cars and gasoline. After their children leave home, older couples typically spend more on vehicles, women's clothing, health care, and long-distance calls.

Marketers should also be aware of the many nontraditional life cycle paths that are common today; these provide insights into the needs and wants of consumers such as divorced parents, lifelong singles, and childless couples. The influx of women into the labour force since the 1950s has transformed family structure so much that in 1997, only 17 percent of households conformed to the traditional model of a wage-earning dad, a stay-at-home mom, and one or more children.[37] Statistics show that between 37 and 50 percent of Canadian marriages end in divorce; this has created a large cohort of single-parent and two-household families.

Personality, Self-Concept, and Lifestyle

personality
Way of organizing and grouping the consistencies of an individual's reactions to situations.

Each consumer has a unique personality. **Personality** is a broad concept that can be thought of as a way of organizing and grouping how an individual typically reacts to situations. Thus personality combines psychological makeup with environmental forces. It includes people's underlying dispositions, especially their

Bally Total Fitness

Does Bally Total Fitness use its Website as a means to connect with consumers via their body image? Does the content and design of the site surprise you? Explain.

www.ballyfitness.com

on line

most dominant characteristics. Personality is one of the least useful concepts in the study of consumer behaviour; that being said, some marketers believe that personality influences the types and brands of products purchased. For instance, the car, clothes, or jewellery a consumer buys may reflect one or more personality traits. Personality traits such as those listed in Exhibit 4.9 may be used to describe a consumer's personality.

Self-concept, or self-perception, refers to how consumers perceive themselves. Self-concept includes attitudes, perceptions, beliefs, and self-evaluations. Self-concept may change; however, the change is often gradual. Through self-concept, people define their identity; this in turn provides for consistent and coherent behaviour.

self-concept
How a consumer perceives himself or herself in terms of attitudes, perceptions, beliefs, and self-evaluations.

Self-concept combines the **ideal self-image** (the way an individual would like to be) with the **real self-image** (how an individual actually perceives himself or herself). Generally, we try to raise our real self-image toward our ideal, or at least narrow the gap. Consumers seldom buy products that jeopardize their self-image. For example, someone who sees herself as a trend setter wouldn't buy clothing that doesn't project a contemporary image.

ideal self-image
The way an individual would like to be.

real self-image
The way an individual actually perceives himself or herself.

Human behaviour depends largely on self-concept. Consumers want to protect their identity as individuals, so they buy products, patronize stores, and carry credit cards that support their self-image. Men's and women's fragrances tend to reflect the self-images of their wearers. Chanel's Egoïste is for the man who has everything, and knows it; likewise, Elizabeth Taylor's White Diamonds is "the fragrance dreams are made of," for all those women who strive for legendary beauty.[38] Lingerie retailer Victoria's Secret recently launched a line of cosmetics for women who want to show and enjoy their sexuality and sensuality.[39]

By influencing the degree to which consumers perceive a good or service to be self-relevant, marketers can affect consumers' motivation to learn about, shop for, and buy a certain brand. Marketers also consider self-concept important because it helps explain the relationship between individuals' perceptions of themselves and their consumer behaviour.

An important component of self-concept is *body image*, that is, the perception people have of the attractiveness of their own physical features. People who undergo cosmetic surgery often experience significant improvement in their overall body image and self-concept. Moreover, an individual's body image can do more to motivate weight loss than either the desire for good health or various social factors.[40] With the median age of Canadians rising, many companies are introducing products aimed at those aging baby boomers who are concerned about their physical appearance. One-third of Canadians were born between 1947

exhibit 4.9

Some Common Personality Traits

- Adaptability
- Need for affiliation
- Aggressiveness
- Need for achievement
- Ascendancy
- Autonomy
- Dominance
- Deference
- Defensiveness
- Emotionalism
- Orderliness
- Sociability
- Stability
- Self-confidence

and 1964, so there is a huge market for products that help individuals look young. Procter & Gamble recently extended its Oil of Olay line with a new ProVital sub-brand aimed at women over fifty. P&G's research showed that many women fifty and older feel more confident, wiser, and freer than ever before. The primary spokesmodels for P&G's ProVital line are older women who have been successful and visible in their professional careers. More male products for skin care and to prevent hair loss are on the market than ever before.

lifestyle
A mode of living as identified by a person's activities, interests, and opinions.

Personality and self-concept are reflected in lifestyle. A **lifestyle** is a mode of living as identified by a person's activities, interests, and opinions. *Psychographics* is the analytical technique used to examine consumer lifestyles and to categorize consumers. Personality characteristics are hard to describe and measure; in contrast, lifestyle characteristics are very useful for segmenting and targeting consumers. Lifestyle and psychographic analysis specifically addresses how consumers outwardly express their inner selves in their social and cultural environment.

Many industries are now using psychographics to better understand their market segments. For example, the auto industry has a psychographic segmentation scheme for classifying car buyers into one of six groups according to their attitudes toward cars and their driving experience. At the two extremes are the "gearheads," true car enthusiasts, who enjoy driving and working on their cars themselves, and the "negatives," who perceive cars as necessary evils they would just as soon do without.

Psychological Influences on Consumer Buying Decisions

8
Identify and understand the *psychological* factors that affect consumer buying decisions

An individual's buying decisions are also influenced by psychological factors such as perception, motivation, learning, and beliefs and attitudes. These are the tools consumers use to recognize their feelings, gather and analyze information, formulate their thoughts and opinions, and take action. Unlike the other three influences on consumer behaviour, psychological influences can be affected by a person's environment because they are applied on specific occasions.[41] For example, you perceive different stimuli and process these stimuli in different ways depending on whether you are sitting in class concentrating on the instructor, sitting outside class talking to friends, or sitting in your dorm room watching television.

Perception

The world is full of stimuli. A stimulus is any unit of input affecting one or more of the five senses: sight, smell, taste, touch, hearing. The process we follow for selecting, organizing, and interpreting these stimuli to form meaningful and coherent pictures is called **perception**. In essence, perception is about how we see the world around us and (from a marketer's perspective) how we recognize we need some help in making a purchasing decision.

perception
The process by which people select, organize, and interpret stimuli to form meaningful and coherent pictures.

selective exposure
The process whereby a consumer notices certain stimuli and ignores other stimuli.

People cannot perceive every stimulus in their environment, so they use **selective exposure** to decide which stimuli to notice and which to ignore. The typical consumer is exposed to more than 250 advertising messages a day but notices only between eleven and twenty.

The familiarity of an object, and its contrast, movement, intensity (such as increased volume), and smell are cues that influence perception. Consumers use these cues to identify and define products and brands. For instance, the shape of a product's packaging, such as Coca-Cola's signature contour bottle, can influwence perception. Colour is another cue, and it plays a key role in consumers' perceptions. Several years ago, Procter & Gamble added bleach to its laundry detergent Oxydol. But people didn't believe it was different because it looked the same. So P&G added blue beads to the normally white detergent. Although the blue beads had nothing to do with the bleaching action, consumers could "see" the difference. Oxydol with Bleach became a successful product because consumers perceived a difference from other detergents.[42]

What consumers perceive may also depend on the vividness or shock value of the stimulus. Graphic warnings of the hazards associated with a product's use are perceived more readily and remembered more accurately than less vivid warnings or warnings that are written in text. "Sexier" ads excel at attracting the attention of younger consumers. Companies like Calvin Klein and Guess use sensuous ads to "cut through the clutter" of competing ads and other stimuli. Similarly, Benetton ads use shock value by alluding to taboo social issues, from racism to homosexuality. A Canadian commercial recommending regular breast self-examinations shocked the country by featuring a young teenage boy offering to conduct breast examinations on women.

Two other concepts closely related to selective exposure are selective distortion and selective retention. **Selective distortion** occurs when consumers change or distort information that conflicts with their feelings or beliefs. Suppose a consumer buys a Chrysler. After the purchase, if she receives new information about a close alternative brand, such as a Ford, she may distort the information to make it more consistent with her prior view that the Chrysler is better than the Ford. Business travellers who fly often distort or discount information about airline crashes because they must use air travel constantly in their jobs. People who smoke and have no plans to quit may distort information from medical reports and the government about the link between cigarettes and lung cancer.

selective distortion
The process whereby a consumer changes or distorts information that conflicts with his or her feelings or beliefs.

Selective retention is remembering only information that supports one's personal feelings or beliefs. The consumer forgets all information that may be inconsistent. For instance, after reading a pamphlet that contradicts his political beliefs, a voter may forget many of the points it makes.

selective retention
The process whereby a consumer remembers only that information which supports his or her personal beliefs.

Which stimuli will be perceived often depends on the individual. People can be exposed to the same stimuli under identical conditions but perceive those stimuli very differently. Two people viewing a TV commercial may have different interpretations of the advertising message. One person may be thoroughly engrossed by the message and become highly motivated to buy the product. The second person may not be able to recall the content of the message thirty seconds after the ad ends—or even the product that was advertised.

Marketing Implications of Perception Marketers must recognize the importance of cues, or signals, in consumers' perception of products. Marketing managers first identify the important attributes (e.g., price, quality) that the targeted consumers want in a product and then design signals to communicate these attributes. For example, consumers will pay more for candy wrapped in expensive-looking foil packages. Yet shiny labels on wine bottles signify less expensive wines; dull labels indicate more expensive wines. Marketers often use price as a signal to consumers that the product is of higher quality than competing products.

Brand names send signals to consumers. For example, the brand names of Close-Up toothpaste, DieHard batteries, and Caress moisturizing soap identify important product qualities. Names chosen for search engines and sites on the Internet, such as Yahoo!, Excite, and Jumbo!, are intended to convey excitement and intensity.

Consumers also perceive quality and reliability with certain brand names. Companies watch their brand identity closely, in large part because a strong link has been established between perceived brand value and customer loyalty. Brand names that consistently enjoy high perceived value from consumers include Kodak, Disney, National Geographic, Mercedes-Benz, and Fisher-Price. Naming a product after a place can also add perceived value by association. Brand names using the words Santa Fe, Kokanee, Rocky Mountain, or Club Monaco convey a

services spotlight

The Science of Music

The shopping experience at Padre Staples Mall in Corpus Christi, TX, changes almost imperceptibly at three p.m. The environmental music shifts from light rock and classical (the morning program) to a mix that is more upbeat but still light. In the sleepy hours after closing time, when the work crews begin their clean-up, the tempo picks up again, to a rock beat.

There is a science to selecting the music for a workplace. Companies are investing in their image by way of their customers' ears. Businesses have always chosen their office locations and furniture carefully; nowadays they are taking just as much care in selecting the sounds that make a first impression on customers or shape an environment for getting work done. Restaurants, apartment complexes, grocery stores, doctors' offices, car dealerships, and gyms all select their music carefully. They use music to make their customers feel more comfortable, their workforce more productive, and their phone customers more willing to stay on hold.

A 1991 study by Muzak LLC, the company whose name has become synonymous with programmed music, found that problem solving improved more than 16 percent in offices with music. A study by the Gallup Organization for environmental music provider AEI Music found that 86 percent of retail customers say music makes a difference where they shop. And according to a study by Service Industry Research Systems, a retail market research firm, 76 percent of customers choose their favourite stores based on emotional factors, including the music. The sales figures show that businesses like what they hear: Muzak reported revenues of US$99.7 million in 1999—an increase of 9.3 percent over the year before.

People also want to take their shopping experience home with them. According to Toni Thomas, spokeswoman for Seattle-based AEI Music, Starbucks and Victoria's Secret are two retailers that not only use music to create a mood, but also sell the same music at their stores. They're also matching their environmental music with the programming that customers hear while on hold and on their Websites: "What a lot of these companies have been doing for the past twenty years is taking it a step farther," says Ms. Thomas.

The gas pump is the latest frontier for music. Exxon stores in Corpus Christi now pipe in music that customers can hear while filling the tank.

Why is background music so important to service businesses such as general retail? Have you ever experienced background music that made your customer experience noticeably better or worse? Visit Muzak's Website (**www.muzak.com**). Why does the company have such a wide range of "audio architecture" solutions?

Source: Adapted from *The National Post,* 3 February 2000, p. C5; "Resistance Was Futile after 'The Sounds of Silence' First Seeped from the Ceiling," Andrea Jares, Scripps Howard News Service.

sense of freedom, adventure, and youth; products named after other locations might conjure up images of pollution and crime.

Marketing managers are also interested in the threshold level of perception—that is, the minimum difference in a stimulus that the consumer will notice. This concept is sometimes referred to as the "just noticeable difference." How much would Sony have to drop the price of a DVD player before consumers recognized it as a bargain—$25? $50? more? One study found that the just noticeable difference in a stimulus is about a 20 percent change. For example, consumers will likely notice a 20 percent price decrease more quickly than a 15 percent decrease. This marketing principle can be applied to other marketing variables as well, such as package size and the loudness of a broadcast advertisement.[43]

Another study found that the bargain-price threshold for a name brand is lower than that for a store brand. In other words, consumers perceive a bargain more readily when stores offer a small discount on a name-brand item than when they offer the same discount on a store brand; for a store brand, a larger discount is needed to achieve a similar effect.[44] Researchers have also found that for low-cost grocery items, consumers typically do not see past the second digit in the price. For instance, consumers do not perceive any real difference between two comparable cans of tuna, one priced at $1.52 and the other at $1.59, because they ignore the last digit.[45]

Health Canada Cigarette Warnings

Look at the health warnings section of the Health Canada tobacco information Website. Does this site use fear to influence people not to smoke? What about the labelling on cigarette packages?

www.infotobacco.com

on line

Besides changing such stimuli as price, package size, and volume, marketers can change the product. How many sporty features will General Motors have to add to a basic two-door sedan before consumers begin to perceive the model as a sports car?

Marketing managers who intend to do business in global markets should be aware of how foreign consumers perceive their products. In Japan, product labels are often written in English or French, even though they may not translate into anything meaningful. But many Japanese associate foreign words on product labels with the exotic and the expensive and with high quality.

Marketers have often been suspected of sending subliminal messages to consumers. The controversy began in 1957, when a researcher claimed to have increased popcorn and Coca-Cola sales at a movie theatre by flashing "Eat popcorn" and "Drink Coca-Cola" on the screen every five seconds for 1/300th of a second. The audience did not consciously recognize the messages. Almost immediately, consumer protection groups became concerned that advertisers were brainwashing consumers, and this practice was banned in Canada and California. Although the researcher later admitted to making up the data and scientists have been unable to replicate the study since, consumers are still wary of hidden messages that advertisers may be sending.

Motivation

By studying motivation, marketers can analyze the main forces influencing consumers to buy or not buy products. When you buy a product, you usually do so to fulfil some kind of need. These needs become motives when they have been sufficiently aroused. Suppose this morning you were so hungry before class that you needed to eat something. In response to that need, you stopped at McDonald's for an Egg McMuffin. In other words, you were motivated by hunger to stop at McDonald's. **Motives** are the driving forces that cause a person to take action to satisfy specific needs.

motive
A driving force that causes a person to take action to satisfy specific needs.

Maslow's hierarchy of needs
A method of classifying human needs and motivations into five categories in ascending order of importance: physiological, safety, social, esteem, and self-actualization.

Why are people driven by particular needs at particular times? One popular theory is **Maslow's hierarchy of needs** (see Exhibit 4.10), which arranges needs in ascending order of importance: physiological, safety, social, esteem, and self-actualization. As a person fulfils one need, a higher-level need becomes more important.

The most basic human needs are *physiological*—that is, the needs for food, water, and shelter. Because they are essential to survival, these needs must be satisfied first. Ads showing a juicy hamburger or a runner gulping down Gatorade after a marathon are examples of appeals to the physiological needs of hunger and thirst.

Safety needs include security and freedom from pain and discomfort. Marketers often exploit consumers' fears and anxieties about safety to sell their products. After environmental groups reported that perchloroethylene, a chemical used in dry cleaning, might be a carcinogen, consumers became worried about toxic substances on their dry-cleaned clothes. Dry cleaners using alternative cleaning methods—such as petroleum-based or water-based methods—sprang up to take advantage of these fears, pitching themselves as safe alternatives to traditional dry cleaners.[46] "Ethics in Marketing" discusses how marketers often play on consumers' fears to sell their products.

After physiological and safety needs have been fulfilled, *social* needs—especially the need for love and the need to belong—become the focus. Love includes acceptance by one's peers as well as sex and romantic love. Marketing managers probably appeal more to this need than to any other. Ads for clothes, cosmetics, and vacation packages typically suggest that buying the product can bring love. The need to belong is also a favourite of marketers. Nike promotes its Air Jordan

exhibit 4.10

Maslow's Hierarchy of Needs

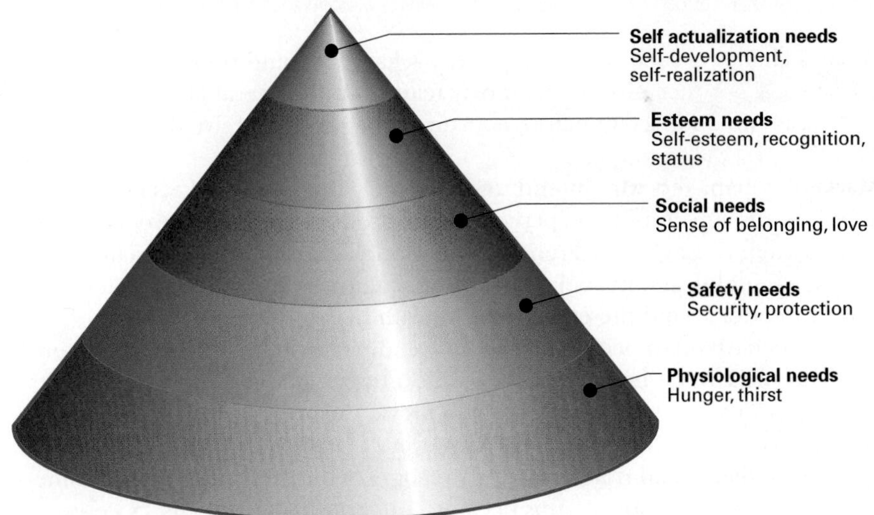

athletic shoes as not just plain old sneakers; they're part fashion statement, part athletic statement. Lace them up and you look cool and play cool—just like Michael Jordan, the shoe's spokesperson and namesake.[47]

Love is acceptance without regard to one's contribution. Esteem is acceptance based on one's contribution to the group. *Self-esteem* needs include self-respect and a sense of accomplishment. Esteem needs also include prestige, fame, and recognition of one's accomplishments. Mont Blanc pens, Mercedes-Benz automobiles, and Harry Rosen stores all appeal to esteem needs. Asian consumers, in particular, are strongly motivated by status and prestige. Asian individuals are always conscious of their place in a group, in an institution, and in society as a whole. Because they attach so much importance to gaining social recognition, Asians are probably the most image-conscious consumers in the world. Status-conscious Asians will not hesitate to spend freely on premium brands such as BMW, Mercedes-Benz, Breitling, and the best Scotch whisky and French cognac.[48] This may explain why jewellery sales at Tiffany's in Japan continue to rise even during Japan's worst economic recession since the Second World War.[49]

The highest human need is for self-actualization. This refers to finding self-fulfilment and self-expression—in other words, reaching the point in life at which "people are what they feel they should be." Maslow felt that very few people ever attain this level. Even so, some advertisements focus on this type of need. American Express ads convey the message that acquiring an Amex card is one of the highest attainments in life.

Even children must satisfy more than just the basic physiological and safety needs. Mattel's Barbie doll fulfils a fundamental need that all girls share—to play out what it might be like in the grown-up world. Through Barbie, girls dream of achievement, glamour, romance, adventure, and nurturing. These dreams touch on many timeless needs, ranging from pride and success to belonging and love. Mattel zeros in on these core needs and addresses them with different Barbie products. Over the years Barbie has been a teacher, a fashion model, a girlfriend, a dentist, an astronaut, a sister, a veterinarian … the list goes on.[50]

Learning

learning
A process that creates changes in behaviour—immediate or expected—through experience and practice.

Almost all consumer behaviour results from **learning**, which is the process that creates changes in behaviour through experience and practice. It is not possible to observe learning directly, but we can infer when it has occurred by a person's actions. Suppose you see an advertisement for a new and improved cold medi-

ethics in marketing

Fear as a Marketing Tool: Does It Sell?

Public health advocates often use fear in their public service advertising to influence public opinion. For example, in Canada cigarette manufacturers have been ordered to provide graphic health warnings, complete with colour photographs, on every cigarette package. One package shows a diseased lung and the message that smoking causes cancer; another, a pregnant woman and the message that smoking hurts babies; another, a limp cigarette and the warning that smoking causes impotence, another, a photograph of a child imitating her smoking mother, with the caption "children see, children do." The photographs of diseased lungs, hearts, and brains are graphic and very upsetting. Some packages display population charts showing that 45,000 Canadians will die from smoking this year. The messages appear in both official languages, one on each side of the package.

These warning labels were created to boost the Canadian government's war against cigarette smoking. Health officials know that if smoking statistics are to decline, people's behaviours and attitudes must change. Most people start smoking in their teens, a time when the behaviour is considered cool and teenagers assume they are immortal. People are aware of the health risks associated with smoking, but they also seek stimulus discrimination to avoid unpleasant messages linking smoking with untimely death. The new, vivid messages are an "in your face" attempt to make it impossible to avoid reminders of the health risk. Even if smokers can ignore the written messages about the ill effects of smoking, the pictures will still act as a reminder.

Before the new messages were required, cigarette manufacturers only had to include print messages about the health risks on their packages. Through focus groups, it was found that as soon as a smoker memorized all the print messages, the messages effectively disappeared (stimulus discrimination). It was determined that the visual messages would be much more effective. Many people are indeed repulsed by the vivid photographs; others simply purchase cardboard cover-ups for their cigarettes and pretend the messages aren't there. Nearly 100 per cent of Canadians are aware of the health risks of smoking, yet young people continue to take up the habit. Can fear reduce these numbers?

Do cigarette package warnings go too far in using fear to get the health message across? Would the use of fear tactics cause you to quit smoking, or at least encourage you to do so? How can behaviours and attitudes toward smoking be changed to stop people from starting?

cine. If you go to the store that day and buy that remedy, we infer that you have learned something about the cold medicine.

There are two types of learning: experiential and conceptual. *Experiential learning* occurs when an experience changes your behaviour. If you try the new cold medicine when you get home and it does not relieve your symptoms, you may not buy that brand again. *Conceptual learning*, which is not a result of direct experience, is the second type of learning. Assume that you are standing at a soft drink machine and notice a new diet flavour with an artificial sweetener. Someone has told you that diet beverages leave an aftertaste, so you choose a different drink. Without even trying it, you have learned that you would not like this new diet drink.

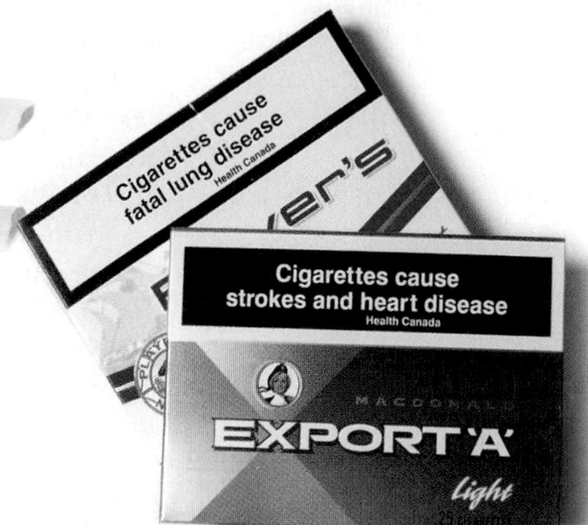

Reinforcement and repetition boost learning. Reinforcement can be positive or negative. If you see a vendor selling frozen yogurt (stimulus), buy it (response), and find the yogurt to be quite refreshing (reward), your behaviour has been positively reinforced. On the other hand, if you buy a new flavour of yogurt and it does not taste good (negative reinforcement), you will not buy that flavour of yogurt again (response). Without positive or negative reinforcement, a person will not be motivated to repeat the behaviour pattern or to avoid it. Thus, if a new brand evokes neutral feelings, some marketing activity—such as a price change or an increase in promotion—may be required to induce further consumption. Learning theory is helpful in reminding marketers that concrete and timely actions are what reinforce desired consumer behaviour.

Repetition is a key strategy in promotional campaigns because it can increase learning. Most marketers use repetitious advertising so that consumers will learn what a product's unique advantage is over the competition. Generally speaking, to heighten learning, advertising messages should be spread over time rather than clustered together.

stimulus generalization
A form of learning that occurs when one response is extended to a second stimulus that is similar to the first.

A related learning concept useful to marketing managers is stimulus generalization. In theory, **stimulus generalization** occurs when one response is extended to a second stimulus that is similar to the first. Marketers often use a successful, well-known brand name for a family of products because it helps consumers familiarize themselves with each product in the family. Brand-name families help companies introduce new products and sell existing items. Jell-O frozen pudding pops rely on the familiarity of Jell-O gelatin; Clorox laundry detergent relies on familiarity with Clorox bleach; and Ivory shampoo relies on familiarity with Ivory soap. Starbucks recently introduced four premium flavours of ice cream in the hope that consumers would transfer their love of Starbucks coffee to ice cream. With only a little publicity and a one-time limited outdoor campaign, Starbucks coffee ice cream flew off the shelves by the quart. The company attributes much of its success with its ice cream brand extension to the strong brand power of Starbucks' 1,500 retail coffee stores nationwide.[51] Branding is examined in more detail in Chapter 9.

Another form of stimulus generalization occurs when retailers or wholesalers design their packages to resemble well-known manufacturers' brands. This sort of imitation often confuses consumers, who buy the imitator thinking it's the original. Many pharmacy chains and department stores package bars of soap to resemble the Body Shop product line. Less expensive soaps are packaged to look like Procter & Gamble's Ivory soap. Counterfeit products that look exactly like the original are also produced. Counterfeit Levi's jeans made in China are hot items in Europe, where Levi Strauss has had trouble keeping up with demand. The knockoffs look so much like the real thing that unsuspecting consumers don't know the difference—until after a few washes, when the belt loops fall off and the rivets begin to rust.

stimulus discrimination
The learned ability to differentiate among stimuli.

The opposite of stimulus generalization is **stimulus discrimination**, which involves learning to differentiate among similar products. Consumers usually prefer one product as more rewarding or stimulating. Some consumers prefer Coca-Cola, others prefer Pepsi; many insist they can taste a difference between the two brands. People will drive an extra distance to one of the 1,900 Tim Hortons stores for a cup of coffee, or for a can of Tim Hortons coffee to take home.

With some types of products—aspirin, gasoline, bleach, paper towels, and so on—marketers rely on promotion to point out brand differences that consumers would otherwise not recognize. This process, called product differentiation, is discussed in more detail in Chapter 9. Usually, product differentiation is based on superficial differences. Bayer tells consumers that it's the aspirin "doctors recommend most."

Tim Hortons has successfully employed stimulus discrimination techniques to gain dedication to their brand of coffee. There are 1,900 Tim Hortons stores across Canada—proof that Tim Hortons coffee is preferable to regular coffee.

Beliefs and Attitudes

Beliefs and attitudes are closely linked to values. A **belief** is an organized pattern of knowledge that an individual holds as true about his or her world. A consumer may believe that Sony's camcorder makes the best home videos, tolerates hard use, and is reasonably priced. These beliefs may be based on knowledge, faith, or hearsay. Consumers tend to develop a set of beliefs about a product and then, through these beliefs, form a *brand image*—a set of beliefs about a particular brand. In turn, the brand image shapes consumers' attitudes toward the product.

belief
An organized pattern of knowledge that an individual holds as true about his or her world.

An **attitude** is a learned tendency to respond consistently toward a given object, such as a brand. Attitudes rest on an individual's value system, which represents personal standards of good and bad, right and wrong, and so on; this is why attitudes tend to be more conplex and enduring than beliefs.

attitude
A learned tendency to respond consistently toward a given object.

Consider how consumers differ around the world in their attitudes toward purchasing on credit. Canadian consumers have long been enthusiastic about charging goods and services and are willing to pay high interest rates for the privilege of postponing payment. Many European consumers consider it absurd to pay for anything—even something small—by taking out what amounts to a loan. Germans especially are reluctant to buy on credit. Italy has a sophisticated credit and banking system that is well suited to handling credit cards, but Italians still prefer to carry cash—often huge wads of it.

If a good or service is meeting its profit goals, positive attitudes toward the product merely need to be reinforced. However, if a brand is not succeeding, the marketing manager must strive to change target consumers' attitudes toward it. Changes in attitude tend to grow out of an individual's attempts to reconcile long-held values with a constant stream of new information. Such changes can be accomplished in three ways: by changing beliefs about the brand's attributes, by changing the relative importance of these beliefs, or by adding new beliefs.

Changing Beliefs about Attributes The first technique is to turn neutral or negative beliefs about products into positive ones. Egg consumption has decreased steadily over the years because consumers believe that eggs contribute to high cholesterol. To counter this the Canadian Egg Marketing Agency has run a series of advertising campaigns outlining the healthy simplicity of eggs. It is trying to remind consumers that eggs can be part of any meal, not just breakfast, and that eggs are "so good, so simple" for people in a hurry who want a nutritious meal. Negative beliefs about eggs are changing to positive beliefs that eggs are part of a well-balanced diet and a good source of protein.

It can be more difficult to change beliefs about a service because service attributes are intangible. Convincing consumers to switch hairstylists or lawyers or to go to a mall dental clinic can be much more difficult than getting them to change brands of razor blades. Image, which is largely intangible, is a significant determinant of service patronage. Canadian banks are working hard to dispel the image that they are dull, rules-driven institutions, with the goal of persuading small businesses to come in the door. Similarly, banks are using giveaways and contests to recruit credit card customers on college and university campuses; their hope is to keep these students' business for life. Service marketing is explored in detail in Chapter 11.

Changing the Importance of Beliefs The second approach to modifying attitudes is to change the relative importance of beliefs about an attribute. For years, consumers have known that bran cereals are high in natural fibre. The primary belief associated with this attribute is that the fibre tends to act as a mild, natural laxative. Today, cereal marketers are promoting the high fibre content of bran cereals as a possible factor in preventing certain types of cancer; this has vastly increased the importance of this attribute in the minds of consumers.

Marketers can also downplay the importance of some beliefs in favour of others. Chrysler Corporation's Jeep unit strives to maintain the Jeep Grand

on line

Canadian Egg Marketing Agency

How is the Egg Marketing Agency using its Website to reinforce beliefs that eggs are "So good, so simple"? How does the site encourage the consumption of eggs as a fast, healthy source of meals?

www.canadaegg.ca

Cherokee's ruggedness: the newest Grand Cherokees have more off-road capability than ever before. Yet only 15 percent of owners ever take them off-road. The Grand Cherokee's marketers have worked hard to play up their product's luxury features. The product's engineers have made more room in the back to carry as many as eight bags of golf clubs. They have also developed a climate-control system with infrared beams to track drivers' and passengers' skin temperature (the air conditioning and heating then automatically adjust). They have even designed his-and-hers key fobs with buttons that remember the settings for power seats and mirrors and that reprogram radio stations for different drivers.[52]

Adding New Beliefs The third approach to transforming attitudes is to add new beliefs. Although changes in consumption patterns often come slowly, cereal marketers are betting that consumers will eventually warm to the idea of cereal as a snack. A print ad for Ralston Purina's Cookie-Crisp cereal features a boy popping the sugary nuggets into his mouth while he does his homework. Boxes of Kellogg's Cracklin' Oat Bran boast that the cereal tastes like oatmeal cookies and makes "a great snack … anytime." Similarly, commercials for Quaker Oats 100% Natural cereal promote eating it straight from the box.

Adding new beliefs is not easy. When Labatt first introduced Labatt Dry beer, consumers were confused, because the word "dry" is commonly used to describe wines. Many consumers have since added the new belief that beer, too, can be described as dry. Volvo faced a similar problem when it introduced its sporty C70 convertible and S80 luxury sedan models. Over a quarter of a century, Volvo had successfully crafted an image for itself as the safest car on the road. Its core market—baby boomers—was aging, and Volvo wanted to appeal to their desire for a fun, powerful, and sexy car that was still safe. Unfortunately, Volvo had done such a good job driving home its safety message that consumers had a difficult time imagining a Volvo as anything other than a boxy, steel-reinforced tank.[53]

LOOKING BACK

You should now be able to see how cultural, social, individual, and psychological factors affect consumer decision-making processes. Station wagons are coming back into vogue as car buyers age, and move through the family life cycle. Beliefs and attitudes about fat and protein in food products are causing sales of foods with more protein to surge and sales of low-fat products to go flat. Increased wealth, better education, and exposure to other cultures—all cultural factors—are making ordinary Canadians more sophisticated, and the anti-establishment attitudes of young people are turning lesser-known brands into marketing successes. Consumer behaviour is a fascinating and often intricate process. An appreciation of consumer behaviour and the factors that influence it will help you identify target markets and design effective marketing mixes.

Summary

1 Explain why marketing managers should understand consumer behaviour. Consumer behaviour describes how consumers make purchase decisions and how they use and dispose of the products they buy. An understanding of consumer behaviour reduces marketing managers' uncertainty when they are defining a target market and designing a marketing mix.

2 **Analyze the components of the consumer decision-making process.** The consumer decision-making process begins with need recognition, when stimuli trigger awareness of an unfulfilled want. If additional information is required to make a purchase decision, the consumer may engage in an internal or external information search. The consumer then evaluates the additional information and establishes purchase guidelines. Finally, a purchase decision is made.

3 **Explain the consumer's postpurchase evaluation process.** Consumer postpurchase evaluation is influenced by prepurchase expectations, the prepurchase information search, and the consumer's general level of self-confidence. Cognitive dissonance is the inner tension that a consumer experiences after recognizing a purchased product's disadvantages. When a purchase creates cognitive dissonance, consumers tend to react by seeking positive reinforcement for the purchase decision, avoiding negative information about the purchase decision, or revoking the purchase decision by returning the product.

4 **Identify the types of consumer buying decisions, and discuss the significance of consumer involvement.** Consumer decision making falls into three broad categories. First, consumers exhibit routine response behaviour for frequently purchased, low-cost items that require very little decision effort; routine response behaviour is typically characterized by brand loyalty. Second, consumers engage in limited decision making for occasional purchases and for unfamiliar brands in familiar product categories. Third, consumers practise extensive decision making when making unfamiliar, expensive, or infrequent purchases. High-involvement decisions usually entail an extensive information search and a thorough evaluation of alternatives. In contrast, low-involvement decisions are characterized by brand loyalty and by a lack of personal identification with the product. The main factors affecting the level of consumer involvement are price, interest, perceived risk of negative consequences, situation, and social visibility.

5 **Identify and understand the *cultural* factors that affect consumer buying decisions.** Cultural influences on consumer buying decisions include culture and values, subculture, and social class. Culture is the essential character of a society that distinguishes it from other cultural groups. Underlying every culture are values, language, myths, customs, rituals, laws, and artifacts (i.e., products); all of these are transmitted from one generation to the next. The most defining element of a culture is its values—the enduring beliefs shared by a society that a specific mode of conduct is personally or socially preferable to other modes of conduct. A culture can be divided into subcultures on the basis of demographic characteristics, geographic regions, national and ethnic background, political beliefs, and/or religious beliefs. A subculture shares elements of the overall culture but also has cultural elements unique to itself. A social class is a group of people who are considered nearly equal in status or community esteem, who regularly socialize among themselves both formally and informally, and who share behavioural norms.

6 **Identify and understand the *social* factors that affect consumer buying decisions.** Social factors include external influences such as reference groups, opinion leaders, and family. Consumers seek out others' opinions for guidance on new products or services, or on products with image-related attributes, or they do so because attribute information is lacking or uninformative. Consumers may use products or brands to identify with or become a member of a reference group. Opinion leaders are members of reference groups who influence others' purchase decisions. Family members also influence purchase decisions; children's shopping patterns tend to be similar to those of their parents.

Do You Know These Terms?

aspirational reference groups 96
attitude 109
belief 109
cognitive dissonance 84
consumer behaviour 79
consumer decision-making process 79
culture 89
direct reference groups 96
evoked set 83
extensive decision making 86
external information search 81
ideal self-image 101
internal information search 81
involvement 85
learning 106
lifestyle 102
limited decision making 86
marketing-controlled information source 82
Maslow's hierarchy of needs 105
motive 105
need recognition 79
nonaspirational reference groups 96
nonmarketing-controlled information source 81
norm 96
opinion leader 97
perception 102
personality 100
primary membership groups 96
real self-image 101
reference group 96
routine response behaviour 85
secondary membership groups 96
selective distortion 103
selective exposure 102
selective retention 103
self-concept 101
social class 94
socialization process 98
stimulus 79
stimulus discrimination 108
stimulus generalization 108

7 Identify and understand the *individual* factors that affect consumer buying decisions. Individual factors that affect consumer buying decisions include gender; age and family life cycle stage; and personality, self-concept, and lifestyle. Beyond obvious physiological differences, men and women differ in their social and economic roles, and this affects consumer buying decisions. How old a consumer is generally indicates what products he or she may be interested in purchasing. Marketers often define their target markets in terms of life cycle stages, and follow changes in consumers' attitudes and behavioural tendencies as they mature. Certain products and brands reflect the personality, self-concept, and lifestyle of individual consumers.

8 Identify and understand the *psychological* factors that affect consumer buying decisions. Psychological factors include perception, motivation, learning, values, beliefs, and attitudes. These factors allow consumers to interact with the world around them, recognize their feelings, gather and analyze information, formulate thoughts and opinions, and take action. Perception allows consumers to recognize their consumption problems. Motivation is what drives consumers to take action to satisfy specific consumption needs. Almost all consumer behaviour results from learning, which is the process that creates changes in behaviour through experience. Consumers with similar beliefs and attitudes tend to react alike to marketing-related inducements.

Discussion and Writing Questions

1. Describe the three categories of consumer decision-making behaviour. Name typical products for which each type of consumer behaviour is used.
2. The type of decision making a consumer uses for a product does not necessarily remain constant. Explain why. Support your answer with an example from your own experience.
3. How do beliefs and attitudes influence consumer behaviour? How can negative attitudes toward a product be changed? How can marketers alter beliefs about a product? Give some examples of how marketers have changed negative attitudes about a product or added or altered beliefs about a product.
4. Recall an occasion when you experienced cognitive dissonance about a purchase. In a letter to a friend, describe the event and explain what you did about it.
5. Family members play many different roles in the buying process: initiator, influencer, decision maker, purchaser, and consumer. In your family, name who might play each of these roles in the purchase of a personal computer system, Froot Loops breakfast cereal, Roots cologne for men, and dinner at McDonald's.
6. You are a new marketing manager for a firm that produces a line of athletic shoes to be targeted to the university subculture. In a memo to your boss, list some product attributes that might appeal to this subculture and the steps in your customers' purchase processes, and recommend some marketing strategies that might influence their decisions.
7. Assume you are involved in the following consumer decision situations: (a) renting a video to watch with your roommates, (b) choosing a fast food restaurant to go to with a new friend, (c) buying a popular music CD, (d) buying jeans to wear to class. List the factors that would influence your decision in each situation, and explain your responses.
8. Visit Land Rover's "Authoritative Guide to SUVs" Website at **www.best4x4.landrover.com**. How does Land Rover help consumers in the evaluation stage of choosing a new sport utility vehicle? Develop your own hypothetical evoked set of three or four SUV models, and present your comparisons. Which vehicle attributes would be most important in your purchase decision?

Application for Small Business

Deli Depot is a new franchise in Halifax that offers cold and hot sandwiches, soup, chili, yogurt, pies, and cookies. It is positioned to compete with Subway and similar sandwich restaurants. Its unique advantages include special sauces on sandwiches, supplementary menu items like soup and pies, and quick delivery within specified zones.

The franchise package offered to franchisees includes information on the factors that typically influence consumers' selection of casual restaurants. These selection factors, in order from most important to least important, include food taste, food variety, value for the money, restaurant reputation, friendliness of employees, and convenience of location.

Robert Powell and a group of investors purchased the right to all franchise locations in the Maritimes. His group estimates that five units can be opened successfully in the first year and that a total of thirty can be opened in the first five years.

Because this is a new franchise, potential customers must first be made aware of Deli Depot and then convinced to try it. Over the long run, a loyal customer base must be established to make each Deli Depot a success.

Questions

1. Are Deli Depot's unique advantages strong enough to attract customers from Subway and other sandwich competitors? Explain.
2. Are all the important customer selection factors for sandwich restaurants included in the list? Do you agree with the importance rankings? Explain.
3. How can Robert and his group make potential customers aware of the new Deli Depot locations and menu selections?
4. How can Robert and his group persuade individuals who try Deli Depot to become regular customers?

CBC VIDEO CASE

Dollars for Disease

When noted Canadian-born celebrity Michael J. Fox revealed his struggle with Parkinson's disease, both the media and foundations raising money for Parkinson's quickly lined up to hear more about the actor's experience with the disease. A Vancouver-born superstar, Fox is best known for his role in the long-running sitcoms *Family Ties* and, more recently, *Spin City* (in which he was paired with the beautiful Heather Locklear). Fox left *Spin City* to concentrate on helping find a cure for the disease that is crippling him.

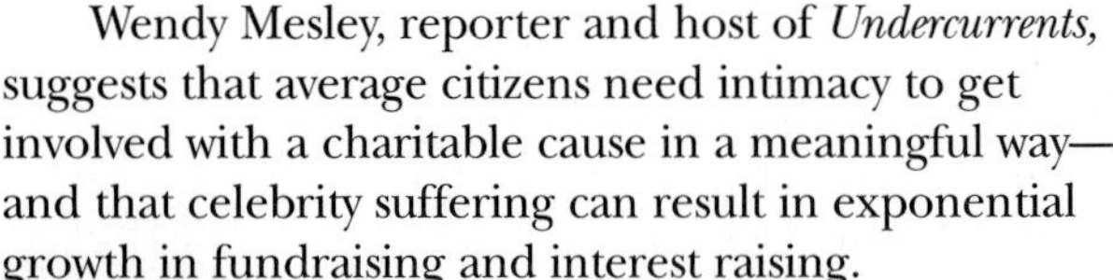

After a cover story in *People*, the North American media were anxious to talk to Fox about his career and his life with Parkinson's disease. It seems that celebrity power makes any topic more interesting. Parkinson's foundations in Canada and the United States scrambled to use Fox's star power to raise money, build awareness, and promote research.

Wendy Mesley, reporter and host of *Undercurrents*, suggests that average citizens need intimacy to get involved with a charitable cause in a meaningful way—and that celebrity suffering can result in exponential growth in fundraising and interest raising.

In an *Undercurrents* segment, she suggested that a $55 million research grant for diabetes was awarded within days of a visit to Ottawa by actress Mary Tyler Moore. Moore has had diabetes all her life, and visited the Canadian government to raise awareness in this country. Are all diseases created equal, or does star power alone dictate what money goes where?

Spokepeople involved in running Parkinson's foundations suggest that the recognition and media time generated by stars like Michael J. Fox can more than double awareness and donations for a disease such as Parkinson's. Fox is even more attractive to them as a spokeperson because he is young, attractive, and

famous, yet is discussing a disease that has traditionally been regarded as an older people's affliction.

Foundations representing diseases that don't have a celebrity spokeperson could benefit equally from star power to move agendas forward; without one, they are at a disadvantage. People and governments pay attention when there is a star attached to a cause. Is glamorizing a disease the way to go for various charity organizations? Parkinson's rapidly became known as the Michael J. Fox disease. How can charities without a famous face compete for their share of charitable donations?

Source:

CBC, *Undercurrents,* "Dollars for Disease," December 26, 1999.

Questions

1. Would you give more money to a charitable cause that has star power attached to it? Explain.
2. Why does celebrity power increase awareness of a cause, and help raise money for it?
3. Discuss how consumer involvement can change when a celebrity lends his or her name to a charitable cause.
4. How does perception play a part in Michael J. Fox's work with Parkinson's?

CHAPTER

5

LEARNING OBJECTIVES

After studying this chapter, you should be able to

1. Describe business marketing
2. Describe the role of the Internet in business marketing
3. Discuss the role of relationship marketing and strategic alliances in business marketing
4. Identify the four major categories of business market customers
5. Explain the North American Industry Classification System
6. Explain the major differences between business and consumer markets
7. Describe the seven types of business goods and services
8. Discuss the unique aspects of business buying behaviour

The success of many corporations today is directly related not only to their relationships with customers but also to the number of their business relationships with other companies, and to the quality of those relationships. The reason is simple: most companies can no longer operate by themselves. Alliances are a key to the future for businesses of all sizes, in every industry, everywhere in the world.

Nowhere is this more true than in the international airline business, where competition for passenger dollars has become cutthroat. The challenge has been to create alliances that offer passengers a seamless travel experience while preserving the unique cultures and products of the individual partners. Fifteen carriers, including Air Canada, United Airlines, Thai Airways, Lufthansa, Air New Zealand, Scandinavian Airlines, Singapore Airlines, and VARIG Airlines, have moved alliance building into a new era by forming the Star Alliance, which presents travellers with a more uniform product while retaining individual brands. This alliance integrates the airlines' frequent flyer programs and offers seamless booking and travel capabilities across all fifteen airlines.

"We believe our alliance helps each of us to secure our place among the successful competitors in a deregulated, liberalized, and highly competitive global air transport market," says Jan Stenberg, president and CEO of SAS, one of the partners. "But it is not our intention to merge our airlines or develop identical product offerings. Our research tells us categorically that our customers enjoy and appreciate our varied cultures. Our strength is in our diversity."

The fifteen carriers combined now serve 892 airports in 129 countries with 7,200 daily departures.

The airlines have been working closely together for some time to develop their relationship. The Star Alliance network is striving to combine fifteen of the world's finest airlines to create an easier flying experience for business travellers, with harmonized schedules and minimal airport and plane-changing hassles. This new initiative not only provides better customer recognition worldwide but also creates a powerful framework for continued future development. It

Star Alliance

How does Star Alliance market itself on the Intenet? How are the benefits of using Star Alliance carriers presented on its Website?

www.star-alliance.com

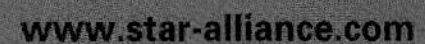

also enables each airline to benefit from considerable synergies, ranging from common utilization of facilities to joint purchasing. The Star Alliance logo will appear as an additional feature on the fuselage of all aircraft in each airline's fleet and on a wide range of information materials. It will also become a familiar sight at airports, ticket offices, and other locations around the world.

The alliance is committed to introducing further benefits for customers, including access to more flights and destinations, simplified ticketing and reservations, more convenient connections, and better baggage and ground services. All of these will combine to create a hassle-free, seamless travel experience. Star Alliance travellers will be able to earn and redeem frequent flyer miles or points on any member airline.

"Our membership in Star Alliance, the world's largest and most solid airline alliance, gives our customers unparalleled access to worldwide markets," says Robert Milton, president and CEO of Air Canada. "We clearly remain Canada's leading airline with the preeminent domestic and international network."

Identify several benefits that members receive from participating in the Star Alliance. In what ways do customers benefit? Does the alliance threaten competition? These issues are addressed in this chapter.

What Is Business Marketing?

1
Describe business marketing

business marketing
The marketing of goods and services to individuals and organizations for purposes other than personal consumption.

Business marketing is the marketing of goods and services to individuals and organizations for purposes other than personal consumption. The sale of an overhead projector to your college or university is an example of business marketing. Business products include those used to manufacture other products, to become part of another product, or to aid the normal operations of an organization. It also includes products acquired for resale without any substantial change in form. The key characteristic distinguishing business products from consumer products is intended use, not physical characteristics. A product purchased for personal or family consumption or as a gift is a consumer good. If that same product, such as a microcomputer or a cellular telephone, is bought for use in a business, it is a business product.

Business Marketing on the Internet

2
Describe the role of the Internet in business marketing

In the twenty-first century, information technology industries will drive economic wealth. The innovations developed by the computing, telecommunications, and electronic media industries will affect every business, large and small.[1] In business marketing, Internet presence is already becoming as common as business cards

Cisco Systems, a network equipment maker, is selling products from its Website at the rate of $20 billion per year. This demonstrates how lucrative business marketing on the Internet can be. Courtesy Cisco Systems

and fax machines. Canada leads the world in Internet adoption. Virtually all large and medium-sized companies in Canada are now using the Internet in one way or another, and 70 percent of Canadian adults have used the Internet. Dell Computer sells $50 million worth of computers every day on the Internet; two-thirds of them are to commercial and industrial customers. Cisco Systems, a network equipment maker, is selling products from its Website at the rate of $20 billion per year.[2]

General Electric purchases $1 billion worth of goods and services per year from its trading process network (TPN). Although the consumer market has received more media attention, e-commerce between businesses is expected to represent 92 percent of the $4 trillion in e-commerce sales expected in 2003.

GE has software that lets its purchasing agents specify to whom they want their bid requests to go and

internet connections

Forrester Research Predicts "Hypergrowth" for On-Line Trade Between Canuck Companies

Business-to-business e-commerce is about to dramatically increase in Canada, according to a report from Forrester Research (**www.forrester.com**). The third quarter of this year will see Canadian B2B on-line trade move into what Forrester calls "hypergrowth," meaning 10 percent of all possible transactions will be done electronically. As usual, we're behind the United States. American businesses hit hypergrowth in B2B trade in the fourth quarter of 2000, according to James Sharp, an analyst in Forrester's Toronto office. In dollar terms, on-line business-to-business trade here will leap from $46 billion this year to $80 billion next year. By 2005, $272 billion of the nation's $1.54 trillion B2B transactions will be done on-line.

Of that, Sharp adds, just over half will be done through e-marketplaces, with goods ranging from office supplies to electronic parts.

Forrester questioned fifty Canadian companies in thirteen industry verticals for the survey, plus 35 "thought leaders" or vendors.

While 80 percent of firms surveyed believe they'll be doing some B2B transactions on-line by next year, Sharp says only 16 percent of all firms have clear strategies on how to do it.

Driving B2B on-line growth will be three sectors, says Sharp: the auto, petrochemical, and computing/electronics industries. All, he adds, will be heavy users of e-marketplaces, which will account for just over half of all B2B on-line transactions by 2005.

Canada's auto supply chain will sell $91 billion on-line five years from now, says Forrester. Much of it will be through Covisint (**www.covisint.com**), the exchange backed by Detroit's Big Three auto makers, although it is one year old and hasn't done any business yet.

The petrochemical sector will do $46 billion on-line in five years, says Sharp, using marketplaces like the Enbridge Petroleum Exchange (**www.electrade.ca**). The exchange, which now moves as much as 2 percent of the country's daily crude trade, is "one of the unsung jewels in Canadian marketplaces," he said.

As much as 40 percent of computing and electronics trade will go on-line by 2005, says the report, through such marketplaces as E2Open (**www.e2open.com**). Almost one-quarter of all trade in office supplies will be done on-line. However, Forrester says that "entrenched practice and e-commerce scepticism" will hold the agricultural sector back from joining on-line marketplaces such as Calgary-based AgriPlace (**www.agriplace.com**). The forest products industry will be another slow joiner.

Why is B2B e-commerce growing faster than B2C e-commerce?

Are some industries more likely to adopt e-commerce applications? Explain.

How do Canadian B2B figures compare to those of the United States? Why?

Source: Plesman Communications Inc. Reprinted with permission.

Xerox
From Xerox's Website, what can you find out about its partnerships?
www.xerox.com

on line

exhibit 5.1

An Internet Guide to Small-Business Exporting

One of the easiest ways to begin exporting is through the Internet. The sites listed below offer valuable resources as well as links to additional information.

www.embpage.org Embassy Web.com is a valuable source of diplomatic information. It provides a window to hundreds of embassies and consulates around the world.

www.exim.gov The Export-Import Bank of the United States was established to help American companies export their goods overseas.

www.ciia.org The Canadian Institute of International Affairs Website helps Canadians enter world trade markets.

www.dfait-maeci.gc.ca On this Website, the Canadian Department of Foreign Affairs and International Trade provides information and resources of assistance to Canadians in world trade.

www.inforexport.gc.ca This is another Government of Canada Website; it provides relevant information to help businesses export products to other countries.

www.royalbank.com/trade This Website, sponsored by the Royal Bank of Canada, helps Canadian businesses make foreign and financial contacts around the globe.

www.fita.org Trade associations are invaluable resources for exporters. The Federation of International Trade Associations Website offers a network of 300,000 companies belonging to 300 international trade associations in North America.

www.tradecompass.com Trade Compass® offers news, information, and sophisticated database products that help companies and individuals navigate the far reaches of trade, importing, exporting, sales, marketing, logistics, research, and e-business in today's global marketplace.

Source: Based on Christopher Farrell and Edith Updike, "So You Think the World Is Your Oyster," *Business Week*, June 9, 1997: ENT8; and research from the Canadian federal government sites and the World Wide Web.

what sort of information, such as drawings, potential vendors should submit. The software then manages the bids as they come back, and ultimately notifies the bidders of the outcome.[3]

Since TPN was launched in 1996, purchasing cycle times have been cut by 80 percent and the costs of purchasing have been reduced by 30 percent. TPN has also made it easier to solicit bids from foreign suppliers. One bid was awarded to a Hungarian firm at a savings of 20 percent.[4] There are 150 GE sales and service locations in Canada, as well as twelve manufacturing plants and 10,000 Canadian employees.

The Internet has made business markets more competitive than ever before. With the Internet, every business in the world is potentially a local competitor.

Relationship Marketing and Strategic Alliances

3
Discuss the role of relationship marketing and strategic alliances in business marketing

Many business marketers now realize that the Internet is a valuable tool for expanding markets and serving customers. Exhibit 5.1 identifies a number of Internet sites that offer important information for firms interested in competing in foreign markets.

As Chapter 1 explained, relationship marketing is about seeking and establishing ongoing partnerships with customers. It involves redefining the fundamental roles of business buyers and sellers. Suppliers are making major adjustments in their thinking, management styles, and methods of responding to purchasers' standards and operational requirements. A satisfied customer is one of the best sources of new business. When a customer knows that its supplier can meet expectations and deliver what is promised, trust is created; and trust is the foundation of most successful relationship marketing efforts.[5]

strategic alliance
A cooperative agreement between business firms.

A **strategic alliance**, sometimes called a strategic partnership, is a cooperative agreement between business firms. Strategic alliances can take the form of licensing or distribution agreements, joint ventures, R&D consortia, or partnerships. They can be between manufacturers, or between manufacturers and customers, manufacturers and suppliers, or manufacturers and channel intermediaries. Recall the Star Alliance of airlines, which has been developed to benefit the fifteen partners as well as their customers. This is an example of a strategic alliance.

The trend toward strategic alliances is accelerating rapidly. In Japan, IBM has a strategic alliance with Ricoh to distribute low-end computers, and another with Fuji Bank to market financial systems. IBM has similar links with other Japanese firms. Ford and Mazda have collaborated on at least ten models. This chapter's "Global Perspectives" box discusses the strategic alliances that one American manufacturer has formed with six Asian producers of home appliances. Cisco Systems lists more than a dozen strategic alliances on its Website.

Companies are realizing that strategic partnerships are more than important—they are critical. Xerox has decided that to maintain its leadership position in the reprographics industry, it must "include suppliers as part of the Xerox family." This strategy often means reducing the number of suppliers, treating the remaining ones as allies, sharing strategic information freely, and drawing on supplier expertise in developing new products that meet the quality, cost, and delivery standards of the marketplace.

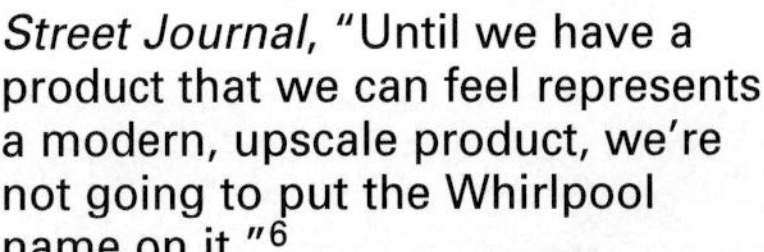

global perspectives

Whirlpool Ventures into a New Frontier

Between 1994 and 1996, Whirlpool Corp. spent $265 million to buy controlling interest in four competitors in China and two in India. Eventually, Whirlpool hopes to become one of Asia's top suppliers of washers, dryers, dishwashers, refrigerators, and household air conditioners.

According to *The Wall Street Journal*, Whirlpool's managers believe that Asia offers very promising market opportunities because of its rapid economic growth and low proportion of households with modern appliances. China has more than 1 billion people, yet fewer than 10 percent of all Chinese households have air conditioners, microwave ovens, or clothes washers.

Whirlpool hopes to export appliances manufactured in China to other Asian countries. To do this successfully, it will have to upgrade substantially the quality of its joint venture partners' products. According to Whirlpool executives, Chinese brands are neither as reliable nor as durable as available Japanese brands. Typically, air conditioners manufactured by Chinese partner firms last only five to eight years, which is half the life expectancy of a Whirlpool unit made in the United States. Whirlpool president and CEO William Marohn has told *The Wall Street Journal*, "Until we have a product that we can feel represents a modern, upscale product, we're not going to put the Whirlpool name on it."[6]

Why would Whirlpool invest $265 million to buy part-ownership in Chinese companies that produce inferior products? Why not just export products made in the United States to Asia, or build Whirlpool manufacturing facilities in China and elsewhere? Assess Whirlpool's joint ventures in terms of general strategic alliance goals, factors that contribute to successful alliances, and the three general problems that commonly plague strategic alliances.

Business marketers form strategic alliances to leverage what they do well. They partner with other companies that have complementary expertise for the following reasons:[7]

- To access markets and technology
- To achieve economies of scale by combining manufacturing, R&D, or marketing activities
- To enter new products to markets more quickly
- To share risk

Some alliances have been extremely successful; others have been dismal failures. Exhibit 5.2 offers six tips for making an alliance successful.

Major Categories of Business Customers

4

Identify the four major categories of business market customers

The business market comprises four major categories of customers: producers, resellers, governments, and institutions.

Producers

The producer segment of the business market includes profit-oriented individuals and organizations that purchase goods and services for incorporating into their own products, or for producing those products, or for use in daily operations. Producers include manufacturers, construction and transportation companies, and finance, real estate, and food service firms. In Canada there are around 40,000 firms in the producer segment of the business market; their shipments total over $450 billion annually. Some of these firms are small; others, such as car makers, are among the world's largest businesses.

In Canada, agribusiness is an important part of the production of goods. Farming is big business, and Canadian farms ship their products around the world. Most large Canadian farms are highly mechanized and are run like large corporations—they bear little resemblance to the family farms of yesteryear.

Individual producers often buy large quantities of goods and services. General Motors spends more than $70 billion annually on business products such as steel, metal components, and tires—more than the GDP of Ireland, Portugal, Turkey, or Greece. Companies like General Electric, Dupont, and IBM spend over $60 million every day on business goods and services.[8]

The producer segment of the business market includes manufacturers—like this globe manufacturer—construction, finance, transportation, and real estate firms, and many others.

Resellers

The reseller market includes retail and wholesale businesses that buy finished goods and resell them for a profit. A retailer sells mainly to final consumers; wholesalers sell mainly to retailers and other organizational customers. There are around 235,000 retailers and 123,000 wholesalers in Canada. Consumer product firms like Procter & Gamble, Kraft General Foods, and Coca-Cola sell directly to large retailers and retail chains; they sell to smaller retail units through wholesalers. Retailing and wholesaling are explored in detail in Chapter 12.

Keebler

What special offers does Keebler have for its business customers? What sectors is it trying to service? Go to the Hollow Tree Website to find out.

www.keebler.com

on line

Business product distributors are wholesalers that buy business products and resell them to business customers. They often carry thousands of items in stock and employ salespeople to call on their customers. Businesses that wish to buy a gross of pencils or 100 pounds of fertilizer typically purchase these items from local distributors rather than directly from, say, Empire Pencil or Dow Chemical.

Governments

A third major segment of the business market is government; this market consists of thousands of federal, provincial, territorial, and local buying units. They make up perhaps the largest single market in Canada for goods and services.

Government contracts are often put out for bid. Interested vendors submit bids—usually sealed—to provide specified products during a particular time. Sometimes the lowest bidder is awarded the contract. When it is not, the government that rejected the lowest bid must present strong evidence to justify its decision. Grounds for rejecting the lowest bid include lack of experience, inadequate financing, or poor past performance. Bidding allows all potential suppliers a fair chance at winning government contracts; it also helps ensure that public funds are spent wisely. For more information about bidding, see this chapter's "Entrepreneurial Insights" box.

Federal Government Name just about any good or service and chances are that someone in the federal government uses it. Canada's federal government is this country's largest customer, spending about $170 billion each year.

Much of the federal government's buying is centralized. However, no single federal agency contracts for all the government's requirements, and no single buyer in any agency purchases everything that agency needs. The federal government is best viewed, perhaps, as a consortium of several large companies and Crown corporations with overlapping responsibilities and thousands of small independent units. Major purchases go through Supply and Services Canada and Public Works and Government Services.

One popular source of information about government procurement is Contracts Canada. Information about bidding for federal contracts can be obtained at **contractscanada.gc.org**.

exhibit 5.2

Tips for Making Strategic Alliances Successful

- Trust one another—alliances break down when one partner becomes greedy.
- Share a common interest in meeting customer needs.
- Bring different skills to the table.
- Share gains, and have a built-in system for ongoing change.
- Understand which party will have direct contact with customers.
- Understand that success and profitability are tied to customer satisfaction.

Source: From "Alliance Highlights," *Fortune*, Best Practices Symposium, March 30, 1998. Reprinted by permission. © *Fortune Magazine*.

Provincial, Territorial, and Municipal Governments For both small and large vendors, selling to provinces, territories, cities, and towns can be less frustrating than selling to the federal government. The paperwork is usually simpler and more manageable than at the federal level. Provincial and local buying agencies include school districts, highway departments, and housing agencies.

Institutions The fourth major segment of the business market consists of those institutions whose goals are not the standard business goals of profit, market share, and return on investment. This segment includes schools, hospitals, churches, foundations, colleges and universities, labour unions, fraternal organizations, civic clubs, and other "nonbusiness" organizations.

5
Explain the North American Industry Classification System

North American Industry Classification System (NAICS)
A detailed numbering system developed by Canada, the United States, and Mexico to classify North American business establishments by their main production processes.

The North American Industry Classification System (NAICS)

The **North American Industry Classification System (NAICS)** was introduced in 1997 to replace the standard industrial classification system (SIC). NAICS (pronounced *nakes*) is an all-new system for classifying North American business establishments. It was developed jointly by Canada, the United States, and Mexico, and provides a common system for classifying industries under the umbrella of the North American Free Trade Agreement (NAFTA). It groups together goods- and service-producing firms that use identical or similar production processes.

NAICS promises to be an extremely valuable tool for business marketers who are analyzing, segmenting, and targeting markets. Each classification group is relatively homogeneous in terms of raw materials required, components used, manufacturing processes employed, and problems faced.[9] The more digits in a code, the more homogenous the group. A supplier who understands the needs and requirements of a few firms within a classification can project requirements for all firms in that category, as well as identify the number, size, and geographic location of firms in that category. This information can used to estimate market potential and market share and to forecast sales. It can also be used to identify potential new customers. NAICS codes will help marketers identify prospective users of a supplier's goods and services.

exhibit 5.3

NAICS Two-Digit Codes and Corresponding Economic Sectors

NAICS code	Economic sector
11	Agriculture, forestry, and fishing
21	Mining
22	Utilities
23	Construction
31–33	Manufacturing
43	Wholesale trade
44–45	Retail trade
47–48	Transportation
51	Information
52	Finance and insurance
53	Real estate and rental and leasing
56	Professional and technical services
57	Management and support services
61	Education services
62	Health and social assistance
71	Arts, entertainment, and recreation
72	Food services, drinking places, and accommodations
81	Other services, except public administration
93	Public administration
98	Estates and trusts
99	Nonclassifiable

Source: US Census Bureau.

exhibit 5.4

Examples of NAICS Hierarchy

NAICS Level	NAICS Code	EXAMPLE #1 Description	NAICS Code	EXAMPLE #2 Description
Sector	31–33	Manufacturing	51	Information
Subsector	334	Computer and electronic product manufacturing	513	Broadcasting and telecommunications
Industry Group	3346	Manufacturing and reproduction of magnetic and optical media	5133	Telecommunications
Industry	33461	Manufacturing and reproduction of magnetic and optical media	51332	Wireless telecommunications carriers, except satellite

Source: U.S. Census Bureau, "New Code System in NAICS," http://www.census.gov/pub/epcd/www/naiscod.htm, 6 March 1998.

Exhibit 5.3 provides an overview of NAICS. Exhibit 5.4 illustrates the six-digit classification system for two of the twenty NAICS economic sectors: manufacturing and information. NAICS's hierarchical structure makes it possible to summarize industry data at several levels of detail.

Business Versus Consumer Markets

6

Explain the major differences between business and consumer markets

The basic philosophy and practice of marketing is the same whether the customer is a business organization or a consumer. That being said, business markets and consumer markets do have different characteristics. Exhibit 5.5 summarizes the main differences.

exhibit 5.5

Major Characteristics of Business Markets Compared to Consumer Markets

Characteristic	Business market	Consumer market
Demand	Organizational	Individual
Purchase volume	Larger	Smaller
Number of customers	Fewer	Many
Location of buyers	Geographically concentrated	Dispersed
Distribution structure	More direct	More indirect
Nature of buying	More professional	More personal
Nature of buying influence	Multiple	Single
Type of negotiations	More complex	Simpler
Use of reciprocity	Yes	No
Use of leasing	Greater	Lesser
Primary promotional	Personal selling	Advertising method

Recent marketing campaigns have highlighted the convenience and recycling benefits of aluminum cans and products. By also mentioning the positive environmental impact of using aluminum, producers hope to influence consumer demand.

Demand

Consumer demand for products is quite different from demand in the business market. Unlike consumer demand, business demand is derived, inelastic, joint, and fluctuating.

Derived Demand The demand for business products is referred to as **derived demand** because organizations buy products to be used in producing consumer products. In other words, the demand for business products is *derived* from the demand for consumer products. The markets for CPUs, hard drives, and DVD-ROMs are derived from the demand for personal computers. These items are only valuable as components of computers. Demand for these items rises and falls with the demand for personal computers.

Because the demand for business products is derived, business marketers must carefully monitor demand patterns and changing preferences in final consumer markets, even though their customers are not in those markets. As well, business marketers must carefully monitor their customers' forecasts, because derived demand is based on expectations of future demand for those customers' products.

Some business marketers not only monitor final consumer demand and customer forecasts but also try to influence final consumer demand. Aluminum producers use television and magazine ads to point out the convenience and recycling opportunities that aluminum offers to consumers, who can choose to purchase soft drinks in either aluminum or plastic containers.

derived demand
The demand for business products.

Inelastic Demand The demand for many business products is inelastic with regard to price. In other words, an increase or decrease in the price of the product will not significantly affect demand for the product.

The price of a product used in the production of a product, or as part of a product, is often a minor portion of the final product's total price, so demand for the final consumer product is not affected. If the price of automobile paint or spark plugs rose significantly—say, 200 percent in one year—would the number of new automobiles sold that year be affected? Probably not.

joint demand
The demand for two or more items used together in a final product.

Joint Demand **Joint demand** occurs when two or more items are used together in a final product. A decline in the availability of memory chips will slow production of microcomputers; in turn, this will reduce the demand for disk drives. Many business products, such as hammer heads and hammer handles, exemplify joint demand.

Fluctuating Demand The demand for business products—especially new plants and equipment—tends to be more unstable than the demand for consumer products. A small change in consumer demand for a product can produce a much larger change in demand for the facilities and equipment needed to make that product. Economists refer to this phenomenon as the **multiplier effect** (or **accelerator principle**).

multiplier effect (accelerator principle)
A phenomenon whereby a small change in consumer demand can produce a much larger change in demand for the facilities and equipment needed to make the consumer product.

Cummins Engine Company, a producer of heavy-duty diesel engines, uses sophisticated surface grinders to make parts. Suppose Cummins is using twenty surface grinders. Each machine lasts about ten years. Purchases have been timed so that two machines will wear out and be replaced annually. If the demand for engine parts does not change, two grinders will be bought in year 1. If the demand for parts declines slightly, only eighteen grinders may be needed in year 2, in which case Cummins won't replace the worn-out ones in year 1. However, suppose that in year 3 the demand returns to previous levels plus a little more. To meet the new level of demand, Cummins will need to replace the two machines that wore out in year 1 and the two that wore out in year 2 and buy one or more additional machines. The multiplier effect works this way in many industries, resulting in highly fluctuating demand for business products.

Purchase Volume

Business customers buy in much larger quantities than consumers. Just think how large an order Post Cereals typically places for the whole-grain wheat it uses to manufacture Shredded Wheat. Imagine the number of tires for Windstar vans that Ford buys at one time for its assembly plant in Oakville.

Number of Customers

Business marketers usually have far fewer customers than consumer marketers. The advantage is that it is a lot easier to identify prospective buyers, monitor current customers' needs and levels of satisfaction, and personally attend to existing customers. The main disadvantage is that each customer becomes crucial—especially for manufacturers that have only one customer. Often, that one customer is the government.

Location of Buyers

Business customers tend to be much more geographically concentrated than individual consumers. Business buyers tend to cluster in specific regions, typically near Canada's major urban centres. The Canadian oil industry is concentrated in Alberta, the Northwest Territories, and Newfoundland. Most Canadian rubber is manufactured in Ontario, and most shoes in the country are made in Quebec. The aircraft industry is concentrated in Ontario and Quebec, and most forestry is on the West Coast.

Distribution Structure

Many consumer products pass through a distribution system that includes the producer, one or more wholesalers, and a retailer. However, because of many of the characteristics already mentioned, channels of distribution are usually shorter in business marketing. Direct channels, through which manufacturers market directly to users, are much more common.

Many businesses that market directly to users are discovering that new media, such as CD-ROMs and the Internet, offer great potential for reaching new and existing customers domestically and around the world. These media also reduce costs to both buyers and sellers.[10]

Nature of Buying

Unlike consumers, business buyers usually approach purchasing rather formally. Businesses use professionally trained purchasing agents who spend their entire careers purchasing a limited number of items. They get to know the items and the sellers well. Some professional purchasers earn the designation certified purchasing manager (CPM) after participating in a rigorous certification program.

Nature of Buying Influence

Typically, more people are involved in a single business purchase decision than in a consumer purchase. Experts from fields as varied as quality control, marketing, and finance, as well as professional buyers and users, may be grouped in a buying centre (discussed later in this chapter).

Type of Negotiations

With some exceptions (e.g., houses, cars), most consumers expect sellers to set the price and other conditions of sale, such as time of delivery and credit terms. In contrast, negotiating is common in business marketing. Buyers and sellers negotiate product specifications, delivery dates, payment terms, and other pricing matters. Sometimes these negotiations require many meetings over several months. Final contracts are often very long and detailed.

on line

Senco Products, Inc.

What kinds of business products does Senco make? Explain your answer. Is Senco only a business marketer? How do you know?

www.senco.com

Use of Reciprocity

reciprocity
A practice where business purchasers choose to buy from their own customers.

Business purchasers often choose to buy from their own customers—a practice known as **reciprocity**. General Motors buys engines for its cars and trucks from Borg Warner, which in turn buys many of the cars and trucks it needs from GM. This practice is neither unethical nor illegal unless one party coerces the other and the result is unfair competition. Reciprocity is generally considered a reasonable business practice.The Canadian Competition Act forbids unfair reciprocity and discrimination in reciprocity agreements.

Use of Leasing

Consumers normally buy products instead of leasing them. But businesses often lease expensive equipment such as computers, construction equipment, and cars and trucks. In doing so they reduce their capital outflow, which allows them to acquire the latest models. They also receive better service, and garner tax advantages.

The lessor—that is, the firm providing the product—can be the manufacturer or it can be an independent firm. The lessor benefits because leasing generates more total revenue than selling outright, and because leasing brings customers into the market who cannot afford to buy goods outright.

Primary Promotional Method

Business marketers tend to emphasize personal selling in their promotion efforts, especially for expensive items, custom-designed products, large-volume purchases, and situations requiring negotiations. Many business sales require a great deal of personal contact. Personal selling is discussed in more detail in Chapter 14.

Types of Business Products

7
Describe the seven types of business goods and services

Business products generally fall into one of the following seven categories, depending on their use: major equipment, accessory equipment, raw materials, component parts, processed materials, supplies, and business services.

Major Equipment

major equipment
Capital goods such as large or expensive machines, mainframe computers, blast furnaces, generators, airplanes, and buildings.

Major equipment includes capital goods such as large or expensive machines, mainframe computers, blast furnaces, generators, airplanes, and buildings. (These items are also commonly called *installations.*) Major equipment is depreciated over time rather than charged as an expense in the year it is purchased. Also, major equipment is often custom-designed. Personal selling is an important part of the marketing strategy for major equipment because distribution channels are almost always direct from the producer to the business user.

Accessory Equipment

accessory equipment
Goods, such as portable tools and office equipment, that are less expensive and shorter-lived than major equipment.

Accessory equipment is generally less expensive than major equipment and has a shorter life. Portable drills, power tools, desktop computers, and fax machines are examples. Accessory equipment is often charged as an expense in the year it is bought instead of being depreciated over its useful life. In contrast to major equipment, accessories are more often standardized; also, they are usually bought by more customers. These customers tend to be widely dispersed—all businesses buy desktop computers, for example.

Local industrial distributors (wholesalers) play an important role in the marketing of accessory equipment. Advertising is a more vital promotional tool for accessory equipment than for major equipment, regard less of where accessories are bought.

Raw Materials

Raw materials are unprocessed extractive or agricultural products—for example, mineral ore, lumber, wheat, corn, fruits, vegetables, and fish. Raw materials become part of finished products. Heavy users of raw materials, such as steel mills, lumber mills, and food canners, generally buy huge quantities of raw materials. Often there are a large number of relatively small sellers of raw materials, so no one seller can greatly influence price or supply. For this reason, the market tends to set the price of raw materials, and individual producers have little pricing flexibility. Promotion is almost always through personal selling, and distribution channels are usually direct from producer to business user.

raw materials
Unprocessed extractive or agricultural products, such as mineral ore, lumber, wheat, corn, fruits, vegetables, and fish.

Component Parts

Component parts are either finished items ready for assembly or products that need very little processing before becoming part of some other product. Examples include spark plugs, tires, and electric motors for cars. A special feature of component parts is that they often retain their identity after becoming part of the final product. For example, automobile tires are clearly recognizable as part of a car. Moreover, because component parts often wear out, they may need to be replaced several times during the life of the final product. Thus, there are two important markets for many component parts: the original equipment manufacturer (OEM) market, and the replacement market.

component parts
Either finished items ready for assembly, or products that need very little processing before becoming part of some other product.

Many of the business features listed in Exhibit 5.5 characterize the OEM market. In OEM markets the difference between unit cost and selling price is often small, but profits can be substantial because of volume buying.

The replacement market includes organizations and individuals buying component parts to replace worn-out parts. Because components often retain their identity in final products, the purchaser often sticks with the same brand the manufacturer used—for example, the same brand of automobile tires or battery. The replacement market operates differently from the OEM market, however. Whether replacement buyers are organizations or individuals, they tend to

Magna International, headquartered in Aurora, Ontario, produces automotive parts, which it ships to car makers around the world. Its customers include the OEMs of cars and trucks in North America, Europe, Mexico, South America, and Asia.

demonstrate the characteristics of consumer markets (see Exhibit 5.5). Consider a replacement part for a car. Purchase volume is usually small, and there are many customers, geographically dispersed, who typically buy from car dealers or parts stores. There are no negotiations, and neither reciprocity nor leasing is usually an issue. Manufacturers of component parts often direct their advertising toward replacement buyers.

Processed Materials

processed materials
Products used directly in manufacturing other products.

Processed materials are used directly in manufacturing other products. Unlike raw materials, they have had some processing. Examples include sheet metal, chemicals, specialty steel, lumber, corn syrup, and plastics. Unlike component parts, processed materials do not retain their identity in final products.

Most processed materials are marketed to OEMs or to distributors servicing the OEM market. Most processed materials—for example, steel and lumber—are bought according to customer specifications or to some industry standard. Price and service are important factors in choosing a vendor.

Supplies

supplies
Consumable items that do not become part of the final product.

Supplies are consumable items that do not become part of the final product—lubricants, detergents, paper towels, pencils, paper, and so on. Typically, supplies are standardized items that purchasing agents buy routinely. They have relatively short lives and are inexpensive compared to other business goods. This category is often referred to as MRO items, which stands for *maintenance, repair,* and *operating* items.

Competition in the MRO market is intense. Bic and PaperMate are in a long-running battle for the business market in cheap ballpoint pens.

Business Services

business services
Expense items that do not become part of a final product.

Business services are expense items that do not become part of a final product. Businesses often retain outside providers to perform janitorial, maintenance, advertising, legal, consulting, research, and other services. Hiring an outside provider makes sense when it costs less than hiring or assigning an employee to perform the task, and when an outside provider is needed for particular expertise.

Business Buying Behaviour

8
Discuss the unique aspects of business buying behaviour

As you probably have already gathered, business buyers don't behave the same way as consumers. Understanding how purchase decisions are made in organizations is an early step in developing a business selling strategy. Five important aspects of business buying behaviour are buying centres, evaluative criteria, buying situations, purchasing ethics, and customer service.

Buying Centres

buying centre
All the people who become involved in the purchase decision.

A **buying centre** includes all the people in an organization who become involved in the purchase decision. Membership and influence vary from company to company. In engineering-dominated firms like Bell Helicopter of Mirabel, Quebec , the buying centre may consist almost entirely of engineers. In marketing-oriented firms like Toyota and IBM, marketing and engineering have almost equal authority. In consumer goods firms like Procter & Gamble, product managers and other marketing decision makers may dominate the buying centre. In a small manufacturing company, almost everyone may be a member.

The number of people involved in a buying centre varies with the complexity and importance of the purchase decision. The buying group will usually change its composition from one purchase to the next and sometimes even from one stage in the buying process to the next. To make matters more complicated, buying centres do not appear on formal organization charts. An IBM executive remembered, "I started out [in the 1980s] selling to the corner office [CEO], then we got moved to the CFO, and then to the data processing manager, and finally to the data center manager."[11]

Roles in the Buying Centre As in family purchasing decisions, several people may play a role in the business purchase process:

- *Initiator:* the person who first suggests making a purchase.
- *Influencers/evaluators:* the people who influence the buying decision. They often help define specifications and provide information for evaluating options. Technical personnel are especially important as influencers.
- *Gatekeepers:* the group members who regulate the flow of information. Often the purchasing agent views the gatekeeping role as a source of his or her power. A secretary may also act as a gatekeeper by determining which vendors get an appointment with a buyer.
- *Decider:* the person who has the formal or informal power to choose or approve the selection of the supplier or brand. In complex situations it is often difficult to determine who makes the final decision.
- *Purchaser:* the person who actually negotiates the purchase. It could be anyone, from the president of the company to the purchasing agent, depending on the importance of the decision.
- *Users:* the members of the organization who will actually use the product. Users often initiate the buying process and help define product specifications. An example illustrating these basic roles is provided in Exhibit 5.6.

exhibit 5.6

Buying Centre Roles for Computer Purchases

Role	Illustration
Initiator	The division general manager proposes to replace the company's computer network.
Influencers/evaluators	The corporate controller's office and the vice-president of data processing have an important say about which system and vendor the company will deal with.
Gatekeepers	The corporate departments for purchasing and data processing analyze the company's needs and recommend likely matches with potential vendors.
Decider	The vice-president of administration, with advice from others, selects the vendor the company will deal with and the system it will buy.
Purchaser	The purchasing agent negotiates the terms of sale.
Users	All division employees use the computers.

on line

Loctite Corporation

What evidence do you see on Loctite's Website that its marketing efforts focus on engineers? Read some of its on-line literature.

www.loctite.com

Implications of Buying Centres for the Marketing Manager Successful vendors understand the importance of identifying who is in the decision-making unit, each member's relative influence in the buying decision, and each member's evaluative criteria. Successful selling strategies often focus on determining the most important influencers and tailoring sales presentations to these members of the buying centre.

Loctite Corporation, the manufacturer of Super Glue and industrial adhesives and sealants, learned that engineers were the most important influencers and deciders in adhesive and sealant purchase decisions. So it focused its marketing efforts on production and maintenance engineers.

Evaluative Criteria

Business buyers evaluate products and suppliers against three important criteria: quality, service, and price—in that order.

- *Quality:* Here, quality refers to technical suitability. A superior tool can do a better job in the production process, and superior packaging can increase dealer and consumer acceptance of a brand. Quality is also evaluated in terms of the salesperson and the salesperson's firm. Business buyers want to deal with reputable salespeople and with companies that are financially responsible. Quality improvement should be part of every organization's marketing strategy.
- *Service:* Almost as much as they want satisfactory products, business buyers want satisfactory service. A purchase offers several opportunities for service. Suppose a vendor is selling heavy equipment. Prepurchase service could include a survey of the buyer's needs. After thorough analysis of the survey findings, the vendor could prepare a report and recommendations in the form of a purchasing proposal. If a purchase results, postpurchase service might consist of installing the equipment and training those who will be using it. Postsale services can also include maintenance and repairs. Another service that business buyers seek is dependability of supply. They must be able to count on sellers to deliver on schedule what was ordered. Buyers also welcome services that help them sell their finished products. Services of this sort are especially appropriate when the seller's product is an identifiable part of the buyer's end product.

Businesses require satisfactory postsales service. This may mean installing the equipment or training employees in its use.

- *Price:* Business buyers want to buy at low prices—usually at the lowest prices. However, a buyer who pressures a supplier to cut prices to a point where the supplier loses money on the sale almost forces shortcuts on quality. The buyer may also in effect be forcing the supplier to stop doing business with him or her. Then a new source of supply will have to be found.

Many international business buyers use similar evaluative criteria. One study of South African buyers of high-tech laboratory instruments found that they use the following evaluative criteria, in descending order: technical service, perceived product reliability, after-sales support, supplier's reputation, ease of maintenance, ease of operation, price, confidence in the sales representative, and product flexibility.[12]

Federal Express

How has FedEx developed a Website to address the service needs of its business customers? Check out the Business Tools on its site.

www.fedex.com

on line

Buying Situations

Often business firms, especially manufacturers, must decide whether to make something or buy it from an outside supplier. The decision is essentially one of economics. Can an item of similar quality be bought at a lower price elsewhere? If not, is manufacturing it in-house the best use of limited company resources? Briggs & Stratton Corp., a major manufacturer of four-cycle engines, might be able to save $150,000 annually on outside purchases by spending $500,000 on the equipment needed to produce gas throttles internally. Yet the company could also use that $500,000 to upgrade its carburetor assembly line, which would save $225,000 annually. When a firm does decide to buy a product instead of making it, the purchase will be a new buy, a modified rebuy, or a straight rebuy.

New Buy A **new buy** is a situation requiring the purchase of a product for the first time. Suppose a law firm decides to replace its word-processing machinery with computers. This situation represents the greatest opportunity for new vendors. No long-term relationship has been established for this product, specifications may be somewhat fluid, and buyers are generally more open to new vendors.

new buy
A situation requiring the purchase of a product for the first time.

If the new item is a raw material or a critical component part, the buyer cannot afford to run out of supply. The seller must be able to convince the buyer that the seller's firm can consistently deliver a high-quality product on time.

Modified Rebuy A **modified rebuy** is usually less critical and less time-consuming than a new buy. In a modified-rebuy situation, the purchaser wants some change in the original good or service. It may be a new colour, greater tensile strength in a component part, more respondents in a marketing research study, or additional services in a janitorial contract.

modified rebuy
A situation where the purchaser wants some change in the original good or service.

Because the two parties are familiar with each other and credibility has already been established, buyer and seller can concentrate on the specifics of the modification. Sometimes, however, modified rebuys are open to outside bidders. The purchaser uses this strategy to ensure that the new terms are competitive. An example would be a law firm deciding to buy more powerful computers. The firm may open the bidding to examine the price and quality of the offers of several suppliers.

ethics in marketing

Gifts from Suppliers: Ford Motor Company's Policy

What policies do firms set regarding accepting gifts from suppliers?

Here's the policy at Ford. Although soliciting gifts and favours is never permissible, if there is a legitimate business purpose, it is permissible to accept gifts and favours that are freely offered by suppliers, dealers, and others with whom Ford does business, subject to the following important limitations:

- The gift must be of nominal value and must involve no more than normal sales promotion or publicity.
- Social amenities must be appropriate and limited and must never give the appearance of impropriety.
- Any discounts on goods or services offered to you by a supplier must be made generally available and cannot be for your benefit only.
- You may never accept cash or gift certificates or gifts of food or alcohol.
- You may not borrow money, except from qualified financial institutions on generally available terms.

Source: From Ford Motor Company's "Standards of Corporate Conduct," 1996. p. 6. Reprinted by permission.

straight rebuy
A buying situation in which the purchaser reorders the same goods or services without looking for new information or investigating other suppliers.

Straight Rebuy A **straight rebuy** is the situation vendors prefer. The purchaser is not looking for new information or other suppliers. It places an order, and the supplier provides the product as in previous orders. Most straight rebuys are routine because the terms of the purchase have been agreed to in earlier negotiations. An example would be the law firm previously cited purchasing printer cartridges from the same supplier on a regular basis.

One common instrument used in straight-rebuy situations is the purchasing contract. Purchasing contracts are used with products that are bought often and in high volumes. Purchasing contracts make the buyer's decision making routine and promise the salesperson a sure sale. The advantage to the buyer is a quick, confident decision; the advantage to the salesperson is reduced or eliminated competition.

Suppliers must remember not to take straight-rebuy relationships for granted. That being said, retaining existing customers is much easier than attracting new ones.

Sears Canada has always been a leader in customer service, with a complete satisfaction or money refunded guarantee. The famous Sears catalogue, and new technologies such as on-line shopping, have enhanced Sears's ability to serve more customers and hold its place in the competitive retail market. www.sears.ca.

Purchasing Ethics

The ethics of business buyer and seller relationships are often scrutinized and sometimes criticized by superiors, associates, other prospective suppliers, the general public, and the news media. Ford Motor Company, mindful of the problems often faced by professional buyers, has developed this chapter's guidelines shown in the "Ethics in Marketing" box.

Customer Service

Increasingly, business marketers are recognizing the benefits of developing formal systems for monitoring customer opinions and perceptions. Companies like McDonald's, Sears, and Lexus build their strategies not only around products but also around a few highly developed service skills. Many firms are finding new ways to enhance customer service through technology. Business marketers are leading the way in adopting new media technologies such as on-line services, CD-ROMs, and the Internet.[13] In November 1994, Federal Express began a service on the Web that offers customers a window directly into its package-tracking database.

LOOKING BACK

Look back at the story about Air Canada and the Star Alliance of airlines at the beginning of this chapter. You now know that a strategic alliance is a cooperative agreement between business firms. General benefits to members of such an alliance include improved access to markets and to technology, economies of scale, faster entry of new products to markets, and reduced risk. Specific benefits relating to the Star Alliance case include world-class opportunities for employees, better customer recognition worldwide, a framework for future development, and synergies such as common use of facilities and joint purchasing. Customers benefit from integrated frequent-flyer programs, access to more flights and destinations, simplified ticketing and reservations, more convenient connections, and better baggage and ground services.

If the alliance is able to deliver the benefits to customers it claims it can, the competition will definitely be threatened. Competitors will likely form alliances to maintain and enhance their market share.

Summary

1 Describe business marketing. Business marketing provides goods and services that are bought for use in business rather than for personal consumption. Intended use, not physical characteristics, distinguishes a business product from a consumer product.

2 Describe the role of the Internet in business marketing. The Internet has made business markets more competitive than ever before. The number of business buyers and sellers using the Internet is rapidly increasing. Firms are seeking new and better ways to expand their markets and sources of supply, increase sales and decrease costs, and better serve customers. With the Internet, every business in the world is potentially a local competitor.

3 Discuss the role of relationship marketing and strategic alliances in business marketing. Relationship marketing involves seeking and establishing long-term alliances or partnerships with customers. A strategic alliance is a cooperative agreement between business firms. Firms form alliances to leverage what they do well by partnering with others who have complementary skills.

4 Identify the four major categories of business market customers. Producer markets include for-profit organizations and individuals that buy products to use in producing other products, as components of other products, or in facilitating business operations. Reseller markets consist of wholesalers and retailers that buy finished products to resell for profit. Government markets include federal, provincial, territorial, and municipal governments that buy goods and services to support their own operations and to serve the needs of citizens. Institutional markets consist of many sorts of nonbusiness institutions whose main goals do not include profit.

5 Explain the North American Industry Classification System. The NAICS provides a way to identify, analyze, segment, and target business and government markets. Organizations can be identified and compared by a numeric code that indicates business sector, subsector, industry group, industry, and country industry.

6 Explain the major differences between business and consumer markets. In business markets, demand is derived, price-inelastic, joint, and fluctuating. Purchase volumes are much larger than in consumer markets, customers are fewer in number and more geographically concentrated, and distribution channels are more direct. Buying is approached more formally using professional purchasing agents, more people are involved in the buying process, negotiations are more complex, and reciprocity and leasing are more common. Finally, selling strategy in business markets usually focuses on personal contact rather than on advertising.

7 Describe the seven types of business goods and services. Major equipment includes capital goods, such as heavy machinery. Accessory equipment is typically less expensive and shorter-lived than major equipment. Raw materials are extractive or agricultural products that have not been processed. Component parts are finished or near-finished items to be used as parts of other products. Processed materials are used to manufacture other products. Supplies are consumable and are not used as part of a final product. Business services are intangible products that many companies use in their operations.

8 Discuss the unique aspects of business buying behaviour. Business buying behaviour is distinguished by five fundamental characteristics. First, buying is usually undertaken by a buying centre consisting of many people who range widely in authority level. Second, business buyers typically evaluate alternative products and suppliers based on quality, service, and price—in that order. Third, business

Do You Know These Terms?

buying falls into three general categories: new buys, modified rebuys, and straight rebuys. Fourth, the ethics of business buyers and sellers are often scrutinized. Fifth, customer service before, during, and after the sale plays a big role in business purchase decisions.

Discussion and Writing Questions

1. How might derived demand affect the manufacturing of an automobile?
2. Why is relationship or personal selling the best way to promote in business marketing?
3. A colleague of yours is trying to sell a new voice-mail system to a local business, and has sent you an e-mail seeking your advice. Send him a return e-mail describing the various people who might influence the customer's buying decision. Include suggestions for dealing with the needs of each of these individuals.
4. Intel Corporation supplies microprocessors to Compaq for use in its computers. Describe the buying situation in this relationship, keeping in mind the rapid advancement of technology in this industry.
5. In small groups, brainstorm examples of companies that feature the products in the different business categories. Compile a list of ten specific business products, including at least one in each category. Then match up with another group. Have each group take turns naming a product, and have the other group identify its appropriate category. Try to resolve all discrepancies by discussion.
6. The Canadian Federation of Independent Business (CFIB) publishes a monthly "green" business registry, links to legislative offices across Canada, and small business news. Visit its Website, and then write a memo to a colleague and explain why he or she should visit this site.
7. What business publications, search facilities, sources, and services are offered at **www.strategis.ic.gc.ca**?
8. How could you use **www.business2business.on.ca** to help plan a business trip?

Application for Small Business

Dan White is an independent video producer whose biggest client is the Province of Manitoba. Although this account is big enough to support the entire business, Dan has developed other lines of business to eliminate the risks involved with having only one customer. Dan has also landed a sizable account through a high school friend who is the vice-president of Good Hands Insurance. This also happens to be the company that underwrites Dan's life insurance. Dan has also been hired to work on various projects for large production companies. Dan generated this business through long-term relationships built by working on projects for the province.

As Dan prepares his business plan for the upcoming year, he is contemplating several strategic changes. The video industry is changing quickly, and Dan has observed two important trends. First, he is finding it harder to own the latest video equipment that his customers are demanding. Second, his clients are finding that they cannot keep up with the recent developments in the industry and would be willing to pay more for his expertise. Dan is looking into a lease for new equipment and is also considering increasing his prices.

Questions:

1. What two-digit NAICS code would you assign to Dan's business?
2. Is Dan's choice to use Good Hands Insurance ethical? Explain.
3. How can Dan use the inelasticity of demand to his advantage?
4. Would you advise Dan to lease or buy the new equipment? Why?

VIDEO CASE

Burke, Inc.: Business-to-Business Alliances

As one of the world's premier international business research and consulting firms, Burke, Inc., provides services to other businesses to help them grow and remain competitive. Burke has offices and affiliates throughout North America as well as an international division, headquartered in London, that operates in eleven European countries and Japan. Burke has four divisions: Burke Marketing Research, Burke Customer Satisfaction Associates, Burke Strategic Consulting Group, and The Training and Development Centre.

Burke owes its success to the number and quality of its business relationships. Today's business environment is so complex that companies can no longer operate independently; strategic alliances offer viable solutions to this. Burke brings more than sixty-five years of industry experience to each business alliance and has joined with companies in a wide variety of industries.

According to Burke's business philosophy, a strategic alliance is especially strong when the two partners bring different strengths to the table. These complementary assets might include access to markets or to technology. Economies of scale are possible by combining R&D or marketing activities. Risks can be shared. Recently, Burke teamed with a publisher to produce a national consumer guide to nonprescription drugs. The publisher and author lacked the experience and sophisticated tools for gathering immediate and accurate information from pharmacists, so they asked Burke Marketing Research to join them. Together, the writer, the publisher, and the researchers produced a very thorough national consumer's guide. Burke was able to provide the timely information that its partner needed to gain a competitive advantage.

Yet Burke does not take a "cookie cutter" approach that offers different partners solutions cut from the same cloth. Rather, working in teams, researchers customize methods for specific industries and product or service categories. Burke's strong belief in teamwork and specialized service influences every alliance and ultimately strengthens its relationships with its partners. Everyone at Burke understands that business clients operate in different marketing environments and have different business objectives, so each business client works with an account team to see that objectives are met efficiently, economically, and on time. The team analyzes each client's business needs and focuses Burke's broad resources on specific requirements.

Recently, the Burke Strategic Consulting Group formed a partnership with Armstrong Laing, a computer software company, to provide consulting support for businesses that purchase Armstrong Laing's management software. Burke will use the software to assist clients in understanding their true costs and in pinpointing the link between long-term strategies and day-to-day decisions. "This partnership allows us to provide innovative solutions to clients who want better financial results through cost management programs," says Diane Salamon, vice-president of Burke, Inc. For its part, Armstrong Laing describes the partnership as a marriage of management expertise and cutting-edge software that will help customers attain leadership positions in their industries. Teaming up with an outside provider of business services made sense for Armstrong Laing because the company did not have management consulting expertise in-house. And like most business-to-business marketers, Armstrong Laing was selling its products in very large quantities to established organizations such as American Express and Blue Cross/Blue Shield, and wanted to offer its clients a comprehensive approach of the highest quality.

Still another element of Burke's alliances is relationship marketing—that is, seeking and establishing ongoing partnerships. For example, one client was a multinational restaurant company that wished to define its strengths and determine the effect of a change in advertising. To provide this information, Burke built a model to show how market share might be affected by different advertising and made predictions based on this model. But the relationship did not end there. Burke continued to set clear priorities for future communication and operating strategies. This long-term relationship allowed the restaurant company to get maximum ROI (return on image) for its advertising dollars. Long-term relationships like this build trust among partners, especially when they share a common interest in meeting customer needs.

Questions

1. Why is Burke, Inc., considered a business marketer?
2. Review Exhibit 5.2. Does Burke follow the tips for making strategic alliances successful?
3. How did Burke's strategic business alliance with Armstrong Laing create a competitive advantage in the marketplace?
4. How does Burke use the principles of relationship marketing?

CHAPTER

6

LEARNING OBJECTIVES

After studying this chapter, you should be able to

1 Describe the characteristics of markets and market segments

2 Explain the importance of market segmentation

3 Discuss the criteria for successful market segmentation

4 Describe the bases commonly used to segment consumer markets

5 Describe the bases for segmenting business markets

6 List the steps involved in segmenting markets

7 Discuss alternative strategies for selecting target markets

8 Explain how and why firms implement positioning strategies, and how product differentiation plays a role

9 Discuss global market segmentation and targeting issues

SEGMENTING AND TARGETING MARKETS

"I want you in my pants."
That was the battle cry for modrobes (pronounced *mode robes*), number 20 on the list of Canada's hottest start-ups, as published in *Profit* magazine in September 2000.

Steven Debus has wanted you in his pants since he came up with the idea of "exam pants" while he was a student at Brock University. Modrobes sells casual clothes that are practical and comfortable. Originally designed for the lifestyle of college and university students, modrobes are wide-legged, stain and wrinkle resistant pants that dry quickly so you don't have to spend valuable beer money on dryers. The concept was loosely based on the medical "scrub" pants worn by operating room physicians.

In 1996 Steve started selling his pants directly over the table in college and university campuses across Canada. "If these aren't the most comfortable pants you've ever had in your life, return them and I'll give you your money back," was the original verbal guarantee he made for each of his customers, and one Steve Debus still stands behind. Modrobes are now available in 400 stores across Canada, but Steve still believes in "in your face" marketing that puts his people directly with the customers at events such as the eight-city Edgefest concert tour and Woodstock '99. Modrobes does limited magazine advertising in publications such as *Vice* and *Access* magazines and *Snowboard* and *Skateboard Canada.* At events, modrobes hands out stickers with company slogans like "I want you in my pants" and "Technology for your ass."

With sales in excess of $3 million in 2000, modrobes's concept of lounge clothing for young, cutting-edge individuals is unique. Debus may want to grow his brand to be as well-known as Levis, but he also wants to maintain the product benefit that young people "want a pant they can wear during the day and go out in at night ... they want to be able to fall asleep in them and go to class the next day without the pant wrinkling ... People are sitting at computers now rather than factories and needed something comfortable, a little more lightweight." The company also produces skirts, long shorts, and microfleece tops.

modrobes

How has modrobes's segmentation and targeting strategy influenced its Website? Do its Web page designs and features make sense in terms of its target market? Does the site tell you much about the target market?

www.modrobes.com

on line

Max Valiquette of NRG Solutions, a youth insight and fulfilment firm, says that a company like modrobes can maintain a relationship with its young market because it's small and meets its customers face to face. Modrobes has two company-owned retail locations in Toronto and one in Vancouver. A three-year retail expansion is underway to develop more stores throughout North America. Large manufacturers have failed to compete with modrobes in the alternative clothing market because they don't have the "cool" or the "wow" authenticity. Valiquette says of authenticity: "Modrobes has that, and it's a massive difference. And young people can smell it from miles away."[1]

What kind of market segment strategy has modrobes adopted? Describe its market segment. Has its strategy been successful?

Market Segmentation

1

Describe the characteristics of markets and market segments

market
People or organizations with needs or wants and the ability and willingness to buy.

market segment
A subgroup of people or organizations sharing one of more characteristics that cause them to have similar product needs.

market segmentation
The process of dividing a market into meaningful, relatively similar, and identifiable segments or groups.

The term market means different things to different people. We are all familiar with terms like supermarket, stock market, labour market, fish market, and flea market. All these types of markets share several characteristics. First, they are composed of people (consumer markets) or organizations (business markets). Second, these people or organizations have wants and needs that can be satisfied by particular product categories. Third, they have the ability to buy the products they seek. Fourth, they are willing to exchange their resources—usually money or credit—for desired products. In sum, a **market** is (1) people or organizations with (2) needs or wants and with (3) the ability and (4) the willingness to buy. A group of people or an organization that lacks any one of these characteristics is not a market.

Within a market, a **market segment** is a subgroup of people or organizations sharing one or more characteristics that cause them to have similar product needs. At one extreme, we can define every person and every organization in the world as a market segment because each is unique. At the other extreme, we can define the entire consumer market as one large market segment and the business market as another large segment. All people have some similar characteristics and needs, as do all organizations.

From a marketing perspective, market segments can be described as somewhere between the two extremes. The process of dividing a market into meaningful, relatively similar, and identifiable segments or groups is called **market segmentation.** The purpose of market segmentation is to enable marketers to tailor their marketing mixes to meet the needs of one or more specific segments.

Exhibit 6.1 illustrates the concept of market segmentation. Each box represents a market consisting of seven people. This market might vary as follows: one homogeneous market of seven people, a market comprising seven individual segments, a market comprising two segments based on gender, a market comprising three age segments, or a market comprising five age and gender market segments. Age and gender and many other bases for segmenting markets are examined later in this chapter.

The Importance of Market Segmentation

2 Explain the importance of market segmentation

Until the 1960s, few firms practised market segmentation, and when they did it was more likely a haphazard effort than a formal marketing strategy. Before 1960 the Coca-Cola Company produced only one beverage and aimed it at the entire soft drink market. Today, Coca-Cola offers over a dozen different products to market segments based on diverse consumer preferences for flavours and calorie and caffeine content. Coca-Cola offers traditional soft drinks, energy drinks (such as Power Ade), flavoured teas, and fruit drinks (Fruitopia).

Market segmentation plays a key role in the strategy of almost every successful organization. It is a powerful tool for several reasons, the main one being that nearly all markets include groups of people or organizations with different product needs and preferences. Market segmentation helps marketers define customer needs and wants more precisely. Because market segments differ in size and potential, segmentation helps decision makers define their marketing objectives more precisely and allocate their resources more efficiently. Also, they can evaluate their own performance with more accuracy when their objectives are more precise.

exhibit 6.1

Concept of Market Segmentation

No market segmentation

Fully segmented market

Market segmentation by gender: M,F

Market segmentation by age group: 1,2,3

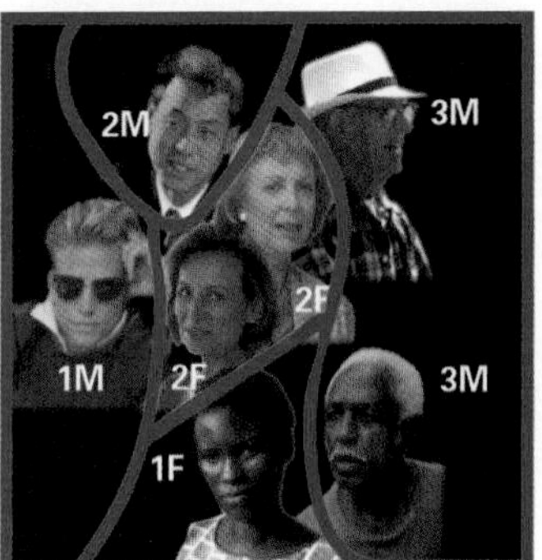

Market segmentation by gender and age group

Casino Niagara in Niagara Falls, Ontario, provides an interesting example of how market segmentation can increase a firm's customer base. The casino employs more than 3,700 people; over 25,000 customers stream through its doors every day. By studying its customers and analyzing its market segments, the casino is able to attract new customers and form strategies to keep current customers interested, happy, and coming back. The Casino bases its advertising appeals on customer profiles, which it builds through ongoing research. It develops its advertising strategy to take geographic and demographic segmentation into account. Its direct marketing efforts are based on usage rate segmentation; typically, customers who spend significant time at the casino tables are presented with special offerings for specific events.

Criteria for Successful Segmentation

3
Discuss the criteria for successful market segmentation

Marketers segment markets for three important reasons. First, segmentation enables them to identify groups of customers with similar needs and to analyze the characteristics and buying behaviours of these groups. Second, segmentation provides marketers with information to help them design marketing mixes specifically matched with the characteristics and desires of one or more segments. Third, segmentation is consistent with the marketing concept of satisfying customer wants and needs while meeting the organization's objectives.

To be useful, a segmentation scheme must produce segments that meet four basic criteria:

- *Substantiality:* A segment must be large enough to warrant developing and maintaining a special marketing mix. This criterion does not necessarily mean that a segment must have many potential customers: marketers of commercial airplanes, large computer systems, and custom-designed homes and business buildings typically develop marketing programs tailored to each potential customer's needs. In most cases, however, a market segment needs many potential customers to make commercial sense. All of Canada's major banks have divisions geared specifically to attracting and servicing the needs of small business.
- *Identifiability and measurability:* Segments must be identifiable, and their size must be measurable. Demographic data—the population in a given geographic area, and the number of people in that area by age, income, marital status, and other characteristics—are often easy to get and provide a fairly concrete measure of segment size. Suppose that a social service agency wants to identify segments by their readiness to participate in a drug and alcohol program or in prenatal care. Unless the agency can measure how many people are willing, indifferent, or unwilling to participate, it will have trouble gauging whether there are enough people to justify setting up the service.
- *Accessibility:* The firm must be able to reach members of targeted segments with customized marketing mixes. Some market segments are hard to reach—for example, senior citizens (especially those with reading or hearing disabilities), individuals who don't speak English, and the illiterate.
- *Responsiveness:* Markets can be segmented using any criteria that seem logical (see Exhibit 6.1). However, unless one market segment responds to a marketing mix differently from other segments, that segment need not be treated separately. When all customers are equally price conscious about a product, there is no need to offer high-, medium-, and low-priced versions to different segments.

Too Faced Cosmetics

Go to the Press Room at the Too Faced Website. What age segment do you think this new cosmetics company is targeting? Defend your answer.

www.toofaced. com

on line

Bases for Segmenting Consumer Markets

4

Describe the bases commonly used to segment consumer markets

Marketers use **segmentation bases,** or **variables,** which are the characteristics of individuals, groups, or organizations, to divide a total market into segments. The choice of segmentation bases is crucial because an inappropriate segmentation strategy can lead to lost sales and missed profit opportunities. The key is to identify bases that will produce substantial, measurable, and accessible segments that will respond differently to different marketing mixes.

segmentation bases (variables)
The characteristics of individuals, groups, or organizations.

Markets can be segmented using a single variable, such as age group, or several variables, such as age group, gender, and education. Single-variable segmentation is less precise but is also easier to use than multiple-variable segmentation. The disadvantages of multiple-variable segmentation are these: it is often harder to use than single-variable segmentation; usable secondary data are less likely to be available; and as the number of segmentation bases increases, the size of individual segments decreases. Nevertheless, the current trend is toward using more rather than fewer variables to segment most markets. Multiple-variable segmentation is obviously more precise than single-variable segmentation. As already noted, Casino Niagara segments its market based on three variables: geography, demographics, and usage rates.

Consumer goods marketers commonly use one or more of the following characteristics to segment markets: geography, demographics, psychographics, benefits sought, and usage rate. A more detailed description of these characteristics follows.

Geographic Segmentation

Geographic segmentation involves segmenting markets by region of the country or world, market size, market density, or climate. Market density is the number of people in a unit of land such as a census tract. Climate is often used to generate geographic segments because of its dramatic effect on consumers' needs and purchasing behaviour. Snowblowers, water and snow skis, and air-conditioning and heating systems are products whose appeal varies sharply with climate.

geographic segmentation
Segmenting markets by region of the country or world, market size, market density, or climate.

Consumer goods companies take a regional approach to marketing, for four reasons. First, many firms need to find new ways to generate sales because of sluggish and intensely competitive markets. Second, computerized checkout stations with scanners enable retailers to assess accurately which brands sell best in their regions. Third, many packaged goods manufacturers are introducing new regional brands intended to appeal to local preferences. Fourth, a more regional approach allows consumer goods companies to react more quickly to competition. One of Quebec's most famous recipes is poutine, a mixture of french fries, gravy, and cheese curds (the average serving contains 60 grams of fat), which was invented in 1957. Poutine is served in some Ontario restaurants and in various locations around the world. It is even on the McDonald's menus in Quebec. But true fans of poutine say the only place to enjoy the real thing is at roadside chip wagons in *la belle province.*

Demographic Segmentation

Marketers often segment markets on the basis of demographic information because that information is widely available and often related to consumers' buying and consuming behaviour. Some common bases of **demographic segmentation** are age,

demographic segmentation
Segmenting markets by age, gender, income, ethnic background, and family life cycle.

on line

Chapters/Indigo

How does Chapters/Indigo target kids? On the Kids' pages of the Website click on the "Wish List" feature. Do you think this feature is a successful way to sell books? Why or why not?

www.chapters.indigo.ca

gender, income, ethnic background, and family life cycle. The following discussion provides some important information about the main demographic segments.

Age Segmentation Children influence a great deal of family consumption. According to Susan Schaefer, YTV's director of marketing, when allowance, earnings, and gifts are included, children between nine and fourteen spend C$1.5 billion each year on food, clothing, and entertainment.[2] In addition, this group has tremendous influence on their parents' spending. A YTV survey found that 90 percent of parents consult their kids when purchasing snack food, 80 percent when planning vacations, and 40 percent when purchasing computers and associated technology. This effect is called "kidfluence." By 2006 there will be 2,155,300 teenagers in Canada.[3] Many companies are making strong efforts to attract children, in the hope of instilling brand loyalty early. Kodak found that kids were inhibited from taking photographs by the need to pester mom to get their film processed. So the company introduced a camera packaged with an envelope for mailing the film back to Kodak for developing.[4] Cosmetics for children—once clearly marketed as make-believe to young girls—are starting to cross the line into real makeup. Children and teens now represent one-fifth of all sales in the cosmetics industry.[5]

A relatively new and somewhat controversial development in marketing to children involves building children's databases on the Net. This chapter's "Ethics in Marketing" box explains the practice and the controversy.

Other age segments are also appealing targets for marketers. There are 4.35 million Canadians born between 1966 and 1976, termed Generation X, and they have considerable spending power.[6]

People between thirty-five and forty-four are likely to have school-age children at home and to outspend all other age groups on housing, clothing, alcohol, and food at home. Those between forty-five and fifty-four spend more than any other group on transportation, entertainment, education, personal insurance, pensions, and food away from home. Research has shown that people over fifty are willing to try new brands. Also, those over fifty-five are going to be passing along C$1 trillion in inheritance to their children and grandchildren in the next few decades.[7]

Seniors (sixty-five and over) are especially attracted to companies that build relationships by taking the time to get to know them and their preferences. As an example, older customers say they prefer catalogue shopping to retail outlets because of dissatisfaction with customer service at retail stores.

Gender Segmentation Marketers of products such as clothing, cosmetics, personal care items, magazines, jewellery, and footwear commonly segment markets by gender. The Score, a twenty-four-hour sports news station, is heavily marketing itself to men between eighteen and twenty-four. The marketing focus is on the station's on-air talent and exciting graphics, and on its Website (**www.TheScore.ca**). It encourages TV viewers to toggle back and forth between their set and the Website.[8]

Brands that have traditionally been marketed to men, such as Gillette razors and Rogaine baldness remedy, are intensifying their efforts to attract women.[9] The National Football League has launched an aggressive effort to retain and add to its female viewership, which on an average football weekend accounts for 43 percent of the league's fan base.[10] As well, "women's" products such as cosmetics, household products, and furniture are being marketed to men.

Income Segmentation Income is a popular demographic variable for segmenting markets because income level influences consumers' wants and determines their buying power. Many markets are segmented by income, including the markets for housing, clothing, automobiles, and food. Value retailers such as

global perspectives

Europe Is Deaf to Snap! Crackle! Pop!

Cereal companies perceive European countries such as Italy as opportunities for growth at a time when the North American cereal market is in decline. However, after years of aggressive marketing campaigns and health awareness programs in Italy, promoting the benefits of cereal, most Italians continue to eat breakfast Italian style: espresso or cappuccino and biscotti dipped into the coffee. North American cereals like corn flakes have been available in Italy since the 1950s, but until this decade they were considered a niche product and relegated to the nation's pharmacies and health food stores. Some progress has been made; a growing number of Italian parents are now giving their children cereal for breakfast.

In the early 1990s, cereal manufacturers began encountering problems at home and looking at markets abroad. Kellogg's started investing heavily in Europe, entering Italy full steam and opening manufacturing plants in Latvia and Denmark. For American cereal companies, Europe offered distinct advantages: higher prices and profit margins, cheaper television time, and fewer competitors. But Kellogg's timing was unfortunate. The fall of European trade restrictions as the European Union moved toward a single market made many plants unnecessary, especially when the number of people eating cereal was not multiplying that rapidly.

In looking for a turnaround, American cereal companies are trying to take advantage of some cultural shifts. The traditional long European lunch is giving way to the North American habit of grabbing a quick bite; this makes a bigger breakfast essential. Also, large North American–style supermarkets with wide aisles are taking over from smaller mom-and-pop stores, which are less inclined to switch to new, untried products.

Kellogg's now dominates Italy's cereal market with an estimated 61 percent market share, but it has recently come under attack from store brands launched by domestic retail chains. Furthermore, North American cereal makers are facing new competition from an Italian food manufacturer, Banila SpA, which recently introduced a pressed cereal breakfast bar. Called Armonie, it is being marketed as a nutritious breakfast food ideal for dipping in milk or coffee, just like biscotti. Ads for Armonie show a young woman flinging open the windows to let the sun shine in and then dipping the cereal bars in milk.[11]

Could cereal companies more effectively segment the Italian cereal market? Which segments might be promising? How should they position their products?

Building Children's Databases on the Net

Mr. Jelly Belly is awfully sweet to kids on line. The rotund mascot at candy maker Herman Goelitz, Inc.'s Website offers visitors free one-ounce samples of jelly beans—so long as they spill the beans about their name, address, gender, age, and where they shop. Only in the fine-print disclaimer does Mr. Jelly Belly reveal what might be done with this personal data: "Anything you disclose to us is ours. So we can do anything we want with the stuff you post. We can reproduce it, disclose it, transmit it, publish it, broadcast it, and post it someplace else."

Millions of kids are going on line, and marketers are in hot pursuit. Eager to reach an enthusiastic audience that is more open to pitches than the typical adult buried in junk mail, companies often entertain tykes on line with games and contests. But to play, these sites often require children to fill out questionnaires about themselves and their families and friends—valuable data to be sorted and stored in marketing databases.

"It's a huge problem. It's deceptive and fraudulent," says Marc Rotenberg, director of the Electronic Privacy Information Center, an on-line privacy rights group. "Kids don't know how their personal information is being used." He adds that typical on-line questionnaires are "much more detailed than the traditional cereal box promotion."

Marketers have been gathering information about kids for decades, dating back to the first decoder ring and proof of purchase. Some experts question whether a raft of new legislation is the right answer; perhaps the current rules on fraudulent and deceptive practices should simply be extended to the on-line market.

Companies are chomping at the bit for details from on-line surfers, no matter how young. At Microsoft Corp.'s Kids pages, when Kyle signs the guest book he is in effect offering up his name, his e-mail address, his home address, and that he is a boy. Kids visiting the site are encouraged to answer questions about what they like to do on line, but they are also asked, "Can a Microsoft representative contact you? [If so,] please include your telephone number including area code." Canadian children can join Zellers' stores' Generation Z points club and shop on line at the Generation Z Website using their points.

Isn't what Herman Goelitz, Inc. is doing with Mr. Jelly Belly just an extension of compiling a mailing list of who ordered decoder rings in the old days? Defend your answer. Do you agree with Marc Rotenberg, or do you think that everyone should simply lighten up? Do you think new legislation is needed to address the building of Jelly Belly–type databases? Explain.

Source: Jared Sandberg, "Ply and Pry: How Business Pumps Kids on Web," *The Wall Street Journal*, 9 June 1997. Reprinted with permission of Dow Jones. Copyright Clearance Center.

on line

M&M/Mars

Does the millennial theme advertising campaign launched by M&M/Mars in 1998 carry over into its Internet marketing? Explain what you find.

www.m-ms.com

dollar stores draw low- and fixed-income customers with easy access, small stores, and rock-bottom pricing.[12] Wal-Mart is moving away from its traditional rural and middle-income markets and targeting higher-income consumers in upscale areas. It is also spending more money on its stores, introducing more high-end merchandise, and upgrading its apparel lines.[13]

Ethnic Segmentation Many companies are segmenting their markets by ethnic groups. In Canada, cultural diversity begins with the French-Canadian and English-speaking Canadian populations, but goes farther than that to target other ethnic populations. According to A.C. Neilson DJC Research in Toronto, the Chinese community is the segment that has been most heavily researched. Advertising to the Asian market is never a simple matter of translation, as more than one language is spoken by Asians in Canada.[14] Many organizations segment this ethnic group by searching last names and creating advertising messages incorporating the colours, symbols, and celebrations thereby identified. At Casino Niagara, marketing executive director Anthony Annunziata has introduced special tables for Baccarat, a popular game among Chinese. The casino also offers Chinese concerts and cuisine.

Some entrepreneurs have built large, enclosed malls that cater specifically to Asian consumers. At the Aberdeen Centre near Vancouver, nearly 80 percent of the merchants are Chinese Canadians, as are 80 percent of the customers. The mall offers fashions made in Hong Kong, a shop for traditional Chinese medicines, and a theatre showing Chinese movies. On weekends the mall offers kung fu martial arts demonstrations and Chinese folk dances.

Family Life Cycle Segmentation The demographic factors of gender, age, and income often do not sufficiently explain variations in consumer buying behaviour. Often, differences in consumption patterns among people of the same age and gender are a result of their being at different stages of the family life cycle. The **family life cycle (FLC)** is a series of stages determined by a combination of age, marital status, and the presence or absence of children.

family life cycle (FLC)
A series of stages determined by a combination of age, marital status, and the presence or absence of children.

Exhibit 6.2 illustrates both traditional and contemporary FLC patterns and shows how families' needs, incomes, resources, and expenditures vary with each stage. The horizontal flow shows the traditional family life cycle. The lower part of the exhibit indicates some of the characteristics and purchase patterns of families at each stage of the traditional life cycle. The exhibit also acknowledges that about half of all first marriages end in divorce. When young marrieds move into the young divorced stage, their consumption patterns often revert back to those of the young single stage. About four out of five divorced people remarry by middle age and re-enter the traditional life cycle, as indicated by the "recycled flow" in the exhibit.

Psychographic Segmentation

Age, gender, income, ethnicity, FLC stage, and other demographic variables are usually helpful in developing segmentation strategies, but often they don't paint the entire picture. Demographics provides the skeleton; psychographics adds meat to the bones. **Psychographic segmentation** is market segmentation on the basis of the following variables:

psychographic segmentation
Market segmentation on the basis of personality, motives, lifestyles, and geodemographics.

- *Personality:* Personality reflects a person's traits, attitudes, and habits. Porsche Cars North America understood well the demographics of the Porsche owner: a forty-something male university graduate earning over $200,000 per year. However, research discovered that there were five personality types within this general demographic category that more effectively segmented Porsche buyers. Exhibit 6.3 describes the five segments. Porsche refined its marketing to reflect the study. After a seven-year slump, sales rose 48 percent.[15]

exhibit 6.2

Family Life Cycle

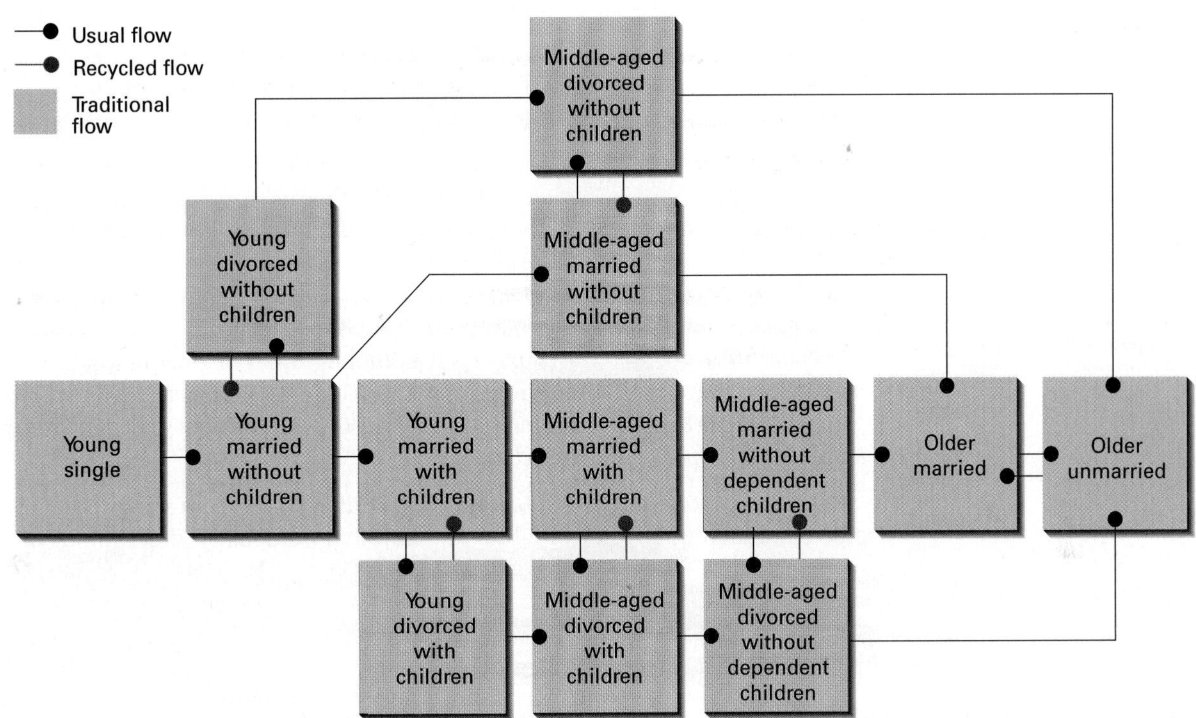

Young single	**Young married without children**	**Young married with children**	**Middle-aged married with children**	**Middle-aged married without children**	**Older married**	**Older unmarried**
Few financial burdens Fashion opinion leaders Recreation-oriented Buy: basic kitchen equipment, basic furniture, cars, equipment for mating game, vacations	Better off financially than they will be in near future Highest purchase rate and highest average purchase of durables Buy: cars, refrigerators, stoves, sensible and durable furniture, vacations	Home purchasing at peak Liquid assets low Dissatisfied with financial position and amount of money saved Interested in new products Like advertised products Buy: washers, dryers, televisions, baby food, chest rubs, cough medicine, vitamins, dolls, wagons, sleds, skates	Financial position still better More wives work Some children get jobs Hard to influence with advertising High average purchase of durables Buy: new and more tasteful furniture, auto travel, unnecessary appliances, boats, dental services, magazines	Home ownership at peak Most satisfied with financial position and money saved Interested in travel, recreation, self-education Make gifts and contributions Not interested in new products Buy: vacations, luxuries, home improvements	Drastic cut in income Keep home Buy: medical appliances, medical care, products that aid health, sleep, and digestion	Drastic cut in income Special need for attention, affection, and security Buy: same medical and product needs as other retired group

- *Motives:* Marketers of baby products and life insurance appeal to consumers' emotional motives—namely, to care for their loved ones. Using appeals to economy, reliability, and dependability, carmakers like Subaru and Suzuki target customers with rational motives. Carmakers like Mercedes-Benz, Jaguar, and Cadillac appeal to customers with status-related motives.
- *Lifestyles:* Lifestyle segmentation divides people into groups according to their beliefs, how they spend their time, the importance they attach to the things around them, and their socioeconomic characteristics such as income and education. Harley-Davidson has divided its customers into seven lifestyle segments, from "cocky misfits" who are most likely to be arrogant troublemakers, to "laid-back camper types" committed to cycling and nature, to "classy capitalists" who have wealth and privilege.[16]

geodemographic segmentation
Segmenting potential customers into neighbourhood lifestyle categories.

- *Geodemographics:* **Geodemographic segmentation** clusters potential customers into neighbourhood lifestyle categories. It combines geographic, demographic, and lifestyle segmentations. Geodemographic segmentation helps marketers tailor marketing programs to consumers who live in small, specific geographic areas (such as neighbourhoods) or who have very specific lifestyle and demographic characteristics.

Psychographic variables can be used individually to segment markets, or they can be combined with other variables to provide more detailed descriptions of market segments. One well-known combination approach, offered by SRI International, is called VALS 2 (version 2 of SRI's Values and Lifestyles program). VALS 2 categorizes consumers by their values, beliefs, and lifestyles rather than by traditional demographic segmentation variables. Many advertising agencies have used VALS segmentation to create effective promotion campaigns.

As Exhibit 6.4 shows, the segments in VALS 2 are classified on two dimensions: vertically by their resources, and horizontally by their self-orientation. Resources include education, income, self-confidence, health, eagerness to buy, intelligence, and energy level. The resources dimension is a continuum ranging from minimal to abundant. Resources generally increase from adolescence

This ad for milk appeals to consumers' emotional motives by associating drinking milk with providing the best nutrition for their growing babies.

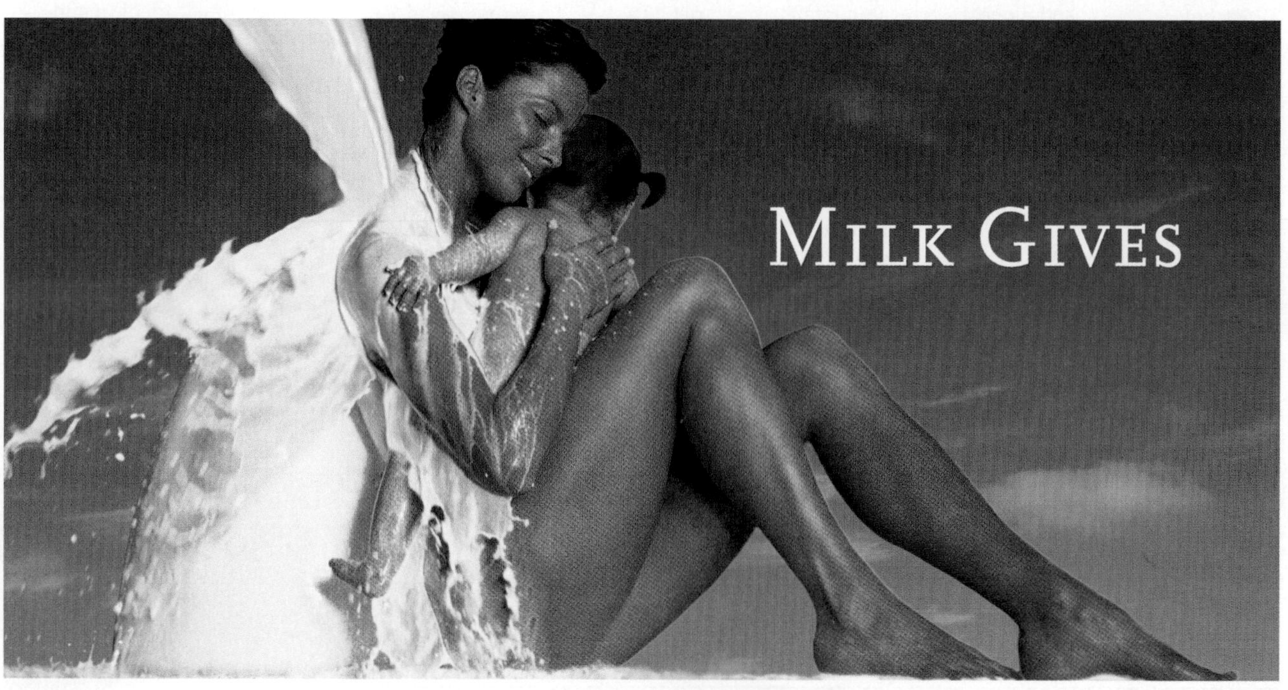

exhibit 6.3

Taxonomy of Porsche Buyers

Type	% of all owners	Description
Top guns	27%	Driven, ambitious types. Power and control matter. They expect to be noticed.
Elitists	24%	Old-money bluebloods. A car is just a car, no matter how expensive. It is not an extension of personality.
Proud patrons	23%	Ownership is an end in itself. Their car is a trophy earned for hard work. Who cares if anyone sees them in it?
Bon vivants	17%	Worldly jetsetters and thrill seekers. Their car heightens the excitement in their already passionate lives.
Fantasists	9%	Walter Mitty types. Their car is an escape. Not only are they uninterested in impressing others with it, but they also feel a little guilty about owning one.

through middle age and decrease with extreme age, depression, financial reverses, and physical or psychological impairment. For its part, the self-orientation dimension classifies three different ways of buying:

- Beliefs or principles—rather than feelings, events, or the desire for approval—guide *principle-oriented* consumers in their choices.
- Other people's actions, approval, and opinions strongly influence *status-oriented* consumers.
- *Action-oriented* consumers are prompted by a desire for social or physical activity, variety, and risk.

exhibit 6.4

VALS 2 Dimensions

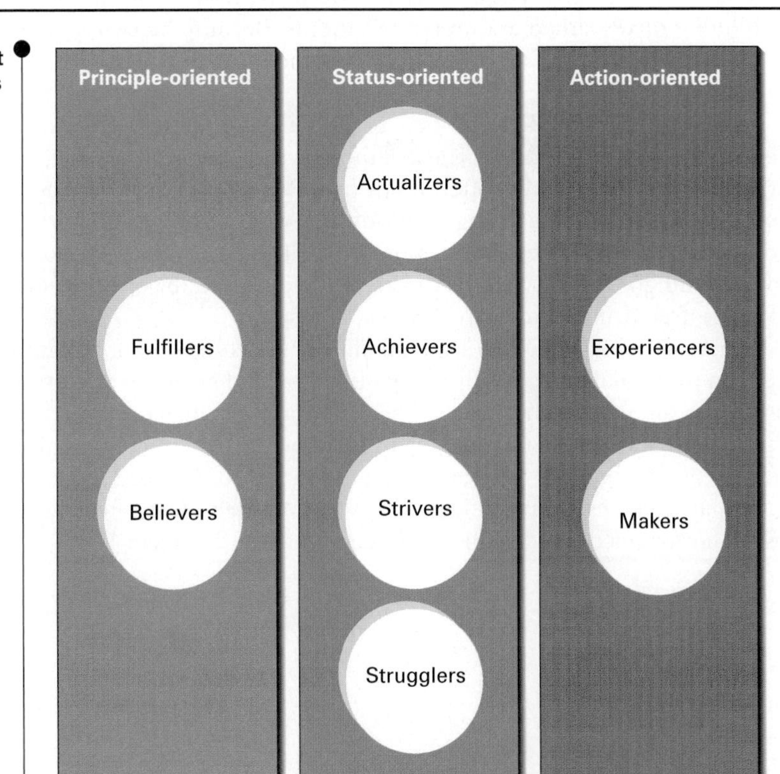

Mead Johnson Nutritionals

How does Mead Johnson, maker of the Boost line of nutritional products, use benefit segmentation on its Website? What other types of segmentation are evident on the site?

www.meadjohnson.ca

on line

Exhibit 6.5 describes the eight VALS 2 psychographic segments. Using only the two key dimensions—resources and self-orientation—VALS 2 defines groups of adult consumers who have distinctive attitudes, behaviour patterns, and decision-making styles.

Benefit Segmentation

benefit segmentation
The process of grouping customers into market segments according to the benefits they seek from the product.

Benefit segmentation is the process of grouping customers into market segments according to the benefits they seek from the product. Most types of market segmentation are based on the assumption that this variable and customers' needs are related. Benefit segmentation is different in that it groups potential customers on the basis of their needs or wants rather than some other characteristic, such as age or gender. The snack food market can be divided into six benefit segments (see Exhibit 6.6).

Marketers can develop customer profiles by examining demographic information associated with people seeking certain benefits. They can then use this information to match marketing strategies with selected target markets. *Reader's Digest* plans to send millions of people with various medical conditions, such as high blood pressure or high cholesterol, booklets filled with articles and prescription drug ads, all about the very condition each subscriber has.[17]

Usage Rate Segmentation

usage rate segmentation
Dividing a market by the amount of product bought or consumed.

Usage rate segmentation divides a market by the amount of product bought or consumed. Categories vary with the product, but they are likely to include some combination of the following: former users, potential users, first-time users, light or irregular users, medium users, and heavy users. Segmenting by usage rates enables marketers to focus their efforts on heavy users or to develop multiple marketing mixes aimed at different segments. Because heavy users often account for a sizable portion of all product sales, some marketers focus on the heavy user segment.

80/20 principle
The principle that 20 percent of customers generate 80 percent of demand.

The **80/20 principle** holds that 20 percent of all customers generate 80 percent of the demand for a product. Although these are not usually the exact percentages, the general idea often holds true. Most businesses depend for their success on maintaining strong relationships with existing customers. Many airline companies derive 80 percent or more of their profits from their business customers and go to great lengths to keep them satisfied, by offering special waiting lounges, free drinks, limousine service, and so on.

In a variant of usage rate segmentation, some companies try to attract nonusers. Using a public database, Menly and James identified arthritis sufferers who did not use their pain reliever, Ecotrin. Three different direct mail packages were sent to these nonusers. The first included a free sample with a 50¢ coupon, the second a $1 rebate coupon, and the third an invitation to send for a free sample. All three promotional offers resulted in at least a 50 percent redemption rate, compared to the usual, nontargeted direct mail response rate of 1 or 2 percent.[18]

exhibit 6.5

VALS™ Psychographic Segments

Actualizers are successful, sophisticated, active, "take-charge" people with high self-esteem and abundant resources. They are interested in growth and seek to develop, explore, and express themselves in a variety of ways. Their possessions and recreation choices reflect a cultivated taste for the finer things in life.

Fulfillers are mature, satisfied, comfortable, reflective people who value order, knowledge, and responsibility. Most are well educated, well-informed about world events, and professionally employed. Fulfillers are conservative, practical consumers; they are concerned about value and durability in the products they buy.

Believers are conservative, conventional people with concrete beliefs and strong attachments to traditional institutions—family, church, community, and nation. As consumers they are conservative and predictable, and favour domestic products and established brands.

Achievers are successful, career- and work-oriented people who like to—and generally do—feel in control of their lives. Achievers live conventional lives, are politically conservative, and respect authority and the status quo. As consumers they favour established goods and services that demonstrate success to peers.

Strivers seek motivation, self-definition, and approval from the world around them. They are easily bored and impulsive. Strivers define success in terms of money, and lack enough of it. They emulate those who own more impressive possessions, but what they wish to obtain is generally beyond their reach.

Experiencers are young, vital, enthusiastic, and impulsive. They seek variety and excitement and combine an abstract disdain for conformity and authority with an outsider's awe of others' wealth, prestige, and power. Experiencers are avid consumers and spend much of their income on clothing, fast food, music, movies, and video.

Makers are practical people who value self-sufficiency. They live within a traditional context of family, practical work, and physical recreation and have little interest in what lies outside that context. They are unimpressed by material possessions other than those with a practical or functional purpose (e.g., tools, pickup trucks, fishing equipment).

Strugglers lead constricted lives; they are ill educated, low skilled, and chronically poor. They lack strong social bonds and are focused on meeting the urgent needs of the present moment. Aging strugglers are concerned about their health. Strugglers are cautious consumers; they represent a very modest demand for most goods and services, but are loyal to favourite brands.

Bases for Segmenting Business Markets

5 Describe the bases for segmenting business markets

The business market has four broad segments: producers, resellers, institutions, and governments (see Chapter 5 for a detailed discussion of these segments). Whether marketers focus on only one or on all four of these segments, they are likely to find diversity among potential customers. Thus, market segmentation offers just as many benefits to business product marketers as it does to consumer product marketers. There are two major categories of business market variables: macrosegmentation variables and microsegmentation variables.

exhibit 6.6 Lifestyle Segmentation of the Snack Food Market

	Nutritional snackers	Weight watchers	Guilty snackers	Party snackers	Indiscriminate snackers	Economical snackers
% of snackers	22%	14%`	9%	15%	15%	18%
Lifestyle characteristics	Self-assured, controlled	Outdoorsy, influential, venturesome	Highly anxious, isolated	Sociable	Hedonistic	Self-assured, price-oriented
Benefits sought	Nutritious, without artificial ingredients, natural	Low in calories, quick energy	Low in calories, good tasting	Good to serve guests, served with pride, go well with beverages	Good tasting satisfies hunger	Low in price, best value
Consumption level of snacks	Light	Light	Heavy	Average	Heavy	Average
Type of snacks usually eaten	Fruits, vegetables, cheese	Yogurt, vegetables	Yogurt, cookies, crackers candy	Nuts, potato chips, crackers, pretzels	Ice cream, cookies, potato chips, pretzels, popcorn	No specific products
Demographics	Better educated, have younger children	Younger, single	Younger or older, female, lower socio-economic status	Middle-aged, nonurban	Teenager	Have large family, better educated

macrosegmentation
A method of dividing business markets into segments based on general characteristics such as geographic location, customer type, customer size, and product use.

Macrosegmentation

Macrosegmentation variables are used to divide business markets into segments according to the following general characteristics:

- *Geographic location:* For some business products, demand varies considerably between regions. Many computer hardware and software companies are located in the Ottawa region and in Ontario's "techno triangle"—Kitchener, Waterloo, and Guelph. Some markets tend to be regional because buyers prefer to purchase from local suppliers and because distant suppliers find it difficult to compete in terms of price and service. So firms that sell to geographically concentrated industries benefit by locating their operations close to the market.
- *Customer type:* Segmenting by customer type enables business marketers to tailor their marketing mixes to the unique needs of particular types of organizations or industries. Many companies are finding this form of segmentation quite effective. The Home Depot, the largest do-it-yourself retail business in North America, has announced plans to begin targeting professional repair and remodelling contractors as well as consumers.[19] Many companies segment the business-to-business market, which is expected to reach C$205 billion by 2005.[20]
- *Customer size:* Business-to-business marketers often use volume of purchases (i.e., heavy, moderate, light) as a basis for segmentation. Or they use the buying organization's overall size, which may affect its purchasing procedures, the types and quantities of products it needs, and its responses to different marketing mixes. Banks often offer different services and lines of credit to commercial customers based on their size.

- *Product use:* Many products—especially raw materials such as steel, wood, and petroleum—have diverse applications. How customers use a product may influence the amount they buy, their buying criteria, and their selection of vendors. The customers of a producer of springs may use that product to manufacture goods as diverse as machine tools, bicycles, surgical devices, office equipment, telephones, and missile systems.

Microsegmentation

Macrosegmentation often produces market segments that are too diverse for targeted marketing strategies. So marketers often find it useful to divide macrosegments based on variables such as customer size or product use into smaller microsegments. **Microsegmentation** is the process of dividing business markets into segments based on the characteristics of decision-making units within a macrosegment. Microsegmentation enables marketers to identify market segments more clearly and to define target markets more precisely. Following are some of the typical microsegmentation variables:[21]

microsegmentation
The process of dividing business markets into segments based on the characteristics of decision-making units within a macrosegment.

- *Key purchasing criteria:* Marketers can segment some business markets by ranking purchasing criteria such as product quality, prompt and reliable delivery, supplier reputation, technical support, and price. Atlas Corporation developed a commanding position in the industrial door market by providing customized products in just four weeks—much faster than the industry average of twelve to fifteen weeks. Atlas's primary market is companies with an immediate need for customized doors.
- *Purchasing strategies:* The purchasing strategies of buying organizations can shape microsegments. Two purchasing profiles that have been identified are satisfiers and optimizers. **Satisfiers** contact familiar suppliers and place the order with the first to satisfy product and delivery requirements. **Optimizers** consider many suppliers (both familiar and unfamiliar), solicit bids, and study all proposals carefully before selecting one. Recognizing satisfiers and optimizers is quite easy. A few key questions during a sales call—such as "Why do you buy product X from vendor A?"—usually produce answers that identify purchaser profiles.

satisfier
The type of business customer that places an order with the first familiar supplier to satisfy product and delivery requirements.

optimizer
The type of business customer that considers many suppliers, both familiar and unfamiliar, solicits bids, and studies all proposals carefully before selecting one.

- *Importance of purchase:* Classifying business customers according to the significance they attach to the purchase of a product is especially appropriate when customers use the product differently. This approach is also appropriate when the purchase is considered routine by some customers but major by others. A small entrepreneur would consider a laser printer a major capital purchase; a large office would find it a normal expense.
- *Personal characteristics:* The personal characteristics of purchase decision makers—their demographic characteristics, decision styles, tolerance for risk, confidence level, job responsibilities, and so on—influence their buying behaviour and thus constitute a viable basis for segmenting some business markets. IBM computer buyers are sometimes characterized as more risk averse than buyers of less expensive clones that perform essentially the same functions. So in its advertising, IBM emphasizes its reputation for high quality and reliability.

one-to-one marketing

She Bytes

She is driven. She is fashionable. She is global. She is with it. Add "She is barely 26" to that list and you've got a pretty accurate description of Natasha Kong, SheNetworks' co-founder and co-director. Kong has spent the past few months flying back and forth between Toronto, home base for the SheNetworks production team, and San Francisco, where her partner, Nicole Blades, runs the company headquarters.

And for Ms. Kong, a co-founder of Shenetworks.com, "she" is one of many young female surfers who feel left out by the larger women's portals on the Internet. Recent surveys by Forrester Research estimate that 41 percent of North American women are on line and that 39 percent of Canadian women are using the Internet. Most Web-surfing women are in their twenties. For Ms. Kong, that's a pretty big demographic to be ignored for long.

"I don't know why they haven't been paying more attention that it's the twenty-something women buying the Kate Spade bag, the Calvin Klein and Gucci's. But we're here to try and make a difference and make people notice," Ms. Blades says.

The SheNetworks.com site is subdivided into categories such as Shefit, Shemoney, Shegrooves, and Shereads. Users of the site can tailor their on-line experience and get the information of interest to them. There's even a cheeky personality survey that lets each visitor leave her mark, and an option to pass on the Website address to a friend to further expand the community.

For potential advertisers, and for sourcing information on this largely ignored demographic, the site is a potential gold mine. Surprisingly, their first round of financing came not from south of the border, but from five Canadian angel investors—all men. "Most people said it was rare to find women in the trenches of technology," says Ms. Kong. But they're out there, and she is hoping their interest in SheNetworks will attract advertisers eager to reach Net-savvy twenty-somethings who are sick of the *Cosmo* worldview.

What sites can you find that are competing with SheNetworks.com, and how do they differ?

How might the site be further developed to expand its value to both advertisers and the target audience?

How might the one-to-one experience be heightened at the site?

Sources: *The Financial Post,* May 2000; *Canadian Business,* May 2000.

Steps in Segmenting a Market

List the steps involved in segmenting markets

In both consumer and business markets, the purpose of segmenting a market is to identify marketing opportunities. Exhibit 6.7 traces the steps in segmenting a market. Note that steps 5 and 6 are actually marketing activities that follow market segmentation (steps 1 through 4).

1. *Select a market or product category for study:* Define the overall market or product category to be studied. It may be a market in which the firm is already competing, or a new but related market or product category, or a totally new market. Molson Breweries studied the values and beliefs of Canadian youth before launching the much applauded "I Am Canadian" rant for the Molson Canadian brand.
2. *Choose one or more bases for segmenting the market:* This step requires insight, creativity, and market knowledge. There are no scientific procedures for selecting segmentation variables. That said, a successful segmentation scheme must produce segments that meet the four basic criteria discussed earlier in this chapter.
3. *Select segmentation descriptors:* After choosing one or more bases, the marketer must select the segmentation descriptors. Descriptors identify the specific segmentation variables to use. If a company selects demographics as a basis of segmentation, it may use age, occupation, and income as descriptors. A company that selects usage segmentation needs to decide whether to go after heavy users, the nonusers, or the light users.

Steps in Segmenting a Market and Subsequent Activities

exhibit 6.7

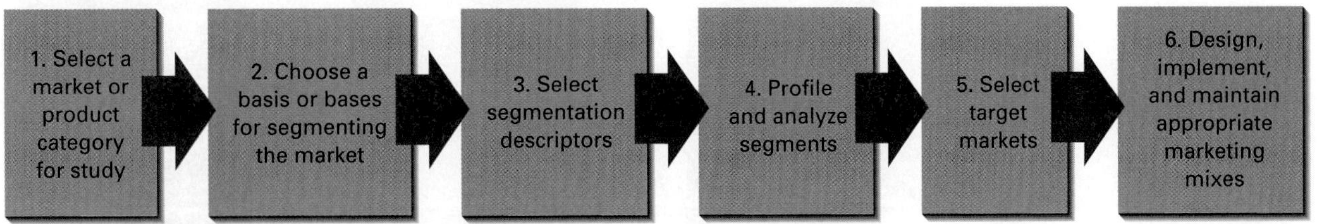

4. *Profile and evaluate segments:* The profile should include each segment's size, expected growth, purchase frequency, current brand usage, brand loyalty, and long-term sales and profit potential. This information can then be used to rank potential market segments by profit opportunity, risk, consistency with organizational mission and objectives, and other factors important to the firm.
5. *Select target markets:* Selecting target markets is not a part of the segmentation process but rather a natural outcome of it. It is a major decision that influences and often directly determines the firm's marketing mix. This topic is examined in greater detail later in the chapter.
6. *Design, implement, and maintain appropriate marketing mixes:* The marketing mix has been described as the product, distribution, promotion, and pricing strategies intended to bring about mutually satisfying exchange relationships with target markets.

Strategies for Selecting Target Markets

7

Discuss alternative strategies for selecting target markets

So far this chapter has focused on the market segmentation process, which is only the first step in deciding whom to approach about buying a product. The next task is to choose one or more target markets. A **target market** is a group of people or organizations for which an organization designs, implements, and maintains a marketing mix intended to meet the needs of that group, resulting in mutually satisfying exchanges. The three general strategies for selecting target markets—undifferentiated, concentrated, and multisegment targeting—are illustrated in Exhibit 6.8. Exhibit 6.9 illustrates the advantages and disadvantages of each targeting strategy.

target market
A group of people or organizations for which an organization designs, implements, and maintains a marketing mix intended to meet the needs of that group, resulting in mutually satisfying exchanges.

Undifferentiated Targeting

A firm that uses an **undifferentiated targeting strategy** is essentially adopting a mass market philosophy—that it, it is approaching the market as one big market with no individual segments. The firm uses one marketing mix for the entire market, on the assumption that individual customers have similar needs that can be met with a common marketing mix.

undifferentiated targeting strategy
A marketing approach that views the market as one big market with no individual segments and thus requiring a single marketing mix.

The first firm in an industry sometimes uses an undifferentiated targeting strategy. With no competition, the firm may not need to tailor marketing mixes to the preferences of market segments. Henry Ford's famous quote about the Model T is a classic example of an undifferentiated targeting strategy: "They can have their car in any colour they want, as long as it's black." At one time, Coca-Cola used this strategy, with a single product and a single size for its familiar green bottle. Marketers of commodity products such as flour and sugar are also likely to use an undifferentiated targeting strategy.

exhibit 6.8

Three Strategies for Selecting Target Markets

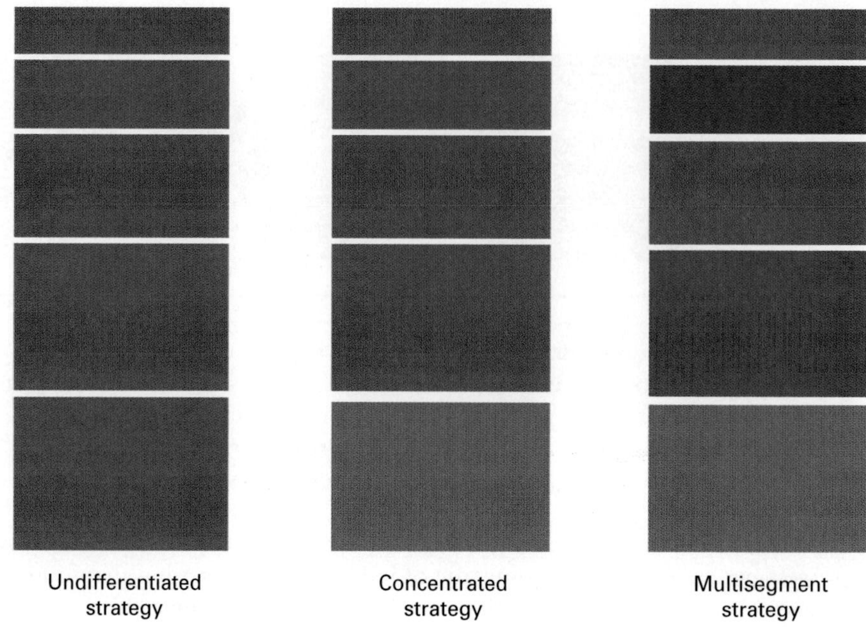

exhibit 6.9

Advantages and Disadvantages of Target Marketing Strategies

Targeting Strategy	Advantages	Disadvantages
Undifferentiated Targeting	• Potential savings on production/marketing costs	• Unimaginative product offerings • Company more susceptible to competition
Concentrated Targeting	• Concentration of resources • Can better meet the needs of a narrowly defined segment • Allows some small firms to better compete with larger firms • Strong positioning	• Segments too small, or changing • Large competitors may more effectively market to niche segment
Multisegment Targeting	• Greater financial success • Economies of scale in production/marketing	• High costs • Cannibalization

One advantage of undifferentiated marketing is that it can reduce production and marketing costs. By producing only one item, the firm should be able to achieve economies of mass production. Also, marketing costs may be lower when there is only one product to promote and a single channel of distribution. Too often, however, an undifferentiated strategy emerges by default rather than by design; this reflects a failure to consider the advantages of a segmented approach. The result is often sterile, unimaginative product offerings that have little appeal to anyone.

Another problem associated with undifferentiated targeting is that it makes a company more vulnerable to competition. Hershey lost a big share of the candy market to Mars and other candy companies before it switched to multisegment marketing. In the late 1950s, Pepsi-Cola began offering several sizes of containers;

Clearly Canadian

Which consumer segments do you think would be most attracted to the Clearly Canadian O+2 and Tre Limone brands? What kind of targeting strategy does the company seem to be following? Why?

www.clearly.ca

as a result, Coca-Cola forfeited its position as the leading seller of cola drinks in supermarkets.

You might think that a firm producing a standard product like toilet tissue would adopt an undifferentiated strategy. However, this market has industrial segments and consumer segments. Industrial buyers want an economical, single-ply product sold in boxes of a hundred rolls. The consumer market demands a more versatile product in smaller quantities. In the consumer market, toilet tissue is differentiated as coloured or white, designer print or no print, cushioned or non-cushioned, economy priced or luxury priced. Fort Howard Corporation, the market share leader in industrial toilet paper, does not even sell to the consumer market.

Concentrated Targeting

With a **concentrated targeting strategy**, a firm selects a market **niche**—that is, one segment of a market—for targeting its marketing efforts. The firm is appealing to a single segment, so it can concentrate on understanding the needs, motives, and satisfactions of that segment's members and on developing and maintaining a highly specialized marketing mix. Some firms find that concentrating resources and meeting the needs of a narrowly defined market segment is more profitable than spreading resources over several different segments.

concentrated targeting strategy
A strategy used to select one segment of a market for targeting marketing efforts.

niche
One segment of a market.

Winners stores were developed to attract working women who wanted designer fashions for less. Some marketers have developed niche malls specifically for working women. Some malls are aimed specifically at Asian Canadians.

Other firms use a concentrated strategy to establish a strong position in a desirable market segment. Porsche targets an upscale automobile market through "class appeal, not mass appeal."

Concentrated targeting violates the old adage, "Don't put all your eggs in one basket." If the chosen segment is too small, or if it shrinks as a result of environmental changes, the firm may suffer. OshKosh B'Gosh, Inc., was highly successful selling children's wear in the 1980s. Unfortunately, the children's line came to define OshKosh to such an extent that it could not sell clothes to anyone else. Attempts at marketing older children's clothing, women's casual clothes, and maternity wear were all abandoned. The company now recognizes that it is in the children's-wear business and is expanding into products such as kids' shoes, children's eyewear, and plush toys.[22]

entrepreneurial insights

Department Store with a Niche?

The new eatons opened with much fanfare in November 2000. The old T. Eaton Company had closed its doors two years earlier. Sears Canada bought the seven urban Eaton's stores and created the new eatons, an upscale emporium with exclusive rights to many high-end clothing collections and dramatically designed decor departments. The new eatons is positioning itself as a collection of upscale boutiques and is targeted at well-off urban dwellers. Exclusive product lines and grander and more spacious interiors are exciting news in retail, but what really sets eatons apart is its level of customer service. Customer perks include carry-to-the-car service, gift-wrapping, courier service, worldwide shipping, free personal shoppers, multilanguage assistance, and in-store cooking and design demonstrations. In the new millennium, the trend in retail is toward in-store specialty areas and superb customer service. It will be interesting to see if the new eatons sets a new standard in department store shopping.

Source: Fawzia Sheikh, "Retail Renaissance," *Marketing*, 11 December 2000.

multisegment targeting strategy
A strategy that chooses two or more well-defined market segments and develops a distinct marketing mix for each.

Procter & Gamble's concentrated strategy to sell its antidandruff shampoo Head & Shoulders has been successful in its narrowly defined target market.

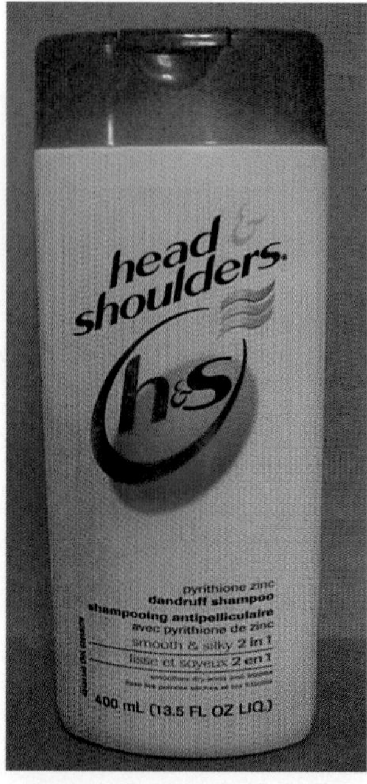

A concentrated strategy can be disastrous for a firm that is not successful in its narrowly defined target market. Before Procter & Gamble introduced Head and Shoulders shampoo, several small firms were already selling antidandruff shampoos. Head and Shoulders was introduced with a large promotional campaign, and the new brand captured over half the market immediately. Within a year, several of the firms that had been focusing on this market segment had gone out of business.

Multisegment Targeting

A firm that chooses to serve two or more well-defined market segments and that develops a distinct marketing mix for each has a **multisegment targeting strategy**. Stouffer's offers gourmet entrees for one segment of the frozen dinner market and Lean Cuisine for another. Cosmetics companies seek to increase sales and market share by targeting multiple age and ethnic groups. Both Maybelline and Cover Girl market different lines to teenage women, young adult women, older women, and African-American women.

Sometimes organizations use different promotional appeals, rather than completely different marketing mixes, when implementing multisegment strategies. Breweries such as Molson and Labatt advertise and promote special events during the hockey play-offs, on the May "two-four" weekend, and throughout the summer, when 40 percent of the beer in Canada's C$11 billion annual beer market is consumed.[23]

Multisegment targeting has many potential benefits, including greater sales volume, higher profits, larger market share, and economies of scale in manufacturing and marketing. Yet it can also involve greater product costs relating to design, production, promotion, inventory, marketing research, and administration. Before deciding to use this strategy, firms should compare the benefits and costs of multisegment targeting to those of undifferentiated and concentrated targeting.

A potential danger of multisegment targeting is **cannibalization**, which happens when sales of a new product cut into the sales of a firm's existing products. Pharmaceutical companies have been introducing over-the-counter medications that block the production of stomach acids as opposed to neutralizing those acids. These firms are well aware that the new heartburn drugs are likely to cannibalize their traditional offerings. In advertising Tagamet HB, SmithKline must avoid comparing it to Tums, the firm's antacid moneymaker.[24]

cannibalization
The situation that arises when sales of a new product cut into sales of a firm's existing products.

Positioning

8
Explain how and why firms implement positioning strategies, and how product differentiation plays a role.

Positioning involves developing a specific marketing mix to influence potential customers' overall perception of a brand, product line, or organization in general. A **position** is the place a product, brand, or group of products occupies in consumers' minds relative to competing offerings. Consumer goods marketers are especially concerned about positioning. Procter & Gamble markets eleven different laundry detergents, each with a unique position (see Exhibit 6.10).

Positioning assumes that consumers compare products on the basis of important features. For this reason, marketing efforts that emphasize irrelevant features are likely to misfire. RootsAir offered a hip, upscale alternative for business travellers at a time when the market was shrinking in fear of recession and fuel costs were at an all-time high.[25]

Effective positioning involves assessing the positions occupied by competing products, determining the important dimensions underlying these positions, and choosing a position in the market where the organization's marketing efforts will

positioning
Developing a specific marketing mix to influence potential customers' overall perception of a brand, product line, or organization in general.

position
The place a product, brand, or group of products occupies in consumers' minds relative to competing offerings.

exhibit 6.10

Positioning of Procter & Gamble Detergents

Brand share	Positioning	Market
Tide	Tough, powerful cleaning	31.1%
Cheer	Tough cleaning and colour protection	8.2%
Bold	Detergent plus fabric softener	2.9%
Gain	Sunshine scent and odor-removing formula	2.6%
Era	Stain treatment and stain removal	2.2%
Dash	Value brand	1.8%
Oxydol	Bleach-boosted formula, whitening	1.4%
Solo	Detergent and fabric softener in liquid form	1.2%
Dreft	Outstanding cleaning for baby clothes, safe for tender skin	1.0%
Ivory Snow	Fabric and skin safety on baby clothes and fine washables	0.7%

Source: Reprinted with permission from the 3 May 1993 issue of *Advertising Age*. Copyright © 1993, Crain Communications Inc.

exhibit 6.11

Perceptual Maps and Positioning Strategies for GM Passenger Cars

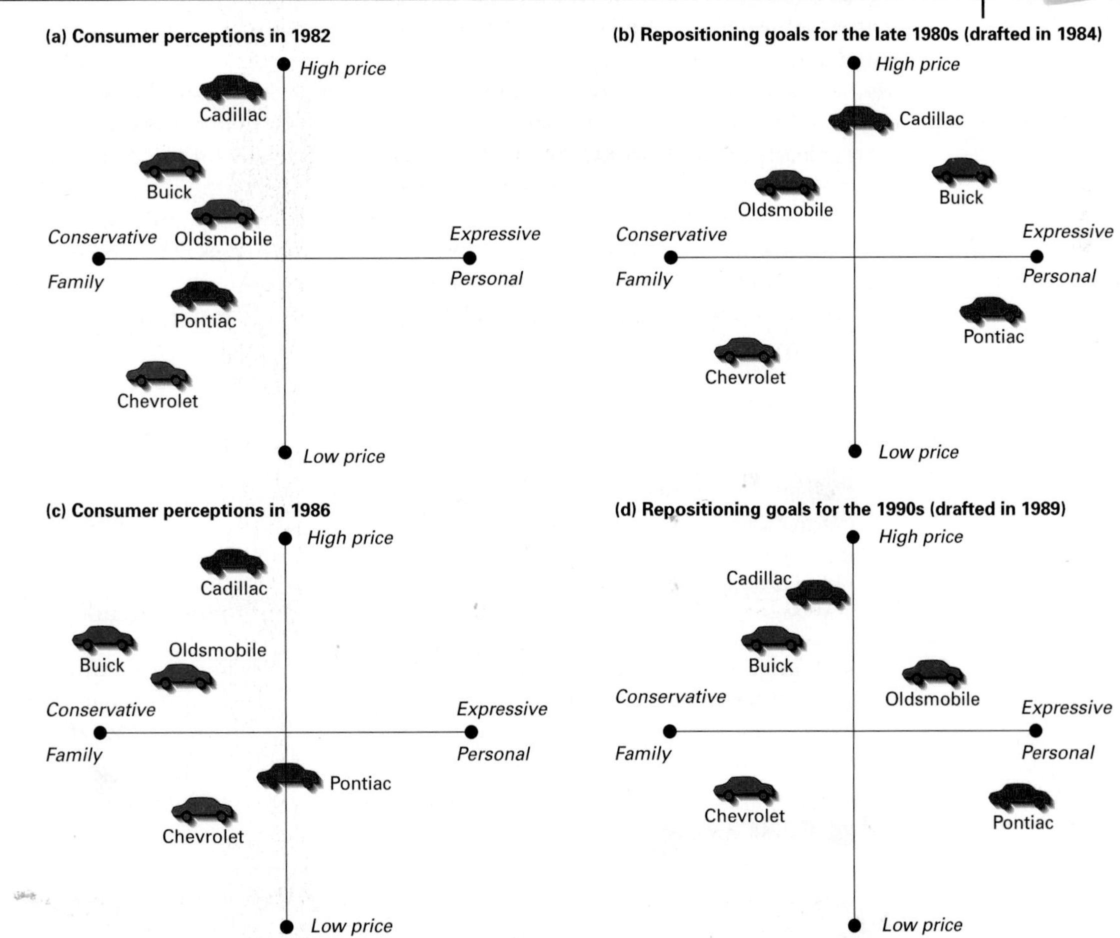

Source: Reprinted with permission from the 3 May 1993 issue of *Advertising Age*. Copyright © 1993, Crain Communications Inc.

have the greatest impact. General Motors recently adopted a strategy for positioning its Sierra trucks against major competitors. The target market was defined as university-educated professionals in their forties with annual incomes of at least $75,000. The company hopes to establish a super-premium position for Sierra.[26]

To distinguish their products from those of competitors, many firms use **product differentiation** as a positioning strategy. The distinctions can be real or perceived. Tandem Computer designed machines with two CPUs and two memories for computer systems that can never afford to be down or lose their databases (e.g., airline reservation systems). Here, Tandem was using product differentiation to create a product with very real advantages for the target market. Many everyday products—bleaches, aspirin, unleaded regular gasoline, some soaps, and so on—are differentiated by trivial means such as brand names, packaging, colour, smell, or "secret" additives. Marketers attempt to convince consumers that a particular brand is distinctive and that they should demand it over competing brands.

product differentiation
A positioning strategy that some firms use to distinguish their products from those of competitors.

Some firms, instead of using product differentiation, position their products as *similar* to competing products or brands. Thus, artificial sweeteners are advertised as tasting like sugar, margarine as tasting like butter.

Perceptual Mapping

Perceptual mapping is a means of displaying or graphing, in two or more dimensions, the location of products, brands, or groups of products in customers' minds. The perceptual map in Exhibit 6.11a is the result of a 1982 study by General Motors of consumers' perceptions of the five GM automobile divisions: Buick, Cadillac, Chevrolet, Oldsmobile, and Pontiac. Consumer perceptions are plotted on two axes. The horizontal axis ranges from conservative and family oriented at one extreme to expressive and personal at the other. The vertical axis is used to rate price perceptions, and ranges from high to low. Note that in 1982 the various GM divisions were not perceived as especially distinctive. Consumers didn't clearly distinguish one brand from another, especially on the conservative/family versus expressive/personal dimension.

perceptual mapping
A means of displaying or graphing, in two or more dimensions, the location of products, brands, or groups of products in customers' minds.

In 1984, General Motors was reorganized to reduce overlap and duplication among divisions and to produce fewer, more distinctive models. The perceptual map in Exhibit 6.11b shows GM's plans for repositioning—that is, changing consumers' perceptions of the various models. As Exhibit 6.11c shows, however, consumer perceptions changed very little between 1982 and 1986.

Positioning Bases

Firms use a variety of bases for positioning, including the following:[27]

- *Attribute:* A product is associated with an attribute, product feature, or customer benefit. Rockport shoes are positioned as an always comfortable brand that is available in a range of styles, from working shoes to dress shoes.[28]
- *Price and quality:* This positioning base may emphasize high price as an indication of quality or low price as an indication of value. Holt Renfrew uses the high-price strategy; Zellers has successfully followed the low-price and value strategy. Cunard's, a London-based cruise liner company that had fallen on hard times, was able to launch a turnaround by repositioning its brand to compete in the affluent consumer market. Changes included a new corporate identity, a series of elegant ad campaigns, and improved customer service.[29]
- *Use or application:* Bell has used the slogan "The next best thing to being there" to promote the use of long-distance calling to friends and loved ones. Emphasizing uses or applications can be an effective way to position a product. The slogan "Orange juice isn't just for breakfast anymore" is an effort to reposition that product as an all-occasion beverage.

- *Product user:* This positioning base focuses on a personality or type of user. Canadian Tire is Canada's number-one hardware retailer, in large part because it has positioned itself as a one-stop source for Canadian families and because of its discounting practices, such as Canadian Tire Money and shopping points for card holders. Forty percent of Canadians make at least one trip a week to a Canadian Tire store.[30]
- *Product class:* The objective here is to associate the product with a particular category of products—for example, a margarine brand with butter.
- *Competitor:* Positioning against competitors is part of any positioning strategy. The Avis rental car positioning as number two behind Hertz is a good example.

Companies often use a mix of positioning bases to reach their target audience. Mountain Dew is one example. This ad combines the elements of youth, outdoor fun, and even irreverence.

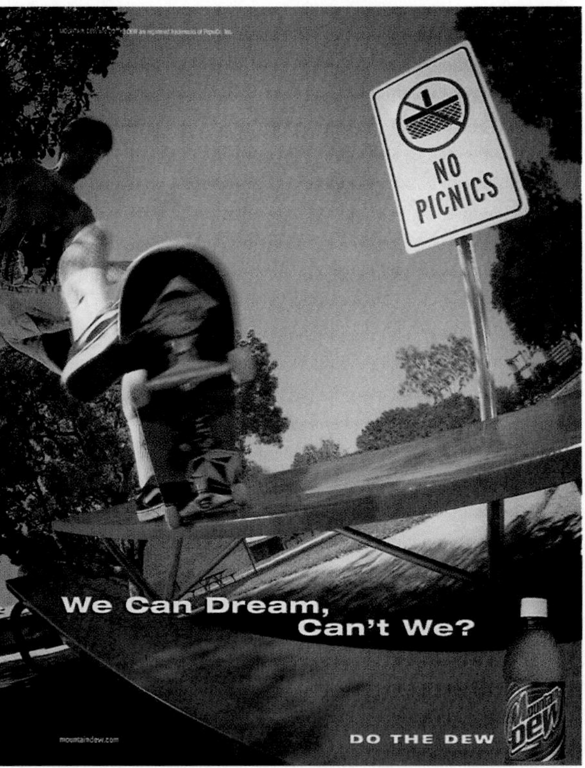
NO PICNICS
We Can Dream,
Can't We?
DO THE DEW
Mtn Dew

It is not unusual for a marketer to use more than one of these bases. The AT&T "Reach Out and Touch Someone" campaign emphasized use but also emphasized the relatively low cost of long-distance calling. Mountain Dew positions its soft drink to the youth market as a thirst-quenching drink, and also associates it with extreme sports and other outdoor fun.[31]

Repositioning

Sometimes products or companies are repositioned in order to sustain growth in slow markets or to correct positioning mistakes. **Repositioning** means changing consumers' perceptions of a brand relative to competing brands. To cope with a stagnant liquor industry, a number of companies are attempting to reposition vodka, a spirit without taste, colour, or aroma, as a fashion icon with a complex taste. This repositioning effort includes higher prices and the use of prestige packaging. Harry Rosen, the Canadian men's clothing retailer, has kept pace with the times by keeping its well-made, high-priced clothing stylish—and sometimes more casual in keeping with modern trends. Midas, a car muffler chain, added brake repairs to its services in 1978. After spending millions of dollars promoting the added service, customer recall was less than 50 percent for brakes. Midas is now repositioning itself as the stop for all car repair needs.[32]

repositioning
Changing consumers' perceptions of a brand in relation to competing brands.

Global Issues in Market Segmentation and Targeting

9
Discuss global market segmentation and targeting issues

The trend toward global market standardization enables firms like Coca-Cola, Colgate-Palmolive, McDonald's, and Nike to market similar products using similar marketing strategies in many different countries. This chapter has also discussed the trend toward targeting smaller, more precisely defined markets.

The tasks involved in segmenting markets, selecting target markets, and designing, implementing, and maintaining appropriate marketing mixes (see Exhibit 6.7) are the same whether the marketer has a local perspective or a global vision. The main difference lies in the segmentation variables commonly used. Countries are often grouped using variables such as per capita GDP, geography, religion, and culture.

Some firms have tried to group countries or customer segments around the world using lifestyle or psychographic variables. In places like Singapore, Taipei,

Tokyo, and Seoul, "Asian yuppies" have substantial spending power and exhibit purchase and consumption behaviours similar to those of their better-known counterparts in North America. To reach these consumers, firms may be able to use a global market standardization approach.

LOOKING BACK

In the story at the beginning of this chapter, modrobes was using various marketing methods to get and keep the attention of its target market. Market segmentation is about dividing a market into segments that are meaningful and identifiable. Targeting involves selecting one or more market segments and then designing, implementing, and maintaining distinctive marketing mixes for them.

Summary

1 Describe the characteristics of markets and market segments. A market is composed of individuals or organizations with the ability and willingness to make purchases to fulfil their needs or wants. A market segment is a group of individuals or organizations with similar product needs as a result of one or more common characteristics.

2 Explain the importance of market segmentation. Before the 1960s, few businesses targeted specific market segments. Today, segmentation is a crucial marketing strategy for nearly all successful organizations. Market segmentation enables marketers to tailor marketing mixes to meet the needs of particular population segments. Segmentation helps marketers identify consumer needs and preferences, areas of declining demand, and new marketing opportunities.

3 Discuss the criteria for successful market segmentation. Successful market segmentation depends on four basic criteria. First, a market segment must be substantial; that is, it must have enough potential customers to be viable. Second, a market segment must be identifiable and measurable. Third, members of a market segment must be accessible to marketing efforts. Fourth, a market segment must respond to particular marketing efforts in a way that distinguishes it from other segments.

4 Describe the bases commonly used to segment consumer markets. There are five commonly used bases for segmenting consumer markets. Geographic segmentation is based on region, size, density, and climate characteristics. Demographic segmentation consists of age, gender, income level, ethnicity, and family life cycle characteristics. Psychographic segmentation includes personality, motives, and lifestyle characteristics. Benefits sought is a type of segmentation that identifies customers according to the benefits they seek in a product. Finally, usage segmentation divides a market by the amount of product purchased or consumed.

5 Describe the bases for segmenting business markets. Business markets can be segmented on two bases. Macrosegmentation divides markets according to general characteristics, such as location and customer type. Microsegmentation focuses on the decision-making units within macrosegments.

6 List the steps involved in segmenting markets. Six steps are involved when segmenting markets: (1) Selecting a market or product category for study; (2) choosing a basis or bases for segmenting the market; (3) selecting segmentation descriptors; (4) profiling and evaluating segments; (5) selecting target markets; and (6) designing, implementing, and maintaining appropriate marketing mixes.

7 Discuss alternative strategies for selecting target markets. Marketers select target markets using three different strategies: undifferentiated targeting, concentrated targeting, and multisegment targeting. An undifferentiated targeting strategy assumes that all members of a market have similar needs that can be met with a single marketing mix. A concentrated targeting strategy focuses all marketing efforts on a single market segment. Multisegment targeting uses two or more marketing mixes to target two or more market segments.

8 Explain how and why firms implement positioning strategies, and how product differentiation plays a role. Positioning is used to influence consumer perceptions of a particular brand, product line, or organization in relation to its competitors. The term position refers to the place the offering occupies in consumers' minds. To establish a unique position, many firms use product differentiation, emphasizing the real or perceived differences between competing offerings. Products can be differentiated on the basis of attribute, price and quality, use or application, product user, product class, or competitor.

9 Discuss global market segmentation and targeting issues. The key tasks in market segmentation, targeting, and positioning are the same regardless of whether the target market is local, regional, national, or multinational. The main differences are the variables used by marketers in analyzing markets and assessing opportunities and the resources needed to implement strategies.

Do You Know These Terms?

benefit segmentation 150
cannibalization 158
concentrated targeting strategy 157
demographic segmentation 143
80/20 principle 150
family life cycle (FLC) 146
geodemographic segmentation 148
geographic segmentation 143
macrosegmentation 152
market 140
market segment 140
market segmentation 140
microsegmentation 153
multisegment targeting strategy 158
niche 157
optimizer 153
perceptual mapping 160
position 158
positioning 158
product differentiation 160
psychographic segmentation 146
repositioning 161
satisfier 153
segmentation bases (variables) 143
target market 155
undifferentiated targeting strategy 155
usage rate segmentation 150

Discussion and Writing Questions

1. Describe market segmentation in terms of the historical evolution of marketing.
2. Choose magazine ads for five different products. For each ad, write a description of the demographic characteristics of the targeted market.
3. Form a team with two other students. Select a product category and brand that are familiar to your team. Using Exhibit 6.9, prepare a market segmentation report and describe a targeting plan.
4. Explain concentrated (niche) targeting. Describe a company not mentioned in the chapter that uses a concentrated targeting strategy.
5. Form a team with two or three other students. Create an idea for a new product. Describe the segment (or segments) you are going to target with the product, and develop a positioning strategy for it.
6. Choose a product category (e.g., blue jeans), and identify at least three different brands and their respective positioning strategies. How is each position communicated to the target audience?
7. Create a perceptual map for the different brands of one of the following products: diet and regular colas, Ford automobiles, fast food hamburger restaurants, or a product of your choice.
8. Investigate how Air Canada uses its Website to cater to its market segments. **www.aircanada.com.**
9. How are visitors to the following Website segmented when seeking relevant job openings? **www.monster.ca**
10. Write a letter to the president of your bank suggesting ways to increase profits and enhance customer service by improving segmentation and targeting strategies. Make your suggestions specific.

Application for Small Business

Judy Brown has always loved working with animals. She has experience in pet grooming, boarding, and in-home pet sitting. She wants to open a full-service business utilizing her skills that is uniquely positioned in relation to the traditional pet grooming/boarding businesses that operate in her town. Customers that use these current pet services deliver their pets to the firms and later pick them up. Most are open between 9 a.m. and 6 p.m. Monday to Friday.

Judy lives in a midsize city close to a major airport. Many high-tech industries are located in or near her city, so there are many men and women in managerial and IT positions, and travel is a regular part of their work. A lot of families have pets, so Judy thinks there is a market for pet-related services, despite the current competition.

Questions

1. How should Judy segment the market for pet services?
2. What targeting strategy should Judy use to start her business? Should this strategy change as her business prospers and grows?
3. How should Judy position her pet services business against her competition?

Creating a Craze

Young girls are spending a lot of time on the Internet these days, and many are talking to their favourite heartthrob popstars. Sony Music is aware of the spending power of children nine to fourteen, and has launched a meticulously manufactured "boy band" to create a buzz that will ensure that these "tween" girls spend heavily on CDs and concerts.

Sony launched the band B4-4 by encouraging on-line relationships between young girls and the band's members, Dan, Ryan, and Ohad. The New Media team at Sony introduced B4-4 through the Internet and promoted its on-line relationship with eight to fourteen year old girls, who are anxious to get to know the objects of their desires—the boy band. In a carefully crafted on-line blitz, the girls were introduced to the B4-4 boys. They can chat with them daily and learn intimate details about them and their lives. They know about the boys' upbringing, their pets, and their hobbies, and they have even seen their baby pictures. The boys make time to say a personalized on-line goodnight to their fans almost every night.

The B4-4 Website became highly interactive for the girl fans. The site provides on-line trading cards for girls to swap with other fans; it also gives easy, step-by step instructions for the girls to create their own grassroots B4-4 Websites, which link to the main corporate site. The B4-4 site even provides craft ideas, prerecorded phone answer messages for girls to use on their answering machines, and lots of information about the boy band. Word-of-mouth promotion of the band was instantaneous, and the fan base has exploded based on the on-line hype created by Sony and the fans themselves.

Sony's New Media Team (most of them in their early twenties) know that many of these girls spend more time on line than off. The girls in the know were happy to circulate information about this great new boy band months before a CD was ever recorded. The New Media Team allowed the girls to develop a relationship with the band, as the boys spent time answering sometimes very personal questions in the on-line chat rooms. So much was happening on the B4-4 Website that the girls really believed they had made friends with the pop stars, and they were happy to tell others about it.

This type of on-line relationship marketing begins a new era of promoting new bands, especially to young markets that are easily influenced. B4-4 had thousands of dedicated fans long before it had a concert, a CD, or a song on the radio. In terms of number of hits, the B4-4 Website was second in Canada only to that of Celine Dion. The result? A number one song for B4-4 within days of its release, and amazing sales and concert success in a very short time. B4-4's first CD went gold in just six weeks.

Source:

CBC, *Undercurrents*, "Creating a Craze," November 5, 2000.

Questions

1. Is Sony using a niche or multiple-segment strategy in promoting this new band? Explain why.
2. What communications strategy has Sony adopted to position its new band to its market?
3. What is the common behaviour pattern that Sony has focused on?

CHAPTER 7

LEARNING OBJECTIVES

After studying this chapter, you should be able to

1 Explain the concept and purpose of a marketing decision support system

2 Define marketing research, and explain its importance to marketing decision making

3 Describe the steps involved in conducting a marketing research project

4 Discuss the growing importance of scanner-based research

5 Explain when marketing research should and should not be conducted

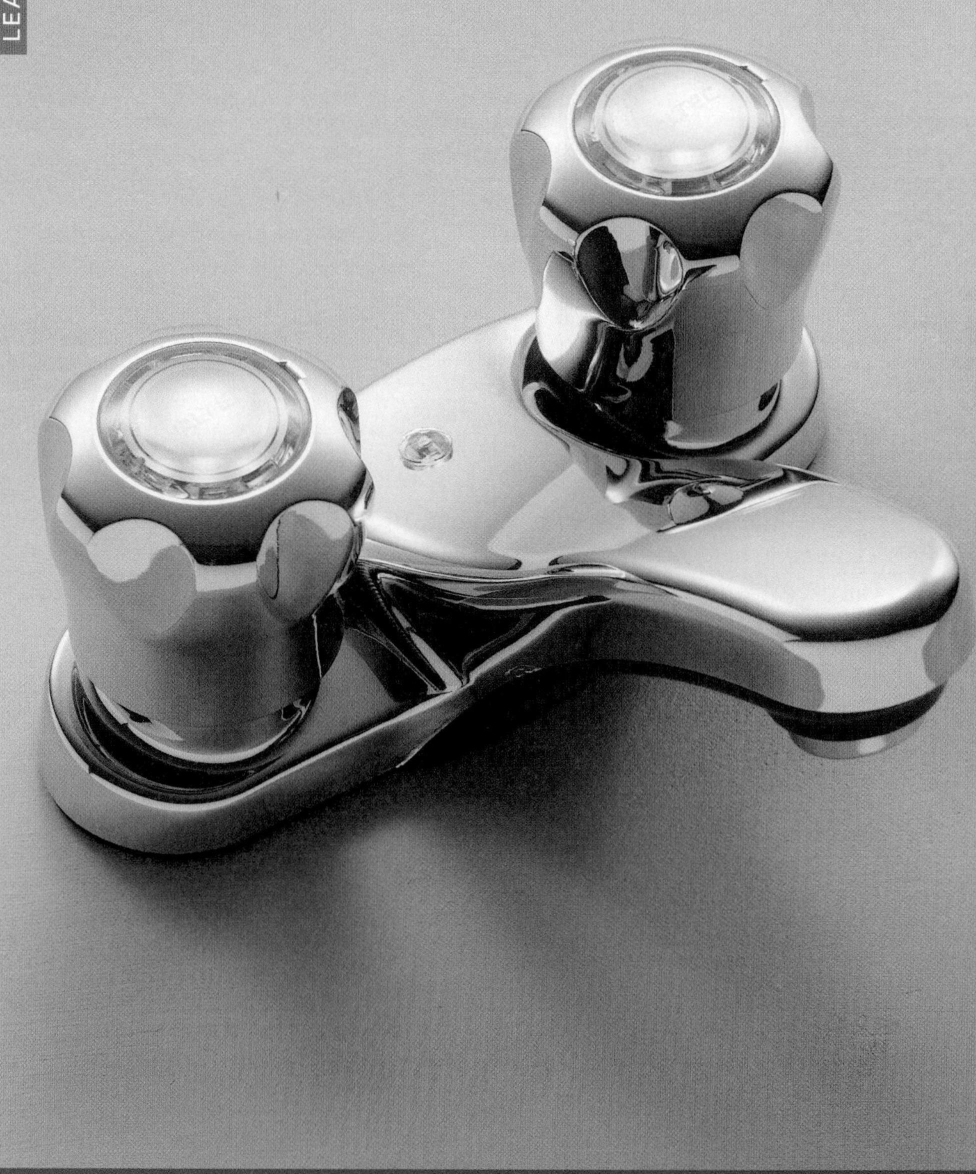

DECISION SUPPORT SYSTEMS AND MARKETING RESEARCH

Waltec Faucets of Wallaceburg, Ontario, a leading manufacturer of kitchen and bathroom faucets, wanted to know the effect that a price increase would have on the sales of its faucets. To test the consumer reaction to price changes, a simulated market test was set up. A simulated market test is similar to a laboratory experiment. In a simulated market test, typical consumers are taken on a shopping trip through a room set up to resemble an area in a typical retail outlet.

For the Waltec simulated market test, a room was set up to resemble the aisles of a home centre or hardware store. On the shelves in the simulated store were Waltec faucets and the faucets of Waltec's leading competitors in the Canadian market. Homeowners who agreed to take part in the test were told to assume that they were in the market to buy either a kitchen or a bathroom faucet. They were to examine all the faucets on display in the simulated store, read the information on the faucet packages, ask questions if they wanted to, and in general do whatever they would normally do if they were in the market to buy a faucet for their homes. Once they had made a product choice, the homeowners were to tell the researcher which brand of faucet they had selected.

To test the reactions of consumers to different prices, on different days of the simulated market test the prices of the Waltec faucets were varied. For example, the basic Waltec bathroom faucet was priced at $39.95, $44.95, $49.95, and $54.95 on different days. However, the prices of all the competitive faucets stayed the same. It was then noted how many homeowners selected the Waltec faucets at the different prices.

It was found that at a price of $39.95, 42 percent of the simulated market test sample selected the Waltec bathroom faucet. However, as the price increased, fewer respondents selected the Waltec faucet. By the time the price reached $54.95, only 17 percent of respondents were selecting the Waltec product. Similar results were found for other Waltec faucets.

It is not surprising that fewer participants in the simulated market test selected the Waltec faucets at higher prices; Waltec's management expected this to

In the past few years, more and more marketing research has been conducted on the Internet. If you are interested in learning more about research on the Web, check any of the following sources.

www.cyberdialogue.com; www.researchinfo.com

happen. What management wanted to learn from the simulated market test was how many consumers it would lose as prices increased—that is, the product's *price elasticity*. (This concept will be discussed in Chapter 15.) Knowledge of a product's price elasticity helps management determine a product's most profitable price.[1]

A simulated market test is one of many types of marketing research. Waltec used marketing research to identify consumer reactions to price changes. What are some other uses of marketing research? What are some techniques for conducting marketing research? How does marketing research relate to decision support systems?

Marketing Decision Support Systems

1

Explain the concept and purpose of a marketing decision support system

marketing intelligence
Everyday information about developments in the marketing environment that managers use to prepare and adjust marketing plans.

decision support system (DSS)
An interactive, flexible computerized information system that enables managers to obtain and manipulate information as they are making decisions.

Accurate and timely information is the lifeblood of marketing decision making. Good information can help an organization maximize its sales and use scarce resources efficiently. To prepare and adjust their marketing plans, managers need a system for gathering everyday information about developments in the marketing environment—that is, for gathering **marketing intelligence**. The system most commonly used these days is called a *marketing decision support system.*

A marketing **decision support system (DSS)** is an interactive, flexible computerized information system that enables managers to obtain and manipulate information as they are making decisions. A DSS bypasses the information-processing specialist and gives managers access to useful data from their own desks. Following are the characteristics of a true DSS system:

- *Interactive*: Managers give simple instructions and see immediate results. The process is under their direct control; no computer programmer is needed. Managers don't have to wait for scheduled reports.
- *Flexible*: A DSS can sort, regroup, total, average, and manipulate the data in various ways. It can also shift gears as the user changes topics, matching information to the problem at hand. For example, the CEO can see highly aggregated figures, and the marketing analyst can view very detailed breakouts.
- *Discovery-oriented:* Managers can probe for trends, isolate problems, and ask "what if" questions.
- *Accessible*: For managers who aren't skilled with computers, DSS systems are easy to learn and use. Novice users can choose a standard or default method for operating the system. For example, they can bypass its optional features and work with the basic system right away; they can learn its more advanced features more gradually.

An example showing how DSS can be used is provided by Charlotte Voorzanger, the marketing manager for Kindred Industries of Midland, Ontario. To evaluate sales of a recently introduced product, Charlotte can "call up" sales by the week, then by the month, breaking them out at her option by, say, customer segments. As she works at her desktop computer, her inquiries can go in several directions, depending on the decision at hand. If her train of thought raises questions about monthly sales last quarter compared to forecasts, she can use her DSS

Quaker Oatmeal
Gatorade
How do these Quaker companies use e-mail to build their databases?
www.quakeroatmeal.com; www.gatorade.com

on line

to analyze problems immediately. Charlotte might see that her new product's sales were significantly below forecast. Were her forecasts too optimistic? She compares other products' sales to her forecasts and finds that the targets were very accurate. Was something wrong with the product? Is her sales department getting insufficient leads, or is it not putting leads to good use? Thinking a minute about how to examine that question, she checks ratios of leads converted to sales product by product. The results disturb her. Only 5 percent of the new product's leads generated orders, compared to the company's 12 percent all-product average. Why? Charlotte guesses that the sales force is not supporting the new product vigorously enough. Quantitative information from the DSS perhaps could provide more evidence to back that suspicion. But already having enough quantitative knowledge to satisfy herself, Charlotte acts on her intuition and experience and decides to have a chat with her sales manager, Peter Arbour.

Perhaps the fastest-growing use of DSS is for **database marketing**, which involves creating a large, computerized file of customers' and potential customers' profiles and purchase patterns. It is usually the key tool for successful micromarketing, which relies on very specific information about a market.

database marketing
The creation of a large, computerized file of customers' and potential customers' profiles and purchase patterns.

Marketing research is the process of planning, collecting, and analyzing data relevant to a marketing decision. The results of this analysis are then communicated to management. Marketing research plays a key role in the marketing system. It provides decision makers with data on the effectiveness of the current marketing mix and with insights for necessary changes. Furthermore, marketing research is a main data source for both management information systems and DSSs.

The Role of Marketing Research

2
Define marketing research, and explain its importance to marketing decision making

Marketing research has three roles: descriptive, diagnostic, and predictive. Its *descriptive* role includes gathering and presenting factual statements. For example, what are the historic sales trends in the industry? What are consumers' attitudes toward a product and its advertising? Its *diagnostic* role includes explaining data. For instance, what was the impact on sales of a change in the design of the package? In its *predictive* function, it addresses "what if" questions. For example, how can the researcher use the descriptive and diagnostic research to predict the results of a planned marketing decision?

Management Uses of Marketing Research

Marketing research can help managers in several ways. It improves the quality of decision making and helps managers trace problems. Most important, sound marketing research helps managers focus on the paramount importance of keeping existing customers, helps them understand the marketplace better, and alerts them to marketplace trends. Marketing research also helps managers gauge the perceived value of their goods and services and the level of customer satisfaction.

marketing research
The process of planning, collecting, and analyzing data relevant to a marketing decision.

Improving the Quality of Decision Making Managers can sharpen their decision making by using marketing research to explore the desirability of various marketing alternatives. To aid managers in their decision making, The Gillette Company, the world leader in men's grooming products, engages in ongoing marketing research. The following are among the types of ongoing studies conducted by Gillette:

- *National consumer studies*—personal interviews to determine current shaving patterns and products used.
- *Brand tracking studies*—monitoring the sales of Gillette and competitor products to determine market patterns and brand switching behaviour.
- *Brand awareness studies*—telephone surveys to determine consumer awareness of Gillette products.
- *Consumer use tests*—studies in which Gillette askes consumers to use selected Gillette products and then gets feedback on their reactions to the products.
- *Retail audits*—an examination of Gillette sales, inventory, product displays, and stockouts by different types of retail outlets.
- *Laboratory research studies*—using potential consumers to test improvements on current products and new Gillette products.

Tracing Problems Managers also use marketing research to find out why a plan has backfired. Was the initial decision incorrect? Did an unforeseen change in the external environment cause the plan to fail? How can the same mistake be avoided in the future?

Keebler introduced Sweet Spots, a shortbread cookie with a huge chocolate drop on it. It has had acceptable sales and is still on the market, but only after marketing research was used to overcome several problems. Soon after the cookie was introduced, Keebler increased the box's size and price. Demand immediately fell. Market research showed that Sweet Spots were now considered more a luxury than an everyday item. Keebler lowered the price and went back to the smaller box. Even though Sweet Spots originally was aimed at upscale adult females, the company also tried to appeal to kids. In later research, Keebler found that the package graphics appealed to mothers but not to children.[2]

Focusing on the Paramount Importance of Keeping Existing Customers An inextricable link exists between customer satisfaction and customer loyalty. Long-term relationships don't just happen; they are grounded in the delivery of service and value by the firm. Customer retention pays big dividends for organizations. Powered by repeat sales and referrals, revenues and market share grow. Costs fall because firms spend less money and energy attempting to replace defectors. Steady customers are easy to serve because they understand the modus operandi and make fewer demands on employees' time. Increased customer retention also drives job satisfaction and pride, which leads to higher employee retention. In turn, the knowledge that employees acquire as they stay longer increases productivity. A Bain & Company study estimated that a decrease in the customer defection rate of 5 percent can boost profits by 25 to 95 percent.[3]

The ability to retain customers is based on an intimate understanding of their needs. This knowledge comes primarily from marketing research. British Airways recast its first-class transatlantic service based on detailed marketing research. Most airlines stress top-of-the-line service in their transatlantic first-class cabins. British Air research found that most first-class passengers simply wanted to sleep. British Air now gives premium flyers the option of dinner on the ground, before takeoff, in the first-class lounge. Once on board, they can slip into British Air pajamas, put their heads on comfortable pillows, slip under blankets, and enjoy an interruption-free flight. On arrival, first-class passengers can have breakfast, use comfortable dressing rooms and showers, and even have their clothes pressed before they set off for business. These changes in British Air's first-class service were driven strictly by marketing research.[4]

Understanding the Ever-Changing Marketplace Marketing research also helps managers understand what is going on in the marketplace and take advan-

exhibit 7.1

Coupon Redemption by Distribution Method in Canada

Distribution method	1998	1999	2000
Free-standing inserts	48%	54%	55%
In store	14	11	14
In/on package	20	17	13
Direct mail	6	6	9
Magazine/newspaper	5	4	3
Charity	5	5	4
Other	2	3	2

Source: Watts NCH Promotional Services Ltd., 160 McNabb Street, Markham, Ontario L3R 4B8, *Monthly Newsletter*, March 2001, p. 2. Reprinted with permission of NCH Promotional Services, Ltd.

tage of opportunities. Marketing research has been practised for as long as marketing has existed. The early Phoenicians carried out market demand studies as they traded in the various ports of the Mediterranean. Marco Polo's diary indicates that he carried out marketing research while travelling to China. There is even evidence that the Spanish systematically conducted market surveys as they explored the New World, and there are examples of marketing research conducted during the Renaissance.

A marketing manager in the present day might consider offering coupons when introducing a new frozen pastry. The coupon would be used along with television advertising to induce trial of the new pastry. The question then arises as to how the coupons should be distributed. Spending on sales promotion is more effective if coupons are distributed so that potential consumers see them and use them. Data from Watts NCH Promotional Services Ltd., a company that monitors coupon distribution and use in Canada, indicate that free-standing inserts are redeemed more often than other types of coupons (see Exhibit 7.1). Free-standing inserts are four-colour, coupon-carrying advertising supplements and are distributed to over 5 million households in Canada inside home-delivered newspa-

global perspectives

Marketing Research Examines Demand for a Prawn-Flavoured Potato Chip

Janjaree Thanma flipped through a fat folder of market research, thinking about a prawn-flavoured potato chip. Janjaree, who directs marketing for Frito-Lay chips in Bangkok, Thailand, had found (based on marketing research) that prawn is the favourite flavour of Thais. But Thais also said they thought a snack with a native flavour such as tom yam, or prawn, is inappropriate. (Frito-Lay people in China, after similar tests, ruled out the most popular flavour in that nation—dog.)

According to Thanna, Thais may "perceive a good snack as a Western snack." After testing 500 flavours, her management team eschewed tom yam for now and stayed with Western flavours such as barbecue.

Such painstaking research has helped Frito-Lay blitz the Thai market, just as it has done in other parts of the world. This blitz began when Frito-Lay bought out its Thai partner, took over a production plant, hired 1,500 farmers to grow potatoes according to its strict criteria, and unleashed a market campaign featuring TV ads and a brigade of "promoter girls" who greeted shoppers in stores. Frito-Lay's sales in Thailand tripled in the first twelve months after the takeover and are forecast at 70 million bags a year.[5]

Do you think that marketing research can be used effectively in most countries of the world? What might be different about conducting marketing research abroad versus in Canada?

pers. So the marketing manager would specify FSIs as the method for distributing coupons for the new frozen pastry product.

Understanding the marketplace is important not only for Canadian and other industrial markets. It is vital for managers everywhere in the world to understand the ever-changing marketplace and their customers. The "Global Perspectives" box illustrates this point.

Steps in a Marketing Research Project

3
Describe the steps involved in conducting a marketing research project

Almost all firms that have adopted the marketing concept engage in some marketing research because it offers decision makers many benefits. Some companies spend millions on marketing research; others, especially smaller firms, conduct informal, limited-scale research studies. When the Mongolian Barbeque first opened in Windsor, Ontario, it drew novelty seekers and was quite successful during the evening dinner hours. However, it never did draw the local business crowd, and sales during the important lunch hour remained low. The owner surveyed businesspeople working within walking distance of the restaurant. He found that they did not know what Mongolian food was like, were confused about the barbeque approach to the food, and assumed that prices were high. In response, the owner began sending out menus to local businesses, and lunch sales quickly picked up.

Whether a research project costs $200 or $2 million, the same general process should be followed. The marketing research process is a scientific approach to decision making that maximizes the chances of getting accurate and meaningful results. Exhibit 7.2 traces the steps: (1) defining the marketing problem, (2) planning the research design and gathering primary data, (3) specifying the sampling procedures, (4) collecting the data, (5) analyzing the data, (6) preparing and presenting the report, and (7) following up.

The research process begins with the recognition of a marketing problem or opportunity. As changes occur in the firm's external environment, marketing managers face these questions: "Should we change the existing marketing mix?" "If we should, how?" Marketing research can be used to evaluate product, promotion, distribution, and pricing alternatives. It can also be used to find and evaluate new market opportunities.

For example, over 3 million babies have been born in Canada since 1990. It is the largest generation since the baby boomers. Even more impressive than their numbers is their wealth. The increase in single-parent and dual-earner households means that kids are making shopping decisions once left to mom. Kids fourteen and under will directly spend several billion dollars this year in allowances, earnings, and gifts, and influence the purchase of many billions more.[6]

For savvy marketers, these statistics represent an opportunity. Marketing research can clarify sharply where the best opportunities lie. Based on its marketing research, Walt Disney is launching a twenty-four-hour kids' radio network. Sometimes research can have unexpected results that require creative uses of the marketing mix. General Motors recently completed an analysis of "backseat consumers"—that is, children between five and fifteen—and found that parents often let their children play a tie-breaking role in deciding which car to purchase. Armed with this information, GM's marketing managers launched several programs. For example, they purchased the inside cover of *Sports Illustrated for Kids,* a magazine targeted to boys from eight to fourteen. The ad featured a brightly coloured two-page spread for the Chevy Venture minivan, a vehicle targeted to young families. They also sent the minivan into malls and showed Disney movies on a VCR inside the van.

exhibit 7.2

The Marketing Research Process

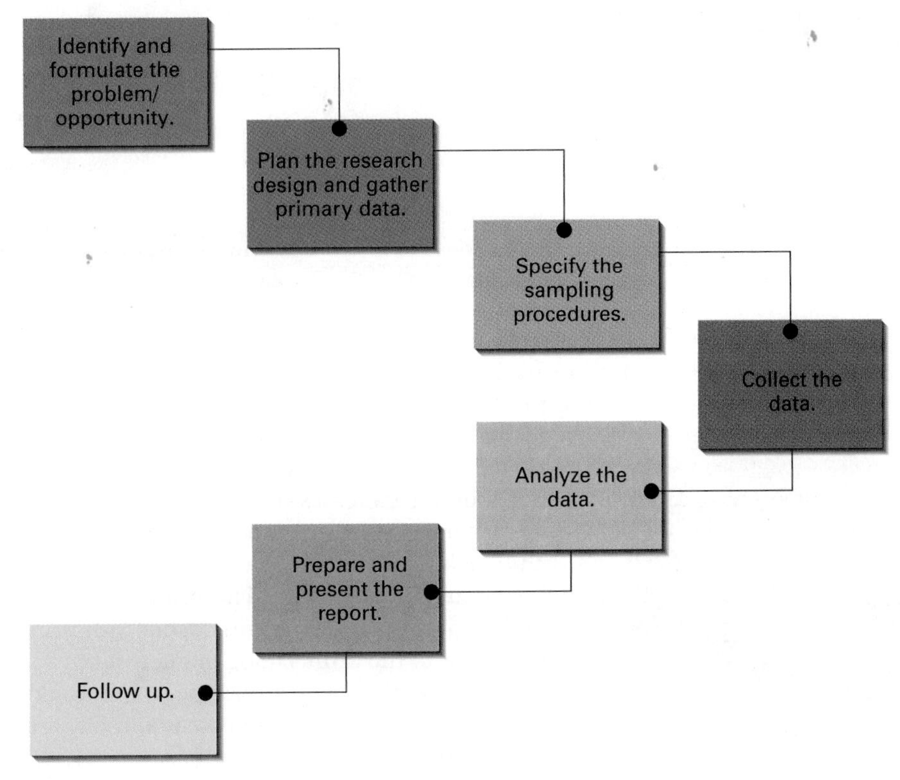

The GM example illustrates an important point about problem/opportunity definition. The **marketing research problem** is information oriented. It involves determining what information is needed and how that information can be obtained efficiently and effectively. The **marketing research objective**, then, is to provide insightful decision-making information. This involves gathering specific pieces of information to answer the marketing research problem. Managers must combine this information with their own experience and other information to make proper decisions. In the GM scenario, the marketing research objective was to determine what role, if any, backseat consumers play in a family's decision to purchase an automobile. In contrast, the **management decision problem** is action oriented. Management problems tend to be much broader in scope and far more general; marketing research problems must be more narrowly defined and specific if the research effort is to be successful. Sometimes several research studies must be conducted to solve a broad management problem. Once GM determined that children within this target market play a tie-breaker role, the question became one of what should be done to influence the tie breakers. GM used marketing research to determine that direct advertising to children in the target market and mall promotions would be the best form of promotion.

marketing research problem
Determining what information is needed and how that information can be obtained efficiently and effectively.

marketing research objective
Specific information needed to solve a marketing research problem; the objective should provide insightful decision-making information.

management decision problem
A broad-based problem that requires marketing research in order for managers to take proper actions.

Secondary Data A valuable tool throughout the research process, but especially in the problem/opportunity identification stage, is secondary data. **Secondary data** are data previously collected for any purpose other than the one at hand. People both inside and outside the organization may have gathered secondary data to meet their needs. Exhibit 7.3 lists some common sources of secondary data. Most research efforts rely at least partly on secondary data, which

secondary data
Data previously collected for any purpose other than the one at hand.

can usually be obtained quickly and inexpensively. The problem is locating relevant secondary data.

Secondary data save time and money if they help solve the researcher's problem. Even if they don't, secondary data are often helpful. For example, they can help formulate the problem statement and suggest research methods and other types of data needed for solving the problem. Also, secondary data can pinpoint the kinds of people to approach and their locations, and newer data can be compared with them. The disadvantages of secondary data stem mainly from any mismatching between the researcher's unique problem and the earlier problem for which the secondary data were originally gathered. In one situation, a major consumer products manufacturer wanted to determine the market potential for a fireplace log made of coal rather than compressed wood by-products. The researcher found plenty of secondary data about total wood consumed as fuel, quantities consumed by section of the country, and types of wood burned. Secondary data were also available about consumer attitudes and purchase patterns relating to wood by-product fireplace logs. The wealth of secondary data provided the researcher with many insights into the artificial log market. Yet nowhere was there any information that would tell the firm whether consumers would buy artificial logs made of coal.

Too often, researchers cannot assess the quality and relevance of secondary data because detailed information about their sources is lacking. A researcher always has to consider the following: Who gathered the data? Why were the data obtained? What methodology was used? How were classifications (such as heavy users versus light users) developed and defined? When was the information gathered?

GM continues to reap the benefits of its marketing research revealing how important kids are in the family decision-making process. In 2000 the company introduced the Warner Bros. Edition Chevy Venture minivan. This model includes a built-in child's restraining seat, a video player, and an ongoing package called VentureTainment! [™ and © Warner Bros. (s01).]

Goes from zero to fun in two shakes of a rabbit's tail.

To find out more, call 1-877-4FUN-VAN or visit us at chevrolet.com.

Introducing the Chevy™ Venture® Warner Bros. Edition,* a minivan that took a left turn at Albuquerque and found its way into the hearts of parents everywhere. With its amazing three-way audio controls, flip-down monitor and built-in video player, you can entertain a small army of kids for miles. And to keep the good times rolling, there's VentureTainment!,℠ a unique ownership package of ongoing benefits from Chevrolet® and Warner Bros. This Venture also

comes with a standard integral child safety seat,† so you won't have to struggle with installing one. Plus flip-and-fold modular bucket seats. All this fun, and more, is standard in the Warner Bros. Edition. After all, it's a Chevy Venture, the most versatile minivan ever.

CHEVY VENTURE

WE'LL BE THERE™

The New Age of Secondary Information—The Internet

At one time, gathering secondary data was always a tedious and boring job. The researcher often had to write to government agencies, trade associations, and other secondary data providers and then wait days or weeks for a reply that might never come. Often, one or more trips to the library were necessary, and the researcher too often found that vital reports were checked out or missing. The rapid development of the Internet and World Wide Web in recent years promises to eliminate the drudgery associated with collecting secondary data.

The Internet is a worldwide telecommunications network that enables people with computers to tap into data of any kind from anywhere in the world. Geographical location doesn't matter, nor does the make of computer. The World Wide Web (or Web) is a part of the Internet that is designed to simplify the transmission of text, images, and sounds. The Web is considered the most popular and user-friendly portion of the Internet.

exhibit 7.3
Traditional Sources of Secondary Data

Source	Description
Internal information	Internal company information can be helpful in solving a particular marketing problem. Examples include sales invoices, other accounting records, data from previous marketing research studies, and historical sales data.
Market research firms	Companies such as A.C. Nielsen, Arbitron, and IMS International are major sources of secondary data regarding market share for consumer products and the characteristics of media audiences.
Trade associations	Many trade associations, such as the Canadian Automotive Dealers' Association and the Automotive Parts Manufacturers' Association of Canada, collect data of interest to members.
National research bureaux, professional associations, foundations	A variety of nonprofit organizations, such as the Conference Board of Canada and the Retail Council of Canada, collect and disseminate data of interest to marketing researchers.
Commercial publications	*Advertising Age, Sales Management, Marketing, Canadian Business, Canadian Consumer,* and many other commercial publications provide useful research data.

Finding Secondary Data on the Internet

If you don't know the address of a particular Website that contains the secondary data you need, you can type a description of what you are looking for directly into your Web browser. (Netscape Navigator and Microsoft Internet Explorer are the most common browsers.) A Web address, or **URL** (**uniform reference locator**), is similar to a street address in that it identifies a particular location (Web server and file on that server) on the Web.

uniform reference locator (URL)
Similar to a street address in that it identifies a unique location on the Web.

A typical Web address might be **www.microsoft.com.** "*www*" is short for World Wide Web. This prefix is not required by all sites and is sometimes replaced with a different prefix, such as *ww2* or no prefix at all. However, most Web addresses begin with *www.* The next item is called the domain name—for example, *microsoft.com.* This is a unique name registered for use on the Internet, much like a trademark is registered and used by a business. The extension (*.com*) tells you that the company is a for-profit company. Other extensions are *.edu* (educational institutions), *.org* (not-for-profit organizations), *.gov* (government sites), *.ca* (Canadian sites) and *.net* (Internet service providers). After the domain name is the information that tells the Web server which document you are requesting. There can be multiple subdirectories that end with a specific file name (*download.htm*), or the path may end with a slash (/) indicating that you want the default document in that directory. (Some Web servers do not provide for default documents; in such cases you will get an error message.)

Search Engines Sites such as AltaVista, Excite, and Google have become popular destinations for Web users seeking information on the Web. A list of popular search engines is provided in Exhibit 7.4. See Chapter 19 for a complete discussion of search engines.

Discussion Groups and Special Interest Groups on the Internet as Sources of Secondary Data

An important means of communicating with other professionals and special interest groups on the Internet is through newsgroups. With an Internet connec-

exhibit 7.4

Popular Search Engines

Search Site	URL	Comments
AOL Search	**search.ad.com**	Allows members to search across the Web. AOL's own content from one place.
AltaVista	**www.alta-vista.com**	Currently the biggest and fastest search engine available.
Ask Jeeves	**www.askjeeves.com**	Human-powered search service that aims to direct you to the exact page that answers your question. If it fails to find a match within its own database, then it will provide matching Web pages from various search engines.
Direct Hit	**www.directhit.com**	Works with other search engines to refine their results. Monitors what users clicked on from the results they see. Sites that get clicked on more than others rise higher in Direct Hit's rankings. Thus, the service dubs itself a "popularity engine."
Excite	**www.excite.com**	Cutting edge, fast, with site reviews and travel guides.
HotBot	**www.hotbot.com**	Uses Inktomi search engine technology, which makes it very fast.
Go/Infoseek	**www.go.com**	Easy-to-use search engine, plus Web directory with site reviews; good place to start for new user.
GoTo	**www.goto.com**	Unlike the other major search engines, GoTo sells its main listings. Companies can pay money to be placed higher in the search results, which GoTo feels improves relevancy. Nonpaid results come from Inktomi.
Google	**www.google.com**	Makes heavy use of link popularity to rank Web sites. Especially helpful in finding good sites in response to general searches such as "cars" and "travel," because users across the Web have in essence voted for good sites by linking to them.
Inktomi	**www.inktomi.com**	Was first used to power HotBot, now also powers several other services. All of them tap into the same index, though results may be slightly different.
Internet Public Library	**www.ipl.org**	Giant cyberlibrary.
LookSmart	**www.looksmart.com**	A human-compiled directory of Websites. Provides directory results to MSN Search, Excite, and many other partners.
Lycos	**www.lycos.com**	An old standard; dated in comparison to some of the new search engines.
MSN Search	**www.search.msn.com**	A LookSmart-powered directory of Websites, with secondary results from AltaVista. RealNames and Direct Hit data also made available.
Netscape Search	**search.netscape.com**	Results come primarily from the Open Directory and Netscape's own "Smart Browsing" data base, which does an excellent job of listing "official" Websites. Secondary results come from Google.
Magellan	**www.mckinley.com**	Family-oriented Web directory and search engine.
World Wide Web Virtual Library	**www.w3.org/vl**	A volunteer effort to organize the World Wide Web by subject.
Yahoo!	**www.yahoo.com**	Very organized and easy to use; another good place to start for the new user.

tion and newsreader software, you can visit any newsgroup supported by your service provider. Chapter 19 provides a detailed discussion illustrating how newgroups can be a valuable source of secondary data.

Planning the Research Design and Gathering Primary Data

Good secondary data can help researchers conduct a thorough situation analysis. With that information, researchers can list their unanswered questions and rank them. Researchers must then decide the exact information required to answer the questions. The **research design** specifies which research questions must be answered, how and when the data will be gathered, and how the data will be analyzed. Typically, the project budget is finalized after the research design has been approved.

research design
Specifies which research questions must be answered, how and when the data will be gathered, and how the data will be analyzed.

Research questions can sometimes be answered by gathering more secondary data; otherwise, primary data will be needed. **Primary data,** or information collected for the first time, can be used for solving the particular problem being investigated. The main advantage of primary data is that they will answer a specific research question that secondary data cannot answer. Suppose Pillsbury has two new recipes for refrigerated dough for sugar cookies. Which one will consumers like better? Secondary data cannot help answer this question. Instead, targeted consumers must try each recipe and evaluate the taste, texture, and appearance of each cookie. Moreover, primary data are current, and researchers know the source. Sometimes researchers gather the data themselves instead of assigning projects to outside companies. Researchers also specify the methodology of the research. Secrecy can be maintained because the information is proprietary. In contrast, secondary data are available to all interested parties for relatively small fees.

primary data
Information collected for the first time; can be used for solving the particular problem under investigation.

Gathering primary data is expensive: costs can range from a few thousand dollars for a limited survey to several million for a nationwide study. A nationwide, fifteen-minute telephone interview with 1,000 adult males can cost $50,000 or more for everything, including a data analysis and the subsequent report. Because primary data gathering is so expensive, firms often cut back on the number of interviews to save money. Larger companies that conduct many research projects use another cost-saving technique: they piggyback studies—that is, they gather data on two different projects using one questionnaire. The drawback is that answering questions about, say, dog food and gourmet coffee may be confusing to respondents. Piggybacking also requires a longer interview—sometimes a half hour or longer—which tires respondents. Typically, the quality of the answers declines, with people giving curt replies and thinking, "When will this end!" Furthermore, a lengthy interview makes people less likely to participate in other research surveys.[7]

The disadvantages of primary data gathering are usually offset by the advantages. It is often the only way of solving a research problem. And because of the variety of techniques available, including surveys, observations, and experiments, primary research can address almost any marketing question.

Survey Research

The most popular technique for gathering primary data is **survey research**, whereby a researcher interacts with people to obtain facts, opinions, and attitudes. Exhibit 7.5 summarizes the characteristics of the most popular forms of survey research.

survey research
The most popular technique for gathering primary data, whereby a researcher interacts with people to obtain facts, opinions, and attitudes.

In-Home Interviews In-home, personal interviews often provide high-quality information, but they tend to be very expensive because of the interviewers' travel

exhibit 7.5 | Characteristics of Various Types of Survey Research

Characteristic	In-home personal interviews	Mall intercept interviews	Central location telephone interviews	Self-administration and one-time mail surveys	Mail panel survey	Executive inteviews	Focus groups
Cost	High	Moderate	Moderate	Low	Moderate	High	Low
Time span	Moderate	Moderate	Fast	Slow	Relatively slow	Moderate	Fast
Use of interviewer probes	Yes	Yes	Yes	No	Yes	Yes	Yes
Ability to show concepts to respondent	Yes (also taste tests)	Yes (also taste tests)	No	Yes	Yes	Yes	Yes
Management control over interviewer	Low	Moderate	High	n/a	n/a	Moderate	High
General data quality	High	Moderate	High to moderate	Moderate to low	Moderate	High	Moderate
Ability to collect large amounts of data	High	Moderate	Moderate to low	Low to moderate	Moderate	Moderate	Moderate
Ability to handle complex questionaires	High	Moderate	High if computer-aided	Low	Low	High	Low

time and travel costs. Therefore, they are rapidly disappearing from the marketing researcher's survey toolbox.

mall intercept interview
Survey research method that involves interviewing people in the common areas of shopping malls.

Mall Intercept Interviews The **mall intercept interview** is conducted in the common area of a shopping mall or in a market research office within that mall. It is the economy version of the door-to-door interview, in that it involves personal contact between interviewer and respondent, but without travel costs for the interviewer. To conduct this type of interview, the research firm rents office space in the mall or pays a significant daily fee. One drawback of mall intercept interviews is that it is hard to get a representative sample of the population.

Mall intercept interviews must be brief. Only the shortest ones are conducted while respondents are standing. Usually researchers invite respondents to their office for interviews, which are rarely over fifteen minutes long. Often, the researchers show respondents concepts for new products or a test commercial, or have them taste a new food product. The overall quality of mall intercept interviews is about the same as for telephone interviews.

computer-assisted personal interviewing
Interviewing method whereby the interviewer reads the questions from a computer screen and enters the respondent's data directly into the computer.

computer-assisted self-interviewing
Interviewing method whereby a mall interviewer directs willing respondents to nearby computer terminals. Repsondents then read questions off the terminal screens and key their answers directly into the computers.

Marketing researchers are applying new technology in mall interviewing. With **computer-assisted personal interviewing**, the researcher conducts in-person interviews, reads questions to the respondent off a computer screen, and directly keys the respondent's answers into the computer. With **computer-assisted self-interviewing**, a mall interviewer intercepts and directs willing respondents to nearby computers. Each respondent reads questions off a computer terminal and directly keys his or her answers into the computer. With fully automated self-interviewing, respondents are guided by interviewers or independently approach a centrally located computer station or kiosk, read questions off a screen, and directly key their answers into the station's computer.

Telephone Interviews Telephone interviews cost less than personal interviews and may provide the best sample of any survey procedure. They are often criticized for providing poorer-quality data than in-home personal interviews; however, studies have shown that this criticism may not be deserved.[8]

Most telephone interviewing is conducted from specially designed phone rooms called **central-location telephone (CLT) facilities**. A phone room has many phone lines, individual interviewing stations, sometimes monitoring equipment, and headsets. The use of wide-area telephone service (WATS) lines enables a research firm to interview people nationwide from a single location.

central-location telephone (CLT) facility
A specially designed phone room used to conduct telephone interviewing.

Many CLT facilities offer computer-assisted interviewing. The interviewer reads the questions from a computer screen and enters the respondent's data directly into the computer. The researcher can stop the survey at any point and immediately print out the survey results. Thus, a researcher can get a sense of the project as it unfolds and fine-tune the research design as necessary. An on-line interviewing system can also save time and money because data entry occurs as the response is recorded rather than as a separate process after the interview. Hallmark Cards found that an interviewer administered a printed questionnaire for its Shoebox greeting cards in twenty-eight minutes. The same questionnaire administered with computer assistance took only eighteen minutes.

Mail Surveys Mail surveys have several benefits: relatively low cost, elimination of interviewers and field supervisors, centralized control, and actual or promised anonymity for respondents (which may draw more candid responses). Some researchers feel that mail questionnaires give the respondent a chance to reply more thoughtfully and to check records, talk to family members, and so forth. However, mail questionnaires usually produce low response rates.

Low response rates pose a problem because certain elements of the population tend to respond more than others. For this reason, the resulting sample may not represent the surveyed population. For example, it may have too many retired people and too few young people with children. In this instance, answers to a question about spending on education may receive less favourable responses than is actually the case. Another serious problem with mail surveys is that no one probes respondents to clarify or elaborate on their answers.

Mail panels like those operated by Market Facts, National Family Opinion Research, and NPD Research offer an alternative to the one-shot mail survey. A mail panel consists of a sample of households recruited to participate by mail for a given period of time. Panel members often receive gifts in return for their participation. Essentially, the panel is a sample used several times. In contrast to one-time mail surveys, the response rates from mail panels are high. Rates of 70 percent (of those who agree to participate) are not uncommon.

Internet Surveys

Advantages of Internet Surveys The popularity of Internet surveys surged in the late 1990s, for several reasons.[9] First, there is the speed with which a questionnaire can be created and distributed to respondents, and the data returned. Since printing, mailing, and data keying delays are eliminated, you can have data in hand within hours of writing a questionnaire. Data are obtained in electronic form, so statistical analysis software can be programmed to process standard questionnaires and return statistical summaries and charts automatically.

A second reason to consider Internet surveys is cost. Printing, mailing, keying, and interviewer costs are eliminated, and the incremental costs of each respondent are typically low, so studies with large numbers of respondents can be done at substantial savings compared to mail or telephone surveys.

Another reason is that by creating respondent panels on the Internet, the researcher can create longitudinal studies by tracking attitudes, behaviour, and perceptions over time. Sophisticated panel tracking software can tailor follow-up questions for the next survey, based on responses from a previous survey; also, missing answers can be filled in.[10]

A fourth reason is that it typically isn't worthwhile to conduct a phone survey to ask two or three questions. On the Internet, however, a survey component could unobtrusively be included within a general site that is used for marketing or business transactions. For example, if a person accesses a banking home page and then goes to the "credit card" link, he or she could be asked a few questions about the features of a credit card that are most important before moving along to the information component.[11]

Yet another benefit of using the Internet for market research is that no other medium can reach so many people so inexpensively. Furthermore, the Internet is an international arena in which many barriers to communication have been erased.

Finally, Internet questionnaires delivered through the Web can be made visually pleasing with attractive fonts and graphics. The graphical and hypertext features of the Web can be used to present products for reaction or to explain service offerings. For respondents with current versions of Netscape Navigator or Internet Explorer—the two most popular Web browsers—audio and video can be added to the questionnaire. This multimedia ability is unique to Web-delivered questionnaires.

Disadvantages of Internet Surveys Despite the advantages of Internet surveys, they still have many drawbacks. Perhaps the biggest problem is that Internet users are not representative of the population as a whole. Not all households use the Internet regularly—although more people are connected, many are infrequent users. Users tend to be male, well educated, technically oriented, and relatively young, and to have above-average incomes. This is changing, however, as more people access the Internet.

The CommerceNet/Nielsen Internet Demographics Study (**www.nielsenmedia.com**) was a World Wide Web survey done in conjunction with a phone survey to assess the biases inherent in Web data. As the discrepancy between the two survey formats decreases, the Web is becoming more of a mass market vehicle. It may not happen completely for several more years, but in this age of rapid change and widespread adoption of new technologies, many are betting that it will happen sooner rather than later.[12]

There are some populations, such as computer product purchasers and home users of Internet services, that are ideal for Internet surveys. Business and professional users of Internet services are also an excellent population to reach with Internet surveys. It is estimated that more than 90 percent of businesses currently to have Internet connections.[13]

A second problem is security on the Internet. Users today are understandably worried about privacy issues. This fear has been fuelled by sensational media accounts of cyberstalkers and con artists preying on Internet users. Given the commercial incentives for ensuring that information such as credit card numbers can be transmitted safely, encryption methodology is going to be at the forefront of Internet developments. This will—it is hoped—resolve the security problem.

unrestricted Internet sample
Anyone with a computer and modem can fill out the questionnaire.

A third problem arises when an **unrestricted Internet sample** is set up on the Internet. In such a sample, anyone who wants can complete the questionnaire. It is fully self-selecting and probably representative of no one except Web surfers. This problem is exacerbated if the same Internet user can access the questionnaire repeatedly. *InfoWorld*, a computer magazine, decided to conduct its Readers Choice survey on the Internet. The results were so skewed by repeat voting for one product that the entire survey was publicly abandoned and the editor asked for readers' help to avoid the problem the next time.[14] A simple solution to repeat respondents is to lock respondents out of the site after they have filled out the questionnaire.

Internet Samples

Internet samples can be classified as unrestricted, screened, or recruited.[15] Unrestricted samples were just discussed. **Screened Internet samples** adjust for the unrepresentativeness of the self-selected respondents by imposing quotas based on some desired sample characteristics. These are often demographic characteristics such as gender, income, and geographic region, or product-related criteria such as past purchase behaviour, job responsibilities, or current product use. The applications for screened samples are generally similar to those for unrestricted samples.

screened Internet sample
Internet sample with quotas based on desired sample characteristics.

Typically, screened sample questionnaires use a branching or skip pattern for asking screening questions to determine whether the full questionnaire should be presented to a respondent. Some Web survey systems make immediate calculations that assign a respondent to a particular market segment based on screening questions, then select the appropriate questionnaire to match the respondent's segment.

Alternatively, some Internet research providers maintain a "panel house" that recruits respondents, who fill out a preliminary classification questionnaire. This information is used to classify respondents into demographic segments. Clients specify the desired segments, and the respondents who match the desired demographics are permitted to fill out the questionnaires of all clients who specify that segment.

Recruited Internet samples are used when more control over the sample is required. Respondents are recruited by telephone, mail, or e-mail or in person. After qualifying, they are sent the questionnaire by e-mail or are directed to a Website that contains a link to the questionnaire. At Websites, passwords are usually used to restrict access to the questionnaire to the recruited sample members. Since the makeup of the sample is known, completions can be monitored and follow-up messages can be sent to those who have not completed the questionnaire, in order to improve the participation rate.

recruited Internet sample
Respondents are prerecruited; after qualifying to participate, they are sent a questionnaire by e-mail or directed to a secure Website to fill out a questionnaire.

For applications that already have a database from which to recruit the sample, recruited samples are ideal. A good application would be, for example, a survey that used a customer database to recruit respondents for a purchaser satisfaction study.

The Internet has been a boon to small businesses and entrepreneurs who wish to conduct marketing research. The reasons why are discussed in the "Entrepreneurial Insights" box.

entrepreneurial insights

The Internet Is a Great Tool for Entrepreneurs Who Want to Conduct Marketing Research

For small business owners who wish to conduct marketing research, the Internet is the "great equalizer." Secondary research is at their fingertips through a search engine. Do they want to know what people are saying about their industry and products? They can go to a chat room.

Small businesses often found it too expensive to hire a marketing research firm. Even when they didn't use a research company, they often found it expensive to hire and train interviewers, and many entrepreneurs simply didn't know how to conduct a survey.

On-line surveys offer a whole new approach for small businesses to conduct survey research inexpensively. The current versions of Microsoft Internet Explorer and Netscape Navigator fully support transparent interactivity for on-line surveys. Entrepreneurs can now create much more sophisticated surveys than mail techniques allow. For example, they can build complicated skip patterns into their on-line surveys. A simple skip pattern would be, "Do you own a dog?" If the answer is no, all the questions pertaining to dog ownership would be skipped.

What pitfalls should entrepreneurs guard against when conducting on-line surveys? When should a small businessperson rely on the expertise of a marketing research firm?

focus group
Seven to ten people who participate in a group discussion led by a moderator.

Focus Groups A **focus group** is a form of personal interviewing. Seven to ten people with certain desired characteristics form a focus group. Often they are recruited by telephone screening. These qualified consumers are usually offered an incentive (typically $30 to $50) to participate in a group discussion. The meeting place (sometimes resembling a living room, sometimes featuring a conference table) has audiotaping and perhaps videotaping equipment. It also likely has a viewing room with a one-way mirror so that clients (manufacturers or retailers) can watch the session. During the session, a moderator hired by the research company leads the group discussion.

group dynamics
Group interaction essential to the success of focus group research.

Focus groups are much more than question-and-answer interviews. There is a difference between "group dynamics" and "group interviewing." The interaction provided in **group dynamics** is essential to the success of focus-group research; this interaction is the reason for conducting group rather than individual research. Central to the whole idea of group sessions is that a response from one person may become a stimulus for another; this generates an interplay of responses that may yield more than if the same number of people had contributed independently.

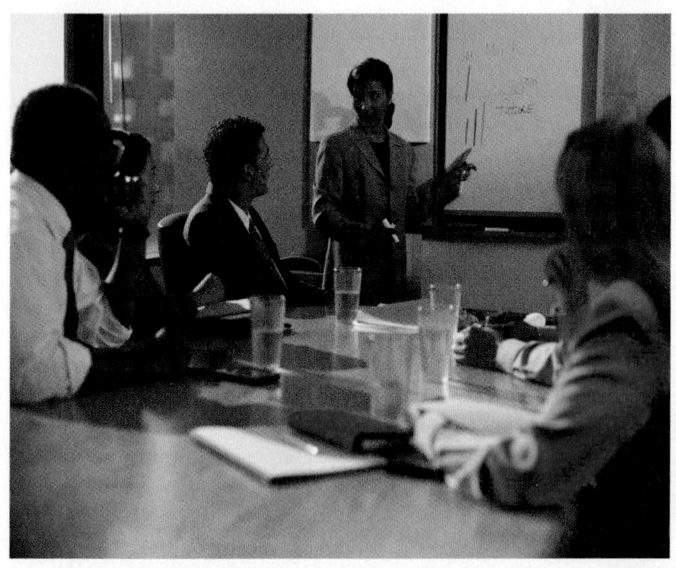
Companies often ask consumers to test their products and then bring them into a focus group to get their feedback.

Focus groups are sometimes used to brainstorm new product ideas or to screen concepts for new products. Ford Motor Company asked consumers to drive several automobile prototypes. These "test drivers" were then brought together in focus groups. During the discussions, consumers complained that they were scuffing their shoes because the rear seats lacked foot room. In response, Ford sloped the floor underneath the front seats, widened the space between the seat adjustment tracks, and made the tracks in the Taurus and Sable models out of smooth plastic instead of metal.

A new system, pioneered by Focus Vision Network, enables client companies and advertising agencies to view live focus groups from distant locations. This private satellite network lets a researcher in Toronto observing a Vancouver focus group control two cameras in the viewing room. The researcher can get a full-group view or a close-up, and can pan over or zoom onto the participants. The researcher can also communicate directly with the moderator through an ear receiver. Ogilvy and Mather—a large advertising agency whose clients include StarKist Sea Foods, Seagrams, Mastercard, and Burger King—has installed this system.

The newest development in qualitative research is the on-line or cyber focus group. A number of organizations are now offering this new means of conducting focus groups. The process is fairly simple:

- The research firm builds a database of respondents via a screening questionnaire on its Website.
- When a client comes to them with a need for a particular focus group, the firm goes to its database and identifies individuals who seem to qualify. It sends an e-mail message to these individuals, asking them to log on to a particular site at a particular time scheduled for the group. The firm pays them an incentive to participate.
- The firm develops a discussion guide similar to one for a conventional focus group.

Greenfield On-line

Find out how on-line focus groups work by signing up to be a participant. Check out some of Greenfield's on-line surveys in the Survey Centre.

www.greenfieldonline.com

on line

- A moderator runs the group by typing in questions on-line for all to see. The group operates in an environment similar to that of a chat room; all participants see all questions and all responses.
- The firm captures the complete text of the focus group and makes it available for review after the group has finished.

Cyber Dialogue, a marketing research company specializing in cyber groups, lists on its Website the following benefits of on-line focus groups:

- *Speed:* Typically, focus groups can be recruited and conducted, with delivery of results, within five days of client approval.
- *Cost effectiveness:* Off-line focus groups incur costs for facility rental, air fare, hotels, and meals. On-line focus groups do not incur these costs.
- *Broad geographic scope:* In a given focus group, you can speak to people in Calgary, Halifax, and San Francisco at the same time.
- *Accessibility:* On-line focus groups offer access to individuals who otherwise might be difficult to recruit (e.g., business travellers, doctors, mothers with infants).
- *Honesty:* From behind their screen names, respondents are anonymous to other respondents, so they tend to talk more freely about certain issues.

Cyber Dialogue prices its focus groups at $3,000. This compares very favourably to the cost for conventional focus groups, which is generally around $7,000 before travel costs.

Unfortunately, no systematic evaluation of on-line focus groups has yet been done. Such groups have some obvious and some not-so-obvious disadvantages. First, if the goal of the research is to quantify the sentiments of a broad segment of the population, cybergroups aren't very helpful. Only a minority of North Americans spend much time on the Internet, and a number of studies have demonstrated that the profile of this on-line population is quite different from that of the broader population. This will become less of an issue as more and more people join the Internet. But at the present time this is a significant problem.

Second, no one has demonstrated whether the group dynamics process—which is so important to the success of conventional focus groups—works in cybergroups. Third, some have hypothesized that cybergroup participants may be more honest about their behaviour, opinions, and feelings than participants in conventional focus groups; others have hypothesized the opposite. At this time, no one knows which hypothesis is correct. Finally, when a cybergroup is used the appearance and body language of participants cannot be observed. The authors of this text conducted an informal survey of moderators; most of them considered this a drawback.

Like many areas, the Internet has revolutionized marketing research. Cyber Dialogue conducts on-line focus groups. With these, discussions take place in a forum similar to that of a chat room. This latest development in qualitative research can mean faster, more cost-effective results for clients.

open-ended question Interview question that encourages an answer phrased in the respondent's own words.

closed-ended question Interview question that asks the respondent to make a selection from a limited list of responses.

scaled-response question A closed-ended question designed to measure the intensity of a respondent's answer.

Questionnaire Design All surveys require a questionnaire. Questionnaires ensure that all respondents will be asked the same questions. There are three basic types of questionnaire questions: open-ended, closed-ended, and scaled-response (see Exhibit 7.6). **Open-ended questions** encourage answers in the respondent's own words. Researchers get a rich array of information based on respondents' frames of reference. In contrast, **closed-ended questions** ask respondents to select from a limited list of responses. Marketing researchers have long differentiated between two-choice questions (referred to as dichotomous questions) and many-item questions (often called multiple choice). **Scaled-response questions** are closed-ended questions designed to measure the intensity of a respondent's answer.

Closed-ended and scaled-response questions are easier to tabulate than open-ended questions because the response choices are fixed. On the other hand, if the researcher is not careful in designing closed-ended questions, important choices may be omitted. Suppose this question were asked on a food study: "What do you normally add to a taco, besides meat, that you have prepared at home?"

The following list seems complete, doesn't it? But consider the following responses: "I usually add a green, avocado-tasting hot sauce"; "I cut up a mixture of lettuce and spinach"; "I'm a vegetarian; I don't use meat at all. My taco is filled only with guacamole." How would you code these replies? Clearly, the question needs an "other" category.

exhibit 7.6

Types of Questions Found on Questionnaires for National Market Research

Open-ended questions	Closed-ended questions	Scaled-response question
1. What advantages, if any, do you think ordering from a mail-order catalogue offers compared to shopping at a local retail outlet? 2. Why do you have one or more of your rugs or carpets professionally cleaned rather than having you or someone else in the household clean them? 3. What is there about the colour of the eye shadow that makes you like it the best?	**Dichotomous** 1. Did you heat the Danish product before serving it? Yes .... 1 No .... 2 2. The federal government doesn't care what people like me think. Agree .... 1 Disagree .... 2 **Multiple choice** 1. I'd like you to think back to the last footwear of any kind that you bought. I'll read you a list of descriptions and would like for you to tell me which category they fall into. (Read list and check proper category.) Dress and/or formal .... 1 Casual .... 2 Canvas/trainer/gym shoes .... 3 Specialized athletic shoes .... 4 Boots .... 5 2. In the last three months, have you used Noxzema skin cream . . . (Check all that apply.) As a facial wash .... 1 For moisturizing the skin .... 2 For treating blemishes .... 3 For cleansing the skin .... 4 For treating dry skin .... 5 For softening skin .... 6 For sunburn .... 7 For making the facial skin smooth 8	Now that you have used the rug cleaner, would you say that you . . (Check one) ____ Would definitely buy it ____ Would probably buy it ____ Might or might not buy it ____ Probably would not buy it ____ Definitely would not buy it

Brand Marketing International
Learn more about mystery shopping by requesting a mystery shopper kit from BMI and reading its shopper application.
www.bmiltd.com

on line

Avocado	1
Cheese (Monterey Jack/cheddar)	2
Guacamole	3
Lettuce	4
Mexican hot sauce	5
Olives (black/green)	6
Onions (red/white)	7
Peppers (red/green)	8
Pimento	9
Sour cream	0

A good question is clear and concise and avoids ambiguous language. Consider the question, "Do you live within ten minutes of here?" The answer depends on the mode of transportation (perhaps the person walks), driving speed, perceived time, and other factors. Respondents should instead be shown a map with certain areas highlighted and asked whether they live within one of those areas.

Clarity also requires that reasonable terminology be used. A questionnaire is not a vocabulary test. Jargon should be avoided, and the language should be geared to the target audience. A question such as "What is the level of efficacy of your preponderant dishwasher powder?" would probably be greeted by a lot of blank stares. It would be much simpler to say "Are you (1) very satisfied, (2) somewhat satisfied, or (3) not satisfied with your current brand of dishwasher powder?"

Stating the survey's purpose at the beginning of the interview also improves clarity. The respondents should understand the purpose of the study and the interviewer's expectations. Of course, to get an unbiased response the interviewer will sometimes have to disguise the study's true purpose. If the interviewer says, "We're conducting an image study for Canadian Imperial Bank of Commerce," and then proceeds to ask a series of questions about the bank, chances are the responses will be biased. Respondents often try to provide answers that they believe are "correct" or that the interviewer wants to hear.

Finally, to ensure clarity the interviewer should avoid asking two questions in one—for example, "How did you like the taste and texture of the Pepperidge Farm coffee cake?" This should be divided into two questions, one about taste and the other about texture.

Clarity is not enough: the questions should also be unbiased. A question such as, "Have you purchased any quality Black & Decker tools in the past six months?" biases respondents to think of the topic in a certain way (in this case, to link quality and Black & Decker tools). Questions can also be leading: "Weren't you pleased with the good service you received last night at the Holiday Inn?" (The respondent is all but instructed to say yes.) These examples are quite obvious; unfortunately, bias is usually more subtle. Even an interviewer's clothing or gestures can create bias.

Observation Research

In contrast to survey research, **observation research** does not rely on direct interaction with people. The three types of observation research are people watching people, people watching an activity, and machines watching people. There are two types of *people watching people* research:

observation research
Research method that relies on three types of observation: people watching people, people watching an activity, and machines watching people.

- *Mystery shoppers*: Researchers posing as customers observe the quality of service offered by retailers. The largest mystery shopper company is Shop 'N Chek, a company that employs over 16,000 anonymous shoppers. Among other things, the firm evaluates salespeople's courtesy for General Motors, flight service for airlines, and the efficiency of hamburger ordering for Wendy's.[16]

- *One-way mirror observations*: At the Fisher-Price Play Laboratory, children are invited to spend twelve sessions playing with toys. Toy designers watch through one-way mirrors to see how children react to Fisher-Price's and other makers' toys. Fisher-Price had difficulty designing a toy lawn mower that children would play with. A designer, observing behind the mirror, noted the children's fascination with soap bubbles. He then created a lawn mower that spewed soap bubbles. It sold over a million units the first year.

audit
A form of observation research that features people examining and verifying the sale of a product.

One form of observation research that features people watching an activity is known as an **audit**—that is, the examination and verification of the sale of a product. Audits generally fall into two categories: retail audits, which measure sales to final consumers, and wholesale audits, which determine the amount of product moved from warehouses to retailers. Wholesalers and retailers allow auditors into their stores and stockrooms to examine the company's sales and order records in order to verify product flows. The retailers and wholesalers receive cash compensation and basic reports about their operations from the audit firms.

All observation techniques offer at least two advantages over survey research. First, bias from the interviewing process is eliminated. Second, observation doesn't rely on the respondent's willingness to provide data.

Observation techniques also have two important disadvantages. First, subjective information is limited because motivations, attitudes, and feelings are not measured. Second, data collection costs may run high unless the observed behaviour patterns occur often, briefly, or somewhat predictably.

experiment
Method a researcher uses to gather primary data.

Experiments

An **experiment** is another method a researcher can use to gather primary data. The researcher alters one or more variables—price, package design, shelf space, advertising theme, advertising expenditures—and observes the effects of those alterations on another variable (usually sales). In the best experiments, all factors are held constant except the ones being manipulated. The researcher can then observe that changes in sales are a result of changes in, say, the amount of money spent on advertising.

Fisher-Price runs a play laboratory in which children are observed through a one-way mirror. Toy designers can see how children react to a variety of toys and get ideas for new creations.

Holding all other factors constant in the external environment is a huge and expensive task, and may be downright impossible. Such factors as competitors' actions, the weather, and economic conditions are beyond the researcher's control. Yet market researchers have ways to account for the ever-changing external environment. Mars, the candy company, was losing sales to other candy companies. The company had reduced the size of its product, and traditional surveys were showing that it was no longer perceived as good value. Mars wondered whether a bigger bar sold at the same price would increase sales enough to offset the higher ingredient costs. The company designed an experiment in which the marketing mix stayed the same in different markets but the size of the candy bar varied. The substantial increase in sales of the bigger bar quickly proved that the additional costs would be more than covered by the additional revenue. Mars increased the bar size, and its market share and profits.

Specifying the Sampling Procedures

Once the researchers decide how they will collect primary data, their next step is to select the sampling procedures they will use. A firm can seldom take a census of all possible users of a new product, nor can it interview all of those potential users. So a firm must select a sample of the group to be interviewed. A **sample** is a subset from a larger population.

Several questions must be answered before a sampling plan can be chosen. First, what is the population or **universe** of interest? This is the group from which the sample will be drawn. It should include all the people whose opinions, behaviour, preferences, attitudes, and so on are of interest to the marketer. For a study whose purpose is to determine the market for a new canned dog food, the universe might be defined to include all current buyers of canned dog food.

After the universe has been defined, the next question is whether the sample must be representative of the population. If the answer is yes, a probability sample is needed. Otherwise, a nonprobability sample may be considered.

Probability Samples A **probability sample** is one in which every element in the population has a known statistical likelihood of being selected. Its most desirable feature is that scientific rules can be used to ensure that the sample represents the population.

One type of probability sample is the random sample. With a **random sample**, every element of the population has an equal chance of being selected as part of the sample. Suppose a university is interested in getting a cross-section of student opinions on a proposed sports complex to be built using student activity fees. If the university can acquire an up-to-date list of all the enrolled students, it can draw a random sample by using random numbers from a table (found in most statistics books) to select students from the list. Common forms of probability and nonprobability samples are shown in Exhibit 7.7.

Nonprobability Samples Any sample in which little or no effort is made to get a representative cross-section of the population can be considered a nonprobability sample. A common form of **nonprobability sample** is the **convenience sample**, which is based on respondents who are convenient or readily accessible to the researcher—for instance, employees, friends, or relatives.

Nonprobability samples are acceptable as long as the researcher understands that they are nonrepresentative. Because of their lower cost, nonprobability samples are the basis of much marketing research.

Types of Errors Whenever a sample is used in marketing research, two major types of error occur: measurement error and sampling error. **Measurement error** occurs when there is a difference between the information desired by the researcher and the information provided by the measurement process. People may tell an interviewer that they purchase Coors beer when they do not. Measurement error generally tends to be larger than sampling error.

Sampling error occurs when a sample somehow does not represent the target population. There are several types of sampling error. Nonresponse error occurs when the sample actually interviewed differs from the sample drawn. This happens because the original people selected to be interviewed either refused to cooperate or were inaccessible. People who feel embarrassed about their drinking habits may refuse to talk about them.

Frame error, another type of sampling error, arises when the sample drawn from a population differs from the target population. Suppose a telephone survey is conducted to find out Calgary beer drinkers' attitudes toward Blue Light. If a Calgary telephone directory is used as the frame (i.e., the device or list from which the respondents are selected), the survey will contain a frame error. Not all Calgary beer drinkers have a phone, and many phone numbers are unlisted. An ideal sample (e.g., a sample with no frame error) matches all the important characteristics of the target population to be surveyed. Could you find a perfect frame for Calgary beer drinkers?

Random error occurs when the selected sample is an imperfect representation of the overall population. Random error reflects how accurately the chosen

sample
A subset of a population.

universe
The population from which a sample will be drawn.

probability sample
A sample in which every element in the population has a known statistical likelihood of being selected.

random sample
A sample arranged so that every element of the population has an equal chance of being selected as part of the sample.

nonprobability sample
Any sample in which little or no attempt is made to get a representative cross-section of the population.

convenience sample
A form of nonprobability sample using respondents who are convenient or readily accessible to the researcher—for example, employees, friends, or relatives.

measurement error
Error that occurs when there is a difference between the information desired by the researcher and the information provided by the measurement process.

sampling error
Error that occurs when a sample somehow does not represent the target population.

frame error
Error that occurs when a sample drawn from a population differs from the target population.

random error
Error that occurs because the selected sample is an imperfect representation of the overall population.

sample's true average (mean) value reflects the population's true average (mean) value. We might take a random sample of beer drinkers in Calgary and find that 11 percent regularly drink Blue Light. The next day we might repeat the same sampling procedure and discover that 14 percent regularly drink Blue Light. The difference is due to random error.

field service firm
A firm that specializes in interviewing respondents on a subcontracted basis.

Collecting the Data

Marketing research field service firms collect most primary data. A **field service firm** specializes in interviewing respondents on a subcontract basis. Many have offices throughout the country. A typical marketing research study involves collecting data in several cities; this requires the marketer to work with a comparable number of field service firms. To ensure uniformity among all subcontractors, detailed field instructions should be developed for every job. Nothing should be open to chance; no interpretations of procedures should be left to subcontractors.

exhibit 7.7
Types of Samples

Probability samples	
Simple random sample	Every member of the population has a known and equal chance of selection.
Stratified sample	The population is divided into mutually exclusive groups (such as gender or age); random samples are then drawn from each group.
Cluster sample	The population is divided into mutually exclusive groups (such as geographic areas); a random sample of clusters is then selected. The researcher collects data from all the elements in the selected clusters or from a probability sample of elements within each selected cluster.
Systematic sample	A list of the population is obtained (i.e., all persons with an account at XYZ Bank), and a skip interval is obtained. The skip interval is obtained by dividing the sample size by the population size. If the sample size is 100 and the bank has 1,000 customers, the skip interval is 10. The beginning number is randomly chosen within the skip interval. If the beginning number is 8, then the skip pattern will be 8, 18, 28, and so on.
Nonprobability samples	
Convenience sample	The researcher selects the easiest population members from which to obtain information.
Judgment sample	The researcher's selection criteria are based on personal judgment that the elements (persons) chosen will likely give accurate information.
Quota sample	The researcher finds a prescribed number of people in several categories (i.e., owners of large dogs versus owners of small dogs). Respondents are not selected on probability sampling criteria.
Snowball sample	The selection of additional respondents is made on the basis of referrals from the initial respondents. This is used when a desired type of respondent is hard to find (e.g., persons who have taken round-the-world cruises in the past three years). This technique employs the old adage "Birds of a feather flock together."

Besides conducting interviews, field service firms provide focus group facilities, mall intercept locations, test product storage, and kitchen facilities to prepare test food products. They also conduct retail audits (counting the amount of a product sold off retail shelves). After in-home interviews are completed, field service supervisors validate surveys by recontacting about 15 percent of the respondents. The supervisors verify that certain responses were recorded properly and that the people were actually interviewed.

After collecting the data, the marketing researcher proceeds to the next step in the research process: data analysis. The purpose of data analysis is to interpret the mass of collected data and draw conclusions from it. The marketing researcher organizes and analyzes the data using one or more of the techniques that are common to marketing research. These include one-way frequency counts, cross-tabulations, and sophisticated statistical analyses. Of these three techniques, one-way frequency counts are the simplest. One-way frequency tables record the responses to a question. For example, the answers to the question, "What brand of microwave popcorn do you buy most often?" would provide a one-way frequency distribution. One-way frequency tables are always done in data analysis, at least as a first step, because they provide the researcher with a general picture of the study's results.

exhibit 7.8

Hypothetical Cross-Tabulation Between Gender and Brand of Microwave Popcorn Purchased Most Often

Brand	Purchase by Gender	
	Male	Female
Orville Redenbacher	31%	48%
Act II	12	6
Pop Rite	38	4
President's Choice	7	23
Weight Watchers	4	18
Other	8	0

A **cross-tabulation**, or "cross-tab," lets the analyst look at the responses to one question in relation to the responses to one or more other questions. What is the association between gender and the brand of microwave popcorn bought most often? Hypothetical answers to this question are shown in Exhibit 7.8. The Orville Redenbacher brand was popular with both males and females, but it was more popular with females. Men strongly preferred Pop Rite, and women were more likely to buy Weight Watchers popcorn.

cross-tabulation
A method of analyzing data that lets the analyst look at the responses to one question in relation to the responses to one or more other questions.

There are many other more powerful and sophisticated statistical techniques available to researchers, such as hypothesis testing, measures of association, and regression analysis. Descriptions of these go beyond the scope of this book but can be found in any good marketing research textbook. Whether these more sophisticated techniques are used depends on the researchers' objectives and the nature of the data gathered.

Preparing and Presenting the Report

After data analysis has been completed, the researcher must prepare the report and communicate the conclusions and recommendations to management. This is a key step in the process. If the marketing researcher wants managers to carry out the recommendations, he or she must convince them that the results are credible and are justified by the data collected.

ethics in marketing

It Seems That I've Heard This Before

When Nissan Motor Co. decided to establish a workplace diversity program, it turned for guidance to one of the leading human resources specialists: Towers Perrin. Towers Perrin had recently built a diversity practice to capitalize on companies' growing concerns about race and gender relations. Towers Perrin's pitch was that it would study a company in detail and then customize a program to fit the client's needs.

Towers Perrin launched its painstaking review of the giant Japanese car maker. Charging up to $360 an hour, the consultants conducted one-on-one interviews with fifty-five executives, analyzed surveys of hundreds of additional workers, and reviewed company antidiscrimination policies and other internal documents. The project, which took four months to complete at a cost to the client of more than $105,000, seemed to reflect Towers Perrin's credo: "Prescription without diagnosis is malpractice." But when the prescription arrived, Nissan officials were far from impressed. "The recommendations were so broad, so generic, we didn't think it reflected what we thought we were going to get," says spokesman Kurt von Zumwalt. The 121-page report "did not seem to be particularly tailored to Nissan."

It wasn't. On the same day that Towers Perrin sent its written findings to Nissan, the consulting firm submitted a strikingly similar report to French-owned Thomson Consumer Electronics, Inc. Except for the companies' names, all nine major recommendations made to Thomson matched Nissan's word for word, as did all fifty-four accompanying "tactics and objectives" and all thirteen elements of a proposed implementation plan.

In offering its services, Towers Perrin had said its recommendations would be based on the company's specific needs, as gleaned from the data Towers Perrin would collect. "No two organizations are identical," the firm wrote in its standard thirty-five-page proposal. "They are all as diverse as their workforces and the markets they serve." Later in the proposal, the firm added that "no textbook solutions exist."

Each client's report contained a long section quoting from the interviews and other research, yet the recommendations didn't refer to any findings that were unique to either company. When Towers Perrin discussed employee polls, it described the results identically. In both instances, it said the polling showed that "women and minorities believe there is little or no understanding by supervisors and managers of how to tap their potential or how to mentor them effectively."

Privately held Towers Perrin, with revenues of just over $1 billion, doesn't dispute that many of its reports use the same language. Indeed, Towers Perrin asserts, it is standard practice for the firm and the industry to give clients with similar problems similar or identical advice. All of Towers Perrin's diversity clients—a total of about sixty companies in recent years—received one of several "templates," says Margaret Regan, co-leader of Towers Perrin's global diversity practice. Clients "do not expect to get something very different from the next client in terms of recommendations." One reason, she says, is that most clients come to the firm precisely because they are at the same early stage of dealing with diversity issues.

Regan says the firm's consultants compose recommendations for clients using a shared word processing file. Similarly, law firms sometimes provide virtually identical memos to different clients facing similar problems, without disclosing that the work has been recycled.[17]

Were the actions of Towers Perrin unethical? Explain. Is there anything wrong with consultants using a shared word processing file from other similar studies to prepare a report? Is this any different from a lawyer giving an identical opinion to different clients for the same problem? Explain.

Usually, researchers are required to present both written and oral reports on the project. These reports should be tailored to the audience. They should begin with a clear, concise statement of the research objectives, followed by a brief and simple but complete explanation of the research design or methodology employed. A summary of the major findings should come next. The conclusion of the report should present recommendations to management.

Most people who enter marketing become research users rather than research suppliers. So they must know what to notice in a report. As with many other items we purchase, quality is not always readily apparent. Nor does a high price guarantee superior quality. The basis for measuring the quality of a marketing research report is the research proposal. Did the report meet the objectives established in the proposal? Was the methodology outlined in the proposal followed? Are the conclusions based on logical deductions from the data analysis? Do the recommendations seem prudent, given the conclusions?

Another criterion is the quality of the writing. Is the style crisp and lucid? It has been said that if readers are offered the slightest opportunity to misunderstand, they probably will. The report should also be as concise as possible.

The vast majority of marketing researchers are highly ethical. That being said, unethical practices and practitioners are sometimes encountered in this profession (as they are in any other). The "Ethics in Marketing" box provides an example.

scanner-based research
A system for gathering information from a single group of respondents by continuously monitoring the advertising, promotion, and pricing they are exposed to and the things they buy.

BehaviorScan
A scanner-based research program that tracks the purchases of 3,000 households through store scanners.

Following Up

The final step in the marketing research process is to follow up. The researcher should determine why management did or did not carry out the recommendations in the report. Was sufficient decision-making information included? What could have been done to make the report more useful to management? A good rapport between the product manager, or whoever authorized the project, and the market researcher is essential. Often they must work together on many studies throughout the year.

Scanner-Based Research

4
Discuss the growing importance of scanner-based research

Scanner-based research is a system for gathering information from a single group of respondents by continuously monitoring the advertising, promotion, and pricing they are exposed to and the things they buy. The variables measured are advertising campaigns, coupons, displays, and product prices. The result is a huge database of marketing efforts and consumer behaviour. Scanner-based research is bringing ever closer the Holy Grail of marketing research: an accurate, objective picture of the direct causal relationship between different kinds of marketing efforts and actual sales.

The two major scanner-based suppliers are Information Resources Incorporated (IRI) and the A.C. Nielsen Company. Each has about half the market. However, IRI is the founder of scanner-based research.

IRI's first product is called **BehaviorScan**. A household panel has been recruited and maintained in each BehaviorScan town. (In total there are 3,000 such panel members.) Panel members shop with an ID card, which they present at the checkout in scanner-equipped grocery stores and drugstores. This card enables IRI to track electronically each household's purchases, item by item, over time. It uses computers to measure TV viewing in each panel household, and can send special commercials to panel member television sets. With such a measure of household purchasing, it is possible to manipulate marketing variables, such as TV advertising or consumer promotions, or to introduce a new product and analyze real changes in consumer buying behaviour.

IRI's most successful product, with sales of over $130 million per year and 740 clients, is InfoScan. InfoScan is a scanner-based sales-tracking service for the consumer packaged-goods industry. Retail sales, detailed consumer purchasing information—including measurement of store loyalty and total grocery basket expenditures—and promotional activity by manufacturers and retailers are monitored and evaluated for all bar-coded products.

Scanner-based research helps marketers identify how successful their marketing efforts actually are. For example, by tracking sample households' purchases, researchers can measure the relationship between an advertising or promotional campaign and actual sales.

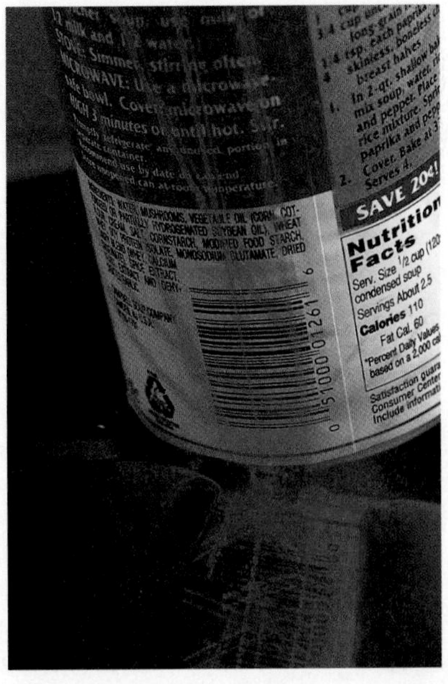

When Should Marketing Research Be Conducted?

5 Explain when marketing research should and should not be conducted

When managers have several possible solutions to a problem, they should not instinctively call for marketing research. In fact, the first decision to make is whether to conduct marketing research at all.

Some companies have been conducting research in certain markets for many years. These firms understand the characteristics of target customers and their likes and dislikes about existing products. In these circumstances, further research would be repetitive and waste money. Procter & Gamble has extensive knowledge of the coffee market. After it conducted initial taste tests with Folgers Instant Coffee, P&G went into national distribution without further research. Consolidated Foods Kitchen of Sara Lee followed the same strategy with its frozen croissants, as did Quaker Oats with Chewy Granola Bars. This tactic does not always work. P&G marketers thought they understood the pain reliever market thoroughly, so they bypassed market research for Encaprin aspirin in capsules. Because it lacked a distinct competitive advantage over existing products, the product failed and was withdrawn from the market.

Managers rarely have such great trust in their own judgment that they would refuse more information if it were available and free. But they might have enough confidence that they would be unwilling to pay very much for the information or wait a long time to receive it. The willingness to acquire additional decision-making information depends on managers' perceptions of its quality, price, and timing. Of course, if perfect information were available—that is, the data conclusively showed which alternative to choose—decision makers would be willing to pay more for it than for information that still left uncertainty. Research should only be undertaken when the expected value of the information is greater than the cost of obtaining it.

LOOKING BACK

Look back at the story about Waltec Faucets that appeared at the beginning of this chapter. A company can use survey research, observations, or experiments to conduct marketing research. Waltec used marketing research (an experiment) to develop a better understanding of how homeowners would react to price changes. This chapter has described a variety of marketing research techniques. In the Waltec example, it might have been possible to use another approach, focus groups, to get the pricing information that Waltec management wanted.

Key marketing data often come from a company's own decision support system, which is constantly gathering data from a variety of sources and funnelling it to decision makers. It then manipulates the data to make better decisions. DSS data are often supplemented by marketing research information.

Summary

1 Explain the concept and purpose of a marketing decision support system. Decision support systems make data instantly available to marketing managers and allow them to manipulate the data themselves to make marketing decisions. Four characteristics of decision support systems make them especially useful to marketing managers: they are interactive, flexible, discovery oriented, and accessible. Decision support systems give managers access to information immediately and without outside assistance. They allow users to manipulate data in a variety of ways and to answer "what if" questions. And, finally, they are accessible to novice computer users.

2 Define marketing research, and explain its importance to marketing decision making. Marketing research is a process of collecting and analyzing data for the purpose of solving specific marketing problems. Marketers use marketing research to explore the profitability of marketing strategies. They can examine why particular strategies failed and analyze characteristics of specific market segments. Managers can use research findings to help keep current customers. Moreover, marketing research allows management to behave proactively rather than reactively by identifying newly emerging patterns in society and the economy.

3 Describe the steps involved in conducting a marketing research project. The marketing research process involves several basic steps. First, the researcher and the decision maker must agree on a problem statement or set of research objectives. The researcher then creates an overall research design to specify how primary data will be gathered and analyzed. Before collecting data, the researcher decides whether the group to be interviewed will be a probability or nonprobability sample. Field service firms are often hired to carry out data collection. Once data have been collected, the researcher analyzes them using statistical analysis. The researcher then prepares and presents oral and written reports, with conclusions and recommendations, to management. As a final step, the researcher determines whether the recommendations were implemented and what could have been done to make the project more successful.

4 Discuss the growing importance of scanner-based research. A scanner-based research system enables marketers to monitor a market panel's exposure and reaction to variables such as advertising, coupons, store displays, packaging, and price. By analyzing these variables in relation to the panel's subsequent buying behaviour, marketers gain useful insights into sales and marketing strategies.

5 Explain when marketing research should and should not be conducted. Marketing research helps managers by providing data to make better marketing decisions. However, firms must consider whether the expected benefits of marketing research outweigh its costs. Before approving a research budget, management also should make sure that adequate decision-making information doesn't already exist.

Discussion and Writing Questions

1. The task of marketing is to create exchanges. What role might marketing research play in facilitating the exchange process?
2. Marketing research has long been associated with manufacturers of consumer goods. Today more and more organizations, both profit and nonprofit, are using marketing research. Why do you think this trend exists? Give some examples.
3. Write a reply to the following statement: "I own a restaurant in the downtown area. I see customers every day whom I know on a first-name basis. I understand their likes and dislikes. If I put something on the menu and it doesn't sell, I know they didn't like it. I also read the magazine *Modern Restaurants*, so I know what the trends are in the industry. This is all the marketing research I need to do."
4. Give an example of (a) the descriptive role of marketing research, (b) the diagnostic role, and (c) the predictive role.
5. Critique the following methodologies and suggest more appropriate alternatives:
   a. A supermarket was interested in determining its image. It dropped a short questionnaire into the grocery bag of each customer before putting in the groceries.
   b. To assess the extent of its trade area, a shopping mall stationed interviewers in the parking lot every Monday and Friday evening.

Do You Know These Terms?

audit 186
BehaviorScan 189
central-location telephone (CLT) facility 179
closed-ended question 184
computer-assisted personal interviewing 178
computer-assisted self-interviewing 178
convenience sample 187
cross-tabulation 189
database marketing 169
decision support system (DSS) 168
experiment 186
field service firm 188
focus group 182
frame error 187
group dynamics 182
mall intercept interview 178
management decision problem 173
marketing intelligence 168
marketing research 169
marketing research objective 173
marketing research problem 173
measurement error 187
nonprobability sample 187
observation research 185
open-ended question 184
primary data 177
probability sample 187
random error 187
random sample 187
recruited Internet sample 181
research design 177
sample 187
sampling error 187
scaled-response question 184
scanner-based research 189
screened Internet sample 181
secondary data 173
survey research 177
uniform reference locator (URL) 175
universe 187
unrestricted Internet sample 180

Interviewers walked up to people after they had parked their cars and asked them for their postal codes.

c. To assess the popularity of a new movie, a major studio invited people to call a 900 number and vote yes, they would see it again, or no, they would not. Each caller was billed a two-dollar charge.

6. You have been charged with determining how to attract more business majors to your school. Write an outline of the steps you would take, including the sampling procedures, to accomplish this task.
7. Why are secondary data sometimes preferred to primary data?
8. In the absence of company problems, is there any reason to develop a marketing decision support system?
9. Discuss when focus groups should and should not be used.
10. Divide the class into teams of eight. Each team will conduct a focus group on the number and quality of services your college or university is providing to its students. One person from each team should be chosen to act as moderator. Remember, it is the moderator's job to facilitate discussion, not to lead discussion. These discussions should last around forty-five minutes. If possible, the groups should be videotaped or recorded. On completion, each team should write a brief report of its results. Consider offering to meet with the dean of students to share the results of your research.
11. Open a Web browser (perhaps Lycos or Yahoo!) and type "marketing research." Out of the thousands of Websites these search words summon, pick one that interests you and report on its content to the class.
12. Why has the Internet been of such great value to researchers seeking secondary data?
13. Go to **www.yankelovich.com**. Explain to the class the nature and scope of the Yankelovich MONITOR. How can marketing researchers use the data from this research?
14. Go to **www.icpsr.umich.edu/gss.** What is the General Social Survey? Compare it with the Yankelovich MONITOR for its usefulness to market researchers.
15. You are interested in home-building trends because your company (Whirlpool) is a major supplier of kitchen appliances. Go to **www.nahb.com** and describe what types of information at this site might be of interest to Whirlpool.
16. What are the advantages and disadvantages of conducting surveys on the Internet?
17. Explain the three types of Internet samples, and discuss why a researcher might choose one over the other.
18. Go to **www.raosoft.com/raosoft** and explain how the company's software lets you distribute questionnaires over the Internet.
19. Go to **www.acop.com** and tell the class about the site and about what type of Internet sample is being drawn. Also, describe the types of surveys being taken.
20. Go to **www.acnielsen.com** and **www.infores.com** and determine what A.C. Nielsen and IRI are saying on the Web about their latest scanner-based technology.
21. Participate in a survey at one of the following URLs, and report your experience to the class:

    GVU Semi-annual Survey on Web Usage
    www.cc.gatech.edu/gvu/user_surveys/
    Personality test
    www.users.interport.net/~zang/personality.html
    Emotional intelligence test
    www.utne.com

Values and Lifestyles (VALS) test
future.sri.com/vals/valshome.html
Various on-line surveys on topics such as politics and consumer trends
www.survey.net
Various surveys
www.dssresearch.com/mainsite/surveys.htm

Application for Small Business

Corinne and Daniel Orset are thinking about opening an independent fast food restaurant specializing in deli-style sandwiches and quiches. Daniel recently ran across some marketing research information, as described here.

Consumers claim that fast service is less important than the convenience of getting to the restaurant in the first place. Twenty-six percent of adults surveyed by Maritz Marketing Research say that a convenient location is the most influential factor in their choice of fast food restaurants. Men are more likely than women to value convenience, by 31 to 23 percent, and younger adults value it more than those over sixty-five.

The thing that average Canadians value most after location is the food itself. Twenty-five percent of respondents say that food quality is the deciding factor in their choice of restaurant. This may mean they consider the food superior, but it could also mean they appreciate the consistency of knowing they'll get the same thing every time, every place. Women, young adults, and seniors are more likely than average to claim that quality is the key ingredient.

Only 12 percent of adults say they make fast food choices based on speed of service, and just 8 percent say price is the key. Adults under twenty-five have lower-than-average incomes and are more likely than those with average incomes to cite price as the most important reason for their restaurant choices.

Middle-aged adults worry less about menu selection, perhaps because they are often accompanied by kids who tend to want the same thing every time. Just 3 percent of those between thirty-five and forty-four claim that their choice is influenced most heavily by children's preferences, yet the presence of offspring may explain why they are less likely than any other age group to care about selection and food quality. They do care about money and time. This age group ranks second after young adults in valuing reasonable prices and second after fifty-five to sixty-four year olds in caring about fast service. The middle-aged are also most likely to make decisions based on brand names—again possibly because of their children.

Questions

1 How might Corinne and Daniel use the preceding information?
2. Is this research performing (a) a descriptive function, (b) a diagnostic function, or (c) a predictive function?
3. Is the preceding research basic or applied? Explain.
4. The above research is part of Maritz Marketing Research's ongoing surveys, which are regularly conducted telephone surveys of a representative sample of 1,000 adults. Visit Maritz's Website at **www.maritz.com/apoll**, and report your findings to the class.

Marketing Research: Science or Hocus Pocus

Accurate and timely information is the lifeblood of marketing decision making. With good information, a company can increase sales and use its resources wisely. But what is the best way to collect good, accurate information?

While marketing is an art, not a science, some aspects of marketing are thought to be more scientific in nature. Marketing research is one of those fields viewed as quite scientific. One of the most important means of gathering marketing research information is consumer surveys. When surveys are used, it is generally assumed by the researcher that survey respondents will give truthful answers to the questions asked. The experience of many researchers suggests, however, that consumers often can't tell or identify their true motivations for purchasing one product over another in the marketplace. As a result, even the most scientifically designed marketing research undertaking may not provide the behavioural information that the study was designed to elicit.

The idea that consumers may not be able to correctly identify purchase motivations has significant implications for marketing managers. If marketing decision makers are misled by the findings from the marketing surveys undertaken, incorrect marketing decisions will be made. Due to the severe consequences of developing and marketing the wrong product, or initiating the wrong promotional campaign, it is important for marketing managers to know what consumers truly feel and think.

To get around the problems inherent in trying to elicit feelings that survey respondents might not be able to give, market researchers have long used approaches other than direct questions. With regard to print advertising, packaging design, and other promotional elements, for example, rather than question people about feelings or interest in different parts of an ad or promotional piece, market research firms have used eye cameras. The eye camera records movements of the eye. It is used to determine which parts of a newspaper or magazine page are read first, or the order and amount of time an individual spends looking at the various parts of an advertisement or package, or which of two competing stimuli receives the most attention.

Another device, the pupilometric camera, photographs eye movements of a different nature and for a different purpose. The dilation and restriction of the pupils has been found to correlate with the degree of interest aroused by visual stimuli. More interesting stimuli result in the dilation of the pupils. An advertisement or a package that is of more interest to the viewer will cause dilation of the pupils, even if the subject is not conscious of this fact.

Yet another device, the psychogalvanometer, is used for measuring an individual's response to a product, package, or advertisement. The principle involved is that the perspiration rate of the body is increased by excitement. The amount of interest or excitement provided by a product or advertisement can, therefore, be measured by recording changes in the perspiration rate. The psychogalvanometer can also be used to measure whether subjects have an emotional reaction to brand names, slogans, or even political candidates.

What else can be done to identify unconscious motivations? Market researchers have long used depth interviews. These are long, probing interviews with one question building on another to delve as deeply as possible into the respondent's motivations. Psychologists, trying to delve deeply into patients' thoughts, have used another approach, hypnosis. Hypnosis, an artificially induced state, is now being used in marketing research as well. As consumers aren't always aware of their true feelings and motives, hypnosis might be used to help subjects explain their real reasons for choosing one product over another. It might also be used to uncover those hidden or subconscious emotions that drive our purchasing behaviour.

According to Hypnosis Insights, a marketing research firm that uses hypnosis on their clients, "Hypnosis shows that consumers or business buyers are more than objective, rational problem solvers—they have essential emotional, sensual aspects to their decision making. Often their choices are much more emotional and impulsive than rational. Properly conducted hypnosis focus groups and personal interviews get people to articulate latent, or underlying, motives, revealing powerful themes and benefits for marketing strategies and advertising campaigns" (see **www.hypnosisinsights.com/whyuse.html**).

Many large firms are using hypnosis in their marketing research. Two examples are Shell Oil and Dewar's Scotch. Most companies, however, don't want it known that they're using this form of research.

Source:
CBC, *Undercurrents,* "Inside Information," January 21, 2001.

Questions

1. What do you think of using hypnosis for collecting marketing research on consumer buying motivations?
2. What might be the benefits of using hypnosis over other forms of marketing research?
3. Why do you think that most companies using hypnosis in their research don't want it generally known?
4. Should market researchers be able to use truth serum drugs, as well as hypnosis, in their efforts to get at true consumer motivations?
5. Check out the Website for Hypnosis Insights (**www.hypnosisinsights.com**). What can you learn about the use of market research using hypnosis from this Website?

CHAPTER

8

LEARNING OBJECTIVES

After studying this chapter, you should be able to

1. Describe the concept of competitive advantage and the three types of competitive advantages
2. Discuss the concept of competitive intelligence
3. Identify the sources of internal competitive intelligence data
4. Identify the non-computer-based external sources of competitive intelligence
5. Explain how the Internet and databases can be used to gather competitive intelligence
6. Discuss the problem of industrial espionage

COMPETITIVE INTELLIGENCE

Richard Teerlink is CEO of one of the most storied brands in the history of business—Harley-Davidson. Customer research drives Harley's strategy. Harley's customers aren't merely buyers of its bikes; they feel like part of the company. "There's a high degree of emotion that drives our success," says Teerlink. "We symbolize the feelings of freedom and independence that people really want in this stressful world." Because of these emotional links to the brand, customers tend to be extremely loyal. Even though the company has boosted capacity, Harley's insistence on top quality means that customers have to wait for bikes. Still, they rarely bolt for the nearest foreign motorcycle dealer to buy a high-speed machine. If anything, scarcity has added to the brand's mystique. To help customers quell their cravings, Harley slaps its logo on merchandise from deodorant to throw pillows.

Harley owners are a diverse bunch, from CEOs to construction workers. How could the company talk to them all? "We needed to give people a reason to use our products, and we needed to be there with them," says Teerlink. So Harley created Harley Owners Groups—HOGs, for short. There are now nearly 360,000 HOG group members, and local chapters organize frequent road rallies. Teerlink and other executives get to as many rallies as possible, and they always carry a pad and pencil. Why? Well, a great new idea might pop up. In the 1970s a rider approached the company about some design changes, and the bikes that emerged as a result are today among Harley's most sought-after models.[1]

Competitive advantages are the key to Harley's long-term success. What is a competitive advantage? What types of competitive advantages has Harley achieved? What role does competitive intelligence play in creating a sustainable competitive advantage? What are the sources of competitive intelligence?

Harley Davidson

Want to learn more about Harley Davidson's competitive advantages? Go to

www.harley-davidson.com

on line

Competitive Advantage

1

Describe the concept of competitive advantage and the three types of competitive advantages

A **competitive advantage**, also called a differential advantage, is the unique features of a company and its products that are perceived by the target market as significant and superior to the competition. It is the factors that cause customers to patronize a firm rather than its competition.

competitive advantage
The unique features of a company and its products that are perceived by the target market as significant and superior to the competition.

Cost Competitive Advantage

There are three types of competitive advantages: cost, product/service differentiation, and niche strategies. Cost leadership can result from obtaining inexpensive raw materials, creating an efficient scale of plant operations, designing products for ease of manufacture, controlling overhead costs, and avoiding marginal customers. DuPont, for example, has an exceptional cost competitive advantage in the production of titanium dioxide. Technicians created a production process using low-cost feedstock, giving DuPont a 20 percent cost advantage over its competitors. The cheaper feedstock technology is complex and can only be accomplished by investing about $100 million and several years of testing time. Having a **cost competitive advantage** means being the low-cost competitor in an industry while maintaining satisfactory profit margins.

cost competitive advantage
Being the low-cost competitor in an industry while maintaining satisfactory profit margins.

A cost competitive advantage enables a firm to deliver superior customer value. Wal-Mart, through its system of regional warehouses and its sophisticated system of electronic information exchange with suppliers, has achieved a significant cost advantage over competitors. Fort Howard Paper's differential advantage lies in its cost-saving manufacturing process. Fort Howard Paper uses only recycled pulp, rather than the more expensive virgin pulp, to make toilet paper and other products. However, the quality of its product is acceptable only to the commercial market—office buildings, hotels, restaurants, and the like. The company does not try to sell to the home market through grocery stores.

Sources of Cost Differential Advantages

Costs can be reduced in a variety of ways. For example, companies can utilize experience curves, use labour more efficiently, provide no-frills goods and services, arrange government subsidies, change product designs, re-engineer their plant, and/or develop new products and new ways of delivering them. Each of these approaches is discussed below.

Experience Curves **Experience curves** tell us that costs decline at a predictable rate as experience with a given product increases (see Exhibit 8.1). With many products, unit costs fall—usually by 20 to 30 percent—as production output doubles. This holds across a broad range of manufacturing, marketing, and administrative costs. Experience curves reflect learning by doing, technological advances, and economies of scale. Firms like Bombardier and Texas Instruments use historical experience curves as a basis for predicting and setting prices. Experience curves allow managers to forecast costs and set prices based on anticipated costs as opposed to current costs.

experience curves
Curves that show costs declining at a predictable rate as experience with a product increases.

Efficient Labour To lower their costs, many companies establish their factories near pools of cheap labour. Magna, Canada's largest auto parts company, has opened plants in Mexico to take advantage of lower-cost labour. In low-skill, labour-intensive industries such as product assembly and apparel manufacturing, labour can be an important component of total costs. Many manufacturers, including Nike, Levi Strauss, and Liz Claiborne, have gone offshore to achieve cheaper manufacturing costs. Many companies are also outsourcing activities such as data entry and other labour-intensive jobs. Other firms are hiring temporary workers, from engineers and systems analysts to production workers and truck drivers, to hold down labour costs.

exhibit 8.1

An Experience Curve

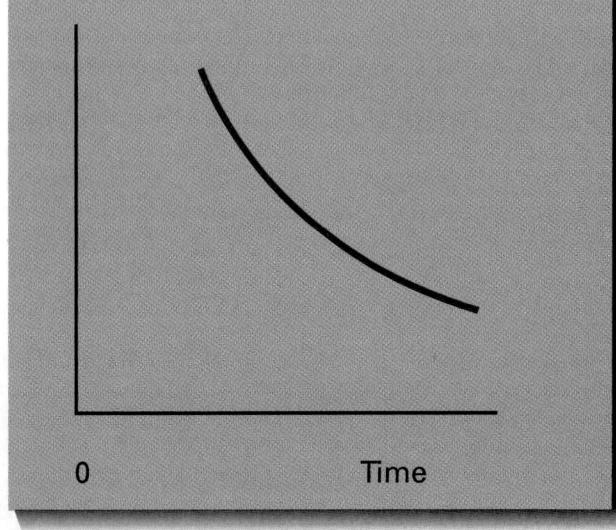

No-Frills Goods and Services Marketers can reduce costs by removing frills and options from a product or service. On many routes, WestJet Airlines offers low fares but no seat assignments or meals. Low prices give WestJet a higher load factor and greater economies of scale; this results in even lower prices.

Government Subsidies Some governments—Japan's is one—routinely provide grants and interest-free loans to "target" industries. Government assistance enabled Japanese semiconductor manufacturers to become global leaders. When a company receives a subsidy, its production costs are in effect lowered by the amount of the subsidy. Bombardier Inc. has received billions of dollars in low-interest loans from the Canada Account, which was set up by the Ministry of Trade and the Ministry of Finance to help Canadian companies bidding on very large contracts. As a result, Bombardier was able to win contracts totalling over $4 billion with Air Wisconsin and Northwest Airlines.[2]

Product Design BMW is a world leader in designing cars for ease of manufacture and assembly. This helps the company offset Germany's high labour costs. Reverse engineering is the process of disassembling a product piece by piece to learn what its components are and how it was manufactured. Reverse engineering a low-cost competitor's product can save research and design costs. Japanese engineers have reversed many North American high-tech products.

Re-engineering Re-engineering to make firms more efficient often leads to downsizing or layoffs of employees. It is especially common in mature industries such as steel and machine parts, and in highly competitive industries such as airlines and telecommunications. Re-engineering can also mean pruning product lines, closing obsolete factories, and renegotiating contracts with suppliers. DaimlerChrysler has recently closed five assembly plants and asked its suppliers to re-engineer parts to reduce costs by 15 percent.

Production Innovations Production innovations such as new technology and simplified production techniques help lower the average cost of production. Technologies such as computer-aided design and computer-aided manufacturing

VIA Rail

For VIA Rail, how important are new methods of service delivery? Examine its "Schedules, Fares and Reservations" link and its travel planner guides and VIA Adventures. Is VIA Rail doing a good job promoting on-line travel arrangements? Explain.

www.viarail.ca

on line

(CAD/CAM) and increasingly sophisticated robots help companies like Bombardier, Honda, and General Electric reduce their manufacturing costs.

New Methods of Service Delivery Medical expenses have been substantially lowered by the use of outpatient surgery and walk-in clinics. Transportation companies like Canadian Airlines and VIA Rail are lowering reservation and ticketing costs by encouraging passengers to use the Internet to book trips and by promoting "ticketless travel."

Reverse engineering can be an effective way to learn a competitor's manufacturing process. It can also result in savings in R&D.

Cost Competitive Advantages Are Rarely Sustainable

Companies very much enjoy achieving a cost-competitive advantage. However, few companies can maintain one in the long term. After all, those advantages are equally available to the competition—for example, technology is transferable. Bell Labs invented fiber-optic cable, which dramatically increased the number of calls that could be transmitted simultaneously through a two-inch cable and thereby reduced the cost of voice and data transmission. Within five years, fiber-optic technology had spread through the industry. Note also that for almost all production processes and product categories, there are alternative suppliers. Over time, high-cost purchasers tend to seek out lower-cost suppliers; ultimately, this enables them to compete more effectively with the industry's low-cost producers.

Differentiation Competitive Advantages

Cost competitive advantages are subject to continual erosion; differential competitive advantages tend to last longer. Because a differential competitive advantage tends to be more durable, many top managers find this strategy more attractive. A product/service **differential competitive advantage** exists when a firm provides something unique (other than a uniquely low price) that is attractive to buyers. Generally, differential advantages relate to brand (Lexus), a strong dealer network (Caterpillar Tractor), product reliability (Maytag), image (Calvin Klein), or

differential competitive advantage
The advantage achieved when a firm provides something that is unique and valuable to buyers beyond simply offering a lower price than the competition.

A product or service with a differential competitive advantage is able to offer consumers a unique and valuable benefit other than a low price. Maytag's reliability has given that company an enduring differential advantage. www.maytag.com

service (Federal Express). Arthur Doppelmayer, an Austrian manufacturer of aerial transport systems, believes that his main differential advantage—besides innovative equipment design—is his service system. This advantage allows his company to come to the assistance of users within twenty-four hours anywhere in the world. Doppelmayer has a worldwide network of warehouses, and his skilled personnel are prepared to respond immediately in emergencies. Similarly, the Japanese service network of Heidelberger Druckmaschinen, the world leader in offset printing, is as comprehensive as Heidelberger's service network in the German home market. The head of the Heidelberger Druckmaschinen subsidiary in Tokyo noted: "How could we afford to offer an inferior service here?"

A brand name with a long-established aura of quality and value offers enduring competitive advantages. Coca-Cola, Leica, BMW, and Breitling stand for quality throughout the world. Continual product and marketing innovation enables these organizations to enhance their differential advantage.

Value Impressions A differential advantage can also be created through **value impressions**. These are features of a product or service that signal value to the customer. A foil package often connotes luxury. The shape of the Joy perfume bottle says "quality" and "exclusivity." Dom Perignon champagne comes in its own special box. Quality sales personnel, such as those found at Harry Rosen, also help create value impressions. Even Wal-Mart's slogan, "Everday Low Prices," leaves an impression of value.

value impressions
The features of a product or service that signal value to the customer.

Augmented Products An augmented product represents another tool for differentiation. When a company adds features to a good or service not expected by the customer, that good or service is referred to as an **augmented product**. When Oscar Mayer took the commodity items of lunch meat, cheese, and crackers and packaged them as "Lunchables," it created an augmented product. When Compaq offers "total computer system solutions," it is selling an augmented product. Sony's efforts to make minicams smaller and more portable have resulted in augmented products. Products that offer "less of something" such as calories, fat, sugar, or alcohol content also can be considered augmented products.

augmented product
A product or service developed when a company adds features not expected by the customer.

The founders of Three Blondes and a Brownie Inc. have been successful in their niche marketing strategy to produce low-fat muffins and brownies. The company sells its Fat-Wise™ products through its distributors across Canada.

Niche Competitive Advantage

A company that has targeted a single segment of the market and intends to serve it well is seeking a **niche competitive advantage**. For small companies with limited resources that potentially face giant competitors, niching may be the only viable option. A market segment that has good growth potential but is not crucial to the success of major competitors is a good candidate for a niche strategy. Once a potential segment has been identified, the firm needs to make certain it can defend the segment against challengers through its superior ability to serve buyers in the segment. Pea-in-the-Pod is a small chain of retail stores that sells clothes for pregnant mothers. Its quality materials, innovative designs, and reasonable prices serve as a barrier against competition.

Many companies using a niche strategy serve only a limited geographic market. Migros is the dominant grocery chain in Switzerland. It has no stores outside that small country. Some companies specialize in a limited range of products—Office Max in office supplies, for example.

niche competitive advantage
The advantage achieved when a firm seeks to target and serve effectively a small segment of the market.

Block Drug Company uses niching by focusing its product line on tooth products. It markets Polident for cleaning false teeth, Poligrip for holding false teeth, and Sensodyne toothpaste for people with sensitive teeth. The Orvis Company manufactures and sells everything that a fly fisherman could ever need. Orvis is a very successful nicher. Three Blondes and a Brownie Inc. of Edmonton (which was founded by three blond women) makes only low-fat cakes and muffins. This company has grown from less than $100,000 in sales in 1994 to over $5 million in 2000, and has opened a second manufacturing plant in Toronto.

Building Tomorrow's Competitive Advantage

The notion of competitive advantage means that a successful firm will stake out a position that is unique in some way relative to that of its rivals. A company that merely imitates its competitors almost certainly lacks a competitive advantage and almost inevitably will perform poorly. Moreover, competitors rarely stand still, so a company that does no more than imitate others will almost certainly find itself trapped in an endless game of catch-up, and will be surprised repeatedly by the accomplishments of its rivals. In a survey of business managers, nearly 80 percent believed that quality would be a fundamental competitive advantage in the new century. In a similar survey in Japan, barely half of Japanese business managers agreed; they saw their main goal as creating new products and businesses.[3] Does this mean that Japanese managers feel that quality is not significant? Absolutely not. It merely indicates that in the future, quality will be the price of market entry, rather than a major source of competitive advantage. Japanese managers well understand that tomorrow's competitive advantages will be different from today's.

Companies need to build their own competitive advantages rather than copy those of their competitors. The sources of tomorrow's competitive advantages are the skills and assets of the organization. *Assets* include patents, copyrights, locations, and technologies that are superior to those of the competition. *Skills* are the functions (e.g., customer service, promotion) that a firm performs better than its competitors. Swissair is well known for its customer service. Marketing managers should continually focus the firm's skills and assets on sustaining and creating competitive advantages. The following questions are helpful: Are the companies skills as assets:

NutraSweet
Stevia

What kind of competitive intelligence could NutraSweet do on-line to assess the threat posed by Stevia, a company that produces a natural, noncaloric sweetener called Stevia? What kind of CI could Stevia do to make inroads into NutraSweet's market share?

www.nutrasweet.com; www.stevia.net

on line

1. ... defined with respect to the competition?
2. ... likely to result in a competitive advantage?
3. ... relevant to the market?
4. ... feasible and cost effective?
5. ... going to result in a sustainable competitive advantage?
6. ... appropriate to the future?

Remember, how long a company can sustain its competitive advantage depends on how quickly competitors can imitate its strategy and plans. Imitation requires a competitor to identify the leader's competitive advantage, determine how it was achieved, and then learn how to duplicate it.

Competitive Intelligence

2
Discuss the concept of competitive intelligence

Competitive intelligence is an important tool for helping firms overcome a competitor's advantage. Specifically, competitive intelligence can help identify the advantage and determine how the advantage was achieved.

Competitive intelligence (CI) involves creating a system that helps managers assess their competitors and their vendors in order to become more efficient and

one-to-one marketing

MyVirtualModel.com Helps Landsend.com Leap over a Prime Web-Shopping Hurdle

Clothing retailers have long viewed the Internet with a mixture of longing and exasperation. The Web provides the chance to sell direct to customers at low cost, but it is difficult to provide them with a realistic enough experience to persuade them to buy without seeing and touching. Some emerging trends are changing that, and growing on-line sales by leaps and bounds.

Driving on-line clothing sales is a burgeoning customer base that's becoming more female and more at ease with Internet shopping. According to IT consulting firm Cap Gemini Ernst & Young, women now comprise 60 percent of on-line buyers in the United States, and 50 percent of on-line buyers in Canada and Australia.

Mail order firm Lands' End has proved that the problem of achieving the right on-line presence is not insurmountable. Its "virtual model" technology helped Internet sales grow by almost 60 percent in the first year after launch.

The technology is from Montreal-based My Virtual Model, which was founded in 2000 and is considered the leading developer of software that lets consumers create and store a virtual version of themselves. Shoppers can visit the partner retailer Website or the myvirtualmodel.com Website and enter their exact measurements and other personal data to build a virtual image of themselves. They can then try clothing on their model, obtain style advice, and make alterations to the model when gaining or losing weight. Working with partner companies such as Landsend.com and Limitedtoo.com, online shoppers can now "try on" clothes right at the Website.

At Landsend.com, those who use My Virtual Model are 19 percent more likely to purchase items and have a 16 percent higher average order value than those who don't use it.

My Virtual Model's software is innovative and has attracted some fairly significant corporate customers, and for company CEO Louise Guay, that spells growth.

What other problems in e-commerce does this type of software help solve?

How might companies such as Lands' End use the Virtual Model data they collect to further enhance the customer experience?

In what other ways is the use of My Virtual Model a competitive advantage for companies such as Lands' End?

Source: Ebusinessforum.com., 4 June 2001.

Faced with an expiring patent for aspartame, NutraSweet used CI to head off any attempts by other companies to erode its market share. The company used the competitive information it gathered to cut costs and improve service. This enabled it to preserve over 80 percent of its market. www.nutrasweet.com

effective. Intelligence is analyzed information. It becomes decision-making intelligence when it has implications for the organization. Say that company A, a primary competitor, has plans to introduce a product with performance standards equal to those of company B but with a 15 percent cost advantage. The new product will reach the market in eight months. This intelligence has important decision-making and policy consequences for company B. Competitive intelligence and environmental scanning (i.e., company B gathers data about the external environment—see Chapter 2) combine to create marketing intelligence. Marketing intelligence is then used as input into a marketing decision support system (see Chapter 7).

Advantages of Competitive Intelligence

CI is one of the hottest areas in marketing today. Many firms, including General Motors, Ford, GTW, P&G Industries, Magna International, Bombardier, and Motorola, have large, well-established CI units. The Ford Taurus was developed after Ford engineers, aided by CI, examined competitors' cars and incorporated the best features of those into one of their own.

competitive intelligence (CI)
An intelligence system that helps managers assess their competition and their vendors in order to become more efficient and effective competitors.

CI helps managers assess their competition and their vendors. This means fewer surprises. CI allows managers to predict changes in business relationships, identify marketplace opportunities, guard against threats, forecast a competitor's strategy, discover new or potential competitors, learn from the success or failure of others, learn about new technologies that can affect the company, and learn about the impact of government regulations on the competition. All of this promotes effective and efficient decision making, which should lead to greater profitability. Sheena Sharp of Sharp Information Research says: "CI gives the company the competitive advantage of foresight and allows it to learn today what will be discovered by others tomorrow."[4]

Several years ago, NutraSweet's patent on the artificial sweetener aspartame was expiring, and the company faced potential disaster. Management was afraid that chemical and food companies would move into the market. NutraSweet analyzed competitors' prices, customer relations, expansion plans, and advertising campaigns. The company used the resulting information to cut costs, improve service, and preserve most of its market. "We maintained over 80 percent of our market," said NutraSweet Co.'s Robert E. Flynn. He added that competitive intelligence practices are worth $50 million a year to his company.

Sources of Internal Competitive Intelligence

3
Identify the sources of internal competitive intelligence data

Many of the sources of data discussed in Chapter 7 can also be used effectively to develop competitive intelligence. Because some of these sources have already been described, we will allude to them only briefly here and in the next two sections, and only from a CI perspective.

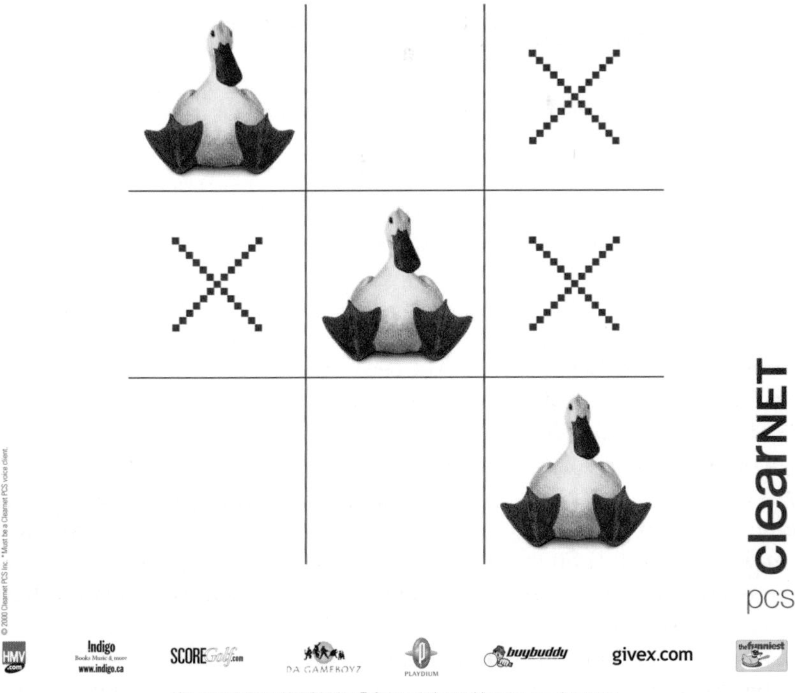

TELUS Corporation's CI group has successfully studied its competition and helped the company become one of Canada's leading telecommunications providers.

It is sales personnel who are best placed to gather CI on a daily basis. They are well positioned to directly observe and ask questions about the competition. Kindred Industries of Midland, Ontario, the largest manufacturer of stainless steel sinks in Canada, found out that a competitor from France, Franke, was entering the Canadian market only after a Kindred salesperson saw a Franke price list on a buyer's desk. The best way to systematically gather CI from the sales force is to formalize the process.

At one very successful packaged goods company, the salespeople are required to fill in a comprehensive form after each sales visit. The form asks for details on rival brands, special promotions, point-of-sale displays, and other merchandising initiatives. At the end of each day, the reports are e-mailed to company headquarters. There they are entered into the company's mainframe computer. Within a day of being filed, the reports are reviewed by top management.

And don't forget about the rest of your company's employees. It is quite likely that your engineering people know something about the engineering capabilities of your competitors. Similarly, your finance and accounting people know something about the financial position of your competitors, and your human resources people know something about their HR activities, and so on. Make sure you tap into the knowledge of *all* of your employees.

CI audit
A competitive intelligence audit of (a) employees, by their type of expertise, (b) independent in-house databases, and (c) marketing research studies available internally.

Companies can uncover internal sources of CI by conducting a CI audit. A **CI audit** should cover the following:

exhibit 8.2

Non-Computer-Based External Sources of Competitive Intelligence

Experts	Newspapers and other publications
CI consultants	Yellow Pages
Government agencies	Trade shows
UCC filings	Speeches by competitors
Suppliers	Neighbours of competitors
Photographs	Advisory boards

- Employees, by areas of expertise such as competitor knowledge, technical competence, market understanding, and other expertise.
- Independent databases maintained on non-network computers.
- Collections of marketing research studies.

CI directory
CI audit data entered into a database management file.

Audit data can then be entered into a database management file, and eventually sorted. The result will be an in-house **CI directory**, cross-indexed by expertise and other topics of interest.

TELUS Corporation, the large Edmonton telecommunications company, was one of the first companies in Canada to establish a CI department. That department is now headed by Carmen Leibel, a 1991 business graduate from the University of Regina. The mission of the TELUS CI group? To learn everything possible about the firm's competitors. For Leibel that means spending many hours studying competitors' product literature and scanning databases and many evenings talking with executives of rival firms. On one occasion, Leibel pulled together enough information to construct a complete profit-and-loss statement on a firm that thought its financial results were private. On another, she pieced together an extensive biography to ascertain whether a rival CEO's past behaviour marked him as a risk taker.[5]

Good information on competitors can be gathered in many ways. When Marriott wanted to enter the economy segment of the hotel market, it sent its CI employees in teams to visit economy hotel chains. Those teams registered in the competitor hotels, where they proceeded to examine the soap, shampoo, towels, and other amenities in the rooms; call the hotel's front desk to request special services; and make loud noises to see if they could be heard in adjacent rooms. Partly on the basis of the information its teams had gathered, Marriott budgeted $500 million to develop Fairfield Inn, which beat the competition in every respect, from soap to service to soundproof rooms, and has been highly successful.

Other internal sources of CI include warranty cards, returned merchandise forms, repair records, customer order files, back order reports, trade show inquiries, accounts receivable histories, and literature requests based on company advertisements, as well as company personnel. Each of these sources can reveal tidbits of CI. If a firm has a large back order for a particular product, it may indicate that its competitors are having a difficult time marketing a similar competing product. CI would then be used to try to determine why this is happening.

Non-Computer-Based External Sources of Competitive Intelligence

4
Identify the non-computer-based external sources of competitive intelligence

Finding external sources of CI is not difficult if one knows where to look. Exhibit 8.2 lists a number of common sources of CI. Each of these is discussed below.

Experts

An **expert** is simply someone with in-depth knowledge of a subject or activity. Experts can be found in a variety of places. Editors and staff writers at technical and trade publications are often quite knowledgeable about a particular field. If you worked in CI for Dell Computer you might want to contact David Kirkpatrick of *Fortune* magazine, who recently wrote an article on the many challenges facing Compaq Computer.[6]

expert
Someone with in-depth knowledge of a subject or activity.

Hands-on experts include people as diverse as computer programmers, systems engineers, master chefs, financial analysts, and fashion designers. These people thoroughly understand their area of expertise. By talking with them, a CI interviewer can usually gather details not found elsewhere. University professors and book authors also have a deep and solid understanding of their fields. To find the names, addresses, and phone numbers of companies, consult Dun & Bradstreet's *Million Dollar Directory*, Standard & Poor's *Register*, or the *Canadian Key Business Directory*. These sources and others can all be found in the library. Once you have a company's address and phone number, you can try to get the information you need by calling its public affairs or public relations office. If the people there don't have the answer, they should be able to refer you to someone who does.

exhibit 8.3

An Advertisement Promoting CI from the Society of Competitive Intelligence Professionals

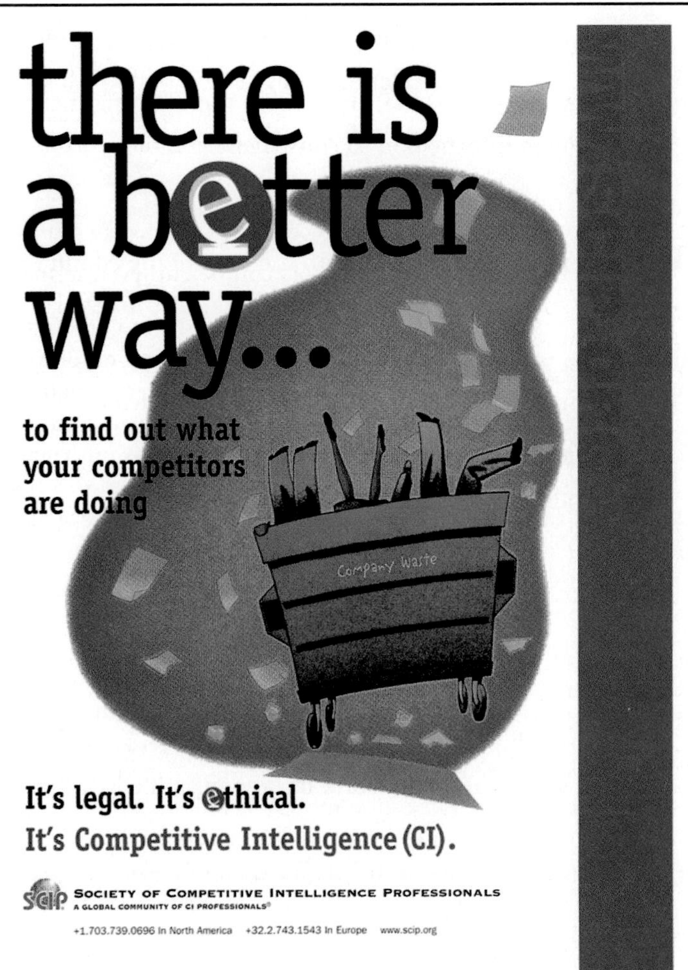

Professional CI consultants use their experience to gather information quickly, so they may be the best resource for learning what the competition is up to. Visit www.scip.org to learn more about CI professionals.
Courtesy Society of Competitive Intelligence Professionals

On-line Yellow Pages

Can you see any advantages to using the on-line Yellow Pages over the traditional Yellow Pages? If so, what are they? If not, why not? Go to the Yahoo! Yellow Pages to find out.

www.yahoo.com

on line

CI Consultants

CI consultants use their experience and expertise to gather needed information quickly and efficiently. Moreover, they know where to find the information or how to extract it. At one company, a manager wanted to confirm that a competitor was experiencing delays in rolling out a new frozen-food product. He hired a CI consultant, who chose to call the competitor directly. The consultant used an interview format to speak with the product manager of the division. That interview went as follows:

> *Interviewer:* "Judd Smith from the Grocer's Association told me you're the expert when it comes to your company's frozen foods." (Rapport-building statement)
> *Source:* "How can I help you?"
> *Interviewer:* "When do you think your new product is going to be available?" (Direct question)
> *Source:* "Not for a while yet."
> *Interviewer:* "Not for a while?" (Restatement)
> *Source:* "Well, we've got some packaging delays ..."
> *Interviewer:* "That's too bad. Do you think it will be ready by March?" (Bracketing)
> *Source:* "Maybe not March, but definitely by May."[7]

The rumour was confirmed. Information about CI professionals can be obtained from the Society of Competitive Intelligence Professionals at **www.scip.org** (see Exhibit 8.3). In Canada there are eight chapters of the Society of Competitive Intelligence Professionals.

Government Agencies

In many parts of the world, governments assist domestic businesses with CI gathering. The French government, with the help of the country's national intelligence agency, runs an ambitious commercial intelligence program. At the behest of the French government, Air France reportedly bugged first-class seats (generally occupied by high-flying business executives) and employed state intelligence operatives as first-class crew.[8] This would be illegal in Canada.

As noted in the previous chapter, Statistics Canada is an excellent source of business data. Especially valuable sources of business information, by product and industry classifications, include the *Census of Manufacturers, Bibliography of Federal Data Sources, Current Publication Index, Historical Catalogue of Statistics Canada Publications,* and many special reports published by the agency. For example, the *Census of Manufacturers* lists Canada's manufacturing firms by size, industry, and value of shipments. Special reports that would be of interest to companies in, say, the transportation industry include *Bus and Urban Transit Statistics* (catalogue number 52-215), *Road Motor Vehicles* (catalogue number 53-219) and *Trucking in Canada* (catalogue number 53-222). Most Statistics Canada publications can now be found through CANSIM, the agency's computerized database.

The province of Quebec created a program called Competitive Intelligence Networks with an initial investment of $7.7 million. At the heart of the program are thirteen "networks," or information services, each covering a specific business sector, such as chemicals or lumber. For each of these industries, expert researchers scour patents, international conference proceedings, specialized magazines, and databases. All of the information gathered is eventually turned into reports.

The goal of this CI project is to encourage Quebec companies to keep abreast of the latest technology. Reports produced by the expert researchers can be purchased for less than $100. If companies want greater detail or additional information, they can hire the experts who put together the original reports.[9]

U.S. government agencies and departments are valuable sources of American CI data. Especially useful are the Occupational Safety and Health Administration (OSHA), the Environmental Protection Agency (EPA), the Federal Communications Commission (FCC), and the Food and Drug Administration (FDA). Under the Freedom of Information Act (FOIA), schematics and source suppliers for many devices that may interfere with radio frequencies—from telephones to microwaves—are available from the FCC. Some OSHA inspection reports reveal critical manufacturing details—often including the machinery involved. EPA regulations require some companies to file reports that indicate production volumes and technologies used. The U.S. Department of Commerce publishes a series of *Current Industrial Reports.* These booklets offer timely data on production, inventories, and orders for approximately 5,000 products representing 40 percent of all American manufacturing. The Securities and Exchange Commission (SEC) is an excellent source for financial information about competitors. Publicly traded companies must file highly detailed reports of their performance and expected risks. Most of these are now available on CD-ROM or through the Internet.

Uniform Commercial Code Filings

Uniform Commercial Code (UCC) filings identify goods that are leased or pledged as collateral. These filings are made by banks or other lending institutions at the local government level. UCC filings are an excellent means for learning about a company's latest additions to plant assets. In one situation, a food-packaging company couldn't understand how a rival was consistently undercutting its prices by 10 percent, and asked a CI firm for help. Through UCC filings, the CI consultant discovered that the competitor's depreciation charges were just 3 percent of sales, compared to 7 percent for its client. A trip to the local Building Department yielded the architectural plans for the rival's plants, as well as the name and phone number of the manufacturer of its machinery. A call to the manufacturer revealed that the company had devised a way to use cheaper machinery in a simpler configuration, which enabled it to reduce its depreciation charges and also its prices.[10]

Uniform Commercial Code (UCC) filings
Filings by banks with government agencies that identify goods that are leased or pledged as collateral.

Suppliers

Unless they have signed a nondisclosure agreement, suppliers will often provide information on products shipped to a competitor. It is easy to estimate a competitor's volume of lipstick production if the tube supplier will tell you how many cases of tubes per month it ships to the competitor's manufacturing facility. One of Procter & Gamble's competitors learned the exact launch date of a concentrated detergent in Europe after a CI consultant visited the factory where a packing machine for the detergent was being made. The delivery date for the machine held the key. Deborah Sawyer, owner of Information Plus of Toronto, a Canadian CI firm, was able to determine the volume of production of a pharmaceutical company's product by discovering the volume of ingredients shipped to the company by its suppliers.[11]

Photographs

It is often said that a picture is worth a thousand words. One firm used a helicopter to take pictures of a rival's manufacturing plant. The firm was trying to decide whether to put more money into an unprofitable elevator division. The key was to figure out what the competition might do. The aerial photos helped determine the competitor's plant capacity, number of employees, and number of shift changes. Trucks with signage helped identify suppliers. As well, on-line databases helped the CI professional construct the competitor's financial statements. In the end it was determined that the competitor had a lower-cost advantage because it offered fewer product options. The CEO, acting on this CI, cut 90 percent of the company's product line and consolidated plants. Profits soared.[12]

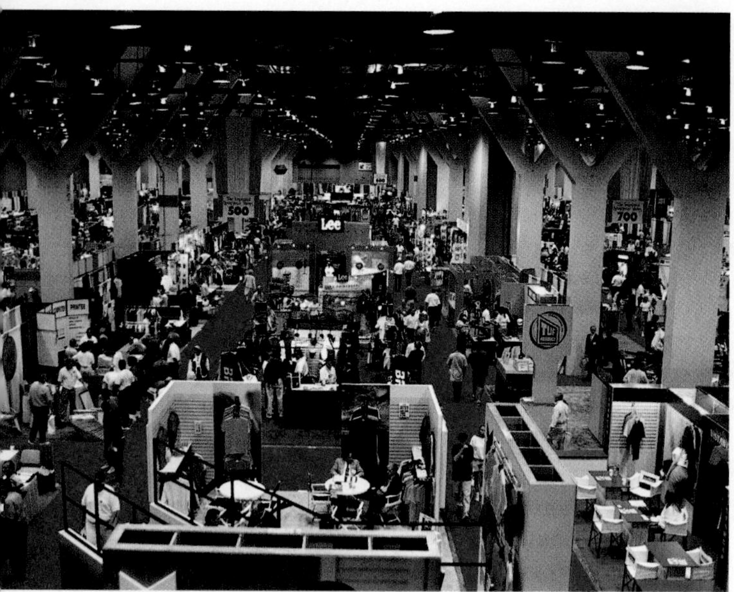

Trade shows are a good source of competitive intelligence. CI professionals can collect sales literature and product brochures, check prices, identify new products, and talk with suppliers.

Newspapers and Other Publications

Newspapers such as the *The Globe and Mail* and *The Financial Post* print timely stories on firms' successes, failures, opportunities, and threats. Business periodicals such as *Canadian Business, Fortune, Canada Commerce,* and *Advertising Age* do the same. Newspaper clipping services scan daily newspapers from around the country and clip all articles on specified topics.

Also, directories can provide a wealth of data. Some excellent directories for CI information are the *Canadian Book of Corporate Management, Blue Book of Canadian Business, Canadian Key Business Directory, Canadian Trade Index, Fraser's Canadian Trade Directory, Scott's Directories* (one for each province), and the *Thomas Register of Canadian Manufacturers.*

Yellow Pages

The Yellow Pages are one of the cheapest and easiest ways to obtain sources of CI. They can be used for CI in the following ways:

- *To locate the number of competitors in a particular market:* For example, under the heading Discount Stores, you can locate all Zellers and Wal-Mart stores in a trading area.
- *To define a realistic trading area:* If you are based on the West Coast and are asked to research a company in the East, how are you to know what a realistic trading area is for that target company? The Yellow Pages for your target's city will provide a map for that trading area.
- *To locate suppliers and distributors:* Let's say you have to locate suppliers for a glass company. You already know that in the glass industry, suppliers of sand, coal, and scrap are situated near the manufacturing plants. The Yellow Pages will provide you with a comprehensive list of these suppliers—some of which probably deal with the target company.
- *To retrieve marketing and product line information*: Take a close look at your typical Yellow Pages display advertisement. It is a highly informative document, almost resembling a miniature D&B credit report. It may list, besides the company's name and address, its product line, the year it was established, its marketing message, and the image it wishes to project to its customers.
- *To determine industry size:* Run your finger down a Yellow Pages column for any category and you will gain a good idea of industry size in the region (i.e., the number of companies and competitors in the market).
- *To understand industry terminology and check your search:* Whenever you search an industry for competitors, suppliers, or any related companies, you want to make sure you haven't left out any categories. Most Yellow Pages now have a fairly thorough cross-index at the back of each volume. Using the cross-index ensures that you will not overlook a crucial category or industry heading.[13]

Trade Shows

Trade shows, sponsored by various trade associations, are very useful for gathering competitive intelligence. COMDEX is the huge computer and electronics industry trade show held each year. A few years ago, Compaq Computer was an also-ran in the PC market. It was producing premium-quality, high-cost machines mainly for engineers. The mass business computer market was passing it by. A potential new management team wanted to know if it could produce PCs to

Compaq's high quality specifications using generic components from a variety of vendors. The team secretly purchased parts at COMDEX and assembled test machines. The quality was excellent, and the cost reductions dramatic. Compaq began restructuring, and the founder and CEO was replaced with a new management team. Compaq charted a completely new strategic course and became the world's largest manufacturer of PCs.

At trade shows, CI professionals can pick up competitors' sales literature and product brochures, talk with competitors' suppliers, check prices, and identify new products, technologies, and industry trends. The Future Shop regularly sends teams to the semiannual Consumer Electronics Show. Each team member is assigned specific CI objectives. Some members may seek operational information, others a particular competitor's marketing strategies. Trade show information can be obtained from a directory called the *Exposition Trade Shows and Fairs Directory*.

Public records can be a great resource for gathering CI, and most of these can be accessed via the Internet or through CD-ROM databases. Check with your university or college librarian to see what kinds of public information are available to your school library.

Speeches by Competitors

People enjoy bragging about their accomplishments. Speeches by company executives often mention new strategic directions, new products, plant openings, and the like. Excellent sources are *The Globe and Mail* and *The Financial Post.* These newspapers contain transcripts of analyst's reports, roundtable discussions of industries, and speeches made before security analysts.

Neighbours to Competitors

A CI professional who wants to know what is happening at a local plant can simply visit the neighbourhood. Employees of a bar or restaurant across the street from a plant will usually have a very good idea of what is happening inside the facility. Waiting around for a shift change will provide a chance to speak with employees as some drop by for refreshment.

Advisory Boards

An advisory board is created to provide information, counsel, or recommendations to an organization's CEO, managers, or board of directors. Basically, it provides expertise and advice and acts as a sounding board in particular areas of management. Advisory boards are nothing new; large multinationals have used them for many years.

An advisory board can provide advice on many topics. Technology, economics, investments, politics, the environment, human resources, and consumer preferences are some of the general areas they cover. Other advisory boards are created to provide expert advice on very specific areas, such as nuclear energy and medicine. Nestle Enterprises Ltd., the Canadian subsidiary of the multinational corporation, created an advisory board focusing on the environment, nutrition, and global marketing.[14]

Using the Internet and Databases for Competitive Intelligence

5

Explain how the Internet and databases can be used to gather competitive intelligence

In Chapter 7 we discussed how to use the Internet to access secondary data. Internet databases are covered in detail in Chapter 19. A CI researcher can use databases to answer these and other questions:

1. What articles have been written about this market?
2. What companies are associated with this product group?
3. What patents have been filed for this technology?
4. What are the most important magazines or books in this industry?

5. What are the chances that I will find something in print on the target company?
6. How many companies are in the same industry as the target company?
7. Who are the reporters studying this industry?
8. How can I be updated on industry and company events without having to constantly request the information?
9. How can I compile a list of the leading experts in the industry and the key institutions they are associated with?[15]

There is no one best database for CI information. Researchers often prefer one database search protocol over another. Some databases contain only government information; others offer only technical data. Dialog is, perhaps, the most user friendly and has excellent technical depth. Paul Owen, vice-president of Information Access Company, a major producer of databases for business, discusses the role of global database producers in this chapter's "Global Perspectives" box.

Many CI professionals rely on CD-ROM databases as well as the Internet. All that is required to access these databases is a CD-ROM drive. Many government databases, such as *CANSIM*, are available on CD-ROM. Perhaps the most comprehensive CD-ROM database of global statistics is Global Data Manager (World Game Institute). This database has over 1,200 separate indicators in time series from the 1960s through 2000, as well as projections into the future. Data categories include food and agriculture, energy, health, demographics, culture, and transportation. The data can be sorted and cross-tabulated using up to fifty indicators at once, projected with a variety of statistical tools, and used in any spreadsheet application.

global perspectives

Global Databases Are an Excellent Source of Competitive Intelligence

The role of global database producers is changing as we move into the next century. Driven by new technologies and increased expectations, new groups of information users are evolving. The result has been rapid change and expansion in the information industry. Search software and interfaces are also evolving in response to these needs, as are delivery systems that provide true "desktop access." All of this is providing both challenges and opportunities for the information industry, which is increasingly turning to alliances to meet user needs.

In the 1980s the vast majority of CI and product and market information passed through information professionals such as librarians and on-line specialists. Today, under the direction of top management or chief information officers (CIOs), companies are seeking ways to distribute more broadly important information, and to do so directly to those who use it. Despite high penetration into major corporations in the 1980s, most decision makers are still unaware of the vast information resources available to them through electronic products.

A primary role of global database producers will be to serve new and existing markets with critical, timely, and comprehensive information—the type of information that drives informed business decision making. These new end-user needs are function-dependent and focused, and are placing new demands on information providers.

One such critical application involves sifting vast amounts of information to identify the few critical pearls of information that answer CI questions; these data are then delivered to the electronic mailboxes of business executives.

Alliances among publishers, database providers, search software designers, and database environment providers will strengthen to meet these needs. We will see linkages among these players to deliver intelligence, not just data, directly to end users.

Global database producers will provide better, not more, information. Value will be added by integrating managed information, both within individual organizations and through alliances. The information industry will make its valuable content the bulk of the traffic on the information superhighway as information users seek ways to increase productivity and profits.[16]

Explain the concept of better, not more, information. Why do you think more database producers are "going global"? Do you see global databases playing a larger role in CI?

BusinessWire
PR Newswire
Check out today's news posted on the BusinessWire and PR Newswire sites. Read an article that interests you. What information in your article could be used for competitive intelligence?
www.businesswire.com; www.prnewswire.com

on line

entrepreneurial insights

Using the Internet to Collect Competitive Intelligence

Our client was an information-systems executive who had contracted with a software development firm to produce mission-critical programs. After several setbacks, the client wanted to better understand the development firm's inner workings and the potential for future problems. Not unexpectedly, the target had a well-stocked Web site with a wealth of pertinent information.

One of the first things we look at on a target company's Web site is press releases. They are also available at BusinessWire (**www.businesswire.com**) and PR Newswire (**www.prnewswire.com**). Press releases are rich in detail that often does not make it into print, due to reporters' limited space. Having access to the original material helps us form "actionable intelligence" from which we can draw solid conclusions. News releases often provide details not published elsewhere—as well as names of people who can comment on some aspect that's important to our client; all it usually takes is a phone call. Press releases can also yield interesting insights into a company's progress (or lack thereof), particularly when we have the better perspective of analyzing two or three years of releases at once.

Another important category of information at the target's Web site in this particular assignment proved to be the officers' biographies. Although the biographies are usually carefully crafted, the information can be telling, especially if there is inconsistency between the biography and other semiofficial documents or public assertions. Our client was dealing with a key executive of the company and wanted a careful evaluation of his capabilities. We took information from the Web site bio, cross-checked it against other official sources, and were able to put together a good overall picture.

In this case we found that two brief stints in executive positions at other companies were not mentioned in his "official" bio. This mismatch between the current bio and other listings in the CorpTech reference library was significant. It provided further insight into the client's original questions regarding the target: management resolve; the resources to complete the task; and the internal communications within the target company.

We knew that our target company had been involved in contract litigation, but we didn't know the details. Although we couldn't access most court records via the Internet, we turned to the federal court's Public Access to Court Electronic Records (PACER). PACER allows any user with a personal computer to dial in to a district or bankruptcy court computer and retrieve official electronic case information and court dockets, usually in less than a minute. User fee charges ($0.60 per minute) for this service have been instituted in most courts. People who want to use this service must first register (call toll-free: 800-676-6856).

A Lexis-Nexis search turned up further court records regarding a recent lawsuit against the target. These records provided the names of the judge and the attorneys for both sides. These names were provided to my client and he had the option of contacting them to discuss the matter, within the bounds of the attorney-client privilege rule of course. Internet access to these types of records may be possible in the future, but for now, both Lexis-Nexis and PACER remain fee-based systems.[18]

Source: From "I Spy: Gathering Business Intelligence" by David Vine. Originally appeared in Mecklermedia Corporation's *Internet World* magazine, Vol. 8, No. 3, March 1997. Copyright ©1997 Mecklermedia Corporation, 20 Ketchum Street, Westport, CT 06880; **www.internet.com**. All rights reserved. Reprinted with permission.

Helene Kassler, Director of Library and Information Services at Field & Company, says that job postings on the Internet are one of her favourite sources of CI: "Companies have to divulge what kind of expertise they want from job applicants. If they don't, they are going to get a million applicants, so it serves the best interest of the company to put in what they want. On the other hand, it is tipping their hand."

Recently, Kassler was gathering information about a privately held high-tech firm. She found little information until the Deja News (**www.dejanews.com**) service yielded a multi-job notice posted on a Usenet group. It included details about the hardware and software with which applicants should be familiar. Later postings revealed information about the company's plans for geographic expansion, the number of additional employees it would require, and the company's strategic focus.[17]

Harley-Davidson
Suzuki Motorcycles

Visit the Web page for Suzuki's cruiser motorcycle line. What kind of CI do you think Suzuki used to enable it to compete effectively against Harley-Davidson? Do you think Suzuki has positioned itself successfully to minimize Harley's competitive advantage? Compare Suzuki's motorcycle site with Harley-Davidson's site to find out.

www.harley-davidson.com; www.suzukicycles.com

www on line

David Vine, a CI consultant, offers an example of how his organization uses the Net to gather CI in this chapter's "Entrepreneurial Insights" box.

Industrial Espionage

6

Discuss the problem of industrial espionage

industrial espionage
Attempting to learn a competitor's trade secrets by illegal or unethical means, or both.

Industrial espionage, commonly called spying, is an attempt to learn a competitor's trade secrets by illegal or unethical means, or both. A discussion of CI would not be complete without alluding to spying. Most often, companies use spying to acquire intellectual property, such as designs for computer chips or other technology patents. More often than not, firms that steal from Canadian companies are foreign. It is sometimes much quicker and cheaper to use espionage to acquire technology than to do it yourself.

It isn't just foreign companies that conduct industrial espionage; governments do the same. The biggest offender seems to be the People's Republic of China:

- A pharmaceutical company, Amgen, discovered that a Chinese spy had infiltrated its organization and was trying to steal a vial of cell cultures for Epogen, a $1.2-billion-a-year drug that treats anemia.
- A Chinese spy in Hong Kong was recently caught using sophisticated telecommunications software to eavesdrop on sensitive phone conversations.
- A Chinese engineer working at a software company allegedly stole a proprietary source code and peddled it to a PRC company.[19]

France, Japan, Israel, and the United Kingdom have all made economic espionage a top priority of their foreign intelligence services.[20] French nationals working at Renaissance Software, Inc. were arrested at an airport for attempting to steal the company's proprietary computer source codes. Marc Goldberg, a French computer engineer, had worked at the company under a program sponsored by France's Ministry of Foreign Affairs that allows French citizens to opt out of military service if they are willing to work at high-tech firms.

A biotech company has genetically engineered hamster ovary cells to produce a protein that boosts the manufacture of red blood cells. These hamster cells are obviously a valuable commodity. An employee and a former company scientist have been charged with stealing a batch of these cells and offering them to a biomedical research firm in India for $300,000.[21] Does Canada carry out this sort of activity? In a survey conducted by the American Society for Industrial Security, Canada was listed as the fifth-biggest espionage threat to American companies, behind China, Japan, France, and the U.K![22]

Not all industrial espionage is conducted by foreign countries

For companies that want to develop an in-house CI team, SpyCompany.Com can furnish all the latest gadgets to help uncover competitors' secrets and to keep the competition from discovering theirs. www.spycompany.com

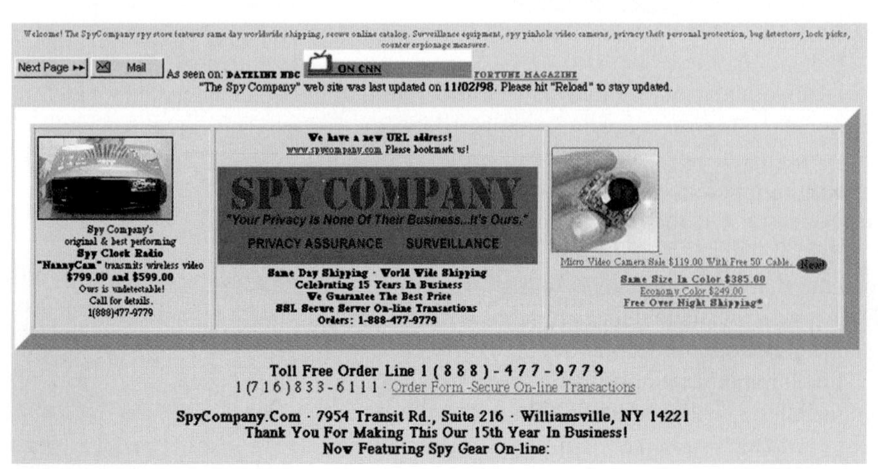

or companies; it is often conducted by domestic companies as well. Fruit of the Loom Inc. has filed a lawsuit against Gildan Activewear of Montreal, alleging that Gilden stole its top-secret marketing plans.[23] It is alleged that David Cherry, executive vice-president at Gildan and a former vice-president at Fruit of the Loom, contacted a former colleague at Fruit of the Loom to obtain its marketing plans. Those plans were then studied by Gildan's top executives and plant managers for the purpose of developing counter-strategies. The Fruit of the Loom employee who supplied the secret marketing plans to Gildan was later hired for a senior position at Gildan.

Magna International of Markham, Ontario, has sued a competitor for hiring away a top Magna executive. Magna is a world leader in hydroforming, a means of shaping metal parts that is far more efficient than stamping. Hydroforming uses high-pressure water to form the parts; the result is better forms and less waste. A major competitor of Magna hired away the head of Magna's hydroforming operations. Magna contends that the competitor hired the Magna executive for the sole purpose of obtaining secret details of Magna's hydroforming operations.

There are many high-tech devices on the market to help thwart espionage, or conduct it. The Truth Phone consists of a desk phone, a microcassette recorder, and a covert lie detector. It records conversations and detects efforts at deception by measuring subaudible microtremors associated with stress and lying. The CC-500 Secure Communication Control Centre is a desk phone that scrambles conversations to foil telephone tappers. To uncover spies, a company can purchase the Counter Surveillance Kit in a briefcase; this includes bug detectors, wiretap alerts, and tape recorder detectors.

The most impressive advances are in video technology. Cameras are being put into every kind of device, including telephones, pagers, motion detectors, ceiling speakers, thermostats, picture frames, desk lamps, eyeglasses, and wristwatches. A basic black-and-white camera not much bigger than a quarter sells for $145 at Spy-Company.Com and can be hidden behind a tie or under a baseball cap. An add-on wireless transmitter for just $299 sends a TV signal to a VCR up to 160 metres away. If you really want portable spyability, $1,100 will get you the world's smallest videotape recorder, the Sony EVO, which fits in a small fanny pack or in the small of your back. Today's cameras can peep through an opening of less than 2 millimetres,

ethics in marketing

Is Competitive Intelligence Ethical?

Almost all scholars who study business ethics agree that the practice of competitive intelligence is ethical. The purpose of CI is to make a business more effective, efficient, and profitable. Efficiency benefits not only the company but society as a whole. Once we can conclude that the end is acceptable, the next issue is means. That is, the question becomes, "Which of the specific methods of collecting and using CI are ethically acceptable, and which are not?"

CI data collection plans that rely on publicly available information, such as in *The Globe and Mail*, are completely acceptable. At the other end of the scale, activities such as theft, bribery, and trespassing are illegal and unethical. Many activities, however, fall in between the extremes. Going through someone's trash is dirty and unappealing but it may not be immoral. Sitting outside a competitor's main gate and counting the number of trucks and rail cars is clandestine, but most agree it is not unethical.[24]

Does a competitor's supplier have an obligation to protect the trade secrets of its customers? Most experts in ethics believe that the supplier does not have that duty unless there is a specific signed agreement to protect such secrets, or unless the supplier voluntarily assumes the duty. The primary responsibility for keeping a trade secret safe lies with the owner of the secret.

Do you agree that CI is ethical? Go over the various ways discussed in this chapter that a researcher can gather CI. Which do you think are generally ethical or unethical? Defend your answer.

making them virtually undetectable. These devices are available to the general public at retailers like SpyCompany.Com (**www.spycompany.com**).

CI is an area of business that has had more than its share of ethics abuses. This chapter's "Ethics in Marketing" box addresses some of the ethical issues relating to CI.

LOOKING BACK

Look back at the story about Harley-Davidson. The company gave its investors an average return of 43 percent per year through the 1990s. In the late 1980s, Harley launched both a rigorous quality control program and a cost reduction program. Although quality and cost control are "the price of admission" for competing in the motorcycle industry, they aren't Harley's competitive advantage. The company's competitive advantage is its brand name. The Harley name is a marketing icon. It stands for freedom, independence, and escape. CI can help Harley remain on top by monitoring competitors and their actions. Harley now has 47 percent of the North American market for heavyweight motorcycles. Heavyweights represent a $5 billion market worldwide. With demand so high, it is little wonder that competitors are springing up. Big Dog Motorcycles is now producing a classic mid-1960s-style cruiser that sells for $22,000, compared to $16,000 for a similar Harley. Big Dog now has fifty-five employees turning out 300 cycles a year. Of more concern to Harley is Polaris, the snowmobile manufacturer, which plans to build 4,000 motorcycles a year in the near future. Polaris is a well-financed company with $1.2 billion in assets. About one-third of Polaris's existing customers are motorcycle enthusiasts, and the company has a dealer network of over 2,000 outlets. Press releases have enabled Harley to determine that the initial motorcycles will not be Harley clones and will be priced significantly lower than Harleys.[25]

Summary

1 **Describe the concept of competitive advantage and the three types of competitive advantages.** A competitive advantage is those unique features of a company and its products that are perceived by the target market as significant and as superior to the competition. It is those factors which cause customers to patronize a firm and not the competition. There are three types of competitive advantages: cost, differentiation, and niche. Cost competitive advantages are usually the most difficult to sustain.

2 **Discuss the concept of competitive intelligence.** Competitive intelligence (CI) involves creating an intelligence system that will help managers assess their competition. Intelligence is analyzed information. It is decision-making intelligence when it has implications for the organization. The notion of CI was derived from military intelligence. CI helps managers assess their competition and vendors. It leads to fewer surprises. CI allows managers to predict changes in business relationships, guard against threats, forecast a competitor's strategy, and develop a successful marketing plan.

3 **Identify the sources of internal competitive intelligence data.** Company personnel, especially sales and service reps, are usually good sources of CI. Many companies require their salespeople to routinely fill out CI reports. Many large companies conduct CI audits, which focus on employees with CI expertise, independent internal databases, and marketing research studies. Once the audit is completed, the data can be entered into a CI database.

4 **Identify the non-computer-based external sources of competitive intelligence.** Non-computer-based external sources of CI include experts, CI consultants, government agencies, UCC filings, suppliers, photographs, newspapers and other publications, the Yellow Pages, trade shows, speeches by competitors, neighbours of competitors, and advisory boards.

5 Explain how the Internet and databases can be used to gather competitive intelligence. The Internet and databases accessed via the Internet offer excellent and rapidly obtained sources of data. CD-ROM databases, such as Global Data Manager, can also prove valuable to CI researchers.

6 Discuss the problem of industrial espionage. Industrial espionage is an attempt to learn a competitor's trade secrets by illegal and/or unethical means. Often foreign companies and governments engage in industrial espionage. Most espionage is directed against high-tech firms.

Do You Know These Terms?

augmented product 203
CI audit 207
CI directory 208
competitive advantage 200
competitive intelligence (CI) 206
cost competitive advantage 200
differential competitive advantage 202
experience curves 200
expert 209
industrial espionage 216
niche competitive advantage 204
Uniform Commercial Code (UCC) filings 211
value impressions 203

Discussion and Writing Questions

1. Explain the three types of competitive advantages, and give examples of companies for each type.
2. Prepare a memo to the company president, who is focusing only on a cost competitive advantage, and explain why this type of advantage is probably not sustainable in the long run.
3. Discuss the relationship between competitive advantage and competitive intelligence (CI).
4. Why do you think CI is so hot in today's business environment?
5. Prepare a memo to your boss at Air Canada outlining why the organization needs a CI unit.
6. List six sources of non-computer-based external CI. What type of data can be obtained from each?
7. Why has the Internet been such an important tool for CI researchers?
8. Form a team with three other students. Each team must choose a firm in the PC manufacturing industry. Next, each team should go to the Website of the firm and acquire as much CI as possible. Each team will then prepare a five-minute oral presentation on its findings.
9. Visit **emporium.turnpike.net** and explain how this site can yield CI.

Application for Small Business

June and Ralph Quark have started a small business in Edmonton that provides on-line data for doctors. It already boasts about 5,000 members. There are people who register by answering a few questions about their identities, including medical specialty, if any. The site is loaded with medical jargon and thus has limited appeal to the general public. After signing in, a person has access to voluminous reports on just about every known disease. The site is already attracting pharmaceutical manufacturers, who spend around $8 billion in North America promoting drugs. Most promotional dollars are aimed at the 300,000 physicians who prescribe drugs. June and Ralph's site is a natural for the drug companies to use as a promotion vehicle.

Questions

1. June and Ralph are concerned that other medical Websites may begin offering the physicians "more something" and siphon off their members. They are also concerned that Microsoft or search engines like Yahoo! may create their own sites. How can June and Ralph use the Internet to gain CI about potential threats and competition?
2. What non-Internet sources could June and Ralph use for CI?

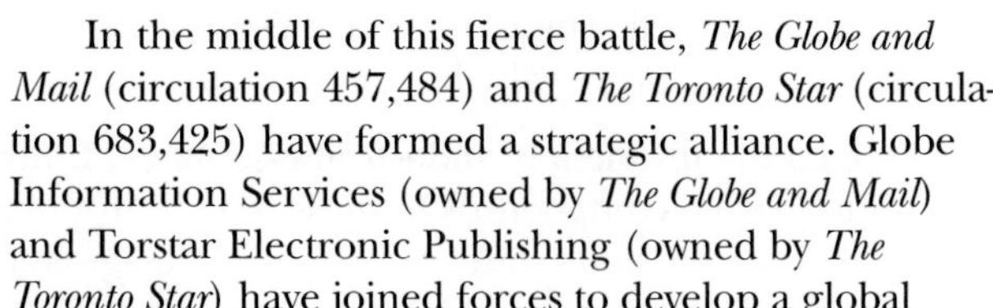

VIDEO CASE

The Newspaper Wars

As the number of companies in most industries continues to shrink, competition among remaining companies has intensified. The level of competition in some industries has been documented in best-selling books such as *The Cola Wars* by J.C. Louis. Yes, competition among rival companies is so fierce that it is referred to as war.

In recent years, competitive intelligence has grown in importance. Information about the growth and importance of competitive intelligence can be obtained on the Website of the Society of Competitive Intelligence Professionals (**www.scip.com**). This is an organization of professionals in the field of competitive intelligence gathering. The Society of Competitive Intelligence Professionals runs courses on intelligence gathering that cost in excess of $10,000.

Flying in the face of the competitive intelligence battles between companies are some recent strategic alliances between competitors. IBM and Dell have joined forces to share information; General Motors is sharing and swapping parts with both Toyota and Honda, who are major rivals for automotive market share; and General Motors and Suzuki are building SUVs based on a common platform at a joint alliance assembly plant in Ingersoll, Ontario. Possibly one of the most interesting strategic alliances between competitors is one recently formed between *The Globe and Mail* and *The Toronto Star,* two major competitors in the Canadian newspaper wars.

The Canadian newspaper market is truly a fierce battleground, as the following will attest: "*The Globe and Mail* and the *National Post* are holding their own in the national newspaper war but rivals *The Toronto Sun* and *The Toronto Star* are losing ground in the heated circulation battle." Since last summer, Toronto has been the site of a heated newspaper war." Aside from the four traditional dailies, three subway papers have been competing for readers and advertisers. "We [*The Toronto Star*] are very satisfied in terms of holding our own in year three of the newspaper war." Toronto's newspaper war claimed its first casualties yesterday with two of the city's so-called subway papers announcing plans to merge operations following heavy financial losses.

In the middle of this fierce battle, *The Globe and Mail* (circulation 457,484) and *The Toronto Star* (circulation 683,425) have formed a strategic alliance. Globe Information Services (owned by *The Globe and Mail*) and Torstar Electronic Publishing (owned by *The Toronto Star*) have joined forces to develop a global help-wanted site called Workopolis.

While operating the Workopolis.com Website as a strategic alliance, the two newspaper giants continue to battle for circulation and advertising revenue. They also continue to steal valued employees from each other. Go figure!

Bibliography

Keith Damsell, "Globe Stays on Top in Circulation Wars," *The Globe and Mail,* 1 May 2001, p. B9.

———, "Subway Papers Merge," *The Globe and Mail,* 14 March 2001, p. B4.

"Globe Holds Wide Lead Over Post," *The Globe and Mail,* 30 October 2001, p. B2.

Source:

CBC, *Venture,* "Strange Bedfellows," February 15, 2000.

Questions

1. Why would two fierce competitors form a strategic alliance?
2. With the formation of the strategic alliance, how can both *The Globe and Mail* and the *Toronto Star* keep competitive secrets from each other? Since forming an alliance, will these two companies continue to compete as fiercely?
3. Visit the Websites of *The Globe and Mail* (**www.globeandmail.com**) and *The Toronto Star* (**www.thestar.com**). What references can you find to Workopolis on each newspaper's Website?
4. Visit the Website of Mercer Management Consulting (**www.mercermc.com**). What can you learn about alliances between competitors on this Website?

2

marketing miscues

General Motors Is Too General

General Motors' top management has gone through a number of shake-ups in the past decade, yet the problem remains the same: GM doesn't create cars that people want, build them effectively, or market them efficiently. To some observers, the company is in a slow-moving time warp that continually lags the competition.

GM has more than twice as many brands and 70 percent more dealerships than Ford, even though GM's unit sales are only 19 percent greater. Critics say GM should stop trying to resuscitate dying divisions and instead spend more on promising newcomers like Saturn Corp. "This is like watching a grade-B movie—you know exactly how it ends," says marketing analyst Mary Ann Keller. "Either Buick or Oldsmobile is going to have to disappear." (General Motors has since announced that Oldsmobile will be phased out after the 2003 model year.) Analysts also would like GM to add more high-profit trucks and new car–truck hybrids like Honda's CR-V and Lexus's RX300. John Zarrella, GM's vice-president of marketing, acknowledges that "we have more cars than we need, and not enough trucks."

Ford, Toyota, Honda, and other rivals long ago moved on—cutting costs, streamlining distribution, raising efficiency, and cranking out innovative models in record time. They have left GM behind, and in key areas it continues to slip: productivity, market-share growth, product development times, overhead expenses, and revenue per vehicle sold. GM's market share—near 50 percent three decades ago—has dropped to 28 percent in 2000. Its spanking-new midsize sedans—among the vaunted successes—weren't selling as well as their lacklustre predecessors. It has taken big rebates just to slow down market share losses. Analysts say that the rebates, which cut into earnings, will have to continue. "The dogs don't like the dog food," says Arthur D. Little Inc. auto consultant John Wolkonowicz. "GM has neither a golden gut (instinct) nor a way of understanding the needs of future customers." A perfect example: although consumers clamour for four-door pickups, such as those produced by Dodge and Ford, GM introduced a three-door.

GM cars that are well conceived sink in the market because of the company's poor brand image, too much competing advertising, and botched manufacturing launches. The new Intrigue sedan is one of the finest cars in its class, but baby boomers never wandered into an Oldsmobile showroom to check it out, thus ending any hopes for the Oldsmobile model.

GM still has factory capacity, marketing structure, and distribution geared to owning 35 percent or more of the market—a share it may never see again. It still has seven marketing divisions with eighty car and truck models. Likewise, there aren't enough sales to support GM's sprawling network of eight-thousand-plus dealers across North America profitably. This excess baggage is crippling. "GM can no longer afford to keep all those car lines current—they don't have the cash flow," explains consultant Wolkonowicz. "They fall further and further behind because the competition can change product more quickly."

Sources: "GM Goes on Ad-fensive with Campaign," *USA Today,* 23 July 1998, p. 3B. Jean Halliday, "GM Pondering Consolidation in Marketing," *Advertising Age,* 11 May 1998, p. 4. Kathleen Kerwin, "GM: It's Time to Face the Future," *Business Week,* 27 July 1998, pp. 25–8. Kathleen Kerwin, "The Shutdown GM Needs?" *Business Week,* 13 July 1998, pp. 34–6. David Kiley, "Optimum Target," *BrandWeek,* 18 May 1998, pp. 38–42.

Questions

1. Using the consumer behaviour model in Chapter 4, explain what variables in the model GM might attack to influence people to buy GM cars.
2. Do you think GM has done a good job segmenting its markets? Defend your answer.
3. Which GM brand appeals the most to you as a consumer? The least? Explain your preferences. How can GM change the latter?
4. If you planned to recommend marketing research to GM, what would be the first four projects you would recommend? Why?
5. Explain how GM might use competitive intelligence to better its position in the marketplace.

Critical Thinking

The Gap Gets It

Mickey Drexler, chief executive of Gap Inc., may have more influence on style than anyone else. Yes, Ralph Lauren embodies a certain look, but how many of us have the money or inclination to imitate the wealthiest of Canada's consumers? Drexler, by contrast, is a mass marketer. He intends to bring style to everyone, from Dawson Creek, British Columbia, to Medicine Hat, Alberta; from Altona, Manitoba, to Codroy, Newfoundland.

"Think about it," Drexler says, over a ham and Swiss cheese sandwich with mustard and a bag of Lay's baked potato chips. "If you go into a supermarket, you would expect to find some fundamental items. You would expect to find milk: nonfat, 1%, 2%, whole milk. You'd expect the dates to be fresh. You want butter. You want certain types of bread. You have your list. I don't know why apparel stores should be any different. I mean, think about it."

What Drexler has done is to transform The Gap from a retail chain into a recognizable global brand. Above all, he is determined to make Gap ubiquitous. If Coke is available in every airport, in every grocery store, in every McDonald's, shouldn't Gap be everywhere too? Since Drexler arrived in 1983, Gap Inc. has grown from 566 stores to over 2,500. In addition to Canada and the United States, The Gap now operates in Japan, the United Kingdom, France, and Germany. One new store opens every day.

"I find clothing very complicated to buy," Drexler says. "It shouldn't be that complicated. It should be simple." Simplicity may be what defines The Gap, but making The Gap work is not so simple. Clothing companies usually depend on the vision and taste of just one person. As soon as that person's vision is tired, it's all over, and the line becomes a parody of itself, which is what happened at Laura Ashley, for example. That's why Paris design houses work so hard to bring in new, young talent. Everything at The Gap depends on Drexler's eye; it isn't like making turbine engines.

Most clothing companies want their products to be a sign of something else—money, power, class, virility, sex, privilege, access. Beneath an unstructured Armani suit lurks a whiff of power, worldliness, competitiveness, *la dolce vita.* Ralph Lauren tries hard to suggest long weekends in exotic locations, ease, trust funds, and other old things. However, Drexler knows instinctively that most consumers aren't all that comfortable with class. The Gap is democratic and familiar—ordinary, unpretentious, understated, almost lowbrow.

Drexler is famous for wandering around The Gap headquarters repeating a sort of mantra: "Think negative five comp. Think negative five comp." Everyone knows he's talking about comparable store sales—that he doesn't want employees to celebrate the 15 percent increase this past June, but to pretend instead that the numbers are down. It's a sort of superstition. He worries constantly about becoming complacent—and he doesn't want to attract the evil eye. The mantra seems to work. "Even after a great quarter everyone in that company comes together and says, 'We didn't do well enough. How can we do better?'" says Rick Lyons, who left last year after thirteen years at The Gap, most recently as an executive vice president. "There's always a grey feeling. I was always grey. Oh sure, we'd celebrate, briefly, after a great quarter, but it was always right back to, 'What did we do wrong?'"

Sometimes things have gone wrong. In 1983, The Gap bought Banana Republic. The company sold jodhpurs, travel trunks, hunting jackets. It was very Indiana Jones, very *Out of Africa.* Which was great, until 1987, when the safari look went out of fashion. To restructure Banana Republic, The Gap took a $6.8 million pretax writeoff. Then, in 1987, Drexler launched Hemispheres, a chain of shops selling expensive "European-inspired" clothes that never caught on.

By 1995, The Gap found many competitors selling "basics." As competition increased, The Gap seemed old, tired, and out of ideas. Drexler responded to this crisis with a bold gamble, an approach to discount marketing that had never been tried before. Out of this experience grew the new business model that now has financial analysts thinking The Gap might be the next Coke.

The gamble was Old Navy, a new division Drexler launched in 1994 to compete with stores like Sears and Pennington's. Discount shopping was the hot growth area in retailing, but, Drexler asked, did it need to be so depressing? Big, loud, fun, and cheap, Old Navy stores are fitted out with exposed pipes and raw concrete floors. There are listening booths where customers can sample CDs and old grocery-store refrigerator cases stocked with T-shirts shrinkwrapped like packages of lean ground beef.

"When we started Old Navy, we sat around and we talked about what we didn't like about discount stores—poor quality, colours that are always just a hair off. We really thought, 'What do we not want to be?' and took it from there," explains Jenny Ming, executive vice president for merchandising at Old Navy.

The pitch was perfect, and Old Navy was an instant success. "There was a time, not so long ago, when people who shopped at department stores wouldn't shop at Wal-Mart—that was déclassé," explains Kurt Barnard, of Barnard's Retail Trend Report. "Then it became chic to shop downscale, to shop for a bargain. People used to pay $10 and they said they paid $20. Now they pay $20 and say they paid $10." Old Navy captures this trend brilliantly. It's discount shopping with an edge, discount shopping that appeals even to people who can afford Gucci. "Old Navy is a concept for a decade. If you create an idea like that once every ten years, you're fine," remarks Baum, the Goldman analyst.

In just three years, The Gap opened over 300 Old Navy stores and sales hit $1 billion. However, as if to confirm how badly this business depends on the vision of just one man, even as Drexler focused on building Old Navy, things at the Gap division went from bad to dreadful. It didn't help that his attention was further distracted by the search for a post-safari identity for Banana Republic.

One day in the summer of 1996, Drexler wandered slowly through a Gap store and was shocked. The clothes were ugly, the carpet was frayed, the fixtures looked cheap. Simplicity and cleanliness had been forgotten. However, what he really hated that summer was a series of new Gap print ads that included a young, androgynous-looking man with long blond hair (unclean?), a pierced lip, and an attitude. It was heroin chic. It was also Calvin Klein—it wasn't The Gap. "It was so incompatible in my mind with what made Gap right," says Drexler. "I think this campaign said more and more, 'If you're a Gap customer, don't come into the Gap.'" The campaign lasted two months. Maggie Gross, The Gap's longtime ad director, promptly took a leave of absence, then resigned. A handful of other Gap advertising people left with her. There were departures in the design department, too.

Drexler didn't go on vacation that summer. Instead he spent two and a half months, from June to August, going through every item of clothing in the line—clothes that were to hit stores in the upcoming spring. He got rid of everything that wasn't pure Gap. Away went the skinny plaid pants and the zip-up men's shirts in '50s orange and brown. Away went the shiny green disco shirts. "It was a good kick," remarks Drexler. "I think the most important thing I learned was the importance of consistency when branding a business." (Did somebody say McDonald's?)

Around the same time, while he was reading a Coca-Cola annual report, Drexler realized that The Gap as a concept wasn't "mature" after all. Coke didn't go out of style. It wasn't superannuated. His reasoning continued: Was a can of Coke any more basic, more fundamental than a white Gap men's shirt? "We started to think about our business in different terms," says Drexler. "We started to think about our brand in a more ubiquitous way. Before, for example, we would have had one store in a particular market. But if you think about great brands around the world, they usually dominate a much larger percent of market share than any apparel company does." Thinking big, thinking in terms of Coca-Cola, Drexler then became obsessed with The Gap's comparatively small market share: "The average per capita expenditure on clothing is approximately $700. We own about $23 of that. So I'm saying, 'Gee, we only have $23 of the $700? You would think Gap should own a lot more of the customer's wardrobe.'"

To multiply that $23, Gap has started opening stores at a quick pace and in towns that Drexler once would have considered too small. In cities where The Gap already exists, stores continue to open. There are Gap, GapKids, Banana Republic, and Old Navy stores in the same shopping centre. Still Drexler feels that the market is far from saturated. In June 1998, The Gap launched Gap-to-go, on the theory that buying clothes should be as easy as ordering in Chinese food. Menus from Gap-to-go list twenty-one basic Gap items; fax your order in and it will be delivered to your office or home by the end of the day. If the original Gap-to-go works, it will be rapidly expanded. Of course there's also the Internet; Gap Online was introduced in November 1997. Banana Republic now mails out catalogues. The Gap is now testing GapBody stores that will sell boxer shorts, cotton panties and bras, pajamas, Gap fragrances, soaps, and candles.

Questions

1. Explain how the safari look could have gone out of style and almost bankrupted Banana Republic. Use the consumer decision-making process in Chapter 4 as the basis for your explanation.
2. Describe the various market segments that each Gap company appeals to.
3. What is the primary form of segmentation used by The Gap? Defend your answer.
4. How can Gap use marketing research to more effectively accomplish its goals?
5. What forms of competitive intelligence would be beneficial to The Gap?
6. Comment on Drexler's management style.

Source: From 'Gap Gets It' by Nina Munk, Fortune, 3 August 1998.

Suggested Readings

Kelly Barron, "Grow Up Already," *Forbes,* 27 July 1998, pp. 58–60.

Becky Ebenkamp, "Extensions: Old Navy Continues to Push Brand Scope with Cosmetics," *Brandweek,* 27 April 1998, pp. 41–2.

Katherine Weisman, "Gap Getting the French Knack," *WWD,* 9 July 1998, pp. 16–17.

3

DECISIONS

CHAPTER

9

LEARNING OBJECTIVES

After studying this chapter, you should be able to

1. Define the term "product"
2. Classify consumer products
3. Define "product item," "product line," and "product mix"
4. Describe marketing uses of branding
5. Describe marketing uses of packaging and labelling
6. Discuss global issues in branding and packaging
7. Describe how and why product warranties are important marketing tools

PRODUCT CONCEPTS

McDonald's has teamed up with ConAgra to test a line of wrapped sandwiches made with Healthy Choice deli meats. The line, which has four varieties, puts McDonald's in the trendy wrap sandwich category and could provide a much needed food item that is low in fat, portable, and convenient. The sandwich is targeted to adult consumers, long a demographic sore spot with the restaurant chain.

For McDonald's, the Healthy Choice brand will provide a good-for-you image that is lacking in many of the restaurant's food items. McDonald's president Alan Feldman is interested in borrowing brand equity from other brands as well. A source close to the company says, "I think you're going to see a lot more of this co-branding at McDonald's."

The McDeli test is part of McDonald's attempt to upgrade its overall food quality and to develop new products that will attract consumer groups other than kids. Its last adult-targeted sandwich line, Deluxe, proved to be an expensive disappointment. The Arch Deluxe burger has been dropped from most stores, and the Fish Deluxe is being redesigned.

The McDeli Wraps, developed by a franchisee, have an average of six to twelve grams of fat. The four varieties—Grilled Chicken Caesar, Turkey & Swiss, Turkey Club, and a no-meat Veggie Wrap—are intended to be a healthier product that mothers can have while the kids eat Happy Meals and that are easy to eat while driving. The wraps have been selling briskly in test markets; one store manager reports sales of 200 wraps daily.

Wrap sandwiches have been growing in popularity and are meant to address three major trends among time-pressed consumers: portability, a growing concern over fat content, and a desire for more freshly made, out-of-home dining solutions. However, wrap sandwiches have a mixed record among fast food restaurants. KFC and Wendy's introduced wrap-style offerings. KFC has since pulled its entry, and Wendy's sales have been below expectations.[1]

Why would a company like McDonald's—which already has a strong brand name and identity—choose to team up with another brand? What are the positives and negatives of such a strategy? Do you think that McDonald's strategy is sound?

McDonald's Healthy Choice

Are McDonald's and Healthy Choice promoting this partnership? Visit their Websites to find out. How can you account for what you discover?

www.mcdonalds.com; www.healthychoice.com

on line

What Is a Product?

1
Define the term "product"

product
Everything, both favourable and unfavourable, that a person receives in an exchange.

The product offering—the heart of an organization's marketing program—is usually the starting point in creating a marketing mix. A marketing manager cannot determine a price, design a promotion strategy, or create a distribution channel until the firm has a product to sell. Moreover, an excellent distribution channel, a persuasive promotion campaign, and a fair price have no value if the product offering is poor or inadequate.

We can define a **product** as everything, both favourable and unfavourable, that a person receives in an exchange. A product can be a tangible good like a pair of shoes, a service like a haircut, an idea like "don't litter," or any combination of these three. Packaging, style, colour, options, and size are some typical product features. Just as important are intangibles such as service, the seller's image, the manufacturer's reputation, and consumers' beliefs about how others will perceive the product.

To most people, "product" means a tangible good. However, services and ideas are also products. (Chapter 11 focuses on the unique aspects of marketing services.) That being said, the marketing process identified in Chapter 1 is the same whether the product is a good, a service, an idea, or some combination of these.

Types of Consumer Products

2
Classify consumer products

business product (industrial product)
A product bought to manufacture other goods or services, to facilitate an organization's operations, or to resell to other customers.

consumer product
A product bought to satisfy an individual's personal wants.

Products can be classified as either business (industrial) or consumer products, depending on the buyer's intentions. The key distinction between the two types of products is their intended use. If the intended use is for business, the product is classified as a business or industrial product. As explained in Chapter 5, a **business product** is used to manufacture other goods or services, to facilitate an organization's operations, or to resell to other customers. A **consumer product** is bought to satisfy an individual's personal wants. Sometimes the same item can be classified as either a business or a consumer product, depending on its intended use. Examples include lightbulbs, pencils, paper, and microcomputers.

We need to know about product classifications because business and consumer products are marketed differently. They are marketed to different target markets and tend to use different distribution, promotion, and pricing strategies.

Chapter 5 examined seven categories of business products: major equipment, accessory equipment, component parts, processed materials, raw materials, supplies, and services. In the current chapter we consider an effective way of classifying consumer products. There are several approaches to this, but the most popular one uses the following four categories: convenience products, shopping products, specialty products, and unsought products (see Exhibit 9.1). This approach classifies products according to how much effort is usually used to shop for them.

Convenience Products

convenience product
A relatively inexpensive item that merits little shopping effort.

A **convenience product** is a relatively inexpensive item that merits little shopping effort. In other words, the consumer is unwilling to shop extensively for such an item. Candy, soft drinks, combs, aspirin, small hardware items, dry cleaning, and car washes fall into the convenience product category.

Consumers buy convenience products regularly, usually without much planning. Even so, consumers do know the brand names of popular convenience

exhibit 9.1

Classification of Consumer Products

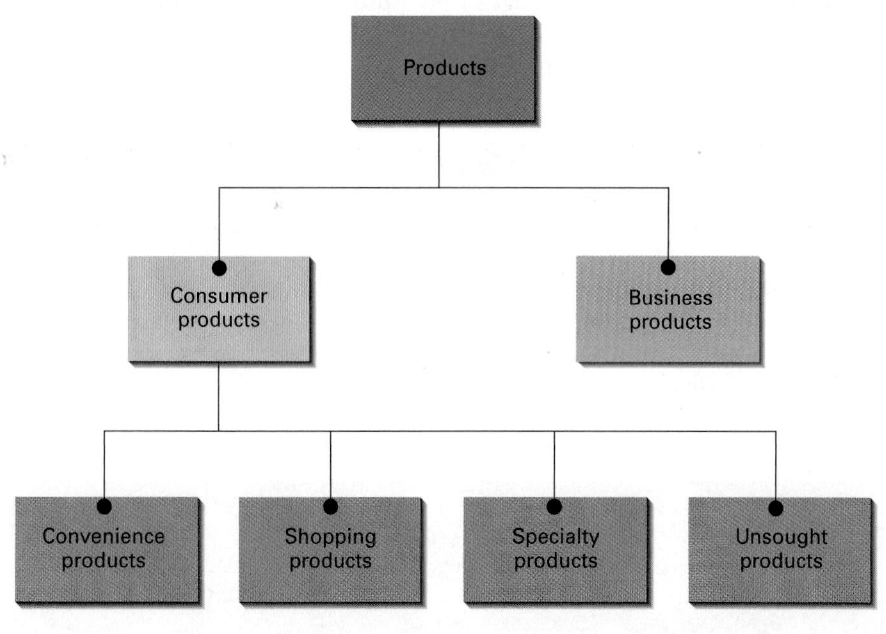

products—Coca-Cola, Bayer aspirin, Right Guard deodorant, and so on. Convenience products usually require wide distribution if sufficient quantities are to be sold to meet profit goals.

shopping product
A product that requires comparison shopping because it is usually more expensive than a convenience product and is found in fewer stores.

specialty product
A particular item for which consumers search extensively and are very reluctant to accept substitutes.

Shopping Products

A **shopping product** is usually more expensive than a convenience product and is found in fewer stores. Consumers usually buy a shopping product only after comparing several brands or stores for style, practicality, price, and lifestyle compatibility. They are willing to invest some effort into this process to achieve the desired benefits.

There are two types of shopping products: homogeneous and heterogeneous. Consumers perceive *homogeneous* shopping products as basically similar—for example, washers, dryers, refrigerators, and TV sets. With homogeneous shopping products, consumers typically look for the lowest-priced brand that has the desired features.

In contrast, consumers perceive *heterogeneous* shopping products as essentially different. Examples are furniture, clothing, housing, and universities. Consumers often have trouble comparing heterogeneous shopping products because their prices and features vary so much, as does their quality. Comparing heterogeneous shopping products is mainly about "finding the best product or brand for *me*"; the resulting decision is often highly individual.

With homogenous products such as washers and dryers, consumers typically buy the lowest-priced brand that has the desired features.

Specialty Products

When consumers search extensively for a particular item and are very reluctant to accept substitutes, that item is a **specialty product**. Breitling watches, Rolls-Royce automobiles, Shaman loudspeakers, Laguiole knives, and Leica cameras might be considered specialty products.

Marketers of specialty products often use selective, status-conscious advertising to maintain the exclusive image of their products. Distribution is often limited to one or a very few outlets in a given geographic area. Brand names and service quality are often very important.

Unsought Products

unsought product
A product unknown to the potential buyer, or a known product that the buyer does not actively seek.

A product unknown to the potential buyer, or a known product that the buyer does not actively seek, is referred to as an **unsought product**. New products fall into this category until advertising and distribution increase consumer awareness of them.

Some goods are always marketed as unsought items—especially needed products that we do not like to think about or care to spend money on. Insurance, burial plots, encyclopedias, and similar items require aggressive personal selling and highly persuasive advertising. Salespeople actively seek leads to potential

Image courtesy of Waterford Crystal

Waterford Crystal is a specialty product that shoppers will spend extra time to locate, and they will be less concerned about price. What challenges do marketers of specialty products face?

buyers. Because consumers usually do not seek out this type of product, the company must go directly to them through salespeople, direct mail, or direct-response advertising.

Product Items, Lines, and Mixes

3 Define "product item," "product line," and "product mix"

Rarely does a company sell a single product. More often, it sells a variety of things. A **product item** is a specific version of a product that can be designated as a distinct offering among an organization's products. Gillette's MACH 3 razor is an example of a product item (see Exhibit 9.2).

product item A specific version of a product that can be designated as a distinct offering among an organization's products.

A group of closely related product items constitutes a **product line**. The "Blades and razors" column in Exhibit 9.2 represents one of Gillette's product lines. Different container sizes and shapes also distinguish items in a product line. Diet Coke is available in cans and in various plastic containers. Each size and each container is a separate product item.

product line A group of closely related product items.

An organization's **product mix** includes all the products it sells. All of Gillette's products—blades and razors, toiletries, writing instruments, lighters—constitute its product mix. Each product item in the product mix may require a separate marketing strategy. Sometimes, however, product lines and even entire product mixes can share some components of a marketing strategy. The Pontiac division of General Motors has promoted all Pontiac items and lines with its theme "We build excitement—Pontiac."

product mix All the products an organization sells.

Organizations benefit in several ways from organizing related items into product lines:

- *Advertising economies:* Product lines provide economies of scale in advertising. Several products can be advertised under the umbrella of the line. Campbell's can talk about its soup being "m-m-good" and promote the entire line.
- *Package uniformity:* A product line can benefit from package uniformity. All packages in the line can have a common look and still keep their individual identities. Again, Campbell's soup is a good example.

Campbell's soup is an excellent example of advertising economies. Without singling out a specific flavour, Campbell's can promote its entire line of soup with the single phrase "m-m-good."

- *Standardized components:* Product lines allow firms to standardize components; this reduces manufacturing and inventory costs. Many of the components that Samsonite uses in its folding tables and chairs are also used in its patio furniture. General Motors uses the same parts on many of its makes and models.
- *Efficient sales and distribution:* A product line enables sales personnel for companies like Procter & Gamble to provide a full range of choices to customers. Distributors and retailers are often more inclined to stock a company's products if it offers a full line. Transportation and warehousing costs are likely to be lower for a product line than for a collection of individual items.
- *Equivalent quality:* Purchasers usually expect and believe that all products in a line are about equal in quality. Consumers expect that all Campbell's soups and all President's Choice cookies are of similar quality.

product mix width The number of product lines an organization offers.

product line depth The number of product items in a product line.

Product mix width (or breadth) refers to the number of product lines an organization offers. In Exhibit 9.2, the width of Gillette's product mix is four product lines. **Product line depth** is the number of product items in a product

on line

Rubbermaid
Go to Rubbermaid's Website and identify its product items, product lines, and product mix. Do any of these surprise you? Explain. How wide do you think Rubbermaid's lines are?
www.rubbermaid.com

exhibit 9.2

Gillette's Product Lines and Product Mix

	Width of the Product Mix			
	Blades and razors	**Toiletries**	**Writing instruments**	**Lighters**
Depth of the product lines	MACH 3	Series	Paper Mate	Cricket
	Sensor	Adorn	Flair	S.T. Dupont
	Trac II	Toni		
	Atra	Right Guard		
	Swivel	Silkience		
	Double-Edge	Soft and Dri		
	Lady Gillette	Foamy		
	Super Speed	Dry Look		
	Twin Injector	Dry Idea		
	Techmatic	Brush Plus		

line. As shown in Exhibit 9.2, Gillette's blades and razors product line includes ten product items; the toiletries product line includes ten product items; the writing instrument and lighter product lines have only two items each.

Firms increase the *width* of their product mix to diversify risk—that is, to spread risk across many product lines instead of gambling on only one or two. Firms also widen their product mix to capitalize on established reputations. In introducing new product lines, Kodak was capitalizing on its image as a leader in photographic products. Kodak's product lines now include film, processing, still cameras, movie cameras, paper, and chemicals. Limited Inc., a company that mostly comprises women's apparel stores (Limited, Limited Too, Victoria's Secret) is experimenting in cosmetics lines—it is developing a line of makeup under the Victoria's Secret brand.[2]

Firms increase the *depth* of their product lines to attract buyers with different preferences, to increase sales and profits by further segmenting the market, to capitalize on economies of scale in production and marketing, and to even out seasonal sales patterns. Since 1970, Timex has increased the depth of its wristwatch line from 300 items to 1,500.[3]

Loblaws has revitalized the PC Green line by focusing more attention on the human element.

Adjustments to Product Items, Lines, and Mixes

Over time, firms change product items, lines, and mixes to take advantage of new technical or product developments or to respond to changes in the environment. They may modify products, reposition products, or extend or contract product lines.

Product Modifications

Marketing managers must decide if and when to modify existing products. **Product modification** changes one or more of a product's characteristics:

product modification
Changing one or more of a product's characteristics.

- *Quality modification*: This involves changing a product's dependability or durability. Reducing a product's quality may let the manufacturer lower the price and appeal to target markets that cannot afford the original product. Conversely, increasing quality can help the firm compete with rival firms.

Increasing quality can also result in stronger brand loyalty, greater leeway to raise prices, and/or new opportunities for market segmentation. To reach consumers who want to buy less expensive, lower-quality film, Eastman Kodak is considering launching a discount film that will not carry Kodak's well-recognized brand name.[4] Michelin has added a higher-quality, higher-priced "run-flat" tire to its product mix. This tire will travel up to 70 kilometres after suffering total air loss.

- *Functional modification:* This involves changing a product's versatility, effectiveness, convenience, or safety. Hostess is introducing a line of fruit-and-grain cereal bars to extend its equity in the snack market beyond the dessert-type products it has traditionally offered. These bars are targeted to higher-income women who want a tastier version of a low-fat, vitamin-fortified breakfast alternative.[5] Lea & Perrins is offering its steak sauce in a value-priced squeeze bottle with a "no mess, stay clean" cap.[6]
- *Style modification:* This involves changing a product's aesthetics rather than its quality or functionality. Clothing manufacturers commonly use style modifications to motivate customers to replace products before they are worn out. **Planned obsolescence** is a term commonly used to describe the practice of modifying products in such a way that those which have already been sold become obsolete before they actually need replacing. Some argue that planned obsolescence is wasteful; some claim it is unethical. Marketers respond that consumers favour style modifications because they like changes in the appearance of goods such as clothing and cars. Marketers also contend that it is consumers, not manufacturers and marketers, who decide when styles are obsolete.

planned obsolescence
The practice of modifying products in such a way that those which have already been sold become obsolete before they actually need replacement.

product line extension
Adding additional products to an existing product line in order to compete more broadly in the industry.

Repositioning

As Chapter 6 explained, repositioning involves changing consumers' perceptions of a brand. "Restaurant-style" has become a popular positioning for soup companies. Pillsbury has launched a line of herb-infused pasta soups for Progresso, and ConAgra will introduce two new Healthy Choice flavours—gumbo with chicken and sausage, and a cheese-based potato soup.[7]

Changing demographics, declining sales, and changes in the social environment often motivate firms to reposition established brands. Eroding market share and the changing demographics of snackers led Frito-Lay to reposition its top-selling brand, Fritos, after fifty-eight years of successfully targeting all ages. This effort included making major changes in the Fritos logo and packaging to focus on consumers between nine and eighteen, and launching a major new radio and TV advertising campaign. Playboy, one of the world's best-known brands, is repositioning itself to better reflect contemporary values and lifestyles. "Our core customers have always been men, but we're trying now to extend the brand attributes to couples," says Christie Hefner. "Playboy is ... a brand that is sexy, romantic, fun, and sophisticated. It should have a broader audience."[8]

Can you think of a scenario where a pair of Levi's jeans, like those being made at this factory in Cape Town, South Africa, would be obsolete? How has Levi's extended its product line to combat any potential obsolescence of its blue jeans?

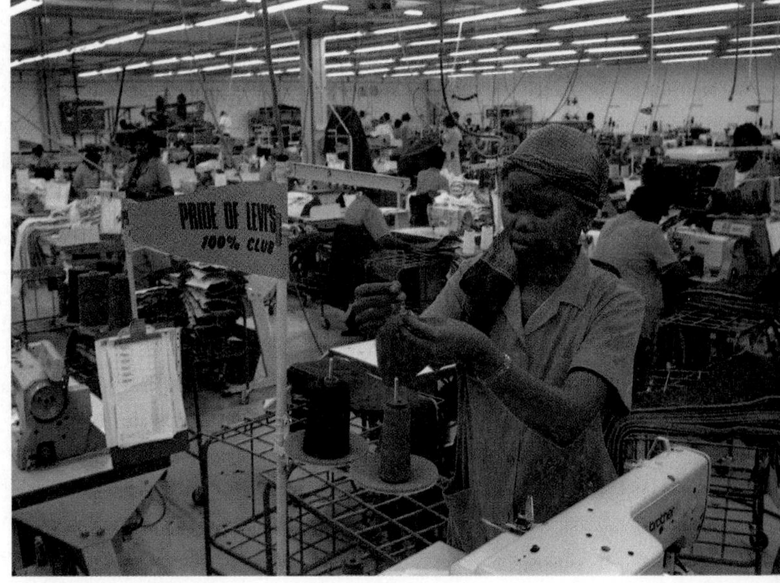

Product Line Extensions

Product line extension occurs when a company's management decides to add products to an existing product line in order to compete more broadly in the industry. Mercedes-Benz AG added eleven cars to its line of passenger vehicles between 1997 and 2000, including two "mini" city cars and a sports utility vehicle.[9] Procter & Gamble is extending its shampoo brand Pantene with its first anti-dandruff product—Pro V Anti-Dandruff—positioned distinctly for women.[10]

Product Line Contraction

Does the world really need thirty-one varieties of Head & Shoulders shampoo? Or fifty-two versions of Crest? Procter & Gamble Co. has decided the answer is no.[11] Procter & Gamble is contracting its product lines by eliminating unpopular sizes, flavours, and other variations to make it easier for customers to find what they are looking for. After decades of introducing new-and-improved this, lemon-flavoured that, and extra-jumbo-size the other thing, P&G has decided that its product lines are overextended.[12] Likewise, Black & Decker has decided to delete a number of household products—Dustbusters, SnakeLight flashlights, and toaster ovens—and concentrate on power tools.[13] Symptoms of product line overextension include the following:

- Some products in the line are not contributing to profits because of low sales, or they are cannibalizing sales of other items in the line.
- Manufacturing or marketing resources are being disproportionately allocated to slow-moving products.
- Some items in the line are obsolete because of new product entries in the line or new products being offered by competitors.

Three major benefits are likely when a firm contracts overextended product lines. First, resources become concentrated on the most important products. Second, managers no longer waste resources trying to improve the sales and profits of poorly performing products. Third, new product items have a greater chance of being successful because more financial and human resources are available to manage them.

Branding

Describe marketing uses of branding

brand
A name, term, symbol, design, or combination thereof that identifies a seller's products and differentiates them from competitors' products.

brand name
That part of a brand that can be spoken, including letters, words, and numbers.

brand mark
The elements of a brand that cannot be spoken.

brand equity
The value of company and brand names.

The success of any business or consumer product depends in part on the target market's ability to distinguish that product from others. Branding is the most valuable tool marketers have for distinguishing their products from the competition's.

A **brand** is a name, term, symbol, design, or combination thereof that identifies a seller's products and differentiates them from competitors' products. A **brand name** is that part of a brand that can be spoken, and can include words (Chevrolet), letters (GM, YMCA), or numbers (WD-40, 7-Eleven). The elements of a brand that cannot be spoken are called **brand marks**—for example, the well-known Mercedes-Benz and McDonald's symbols.

Benefits of Branding

Branding has three main end-purposes: product identification, repeat sales, and new-product sales. The most important of these is *product identification.* Branding allows marketers to distinguish their products from all others. Many brand names are extremely familiar to consumers. Examples include Coca-Cola, McDonald's, Kodak, Hallmark, and Disney. According to teenagers, the coolest brands are Nike, Levi's, Guess?, Gap, Coke, Pepsi, and Sega.[14]

The term **brand equity** refers to the value of company and brand names. A brand that has high awareness, perceived quality, and brand loyalty among customers has high brand equity. A brand with strong brand equity is a valuable

exhibit 9.3

Estimated Value of Selected World Brands

Brand	Current value in billions (C$)
Coca-Cola	$71.5
Marlboro	$69.6
IBM	$31.3
Motorola	$28.1
Hewlett-Packard	$24.2
Microsoft	$21.4
Kodak	$21.2
Budweiser	$20.9
Kellogg's	$20.1
Nescafe	$18.8

Source: *Financial World,* July 1999.

exhibit 9.4

Master Brands in Selected Product Categories

Product category	Master brand
Baking soda	Arm & Hammer
Adhesive bandages	Band-Aid
Rum	Bacardi
Antacids	Alka-Seltzer
Gelatin	Jell-O
Soup	Campbell's
Toy trains	Lionel
Cream cheese	Philadelphia
Crayons	Crayola
Petroleum jelly	Vaseline

Source: From "Strategies for Leveraging Master Brands" by Peter H. Farquhar et al., *Marketing Research,* September 1992, pp. 32–43. Reprinted by permission of the American Marketing Association.

asset. The value of some major brands, according to *Financial World* magazine is shown in Exhibit 9.3.

The term **master brand** has been used to refer to a brand so dominant in consumers' minds that they think of it immediately when a product category, use, attribute, or customer benefit is mentioned. Exhibit 9.4 lists the master brands in several product categories. How many other brands can you name in these eleven categories? Can you name any other product categories in which the master brands listed in Exhibit 9.4 compete? Probably not many. Campbell's means soup to consumers; it doesn't mean high-quality food products.

master brand
A brand so dominant in consumers' minds that they think of it immediately when a product category, use situation, product attribute, or customer benefit is mentioned.

What constitutes a good brand name? An effective brand name usually has several of these features:

- It is easy to pronounce (by both domestic and foreign buyers).
- It is easy to recognize.
- It is easy to remember.
- It is short.
- It is distinctive, unique.

- It describes the product.
- It describes product use.
- It describes product benefits.
- It has a positive connotation.
- It reinforces the desired product image.
- It is legally protectable in home and foreign markets of interest.

Obviously, no brand exhibits all of these characteristics. What is most important is that the owner can protect the brand for its exclusive use.

Well-known brands command substantial premiums in many places around the world. In India, Gillette disposable razors sell for twice the price of local brands. However, companies need to make sure their brand names translate appropriately in other languages—see the "Global Perspectives" box.

The best generator of repeat sales is satisfied customers. Branding helps consumers identify products they wish to buy again and avoid those they do not. **Brand loyalty**, a consistent preference for one brand over all others, is quite high in some product categories. Over half the users in product categories such as cigarettes, mayonnaise, toothpaste, coffee, headache remedies, photographic film, bath soap, and ketchup are loyal to one brand. One annual Monitor poll conducted by Yankelovich Partners reported that 74 percent of respondents "find a brand they like, then resist efforts to get them to change." Once consumers are convinced of the quality and value of a particular brand, it takes a lot of money and effort to change their minds.[15] Brand identity is essential to developing brand loyalty.

brand loyalty
A consistent preference for one brand over all others.

The third main purpose of branding is to facilitate new product sales. Company and brand names like those listed in Exhibit 9.3 and Exhibit 9.4 are extremely useful when introducing new products.

The Internet is providing firms with new means of generating brand awareness, promoting a desired brand image, stimulating new and repeat brand sales, enhancing brand loyalty, and building brand equity. A number of packaged goods firms, including Procter & Gamble, Campbell's Soup, and Gerber, have developed an on-line presence. Unilever's Lipton Recipe Secrets has launched a Website that will be a part of an interactive test that the company plans to use to measure brand awareness, attitudes, and product use.[16]

global perspectives

The Name Game Heats Up

As the world goes global, it is more important than ever that companies screen their brand names for multilingual suitability. Here are a few examples of companies that ran into brand name problems overseas:

- General Motors named a new Chevrolet the Beretta without getting permission from the Italian arms manufacturer. It cost GM $500,000 to settle the lawsuit.
- Estee Lauder was set to export its Country Mist makeup when German managers pointed out that "mist" in German is slang for "manure." The name became Country Moist in Germany.
- A food company advertised its giant burrito as Burrada. In Spanish, the colloquial meaning of that word is "big mistake."

Foreign companies selling here often make the same mistakes.

Consider:

- Creap (Japanese coffee creamer)
- Bimbo (Mexican bread)
- Darkie (Asian toothpaste)[17]

What should companies do to avoid these kinds of mistakes? What would also be some important considerations for brand names used in other countries?

Fuji
Tylenol
What elements on Fuji film's Website seem to encourage brand loyalty? Be sure to check out the list of services. What about the elements on Tylenol's site? Why do you think so?
www.fujifilm.net; www.tylenol.com

exhibit 9.5
Major Branding Decisions

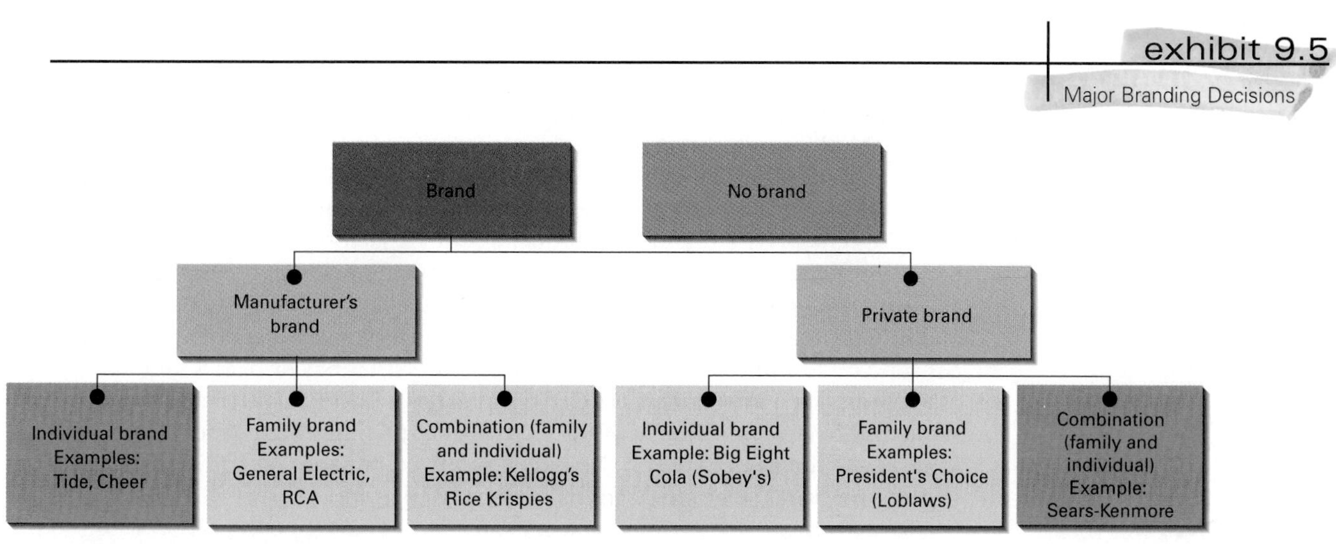

Branding Strategies

Firms face complex branding decisions. As Exhibit 9.5 illustrates, the first decision is whether to brand at all. Some firms actually use the lack of a brand name as a selling point. Unbranded products are called generic products. Firms that decide to brand their products must decide whether to follow a policy of using manufacturers' brands, or private (distributor) brands, or both. In either case, they must then decide whether to go with individual branding (different brands for different products), or family branding (common names for different products), or a combination of the two.

Generic Products Versus Branded Products

The typical **generic product** is a no-frills, no-brand-name, low-cost product identified simply by its product category. (Note that a generic product is not the same thing as a brand name that has become generic, such as cellophane.) Generic products have captured significant market shares in some product categories, such as canned fruits, canned vegetables, and paper products. These unbranded products are often identified only by black stencilled lettering on white packages.

generic product
A no-frills, no-brand-name, low-cost product that is identified simply by its product category.

The main appeal of generics is their low price. Generic grocery products are usually 30 to 40 percent less expensive than manufacturers' brands in the same product category and 20 to 25 percent less expensive than retailer-owned brands.

Pharmaceuticals are another product category in which generics have made inroads. When patents on successful pharmaceutical products expire, low-cost generics rapidly appear on the market. When the patent on Merck's popular antiarthritis drug Clinoril expired, sales declined by 50 percent almost immediately.

Brand names are also important in the service industry; see this chapter's "Entrepreneurial Insights" box.

Manufacturers' Brands Versus Private Brands

The brand name of a manufacturer (e.g., Kodak, Lazy Boy, Fruit of the Loom) is called a **manufacturer's brand**. Sometimes the term "national brand" is used instead, but often this isn't accurate, as many manufacturers serve only regional markets.

manufacturers' brand
The brand name of a manufacturer.

private brand
A brand name owned by a wholesaler or a retailer.

A **private brand** is a brand name owned by a wholesaler or a retailer. Craftsman (a Sears brand), President's Choice (Loblaws), Mastercraft (Canadian Tire), Beaumark (The Bay), Big Eight (Sobey's), Select (Safeway), and Life Brand (Shoppers Drug Mart) are all private brands. Private labels currently account for about 19.1 percent of retail sales in Canada, but the figures vary significantly by province. Thus, they account for 25.2 percent of sales in Ontario but only 11.4 percent of sales in Quebec. Canada ranks fourth in the world in private label sales, behind Switzerland (41.8 percent), Great Britain (29.7 percent), and Belgium (25.8 percent). The biggest-selling product categories for private labels are butter and dairy products (62.1 percent) and frozen vegetables (53.7 percent).[18]

Who buys private brands? According to one expert, "the young, discerning, educated shopper is the private label buyer." These individuals are willing to purchase private brands because they have confidence in their ability to assess quality and value.[19] Exhibit 9.6 illustrates key issues that wholesalers and retailers should consider in deciding whether to sell manufacturers' brands or private brands. Many firms, such as Wal-Mart, The Bay, and Safeway, offer a combination of both. In fact, Wal-Mart and Sears have turned their low-priced, private-label jeans into some of the most popular brands around, thanks to hip marketing campaigns featuring rock bands, Websites, and imagery targeted at teens.[20]

Individual Brands Versus Family Brands

individual branding
Using different brand names for different products.

Many companies use different brand names for different products; this practice is referred to as **individual branding**. Companies use individual brands when their products vary greatly in use or performance. It would not make sense to use the same brand name for a pair of dress socks and a baseball bat. Procter & Gamble targets different segments of the laundry detergent market with Bold, Cheer, Dash, Dreft, Era, Gain, Ivory Snow, Oxydol, Solo, and Tide. Canada Packers sells its food products under the names Maple Leaf, York, Domestic, Dial, and Devon.

family brand
Marketing several different products under the same brand name.

A company that markets several different products under the same brand name is using a **family brand.** Sony's family brand includes radios, TV sets, stereos, and other electronic products. But a brand name can only be stretched so far. Do you know the differences among Holiday Inn, Holiday Inn Express, Hol-

entrepreneurial insights

Brand Names Mean More Profits in the Service Industry

Three years ago, the sign came down on the Orchard Park Hotel in Toronto and a Days Inn sign was erected in its place. The hotel, in the city's east end near the Beaches neighbourhood, was still owned and managed by Ron Chemij and his family, but they had decided they could make more money with a well-known name.

"People used to come in and say 'Can I look at a room and how much?'" says Mr. Chemij. "With the Days Inn sign, they come in and say, 'How much?' They know what they're getting with a Days Inn."

Across Canada, more and more independent hotel and motel owners have been going to brand-name chains. The hotels and motels are still independently owned, but the owners enter a marketing or franchise agreement to use the well-known brand name. According to the Hotel Association of Canada, the number of brand-name hotels in the country has risen by 47 percent in the past five years with virtually no new construction. "It's existing properties that are going to the name chains," says Anthony Pollard, president of the association.

The trend has been driven by the realities of the market. An analysis of 8,013 hotels and motels by Dun & Bradstreet Canada shows extremely weak profits for the independents. Brand-name hotels have been performing much better. D&B believes that a recognizable name offers hotel owners significant advantages. "We track market share numbers and we see about a 15 percent market share premium for a well-known name," says Robert Ortt of Dun & Bradstreet.

Profitable hotels often make a positive return on only the last 15 to 20 percent of the business they bring in. Mr. Chemij says the first years of his hotel's life were a struggle. But he adds that his occupancy rate has jumped 15 percent each year since the switch to Days Inn.[21]

iday Inn Select, Holiday Inn Sunspree Resort, Holiday Inn Garden Court, and Holiday Inn Hotel & Suites? Neither do most travellers.[22] Loblaws has a very successful family brand name in President's Choice, which is carried on cookies, soft drinks, bottled water, paper products, and many other items. Loblaws is now considering adding the President's Choice name to the insurance, mutual fund, and travel businesses it operates.[23] Do you think this will work, or is it a case of extending the name too far?

Co-branding

Co-branding involves placing two or more brand names on a product or its package. There are three types of co-branding. *Ingredient branding* identifies the brand of a part that makes up the product. Examples of ingredient branding include a microprocessor (Intel) in a personal computer (Compaq), and a premium leather interior (Coach) in an automobile (Lincoln). *Cooperative branding* is where two brands receiving equal treatment borrow on each other's brand equity; examples include Second Cup and Air Canada, and American Express and Sheraton. Finally, there is *complementary branding*, where products are advertised or marketed together to suggest use, such as a spirits brand (Seagram's) and a compatible mixer (7-Up).

co-branding
Placing two or more brand names on a product or its package.

Co-branding is a useful strategy when a combination of brand names enhances the prestige or perceived value of a product or when it benefits brand owners and users. Costco Wholesale outlets are co-branded with American Express; this allows cardholders to earn dollars off on purchases at Costco outlets in Canada.

Co-branding can also be used when two or more organizations wish to collaborate on a product. Frito-Lay and McIllhenny's have joined together to market The Original Tabasco Chips.[24] Nabisco and Kraft Foods' Post cereal have teamed up to offer Oreo O's cereal.[25]

exhibit 9.6

Comparing Manufacturers' and Private Brands from the Reseller's Perspective

Key advantages of carrying manufacturer's brands	Key advantages of carrying private brands
• Heavy advertising to the consumer by manufacturers like Procter & Gamble helps develop strong consumer loyalties.	• A wholesaler or retailer can usually earn higher profits on its own brand. Also, because the private brand is exclusive, there is less pressure to mark the price down to meet competition.
• Well-known manufacturers' brands, such as Kodak and Fisher-Price, can attract new customers and enhance the dealer's (wholesaler's or retailer's) prestige.	• A manufacturer can decide to drop a brand or a reseller at any time or even to become a direct competitor to its dealers.
• Many manufacturers offer rapid delivery, enabling the dealer to carry less inventory.	• A private brand ties the customer to the wholesaler or retailer. A person who wants a Die-Hard battery must go to Sears.
• If a dealer happens to sell a manufacturer's brand of poor quality, the customer may simply switch brands but remain loyal to the dealer.	• Wholesalers and retailers have no control over the intensity of distribution of manufacturers' brands. Canadian Tire store managers don't have to worry about competing with other sellers of Mastercraft or MotoMaster products. They know that these brands are sold only in Canadian Tire stores.

trademark
The exclusive right to use a brand or part of a brand.

service mark
Trademark for a service.

Trademarks

A **trademark** is the exclusive right to use a brand or part of a brand. Others are prohibited from using the brand without permission. A **service mark** performs the same function for services, such as H&R Block and Weight Watchers. Parts of a brand or other product identification may qualify for trademark protection. Examples:

- Shapes, such as the Jeep front grille and the Coca-Cola bottle.
- Ornamental colour or design, such as the decoration on Nike tennis shoes, the black-and-copper colour combination of a Duracell battery, Levi's small tag on the left side of the rear pocket of its jeans, and the cutoff black cone on the top of Cross pens.
- Catchy phrases, such as Prudential's "Own a piece of the rock" and Timex's "Takes a licking and keeps on ticking."
- Abbreviations, such as Blue, CN, and Coke.

In Canada, trademarks are registered under the Trademarks Act. Rights to a trademark last as long as the mark is used. Usually, if a firm does not use a trademark for two years, the trademark is considered abandoned. If a new user picks up the abandoned trademark, that new user can claim exclusive ownership of the mark. The Trademarks Act specifies the types of marks that can be protected and the remedies available for trademark violations. Businesses planning to introduce new brands, trademarks, or packages should consider the following:[26]

generic product name
Identifies a product by class or type and cannot be trademarked.

- Check carefully before adopting a trademark or packaging style to make sure you're not infringing on someone else's.
- After a thorough search, consider registering your trademark.
- Make your packaging as distinctive as possible.
- Police your trademark.

Procter & Gamble uses individual branding to target different segments of the laundry detergent market. How successful do you think the company would be if it shifted to a family branding strategy? Do you think Era would compete as effectively? More effectively? Less effectively? Explain.

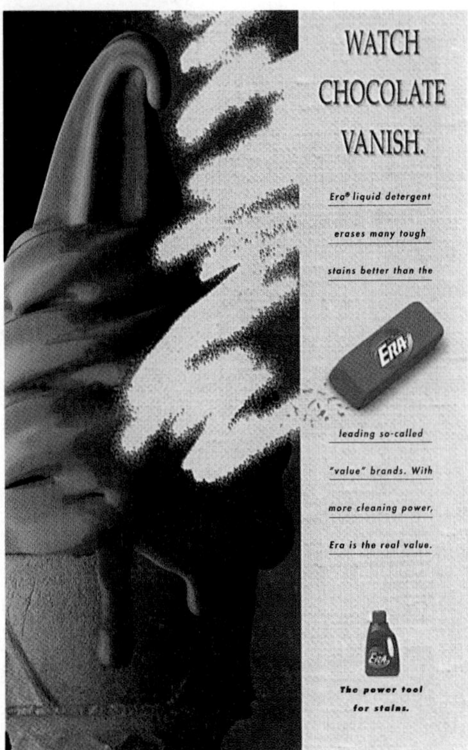

WATCH
CHOCOLATE
VANISH.
Era® liquid detergent
erases many tough
stains better than the
leading so-called
"value" brands. With
more cleaning power,
Era is the real value.
ERA
The power tool
for stains.

Sometimes it is difficult to determine whether a particular brand or package design is infringing on another's trademark. GolfGear International's new product branding strategy, described in this chapter's "Ethics in Marketing" example, illustrates this point.

Companies that fail to protect their trademarks face the problem of their product names becoming generic. A **generic product name** identifies a product by class or type and cannot be trademarked. Former brand names that were not sufficiently protected by their owners and that subsequently became generic product names include aspirin, cellophane, linoleum, thermos, kerosene, monopoly, cola, and shredded wheat.

Companies like Rolls-Royce, Cross, Xerox, Levi Strauss, Frigidaire, and McDonald's aggressively enforce their trademarks. Rolls-Royce, Coca-Cola, and Xerox even run newspaper and magazine ads stating that their names are trademarks and should not be used as descriptive or generic terms. Some ads threaten lawsuits against competitors that violate trademarks.

Despite severe penalties for trademark violations, trademark infringement lawsuits are not uncommon. One of the major battles is over brand names that closely resemble another brand name. Donna Karan filed a lawsuit against Donnkenny Inc., whose Nasdaq trading symbol—DNKY—is too close to Karan's DKNY trademark.[27] Polo Ralph Lauren is concerned about the potential confusion with a magazine named *Polo,* a twenty-three-year-old publication aimed at eques-

ethics in marketing

Ti-Gear: Owning Up to a Name

The name of GolfGear International Inc.'s new product offering, the "Ti-Gear" wood, is raising a few eyebrows. On the one hand, "They [GolfGear International] don't have Tiger [Woods'] authorization, and we can't give further comment on the advice of our attorneys," says Bev Norwood, spokesperson for International Management Group, the sports representative's agency working on behalf of Woods. On the other hand, the golf club is made with a patented "forged titanium insert" intended to help the ball travel farther.

GolfGear International's president and chairman, Don Anderson, noted in a written statement that his company has been using the name Titanium Gear since 1990 or 1991.

"We shortened it to Ti-Gear," his statement read. "'Ti' is the symbol of Titanium, and 'Gear' follows our family of products since we started in business nearly ten years ago. The name ... clearly has nothing to do with Tiger Woods." He also noted that other GolfGear products use similar names that reflect their components, such as "Carbon Gear."

"Determining whether or not the use of a particular mark is likely to cause confusion with another mark is based on a number of factors," says Bart Lazar, a partner specializing in the protection and enforcement of trademark rights with the Seyfarth, Shaw, Fairweather and Geraldson law firm. "The fact that two marks may look or sound similar is important, but it's only one factor." Among the criteria that would factor into a trademark infringement case would be whether GolfGear knew of Tiger Woods at the time the company adopted the mark, and whether consumers are likely to be confused.[28]

Is the Ti-Gear brand a trademark violation? Is the branding strategy ethical? Discuss.

trians. The company is worried that readers will mistake the magazine for something associated with the designer.[29]

Companies must also contend with fake or unauthorized brands, such as fake Levi's jeans, Microsoft software, Rolex watches, Reebok and Nike footwear, and Louis Vuitton handbags. Copycat golf clubs, such as Big Bursa, a knockoff of Callaway's popular Big Bertha, are growing in sales.[30]

In Europe you can sue counterfeiters only if your brand, logo, or trademark is formally registered. Until recently, formal registration was required in each country in which a company sought protection. A company can now register its trademark in all European Union (EU) member countries with one application.[31]

Packaging

5
Describe marketing uses of packaging and labelling

Packages have always served a practical function, which is to hold contents together and protect goods as they move through the distribution channel. Today, packaging is also a container for promoting the product and making it easier and safer to use.

Packaging Functions

The three most important functions of packaging are to contain and protect products, to promote products, and to facilitate the storage, use, and convenience of products. A fourth function of packaging that is becoming increasingly important is to facilitate recycling and reduce environmental damage.

Containing and Protecting Products The most obvious function of packaging is to contain products that are liquid, granular, or otherwise divisible. Packaging also enables manufacturers, wholesalers, and retailers to market products in specific quantities, such as grams.

Physical protection is another obvious function of packaging. Most products are handled several times between the time they are manufactured, harvested, or otherwise produced and the time they are consumed or used. Many products are

Nabisco started a trend in snack food packaging with its resealable foil bag. The resealable packaging (also known as the doyne packaging) helped increase consumer consumption of the product and also led the company to roll the packaging out with other brands such as CRISPERS Crackers.

shipped, stored, and inspected several times between production and consumption. Some, like milk, need to be refrigerated. Others, like beer, are sensitive to light. Still others, like medicines and bandages, need to be kept sterile. Packages protect products from breakage, evaporation, spillage, spoilage, light, heat, cold, infestation, and many other conditions. Mission Foods is using modified-atmosphere packaging for tortillas, which are usually refrigerated. Oxygen-collecting films now in development could improve shelf-life for refrigerated pastas.[32]

Promoting Products Packaging does more than identify the brand, list ingredients, specify features, and give directions. A package differentiates a product from competing products and may associate a new product with a family of other products from the same manufacturer. Welch's spent over $1 million to repackage its line of grape juice-based jams, jellies, and juices to unify the line and get more impact on the shelf.[33]

Packages use designs, colours, shapes, and materials to try to influence consumers' perceptions and buying behaviour. Health-conscious consumers are likely to think that any food is probably good for them as long as it comes in green packaging. Two top brands of low-fat foods—SNACKWELL'S and Healthy Choice—use green packaging.[34] Kimberly-Clark Corp. and Procter & Gamble Co. recently introduced a wide array of more appealing boxes for Kleenex and Puffs tissues. The idea is that if boxes are more attractive, people won't mind sticking them in every room of the house. So far the strategy seems to be working. Almost 25 percent of the money spent on this $1.5 billion market goes for premium varieties.[35]

Packaging has a measurable effect on sales. Quaker Oats revised its package for Rice-a-Roni without making any other changes in marketing strategy and experienced a 44 percent increase in sales in one year.

Facilitating Storage, Use, and Convenience Wholesalers and retailers prefer packages that are easy to ship, store, and stock on shelves. They also like packages that protect products, prevent spoilage or breakage, and extend the product's shelf life.

Consumers' requirements for convenience cover many dimensions. Consumers are constantly seeking items that are easy to handle, open, and reclose. Some consumers want packages that are tamperproof or childproof. Consumers also want reusable and disposable packages. Surveys conducted by *Sales & Marketing Management* revealed that consumers dislike—and avoid buying—leaky ice cream boxes, overly heavy or fat vinegar bottles, immovable pry-up lids on glass bottles, key-opener sardine cans, and hard-to-pour cereal boxes. Such packaging innovations as zipper tear strips, hinged lids, tab slots, screw-on tops, and pour spouts were introduced to solve these and other problems. C&H Sugar designed a new carton with an easy-to-pour, reclosable top.[36]

Some firms use packaging to segment markets. The C&H carton is targeted at consumers who don't do a lot of baking and are willing to pay at least twenty cents more for the package. Different-size packages appeal to heavy, moderate, and light users. Salt is sold in package sizes ranging from single serving to picnic size to giant economy size. Campbell's soup is packaged in single-serving cans aimed at the elderly and singles markets. Beer and soft drinks also are marketed in various package sizes and types. Packaging convenience can increase a product's utility and, therefore, its market share and profits.

Facilitating Recycling and Reducing Environmental Damage One of the most important current packaging issues is compatibility with the environment. According to one study, 90 percent of surveyed consumers say that no more packaging material should be used than is necessary. The ability to recycle is also important.[37]

Hewlett-Packard

Visit Hewlett-Packard's Website to find out how it facilitates the recycling and refurbishing of its products. What role do environmental concerns play in HP's packaging?

www.hp.com/abouthp/environment

on line

Some firms use their packaging to target environmentally concerned market segments. Brocato International markets shampoo and hair conditioner in biodegradable bottles. Procter & Gamble markets Sure Pro and Old Spice in "eco-friendly" pump-spray packages that do not rely on aerosol propellants. Other firms that have introduced pump sprays include S.C. Johnson (Pledge furniture polish), Reckitt & Coleman Household Products (Woolite rug cleaner), Rollout L.P. (Take 5 cleanser), and Richardson-Vicks (Vidal Sassoon hair spray).[38]

Many marketers of hair care products are packaging their products in bottles that do not rely on aerosol propellants. Can you think of other industries that have addressed environmental concerns when packaging or promoting their products?

Labelling

An integral part of any package is its label. Labelling generally takes one of two forms: persuasive or informational. **Persuasive labelling** focuses on a promotional theme or logo; consumer information is secondary. Price Pfister developed a new, persuasive label, featuring a picture of a faucet, the brand name, and the logo, with the goal of strengthening brand identity and becoming known as a brand instead of as a manufacturer.[39] Note that the standard promotional claims—"new," "improved," "super," and so on—are no longer very persuasive. Consumers have been saturated with "newness" and thus discount these claims.

Informational labelling is designed to help consumers make proper product selections and lower their cognitive dissonance after purchase. Sears attaches a "label of confidence" to all its floor coverings. This label gives product information such as durability, colour, features, cleanability, care instructions, and construction standards. Most of the major furniture manufacturers affix labels to their wares that explain their construction features: type of frame, number of coils, fabric characteristics, and so on. The Consumer Packaging and Labelling Act and the Food and Drugs Act state the minimum information that must appear on food products and set the standards for health care claims on food packaging. An important outcome of these acts is that guidelines now exist for terms such as *low fat, light, reduced cholesterol, low sodium, low calorie,* and *fresh.*

persuasive labelling
Labelling that focuses on a promotional theme or logo; consumer information is secondary.

informational labelling
Labelling designed to help consumers make proper product selections and lower their cognitive dissonance after the purchase.

Universal Product Codes

The **universal product codes (UPCs)** that appear on many items in supermarkets and other high-volume outlets were first introduced in 1974. The numerical codes appear as a series of thick and thin vertical lines, so they are often called bar codes. The lines are read by computerized optical scanners that match codes with brand names, package sizes, and prices. They also print information on cash register tapes and help retailers control inventories, track sales, and rapidly and accurately prepare records of customer purchases. The UPC system and scanners are also used in single-source research (see Chapter 7).

universal product codes (UPCs)
Series of thick and thin vertical lines (bar codes), readable by computerized optical scanners, that represent numbers used to track products.

Global Issues in Branding and Packaging

6
Discuss global issues in branding and packaging

International marketers must address several concerns regarding branding and packaging.

Branding

When planning to enter a foreign market with an existing product, a firm has three options for handling the brand name:

- *One brand name everywhere:* This strategy is useful when the company markets mainly one product and the brand name does not have negative connotations in any local market. The Coca-Cola Company uses a one-brand-name strategy in 195 countries around the world. The advantages of a one-brand-name strategy are greater identification of the product from market to market and ease of coordinating promotion from market to market.

- *Adaptations and modifications:* A one-brand-name strategy is not possible when the name cannot be pronounced in the local language, when the brand name is owned by someone else, or when the brand name has a negative or vulgar connotation in the local language. The Iranian detergent "Barf," for example, might encounter some problems in the North American market.[40]
- *Different brand names in different markets:* Local brand names are often used when translation or pronunciation problems occur, when the marketer wants the brand to appear to be a local brand, or when regulations require localization. Gillette's Silkience hair conditioner is called Soyance in France and Sientel in Italy. The adaptations were deemed to be more appealing in the local markets. Coca-Cola's Sprite brand had to be renamed Kin in Korea to satisfy a government prohibition on the unnecessary use of foreign words. Snuggle fabric softener is called FaFa in Japan, Cajoline in France, and other cuddly names elsewhere in the world.[41]

Packaging

Three aspects of packaging that are especially important in international marketing are labelling, aesthetics, and climate considerations. The major labelling concern is properly translating ingredient, promotional, and instructional information on labels. In Eastern Europe, packages of Ariel detergent are printed in fourteen languages, from Latvian to Lithuanian.[42] Care must be employed to meet all local labelling requirements. Several years ago an Italian judge ordered that all bottles of Coca-Cola be removed from retail shelves because the ingredients were not properly labelled. Labelling is also harder in countries that require bilingual labelling. This includes Belgium and Finland as well as Canada.

Package *aesthetics* may also require some attention. The key is to stay attuned to cultural traits in host countries. Often colours have different connotations: red is associated with witchcraft in some countries, green with danger, white with death. In countries where few people own a refrigerator, soft drinks are not sold in six-packs. In some countries, products like detergent may be bought only in small quantities because of a lack of storage space. Other products, like cigarettes, may be bought in small quantities, or even single units, because of the low purchasing power of buyers.

On the other hand, the simple visual elements of a brand, such as its symbol or logo, can become a standardizing element across products and countries. When Scott Paper wanted to establish a global brand identity for its product line, it used a single brand mark for all product lines that was flexible enough to accommodate such variables as country-specific product names.[43]

Products facing extreme climates or that must be shipped long distances require sturdier and more durable packages. Spillage, spoilage, and breakage are all important concerns when products are shipped long distances or handled often during shipping and storage. Packages may also have to ensure a longer product life if the time between production and consumption lengthens significantly.

warranty
Confirms the quality or performance of a good or service.

express warranty
A written guarantee.

Product Warranties

7
Describe how and why product warranties are important marketing tools

A package protects the product; a **warranty** protects the buyer and provides essential information about the product. A warranty confirms the quality or performance of a good or service. An **express warranty** is a written guarantee. Express warranties range from simple statements—such as "100 percent cotton" (a guarantee of quality) or "complete satisfaction guaranteed" (a statement of performance)—to extensive documents written in technical language. In contrast, an **implied warranty** is an unwritten guarantee that the good or service is fit for the purpose for which it was sold. Court rulings would suggest that all sales in Canada carry an implied warranty.

implied warranty
An unwritten guarantee that the good or service is fit for the purpose for which it was sold.

LOOKING BACK

Look back at the story that opened the chapter about McDonald's introducing a new wrap sandwich to its product line. McDonald's has chosen to co-brand with Healthy Choice because of the latter's low fat content, which is important to the adult market that McDonald's is trying to reach. McDonald's has been criticized in the past for its high-fat foods. With more and more adults wanting lower-fat, healthier foods, the Healthy Choice brand should be an attractive partner for McDonald's. A potential negative is that the emphasis on the Healthy Choice brand may serve to confirm adult consumers' perceptions that McDonald's traditional menu items are less healthy. The company hopes to boost overall sales by attracting adult consumers—a market segment that has been a challenge in the past. Healthy Choice has strong brand recognition as a low-fat product line. Given that more adults are health-conscious, the co-branding strategy seems to be sound.

Summary

1 **Define the term "product."** A product is anything, desired or not, that a person or organization receives in an exchange. The basic goal of purchasing decisions is to receive the tangible and intangible benefits associated with a product. Tangible aspects include packaging, style, colour, size, and features. Intangible aspects include service, the retailer's image, the manufacturer's reputation, and the social status associated with a product. An organization's product offering is the crucial element in any marketing mix.

2 **Classify consumer products.** Consumer products are classified into four categories: convenience products, shopping products, specialty products, and unsought products. Convenience products are relatively inexpensive and require limited shopping effort. Shopping products are of two types: homogeneous and heterogeneous. Because of the similarity of homogeneous products, they are differentiated mainly by price and features. In contrast, heterogeneous products appeal to consumers because of their distinct characteristics. Specialty products possess unique benefits that are highly desirable to certain customers. Finally, unsought products are either new products or products that require aggressive selling because they are generally avoided or overlooked by consumers.

3 **Define the terms "product item," "product line," and "product mix."** A product item is a specific version of a product that can be designated as a distinct offering among an organization's products. A product line is a group of closely related products offered by an organization. An organization's product mix includes all the products it sells. Product mix width refers to the number of product lines an organization offers. Product line depth is the number of product items in a product line. Firms modify existing products by changing their quality, functional characteristics, or style. Product line extension occurs when a firm adds new products to existing product lines.

4 **Describe marketing uses of branding**. A brand is a name, term, or symbol that identifies and differentiates a firm's products. Established brands encourage customer loyalty and help new products succeed. Branding strategies require decisions about individual, family, manufacturers', and private brands.

Do You Know These Terms?

5 **Describe marketing uses of packaging and labelling.** Packaging has four functions: to contain and protect products; to promote products; to facilitate product storage, use, and convenience; and to facilitate recycling and reduce environmental damage. As a tool for promotion, packaging identifies the brand and its features. It also serves the critical function of differentiating a product from competing products and linking it with related products from the same manufacturer. A label is an integral part of a package and has persuasive and informational functions. In essence, the package is the marketer's last chance to influence buyers before they make a purchase decision.

6 **Discuss global issues in branding and packaging.** Besides brand piracy, international marketers must address a variety of concerns relating to branding and packaging: choosing a brand name policy, translating labels, meeting host country labelling requirements, making packages aesthetically compatible with host country cultures, offering the sizes of packages preferred in host countries, and so on.

7 **Describe how and why product warranties are important marketing tools.** Product warranties are important tools because they offer consumers protection and help them gauge product quality.

Discussion and Writing Questions

1. Break into groups of four or five. Have each group place each of the following products in the category (convenience, shopping, specialty, unsought) that they think fits best from their perspective as consumers (i.e., if they were buying the product): Coca-Cola (brand), car stereo, winter coat, a pair of shoes, life insurance, blue jeans, hamburgers.
2. A local civic organization has asked you to give a luncheon presentation about planned obsolescence. Instead of pursuing a negative approach by talking about how businesses exploit customers by resorting to planned obsolescence, you have decided to talk about the benefits of producing products that do not last forever. Prepare a one-page outline of your presentation.
3. A local supermarket would like to introduce its own brand of paper goods (paper towels, facial tissue, etc.) to sell alongside its current inventory. The company has hired you to generate a report outlining the advantages and disadvantages of doing so. Write the report.
4. Identify five outstanding brand names, and explain why each is included in your list.
5. Break into small groups, and discuss the packaging of a product familiar to all of your group members. Make a brief presentation to your class describing the pros and cons of this package.
6. How have several snack food companies modified their products to serve the emerging needs of their customers?
7. What is the product mix offered at the following Website? **www.marriott.com**
8. List the countries to which Levi Strauss markets through **www.levi.com**. How do the product offerings differ between the North American and European selections?

Application for Small Business

The Baker family owns a trout farm in southern Ontario and is known for raising the best trout in the area. After graduating from the University of Windsor with a degree in marketing, Frank Baker returned to the farm with a mind full of new ways to cash in on the farm's reputation. At the time, the family was allowing several local supermarkets and restaurants to use the Baker name on their trout. In southern Ontario, eating Baker Farms trout was a sign of status. Frank, eager to put his degree to work, convinced his family they could make money off their name by selling their products already packaged to supermarkets. After hearing the idea, the family quickly met to formulate a plan to begin selling Baker Farms trout.

Questions

1. What type of product is the Baker family selling? Explain.
2. What type of branding is the Baker family using? Explain.
3. How should Baker Farms trout be packaged?
4. Assuming that the Bakers want to reposition their products, what would be the optimal strategy?

VIDEO CASE

Ben & Jerry's: Taste and Innovation

What's in a name? Everything at Ben & Jerry's, makers of mouth-watering ice cream in smooth and chunky flavours. Produced from local, family farm dairy products and spring water, Ben & Jerry's strong brand image is one of high quality, innovative flavours, and barrel-of-laughs names. Products like Chunky Monkey, Vanilla Like It Oughta Be, Chubby Hubby, and Chocolate Chip Cookie Dough delight the palette and underscore the whimsical image of the company. To honour Grateful Dead icon Jerry Garcia, and to appeal to youthful audiences, the company created Cherry Garcia ice cream in 1987. One of their newest flavours is Dilbert: Totally Nuts, named for the hapless comic strip hero of today's workaday world.

But the names aren't only funny. They carry a lot of weight supporting the company's brand equity. They have also created value based on customer recognition of the brand and loyalty among customers who like both the ice cream and the company mandate to improve society and the environment. Actually, Ben & Jerry's social philosophy plays a major role in making the company name well known. For example, Phish Food, chocolate ice cream with fish-shaped chocolate chunks, is named for the rock band Phish. On each container of Phish Food, the band pledges, "Our share of the proceeds goes to environmental efforts, so enjoy the good taste and karma." In 1997, sales of Phish Food generated royalties of $159,000.

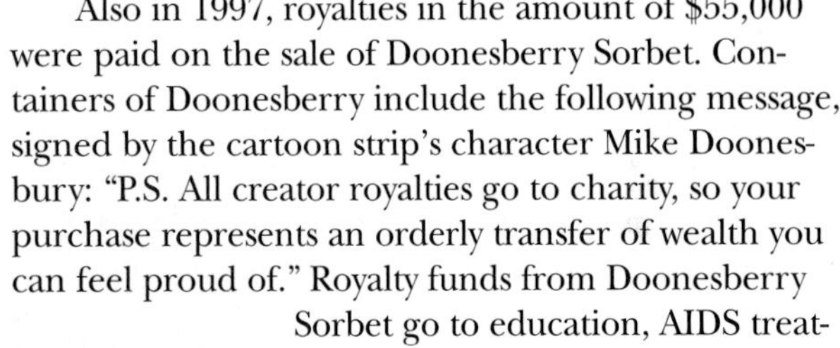

Also in 1997, royalties in the amount of $55,000 were paid on the sale of Doonesberry Sorbet. Containers of Doonesberry include the following message, signed by the cartoon strip's character Mike Doonesbury: "P.S. All creator royalties go to charity, so your purchase represents an orderly transfer of wealth you can feel proud of." Royalty funds from Doonesberry Sorbet go to education, AIDS treatment and prevention, reducing poverty, and human rights.

Though premium ice cream is still the company favourite, Ben & Jerry's has expanded the product mix because the original product is high in fat and today's consumers want low-fat, healthier products with more nutritional value. Product lines now include low-fat ice cream, low-fat and nonfat frozen yogurts, and fat-free sorbet. The idea is "to blend flavour that tastes very fattening into ice cream that isn't." All the product lines share the same marketing strategy, complete with offbeat humour and catchy names. For its twentieth birthday, Ben & Jerry's has introduced new, low-fat flavours—Coconut Cream Pie Low Fat, S'Mores, and Blackberry Cobbler. Within each product line, some flavours have become so well known that they constitute brands unto themselves. For example, Cherry Garcia is available in both the premium and frozen yogurt categories.

Catchy names and expanded product lines are not the only marketing strategies followed at Ben & Jerry's, where even the packaging is considered a promotional element. That's why all product lines are packaged in similarly designed and illustrated containers. Because consumers often believe that different product lines made by the same manufacturer are equal in quality, those who love the ice cream may try the yogurt, especially because their packaging looks alike.

To celebrate its twentieth birthday, Ben & Jerry's redesigned its package to be fun and colourful and to have an appetizing look. However, packaging at Ben & Jerry's also conveys important messages about the ingredients. Besides information on charitable contributions, the labels on the cartons state, "We oppose rBGH, Recombinant Bovine Growth Hormone. The family farmers who supply our milk and cream pledge not to treat their cows with rBGH ..." The company's overarching belief in social responsibility—whether it be the consumers' right to know what they are eating or the corporate call to social giving—is reflected in its package designs.

The packaging materials themselves have become a test of the company's pledge to improve the environment. One goal is to make the transition to totally chlorine-free paper for containers because the bleaching process releases pollutants into the air. These kinds of measures seem on the surface to be great marketing hooks; still, the public does not always favour company initiatives. The packaging for Peace Pops ice cream bars was redesigned, with this message added: "We package our Peace Pops in bags, not individual boxes, because it puts less trash in the landfill." But sales declined because customers wanted the packaging of their premium ice cream to reflect its high quality and high price. Reluctantly, the company changed packaging back to boxes. As a compromise, the new Peanut Butter & Jelly bar is in a plastic bag inside a chlorine-free box.

Bibliography

Ben & Jerry's annual report
www.benjerry.com

Questions

1. What are the tangible and intangible dimensions of Ben & Jerry's products?
2. Why did Ben & Jerry's develop several product lines?
3. Describe Ben & Jerry's brand equity.
4. What is the advantage of Ben & Jerry's using one marketing strategy for the entire product mix?

CHAPTER

10

LEARNING OBJECTIVES

After studying this chapter, you should be able to

1 Explain the importance of developing new products, and describe the six categories of new products

2 Explain the steps in the new product development process

3 Explain why some products succeed and others fail

4 Discuss global issues in new product development

5 Describe the organizational groups or structures used to facilitate new product development

6 Explain the diffusion process through which new products are adopted

7 Explain the concept of product life cycles

DEVELOPING AND MANAGING PRODUCTS

A four-year-old asked her mom if she could put coloured cake sprinkles in her favourite ketchup. The intrigued mom said it was okay, and thus came about a new product, later to be named Sparky, from the H.J. Heinz Co.

It happens that the mom works for the worldwide, multi-billion-dollar H.J. Heinz Company of Canada Ltd. in Leamington, Ontario. When the mom related the story of her daughter's request to the marketing people in the Leamington office, they too were intrigued. The product concept was tested with consumers, and the research/test kitchen crew in Leamington invented sprinkles that not only appealed to the taste of young kids but could withstand sitting in ketchup bottles and still look good. For consumer testing, the product was given to 250 households with children.

Thus was born Sparky. In short order, Sparky was on supermarket shelves supported by a new advertising campaign featuring Sparky and dancing french fries. Unfortunately, Sparky didn't sell as well as Heinz had hoped and the product was withdrawn from the market. It was a product failure. For companies like Heinz, and just about every other company, some new products fail. However, for every new product failure, companies that do their homework will have several successes.

For Heinz, while Sparky was failing, Blastin' Green ketchup became a big success. Blastin' Green was selling at a rate of 1 million bottles per month in Canada and the U.S. in its first ten months on the market. Blastin' Green was so successful, in fact, that it raised Heinz's share of the ketchup market by 5 percentage points to 59 percent, its highest share ever.[2]

Shortly to follow Blastin' Green into the market is Funky Purple. Funky Purple will hit supermarket shelves in Canada in February 2002.[2] Why purple? After the success of Blastin' Green, Heinz asked thousands of kids what other ketchup colours they would like to see. The most often requested colour was purple.

The colourful ketchups from Heinz are specifically designed for kids, the segment of the market who consume more than half of all the ketchup produced. Heinz also designed new "EZ Squirt" plastic bottles for the ketchup with smaller openings that allow kids to write their names and draw designs on their food.

H.J. Heinz of Canada

How does Heinz's Website support its new products? What can you find out about new Heinz products on that Website? What can you find out about product testing?

www.heinz.com

on line

"New products are our lifeblood," states Murray Pennell, director of research and development for Heinz of Canada.[3] The H.J. Heinz Company of Canada expects anywhere from $15 to $50 million in new product sales each year.

Why do you think Sparky failed while Blastin' Green was a huge success? Are you surprised at where the idea for Sparky came from? Where might other new product ideas come from? Why do big companies like Heinz have product failures? Do you think Funky Purple will be as successful as Blastin' Green?

The Importance of New Products

1

Explain the importance of developing new products, and describe the six categories of new products

New products sustain growth and profits; they also replace obsolete items. 3M Corp. introduces around 500 new products each year.[4] Colgate-Palmolive Company credits new products launched over the past five years for bringing in $2.8 billion—almost one-third of its total sales revenue. Johnson & Johnson and Gillette Co. expect products launched in the past five years to account for 36 and 50 percent of annual revenue, respectively[5] In the past ten years, new brands have accounted for 80 percent of the sales increase in cereals.[6]

Categories of New Products

new product
A product that is new to the world, the market, the producer, the seller, or some combination of these.

The term **new product** is somewhat confusing, because it can mean so many things. There are several "correct" definitions of the term. A product can be new to the world, to the market, to the producer or seller, or to some combination of these. There are six categories of new products:

- *New-to-the-world products* (also called *discontinuous innovations*): These products create an entirely new market. The telephone, television, computer, and fax machine are commonly cited examples of new-to-the-world products.
- *New product lines*: These products allow a firm to enter an established market. When Ballard Power Systems of Vancouver added fuel cells to its battery line, it entered the efficient, nonpolluting auto engine segment of the market.
- *Additions to existing product lines:* This category includes new products that supplement a firm's established lines. Hallmark recently announced that it was adding 117 new greeting cards to its line—for pets. According to Hallmark's research, 75 percent of pet owners give Christmas presents to their pets, and 40 percent celebrate their pets' birthdays.[7]
- *Improvements or revisions of existing products:* "New and improved" products can be significantly or only slightly changed. Breyers Soft 'n Creamy! ice cream "scoops right out without bending the spoon."[8] Anyone who has ever sat around for fifteen minutes waiting for ice cream to thaw would certainly agree that this is a product improvement. The new green ketchup described at the beginning of this chapter also fits into this category.

  Most new products fit into the *improvement or revision* category. According to one expert, "companies are making low-risk launches—a lot of line extensions, new colours and flavours."[9]

Keebler

Visit Keebler's on-line newsroom to read about new product offerings. What categories of new products are represented?

www.keebler.com

on line

- *Repositioned products:* These are existing products targeted at new markets or market segments. Quaker Oats abandoned its fat-free positioning strategy for Rice Cakes following an 11 percent drop in sales over two years. The new strategy focuses on great taste and includes Chocolate Chip and Peanut Butter flavours.[10]
- *Lower-priced products:* This category includes products that provide performance similar to that of competing brands but at a lower price. Hewlett-Packard developed the Laser Jet 3100, a combination scanner, copier, printer, and fax machine. When introduced, this new product was priced lower than many conventional colour copiers, and much lower than the combined price of the four items purchased separately.

ethics in marketing

Responding to a Declining Beer Market

In 1986, Canadians drank an average of 76.88 litres of beer. That figure has since slipped below 65 litres. Canada now stands seventeenth in the world in beer consumption, behind such countries as the United Kingdom, the United States, and Ireland. Worse still, the number of Canadians between nineteen and thirty-four—the biggest beer drinkers—is declining.[11]

In response to the stagnant market, Canadian breweries are chasing consumers up the age chain, trying to get younger consumers to drink more beer, and trying to appeal to groups who have not traditionally been beer drinkers. "Your taste buds change as you get older," says Mike Bradica, vice-president and general manager of Guinness Canada, which sells beers like Guinness, Kilkenny, and Harp to please the changing tastes of beer drinkers. "It's like drinking wine. When you first start drinking wine, you drink sweeter ones. As you get older, you tend toward drier ones."[12]

Molson and Labbatt are targeting the twenty to thirty-five market with imports such as Boddingtons, Leffe, and Belle-Vue Kriek. These beers are sold exclusively through bars catering to the young and are promoted to this audience. Microbreweries have been penetrating this market with specialty products such as Upper Canada's Rebellion. Not to be left out, Molson has opened a brew pub in the Air Canada Centre, home of the Maple Leafs and Raptors. Molson is looking to open a second brew pub in Vancouver's GM Place.

Since the 1980s, Canadian breweries have been targeting women, not traditionally a beer-drinking audience, by introducing light and ice beers and through trendy advertising of these products.

Can existing beers with slight modifications be considered new products? Explain. What category of new products might these beers fall into? Should breweries be targeting new market segments to get these consumers to drink beer? Should breweries be targeting traditional markets to get them to drink more?

The New Product Development Process

2

Explain the steps in the new product development process

The management and technology consulting firm Booz, Allen, and Hamilton has studied the new product development process for over thirty years. The firm has analyzed five major studies undertaken during this period and has concluded that the companies most likely to succeed in developing and introducing new products are the ones that take the following actions:

- They make the long-term commitment needed to support innovation and new product development.
- They take a company-specific approach, driven by corporate objectives and strategies, with a well-defined new product strategy at its core.

- They capitalize on experience to achieve and maintain a competitive advantage.
- They establish an environment—a management style, an organizational structure, and a degree of support from top management—that is conducive to achieving company-specific new product and corporate objectives.[13]

Most companies follow a formal process for developing new products, a process that usually starts with a new product strategy. Exhibit 10.1 traces this seven-step process, which is discussed in detail in this section. The exhibit is funnel-shaped to highlight the fact that each stage acts as a screen. The purpose of screening is to filter out unworkable ideas.

exhibit 10.1
New Product Development Process

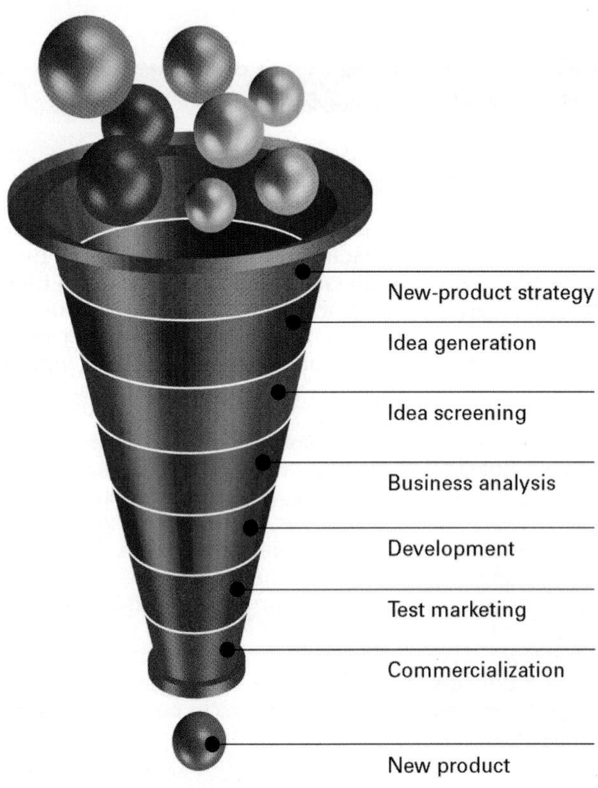

New Product Strategy

new product strategy
Linking the new product development process with the objectives of the marketing department, the business unit, and the corporation.

A **new product strategy** links the new product development process with the objectives of the marketing department, the business unit, and the corporation. A new product strategy must be compatible with these objectives, and all three objectives must be consistent with one another.

New product strategy is part of the organization's overall marketing strategy. It sharpens the organization's focus and provides general guidelines for generating, screening, and evaluating new product ideas. The new product strategy specifies the roles that new products must play in the organization's overall plan; it also describes the characteristics of the products the organization wants to offer and of the markets it wants to serve.

Healthy Choice
How does Healthy Choice use its Website to generate new product ideas? Go to "Table One" on its Website to find out.
www.healthychoice.com

Idea Generation

New product ideas have many sources, including customers, employees, distributors, competitors, R&D, and consultants.

- *Customers:* The marketing concept suggests that customers' wants and needs should be the springboard for developing new products. Thermos, the vacuum bottle manufacturer, provides an interesting example of how companies tap customers for ideas. The company's first step in developing an innovative home barbecue grill was to send ten members of its interdisciplinary new product team into the field for a month. Their assignment was to learn all about people's cookout needs and to invent a product to meet them. The team conducted focus groups, visited people's homes, and even videotaped barbecues.
- *Employees:* Marketing personnel—advertising and marketing research employees as well as salespeople—often generate new product ideas, because they analyze and are involved in the marketplace. Firms should encourage their employees to submit new product ideas, and should reward them if their ideas are adopted. Post-it® Notes started with an employee's idea. A number of years ago the R&D department of 3M's commercial tape division developed and patented the adhesive component of Post-it® Notes. However, it was a year before an employee of the commercial tape division identified a use for the adhesive. He sang in a church choir and had been using paper clips and slips of paper to mark places in hymn books. But the paper clips damaged his books, and the slips of paper fell out. The solution, as we now all know, was to apply the adhesive to small pieces of paper and sell them in packages. The product was wildly successful.

Going direct to the customer to learn about people's cookout needs is what helped the Thermos work team create a new type of outdoor grill. Tapping customers can be a very effective method of generating new product ideas.

- *Distributors:* A well-trained sales force routinely asks distributors about needs that are not being met. Because they are closer to end users, distributors are often more aware than manufacturers of customer needs. The inspiration for Rubbermaid's litter-free lunch box, named Sidekick, came from a distributor. The distributor suggested that Rubbermaid place some of its plastic containers inside a lunch box and sell the box as an alternative to plastic wrap and paper bags.
- *Competitors:* No firm relies solely on internally generated ideas for new products. A big part of any organization's marketing intelligence system should be monitoring the performance of competitors' products. One purpose of competitive monitoring is to determine which, if any, of the competitors' products should be copied (see Chapter 8). Competitive monitoring includes tracking products sold by a company's own customers. This chapter's "Global Perspectives" box illustrates how Coca-Cola has followed this strategy successfully in Japan.

There is plenty of information about competitors on the Internet.[14] AltaVista (**www.altavista.digital.com**) is a powerful index tool that can be used to locate information about products and companies. Fuld & Co.'s competitive intelligence guide provides links to a variety of market intelligence sites.

- *Research and development (R&D)*: R&D is carried out in four distinct ways. *Basic research* is scientific research aimed at discovering new technologies. *Applied research* takes these new technologies and tries to find useful applications for them. **Product development** goes one step further by converting applications into marketable products. *Product modification* involves making cosmetic or functional changes in existing products. Many new product breakthroughs come from R&D activities. Pert Plus, Procter & Gamble's combination shampoo and conditioner, was invented in the laboratory.

product development
A marketing strategy that entails creating marketable products and converting new technologies into marketable products.

- *Consultants:* Outside consultants are always available to examine a business and recommend product ideas. These firms include the Weston Group; Booz, Allen, and Hamilton; and Management Decisions. Traditionally, consultants like these have determined whether a company has a balanced portfolio of products and, if not, what new product ideas it needs in order to offset the imbalance. An outside consultant conceived Airwick's highly successful Carpet Fresh carpet cleaner.

Creativity is the wellspring of new product ideas, regardless of who comes up with them. A variety of approaches and techniques have been developed to stimulate creative thinking. The two considered most useful for generating new product ideas are brainstorming and focus group exercises. The goal of **brainstorming** is to get a group to think of unlimited ways to vary a product or solve a problem. Group members avoid criticizing an idea, no matter how ridiculous it seems. Objective evaluation is postponed—the sheer quantity of ideas is what matters. As noted in Chapter 7, an objective of focus group interviews is to stimulate insightful comments through group interaction. Focus groups usually consist of seven to ten people. Consumer focus groups have generated excellent new product ideas—for example, Cycle dog food, Stick-Up room deodorizers, Dustbuster vacuum cleaners, and Wendy's salad bar. In the industrial market, machine tools, keyboard designs, aircraft interiors, and backhoe accessories have evolved from focus groups.

brainstorming
Getting a group to think of unlimited ways to vary a product or solve a problem.

A study conducted recently by the Product Development and Management Association found that it took seven ideas to generate a new commercial product, down from eleven ideas in 1990. In 1967 it took fifty-eight ideas for one new item. Today, companies do more work at the beginning of the development process—such as identifying final users—and sometimes use computer simulation tools to speed up the design stage.[15]

Idea Screening

After new ideas have been generated, they pass through the first filter in the product development process. This stage, called **screening**, eliminates ideas that are inconsistent with the organization's new product strategy or that are obviously inappropriate for some other reason. The new product committee, the new product department, or some other formally appointed group conducts the screening review. Most new product ideas are rejected at the screening stage.

screening
The first filter in the product development process, which eliminates ideas that are inconsistent with the organization's new product strategy or are obviously inappropriate for some other reason.

Concept tests are often used during the screening stage to rate concept (or product) alternatives. A **concept test** evaluates a new product idea, usually before any prototype has been created. Typically, researchers get consumer reactions to descriptions and visual representations of a proposed product.

concept test
A test to evaluate a new product idea, usually before any prototype has been created.

Concept tests are considered fairly good predictors of success for line extensions. They have also been relatively precise predictors of success for new products that are not copycat items, that are not easily classified into existing product categories, and that do not require major changes in consumer behaviour—such as Betty Crocker Tuna Helper, Cycle dog food, and Libby Fruit Float. However, concept tests are usually inaccurate in predicting the success of new products that create new consumption patterns and that require major changes in consumer behaviour—such as microwave ovens, videocassette recorders, computers, and DVDs.

global perspectives

Monitoring Competition Pays Off

In 1990 the Coca-Cola Company dominated the soft drink market in Japan. Coke controlled 90 percent of the carbonated drink market and over 30 percent of the entire soft drink market, including noncarbonated drinks.

But consumer preferences began changing rapidly. Demand for less-sweet noncarbonated drinks rose quickly. Japanese companies such as Suntory, Asahi Soft Drinks, and Calpis Food Industry began attracting large numbers of purchasers with new products such as Asian teas, fruit-flavoured sodas, teas, coffees, and fermented milk drinks. Coke's market share began falling rapidly. According to one industry analyst, "Coke used to have trouble with product development—with its speed and coming up with new localized products—but they've gotten faster and smarter.[16]

Since 1994 Coke has reversed its declining market share by introducing more than thirty new drinks, including an Asian tea called Sokenbicha, an English tea called Kochakaden, a coffee drink called Georgia, and a fermented milk drink called Lactia.

"Coca-Cola is mean and scary," says one competitor. "They have deep pockets, and these days they study us closely and challenge us with all these me-toos. That's something they never did before."[17]

A Coca-Cola representative, when asked to respond to this charge, said that the company does not follow a copy-cat strategy. Instead, it improves on competitors' product ideas and introduces superior products.

What category of new products is the Coca-Cola Company introducing into Japan? Is its strategy of monitoring competitors' new products and introducing similar items ethical? Does it make good business sense?

Business Analysis

New product ideas that survive the initial screening process move to the **business analysis** stage, where preliminary figures for demand, cost, sales, and profitability are calculated. For the first time, costs and revenues are estimated and compared. Depending on the nature of the product and the company, this process may be simple or complex.

business analysis
The second stage of the screening process, when preliminary figures for demand, cost, sales, and profitability are calculated.

The newness of the product, the size of the market, and the nature of the competition all affect the accuracy of revenue projections. In an established market such as soft drinks, industry estimates of total market size are available. Forecasting market share for a new entry is a bigger challenge.

Analyzing overall economic trends and their impact on estimated sales is especially important in product categories that are sensitive to fluctuations in the business cycle. If consumers view the economy as uncertain and risky, they will put off buying durable goods like homes, cars, and appliances. Likewise, business buyers postpone major equipment purchases if they expect a recession.

The following questions are commonly asked during the business analysis stage:

- What is the likely demand for the product?
- What impact would the new product probably have on total sales, profits, market share, and return on investment?
- How would the introduction of the product affect existing products? Would the new product cannibalize existing products?
- Would current customers benefit from the product?
- Would the product enhance the image of the company's overall product mix?
- Would the new product affect current employees in any way? Would it lead to hiring more people or reducing the size of the workforce?
- What new facilities, if any, would be needed?
- How would competitors be likely to respond?
- What is the risk of failure? Is the company willing to take the risk?

Answering these and related questions may require studies of markets, costs, technical capabilities, and the competition. But at the end of this stage, management should have a good understanding of the product's market potential. This full understanding is important, because costs increase dramatically once a product idea enters the development stage.

This chapter's "Entrepreneurial Insights" box provides a checklist that small businesses can use for evaluating new product ideas.

Development

development
The stage in the product development process when a prototype is developed and a marketing strategy is outlined.

In the early stages of **development**, the R&D department or engineering department may develop a prototype of the product. During this stage, the firm should start sketching a marketing strategy. The marketing department should decide on the product's packaging, branding, labelling, and so on. Also, it should map out preliminary promotion, price, and distribution strategies. The technical feasibility of manufacturing the product at an acceptable cost should also be thoroughly examined.

The development stage can last a long time and thus be very expensive. Crest toothpaste was in the development stage for ten years. It took eighteen years to develop Minute Rice, fifteen years to develop the Polaroid Colourpack camera, fifteen years to develop the Xerox copy machine, and fifty-five years to develop television. Gillette spent six years and more than $750 million developing the MACH 3 razor.[18] Preliminary efforts to develop a three-bladed razor began twenty-eight years before the MACH was launched.[19]

The development process works best when all the involved parties (R&D, marketing, engineering, production, and even suppliers) work together rather than sequentially—a process called simultaneous product development (discussed later in this chapter). The Internet is useful for improving communications between marketing personnel, advertising agencies, graphic designers, and others

entrepreneurial insights

Checklist for Evaluating New Product Concepts

If a small business is lucky enough to have stable or increasing sales, new product additions can boost profits and market share. Small business managers must be careful, however, not to expand beyond the firm's financial capacity. A new product will require shelf space, investment in inventory, perhaps spare parts, and maybe even a new salesperson; all of these cost money.

A new small business usually has only one chance to "do it right." A failure in introducing a new product can mean bankruptcy. Conversely, for the owner of an established small business who suddenly finds that his or her source of livelihood has evaporated, the right new product can help offset declining demand.

The product development process is generally the same no matter how small or large the firm. However, many entrepreneurs must undertake most steps in the process themselves; they cannot rely on specialists or outside consultants.

Here's a simple checklist that small businesses can use for evaluating new product concepts. By adding up the points, a small business owner can more accurately estimate success.

1. Contribution to before-tax return on investment:
   - More than 35 percent +2
   - 25–35 percent +1
   - 20–25 percent –1
   - Less than 20 percent –2
2. Estimated annual sales:
   - More than $10 million +2
   - $2–$10 million +1
   - $1–$1.99 million –1
   - Less than $1 million –2
3. Estimated growth phase of product life cycle:
   - More than three years +2
   - Two or three years +1
   - One or two years –1
   - Less than one year –2
4. Capital investment payback:
   - Less than one year +2
   - One to two years +1
   - Two to three years –1
   - More than three years –2
5. Premium price potential:
   - Weak or no competition, making entry easy +2
   - Mildly competitive entry conditions +1
   - Strongly competitive entry conditions –1
   - Entrenched competition that makes entry difficult –2

This checklist is by no means complete, but a neutral or negative total score should give an entrepreneur reason to consider dropping the product concept.

involved in developing products. On the Internet, multiple parties from a number of different companies can meet regularly with new ideas and information at their fingertips—an inexpensive way to get products to the shelf faster.[20]

Scuba Barbie has to swim and kick for fifteen hours to satisfy Mattel that she'll last at least a year.

During the development stage, laboratory tests are often conducted on prototype models. User safety is an important aspect of lab testing, which subjects products to much more severe treatment than they are expected to receive from end users. Kindred Industries of Midland, Ontario, tests kitchen faucets by running water through them at much higher pressure and for much longer periods than would ever occur in someone's kitchen.

Many products that test well in the lab are also tried out in homes or businesses. Product categories well suited for use tests include human and pet food products, household cleaning products, and industrial chemicals and supplies. These products are all relatively inexpensive, and their performance characteristics are apparent to users. At a factory that Gillette Co. calls "World Shaving Headquarters," about 200 male and 30 female employee volunteers evaluate potential new razors and blades each weekday morning. They assess features such as sharpness, smoothness, and ease of handling.[21] In addition to to this, research teams count razor strokes, clock the length of dewhiskerization, and observe split-face shaving, in which dueling products are tested on opposite sides of a subject's face. Gillette also employs 2,700 off-site shavers, who evaluate products at home.

Most products require some refinement based on the results of laboratory and use tests. A second stage of development often takes place before test marketing.

Test Marketing

After products and marketing programs have been developed, they are usually tested in the marketplace. **Test marketing** is the limited introduction of a product and a marketing program to determine the reactions of potential customers in a market situation. Test marketing allows management to evaluate alternative strategies and to assess how well the various aspects of the marketing mix fit together. Febreze, Procter & Gamble Co.'s new spray that permanently removes odors such as cigarette smoke and pet odors from garments, was test marketed for nearly a year.[22]

test marketing
The limited introduction of a product and a marketing program to determine the reactions of potential customers in a market situation.

The cities chosen as test sites should reflect market conditions in the new product's projected market area. No "magic city" exists that can universally represent market conditions; a product's success in one city can never guarantee that it will be a nationwide hit. So when selecting test market cities, researchers should find locations where the demographics and purchasing habits mirror the overall market. The company should also have good distribution in the test cities. Moreover, the test locations should be isolated from the media. If the TV stations in a particular market reach a very large area outside that market, the advertising used for the test product may pull in many consumers from outside the market. The product may then look more successful than it really is. Exhibit 10.2 provides a useful checklist of criteria for selecting test markets.

The High Costs of Test Marketing

Test marketing often takes a year or longer, and costs can exceed $1 million. Some products remain in test markets even longer. McDonald's spent twelve years developing and testing salads before introducing them. Despite the cost, many firms believe it is a lot better to fail in a test market than in a national introduction.

on line

What can you find out on the Internet about current test marketing? Use the AltaVista search engine and type in "Test Marketing."

www.altavista.com

exhibit 10.2

Checklist for Selecting Test Markets

In choosing a test market, many criteria need to be considered, but especially the following:
Similarity to planned distribution outlets
Relative isolation from other cities
Availability of advertising media that will cooperate
Diversified cross-section of ages, religions, cultural-societal preferences, etc.
No atypical purchasing habits
Representative population size
Typical per capita income
Good record as a test city, but not overly used
Not easily "jammed" by competitors
Stability of year-round sales
No dominant television station; multiple newspapers, magazines, and radio stations
Availability of retailers that will cooperate
Availability of research and audit services
Freedom from unusual influences, such as one industry's dominance or heavy tourism

Because test marketing is so expensive, some companies do not test line extensions of well-known brands. Because the Folger's brand is well known, Procter & Gamble faced little risk in distributing its instant decaffeinated version nationally. Consolidated Foods Kitchen of Sara Lee followed the same approach with its frozen croissants. Other products that were introduced without being test marketed include General Foods' International Coffees, Quaker Oats' Chewy Granola Bars and Granola Dipps, and Pillsbury's Milk Break Bars.

The high cost of test marketing is not purely financial. One unavoidable problem is that test marketing exposes the new product and its marketing mix to competitors before it is introduced. Thus, the element of surprise is lost. Several years ago, Procter & Gamble began testing a ready-to-spread Duncan Hines frosting. General Mills took note and rushed to market with its own Betty Crocker brand, which now is the best-selling brand of ready-to-spread frosting. Competitors can also sabotage or "jam" a testing program by introducing their own sales promotion, pricing, or advertising campaigns. The purpose is to hide or distort the normal conditions that the testing firm might expect in the market. When Coca-Cola tested its contour can (a curvy can inspired by Coke's trademark bottle) at a premium price, PepsiCo counterattacked furiously by offering discounts on its cola products.[23]

Alternatives to Test Marketing

Many firms are looking for cheaper, faster, safer alternatives to traditional test marketing. In the early 1980s, Information Resources Incorporated pioneered one alternative: single-source research using supermarket scanner data (see Chapter 7). A typical supermarket scanner test costs around $300,000. Another alternative to traditional test marketing is **simulated (laboratory) market testing.** Advertising and other promotional materials for several products, including the test product, are shown to members of the product's target market. These people are then taken to shop at a mock or real store, where their purchases are recorded. Shopper behaviour, including repeat purchasing, is monitored to assess the product's likely performance under true market conditions. Research firms offer simulated market tests for $25,000 to $100,000, compared to $1 million or more for full-scale test marketing.

Procter & Gamble used Canada as a test market for its battery-operated floor cleaner, the Swiffer WetJet.

Despite these alternatives, most firms still consider test marketing essential for most new products. The high price of failure simply prohibits the widespread introduction of most new products without testing. Sometimes, however, when risks of failure are estimated to be low, it is better to skip test marketing and move directly from development to commercialization.

simulated (laboratory) market testing
The presentation of advertising and other promotion materials for several products, including a test product, to members of the product's target market.

Commercialization

The final stage in the new product development process is **commercialization**, that is, the decision to market a product. The decision to commercialize the product sets several tasks in motion: ordering production materials and equipment, starting production, building inventories, shipping the product to field distribution points, training the sales force, announcing the new product to the trade, and advertising to potential customers.

commercialization
The decision to market a product.

The time from the initial commercialization decision to the product's actual introduction varies. It can range from a few weeks for simple products that use existing equipment to several years for technical products that require custom manufacturing equipment.

The total cost of development and initial introduction can be staggering. Kodak spent over $1 billion developing its Advanced Photo System (APS) and another $100 million for first-year promotion. Gillette spent $750 million developing MACH 3, and the first-year marketing budget for its new three-bladed razor was $300 million.[24]

A well-planned Internet campaign can provide information on a particular new product for people who are looking for the solutions it offers. Attempting to reach customers at the point in time when they need a product is much more efficient and cost-effective than communicating with a target market that may eventually have a need for the product.[25]

Despite the high cost of developing and testing new products, 85 percent of all new product introductions fail.[26] Products fail for a number of reasons. A common one is that they simply don't offer any discernible benefit relative to

3
Explain why some products succeed and others fail

existing products.[27] Another is a poor match between product features and customer desires. There are telephone systems on the market with over 700 different functions, although the average user is happy with just ten.[28] Other reasons for failure include overestimation of market size, incorrect positioning, a price too high or too low, inadequate distribution, poor promotion, or simply an inferior product compared to those of competitors.

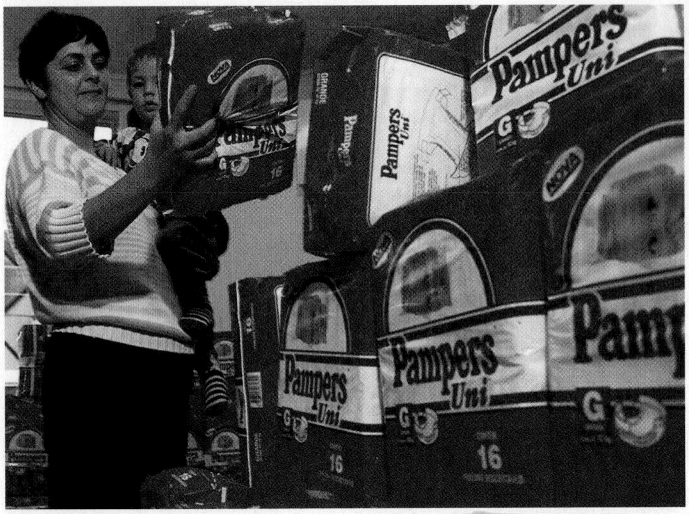

Procter & Gamble's aggressive global marketing strategy included a plan to have Pampers Phases on store shelves in ninety countries within a year. Do you think that Pampers sold in Brazil are different from those sold in Canada or other countries? Explain.

Failure can be a matter of degree. Absolute failure occurs when a company cannot recoup its development, marketing, and production costs. The product actually loses money for the company. A relative product failure results when the product returns a profit but fails to achieve sales, profit, or market share goals.

The high costs and other risks of developing and testing new products do not stop many companies, such as Rubbermaid, Colgate-Palmolive, Campbell's Soup, Bombardier, 3M Corp., and Procter & Gamble, from aggressively developing and introducing new products.

The most important factor in a successful new product introduction is a good match between the product and market needs—as the marketing concept would predict. Successful new products deliver meaningful and perceivable benefits to sizable numbers of people or organizations and are different in some meaningful way from their intended substitutes.[29] Firms that routinely succeed at introducing new products tend to share the following characteristics:

- A history of carefully listening to customers
- An obsession with producing the best product possible
- A vision of what the market will be like in the future
- Strong leadership
- A commitment to new product development
- A team approach to new product development[30]

Global Issues in New Product Development

4
Discuss global issues in new product development

The increasing globalization of markets and of competition provides a reason for multinational firms to consider new product development from a worldwide perspective. A firm that starts with a global strategy is better able to develop products that are marketable worldwide. In many multinational corporations, every product is developed for potential worldwide distribution, and unique market requirements are built in whenever possible. Procter & Gamble introduced Pampers Phases into global markets within one month of introducing the product in Canada. P&G's goal was to have the product on the shelf in ninety countries within one year. The objective was to establish brand loyalty among dealers and consumers before foreign competitors could react.

Some global marketers design their products to meet regulations and other key requirements in their major markets and then, if necessary, meet smaller markets' requirements country by country. Nissan develops lead-country car models that can, with minor changes, be sold in most markets. For the remaining markets, Nissan provides other models that can readily be adapted. Using this approach, Nissan has been able to reduce the number of its basic models from forty-eight to eighteen. There are, however, exceptions to this approach.

Organization for New Product Development

5
Describe the organizational groups or structures used to facilitate new product development

To cultivate a steady stream of new products, an organized structure is essential. Yet in many firms, top managers tend to receive new product ideas passively instead of actively soliciting them. Moreover, managers often process poorly the ideas they do receive, so that chance determines whether these ideas are fully considered.

One of the main requirements for generating ideas for new products and successfully introducing them is support from top management. In addition to this, several kinds of groups or structures within an organization can facilitate the development of new products. These include new product committees and departments, venture teams and intrapreneurs, and parallel engineering.

New Product Committees and Departments

A **new product committee** is an ad hoc group whose members manage the new product development process. The members usually represent functional interests, such as manufacturing, R&D, finance, and marketing. Many organizations use new product committees to screen ideas.

new product committee
An ad hoc group whose members manage the new product development process.

One alternative to a new product committee is a **new product department**, which performs the same functions as a new product committee but on a full-time basis. New product departments typically recommend new product objectives and programs, plan exploratory studies, evaluate concepts and ideas for new products, coordinate testing, and direct interdepartmental teams. Ideally, people in the product development department communicate regularly with their peers in the operating departments.

new product department
Performs the same functions as a new product committee but on a full-time basis.

Setting up a formal department helps ensure that authority and responsibilities are well defined and are delegated to specific individuals. A separate department with the authority to develop new products can be free from the undue influence of the production, marketing, and other departments. A separate department also has the authority to accomplish its tasks. In these circumstances the new product development manager is able to rely less on people outside his or her sphere of influence.

Venture Teams and Intrapreneurs

A **venture team** is a market-oriented group staffed by a small number of representatives from different disciplines. Team members from marketing, R&D, finance, and other areas focus on a single objective: planning their company's profitable entry into a new business. Usually, venture groups are used to handle important business and product tasks that do not fit neatly into the existing organization, that demand more financial resources and longer times to mature than other organizational units can provide, and that require creativity neither sheltered nor inhibited by the larger organization. Unlike new product committees, venture teams require a full-time commitment. In contrast to new product departments, venture teams are not stable departments but rather are formed and disbanded as the organization's circumstances dictate. Successful products that were planned by venture teams include the Boeing 757 and the IBM line of personal computers.[31]

venture team
A market-oriented group staffed by a small number of representatives from different disciplines.

An *intrapreneur* is defined here as an entrepreneur working inside a large organization. Many companies eager to foster innovation among employees have intrapreneurship programs. Colgate-Palmolive has an internal entrepreneurship program called Colgate Venture. It provides seed money, guidance, and training to potential entrepreneurs from any level of the company who propose new product ideas. They can invest a portion of their wages in the project in exchange for a stake in the product when it is marketed.[32] For an intrapreneurship program to work, top management must support the program and the company's culture must accept the proposition that many good ideas never make it to market.

Simultaneous Product Development

The earlier a product is brought to market, the greater the chance that its profits will be strong. Delays lead to lost sales. Xerox learned that lesson the hard way: its executives were stunned to discover that Japanese competitors were developing new copier models twice as quickly as Xerox and at half the cost. Many firms are trying to find new ways to shorten their development cycles to ensure they are the first to market new products.

simultaneous product development
A new, team-oriented approach to new product development.

A new, team-oriented approach to new product development is **simultaneous product development.** This approach enables firms to shorten the development process and reduce its costs. With simultaneous product development, all relevant functional areas and outside suppliers participate in all stages of the development process. Instead of proceeding through highly structured stages, the cross-functional team operates in unison.[33] By involving key suppliers early in the process, a firm capitalizes on their specialized knowledge. Also, those suppliers are well positioned to design and develop critical component parts.

The Spread of New Products

6
Explain the diffusion process through which new products are adopted.

Managers have a better chance of successfully marketing products when they understand how consumers learn about and adopt products. A person who buys a new product never before tried may ultimately become an **adopter**—that is, a consumer who was happy enough with his or her trial experience with a product to use it again.

adopter
A consumer who was happy enough with his or her trial experience with a product to use it again.

innovation
A product perceived as new by a potential adopter.

diffusion
The process by which the adoption of an innovation spreads.

Diffusion of Innovation

An **innovation** is a product perceived as new by a potential adopter. It really doesn't matter whether the product is "new to the world" or some other category of new product. If it is new to a potential adopter, it is an innovation in this context. **Diffusion** is the process by which the adoption of an innovation spreads.

Five categories of adopters participate in the diffusion process:

- *Innovators:* the first 2.5 percent of all those who adopt the product. Innovators are eager to try new ideas and products, almost as an obsession. Besides having higher incomes, they are more worldly and more active outside their communities than people who are not innovators. They rely less on group norms and are more self-confident. Because they are well educated, they are more likely to get their information from scientific sources and experts. Innovators are characterized as being venturesome.
- *Early adopters:* the next 13.5 percent to adopt the product. Although early adopters are not the very first, they do adopt early in the product's life cycle. Compared to innovators, they rely much more on group norms and values.

3Com, Palm

Who do you think the adopters of PalmPilot organizers are? Read the "Customer Testimonials" on the 3Com Website. According to 3Com, who are the innovators, the early majority, and the late majority? What other clues on the site can help you determine what kinds of people are adopting PalmPilots?

www.palm.com/newspromo/index.html

on line

They are also more oriented to their communities, in contrast to innovators, whose outlook is more worldly. Early adopters are more likely than innovators to be opinion leaders, because they are more closely affiliated with groups. The respect of others is a dominant characteristic of early adopters.

- *Early majority:* the next 34 percent to adopt. These people weigh the pros and cons before adopting a new product. They are likely to collect more information and to evaluate more brands than early adopters, which serves to extend the adoption process. They rely on the group for information and are unlikely to be opinion leaders themselves. Instead, they tend to be opinion leaders' friends and neighbours. They constitute an important link in the process of diffusing new ideas, because they are positioned between earlier and later adopters. A dominant characteristic of the early majority is deliberateness.
- *Late majority:* the next 34 percent to adopt. The late majority adopt a new product because most of their friends already have. Because they also rely on group norms, their adoption is a result of pressure to conform. These people tend to be older, and also below average in income and education. They depend mainly on word-of-mouth communication rather than on the mass media. The dominant characteristic of the late majority is scepticism.
- *Laggards:* the final 16 percent to adopt. Like innovators, laggards do not rely on group norms. Their independence is rooted in their ties to tradition. Thus, the past heavily influences their decisions. By the time laggards adopt an innovation, it has probably been outmoded and replaced by something else. For example, they may have bought their first black-and-white TV set after colour TV was already widely diffused. Laggards have the longest adoption times and the lowest socioeconomic status. They tend to be suspicious of new products and alienated from a rapidly evolving society. The dominant value of laggards is tradition. Marketers typically ignore laggards, who do not seem to be motivated by advertising or personal selling.

Product Characteristics and the Rate of Adoption

Five product characteristics can be used to predict and explain the rate of acceptance and diffusion of a new product:

- *Complexity:* the degree of difficulty involved in understanding and using a new product. The more complex the product, the slower is its diffusion. Before many of their functions were automated, 35mm cameras were used mainly by hobbyists and professionals. They were just too complex for most people to learn to operate.
- *Compatibility:* the degree to which the new product is consistent with past experiences, current needs, and existing values and product knowledge. Incompatible products diffuse more slowly than compatible products. The introduction of contraceptives is incompatible in countries where religious beliefs discourage the use of birth control.
- *Relative advantage:* the degree to which a product is perceived as superior to existing substitutes. Because it reduces cooking time, the microwave oven has a clear relative advantage over conventional ovens.
- *Observability:* the degree to which the benefits or other results of using the product can be observed by others and communicated to target customers.

Schick is generating product awareness by offering a free razor on its Website. The company has already received thousands of requests for free razor samples.

Fashion items and automobiles are highly visible and more observable than personal care items.

- *"Trialability"*: the degree to which a product can be tried on a limited basis. It is much easier to try a new toothpaste or breakfast cereal than a new automobile or microcomputer. Demonstrations in showrooms and test drives are different from in-home trial use. To stimulate trials, marketers use free-sampling programs, tasting displays, and small package sizes.

Marketing Implications of the Adoption Process

Two types of communication aid the diffusion process: word-of-mouth communication among consumers, and communication from marketers to consumers. *Word-of-mouth communication* within and across groups speeds diffusion. Opinion leaders discuss new products with their followers and with other opinion leaders. Marketers must therefore ensure that opinion leaders have the types of information desired in the media that they use. Suppliers of some products, such as professional and healthcare services, rely almost entirely on word-of-mouth communication for new business.

The second type of communication aiding the diffusion process is *communication directly from the marketer to potential adopters.* Messages directed at early adopters should normally use different appeals than messages directed toward the early majority, the late majority, or the laggards. Early adopters are more important than innovators because they make up a larger group, are more socially active, and are usually opinion leaders.

As the focus of a promotional campaign shifts from early adopters to the early majority and the late majority, marketers should study the dominant characteristics, buying behaviour, and media characteristics of these target markets. Then they should revise their messages and media strategies to fit. The diffusion model helps marketers develop and implement promotion strategies.

Product Life Cycles

7

Explain the concept of product life cycles

product life cycle
A concept that provides a way to trace the stages of a product's acceptance, from its introduction (birth) to its decline (death).

product category
All brands that satisfy a particular type of need.

The product life cycle (PLC) is one of the most familiar concepts in marketing. Few other general concepts have been so widely discussed. Although some researchers have challenged the theoretical basis and managerial value of the PLC, most believe it has great potential as a marketing management tool.

The **product life cycle** concept provides a means to trace the stages of a product's acceptance, from its introduction (birth) to its decline (death). As Exhibit 10.3 shows, a product progresses through four main stages: introduction, growth, maturity, and decline. Note that the product life cycle illustrated does not refer to any one brand; rather, it refers to the life cycle for a product category or product class. A **product category** includes all brands that satisfy a particular type of need. Product categories include passenger cars, cigarettes, soft drinks, and coffee.

exhibit 10.3

Four Stages of the Product Life Cycle

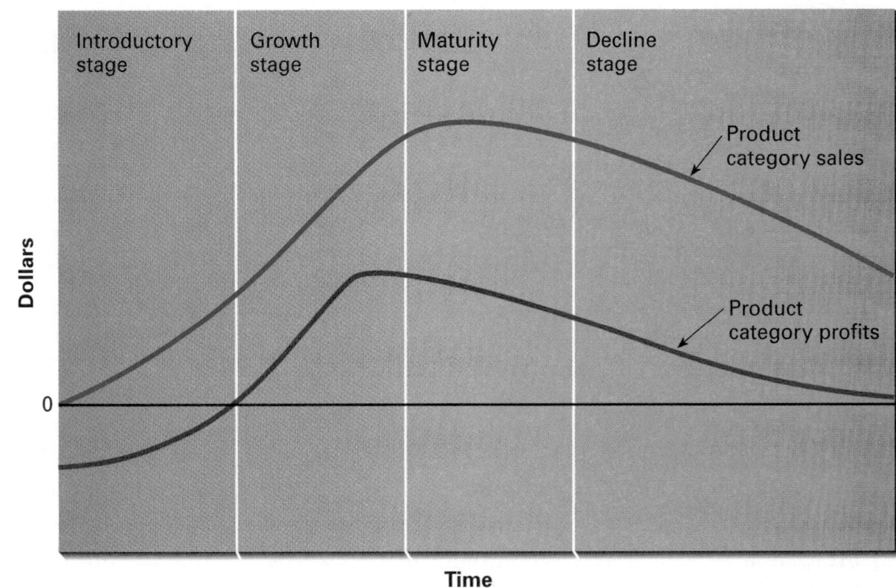

The time a product spends at any one stage of its life cycle can vary dramatically. Some products, such as fad items, move through the entire cycle in weeks. Others, such as electric clothes washers and dryers, stay in the maturity stage for decades. Exhibit 10.3 illustrates the typical life cycle for a consumer durable good, such as microwave ovens. Exhibit 10.4 illustrates typical life cycles for styles (such as formal, business, and casual clothing), fashions (such as miniskirts and stirrup pants), and fads (such as leopard-print clothing). Changes in a product, its uses, its image, and its positioning can extend its life cycle.

The product life cycle concept does not tell managers the length of a product's life cycle or of its various stages. It does not dictate marketing strategy. It is simply a tool to help marketers forecast future events and suggest appropriate strategies.

introductory stage
The full-scale launch of a new product into the marketplace.

Styles, fashions, and fads tend to follow different product life cycles. Based on what you see in Exhibits 10.3 and 10.4, what do you think the life cycle is for Pokemon cartoons, movies, and products?

Introductory Stage

The **introductory stage** of the product life cycle represents the full-scale launch of a new product into the marketplace. Computer databases for personal use, room-deodorizing air-conditioning filters, and wind-powered home electric generators are all product categories that have recently entered the product life cycle. The introduction stage of the PLC is characterized by high failure rates, little competition, frequent product modification, and limited distribution.

Marketing costs during the introductory stage tend to be high, for several reasons. High dealer margins are often needed to obtain adequate distribution, and incentives must be offered to get consumers to try the new product. Advertising expenses are high because of the need to educate consumers about the new product's benefits. Also, production costs are often high during this stage, as product and manufacturing flaws are identi-

exhibit 10.4

Product Life Cycles for Styles, Fashions, and Fads

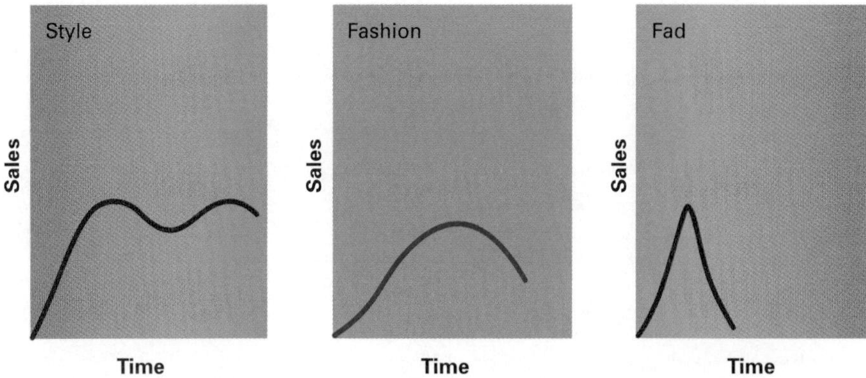

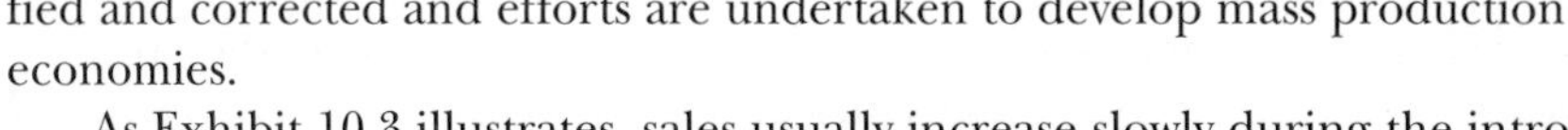

fied and corrected and efforts are undertaken to develop mass production economies.

growth stage
The second stage of the product life cycle, when sales typically grow more quickly, many competitors enter the market, and profits are healthy; also, large companies may begin acquiring small, pioneering firms.

As Exhibit 10.3 illustrates, sales usually increase slowly during the introductory stage. Moreover, profits are usually negative because of R&D costs, factory tooling, and high introduction costs. The length of the introductory phase is determined largely by the product's characteristics, such as its advantages over substitute products and the effort required to make it known to consumers. A short introductory period is usually preferred to help reduce the impact of negative earnings and cash flows. As soon as the product gets off the ground, the financial burden should begin to diminish. Also, a short introduction helps dispel some of the uncertainty as to whether the new product will succeed.

Coffee is an example of a product in the maturity stage, during which niche marketers emerge. Starbucks targets its gourmet products at newer, younger, more affluent coffee drinkers.

In the introductory stage, promotion focuses on developing product awareness and informing consumers about the product category's potential benefits. At this stage, the communication challenge is to stimulate primary demand—that is, demand for the product in general rather than for a specific brand. Intensive personal selling is often required to gain acceptance for the product among wholesalers and retailers. The promotion of convenience products often requires heavy consumer sampling and couponing. Shopping and specialty products demand educational advertising and personal selling to the final consumer.

Growth Stage

If a product category survives the introductory stage, it advances to the **growth stage** of the life cycle. During this stage, sales typically grow more quickly, many competitors enter the market, and large companies may start to acquire small pioneering firms. Profits rise rapidly during the growth stage, reach their peak, and begin declining as competition intensifies. The emphasis switches from primary demand promotion (e.g., promoting CD players) to aggressive brand advertising and communication of the differences between brands (e.g., promoting Rotel versus Rega and Naim).

During the growth stage, distribution becomes a key to success (as it will be in later stages as well). Manufacturers scramble to sign up dealers and distributors and to build long-term relationships. Without adequate distribution, it is impossible to establish a strong market position.

Wendy's

Follow Wendy's advertisements from the first network commercials to present-day ads. How has Wendy's developed and promoted new products to successfully compete in the maturity stage?

www.wendys.com/the_ads/ads_frame.html

on line

Maturity Stage

A period during which sales increase less quickly signals the beginning of the **maturity stage** of the life cycle. New users cannot be added indefinitely, and sooner or later the market approaches saturation. Usually this is the longest stage of the product life cycle. Many common major household appliances are now in the maturity stage of their life cycles.

maturity stage
A period during which sales increase less quickly.

For shopping products and many specialty products, annual models begin to appear during the maturity stage. Product lines are lengthened to appeal to additional market segments. Service and repair take on more importance as manufacturers strive to distinguish their products from those of other firms. Product design changes tend to become stylistic (How can the product be made different?) rather than functional (How can the product be made better?).

As prices and profits continue to fall, marginal competitors start dropping out of the market. Dealer margins also shrink, resulting in less shelf space for mature items, lower dealer inventories, and a general reluctance to promote the product. Thus promotion to dealers often intensifies during this stage, in order to retain loyalty.

Heavy consumer promotion by the manufacturer is also required to maintain market share. Consider these well-known examples of competition in the maturity stage: the so-called "cola war" featuring Coke and Pepsi, the "beer war" featuring Molson brands and Labatt brands, and the "burger wars" pitting leader McDonald's against challengers Burger King and Wendy's.

Another characteristic of the maturity stage is the emergence of "niche marketers" targeting narrow, well-defined, underserved segments of a market. Starbucks Coffee targets its gourmet line at the only segment of the coffee market that is growing: new, younger, more affluent coffee drinkers.

Decline Stage

A long-run drop in sales signals the beginning of the **decline stage**. The rate of decline is governed by how rapidly consumers change their tastes or adopt substitute products. Many convenience products lose their market overnight, leaving large inventories of unsold items. This is also common with fad items such as designer jeans. Other products, like citizen band (CB) radios, black-and-white TV sets, and analog wristwatches, die more slowly.

decline stage
A long-run drop in sales.

Sales of music cassette tapes have declined from 29 percent of all retail music sales in 1991 to under 15 percent today.[34] Retailers like Sam the Record Man and HMV have reduced the space allocated to cassettes by 50 percent over this time period. Is the music cassette dead? No, but it is clearly in the decline stage. Music cassettes are still quite profitable to some marketers.

Some firms have developed successful strategies for marketing decline-stage products. They eliminate all nonessential marketing expenses and let sales decline as more and more customers stop purchasing the products. Eventually, the product is withdrawn from the market.

Implications for Marketing Management

The product life cycle concept encourages marketing managers to plan so that they can take the initiative instead of reacting to past events. The product life cycle is especially useful as a predicting or forecasting tool. Products pass through distinctive stages, so it is often possible to estimate a product's location on the curve using historical data. Profits, like sales, tend to follow a predictable path over a product's life cycle.

exhibit 10.5

Typical Marketing Strategies During the Product Life Cycle

Marketing	Product Life Cycle Stage: Introduction	Growth	Maturity	Decline
Product strategy	Limited number of models; frequent product modifications	Expanded number of models; frequent product modifications	Large number of models	Elimination of unprofitable models and brands
Distribution strategy	Distribution usually limited, depending on product; intensive efforts and high margins often needed to attract wholesalers and retailers	Expanded number of dealers; intensive efforts to establish long-term relationships with wholesalers and retailers	Extensive number of dealers; margins declining; intensive efforts to retain distributors and shelf space	Unprofitable outlets phased out
Promotion strategy	Develop product awareness; stimulate primary demand; use intensive personal selling to distributors; use sampling and couponing for consumers	Stimulate selective demand; advertise brand aggressively	Stimulate selective demand; advertise brand aggressively	Phase out all promotion
Pricing strategy	Prices are usually high to recover development costs	Prices begin to fall toward end of growth stage as a result of competitive pressure	Prices continue to fall	Prices stabilize at relatively low levels; small price rises are possible if competition is negligible

exhibit 10.6

Relationship Between the Diffusion Process and the Product Life Cycle

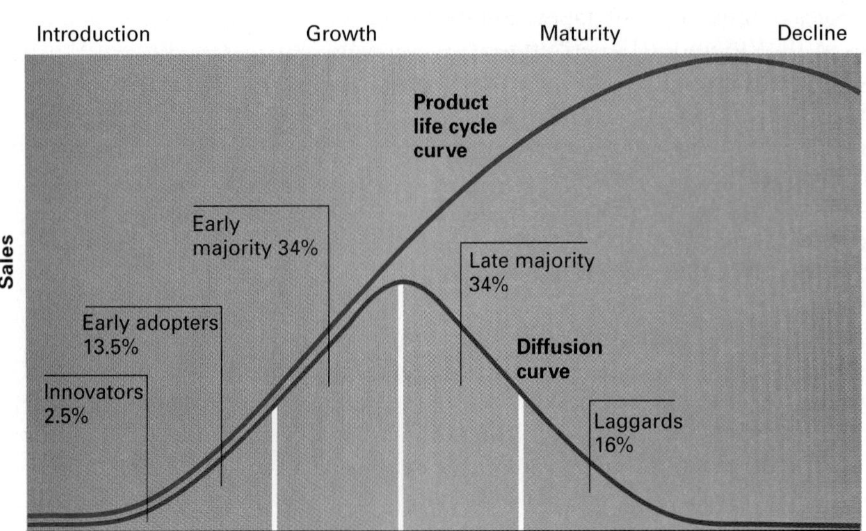

LOOKING BACK

Look back at the story at the beginning of this chapter about the H.J. Heinz Company. Did the source of the idea for the new products surprise you? In fact, many ideas for new products come from customers and company employees, from both inside and outside the company. It is important that a company be aware of sources of new product ideas and actively encourage these sources to contribute ideas. Without ideas, companies will never develop new products.

Like all companies, Heinz cannot succeed without new products. Some new products will fail, of course, but if a company does not take risks with new product concepts, the company as a whole will surely fail.

Summary

1 Explain the importance of developing new products, and describe the six categories of new products. New products are important to sustain growth and profits and to replace obsolete items. New products can be classified as new-to-the-world products (discontinuous innovations), new product lines, additions to existing product lines, improvements or revisions of existing products, repositioned products, or lower-cost products. To sustain or increase profits, a firm must introduce at least one new successful product before a previous product advances to the maturity stage and profit levels begin to drop. Several factors make it more important than ever for firms to consistently introduce new products: shortened product life cycles, rapidly changing technology, changing consumer priorities, the high rate of new product failures, and the length of time needed to implement new product ideas.

2 Explain the steps in the new product development process. First, a firm formulates a new product strategy by outlining the characteristics and roles of future products. Then new product ideas are generated by customers, employees, distributors, competitors, and internal R&D personnel. Once a product idea has survived initial screening by an appointed screening group, it undergoes business analysis to determine its potential profitability. If a product concept seems viable, it progresses into the development phase, during which the technical and economic feasibility of the manufacturing process is evaluated. The development phase also includes laboratory and use testing of the product for performance and safety. Following initial testing and refinement, most products are introduced in a test market to evaluate marketing strategies and customer responses. Finally, test market successes are propelled into full commercialization. The commercialization process involves starting up production, building inventories, shipping to distributors, training a sales force, announcing the product to the trade, and advertising to consumers.

3 Explain why some products succeed and others fail. The most important factor in the success of a new product relates to whether the product matches the needs of the market. Good matches are often successful; poor matches are not.

4 Discuss global issues in new product development. A marketer with global vision seeks to develop products that can easily be adapted to suit local needs. The goal is not simply to develop a standard product that can be sold worldwide.

5 Describe the organizational groups or structures used to facilitate new product development. Firms facilitate the development of new products with new product committees or departments or with venture teams. New product committees are composed of representatives of various branches of an organization and play mainly an advisory role. A new product department may be a separate

Do You Know These Terms?

adopter 266
brainstorming 258
business analysis 259
commercialization 263
concept test 258
decline stage 271
development 260
diffusion 266
growth stage 270
innovation 266
introductory stage 269
maturity stage 271
new product 254
new product committee 265
new product department 265
new product strategy 256
product category 268
product development 258
product life cycle 268
screening 258
simulated (laboratory) market testing 263
simultaneous product development 266
test marketing 261
venture team 265

department, a high-level staff function, a part of marketing, or a part of R&D. Venture team members are recruited from within an organization to work full-time on specific projects and are encouraged to take an "intrapreneurial" approach to new product development. Some firms use an organizational structure popular in Japan, called simultaneous product development, whereby all departments work together to develop new products.

6 **Explain the diffusion process through which new products are adopted.** The diffusion process is the spread of a new product from its producer to ultimate adopters. Adopters in the diffusion process belong to five categories: innovators, early adopters, the early majority, the late majority, and laggards. Product characteristics that affect the rate of adoption include product complexity, compatibility with existing social values, relative advantage over existing substitutes, visibility, and "trialability." The diffusion process is facilitated by word-of-mouth communication and communication from marketers to consumers.

7 **Explain the concept of product life cycles.** All product categories undergo a life cycle with four stages: introduction, growth, maturity, and decline. The rate at which products move through these stages varies dramatically. Marketing managers use the product life cycle concept as an analytical tool to forecast a product's future and devise effective marketing strategies.

Discussion and Writing Questions

1. What is the difference between a new product committee and a venture team?
2. List the advantages of simultaneous product development.
3. In small groups, brainstorm ideas for a new wet-weather clothing line. What type of product would potential customers want and need? Prepare and deliver a brief presentation to your class.
4. You are a marketing manager for Nike. Your department has come up with the idea of manufacturing a baseball bat for use in high schools across the country. Assuming you are in the business analysis stage, write a brief analysis based on the questions in the "Business Analysis" section of the chapter.
5. What are the major disadvantages to test marketing, and how could they be avoided?
6. Describe some products whose adoption rates have been affected by complexity, compatibility, relative advantage, observability, and/or "trialability."
7. What type of adopter behaviour do you typically follow? Explain.
8. Place the personal computer on the product life cycle curve, and give reasons for placing it where you did.
9. How could information from customer orders at the following site help the company's marketers plan new product developments? **www.pizzahut.com**
10. How is customer input affecting the development of Baked Lay's potato chips? **www.fritolay.com**

Application for Small Business

Joyce Strand went to the oven to remove the newest batch of beef jerky that she would later sell to the Frontenac Central Store. To her surprise, she had turned the oven up too high, and the beef jerky had dried to a crisp. Although the texture was much different, the jerky still had its unmistakable taste. Joyce decided to take it to the store anyway and let the customers decide. The new snack became a huge success in the snack food section of the store. So Joyce began experimenting with different tastes and textures of snack foods. Realizing that innovation can be very profitable, she now actively looks for new ways to please her customers.

Questions

1. How might Joyce ensure that she pays proper attention to developing new products?
2. What factors should she be aware of that might lead to product failure?
3. Prepare a list of criteria similar to those in the "Entrepreneurial Insights" box in this chapter that Joyce might use to evaluate her new product ideas.

VIDEO CASE

AutoCite: Traffic Ticket and Parking Citation System

For decades, the writing of a ticket was only the first step in a long, manual process. An officer dropped off the ticket at the station, and from there it went to the records department for sorting and batching. It was then transmitted to the judicial system and data processing. The handwritten information was keypunched into the mainframe and then returned for filing. At each step, tickets were flagged for errors, but mistakes regularly surfaced, resulting in an inefficient process.

This situation prompted companies such as Epson, Grid, Husky, Symbol, and Telxon to market general-purpose, hand-held computers to police departments. But these devices required officers to wear a clumsy printer on their belts or strapped over their shoulders, and such computer configurations were not designed for citation management.

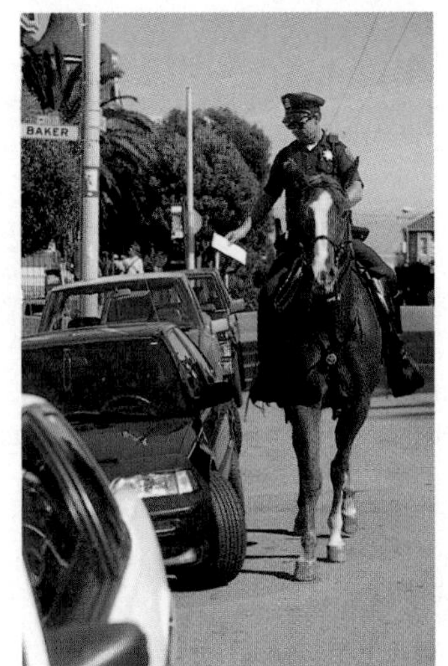

Enforcement Technology, Inc. (ETEC) recognized an unsatisfied need and set out to develop a new product that would deal the final blow to the bulky, inefficient computers. ETEC focused on developing a product so unique that once introduced, it would outdate the competition. The new product, called AutoCite, is a portable, lightweight, hand-held computer with a built-in printer, specialized for issuing traffic tickets and parking citations.

ETEC's new product strategy was to carve out a market niche through specialization. Competitors sold general-purpose computers—hardware only—and this required customers to purchase obligatory software from other companies. To distinguish AutoCite from other brands, ETEC produced a complete package of hardware and software. Also, ETEC provided product training and totally maintained AutoCite at every level. Customers found it highly convenient to look to a single supplier for both sales and service.

AutoCite's success encouraged ETEC to analyze other needs in the citation process and develop the technology to meet them. The result is a fully automated system of products that work in harmony. AutoCite is now updated to include a magnetic stripe and bar code reading capability so that information is entered automatically from the magnetic stripe on the back of a driver's licence. Using a prestored "hotsheet," AutoCite alerts the officer with "Wants or Warrants" keyed to the driver's licence number. AutoPROCESS processes citations through on-line court and hearing scheduling. AutoALARM is a false alarm management system, which includes citation issuance computers, window decal distribution, alarm permit updates and payments, and billing statements. The AutoCite Patrol Car System is an AutoCite unit that adapts to the notebook (laptop) computer in a patrol car to issue traffic tickets; it is especially useful for issuing moving citations and preparing interviews and crime, accident, and arrest reports.

This product line is fully supported by ETEC's cash management and delinquent collection services. The company has parking enforcement centres to process tickets for its customers and has implemented a follow-up service to collect delinquent citations. But these services are only part of the benefits. Cities, universities, and agencies are saving money in processing costs and recovery of delinquent fines. In one year, ETEC collected $600,000 for one city by taking a backlog of 60,000 citations and going back as far as two years for collections. ETEC now processes around 3,000 delinquent parking citations each month for roughly $50,000 in new revenue. With results like this, AutoCite can pay for itself within a year.

Revenue generation is complemented by an additional benefit: The use of AutoCite has been shown to reduce the indirect costs associated with low staff productivity. Data entry, which used to eat into staff and clerical time, is now a memory in departments and agencies. And the error rate is smaller. There's also an intangible benefit—better employee morale. Officers have been pleased with ETEC's reliable computers and high-quality customer service. Their increased efficiency has led to greater job satisfaction.

By creating a fully automated citation management process, ETEC has police departments and agencies singing its praises. AutoCite has been adopted by over 300 police agencies, over 50 colleges and universities, and agencies in 8 foreign countries, and is well positioned to build on its resounding success.

Questions

1. Describe the product development process for AutoCite.
2. Why has AutoCite been successful?
3. How did ETEC develop the product line?
4. What strategy should ETEC follow in introducing new products for law enforcement?

CHAPTER

11

LEARNING OBJECTIVES

After studying this chapter, you should be able to

1. Discuss the importance of services to the economy
2. Discuss the differences between services and goods
3. Explain why services marketing is important to manufacturers
4. Describe the components of service quality and the gap model of service quality
5. Develop marketing mixes for services
6. Discuss relationship marketing in services
7. Explain internal marketing in services
8. Discuss global issues in services marketing
9. Describe nonprofit organization marketing
10. Explain the unique aspects of nonprofit organization marketing

SERVICES AND NONPROFIT ORGANIZATION MARKETING

"My kids haven't seen Santa Claus since we've arrived," lamented a Middle Eastern traveller who recently took his family to the Four Seasons Hotel in Washington, D.C. Coming quickly to the rescue, Liliana Vidal-Quadras, the hotel's assistant front office manager, found an employee to gather a costume and play Santa for a few hours. Afterwards, the guest rewarded the staff member and the hotel kicked in a bonus for her efforts.

Service like that has made Four Seasons one of the top luxury hotel chains in the world. The secret to its success may have everything to do with how it treats its employees.

Profit sharing, frequent promotion, retirement contribution plans, tuition reimbursement, and travel opportunities are some of the perks that the Toronto-based company offers its 25,000 employees. These benefits have resulted in low turnover (around 24 percent, compared with the industry average of 40 percent) and earned it a reputation for being one of North America's top employers. Four Seasons recently made *Fortune*'s prestigious list of the 100 best companies to work for in the United States for the fourth consecutive year. It is the only Canadian company ever to make the *Fortune* list.

The payoff for being a top employer is a loyal following. It is not uncommon for staff to go beyond the call of duty for guests, who spend an average of US$200 a night—up to US$680 at hotels in bigger cities. One employee in Washington jumped on a plane to deliver a briefcase left by a corporate executive; another in the Caribbean lit candles and laid a trail of rose petals for a couple on their honeymoon.

At Four Seasons beach resorts, attendants spritz water on guests every hour as they lounge by the pool. Swimmers are greeted with fluffed towels and robes. Room service includes delivering Christmas trees and providing dog amenities (with compliments). If toilet paper is not of the desired quality, it is quickly replaced. "We're not just selling food and beverages," says Ms. Vidal-Quadras, a hospitality graduate recently hired to work in Washington. "We're selling our service and that's the secret behind the Four Seasons name."

Four Seasons Hotels and Resorts

At which different customer segments does Four Seasons target its hotels and resorts? How do their service needs differ? What special facilities and staff training must Four Seasons provide to meet the different segments' needs?

www.fourseasons.com

on line

Money is not the first reason Ms. Vidal-Quadras wants to stick around—in fact, most of the hotel's entry-level staff earn modest salaries. In the United States, its largest market, services employees make from US$18,350 to $32,411. And the work they do is not always easy, as guests who wish to be pampered can sometimes be terribly demanding. What, then, is the appeal?

Beginning on day one, new hires are hustled through a rigorous training program. Most of them are assigned both a mentor, whose job it is to map out career prospects, and a "buddy," who familiarizes them with the immediate tasks at hand. Workers have a direct stake in the company, receiving up to 5 percent of their salaries through a profit-sharing plan. They also receive between five and twenty free nights at any Four Seasons resort and a 50 percent discount on food and drink.

Four Seasons has come a long way since it opened a motor hotel in Toronto's red light district in 1961. Today the publicly traded company manages more than forty-seven luxury hotel and resort properties in nineteen countries. Its fiscal 1999 revenues topped $2.3 billion, and its net earnings increased more than 24 percent to $86 million. Its operating record is enviable, according to most analysts. Since 1995 the company's share price has generated a compound annualized rate of return of around 40 percent, outpacing McDonald's, Coca-Cola, and Gucci. Four Seasons is still controlled by founder Isadore Sharp and his family. Saudi Prince Alwaleed bin Talal, the world's fifth-richest man, owns a 25 percent stake in the chain.

At Cornell University in Ithaca, New York, which has one of the top-rated hotel schools in North America, dozens of graduates have dreams of working in faraway places. Four Seasons is clearly one of the most desirable places to work, said Millie Reed, head of the university's career placement program.

"It's just that aura of Four Seasons," she says. "Students just really seem to enjoy working there."[1]

How do services, such as hotel accommodation, differ from goods (e.g., cars, clothing, and food items)? Why does Four Seasons go to such lengths to develop and keep its employees? Why has Four Seasons been so successful?

The Importance of Services

A **service** is the result of applying human or mechanical efforts to people or objects. Services are enacted through deeds, performances, or processes. Industries providing services are widespread. Exhibit 11.1 offers some examples.

1

Discuss the importance of services to the economy

service
The result of applying human or mechanical efforts to people or objects.

Given the pervasiveness of services in modern Canada, the services sector strongly influences the economy. More than seven in ten workers currently work in services. The service sector accounts for 66 percent of Canada's GNP. Service employees can also be found in manufacturing industries such as computer and engineering firms, which provide value-added services on top of their basic products. According to Statistics Canada, service occupations have been responsible for almost all net job growth over the past two decades (see Exhibit 11.2). The huge demand for services in Canada is expected to continue.[2]

Services are also important to the world economy. For example, 74 percent of the American GDP is accounted for by services. In Great Britain, 73 percent of jobs are in services; 57 percent of German workers and 62 percent of Japanese workers are in services.[3]

The marketing process outlined in Chapter 1 is the same for all types of products, whether they are goods or services. Many ideas and strategies discussed in this book are illustrated with service examples. In many ways, marketing is marketing, whatever the product's characteristics. That being said, services have some unique characteristics that distinguish them from goods, and marketing strategies need to be adjusted for these characteristics.

How Services Differ from Goods

2

Discuss the differences between services and goods

Services have four unique characteristics that distinguish them from goods: intangibility, inseparability, heterogeneity, and perishability.

Intangibility

The basic difference between services and goods is that services are intangible. Because of their **intangibility**, they cannot be sensed—that is, touched, seen, tasted, heard, or felt—in the same manner that goods can be sensed. Services cannot be stored and are often easy to duplicate.

intangibility
Services cannot be sensed—that is, touched, seen, tasted, heard, or felt—in the same manner that goods can be sensed.

exhibit 11.1

Common Examples of Service Industries

Category	Example
Communication	Telephone, Internet, cable TV services
Transportation	Air transportation, car rental
Trade	Retailing, wholesaling
Finance	Banking, accounting, insurance
Miscellaneous	Government, education, health care, recreation services, hotels, restaurants, repair services, legal services, business services, personal and household services

exhibit 11.2

The Impact of the Service Sector on Job Growth

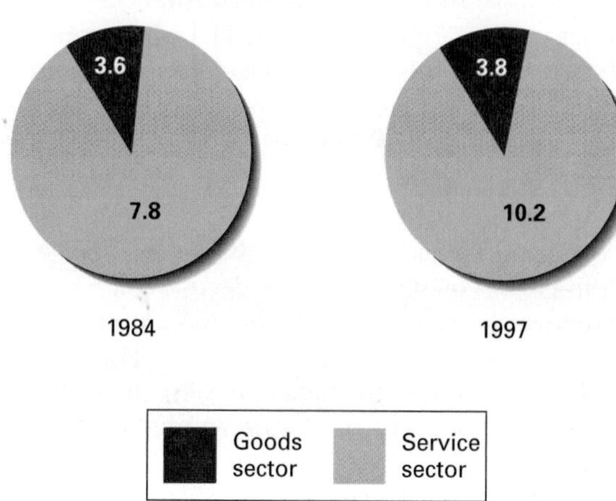

search quality
A characteristic that can be easily assessed before purchase.

experience quality
A characteristic that can be assessed only after use.

credence quality
A characteristic that consumers may have difficulty assessing even after purchase because they do not have the necessary knowledge or experience.

It is harder to evaluate the quality of services than of goods, before or even after a purchase, because compared to goods, services tend to have fewer search qualities. A **search quality** is a characteristic that can be easily assessed before purchase—for instance, the colour of an appliance or car. At the same time, services tend to exhibit more experience and credence qualities. An **experience quality** is a characteristic that can be assessed only after use, such as the quality of a meal in a restaurant or the actual experience of a vacation. A **credence quality** is a characteristic that consumers may have difficulty assessing even after purchase because they do not have the necessary knowledge or experience. Medical and consulting services exhibit credence qualities.

All of this means that it is harder for marketers to communicate the benefits of services than to communicate the benefits of goods. So they often rely on tangible cues to communicate a service's nature and quality. On-line grocery retailer Grocery Gateway incorporates the image of a delivery van in its logo to help make tangible its benefit of home delivery.

The facilities that customers visit, or from which services are delivered, are a critical tangible part of the total service offering. Messages about the organization are communicated to customers through elements such as the decor, the neatness of service areas, and the staff's manners and dress. Flight Centre has deliberately designed its stores to be different from those of typical travel agents. The stores are clean and brightly lit inside and out and have a minimalist red-and-white colour scheme. Staff serve customers from behind counters similar to those found in retail banks. The stores have been designed with a very clear objective: to attract and process as many customers as possible who want to buy no-frills plane tickets as quickly as possible.[4]

Inseparability

inseparability
A characteristic of services that allows them to be produced and consumed simultaneously.

Goods are produced, sold, and then consumed. In contrast, services are often sold, produced, and consumed at the same time. In other words, their production is inseparable from their consumption. **Inseparability** means that because consumers must be present during the production of the services they are buying (e.g., haircuts, surgery), they are actually involved in that production. In many fast food restaurants there are touch-activated video screens that display words and/or pictures; customers can thus order their own meals, which speeds up the

Air Canada's Aeroplan Program

Read about Air Canada's highly successful frequent flyer program, Aeroplan. How do Aeroplan points make the benefits of flying with Air Canada more tangible? How is the program paid for? Why has Aeroplan been so successful?

www.aircanada.ca

on line

ordering process.[5] This type of consumer involvement is rare in goods manufacturing.

Inseparability also means that services cannot usually be produced in a centralized location and consumed in decentralized locations, as goods typically are. Services are also inseparable from the perspective of the service provider. This means that quality of service depends on the quality of the firm's employees.

Heterogeneity

One great strength of McDonald's is its consistency. Customers know exactly what they are going to get, whether they are ordering a Big Mac and fries in Seattle, Halifax, or Tokyo. This is not the case with many service providers. Services exhibit **heterogeneity** in the sense that they tend to be less uniform than goods. The physicians in a group practice tend to vary among each other in their technical and interpersonal skills. The same with the stylists in a salon. A given physician's or hair stylist's performance may even vary with the time of day, physical health, or some other factor. Services tend to be labour intensive, and production and consumption are inseparable; as a result, consistency and quality control can be hard to achieve in service industries.

heterogeneity
A characteristic of services that makes them less standardized and uniform than goods.

Standardization and training help increase consistency and reliability. Limited menu restaurants like Pizza Hut and KFC offer customers high consistency from one visit to the next because of standardized preparation procedures. Another way to increase consistency is to mechanize the process. Banks have reduced the inconsistency of teller services by providing ATMs. Automatic coin receptacles on toll roads have replaced human collectors.

Because KFC uses standardized preparation procedures, the meal you order at its restaurant in the Itae Won shopping area of Seoul, South Korea, will be consistent with what you would get at the KFC in the smallest of Canadian towns.

Perishability

Perishability means that services cannot be stored, warehoused, or inventoried. An empty hotel room or airplane seat produces no revenue that day—the revenue is lost. Yet during peak periods, service organizations are often forced to turn away full-price customers.

In many service industries, one of the biggest challenges is to find ways to synchronize supply and demand. The philosophy that some revenue is better than none has prompted many hotels to offer deep discounts on weekends and during the off-season, and has prompted airlines to adopt similar pricing strategies during off-peak hours. Car rental agencies, movie theatres, and restaurants also use discounts to encourage demand during nonpeak periods.

perishability
A characteristic of services that prevents them from being stored, warehoused, or inventoried.

Services Marketing in Manufacturing

3
Explain why services marketing is important to manufacturers

It is useful to compare goods marketing with services marketing. That being said, it can be hard to distinguish between manufacturing firms and service firms. Many manufacturing firms point to service as a major factor in their success. For example, maintenance and repair services are important to buyers of copy machines.

Chrysler Canada has made its 5/100 Powertrain warranty, which is available on all of its products including the Jeep Liberty, a cornerstone of both its marketing strategy and its Website.

Goods manufacturers often stress service in the hope it will give them a strong competitive advantage, especially in industries in which products are perceived as similar. In the car industry, consumers perceive few quality differences between car brands.

In recent years, car makers such as GM and DaimlerChrysler have found themselves competing more and more through value-added services such as extended warranties and roadside assistance packages. In the industry these efforts have been dubbed the "warranty wars" (a play on the old term "price wars"). For decades, Japanese car makers like Honda had the most extensive warranties. Some experts believe that though American manufacturers are not yet producing more reliable cars, they can at least match the competition's warranties.[6]

Service Quality

4

Describe the components of service quality and the gap model of service quality

Because of the four unique characteristics of services, the quality of services is more difficult to define and measure than the quality of tangble goods. Business executives consider improving service quality one of the most critical challenges facing them today.

Customers evaluate service quality by the following five components:[7]

reliability
The ability to perform a service dependably, accurately, and consistently.

responsiveness
The ability to provide prompt service.

assurance
The knowledge and courtesy of employees and their ability to convey trust.

empathy
Caring, individualized attention to customers.

- ***Reliability:*** the ability to perform the service dependably, accurately, and consistently. Reliability means performing the service right the first time. Because this attribute is so important to consumers, service firms often compete on it. In the high-speed Internet service provider market, firms such as Rogers@Home and Bell Sympatico promote themselves as providing reliable and fast Web access.
- ***Responsiveness:*** the ability to provide prompt service. Examples of responsiveness include calling the customer back quickly, serving lunch quickly to someone in a hurry, and mailing a transaction slip immediately.
- ***Assurance:*** the knowledge and courtesy of employees and their ability to convey trust. Skilled employees who treat customers with respect and make customers feel they can trust the firm exemplify assurance.
- ***Empathy:*** caring, individualized attention to customers. Firms whose employees recognize customers, call them by name, and learn their specific requirements are providing empathy.

exhibit 11.3

Gap Model of Service Quality

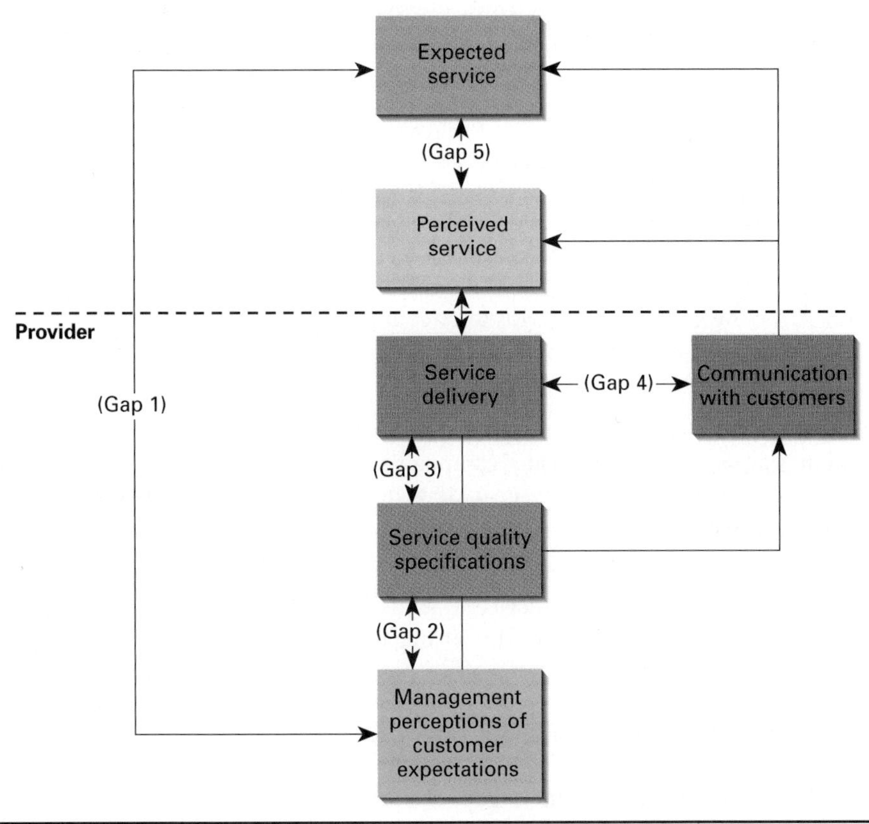

Source: Reprinted with permission of The Free Press, a Division of Simon & Schuster, Inc. from *Delivering Quality Service: Balancing Customer Perceptions and Expectations* by Valerie A. Zeithaml, A. Parasuraman, and Leonard L. Barry. Copyright © 1990 by The Free Press.

- ***Tangibles:*** the physical evidence of the service. The tangible parts of a service include the physical facilities, tools, and equipment used to provide the service—such as a doctor's office or an ATM—and the appearance of personnel.

tangibles
The physical evidence of a service, including the physical facilities, tools, and equipment used to provide the service.

Overall service quality is measured by combining customers' evaluations for all five components.

The Gap Model of Service Quality

A model of service quality called the **gap model** identifies five gaps that can cause problems in service delivery and influence customer evaluations of service quality.[8] These gaps are illustrated in Exhibit 11.3.

gap model
A model identifying five gaps that can cause problems in service delivery and influence customer evaluations of service quality.

- *Gap 1*: the gap between what customers want and what management thinks customers want. This gap results from a lack of understanding or a misinterpretation of the customers' needs, wants, or desires. A firm that does little or no customer satisfaction research is likely to experience this gap. An important step in closing gap 1 is to keep in touch with what customers want by doing research on customer needs and customer satisfaction.
- *Gap 2*: the gap between what management thinks customers want and the quality specifications that management develops to provide the service.

Essentially, this gap is the result of management's inability to translate customers' needs into delivery systems within the firm. Kentucky Fried Chicken once rated its managers' success according to "chicken efficiency," or how much chicken they threw away at the end of the night. Consumers who came in late at night would either have to wait for chicken to be cooked or settle for chicken several hours old. The "chicken efficiency" measurement did not take customers into account, and financial performance suffered.[9]

- *Gap 3:* the gap between the service quality specifications and the service that is actually provided. If both gaps 1 and 2 have been closed, then gap 3 is a result of the inability of management and employees to do what should be done. Poorly motivated workers can cause this gap. Management needs to ensure that employees have the skills and the proper tools to perform their jobs. To close gap 3, it also helps to encourage teamwork and to train employees so they know what management expects.
- *Gap 4:* the gap between what the company provides and what the customer is told it provides. This is clearly a communication gap. It may include misleading or deceptive advertising campaigns promising more than the firm can deliver, or firms doing "whatever it takes" to get the business. To close this gap, a company needs to create realistic customer expectations through honest, accurate communication about what it can provide.
- *Gap 5:* the gap between the service that customers receive and the service they want. This gap can be positive or negative. If a patient expects to wait twenty minutes in the physician's office before seeing the physician but waits only ten minutes, the patient's evaluation of service quality will be high. A forty-minute wait would result in a lower evaluation.

When one or more of these gaps are large, service quality is perceived as low. As the gaps shrink, service quality improves.

Marketing Mixes for Services

5

Develop marketing mixes for services

The unique characteristics of services—intangibility, inseparability, heterogeneity, and perishability—make marketing services more challenging. The elements of the marketing mix (i.e., product, distribution, promotion, pricing) need to be adjusted to meet the special needs created by these characteristics.

Product (Service) Strategy

The development of "product" strategy in services marketing requires planning focused on the service process.[10] Three types of processing occur:

- *People processing* takes place when the service is directed at a customer. Examples are transportation services, hairstyling, health clubs, and dental care.
- *Possession processing* occurs when the service is directed at something a customer owns. Examples are lawn care, car repair, dry cleaning, and veterinary services.
- *Information processing* involves the use of technology (e.g., computers) or brainpower. Examples are accounting, education, and legal and financial services.

Because customers' experiences and involvement differ for each of these types of services, marketing strategies may also differ. People-processing services require more customer participation than possession-processing services; this

exhibit 11.4

Core and Supplementary Services for Federal Express

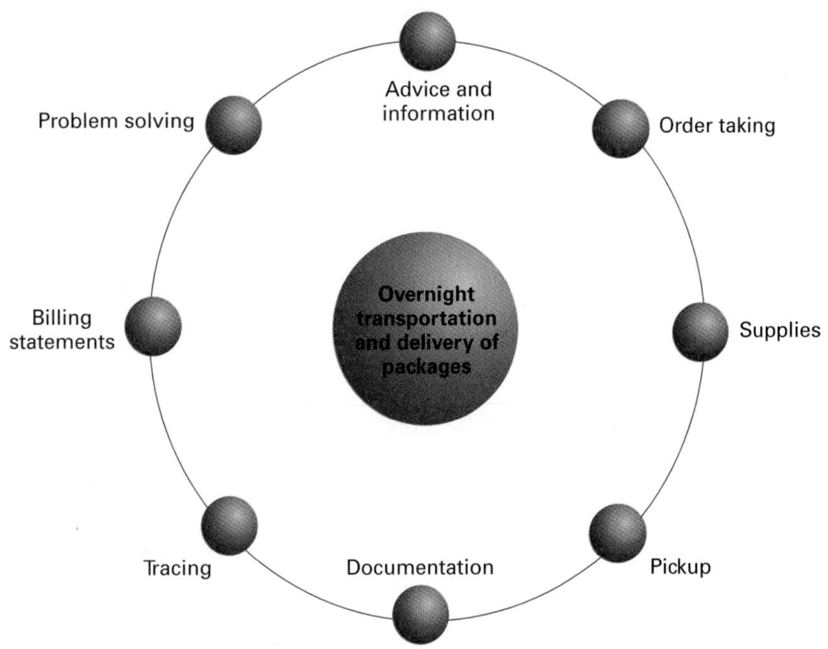

Source: From *Services Marketing*, 3rd ed. by Christopher H. Lovelock, © 1996. Reprinted by permission of Pearson Education Inc., Upper Saddle River, N.J.

means that marketing strategies for the former will need to focus more on inseparability and heterogeneity issues.

Core and Supplementary Services

The service offering can be viewed as a bundle of activities. This bundle will include the **core service**, which is the most basic benefit the customer is buying, and a group of **supplementary services** that support or enhance the core service. Exhibit 11.4 illustrates these concepts for FedEx. The core service is overnight transportation and delivery of packages, which involves possession processing. The supplementary services—some of which involve information processing—include problem solving, providing advice and information, sending billing statements, and taking orders.

core service
The most basic benefit the consumer is buying.

supplementary services
A group of services that support or enhance the core service.

In many service industries the core service becomes a commodity as competition increases. Thus firms usually emphasize supplementary services to create a competitive advantage.

In the highly competitive Toronto–London market, major airlines are inventing new ways to build the loyalty of their most valuable customers. For its top-spending customers Air Canada offers special departure and arrival lounges as well as a preboarding concierge, who for no extra charge takes care of personal requests such as theatre bookings. British Airways targets first-class passengers with complimentary pre-flight gourmet meals and on-board seats that can be transformed into fully reclining beds. The newest entrant into this crowded market, which also includes Air Transat, is Virgin Atlantic. This airline, which has won many service quality awards on other international routes, offers free on-board massages and complimentary limousine service at both ends for business and first-class passengers.[11]

In contrast, some firms position themselves by greatly reducing their supplementary services and offering a valuable core service at low cost. Fashion retail chain Winners Apparel competes by selling popular brand names at reduced

entrepreneurial insights

Sport Hawk Finds Big Money in Ferrying Athletes

Neil Jamieson has been building perhaps the fastest-growing airline in Canada, but few people have ever set foot on board one of his planes. That's because the Toronto businessman's company, Sport Hawk International, caters to only the most elite of clientele, flying professional sports teams to games across North America. "The teams pay us well and they demand a lot. I think we're in the ultimate customer service business," says the forty-two-year-old former Bay Street mergers and acquisition expert.

Since his family firm, Scocan RSA Ltd., bought a majority interest in Sport Hawk in 1997, revenues have grown from US$2 million to a projected US$30 million. Along the way, the airline has expanded from one aircraft to a fleet of four Boeing 727 jets carrying sixteen teams. Its customers include the Toronto Maple Leafs and Raptors, the Chicago Bulls, White Sox, and Cubs, the New York Islanders, and the Montreal Expos. The company is working on a contract to fly golfers for the Professional Golf Association tour. Each team pays about US$1.5 million a year for a season's worth of travel, or about 100 hours of flying time. For their money, teams are treated to comfort and—something of prime concern to passengers like Keon Clark, the six-foot-eleven centre for the Raptors—lots of cabin space.

Usually a 727 seats 150 people, but Sport Hawk has its planes configured with only sixty-six first-class seats. Between each seat is 140 centimetres of space, compared with 80 to 85 centimetres in a normal plane's economy section. The cabin is divided into three compartments. There is a front area for coaches, complete with facilities to review game tapes, a middle section where players sit and can watch a movie with radio headphones, and a back portion outfitted with club seating and tables so that people can play cards and talk. The cabin is also decorated with interchangeable logos to create a home team atmosphere.

Sport Hawk tries to provide upscale food, but passengers sometimes demand special requests. When leaving Montreal, teams often ask for Bar-B-Barn ribs, and in Los Angeles, Aunt Kizzy's soul food is always a hit with the basketball teams. Though the pampering is an expected perk of being a professional athlete, the comfort and convenience also serve a practical purpose. "I think travelling is one of the biggest stresses," said Brian James, the Raptors' equipment and travel manager. "Definitely, it wears on the teams. There are games that are that much tougher just because of your schedule leading up to them."

Years of rapid growth have had a downside. "Sport Hawk has grown in leaps and bounds in the last few years, some would say too quickly," says Jamieson. "It's good for every business to grow, and everyone wants their business to get bigger and bigger, but at the same time you start to lose those personal touches." Recognizing this, Sport Hawk is hiring more professional management and deferring further growth.

How has Sport Hawk customized its service to attract a loyal clientele? What are the dangers of growing a service such as Sport Hawk's too quickly?

Source: Adapted from Peter Fitzpatrick, "Sport Hawk Finds Big Money in Ferrying Athletes," *The National Post*, 28 March 2001, p. C7.

prices, in no-frills stores that provide minimal customer service. In Canada in May 2001 the store launched HomeSense, a new home furnishings chain, with a similar positioning: "Home fashions for less. Every day."[12]

Mass Customization

An important issue in developing the service offering is whether to customize or standardize it. Customized services are more flexible and respond to individual customers' needs. They also usually command a higher price. The traditional law firm, which treats each case differently according to the client's situation, offers customized services. Standardized services are more efficient and cost less. Unlike traditional banks, virtual bank Citizens Bank of Canada (**www.citizensbank.ca**) offers only one type of bank account: a combined chequing and savings account, for which its customers pay a low monthly fee.[13]

mass customization
A strategy that uses technology to deliver customized services on a mass basis.

Instead of choosing to either standardize or customize its services, a firm may adopt **mass customization**. Mass customization is a new strategy that involves using technology to deliver customized services on a mass (i.e., standardized) basis. That way each customer gets whatever she or he asks for. On-line retailer Amazon.com (**www.amazon.com**) customizes its home page with book recommendations for each customer based on past purchases.[14]

Mountain Equipment Co-Op

How does MEC promote its products? What are the different ways it tries to connect with its customers? How does being a co-op affect the level of customer service it provides?

www.mec.ca

on line

Would you trade a pizza for your pet's health?

The sad fact is that the majority of Canadians cannot afford the best possible healthcare for their dogs and cats.

It doesn't have to be this way.

PetCare, Canada's leading provider of pet insurance, offers affordable coverage for unexpected accidents and illnesses. Plans start as low as **$8.50/month for cats** and **$9.95/month for dogs**. And there's still something left over for pizza.

Protect your pet, your peace of mind and your budget.

Call or visit our Web site today.

PetCare
INSURANCE BROKERS LTD

petcareinsurance.com

Toll-free: 1-866-275-PETS (7387)

Insure your dog or cat for less than $10 a month.

PetCare (www.petcareinsurance.com) partners with established retail brands in Canada and the United States and uses the Internet and a toll-free phone number to sell affordable pet insurance directly to Canadian and American pet owners.

McDonald's is introducing the "Made for You" system that allows customers to order sandwiches the way they like them.[15]

The Service Mix

Most service organizations market more than one service. Rogers offers a range of multimedia services including cable TV, cell phone services, the Internet, video and DVD rentals, and television and radio programming. An organization's service mix represents a set of opportunities, risks, and challenges. Each part of the service mix should make a different contribution to the firm. To succeed, each service may need a different level of financial support.

So designing a service strategy entails deciding which new services to introduce to which target markets, which existing services to maintain, and which services to eliminate.

internet connections

Canada's E-gov Efforts Put Us in Front, but We May Not Be Able to Win the Race

We're No. 1, but don't uncork the champagne just yet. Canada ranked first in Accenture's (**www.accenture.com**) second annual e-government study, which examined on-line service delivery practices in twenty-two countries. But it's too early to claim victory.

"This is a point-in-time survey and a year from now it could be very different," says Graeme Gordon, an Ottawa-based partner with Accenture's Canadian e-government practice. "The race has really just begun."

While everyone is just out of the gates, some departments are setting the pace. Gordon says that public works, the defence department, and Revenue Canada are out in front.

"The revenue agencies worldwide are the ones that are really making the big headway in terms of progress," Gordon says. "Canada, Ireland, Singapore, Australia, Spain, all of them have very good examples of being able to pay taxes and look at your taxes on-line and submit on-line."

Gordon says the rankings were determined by two criteria: service maturity and delivery maturity. For service, Accenture went to each government's Website and checked to see how many of the 165 services could be done on-line. The level of interaction—whether users could complete a transaction or just get information—determined the score. This was worth 70 percent of the grade.

The other 30 percent was decided by a variety of factors influencing how services were delivered. Whether the federal government will reach its goal of having all of its services on-line by 2004 remains to be seen. The early returns are encouraging, but the meltdown in the high-tech industry could influence the timetable. Gordon says a stick in the economic wheel will most likely affect the government, but "right now the commitments haven't changed."

A report released on 17 April by Forrester Research (**www.forrester.com**) agrees that government agencies are introducing on-line services, but adds that their efforts won't fulfil Canada's ambition for seamless government. Forrester interviewed officials from twenty-nine federal agencies and various provinces and territories. Quebec refused to participate in the study.

What is meant by the term "digital divide"? Why is it of concern to practitioners of e-government? What are the barriers faced by government in the delivery of on-line services? By consumers in adopting on-line government services?

Source: Geoffrey Downery, "Leader of the Pack, for Now," *EBusiness Journal* 3(5) (May 2001), p. 6.

Distribution Strategy

Distribution strategies for service firms must consider issues like convenience, location, scheduling, number of outlets, and direct versus indirect distribution. A key factor influencing the selection of a service provider is convenience, so firms must offer that. Shoppers Drug Mart has late-night opening hours for many of its downtown stores. Some stores are open twenty-four hours to provide maximum convenience.

For many service firms, an important question is how many outlets to provide and what their hours should be. Distribution should meet but not exceed the target market's needs and preferences. Having too few outlets may inconvenience customers; having too many may boost costs unnecessarily. Intensity of distribution also depends on the image the firm wants to maintain. Having only a few outlets may make the service seem more exclusive or selective.

The next service distribution decision is whether to distribute services to end users *directly*, or *indirectly* through other firms. Because services are intangible, many service firms must use direct distribution or franchising. Examples include legal, accounting, and personal care services. The newest form of direct distribution is the Internet. Most major airlines are now providing on-line services to sell tickets directly to consumers; this results in lower distribution costs for the airline companies. Similarly, most of Canada's major retail banks now offer on-line banking services.

CIBC has gone one step beyond most of its competitors by teaming up with Loblaws to create a new Canadian bank, President's Choice Financial. Launched in 1997, PC Financial enjoys in-store promotion of its high-interest savings account, which also offers discounts on groceries. The bank is attracting a younger, more affluent customer base than it is used to. PC Financial has over 350,000 customers to date and is growing at the rate of 4,000 new households a week. It has added mortgages, mutual funds, and credit cards to its product offering.[16]

The *location* of a service most clearly reveals the relationship between its target market strategy and its distribution strategy. Conrad Hilton is reported to have claimed that the three most important factors in determining a hotel's success are "location, location, and location."

Flight Centre, whose business model is based on volume sales, situates its stores near areas of heavy pedestrian flow such as subway stations.[17]

For time-dependent service providers like airlines, physicians, and dentists, scheduling is often a more important factor. Scheduling is sometimes the most important factor in a customer's choice of airline.

Promotion Strategy

Consumers and business users have more trouble evaluating services than goods, because services are less tangible. For their part, marketers have more trouble promoting intangible services than tangible goods. Here are four promotion strategies they can try:

To communicate the benefits of intangible services, marketers often rely on concrete symbols. The delivery van used by on-line retailer Grocery Gateway as part of its logo and in all its advertising visually demonstrates the company's main benefit of convenience.

- *Stressing tangible cues:* A tangible cue is a concrete symbol of the service offering. To make their intangible services more tangible, hotels turn down the bedcovers and place mints on the pillows. Department stores like Eatons and The Bay often pick a specific product or line of products to spotlight in each piece of advertising to help make their intangible services seem more tangible. Merrill Lynch uses a bull to help give its financial services substance.
- *Using personal information sources:* A personal information source is someone consumers are familiar with (such as a celebrity) or someone they know or can relate to personally. Celebrity endorsements are sometimes used to reduce customers' perceived risk in choosing a service. Service firms may also seek to stimulate positive word-of-mouth communication among present and prospective customers by using real customers in their ads.
- *Creating a strong organizational image:* One way to create an image is to manage the evidence, including the physical environment of the service facility, the appearance of the service employees, and the tangible items associated with the service (e.g., stationery, bills, business cards). McDonald's has created a strong organizational image with its Golden Arches, relatively standardized interiors, and employee uniforms. Another way to create an image is through branding. IBM promotes its value-added services to businesses through sub-brand names such as E-Business and Blue Velocity.
- *Engaging in postpurchase communication:* Postpurchase communication refers to the follow-up activities that a service firm might engage in after a customer transaction. Postcard surveys, telephone calls, brochures, and various other types of follow-up show customers that their feedback matters and that their patronage is appreciated.

Price Strategy

The considerations in pricing a service are similar to the pricing considerations discussed in Chapter 15. However, the unique characteristics of services present two special pricing challenges.[18]

First, before a service can be priced, the unit of service consumption must be defined. Should pricing be based on completing a specific service task (e.g., cutting a customer's hair), or should it be based on time (e.g., how long it takes to cut a customer's hair)? Some services include the consumption of goods, such as food and beverages. Restaurants charge customers for food and drink rather than for the use of a table and chairs. Some transportation firms charge by distance; others charge a flat rate.

Second, for services that comprise multiple elements, the issue is whether pricing should be based on a "bundle" of elements or whether each element should be priced separately. A bundled price may be preferable when consumers dislike having to pay "extra" for every part of the service (e.g., paying extra for baggage handling or food on an airplane). Also, bundled prices are easier for firms to administer.

Some customers may not want to pay for service elements they do not use. Many furniture stores have "unbundled" delivery charges from the price of the furniture. Customers can choose to pick up the furniture at the store, thus saving on the delivery fee.

Similarly, cable, satellite, and digital TV companies are offering consumers more choice than ever before in terms of which channels they choose to be provided with. No longer are all available channels simply bundled together.

Marketers should set performance objectives when pricing each service. Three categories of pricing objectives have been suggested:

- *Revenue-oriented pricing* focuses on maximizing the surplus of income over costs. A limitation of this approach is that for many services it can be difficult to determine costs.
- *Operations-oriented pricing* seeks to match supply and demand by varying prices. Matching hotel demand to the number of available rooms can be achieved by raising prices at peak times and decreasing them during slow times.
- *Patronage-oriented pricing* strives to maximize the number of customers using the service. Thus, prices vary with different market segments' ability to pay, and methods of payment (such as credit) are offered that increase the likelihood of a purchase.

A firm may need to use more than one type of pricing objective. In fact, all three objectives probably need to be included to some degree in pricing strategies, although the importance of each type will vary depending on the type of service provided, the prices competitors are charging, the differing ability of various customer segments to pay, and/or the opportunity to negotiate price. For customized services (e.g., legal services and construction services), customers may also be in a position to negotiate a price.

Relationship Marketing in Services

6
Discuss relationship marketing in services

Many services involve ongoing interaction between the service organization and the customer. Such services can benefit from relationship marketing, a strategy that was described in Chapter 1. Relationship marketing is an approach to attracting, developing, and retaining customers. The idea is to develop strong loyalty by creating satisfied customers who will buy additional services from the firm and who are unlikely to switch to a competitor. Satisfied customers are likely to praise the company to others, which in turn will bring in new customers.

Many businesses have found it more cost effective to hang on to the customers they have than only to try to attract new ones. One bank found that increasing customer retention 2 percent had the same effect on profits as reducing costs 10 percent.

It has been suggested that relationship marketing can be practiced at three levels (see Exhibit 11.5):[19]

exhibit 11.5

Three Levels of Relationship Marketing

Level	Type of bond	Degree of service customization	Main element of marketing mix	Potential for long term advantage over competitors
1	Financial	Low	Price	Low
2	Financial, social	Medium	Personal communication	Medium
3	Financial, social, structural	Medium to high	Service delivery	High

Source: Reprinted with permission of The Free Press, a Division of Simon & Schuster, Inc. from *Marketing Services: Competing Through Quality* by Leonard L. Barry and A. Parasuraman. Copyright © 1991 by The Free Press.

- *Level 1:* The firm uses pricing incentives to encourage customers to continue doing business with it. Many firms use loyalty cards that provide frequent users with free or discounted services. In the long term this level of relationship marketing is the least effective because its price-based advantage is easily imitated by other firms.
- *Level 2:* This level of relationship marketing also uses pricing incentives, but it seeks as well to build social bonds with customers. The firm stays in touch with customers, learns about their needs, and designs services to meet those needs. At fitness centers such as The Good Life, personal trainers get to know their clients over time and build customized exercise regimens for them. Level 2 relationship marketing has a greater potential than level 1 for keeping the firm ahead of the competition.
- *Level 3:* At this level the firm uses financial and social bonds as at level 2, but adds structural bonds to the formula. Structural bonds are developed by offering value-added services that are not readily available from other firms. Four Seasons operates a chainwide program called "Do Leave Home Without It" where guests are told not to worry about having the correct formal wear for functions. Each hotel stocks a complete ensemble for business or casual wear, for both men and women, in a wide range of styles and sizes. These clothes are lent to guests at no charge. Four Seasons Singapore stocks the latest fashions from the Italian designer Ermenegildo Zegna.[20]

The creation of corporate daycare facilities is one way a company can market itself and its internal services to its employees. Internal marketing efforts like this can help employers attract and retain valuable employees.

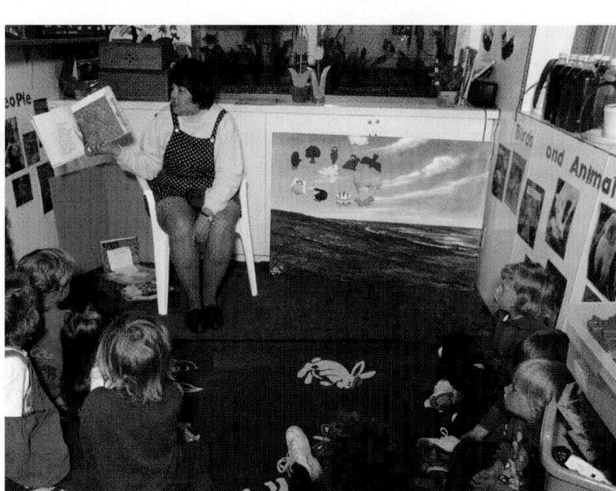

Programs like this one have the strongest potential for sustaining long-term relationships with customers.

Internal Marketing in Service Firms

7

Explain internal marketing in services

Services are performances, so the quality of a firm's employees is an important part of building long-term relationships with customers. Employees who like their jobs and are satisfied with the firm they work for are more likely to deliver superior service to customers. In other words, a firm that makes its employees happy has a better chance of keeping its customers coming back. So it is critical that service firms practise **internal marketing**, which means treating employees as customers and developing systems and benefits that satisfy their needs. The following activities are involved in internal marketing: competing for talent, offering a vision, training employees, stressing teamwork, giving employees more freedom to make decisions, measuring and rewarding good service performance, and knowing employees' needs.[21]

internal marketing
Treating employees as customers and developing systems and benefits that satisfy their needs.

Global Issues in Services Marketing

8
Discuss global issues in services marketing

The international marketing of services is a major part of global business, but one that is also fraught with difficulty.

To be successful in the global marketplace, service firms must first determine the nature of their core product. Then the marketing mix elements (additional services, pricing, promotion, distribution) should be designed to take into account each country's local environment. Because customers and employees interact so much in the delivery of services, special attention must be paid to cultural norms. As highlighted in the "Global Perspectives" box, failure to respect the local culture can lead to disaster for the service exporter.

Wal-Mart's Famous Service with a Smile? Not in Germany

In stores the world over, the American maxim that "the customer is king" has long been taken as gospel—but not in highly conservative Germany. The rules of German retailing are "the grumpier the better" and "the customer comes last"—an approach that seems to work wonders with shoppers. Anyone who suspects this to be an overly harsh assessment should examine the disastrous foray by Wal-Mart, the world's biggest and most service-conscious supermarket chain, into the cheerless arena of German shopping. U.S.-owned Wal-Mart arrived in Germany in January 1998, bubbling with confidence and determined to pamper every shopper in sight. Staff in all of its ninety-five German stores were specially trained and ordered to apply the company's golden rules. If a customer came within ten feet, they should smile sweetly and offer to help. And customers' bags had to be packed at the checkout—a service painfully absent in leading German supermarkets. The result was a culture clash of huge proportions. Instead of charming the Germans, the Wal-Mart tactics infuriated shoppers and aroused their suspicions. "German customers cannot handle this kind of service," said Barbara Schnappauf, a researcher at GFK, Germany's biggest research institute. "If someone tries to put things in a bag for them, they say to themselves, 'Hey, I just paid for that. That's mine.' If someone takes hold of their possessions at the checkout, they think they are trying to steal them."

Wal-Mart's alien service culture and its teething difficulties with German suppliers are being cited as the reasons for catastrophic results. Losses are estimated by analysts at more than $222 million a year. And things are said to be getting worse. In an annual survey of customer sentiment, Wal-Mart ranked bottom of all retailers surveyed. It is not just German customers who can't stomach Wal-Mart's ways. Stories abound of staff hiding in washrooms to avoid the morning ritual, the Wal-Mart chant: "Give us a W... Give us an A...Wadduya get? Yeah ...WAAAL-MART." Or the finale to the morning meeting: "Who is number one?" they ask. "The customer, of course!" "German customers do not understand what the point of this service is," says Martin Kaldik, an expert on German retailing.

Evaluate Wal-Mart's entry into Germany. What has gone wrong? Why? How could Wal-Mart have had a successful launch in the country? Assuming that withdrawal is not an option, what would you recommend the company do next?

Source: "Wal-Mart's Famous Service with a Smile? Not in Germany" by *The Daily Telegraph, The National Post,* 31 October 2000, p. B5.

Heart and Stroke Foundation of Canada

What are the marketing objectives of the Heart and Stroke Foundation? In other words, what are the different audiences for this charity, and what does it want to say to them? How does the foundation raise money? What proportion of its annual income does the foundation get from government? How does this level affect it?

www.na.heartandstroke.ca

on line

Nonprofit Organization Marketing

9

Describe nonprofit organization marketing

A **nonprofit organization** is an organization that exists to achieve some goal other than the usual business goals of profit, market share, and return on investment. Nonprofit organizations share important characteristics with service firms in the private sector. Both market intangible products. Both often require the customer to be present during the production process. Both for-profit and nonprofit services vary greatly from producer to producer and from day to day, even within the same producer. Neither for-profit nor nonprofit services can be produced and stored, the way tangible goods can.

nonprofit organization
An organization that exists to achieve some goal other than the usual business goals of profit, market share, or return on investment.

Few people realize that nonprofit organizations account for a large percentage of Canada's economic activity. Moreover, government organizations employ a large proportion of Canada's workers. Nonprofit organizations include tens of thousands of charities, schools, colleges and universities, and arts and cultural groups.

What Is Nonprofit Organization Marketing?

Nonprofit organization marketing is the effort by nonprofit organizations to bring about mutually satisfying exchanges with target markets. These organizations vary greatly in size and purpose and operate in different environments. That being said, most perform the following marketing activities:

nonprofit organization marketing
The effort by nonprofit organizations to bring about mutually satisfying exchanges with target markets.

- They identify the customers they wish to serve or attract (although they usually use another term, such as *clients, patients, members,* or *sponsors*).
- They explicitly or implicitly specify objectives.
- They develop, manage, and eliminate programs and services.
- They decide on prices to charge (although they use other terms such as *fees, donations, tuition, fares, fines,* or *rates*).
- They schedule events or programs, and determine where they will be held or offered.
- They communicate their availability through brochures, signs, public service announcements, and advertisements

Often, nonprofit organizations that carry out these functions don't realize they are engaged in marketing.

Unique Aspects of Nonprofit Organization Marketing Strategies

10

Explain the unique aspects of nonprofit organization marketing

Like their counterparts in business, nonprofit managers develop marketing strategies to bring about mutually satisfying exchanges with target markets. However, marketing in nonprofit organizations is unique in many respects. It sets marketing objectives differently, selects its markets differently, and develops appropriate marketing mixes differently.

This ad attempts to break through the ignorance surrounding low literacy levels in Canada. What segment of the population do you think it is targeting? Do you think it is effective? Why? www.abc-canada.org

WHEN YOU STRUGGLE
TO READ AND WRITE,
WORDS CAN'T DESCRIBE IT.
Incredibly, 5 million Canadians have serious problems with reading, writing and math. You can help. To learn more, visit www.abc.canada.org or call 1-800-303-1004
ABC
CANADA

Objectives

In the private sector the profit motive is both an objective for guiding decisions and a criterion for evaluating results. Nonprofit organizations do not seek to make a profit for redistribution to owners or shareholders. Often they focus instead on generating enough funds to cover expenses. The Salvation Army does not gauge its success by the amount of money it raises in donations. The Canadian Film Centre does not base its performance evaluations on the dollars in revenue it takes in.

Most nonprofit organizations are expected to provide equitable, effective, and efficient services that respond to the wants and preferences of multiple constituencies. These include users, payers, donors, politicians, appointed officials, the media, and the general public. Nonprofit organizations cannot measure their success or failure in strictly financial terms.

The lack of a financial "bottom line" and the existence of multiple, diverse, intangible, and sometimes vague or conflicting objectives makes it difficult for nonprofit managers to prioritize objectives, make decisions, and evaluate performance. They must often use approaches that are different from the ones commonly taken by the private sector.

Target Markets

Three issues relating to target markets are unique to nonprofit organizations:

- *Apathetic or strongly opposed targets:* Private sector organizations usually give priority to developing those market segments which are most likely to respond to particular offerings. In contrast, nonprofit organizations must often target those who are apathetic about or strongly opposed to receiving their services. This is the case, for example, with vaccinations, family-planning guidance, help for problems of drug or alcohol abuse, and psychological counselling.
- *Pressure to adopt undifferentiated segmentation strategies:* Nonprofit organizations often adopt undifferentiated strategies by default (see Chapter 6). Sometimes

Vancouver Aquarium

How does the Vancouver Aquarium promote itself to its different customer audiences, including tourists and school parties? How does it fund itself?

www.vanaqua.org

on line

entrepreneurial insights

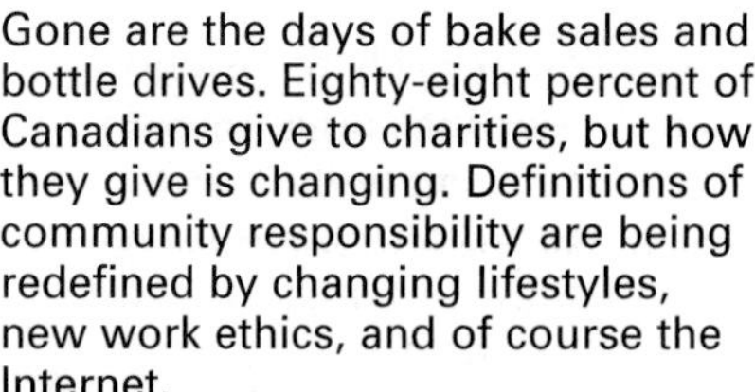

A Virtual Community of Giving: Charity.ca

Gone are the days of bake sales and bottle drives. Eighty-eight percent of Canadians give to charities, but how they give is changing. Definitions of community responsibility are being redefined by changing lifestyles, new work ethics, and of course the Internet.

One new vision of social responsibility is Charity.ca, a Web portal that is connecting donors and charities and creating a virtual community of giving. This innovative approach to on-line charity is the brainchild of Richard Ivey, the founder of Charity.ca. After more than twenty years of involvement in philanthropy, Ivey recently became involved in a series of Internet initiatives. Last November these two interests merged.

"I thought it would be great to bring the Internet to the nonprofit world," he said in an interview. With capital and support from NRG, a Web incubator that has fostered many successful Web ventures, Charity.ca was launched last spring.

The way Ivey talks about Charity.ca, you'd think he was marketing a new brand of beer, not charity. He makes it sound exciting and new, and then you realize it actually is.

With savvy talk about broadening demographics and diversifying giving, he is taking the image of charity and turning it on its head. This different approach is evident when you arrive at Charity.ca's home page. Instead of inundating visitors with grim statistics and pleas for assistance, Charity.ca provides information on a wide range of current issues and events, both in Canada and around the planet. These issues, in turn, link to associated charities.

"So many of the donations that people make are based on a compelling story and not the charity names themselves," says Vaughn McIntyre, the CEO of Charity.ca, which is capitalizing on the fact that the Web allows people to get through huge amounts of information in a short time and make informed decisions on where they want to put their money.

It's straightforward, it's informative, and it puts people in control. The most innovative sections offered by Charity.ca are Tributes and In Memoriam. These provide donors with access to newspaper obituaries from across Canada, and make it easier to give gifts in memory of loved ones. Though it sounds a little grim, these sections recognize a market with great potential.

"Based on our research, 50 percent of all donations that people intend to make from reading the obituaries in newspapers are lost because the people can't find the address or don't have time to write the cheque," says Ivey. "If they can go to the Charity.ca and do it in thirty seconds, we hope to dramatically increase the number of memorial gifts in the country."

Charities recognize that they must pursue new ways of generating revenue on the Web, and have been responding quickly to Charity.ca. They can link their own pages to Charity.ca, complete with all their background information. They can also place Charity.ca's on-line donation button on their own home page, generating even more exposure and revenue. On-line giving is less expensive to administer than traditional methods of fundraising—an important factor. According to the Centre for Voluntary Sector Services at Ryerson Polytechnic University, the average cost to raise a dollar of charity is 26 cents. At Charity.ca the cost is 8 cents.

How does Ivey's Website generate revenue? It charges charities that have joined up 8 percent for transferring monies and for paying credit card fees and issuing tax receipts.

Visit www.charity.ca. What gap in the charity market is Charity.ca filling? Considering that the largest charity donors tend to be middle-aged or older, how easy do you think the site is to navigate for older people? How could Charity.ca improve its service?

Sources: Adapted from Jill Toombs, "A Virtual Community of Giving," *The National Post: eWorld*, 31 October 2000, p. C6.

they fail to recognize the advantages of targeting, or an undifferentiated approach may seem to offer economies of scale and low per capita costs. Other times, nonprofit organizations are pressured or required to serve the maximum number of people by targeting the average user. The problem with developing services targeted at the average user is that there are few "average" users. So such strategies typically fail to fully satisfy any market segment.

- *Complementary positioning:* The main role of many nonprofit organizations is to provide services, with available resources, to those who are not adequately served by private sector organizations. As a result, nonprofit organizations must often complement rather than compete with the efforts of others. The positioning task is to identify underserved market segments and to develop marketing programs that match their needs, rather than to target the niches that may be most profitable. A university library may see itself as complementing the services of the public library, rather than as competing with those services.

Product Decisions

There are three product-related distinctions between business and nonprofit organizations:

- *Benefit complexity:* Instead of simple product concepts, like "Fly the friendly skies" or "We earn money the old-fashioned way," nonprofit organizations often market complex behaviours or ideas. Examples include the need to eat right, not to drink and drive, and not to smoke tobacco. The benefits consumers receive are complex, long-term, and intangible, and so are more difficult to communicate to consumers.
- *Benefit strength:* With many nonprofit offerings the benefit strength is quite weak or indirect. What are the direct, personal benefits to you of driving 80 kilometres an hour, donating blood, or asking your neighbours to contribute money to a charity? In contrast, most private sector service organizations offer customers direct, personal benefits in an exchange relationship.
- *Involvement:* Many nonprofit organizations market products that call for very low involvement ("Prevent forest fires," "Don't litter") or very high involvement ("Join the military," "Stop smoking"). For private sector goods the typical range is much narrower. Traditional promotional tools may be inadequate to motivate the adoption of either low- or high-involvement products.

Distribution Decisions

The nonprofit organization's capacity to distribute its service offerings to potential customer groups when and where they want them is often a key factor in its success. Many colleges and universities have one or more satellite campuses to provide easier access for distant students. Some institutions also offer classes to off-campus students through interactive video technology.

The extent to which a service depends on fixed facilities has important implications for distribution decisions. Obviously, services such as rail transit and lake fishing can be delivered only at specific points. Many nonprofit services, however, do not depend on special facilities. Counselling need not take place in agency offices; it can be done wherever counsellors and clients can meet. Probation services and outreach youth programs are other examples of deliverable services.

Nonprofit organizations must often be creative in their marketing and promotions. To spread the word about the Catholic Church, the Vatican is licensing images it owns for use on salable merchandise.

Promotion Decisions

Unlike government agencies, many nonprofit organizations are small and simply don't have the resources to retain advertising agencies, promotion consultants, or marketing staff. However, nonprofit organizations have a few special promotion resources they can call on:

- *Volunteers:* Nonprofit organizations often seek out marketing, sales, and advertising professionals to help them develop and implement promotion strategies. Some ad agencies donate their services in exchange for potential long-term benefits. Donated services create good will, personal contacts, and general awareness of the donor's organization, reputation, and competency.

- *Sales promotion activities*: Sales promotion activities that utilize existing services or other resources are being used more and more often to draw attention to the offerings of nonprofit organizations. Charity.ca (see entrepreneurial spotlight) used a prize draw, including the chance to win a golf vacation to Florida, to successfully launch its site.[22]

- *Public service advertising*: A **public service advertisement (PSA)** is an announcement that promotes a program of a federal, provincial, or local government or of a nonprofit organization. The sponsor of a PSA does not pay for the time or space, which instead is donated by the medium.

public service advertisement (PSA)
An announcement that promotes a program of a federal, provincial, or local government or of a nonprofit organization.

- *Licensing:* Some nonprofit organizations have found that licensing is an effective way to communicate to a large audience. The Vatican is trying to raise money and spread the word about the Catholic Church through a licensing program. This program will put images from the Vatican—its art collections, manuscripts, frescoes, and architecture, and so on—on T-shirts, glassware, candles, and ornaments.[23]

Pricing Decisions

Five key characteristics distinguish the pricing decisions of nonprofit organizations from those of the profit sector:

- *Pricing objectives:* Revenue is the main pricing objective in the profit sector—more specifically, profit maximization, sales maximization, or target return on sales or investment. Many nonprofit organizations must also be concerned about revenue. However, nonprofit organizations often seek to either partially or fully defray costs rather than to achieve a profit for distribution to stockholders. Nonprofit organizations also seek to redistribute income—for instance, through taxation and sliding-scale fees. Moreover, they strive to allocate resources fairly among individuals or households or across geographic or political boundaries.

- Nonfinancial prices: In many nonprofit situations, consumers are not charged a monetary price but instead must absorb nonmonetary costs. The importance of those costs is illustrated by the large number of eligible citizens who do not take advantage of "free" services for the poverty stricken. In many public assistance programs, about half the people who are eligible don't participate. Nonmonetary costs consist of the opportunity cost of time, embarrassment costs, and effort costs.

- *Indirect payment:* Indirect payment through taxes is common to marketers of "free" services, such as libraries, fire protection, and police protection. Indirect payment is not a common practice in the profit sector.

- *Separation between payers and users:* By design, many charitable organizations provide services to those who are relatively poor, and those services are paid for mainly by those who have more money. Examples of the same thing can be found in the profit sector (such as insurance claims); however, the practice is much less prevalent there.

- *Below-cost pricing:* An example of below-cost pricing is university tuition. Almost all private and public colleges and universities price their services below full cost. This practice also exists in the profit sector, although it is generally an undesirable, temporary situation.

LOOKING BACK

Look back at the story about Four Seasons Hotels and Resorts that appeared at the beginning of this chapter. After reading the chapter, you should know the answers to the questions posed at the end of the story. Services, like hotels, differ from goods on four characteristics: intangibility, inseparability, heterogeneity, and perishability. Four Seasons invests a great deal of time and money in its employees because it knows that quality employees are critical to quality service delivery. The chain's prosperity can be attributed to its successful delivery of consistently high service quality. Service quality can be measured by looking at a firm's responsiveness, assurance, empathy, and tangibles. In all four of these areas, Four Seasons delivers excellence.

Summary

1 Discuss the importance of services to the economy. The service sector plays a crucial role in the Canadian economy, employing about seven out of ten workers and accounting for more than two-thirds of GDP.

2 Discuss the differences between services and goods. Services are distinguished by four characteristics: intangibility, inseparability, heterogeneity, and perishability. Services are intangible in that they lack clearly identifiable physical characteristics, which makes it difficult for marketers to communicate their specific benefits to potential customers. Typically, it isn't possible to separate service production from service consumption. Services are heterogeneous in that their quality depends on such variables as the service provider, the individual consumer, location, and so on. Finally, services are perishable in the sense that they cannot be stored or saved. As a result, synchronizing supply with demand is especially challenging in the service industry.

3 Explain why services marketing is important to manufacturers. Although manufacturers are marketing mainly goods, the related services they provide often give them a competitive advantage, especially when competing goods are quite similar.

4 Describe the components of service quality and the gap model of service quality. There are five components of service quality: reliability (ability to perform the service dependably, accurately, and consistently), responsiveness (providing prompt service), assurance (knowledge and courtesy of employees and their ability to inspire trust), empathy (caring, individualized attention), and tangibles (physical evidence of the service).

The gap model identifies five key discrepancies that can influence customer evaluations of service quality. When the gaps are large, service quality is low. As the gaps shrink, service quality improves. Gap 1 is the gap between customer expectations and management's perceptions of those expectations. Gap 2 is the gap between management's perception of what the customer wants and specifications for service quality. Gap 3 is the gap between service quality specifications and delivery of the service. Gap 4 is the gap between service delivery and what the company promises to the customer through external communication. Gap 5 is the gap between customers' service expectations and their perceptions of service performance.

5 Develop marketing mixes for services. "Product" (service) strategy issues include what is being processed (people, possessions, information), core and supplementary services, customization versus standardization, and the service mix or portfolio. Distribution decisions involve convenience, number of outlets, direct versus indirect distribution, and scheduling. Stressing tangible cues, using personal sources of information, creating strong organizational images, and engaging in postpurchase communication are effective promotion strategies. Pricing objectives for services can be revenue oriented, operations oriented, patronage oriented, or any combination of the three.

6 Discuss relationship marketing in services. Relationship marketing in services involves attracting, developing, and retaining customer relationships. There are three levels of relationship marketing: level 1 focuses on pricing incentives; level 2 uses pricing incentives and social bonds with customers; and level 3 uses pricing, social bonds, and structural bonds to build long-term relationships.

7 Explain internal marketing in services. Internal marketing means treating employees as customers and developing systems and benefits that satisfy their needs. Employees who like their jobs and are happy with the firm they work for are more likely to deliver good service. Internal marketing activities include competing for talent, offering a vision, training employees, stressing teamwork, giving employees freedom to make decisions, measuring and rewarding good service performance, and knowing employees' needs.

8 Discuss global issues in services marketing. To be successful globally, service firms must adjust their marketing mix for the environment of each target country. Cultural adaptation plays a major role in the successful transplanting of services internationally.

9 Describe nonprofit organization marketing. Nonprofit organizations pursue goals other than profit, market share, and return on investment. Nonprofit organization marketing facilitates mutually satisfying exchanges between nonprofit organizations and their target markets.

10 Explain the unique aspects of nonprofit organization marketing. Several unique characteristics distinguish nonbusiness marketing strategy, including a concern with services and social behaviours rather than manufactured goods and profit; a difficult, undifferentiated, and in some ways marginal target market; a complex product that may have only indirect benefits and elicit very low involvement; a short, direct, immediate distribution channel; a relative lack of resources for promotion; and prices only indirectly related to the exchange between the producer and the consumer of services.

Do You Know These Terms?

assurance 284
core service 287
credence quality 282
empathy 284
experience quality 282
gap model 285
heterogeneity 283
inseparability 282
intangibility 281
internal marketing 294
mass customization 288
nonprofit organization 295
nonprofit organization marketing 295
perishability 283
public service advertisement (PSA) 299
reliability 284
responsiveness 284
search quality 282
service 281
supplementary services 287
tangibles 285

Discussion and Writing Questions

1. Explain what the search, experience, and credence qualities are for medical services.
2. Assume that you are the manager of a restaurant. Write a list of implications of inseparability for your firm.
3. Analyze a recent experience you have had with a service business (e.g., a hairdresser, a movie theatre, a car mechanic, a restaurant) in terms of your expectations and perceptions about each of the five components of service quality.
4. Apply what you have learned about service quality to your university food service, and write a memo to the food service manager making recommendations for change, if necessary.
5. Form a team with at least two other classmates, and come up with an idea for a new service. Develop a marketing mix strategy for the new service.
6. Regarding the service developed in question 5, design with the other members of your team a relationship marketing strategy.
7. List some of the issues you would have to consider in taking your new service (from question 5) global. How would you change your marketing mix to address those issues?

8. Form a team with two or three classmates. Using the promotion strategies discussed in the chapter, design a promotion strategy for your college or university.
9. Your nonprofit community theatre is having difficulty attracting new patrons. Most of its present patrons are fifty or older. What other target markets might be viable? For each target market you choose, identify the promotion activities you would use to attract it.
10. What services does **www.exit.ca** offer? How do visitors use the deals section?
11. Visit **www.airmiles.ca**. How does Airmiles make the services it partners with more tangible and attractive? How is the program similar to and different from Air Canada's Aeroplan program, which was discussed earlier? Which one is more effective? Explain why.

Application for Small Business

Amanda Baker has decided she wants to start a marketing consulting business. She has been able to generate solid financial backing for her venture because she already has developed an outstanding reputation as a creative and successful marketer, so start-up resources are not a large problem. Amanda will target small companies with her services. Her business will be located in a medium-sized community not far from a large city.

Questions

1. How can Amanda tangibilize her service for potential clients?
2. What can Amanda do to ensure she will offer a quality service to her clients?
3. What marketing strategies can Amanda use to help her develop long-term relationships with her clients?

The Wickaninnish Inn

The Wickaninnish Inn near Tofino, British Columbia, has found a unique way of positioning itself as a leading service provider among the province's competing hotels.

Cold and stormy winters can be the bane of many coastal resorts. Not so for Wickaninnish, which has made unparalleled views of the storms a major service feature. The inn has been designed from the ground up for the specific purpose of providing the most comfortable location on North America's west coast for storm watching. Wickaninnish is built on a rocky promontory on the rugged west coast of Vancouver Island. With the inn surrounded by water on three sides, every one of the forty-six guest rooms has an ocean view, as well as a fireplace and other amenities you would find in a luxury hotel.

By getting to know intimately its key target audience of busy city dwellers, Wickaninnish has been able to devise a range of service packages for different tastes. Those wanting a fast, hassle-free escape are directed to the No Stress Express package, which bundles a convenient flight with a weekend stay at the Inn. The Nature Lover's package includes guided nature walks, while the Gourmet Trail offers excursions to the finest dining spots around Vancouver Island.

And for those guests who don't want to preplan their stay, the Wickaninnish Inn offers dedicated guest service representatives. These concierges act as personal assistants to guests, helping them organize any itinerary of activities at short notice, such as a visit to the nearby hot springs.

Watch the video case and explore the Wickaninnish Inn's Website (**www.wickinn.com/Press**) to find out more about how the McDiarmid family have gone about successfully marketing their unique and luxurious little hotel.

Source:

CBC, *Venture*, "Storm Inn," February 3, 1998.

Questions

1. Services are intangible, inseparable from the provider, perishable, and heterogeneous. How do these characteristics apply to the Wickaninnish Inn's services?
2. Lodging is a fiercely competitive service industry. What are the different elements of Wickaninnish's promotional strategy, and how are they helping it attract customers the year round? What could the hotel do to improve in terms of its promotional strategy?
3. The five components of service quality are reliability, responsiveness, assurance, empathy, and tangibles. What evidence can you cite that the Wickaninnish Inn delivers on these components? What could the hotel do to improve its service quality?

CHAPTER

12

LEARNING OBJECTIVES

After studying this chapter, you should be able to

1. Explain what a marketing channel is and why intermediaries are needed
2. Define the types of channel intermediaries, and describe their functions and activities
3. Describe the channel structures for consumer and business-to-business products, and discuss alternative channel arrangements
4. Discuss the issues that influence channel strategy
5. Explain channel leadership, conflict, and partnering
6. Identify the special problems and opportunities associated with distribution in service organizations
7. Discuss channel structure and logistics issues in global markets

MARKETING CHANNELS AND WHOLESALING

Shell Oil Products, a division of Shell Oil Company, used to buy all its personal computers from Compaq or IBM. Two years ago it switched its allegiance and its $26 million in annual PC purchases to Dell. The reason had less to do with the computers than with the way Dell sells them. Unlike Compaq and IBM, Dell sells directly to customers, thus eliminating distributors and resellers, who bring up the price and lengthen the time it takes to get the hardware. On top of that, Dell only sells custom-made machines, which it builds to the customer's exact specifications. Its competitors build machines first and then wait for customers to order a particular model.

Dell, which Michael Dell founded as a mail-order company when he was still a university student, deploys a direct sales force to cut out retailers, specialty stores, and distributors. The success of Dell's marketing model—selling through direct sales channels, building custom-made PCs, and streamlining the distribution process—is amply reflected on the stock market. Since 1990, Dell stock has increased by 29,600 percent! Today, the $13 billion company is the world's largest direct seller of computers.

To really understand Dell's eye-popping growth, you need only to look at how good it is at selling custom-made machines directly to buyers. First, Dell has no finished inventory because it builds its PCs on demand. As soon as a computer is built it is shipped to the customer. The entire process, from phone call to loading onto a delivery truck, takes just thirty-six hours. Orders are relayed instantly to one of Dell's three plants. Once an order is received, a Dell PC can be custom-built to the customer's exact specifications within eight hours, with software installed, tested, and packed.

Second, Dell can ship machines with the latest high-margin components. Because of its close relationships with component suppliers such as Intel for chips and Maxtor for hard drives, these components arrive just in time to be installed in its machines. This practically eliminates any stockpiling of raw materials, which can quickly become obsolete in the rapidly changing computer industry. This saves money, too, because component prices tend to fall many times throughout the year.

Third, in contrast to IBM and Compaq, which use resellers to sell their PCs, Dell has direct

Dell Computer

Visit Dell's Website. How is it set up to sell in a marketing channel that goes directly to the customer?

www.dell.ca

on line

contact with its customers. When customers start requesting 8.4 gigabyte drives, Dell knows about it immediately; this knowledge enables it to make split-second procurement decisions. Also, knowing its customers personally gives Dell considerable leverage the next time customers have hardware needs or want to upgrade their entire stock of computers. Fourth and finally, selling directly means that Dell isn't getting paid by resellers but by large corporations such as Ford and Shell Oil. Not surprisingly, Dell receivables have a great credit rating—Dell typically has its money in the bank before the computer is even built.

Dell is now striving to boost sales over the Internet, the ultimate direct channel. It is already the biggest on-line seller of computers, selling more than $6 million in computers every day from its Website. Dell even sells computers on-line in China.

Compaq (which recently merged with Hewlett-Packard) and IBM are dabbling in direct sales, but risk losing relationships with dealers if they go too far. Compaq and IBM depend on resellers for 90 percent of their sales, and resellers can easily retaliate against suppliers that get too aggressive about selling direct. Giving in to this reality, Compaq and IBM have been trying to make their three-step distribution process—manufacturer to distributor to reseller to customer—work as efficiently as Dell's one-step model. Both have enlisted distributors to do part of the assembly of their computers as a way to lower costs. Distributors can also assemble customized PCs based on what customers want, as Dell does. However, because they must still pay dealers, they must either charge slightly more or accept lower profit margins.[1]

What advantages does Dell derive from selling in marketing channels directly to customers? Is there any way that Compaq or IBM can expand the use of direct channels without alienating current networks of resellers? What areas of distribution, such as inventory, materials handling, and transportation, could they streamline to compete with Dell more effectively? Similar questions will be addressed throughout this chapter, which considers marketing channels.

Marketing Channels

1

Explain what a marketing channel is and why intermediaries are needed

The term *channel* is derived from the Latin word *canalis,* which means canal. A marketing channel can be viewed as a large canal or pipeline through which products, their ownership, communication, financing, and payment, and the accompanying risk, flow to the consumer. In formal terms, a **marketing channel** (also called a **channel of distribution**) is a business structure of interdependent organizations that extends from the point of product origin to the consumer for the purpose of moving products to their final consumption destination.

marketing channel (channel of distribution)
A set of interdependent organizations that ease the transfer of ownership as products move from producer to business user or consumer.

Many different types of organizations participate in marketing channels. **Channel members** (also called intermediaries, or resellers, or middlemen) negotiate with one another, buy and sell products, and facilitate the change of ownership between buyer and seller in the course of moving products from the manufacturer into the hands of the final consumer. As products move through the marketing channel, channel members provide economies to the distribution process in the form of specialization and division of labour. They also overcome discrepancies and provide contact efficiency.

channel members
All parties in the marketing channel that negotiate with one another, buy and sell products, and facilitate the change of ownership between buyer and seller in the course of moving the product from the manufacturer into the hands of the final consumer.

Providing Specialization and Division of Labour

According to the concept of specialization and division of labour, breaking down a complex task into smaller, simpler ones and allocating those smaller tasks to specialists creates greater efficiency and lower average production costs. Manufacturers achieve economies of scale through the use of efficient equipment capable of producing large quantities of a single product.

Marketing channels can also attain economies of scale through specialization and division of labour by aiding producers who lack the motivation, financing, or expertise to market directly to end users or consumers. Sometimes, as with most consumer convenience goods such as soft drinks, the cost of marketing directly to millions of consumers—taking and shipping individual orders—is prohibitive. Producers hire channel members such as wholesalers and retailers to do what they as producers are not equipped to do or what channel members are better able to do. Channel members can do some things more efficiently than producers because they have built good relationships with their customers. Their specialized expertise enhances the overall performance of the channel.

Overcoming Discrepancies

Marketing channels also aid in overcoming discrepancies of quantity, assortment, time, and space created by economies of scale in production. Assume that Quaker Oats of Canada can efficiently produce its frozen Aunt Jemima Waffles only at a rate of 5,000 units in a typical day. Not even the most ardent waffle fan could consume that amount in a year, much less in a day. The quantity produced to achieve low unit costs has created a **discrepancy of quantity**, which is the difference between the amount of product produced and the amount an end user wants to buy. Marketing channels store the product and distribute it in the appropriate amounts; in other words, they overcome quantity discrepancies by making products available in the quantities that consumers desire.

discrepancy of quantity
The difference between the amount of product produced and the amount a customer wants to buy.

Mass production creates not only discrepancies of quantity but also discrepancies of assortment. A **discrepancy of assortment** arises when a consumer does not have all the items necessary to receive full satisfaction from a product. For waffles to provide maximum satisfaction—that is, for the assortment to be completed—several other products are required. At the very least, most people want a knife, a fork, a plate, butter, and syrup. Others might add orange juice, coffee, cream, sugar, eggs, and bacon or sausage. Quaker Oats is a large consumer products company, but it does not come close to providing the optimal assortment to go with its Aunt Jemima Waffles. To overcome discrepancies of assortment, marketing channels assemble in one place many of the products necessary to complete a consumer's needed assortment.

discrepancy of assortment
The lack of all the items a customer needs to receive full satisfaction from a product or products.

A **temporal discrepancy** is created when a product is produced but the consumer is not ready to buy it. Marketing channels overcome temporal discrepancies by maintaining inventories in anticipation of demand. Manufacturers of seasonal

temporal discrepancy
The difference between when a product is produced and when a customer is ready to buy it.

merchandise such as Christmas decorations are in operation all year, even though consumer demand is concentrated during certain months of the year.

spatial discrepancy
The difference between the location of the producer and the location of widely scattered markets.

Furthermore, because mass production requires many potential buyers, markets are usually scattered over large geographic regions, creating a **spatial discrepancy**. Often, global or at least nationwide markets are needed to absorb the outputs of mass producers. Marketing channels overcome spatial discrepancies by making products available in locations convenient to consumers. Automobile manufacturers overcome spatial discrepancies by franchising dealerships close to consumers.

Providing Contact Efficiency

Consider your extra costs if supermarkets, department stores, shopping centres, and malls did not exist. Suppose you had to buy your milk at a dairy and your meat at a stockyard. Imagine buying your eggs and chicken at a hatchery and your fruits and vegetables at various farms. You would spend a great deal of time, money, and energy just shopping for a few groceries. Channels simplify distribution by cutting the number of transactions that consumers have to make to get products from manufacturers and by making an assortment of goods available in one location.

Consider another example, which is illustrated in Exhibit 12.1. Four students in your class each want to buy a television set. Without a retail intermediary like Future Shop, television manufacturers Magnavox, Zenith, Sony, Toshiba, and RCA would each have to make four contacts to reach the four buyers who are in the target market, for a total of twenty transactions. However, each producer only has to make one contact when Future Shop acts as an intermediary between producers and consumers; this reduces the number of transactions to nine. Each producer sells to one retailer instead of four consumers; your classmates buy from one retailer instead of five producers.

exhibit 12.1
How Marketing Channels Reduce the Number of Required Transactions

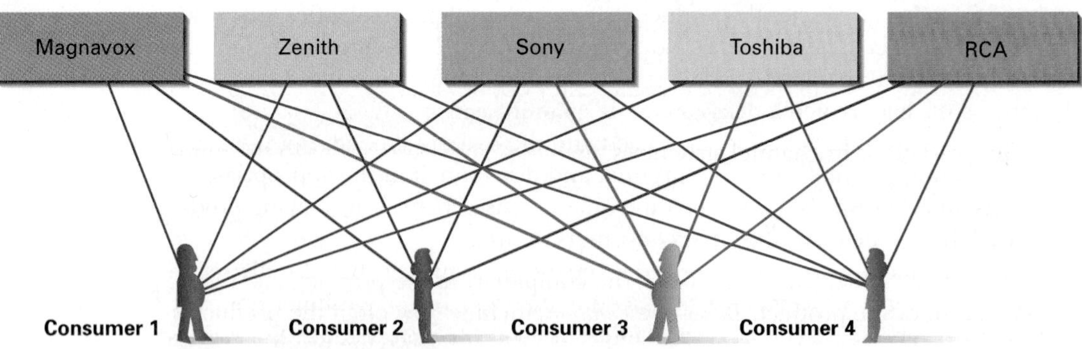

Without an intermediary: 5 producers x 4 consumers = 20 transactions

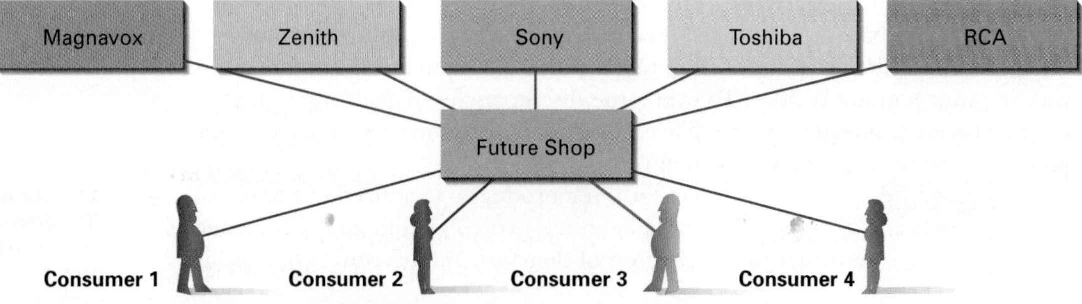

With an intermediary: 5 producers + 4 consumers = 9 transactions

This simple example illustrates the concept of contact efficiency. Canadian manufacturers sell to millions of individuals and families. Channel intermediaries greatly reduce the number of required contacts. As a result, producers are able to offer their products cost effectively and efficiently to consumers all over the world.

Channel Intermediaries and Their Functions

A marketing channel provides countless efficiencies in bringing a product to the consumer. Next we discuss who the intermediaries in a channel are, and the specific functions they provide.

2
Define the types of channel intermediaries, and describe their functions and activities

Types of Channel Intermediaries

Intermediaries in a channel negotiate with one another, facilitate changes of ownership between buyers and sellers, and physically move products from the manufacturer to the final consumer. Some intermediaries take title to the product; others don't. This is the easiest way to differentiate them. Taking title involves owning the merchandise and controlling the terms of the sale—for example, the price and the delivery date. Retailers and merchant wholesalers are examples of intermediaries that take title to products in the marketing channel and resell them. **Retailers** are firms that sell mainly to consumers. Retailers will be discussed in more detail in Chapter 14.

retailers
Channel intermediaries that sell mainly to consumers.

Merchant wholesalers are organizations that facilitate the movement of products and services from the manufacturer to producers, resellers, governments, institutions, and retailers. Merchant wholesalers take title to the goods they sell. Most of them operate one or more warehouses where they receive, store, and reship goods. Most of their customers are small- or moderate-size retailers, but merchant wholesalers also market to manufacturers and institutional clients.

merchant wholesalers
Institutions that buy goods from manufacturers and resell them to businesses, government agencies, and other wholesalers or retailers; they receive and take title to goods, store them in their own warehouses, and later ship them.

Other intermediaries do not take title to goods and services; instead they facilitate the exchange of ownership between sellers and buyers. **Agents and brokers** simply facilitate the sale of a product from producer to end user by representing retailers, wholesalers, or manufacturers. Title reflects ownership, and ownership usually implies control. Unlike wholesalers, agents or brokers generally have little input into the terms of the sale. They do, however, get a fee or commission based on sales volume.

agents and brokers
Wholesaling intermediaries that facilitate the sale of products from producer to end user by representing retailers, wholesalers, or manufacturers; they do not take title to the product.

Most variations in channel structures are a function of variations in the numbers and types of wholesaling intermediaries. Generally, product characteristics, buyer considerations, and market conditions determine which type of intermediary the manufacturer should use. *Product characteristics* include whether the product is standardized or customized, the complexity of the product, and the gross margin of the product. *Buyer considerations* include how often the product is purchased and how long the buyer is willing to wait to receive the product. *Market characteristics* include how many buyers are in the market and whether they are concentrated in a general location or are widely dispersed. Exhibit 12.2 shows these determining factors.

Channel Functions Performed by Intermediaries

Retailing and wholesaling intermediaries in marketing channels perform several essential functions that make possible the flow of goods between producer and buyer. The three basic functions that intermediaries perform are summarized in Exhibit 12.3.

Transactional functions involve contacting and communicating with prospective buyers to make them aware of existing products and explain their features,

exhibit 12.2

Factors Suggesting the Type of Wholesaling Intermediary to Use

Factor	Merchant wholesalers	Agents or brokers
Nature of product	Standard	Nonstandard, custom
Technicality of product	Complex	Simple
Product's gross margin	High	Low
Frequency of ordering	Frequent	Infrequent
Time between order and shipment	Buyer desires shorter lead time	Buyer satisfied with long lead time
Number of customers	Many	Few
Concentration of customers	Dispersed	Concentrated

Source: Reprinted from *Industrial Marketing Management,* February 1989, Donald M. Jackson and Michael F. D'Amico, "Products and Markets Served by Distributors and Agents," 27–33. Copyright 1989, with permission from Elsevier Science.

advantages, and benefits. *Logistical* functions include transporting, storing, sorting out, accumulating, and allocating products as well as assorting them into either homogeneous or heterogeneous collections. Grading agricultural products is an obvious sorting-out process; consolidating many lots of grade A eggs from different sources into one lot is an example of the accumulation process. Supermarkets and other retailers perform the assorting function by assembling thousands of different items that match their customers' desires.

The third basic channel function, *facilitating,* includes research and financing. Research provides information about channel members and consumers by getting answers to questions such as these: Who are the buyers? Where are they located? Why do they buy? Financing ensures that channel members have the money to keep products moving through the channel to the ultimate consumer.

The agricultural process of grading is a logistical function. This heterogenous collection of eggs is being sorted into separate homogenous groupings that meet the different needs of supermarkets and other retailers.

A single company may provide one, two, or all three functions. Westburne Supply of British Columbia, a wholesaler of plumbing products, serves all of Western Canada. As a full-service wholesaler, Westburne provides transactional, logistical, and facilitating channel functions. Westburne's salespeople contact retailers, contractors, and plumbers in the firm's service area. They negotiate prices and arrange for product delivery. The company also provides facilitating functions such as supplying credit to its customers. It assists its retail customers by providing point-of-purchase materials and helping with in-store displays. It also performs logistical functions by acquiring many types, sizes, and styles of sinks, faucets, and other plumbing products from various manufacturers in Canada and storing those products in its warehouses as inventory. When an order is to be filled, Westburne ships the required products directly to its customers.

Although individual members can be added to or deleted from a channel, someone must still perform these essential functions. They can be performed by producers, by end users or consumers, by channel intermediaries such as wholesalers and retailers, or (sometimes) by nonmember channel participants. A manufacturer that decides to eliminate its private fleet of trucks must be able to move its goods to the wholesaler. Perhaps the wholesaler has its own fleet of trucks, or perhaps transportation will be provided by a nonmember channel participant such as an independent trucking firm. Non-

What kind of marketing channel functions can be performed over the Internet?

on line

exhibit 12.3

Marketing Channel Functions Performed by Intermediaries

Type of function	Description
Transactional functions	**Contacting and promoting:** Contacting potential customers, promoting products, soliciting orders **Negotiating:** Determining how many goods or services to buy and sell, type of transportation to use, when to deliver, and method and timing of payment **Risk taking:** Assuming the risk of owning inventory
Logistical functions	**Physically distributing:** Transporting and sorting goods to overcome temporal and spatial discrepancies **Storing:** Maintaining inventories and protecting goods **Sorting:** Overcoming discrepancies of quantity and assortment by *Sorting out:* Breaking down a heterogeneous supply into separate homogeneous stocks *Accumulation:* Combining similar stocks into a larger homogeneous supply *Allocation:* Breaking a homogeneous supply into smaller and smaller lots ("breaking bulk") *Assortment:* Combining products into collections or assortments that buyers want available at one place
Facilitating functions	**Researching:** Gathering information about other channel members and consumers **Financing:** Extending credit and other financial services to facilitate the flow of goods through the channel to the final consumer

members may provide many other essential functions that channel members used to provide. Research firms may perform the research function; advertising agencies, the promotion function; transportation and storage firms, the physical distribution function; and banks, the financing function.

Channel Structures

3
Describe the channel structures for consumer and business-to-business products, and discuss alternative channel arrangements

A product can take many routes to reach its consumer. Marketers search for the most efficient channel from the many alternatives available. Marketing a consumer convenience good like gum or candy differs from marketing a specialty good like a Mercedes-Benz. These two products require very different distribution channels. Likewise, the appropriate channel for a major equipment supplier like Boeing Aircraft would be unsuitable for an accessory equipment producer like Black & Decker. To illustrate the differences in typical marketing channels for consumer and business-to-business products like these, the next sections discuss the structures of marketing channels for each product type. Alternative channel structures are also discussed.

Channels for Consumer Products

Exhibit 12.4 illustrates the four ways manufacturers can route products to consumers. Producers use the **direct channel** to sell directly to consumers. Direct marketing activities—including telemarketing, mail order and catalogue shopping,

direct channel
A distribution channel in which producers sell directly to consumers.

on line

Oneida Limited

Visit Oneida's home page to see how and where it sells its products. Are there different channels for its consumer products and its business products?

www.oneida.com

and electronic retailing (e.g., on-line shopping and shop-at-home TV)—are good examples of this type of channel structure. Home computer users can purchase Dell computers directly over the telephone or directly from Dell's Internet Website. There are no intermediaries. Producer-owned stores and factory outlet stores—Sherwin-Williams, Polo/Ralph Lauren, Club Monaco, Nike, Body Shop, and so on—are also direct channels. Farmers' markets are direct channels. Direct marketing and factory outlets are discussed in more detail in Chapter 14.

At the other end of the spectrum, *agent/broker channels* are fairly complicated. Agent/broker channels are typically used in markets with many small manufacturers and many retailers. These entities lack the resources to find each other. Agents or brokers bring manufacturers and wholesalers together for negotiations but do not take title to the merchandise. Ownership passes directly to one or more wholesalers and then to retailers. Retailers then sell to the product's ultimate consumer. A food broker represents buyers and sellers of grocery products. The broker acts on behalf of many different producers and negotiates the sale of their products to wholesalers that specialize in foodstuffs. These wholesalers in turn sell to grocers and convenience stores.

Most consumer products are sold through distribution channels similar to the other two alternatives: the retailer channel, and the wholesaler channel. A *retailer channel* is most common when the retailer is large and can buy in large quantities directly from the manufacturer. Wal-Mart, Canadian Tire, Sears, and car dealerships are examples of retailers that often bypass a wholesaler. A *wholesaler channel* is often used for low-cost items that are purchased often, such as candy, cigarettes, and magazines. M&M/Mars sells candies and chocolate bars to wholesalers in large quantities. The wholesalers then break these quantities into smaller quantities to satisfy individual retailer orders.

exhibit 12.4

Marketing Channels for Consumer Products

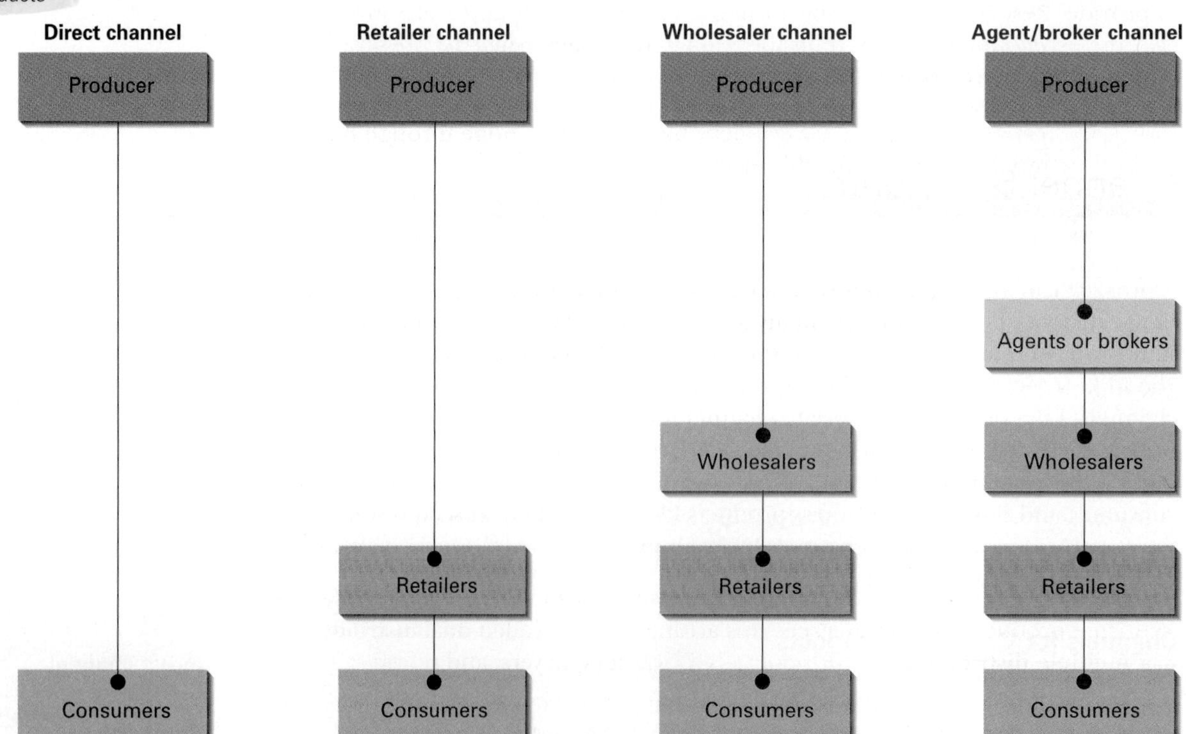

exhibit 12.5

Channels for Business-to-Business and Industrial Products

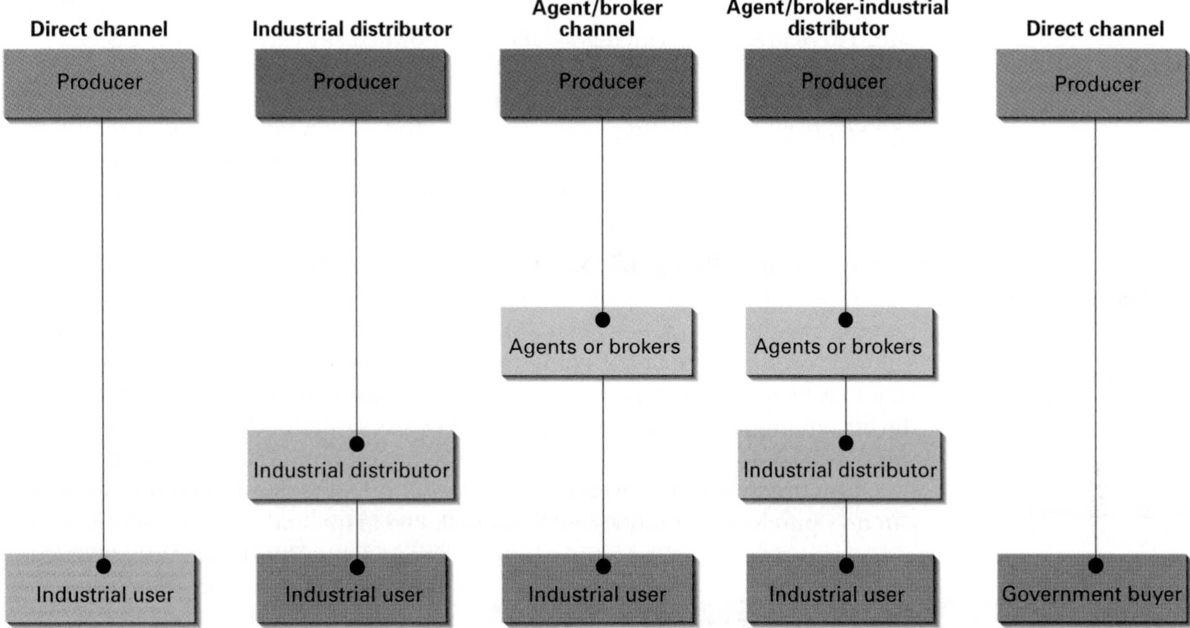

Channels for Business-to-Business and Industrial Products

As Exhibit 12.5 illustrates, five channel structures are common in business-to-business and industrial markets. First, direct channels are typical in business-to-business and industrial markets. Manufacturers buy large quantities of raw materials, major equipment, processed materials, and supplies directly from other manufacturers. Manufacturers that require suppliers to meet detailed technical specifications often prefer direct channels. DaimlerChrysler Canada must communicate directly with its suppliers, and its orders are huge; this makes anything but a direct channel impractical. The channel from producers to government buyers is also a direct channel. Because government buying is often done through bidding, a direct channel is attractive for this market.

Companies selling standardized items of moderate or low value often rely on *industrial distributors.* In many ways, industrial distributors are like supermarkets for organizations. They are wholesalers that buy and take title to products. Moreover, they usually keep inventories of their products and sell and service them. Many small manufacturers cannot afford to employ their own sales forces. Instead, they rely on manufacturers' representatives or selling agents to sell to either industrial distributors or users.

Alternative Channel Arrangements

Rarely does a producer use just one type of channel to move its products. Usually it employs several different or alternative channels, which include multiple channels, nontraditional channels, adaptive channels, and strategic channel alliances.

Multiple Channels When a producer selects two or more channels to distribute the same product to target markets, this arrangement is called **dual distribution** (or **multiple distribution**). Whirlpool sells its washers, dryers, and refrigerators directly to home and apartment builders and contractors, but it also sells these same appliances to retail stores that sell to consumers. J. Crew, which has

dual distribution (multiple distribution)
The use of two or more channels to distribute the same product to target markets.

on line

Autobytel.ca
CarPoint

Visit Autobytel.ca and CarPoint to see what advantages they have over traditional car lots. If you were in the market for a new or used car, would you use an Internet broker? Explain.

www.autobytel.ca; carpoint.msn.com

traditionally used direct mail channels, has now opened retail and outlet stores. Multiple channels are also employed by producers with unique second brands. The Walt Disney Company routinely releases first-run animated films to movie theatres and then releases their sequels directly to the home DVD market. Sequels such as *Aladdin and the King of Thieves* and *Pocahontas: Journey to a New World* follow up its theatre blockbusters. Computer maker Gateway had always sold PCs to consumers over the telephone and the Internet; recently, however, it has forged new dealer channels to reach the business market through a program called Gateway Partners. The company is also opening retail stores in Canada through which customers can purchase custom-built systems.[2]

Nontraditional Channels Nontraditional channel arrangements often help differentiate a firm's products from those of the competition. Some manufacturers use nontraditional channels such as the Internet, mail order, and infomercials to sell their products instead of going through traditional retailers. Nontraditional channels limit a brand's coverage, but they are also a possible means for producers serving niche markets to gain market access and customer attention without having to establish channel intermediaries. For larger firms, nontraditional channels provide new avenues of sales. In many school cafeterias, students can now purchase fast food from Taco Bell, Pizza Hut, and Subway Sandwiches & Salads. Pizza Hut delivers pizzas ready-made to schools; it also sells frozen pizza-making kits to school cafeterias, sending out trainers to teach cafeteria workers how to make the pizzas.[3] Many Wal-Mart stores now let customers order McDonald's burgers and fries as they check out. The order is sent from Wal-Mart's cash register to the McDonald's kitchen located within the store. The food is then whisked up to the departing customer.

The Internet has had a drastic impact on retail channels in many industries. Internet purchasing is now moving into the car industry. Would you buy a car over the Internet? Go to Autobytel.ca to see what it is all about. (This Web page is the property of autobytel.ca inc., a subsidiary of Autobytel Inc. and is reproduced herein with its express permission.)

Consumers looking for a new car can now purchase one over the Internet. In the "Entrepreneurial Insights" box, read about how companies are transforming the way cars are sold.

Adaptive Channels Many companies are now realizing that they don't always have the capacity to serve their customers. Innovative channel members have come to recognize that by sharing their resources with others in the channel, they can take advantage of profit-making opportunities. A flexible and responsive channel of distribution is called an **adaptive channel**. Adaptive channels are often initiated when a firm identifies a customer requirement that it does not have the capacity to fulfil. Volvo was having difficulties providing replacement parts for emergency repairs. So it united with FedEx. Now a Volvo dealer that needs a part calls a toll-free number, and FedEx ships the part immediately.

adaptive channel
An alternative channel initiated when a firm identifies critical but rare customer requirements that it does not have the capability to fulfil.

Strategic Channel Alliances Producers often form **strategic channel alliances**, which use another manufacturer's already established channel. Alliances are used most often when marketing channel relationships are too expensive to create, and too time consuming. Starbucks and Kraft recently announced a long-term

strategic channel alliance
A cooperative agreement between business firms to use each other's already established distribution channels.

Kraft Foods
Starbucks Coffee

Visit the Websites for Kraft and Starbucks for information on their strategic channel alliance. Does what you find (or don't find) surprise you? Why have they decided not to publicize this alliance on the Web?

www.kraftfoods.com; www.starbucks.com

on line

entrepreneurial insights

The Internet Shakes Up Traditional Car-Buying Channels

Is traditional car buying as we know it about to end? Savvy customers in Canada, the United States, and Australia can now purchase a car over the Internet without ever haggling with a car salesperson, and visit the dealership only to pick up the keys and the car. Some can even get the car delivered to their door without ever setting foot inside a dealership.

Many car buyers are now using the Internet for research. According to J.D. Power and Associates, over 25 percent of all new vehicle buyers are using the Internet for vehicle product and pricing information. This number is expected to jump to over 50 percent in the coming year. Internet car brokers like Autobytel.com and Microsoft's CarPoint are now allowing car buyers to go the next step: securing financing and completing the purchase of a new car on-line. The highest-volume car brokerage services estimate that their sites are generating over 700,000 new car sales annually—nearly 5 percent of the total 16 million-plus new vehicles sold annually in North America. Autobytel.com was recently ranked as one of the fastest-growing small businesses by *Entrepreneur* magazine and Dun & Bradstreet.

Here's how an Internet sale works. Car buyers browse Autobytel's site (**www.autobytel.ca**) to find the precise make of car they want, read on-line reviews, and compare models. Once a customer chooses a make and model, he or she fills out a form on the Autobytel.ca Website. Financing or leasing and insurance can also be arranged at the Website. The information is automatically routed to the closest Autobytel.com-accredited dealer. After receiving the purchase order, the dealer calls or e-mails the customer within forty-eight hours to confirm the features wanted. Later the dealer calls the customer back with a price. The price quoted starts with the dealer's invoice rather than with the sticker price used by showroom salespeople. After a price is finalized, the customer drops by the dealer to pick up the new car.

Internet brokers appeal to those consumers—and there are many of them—who are frustrated with the traditional horse-trading, time-wasting, and ritual haggling that have been part of the car industry since the Model T. The lure of buying a car over the Internet is convenience, along with low, fixed prices and a fast, pain-free transaction. Internet car purchasers tend to be wealthier and better educated.

Dealers are overcoming their scepticism about Internet brokering. Even with the monthly fees they pay to auto brokers like Autobytel.com and CarPoint, dealers get hot prospects at lower cost than through traditional advertising. For the monthly dues it pays, the dealer is guaranteed to be the exclusive dealer for the brand in a particular region.

The number of new cars being sold over the Internet has caught the attention of the big car makers. Most on-line car shoppers start with the manufacturers' sites, then move to other sites for more specific price and availability information. GM's new site, GM BuyPower, offers consumers access to dealer inventory information. Customers who visit GM's main Website can select options and then find a showroom in their area with the exact car they want. They can then schedule a test drive on-line, and even ask the dealer to hold the car until they can come in. Area dealers respond with best-price quotes. Similar Website services are in the works at Ford and DaimlerChrysler.[4]

licensing arrangement to begin stocking Starbucks coffee on supermarket shelves nationwide. Under the arrangement, Starbucks will roast and package the coffee, and Kraft will market and distribute it in supermarkets. Starbucks's coffee will be sold by Kraft's 3,500 salespeople, who comprise one of the largest direct-selling teams in the food industry. This alliance will allow Starbucks to distribute its coffee through grocery stores much more quickly than if it had gone it alone.[5]

Strategic channel alliances are also common for selling in global markets, where cultural differences, distance, and other barriers can inhibit the establishment of channels. Oracle, the software giant, recently formed a strategic alliance with Japanese computer giant Fujitsu in the Asia-Pacific region. Under the alliance, Fujitsu will distribute and market Oracle's information management software on Fujitsu servers in Australia, China, Hong Kong, Thailand, and Vietnam.[6] Cott Corp. of Toronto, the largest supplier of private label soft drinks in the world, has established a strategic alliance with Sainsbury, the largest supermarket chain in the United Kingdom. This arrangement gives Cott Cola distribution throughout the country.

Channel Strategy Decisions

4

Discuss the issues that influence channel strategy

Devising a marketing channel strategy requires several critical decisions. Marketing managers must decide what role distribution will play in the overall marketing strategy. They must also be sure that the channel strategy chosen is consistent with product, promotion, and pricing strategies. In making these decisions, marketing managers must consider which factors will influence the choice of channel and which level of distribution intensity will be appropriate.

Factors Affecting Channel Choice

Marketers must answer many questions before choosing a marketing channel. The final choice depends on several factors, which often interact. These factors can be categorized as follows: market factors, product factors, producer factors.

Market Factors Among the most important market factors affecting the choice of distribution channel are target customer considerations. Specifically, marketing managers must ask the following questions: Who are the potential customers? What do they buy? Where do they buy? When do they buy? How do they buy? The choice of channel depends as well on whether the producer is selling to consumers or to industrial customers. Industrial customers' buying habits are very different from those of consumers. Industrial customers tend to buy in larger quantities; they also require more customer service. Consumers usually buy in very small quantities and sometimes don't mind if they get no service at all, as in a discount store.

Location and market size are also important to channel selection. As a rule, if the target market is concentrated in one or more specific areas, then direct selling through a sales force is appropriate. When markets are more widely dispersed, intermediaries are less expensive. Also, the size of the market influences channel choice. Typically, a very large market requires more intermediaries. Procter & Gamble has to reach millions of consumers with its many brands of household goods. So it needs many intermediaries, including wholesalers and retailers.

Product Factors Products that are more complex, customized, and expensive tend to benefit from shorter and more direct marketing channels. Products like these sell better through direct sales forces. Examples include pharmaceuticals, scientific instruments, airplanes, and mainframe computer systems. The more standardized a product is, the longer its distribution channel can be and the more intermediaries can be involved. The formula for chewing gum is about the same from producer to producer; usually, only flavour and shape differ. Chewing gum is also very inexpensive. So the distribution channel for gum tends to involve many wholesalers and retailers.

A product's life cycle is also an important factor. In fact, the choice of channel may well change over the product's life. When photocopiers were first available, they were typically sold by direct sales forces. Nowadays photocopiers can be found in several places, including warehouse clubs, electronics superstores, and mail order catalogues. As products become more common and less intimidating, producers tend to look for alternative channels. Gatorade was originally sold to sports teams, gyms, and fitness clubs. As the drink became more popular, mainstream supermarket channels were added, then convenience stores and drugstores. Now Gatorade can be found in vending machines and even in some fast food restaurants.

Another factor is the delicacy of the product. Perishable products like vegetables and milk have a relatively short life span. Fragile products like china and crystal must be handled as little as possible. Both require fairly short marketing channels.

Producer Factors In general, producers with extensive financial, managerial, and marketing resources are in a better position to use direct channels. These producers can hire and train their own sales forces, warehouse their own goods, and extend credit to their customers. Smaller or weaker firms must rely on intermediaries to provide these services for them. Relative to producers with only one or two product lines, producers that sell several products in a related area are able to choose channels that are more direct. Sales expenses can then be spread over more products.

Another factor is that the producer may want to control pricing, positioning, brand image, and customer support. Firms that sell "exclusive" products, such as designer perfumes and clothing, usually avoid channels in which discount retailers are present. Manufacturers of upscale products—Gucci (handbags), Godiva (chocolates), Laguiole (knives), and so on—may sell their wares only in carriage trade stores in order to maintain an aura of exclusivity. That being said, many producers have opted to risk their image and test sales in discount channels. Levi Strauss has expanded its distribution to include Wal-Mart and Sears.

Levels of Distribution Intensity

Organizations have three options when it comes to intensity of distribution: intensive distribution, selective distribution, or exclusive distribution (see Exhibit 12.6).

one-to-one marketing

TV Gets Personal

Contrary to popular belief, interactive TV (iTV) is not a convergence between the Internet and TV, nor is it the Internet *on* TV. Rather, iTV is radically enhanced television that allows the viewer to interact with new forms of programming and advertising using that familiar interface, the remote control.

With iTV, viewers will be able to time-shift programming, create their own channels, watch more TV when they want to watch it, and—oh my—skip commercials. Media Experts forecast that by 2004, these devices will reach critical mass and be present in more than 35 percent of Canadian households.

This technology will bring advertisers new tools and new challenges. One tool is addressability. Like a personal computer's IP address, digital set-top boxes have a digital signature that allows a signal to be sent back to the broadcaster. This signal confirms delivery of a TV message to a specific set, at a specific household, in real or shifted time. So no more estimates of audience exposure, but real verification of commercial delivery to the set.

As well, personalization software will analyze viewing habits and suggest relevant programming. More importantly, it will segment viewers into predefined marketing segments based on their viewing habits. These segments will then be targeted by advertisers.

Interactivity will also be a key tool. The two-way capabilities and larger bandwidth of digital cable will allow the consumer to voluntarily feed back to the advertiser. Viewers will be able to ask for more product information, click on a product—say, a must-have sweater worn by Jennifer Aniston of *Friends*—and add it to their shopping cart.

Says Sarah Ross-Schlatter, Internet marketing manager at HMV.com, "People don't want more ads and they don't want more sells focused at them. If you feel that there's a value proposition around a certain product, why not let that product get closer to you and give you more of the good stuff that you'd expect? And that's where we believe there's a lot of benefit in iTV."

What can you find out about the current success of iTV in Canada and abroad? What are some of the potential negative aspects of iTV? What will iTV advertising campaigns need that many traditional media campaigns don't?

Source: Mark Sherman, *Marketing*, 7 May 2001.

exhibit 12.6

Intensity of Distribution Levels

Intensity level	Distribution intensity objective	Number of intermediaries in each market	Examples
Intensive	Achieve mass market selling; popular with health and beauty aids and convenience goods that must be available everywhere	Many	Pepsi-Cola, Frito-Lay potato chips, Huggies diapers, Alpo dog food, Crayola crayons
Selective	Work closely with selected intermediaries who meet certain criteria; typically used for shopping goods and some specialty goods	Several	Donna Karan clothing, Hewlett-Packard printers, Burton snowboards, Aveda aromatherapy products
Exclusive	Work with a single intermediary for products that require special resources or positioning; typically used for specialty goods and major industrial equipment	One	BMW

intensive distribution
A form of distribution aimed at having a product available in every outlet at which target customers might want to buy it.

Intensive Distribution **Intensive distribution** is distribution aimed at maximum market coverage. The manufacturer tries to have the product available in every outlet from which potential customers might want to buy it. If buyers are unwilling to search for a product—as is true of convenience goods and operating supplies—the product must be very accessible to buyers. A low-value product that is purchased frequently may require a lengthy channel. Candy is found in almost every type of retail store imaginable. It is typically sold to retailers in small quantities by a food or candy wholesaler. Wrigley cannot afford to sell its gum directly to every service station, drugstore, supermarket, and discount store. The cost would be too high.

Most manufacturers pursuing an intensive distribution strategy sell to a large percentage of the wholesalers that are willing to stock their products. The willingness (or unwillingness) of retailers to handle items tends to restrict the ability of manufacturers to achieve intensive distribution. A retailer already carrying ten brands of gum may show little enthusiasm for one more brand.

selective distribution
The form of distribution achieved by screening dealers to eliminate all but a few in any given area.

Selective Distribution **Selective distribution** is achieved by screening dealers to eliminate all but a few in any single area. Maytag selects a handful of appliance dealers in a geographic area to sell its washers, dryers, and other appliances. DKNY clothing is sold only in select retail outlets. Because only a few retailers are chosen, the consumer must seek out the product. Shopping goods and some specialty products are distributed selectively. Accessory equipment manufacturers in the business-to-business market also tend to follow a selective distribution strategy.

Firms apply several screening criteria to find the right dealers. Accessory equipment manufacturers (e.g., NEC) may seek dealers that can service their products properly. Makers of TV sets (e.g., Zenith) may look for service ability and a quality dealer image. If the manufacturer expects to move a large volume of merchandise through each dealer, it will choose only those dealers that can handle large volumes. These manufacturers may not even consider smaller retailers.

Exclusive Distribution The most restrictive form of market coverage is **exclusive distribution**—that is, only one or two dealers in a given area. Because buyers may have to search or travel extensively to buy the product, exclusive distribution is usually confined to consumer specialty goods, a few shopping goods, and major industrial equipment. Products such as Ferraris, Chris-Craft power boats, and Pettibone tower cranes are distributed under exclusive arrangements. New companies sometimes grant exclusive territories to achieve market coverage in a particular area. Limited distribution may project an exclusive image for the product.

exclusive distribution
The form of distribution that establishes one or a few dealers in a given area.

Retailers and wholesalers may be unwilling to commit the necessary time and money to promote and service a product unless the manufacturer guarantees them an exclusive territory. This shields the dealer from direct competition and enables it to be the main beneficiary of the manufacturer's promotion efforts in the geographic area. With exclusive distribution, channels of communication are usually well established; the manufacturer works with a limited number of dealers rather than with many accounts.

Exclusive distribution has been part of retailing for years. In the toy industry, Hasbro makes certain Star Wars series characters exclusively for selected retailers, including Toys 'R' Us, Wal-Mart, and KB Toys. F.A.O. Schwarz estimates that as much as 30 percent of all toys it sells are unavailable in other stores. In an era when a few big toy makers are making lots of similar-looking toys, exclusive offerings help stores stand out from the crowd and draw more customers.[7]

Exclusivity has advantages; it also has pitfalls. An exclusive network may not be large enough if demand is brisk. Manufacturers and retailers run the risk of angering customers who can't get the product. The producer's insistence on exclusivity may place the channel in financial jeopardy during times of weak demand. Honda's Acura division uses an exclusive distribution strategy to create a distinctive image for its high-priced cars. Acura dealers struggled initially because of the car's small niche market, low resale demand, and, ironically, infrequent need for follow-up service and repair. After several years, Acura dealerships became very strong competitors on the basis of their quality and service.

Honda's Acura dealerships have become strong competitors in the increasingly competitive automobile marketplace. The company's exclusive distribution strategy has successfully created a distinctive image for its cars.

Managing Channel Relationships

5
Explain channel leadership, conflict, and partnering

A marketing channel is more than a set of institutions linked by economic ties. Social relationships play an important role in building unity among channel members. The basic social dimensions of channels are power, control, leadership, conflict, and partnering.

Channel Power, Control, and Leadership

Channel power is a channel member's capacity to control or influence the behaviour of other channel members. **Channel control** occurs when one channel member affects another member's behaviour. To achieve control, a channel member assumes channel leadership and exercises authority and power. This member is termed the **channel leader**, or **channel captain**. In one marketing channel, the manufacturer may be the leader because it controls new product designs and product availability. In another, the retailer may be the channel

channel power
The capacity of a particular marketing channel member to control or influence the behaviour of other channel members.

channel control
A situation that occurs when one marketing channel member intentionally affects another member's behaviour.

channel leader (channel captain)
The member of a marketing channel that exercises authority and power over the activities of other channel members.

leader because it wields power and control over the retail price, inventory levels, and postsale service. Read about how some retailers are wielding their power in the "Ethics in Marketing" box.

The exercise of channel power is a routine element in many business activities in which the goal is cost savings and greater efficiency. For years, distributing magazines was a simple, inefficient business. Most cities had one wholesaler, who purchased magazine titles from publishers for 60 percent of the magazine's cover price. The wholesaler delivered new issues to retail stores, which purchased the magazines from the wholesaler at 80 percent of the magazine's cover price. The retailer, the wholesaler, and the publisher each got a cut from every magazine sold. The wholesalers sent unsold magazines back to the publisher. Then supermarket giant Safeway, in an effort to control costs, decided to reduce the number of single-city magazine wholesalers it traditionally dealt with by opening up several large regions to competitive bidding. Other big retailers, such as Wal-Mart, soon followed suit. To win contracts for larger regions, wholesalers were forced to offer better terms and to expand their operations or go out of business. Now retailers typically pay just 70 to 75 percent of a magazine's cover price, and the number of wholesalers they deal with has been drastically reduced. In turn, many wholesalers are exerting their own power over magazine publishers in an effort to remain profitable. One wholesaler, in an effort to reduce returns—an expensive and unprofitable part of the business—now requires publishers of new titles to provide a "minimum discount" from the cover price of 44 percent (meaning it will pay no more than 56 percent, compared with the current 60 percent norm). Other wholesalers are demanding new fees from publishers for magazines deemed unprofitable.[8]

Channel Conflict

channel conflict
A clash of goals and methods between distribution channel members.

Inequitable channel relationships often lead to **channel conflict**, which is a clash of goals and methods among the members of a distribution channel. Broadly speaking, conflict is not necessarily bad. Often it arises because staid, traditional channel members refuse to keep pace with the times. Removing an outdated intermediary may result in reduced costs for the entire supply chain.

There are many possible sources of conflict among channel members. Conflict often arises because channel members have conflicting goals. Athletic footwear retailers want to sell as many shoes as possible in order to maximize profits, whether the shoe is manufactured by Nike, Adidas, or Saucony; for its part, Nike wants a certain sales volume and market share in each market.

Conflict can also arise when channel members fail to meet the expectations of other channel members. For example, the franchisee may not follow the rules set down by the franchiser, or communications may break down between channel members. If a manufacturer reduces the length of warranty coverage and fails to communicate this change to dealers, conflict may occur when dealers make repairs in the expectation of being reimbursed. Furthermore, ideological differences and different perceptions of reality can generate conflict. Retailers tend to assume that "the customer is always right" and typically have very liberal return policies. Wholesalers and manufacturers are more likely to feel that people "try to get something for nothing" or don't follow product instructions carefully. Their approach to allowable returns obviously conflicts with that of most retailers.

When Ethan Allen began to sell direct through its Website, its independent licensees strongly resisted. This vertical conflict was resolved when the company recruited dealers to deliver merchandise and handle returns, and gave them a percentage of the revenue generated by on-line sales.

Conflict within a channel can be horizontal or vertical. **Horizontal conflict** is the kind that

ethics in marketing

Retailers Gain the Upper Hand

Marketing channels lend themselves to conflict. More often than not, the largest player in the channel makes the rules. At one time the manufacturers were the big guys, directing retailers from above as if they were pieces on a chess board; nowadays the channel leader is just as likely to be the retailer. Mega-retailers like Wal-Mart and the large, consolidated department store chains can make life hard for manufacturers and suppliers. Toys 'R' Us was recently charged for pressuring manufacturers—in particular Mattel and Hasbro—to deny popular toys to warehouse clubs and other discounters. Because Toys 'R' Us has such huge clout in its marketing channels, it was able to demand exclusive arrangements with manufacturers of hot toys, such as Mattel's Holiday Barbie doll, so that they could not be sold by discounters at prices lower than those of Toys 'R' Us.[9]

To reduce their risk of stocking new products, many large retailers are now charging slotting allowances—that is, they are demanding that manufacturers buy space for their new products on retail shelves. In some markets slotting fees are as high as thousands of dollars per store. Retailers say the fees are justified, considering how uncertain they are to make a profit on the ever-growing number of new products. Some retailers are even demanding slotting allowances to keep established products on the shelves.

Many manufacturers, especially smaller ones, consider slotting allowances extortion. They may find it impossible to get their new products into major supermarkets because they cannot afford the slotting fees. As a result of slotting, some products are never introduced to the market; other good products fail because slotting prevents them from getting good distribution to potential customers.

Many large department stores are demanding that their apparel suppliers cover the costs of heavy discounts and markdowns on their own selling floors. They are increasingly demanding that suppliers guarantee their stores' profit margins, and they are insisting on cash rebates if the guarantees aren't met. In addition, large department store chains are increasingly levying fines for violating ticketing, packing, and shipping rules. Department stores say that suppliers in today's market have to bear their share of the risk of selling fashion. Hardest hit have been smaller apparel companies, whose payments to retailers often outweigh profits. Some small and midsize suppliers are banding together to consider what they can do about retailers' demands.[10]

How can power struggles among channel members affect the ultimate consumer? Should retailers be permitted to charge slotting fees, which prevent small manufacturers from using the best channels to reach their potential customers? Do you agree with retailers that apparel suppliers should bear some of the risk of fashion?

arises among channel members on the same level that handle the same manufacturer's brands, such as two or more different wholesalers, or two or more different retailers. This type of channel conflict is most often encountered when manufacturers are practising dual or multiple distribution strategies. There was considerable channel conflict after computer manufacturers began distributing their computers beyond the traditional resellers, through discount stores, department stores, warehouse clubs, and electronic superstores. Upscale department stores threatened not to stock Elizabeth Taylor's Black Pearls fragrance after they learned that the product was also being offered to some mass merchandisers.

horizontal conflict
Channel conflict among members on the same level.

Many regard horizontal conflict as healthy competition. Vertical conflict is much more serious. **Vertical conflict** is the kind that arises between different levels in a marketing channel, most typically between manufacturer and wholesaler or manufacturer and retailer. Producer versus wholesaler conflict arises when the producer chooses to bypass the wholesaler and deal directly with consumers or retailers. Conflict arose when several producers agreed to Wal-Mart's request that they deal with it directly, bypassing middlemen altogether.

vertical conflict
Channel conflict that occurs between different levels in a marketing channel, typically between manufacturer and wholesaler or manufacturer and retailer.

Dual distribution strategies can also cause vertical conflict in the channel. Wireless telephone carriers traditionally sold cell phone service through local dealers—usually small electronics stores. Faced with heavier competition from upstarts, carriers have recently begun opening their own stores and mall kiosks, and resorting to special prices and telemarketing to reach potential customers at home. Local dealers, who helped build the cell phone market in the early 1980s, say the carriers are trying to squeeze them out of business.[11] Similarly, manufacturers that are experimenting with selling to customers directly over the Internet are creating conflict with their traditional retailing intermediaries. Experts predict that total on-line travel sales will increase to over $11 billion by 2002 and will threaten the livelihood of thousands of travel agents.[12]

Producers and retailers can also disagree over terms of sale or other aspects of the business relationship. When Procter & Gamble introduced "everyday low pricing" to its retail channel members—a strategy designed to standardize wholesale prices and eliminate most trade promotions—many retailers retaliated. Some reduced the number of P&G sizes they carried; others eliminated marginal brands; still others moved P&G brands from prime shelf space to less visible shelves.

Channel Partnering

Whatever the locus of power, channel members rely heavily on one another. Even the most powerful manufacturers depend on dealers to sell their products; even the most powerful retailers require the products provided by suppliers. In sharp contrast to the adversarial relationships of the past between buyers and sellers, contemporary management thought emphasizes the development of close working partnerships among channel members. **Channel partnering**, or **channel cooperation**, is the joint effort of all channel members to create a supply chain that serves customers and creates a competitive advantage. Channel partnering is vital if each member is to gain something from other members. By cooperating, retailers, wholesalers, manufacturers, and suppliers can speed up inventory replenishment, improve customer service, and reduce the total cost of the marketing channel. In global markets, partnering can often work to the benefit of two companies. The "Global Perspectives" box shows how.

channel partnering (channel cooperation)
The joint effort of all channel members to create a supply chain that serves customers and creates a competitive advantage.

Channel alliances and partnerships can be traced, in part, directly to attempts by firms to leverage the intellectual, material, and marketing resources of their business partners worldwide to make entry into far-flung markets easier and more cost effective. The growth of channel partnering is also due to the growth of information infrastructures that foster cooperation and sharing of information in both national and global markets.[13] A comparison between companies that approach the marketplace unilaterally and those that form partnerships and engage in channel cooperation is provided in Exhibit 12.7.

Collaborating channel partners meet the needs of consumers more effectively by ensuring that the right products reach the shelves at the right time and at a lower cost. Forced to become more efficient in a highly competitive environment, many retailers and vendors are turning formerly adversarial relationships into partnerships. Wal-Mart's Retail Link technology provides some 3,200 vendors with access to point-of-sale data; this makes it easier for them to replenish inventories at Wal-Mart's 2,000 stores. Based on sales data, vendors are customizing Wal-Mart's workwear clothing inventory at each store on the basis of demographics, regional tastes, and weather patterns. As a result of vendor partnerships, Wal-Mart has reduced its overall inventory by 25 percent even while sales have risen 15 percent.[14]

Channels and Distribution Decisions for Services

6
Identify the special problems and opportunities associated with distribution in service organizations

The fastest-growing part of our economy is the service sector. Although distribution in the service sector is difficult to visualize, the same skills, techniques, and strategies used to manage inventory can also be used to manage service inventory—hospital beds, bank accounts, airline seats, and so on. The quality of the planning and execution of distribution can have a major impact on costs and customer satisfaction.

exhibit 12.7

Transaction versus Partnership Based Firms

Transaction based	Partnership based
Short-term relationships	Long-term relationships
Multiple suppliers	Fewer suppliers
Adversarial relationships	Cooperative partnerships
Price dominates	Value-added services dominate
Minimal investment from suppliers	High investment for both buyer and supplier
Minimal information sharing	Extensive product, marketing, and logistics information sharing
Firms are independent	Firms are interdependent, with joint decision making.
Minimal interaction between respective functional areas	Extensive interaction between buyer and supplier functional areas

Source: From *Competing Through Supply Chain Management: Creating Market-Winning Strategies Through Supply Chain Partnerships* by David Frederick Ross (New York: Chapman & Hall, 1998), p. 61. Reprinted by permission of the publisher.

global perspectives

Cereal Partners Worldwide

General Mills is one of the largest makers of cereal in the world, with sales in excess of $7 billion. The company is well known to most of us for its brand name products such as Cheerios, Honey Nut Cheerios, Total, Wheaties, Lucky Charms, and Trix. But when it wanted to move many of its cereals into global markets, it wasn't sure it had the distribution capabilities to be as successful outside North America.

In 1991, to handle worldwide distribution for General Mills cereals, Cereal Partners Worldwide (CPW) was established. CPW is a partnership between General Mills and Nestlé. Nestlé is another well-known international company and offers a wide range of coffee brands, dairy products, infant foods, ice creams, confectioneries, and frozen foods. CPW was created to bring together the cereal-making capabilities of General Mills with the worldwide distribution skills of Nestlé.

CPW, which is headquartered in Geneva, Switzerland, began selling General Mills cereals under the Nestlé label in France, the United Kingdom, Spain, and Portugal in 1991. CPW is now distributing cereals in over seventy-five countries around the world and has achieved sales in excess of $1.5 billion.

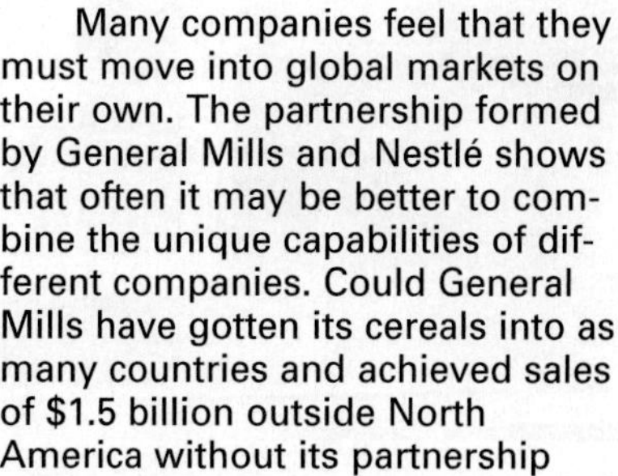

Many companies feel that they must move into global markets on their own. The partnership formed by General Mills and Nestlé shows that often it may be better to combine the unique capabilities of different companies. Could General Mills have gotten its cereals into as many countries and achieved sales of $1.5 billion outside North America without its partnership with Nestlé?

Source: Developed from the following Websites: **www.generalmills.com; www.nestle.com; www.adpaccorp.com.**

One thing that sets service distribution apart from traditional manufacturing distribution is that in a service environment, production and consumption are simultaneous. In manufacturing, a production setback can often be remedied by using safety stock or a faster mode of transportation. Such substitution is not possible with a service. Also, the benefits of a service are relatively intangible—that is, you can't normally see the benefits of a service, such as a doctor's physical exam. A consumer can, however, usually see the benefits provided by a product—for example, a vacuum cleaner removing dirt from the carpet.

Because service industries are so customer oriented, customer service is a priority. Service distribution focuses on three main areas:

- *Minimizing wait times:* Minimizing the amount of time customers wait in line to make a deposit at a bank, wait for their food at a restaurant, or wait in a dentist's office for an appointment is a key factor in maintaining the quality of service. People tend to overestimate the amount of time they spend waiting in line, researchers report, and unexplained waits seem longer to them than explained ones. Some restaurants give patrons pagers that allow them to roam around or go to the bar. Some banks have installed electronic boards displaying stock quotes or sports scores. Car rental companies reward repeat customers by eliminating their waits altogether.[15] Airports have designed comfortable sitting areas with televisions and children's play areas for those waiting to board planes.
- *Managing service capacity:* A product manufacturer's inventory acts as a buffer, enabling it to provide the product during periods of peak demand without extraordinary effort. Service firms don't have this luxury: if they don't have the capacity to meet demand, they must either turn down some prospective customers, let service levels slip, or expand capacity. At tax time a tax preparation firm may have so many customers desiring its services that it has to either turn business away or add temporary offices or preparers. Popular restaurants risk losing business when seating is unavailable or waits are too long.
- *Improving delivery through new distribution channels:* Like manufacturers, service firms are experimenting with distribution channels. These new channels can increase the time that services are available (e.g., using the Internet to disseminate information and services twenty-four hours a day), or they can increase customer convenience (e.g., pizza delivery, walk-in medical clinics, or a dry cleaner located in the supermarket). Banks offer ATM machines in many high customer-traffic locations. Telephone banking is further expanding customer service.[16]

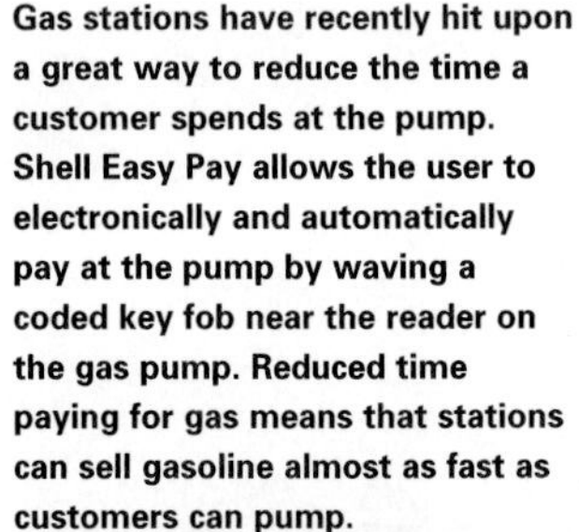

Gas stations have recently hit upon a great way to reduce the time a customer spends at the pump. Shell Easy Pay allows the user to electronically and automatically pay at the pump by waving a coded key fob near the reader on the gas pump. Reduced time paying for gas means that stations can sell gasoline almost as fast as customers can pump.

The Internet is quickly becoming an alternative channel for delivering services. Consumers can now purchase plane tickets, plan vacation cruises, reserve hotel rooms, pay bills, purchase mutual funds, and receive electronic newspapers in cyberspace. It is expected that by 2004, Canadians will be spending over $5 billion a year booking travel arrangements on the Internet.[17]

Channel Decisions for Global Markets

7
Discuss channel structure and logistics issues in global markets

The world is becoming a friendlier place for marketers. In the past decade the processes of globalization have swept away many barriers. Businesses are finding the world market more appealing than ever. This means that global marketing channels are important to Canadian corporations that export their products or that manufacture abroad.

Developing Global Marketing Channels

Before trying to design marketing channels in foreign countries, executives should recognize the unique cultural, economic, institutional, and legal aspects of each market. Manufacturers introducing products in global markets face a tough decision: what type of channel structure to use. Specifically, should the product be marketed directly, mostly by company salespeople, or should it be marketed through independent foreign intermediaries such as agents and distributors? Using company salespeople generally provides more control and less risk. However, setting up a sales force in a foreign country also involves greater financial and organizational commitment.

Marketers should realize that foreign channel structures can be very different from domestic ones. Canadian firms wishing to sell goods in Japan often must go through three layers of wholesalers and subwholesalers: the national or primary wholesalers, the secondary or regional wholesalers, and the local wholesalers. When Gillette entered the Japanese market, it tried to use a sales force to call directly on retailers, just as it does in Canada. Warner-Lambert, on the other hand, sold its Schick razors through traditional wholesale channels in Japan. What happened? Schick has a commanding lead in the razor and blade market in Japan.[18]

The channel types available in foreign countries usually differ as well. The more highly developed a nation is economically, the more specialized its channel types will be. So a marketer who wants to sell in Germany or Japan will have several channel types to choose from. Conversely, developing countries like India, Ethiopia, and Venezuela offer few channel types; typically, there are few mail order channels, vending machines, or specialized retailers and wholesalers.

Marketers must also be aware of "gray" marketing channels in many foreign countries, within which products are distributed through unauthorized channel intermediaries. GM imports only a handful of its Chevy Astro vans into Japan; more than 80 percent of the van's sales in that country are through a shadowy network of independent grey market importers, whose prices are much lower. Astros sold in Japan through official channels start at $41,000. Because grey market dealers keep inventories low and avoid costly overhead, their prices start at around $35,000; dickering can knock off another 5 to 10 percent. But because the vehicles aren't sold through proper channels, grey market cars aren't covered by factory warranties. Also, services and repairs can be a hassle because grey market dealers aren't equipped to handle them. Grey market sales divert business from GM's official importers, and GM occasionally has to deal with angry grey market customers who complain when they can't get service.[19]

LOOKING BACK

As you complete this chapter, you should be able to see how marketing channels operate and how channel intermediaries work together to move goods from the manufacturer to the final consumer. Companies can choose among several different marketing channels to sell their products or sell in several channels. As the opening story discussed, computer manufacturers can use direct channels, like Dell has done, or indirect channels that involve one or more resellers. Computer manufacturers Hewlett-Packard and IBM have been experimenting with direct channels. Dell and Gateway utilize the Internet to distribute their products.

Summary

1 Explain what a marketing channel is and why intermediaries are needed. Marketing channels are composed of members that perform negotiating functions. Some intermediaries buy and resell products; others facilitate the exchange of ownership between buyers and sellers without taking title. Nonmember channel participants do not engage in negotiating activities and function as auxiliary parts of the marketing channel structure. Intermediaries are often included in marketing channels for three important reasons. First, the specialized expertise of intermediaries may improve the overall efficiency of marketing channels. Second, intermediaries may help overcome discrepancies by making products available in quantities and assortments desired by consumers and business buyers and at locations convenient to them. Third, intermediaries reduce the number of transactions required to distribute goods from producers to consumers and end users.

2 Define the types of channel intermediaries, and describe their functions and activities. The main point here is that some intermediaries take title to the product, and others don't. Retailers sell mainly to consumers. Merchant wholesalers facilitate the movement of products and services from the manufacturer to producers, resellers, governments, institutions, and retailers. Agents and brokers do not take title to the goods and services they market but do facilitate the exchange of ownership between sellers and buyers. Channel intermediaries perform three basic types of functions. Transactional functions include promoting, negotiating, and risk taking. Logistical functions include physical distribution, storing, and sorting. Facilitating functions include researching and financing.

3 Describe the channel structures for consumer and business-to-business products, and discuss alternative channel arrangements. Marketing channels for consumer and business-to-business products vary in degree of complexity. The simplest consumer product channel involves direct selling from the producer to the consumer. Businesses may sell directly to business or government buyers. Marketing channels grow more complex as intermediaries become involved. Consumer product channel intermediaries include agents, brokers, wholesalers, and retailers. Business product channel intermediaries include agents, brokers, and industrial distributors. Marketers often use alternative channel arrangements to move their products to consumers. With dual distribution or multiple distribution, they choose two or more different channels to distribute the same product. Nontraditional channels help differentiate a firm's products from those of competitors, or they provide a manufacturer with another avenue for sales. Adaptive channels are flexible and responsive channels of distribution that a firm initiates when it identifies critical but rare customer requirements that it does not have the capability to fulfil. Once the requirements are identified, arrangements with other channel members are made to help satisfy these requests. Finally, strategic channel alliances are arrangements that use another manufacturer's already established channels.

4 Discuss the issues that influence channel strategy. When determining marketing channel strategy, the marketing manager must determine which market, product, and producer factors will influence the choice of channel. The manager must also determine the appropriate level of distribution intensity. Intensive distribution is distribution aimed at maximum market coverage. Selective distribution is achieved by screening dealers to eliminate all but a few in any single area. The most restrictive form of market coverage is exclusive distribution, which entails only one or a few dealers within a given area.

5 **Explain channel leadership, conflict, and partnering.** Power, control, leadership, conflict, and partnering are the main social dimensions of marketing channel relationships. Channel power refers to the capacity of one channel member to control or influence other channel members. Channel control occurs when one channel member intentionally affects another member's behaviour. Channel leadership is the exercise of authority and power. Channel conflict arises when there is a clash of goals and methods among the members of a distribution channel. Channel conflict can be horizontal, among channel members at the same level, or it can be vertical, among channel members at different levels of the channel. Channel partnering is the joint effort of all channel members to create a supply chain that serves customers and creates a competitive advantage. Collaborating channel partners meet the needs of consumers more effectively by ensuring that the right products reach shelves at the right time and at a lower cost, boosting sales and profits.

6 **Identify the special problems and opportunities associated with distribution in service organizations.** Managers in service industries use the same skills, techniques, and strategies to manage distribution functions as managers in goods-producing industries. The distribution of services focuses on three main areas: minimizing wait times, managing service capacity, and improving delivery through new distribution channels.

7 **Discuss channel structure and logistics issues in global markets.** Global marketing channels are becoming more important to Canadian companies seeking growth abroad. Manufacturers introducing products in foreign countries must decide what type of channel structure to use—in particular, whether the product should be marketed through direct channels or through foreign intermediaries. Marketers should be aware that channel structures in foreign markets may be very different from what they are accustomed to in Canada.

Do You Know These Terms?

adaptive channel 314
agents and brokers 309
channel conflict 320
channel control 319
channel leader (channel captain) 320
channel members 307
channel partnering (channel cooperation) 322
channel power 319
direct channel 321
discrepancy of assortment 307
discrepancy of quantity 307
dual distribution (multiple distribution) 313
exclusive distribution 319
horizontal conflict 321
intensive distribution 318
marketing channel (channel of distribution) 307
merchant wholesalers 309
retailers 309
selective distribution 318
spatial discrepancy 308
strategic channel alliance 314
temporal discrepancy 307
vertical conflict 321

Discussion and Writing Questions

1. Describe the most likely marketing channel structure for each of these consumer products: candy bars, Tupperware products, nonfiction books, new cars, farmer's market produce, and stereo equipment. Construct alternative channels for these same products.
2. Discuss why intermediaries are important to the distribution of most goods. What important functions do they provide?
3. Amazon.com successfully uses a direct channel to sell books and music to consumers over the Internet. How has Amazon affected traditional book retailers? How are giant booksellers like Indigo countering Amazon's competitive advantage?
4. Which distribution intensity level—intensive, selective, or exclusive—is used for the following products? Breitling watches, Land Rover SUVs, M&Ms, special edition Barbie dolls, Crest toothpaste. Explain why.
5. You have been hired to design an alternative marketing channel for a firm specializing in manufacturing and marketing novelties for university student organizations. In a memo to the firm's president, describe how the channel operates.
6. What is the difference between horizontal and vertical channel conflict? Give an example of each.
7. What is meant by channel partnering? What are the potential benefits of channel partnering?
8. What are some of the unique problems encountered by companies going into global distribution?

9. Assume that you are the marketing manager of a hospital. Write a report indicating the distribution functions that concern you. Discuss the similarities and dissimilarities of distribution for services and for goods.
10. Visit **www.viarail.ca**. How does Via Rail help customers with their entire travel planning?

Application for Small Business

Boudreaux has owned and operated a small spice-manufacturing business in Montreal for around ten years. Boudreaux has also experimented with preparing and selling several sauces, mostly for meats and salads. Generally, his firm has sold its products locally. Sometimes, however, distributors have signed contracts to sell Boudreaux's products regionally.

Boudreaux's most recent product—a spicy Cajun mayonnaise—has been a huge success locally, and several inquiries have come from large distributors regarding the possibility of selling the mayonnaise regionally and perhaps nationally. No research has been conducted to determine the demand for the mayonnaise. Also, it is being packaged and sold only in 340 gram bottles. The red-and-white label simply says "Boudreaux's Cajun Mayonnaise" and lists the main ingredients.

Questions

1. What should Boudreaux do to help the firm decide how best to market the new Cajun mayonnaise?
2. Should Boudreaux sign a contract with one of the distributors to sell the Cajun mayonnaise, or should his firm try to sell the product directly to one or more of the major supermarket chains?

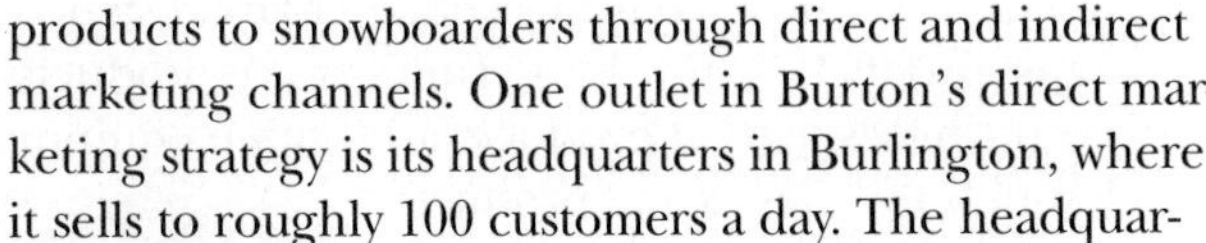

Burton Snowboards: Going Global

Burton Snowboards is a designer and manufacturer of premier snowboarding equipment. Since its somewhat humble start in 1977, the company has grown from a single workshop into an international retailer. Higher sales require a more involved distribution system, so in 1992, Burton relocated its offices to Burlington, Vermont, which offered easy access to an international airport, a larger workforce, and more business services. Burton expected to achieve better distribution of its products from its new headquarters. In conjunction with smaller offices in Austria and Japan, the Burlington office links Burton to retailers and consumers in the United States, Canada, and abroad. Burton does all its manufacturing in Vermont but has warehouses in Vermont, New York, Europe, and Asia.

To reach the maximum number of customers, Burton uses dual distribution. That is, it sells the same products to snowboarders through direct and indirect marketing channels. One outlet in Burton's direct marketing strategy is its headquarters in Burlington, where it sells to roughly 100 customers a day. The headquarters houses the manufacturing facility, offices, and a factory showroom, whose retail store sells everything Burton makes, from hard goods to soft goods. The hard goods line includes snowboards, bindings, boots, board and travel bags, and backpacks. The soft goods line includes five categories of specially designed clothing made from highly breathable and highly waterproof insulated fabrics. Direct marketing of products is also handled through mail order, catalogue shopping, and on-line Internet retailing.

The Burton Website is the latest addition to the company's direct marketing efforts. It offers detailed descriptions of all the company's products and explains the many different kinds of snowboards and gear available each season. Internet users can then order the catalogue from any Burton location.

The Internet and Burton's dual distribution strategy have made it easy for customers around the world to buy Burton products, but this has not always been the case. Before 1985, Burton was sending snowboards to Europe based on individual requests. The company eventually realized it could simplify distribution by cutting the number of transactions required to get products from the factory to the rider. It decided to develop a marketing channel using intermediaries, dealers, and distributors.

Burton intermediaries provide the specialized expertise necessary for efficient product education and distribution. Distributors and dealers communicate with new and repeat customers to create awareness of Burton's product features, advantages, and benefits. Perhaps more importantly, intermediaries ensure that the right quantities, proportions, and assortments of products are available at one location so that riders have the right number and kind of items they need when they need them. After all, having a great snowboard doesn't mean much unless you have the bindings to go with it. Burton's supply chain connects all the business entities that move company products to the right place at the right time. This chain allows Burton to avoid discrepancies that could reduce customer satisfaction, cost the company repeat business, or compromise its reputation. To support its extensive distribution network, Burton uses a supply chain information system to track every piece of inventory throughout the world and to monitor ordering, delivery, and bill payment.

When the company first decided to use intermediaries, Jake Burton, the company founder and owner, had to choose a marketing channel strategy that took the particulars of the market, his company, and its products into consideration. He had to ask the question, "Where are the potential snowboarders?" The answer to that primary question has been constantly evolving since it was first asked. When the company started, it advertised in major publications and filled orders as they came in directly to the Burton head office. As the popularity of snowboarding increased to the point of being accepted at most ski resorts, wider distribution began to make more sense. When Burton saw the untapped potential of the European market, he opened up shop in Austria. By the late 1990s, Burton was doing business in twenty-seven countries.

Product factors also influenced the company's channel decisions. Burton snowboards are highly customized, varying in length, type of ride (freestyle, freeride, or carving), and graphic design. For such specialized products, a shorter, more direct marketing channel is preferable. Channel selection is also influenced by the type of manufacturer. Jake Burton's investment in Burton Snowboards is reflected in the distribution strategy the company has pursued. Because he personally spent years developing the sport of snowboarding and the products that go with it, Burton wanted to control his company's pricing, positioning, brand image, and customer support initiatives.

Another issue affecting Burton's channel strategy was the level of distribution intensity—that is, the number of outlets available to customers for buying snowboards and other Burton products. Jake Burton chose selective distribution, screening dealers to eliminate all but a few retailers in any single area and having the company's outside sales force and internal distribution management staff work closely with this focused group of retailers. In Europe, the challenge of screening prospective distributors was more difficult, so Jake Burton carefully selected only dealers who were dedicated to the sport of snowboarding.

Burton Snowboards has risen to be the industry leader in its market, and its multipronged distribution strategy that uses both direct and indirect channels is what allows the company to provide top-of-the-line snowboards, bindings, boots, and clothing to snowboarders worldwide.

Bibliography

Reade Bailey, "Jake Burton, King of the Hill," *Ski*, February 1998, pp. 67–8.

Burton Snowboards Press Kit

www.burton.com

Questions

1. Describe Burton Snowboards' dual distribution.
2. What advantages does Burton gain from using a channel of distribution?
3. How do marketing channels help Burton overcome discrepancies?
4. Explain the intensity of distribution levels. Why did Burton choose selective distribution?

CHAPTER

13

LEARNING OBJECTIVES

After studying this chapter, you should be able to

1 Discuss logistics and supply chain management and their evolution into distribution practice

2 Discuss the concept of balancing logistics service and cost

3 Describe the integrated functions of the supply chain

4 Discuss new technology and emerging trends in logistics

Cupboard starting to look bare?
g
TM
grocerygateway.com

SUPPLY CHAIN MANAGEMENT

A green truck pulls up to the curb in front of your house and delivers the week's groceries that you ordered on line from your office this morning. The groceries cost no more than usual, although you pay an eight-dollar delivery charge. The best part is that you didn't have to go grocery shopping.

Grocery Gateway.com is a grocery retailer that sidesteps the usual bricks-and-mortar grocery stores, and through the wonders of e-commerce and a chain of suppliers and logistics makes quick, affordable deliveries to your door. And it's not just your bread, meat, and vegetables. Grocery Gateway can also bring you wine, beer, books, drugstore products, and household items.

"Everyone has better things to do in life than shop for groceries," is the premise on which Grocery Gateway was created. Customers can be registered and shopping for the first time in fifteen minutes, and immediately on subsequent shopping experiences. Customers are able to do their grocery shopping in about the time it takes the average person to write up a grocery list ... or they can spend more time on the Website, comparison shopping or checking out its recipes.

In your personal computer you can immediately start shopping—the Website is organized into logical "aisles" much like a traditional grocery store, and you select the brands and sizes of products that you need. To save time you can choose a preset list created by Grocery Gateway that features the products most customers purchase. At any time on your on-line shopping trip you can view your shopping cart to see what you've got. A subtotal always appears on the screen to let you know exactly how much you have spent. You can choose from grocery and drugstore items, research beers and wines, and even look up recipes while you shop. At "checkout" you choose a window of time within which you wish to have your groceries delivered.

The delivery person will call you fifteen minutes before arriving at your home and will carry the groceries into your kitchen, accepting credit cards, cheques, or Interac payments ... but not tips.

The system works through partnerships with food suppliers, Web and digital special-

Grocery Gateway

How easy is it to navigate Grocery Gateway's site? Would you buy groceries through this site if it served your area?

www.grocerygateway.com

on line

ists, financial partners, and hardware and software suppliers—with companies like IBM, the Royal Bank, and Longo's supermarkets. Logistics are handled with special software. Orders and schedules are created and maintained with state-of-the-art technology. Grocery Gateway doesn't have a grocery store per se, but it does have a 280,000-square-foot distribution centre called the Grocery Gateway Market Centre. Here products are accepted and orders are hand-picked and packed into insulated totes, which are delivered in refrigerated trucks.

In the grocery business since 1996, Grocery Gateway makes as many as 8,000 deliveries each week. That is still a fraction of the $9 billion per year grocery market in Canada, but it represents consistent growth. Seventy-five percent of the firm's home home delivery customers become repeat customers.[1]

What advantages does Grocery Gateway gain by selling in marketing channels direct to the customer, thus bypassing traditional intermediaries?

Competitors have taken note of Grocery Gateway's success and are experimenting with on-line grocery ordering and direct delivery. What areas of distribution, such as inventory, materials handling, logistics, and transportation, could be streamlined to compete more effectively in today's wired world? Similar questions will be addressed throughout this chapter, which is about logistics and supply chain management.

Logistics Decisions and Supply Chain Management

1

Discuss logistics and supply chain management and their evolution into distribution practice

logistics
The process of strategically managing the efficient flow and storage of raw materials, in-process inventory, and finished goods from point of origin to point of consumption.

supply chain
The connected chain of all of the business entities, both internal and external to the company, that perform or support the logistics function.

Now that you are familiar with the structure and strategy of marketing channels, it is important to also understand how products are physically moved through a channel of distribution, or the supply chain. **Logistics** is a term borrowed from the military that describes the process of strategically managing the efficient flow and storage of raw materials, in-process inventory, and finished goods from point of origin to point of consumption. Logistics is an integral part of marketing strategy; it represents "place" in the marketing mix (product, price, promotion, and place) and encompasses the processes involved in getting the right product to the right place at the right time.

The **supply chain** is the connected chain of all of the business entities, both internal and external to the company, that perform or support the logistics function. It incorporates all of the logistical activities associated with moving goods from the raw materials stage through to the end user. These include sourcing and procuring raw materials, scheduling production, processing orders, managing inventory, arranging transportation and warehousing, serving customers, establishing the information systems required to monitor these activities, and dealing with external partners such as vendors, carriers, and third-party companies.[2]

Supply chain management or **integrated logistics** coordinates and integrates all these activities into a seamless process. It seeks to unify the competencies and resources of business functions both within the firm and outside among the firm's allied channel partners. The result is a highly competitive, customer-satisfying supply system focused on developing innovative solutions and synchronizing the flow of goods, services, and information to create enhanced customer value.[3] Bernard J. LaLonde, professor emeritus of logistics at Ohio State University, defines supply chain management as "the delivery of enhanced customer and economic value through synchronized management of the flow of physical goods and associated information from sourcing to consumption."[4] Exhibit 13.1 depicts the supply chain process.

supply chain management (integrated logistics)
A management system that coordinates and integrates all the activities performed by supply chain members from source to the point of consumption; the result is enhanced customer and economic value.

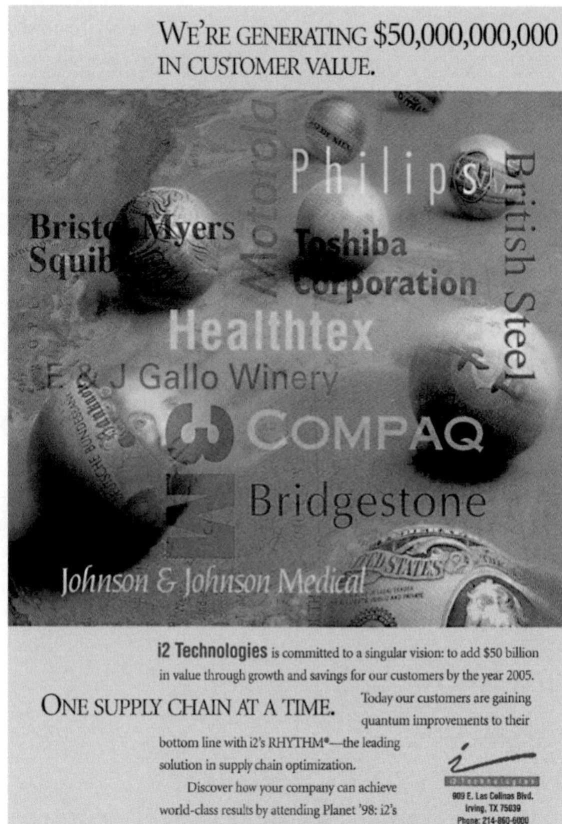

i2 Technologies is a global supply chain management company with offices in Canada, the United States, and around the world that helps its clients coordinate and integrate all logistical functions into a seamless process. Visit www.i2.com to learn more about how it does this.

It is critical to remember that supply chain management is completely customer driven. In the era of mass production, manufacturers produced standardized products that were "pushed" down through the supply channel to consumers. In contrast, in today's marketplace, products are being driven by the customers, who expect to receive product configurations and services matched to their unique needs.[5]

This reversal of the flow of demand—from "push" to "pull"—has resulted in a radical reformulation of market expectations and traditional marketing, production, and distribution functions. Supply chain management utilizes partnership channels of suppliers, manufacturers, wholesalers, and retailers; these work together to create customer value—that is, to deliver the product configurations and mixes of services demanded by customers. Supply chain management today has two roles: to *communicate* customer demand from the point of sale all the way back to the supplier; and to *engineer* the timely and cost-effective movement of goods through the entire supply pipeline.[6]

Supply chain management includes the following activities:

- Managing the movement of information and customer requirements up and down the supply chain.
- Managing the movement and storage of raw materials and parts from their sources to the production site.
- Managing the movement of raw materials, semimanufactured products, and finished products within and among plants, warehouses, and distribution centres.
- Planning production in response to consumer demand.
- Planning and coordinating the physical distribution of finished goods to intermediaries and final buyers.
- Cultivating and coordinating strategic partnerships with supply chain members to meet the unique needs of customers and to create customer value.

In summary, it is the task of supply chain management logisticians to direct raw materials and parts to production departments and finished or semifinished products through warehouses and eventually to intermediaries or end users. Remember above all that supply chain management begins and ends with the customer. Instead of forcing into the market products that may or may not sell quickly, supply chain management logisticians react to actual customer demand. When they do, the flows of raw materials, finished products, and packaging mate-

on line

EXE Technologies

What tools can EXE provide a company to help with its supply chain management functions? Which of EXE's services and products do you think would be the most valuable to a company?

www.exe.com

rials are minimized at every point along the supply chain; the result is lower costs and increased customer value.

The Evolution of Integrated Logistics and Supply Chain Management

Only recently have integrated supply chains been treated with much prominence by corporate managers. However, their roots go back to a process known simply as *physcial distribution.*[7] In the early 1900s, much economic activity in North America focused on moving agricultural products to market. Production output was cascaded, or pushed, down the channel, and the emphasis was on transporting fin-

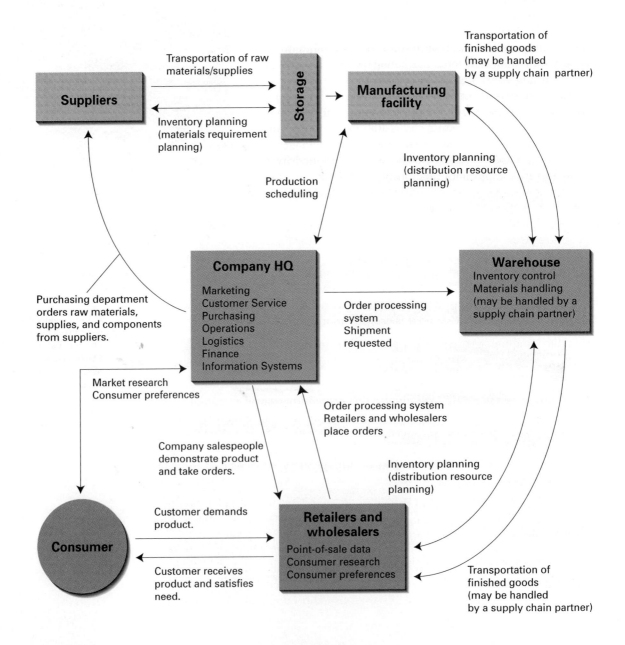

exhibit 13.1

The Supply Chain

ished goods from the manufacturer to the next member in the channel and storing them once they got there. Until the late 1950s, businesses viewed physical distribution as a subset of marketing and approached it from a functional perspective. Warehousing, materials handling, wholesaling, transportation, and inventory control were treated as distinct and independent parts of the distribution process. The process only concerned those activities directly related to physically moving the product. Distribution or "traffic" managers were responsible only for knowing the tariff and regulatory mysteries of moving outbound freight.

In the early 1960s the focus shifted toward systems of activities with interconnected components. Costs along the entire logistics system were analyzed and streamlined in an attempt to balance cost with efficiency of distribution. Management was consolidated for warehousing, inventory control, materials handling, and inbound and outbound transportation.

In the early 1970s the concept of logistics management was broadened so as to focus mainly on the customer. Customer service, of which physical distribution is a component, became a significant issue. Minimizing costs gave way to maximizing profits; logistics came to be perceived as a way to create customer value. As power began to move downstream to customers, more progressive companies began migrating from inventory "push" to customer "pull" channels.

As the 1980s drew to a close, logistics came to be perceived as a critical component in marketing and in corporate strategy generally, and as an important means for firms to differentiate themselves from the competition. The globalization of markets and advances in information technology greatly influenced supply chain partnering. During this phase, integrated supply chains, information sharing, and working together to satisfy customers became central issues in distribution. Integrated logistics, supply chain management, global logistics, and information technology became important to the success of firms. Advocates of this focus on distribution realize that significant productivity increases can only come by managing supply chain relationships, information, and material flows across enterprise borders—that is, by developing truly integrated supply chains whose components share information and work together to increase customer value.

The future of logistics lies in achieving a better understanding of customer behaviour and of customers' perceptions of firms. Specifically, how do customers react when companies change their logistics? As the boundaries between supply chain partners partially disappear, it becomes more and more important to understand all the components of the supply chain. Firms that can foster greater cooperation between supply chain partners to create value for customers will succeed. Supply chain management is growing more sophisticated, and technology is spreading rapidly, so Internet organizations that can provide delivery services and warehousing are enjoying tremendous growth.

Benefits of Supply Chain Management

Companies are beginning to recognize the tremendous payoff potential of supply chain management. Wal-Mart leveraged the supply chain to achieve dominance in the retail marketplace; Dell has reconfigured the supply chain so that it can respond almost instantly to customer orders; various companies are taking bold measures to eliminate standing inventory, thus creating efficiencies throughout the supply chain.

The benefits of an integrated supply chain are many.[8] A study conducted at the Massachusetts Institute of Technology found that the most commonly reported benefits related to the following: reduced costs in inventory management, transportation, warehousing, and packaging; improved service through techniques such as time-based delivery and make-to-order; and enhanced revenues resulting from greater product availability and more customized products. The companies studied recorded a number of impressive supply chain accomplishments:

- A 50 percent reduction in inventory
- A 40 percent increase in on-time deliveries
- A 27 percent decrease in cumulative cycle times (length of time from customer placing order to customer receiving order)
- A doubling of inventory turns, coupled with a ninefold reduction in out-of-stock rates
- A 17 percent increase in revenues

Another study, by A.T. Kearney, looked at supply chain management from another angle—specifically, the costs of not paying careful attention to the supply chain. It was found that supply chain inefficiencies such as late deliveries, stagnant inventories, and the higher costs these produce, could waste as much as 25 percent of a company's operating costs. Assuming even a relatively low profit margin of 3 to 4 percent, a 5 percent reduction in supply chain waste could double a company's profits. Yet another recent study found that companies following the best practices in supply chain management enjoyed a 45 percent total supply chain cost advantage over their median competitors. Specifically, their supply chain costs as a percentage of revenues were 3 to 7 percent less than the median, depending on the industry.

2
Discuss the concept of balancing logistics service and cost

logistics service
Interrelated activities performed by a member of the supply chain to ensure that the right product is in the right place at the right time.

Logistics service is the package of activities performed by a supply chain member to ensure that the right product is in the right place at the right time. Customers are rarely interested in the activities themselves; instead, they are interested in the results or the benefits they receive from those activities—namely, efficient distribution. At the most basic level, customers demand availability, timeliness, and quality. Specifically, customers expect the following:

- The product will be available when they want it.
- The product will be easy to order.
- The company will be able to provide the order promptly and consistently.
- The good will be received in good order (i.e., undamaged).

Most logistics managers try to maximize service while minimizing costs. To this end, they must examine the total costs of the supply chain—sourcing and procurement of raw materials, warehousing and materials handling, inventory control, order processing, and transportation—using the total cost approach. The *total cost approach* involves examining how factors such as cost of raw materials, number of warehouses, size of finished goods inventory, and transportation expenses relate to one another. Of course, the cost of each of these separate elements should also be examined in relation to the level of customer service. When this approach is taken, the supply chain is viewed as a whole, not as a series of unrelated activities.

Ideally, the logistics manager will want to optimize overall logistics performance so that overall costs are minimized while the desired level of supply chain service is maintained. Put more simply, implementing the total cost approach requires trade-offs. A supplier that wants to provide next-day delivery to its customers and also to minimize transportation costs must make a trade-off between the desired level of service (expensive next-day delivery) and the transportation goal (minimal costs).

Under the total cost approach, the high cost of air transportation often can be justified. Rapid delivery can drastically reduce the number of warehouses required at distant locations. So the higher cost of using air freight may be more than justified by the savings in inventory and warehouse expenses (see Exhibit 13.2). The Limited uses a quick-response logistics infrastructure to respond to

exhibit 13.2

How Using Air Freight Lowers Logistics Cost under the Total Cost Approach

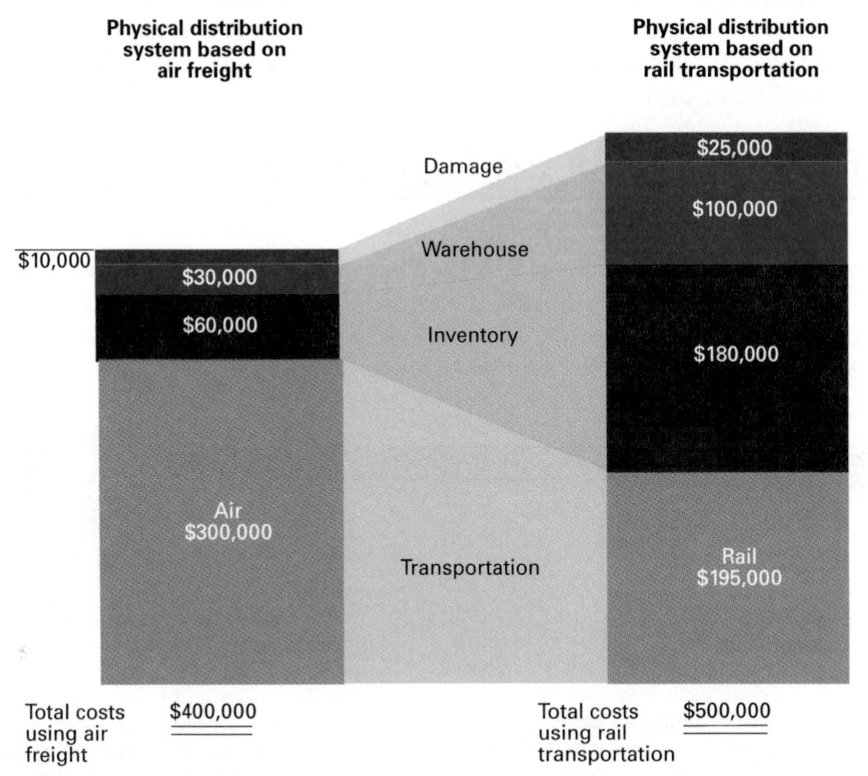

market information collected from point-of-sale data. Air transportation is used for time-sensitive fashions to ensure immediate market availability; basic articles of clothing are shipped by less costly means. The savings arising from reduced inventory levels make this a cost-effective solution.[9]

Some logistics managers are no longer focusing on reducing logistics costs as much as possible. Instead, they are trying to exploit their logistics capabilities to increase customer satisfaction and maintain customer demand. According to the Global Logistics Research Team at Michigan State University, many firms are using their logistics capabilities to achieve business success. These firms are developing competencies that are "superior to competition in terms of satisfying customer expectations and requirements." They define world-class logistical competencies as including the following:

- Devising logistics service strategies to meet the specific requirements of customers as a way to position and differentiate themselves from the competition.
- Integrating all members of the supply chain to achieve internal logistical operating excellence and to develop external supply chain relationships.
- Determining and responding quickly to changing logistical requirements.
- Constantly monitoring all internal and external aspects of the supply chain to ensure that the right product is in the right place at the right time.[10]

For example, warehousing facilities are increasingly providing value-added services that go well beyond mere storage. In the past, overnight delivery was considered an extra service for a warehouse to provide. Warehouses today are more likely to engage in product transformation services, such as custom palletization, kitting, repackaging, even final product assembly.[11] A recent study by KPMG Management

Consulting found that more and more executives believe that the supply chain can contribute to corporate success as much as or more than branding. Specifically, these companies believe that an efficiently managed supply chain can result in service excellence and that this will ultimately mean more to customers than branding.[12]

Integrated Functions of the Supply Chain

3 Describe the integrated functions of the supply chain

The logistics supply chain consists of several interrelated and integrated functions: (1) procuring supplies and raw materials, (2) scheduling production, (3) processing orders, (4) managing inventories of raw materials and finished goods, (5) warehousing and materials handling, and (6) selecting modes of transporta-

services spotlight

All zarage

It's near the end of Zara's winter sale, a Saturday on Bloor Street in Toronto. Most of the store's stock is gone, and the racks stand stark and barren. What remains is a mismatch of knee-length skirts, tweed suit jackets, and a few wool coats, all marked down from good prices to better ones—$29, $49, $99. But customers are walking the ruins, worried. "You're not closing down, are you?" a woman asks a cashier, shouting above the Euro-pop (shipped from Zara's head office in Spain). No, says the clerk, they've just sold out. They expect to see a new spring shipment the following week. For now, it's grab what you can.

Zara has also cleared its shelves in Vancouver and Montreal, the two other Canadian cities where it opened in 1999. The Zara chain is just as wildly successful in its other 450 outlets, from Tokyo to Bahrain—especially in label-obsessed France, where Zara clearly doesn't play by the rules.

In a survey of *Vogue* readers, young Parisian women voted Zara their favourite store, even though Zara doesn't believe in big-name designers or catwalks or collections. *Vogue* wanted to know how Zara had made such a splash without spending a single *sou* on billboards or glossy ads.

Zara has introduced the concept of "live collections," which can be designed, manufactured, distributed, and sold almost as quickly as its customers' fleeting fads. The company takes, on average, ten to fifteen days from sketching a new piece of clothing to delivering it to its stores. Production is in small batches. Zara does not overstock. If an item doesn't sell, production is scrapped.

Zara's managers are its intelligence gatherers. Every day, they report from four continents on what shoppers are demanding and what they do not like. Jose Maria Castellano, CEO of Zara's parent company, Inditex, adds, "We can create a new fashion line in days. Our competitors manufacture most of their collections in advance. But that involves guessing what customers will want six or nine months down the line. Our model minimizes the risk of being saddled with lots of unsold stock, and it maximizes full prices because very little gets remaindered."

Tailors in Galicia, Spain, created more than 11,000 different designs for Zara last year. Most of them were manufactured in-house. Such integration is unusual in the garment industry, where retailers tend to outsource production to cheap-labour countries in Asia and Latin America. But proximity, Castellano says, is vital to Zara's rapid reflexes. Zara, for example, is three times as efficient at moving inventory as the Gap or H&M.

The concept of finding something new every week is familiar to Spaniards, who have been shopping at Zara since it opened in 1975. Astute shoppers even know the days when Zara's trucks deliver new merchandise. The keenies plunge into the boxes as if they were diving for chocolates. Shop assistants complain they rarely have time to put the new merchandise on the shelves.

Abroad, customers have needed some coaching in the Zara shopping experience. Castellano recalls that when Zara opened its first store in the United Kingdom three years ago, on London's Regent Street, shoppers would come in to browse and then leave. "They would tell our assistants they would come back when the sales started, and we would have to explain that what they liked would not be in the sales because the stock changed every week."

"Zara's concept is different and it's working," says Toronto retail consultant Len Kubas. "It's quite unlike the usual American fare. In Canada, the company has generated a terrific, positive buzz considering the size of its presence. The feeling is, if you go to Toronto, Montreal, and Vancouver, you have to check out Zara." Goldman Sachs has singled out Zara among the three "global winners" of the fashion industry (the others: The Gap and H&M).[13]

How does Zara differ in terms of its supply chain management compared to other major fashion retailers? Why do you think it doesn't follow the standards set by the biggest American chains such as The Gap? As a fashion customer, what do you think of Zara's philosophy of delivering a limited supply of "live collections" to its stores? What are the benefits to customers of this approach? What are the disadvantages?

Source: Adapted from *Report on Business Magazine*, April 2001, pp. 88–90, 92. Reprinted with permission of *The Globe and Mail.*

tion. These components are shown in Exhibit 13.3. Although these components are discussed here separately, they are, of course, highly interdependent.

Integrating and linking all of these logistics functions is the **logistics information system**. Today's supply chain logisticians are at the forefront of information technology. Information technology is not just a functional affiliate of supply chain management. Rather, it is the enabler, the facilitator, the link that connects the various components and partners of the supply chain into an integrated whole. Electronic data interchange, on-board computers, satellite and cellular communications systems, materials handling and warehouse management software, enterprisewide systems solutions, and the Internet are among the information enablers of successful supply chain management.[14]

logistics information system
Information technology that integrates and links all the logistics functions of the supply chain.

The **supply chain team**, in concert with the logistics information system, orchestrates the movement of goods, services, and information from the source to the consumer. Typically, supply chain teams cut across organizational boundaries, embracing all parties who participate in moving products to market. The best supply chain teams also move beyond the organization to include the external participants in the chain, such as suppliers, transportation carriers, and third-party logistics suppliers. Members of the supply chain communicate, coordinate, and cooperate extensively.[15]

supply chain team
An entire group of individuals who orchestrate the movement of goods, services, and information from the source to the consumer.

Sourcing and Procurement

One of the most important links in the supply chain is the one between the manufacturer and the supplier. Purchasing professionals are on the front lines of supply chain management. Purchasing departments plan purchasing strategies, develop specifications, select suppliers, and negotiate price and service levels.

The goal of most sourcing and procurement activities is to reduce the costs of raw materials and supplies. Purchasing professionals have long relied on tough negotiations to get the lowest prices possible from suppliers of raw materials, supplies, and components. However, this old approach of simply negotiating the lowest prices doesn't always fit well with the practice of supply chain management. Because purchasing is at the top of the supply chain, it is crucial to the manufac-

exhibit 13.3

Integrated Components of the Logistics Supply Chain

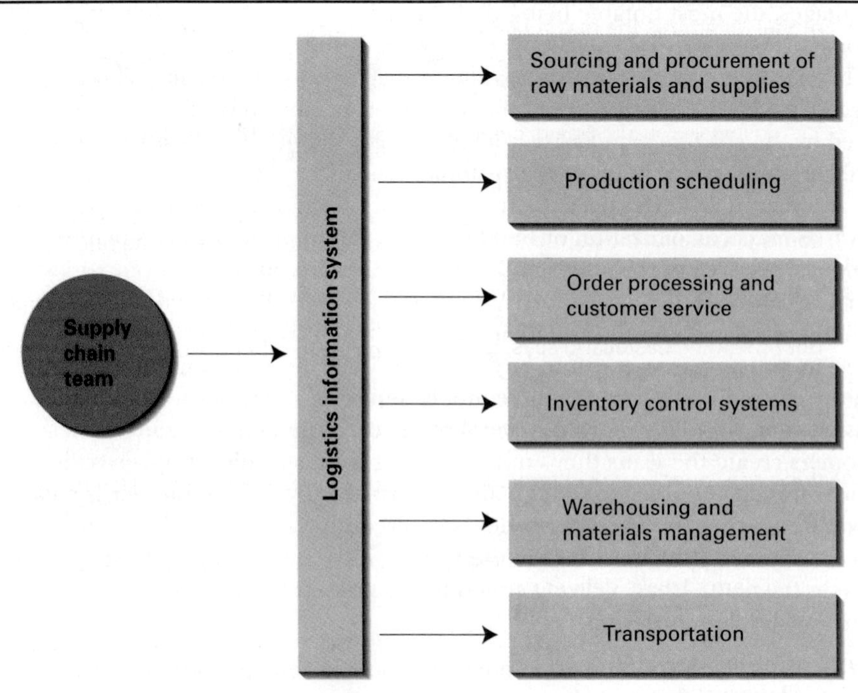

turer's relationship with its customers down the line. Yet purchasing efforts rarely look toward the bottom of the chain, to the customers.[16]

Perhaps the biggest contribution that purchasing can make to supply chain management is in the area of vendor relations. Companies can use the purchasing function to strategically manage suppliers in order to reduce the total cost of materials and services. Through enhanced vendor relations, buyers and sellers can develop cooperative relationships that reduce costs and improve efficiency with the aim of lowering prices and enhancing profits.[17] By integrating suppliers into their companies' businesses, purchasing managers are better able to streamline purchasing processes, manage inventory levels, and reduce overall costs of the sourcing and procurement.[18]

An excellent example of a company whose supply chain management involves many suppliers—whose contributions to the company's success are much appreciated, and recognized in annual awards—is Celistica Inc, which is headquartered in Toronto. Celestica is a worldwide leader in electronics manufacturing services (EMSs). The company is committed to customer service and to providing seamless and efficient service on a global scale. The company has extensive supply chain contacts with leading technology and carrier companies and ensures that its products are distributed worldwide quickly and easily with track and trace capabilty. Experts in international export and import compliance ensure that products travel across borders quickly and efficiently. Celestica uses supply chain software and a large team of logistic experts to ensure supply chain management leadership, purchasing finesse, and leading-edge technology. "Celestica's supply chain management capabilities are essential to its ability to act as a seamless extension of its customers' organizations, " said Andrew Gort, Celestica's senior vice-president of global supply chain management.[19]

Production Scheduling

In traditional mass market manufacturing, production begins when forecasts call for more product to be made or when inventory control systems signal low inventory levels. The firm then makes product and transports it to its warehouses or those of intermediaries; there it awaits orders from retailers or customers. Production scheduling based on pushing product down to the consumer has obvious disadvantages, the most notable being that companies risk making products that may become obsolete or that consumers don't want in the first place.

In a customer "pull" manufacturing environment—a newer model, and growing in popularity—goods or services are not produced until an order is placed by the customer specifying the desired configuration. At Gateway a personal computer is not built until a customer has selected the desired configuration and placed an order over the telephone or on the Internet. This process, known as **mass customization** or **build-to-order**, uniquely tailors mass market goods and services to the needs of the individuals who buy them. Companies as diverse as BMW, Dell, Levi Strauss, Mattel, and a slew of Web-based businesses are adopting mass customization to maintain or obtain a competitive edge.

mass customization (build-to-order)
A production method whereby products are not made until an order is placed by the customer and products are made according to customer specifications.

As more companies move toward mass customization, continuous dialogue with the customer is becoming increasingly important. Levi Strauss has made measure-to-fit women's jeans for several years. With the help of a sales associate, customers create the jeans they want by picking from six colours, three basic models, five different leg openings, and two types of fly. Each customer is measured for a correct fit. Then the order is entered into a Web-based terminal linked to the stitching machines in the factory. Two to three weeks later the jeans arrive in the mail. A bar code tag sealed to the pocket lining stores the measurements for simple reordering.[20]

just-in-time production (JIT)
Redefining and simplifying manufacturing by reducing inventory levels and delivering raw materials just when they are needed on the production line.

Just-in-Time Production An important approach to manufacturing that is common today is a Japanese innovation called **just-in-time production (JIT)**, sometimes called lean production. It requires manufacturers to work closely with suppliers and transportation providers to get required items to the assembly line or factory floor at the precise time they are needed for production. For the manufacturer, JIT means that raw materials arrive at the assembly line in guaranteed working order just in time to be installed, and that finished products are generally shipped to the customer immediately after completion. For the supplier, JIT means supplying customers with products in just a few days, or even a few hours, rather than weeks. For the ultimate consumers, JIT means lower costs, shorter lead times, and products that more closely meet their needs. In Canada, Celestica has inventory hubs operating on JIT schedules to provide its OEM customers with reliable materials close to their facilities.

JIT benefits manufacturers by reducing raw materials inventories. At Dell Computer's Texas plant, computer components are often delivered just minutes before they are needed. Chips, boards, and drives are kept in trucks backed up into bays fifty feet from the beginning of the production line. On average, Dell takes only eight days to turn new parts into finished products.[21] At Saturn's assembly plant in Spring Hill, Tennessee, the inventory at any given time is barely two hours; for other other car makers it is two weeks!

JIT involves less paperwork. It also results in shorter lead times—that is, the time it takes to get parts from a supplier after an order has been placed. Manufacturers that use JIT enjoy better relationships with suppliers and can lower their production and storage costs. However, there is little safety stock and therefore no margin for error, so the manufacturer cannot afford to make a mistake. A manufacturer using JIT must be confident that supplier will provide it with high-quality parts, and will meet all delivery commitments.

order processing system
System whereby orders are entered into the supply chain and filled.

Many companies have adopted JIT II, an updated form of JIT. JIT II involves sharing up-to-the-minute internal, proprietary data such as sales forecasts with suppliers. Also, suppliers' agents may be allowed to set up offices in the manufacturer's facility; in fact, they may be asked to replace purchasing agents and place orders for themselves.

Order Processing

Often the order is the catalyst that sets the supply chain in motion, especially in the build-to-order environments of leading computer manufacturers such as Dell and Gateway. The **order processing system** processes customers' requirements and sends that information into the supply chain via the logistics information system. The order goes to the manufacturer's warehouse, where it is checked whether the product is in stock. If it is, the order is filled and arrangements are made to ship. If the product is not in stock, a replenishment request is triggered that finds its way to the factory floor.

Fast and accurate order processing is vital to good service. As an order enters the system, management must monitor two flows: the flow of goods, and the flow of information. Often the best-laid plans of marketers can get entangled in the order processing system. Obviously, good communication among sales representatives, office personnel, and warehouse and shipping personnel is essential to correct order pro-

Mass customization is a way for companies to meet each individual customer's needs. Levi Strauss has been using this type of build-to-order strategy in the United States in the manufacture of women's jeans. Custom orders are transmitted to production at the point of sale; the measured-to-fit jeans arrive two or three weeks later.

GE Information Systems

Learn more about EDI by visiting the Products and Services page of its Website. What are the newest articles saying about EDI technology? Link to them through the GE IS page.

www.geis.com

on line

cessing problems. Shipping the wrong merchandise or an incomplete order can create just as much dissatisfaction as stockouts or slow deliveries. The flow of goods and information must be monitored constantly so that mistakes can be corrected before an invoice is prepared and the merchandise shipped.

electronic data interchange (EDI)
Information technology that replaces paper documents with electronic transmission.

Order processing is becoming more automated as a result of **electronic data interchange (EDI)**. The point of EDI is to replace the paper documents that usually accompany business transactions (e.g., purchase orders and invoices) with electronic documents. Companies that use EDI can reduce their inventory levels, improve their cash flow, streamline their operations, and transmit information more quickly and accurately. EDI is also believed to create a closer relationship between buyers and sellers.

It should not be surprising that retailers are quickly embracing EDI. For Wal-Mart, Zellers, The Bay, Canadian Tire, and the like, logistics speed and accuracy are crucial competitive tools in an overcrowded retail environment. Many big retailers are helping their suppliers acquire EDI technology so that they can be linked to the system. EDI works hand in hand with retailers' consumer response programs, which are designed to place the right products on the shelves, in the right styles and colours, through improved inventory, ordering, and distribution techniques. (See Chapter 13 for more discussion of retailers' use of EDI techniques.) The Bay has merged its customer databases with those of Zellers and has combined the two chains' rewards programs and Websites to improve customer loyalty and to maintain a supply chain that includes customer relationship management and supply chain efficiencies.[22]

Inventory Control

inventory control system
A method of developing and maintaining an adequate assortment of products to meet customer demand.

Closely related to the procurement, manufacturing, and ordering processes are inventory control systems. An **inventory control system** develops and maintains an adequate assortment of materials or products to meet a manufacturer's or a customer's demands.

Inventory decisions, for both raw materials and finished goods, have a big impact on supply chain costs and on the level of service provided. If too many products are kept in inventory, costs increase, and so do risks of obsolescence, theft, and damage. If too few products are kept on hand, the company risks product shortages and angry customers, and ultimately lost sales. A study by Procter & Gamble found that out-of-stock products reduced consumer purchases by more than 3 percent per shopping trip and that 48 percent of P&G's products were out of stock at least once a month. This cost the company valuable sales and customer satisfaction.[23] The goal of inventory management is to keep inventory levels as low as possible while maintaining an adequate supply of goods to meet customer demand.

Sleep Right is planning a promotion on the Great Mattress Company's Gentle Rest mattress. The sales forecast is fifty units. Sleep Right has ten open Gentle Rest orders with its distribution centre. New mattresses must be delivered in two weeks, in time for the promotion.

Sleep Right's distribution centre is notified electronically of the order of fifty new Gentle Rest mattresses. It currently has twenty Gentle Rest mattresses in inventory and begins putting together the transportation plans to deliver these to the Sleep Right store. Delivery takes one day. It orders forty new mattresses from its mattress wholesaler to make up the difference.

ABC Mattress Wholesaling Company is notified electronically of Sleep Right's order of forty new Gentle Rest mattresses. It currently does not have any of these in stock but orders electronically forty from the Great Mattress Company's factory.

Once it receives the new mattresses, it can have them delivered to the Sleep Right in two days.

The Great Mattress Company receives ABC's order electronically and forwards it to the factory floor. Production of a new mattress takes twenty minutes. The total order of forty mattresses will be ready to be shipped to ABC in two days. Delivery takes one day. Raw material supplies for this order are requested electronically from Great Mattresses's supply partners, which deliver the needed materials just-in-time to its stitching machines.

The process of managing inventory from the supplier to the manufacturer is referred to as **materials requirement planning (MRP)**, or materials management. This system also encompasses sourcing and procurement operations—that is, it signals the purchasing department that raw materials, supplies, or components need to be replenished to produce more goods. Systems that manage the finished goods inventory from manufacturer to end user are commonly referred to as **distribution resource planning (DRP)**. Both inventory systems use various inputs—sales forecasts, available inventory, outstanding orders, lead times, mode of transportation to be used, and so on—to determine what actions must be taken to replenish goods at all points along the supply chain. Demand in the system is collected at each level in the supply chain, from the retailer back up the chain to the manufacturer. When EDI is used, the transmission speed of the information can be greatly accelerated, which is always helpful.[24] Exhibit 13.4 provides an example of inventory replenishment using distribution resource planning from the retailer to the manufacturer.

materials requirement planning (MRP)
An inventory control system that manages the replenishment of raw materials, supplies, and components from the supplier to the manufacturer.

distribution resource planning (DRP)
An inventory control system that manages the replenishment of goods from the manufacturer to the final consumer.

Enhanced versions of DRP have emerged, especially in the retailing and supermarket industries, under the names *continuous replenishment* (CR), *efficient consumer response* (ECR), and *vendor managed inventory* (VMI). These systems are beyond the scope of this discussion; but note that all use information technology to increase the speed at which inventory needs can be communicated throughout the supply chain. This hastens the flow of product from the manufacturer to the point of sale. Procter & Gamble estimates that it has saved its retail partners, such as retail giant Wal-Mart, more than $65 million through such inventory control methods.[25]

Just-in-time manufacturing processes have had a strong impact on inventory levels. Because JIT requires supplies to be delivered at the time they are needed on the factory floor, little inventory is needed. With JIT the purchasing firm can reduce the amount of raw materials and parts it keeps on hand by ordering more often and in smaller amounts. Lower inventory levels can give firms a competitive edge by making it possible for them to halt the production of some products in favour of others that are gaining popularity with consumers. Additional savings arise from the fact that less capital is tied up in inventory and that less storage space is needed.[26]

In a true supply chain management environment in which all members of the supply chain are working closely together, companies are substituting information for inventory. Cisco Systems recently formed a partnership with UPS Worldwide Logistics to develop a more efficient process for sending its routers to Europe. Of the tons of routers it ships to European markets each week, Cisco needed to know where each box was at all times; it also had to be able to reroute orders to fill urgent requests. With its knowledge of international plane, train, and trucking schedules, UPS can ship Cisco's routers from the company's manufacturing facility in California and track them to European customers in under four days. When Cisco did the job on its own, deliveries took up to three weeks. The partnership with UPS saves Cisco precious dollars once tied up in inventory.[27]

Warehousing and Materials Handling

Supply chain logisticians oversee the constant flow of raw materials from suppliers to the manufacturer and finished goods from the manufacturer to the ultimate

exhibit 13.4

Inventory Replenishment Example

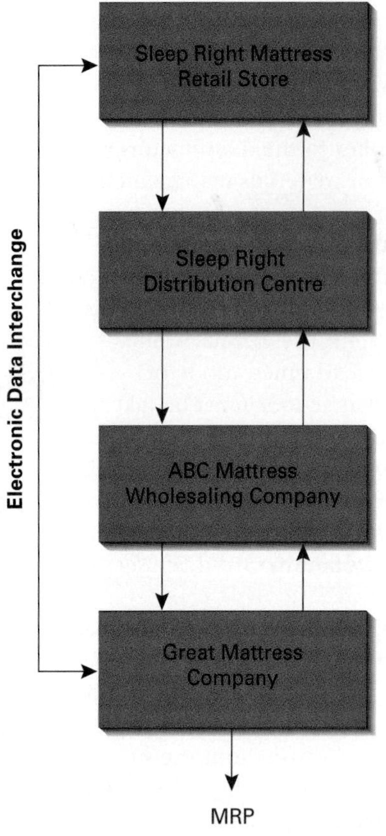

Sleep Right is planning a promotion on the Great Mattress Company's Gentle Rest mattress. Sales forecast is for fifty units to be sold. Sleep Right has ten open Gentle Rest orders with its distribution centre. New mattresses must be delivered in two weeks, in time for the promotion.

Sleep Right's Distribution Centre is electronically notified of the order of fifty new Gentle Rest mattresses. It currently has twenty Gentle Rest mattresses in inventory and begins putting together the transportation plans to deliver these to the Sleep Right Store. Delivery takes one day. It orders forty new mattresses from its mattress wholesaler to make up the difference.

ABC Mattress Wholesaling Company is electronically notified of Sleep Right DC's order of forty new Gentle Rest mattresses. It currently does not have any of these in stock but electronically orders forty from the Great Mattress Company's factory. Once it receives the new mattresses, it can have them delivered to the Sleep Right DC in two days.

The Great Mattress Company electronically receives ABC's order and forwards it to the factory floor. Production of a new mattress takes twenty minutes. The total order of forty mattresses can be ready to be shipped to ABC in two days. Delivery takes one day. Raw material supplies for this order are electronically requested from Great Mattress's supply partners, who deliver the needed materials just-in-time to its stitching machines.

consumer. Just-in-time manufacturing processes may eliminate the need to warehouse many raw materials; even so, manufacturers often keep some safety stock on hand in the event of an emergency, such as a strike at a supplier's plant or a catastrophic event that temporarily stops the flow of raw materials to the production line. Likewise, the final user may not need or want the goods at the same time the manufacturer produces and wants to sell them. Products such as grain and corn are produced seasonally, but consumers demand them the year round. Other products such as Christmas ornaments and turkeys are produced the year round, but consumers do not want them until autumn or winter. So management must have a storage system to hold these products until they are shipped.

Storage is what helps manufacturers manage supply and demand, or production and consumption. It provides time utility to buyers and sellers, in the sense that the seller stores the product until the buyer wants or needs it. Even when products are used regularly, not seasonally, many manufacturers store excess products in case demand surpasses the amount produced at a given time. However, there are costs involved in storing additional product, including taxes, insurance costs, warehouse operating costs, and losses from theft, obsolescence, or spoilage. Another drawback is opportunity costs—that is, while money is tied up in stored product, it can't be used for something else.

materials handling system
A method of moving inventory into, within, and out of the warehouse.

A **materials handling system** moves inventory into, within, and out of the warehouse. Materials handling includes these functions:

- Receiving goods into the warehouse or distribution centre
- Identifying, sorting, and labelling the goods

- Dispatching the goods to a temporary storage area
- Recalling, selecting, or picking the goods for shipment (which may include packaging the product in a protective container for shipping)

The goal of a materials handling system is to move items quickly with minimal handling. With a manual, nonautomated system, a product may be handled more than a dozen times. Each time it is handled, costs increase, and so does the risk of damaging it; each lifting of a product stresses its package. That is why most manufacturers have moved to automated systems. With these, scanners read bar codes to identify quickly goods entering and leaving the warehouse. Automatic storage and retrieval systems automatically store and pick goods in the warehouse or distribution centre. Automated materials handling systems decrease product handling and ensure that products are placed accurately; they also improve the accuracy of order picking and the rates of on-time shipment.

Baxter Health Care, a leading manufacturer and marketer of health care products, uses a sophisticated materials handling system to reduce product handling and keep costs to a minimum. As goods are received into the warehouse, bar-coded labels are affixed to the pallets of incoming product; these are then placed on a fully automated conveyor, which carries them the storage area. There, truck operators scan the labels while an on-board, radio-controlled computer tells the operator exactly where to drop off the load. When the items to fill an order are picked off the shelves and placed in a carton, another bar-coded label is applied, and the carton is placed on the conveyor system. Automatic scanners posted throughout the intricate conveyor system read each bar code and divert each carton to the proper shipping lane. This automated system gives Baxter a high degree of control over how orders are handled, placed, picked, and sequenced for shipping.

Transportation

Transportation typically accounts for 5 to 10 percent of the price of goods.[28] Supply chain logisticians must decide which mode of transportation to use to move products from supplier to producer and from producer to buyer. These decisions are, of course, related to all other logistics decisions. The five main modes of transportation are railways, motor carriers, pipelines, water transportation, and airways. Logistics managers generally choose a mode of transportation on the basis of several criteria:

- *Cost:* the total amount a specific carrier charges to move the product from the point of origin to the destination.
- *Transit time:* the total time a carrier has possession of the goods, including the time required for pickup and delivery, handling, and movement between the point of origin and the destination.
- *Reliability:* the consistency with which the carrier delivers goods on time and in acceptable condition.
- *Capability:* the ability of the carrier to provide the appropriate equipment and conditions for moving specific kinds of goods, such as those that must be transported in a controlled environment (e.g., under refrigeration).
- *Accessibility:* the carrier's ability to move goods over a specific route or network.
- *Traceability:* the relative ease with which a shipment can be located and transferred.

The mode of transportation used depends on the needs of the shipper as they relate to the six criteria noted above. Exhibit 13.5 compares the basic modes of transportation on these criteria.

In just-in-time manufacturing, the transportation network often replaces the warehouse or eliminates the expense of storing inventories; this is because goods are timed to arrive the moment they're needed on the assembly line or for shipment to customers. Dell Computer has gone even farther to trim inventory of parts by, for instance, taking delivery of components just minutes before they are needed. Monitors, instead of going to a Dell distribution centre, are shipped from the supplier's factory in Mexico at the same time that a finished computer is leaving Dell's factory in Texas. The two components meet for the first time in a delivery van just before reaching the customer.[29]

Trends in Logistics

4
Discuss new technology and emerging trends in logistics

Several technological advances and business trends are affecting today's logistics industry . Three of the most important ones are increased automation, outsourcing of logistics functions, and electronic distribution.

Automation

Computer technology has boosted the efficiency of logistics dramatically. One of the main goals of automation is to bring up-to-date information to the logistics manager's desk. For instance, logisticians have long referred to the transportation system as the "black hole," where products and materials fall out of sight until they reappear some time later in a plant, store, or warehouse. Now carriers have systems that track freight, monitor the speed and location of carriers, and make routing decisions on the spur of the moment. Over three-quarters of North America's major trucking companies now use computers to help plan routes, and over half have computers aboard each truck to monitor location by satellite. These systems help transportation firms compete in today's demanding economy. With retailers and manufacturers keeping less inventory, deliveries must often be made at exact times to avoid shutting down a plant or forcing a store to run out of a popular product.[30]

The rapid exchange of information that automation brings to the distribution process helps each supply chain partner plan more effectively. The links among suppliers, buyers, and carriers open up opportunities for joint decision making. As more companies compete in global markets, timely information becomes even

exhibit 13.5

Criteria for Ranking Modes of Transportation

	Highest			Lowest
Relative cost	Air	Truck	Rail	Pipe	Water
Transit time	Water	Rail	Pipe	Truck	Air
Reliability	Pipe	Truck	Rail	Air	Water
Capability	Water	Rail	Truck	Air	Pipe
Accessibility	Truck	Rail	Air	Water	Pipe
Traceability	Air	Truck	Rail	Water	Pipe

global perspectives

The Internet Brings Global Logistics Closer Together

Internet technologies are making it easier for global supply chain managers to ship products around the world, helping companies large and small manage their increasingly complex global fulfilment strategies. More and more, global logistics strategies will intertwine traditional distribution methods with the real-time capabilities of the Internet, allowing global supply chain managers to more efficiently move products around the world. Two such Internet technologies that are causing a stir in the world of global supply chain management are Web-enabled supply chain management systems and global transportation exchanges.

While large companies still rely heavily on electronic data interchange (EDI) to transmit and receive order requests along the supply chain, small and midsize manufacturers in the far reaches of Asia, Latin America, and the Caribbean are relatively low-tech companies and don't possess the financial means or the technological sophistication to handle EDI. Internet technologies, such as Java and the Extensible Markup Language (XML), are playing a larger role in developing systems to exchange information among global companies and their partners in the far-flung reaches of the world. Home Depot, the home-improvement retailer, for instance, partners with some 300 overseas manufacturers. The retailer uses a payment system accessible from the Internet that caters to its small suppliers who don't have the capability to use EDI. Another example is Stride Rite Corporation, retailer of children's athletic and casual footwear. The shoe company buys nearly all of its shoes from overseas manufacturers, mostly independently owned footwear makers in China. Its online order management system allows Stride Rite service reps to track specific orders for their customers from the time the shipment leaves the Far East until it arrives at the warehouse doors.

Global transportation exchanges are another recent phenomenon credited to today's increasingly connected world. With the explosion of worldwide trade, due in large part to the explosion of Internet-based companies, organizations that exist primarily or entirely on the Internet, supply chain managers more than ever need the information necessary to determine the most cost-effective shipping method. By leveraging the near universal reach of the Internet, transportation exchanges seek to match carriers and their available space to manufacturers and distributors looking to keep goods flowing seamlessly through the supply chain. On the Celarix.com transportation exchange, for instance, more than seventy shippers and ten ocean carriers actively post real-time cargo and available space.

What other global supply chain components could be streamlined using Internet applications? What are the benefits of an Internet exchange that brings shippers and transportation carriers around the world together? What might be some disadvantages?

Source: Adapted from Eric Chabrow, "Supply Chains Go Global—The Internet Levels the Geographic Playing Field and Lets Companies Reach into the Farthest Corners of the Planet for Partners and Customers," *Information Week,* 3 April 2000, p. 50; John Day, "They Do More Than Carry the Load—Third Party Logistics Providers Evolve into Supply-Chain Partners," *Electronic Buyers' News,* 10 January 2000, p. 57; Rick Gunn, "Global Communities Seek Even Tighter Bonds: The Internet Is Playing a Key Role as Companies Seek to Adjust World-wide Fulfilment Strategies," *Automatic I.D. News,* November 1999, p. 51.

more important. Some 17,500 UPS employees are now equipped with "ring scanners"—small, electronic devices worn on their index finger and wired to a small computer on their wrist. When a handler holds a package, the ring shoots a pattern of photons at a bar code on the package. Within moments, its location flashes to customers trolling the Internet. The Internet service can also zap the signature of whoever signs for a shipment anywhere in the world.[31]

Outsourcing Logistics Functions

External partners are becoming more and more important to efficient supply chain management. **Outsourcing**, or **contract logistics**, is a rapidly growing segment of the distribution industry. It involves a manufacturer or supplier turning over the entire function of buying and managing transportation—or another function of the supply chain, such as warehousing—to an independent third party. In an effort to focus on their core competencies, many manufacturers are turning to outside partners for their logistics expertise. Partners create and manage entire solutions for getting products where they need to be, when they need to be there. Logistics partners offer staff, an infrastructure, and services that reach consumers virtually anywhere in the world. Because a logistics provider is

outsourcing (contract logistics)
A manufacturer's or supplier's use of an independent third party to manage an entire function of the logistics system, such as transportation, warehousing, or order processing.

Grand & Toy

What kind of e-commerce services described on the Grand & Toy Website have allowed the company to increase its business-to-business services?

www.grandandtoy.com

on line

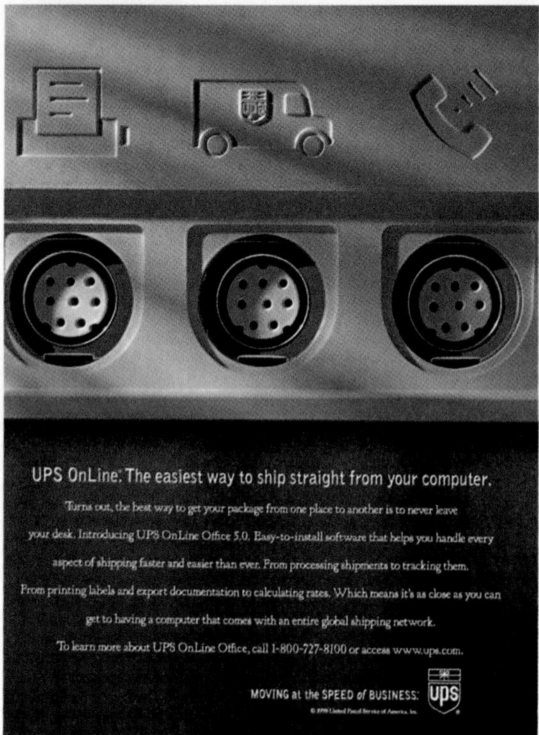

UPS On-Line increases its clients' self-sufficiency in processing and tracking shipments. UPS customers can take more ownership of their logistics functions without having to invest in customized logistics technology.

focused, clients receive service in a timely and efficient manner; this increases customer satisfaction and raises the company's reputation generally.[32] Most North American manufacturers and suppliers are either using or considering using third-party logistics services.[33]

Third-party contract logistics allows a company to cut inventories, and locate stock at fewer plants and distribution centres, while providing the same or better service. It can then focus on its core business. Whirlpool decided to use a third-party logistics provider after it realized it was spending too much on moving products. Originally, each of Whirlpool's eleven American plants handled its own logistics; the result was a tangle of routes and inefficiencies and out-of-control costs. On a single day, two or more Whirlpool trucks might make stops to pick up goods from a supplier when a single truck could have done the job. Whirlpool decided that outsourcing was the best option, in part because it would allow the company to concentrate on what it does best: make appliances. The company selected Ryder Dedicated Logistics, which soon untangled the transport routes. Ryder now runs warehouses for Whirlpool and collects data that let it analyze supplier performance and spot new cost-cutting opportunities.[34]

Many firms are taking outsourcing a step further by allowing business partners to take over the final assembly of their products or their packaging. Usually the point of this is to reduce inventory costs, speed up delivery, or meet customer requirements better. Ryder assembles and packages twenty-two different combinations of shrink-wrapped boxes that contain the ice trays, drawers, shelves, doors, and other accessories for the various refrigerator models Whirlpool sells. Before, Whirlpool would install the accessories in the refrigerators at the plant—a source of considerable confusion on the factory floor.[35]

IBM is allowing some of its distributors to do more final product assembly. Today, around 31 percent of its desktop PCs are assembled by eleven business partners, many of whom may install non-IBM components. One reseller actually assembles some of its IBM orders in a warehouse right next to IBM's factory in North Carolina, which saves on distribution costs.[36] For Nike's new athletic equipment division, contract logistics provider Menlo Logistics inflates basketballs, soccer balls, and footballs, which come in half-inflated because they take up less room that way. For some retailers, the logistics company also puts the balls in colourful packages and sticks on price tags.[37]

Electronic Distribution

electronic distribution
A distribution technique that involves any kind of product or service that can be distributed electronically, for example, through fiber-optic cable or satellite transmission.

Electronic distribution is the most recent development in the logistics arena. Broadly defined, **electronic distribution** involves any kind of product or service that can be distributed electronically, for example, through fiber-optic cable or satellite transmission. The Internet Shopping Network (**www.isn.com**), the largest on-line seller of computer hardware and software, just added a Downloadable Software division. Customers access the ISN over the Internet, select the software they wish to purchase, transfer their credit card information, and have the software available for use immediately. With the advent of technology that compresses data much more than in the past, movies and music CDs are now downloadable and playable on computerized home entertainment systems. This will revolutionize physical distribution as we know it today for any product that can be transmitted through electronic means, including newspapers, books, magazines, and audio and video entertainment.

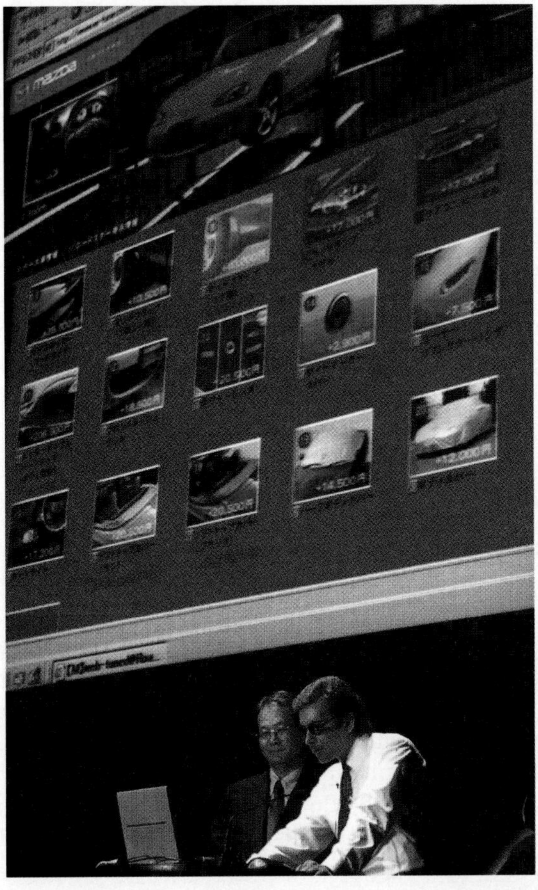

Mazda Motor Corporation President Mark Fields demonstrates its Internet Build-To-Order system, which enables customers to order special cars from a combination of engines, transmissions, frames, and interiors and exteriors (www.mazda.ca). Read the "Internet Connections" boxed feature to see how choiceboards are putting customers in the driver's seat.

internet connections

Choiceboards Are Redefining the Supply Chain and Putting Customers in Command

Buying a car today is an exercise in frustration. You have to look at dozens of models on dealer lots, but not one of them meets your needs precisely. The car you ultimately purchase represents a compromise, providing some of the features you want (antilock brakes and a sunroof) and a slew of others you don't (fog lamps and heated seats).

This sort of frustration is designed into business systems. Companies create fixed product lines that represent their best guesses about what buyers want, and buyers make do with the choices they're offered. Fixed product line systems frustrate suppliers as well. Predictions of future demand, no matter how well grounded, are inevitably inaccurate. That's why newspaper pages teem with announcements of sales, factory rebates, and dealer incentives—they're sure signs of manufacturing guesses gone awry.

Thanks to the Internet, there is an alternative to the traditional, unhappy mismatch of customer needs and supplier performance. In all sorts of markets, customers will soon be able to describe more accurately what they want, and suppliers will be able to deliver the desired product or service without compromise or delay.

Catalyzing this shift is an innovation we call a "choiceboard"—an interactive, on-line system that lets customers design their own products by choosing from a dynamic menu of attributes, components, prices, and delivery options. The customer's selections send signals to the supplier, and this sets in motion the wheels of procurement, assembly, and delivery.

It's impossible to predict how this war of the choiceboards will play out, but it seems clear that the victors will be those with the best-designed choiceboards, supplier networks, and customer relationships. One-stop shopping will take on a whole new meaning, and e-commerce will take on a whole new look.

What is the value proposition of choiceboards for buyers? For sellers? Do you think choiceboards will continue to be a determinant of competitive advantage, or are they likely to become a strategic necessity? Explain. Do choiceboards create an environment where disintermediation is likely to occur? If so, are new "cyber-intermediaries" likely to emerge?

Source: Adapted from Adrian J. Slywotzky and David J. Morrison, "The Missing Link," *The Industry Standard*, 10 July 2000.

LOOKING BACK

Think back to opening story about Grocery Gateway's on-line grocery delivery plan. The company is turning the traditional grocery industry upside down as it revolutionizes selling groceries and other goods through the Internet. The company maintains a focus on providing cost-effective, scheduled delivery to the home. Shoppers can surf Grocey Gateway's Website to purchase milk and bread instead of travelling to their nearest grocery or convenience store, thus eliminating traditional retailing intermediaries. The company also provides a pick-up service for vacationers on their way to cottage country and logistics services for SERCA Foodservice.

Summary

1 Discuss logistics and supply chain management and their evolution into distribution practice. Logistics is the process of strategically managing the efficient flow and storage of raw materials, in-process inventory, and finished goods from point of origin to point of consumption. The supply chain connects all of the business entities, both internal and external to the company, that perform or support the logistics function. Supply chain management, or integrated logistics, coordinates and integrates all the activities performed by supply chain members into a seamless process that delivers enhanced customer and economic value through synchronized management of the flow of goods and information from sourcing to consumption. The concept of supply chain management evolved from the physical distribution of agricultural goods in the early 1900s, which focused on pushing products to market. Today, logistics and supply chain management are viewed as a key means of differentiation for a firm and as a critical component in marketing and corporate strategy. The focus is on pulling products into the marketplace and partnering with members of the supply chain to work together and share information.

2 Discuss the concept of balancing logistics service and cost. Today, logistics service is recognized as an area in which a firm can distinguish itself from the competition. Many logisticians strive to achieve an optimal balance of customer service and total distribution cost. Important aspects of service are availability of product, timeliness of deliveries, and quality (accuracy and condition) of shipments. In evaluating costs, logistics managers examine all parts of the supply chain—sourcing and procurement of raw materials, warehousing and materials handling, inventory control, order processing, and transportation—using the total cost approach. Many logisticians are decreasing their emphasis on reducing logistics costs to the lowest possible level in favour of exploiting logistics capabilities to increase customer satisfaction and maintain customer demand.

3 Describe the integrated functions of the supply chain. The logistics supply chain consists of several interrelated and integrated functions: (1) procuring supplies and raw materials, (2) scheduling production, (3) processing orders, (4) managing inventories of raw materials and finished goods, (5) warehousing and materials handling, and (6) selecting modes of transportation. Integrating and linking all of the logistics functions of the supply chain is the logistics information system. Information technology connects the various components and partners of the supply chain to make an integrated whole. The supply chain team, in concert with the logistics information system, orchestrates the movement of goods, services, and information from the source to the consumer. Supply chain teams typically cut across organizational boundaries, embracing all parties who participate in moving product to market. Procurement deals with the purchase of raw materials, supplies, and components according to production scheduling. Order processing monitors the flow of goods and information (order entry and order handling). Inventory control systems regulate when and how much to buy (order timing and order quantity). Warehousing provides storage of goods until needed by the customer, while the materials handling system moves inventory into, within, and out of the warehouse. Finally, the major modes of transportation include railways, motor carriers, pipelines, waterways, and airways.

4 Discuss new technology and emerging trends in logistics. Several trends are emerging in today's logistics industry. Technology and automation are bringing up-to-date distribution information to the decision maker's desk. Technology is also linking suppliers, buyers, and carriers for joint decision making and has created a new electronic distribution channel. Many companies are saving money and time by out-sourcing third-party carriers to handle some or all aspects of the distribution process.

Discussion and Writing Questions

1. Discuss the benefits of supply chain management. How does supply chain management result in enhanced customer value?
2. Discuss the trade-offs between logistics service and cost. How can the high cost of expensive air transportation to enhance service be offset? How does logistics service affect customer satisfaction?
3. Discuss how just-in-time production affects the entire supply chain. Specifically, how does JIT affect suppliers, procurement planning, inventory levels, mode of transportation selected, and warehousing? What are the benefits of JIT to the end consumer?
4. Assume you are the logistics manager for a producer of expensive, high-tech computer components. Identify the most suitable method(s) of transporting your product in terms of cost, transit time, reliability, capability, accessibility, and traceability. Now assume that you are the logistics manager for a producer of milk. How does this change your choice of transportation?

Application for Small Business

Joe Kelly has a restaurant supply business in Saskatchewan that serves all of Saskatchewan and west to Vancouver Island. Joe sells small appliances (toasters, coffee machines, cappucino makers) and dishes for restaurant use. He has a sales force of ten people on the road constantly and delivers from his Regina warehouse across the West once each month. Most of his product is shipped by ship and then train from other continents. Invoicing and orders are sent mainly via Canada Post.

Questions

1. How could Joe make his sales and distribution functions more efficient?
2. Should Joe consider using different techniques to improve his supply chain management? What would you recommend for his sales and supply chain management process?

Do You Know These Terms?

distribution resource planning (DRP) 343
electronic data interchange (EDI) 342
electronic distribution 348
inventory control system 342
just-in-time production (JIT) 340
logistics 332
logistics information system 339
logistics service 336
mass customization (build-to-order) 340
materials handling system 344
materials requirement planning (MRP) 343
order processing system 341
outsourcing (contract logistics) 347
supply chain 332
supply chain management (integrated logistics) 333
supply chain team 339

Organics to You

Supply chain management is all about getting the right products to the right people at the right place at the right time. British Columbia's Organics to You (OTY) learned the long, hard way that the order process and delivery systems that make this possible are critical to a company's success and growth.

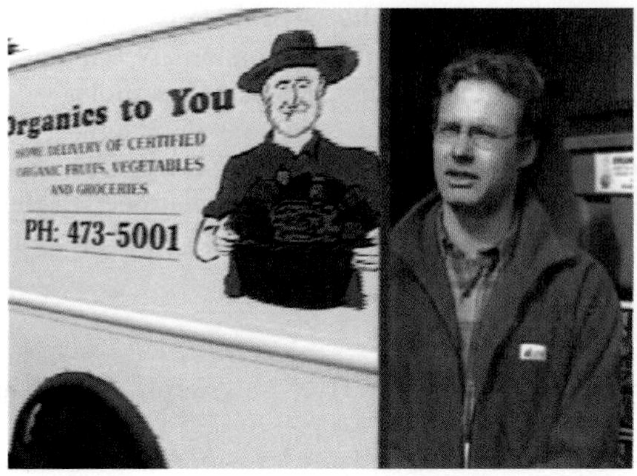

Organics To You is a small company that specializes in putting together bins of organic produce and delivering them fresh to customers. Its business goal is to get good, fresh, organic food to people at a reasonable cost. OTY was the first company in British Columbia to offer delivered organic produce, but its success was soon followed by as many as twenty competitors. To keep its leading position in the organic produce business, OTY knew it needed to allow custom orders for its customers, so they could select specifically which fruits and vegetables would be delivered to their homes. Sound easy? Not without a communications system that allowed for ordering, invoicing, and inventory systems as well as telephone systems that allowed customer orders and fulfilment to happen seamlessly. OTY did not have such a system in place. In fact, its systems could not accommodate its customers' needs.

The company knew it needed to reorganize its systems in order to stay competitive—it knew it needed to be a leader in computerized, customized home delivery of organic food in order to maintain its lead position. It needed a technology makeover—a new, touch-tone phone order system and reliable voicemail system—and it needed it fast. OTY immediately looked to consultants who specialize in logistics management and ordering systems, but decided they cost too much money. The managers at OTY decided to spearhead the changes themselves, and over a period of almost two years made mistakes with technology suppliers who could not make the logistics systems work together.

OTY's piecemeal efforts at hiring programmers and buying phone systems resulted in its staff feeling as if they were prisoners to a computer program that wasn't working and a phone system that didn't do its job. They felt stuck and stressed and unable to grow their company. Ultimately, OTY started again at the beginning and had consultants install an integrated communications program that allowed orders by phone, on-line, and through a catalogue, along with an inventory system that worked. It was expensive, but it allowed OTY to introduce custom orders and stay competitive. But the two years of stress took its toll internally, with staff and management problems.

Sources:

CBC, *Venture*, "Organics to You," February 1, 2000.
www.spud.ca

Questions:

1. How does customer service relate to supply chain management for the British Columbia business Organic to You?
2. What did Organics to You learn about the balance of logistics and costs throughout the two-year communications overhaul at its company?
3. How does the nature of the OTY product offering make supply chain management even more critical?
4. Why was Organics to You unable to launch its "custom bin" without integration of ordering, inventory, and communications systems?

3

marketing miscues

Roots Air

A short-lived experiment in high-style flying came to an end in May 2001 with the final flight of Roots Air. Skyservice Airlines Inc., the parent of the Toronto-based Roots, stopped flying after less than six weeks. "Recently, a lot of capacity has been added to the routes we fly, which would mean that we would have had to wage the same kind of competitive war that Canadian Airlines did," said Russell Payson, chairman, chief executive, and president of Skyservice. "Suspending flights was the fiscally responsible thing to do for our customers, shareholders, and employees."

Roots, which was 80 percent owned by Skyservice, with the clothier Roots Canada holding a minority stake, launched 26 March 2001 amid much fanfare and an aggressive marketing campaign that promised deluxe service. Its game plan was to attract high-paying business customers with stylish amenities, while charging them slightly less than Air Canada's full fare.

There was much skepticism in the analyst community, with most industry professionals predicting the carrier would die by June, or early fall at the latest. The main concern was that the business travellers Roots was targeting also demand high frequency, which the three-plane company could not deliver. "It's astonishing that it pulled out this quickly—it must have had a dreadful first month," said Douglas Reid of the Queen's University School of Business.

Roots may be best remembered as the shortest-lived airline in Canada. Vistajet, a London-based carrier, closed after 109 days in 1997, while Greyhound Air managed to keep flying for more than a year before shutting down in the same year. From the outset, Roots had difficulty filling seats, and was forced to respond with deep discounts that overturned the high-cost economics of the business. Industry sources speculate it was losing about $200,000 a day. Avi Dalfen, an analyst at Research Capital, whose firm raised the initial $35 million in private equity for the startup, said the company's business plan was sound but that the environment changed. Most significant was Canada 3000's decision to begin offering low-fare business seats, which fractured Roots' market. "The model is not only what you're doing, it's what everybody else is doing in your space. There's no question that it's radically different today than it was a year ago," he said.

Source:

Peter Fitzpatrick, "Airline Never Had a Chance, Say Analysts," *The National Post— National Financial Post,* 4 May 2001, p. C1; files from Canadian Press DOC# 20010504NP0400144.

Questions

1. What do you see as the major problems faced by Roots Air prior to closing?
2. What were the airline's main strengths?
3. What could the airline have done to better weather the market?
4. Assume you are launching a new airline service in Canada? How would you position and promote it? What service strategies would you adopt?

Critical Thinking

Coke: Leveraging the Brand

Douglas Daft, CEO of Coca-Cola, may have to tackle what could be one of the biggest questions surrounding his company's core product. Is the Coke brand still as special in the new millennium as it was back at the start of the twentieth century?

John S. Pemberton, a pharmacist in Atlanta, made his first batch of Coca-Cola syrup in 1886. Today, the Coca-Cola Company has become a major multinational company, with more than 16 million consumers worldwide and 31,000 employees. Headquartered in Atlanta, the company consists of five geographic groups: (1) North America, (2) Latin America, (3) Greater Europe, (4) Africa and the Middle East, and (5) Asia Pacific. Additionally, Coca-Cola owns Minute Maid Company, the world's leading marketer of juices and juice drinks.

Coca-Cola's corporate mission is to maximize shareowner value over time by increasing volume, expanding sales worldwide, maximizing long-term cash flows, and improving economic profit. The company attempts to execute its strategy through its six key premises:

- Consumer demand drives the company's decision making.
- The Coca-Cola brand is the core product.
- The company offers a broad selection of nonalcoholic ready-to-drink beverages.
- Coca-Cola will be the best marketer in the world.
- The company thinks and acts locally.
- The company will serve as a model for what a corporate citizen should represent.

Coca-Cola's Brands

Two factors have contributed strongly to Coca-Cola's success: (1) its direct marketing approach (often referred to as "from the TV set to the store shelf") and (2) the company's distribution system of independent local franchisees. However, it has been the company's core brands that have actually touched the lives of consumers around the world. These core brands include Coca-Cola (developed in 1886), Fanta (revived as we now know it in 1955), Sprite (debuted in 1961), and Diet Coke (introduced in 1982). Additionally, there are over 500 flavour combinations marketed worldwide, including such products as coffee, tea, bottled water, and fruit drinks.

The "Soft" Drink Market

Unfortunately for soft drink producers, 1999 was not a good year for the beverage industry. As we enter the twenty-first century, the soft drink market is very mature and growing very slowly. Consumption of orange juice was on the rise in the late 1990s into 2000. At the same time, the bottled water market grew from a $200 million market in the 1970s to a $5 billion growth industry in 2000. This growth has been attributed to three major factors: (1) health concerns, (2) the convenience/portability of small bottles, and (3) the opportunity to try something different.

Who would have thought that drinking water would be seen as "trying something different"? Interestingly, however, taste is defining the market. There are juice- flavored waters, sweet waters, and waters that taste strong and chalky, as well as waters with no taste at all. Add to this the waters enhanced with herbal preparations (e.g., St. John's wort, echinacea, ginseng) and nutrients (calcium) and one finds a market that appears to be offering a healthy alternative to carbonated drinks! Douglas Daft is set for battle and thinks Coca-Cola can become a product leader in this alternative beverage segment.

Daft's interest in the alternative beverage market is fuelled by a mass exodus from the soda market. Consumers are worried about the harmful effects of ingredients such as caffeine and aspartame. However, Coca-Cola has never focused much attention on its noncarbonated offerings. Rather, the company has allowed these noncarbonated products to follow "me-too" strategies—it has developed products and entered markets after other companies have shown the success of such diverse product offerings. Becoming a leader in the beverage market, rather than the soft-drink leader, has some observers questioning the strength of Coke's brand equity.

Coca-Cola's Brand Equity

Coca-Cola has built its brand equity on a limited number of core brands. The strength of the Coke brand, however, has not left room for any trial and error in experimenting with new products. Many consumers still remember the company's unsuccessful attempt in the early 1980s to change the taste of its original Coke product. To avoid possibly diluting its brand equity with product mistakes, Coca-Cola has not put the Coke name on its me-too products. The company has utilized a global branding strategy only for its major brand—basically assuming that there is worldwide desire for a single product.

With consumer preferences changing the nature of the beverage marketplace, Daft's tenure at Coca-Cola may be remembered according to whether he allows the Coke brand name to be put on all Coca-Cola products (e.g., water, mango juice in Latin America, rice drinks in Asia) in an attempt to be all things to all people. If he does, and the results are positive, Daft will have allowed the company and its shareholders to reap the benefits of brand equity. If the results are less than favourable, Daft risks being blamed for diluting the company's brand equity.

Bibliography

Carol L. Bowers, "Bottled Water Business Take Off," *Utility Business,* March 2000, pp. 36–7.

Dean Foust and Debora Rubin, "Now, Coke Is No Longer 'It'," *Business Week,* 28 February 2000, pp. 148–51.

Kate MacArthur, "Coke Crisis: Equity Erodes as Brand Troubles Mount," *Advertising Age,* 24 April 2000, p. 3.

Greg W. Prince, "The Year of Living Dangerously," *Beverage World,* 15 March 2000, pp. 34–51.

Rupert Wright, "Coca-Cola: Ice-Cold Times for an Icon," The *Independent—London,* 30 January 2000, p. 27.

www.thecolacompany.com.

Questions

1. What does the term "brand equity" mean in relation to the Coca-Cola Company?
2. Describe Coca-Cola's branding strategy.
3. Why might the company's move into alternative beverages dilute its core brand?
4. Where are Coca-Cola's core brands on the product life cycle?
5. Should Coca-Cola put the Coke brand on alternative beverages?

4

CHAPTER 14

LEARNING OBJECTIVES

After studying this chapter, you should be able to

1. Discuss the importance of retailing in the Canadian economy
2. Explain the dimensions by which retailers can be classified
3. Describe the major types of retail operations
4. Discuss nonstore retailing techniques
5. Define e-tailing, and outline the issues surrounding its use
6. List the major tasks involved in developing a retail marketing strategy
7. Discuss the challenges of expanding retailing operations into global markets
8. Describe future trends in retailing

RETAILING

As athletes of the 1998 Canadian Winter Olympic team marched into the Olympic Stadium in Nagano, Japan, Canadians around the globe watched with pride, but two individuals—Michael Budman and Don Greene—stood especially proud. For the first time, curling, snowboarding, and women's ice hockey were being recognized as events at the Olympic Games, and for the first time, the Canadian team had been outfitted by Canadian retailer Roots, a company that Greene and Budman founded in 1973.

Roots, which started out as a family-owned shoe business, has grown to be Canada's number one brand, recognized around the world. Since opening its doors in 1973 as a single-product retail store selling Roots negative-heel shoes, it has expanded into an international lifestyle brand with over 150 stores in Canada, the United States, and Asia, as well as an on-line store. Company founders Budman and Green choose their products based on their personal inspiration: the natural beauty of Canada, their families, their passion for great style, and their love of sports. According to retail analyst Strapagiel, Roots' commitment to lifestyle has allowed it to cater to a niche market.[1]

Roots introduced its first sweatshirt, Roots Beaver Athletics, in 1975. Since that time it has expanded its product offerings to include items such as Roots Leathers, Roots Athletics, Roots Passport, Roots Kids and Baby Roots, Roots Time, Roots Vitamins, Roots Uniscent, and Roots Vision. Though Roots has diversified its product lines, all the items it sells remain true to its logo: "Quality, Integrity, Longevity." Despite the diversity of its product lines, and despite its global expansion, over 90 percent of Roots products are manufactured in Canada, as a reflection of the management team's Canadian roots.[2]

Since the 1998 Winter Olympics, Roots has outfitted the 2000 Canadian Summer Olympic team for the Sydney games and has been contracted by the Canadian and U.S. Olympic committees to outfit both nations' teams until 2012. "We are thrilled to have the opportunity to outfit the U.S. Olympic Team [in Salt Lake City], the host country, in Roots style. Our philosophy is if you look great you will feel good and perform better."[3]

Roots
How would you like to buy your clothes on-line? Go to the Roots Website and see what you think of the on-line clothes shopping experience.
www.roots.ca

on line

Roots has over $135 million in retail sales. The company is proud of its history and is striving to continue its legacy as one of Canada's greatest retail success stories.

The Role of Retailing in Canada

1

Discuss the importance of retailing in the Canadian economy

retailing
All the activities directly related to the sale of goods and services to the ultimate consumer for personal, nonbusiness use.

Retailing—all the activities directly related to the sale of goods and services to the ultimate consumer for personal, nonbusiness use—enhances the quality of our daily lives. Whenever we shop for products or services, we are involved in retailing. As businesspeople, if the transactions we complete within our activities are the final link between producer and end user, we are involved in retailing. The millions of goods and services provided by retailers reflect the needs, styles, and desires of Canadian society. As lifestyles and demographics change, retailers must adjust the products and services they offer. In this way new opportunities are always being presented to the retail market. Retailers must always be aware of changes in their customer bases.

Retailing affects all of us directly or indirectly. Retailing represents approximately $250 billion annually to the Canadian economy. The retail sector is one of this country's largest employers, providing 12 percent of Canada's 14 million jobs.[4]

Independent retailers, including franchises, account for 75 percent of Canada's 180,000 retail businesses. Revenues from this group comprise over 60 percent of the country's retail operations. Even so, chains tend to dominate certain retail categories in Canada, including clothing and general merchandising. In terms of retail categories, the automotive and food sectors account for 38 percent and 24 percent of annual Canadian retail revenues respectively.[5]

In the United States, most retailers are quite small and a few giant organizations dominate the industry. In that country fewer than 10 percent of all retail establishments account for over half of total retail sales and employ about 40 percent of all retail workers. Exhibit 14.1 lists the top private retail chains in Canada by revenue.

exhibit 14.1

Largest Private Canadian Retailers[6]

1998 Rank	Company	Major category	Revenue ($000)
1	Zellers	Department stores	4,598,000
2	Costco Canada	Warehouse clubs	3,087,962
3	Katz Group	Drug stores	1,700.000
4	Rona	Hardware/home	988,385
5	Reno-Depot	Hardware/home	588,000
6	Grand & Toy	Office supplies	568,195
7	Black's Photo	Photography	137,586

NOTE: This list of Canadian retail chains may not include certain privately held retail outlets.

Classification of Retail Operations

A retail establishment can be classified according to its ownership, level of service, product assortment, and price. Specifically, retailers use the latter three variables to position themselves in the marketplace. (As noted earlier, positioning is the strategy used to influence how consumers perceive one product in relation to all competing products.) These three variables can be combined in various ways to create distinctly different retail operations. Price and product assortment are also two of the four elements comprising the retail marketing mix; these will be discussed in this context later in the chapter. Exhibit 14.2 identifies the main types of retail stores discussed in this chapter and classifies them by level of service, product assortment, price, and gross margin.

2
Explain the dimensions by which retailers can be classified

Ownership

In terms of ownership, retailers can be broadly classified as independents, or franchises, or members of a chain. Retailers owned by a single person or partnership and not operated as part of a larger retail institution are **independent retailers**. Most of the world's retailers are independent—that is, they operate one or a few stores in their community. In Canada, independent retailers comprise over 60 percent[7] of retailing operations. Many of the businesses listed in your local telephone book—from florists to mechanics to restaurants—would fall into this category.

independent retailers
Retailers owned by a single person or partnership and not operated as part of a larger retail institution.

Chain stores are groups of stores in the same retail industry owned and operated by a single organization. The home or central office assumes responsibility for many administrative tasks for the entire chain. Often it is the home office that procures the merchandise sold in all the stores, with corresponding economies of scale. Chain stores can be very large, such as the Zellers chain of department

chain stores
Stores owned and operated as a group by a single organization.

exhibit 14.2

Types of Stores and Their Characteristics

Type	Level of service	Product assortment	Price	Gross margin
Department store	Moderately high to high	Broad	Moderate to high	Moderately high
Specialty store	High	Narrow	Moderate to high	High
Supermarket	Low	Broad	Moderate	Low
Convenience store	Low	Medium to narrow	Moderately high	Moderately high
Full-line discount store	Moderate to low	Medium to broad	Moderately low	Moderately low
Discount specialty store	Moderate to low	Medium to broad	Moderately low to low	Moderately low
Warehouse clubs	Low	Broad	Low to very low	Low
Off-price retailer	Low	Medium to narrow	Low	Low
Restaurant	Low to high	Narrow	Low to high	Low to high

franchise
A licensed agreement between a parent company and an independent merchant that gives the merchant the right to operate under the trademark of the parent company in exchange for financial returns.

stores, or they can be smaller, more regionally based chains, such as Kent Building Supplies in Atlantic Canada.

Franchises are owned and operated by individual merchants but are licensed by a larger supporting organization or parent company. Under franchise agreements, the franchiser exchanges branding, trademarks, and management support for a portion of the financial returns secured by the franchisee. Franchising combines the advantages of independent ownership with those of the chain store organization.

There are two basic forms of franchises today: product and trade name franchising, and business format franchising. In the former a dealer agrees to sell certain products provided by a manufacturer or a wholesaler. This approach is used widely in the automobile, soft drink, and gasoline industries. For example, a local tire retailer may hold a franchise to sell Michelin tires. In the same vein, the Coca-Cola bottler in a particular area is a product and trade name franchisee licensed to bottle and sell Coca-Cola's soft drinks.

Business format franchising involves an ongoing business relationship between a franchiser and a franchisee. Typically, a franchiser "sells" a franchisee the right to use the franchiser's format or approach to doing business. This form of franchising has expanded rapidly since the 1950s in the restaurant, apparel, hotel/motel, and real estate industries. Fast food restaurants like McDonald's, Wendy's, and Burger King, and service companies like First Choice Haircutters, use this kind of franchising.

Level of Service

The level of service that retailers provide can be classified along a continuum, from full service to self-service. Some retailers—typically those selling high-end or luxury goods—offer high levels of service. Exclusive clothing dealers and your local bridal boutique typically provide many value-added services such as alterations, credit, delivery, consulting, liberal return policies, layaway, gift-wrapping, and personal shopping. Discount stores like A Buck or Two usually offer fewer individualized services to customers, although some discount retailers such as Wal-Mart do place a high value on customer satisfaction. "Sam Walton changed the landscape of American retailing. How did he do it? By building a culture based on one simple principle: making the customer No. 1."[8] Retailers such as factory outlets and warehouse clubs offer virtually no services; the customer benefits from lower purchasing costs.

Product Assortment

The third basis for positioning or classifying stores is by the breadth and depth of their product lines. Specialty stores—Cotton Ginny, Hallmark, The Second Cup, and others—are the most concentrated in their product assortment, usually carrying single or narrow product lines but in considerable depth. Other retailers, such as factory outlet stores, may carry only part of a single line. Roots, a Canadian clothes manufacturer, sells only certain items of its own brand in its many outlet stores.

At the other end of the spectrum, full-line discounters typically carry broad assortments of merchandise with limited depth. Canadian Tire carries automotive supplies, hardware, household cleaning products, and gardening tools. However, it may carry only a handful of brands of each item, whereas supermarkets and specialty stores may carry many more. Discount specialty stores like Reno Depot, Toys 'R' Us, and IKEA carry a broad assortment in concentrated product lines, in these cases building/home supplies, toys, and furniture/housewares respectively.

Price

Price is a fourth way to position retail stores. Traditional department stores and specialty stores typically charge the full "suggested retail price." In contrast, discounters, factory outlets, and off-price retailers use low prices to lure shoppers.

The last column in Exhibit 14.2 showed the typical gross margin for each type of store. **Gross margin** is the amount the retailer makes as a percentage of sales after the cost of goods sold is subtracted. The gross margin and the price generally follow the same trend. A traditional jewellery store, which typically has a lower volume of sales, tends to have both high prices and high gross margins. In contrast, a factory outlet, which tries to move larger volumes of inventory, is likely to have both low prices and low gross margins.

gross margin
The amount of money the retailer makes as a percentage of sales after the cost of goods sold is subtracted.

During sale periods and price wars, stores mark down their prices on certain items in an effort to win customers. Typically this causes gross margins across an industry to decline. One recent example in Canada involves the laser eye surgery market. In 1999, industry pioneers such as TLC chain charged between $2,000 and $2,500 per eye; new entrants then began charging less than $1,000 for both. This has placed the entire industry in a vulnerable situation in terms of profitability.[9]

Major Types of Retail Operations

3
Describe the major types of retail operations

There are several types of retail stores. Each offers a different product assortment, type of service, and price level, according to its customers' shopping preferences.

Department Stores

Housing several departments under one roof, a **department store** carries a wide variety of shopping and specialty goods, including apparel, cosmetics, housewares, electronics, and sometimes furniture. Usually, purchases are made within each department rather than at one central check-out area. Each department is treated as a separate buying centre to achieve economies in promotion, buying, service, and control. Each department is usually headed by a **buyer**, who not only selects the merchandise for his or her department but may also be responsible for promotions and personnel. For a consistent, uniform store image, central manage-

department store
A store housing several departments under one roof.

buyer
A department head who selects the merchandise for his or her department and may also be responsible for promotions and personnel.

TLC Laser Eye Center, which now operates over 50 centres across North America, has a strong reputation in the eye surgery market. Would you choose an eye centre based on reputation or price?

Mountain Equipment Co-op

What benefits could consumers gain by purchasing athletic wear through the MEC Website that they might not gain by purchasing through traditional channels? How do the prices of comparable goods compare to those of traditional retail outlets?

www.mec.ca

on line

ment sets broad policies about the types of merchandise carried and their price ranges. Central management is also responsible for credit policies, store expansion, customer service, the overall advertising program, and so on.

Large, independent department stores are rare today. Most department stores today are owned by national chains. Among the largest Canadian department store chains are Sears Canada and The Bay. After a lengthy battle, one of Canada's most widely recognized chains, the Timothy Eaton Company, sold its remaining stores to Sears in December 1999. Sears will maintain the Eaton marketing entity for seven of its choice urban stores, and will merge the remaining fifty-seven with Sears department stores. Under the new ownership, Toronto's Eaton Centre and Yorkdale Shopping Centre, Calgary's Eaton Centre, Vancouver's Pacific Centre, Ottawa's Rideau Centre, and the Eatons stores in Winnipeg and Victoria will continue to be run as Eatons stores. These stores range in size from 300,000 to 700,000 square feet and in 1998 accounted for more than 30 percent of the chain's $1.6 billion in sales. Sears plans to position these seven stores as high-end department stores, comparable to international industry leaders such as London's Harrods and Berlin's Kaufhaus des Westens.[10]

In recent years, consumers have become more cost conscious and value oriented. Specialty retailers like Cotton Ginny, along with discounters, catalogue outlets, and e-tailing Websites, are offering sharper pricing, greater convenience, and superior merchandise selection; in doing so they are taking sales away from department stores. They have also been quicker to adopt new technologies and to invest in labour-saving strategies. In addition, their leaner cost structures typically translate into lower prices for customers. At the same time, manufacturers like Liz Claiborne, Roots, Calvin Klein, and Polo/Ralph Lauren are opening outlet stores of their own. Furthermore, discount stores such as Wal-Mart and Zellers (which has adopted the Martha Stewart Living collection) are upgrading their assortments, taking still more sales away from department stores.

Department store managers are following several strategies to preserve their market share. For example, they are repositioning their stores as specialty outlets by dividing their departments into series of miniboutiques, each appealing to a distinct fashion taste. Eaton's plans to feature Tommy Hilfiger and Anne Klein boutiques in its stores. Furthermore, department stores are enhancing customer service to shift the focus away from price. Services include complimentary alterations, longer store hours, personalized attention, after-sale follow-up, and personal wardrobe planning. Finally, they are expanding, remodelling, and revitalizing themselves to show off new merchandising directions.

Specialty Stores

specialty store
A retail store specializing in a given type of merchandise.

Specialty stores allow retailers to refine their segmentation strategies and tailor their merchandise to specific target markets. A specialty store is a type of store, but it is also a retail method, in the sense that such stores specialize in a given type of merchandise. Examples of specialty stores include children's clothing, men's clothing, candy, baked goods, gourmet coffee, sporting goods, and pet supplies. A typical specialty store carries a deeper but narrower assortment of specialty merchandise than does a department store. Generally, specialty stores' sales clerks are highly knowledgable and can offer more attentive customer service. This format has become very powerful in the apparel market and other areas. Tim Hortons, Fairweather, M&M Meat Shops, Athlete's World, and Mountain Equipment Co-op are all successful chain specialty retailers.

Consumers in specialty outlets usually perceive price as secondary. The distinctive merchandise, the store's physical appearance, and the caliber of the staff

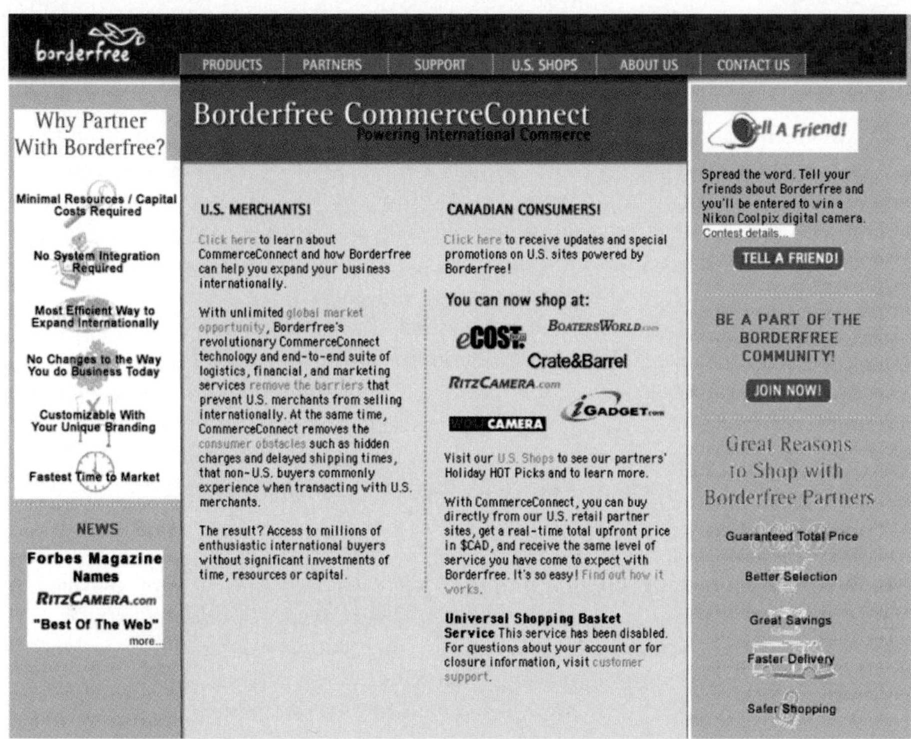

On-line shopping has given consumers an alternative to the often high-priced, stale merchandise offered in department stores. Borderfree Inc. (www.borderfree.com), a full-service facilitator of international e-commerce, allows Canadian consumers to shop directly at the most popular U.S. retail sites in Canadian dollars. Shoppers are given a guaranteed total purchase price, including currency exchange, taxes, duties, and shipping and handling costs, eliminating any postdelivery sticker shock. This has capitalized on consumers' desire for high quality, low prices, better choice, and convenience.

are what determine the store's popularity. Independent specialty toy stores often shun mass-produced toys such as are sold in Zellers or Toys 'R' Us, in favour of more educational toys or toys that are hard to find, for example, Brio's wooden train sets. Because they cannot compete on price with the big toy stores, independent toy retailers offer enhanced services such as personal shopping and free gift wrapping.[11] Manufacturers often prefer to introduce new products in small specialty stores before moving on to larger retail and department stores. Athlete's World has been a top Canadian retailer of athletic footwear for years, and its full-price shopping mall stores offer a venue for brands such as ecko, Fila, Champion, and Lugz. Athlete's World stores are also home to the Nike Shop. Introducing new sport shoes through specialty retailers like Athlete's World creates an image of exclusivity for Nike.[12] Small specialty stores also provide a low-risk testing ground for many new product concepts.

One specific form of specialty store is a restaurant. Restaurants straddle the line between retailing establishments and service establishments. This is because they sell tangible products—food and drink—but also provide valuable service in the form of food preparation and food service. Most restaurants could even be considered specialty retailers, since most of them try to provide a distinctive type of cuisine—for example, Red Lobster seafood restaurants, Il Fornello Italian restaurants, Tim Hortons coffee shops, Kentucky Fried Chicken, and Pizza Delight pizza restaurants. Canadians spend over $28 billion annually in restaurants. [13]

As retailing institutions, restaurants must deal with many of the same issues as more traditional retailers, such as personnel, distribution, inventory management, promotion, pricing, and location. Restaurants and food service retailers run the spectrum: some offer limited service and inexpensive food (e.g., fast food chains, the local diner), others offer sit-down service and moderate to high prices (e.g., Mexicali Rosa's Mexican restaurants or the local, trendy Italian bistro).

Restaurants are among the most entrepreneurial of businesses and also among the most competitive. Because barriers to starting a restaurant are low, the opportunity appeals to many people. However, the risks are great: it is estimated that around 50 percent of all new restaurants fail during their first year. Restaurants face competition not only from other restaurants but also from consumers,

on line

Dineaid.com

Dineaid.com is striving to promote Atlantic Canadian restaurateurs. Recently it introduced an on-line ordering service for some of its clients. Visit its Website and then write a short proposal discussing the pros and cons of ordering meals over the Internet, identifying the major incentives for companies to take advantage of this service.

www.dineaid.com

who can easily choose to cook at home. Competition has fostered innovation in the restaurant industry and has led to trends such as the introduction of more nutritious choices for health-conscious consumers. Restaurants are also competing with one another by seeking out and targeting underserved distribution niches. More and more fast food operators are looking to provide service at hospitals, airports, schools, and highway rest stops.[14] Some Esso gas stations now feature Tim Hortons coffee shops and McDonald's franchises. These pairings save money on property leases, lure more customers, and foster innovation.[15]

More restaurants are competing directly with supermarkets by offering take-out and delivery. M&M Meat Shops, Canada's largest retailer of frozen foods with over 270 franchises across the country, offers "hundreds of meal ideas in one aisle"—another convenient and efficient alternative to dining out.[16]

supermarket
A large, departmentalized, self-service retailer that specializes in food and some nonfood items.

Supermarkets

Canadians spend roughly one-tenth of their disposable income in supermarkets.[17] A **supermarket** is a large, departmentalized, self-service retailer specializing in food and some nonfood items. According to 1996 Statistics Canada census data, Canadians spend about three-quarters their food money in retail grocery stores and supermarkets. There are some regional differences: Atlantic Canadians spend almost four-fifths of their food money in stores, British Columbians only around two-thirds.[18] A decade ago, industry experts predicted a decline of the supermarket industry, assuming that slim profit margins of just 1 to 2 percent of sales left it vulnerable. For various reasons, they were not quite right. They had misread the demographic trends.

Tim Hortons locations range from full standard stores to combo units with Wendy's and Tim Hortons kiosks in numerous Esso Tiger Express outlets. Tim Hortons has locations in shopping malls, universities, and hospitals.

For example, there are now more dual-income and single-parent families than ever before; as a result, consumers are eating out more or are too busy to prepare meals at home. The growth in the away-from-home food market has been driven by the entry of more women into the workforce and their need for convenience and time-saving products. Working couples need one-stop shopping, and the number of affluent customers willing to pay for specialty and prepared foods is increasing. This is expanding the market opportunities for both restaurants and prepared food stores such M&M Meats. It is also changing the product assortments found in supermarkets; for example, Loblaws now offers the President's Choice line of prepared meals, and Sobey's offers the Our Best line.

Another demographic trend affecting supermarkets is ethnicity. Canada's population of Asians is growing, especially in the West. Over one-third of immigrants to Canada are from Hong Kong, India, China, Taiwan, and the Philippines.[19] It is becoming more and more important for supermarkets to tailor their stores' product mixes to reflect that fact.

In the increasingly competitive marketplace, many supermarket chains are tailoring their marketing strategies to appeal to specific consumer segments. Most notable in this regard is the shift toward loyalty marketing programs, which reward loyal customers with discounts or gifts. Supermarket retailers pass out frequent shopper cards,

services spotlight

A Licence to Print Money

It's springtime. You decide to rid your wallet of the paper junk that has grown there like a fungus since mid-November. Out go the gum wrappers, the ABM receipts, and the long-expired 2-for-1 coupons. But for some reason, you can't bear to toss out that $1.80 in Canadian Tire money that is broadening your billfold's girth. "People don't like to throw away currency. The coupons themselves remind people of money and so they find it very hard to toss them out," says Adrienne Simmons, a researcher at Toronto-based Kubas Consultants, pointing to a key reason for the success of Canadian Tire money.

Canadian Tire money is the oldest and most successful loyalty program in Canada. It has spawned many imitations, but none as widely known, and none that can boast of having a sentimental connection to this country's culture. Canadian Tire now allows customers to collect virtual money on the company's house credit card, its Website, and its affiliate MasterCard—moves that have broken the chain's loyalty initiative out of its original mold.

Despite the program's timeless popularity, doling out coupons with every customer purchase yields none of the consumer information that is now so desired by retailers. The blue Air Miles card accepted at many retail chains across the country automatically tracks users' purchase patterns. In a Kubas study of major Canadian cities, Air Miles ranked No. 2 in consumer popularity behind Canadian Tire money. Almost 49 percent of respondents were Air Miles cardholders, while 50 percent collected Canadian Tire money.

"Loyalty programs started off years ago as purely an incentive and became a really successful way to encourage customer loyalty, and with Canadian Tire money, you can essentially buy something for free," says Steve Boase, a retail consultant at J.C. Williams Group. "The trouble is, how can you change longstanding programs in a way that, in the long run, leads to a better in-store experience for customers?" A knowledge of consumer buying patterns helps retailers deploy more effective promotions, and ideally makes customers more loyal. However, Canadian Tire's original program—which dispenses coupons equalling 2.5 percent of the subtotalled value of goods purchased at the cash register—has changed little, Mr. Bonikowsky notes, because "first and foremost, Canadian Tire money is about rewarding people. It's not about tracking customer buying patterns."

Mr. Bonikowsky would not reveal how much of the promotional money it doles out every year, but he estimates that $100 million worth of coupons are out there in customers' pockets—much of which will be redeemed. The relative simplicity of the veteran plan may be what consumers find most appealing in a retail marketplace saturated with competing loyalty programs. "It's successful because of the ease of use. There is no expiry date and there are no restrictions. People get the money, keep it, and spend it," says Ms. Simmons. The central program's failure to keep tabs on its consumers may not be too much of an impediment to overall sales, she adds. "People see the money in their wallets and it reminds them of going to Canadian Tire." That, she says, is marketing at its most effective.

Visit **www.canadiantire.ca** and read more about the Canadian Tire Money program under "Company Info." How is its success measured? What are the advantages and disadvantages of this loyalty program compared to ones that capture data on customers such as Air Miles?

Source: Adapted from Hollie Shaw, "A Licence to Print Money," *The National Post*, 30 April 2001, p. C5.

which are scanned at checkout time; this helps them track shoppers' buying habits. They can then use the information to "microtarget" customers through direct mail.

As stores seek to meet consumer demand for one-stop shopping, conventional supermarkets are being replaced by bigger superstores, which are usually twice the size of supermarkets. Superstores meet the needs of today's consumers for convenience, variety, and service. They offer one-stop shopping for many food and nonfood needs, as well as many services, including pharmacies, flower shops, salad bars, in-store bakeries, take-out food sections, sit-down restaurants, health food sections, video rentals, dry-cleaning services, shoe repair, photo processing, and banking. Some even offer family dentistry or optical shops. This tendency to offer a wide variety of nontraditional goods and services under one roof is called **scrambled merchandising**. Loblaws, an Ontario supermarket chain that operates supermarkets under various marketing entities across the country and in nine other countries, sells seasonal decorations, lawn furniture, various household items, and gift items such as candles.

scrambled merchandising
The tendency to offer a wide variety of nontraditional goods and services under one roof.

Convenience Stores

convenience store
A miniature supermarket that carries only a limited line of high-turnover convenience goods.

A **convenience store** can be defined as a miniature supermarket that carries only a limited line of high-turnover convenience goods. These self-service stores are typically located near residential areas and are generally open twenty-four hours a day, seven days a week. Convenience stores offer exactly what their name implies: convenient location, long hours, fast service. But prices are usually higher at convenience stores than at supermarkets. Thus the customer pays for the convenience.

From the mid-1970s to the mid-1980s, hundreds of new convenience stores opened across the country, many with self-service gas pumps. Full-service gas stations fought back by closing service bays and opening miniature stores of their own, selling convenience items such as cigarettes, sodas, and snacks. Supermarkets, drug stores, and discount stores also wooed customers with one-stop shopping, 24/7 hours, and express checkouts. To combat competition from gas stations and supermarkets, convenience store operators have changed their strategy: they have expanded their offerings of nonfood items to include video rentals, health and beauty aids, upscale sandwich and salad lines, coffee bars, and more fresh produce. Some convenience stores are even branded or offer franchised goods—for example, Esso stores now sell Tim Hortons coffee.

Discount Stores

discount store
A retailer that competes on the basis of low prices, high turnover, and high volume.

A **discount store** is a retailer that competes on the basis of low prices, high turnover, and high volume. There are four major categories of discounters: full-line discount retailers, discount specialty retailers, warehouse clubs, and off-price retailers.

full-line discount stores
A retailer that offers consumers very limited service and carries a broad assortment of well-known, nationally branded "hard goods."

mass merchandising
A retailing strategy using moderate to low prices on large quantities of merchandise and lower service to stimulate high turnover of products.

Full-Line Discounters Compared to traditional department stores, **full-line discount stores** offer consumers very limited service and carry a much broader assortment of well-known, nationally branded "hard goods," including housewares, toys, automotive parts, hardware, sporting goods, and garden items, as well as clothing, bedding, and linens. Some even carry limited nonperishable food items, such as soft drinks, canned goods, and potato chips. As with department stores, national chains dominate the discounters. Full-line discounters are often called mass merchandisers. **Mass merchandising** is the retailing strategy whereby retailers use moderate to low prices on large quantities of merchandise and lower service to stimulate high turnover of products.

Wal-Mart is the largest full-line discount organization in terms of sales. With over 3,400 stores in ten countries, including 178 in Canada, Wal-Mart has expanded rapidly by locating on the outskirts of small towns and absorbing business for miles around. Much of Wal-Mart's success has been attributed to its merchandising foresight, cost consciousness, efficient communication and distribution systems, and involved, motivated employees. Wal-Mart is credited with pioneering the retail strategy of "every-day low pricing," a strategy now widely copied by retailers the world over. Besides expanding throughout all fifty states, Wal-Mart has expanded globally into Mexico, Canada, Puerto Rico, Brazil, Argentina, China, and Indonesia. Most recently, it has entered Germany by acquiring the German hypermarket chain Wertkauf, and Korea by acquiring the Korea Makro chain.[20] Retailing abroad has proved to be quite a challenge for the giant discounter.

In an attempt to compete against the American giant's expansion into Canada, Zellers has been aggressively trying to position its chain of over 350 stores as *the* Canadian full-line discounter. Owned and operated by the Canada's Hudson's Bay Company, Zellers has developed some proprietary labels and has sole distribution rights for a number product labels, including Levi's Orange Tab. It has also adopted several celebrity labels, including Gloria Vanderbilt's "wear-to-work," Delta Burke's Plus Sizes, and the Martha Stewart Living collection.[21]

A hybrid of the full-line discounter is the hypermarket, a concept adapted from the Europeans. The flashy **hypermarket** format combines a supermarket and full-line discount store in a space ranging from 200,000 to 300,000 square feet. Although they have enjoyed widespread success in Europe, where consumers have fewer retailing choices, hypermarkets have been much less successful in North America.

hypermarket
A retail store that combines a supermarket and full-line discount store in a space ranging from 200,000 to 300,000 square feet.

Similar to hypermarkets but only half the size are **supercentres,** which combine groceries and general merchandise with a wide range of services including pharmacies, dry cleaners, portrait studios, film developers, hair salons, opticians, and restaurants—all in one location. For supercentre operators like Wal-Mart, food is a customer magnet that sharply increases the store's overall volume, while taking customers away from traditional supermarkets.[22] Though it isn't doing so yet in Canada, Wal-Mart now operates over 900 SuperCentres in the United States and plans to replace many older Wal-Marts with this format. Loblaws operates supercentres across the country under umbrellas such as The Real Canadian Superstore and Atlantic Superstore. Over and above their full line of President's Choice convenience products, the Loblaws superstores provide photolabs, dry cleaners, garden centres, and various other value-added services.

supercentres
Retail stores that combine groceries and general merchandise goods with a wide range of services.

Supercentres are threatening to push Europe's traditional small and medium-size food stores into extinction. Old-fashioned corner stores and family businesses are giving way to larger chains offering food, drugs, services, and general merchandise all in one place. Many European countries are passing legislation to make it more difficult for supercentres to open. In France, laws have been passed banning new supercentres over 1,000 square meters (10,800 square feet). Belgium and Portugal have passed similar bans. In Britain and the Netherlands, areas outside towns and cities are off limits to superstores. By imposing planning and building restrictions for large stores, these countries are trying to accommodate environmental concerns, movements to revive city centres, and the worries of small shopkeepers.

An increasingly popular variation of full-line discounting is *extreme value retailing*. Two excellent examples are the Great Canadian Dollar Store and A Buck or Two. Major discounters are shifting toward the supercentre format. In doing so they are increasing their offerings of higher-priced goods aimed at higher-income consumers. This has created an opening for extreme value retailers to entice low-income shoppers. Low and fixed income customers are drawn to extreme value retailers, which offer easy access, small stores, a narrow selection of basic merchandise, and rock-bottom prices.[23]

Discount Specialty Stores Another discount niche is the single-line **specialty discount stores**, which can be, say, sporting goods stores, electronics stores, auto parts stores, office supply stores, or toy stores. These stores offer a nearly complete selection of single-line merchandise and use self-service, discount prices, high volume, and high turnover to their advantage. Discount specialty stores are often termed **category killers** because they so heavily dominate their narrow merchandise segments. Examples include Toys 'R' Us in toys, Future Shop in electronics, Staples and Office Depot in office supplies, Home Depot and Kent Building Supplies in home improvement supplies, and IKEA in home furnishings.

specialty discount store
A retail store that offers a nearly complete selection of single-line merchandise and uses self-service, discount prices, high volume, and high turnover.

category killers
The term often used to describe specialty discount stores because they dominate so heavily their narrow merchandise segment.

Toys 'R' Us was the first category killer, offering a giant selection of toys—usually over 15,000 different items per store—at prices usually 10 to 15 percent less than competitors'. When Toys 'R' Us came on the retail scene, department stores were generally limiting their toy assortments to the Christmas season. Toys 'R' Us offered a broad assortment of inventory all year long. Also, the playing field was scattered with many small toy chains or mom-and-pop stores. With its bright, warehouse-style stores, Toys 'R' Us gobbled up market share; as a result, many small toy stores failed and many department stores eliminated their toy departments. The Toys 'R' Us chain—currently a $10 billion company with about 1,400

on line

Toys 'R' Us

Who seems to be the marketing audience for the Toys 'R' Us Website? Is the site as kid friendly as you expected it to be?

www.toysrus.com

stores worldwide—now commands roughly one-quarter of the American retail toy business. Toys 'R' Us first went international in 1984—initially in Canada, then in Europe, Hong Kong, and Singapore. Since then the company has opened over 450 stores in over two dozen foreign countries.

Other specialty segments have followed the lead of Toys 'R' Us, hoping to build similar retailing empires in highly fragmented mom-and-pop markets. The home improvement industry was once dominated by professional builders and small hardware stores offering basic stables of products. Now several large big box players are capturing the market. Similarly, before the PETsMART pet supplies chain was established, the pet industry was dominated by thousands of independent neighborhood pet stores. Another highly fragmented industry was the office products industry. As more people began working from home, replacing their typewriters with personal computers and purchasing fax machines, the local stationery store, with its limited selection of paper and writing materials, quickly became obsolete. The industry is now dominated by Office Depot and Staples, each of which stocks some 5,000 to 7,000 different types of products. Category-dominant retailers like these serve their customers by offering an unequalled selection of merchandise, stores that make shopping easy, and low prices every day; this eliminates the need for time-consuming comparison shopping.[24]

warehouse membership clubs
Limited service merchant wholesalers that sell limited selections of brand name appliances, household items, and groceries on a cash-and-carry basis to members—usually small businesses and groups.

Warehouse Clubs **Warehouse membership clubs** sell a limited selection of brand-name appliances, household items, and groceries. Sometimes referred to as "big-box stores," they usually sell items in bulk from warehouse outlets on a cash-and-carry basis to members only. Individual members of warehouse clubs are charged low membership fees or none at all.

Warehouse clubs such as Costco have had a big impact on supermarkets. With 90,000 square feet or more, warehouse clubs offer 60 to 70 percent general merchandise and health and beauty care products, with grocery-related items making up the difference.[25] Customers typically use warehouse clubs to stock up on staples; then they go to specialty outlets or food stores for perishables.

Fierce competition is typical of the warehouse club industry. Common practices include price slashing, selling below cost, locating outlets to compete directly, and sometimes hiring away rivals' employees to gain an edge in local markets.

off-price retailer
A retailer that sells at prices 25 percent or more below traditional department store prices because it pays cash for its stock and usually does not ask for return privileges.

Off-Price Discount Retailers An **off-price retailer** sells at prices 25 percent or more below traditional department store prices because it pays cash for its stock and usually doesn't ask for return privileges. Off-price retailers buy manufacturers' overruns at cost or even less. They also absorb goods from bankrupt stores, irregular merchandise, and unsold end-of-season output. Nevertheless, much off-price retailer merchandise is first-quality, current goods. Because buyers for off-price retailers purchase only what is available or what they can get a good deal on, merchandise styles and brands often change monthly. Today there are hundreds of off-price retailers, including Winners.

factory outlet
An off-price retailer owned and operated by a manufacturer.

Factory outlets are an interesting variation on the off-price concept. A **factory outlet** is an off-price retailer owned and operated by a manufacturer. Thus it carries only one line of merchandise—its own. Each season, between 5 to 10 percent of a manufacturer's output does not sell through regular distribution channels due to close-outs (merchandise being discontinued), factory seconds, and cancelled orders. Using factory outlets, manufacturers can regulate where their surplus is sold, and they can realize higher profit margins than they would by disposing of the goods through independent wholesalers and off-price retailers. Factory outlet malls are typically located in out-of-the-way rural areas or near vacation destinations. Most are situated at least 50 kilometres from urban or suburban shopping areas so that manufacturers don't alienate their department store accounts by selling the same goods virtually next door at a discount.

A number of manufacturers are reaping the benefits of the popularity of outlet malls, including Roots, Liz Claiborne, and Nike (apparel), Oneida (silversmiths), and Dansk (kitchenware). Several outlet malls have opened in Canada in recent years. The Canada One Factory Outlet mall in Niagara Falls boasts almost forty stores, from Danier Leather Goods to Cambridge Towels.

Nonstore Retailing

The retailing methods discussed so far have been in-store methods; that is, customers must physically shop at stores. **Nonstore retailing** involves shopping without visiting a store. Because consumers demand convenience, nonstore retailing is growing faster than in-store retailing. The main forms of nonstore retailing are automatic vending, direct retailing, and direct marketing.

4
Discuss nonstore retailing techniques

nonstore retailing
Shopping without visiting a store.

Automatic Vending

A low-profile yet important form of retailing is automatic vending. **Automatic vending** involves using machines to offer goods and services for sale. The soft drink, candy, and snack vending machines found in cafeterias and office buildings are examples. The British were the first to introduce coin-operated vending machines when they began selling postcards through them in the early 1880s.[26] Since then, vending machines have become a retail outlet for many products and services, including snacks, toiletries, stationery items, and videos.

automatic vending
The use of machines to offer goods for sale.

direct retailing
Representatives sell products door to door, office to office, or at home parties.

Retailers are constantly seeking new opportunities to sell through vending. In an attempt to expand its distribution beyond supermarkets, convenience stores, and delicatessens, Snapple has developed a glass-front vending machine capable of offering fifty-four different flavours simultaneously. Many vending machines today also sell nontraditional merchandise, such as videos, toys, stickers, and sports cards. Vending machines in college and university libraries sell computer diskettes, pens and highlighters, and other office-type supplies. Kodak cameras and films can now be purchased from vending machines in sports stadiums and tourist areas. Vending machines in theatre lobbies are selling T-shirts with movie themes. Moviegoers were able to buy a *Lost in Space* T-shirt for $16.95 by inserting a credit card into a vending machine.[27] Marketers are also experimenting with fresh foods in vending machines. Wireless technologies are providing new opportunities for vending machines by allowing consumers to purchase products directly from their bank accounts through their cellular phones or other electronic devices.

Because of the convenience, consumers are generally willing to pay higher prices at vending machines. On the other hand, vending machines are sometimes out-of-order, and there is little customer service if there are problems with the merchandise.

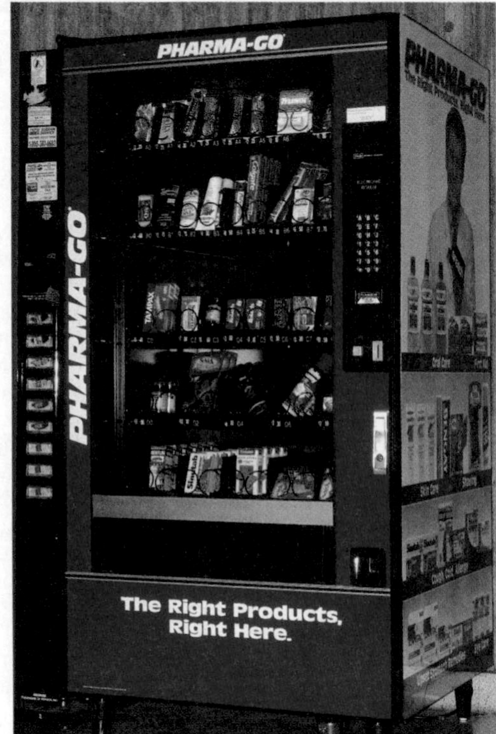

Direct Retailing

In **direct retailing**, representatives sell products door to door, office to office, or at parties in private homes. Companies such as Mary Kay Cosmetics, Parti-Lite candles, Melaleuca wellness products, and World Book Encyclopedia depend on direct retailing. Even personal computers are now being sold this way.

Nowadays, most direct retailers favour parties instead of door-to-door canvassing. Parties call for one person, the host, to gather together as many prospective buyers as possible. Most parties are combination social affairs and sales demonstrations. PartyLite, the Massuchusetts-based direct-sales company, sells its candles and accessories across North America and Europe through consultants, who organize parties at customers' homes. The hostesses open up their homes to friends and family for showings of PartyLite products; in return, the company offers them special deals.

Sales by direct retailers have fallen as women have entered the workforce. Working women are not home during the day and have little time to attend selling parties. Most direct sellers such as Avon and Tupperware still advocate the party method, but the realities of the marketplace are such that they have had to be more creative in reaching their target customers. Direct sales representatives now hold parties in offices, parks, and even parking lots. Others hold informal gatherings where shoppers can just drop in at their convenience, or they offer self-improvement classes. Many direct retailers are turning to direct mail, telephone orders, and Internet sales to find new customers and increase sales. Others, like Avon, are turning to more traditional retailing venues. Tupperware recently opened Tupperware Showcases, small kiosks located in major shopping centres throughout North America. Melaleuca has introduced the Melacart to its Website; consumers can purchase directly from this channel.

Direct Marketing

direct marketing (direct response marketing)
Techniques used to get consumers to make a purchase from their home or office or some other nonretail setting.

Direct marketing, sometimes called *direct response marketing*, refers to the techniques used to get consumers to make purchases from their home or office or some other nonretail setting. These techniques include direct mail, catalogues and mail order, telemarketing, and e-retailing. Shoppers using these methods are less bound by traditional shopping situations. Direct response shoppers tend to be time-strapped and to live in rural or suburban areas. These people value the convenience and flexibility of direct marketing.

entrepreneurial insights

My Favourite Doll is Barbie's Canadian Marketing Queen

My Favourite Doll, founded in 1994 by Margaret Matsui of Mississauga, Ontario, is a leading retailer and mail order distributor of collectible dolls, especially the Barbie collection. My Favourite Doll is listed in *Profit Guide* magazine's 2001 *Profit* 100, which is a list of Canada's fastest-growing companies. Matsui has grown her business into a 3.8 million enterprise in less than a decade.[28] Over 80 percent of her revenue is generated through the sale of special edition products that aren't generally available through other, larger retail channels.

Matsui is an expert in everything Barbie. Mattel has chosen her company to be an authorized dealer for the Official Barbie Collectors Club of Canada.[29]

My Favourite Doll's Website, **www.mfd.net**, provides a retail channel for the products; it is also a value-added portal to everything about Barbie. The site provides links to other doll distributors, tracks news within the industry, and provides profiles and updates on new specialty products.

Matsui has succeeded in large part because she has been able to capture a niche market, and also because she is deeply committed to customer service—she pays for return shipments of damaged products. To complement her retail showroom in Mississauga, Ontario, she accepts and fills orders by telephone, fax, and the Internet. This has allowed her to expand into broader national and international markets.

Matsui plans to penetrate even more deeply the Canadian market—which currently represents 25 percent of her revenues—and to expand her non-Barbie product lines. Building on a lifelong passion—her Website showcases a picture of her as a child opening up a doll at Christmas—she has been able to capitalize on various retail channels to establish a successful and growing Canadian company.

What are the benefits of retailing to a niche market? What hurdles need to be overcome? How can the Internet contribute to the success of such a venture?

Direct Mail Direct mail can be the most efficient or the least efficient retailing method, depending on the quality of the mailing list and the effectiveness of the mailing piece. With direct mail, marketers can target their customers precisely according to demographics, geographics, and even psychographics. Good mailing lists come from an internal database or are available from list brokers for around $35 to $150 per thousand names. A Calgary-based sales representative from a pharmaceutical company may buy a list of all the physicians in the area. The sales representative may then design a direct mail piece that explains the benefits of the company's products and highlights any pertinent special offers. Direct mailers can also deliver sales messages to consumers by videocassette, CD-ROM, or e-mail brochure.

Direct mailers are becoming more sophisticated in their customer targeting. Using statistical methods to analyze census data, lifestyle and financial information, and past-purchase and credit history, they can pick out those most likely to buy their products. Using this technique, a direct marketer like Dell Computers can target 500,000 people with the right spending patterns, demographics, and preferences. Without this technique, Dell could easily mail millions of solicitations annually. Solicitations can be targeted to as few as 10,000 prospects; if they are the right prospects, the company can save millions in postage while preserving sales. Customer relationship management (CRM) software is now available that allows for increased efficiencies.

Catalogues and Mail Order Consumers can now buy just about anything through the mail, from the mundane, such as books, music, and T-shirts, to the outlandish, such as the $5 million diamond-and-ruby-studded bra available through Victoria's Secret. Although most catalogue shoppers are women, the percentage of men who shop this way has been growing in recent years. Demographic changes have shifted more of the responsibility for shopping onto men; to them, it makes more sense to shop by catalogue or mail order than to trek to the mall.[30]

The most successful catalogues tend to be those aimed at highly segmented markets. Sears' catalogue sales had dropped off; then it replaced its "big book" with a series of specialty catalogues and aimed those at specific market segments, and its catalogue sales rose again. Some retailers are using mail order to good effect. IKEA, the Swedish furniture company, issues three separate catalogues (general, kitchen, work); each allows customers to order products through toll-free numbers twenty-four hours a day, seven days a week. IKEA's reasonable prices and quick delivery have also contributed to its success.[31] Other successful mail order catalogues, including those from Mountain Equipment Co-op, Victoria's Secret, and Lee Valley, target hard-working, home-oriented baby boomers who do not have time to visit retail stores, or don't have access to them. To remain competitive and to save their customers' time, catalogue companies are building computer databases containing customer information; customers who are listed in these don't have to repeatedly provide their addresses, credit card information, and so on.

Telemarketing **Telemarketing** involves using the telephone to sell directly to consumers. Telemarketing includes outbound sales calls, usually unsolicited (i.e., cold calls), and inbound calls (i.e., placing/receiving orders through toll-free 800 numbers or fee-based 900 numbers).

telemarketing
Using the telephone to sell directly to consumers.

Outbound telemarketing is an attractive direct-marketing technique because of rising postage rates and decreasing long-distance phone rates. Also, skyrocketing field sales costs have placed pressure on marketing managers to use outbound telemarketing. In their search for ways to keep costs under control, marketing managers are discovering how to pinpoint prospects quickly, zero in on serious buyers, and keep in close touch with regular customers. Meanwhile, they are reserving expensive, time-consuming, in-person calls for closing sales.

on line

Lee Valley Tools

How do companies like Lee Valley benefit from using catalogues as their primary retail channel? Are these benefits similar to or different from those derived from the use of on-line ordering channels? Explain.

www.leevalley.ca

Though outbound telemarketing has its advantages from a corporate perspective, consumers are growing increasingly aware of the potential for fraud, and are becoming less tolerant of unsolicited phone calls. Outbound telemarketing is now regulated through the federal Competition Act. Companies must now disclose fully the purpose of the call at the beginning of the conversation.[32] In an effort to combat telemarketing fraud, which accounted for over $1.5 million in personal losses nationwide in 2000, the Ontario Provincial Police now operate a service called Phonebusters. This provides an avenue for consumers to learn about and report fraudulent activities.[33]

Inbound telemarketing programs, which use 800 and 900 numbers, are used mainly to take orders, generate leads, and provide customer service. Inbound 800 telemarketing has been supplementing direct response TV, radio, and print advertising campaigns for over twenty-five years. The 900 numbers, which were introduced only recently, charge a toll to customers. These are gaining popularity as a cost-effective retail channel. One of the biggest benefits of 900 numbers is that they allow marketers to generate qualified responses. The phone charge may well reduce the total volume of calls; but the calls that do come in are from customers who are truly interested in the product or service.

Electronic Retailing

Electronic retailing includes the television shopping networks and on-line retailing, or e-tailing. Both these channels offer the convenience of shopping twenty-four hours a day, seven days a week.

Television Shopping Networks Shop-at-home networks are specialized forms of direct response marketing. These dedicated TV channels offer a variety of products and services, which are targeted to specific market segments. Home viewers can phone in their orders directly on a toll-free line and shop with a credit card. The shop-at-home industry is now a billion-dollar business with a loyal customer following. Television shopping networks have extremely broad market reach—they can reach every home that has cable TV service.

Most TV shopping networks are converging their services with the Internet to provide a comprehensive and interactive shopping experience for consumers.

The Shopping Network, based in Toronto, has tied its on-air activities to an interactive, e-commerce-enabled Website. Through **www.tsc.ca**, customers can purchase items they have seen on TV. They also have access to daily broadcast schedules. They can even view the actual show through streaming video players.

Home shopping networks are now beginning to offer products that appeal to more affluent audiences. The average home-shopping viewer is thirty-one and has a household income over $60,000. Food marketers such as Hershey Foods, Campbell Soup, and Kellogg's are the latest companies to test the potential of shop-at-home networks, especially with new product introductions. Hershey introduced its Pot of Gold candy line on QVC, an American network, and sold 1,600 boxes of candy in four minutes. Campbell plans a full hour on the QVC network to sell reproductions of the first Campbell Kid dolls. Campbell will also showcase historical advertising and videos related to the merchandise being sold. Kellogg's introduced Cocoa Frosted Flakes on home shopping channels rather than through traditional channels.[34]

5
Define e-tailing, and outline the issues surrounding its use

On-line Retailing The Internet has spread rapidly in the past few years, and this has opened up a new retailing channel for businesses. E-tailing builds on traditional retailing channels to enable companies to service the rapidly growing market segment that is comfortable with the Internet as a business channel.

There are some who suggest that e-tailing has not met its original projections, which ranged upwards of several billion dollars by the year 2000; that being said, Canadians spent $417 million in on-line purchases in 1999, and 60 percent of this amount was spent within Canada.[35] More than two-thirds of large Canadian retailers expect that within the next couple of years, the Internet will be their main nonstore channel.[36]

In both theory and practice, e-tailing is a natural extension of traditional retailing. It can capitalize on existing distribution and supply chain networks, but it can also be a cost-effective means of incorporating new, value-added features to enhance consumers' experiences. So far, the most successful product and services in on-line retailing have been travel, books, digital products (e.g., music and software), and luxury or niche products. According to Statistics Canada data, books, magazines, newspapers, travel arrangements, computer software, and automotive parts were the most widely purchased items in 1999.[37]

Even consumers who do not buy things over the Internet have found it to be an efficient research tool. Information about product options, product substitutes, quality, and pricing are easy to find on the Internet before any purchase is made. This gives consumers much more bargaining power. This trend toward consumer "enlightenment" will affect all retailers, both traditional and electronic.

portal
A Website that provides a starting point and home base for Web-based activities.

On the Internet, consumers can visit various on-line shopping **portals**—essentially virtual malls—or they can shop directly from their favourite sites. Yahoo Canada Shopping, **ca.shopping.yahoo.com**, offers products and services from over thirty-five merchants. Consumers can shop for anything from beauty products to computers to antiques at all of the participating merchant stores using the Yahoo Wallet. This is essentially a purchaser profile that enables customers to shop at multiple stores without having to fill out the same information over and over. Retail Canada's shopping portal, **www.retailcanada.com**, categorizes participating merchants by province and then by product category. This portal offers relatively small businesses the opportunity to showcase their Websites through a nationally branded site.

A shopper who is seeking a specific product can visit a specific Website instead of going through a portal. Some sites, such as the Chapters/Indigo site, are designed specifically for the on-line environment. Other sites are designed to complement existing retail channels. Most companies nowadays have some sort of presence on the Web, although not all their sites have e-tailing transaction capabilities.

For books, music, and DVDs, **www.chapters.indigo.ca**, is one of Canada's most comprehensive on-line sources. Some of the value-added features available on this site include a "wish list," which allows users to identify books they would like to receive as gifts; search by author/artist, subject, or title; and rewards programs and gift certificates. Examples of specialty e-tailers in Canada include Mountain Equipment Co-op sporting equipment and apparel (**www.mec.ca**), and From Here to Maternity clothing for pregnant women (**www.fromheretomaternity.com**).

RETAIL CANADA.com offers Canadian consumers and merchants a wide variety of products, ranging from books to clothing to music, and home decor available from its 5,000-plus merchant members.

Despite the benefits of e-tailing for both consumers and retailers, there are several reasons why consumers are not adopting this shopping option more quickly. Many consumers are hesitant to provide personal and financial data to companies through the Internet. As of 1999, more than three-quarters of Internet-linked households were reluctant to provide credit card information over the Internet; these people preferred to use the Internet only for window shopping and customer service. To address this issue, e-tailing sites are developing comprehensive privacy and security policies. In Canada, the Personal Information Protection and Electronic Documents Act has been introduced to protect both consumers and businesses in this new and expanding commercial environment. The Canadian Working Group on Electronic Commerce and Consumers has developed eight consumer protection principles to guide businesses in their e-tailing efforts, with the goal of ensuring that all stakeholders' rights are upheld.[38]

Also, e-tailers must find ways to personalize the e-commerce experience so that it resembles face-to-face contact with a sales representative. To this end, many e-tailers are capitalizing on interactive technologies. The Website of clothing retailer Lands' End, **www.landsend.com**, offers features that enable consumers to "see" how the clothing would look on them. Cosmetics e-tailer Reflect.com, **www.reflect.com**, customizes all its orders to the features and desires of each customer.

fulfilment
The capability to fill orders in accordance with customer expectations.

Fulfilment of orders is another major concern for e-tailers. For companies with established distribution networks direct to consumers, such as Mountain Equipment Co-op and IKEA, this concern may not be as big. However, retailers that traditionally only dealt with customers in stores must make sure they are capable of meeting customers' past expectations. This may involve revamping the company's total operations. Many companies are developing strategic alliances with shipping companies that have specialized competence in this area. The inability of Toys 'R' Us' to fill orders during the 1999 Christmas season resulted in a class action lawsuit being filed against that company.[39]

Retail Marketing Strategy

Retailers must develop marketing strategies based on overall goals and strategic plans. Retailing goals may include more traffic, higher sales of a specific item, a

internet connections

E-tailers Should Pick a Niche

Despite the economic slowdown, the plunge in financing for business-to-consumer startups, and the failure of dot.coms like eToys, on-line retailing has a good future in Canada—but only for those who think small, says a consulting firm.

"If you told me you wanted to be a large-scale Web-based [retail] player in Canada I would fully advise against it," says Peter Stanger, vice-president and leader of the business-to-consumer area for the Boston Consulting Group's Toronto office (**www.bcg.com**).

Only e-tailers that carve out a niche or strike a partnership to get purchasing deals are going to make it in the face of competition from giants like Sears Canada (**www.sears.ca**), Futureshop (**www.Futureshop.ca**), and Indigo (**www.chapters.indigo.ca**), says Stanger. A new study by BCG concludes that only 28 percent of Canadians with Internet access have bought anything on the Web, compared to 54 percent of Americans. Stanger says that's partly because there are fewer Canadian retail sights, or foreign sites offering Canadian prices and shipping. Also, "bricks and clicks" retailers are stealing market share from Web-based retailers, and will continue to do so.

Though Web-based retailers have improved their profitability, they are still incurring operating losses of 96 percent of revenues. In comparison, store-based e-tailers are generating operating losses of 36 percent of revenues. Furthermore, managing relationships with customers and having a cost-effective fulfilment structure are vital to profitability.

How are bricks-and-clicks retailers stealing market share from Web-based retailers? Why are Canadian consumers buying less on-line than their American counterparts? According to the Canadian Retail Council, where is the greatest growth in on-line Canadian retailing likely to be in the next five years?

Source: Howard Solomon, "Pick a Niche, Study Warns E-tailers," *EBusiness Journal* 3(6), June 2001, p. 7.

more upscale image, or heightened public awareness of the retail operation. The strategies retailers use to achieve their goals may include a sale, updated decor, the introduction of a new channel, or a new advertisement. The key tasks in strategic retailing are defining and selecting a target market and developing a retailing mix to successfully meet the needs of the chosen target market.

6
List the major tasks involved in developing a retail marketing strategy

Defining a Target Market

The foremost task in developing a retail strategy is to define the target market. This process begins with market segmentation (review Chapter 6). Successful retailing has always been based on knowing the customer. Retail chains sometimes founder when management loses sight of the customers the stores should be serving. More women are entering the corporate world, and casual clothing is tolerated in offices more than it used to be. The product assortments of retail clothing stores must take this into account. A number of trendy women's clothing chains, including Fairweather, have adapted their product lines to meet the changing lifestyles and career paths of their target markets.

In retailing, target markets are often defined by demographics, geographics, and psychographics. To appeal to their target markets, fast food chains like McDonalds are tracking children's trends and tastes and incorporating into their product offerings toys and themes based on these.

Before the retail mix can be created, the target market must be determined. Merchandisers like Sears and Canadian Tire adapt their product offerings and their individual stores to local and regional demographics. Sears stores in the upscale shopping districts of Toronto and Vancouver carry more luxury goods and designer fashions than stores in rural or less affluent areas.

Choosing the Retailing Mix

Retailers combine the elements of the retailing mix to arrive at a single retailing method to attract the target market. The six Ps of the **retailing mix** are the traditional four "Ps" of the marketing mix (*product, price, position, place*), and, in addition, *personnel* and *presentation.*

retailing mix
The traditional four "Ps" of the marketing mix (product, price, position, place), and, in addition, personnel and presentation.

The six Ps in combination constitute a retailer's image; this image then influences consumers' perceptions. Using their impressions, shoppers position stores against one another. A retail marketing manager must make sure the store's positioning is compatible with the target customers' expectations. As discussed early in this chapter, retail stores can be positioned on three broad dimensions: product assortment, price, and personnel. Management should use the other factors—place, presentation, and promotion—to fine tune the basic positioning of the store.

The Product Offering

The first element in the retailing mix is the **product offering**, also called the product assortment or merchandise mix. Retailers decide what to sell on the basis of what their target market wants to buy. They base their decision on market research, past sales, fashion trends, customer requests, and other sources. After more companies began promoting office casual days, Tip Top Tailors introduced its Business Casual line. Tip Top targets another specific market segment with its Big and Tall line.[40]

product offering
The mix of products offered to the consumer by the retailer, also called the product assortment or merchandise mix.

Developing a product offering essentially involves making decisions about the width and depth of the product assortment. *Width* refers to the assortment of products offered; *depth* refers to the number of different brands offered within each assortment. Price, store design, displays, and service are important to consumers in determining where to shop, but the most critical factor is merchandise selection. In an ambitious program to reposition itself as a competitive, moderate-priced department store, Sears increased the amount of space it devoted to

exhibit 14.3

The Retailing Mix

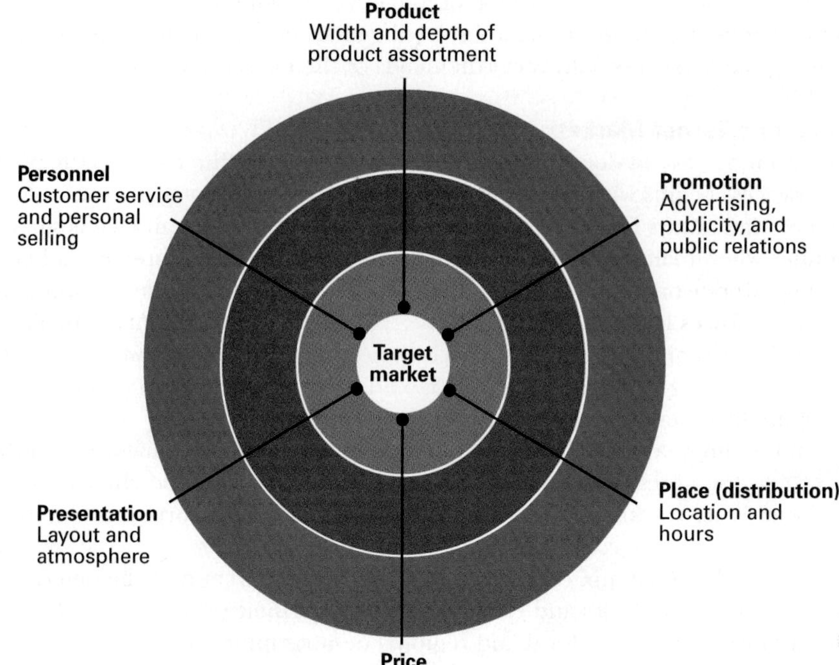

clothes and home fashions and de-emphasized tools and appliances. Sears's has also remodelled its stores and is pushing to bring women into the stores to shop for apparel and cosmetics. For example, Sears now carries a line of Benetton apparel.[41]

After determining which products will satisfy target customers' desires, a retailer must find sources of supply and evaluate the products. Once it finds the right products, the retail buyer negotiates purchase contracts. The buying function can be performed in-house, or it can be delegated to an outside firm. The goods must then be moved from the seller to the retailer, which means shipping, storing, and stocking the inventory. Inventory management involves cutting prices to move slow goods and keeping adequate supplies of hot-selling items in stock. Finally, as in all good systems, the entire process is evaluated to eliminate problems and bottlenecks.

One of the more efficient new methods of managing inventory and streamlining how products are moved from supplier to distributor to retailer is called *efficient consumer response,* or ECR. At the heart of ECR is *electronic data interchange,* or EDI, the computer-to-computer exchange of information. When ECR is fully implemented, products are scanned at the retail store when purchased; this updates the store's inventory lists. Headquarters then polls the stores to retrieve the data needed to produce an order. The vendor confirms the order, shipping date, and delivery time and then ships the order and transmits the invoice electronically. The item is received at the warehouse, scanned into inventory, and then sent to the store. The invoice and receiving data are reconciled. Payment via an electronic transfer of funds completes the process.

Many large companies have also implemented enterprise resource planning (ERP) solutions—software programs that integrate all business operations, including inventory management. New, Internet-based, user-friendly interfaces for these systems are providing cost-effective and efficient tracking mechanisms for companies' suppliers, large or small. Integrated systems also allow for the streamlining of production cycles, which can improve the responsiveness of the retail

Loblaws

How extensive are Loblaws private label brands? How do they compare in scope and price to other brands? Visit the company's Website to find out.

www.loblaw.com

on line

sector. New styles can be recreated on a computer, and the designs can be transmitted electronically to manufacturers for production. New merchandise can be produced and put on store shelves in weeks rather than months.

As margins drop and competition intensifies, retailers are becoming ever more aware of the advantages of **private label brands**—that is, brands designed and developed using the retailer's name. Because goods themselves typically make up between 70 and 85 percent of a retailer's expenses, eliminating middlemen can shave costs. That is why the prices of private label goods are typically lower than for national brands, and offer greater greater value to customers. Marks Work Wearhouse conducts 70 percent of its business through its private label brands, Windriver and Denver Hayes.[42] Private label brands can be seen in most retail sectors. Atlantic Canada's supermarket chain Sobey's offers its Our Best line of prepared foods; while Loblaws offers its President's Choice brand label for comparable products. Zellers has recently introduced its "Truly" brand, which encompasses more than 200 products, including apparel, household items, and beauty aids.[43]

private label brands
Brands that are designed and developed using the retailer's name.

Promotion Strategy

Retail promotion strategy includes advertising, public relations and publicity, and sales promotion. The goal is to help position the store in consumers' minds. Retailers design intriguing ads, stage special events, and develop promotions aimed at their target markets. Today's grand openings are carefully orchestrated blends of advertising, merchandising, good will, and glitter. All the elements of an opening—press coverage, special events, media advertising, and store displays—are carefully planned.

Retailers' advertising is carried out mainly at the local level, although retail giants like Sears and Zellers may advertise nationally. Local advertising by retailers involves specific communication about their stores, such as location, merchandise, hours, prices, and special sales. National advertising by retailers, to the extent it is done, generally focuses on image. The "Softer Side of Sears" national ad campaign was used to help reposition Sears as a low-priced but fashion-conscious apparel retailer. An accompanying campaign, "Come See the Many Sides of Sears," was used to promote the retailer's nonapparel merchandise, such as tools, paint, and car parts.

Often large retailers and well-known clothing designers or manufacturers of exclusive specialty products share the spotlight in ads. Ads linking Nike and Athlete's World—a Canadian athletic clothing and footwear chain—let everyone know that the latter sells the former's latest styles. In turn, these ads expand the reach of Nike's advertising. This type of arrangement, called *cooperative advertising*, is common in the apparel industry but is only starting to become common with packaged goods companies. Traditionally, marketers would simply pay retailers to feature their products in store mailers, or they would develop TV campaigns and simply tack on several retailers' names at the end of product commercials or at the bottom of print ads. The present trend is toward spots becoming more collaborative, with clear dual objectives.

Many retailers are forgoing media advertising these days in favour of direct mail or frequent shopper programs. Direct mail, e-mail, and catalogue programs are luring many retailers, who believe these may be a cost-effective means of increasing their core customers' brand loyalty and spending. Integrated advertising strategies using e-mail and mail order coupons are becoming more common. Each quarter, Greenhawk Equestrian and Harness Supplies mails catalogues to the equestrian community across the country. Home repair outlets such as Home Depot have been using direct mail, often around holidays when people have time off to carry out repairs. Restaurants and small retailers, such as Carlton Cards, have been using frequent diner or frequent shopper programs for years. Now many big retailers, like mass merchandiser Sears, are offering frequent shopper programs or loyalty programs that shower top shoppers with perks ranging from advance notice of sales and free gift wrapping to store discounts based on spending. By shopping with a Sears credit card, a Sears customer can amass Sears points that are redeemable for Sears gift certificates.

The Proper Location

Another element in the retailing mix is place, or site location. Selecting a proper site is critical. For one thing, it involves a large, long-term commitment of resources. Whether the retailer leases or purchases, location implies some degree of permanence. For another, location affects growth. The chosen area should be growing economically so that it can sustain the original store and any future stores. Furthermore, the local business environment may change over time. If the location's value deteriorates, the store may have to be closed or relocated.

The first location decision is *which community?* Here are four of the factors at play: stability, the potential for economic growth, the competition, the political climate. Toys 'R' Us usually establishes its stores in rapidly growing areas where the population closely matches its customer base.

Sometimes it is not the economic profile or political climate that makes a community a good location but rather its geographic location. Companies targeting the teen market, like the Garage Clothing Company, benefit from locating their stores in large shopping centres frequented by youth. Most major shopping centres are easily accessible by public transit and are popular hangouts for teenagers. Wal-Mart has usually refrained from locating in major urban areas; it prefers to locate in suburbs and small towns.[44]

After settling on a geographic region or community, retailers must choose a specific site. Besides growth potential, the important factors here are neighbourhood socioeconomic characteristics, traffic flows, land costs, zoning regulations, and public transportation. Retailers should also consider where competitors are located, not to mention their own stores. A particular site's visibility, parking, entrance and exit locations, accessibility, and safety and security are other variables to consider. Finally, retail synergy—that is, how well a store's format meshes with the surrounding retail environment—is also important.[45] Retail decision makers probably would not locate a Great Canadian Dollar store next door to an Eatons department store.

"Location, location, location" has long been a retailing axiom. Wal-Mart has become the largest retailer in North America by locating in underserved small towns. Wal-Marts offer hair salons, mail centres, optometrists, travel agencies, pharmacies, and food outlets—every retail destination that the average small town has, translated to a single site. One final decision about location faces retailers: whether to have a freestanding unit or to become a shopping centre or mall tenant.

Freestanding Stores Large retailers such as Wal-Mart, Canadian Tire, Costco, and furniture and car retailers can use isolated, freestanding locations because they are "destination" stores—that is, stores that consumers make deliberate plans to visit. In other words, customers seek out stores like these. Isolated stores often enjoy the advantages of low site cost (or rent) and no nearby competitors. On the other hand, it can be hard to attract customers to freestanding stores, and no other retailers are around to share costs.

Freestanding units are growing in popularity among retailers as they strive to make their stores more convenient, more enticing, and more profitable. Perhaps the great advantage to freestanding sites is their high visibility. Retailers can easily feel lost in huge shopping centres and malls; in contrast, freestanding units can help stores develop an identity with shoppers. Store chains that opt for freestanding are often able to grow faster, and this has strengthened the trend toward stand-alone units. Retailers such as Indigo and IKEA have chosen to be freestanding, for the sake of achieving their expansion objectives. Waiting for shopping centres to be built can slow down an aggressive expansion plan.[46]

Shopping Centres The tremendous boom in shopping centres began after the Second World War, as North Americans started migrating to the suburbs. The first shopping centres were *strip centres*, which were typically located along busy streets. They usually included a supermarket, a variety store, and perhaps a few specialty stores. Strip malls are essentially unplanned business districts, and they remain popular.

Next, small *community shopping centres* emerged, with one or two small department store branches, more specialty shops, one or two restaurants, and several apparel stores. These centres offer a broader variety of shopping, specialty, and convenience goods, provide large, off-street parking lots, and usually span 75,000 to 300,000 square feet of retail space.

Finally came the huge *regional malls*. Regional malls are entirely enclosed, or at least roofed to allow shopping in any weather. Many are landscaped with trees, fountains, and sculptures. They have acres of free parking. They have *anchor stores* or *generator stores* (e.g., Wal-Mart, Sears, or Dominion), which are usually located at opposite ends of the mall to create heavy foot traffic for the stores in the central section.

Community shopping centres and regional malls offer several advantages to retailers. First, the facilities are designed to attract shoppers. Second, the shopping environment, anchor stores, and "village square" activities draw customers. Third, ample parking is available. Fourth, the centre or mall projects a unified image. Fifth, tenants share the expenses of the mall's common areas and promotions for the entire mall. Finally, malls can target different demographic groups. Some malls are considered upscale; others are aimed bargain hunters.

Locating in a shopping centre or mall does have disadvantages. Leases tend to be expensive, and common promotion efforts may not attract customers to a particular store. There may be lease restrictions relating to hours of operation and the merchandise that can be carried. The anchor stores may dominate the tenants' association. Finally, there may be direct competition within the same facility.

Retail analysts expect that in the coming years, consumers will do even more of their shopping at neighbourhood strip shopping centres. Faced with more and more demands on their time, they will choose speed and convenience over the elegance and variety offered by large regional malls. Many of the nation's shopping malls are anticipating this and are reinventing themselves to resemble open strip malls. This move to redevelop malls is sometimes referred to as *demalling*.

Retail Prices

Another important element in the retailing mix is price. Retailing's ultimate goal is to sell products to consumers, and the right price is critical to sales. Because retail prices are usually based on the cost of the merchandise, an essential part of pricing is efficient and timely buying.

Price is also key to a retail store's positioning strategy. Higher prices often suggest both quality and prestige; certainly they do this for Birks and Holt Renfrew. In contrast, discounters and off-price retailers such as Wal-Mart and Winners offer good value for the money. There are even stores, such as the Great Canadian Dollar stores, where everything costs shoppers one dollar. This single-price-point strategy is aimed at getting higher-income customers to make impulse purchases through what analysts call the "wow factor"—the excitement of discovering an item costs only a dollar.[47]

A pricing trend among North American retailers that seems to be here to stay is *every-day low pricing*, or EDLP. Introduced to the retail industry by Wal-Mart, EDLP offers consumers low prices all the time instead of only during occasional sales. The Gap reduced its prices on denim jeans, denim shirts, socks, and other items to protect and broaden its share of the casual clothes market. Even some supermarkets have found success in EDLP.

Rent-to-own retailers offer ownership of merchandise after the customer fulfils his or her obligation under a rental agreement. These agreements have come under close scrutiny lately for their high ultimate retail prices and their target marketing practices. Read about the ethical dilemmas facing the rent-to-own industry in this chapter's "Ethics in Marketing" box.

Presentation of the Retail Store

A retail store's presentation helps determine its image; it also positions the store in the minds of consumers. A retailer that wants to position itself as an upscale store will use a lavish or sophisticated presentation.

atmosphere
The overall impression conveyed by a store's physical layout, decor, and surroundings.

The main element of a store's presentation is its **atmosphere**—defined in this context as the overall impression conveyed by a store's physical layout, decor, and surroundings. The atmosphere can create a relaxed feeling or a busy one, a sense of luxury or of efficiency, a friendly attitude or a cold one, a sense of organization or of clutter, a mood of fun or a serious mood. The look at Disney stores is designed to make children feel they are actually in an amusement park. HMV music stores have a recording studio feel, with areas for private listening. Theme restaurants such as Rainforest Café, with its moving animals and jungle décor, make customers feel as if they are part of an adventure instead of merely eating a meal. Roots clothing stores, with their log walls, project a sense of the rustic outdoors.

More often these days, retailers are adding an element of entertainment to their stores. The Nike Town store in Chicago looks more like a museum than a traditional retail store. The three-storey space displays its products amidst life-size Michael Jordan statues and glassed-in relics such as Nolan Ryan's baseball shoes. A History of Air exhibit explains the pockets of air in the soles of some Nike shoes. A video theatre plays Nike commercials and short films featuring Nike gear.

The layout of retail stores is a key factor in their success. Layout is planned so that all space in the store is used effectively, including aisles, fixtures, merchandise displays, and nonselling areas. Effective store layout ensures the customer's shopping ease and convenience; it also has a powerful influence on customer traffic patterns and on purchasing behaviour.

This enormous frog sculpture crowns the entrance to the Rainforest Cafe. Coupled with the giant toadstools that flank the doors, the sculptures that decorate the outside of the restaurant create an impression of fun and whimsy.

Layout includes product placement. Many technologically advanced retailers are using a technique called *market-basket analysis* to analyze the huge amounts of data collected through their point-of-purchase scanning equipment. This analysis looks for products that are commonly purchased together to help retailers place products in the right places.[48] Wal-Mart uses market-basket analysis to determine where to stock products. Bananas are placed not only in the produce section but also in the cereal aisle. Kleenex tissues are in the paper goods aisle but are also mixed in with the cold medicines. Measuring spoons are in the housewares and also hanging next to Crisco shortening. In October, flashlights are not only in the hardware aisle but also with the Halloween costumes.[49]

How can a company create an atmosphere on its Website? Visit some of your favourite retailers to see if they have been able to recreate the atmosphere of their stores on the Internet. Is it easier to create an on-line atmosphere for certain products, services, or industries?

on line

ethics in marketing

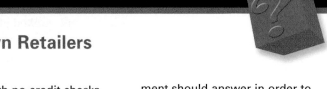

The Ethical Dilemma of Rent-to-Own Retailers

There are more than 7,500 rent-to-own outlets in the United States. RTO retail outlets provide a variety of products to their customers, including furniture, appliances, electronics, and jewellery. RTO contracts allow customers to take ownership of the merchandise at the end of a specified series of payments. However, the $4 billion RTO retailing industry has been under fire lately from critics who allege that these stores charge exorbitant interest rates on consumer goods and unfairly target poor and minority consumers who don't have credit cards. Several lawsuits have already been decided in favour of customers who dealt with rent-to-own retailers.

Most often, rent-to-own customers are the consumers who can least afford the interest rates and fees charged—low-income individuals whose credit is not good or who have difficulty establishing credit. Sometimes these individuals believe they have nowhere else to turn to buy the goods they want, or they simply don't understand how much they are being charged in the long run. RTO outlets are generally located in or near less affluent communities. Promotions are targeted toward members of these communities, and offer the opportunity to rent to own at weekly or monthly rental rates with no credit checks. Because of their lower socioeconomic status, these customers generally lack cash to purchase outright from ordinary retailers and are therefore especially sensitive to no-credit check pitches.

At the heart of the RTO dispute is a single question: Are rent-to-own transactions instalment sales at usurious interest rates, or are they, as the industry suggests, unique transactions with exceptionally high costs to justify the high prices? To decide, readers must first understand how RTO deals work. At the onset of the agreement, the customer signs a contract spelling out the cost of the weekly or monthly payments, the number of payments to be made, and the total that will be paid. If the consumer makes all payments as scheduled, he or she keeps the item at the end of the deal. If the consumer is late or misses a payment, the property can be repossessed and any equity that the consumer thought was built up in the item is gone. In some cases, if the payment is simply late, the contract allows the consumer to "reinstate" the existing contract for a fee.

The *Canadian Consumer Handbook*[50] lists the following questions that a consumer considering entering into a rent-to-own agreement should answer in order to avoid unexpected pitfalls:

- What is the total cost of the item?
- Am I getting a new or used item?
- Can I purchase the item before the end of the rental term? If so, how is this price calculated?
- Will I get credit for all of my payments if I decide to purchase the item?
- Is there a charge for repairs during the rental period? Will I get a replacement while the rented item is not in my possession?
- What happens if I am late on a payment? Will the item be repossessed?
- Will I pay a penalty if I return the item before the end of the contract period?

What do you think needs to be done to resolve the ethical dilemmas in the rent-to-own industry? What consumer education programs could be developed to help lower-income consumers purchase the goods they want without having to pay the higher prices charged by RTO retailers? Are there some programs that other retailers could develop that would provide low-income consumers with less costly retail options?

The following are the strongest factors influencing a store's atmosphere:

- *Employee type and density:* Employee type refers to employees' general characteristics—for instance, neat, friendly, knowledgeable, service oriented. Density is the number of employees per thousand square feet of selling space. A discounter like Kmart has a low employee density; this creates a casual, "do-it-yourself" atmosphere. Holt Renfrew's density is much higher, denoting readiness to serve the customer's every whim. Too many employees and not enough customers can suggest desperation, and can intimidate customers.
- *Merchandise type and density:* The type of merchandise carried and how it is displayed affect the atmosphere. A prestigious retailer like Eatons carries the

best brand names and displays them in neat, uncluttered arrangements. Discounters and off-price retailers may sell some well-known brands, but many carry seconds or out-of-season goods. Often they stack their merchandise so high that it falls into the aisles; this helps create the impression that "We've got so much stuff, we're practically giving it away."

- *Fixture type and density:* Fixtures can be elegant (rich woods), or trendy (chrome and smoked glass), or they can consist of old, beat-up tables, such as in antique stores. The fixtures should be consistent with the general atmosphere the store is trying to create. The Gap creates a relaxed and uncluttered atmosphere by displaying its merchandise on tables and shelves rather than on traditional pipe racks; this allows customers to see and touch the merchandise more easily. Some cafés and drinking establishments are now providing PCs with Internet access to get customers to stay longer.
- *Sound:* Sound can be pleasant or unpleasant for customers. Classical music at a nice Italian restaurant helps create ambiance, just as country-and-western music does at a truck stop. Music can also entice customers to stay in the store longer and buy more, or eat quickly and then leave the table for others. Researchers have found that rapid music tends to make people eat more, chew less, and take bigger bites, whereas slow music prompts people to dine more slowly and eat less.[51] Retailers can tailor their musical atmosphere to their shoppers' demographics and to the merchandise they are selling. Music can be used to create an image, control the pace of the store traffic, and attract or direct the shopper's attention. Harrods in London features music by live harpists, pianists, and marching bagpipers to create different atmospheres in different departments. Coffee shops are also getting into the music business, as are theme restaurants like the Hard Rock Cafe, Planet Hollywood, the Harley-Davidson Cafe, and the Rainforest Cafe; all of these establishments turn eating a hamburger and fries into an experience. Au Bon Pain, Starbucks, and Victoria's Secret have all sold copies of their background music, in the hope that the music will remind consumers of the feeling of being in their stores.
- *Odours:* Smell can stimulate or depress sales. The wonderful aroma of pastries and breads entices bakery customers. If a grocery store pumps in the smell of baked goods, sales in that department increase dramatically. Department stores have pumped in fragrances that are pleasing to their target markets, with favourable results. Not surprisingly, more and more retailers are using fragrance as a key design element, as important as layout, lighting, and background music. Research suggests that people evaluate merchandise more positively, spend more time shopping, and are generally in a better mood when an agreeable odour is present. Retailers are using fragrances as an extension of their retail strategy. The Rainforest Café pumps fresh-flower extracts into its retail sections.
- *Visual factors:* Colours and lighting can create a mood and focus attention. Red, yellow, and orange are considered warm colours and are used when a feeling of warmth and closeness is desired. Cool colours such as blue, green, and violet are used to open up closed-in places and create an air of elegance and cleanliness. Some colours are better for display. Diamonds are most striking to look at against black or dark-blue velvet. Lighting can also strongly affect the store's atmosphere. Jewellery is best displayed under high-intensity spotlights, cosmetics under more natural light. Many retailers have found that natural lighting, either from windows or skylights, can increase sales. The lighting outside the store is also important: the store's façade can create a favourable first impression with shoppers.

Personnel and Customer Service

People are a unique aspect of retailing. Most retail sales involve a customer–salesperson relationship, if only briefly. When customers shop at a grocery store, the cashiers check and bag their groceries. When customers shop at a prestigious clothier, the sales clerks may help select the styles, sizes, and colours. They may also help in the fitting process, offer alteration services, wrap purchases, and even offer a glass of champagne. Sales personnel provide their customers with the amount of service prescribed in the retail strategy of the store.

A recent study found that 35 percent of consumers have had negative shopping experiences, with nearly one in ten switching retailers afterwards.[52] Good service is even more important when the economy is growing slowly, when companies survive by keeping the customers they have. Studies show that customer retention results in above-average profits and superior growth. Home Depot has embraced this philosophy and provides its customers with excellent service. Home Depot salespeople, often recruited from the ranks of carpenters and electricians, are encouraged to spend all the time needed with customers, even if it's hours.

Retail salespeople serve another important selling function: they persuade shoppers to buy. So they must be able to persuade customers that what they are selling is what the customer needs. Salespeople are trained in two common selling techniques: trading up and suggestion selling. Trading up means persuading customers to buy higher-priced items than they originally intended to buy. To avoid selling customers things they don't need or want, salespeople should take care when applying trading-up techniques. Suggestion selling, a common practice with most retailers, seeks to broaden customers' original purchases with related items. The cashiers at Staples often ask customers whether they would like to include the weekly stationery specials with their purchases. Suggestion selling and trading up should always help shoppers recognize true needs; it should not be used to sell merchandise that customers don't want.

Global Retailing

7 Discuss the challenges of expanding retailing operations into global markets

It is no accident that Canadian retailers are now testing their store concepts on a global basis. With the battle for market share among domestic retailers showing no signs of abating, and with growth prospects dismal, mature retailers are looking for growth opportunities in the growing consumer economies of other countries. In terms of domestic operations, over half of Canadian on-line retailers view their main competition as coming from American retailers.[53]

Several events have made international expansion more feasible. First, the spread of communication networks and mass media is homogenizing tastes and product preferences around the world. As a result, the casual North American lifestyle and the products that symbolize it, such as Levi's jeans and Roots headgear, are becoming more appealing. Second, trade agreements such as the North American Free Trade Agreement (NAFTA) and the European Union (EU) have lowered tariffs and made it easier for Canadian retailers to expand into Mexico, the United States, and Europe.[54] Last, high growth potential in underserved markets is luring foreign retailers into Latin America, South America, and Asia. China has one-quarter of the world's people but has only recently opened its markets to outsiders. Although most Chinese still have weak spending power, it is expected that China's economy will eclipse all others in the next twenty-five years.[55]

Before plunging into the international arena, retailers need to do their homework. According to analysts at the consulting firm Ernst & Young, retailers should not expand abroad until they have achieved a secure and profitable position domestically. Also, they must take a long-term perspective: many foreign

Auchan

Visit the Website of one of France's largest retailers. How well is Auchan reaching global customers with its site? Click on "anglais" for the English version.

www.auchan.com

on line

operations take longer to set up and longer to turn a profit. Finally, a retailer's global strategy must be made to mesh with its overall strategy. Retailers should begin by determining what their core competency is (e.g., low prices, a distinctive look, excellent customer service), and then determine whether the local market would respond to it. The Gap can attribute its international success to its allegiance to the "American casual" formula. Similarly, wherever shoppers travel, they can reasonably expect to experience Wal-Mart's friendliness, the quality, service, and cleanliness of McDonald's, and the brand statements of Marks & Spencer, The Body Shop, and IKEA.[56]

Besides keeping their core strengths when going global, retailers need to be prepared to make any necessary adjustments. So a big part of a retailer's advance "homework" involves learning which products will sell in foreign markets. Colour preferences, taste preferences, promotional campaigns, service expectations, the

exhibit 14.4

Factors Used to Analyze Global Retail Markets

- *Market size and economics:* This involves analyzing factors such as population and demographic trends, economics (including GDP and consumer spending), and political trends that could make or break the success of a retailer in a foreign country. The central government in China has been urging middle-income Chinese to buy their own housing. For retailers, this means plenty of new apartments and homes to fill with more electronics, bigger refrigerators and kitchens, and clothes (because of bigger closets).
- *Infrastructure and distribution*: This involves building global supply chains and securing qualified labour—often a particular challenge in emerging markets. In logistical terms, expansion within North America is simpler. In many developing countries such as China, underdeveloped transportation infrastructures and other logistical weaknesses pose daunting distribution challenges to retailers.
- *Competition*: This involves assessing the current competitive landscape and how the retailer could bring innovations to the market. Compared to the United States, Mexico is grossly understored. That country has less than 550 square feet of food and apparel stores per thousand people, compared to 20,000 square feet per thousand in the United States. Similarly, Europe has a higher percentage of independent, mom-and-pop operations. The highly fragmented European market appears ripe for invasion by well-capitalized big-box retailers.
- *Operations*: This involves assessing how operational concerns such as those relating to real estate, labour, and inventory will affect the success of overseas units. Labour laws vary drastically from country to country. Cultural differences affect holidays, the number of vacation days per employee, and hours of operation. Canadian retail stores are open an average of seventy hours a week; in Greece, retail stores are open only about forty-six hours a week.
- *Financial and tax reporting:* This involves addressing issues such as currency fluctuations, the hedging of risks, and taxation. A number of retailers are entering Argentina, Brazil, and Chile because their markets are open and their business economies and financial systems are more "Western-like."
- *Merchandise acceptability*: This involves retailers researching local consumer needs, preferences, and buying habits, and then adjusting their assortments to match the region's culture. In Japan, back-to-school sales are held in April. In Europe, August is a traditionally slow retailing month because most Europeans are on vacation. When IKEA came to North America it learned that it needed to offer larger beds, furniture with larger drawers, and different assortments of kitchen utensils.
- *Partnering capability*: This involves considering the availability of suitable partners in the foreign country or region. Starbucks typically picks distribution and supply partners before entering a new a country or region. Poor strategic alliances ruin a retail operation.

Source: Adapted from "Global Retailing '97," Ernst & Young special report for *Chain Store Age*, December 1997. Reprinted by permission from *Chain Store Age*. Copyright 1998 Lebhar-Friedman, Inc., 425 Park Avenue, NY, NY 10022.

global perspectives

Japan Wakes Up and Smells Starbucks

Starbucks is giving Japanese coffee bar chains the jitters. When a billboard proclaiming "Opening Soon: Starbucks Coffee" appeared in Tokyo's fashionable Omotesando district, local coffee bars went into a flurry of activity. One nearby coffee bar enlisted real estate agents to help determine where the new Starbucks might open shop. Other Japanese coffee bars began offering "Seattle Coffee" or remodelled their shops to resemble Starbucks outlets. Starbucks' ambitious expansion plans for the Pacific Rim could indeed make it one of the world's largest coffee shop chains.

Starbucks opened its first Japanese coffee bar in Tokyo's swank Ginza shopping district. Japanese coffee purveyors fear Starbucks, which has a reputation for knowing how to create a thirst. Starbucks's entrance in the Japanese market worries Japanese coffee executives because they do not know how to replicate it. Starbucks may be able to create new coffee markets in Japan where the Japanese themselves have failed.

Japanese consumers may need a little hand holding at first to guide them through the thicket of grandes and frappucinos. However, Yuji Tsunoda, president of Starbucks Coffee Japan, thinks they'll catch on fast. "Four years ago, how many Americans knew what a latte, doppio espresso, or cappucino were?" he says. "It's up to us to help our customers understand coffee better."

The coffee is cheaper at the coffee bars down the street (just 160 yen, or $1.50, versus 250 yen, about $2.30), but with their low ceilings, somber interiors, and cafeteria-style trays, they hardly evoke a gourmet ambiance. Neither does the food. The snacks on offer at the older coffee bars include fried chicken with spaghetti on a hot dog bun and a salty fried noodle sandwich with seaweed on top. Starbucks takes a more epicurean tack, offering cookies, muffins, and croissants, along with sandwiches made from pita bread and sesame seed bagels.[57]

What retailing strategies would you suggest local Japanese coffee retailers consider to compete with Starbucks? Do you think Starbucks's cookie-cutter approach to selling coffee and snacks in global markets will be successful? Explain.

preferred cut of a garment, and shopper's physiques vary worldwide; so does the acceptance by customers of foreign brands and private label merchandise. Differences also dictate where goods should be placed within stores. In some cultures, men's and women's clothing should not be displayed side by side. Latin Americans want fruits and vegetables located at the front of a store. In North America it is standard practice to place lower-priced private label merchandise to the right of name brands, because "natural" eye flow causes shoppers to comparison shop to the right. That merchandising approach does not necessarily hold true in countries where people read up and down or right to left.[58]

Read about Starbucks's adventures breaking into the Japanese market in this chapter's "Global Perspectives" box.

Trends in Retailing

8
Describe future trends in retailing

Predicting the future is always risky, but there are four broad trends in retailing: the use of entertainment to lure customers; an effort to provide greater convenience for today's "precision shoppers"; the provision of customer management programs; and multiple channel integration.

Entertainment

Adding entertainment to the retail environment has been one of the most popular strategies in retailing in recent years. Both small retailers and national chains are using entertainment to distinguish themselves from the competition.

Entertainment is not limited to music, videos, fashion shows, or guest appearances by soap opera stars and book authors. Entertainment includes anything that offers shoppers a good time, that stimulates their senses or emotions, and that gets them into the store, keeps them there, and encourages them to buy and later come back. The quiet, comfortable couches and cafes of bookstores and book-and-music retailers like Indigo add entertainment value. To catch the attention of younger consumers, some apparel stores and theme restaurants are showing music videos on giant screens. Future Shop lets customers listen to music and play video games before purchasing these products.

Convenience and Efficiency

Today's consumers are looking for ways to shop more quickly and efficiently. Around 75 percent of women are now working full- or part-time, so consumers no longer have the hours they once did to devote to shopping. One study found that consumers are going to malls half as often as they used to the early 1990s; once there, they visit one-third as many stores as they used to.[59] Today, the average mall visit lasts only an hour, down from ninety minutes in 1982.[60]

In part, this decline reflects the increase in the numbers of working women; however, all consumers are more stretched for time. In trying to balance work with entertainment and family activities, they have become "precision shoppers." Today's consumers are more purposeful in their shopping—that is, they are visiting fewer stores and spending less time in them. They are also less likely to buy on impulse.[61]

HMV listening posts have become a fundamental in-store component. The retailer recently debuted HMV.com interactive kiosks at two locations where consumers can research and order music on-line, thus allowing the company to capitalize on today's technology.

All of this means that retailers must learn to better manage their patrons' experiences. Consumers are no longer satisfied because a store merely met their expectations. They want retailers to provide delightful experiences, to anticipate their expectations, and to go the extra mile to exceed those expectations. To this end, retailers can provide shopping assistance, deliver and install products, service them well after the sale, and dispose of and renew the products.

Retailers can do all this by offering baby-sitting services, free drinks and refreshments, preferred parking spaces, and pick-up for shoppers who do not want to fight traffic. Supermarkets and drugstores are now providing drive-through windows, flu shots, cholesterol screenings, and even in-store health clinics.[62] In addition, retailers are maintaining records of consumers' preferences, the better to provide individualized attention. Perhaps the store's records indicate that a consumer prefers a particular style of suit; the sales associate can then show the consumer the new suits for the season in that style.[63]

Experts predict that retailers—especially supermarkets—are about to become true marketers rather than merely distribution centres. For instance, packaged goods and staples will no longer be sold in supermarkets. Instead they will be delivered directly to consumers at home, within fifteen minutes of the order' being placed; this will free shoppers to visit stores for things they enjoy buying—fresh produce, meats, the ingredients for a dinner party, and so on. Consumers who need staples will use hand scanners to record products' bar codes and update electronic shopping lists. Magazine ads will also carry bar codes so that consumers will be able to scan pages to put new products on their lists. The Gap is testing a program, called Gap to Go, that offers quick home or office delivery of apparel. Customers fill out a form listing items such as socks, caps, belts, and jeans, and fax it or submit it on line; they can then have their order delivered within an hour for a delivery fee.[64]

Customer Management

In today's retailing environment, a prime location and unique merchandise are not the keys to success that they used to be.[65] Retailers are now recognizing that customer equity is one of the only ways to sustain true competitive advantage. Through customer management strategies, leading retailers are intensifying their efforts to identify, satisfy, and retain their best customers and maximize value for them. Utilizing database technology to manage customer relationships is called one-to-one marketing and is the topic of Chapter 18.

Three emerging customer management strategies that retailers are embracing are customer relationship marketing, loyalty programs, and clienteling. Regardless of the strategy used, the intent is the same—to foster loyalty and develop an ongoing dialogue with the retailer's best customers. *Customer relationship management* (CRM) arose from the need to target more accurately a fragmented customer base that was becoming more and more difficult to reach through mass advertising vehicles such as television and newspapers. True CRM links customer information to transaction data collected through point-of-sale scanning systems to glean knowledge about customer purchase histories, shopping preferences, and motivations; it then transmits that knowledge throughout the organization to make customer-centred business decisions.

Armed with richer customer databases and the technology to gather and analyze customer and sales data, retailers are now developing *loyalty programs.* These programs identify and reward the retailer's best customers. Sears' KidVantage program provides savings to members with young children.

Another approach to managing and building long-term relationships with best customers is *clienteling.* Saks Fifth Avenue strongly emphasizes personal contact between staff and customers. Associates collect and maintain detailed electronic client profiles, which are then used to provide enhanced service. Sales associates are encouraged to serve clients across all departments so that the associates, already familiar with size and style preferences, can address clients' complete wardrobe needs instead of merely selling merchandise from their assigned departments.

Channel Integration

Many retailers are adopting the Internet as a commerce channel; as a result, companies are having to find ways to integrate their various retail channels. Some now allow customers to order items on line but pick them up at the nearest retail outlet. Trends like these are allowing companies to capitalize on today's technology.

LOOKING BACK

Think back to the opening vignette about Roots's newest retailing adventures. Retailers are no longer simply competing with other retailers such as discounters, specialty stores, and department stores, and with other forms of retailing such as direct mail; they are having to identify ways to attract customer attention. Retailers are realizing that they must give consumers a good reason to shop in their stores. To this end, many stores are transforming their retailing strategies to reflect what the consumer wants: more for less.

Summary

1 **Discuss the importance of retailing in the Canadian economy.** Retailing plays a vital role in the Canadian economy for two main reasons. First, retail businesses contribute to our high standard of living by providing a vast number and diversity of goods and services. Second, retailing employs a large part of the Canadian working population—over fourteen million people.

2 **Explain the dimensions by which retailers can be classified.** Many different kinds of retailers exist. A retail establishment can be classified according to its ownership, level of service, product assortment, and price. On the basis of ownership, retailers can be broadly differentiated as independent retailers, chain stores, or franchise outlets. The level of service retailers provide can be classified along a continuum of high to low. Retailers also classify themselves by the breadth and depth of their product assortment; some retailers have concentrated product assortments whereas others have extensive product assortments. Last, general price levels also classify a store, from discounters offering low prices to exclusive specialty stores where high prices are the norm. Retailers use the latter three variables to position themselves in the marketplace.

3 **Describe the major types of retail operations**. The major types of retail stores are department stores, specialty retailers, supermarkets, convenience stores, discount stores, and restaurants. Department stores carry a wide assortment of shopping and specialty goods, are organized into relatively independent departments, and offset higher prices by emphasizing customer service and decor. Specialty retailers typically carry a narrower but deeper assortment of merchandise, emphasizing distinctive products and a high level of customer service. Supermarkets are large, self-service retailers that offer a wide variety of food products and some nonfood items. Convenience stores carry a limited line of high-turnover convenience goods. Discount stores offer low-priced general merchandise and consist of four types: full-line discounters, discount specialty retailers, warehouse clubs, and off-price retailers. Finally, restaurants straddle the line between the retailing and services industries; though restaurants sell a product, food and drink, to final consumers, they also can be considered service marketers because they provide consumers with the service of preparing food and providing table service.

4 **Discuss nonstore retailing techniques**. Nonstore retailing, which is shopping outside a store setting, has three major categories. Automatic vending uses machines to offer products for sale. In direct retailing, the sales transaction occurs in a home setting, typically through door-to-door sales or party plan selling. Direct marketing refers to the techniques used to get consumers to buy from their homes or places of business. Such techniques include direct mail, catalogues and mail order, telemarketing, and electronic retailing (e.g., home shopping channels and on-line shopping over the Internet).

5 **Define e-tailing, and outline the issues surrounding its use.** E-tailing allows companies to service the rapidly growing market segment that is comfortable with technology and the Internet as a business channel. It is a natural extension to traditional retailing that can capitalize on existing distribution and supply chain networks, but can also be a cost-effective means of incorporating new, value-added features to enhance the consumer experience. Several issues continue to impede the rapid adoption of this shopping option. These include consumers who remain hesitant to provide personal and financial data to companies via the Internet, and the impersonal shopping experience.

6 **List the major tasks involved in developing a retail marketing strategy**. Retail management begins with defining the target market, typically on the basis of demographic, geographic, or psychographic characteristics. After determining the

target market, retail managers must develop the six variables of the retailing mix: product, promotion, place, price, presentation, and personnel.

7 Discuss the challenges of expanding retailing operations into global markets. With increased competition and slow domestic growth, mature retailers are looking for growth opportunities in the developing consumer economies of other countries. The homogenization of tastes and product preferences around the world, the lowering of trade barriers, and the emergence of underserved markets have made the prospects of expanding across national borders more feasible for many retailers. Retailers wanting to expand globally should first determine what their core competency is and determine whether this differentiation is what the local market wants. Retailers also need to skilfully make adjustments in product mix to meet local demands.

8 Describe future trends in retailing. Three major trends are evident in retailing today. First, adding entertainment to the retail environment is one of the most popular strategies in retailing in recent years. Small retailers as well as national chains are using entertainment to set themselves apart from the competition. Second, retailers of the future will offer more convenience and efficiency to consumers as consumers become more precise on their shopping trips. Staples won't be sold in stores but instead will be delivered directly to the consumer, freeing shoppers to visit stores for products they enjoy buying. Advances in technology will make it easier for consumers to obtain the products they want. Last, more and more retailers are using the information they collect about their customers at the point of sale to develop customer management programs, including customer relationship marketing, loyalty programs, and clienteling.

Discussion and Writing Questions

1. Discuss the possible marketing implications of the recent trend toward supercentres, which combine a supermarket and a full-line discount store. How does this affect small local retailers?
2. Identify and explain the major strengths and weaknesses of the Internet as a retailing channel.
3. Study the marketing of a major Canadian retailer, and discuss the elements you feel led to its success.
4. You want to convince your boss, the owner of a bookstore, of the importance of store atmosphere. Write a memo citing specific examples of how a store's atmosphere affects your own shopping behaviour.
5. Write a brief article about how consumer demand for convenience and efficiency is influencing the future of retailing, and what retailers must do to address this. Substantiate your answer with articles and other outside sources.
6. Your retail clothing company is considering expanding into Mexico. What information about the country and its customs should you collect before opening a store in Mexico?
7. Form a team of three classmates. Identify at least three different retail stores in your city where pet supplies are sold. Include nonstore forms of retailing such as catalogues, the Internet, and veterinarian offices. Team members should divide up and visit all the different retailing outlets. Prepare a report describing the differences in brands and products sold at each of the retailing formats, and the differences in store characteristics and service levels. For example, which brands are sold through mass merchandisers? independent specialty stores? other venues? Why are different products and brands distributed through different types of stores?
8. Go to the Gift.ca gift shop (**www.thegift.ca**). How is this site helping both soon-to-be-married couples and their guests? What are the benefits to this approach to gift registries?

Do You Know These Terms?

9. How much does the most powerful computer with the fastest modem, most memory, largest monitor, biggest hard drive, and all the available peripherals cost at **www.dell.com**? How does this price compare with the Future Shop at **www.futureshop.ca**? How can you explain price differences between the two retail operations?
10. Visit **www.roots.ca**. How is the company trying to create an atmosphere on its site? Are these efforts effective?

Application for Small Business

Ron Johnson is developing a retail strategy to open up his new athletic shoe and sports equipment store. He has decided to carry Nike and Converse as his two lines of athletic shoes. This will give him top-of-the-line merchandise (Nike) and a lower-priced, high-quality alternative (Converse). He has obtained permission from one of his former professors to hold brainstorming sessions in a couple of her classes. From these sessions, he has identified the following criteria that customers might apply in selecting a particular athletic shoe: (1) attractiveness/style/colour, (2) brand name, (3) comfort, (4) price, (5) endorsement, and (6) quality. He has also determined that location, friends' recommendations, brands carried, and store atmosphere are important in selecting a place to purchase athletic shoes.

Questions

1. What type of retailing strategy should Ron use?
2. Which elements of the retailing mix are relatively more important?

CBC VIDEO CASE

Pushing Pop

A new trend among major soft drink retailers is the establishment of programs aimed at securing exclusive marketing relationships with various youth institutions, including public schools. Throughout British Columbia, Coca-Cola and Pepsi-Cola maintain exclusive marketing contracts with many public schools, from elementary through to secondary institutions. Generally, under these contracts, the schools are only allowed to sell milk and the product lines of the soft drink company with which they have the contract. However, the contracts tend to extend beyond product offerings and to filter into all aspects of school life, and are being directly linked to such things as school pride. In return for pushing the drink company's products, the school administration obtains revenues and other monetary benefits from the relationship. The scenario has spurred a debate over whether the public school system should become a new marketing channel for products targeted at teens. The following accounts outline some British Columbia examples.

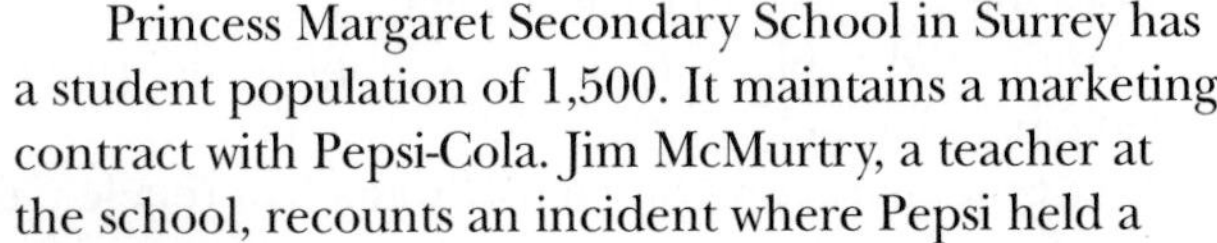

Princess Margaret Secondary School in Surrey has a student population of 1,500. It maintains a marketing contract with Pepsi-Cola. Jim McMurtry, a teacher at the school, recounts an incident where Pepsi held a contest for a student to win a pager. To be eligible for the contest, students had to name various Pepsi products. Pepsi photographed the winners, who were of course holding Pepsi products in such a way that the labels were visible.

Robert Bateman Secondary School in Abbotsford has a student population of 1,000 and maintains a marketing contract with Coca-Cola. As with other cases, the contract stipulates that the school is not allowed to market and sell other drink products. A class project that involved marketing students developing a mock marketing plan for a local soft drink company contradicted these terms; this led to Coke asking the school administration to have all reference to the competing soda company removed from the school. The conflict arose when a Coca-Cola service person saw student-made signs advertising Jones Soda in the school halls. Within two days, the posters were removed. Since the episode, both sides have conceded that there was some overreaction and misunderstanding. The teacher in this case took the stand that the marketing efforts had moved from vending machines directly into the classroom environment.

Como Lake Middle School in Coquitlam has a student population of 560 and holds an exclusive marketing contract with Coca-Cola. One teacher from the school recounted an incident where an announcement over the PA system informed the students that students who arrived at the administration office bearing a Coke product would be eligible to win a prize. The school administration, in its efforts to counteract the claim that they were actively promoting the brand within the school, brought in a senior representative from Coke to address the student population. During the address, students were informed about the healthy aspects of Coke's products.

Vancouver Technical School has a student population of 1,800 and maintains a marketing contract with Coca-Cola. Under the nondisclosure clause signed between the school and the company, the school administration was not allowed to divulge the specifics of the contract, which conflicted with some groups who felt that public institutions should not enter into such agreements. The principal did reveal that the school received a cash lump sum for exclusivity as well as a commission on sales from vending machines throughout the building. His argument for entering into the relationship was that schools are in an unfortunate predicament of being underfunded yet expected to deliver a quality product.

Some common themes of these cases were that the contracts were justified by the school administrations and that the schools were financially rewarded for selling the soft drink products. In some of the cases, teachers were hesistant to come forward with specific stories. The soft drink companies believe they are providing a service to students and contributing to the educational process by sponsoring school events and promoting school pride.

Source:

CBC, *Undercurrents*, "Pushing Pop," October 8, 2000.

Questions

1. Why would major soft drink retailers want to obtain exclusive rights to sell their products within a school?
2. Should school administrations be allowed to market and promote certain products to students?
3. Why are vending machines an appropriate retail channel to use for selling products in a school? Are there any other retail options available for soft drink companies?

CHAPTER

15

LEARNING OBJECTIVES

After studying this chapter, you should be able to

1. Discuss the importance of pricing decisions to the economy and to the individual firm
2. List and explain a variety of pricing objectives
3. Explain the role of demand in price determination
4. Describe cost-oriented pricing strategies
5. Demonstrate how the product life cycle, competition, distribution and promotion strategies, customer demands, the Internet and extranets, and perceptions of quality can affect price
6. Describe the procedure for setting the right price
7. Identify the legal and ethical constraints on pricing decisions
8. Explain how discounts, geographic pricing, and other special pricing tactics can be used to fine tune the base price

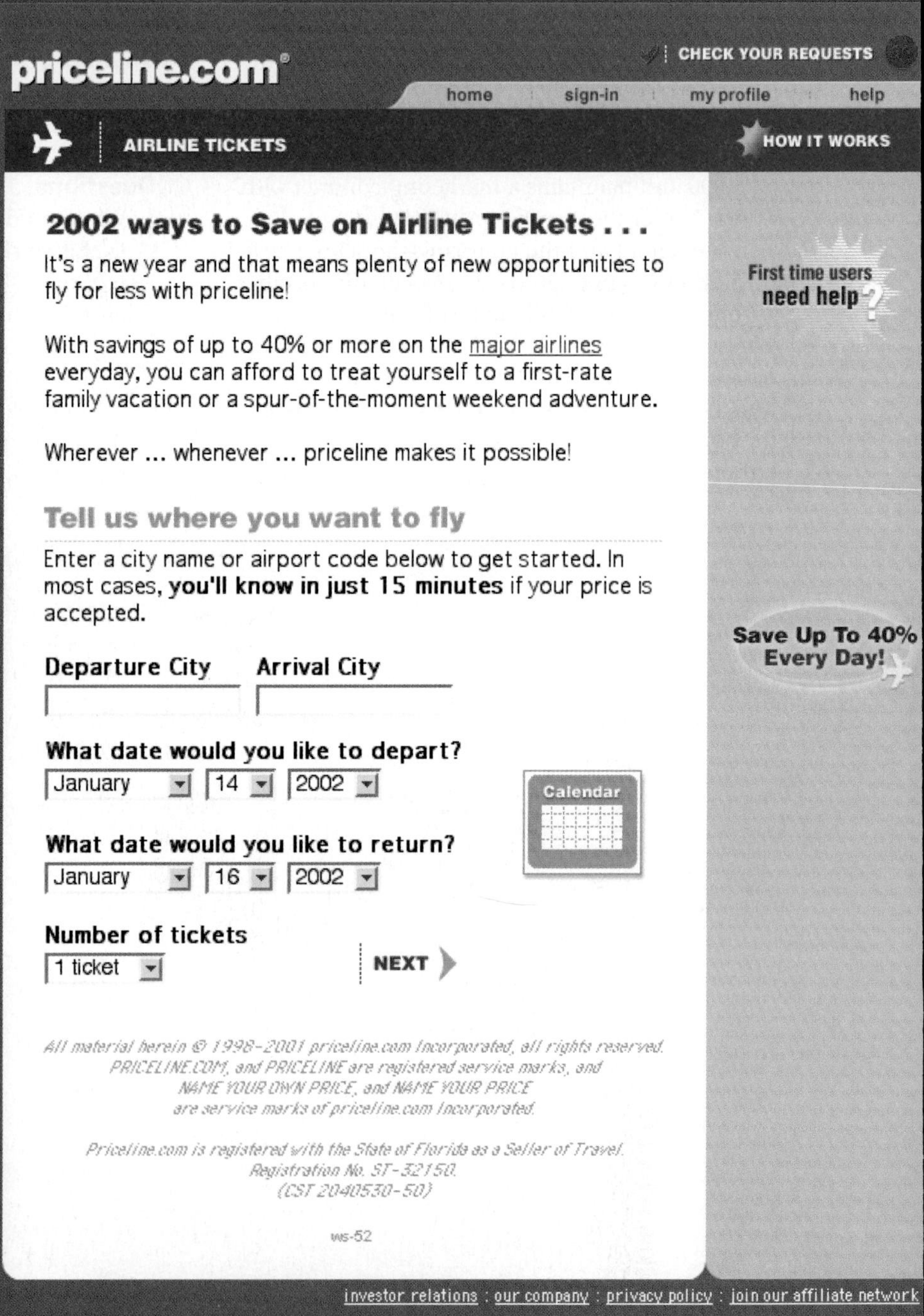

priceline.com
CHECK YOUR REQUESTS
home
sign-in
my profile
help
AIRLINE TICKETS
HOW IT WORKS
2002 ways to Save on Airline Tickets . . .
It's a new year and that means plenty of new opportunities to fly for less with priceline!
With savings of up to 40% or more on the major airlines everyday, you can afford to treat yourself to a first-rate family vacation or a spur-of-the-moment weekend adventure.
Wherever ... whenever ... priceline makes it possible!
Tell us where you want to fly
Enter a city name or airport code below to get started. In most cases, you'll know in just 15 minutes if your price is accepted.
Departure City
Arrival City
What date would you like to depart?
January
14
2002
Calendar
What date would you like to return?
January
16
2002
Number of tickets
1 ticket
NEXT
All material herein © 1998–2001 priceline.com Incorporated, all rights reserved. PRICELINE.COM, and PRICELINE are registered service marks, and NAME YOUR OWN PRICE, and NAME YOUR PRICE are service marks of priceline.com Incorporated.
Priceline.com is registered with the State of Florida as a Seller of Travel. Registration No. ST-32150. (CST 2040530-50)
ws-52
First time users need help?
Save Up To 40% Every Day!
investor relations : our company : privacy policy : join our affiliate network

PRICING AND SETTING THE RIGHT PRICE

The full-page newspaper ads trumpeting the debut of Priceline.com showed *Star Trek* captain William Shatner wearing an expression so intense that he seemed to be contemplating a Klingon attack rather than a new way to buy airline tickets. Or perhaps he was simply trying to decide whether this new Website, which allows people to name their own prices on airline tickets, hotels, and many other items, is a good deal or a science fiction fantasy.

Here's how it works. A customer who wants to take a vacation, for example, logs on to **www.priceline.com** and types in when and where she wants to travel, what she wants to pay, and her credit card number. Priceline then sends this "bid" to the airlines. If a carrier accepts it, a ticket is issued within one hour (or one day for international flights), and the credit card is charged.

According to CEO Jay Walker, the scheme is based on the fact that the major airlines fly with some 500,000 seats empty every day. For them, "Priceline is a dream come true. When was the last time an airline had customers take out their credit card and say, 'Put me on any flight where you've got room?'"

Having begun with airline tickets, Priceline is now adding long-distance telephone services, home financing, new cars, rental cars, and hotel rooms to its Internet service. It is intent on boldly going where no on-line shopping service has gone before.[1]

The Priceline concept illustrates how demand and supply determine price. The consumer puts the price he or she is willing to pay (demand) into the system, and sellers decide whether they want to provide the product or service at that price (supply). Will the Internet have a big impact on pricing? How does cost fit into the pricing equation? Can price influence the perceived quality of a product? How does competition affect price?

Priceline

Learn more about how Priceline works by visiting its Website. Would you be willing to book your next flight this way? Which of Priceline's services would you be willing to try? Can you think of other markets that Priceline could enter?

on line

The Importance of Price

1

Discuss the importance of pricing decisions to the economy and to the individual firm

Price means one thing to the consumer and something else to the seller. To the consumer, it is the cost of something. To the seller, price is revenue, the main source of profits. In the broadest sense, price allocates resources in a free market economy. With so many ways of looking at price, it's no wonder marketing managers find it a challenge to set prices.

What Is Price?

price
That which is given up in an exchange to acquire a good or service.

Price is that which is given up in an exchange to acquire a good or service. Price is typically the money exchanged for the good or service.

Price, however, can relate to anything with perceived value, not just money. When goods and services are exchanged for each other, with no money changing hands, the trade is called barter. If you exchange this book for a chemistry text at the end of term, you have engaged in barter. The price you paid for the chemistry book was this textbook.

The Importance of Price to Marketing Managers

revenue
The price charged to customers multiplied by the number of units sold.

profit
Revenue minus expenses.

Prices determine revenues, which are the main sources of profit for an organization. **Revenue** is the price charged to customers multiplied by the number of units sold. Revenue is what pays for every activity of the company: production, finance, sales, distribution, and so on. What's left over (if anything) is **profit**. Managers usually strive to charge a price that will earn a fair profit.

To earn a profit, managers must set a price that is neither too high nor too low, and that equals the perceived value to target consumers. If a price is set too high, many consumers will perceive the value as less than the cost, and sales opportunities will be lost. Many mainstream purchasers of cars, sporting goods, CDs, tools, wedding gowns, and computers are buying "used" or "preowned" items to get a better deal. When the price of a new product is set too high, this may encourage some shoppers to go to a "preowned" or consignment retailer.

Conversely, if a price is too low, many consumers will perceive the good or service as a great value, but the firm will be losing revenue it could have earned. Furthermore, setting prices too low may not attract as many buyers as managers expect. Companies that price too low may lose profits because the lower margins on the products are not recouped by the increased sales.

Pricing Objectives

2

List and explain a variety of pricing objectives

To survive in today's highly competitive marketplace, companies need pricing objectives that are specific, attainable, and measurable. Realistic pricing goals then require monitoring to determine the effectiveness of the company's strategy. For convenience, pricing objectives can be divided into three categories: profit oriented, sales oriented, and status quo.

Profit-Oriented Pricing Objectives

Profit-oriented objectives include profit maximization, satisfactory profits, and target return on investment. A brief discussion of each of these objectives follows.

Profit Maximization *Profit maximization* means setting prices so that total revenue is as large as possible relative to total costs. Profit maximization does not always signify unreasonably high prices. Both price and profits depend on the type of competitive environment a firm faces—for example, does it hold a monopoly or is it selling in a much more competitive situation? Many firms do not have the necessary accounting data to maximize profits. It sounds simple to say that a company should keep producing and selling goods or services as long as revenues exceed costs. Yet it can be difficult to set up an accurate accounting system to determine the point of profit maximization. Although profit maximization may sound like an excellent objective to stockholders, it is not good enough for planning. The statement "We want to make as much money as we can" is vague and lacks focus.

Satisfactory Profits *Satisfactory profits* means a reasonable level of profits. Many organizations, instead of maximizing profits, strive for profits that are satisfactory to the stockholders and management—in other words, a level of profit that is consistent with the level of risk. In a risky industry a satisfactory profit might be 35 percent; in a low-risk industry it might be 7 percent. To maximize profits, a small business owner might have to keep his or her store open seven days a week. However, the owner might not want to work that hard and might be satisfied with less profit.

Target Return on Investment The most common profit objective is a target **return on investment (ROI),** sometimes called the firm's return on total assets. ROI measures how effective management is at generating profits with the assets available. The higher the firm's ROI, the better off it is. Many companies, including Du Pont, General Motors, Navistar, Exxon, and Magna, use target ROI as their main pricing goal.

return on investment (ROI)
Net profit after taxes divided by total assets.

Return on investment is calculated as follows:

$$\text{Return on investment} = \frac{\text{Net profits after taxes}}{\text{Total assets}}$$

Assume that in 2002 Johnson Controls had assets of $4.5 million and net profits of $550,000. Johnson Controls' ROI is:

$$\begin{aligned} \text{ROI} &= \frac{550{,}000}{4{,}500{,}000} \\ &= 12.2 \text{ percent} \end{aligned}$$

Comparing this 12.2 percent ROI with the industry average provides a good standard for measuring Johnson's performance. Any ROI needs to be evaluated in terms of the competitive environment, risks within the industry, and economic conditions. Usually, firms seek ROIs in the 10 to 30 percent range. General Electric seeks a 25 percent ROI; Alcoa, Rubbermaid, and most major pharmaceutical companies strive for a 20 percent ROI. In some industries, such as the grocery industry, an ROI of under 5 percent is common and acceptable.

Sales-Oriented Pricing Objectives

Sales-oriented pricing objectives are based either on market share or on dollar or unit sales. Marketing managers should be familiar with these pricing objectives.

Market Share **Market share** is a company's product sales as a percentage of total sales for that industry. Sales can be reported in dollars or in units. It is vital to know whether market share is being expressed in revenue or units. Consider four companies competing in an industry with 2,000,000 total unit sales and total industry revenue of $4 million (see Exhibit 15.1). Company A has the largest unit market share at 50 percent, but it has only 25 percent of the revenue market share. In contrast, company D has only a 15 percent unit share, but the largest revenue share with 30 percent.

market share
A company's product sales as a percentage of total sales for that industry.

Many companies believe that maintaining or increasing market share is an indicator of the effectiveness of their marketing mix. A larger market share often

Kraft General Foods
Visit the Kraft pantry. Does Maxwell House emphasize taste in its Web advertising? If so, how?
www.kraftfoods.com

on line

exhibit 15.1

Two Ways to Measure Market Share (units and revenue)

Company	Units sold	Unit price	Total Revenue	Unit market share	Revenue market
A	1,000,000	$1.00	$1,000,000	50%	25%
B	200,000	4.00	800,000	10	20
C	500,000	2.00	1,000,000	25	25
D	300,000	4.00	1,200,000	15	30
Total	2,000,000		$4,000,000		

does mean higher profits, thanks to greater economies of scale, market power, and the ability to compensate top-quality management. Conventional wisdom also says that market share and ROI are strongly related. For the most part they are; however, many companies with low market share survive and even prosper.

The 1990s proved that the conventional wisdom about market share and profitability isn't always reliable. Because of extreme competition in some industries, many market share leaders either did not reach their target ROIs or actually lost money. The airline, personal computer, and food industries had this problem. Procter & Gamble switched from market share to ROI objectives after realizing that profits don't automatically follow from a large market share. PepsiCo says its new Pepsi challenge is to be No. 1 in share of industry profit, not in share of sales volume.

A common example of sales maximization is the post-holiday sales blitz in late December. Designed to move excess inventory, this strategy is used on a temporary basis.

Sales Maximization Instead of striving for market share, sometimes companies try to maximize sales. The objective of maximizing sales ignores profits, competition, and the marketing environment as long as sales are rising.

If a company is strapped for funds or faces an uncertain future, it may try to generate a maximum amount of cash in the short run. Management's task when using this objective is to calculate which price–quantity relationship generates the greatest cash revenue. Sales maximization can also be effectively used on a temporary basis to sell off excess inventory. It is not uncommon to find Christmas cards, ornaments, and so on discounted at 50 to 70 percent off retail prices after the holiday season. Maximization of cash should never be a long-run objective, because cash maximization may mean little or no profitability.

Status Quo Pricing Objectives

status quo pricing
Pricing objective that maintains exisiting prices or meets the competition's prices.

Status quo pricing seeks to maintain existing prices or to meet the competition's prices. This third category of pricing objectives has the big advantage of requiring little planning. It is essentially a passive policy.

Often, firms competing in an industry with an established price leader simply meet the competition's prices. These industries typically have fewer price wars than those with direct price competition. Often, managers regularly shop competitors' stores to ensure that their prices are comparable. Fast food chains such as McDonald's, Wendy's, and Burger King monitor one another's prices and try to follow a status quo pricing strategy. If someone comes along, however, and lowers fast food prices, as Taco Bell has done in recent years, the companies must return to competitive pricing strategies.

The Demand Determinant of Price

3
Explain the role of demand in price determination

After marketing managers establish pricing goals, they must set specific prices to reach those goals. The price they set for each product depends mainly on two factors: the demand for the good or service, and the cost to the seller for that good or service. When pricing goals are mainly sales oriented, demand considerations usually dominate.

The Nature of Demand

demand
The quanity of a product that will be sold in the market at various prices for a specified period.

Demand is the quantity of a product that will be sold in the market at various prices for a specified period. The quantity of a product that people will buy depends on its price. The higher the price, the fewer goods or services consumers will demand. Conversely, the lower the price, the more goods or services they will demand.

This trend is illustrated in Exhibit 15.2a, which graphs the demand per week for gourmet popcorn at a local retailer at various prices. This graph is called a *demand curve.* The vertical axis of the graph shows different prices for gourmet popcorn, measured in dollars per package. The horizontal axis measures the quantity of gourmet popcorn that will be demanded per week at each price. For example, at a price of $2.50, 50 packages will be sold per week; at $1.00, consumers will demand 120 packages—as the *demand schedule* in Exhibit 15.2b shows.

supply
The quantity of a product that will be offered to the market by a supplier at various prices for a specified period.

The demand curve in Exhibit 15.2 slopes downward and to the right, indicating that more gourmet popcorn is demanded as the price is lowered. One reason why more is sold at lower prices than at higher prices is that lower prices bring in new buyers. This fact might not be so obvious with gourmet popcorn, but consider the example of steak. As the price of steak drops lower and lower, some people who have not been eating steak will probably start buying it rather than hamburger. Also, with each reduction in price, existing customers may buy extra amounts. Similarly, if the price of gourmet popcorn falls low enough, some people will buy more than they have bought in the past.

As price decreases, the demand for gourmet popcorn increases. One reason is that lower prices generally attract new buyers.

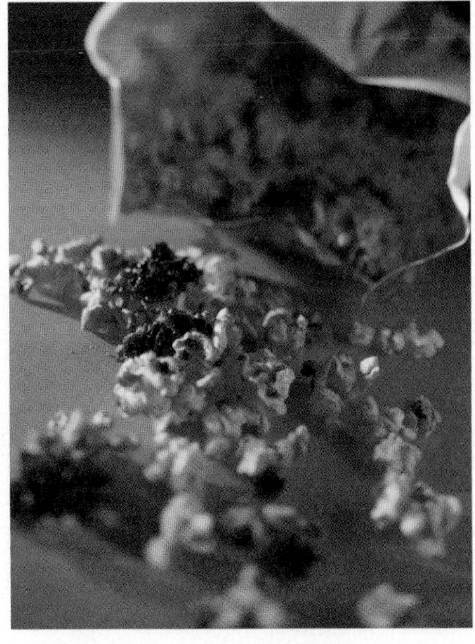

Supply is the quantity of a product that will be offered to the market by a supplier or suppliers at various prices. Exhibit 15.3a illustrates the *supply curve* for gourmet popcorn. Unlike the demand curve, which falls, the supply curve for gourmet popcorn slopes upward and to the right. At higher prices, gourmet popcorn manufacturers will obtain more resources (popcorn, flavourings, salt) and produce more. If the price consumers are willing to pay for gourmet popcorn increases, producers can afford to buy more ingredients.

Output tends to increase at higher prices because manufacturers can sell more packages of gourmet popcorn and earn greater profits. The *supply schedule* in Exhibit 15.3b shows that at $2 suppliers are willing to place 110 packages of gourmet popcorn on the market; at a price of $3, they will offer 140 packages.

How Demand and Supply Establish Prices At this point, let's combine the concepts of demand and supply to see how competitive market prices are determined. So far, the premise is that if the price is X, then consumers will purchase Y amount of gourmet popcorn. How high or low will prices actually go? How many packages of gourmet

exhibit 15.2

Demand Curve and Demand Schedule for Gourmet Popcorn

(a) Demand curve

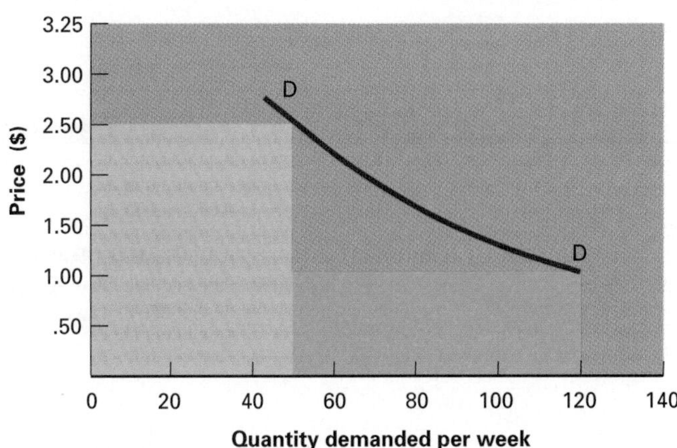

(b) Demand schedule

Price per package of gourmet popcorn ($)	Packages of gourmet popcorn demanded per week
3.00	35
2.50	50
2.00	65
1.50	85
1.00	120

exhibit 15.3

Supply Curve and Supply Schedule for Gourmet Popcorn

(a) Supply curve

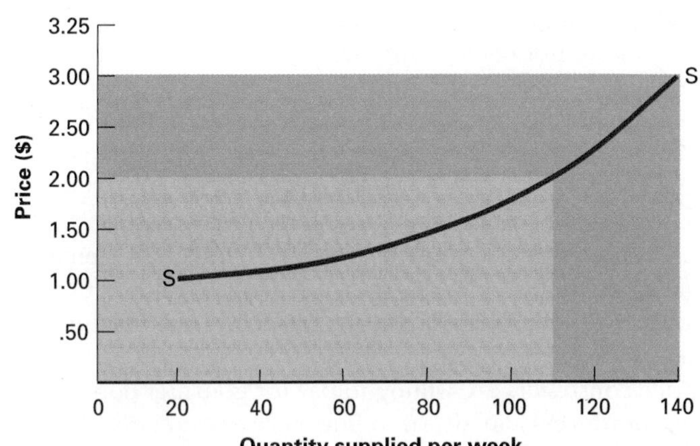

(b) Supply schedule

Price per package of gourmet popcorn ($)	Packages of gourmet popcorn supplied per week
3.00	140
2.50	130
2.00	110
1.50	85
1.00	25

Columbia House

How can Columbia House offer so many CDs or videos for one cent? Go to the Website to see what kind of deals Columbia House is offering right now. Compare the introductory offers to the pricing for subsequent purchases. What conclusions can you draw about Columbia House's elasticity of demand for CDs, based on the posted pricing for the initial sign-up and for subsequent purchases?

www.columbiahouse.com

on line

popcorn will be produced and consumed? The demand curve cannot predict consumption, nor can the supply curve alone forecast production. Instead, we need to look at how supply and demand interact. For this, see Exhibit 15.4.

At a price of $3, the public would demand only 35 packages of gourmet popcorn. Suppliers, however, stand ready to place 140 packages on the market at this price (see data from the demand and supply schedules). This would create a surplus of 105 packages of gourmet popcorn. How does a merchant eliminate a surplus? By lowering the price.

At a price of $1, 120 packages would be demanded, but only 25 would be supplied. A shortage of 95 units would be created. If a product is in short supply and consumers want it, how do they entice the dealer to supply more? They offer more money—that is, they pay a higher price.

Now let's examine a price of $1.50. At this price, 85 packages are demanded and 85 are supplied. When demand and supply are equal, a state called **price equilibrium** is achieved. A temporary price below equilibrium—say $1.00—results in a shortage, because at that price the demand for gourmet popcorn is greater than the available supply. Shortages put upward pressure on price. At equilibrium, there is no inclination for prices to rise or fall.

price equilibrium
The price at which demand and supply are equal.

Elasticity of Demand

To appreciate demand analysis, you should understand the concept of elasticity. **Elasticity of demand** refers to consumers' responsiveness or sensitivity to changes in price. **Elastic demand** occurs when consumers buy more or less of a product when the price changes. Conversely, **inelastic demand** means that an increase or a decrease in price will not significantly affect demand for the product.

Elasticity over the range of a demand curve can be measured using this formula:

$$\text{Elasticity } (E) = \frac{\text{Percentage change in quantity demanded of good A}}{\text{Percentage change in price of good A}}$$

If E is greater than 1, demand is elastic.
If E is less than 1, demand is inelastic.
If E is equal to 1, demand is unitary.

Unitary elasticity means that an increase in sales exactly offsets a decrease in prices so that total revenue remains the same.

elasticity of demand
Consumers' responsiveness or sensitivity to changes in price.

elastic demand
A situation in which consumer demand is sensitive to changes in price.

inelastic demand
A situation in which an increase or a decrease in price will not significantly affect demand for the product.

unitary elasticity
A situation in which total revenue remains the same when prices change.

exhibit 15.4

Equilibirum Price for Gourmet Popcorn

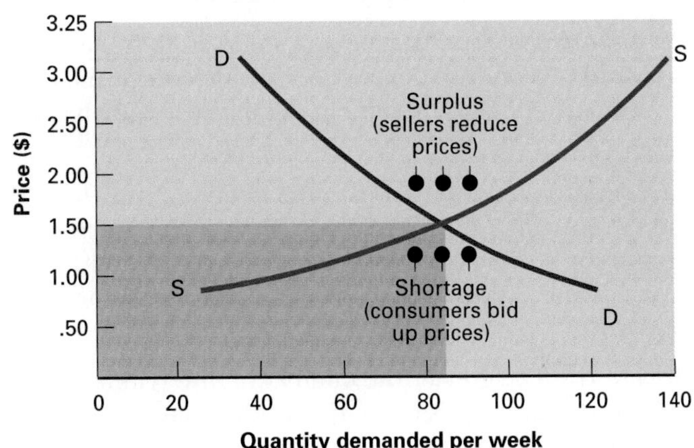

Elasticity can be measured by observing these changes in total revenue:

- If price goes down and revenue goes up, demand is elastic.
- If price goes down and revenue goes down, demand is inelastic.
- If price goes up and revenue goes up, demand is inelastic.
- If price goes up and revenue goes down, demand is elastic.
- If price goes up or down and revenue stays the same, elasticity is unitary.

Exhibit 15.5a shows a highly elastic demand curve. Decreasing the price of a Sony VCR from $300 to $200 increases sales from 18,000 units to 59,000 units. Revenue increases from $5.4 million ($300 x 18,000) to $11.8 million ($200 x 59,000). The price decrease results in a large increase in sales and revenue.

Exhibit 15.5b shows a completely inelastic demand curve. Let's assume that the cost of used-car vehicle inspection fees is increased from $10 to $20. There is no change in the number of used cars inspected. Increasing the price of the inspection fee by 100 percent does not cause people to stop buying used cars. Demand is completely inelastic for inspection fees. People won't quit buying used cars if the inspection fee increases—within a reasonable range.

exhibit 15.5

Elasticity of Demand for Sony VCRs and Auto Inspection Stickers

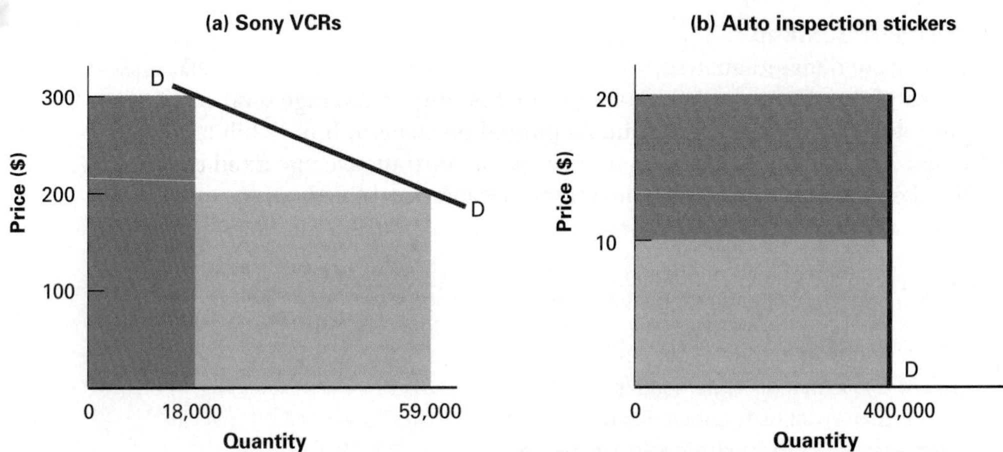

Factors That Affect Elasticity Several factors affect elasticity of demand, including the following:

- *Availability of substitutes:* When many substitute products are available, the consumer can easily switch from one product to another, making demand elastic.
- *Price relative to purchasing power:* If a price is so low as to be an inconsequential part of an individual's budget, demand will be inelastic. If the price of salt doubles, consumers will not stop putting salt on their eggs, because salt is cheap anyway.
- *Product durability:* Consumers often have the option of repairing durable products instead of replacing them. If a person plans to buy a new car but prices suddenly begin to rise, he or she may elect to fix the old car and drive it for another year. In other words, if people are sensitive to the price increase, demand is elastic.
- *A product's other uses:* The greater the number of different uses for a product, the more elastic demand tends to be. If a product has only one use, as may be true for a new medicine, the quantity purchased will not vary as price varies.

A person will consume the prescribed quantity, regardless of price. On the other hand, a product like steel has many possible applications. As its price falls, steel becomes more economically feasible in a wider variety of applications. This means that the demand for steel is relatively elastic.

The Cost Determinant of Price

Describe cost-oriented pricing strategies

Sometimes companies minimize or ignore the importance of demand and price their products largely or solely on the basis of costs. Prices determined strictly on the basis of costs may be too high for the target market, thereby reducing or eliminating sales. On the other hand, cost-based prices may be too low, causing the firm to earn a lower return than it should. However, costs should generally be part of any price determination, if only as a floor below which a good or service must not be priced in the long run.

The idea of cost may seem simple, but it is actually a multifaceted concept, especially for producers of goods and services. **Variable costs** are those which deviate with changes in the level of output; an example of a variable cost is the cost of materials. In contrast, **fixed costs** do not change as output is increased or decreased. Examples include rent and executives' salaries.

variable costs
Costs that vary with changes in the level of output.

fixed costs
Costs that do not change as output is increased or decreased.

To compare the cost of production to the selling price of a product, it is helpful to calculate costs per unit, or average costs. **Average variable cost (AVC)** equals total variable costs divided by quantity of output. **Average total cost (ATC)** equals total costs divided by output. As plotted on the graph in Exhibit 15.6a, AVC and ATC are basically U-shaped curves. In contrast, average fixed costs (AFC) decline steadily as output increases, because total fixed costs are constant.

average variable cost (AVC)
Total variable costs divided by quantity of output.

average total cost (ATC)
Total costs divided by quantity of output.

Marginal cost (MC) is the change in total costs associated with a one-unit change in output. Exhibit 15.6b shows that when output rises from 7 to 8 units, the change in total cost is from \$640 to \$750; it follows that marginal cost is \$110.

marginal cost (MC)
Change in total costs associated with a one-unit change in output.

All the curves illustrated in Exhibit 15.6a have definite relationships:

- AVC plus AFC equals ATC.
- MC falls for a while and then turns upward, in this case with the fourth unit. At that point diminishing returns set in, meaning that less output is produced for every additional dollar spent on variable input.
- MC intersects both AVC and ATC at their lowest possible points.
- When MC is less than AVC or ATC, the incremental cost will continue to pull the averages down. Conversely, when MC is greater than AVC or ATC, it pulls the averages up, and ATC and AVC begin to rise.
- The minimum point on the ATC curve is the least cost point for a fixed capacity firm, although it is not necessarily the most profitable point.

Because steel has many possible applications, price changes have a great impact on demand. As its price falls, steel becomes a more economically feasible alternative, so the demand for it is relatively elastic.

Markup Pricing

Markup pricing, the most popular method used by wholesalers and retailers to establish a selling price, does not directly analyze the costs of pro-

markup pricing
The cost of buying the product from the producer, plus amounts for profit and for expenses not otherwise accounted for.

duction. Instead, **markup pricing** is the cost of buying the product from the producer, plus amounts for profit and for expenses not otherwise accounted for. The total determines the selling price.

A retailer, for example, adds a certain percentage to the cost of the merchandise received to arrive at the retail price. An item that costs the retailer $1.80 and is sold for $2.20 carries a markup of 40¢, which is a markup of 22 percent of the cost (40¢/$1.80). Retailers tend to discuss markup in terms of its percentage of the retail price—in this example, 18 percent (40¢/$2.20). The difference between the retailer's cost and the selling price (40¢) is the gross margin.

keystoning
The practice of marking up prices by 100 percent, or doubling the cost.

Markups are often based on experience. Many small retailers mark up merchandise 100 percent over cost. (In other words, they double the cost.) This tactic is called **keystoning.** Some other factors that influence markups are the merchandise's appeal to customers, past response to the markup, the item's promotional

exhibit 15.6

Hypothetical Set of Cost Curves and a Cost Schedule

(a) Cost curves

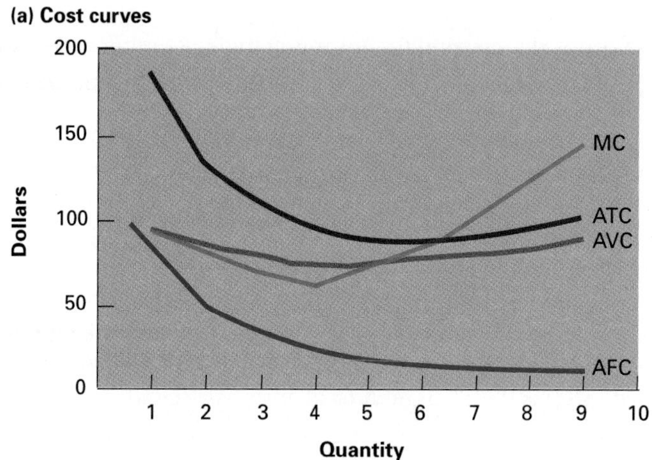

(b) Cost schedule

Total-cost data, per week				Average-cost data, per week			
(1) Total product (Q)	(2) Total fixed cost (TFC)	(3) Total variable cost (TVC)	(4) Total cost (TC)	(5) Average fixed cost (AFC)	(6) Average variable cost (AVC)	(7) Average total cost (ATC)	(8) Marginal cost (MC)
			TC = TFC + TVC	$AFC = \frac{TFC}{Q}$	$AVC = \frac{TVC}{Q}$	$ATC = \frac{TC}{Q}$	$MC = \frac{\text{change in TC}}{\text{change in Q}}$
0	$100	$ 0	$ 100	—	—	—	—
1	100	90	190	$100.00	$90.00	$190.00	$ 90
2	100	170	270	50.00	85.00	135.00	80
3	100	240	340	33.33	80.00	113.33	70
4	100	300	400	25.00	75.00	100.00	60
5	100	370	470	20.00	74.00	94.00	70
6	100	450	550	16.67	75.00	91.67	80
7	100	540	640	14.29	77.14	91.43	90
8	100	650	750	12.50	81.25	93.75	110
9	100	780	880	11.11	86.67	97.78	130
10	100	930	1030	10.00	93.00	103.00	150

value, the seasonality of the goods, their fashion appeal, the product's traditional selling price, and competition.

The biggest advantage of markup pricing is its simplicity. The main disadvantage is that it ignores demand and may result in overpricing or underpricing the merchandise. Sometimes companies charge different markups to different customers. One example of this practice is ethnic pricing as practised by some airlines. This concept is discussed in this chapter's "Ethics in Marketing" box.

Profit Maximization Pricing

Producers tend to use more complicated methods of setting prices than distributors. One is **profit maximization**, which results when marginal revenue equals marginal cost. You learned earlier that marginal cost is the change in total costs associated with a one-unit change in output. Similarly, **marginal revenue (MR)** is the extra revenue associated with selling an extra unit of output. As long as the revenue of the last unit produced and sold is greater than the cost of the last unit produced and sold, the firm should continue manufacturing and selling the product.

profit maximization
When marginal revenue equals marginal cost.

marginal revenue (MR)
The extra revenue associated with selling an extra unit of output, or the change in total revenue with a one-unit change in output.

Exhibit 15.7 shows the marginal revenues and marginal costs for a hypothetical firm, using the cost data from Exhibit 15.6b. The profit-maximizing quantity,

ethics in marketing

There Are No Ethics in Ethnic Pricing

Brendan McInerney, who lives in Frankfurt, Germany, could hardly believe his ears. His wife could fly to Osaka, Japan, for Christmas for 1,700 marks ($965) on Lufthansa, but he would have to pay 2,700 marks on the same flight. The reason: Mr. McInerney's wife, Kyoko, is Japanese, Mr. McInerney isn't. "This is discrimination," McInerney says, fuming, even after Lufthansa eventually offered him the same fare as his wife. "It's illegal. It's unfair."

It *is* illegal in Germany, and it is undoubtedly unfair. It goes on, however, fuelled by increasing rivalry among carriers—and not only in Germany. Throughout Europe, lots of people are getting special deals on airline tickets and other items because of their passports or those of their employers. Mr. McInerney works for a German bank, but according to his travel agent, he would automatically qualify for the same cut-rate fare as his wife if he worked for a Japanese bank.

Commonly called "ethnic pricing," the practice of giving discounts to people of certain nationalities has long been routine in developing countries such as India, China, and Russia. However, in Europe and especially in Germany, the practice is generally kept hush-hush because of the ethical and legal questions it raises.

Christian Hofer, an expert on air traffic fares with the German Freight Agency, which is invested with the authority to approve special fares, says ethnic pricing such as that being offered by Lufthansa, Air France, and other carriers in Germany is against the law. "For all flights out of Germany," Hofer says, "there can't be any discrimination on the basis of nationality." Nevertheless, Hofer says he routinely hears about such deals being offered on the grey market and is essentially powerless to do anything about it. "We don't have the police powers to intervene as we'd like," he says.

The grey market comprises travel agencies specializing in long-distance economy flights. Indeed, Lufthansa itself doesn't even advertise the special fares. Instead, it hammers them out in individual contracts with select travel offices, which offer the special fares only on request. Thus, even in Germany ethnic pricing has largely remained a well-kept secret.

Lufthansa doesn't deny its involvement with ethnic pricing. It says the practice is common in Germany and argues that it is only reacting to competition from the national carriers of Japan, South Korea, China, and Iran. "The others started it," says Dagmar Rotter, a Lufthansa spokeswoman. "We only offered it after the market forced us to do so."

For McInerney, the ethnic pricing issue in Germany is academic. After being confronted with the absurdity of charging a husband and wife different prices, Lufthansa said it was changing its policy to include spouses travelling together and would make an exception for McInerney in advance. Best of all, McInerney says, is the frequent flyer mileage: "I get Lufthansa miles." Otherwise, he says, he would have flown with All Nippon Airways to begin with.[2]

Do you think Lufthansa's response that it was "simply meeting competition" is sufficient justification for "ethnic pricing"? Does letting spouses both receive the ethnic fare solve the problem? Some airlines offer ethnic fares to their citizens when they are living abroad. The airlines say that this is the only way some workers can afford to go home to visit their families. How would you respond to this logic?

where MR = MC, is six units. You might say, "If profit is zero, why produce the sixth unit? Why not stop at five?" In fact, you would be right. The firm, however, cannot know that the sixth unit will produce zero profits until it determined that profits are no longer increasing. Economists suggest producing up to the point where MR = MC.

Break-Even Pricing

break-even analysis
A method of determining what sales volume must be reached before total revenue equals total costs.

Break-even analysis determines what sales volume must be reached before the company breaks even (its total costs equal total revenue). The typical break-even model assumes a given fixed cost and a constant average variable cost. Suppose that Universal Sportswear, a hypothetical firm, has fixed costs of $2,000 and that the cost of labour and materials for each unit produced is 50¢. Assume that it can sell up to 6,000 units of its product at $1 without having to lower its price.

Exhibit 15.8a illustrates Universal Sportswear's break-even point. As Exhibit 15.8b indicates, Universal Sportswear's total variable costs increase by 50¢ every time a new unit is produced, and total fixed costs remain constant at $2,000 regardless of the level of output. Thus, 4,000 units of output give Universal Sportswear $2,000 in fixed costs and $2,000 in total variable costs (4,000 units x 50¢), or $4,000 in total costs. Revenue is also $4,000 (4,000 units x $1), giving a net profit of zero dollars at the break-even point of 4,000 units.

The formula for calculating break-even quantities is simple:

$$\text{Break-even quantity} = \frac{\text{Total fixed costs}}{\text{Fixed cost contribution}}$$

Fixed cost contribution is the price less the average variable cost. So for Universal Sportswear,

$$\text{Break-even quantity} = \frac{\$2{,}000}{(\$1.00 - 50¢)} = \frac{\$2{,}000}{50¢}$$

$$= 4{,}000 \text{ units}$$

The advantage of break-even analysis is that it provides a quick estimate of how much the firm must sell to break even and how much profit can be earned if higher sales volumes are obtained. If a firm is operating close to the break-even point, it may want to see what it can do to reduce costs or increase sales. Break-

exhibit 15.7

Point of Profit Maximization

Quantity	Marginal revenue (MR)	Marginal cost (MC)	Cumulative total profit
0	—	—	—
1	140	90	50
2	130	80	100
3	105	70	135
4	95	60	170
5	85	70	185
*6	80	80	185
7	75	90	170
8	60	110	120
9	50	130	40
10	40	150	(70)

exhibit 15.8

Costs, Revenues, and Break-Even Point for Universal Sportswear

(a) Break-even point

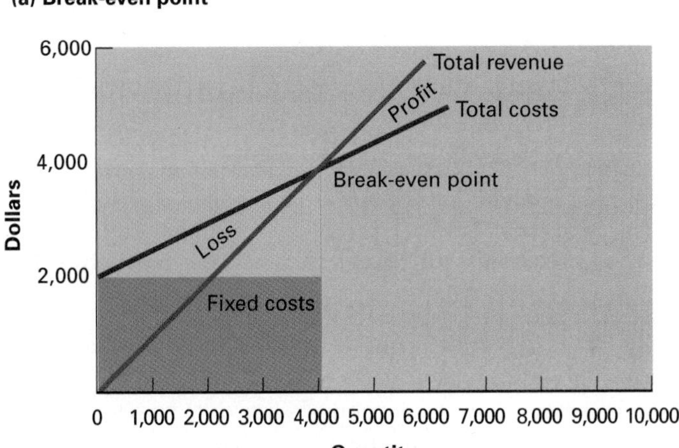

(b) Costs and revenues

Output	Total fixed costs	Average variable costs	Total variable costs	Average total costs	Average revenue (price)	Total revenue	Total costs	Profit or loss
500	$2,000	$0.50	$ 250	$4.50	$1.00	$ 500	$2,250	($1,750)
1,000	2,000	0.50	500	2.50	1.00	1,000	2,500	(1,500)
1,500	2,000	0.50	750	1.83	1.00	1,500	2,750	(1,250)
2,000	2,000	0.50	1,000	1.50	1.00	2,000	3,000	(1,000)
2,500	2,000	0.50	1,250	1.30	1.00	2,500	3,250	(750)
3,000	2,000	0.50	1,500	1.17	1.00	3,000	3,500	(500)
3,500	2,000	0.50	1,750	1.07	1.00	3,500	3,750	(250)
*4,000	2,000	0.50	2,000	1.00	1.00	4,000	4,000	(0)
4,500	2,000	0.50	2,250	.94	1.00	4,500	4,250	250
5,000	2,000	0.50	2,500	.90	1.00	5,000	4,500	500
5,500	2,000	0.50	2,750	.86	1.00	5,500	4,750	750
6,000	2,000	0.50	3,000	.83	1.00	6,000	5,000	1,000

even analysis has several important limitations. Sometimes it is hard to know whether a cost is fixed or variable. If labour wins a tough guaranteed employment contract, are the resulting expenses a fixed cost? More important than cost determination is the fact that simple break-even analysis ignores demand. How does Universal Sportswear know it can sell 4,000 units at $1? Could it sell the same 4,000 units at $2 or even $5? Obviously, this information would profoundly affect the firm's pricing decisions.

Other Determinants of Price

Other factors besides demand and costs can influence price. For example, the stage of the product's life cycle, the competition, and the product's distribution strategy, promotion strategy, and perceived quality can all affect pricing.

on line

Fragrance Net

Compare the effect of product life cycle on pricing. Go to Fragrance Net and compare the prices of White Shoulders (introduced in 1935) to those of Narcisse (introduced in 1992). Do the prices surprise you? What can you conclude about the product life cycle of each fragrance? Does the cycle even apply to perfumes?

www.fragrancenet.com

5

Demonstrate how the product life cycle, competition, distribution and promotion strategies, customer demands, the Internet and extranets, and perceptions of quality can affect price

Stages in the Product Life Cycle

As a product moves through its life cycle, the demand for it tends to change, and so do competitive conditions:

- *Introductory stage:* Management usually sets prices high during the introductory stage. One reason is that it hopes to recover its development costs quickly. Also, demand originates in the core of the market (the customers whose needs ideally match the product's attributes) and so is relatively inelastic.
- *Growth stage:* Prices generally begin to stabilize as the product enters the growth stage. There are several reasons why. First, competitors have entered the market, increasing supply. Second, the product has begun to appeal to a broader market, often lower income groups. Finally, economies of scale are lowering costs, and the savings can be passed on to the consumer.
- *Maturity stage:* Maturity usually brings further price decreases as competition increases and inefficient, high-cost firms are eliminated. The manufacturers that remain in the market toward the end of the maturity stage typically offer similar prices. Usually only the most efficient remain, and they have comparable costs. At this stage, price increases are usually cost initiated, not demand initiated. Also, price reductions in the late phase of maturity don't stimulate demand much. Because demand is limited and producers have similar cost structures, the remaining competitors will probably match price reductions.
- *Decline stage:* The final stage of the life cycle may see further price decreases as the few remaining competitors try to salvage the last vestiges of demand. When only one firm is left in the market, prices begin to stabilize. In fact, prices may eventually rise dramatically if the product survives and moves into the specialty goods category, as with horse-drawn carriages and vinyl records.

The Competition

Competition varies during the product life cycle and strongly affects pricing decisions. Although a firm may not have any competition at first, the high prices it charges may induce other firms to enter the market. As they do, intense competition can lead to price wars. What pulls companies into self-defeating price wars? Often they make the mistake of measuring their success by market share rather than by profitability.

Recently, one company outsmarted its competition to avoid a calamitous price war. Company A heard that company B was trying to steal some business by offering a low price to one of A's best customers. Instead of immediately cutting its prices, A visited three of B's best clients and told each that it must be paying *x*, the same price that B had quoted to A's own customer. Within days, B had retracted its low-price offer to A's client. Presumably, B had received calls from three angry clients asking for the same special deal.

Sometimes governments intervene to control actions that could lead to price wars. Price wars often begin when one company offers a "sale."

Unless a product in the decline stage becomes a specialty item, like vinyl records, its price will tend to decrease.

However, that's not so easily done in France, as this chapter's "Global Perspectives" reveals.

Distribution Strategy

Often, an effective distribution network can overcome minor flaws in the marketing mix. For example, consumers may perceive a price as being slightly higher than normal, but may buy the product anyway if it is being sold at a convenient retail outlet.

A firm can often attain adequate distribution for a new product by offering a larger-than-usual profit margin to distributors. A variation on this strategy is to offer dealers a large trade allowance; this helps offset the costs of promotion and further stimulates demand at the retail level.

Gradually, manufacturers have been losing control within distribution channels to wholesalers and retailers, which often adopt pricing strategies that serve their own purposes. For instance, some distributors are **selling against the brand**—that is, they are placing well-known brands on the shelves at high prices while offering other brands (typically, their private label brands, such as Craftsman tools, Mastercraft auto parts, or Life Brand cosmetics) at lower prices.

selling against the brand
Stocking well-known branded items at high prices in order to sell store brands at discounted prices.

Wholesalers and retailers sometimes go outside traditional distribution channels to buy grey-market goods. Distributors obtain the goods through unauthorized channels for less than they would usually pay; this means they can sell the goods with bigger-than-normal markups or at reduced prices. Imports are especially susceptible to grey marketing. Porsche cars, JVC stereos, and Seiko watches are among the brand name products that have suffered from grey marketing.

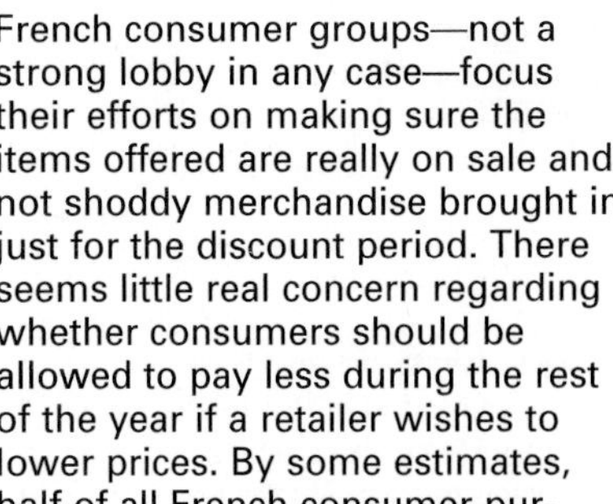

global perspectives

Want to Have a Sale in France? Hey, Not So Fast

Mark this down: The French government says that holiday sales can begin on 6 January. In France, the government not only owns the airline, runs the railway, and operates a bank, but is also in charge of post-Christmas sales.

Price cutting after the holidays is common practice around the world, but here it is the political heirs of Louis XIV who determine when and how merchandise can be discounted. By law, stores are allowed to offer merchandise below cost only twice a year—during the post-Christmas period, and in the six-week summer sale season. A law passed in 1996 set even stricter terms for what constitutes a sale: the goods must have been bought by the store at least thirty days before, not brought in and instantly marked down.

Around 2,000 inspectors from the Competition, Consumption, and Repression of Fraud Directorate go to the stores, making sure the labels on sale products are genuine discounts, that only previously offered merchandise is on sale, and that the time limit has been adhered to. Every year, dozens of fines are issued to stores that started their sales too early. Violators of the starting date or merchandise rules can be fined $5,000 to $20,000. "If a government inspector came in the day before a sale can begin and we had articles on sale, we would have been charged a fine," said a spokeswoman for Le Bon Marché, a major department store.

The regulation of sales is just one example of how France's approach to capitalism diverges sharply from the approach taken by its Anglo-Saxon neighbours and allies. The law "is to avoid too much competition between merchants," said Bernard Chartier of the city administration office in Paris, which is responsible for setting the kickoff date for the sale season. The date is carefully selected in consultation with merchant and consumer associations.

French consumer groups—not a strong lobby in any case—focus their efforts on making sure the items offered are really on sale and not shoddy merchandise brought in just for the discount period. There seems little real concern regarding whether consumers should be allowed to pay less during the rest of the year if a retailer wishes to lower prices. By some estimates, half of all French consumer purchases are made during the two sale seasons.[3]

Should Canada adopt the French law? Explain. Do you feel that the law hurts competition? Why aren't French consumers more upset by this law?

Source: Adapted from Anne Swardson, "In France, It's On Sale When the State Says So," *International Herald Tribune*, 6 January 1998.

on line

Foot Locker

Check out the price of your favourite brand of gym shoes on the Foot Locker site. How does supply and demand work in this market? Is supply tight? If not, can you explain the prices you find?

www. footlocker.com

Manufacturers can regain some control over price by using an exclusive distribution system, by franchising, or by avoiding doing business with price-cutting discounters. They can also package merchandise with the selling price marked on it, or place goods on consignment. All of that aside, the best way for manufacturers to control prices is to develop brand loyalty among consumers by delivering quality and value.

The Impact of the Internet and Extranets

The Internet, corporate networks, and wireless setups are linking people, machines, and companies around the globe—and connecting sellers and buyers as never before. Buyers can now quickly and easily compare products and prices, which places them in a better bargaining position. At the same time, these technologies are enabling sellers to collect extensive data about customers' buying habits and preferences, and even their spending limits; this information can then be used to adjust products and prices. The first signs of this new, fluid pricing are to be found on the Internet. On-line auctions are allowing cybershoppers to bid on everything from collectibles to treadmills. In contrast, electronic exchanges act as middlemen.

extranet
A private electronic network that links a company with its suppliers and customers.

But the pricing revolution is reaching beyond the Internet. Companies are now creating private networks, or **extranets**, that link them with their suppliers and customers. These systems make it possible to get a precise handle on inventory, costs, and demand at any given point in time—and to adjust prices instantly. In the past there was a significant cost (known as the "menu cost") associated with changing prices. For a company with a large product line, it could take months for price adjustments to filter down to distributors, retailers, and salespeople. Now that networks are being streamlined, menu costs and times are being reduced almost to zero.[4]

Shopping over the Internet is on the rise, and as part of that trend Internet auctions are becoming increasingly popular. At sites like ebay.com, consumers can purchase anything from computers to collectibles. How interested would you be in participating in an Internet auction, either as a buyer or a seller?

Two trailblazers in Internet commerce are Covisint and Priceline. Covisint includes many major auto assemblers (e.g., General Motors, Ford, DaimlerChrysler, Renault, and Nissan) and hundreds of auto parts suppliers. Covisint is a Web-based exchange that lets customers shop for the best prices on auto parts and other materials (e.g., steel, plastic, rubber). Business buyers save money by shopping for the best prices or by locking in long-term deals when prices are low. Priceline lets anyone bid on all kinds of goods and services: airline tickets, hotel rooms, mortgages, new cars, rental cars, and so on.[5] The Priceline story was discussed in more detail in this chapter's opening vignette.

Internet auctions are also expanding. Presently at AucNet, dealers and wholesalers are buying and selling around 6,000 cars per month.[6] Auction sites are selling everything from electronics, old books, and furniture to Samurai swords and real estate. Check out **ebay.com**, **onsale.com**, or **eworldauction.com** to get a feel for auction sites.

Promotion Strategy

Price is often used as a promotional tool to increase consumer interest. The weekly grocery section of your newspaper advertises many products with special low prices. Crested Butte Ski Resort in Colorado tried a unique twist on price promotions: it made the unusual offer of free skiing between Thanksgiving and Christmas. Its only revenues were voluntary contributions from lodging and restaurant owners, who benefited from the droves of skiers taking advantage of the promotion. Lodging during the slack period is now booked solid, and on the busiest days 9,000 skiers jam slopes designed for around 6,500. Crested Butte Resort no longer loses money during this time of the year.

Pricing also can be a tool for trade promotions. Levi's Dockers (casual men's slacks) are very popular with white-collar men between twenty-five and forty-five, a growing and lucrative market. Sensing an opportunity, Bugle Boy began offering similar pants at cheaper wholesale prices; this gave retailers a bigger gross margin than they were getting with Dockers. Levi Strauss had to either lower prices or risk its $400 million annual Docker sales. Although Levi Strauss meant for its cheapest Dockers to retail for $35, it started selling Dockers to retailers for $18 a pair. Retailers could then advertise Dockers at a very attractive retail price of $25.

Demands of Large Customers

Large customers of manufacturers—for example, Wal-Mart and Zellers—often make specific pricing demands on suppliers. For example, department stores are placing heavier and heavier demands on suppliers to cover their discounts and markdowns. They want suppliers to guarantee their stores' profit margins, and they are insisting on cash rebates if such guarantees aren't met.

In the past, when a garment maker sold to a store, the two parties agreed on a retail price, and at the end of the season the supplier rebated some of the cost of markdowns. Discounts and markdowns were far rarer then than they are today: department stores could afford plenty of sales help to push products. However, as stores cut labour costs, they came to rely on promotional markdowns and sales to move goods—with suppliers covering any shortfalls in profit margins.

The Relationship of Price to Quality

Consumers tend to rely on price as a predictor of quality when there is great uncertainty involved in the purchase decision. That is, the higher the price, the better the quality. This seems to be true for all products, but more for some than for others.[7] Among the products that benefit from this phenomenon are coffee, stockings, aspirin, salt, floor wax, shampoo, clothing, furniture, perfume, whiskey, and many services. As consumers obtain additional information—for instance, about the brand or the store—their reliance on price as an indicator of quality decreases.[8]

In the absence of other information, people typically assume that a price is higher because the product contains better materials, or is made more carefully, or—in the case of professional services—because the provider has more expertise. Consumers tend to be more accurate in their price–quality assessments for nondurable goods (e.g., ice cream, frozen pizza, oven cleaner) than for durable goods (e.g., coffeemakers, gas grills, ten-speed bikes).[9] Knowledgeable merchants take these consumer attitudes into account when devising their pricing strategies. **Prestige pricing** involves charging a high price to help promote a high-quality image.

prestige pricing
Charging a high price to help promote a high-quality image.

How to Set a Price on a Product

6
Describe the procedure for setting the right price

Setting the right price on a product is a four-step process (see Exhibit 15.9):

1. Establish pricing goals.
2. Estimate demand, costs, and profits.
3. Choose a price strategy to help determine a base price.
4. Fine tune the base price with pricing tactics.

Establish Pricing Goals

The first step in setting the right price is to establish pricing goals. Recall that pricing objectives fall into three categories: profit oriented, sales oriented, and status quo. These goals are derived from the firm's overall objectives.

All pricing objectives have trade-offs, which managers must weigh. The objective of maximizing profits may require a bigger initial investment than the firm can commit. Reaching the desired market share often means sacrificing short-term profit, because without careful management, long-term profit goals may not be met. Meeting the competition is the easiest pricing goal to implement. However, can managers really afford to ignore demand and costs, the life cycle stage, and other considerations? When developing pricing objectives, managers must consider these trade-offs in light of the target customers and the environment.

Estimate Demand, Costs, and Profits

After establishing pricing goals, managers should estimate total revenue at a variety of prices. Then they should determine corresponding costs for each price. At this point they are ready to estimate how much profit, if any, and how much market share can be earned at each possible price. These data become the heart of the developing price policy. Managers can study the options in light of rev-

exhibit 15.9

Steps in Setting the Right Price on a Product

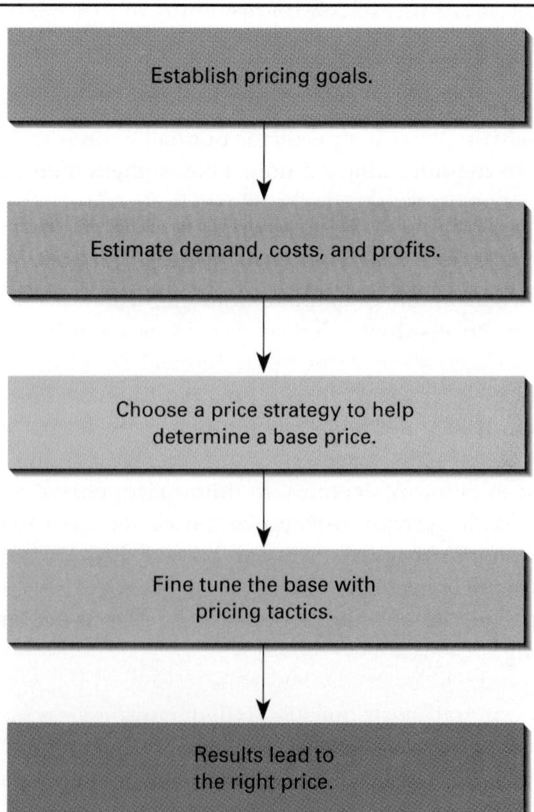

Genentech, Incorporated

How does Genentech position and promote its products in light of the high prices often charged?

www.gene.com

on line

enues, costs, and profits. In turn, this information can help determine which price will best meet the firm's pricing goals.

Choose a Price Strategy

The basic, long-term pricing framework for a good or service should be a logical extension of the pricing objectives. The marketing manager's chosen **price strategy** defines the initial price and gives direction for price movements over the product life cycle.

price strategy
The basic, long-term pricing framework, which establishes the initial price for a product and the intended direction for price movements over the product life cycle.

The price strategy sets a competitive price in a specific market segment, based on a well-defined positioning strategy. Changing a price level from premium to superpremium may require a change in the product itself, in the target customers served, in the promotional strategy, or in the distribution channels. Thus, changing a price strategy can require dramatic alterations in the marketing mix. A carmaker cannot successfully compete in the superpremium category if the car looks and drives like an economy car.

In pricing a new product and devising a price strategy, a company's freedom depends on the market conditions and the other elements of the marketing mix. If a firm launches a new item resembling several others already on the market, its pricing freedom will be restricted. To succeed, the company will probably have to charge a price close to the average market price. In contrast, a firm that introduces a totally new product with no close substitutes will have considerable pricing freedom.

The three basic strategies for setting a price on a good or service are price skimming, penetration pricing, and status quo pricing. A discussion of each type follows.

Price Skimming Price skimming is sometimes called a "market-plus" approach to pricing, because it denotes a high price relative to the prices of competing products. Radius Corp. produces unique, oval-headed toothbrushes made of black neoprene that look like scuba-diving accessories. Radius uses a skimming policy, pricing the toothbrushes at $9.95, compared to around $2.95 for a regular toothbrush.

The term **price skimming** is derived from the phrase "skimming the cream off the top." Companies often use this strategy for new products when the product is perceived by the target market as having unique advantages. For example, Caterpillar sets premium prices on its construction equipment to support and capture its high perceived value. Genzyme Corp. introduced Ceredase as the first effective treatment for Gaucher's disease. This pill allows patients to avoid years of painful physical deterioration and lead normal lives. A year's supply for one patient can exceed $300,000.

price skimming
A pricing policy whereby a firm charges a high introductory price, often coupled with heavy promotion.

Price skimming works best when the market is willing to buy the product even though it carries an above-average price. If some purchasing agents feel that Caterpillar equipment is far superior to competitors' products, then Caterpillar can charge premium prices successfully. Firms can also effectively use price skimming when a product is well protected legally, when it represents a technological breakthrough, or when it has in some other way blocked entry to competitors. Managers may follow a skimming strategy when production cannot be expanded rapidly because of technological difficulties, shortages, or constraints imposed by the skills and time required to produce a product. As long as demand is greater than supply, skimming is an attainable strategy.

A successful skimming strategy enables management to recover its product development or "educational" costs quickly. (Often, consumers must be "taught" the advantages of a radically new item, such as high-definition TV.) Even if the market perceives an introductory price as too high, managers can easily correct the problem by lowering the price. Firms often feel it is better to test the market

Southwest Airlines Home Gate
How does Southwest promote its fare advantage on the Web?
www.iflyswa.com

on line

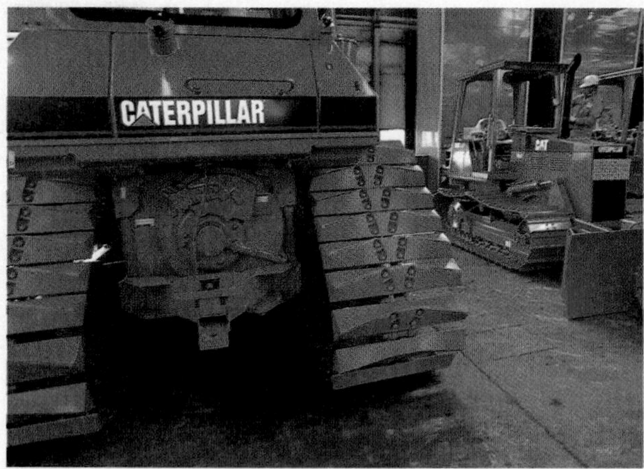

As long as Caterpillar equipment is considered a superior value, the company can successfully implement a price-skimming strategy. Were the quality or perceived value of the product to decrease, skimming would not be a viable strategy.

at a high price and then lower the price if sales are too slow. They are tacitly saying, "If there are any premium-price buyers in the market, let's reach them first and maximize our revenue per unit."

Penetration Pricing Penetration pricing is at the other end of the spectrum from skimming. **Penetration pricing** involves charging a relatively low price for a product as a way to reach the mass market. The low price is designed to capture a large share of a substantial market, resulting in lower production costs. If a marketing manager has made obtaining a large market share the firm's pricing objective, penetration pricing is a logical choice.

However, penetration pricing does mean lower profit per unit. Relative to a skimming policy, it requires higher-volume sales to reach the break-even point. If reaching a high volume of sales takes a long time, the recovery of product development costs will also be slow. As you might expect, penetration pricing tends to discourage competition.

penetration pricing
A pricing policy whereby a firm charges a relatively low price for a product initially as a way to reach the mass market.

A penetration strategy tends to be effective in a price-sensitive market. Price should decline more rapidly when demand is elastic, because the market can be expanded through a lower price. Also, price sensitivity and greater competitive pressure should lead to a lower initial price and a relatively slow decline in the price later.

For some years Fuji and Kodak battled it out in overseas film markets. In Canada, the situation was quite different: Kodak and Fuji treated this market like a cozy, mutually profitable duopoly. Both enjoyed large margins. Kodak had most of the market for film, and distant #2 Fuji always priced its films just a bit lower.

Then in 1997, Fuji began slashing prices by as much as 25 percent. Fuji's explanation was that Costco, one of its five largest distributors, had dropped Fuji for Kodak, and that the company had thus been stuck with 2.5 million rolls of film. Fuji sold the film at a steep discount to other distributors. When consumers saw that the familiar red, white, and green boxes were a dollar or two cheaper, many switched brands, and this increased Fuji's share of the market.[10]

Status Quo Pricing The third basic price strategy a firm can choose is status quo pricing, or meeting the competition. It means charging a price identical to or very close to the competition's price. Status quo pricing has the advantage of simplicity; its disadvantage is that the strategy may ignore demand, or cost, or both. However, meeting the competition may be the safest route to long-term survival if the firm is comparatively small.

The Legality and Ethics of Price Strategy

7
Identify the legal and ethical constraints on pricing decisions

As we noted in Chapter 3, some pricing decisions are subject to government regulation. Before marketing managers establish any price strategy, they should know the laws that limit their scope for decision making. The law has much to say about resale price maintenance, price fixing, price discrimination, and predatory pricing.

Smith & Hawken

What kind of pricing strategy does Smith & Hawken employ on its Website? What about the mix of products? Do these two marketing elements—pricing and product mix—seem different from what you find in the store or the catalogue? Explain why.

www.smithhawken.com; www.smithandhawken.com

on line

Resale Price Maintenance

Many producers would like to be able to control the prices of their products on retail store shelves. However, resale price maintenance is illegal in Canada. Section 50 of the Competition Act prohibits a manufacturer from requiring a retailer to sell a product at a particular price or below a particular price. The act allows a manufacturer to set a *suggested retail price* as long as it is clear that the retailer will not be discriminated against if it does not maintain that suggested price.

Price Fixing

price fixing
An agreement between two or more firms on the price they will charge for a product.

Price fixing is an agreement between two or more firms on the price they will charge for a product. Suppose that two or more executives from competing firms meet to decide how much to charge for a product, or to decide which of them will submit the lowest bid on a certain contract. Such practices are illegal under the Competition Act. Offenders can receive fines and prison terms. Canada's three largest flour milling companies—Robin Hood Multifoods, Maple Leaf Mills, and Ogilvie Mills—were fined $1 million each for rigging bids to supply flour to the federal government.

Price Discrimination

The Competition Act prohibits any firm from selling to two or more different buyers, within a reasonably short time, commodities (not services) of like grade and quality at different prices where the result would be substantially reduced competition. Note that not all price differences represent price discrimination. For example, children and seniors pay lower prices for movie tickets. For price discrimination to exist, the following conditions must be present:

- There must be price discrimination; that is, the seller must charge different prices to different customers for the same product.
- The two customers must be competitors.
- The seller must discriminate by price among two or more purchasers; that is, the seller must make two or more actual sales within a reasonably short time.
- The products sold must be commodities or other tangible goods.
- The products sold must be of like grade and quality, not necessarily identical. If the goods are truly interchangeable and substitutable, then they are of like grade and quality.
- The act of discrimination must be part of an ongoing practice of discrimination.

Predatory Pricing

predatory pricing
The practice of charging a very low price for a product with the intent of driving competitors out of business or out of a market.

Predatory pricing is the practice of charging a very low price for a product with the intention of driving competitors out of business or out of a market. Once competitors have been driven out, the firm raises its prices. This practice is illegal under section 34(b) of the Competition Act. However, it is difficult to prove. It must be shown that the predator (i.e., the destructive company) explicitly tried to ruin a competitor and that the predatory price was below the defendant's average cost.[11] Some provinces, such as British Columbia, Alberta, and Manitoba, have provincial legislation that prohibits companies from selling below cost plus some reasonable markup, such as 5 percent.

Price fixing

To learn about current price-fixing cases, type "price fixing" into your favourite search engine and compare a few company Websites. How do companies deal with this type of scandal on their sites? Does this surprise you?

Tactics for Fine-Tuning the Base Price

8

Explain how discounts, geographic pricing, and other special pricing tactics can be used to fine tune the base price

After managers understand both the legal and the marketing consequences of price strategies, they should set a **base price**—that is, the general price level at which the company expects to sell the good or service. The general price level is correlated with the pricing policy: above the market (price skimming), at the market (status quo pricing), or below the market (penetration pricing). The final step, then, is to fine tune the base price.

base price
The general price level at which the company expects to sell the good or service.

Fine tuning techniques are short-run approaches that do not change the general price level. They do, however, result in changes within a general price level. These pricing tactics allow the firm to adjust for competition in certain markets, meet ever-changing government regulations, take advantage of unique demand situations, and meet promotional and positioning goals. Fine tuning pricing tactics include various sorts of discounts, geographic pricing, and special pricing tactics.

Discounts, Allowances, Rebates, and Value Pricing

A base price can be lowered through the use of discounts and the related tactics of allowances, rebates, and value pricing. Managers use the various forms of discounts to encourage customers to do what they would not ordinarily do, such as pay cash or take delivery out of season. Following is a summary of common tactics:

quantity discount
A price reduction offered to buyers buying in multiple units or above a specified dollar amount.

cumulative quantity discount
A deduction from list price that applies to the buyer's total purchases made during a specific period.

noncumulative quantity discount
A deduction from list price that applies to a single order rather than to the total volume of orders placed during a certain period.

cash discount
A price reduction offered to a buyer in return for prompt payment of a bill.

functional discount (trade discount)
A discount to wholesalers and retailers for performing channel functions.

seasonal discount
A price reduction for buying merchandise out of season.

promotional allowance (trade allowance)
A payment to a dealer for promoting the manufacturer's products.

- *Quantity discounts:* When buyers get a lower price for buying in multiple units or above a specified dollar amount, they are receiving a **quantity discount.** A **cumulative quantity discount** is a deduction from list price that applies to the buyer's total purchases made during a specific period; it is intended to encourage customer loyalty. A **noncumulative quantity discount** is a deduction from list price that applies to a single order rather than to the total volume of orders placed during a certain period. It is intended to encourage orders in large quantities.
- *Cash discounts:* A **cash discount** is a price reduction offered to a buyer in return for prompt payment of a bill. Prompt payment saves the seller carrying charges and billing expenses.
- *Functional discounts:* When distribution channel intermediaries, such as wholesalers or retailers, perform a service or function for the manufacturer, they must be compensated. This compensation—typically a percentage discount from the base price—is called a **functional discount** (or **trade discount**). Functional discounts vary greatly from channel to channel, depending on the tasks performed by the intermediary.
- *Seasonal discounts:* A **seasonal discount** is a price reduction for buying merchandise out of season. It shifts the storage function to the purchaser. Seasonal discounts also enable manufacturers to maintain a steady production schedule year-round.
- *Promotional allowances:* A **promotional allowance** (also known as a **trade allowance**) is a payment to a dealer for promoting the manufacturer's products. It is both a pricing tool and a promotional device. As a pricing tool, a promotional allowance is like a functional discount. If, for example, a retailer runs an ad for a manufacturer's product, the manufacturer may pay half the cost. If a retailer sets up a special display, the manufacturer may include a certain quantity of free goods in the retailer's next order.

services spotlight

Discounting Dilemma

Traditional department stores such as The Bay and Sears Canada are increasingly feeling the pinch of competition from mass discount chains such as Wal-Mart Canada. That message was clear in June 2001 as the heads of Canada's two largest department stores faced off at a Retail Council of Canada seminar on customer loyalty. "The mass [merchants] basically set the pricing in this country," said George Heller, CEO of Hudson's Bay Co., which operates The Bay and Zellers chains. "The amount of full-price merchandise being sold year over year is declining, no doubt about it, and we have nobody to blame but ourselves." Heller said that years of aggressive price wars between The Bay and the former Eatons retail empire trained Canadian consumers—now more retail savvy than ever before—to buy goods only when they were on sale. While those two duked it out in the mid-price market, Sears flourished in the suburbs and Wal-Mart swept into Canada, establishing itself within five years as the number one discount merchant in the country.

"Mass channel prices are getting lower and lower and it puts enormous pressure on the others," said Heller. If the price gap between traditional and mass merchandisers keeps growing, he said, it will become harder for customers to believe that a plain T-shirt costing three to four times more in a department store is actually worth the higher price because of its quality. "I think Canadian consumers have always been value conscious, but department stores were the value shop twenty years ago," noted retail consultant Richard Talbot. "Now they are under attack." Department stores are therefore faced with a dilemma: they must discount more aggressively in order to see a bounce in sales, but slashing prices eats into their profit margins.

Mark Cohen, CEO of Sears Canada Inc., believes that department stores will never be replaced by single-category big boxes or specialty retailers as long as they stand out by offering customers superior service. Today's time-strapped female shopper might ultimately side with a retailer that allows her to return merchandise without a hassle, he said. "The struggle is to be able to afford that [service] and do it reliably," Cohen said. Both he and Heller agreed that boosting the level of in-house brands will allow department stores to be price competitive and still make money. In the past three years, Zellers' private label business has grown from nil to about 22 percent of sales. That could reach 35 percent in the next couple of years depending on customer response. Less than 30 percent of The Bay's sales come from private label products, but that could grow to 35 percent in two to three years, and as high as 70 percent in some subcategories of apparel such as lingerie, Heller said. At Sears, about 65 percent of the chainwide sales come from private label goods.

Why are The Bay and Sears finding it so hard to determine a profitable pricing strategy? How does their strategy differ from Wal-Mart's? Do you agree that customers will pay higher prices for better service in department stores versus discount stores? What are the benefits to the stores of selling more private label goods? What are the benefits (and downsides) for customers?

Source: Adapted from Holly Shaw, "Sears, The Bay Paying Price for Past Price Wars," *The National Post,* 20 June 2001, p. C6.

- *Rebates:* A **rebate** is a cash refund given for purchasing a product during a specific period. The advantage of a rebate over a simple price reduction for stimulating demand is that a rebate is a temporary inducement that can be taken away without altering the basic price structure.

rebate
A cash refund given for the purchase of a product during a specific period.

Value-Based Pricing

Value-based pricing is a strategy that has grown out of the quality movement. It does not establish prices based on costs or competitors' prices. Rather, it starts with the customer, considers the competition, and then determines the appropriate price. Firms that use this strategy are customer driven. They are seeking to understand the attributes that customers want in the goods and services they buy, and the value of those attributes to those customers. Because very few firms operate in a pure monopoly, a marketer using value-based pricing must also determine the value of competitors' offerings to customers. Customers determine the value of a product (not just its price) relative to the value of alternatives. So in value-based pricing, the price of the product is set at a level that seems to the customer to be a good price compared with the prices of other options.

value-based pricing
The price is set at a level that seems to the customer to be a good price compared to the prices of other options.

An important type of value pricing is everyday low prices. This form has evolved because of trade loading. **Trade loading** occurs when a manufacturer tem-

trade loading
The practice of temporarily lowering the price to induce wholesalers and retailers to buy more goods than can be sold in a reasonable time.

Christmas Depot

What kinds of discounts would you expect to find at a year-round Christmas store? Go to the on-line Christmas Depot and check some of the prices. Did you find any deals?

www.christmasdepot.com

on line

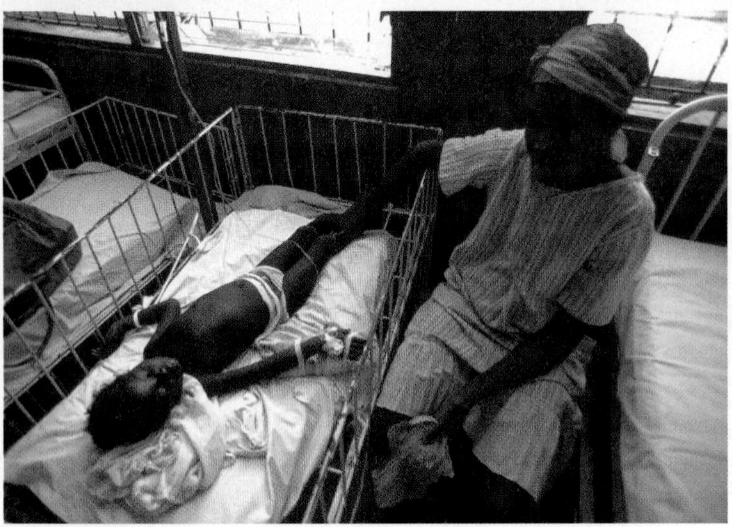

Glaxo-Wellcome offers a discount on AZT for AIDS patients in impoverished nations. This discount, which might be termed a "social responsibility discount," can help infected infants but is not available for the long-term care of their mothers. Do you think this is ethical? Explain.

porarily lowers the price to induce wholesalers and retailers to buy more goods than can be sold in a reasonable time. Say that Procter & Gamble offers Shoppers Drug Mart an extra thirty cents off the normal price for a bottle of Prell. The chain's buyer jumps at the bargain and buys a three-month supply of Prell. Typically, Shoppers Drug Mart will pass along the discount to customers for about a month, but then return to the original price for the last two months, thereby reaping some extra profit.

Trade discounts like these have more than tripled in the past decade. The practice is most common in the packaged goods industry. Many billions of dollars in grocery products—mostly nonperishables—sit at any one time on trucks and railcars or stacked inside distribution centres, caught in gridlock because of trade loading. This idle inventory adds to the nation's grocery bill. However, it is estimated that such practices generate about 70 percent of wholesalers' profits and 40 percent of supermarkets' profits.[12] Understandably, wholesalers and retailers have become addicted to trade-loading deals.

Procter & Gamble has decided to attack the trade-loading problem with **everyday low prices (EDLP),** which is the tactic of offering lower prices (typically 10 to 25 percent lower) and maintaining those prices while eliminating the functional discounts that result in trade loading. So instead of selling, say, a case of cake mix for $10.00 most of the time and then for $7.00 to load the trade, P&G will sell the case for $8.50 all the time. Since 1994, P&G has reduced its list prices by 12 to 24 percent on all its brands.[13]

everyday low prices (EDLP)
The price tactic of permanently reducing prices 10 to 25 percent below the traditional levels while eliminating trade discounts that create trade loading.

Geographic Pricing

Because many sellers ship their wares to a nationwide or even a worldwide market, the cost of freight can greatly affect the total cost of a product. Sellers may use several different geographic pricing tactics to moderate the impact of freight costs on distant customers. Following are the most common methods of geographic pricing:

- *FOB origin pricing:* **FOB origin pricing**, also called FOB factory or FOB shipping point, is a price tactic that requires the buyer to absorb the freight costs from the shipping point. The farther buyers are from sellers, the more they pay, because transportation costs increase with distance.
- *Uniform delivered pricing:* If the marketing manager wants total costs, including freight, to be equal for all purchasers of identical products, the firm will adopt uniform delivered pricing, or "postage stamp" pricing. With **uniform delivered pricing**, the seller pays the actual freight charges and bills every purchaser an identical, flat freight charge.
- *Zone pricing:* A marketing manager who wants to equalize total costs among buyers within large geographic areas—but not necessarily all of the seller's market area—may modify the base price with a zone-pricing tactic. **Zone pricing** is a modification of uniform delivered pricing. Instead of placing the entire country (or its total market) under a uniform freight rate, the firm

FOB origin pricing
A price tactic that requires the buyer to absorb the freight costs from the shipping point ("free on board").

uniform delivered pricing
A price tactic in which the seller pays the actual freight charges and bills every purchaser an identical, flat freight charge.

zone pricing
A modification of uniform delivered pricing that divides the country (or the total market) into segments or zones and charges a flat freight rate to all customers in a given zone.

United Parcel Service

Go to UPS's Website and do some quick cost comparisons on sending the same package to a friend in town and to a friend located at some distance. Does the difference in cost surprise you? Is it justified? Explain.

www.ups.com

on line

divides the market into segments or zones and charges a flat freight rate to all customers in a given zone.

- *Freight absorption pricing*: In **freight absorption pricing**, the seller pays all or part of the actual freight charges and does not pass them on to the buyer. The manager may use this tactic in intensely competitive areas or as a way to break into new market areas.

freight absorption pricing
A price tactic in which the seller pays all or part of the actual freight charges and does not pass them on to the buyer.

- *Basing point pricing*: With **basing point pricing**, the seller designates a location as a basing point and charges all buyers the freight cost from that point, regardless of the city from which the goods are shipped.

basing point pricing
A price tactic that charges freight from a given (basing) point, regardless of the city from which the goods are shipped.

Special Pricing Tactics

Special pricing tactics defy neat categorization. Managers use these tactics for various reasons—for example, to stimulate demand for specific products, to increase store patronage, or to offer a wider variety of merchandise at a specific price point. Special pricing tactics include a single-price tactic, flexible pricing, professional services pricing, price lining, leader pricing, bait pricing, odd–even pricing, price bundling, and two-part pricing. A brief overview of each of these tactics follows.

Single-Price Tactic A merchant using a **single-price tactic** offers all goods and services at the same price (or perhaps two or three prices). Retailers using this tactic include Dollar Stores, One Price Clothing Stores, Dre$$ to the Nine$, Your $10 Store, and Fashions $9.99. One Dollar Stores, located in malls across Canada, sell all products at prices of one or two dollars.

single-price tactic
When a merchant offers all goods and services at the same price or prices.

Flexible Pricing **Flexible pricing** (or **variable pricing**) means that different customers pay different prices for essentially the same merchandise bought in equal quantities. This tactic is often found in the sale of shopping goods, specialty merchandise, and most industrial goods except supply items. Car dealers, many appliance retailers, and manufacturers of industrial installations, accessories, and component parts commonly follow the practice. It allows the seller to adjust for competition by meeting another seller's price. Flexible pricing also enables the seller to close a sale with price-conscious consumers. If buyers show promise of becoming large-volume shoppers, flexible pricing can be used to lure their business.

flexible pricing (variable pricing)
A price tactic in which different customers pay different prices for essentially the same merchandise bought in equal quantities.

The obvious disadvantages of flexible pricing are the lack of consistent profit margins, the potential ill will of purchasers who paid "too much," the tendency for salespeople to automatically lower the price to make a sale, and the possibility of a price war among sellers. The disadvantages of flexible pricing have led the automobile industry to experiment with one price for all buyers. Ford started offering the Cougar at one price and has seen an 80 percent increase in sales. General Motors uses a one-price tactic for some of its models, including the Saturn and the Buick Regal.

Professional Services Pricing Professional services pricing is used by people with lengthy experience and training; also, they have often been certified by a licensing board. Lawyers, psychologists, business consultants, and family counsellors fall into this category. Many professionals charge customers an hourly rate, but sometimes they base their fees on the solution of a problem or on the performance of an act. For example, a lawyer might charge $1,000 for completing a divorce but only $150 for handling a traffic ticket.

Price Lining When a seller establishes a series of prices for a type of merchandise, it creates a price line. **Price lining** is the practice of offering a product line with several items at specific price points. Hon, an office furniture manufacturer,

price lining
The practice of offering a product line with several items at specific price points.

leader pricing (loss leader pricing)
A price tactic in which a product is sold near or even below cost in the hope that shoppers will buy other items once they are in the store.

bait pricing
A price tactic that tries to get consumers into a store through false or misleading price advertising and then uses high-pressure selling to persuade consumers to buy more expensive merchandise.

odd–even pricing (psychological pricing)
A price tactic that uses odd-numbered prices to connote bargains and even-numbered prices to imply quality.

price bundling
Marketing two or more products in a single package for a special price.

unbundling
Reducing the bundle of services that comes with the basic product.

may offer its four-drawer file cabinets at $125, $250, and $400. The Limited may offer women's dresses at $40, $70, and $100, with no merchandise marked at prices between those figures. Price lining reduces confusion for both the salesperson and the consumer. Also, the buyer may be offered a wider variety of merchandise at each established price. Price lines may also enable a seller to reach several market segments.

Leader Pricing **Leader pricing** (or **loss leader pricing**) is an attempt by the marketing manager to attract customers by selling a product near or even below cost, in the hope that shoppers will buy other items once they are in the store. This type of pricing appears every week in the newspaper ads of supermarkets, specialty stores, and department stores. Leader pricing is typically used on well-known items that consumers can easily recognize as bargains at the special price. The goal is not necessarily to sell large quantities of leader items, but rather to appeal to customers who otherwise might shop elsewhere.

Bait Pricing In contrast to leader pricing, which is a genuine attempt to give the consumer a reduced price, bait pricing is deceptive. **Bait pricing** gets the consumer into a store through false or misleading price advertising and then uses high-pressure selling to persuade the consumer to buy more expensive merchandise.

A retailer may advertise a computer for only $599. That is the bait. When a customer goes in to see the computer, the salesperson says they are out of stock, or points out all of the disadvantages of the low-priced computer to the prospective buyer and then tries to sell a more expensive model. Bait pricing can be illegal under the Competition Act.

Odd–Even Pricing **Odd–even pricing** (or **psychological pricing**) involves pricing at odd-numbered prices to connote a bargain and pricing at even-numbered prices to imply quality. For years, many retailers have used this tactic, pricing their products in odd numbers—for example, $99.95 or $49.95. Some retailers favour odd-numbered prices because they believe that $9.99 sounds less imposing to customers than $10.00. Other retailers believe that the use of an odd-numbered price signals to consumers that the price is at the lowest level possible. Neither theory has ever been conclusively proved, although one study found that consumers perceive odd-priced products as being on sale.[14] The most recent research shows that consumers do purchase more at odd prices.[15]

Even-numbered pricing is sometimes used to denote quality. Examples include a fine perfume at $500 a bottle, a good watch at $1,500, or a mink coat at $8,000.

Services, such as hotels, use price bundling to stimulate demand. (© 2001 Marriott International, Inc. All rights reserved. Reprinted with permission of Marriott International, Inc.)

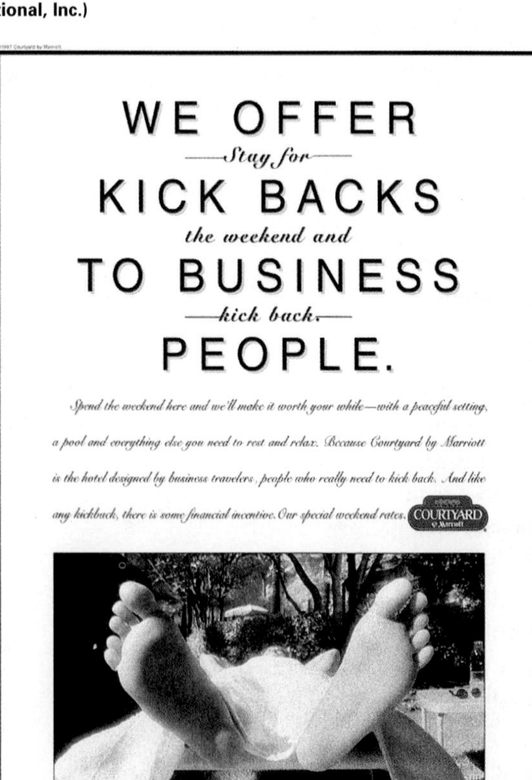

Price Bundling **Price bundling** involves marketing two or more products in a single package for a special price. Examples include packages of stereo equipment or office furniture, packages of options on cars, weekend hotel packages that include a room and several meals, and airline vacation packages. Microsoft now offers "suites" of software that bundle spreadsheet, word processing, graphics, e-mail, and Internet access programs, along with groupware for networks of computers. Price bundling can stimulate demand for the bundled items if the target market perceives the price as a good value.[16]

A related price tactic is **unbundling**, or reducing the bundle of services that comes with the basic product. Instead of raising the price of hotel rooms, some hotel chains have started charging registered guests for parking. To help hold the line on costs, some department stores now require customers to pay for gift wrapping.

Two-Part Pricing **Two-part pricing** involves establishing two separate charges to consume a single good or service. Tennis clubs and health clubs charge a membership fee, as well as a flat fee each time a person uses certain equipment or facilities. Or, alternatively, they charge a base rate for a certain level of use, such as ten racquetball games per month, and a surcharge for anything over that amount.

two-part pricing
A price tactic that charges two separate amounts to consume a single good or service.

LOOKING BACK

Look back at the vignette about Priceline. There is no doubt that the Internet will have a big impact on pricing. Buyers will be able to quickly compare prices and products. Sellers will learn more about potential buyers and tailor their products accordingly. Extranets will lower costs and enable sellers to deliver better value to purchasers.

Cost determines the floor below which a price should not be set in the long run. A price set solely on cost may be too high and therefore not attract customers. Conversely, a price based on cost alone that is too low results in lost revenues and profits.

Price can have an impact on perceived quality, depending on a number of issues, such as the type of product, advertising, and the consumer's personality. A well-known brand is usually more important than price in consumers' quality perceptions.

Competition can help hold down prices in the marketplace. A firm without competition that charges a high price will soon find competitors attracted to that market. As competitors enter the market, prices typically fall, because firms compete for market share by lowering prices.

Summary

1 Discuss the importance of pricing decisions to the economy and to the individual firm. Pricing plays an integral role in the Canadian economy by allocating goods and services among consumers, governments, and businesses. Pricing is essential in business because it creates revenue, which is the basis of all business activity. In setting prices, marketing managers strive to find a level high enough to produce a satisfactory profit.

2 List and explain a variety of pricing objectives. Establishing realistic and measurable pricing objectives is a critical part of any firm's marketing strategy. Pricing objectives are commonly classified into three categories: profit oriented, sales oriented, and status quo. Profit-oriented pricing is based on profit maximization, a satisfactory level of profit, or a target return on investment. The goal of profit maximization is to generate as much revenue as possible in relation to cost. Often, a more practical approach than profit maximization is setting prices to produce profits that will satisfy management and stockholders. The most common profit-oriented strategy is pricing for a specific ROI relative to a firm's assets. The second type of pricing objective is sales oriented, and focuses on either maintaining a percentage share of the market or maximizing dollar or unit sales. The third type of pricing objective aims to maintain the status quo by matching competitors' prices.

3 Explain the role of demand in price determination. Demand is a key determinant of price. When establishing prices, a firm must first determine demand for its product. A typical demand schedule shows an inverse relationship between quantity demanded and price: when price is lowered, sales increase; and when price is increased, the quantity demanded falls. However, for prestige products, there may be a direct relationship between demand and price: the quantity demanded will increase as price increases.

Marketing managers must also consider demand elasticity when setting prices. Elasticity of demand is the degree to which the quantity demanded fluctuates with changes in price. If consumers are sensitive to changes in price, demand is elastic; if they are insensitive to price changes, demand is inelastic. Thus, an increase in price will result in lower sales for an elastic product and little or no loss in sales for an inelastic product.

4 Describe cost-oriented pricing strategies. The other major determinant of price is cost. Marketers use several cost-oriented pricing strategies. To cover their own expenses and obtain a profit, wholesalers and retailers commonly use markup pricing: that is, they tack an extra amount onto the manufacturer's original price. Another pricing technique is to maximize profits by setting price where marginal revenue equals marginal cost. Still another pricing strategy determines how much a firm must sell to break even and uses this amount as a reference point for adjusting price.

5 Demonstrate how the product life cycle, competition, distribution and promotion strategies, customer demands, the Internet and extranets, and perceptions of quality can affect price. The price of a product normally changes as it moves through the life cycle and as demand for the product and competitive conditions change. Management often sets a high price at the introductory stage, and the high price tends to attract competition. The competition usually drives prices down, because individual competitors lower prices to gain market share.

Adequate distribution for a new product can sometimes be obtained by offering a larger-than-usual profit margin to wholesalers and retailers. The Internet enables consumers to compare products and prices quickly and efficiently. Extranets help control costs and lower prices. Price is also used as a promotional tool to attract customers. Special low prices often attract new customers and entice existing customers to buy more. The demands of large customers can squeeze the profit margins of suppliers.

Perceptions of quality also can influence pricing strategies. A firm trying to project a prestigious image often charges a premium price for a product. Consumers tend to equate high prices with high quality.

6 Describe the procedure for setting the right price. The process of setting the right price on a product has four main steps: (1) establishing pricing goals; (2) estimating demand, costs, and profits; (3) choosing a price policy to help determine a base price; and (4) fine tuning the base price with pricing tactics.

7 Identify the legal and ethical constraints on pricing decisions. Government regulation helps monitor four main areas of pricing: resale price maintenance, price fixing, predatory pricing, and price discrimination. Regardless of the wishes of producers, resellers can charge whatever price they wish for products; price fixing between competive sellers is illegal; pricing to put a competitor out of business is illegal; and charging a different price for commodities of like grade and quality when the effect is to cause competitive injury is illegal. Resale price maintenance, price fixing, predatory pricing, and price discrimination are all covered by the Competition Act.

8 Explain how discounts, geographic pricing, and other special pricing tactics can be used to fine tune the base price. Several techniques enable marketing managers to adjust prices within a general range in response to changes in competition, government regulation, consumer demand, and promotional and positioning goals. Techniques for fine tuning a price can be divided into three main categories: discounts, allowances, rebates and value pricing; geographic pricing; and special pricing tactics.

The first type of tactic gives lower prices to those who pay promptly, order a large quantity, or perform some function for the manufacturer. Value-based pricing starts with the customer, considers the competition and costs, and then determines a price. Everyday low pricing, a form of value-based pricing, arose from trade loading. Trade loading is a manufacturer's temporary functional discount to induce wholesalers and retailers to buy more goods than can be sold in a reasonable length of time. Trade loading increases inventory expenses and channel expenses and lowers the manufacturer's profits. A tactic meant to overcome these problems is "everyday low pricing," or maintaining low prices over time while eliminating the discounts that result in trade loading. Other tactics in this category include seasonal discounts, promotion allowances, and rebates (cash refunds).

Geographic pricing tactics—such as FOB origin pricing, uniform delivered pricing, zone pricing, freight absorption pricing, and basing-point pricing—are ways of moderating the impact of shipping costs on distant customers.

Discussion and Writing Questions

1. Why is pricing so important to the marketing manager?
2. Explain the role of supply and demand in determining price.
3. Explain the concepts of elastic and inelastic demand. Why should managers understand these concepts?
4. Your firm has based its pricing strictly on cost in the past. As the newly hired marketing manager, you believe this policy should change. Write the president a memo explaining your reasons.
5. Give an example of each major type of pricing objective.
6. How does the stage of a product's life cycle affect price? Give some examples.
7. Go back to Priceline.com. Can you research a ticket's price before purchasing it? How comfortable are you with naming your own price? Relate the supply and demand curves to customer-determined pricing.
8. A manufacturer of office furniture decides to produce antique-style rolltop desks, but formatted for personal computers. The desks will have built-in surge protectors, a platform for raising or lowering the monitor, and a number of other features. The quality, solid-oak desks will be priced far below comparable products. The marketing manager says, "We'll charge a low price and plan on a high volume to reduce our risks." Comment.
9. Develop a price line strategy for each of these firms:
   a. a university bookstore
   b. a restaurant
   c. a DVD rental firm
10. Explain the difference between freight absorption pricing and uniform delivered pricing. When would it be appropriate to use each?
11. Divide into teams of four. Each team should choose one of the following topics: skimming, penetration pricing, status quo pricing, price fixing, EDLP, geographic pricing, adopting a single-price tactic, flexible pricing, or professional services pricing. Each team should then pick a retailer that it feels most closely follows the team's chosen pricing strategy. Go to the store and write down examples of the strategy. Interview the store manager and get his or her views on the advantages and disadvantages of the strategy. Each team should then make an oral report in class.
12. What pricing advantages does the Auto Connection (**www.autoconnection.com**) seem to offer compared to traditional auto dealers?
13. What kind of pricing strategies are being offered by the following four telecommunication competitors?
    www.att.com
    www.mci.com
    www.sprint.com
    www.gte.com

Do You Know These Terms?

Application for Small Business

Northern Lights Perfume of North Bay, Ontario, is a small manufacturer that distributes a line of quality women's perfumes to intermediate- and high-priced department and specialty stores. It has recently decided to add a new, lower-priced line to its product mix to capture a slightly different segment of the market. The new product is called "Passion Flower." A recent market test revealed the following estimated total demand for the product at the quoted prices:

Price ($)	Number of units
15.00	25,000
20.00	20,000
22.50	19,000
25.00	11,000
27.50	10,000

The accounting department figures that the average variable cost for the new perfume would be $13 per unit. Fixed costs are estimated at $40,000.

Questions

1. Assuming that the market research studies are accurate, what price should be charged for the perfume?
2. What kind of market research study could have been done to determine the demand schedule for the perfume? Assume that fixed costs are $140,000 rather than $40,000. Should the company have produced for the short run? For the long run?
3. Discuss the advantages and disadvantages of break-even analysis.
4. What is the break-even point for this perfume? Of what significance is that point?

VIDEO CASE

Toronto Blue Jays: Ballpark Pricing

The opening pitch of 2002 marked the start of the Toronto Blue Jays' twenty-sixth season in the American League. Over the past five seasons the Jays have won a little fewer than half the games they've played (162 each year). For home games the Jays play in the SkyDome, the world's most advanced retractable-roof stadium, which seats 50,516. The club has invested $5 million in it for preferred supplier status and a Sky Box.

With their state-of-the-art stadium, the Jays feel that if they can field a winning team, their tickets are a great value because of the satisfaction that baseball lovers can expect to receive. Tickets to games range from $7 to $35. This pricing structure is based on the perceived value of the entertainment offered. Every season the Blue Jays have to balance two key economic factors when determining their ticket prices: the demand for seats, and the skyrocketing costs of running a major league baseball club.

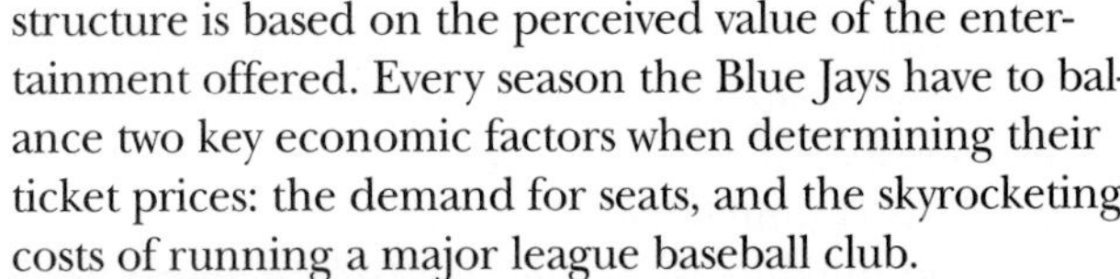

The Jays' front office does not expect consumers to be highly sensitive to fluctuations in price: they expect Jays fans to turn out in great numbers despite rising ticket prices. This inelastic demand for Jays tickets can be attributed greatly to the fact that the team has played well, but also to the fact that loyal Jays fans can never stay away. They are willing to pay the price to support their team.

Another reason for the inelastic demand for Blue Jays tickets is that there is no locally available substitute. Sports fans can support any number of professional sports, from baseball to tennis; and they can always watch amateurs play; but for major league baseball in Toronto, the Jays are the only game in town. The purchasing power of Torontonians is also an important factor in the inelastic demand for Jays tickets. The Jays' front office provides a wide range of ticket options—preferred or general seating, a season's subscription or a single ticket—so that even if prices increased, most residents in the Toronto area could still come to the games.

For the Blue Jays, pricing strategies are not just a financial necessity, they are also a promotional tool for increasing fan attendance. At all Saturday home games and nonholiday weekday games, senior citizens and youths under fourteen can purchase tickets (except the most expensive ones) for half-price. Season ticket holders receive special benefits: the same seats for every game, guaranteed tickets for postseason games played at home, a complimentary Blue Jays media guide and calendar; and the convenience of entering the SkyDome on game day without having to wait in line at the ticket window. Fans with group tickets also receive special treatment: preferred seating; personal services from the group sales staff; and promotional posters, pocket schedules, and stickers. These perks help persuade large groups (five hundred or more) to use games as social events; as fundraisers; or as ways to promote a business, a social group, or a sports organization.

Ticket sales provide a large portion of the Blue Jays' revenue. Merchandising contributes a large part as well. Blue Jays souvenirs and gifts are sold at the ballpark, at Blue Jays Bullpen souvenir stores, and at upscale department stores across Canada. Also, free catalogues are available by calling a toll-free number, and the complete line of Jays merchandise is available on-line from a wholly owned Jays subsidiary. Caps, jerseys, and jackets like those worn on the field by the players are all available for sale; so are accessories, novelties, and collectibles.

The Blue Jays merchandising machine uses a prestige pricing strategy. Charging high prices helps promote the Jays' high-quality image. Although jackets range from $107.78 to $184.82 and jerseys from $92.37 to $215.63, consumers are willing to pay a high price for official, authentic merchandise that has been approved by the Blue Jays and by Major League Baseball.

Inelastic ticket demand and the prestige pricing of merchandise are fuelled by the success of the ball team. Because the Toronto Blue Jays are a winning team, their fans are willing to pay the price to see them play ball.

Bibliography

www.bluejays.ca

Questions

1. What considerations are included in the Jays' ticket pricing?
2. Why is demand for Blue Jays tickets inelastic?
3. How do the Jays use price as a promotional tool?
4. What pricing strategy is used for Blue Jays merchandise?

CHAPTER

16

LEARNING OBJECTIVES

After studying this chapter, you should be able to

1 Discuss the role of promotion in the marketing mix

2 Discuss the elements of IMC

3 Describe the communication process

4 Explain the goals and tasks of IMC

5 Discuss the AIDA concept and its relationship to the IMC program

6 Describe the factors that affect IMC

7 Describe personal selling

8 Discuss the key differences between relationship selling and traditional selling

9 List the steps in the selling process

10 Describe the functions of sales management

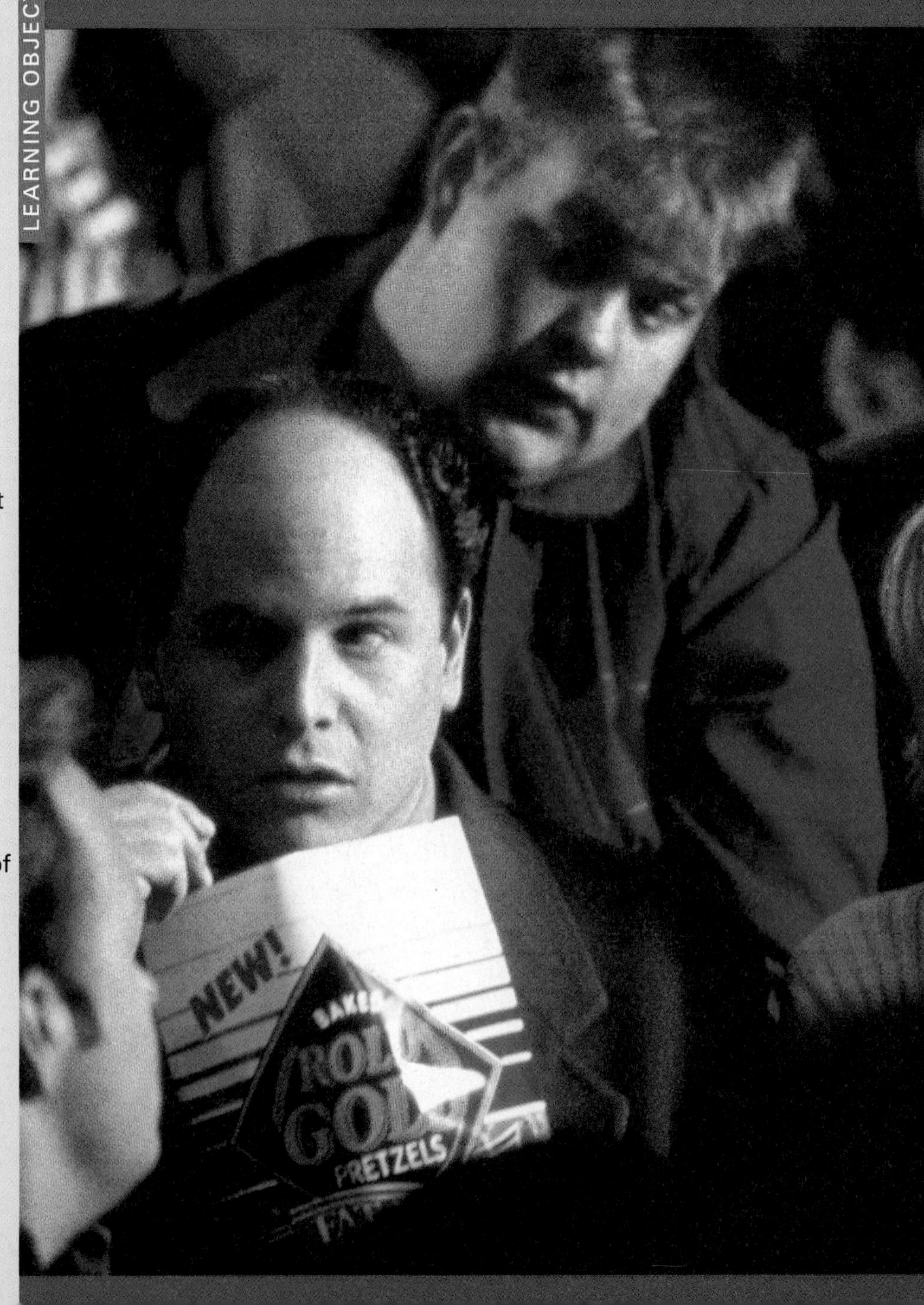

MARKETING COMMUNICATION AND PERSONAL SELLING

Most people don't think twice about the bag of chips or cheese snacks they throw into their shopping carts. Consumers just know that the Frito-Lay name and its brands mean good-quality, good-tasting salty snacks. Revenues at Frito-Lay North America, a subsidiary of PepsiCo, grew 7 percent and market share grew by 2 percent to 58 percent in 2000. Annual worldwide sales of Frito-Lay snacks are over $11 billion. Imagine selling billions of dollars in chips a year!

Canadians know Frito-Lay brands at sight: Doritos, Fritos, Lay's, Cheetos, Ruffles, Rold Gold, Wavy Lay's, and Baked Lay's, to name the company's most popular. But how did Frito-Lay get to where it is today? How has the company developed such astounding sales and loyalty among chip aficionados? Much of it has to do with Frito-Lay's promotional plan, which encompasses advertising, sales promotion, public relations, and personal selling.

With a multimillion dollar ad budget, Frito-Lay has plenty of opportunity to get its message of great-tasting snacks across to consumers. Frito-Lay has been a long-time repeat advertiser during the annual Super Bowl. The vast audience provided by the Super Bowl telecast has proved to be an excellent launching pad for Frito-Lay's new brands, such as Wavy Lay's in 1995 and Doritos 3Ds in 1998.

Realizing the natural link between salty snacks and soda, Frito-Lay is continuing its successful sales promotional strategy of offering supermarket-friendly promotions with Pepsi-Cola products, its sister company. Its combined promotion with Pepsi included a "Halloween House Party" with joint Pepsi and Frito-Lay displays at retailers, special packaging, and coupons offering $1 off a purchase of Doritos with the purchase of Pepsi.

Kids' lunches represent a sizable opportunity for Frito-Lay snacks. Frito-Lay has developed the Planet Lunch program, which is targeted specifically to kids and teens. Planet Lunch focuses on single-serving variety packs of its chips and snacks, which it promotes through some 15,000 in-store displays and its Lunch of a Lifetime contest. To enter the Lunch of a Lifetime contest, consumers must collect and submit by mail four pictures from the back of specially marked Planet Lunch™ 28 g bags of Lay's, Doritos, or Cheetos products; the contest can also be entered on-line through the Planet Lunch Website

Frito-Lay

For more information on Frito-Lay's snack brands and its promotional strategies, to learn more about olestra, or to peruse the company's annual report, visit Frito-Lay's Website.

www.fritolay.com

on line

(**www.planetlunch.ca**). Prizes include lunch with a cowboy at the Calgary Stampede, lunch at a Lunar Lunch Mission at the Cosmo Dome® in Montreal, lunch at the ICE Hotel® in Quebec City, or lunch on top of the Canadian Rockies!

Wow! fat-free snacks, made with the controversial fat substitute olestra, have created a formidable public relations task for Frito-Lay. Fat calories from foods fried with olestra (which was developed by Procter & Gamble under the brand name Olean) are not digested by the human body because the additive's fat molecules are too large. This means that consumers get the taste of fat without the added baggage of unwanted calories. The two companies have released countless press releases to back up their research into the safety of olestra and to detail the U.S. Food and Drug Administration's approval of the additive. The Wow! brand is not yet accepted in Canada because it is suspected of causing gastrointestinal problems and potentially serious health risks.

Frito-Lay has invested heavily in advertising and sales promotions. That said, the backbone of the company is its 18,000-strong sales force, which consumers rarely notice but which in 1998 was voted one of America's best sales forces by *Sales & Marketing Management* magazine. Senior executives at Frito-Lay understand that continued growth is more than the result of good advertising campaigns; it is also the culmination of the thousands of face-to-face conversations that their individual sales reps have every day with store managers at supermarkets and convenience stores. Frito-Lay's route service reps (RSRs) use technology and selling skills to convince store managers to stock more Frito-Lay products and position them prominently on their shelves. With handheld computers, RSRs track how products are selling in each store. The company does a monthly analysis of which sizes and flavours sell well in each sales territory. Frito-Lay then uses these data to optimize what it stocks on shelves and to plan promotions tied around certain brands.[1]

As you can see, Frito-Lay strongly emphasizes promotion in its marketing mix. What is the role of promotion in the marketing mix? What types of promotional tools are available to companies, and what factors influence the choice of tools? How is the promotion plan created? The rest of the chapter answers these questions.

The Role of IMC in the Marketing Mix

Few goods or services, no matter how well developed, priced, or distributed, can survive in the marketplace without effective promotion. **Promotion**—the "p" of marketing—is communication by marketers that informs, persuades, and reminds potential buyers about a product in order to influence their opinion or elicit a response. Another term for promotion is integrated marketing communication (IMC). As part of the marketing plan, IMC is a plan for coordinating the elements of promotion: advertising, public relations, personal selling, and sales promotion.

One of the main objectives of an IMC plan is to communicate product benefits to the target audience. A **differential advantage** is those unique features of a company and its products that are perceived by the target market as superior to the competition. These features can include high product quality, rapid delivery, low prices, excellent service, or a feature not offered by the competition. Oil of Olay offers daily lathering cleansing cloths that exfoliate, tone, and condition skin like a facial. By effectively communicating this differential advantage through advertising, Oil of Olay is able to stimulate demand for its skin care products. Clearly, then, promotion is a vital part of the marketing mix, informing consumers of a product's benefits and thereby positioning the product in the marketplace.

1

Discuss the role of promotion in the marketing mix

promotion
Communication by marketers that informs, persuades, and reminds potential buyers about a product in order to influence an opinion or elicit a response.

differential advantage
One or more unique aspects of an organization that influence target consumers to purchase its products or services

The Promotional Mix

Most IMC plans use several elements to reach the target market. These may include personal selling, advertising, sales promotion, and public relations. This combination is referred to as the **promotional mix** (or **IMC plan**). The promotional mix is one that management believes will meet the needs of the target market and achieve the organization's overall goals. The more funds a firm allocates to a given promotional element, the more importance that firm attaches to that element in the overall mix.

2

Discuss the elements of IMC

promotional mix (IMC plan)
Plan for integrating the elements of promotion: advertising, public relations, personal selling, and sales promotion.

Personal Selling

Personal selling is a purchase situation in which two people communicate in an attempt to influence each other. Both the buyer and the seller have specific objectives. Typically, the buyer wants to buy the best product for the least amount; the salesperson often needs to reach monthly sales goals.

Traditional methods of personal selling include a planned presentation to one or more prospective buyers for the purpose of making a sale. Whether it takes place face to face or over the phone, personal selling attempts to persuade the buyer to take some action. A car salesperson may try to persuade a car buyer that a particular model is superior to a competing model in certain features, such as fuel efficiency, roominess, and interior styling. Once the buyer has been somewhat convinced, the salesperson may try to elicit some action from the buyer, such as a test drive or a purchase. Once an action has been taken, the salesperson will follow up with the customer, even after the sale is made. This entire process, including follow-up,is called relationship selling.

Relationship selling emphasizes a win-win outcome so that both buyer and seller reach their objectives in the long term. Relationship selling attempts to create loyalty between the customer and salesperson.[2] Personal selling and relationship selling are discussed later in this chapter.

personal selling
Planned presentation to one or more prospective buyers for the purpose of making a sale.

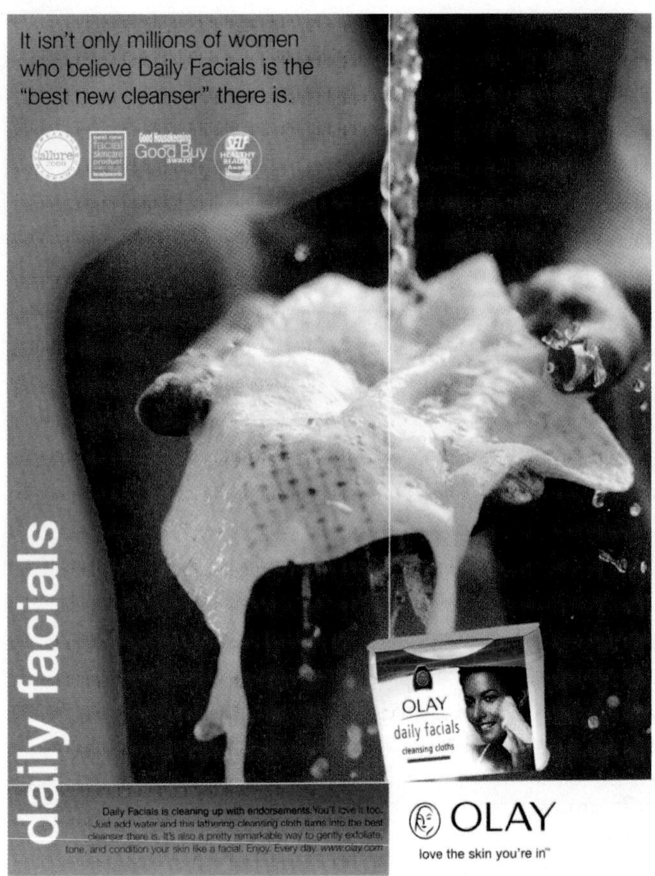

It isn't only millions of women who believe Daily Facials is the "best new cleanser" there is.
Good Buy
daily facials
OLAY
daily facials
cleansing cloths
Daily Facials is cleaning up with endorsements. You'll love it too. Just add water and this lathering cleansing cloth turns into the best cleanser there is. It's also a pretty remarkable way to gently exfoliate, tone, and condition your skin like a facial. Enjoy. Every day. www.olay.com
OLAY
love the skin you're in™

Olay is promoting its Daily Facials Cleansing Cloths through endorsements from its "millions of users" and awards that it has received from magazines, such as the Good Buy Award from *Good Housekeeping* and the Health Beauty Award from *Self*. By effectively communicating its endorsements through advertising, Olay can stimulate demand for its facial products.

Advertising

Almost all companies selling a good or a service use some form of advertising, whether it involves a multimillion-dollar campaign or a simple classified ad in a newspaper. **Advertising** is any form of paid communication in which the sponsor or company is identified. Traditional media—television, radio, newspapers, magazines, books, direct mail, billboards, transit cards (advertisements on buses and taxis and at bus stops), and so on—are the most common approaches to consumer advertising. That being said, marketers are finding many new ways to send their advertisements, most notably through electronic means such as the Internet.

One of advertising's main benefits is that it can communicate to large numbers of people at once. Cost per contact, therefore, is typically very low. Advertising can reach the masses (e.g., through national TV networks), but it can also be microtargeted to small groups of potential customers (e.g., through trade magazines or specialty TV channels).

exhibit 16.1

Role of Promotion in the Marketing Mix

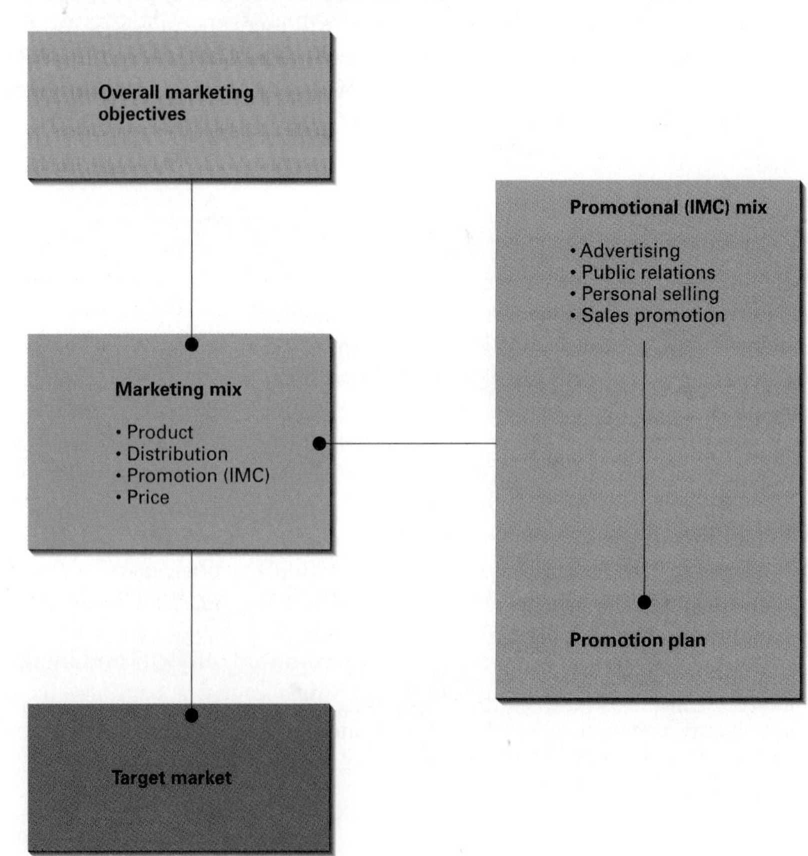

Nabisco

Nabisco lists its promotions on its Website. What are the advantages and disadvantages of this? Visit the site to get more information.

www.nabisco.com

on line

Although the cost per contact in advertising is very low, the total cost to advertise is usually very high. This tends to restrict national advertising to those companies with very deep pockets for this sort of promotion. The Ontario Lottery and Gaming Corporation spent approximately $7 million on advertising for Lotto 6/49 out of its entire lottery budget of $23 million on all media, including TV and radio commercials and print advertisements. Few small companies can match this level of spending for a national campaign.

For smaller companies, advertising costs can sometimes be prohibitive. Few small companies can match the $60 million spent by the Ontario government.

Sales Promotion

Sales promotion consists of all marketing activities, other than personal selling, advertising, and public relations, that stimulate consumer purchasing. Sales promotion is a short-run tool used to stimulate immediate product or service demand. Sales promotion can be aimed at end users, trade customers, or a company's employees. Sales promotions include free samples, contests, premiums, trade shows, vacation give-aways, and coupons. A major promotional campaign might use several of these tools. Nabisco routinely issues coupons for cents off its Oreo sandwich cookies. To celebrate holidays and grab shoppers' attention, the same company uses red food dye at Christmas and blue at Easter, giving Oreos a holiday twist.[3]

Marketers often use sales promotion to improve the effectiveness of other ingredients in the promotional mix, especially advertising and personal selling. Sales promotion complements advertising by yielding faster sales responses. Pizza Hut handed out over 1 million reformulated pizzas at special events or offered coupons for a complimentary pie. In markets where the coupons were distributed, nearby restaurants saw an instant spike in traffic. The sampling and coupons were critical to Pizza Hut's goal of encouraging trials and drawing back people who had migrated to other pizza chains.[4] Sales promotion is discussed in more detail in Chapter 17.

advertising
Impersonal, mass communication about a product or organization that is paid for by a marketer.

sales promotion
Marketing activities—other than personal selling, advertising, and public relations—that stimulate consumer buying.

Public Relations

Organizations that are concerned about how their target markets perceive them often spend large sums to build a positive public image. **Public relations** involves evaluating public attitudes, identifying areas within the organization that the public may be interested in, and executing a program to earn public understanding and acceptance. Public relations helps an organization communicate with its customers, suppliers, stockholders, government officials and employees, and with the community in which it operates. Marketers use public relations not only to maintain a positive image but also to educate the public about the company's goals and objectives, introduce new products, and support the sales effort.

A solid public relations program can generate favourable publicity. **Publicity** is public information about a good or service for which the company doesn't have to pay. The organization is not generally identified as the source of the information. The wine industry received favourable publicity and increased its sales after several medical studies found a link between good health and the consumption of red wine. This underscores a peculiar reality of marketing: no matter how many millions are spent on advertising, nothing sells a product better than free publicity.

public relations
Marketing function that evaluates public attitudes, identifies areas within the organization that the public may be interested in, and executes a program of action to earn public understanding and acceptance.

publicity
Information about a good or service for which the company doesn't pay.

Although an organization does not pay for this kind of mass media exposure, publicity should not be viewed as free. Preparing news releases, staging special events, and persuading the media to print or broadcast them costs money. Shoppers Drug Mart/Pharmaprix participated in the "Caring Star" campaign. During the campaign, public service announcements (unpaid advertising) were run in *Time*, *People*, and *Glamour* magazines encouraging customers to visit their local Shoppers Drug Mart retailer and purchase a "caring star" for $1. The campaign was used to raise awareness, provide education, and support research around colorectal cancer. The press was invited to attend the presentation of the campaign's proceeds to the co-chairs of the Colorectal Cancer Screening Initiative Foundation. Public relations and publicity are considered in more detail in Chapter 17.

Marketing Communication

3
Describe the communication process

People assign meanings to feelings, ideas, facts, attitudes, and emotions. IMC involves **communication**, which is the process by which we exchange or share meanings through a common set of symbols. A company that has developed a new product, or changed an old one, or that is simply trying to increase sales of an existing good or service, must communicate its selling message to potential customers. Marketers communicate information about their firm and its products to various audiences through IMC programs. Pepsi commercials send messages to their target audience of kids through sports figures such as basketball star Shaquille O'Neal.

communication
The process by which we exchange or share meanings through a common set of symbols.

There are two main categories of communication: interpersonal communication and mass communication. **Interpersonal communication** is direct, face-to-face communication between two or more people. People who are communicating face to face can see each other's reactions and respond almost immediately. A salesperson speaking directly with a client is an example of marketing communication that is interpersonal.

interpersonal communication
Direct, face-to-face communication between two or more people.

Mass communication involves communicating to large audiences. A great deal of marketing communication is directed to consumers as a whole, usually through a mass medium such as television or newspapers. When a company advertises, it does not personally know the people it is trying to communicate with. Also, it is unable to know immediately what consumers' reactions to its message are. Competitors' messages or other distractions in the environment can reduce the effectiveness of a company's mass communication effort.

mass communication
Communication to large audiences.

The Communication Process

Marketers are both senders and receivers of messages. As senders, marketers attempt to inform people about their goods or services, and persuade or remind those people to buy them. As receivers, marketers try to understand their target market so that they can send messages people can respond to positively. In other words, marketing communication is two-way, not one-way.[5] Exhibit 16.2 illustrates the two-way nature of the communication process.

In the communication process, the **sender** is the originator of the message. In an interpersonal conversation, the sender might be a parent, a friend, or a salesperson. With an advertisement or press release, the sender will be the company itself.

sender
The originator of the message in the communication process.

A basic principle of encoding is that what matters most is what the receiver hears. So it is essential for the receiver to get the message intended by the sender. One way of conveying a message is to use concrete words and pictures. Microsoft uses television and print advertising to communicate a message using images and dialogue. It is important that the advertiser do research to ensure that the audience is receiving the intended message.

exhibit 16.2

Communication Process

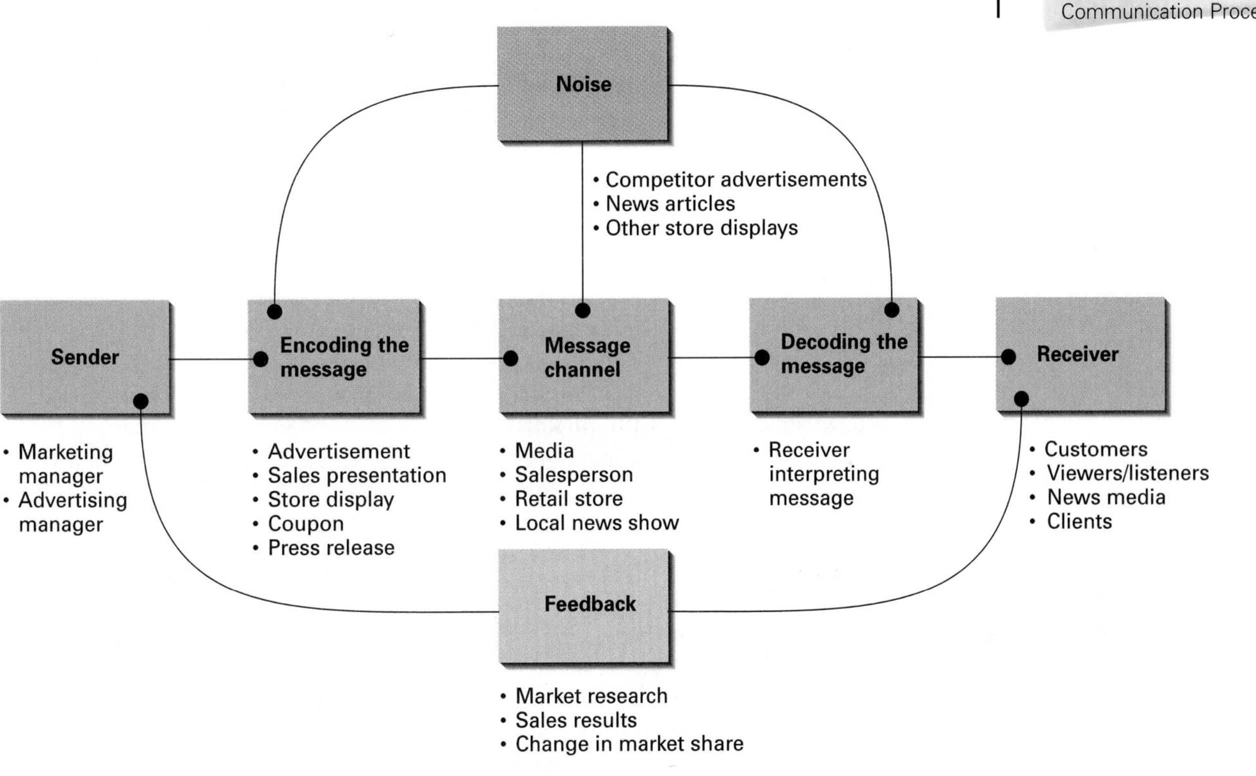

Every communication needs a sender and a receiver. Chanel sends image-related messages associated with its fragrances. The Hudson's Bay Company, which sells the fragrance, is also mentioned in the ad. Can The Bay also be a sender along with Chanel? Explain.

encoding
Conversion of the sender's ideas and thoughts into a message, usually in the form of words or signs.

The process of converting the sender's ideas and thoughts into a message—usually in the form of words or signs—is known as **encoding**. Microsoft might encode its message into an advertisement, or a Microsoft salesperson might encode the message into a sales presentation. A basic principle of encoding is that what matters most is what the receiver hears. So the receiver must get the message intended by the sender. One way of conveying a message is to use concrete words and pictures.

channel
A medium of communication—such as TV, radio, a newspaper, a magazine, or a salesperson's facial expressions and gestures—for transmitting a message.

noise
Anything that distorts, interferes with, or slows down the transmission of information.

Message Transmission To be transmitted, a message requires a **channel**—TV, radio, a newspaper, a magazine, or some other communication medium. A salesperson's facial expressions and gestures can also be considered a channel.

Reception takes place when the message is received. In a two-way conversation between a sales representative and a potential client, reception is usually high. In contrast, receivers may or may not detect the message when it is mass communicated, because most media are cluttered by "noise." **Noise** is anything that distorts, interferes with, or slows down the transmission of information. In some media, such as newspapers and television, the noise level is high and the reception level is low. The reception of Calvin Klein ads can be hampered by competing fragrance ads or by stories in a magazine or newspaper. Transmission can also be hindered by situational factors such as the physical environment, the weather, the presence of other people, or the consumer's mood at the time. Mass communication may not even reach all the right consumers. Some members of the target audience may be reading magazines other than the ones the Calvin Klein ads are appearing in.

receiver
The person who decodes a message.

decoding
Interpretation of the message the source has sent through a channel.

The Receiver and Decoding Marketers communicate their message through a channel to customers, or **receivers**, who then decode the message. **Decoding** is the interpretation of the message that the source has sent through a channel. Effective communication requires common understanding between the sender and receiver, or a common frame of reference. So marketing managers must ensure a proper match between the message being conveyed and the target market's attitudes and ideas.

Even when a message has been received, it will not necessarily be properly decoded because of selective exposure, distortion, and retention (refer to Chapter 4).[6] When people receive a message, they tend to interpret it to reflect their own biases, needs, knowledge, and culture. Factors that can lead to miscommunication are differences in age, social class, education, culture, and ethnicity. Also, people don't always listen or read carefully, and this increases the likelihood that a message will be misinterpreted. A large proportion of both printed and televised advertisements are misunderstood by consumers. Bright colours and bold graphics have been shown to increase consumers' comprehension of marketing communication. However, even these techniques are not foolproof. A classic example of miscommunication occurred when Lever Brothers mailed out samples of its new dishwashing liquid, Sunlight, which contains real lemon juice. The package clearly stated that Sunlight was a household cleaning product. However, many people saw the word sunlight, the large picture of lemons, and the phrase "with real lemon juice" and thought the product was lemon juice.

feedback
The receiver's response to a message.

Feedback In interpersonal communication, the receiver's response to a message is direct **feedback** to the source. Feedback can be verbal, as in saying "I agree," or nonverbal, as in nodding, smiling, or frowning.

Mass communicators like Calvin Klein are often cut off from direct feedback, which means they must rely on indirect feedback gathered through market research or sales trend analysis. Calvin Klein might use the percentage of television viewers or magazine readers who recall that they have been exposed to Calvin Klein's message. On the basis of indirect feedback, mass communicators decide whether to continue, modify, or drop a message.

The Communication Process and the Promotional Mix

The four elements of the IMC program vary in their capacity to affect the target audience. For instance, promotional mix elements may communicate with the consumer directly or indirectly. The message may flow one way or two ways. Feedback may be fast or slow, strong or weak. Likewise, the communicator may have varying degrees of control over message delivery, content, and flexibility. Exhibit 16.3 outlines differences among the IMC elements.

From Exhibit 16.3, you can see that most elements of IMC are indirect and impersonal, and provide only one direction of message flow. Generally speaking, advertising, public relations, and sales promotion are impersonal, one-way means of mass communication. Because they provide no opportunity for direct feedback, they cannot adapt easily to consumers' changing preferences, individual differences, and personal goals.

Personal selling, on the other hand, involves personal, two-way communication. The salesperson is able to receive immediate feedback from the consumer and adjust the message accordingly. Because a salesperson can only communicate with one person at a time—or at most a small group—personal selling is a poor choice if the marketer wants to send a message to many potential buyers.

Integrated Marketing Communications

Ideally, marketing communications from each element in the promotional mix (personal selling, advertising, sales promotion, and public relations) will be integrated—that is, the message reaching the consumer will be the same whether it is conveyed through an advertisement, a salesperson in the field, a magazine article, or a coupon in a newspaper insert.

Every communication that a company sends to the customer says something about the company. Unfortunately, many marketers forget this when planning promotional messages, and fail to integrate their communication efforts. Most often, the rifts develop between personal selling and sales promotion.

The problems arising from an unintegrated, disjointed approach to communication have propelled many companies to adopt **integrated marketing commu-**

integrated marketing communications (IMC)
The method of carefully coordinating all promotional activities to produce a consistent, unified message that is customer focused.

exhibit 16.3

Characteristics of the Elements in the Promotional Mix

	Personal selling	Advertising	Sales promotion	Public relations
Mode of communication	Direct and face-to-face	Indirect and nonpersonal	Usually indirect and nonpersonal	Usually indirect and nonpersonal
Communicator control over situation	High	Low	Moderate to low	Moderate to low
Amount of feedback	Much	Little	Little to moderate	Little
Speed of feedback	Immediate	Delayed	Varies	Delayed
Direction of message flow	Two-way	One-way	Mostly one-way	One-way
Control over message content	Yes	Yes	Yes	No
Identification of sponsor	Yes	Yes	Yes	No
Speed in reaching large audience	Slow	Fast	Fast	Usually fast
Message flexibility	Tailored to prospective buyer	Same message to all audiences	Same message to varied target audiences	Usually no direct control over message

on line

Burger King

Do Burger King's "Burger Bucks" qualify as a promotion? Explain. Visit the Website to formulate an answer.

www.burgerking.com

nications (IMC). IMC involves carefully coordinating all promotional activities—advertising, sales promotion, personal selling, and public relations, as well as other communication activities—to produce a consistent, unified message that is customer focused. Marketing managers carefully work out the roles that various IMC elements will play in the marketing mix. The timing of promotional activities is coordinated, and the results of each IMC program are carefully monitored to improve future use of the IMC tools. Typically, a marketing communications director is appointed who has overall responsibility for integrating the company's communications.

The Goals and Tasks of IMC

4 Explain the goals and tasks of IMC

IMC seeks to modify behaviour and thoughts in some positive way for the company. Thus, promoters can try to persuade consumers to eat at Burger King instead of McDonald's. IMC also strives to reinforce existing behaviour—for instance, to get customers to keep eating at Burger King. Through its IMC program, the company hopes to project a favourable image and to motivate consumers to buy its goods and services.

IMC can *inform* the target audience, or *persuade* that audience, or *remind* it. Often a marketer will try to accomplish two or three of these at once. Exhibit 16.4 lists the three tasks of IMC and some examples of each.

Informing

informative promotion Increasing the awareness of a new brand, product class, or product attribute; explaining how the product works; suggesting new uses for a product; building a company image.

Informative promotion may try to stimulate interest in purchasing a product or service. Such messages are generally more prevalent in the early stages of the product life cycle. People typically will not buy a product or service or support a nonprofit organization until they can see its benefits to them. Informative messages are important for promoting complex, highly technical products such as automobiles, computers, and investment services. Informative promotion is also important for a "new" brand being introduced into an established product class—

exhibit 16.4

Promotion Tasks and Examples

Informative promotion
Increasing the awareness of a new brand, product class, or product attribute
Explaining how the product works
Suggesting new uses for a product
Building a company image

Persuasive promotion
Encouraging brand switching
Changing customers' perceptions of product attributes
Influencing customers to buy now
Persuading customers to call

Reminder promotion
Reminding consumers that the product may be needed in the near future
Reminding consumers where to buy the product
Maintaining consumer awareness

for example, a new brand of detergent entering the well-established laundry detergent product category, which is dominated by well-known brands such as Tide and Cheer. A new product cannot establish itself against more mature products unless potential buyers are aware of it, understand its benefits, and understand its positioning in the marketplace.

Persuading

Persuasive promotion is designed to stimulate a purchase—to stimulate consumers to drink more Coca-Cola or use H&R Block tax services. Usually, persuasion becomes the main goal of IMC once the product has entered the growth stage of its life cycle. By this time the target consumers should have general product awareness and some knowledge of how the product can fulfil their needs. So the promotional task switches from informing consumers about the product category to persuading them to buy the company's brand. Here the message emphasizes the product's real and perceived differential advantages; it often appeals to emotional needs such as love, belonging, self-esteem, and ego satisfaction.

Persuasion can also be important in very competitive mature product categories such as household items, soft drinks, beer, and banking services. Here the promotional message often encourages brand switching and aims to convert occasional buyers into loyal ones.

persuasive promotion
Encouraging brand switching; changing customers' perceptions of product attributes; influencing customers to buy now; persuading customers to call.

Reminding

Reminder promotion is used to keep the product and brand name in the public's mind. This type of promotion prevails in the maturity stage of the life cycle. It assumes that the target market has already been persuaded of the merits of the product or service. Its purpose is simply to trigger a memory. Crest toothpaste, Tide laundry detergent, Molson beer, and many other consumer products often use reminder promotion.

reminder promotion
Reminding consumers that the product may be needed in the near future; reminding consumers where to buy the product; maintaining consumer awareness.

IMC Goals and the AIDA Concept

5
Discuss the AIDA concept and its relationship to the IMC program

The ultimate goal of any IMC program is to get the target audience to buy a good or service or—in the case of nonprofit organizations—to take some action (e.g., donate blood). A classic model for reaching IMC goals is called the **AIDA concept.**[7] The acronym stands for Attention, Interest, Desire, and Action—the stages of consumer involvement with an IMC message.

AIDA concept
Model outlining the process for achieving IMC goals in terms of stages of consumer involvement with the message; stands for Attention, Interest, Desire, and Action.

In this model, consumers respond to marketing messages in a cognitive (thinking), affective (feeling), and conative (doing) sequence. First, the IMC message attracts a person's attention. In personal selling, a greeting attracts the customer's attention; in advertising and sales promotions, the attraction may be loud volume, unusual contrasts, bold headlines, movement, bright colours, and so on. Next, a good sales presentation, demonstration, or advertisement creates interest in the product. Then desire is created by illustrating how the product's features will satisfy the consumer's needs. Finally, a special offer or a strong closing sales pitch is used to obtain purchase action.

The AIDA concept assumes that promotion propels consumers along the following four steps in the decision to purchase a product:

1. *Awareness:* The advertiser must first make the target market aware of its messages. A firm can't sell a good or service if the market doesn't know it exists. When Proctor & Gamble first introduced the Swiffer Sweeper, it advertised heavily on TV and in magazines; it also conducted live demonstrations at malls.

2. *Interest:* On its own, brand awareness rarely leads to a sale. The next step is to create interest in the product. A print ad or TV commercial can't actually tell people to go and buy the product. Proctor & Gamble had to make clear how the Swiffer would benefit users. Live promotions helped accomplish this.
3. *Desire:* Potential customers may not see a given product as having any advantage over others. Proctor & Gamble had to create brand preference for the Swiffer by explaining its differential advantage over the competition. The Swiffer was shown to clean floors better and more efficiently than other floor-cleaning tools. At this stage, Proctor & Gamble could have offered other reasons to purchase the product.
4. *Action:* Some members of the target market will now be willing to buy the product though they haven't actually done it yet. Coupons, premiums, displays in grocery stores, and trial-size packages can often push the customer into making a purchase.

Most buyers involved in high-involvement purchase situations pass through the four stages of the AIDA model on the way to making a purchase. The promoter's task is to determine where on the purchase ladder most of the target consumers are and design an IMC program to meet their needs. If Proctor & Gamble has determined that about half its buyers are in the preference or conviction stage but for some reason have not yet bought the Swiffer, the company may mail money-off coupons to prompt them to buy.

The AIDA model does not explain how communications influence purchase decisions. It does suggest that IMC's effectiveness can be measured in terms of consumers progressing from one stage to the next. However, the order of stages in the model has been much debated, and so has the question of whether consumers go through all the steps. For example, purchase can occur without interest or desire, as when a low-involvement product is bought on impulse. Whatever the order of the stages, and however consumers progress through them, AIDA helps marketers by suggesting which IMC elements will be most effective.[8]

AIDA and the Promotional Mix

Exhibit 16.5 depicts the relationship between the IMC program and the AIDA model. Advertising is best at creating awareness about goods or services. In contrast, personal selling reaches fewer people at first. Salespeople are more effective at creating customer interest for a product or service and at gaining desire. Advertising can help a potential computer purchaser gain knowledge about competing brands, but the salesperson in an electronics store may be the one who actually encourages the buyer to purchase a specific brand. The salesperson also has the advantage of being able to demonstrate the product's benefits to the buyer.

exhibit 16.5

When the Elements of IMC Are Most Useful

	Attention	Interest	Desire	Action
Personal selling	Somewhat effective	Very effective	Very effective	Somewhat effective
Advertising	Very effective	Very effective	Somewhat effective	Not effective
Sales promotion	Somewhat effective	Somewhat effective	Very effective	Very effective
Public relations	Very effective	Very effective	Very effective	Not effective

Sales promotion is best at creating strong desire and purchase intent. Coupons and other price-off promotions are used to persuade customers to buy products. Frequent-buyer sales promotion programs are popular among retailers and coffee companies, and allow consumers to accumulate points or dollars that they can later redeem for goods. Frequent-buyer programs tend to increase purchase intent and to encourage repeat purchases. Canadian Tire stores reward loyal shoppers with Canada Tire money, which can be used to purchase more products at the retailer.

Public relations has its greatest impact in building awareness about a company, good, or service. Many companies can attract attention and build good will by sponsoring community events that benefit a worthy cause. Sponsorships develop a positive image of the firm and its products in the minds of the target audience. Good publicity can also help develop consumer desire for a product. Also, book authors make appearances on talk shows and at bookstores to sign books and speak to fans. Similarly, movie marketers use prerelease publicity to raise the profile of their movies and to increase initial box office sales. Most major motion picture studios have their own Websites, where they provide viewers with multimedia clips and publicity photos of their current movies. And, of course, movie promoters include in their advertising the publicity they have garnered through reviewers' quotes and Academy Award nominations.

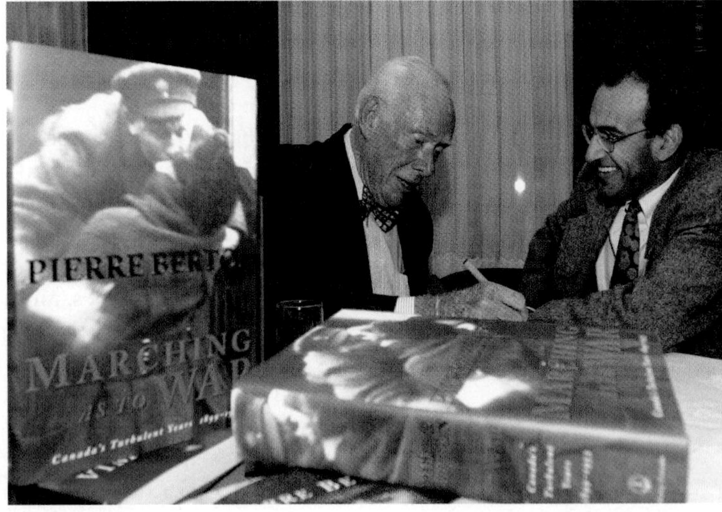

Pierre Berton signs a copy of his book *Marching As To War* for fellow author and friend Ted Barris. This is but one of a string of stops Mr. Berton made to promote his book.

Factors Affecting IMC

6

Describe the factors that affect IMC

IMC programs vary a great deal from one product and one industry to the next. Normally, advertising and personal selling are used to promote goods and services; these are supported and supplemented by sales promotion. Public relations helps develop a positive image for the organization and the product line. However, a firm may choose not to use all four promotional elements in its IMC program, or it may choose to use them in varying degrees. The particular promotional mix a firm chooses for a product or service depends on several factors, including the nature of the product, the stage in the product life cycle, the target market's characteristics, the type of buying decision, the funds available for promotion, and whether a push or a pull srategy is used.

Nature of the Product

A product's characteristics can influence its IMC program. Products can be classified as either business products or consumer products (see Chapter 9). Often, business products are not suited to mass promotion and are custom tailored to the buyer's exact specifications. Most producers of business goods, such as network software and industrial machinery, rely more heavily on personal selling than on advertising. Yet advertising still serves a purpose in promoting business goods. Advertisements in the trade media can be used to create general buyer awareness and interest. And advertising in the print media can help salespeople locate potential customers if there are reply card inserts that solicit customer information.

Consumer products do not require the selling efforts of a company representative. Consumer goods are promoted mainly through advertising to create brand familiarity. Ads on TV and radio and in newspapers and consumer magazines are used extensively to promote consumer goods, especially nondurables. For shopping goods such as automobiles and appliances, personal selling is important at the retail level.

The costs and risks associated with a product also influence the IMC program. As a general rule, the greater the costs or risks of using a product, the more important personal selling becomes. Convenience products do not require a salesperson to close the sale. In fact, inexpensive items cannot support the cost of a salesperson's time and effort unless the volume is high. On the other hand, cars, new buildings, new homes, and expensive and complex machinery represent a considerable investment. A salesperson must assure buyers that they are spending their money wisely and not taking an undue financial risk.

Stage in the Product Life Cycle

The product's stage in its life cycle is a big factor in designing an IMC program (see Exhibit 16.6.) In the introduction stage, the basic goal of IMC is to inform the target audience that the product is available. At first the emphasis is on the general product class—for example, personal computers. This emphasis gradually changes to awareness of specific brands, such as IBM, Apple, and Compaq. Typically, extensive advertising and public relations are used to inform the target audience of the product class or brand and to heighten awareness levels. Consumer promotion encourages early trial of the product, and personal selling and trade promotions get retailers to carry the product.

Once the product reaches the growth stage of the life cycle, the IMC blend often shifts because different types of potential buyers are being targeted and competition is becoming fiercer. There is more emphasis on persuasive and reminder advertising. Advertising and public relations continue to be major elements in the IMC program, but sales promotion can be reduced because consumers need fewer incentives to purchase. During the growth stage, persuasive and reminder messages are used to build and maintain brand loyalty. By this stage, personal selling has usually succeeded in getting adequate distribution for the product.

As the product approaches the maturity stage, brand loyalty is encouraged through heavy use of sales promotions and reminder advertisements.

exhibit 16.6

Product Life Cycle and IMC

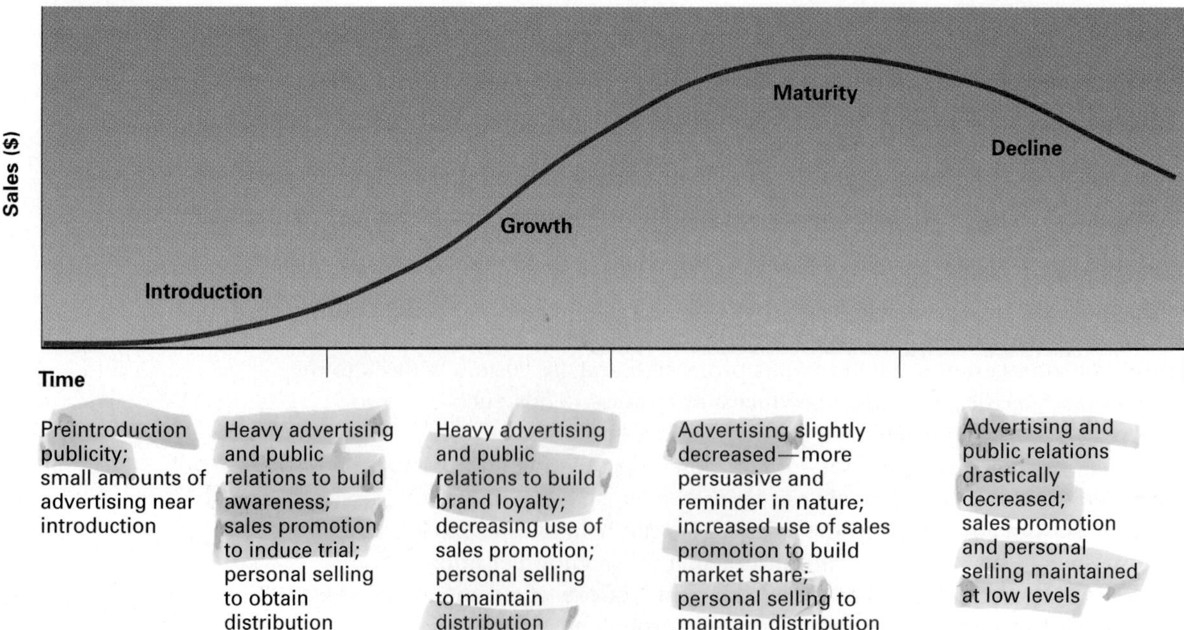

The Globe and Mail
The National Post
From their respective Websites, what can you tell about the target markets for *The Globe and Mail* and *The National Post*? How will this information influence any promotions either newspaper might want to do?
www.globeandmail.ca; www.nationalpost.com

on line

All IMC activities, especially advertising, are reduced as the product enters the decline stage. However, personal selling and sales promotion efforts may be maintained, especially at the retail level.

Target Market Characteristics

A target market characterized by widely scattered customers, highly informed buyers, and brand-loyal repeat purchasers generally requires a promotional mix with more advertising and sales promotion and less personal selling. Sometimes, however, personal selling is required even when buyers are well informed and geographically dispersed. Typically, heavy machinery is sold to extremely competent people with extensive product knowledge; even so, the salespeople involved must still be present to work out the details of the purchase agreement.

Print advertising can be used to find potential customers who are hard to locate. The reader is invited to call or mail in a reply card for more detailed information. Having made customer contact in this way, salespeople can approach these potential customers.

Type of Buying Decision

An IMC program is also affected by the type of buying decision—for example, by whether the decision is routine or complex. With routine consumer decisions like buying toothpaste or soft drinks, the most effective communication brings attention to the brand or reminds the consumer about the brand. Advertising and especially sales promotion are the most productive promotion tools for products requiring routine decisions.

If the decision is neither routine nor complex, advertising and public relations help establish awareness for the good or service. Suppose a man is looking for a bottle of wine to serve his dinner guests. As a beer drinker, he is not familiar with wines, yet he has seen advertising for Hillside Estates wines and has also gone to the company's Website to find out more about the winery. He may be more likely to buy this brand because he is already aware of it.

Consumers making complex buying decisions are more extensively involved. They rely on large amounts of information to help them reach a purchase decision. Personal selling is most effective in helping these consumers decide. Consumers thinking about buying a car usually depend on a salesperson to provide the information they need to reach a decision. Also, print advertising is often used for high-involvement purchase decisions because it can provide a large amount of information to the consumer.

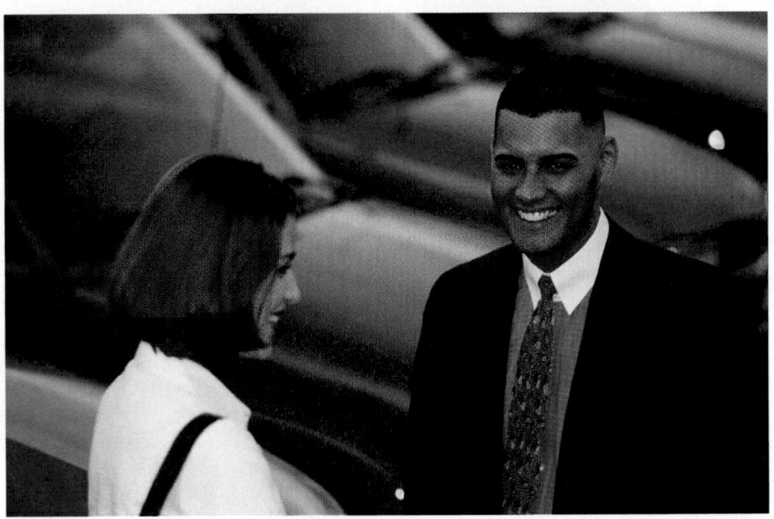

Consumers making complex buying decisions often depend on the salesperson to provide important product information. Purchasing a car is one such example. Can you think of others?

Available Funds

Money may well be the most important factor in determining an IMC program. A small, undercapitalized manufacturer may have to rely heavily on inexpensive print ads. Even well-capitalized organizations may not be able to afford the advertising rates of publications like *Maclean's, Reader's Digest,* and *Maxim.* The price of a single high-profile advertisement in these magazines could support a salesperson for a year.

A firm will generally try to optimize its return on promotion dollars while mini-

Upjohn

Is Upjohn using its Website for direct-to-consumer advertising? What makes you think so? How is the company promoting its latest drugs on its Website? What is your opinion of how Upjohn is informing or promoting its products?

www.upjohn.com

on line

mizing the *cost per contact*—that is, the cost of reaching one member of the target market. In personal selling, public relations, and sales promotions such as sampling and demonstrations, cost per contact tends to be very high. Advertising typically reaches a large number of people, so its cost per contact is very low.

Usually a trade-off must be made among the funds available, the size of the target market, and the relative costs of the promotional elements. A company may have to forgo a full-page colour advertisement in *People* magazine to pay for a personal selling effort. The ad in *People* would reach more consumers than personal selling, but the company just can't afford to buy the space.

Push and Pull Strategies

The last factor that affects the promotional mix is whether a push or a pull promotional strategy will be used. Manufacturers may use aggressive personal selling and trade advertising to convince wholesalers or retailers to carry and sell their merchandise. This approach is known as a **push strategy** (see Exhibit 16.7.) Wholesalers, in turn, must push the merchandise forward by persuading retailers to handle the goods. Retailers then use advertising, displays, and other forms of promotion to convince consumers to buy the "pushed" products. This concept also applies to services. Sony Canada Ltd. may offer a trip to Hawaii to the top Sony salesperson in Canada in the first quarter. As a result, salespeople at the various retailers will be more more likely push Sony products over those of competitors.

push strategy
A marketing strategy that uses aggressive personal selling and trade advertising to convince a wholesaler or a retailer to carry and sell particular merchandise.

pull strategy
A marketing strategy that stimulates consumer demand to obtain product distribution.

At the other extreme is a **pull strategy**, which stimulates consumer demand to obtain product distribution. A manufacturer using a pull strategy focuses its efforts on end consumers or opinion leaders. Say, for example, that Clinique decides to offer a free gift with every purchase. Consumers will then demand Clinique products at retailers in order to receive this limited time offer. As demand increases, the retailers will order the merchandise from the wholesalers. The wholesalers, confronted with rising demand, will then place an order for the

exhibit 16.7

Push Strategy versus Pull

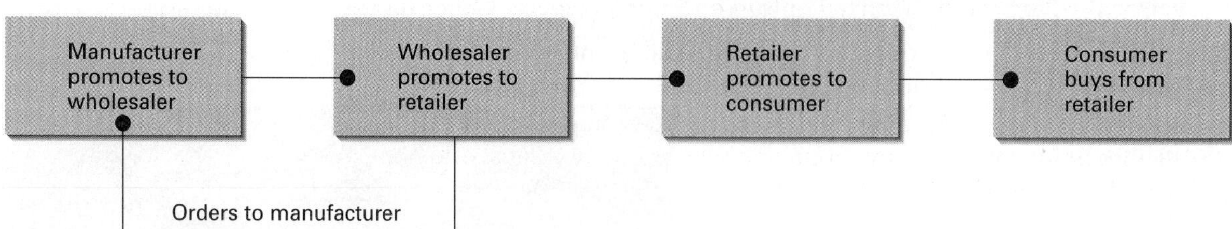

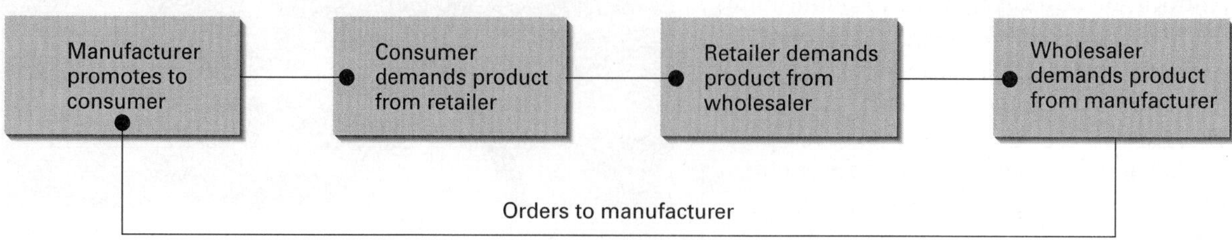

"pulled" merchandise from the manufacturer. In this way, consumer demand pulls the product through the channel of distribution (see Exhibit 16.7.) Heavy sampling, introductory consumer advertising, and couponing are all part pull strategies.

Rarely does a company use a pull or a push strategy exclusively. Instead, the IMC program will emphasize one of these strategies. Pharmaceutical companies generally use a push strategy—personal selling and trade advertising—to promote their drugs and therapies to physicians. Sales presentations and advertisements in medical journals give physicians the detailed information they need to prescribe medications to their patients. Most pharmaceutical companies supplement their push strategy with a pull strategy targeted directly at potential patients through ads in consumer magazines and on television. Many physicians are expressing concern about the increasing amount of direct-to-consumer advertising that is prompting many patients to demand drugs they do not need or that may cause adverse reactions. Read this chapter's "Ethics in Marketing" article to learn more about this controversial promotional practice.

Personal Selling

7
Describe personal selling

Personal selling is direct communication between a sales representative and prospective buyers.

In a sense, we are all salespeople. During a job search, applicants must "sell" themselves to prospective employers in an interview. To reach the top in most organizations, people need to sell ideas to peers, superiors, and subordinates. Most important, they must sell themselves to just about everyone with whom they interact.

Personal selling offers several advantages over other forms of promotion:

- The consumer can be given a detailed explanation or demonstration of the product. This is especially useful for new or complex goods and services.
- The sales message can be tailored according to the needs of the customer at hand. When the customer has questions or raises objections, the salesperson is there to provide explanations.
- Personal selling can be directed only to qualified prospects. Other forms of IMC involve some unavoidable waste because many people receiving the message are not in the target market.
- The costs of personal selling can be controlled by adjusting the size of the sales force. In contrast, advertising and sales promotion must often be purchased in large amounts to be effective.
- Personal selling is much more effective than other forms of promotion in closing a sale and gaining a satisfied customer "for life."

Generally speaking, personal selling becomes more important as the number of potential customers decreases, as the complexity of the product increases, and as the value of the product increases (see Exhibit 16.8.) For highly complex goods such as company airplanes or corporate telecommunications systems, a salesperson is needed to determine the prospective customer's needs, explain the product's basic advantages, and propose the exact features and accessories that will meet the client's needs.

ethics in marketing

Pull Strategy for Prescription Drugs Puts Doctors in the Hot Seat

During the diet-drug debacle, doctors wrote millions of prescriptions for the fenphen drug to patients wanting to lose weight, even though there was little hard scientific evidence that the drug worked. Doctors also prescribed Redux, a drug intended only for dangerously obese patients, to many patients who wanted to trim ten or twenty pounds. And they wrote some 15,000 to 20,000 prescriptions for the impotency drug Viagra when it first appeared on the market for many men who were not clinically impotent but who wanted a boost. Fenphen and Redux were eventually called off the market; it has been found that Viagra is potentially dangerous for men with certain types of heart disease.

Physicians don't like it that more advertising is being directed at their patients. Too often, that information is limited; the patients then diagnose themselves and come to them with a particular therapy in mind, without knowing its drawbacks or even if the drug is right for them. Also, drug ads tend to present pharmaceutical products as wonder drugs. Ads for allergy medicine are especially dramatic, offering allergy sufferers visions of happiness and serenity.

But many people believe that the benefits of consumer advertising of prescription drugs far outweigh any disadvantages. Drug ads result in more informed patients who can ask their physicians better questions. Consumers are presented with information about treatments they might have never known existed. These ads may also help consumers determine whether they have a medical problem. Many serious medical conditions remain undiagnosed because Americans don't know about the symptoms or don't regularly see a doctor. For instance, it is estimated that only half of diabetics even know they have the disease. In the end, proponents claim, the doctor makes the prescribing decision based on what is best for the patient.[9]

What is your opinion on the advertising of prescription drugs to consumers? Should there be restrictions on what drug advertisers can do? How can doctors cope with the increased pressure from patients due to drug advertising?

exhibit 16.8

Comparison of Personal Selling and Advertising / Sales Promotion

Personal selling is more important if	Advertising and sales promotion are more important if
The product has a high value.	The product has a low value.
It is a custom-made product.	It is a standardized product.
There are few customers.	There are many customers.
The product is technically complex.	The product is simple to understand.
Customers are concentrated.	Customers are geographically dispersed.
Examples: insurance policies, windows, airplane engines	Examples: soap, magazine subscriptions, custom cotton T-shirts

8

Discuss the key differences between relationship selling and traditional selling

Relationship Selling

Until recently, personal selling focused on making planned presentations to prospective customers and chalking up a sale. Marketers concerned themselves mainly with making a one-time sale and then moving on to the next prospect. Whether the sales pitch was made face to face (during a personal sales call) or over the telephone (through telemarketing), traditional personal selling methods tried to convince buyers to take some action. Once the customer was somewhat convinced, the salesperson used a variety of techniques to elicit a purchase. Often the salesperson and the buyer had mismatched objectives, and the result was a win-lose situation.[10] This type of sales approach has not disappeared entirely, but it is being used less often by professional salespeople.

exhibit 16.9

Key Differences Between Traditional Selling and Relationship Selling

Traditional personal selling	Relationship selling
Sell products (goods and services)	Sell advice, assistance, and counsel
Focus on closing sales	Focus on improving the customer's bottom line
Limited sales planning	Consider sales planning as top priority
Spend most contact time telling customers about product	Spend most contact time attempting to build a problem-solving environment with the customer
Conduct "product-specific" needs assessment	Conduct discovery in the full scope of the customer's operations
"Lone wolf" approach to the account	Team approach to the account
Proposals and presentations based on pricing and product features	Proposals and presentations based on profit impact and strategic benefits to the customer
Sales follow-up is short term, focused on product delivery	Sales follow-up is long term, focused on long-term relationship enhancement

Source: Robert M. Peterson, Patrick L. Schul, and George H. Lucas, Jr., "Consultative Selling: Walking the Walk in the New Selling Environment," *National Conference on Sales Management, Proceedings,* March 1996.

Nowadays, personal selling emphasizes the relationship between the salesperson and the buyer. **Relationship selling**, or **consultative selling**, is a multistage process that emphasizes developing long-term, satisfied customers. The focus is on building mutual trust between buyer and seller; this is accomplished when the seller delivers long-term, value-added benefits to the buyer.[11] Relationship salespeople act as consultants, partners, and problem solvers for their customers. They strive to develop trust over time. They no longer focus on one-time sales, but rather on establishing long-term relationships with buyers. When done right, the result is a win–win situation.[12]

relationship selling (consultative selling)
Sales practice of building, maintaining, and enhancing interactions with customers in order to develop long-term satisfaction for both buyer and seller.

Relationship selling results in loyal customers who purchase from the company over and over again. A relationship selling strategy is less expensive than constantly prospecting and selling to new customers. One consulting firm estimates that if a small to midsize company were to increase its customer retention rate by just 5 percent, its profits would double in about ten years.[13]

Exhibit 16.9 lists the key differences between traditional personal selling and relationship or consultative selling. These differences will become more apparent when we explore the personal selling process later in the chapter.

Advances in e-commerce are threatening the buyer–seller relationship. In this chapter's "Entrepreneurial Insights" box, we discuss a start-up Internet company whose mission is to bring together buyers and sellers in bidding wars.

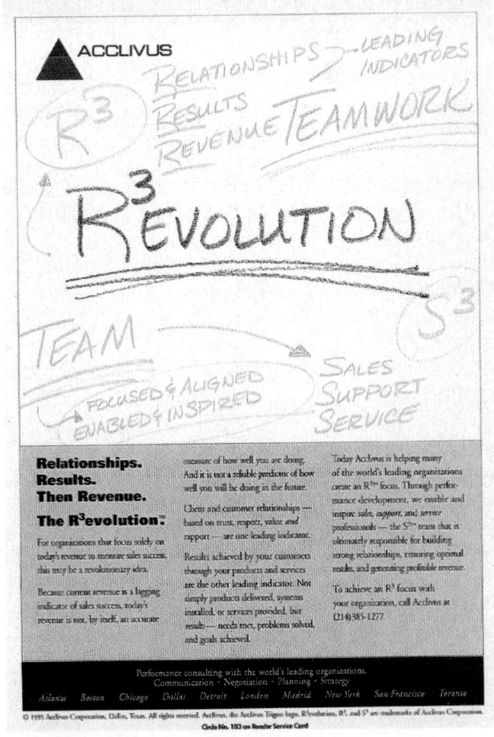

A multistage process focusing on developing trust over time, relationship selling emphasizes a win–win outcome.

Steps in the Selling Process

9
List the steps in the selling process

sales process (sales cycle)
The steps a salesperson goes through in a particular organization to sell a particular product or service.

Personal selling may sound like a relatively simple task; in fact, completing a sale involves several steps. The **sales process, or sales cycle**, is simply the set of steps a salesperson goes through to sell a particular product or service. Every product or service has its own unique sales process; the variations relate to the features of the product or service, the characteristics of the market, and the processes inside the firm—for example, how it gathers leads.

Some sales take a few minutes to complete; others take months or years. For Eastman Kodak's line of high-speed motion analysis cameras, the typical sale takes between nine and eighteen months to close.[14] At the other end of the spectrum, sales of that firm's more basic cameras to retailers are generally more routine, and may take only a few days. Whether a salesperson spends a few minutes or a few years on a sale, these are the seven basic steps in the personal selling process:

1. Generating leads
2. Qualifying leads
3. Approaching the customer and probing needs
4. Developing and proposing solutions to the customer
5. Handling customer objections
6. Closing the sale
7. Following up

Like other forms of marketing communication, these selling steps follow the AIDA concept discussed in the first half of the chapter. Think of the retailer in the mall. The salesperson first evaluates whether a shopper in the store is able to buy. He then gets her attention. After questioning her and assessing her needs, he

entrepreneurial insights

Web Service Helps Buyers Get Right Price at the Expense of Relationships

A new type of commerce is emerging on the Internet that is endangering the traditional buyer–seller relationship. TD Waterhouse (**www.Tdwaterhouse.ca**) is a subsidiary of TD Canada Trust. It is one of many Canadian on-line brokers that is enabling individual investors to purchase and sell their own stocks and bonds on the Internet. In doing so, investors avoid paying any up-front brokerage commissions. More and more people are using the Internet to make their own investments without going through a broker.

TD Waterhouse provides many of the services required for on-line trading. It provides daily morning market updates as well as research on companies and press releases on potentially good investments. On-line security is an issue for some, but less so than in the past.

With electronic trading, individuals can save money on their sales and purchases by cutting out the salesperson (broker). There are other advantages to e-trading besides this. It's faster—in fact, it's instantaneous, and ensures an immediate place in the cue for making a trade at a specific price. Also, the broker's own interests don't come into play. Furthermore, e-trading expands the investor's available universe of potential stocks and bonds, and forces companies that are traded on the market to communicate better with investors.

The implications of e-trading are especially frightening for investment companies that rely heavily on stockbrokers to buy and sell for their clients. E-trading could easily drive out of business those brokers who have long relied on the relationships they have cultivated so painstakingly with individual investors. On-line bidding may actually help some companies—especially smaller ones—broaden their customer base, but those same companies may lose the opportunity to enhance their sales by cultivating win–win relationships. Also, e-trading means that buyers give up the satisfaction of meeting with suppliers face to face.[15]

In this age of e-commerce, has the salesperson become an endangered species? How can salespeople take advantage of this information technology that threatens their existence?

exhibit 16.10

Relative Amount of Time Spent in Key Steps of the Selling Process

Key selling	Traditional selling	Relationship/ consultative
Generating leads	High	Low
Qualifying leads	Low	High
Approaching the customer and probing needs	Low	High
Developing solutions	Low	High
Proposing solutions through a sales presentation	High	Low
Closing the sale	High	Low
Following up	Low	High

presents products that should interest her. He then trys to get an agreement from her to buy. Follow-up after the sale—the final step in the selling process—not only lowers her post-purchase anxiety, but also opens up opportunities for him to discuss future sales. Effective follow-up leads to repeat business, in which case the process may start all over again at the needs assessment step.

Traditional selling and relationship selling follow the same basic steps. The two differ mainly in the relative importance they place on key steps in the process (see Exhibit 16.10.) Traditional selling is transaction oriented and emphasizes generating as many leads as possible, making as many presentations as possible, and closing as many sales as possible. Little effort is made to identify customer needs or to match those needs to the benefits of the product or service. In contrast, the salesperson practising relationship selling emphasizes uncovering each customer's specific needs and matching those needs with a product or service.

Generating Leads

Initial groundwork must precede communication between the potential buyer and the salesperson. **Lead generation**, or **prospecting**, involves identifying those firms and people most likely to buy the seller's offerings. These firms or people become "sales leads" or "prospects."

lead generation (prospecting)
Identifying those firms and people most likely to buy the seller's offerings.

Sales leads can be secured in various ways, most notably through advertising, trade shows, conventions, and direct-mail and telemarketing programs. Favourable publicity also helps create leads. Company records of past client purchases are another excellent source of leads. Many sales professionals are securing valuable leads from their firm's Website. Today about 55 percent of all Websites are used for some sort of lead generation.[16]

Another way to gather a lead is through a **referral**—that is, a recommendation from a customer or business associate. The advantages of referrals over other forms of prospecting include highly qualified leads, higher closing rates, larger initial transactions, and shorter sales cycles. Simply put, the salesperson and the company can earn more money in less time when prospecting using referrals. To increase the number of referrals they receive, some companies pay or send small gifts to customers or suppliers who provide referrals. Research has suggested that one referral can be as valuable as twelve cold calls. Yet although 80 percent of clients are willing to give referrals, only 20 percent are ever asked.[17]

referral
A recommendation to a salesperson from a customer or business associate.

Networking, which is similar to referrals, involves using friends, business contacts, co-workers, acquaintances, and fellow members of professional or civic organizations to find out about potential clients. Salespeople for SMED, an office furniture supplier in Canada, regularly visit with local architects and designers who build new office space in the area. They also network with people in other

networking
The process of finding out about potential clients from friends, business contacts, co-workers, acquaintances, and fellow members of professional or civic organizations.

industries, such as telecommunications. If a company is buying a new phone system for a facility, for example, it will probably need office furniture as well.[18]

Before the advent of more sophisticated methods of lead generation, such as direct mail and telemarketing, most prospecting was done through cold calling. With **cold calling** the salesperson approaches potential buyers without any prior knowledge of their needs or financial status. Although this method is still used, many sales managers realize how inefficient it is for their top salespeople to spend their time searching for the "needle in a haystack." When the job of cold calling is assigned to lower-cost employees, such as sales support people, the more experienced salespeople can apply their relationship-building skills to prospects that have already been identified.[19]

cold calling
Form of lead generation in which the salesperson approaches potential buyers without any prior knowledge of the prospects' needs or financial status.

Qualifying Leads

After a prospect shows interest in learning more about a product, the salesperson qualifies the lead. Visiting unqualified prospects wastes a salesperson's time and the company's resources. One study surveyed 400 marketers whose companies advertise in trade publications and found that almost 40 percent of leads went completely unanswered—most likely because they were unqualified.[20]

Lead qualification consists of determining whether the prospect has three things:[21]

lead qualification
Determining a sales prospect's authority and ability to buy.

- *A recognized need:* The salesperson should start by considering prospects that know they have a need, but should not discount prospects that don't know it yet. Preliminary interviews often provide the salesperson with enough information to determine whether the purchaser has a need.
- *Buying power:* Buying power involves both the authority to make purchase decisions and access to funds to pay for purchases. To avoid wasting time and money, before making a presentation the salesperson needs to determine whether the purchaser has the authority and ability to pay.
- *Receptivity and accessibility:* The prospect must be accessible to the salesperson. Some prospects simply refuse to see salespeople.

Lead qualifications are often performed by telemarketers or sales support staff. Such a system frees sales representatives from the time-consuming task of determining a prospect's need, buying power, and receptiveness. Prequalification systems can even arrange initial meetings between the prospect and the salesperson. The result is that the salesperson spends more time in front of interested customers.

With more and more companies setting up Websites, attention is being paid to methods for qualifying on-line leads. The object of a company's Website should be to get visitors to register, indicate which products they are interested in, and offer some information on their time frame and resources. Leads from the Internet can then be prioritized (e.g., to give higher priority to those indicating a short time frame) and transferred to salespeople. Often, Website visitors can be enticed to answer questions by offers of free merchandise or information. Enticing visitors to register also allows companies to customize future electronic interactions—for example, by giving prospects who visit the Website their choice from an electronic menu of products tailored specifically to their needs.[22]

Before making an approach, the salesperson should learn as much as possible about the prospect. This "homework" is often referred to as the **preapproach**. Another preapproach task is to determine whether the approach should involve a personal visit, a phone call, a letter, or some other form of communication.

preapproach
The "homework" that must be done by the salesperson before he or she contacts the prospect.

During the sales approach, the salesperson either talks to the prospect or secures an appointment in order to fully discuss the prospect's needs. Relationship selling theorists suggest that at this stage salespeople should begin developing mutual trust. They must sell themselves before they can sell the product.

Dominion Bond Rating Service (DBRS)

How can you use DBRS's Website for preapproach work? Would DBRS be best used for certain companies and not others? Explain.

www.dbrs.com

on line

Small talk that introduces sincerity and some suggestion of friendship is encouraged as a means of building rapport with the prospect; however, remarks that could be construed as insincere should be avoided.

The salesperson should be determining how to maximize the fit between the company's offerings and what the prospective customer wants. As part of the **needs assessment**, the consultative salesperson must know everything there is to know about the following:[23]

needs assessment
Determining the customer's specific needs and the options that customer has for satisfying them.

- *The product or service*: Product knowledge is the cornerstone for conducting a successful needs analysis.
- *Customers and their needs*: The salesperson should know more about customers than customers know about themselves.
- *The competition*: Salespeople must know as much about the competitor's company and products as they know about their own company
- *The industry:* Knowing the industry requires active research by the salesperson.

Customer profiles help salespeople optimize their time and resources. The salesperson uses such a profile to develop an intelligent analysis of the prospect's needs in preparation for the next step, which is developing and proposing solutions.

The salesperson should wrap up the sales approach and needs assessment with a commitment from the customer to some kind of action. This commitment qualifies the prospect further, and also justifies investing further sales time.

Developing and Proposing Solutions

Once the salesperson has gathered the appropriate information, he or she tries to match product or service offerings to the prospect's needs. Usually, these solutions are presented to the client at a sales presentation in the form of a sales proposal. A **sales presentation** is a formal meeting at which the salesperson has an opportunity to present a sales proposal. A **sales proposal** is a written document or professional presentation that outlines how the company's product or service will meet or exceed the client's needs.

sales presentation
A face-to-face explanation of the sales proposal to a prospective buyer.

sales proposal
A formal written document or professional presentation that outlines how the salesperson's product or service will meet or exceed the prospect's needs.

For many salespeople, technology has become an important part of the sales presentation. Salespeople for Dell Computer don't just tell potential clients how much money they will save by buying Dell PCs—they prove it. Using a sophisticated software program called Product Expert, Dell's corporate account reps show clients how much it costs to buy, deploy, and maintain a Dell PC over its lifetime. The reps download the software onto their laptop PCs before going on their sales calls. That software allows a client to plug in variables specific to its business, such as how many employees use PCs and how many desktop units it purchases annually. After manipulating the data, the client can then print out an executive summary. Because the savings information is presented to clients in a tangible format, the software is now an integral part of Dell's sales proposals.[24]

The quality of the sales proposal and presentation can make or break a sale. Salespeople must be able to present the proposal and handle customer objections confidently and professionally.

Handling Objections

Rarely does a prospect say "I'll buy it" right after a presentation. Often objections are raised, or perhaps questions about the proposal and the product. The potential buyer may insist that the price is too high, or that he or she does not have

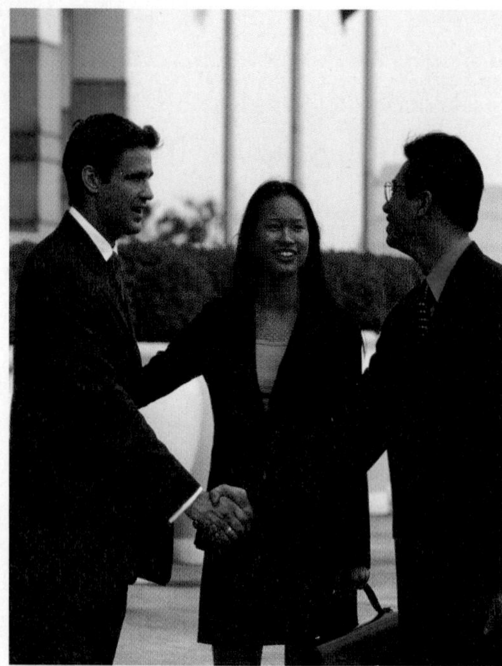

Closing the sale is the result of thorough preparation, a professional presentation, and skilful negotiation. But it is only the first step in building and maintaining a good customer relationship.

enough information to make a decision, or that the good or service will not satisfy the present need.

One of the first lessons every salesperson learns is that objections to the product should not be taken personally but should be viewed as requests for information. Before a crucial sales presentation with an important prospect, Dell salespeople anticipated that the customer would have doubts that Dell's direct-selling model would provide them with the same level of service and dedication they could get from a reseller. Being prepared to deal with these objections helped Dell win the contract.[25]

Often, the salesperson can use the objection to close the sale. If the customer tries to pit suppliers against each other to drive down the price, the salesperson should be prepared to point out weaknesses in the competitor's offer and stand by the quality of his or her own proposal.[26]

Closing the Sale

At the end of the presentation, the salesperson should ask the customer how he or she would like to proceed—for example, "How would you like to pay?" Customers often give signals during or after the presentation that they are ready to buy or are not interested. Signals include changes in facial expressions, gestures, and questions asked. The salesperson should look for these signals and respond appropriately.

Closing requires courage and skill. Naturally, the salesperson wants to avoid rejection, and asking for a sale carries with it the risk of a negative answer. Building a good relationship with the customer is very important. If the salesperson has developed a strong relationship with the customer, only minimal efforts will be needed to close a sale.

negotiation
The process of the salesperson and the prospect offering special concessions in an attempt to arrive at a sales agreement.

Negotiation often plays a key role in the closing. **Negotiation** involves the salesperson and the prospect offering special concessions to each other in an attempt to arrive at a sales agreement. Effective salespeople should emphasize value to the customer; this can render the price a nonissue. Salespeople should also try to avoid giving unilateral concessions. If the customer asks for a 5 percent discount, the salesperson should be ready to ask for something in return, such as more flexibility with a delivery schedule.[27]

Salespeople working in foreign markets should tailor their presentations and closing styles to each market. Any given personality and set of skills will be successful in some countries but an absolute failure in others. A salesperson who is an excellent closer and who is always focused on the next sale will find it difficult to do business in Latin America. Generally, in Latin America people like to take a long time building personal relationships with their suppliers.[28] Read about other global *dos* and *don'ts* of selling in the "Global Perspectives" box.

Following Up

follow-up
The final step of the selling process, in which the salesperson ensures that delivery schedules are met, that the goods or services perform as promised, and that the buyer's employees are properly trained to use the products.

Many salespeople think that the end goal of selling is to close the sale—that making the sale is all that's important. But **follow-up** is very important. Salespeople must ensure that delivery schedules are met, that the goods or services perform as promised, and that the buyers' employees are properly trained to use the products.

A basic goal of relationship selling is to motivate customers to come back again and again. Most businesses depend on repeat sales, and repeat sales depend on thorough and continued follow-up by the salesperson. Finding a new customer is far more expensive than retaining an existing customer. When customers feel abandoned, they don't return. Today this issue is more pertinent than ever,

global perspectives

Global *Dos* and *Don'ts* in Selling

Most large companies with operations on foreign soil employ locals to sell their products. Most selling skills that are successful in North America also will work overseas. However, knowing how to act in certain cultures can be the difference between closing the deal and losing a customer.

Arab countries: Don't use your left hand to hold, offer, or receive materials because Arabs use their left hand to touch toilet paper. If you must use your left hand to write, apologize for doing so. Handshakes in Arab countries last longer than typical North American handshakes.

China: Never talk business on the first meeting—it's disrespectful. Don't refuse tea during a business discussion. Always drink it, even if you're offered a dozen cups a day. Never begin to eat or drink before your host does. Also, printed materials presented to Chinese business leaders should be in black and white, because colours have great significance for the Chinese. The Chinese tend to be extremely meticulous, and look to create long-term relationships with a supplier before agreeing to buy anything. Chinese are more intradependent and tend to include more people in on a deal. Most deals in China are finalized in a social setting, over drinks or dinner. Also, getting to know the businessperson's family will personalize and strengthen the relationship.

European countries: Western and Eastern Europeans shake hands again whenever they're apart for even a short period of time, for example, lunch.

France: Don't schedule a breakfast meeting—the French tend not to meet until after 10 a.m. The French know far more about wine than most Americans, so avoid giving wine or wine-related gifts to French clients. The French also prefer gifts that are of French origin.

Germany: Don't address a business associate by his or her first name, even if you've known each other for years. Always wait for an invitation to do so. Also, breakfast meetings are unheard of here, too. Salespeople should expect a sober, rigid business climate and negotiations that lack flexibility and compromise.

Central and South America: People here don't take the clock too seriously—scheduling more than two appointments in one day can prove disastrous. Latin Americans also tend to use a lighter, lingering handshake. Negotiations with Central and South American customers typically include a great deal of bargaining. Personal relationships are important in Central and South America, so salespeople should make face-to-face contact with their clients during meetings and presentations.

Japan: Don't bring up business on the golf course—always wait for your host to take the initiative. Don't cross your legs in Japan—showing the bottom of the foot is insulting. Japanese businesspeople shake hands with one firm gesture combined with a slight bow, which should be returned. Japanese prefer gifts from well-known American stores, such as Tiffany's or Saks Fifth Avenue. Also, the higher the position of the recipient, the more elaborately wrapped the gift should be.

Mexico: Don't send a bouquet of red or yellow flowers as a gift—Mexicans associate those colours with evil spirits and death. Instead, send a box of premium chocolates. Including a small gift for the client's children creates a positive impression.

Vietnam: When meeting a Vietnamese woman, wait for her to extend a hand first—she may simply nod or bow slightly, the most common form of greeting in Vietnam. Vietnamese do not like to be touched or patted on the back or shoulders in social situations.

Miscellaneous: The thumbs-up gesture is considered offensive in the Middle East, rude in Australia, and a sign of "OK" in France. It's rude to cross your arms while facing someone in Turkey. In the Middle East, don't ask, "How's the family?"—it's considered too personal. In most Asian countries, staring directly into a person's eyes is considered discourteous.[29]

because customers are far less loyal. Buyers are more inclined to look for the best deal, especially when follow-up after the sale has been poor. More and more buyers favour building a relationship with sellers.

Dell Computer is committed to enhancing its customers' satisfaction through effective follow-up and customer support. Dell has developed an extensive extranet system, Premier Pages, which is designed to give Dell's contract customers product, pricing, and service information at the touch of a mouse. Each Dell customer gets its own password-protected Premier Page. Access provides product information, pricing structures, an employee purchase plan, on-line product ordering, and up-to-date purchase history reports. The costs to Dell have been justified in customer satisfaction alone. One customer estimated that it had saved $2 million on technical support costs thanks to Premier Pages.

Sales Management

10
Describe the functions of sales management

Selling is a personal relationship, and so is sales management. The tasks of sales management are as follows:

1. Define sales goals and the sales process
2. Determine the sales force structure
3. Recruit and train the sales force
4. Compensate and motivate the sales force
5. Evaluate the sales force

Defining Sales Goals and the Sales Process

Effective sales management begins with a clear statement of sales goals. Sales goals should be stated in clear, precise, and measurable terms and should always specify a time frame. A life insurance company may have as a goal to sell $50 million in life insurance policies annually, to attain a 12 percent market share, or to achieve $1 million in profits. Individual salespeople are assigned goals in the form of quotas. A **quota** is simply a statement of the salesperson's sales goals—usually based on sales volume.

quota
Statement of the individual salesperson's sales objectives, usually based on sales volume alone but sometimes including key accounts (those with greatest potential), new accounts, and specific products.

Successful sales managers focus not only on sales goals but also on the entire sales process. An important responsibility of the sales manager is to determine the most effective and efficient sales process to follow in selling each different product and service. Although the basic steps of the sales process are the same as discussed earlier, a manager must formally define the specific procedures salespeople go through to do their jobs—for example, where leads are generated, how they are qualified, the best way to approach potential clients, and what terms can be negotiated during closing.

Determining the Sales Force Structure

Because personal selling is so costly, no sales department can afford to be disorganized. Proper design helps the sales manager delegate sales duties and provide direction for salespeople. Sales departments are most commonly organized by geographic regions, by product lines, by marketing functions performed (account development, account maintenance, and so on), by market or industry, or by individual clients or accounts. IBM's Canadian sales force could be organized into sales territories covering the Maritimes, Quebec, Ontario, the Prairies, and British Columbia, or it could be organized into distinct groups—for example, a personal computer group and a mainframe group. IBM salespeople can also be assigned to specific industries or markets—for example, the telecommunications industry—or to key clients such as the federal government.

Market or industry based structures and key account structures are gaining popularity in today's competitive selling environment, especially with the emphasis on relationship selling. Familiarity with one industry or market enables sales reps to become experts and thereby offer better solutions and service. Many companies are organizing their sales forces around specific customers in the hope of improving customer service, encouraging collaboration with other divisions of the company, and uniting salespeople in customer-focused sales teams. Hewlett-Packard, which recently merged with Compaq, realigned its sales force to focus on industries rather than regions. HP reps are now trained and deployed to be experts in key customer segments such as manufacturing and financial services. HP found that its customers prefer having access to all of HP's products and dealing with only one salesperson.[30]

Mary Kay Cosmetics

What can you find out about Mary Kay's sales network from the company Website? What can you find out about the compensation of Mary Kay's sales force? How else does the company use the site to promote itself to future salespeople?

www.marykay.com

on line

Recruiting and Training the Sales Force

Sales force recruitment should be based on a detailed description of the sales task as defined by the sales manager. Top performers are driven by their own high goals. They are also self-confident and achievement oriented, and they like to talk about their sales accomplishments. Effective salespeople keep close tabs on their own performance and compare it with their past performance. They are optimistic, assertive, and highly knowledgeable about the product. They know how to listen to customers. They are team players who support their co-workers. They are self-trainers and are always upgrading their selling skills. Effective salespeople always plan the next step before they leave the client's office.

After the sales recruit has been hired, training begins. A new salesperson generally receives information about the company and its products and customers, as well as training in selling techniques. Most successful sales organizations have learned that training is not just for newly hired salespeople. Training is offered to all salespeople in an ongoing effort to hone selling skills and relationship building.

Compensating and Motivating the Sales Force

Compensation planning is one of the sales manager's toughest jobs. Only good planning will ensure that compensation attracts, motivates, and retains good salespeople. Generally, companies and industries with lower levels of compensation suffer higher turnover rates; this increases costs and decreases effectiveness. Some firms take profit into account when developing their compensation plans: instead of paying salespeople according to overall volume, they pay according to the profits generated from selling each product. Still other companies tie a part of the salesperson's total compensation to customer satisfaction, which is assessed through periodic customer surveys.

The three basic compensation methods for salespeople are commission, salary, and combination plans. A typical commission plan gives salespeople a specified percentage of their sales revenue. A **straight commission** system compensates the salesperson only when a sale is made. At the other end of the spectrum, a **straight salary** system compensates a salesperson with a stated salary regardless of sales productivity. Most companies offer a compromise between straight commission and straight salary plans. A *combination system* offers a base salary plus an incentive—usually a commission or a bonus. Combination systems have benefits for both the sales manager and the salesperson. The salary portion helps the manager control the sales force; the incentive provides motivation. For the salesperson, a combination plan offers an incentive to excel while minimizing the extremely wide swings in earnings that may occur when the economy slows down.

straight commission
A method of compensation in which the salesperson is paid some percentage of sales.

straight salary
A method of compensation in which the salesperson receives a salary regardless of sales productivity.

With the growing emphasis on relationship selling, many sales managers are beginning to find that relationship building is fostered when a portion of the salesperson's compensation is tied to clients' satisfaction with that salesperson. At GE Aircraft Engines, a portion of salespeople's total compensation is tied to customer service and satisfaction, which is measured through surveys.

Compensation plans motivate salespeople to sell, but sometimes they are not enough. Sales managers often offer incentives as well. The most popular incentives are cash rewards, which are used in over 60 percent of sales organizations.[31] Rewards can help increase overall sales volume, add new accounts, improve morale and good will, move slow items, and bolster slow sales. They also can be used to achieve long-term or short-term objectives, such as unloading overstocked inventory and meeting monthly or quarterly sales goals.

An effective sales manager inspires the salespeople, and encourages them to achieve their goals through clear and enthusiastic communications. A recent study that assessed the attributes of sales leaders found that the best of them shared a number of key personality traits (see Exhibit 16.11), such as a sense of urgency, openness to new ideas, and a desire to take risks. These traits separate motivational sales leaders from mere sales managers.

Evaluating the Sales Force

The final task of a sales manager is to evaluate the effectiveness of the sales force. For this, the sales manager needs feedback—that is, regular information from salespeople. Typical performance measures include sales volume, contribution to profit, calls per order, sales or profits per call, and percentage of calls achieving specific goals such as sales of products that the firm is heavily promoting.

exhibit 16.11

Seven Key Leadership Traits of Effective Sales Leaders

Effective sales leaders ...	
... are assertive	Assertive sales leaders know when and how to get tough and how to assert their authority.
... possess ego drive	Sales leaders with ego drive have the desire and ability to persuade their reps to take action.
... possess ego strength	Sales leaders with ego strength are able to not only make sure they bounce back from rejection but also make sure their reps rebound, too.
... take risks	Risk-taking sales leaders are willing to go out on a limb in an effort to make a sale or enhance a relationship.
... are innovative	Innovative sales leaders stay open to new ideas and new ways of conducting business.
... have a sense of urgency	Urgent sales leaders understand that getting things done now is critical to winning and keeping business.
... are empathetic	Empathetic sales leaders help their reps grow by listening and understanding.

Source: Table adapted from Geoffrey Brewer, "The 7 Traits of Great Sales Leaders," *Sales & Marketing Management*, July 1997: 38–46. Reprinted with permission.

Performance information helps the sales manager monitor a salesperson's progress throughout the sales cycle and pinpoint where breakdowns may be occurring. For example, if a sales manager notices a sales rep letting too many prospects slip away after presenting proposals, it may mean the sales rep needs help with developing proposals, handling objections, or closing sales.

LOOKING BACK

Snack maker Frito-Lay does not use just one element of the promotional mix to promote its many brands of salty snacks. Rather, it uses a mix of promotional elements: advertising, public relations and publicity, and sales promotion. Promotion proved crucial to Frito-Lay's successful launch of brands such as Baked Lay's. As you read the next chapter, keep in mind that marketers try to choose the mix of promotional elements that will best promote their good or service. Rarely will a marketer rely on just one method of promotion.

Summary

1 Discuss the role of promotion in the marketing mix. The promotion "p" of marketing is internal marketing communication that informs, persuades, and reminds potential buyers of a product in order to influence an opinion or elicit a response. The IMC program outlines how the elements of promotion become a coordinated IMC plan to meet the firm's overall objectives and marketing goals. The IMC program is an integral part of the total marketing plan along with its product, distribution, and place. It is the plan for using the elements of promotion—personal selling, advertising, sales promotion, and public relations—to meet the firm's overall objectives and marketing goals. Based on these objectives, the elements of the promotional strategy become a coordinated promotion plan. The promotion plan then becomes an integral part of the total marketing strategy for reaching the target market, along with product, distribution, and place.

2 Discuss the elements of IMC. The elements of the promotional mix include personal selling, advertising, sales promotion, and public relations. Personal selling typically involves direct communication, in person or by telephone; the seller tries to initiate a purchase by informing and persuading one or more potential buyers. More current notions of personal selling focus on the relationship developed between the seller and the buyer. Advertising is a paid form of impersonal, one-way mass communication. Sales promotion backs up other components of the promotional mix by stimulating purchasing. Finally, public relations is the function of promotion concerned with a firm's public image. Firms can't buy good publicity, but they can take steps to create a positive company image.

3 Describe the communication process. When an individual or organization has a message it wishes to convey to a target audience, it encodes that message using language and symbols and sends the message through a channel of communication. Noise in the transmission channel distorts the source's intended message. Reception occurs when the message falls within the receiver's frame of reference. The receiver decodes the message and provides feedback to the source. Normally, feedback is direct for interpersonal communication and indirect for mass communication.

4 Explain the goals and tasks of IMC. The fundamental goals of IMC are to inform, persuade, and remind. Informative promotion explains a product's/service's purpose and benefits. Typically, promotion that informs the consumer is used to increase demand for a product category or to introduce a new good or service. Persuasive promotion is designed to stimulate a purchase or an action. Promotion that persuades the consumer to buy is essential during the growth stage of the product life cycle, when competition becomes fierce. Reminder promotion is used to keep the product and brand name in the public's mind. Promotions that remind are generally used during the maturity stage of the product life cycle.

5 Discuss the AIDA concept and its relationship to the IMC program. The AIDA model outlines the four basic stages in the decision to make a purchase: (1) awareness, (2) interest, (3) desire, and (4) action. The components of IMC have varying levels of influence at each stage of the AIDA model. Advertising is a good tool for increasing product awareness and knowledge. Sales promotion is effective when consumers are at the desire and action (purchase) stages of the decision-making process. Personal selling is most effective in developing customer interest and desire.

6 Describe the factors that affect IMC. Promotion managers consider many factors when creating promotional mixes. These factors include the nature of the product, the product life cycle stage, the characteristics of the target market, the type of buying decision involved, the availability of funds, and the choice of push or pull strategies. Because most business products tend to be custom tailored to the buyer's exact specifications, for these the marketing manager may choose a promotional mix that relies more heavily on personal selling. Most consumer products are mass produced and lend themselves better to mass promotional efforts such as advertising and sales promotion. As products move through different stages of the product life cycle, marketers emphasize different IMC elements. Advertising is emphasized more in the introductory stage of the product life cycle than in the decline stage. Characteristics of the target market, such as brand loyalty and the geographic location of potential buyers, influence the IMC program, and so does the complexity of the buying decision. The IMC budget also determines the promotional mix. Small firms with limited funds rely more heavily on public relations; larger firms can afford broadcast or print advertising. Finally, if a firm uses a push strategy to promote its product or service, the marketing manager may use aggressive advertising and personal selling to wholesalers and retailers. If a pull strategy is chosen, the manager often relies on aggressive mass promotion, such as advertising and sales promotion, to stimulate consumer demand.

7 **Describe personal selling**. Personal selling is direct communication between a sales representative and one or more prospective buyers. Broadly speaking, all businesspeople use personal selling to promote themselves and their ideas. Personal selling offers several advantages over other forms of IMC. Personal selling allows salespeople to thoroughly explain and demonstrate a product. Salespeople have the flexibility to tailor a sales presentation to the needs and preferences of individual customers. Personal selling is more efficient than other forms of promotion because salespeople target qualified prospects and avoid wasting efforts on unlikely buyers. Personal selling gives greater managerial control over promotion costs. Finally, personal selling is the most effective method of closing a sale and producing satisfied customers.

8 **Discuss the key differences between relationship selling and traditional selling**. Relationship selling is the practice of building, maintaining, and enhancing interactions with customers in order to develop long-term satisfaction through mutually beneficial partnerships. Traditional selling is transaction focused; that is, the salesperson is most concerned with making one-time sales and moving on to the next prospect. Salespeople practising relationship selling spend more time understanding a prospect's needs and developing solutions to meet those needs.

9 **List the steps in the selling process**. The selling process comprises seven basic steps: (1) generating leads, (2) qualifying leads, (3) assessing approach and needs, (4) developing and proposing solutions, (5) handling objections, (6) closing the sale, and (7) following up.

10 **Describe the functions of sales management**. Sales managers perform several important functions. They set overall company sales goals and define the sales processes most effective for achieving those goals. They determine the structure of the sales force based on geographic, product, function, and customer variables. They develop the sales force through recruiting and training. They motivate the sales force through compensation planning, motivational tools, and effective sales leadership. Finally, they evaluate the sales force through salesperson feedback and other performance measures.

Discussion and Writing Questions

1. What is an IMC program? Explain the concept of differential advantage in relation to IMC.
2. Why is understanding the target market a crucial aspect of the communication process?
3. Discuss the importance of IMC. Give some current examples of companies that are and are not practising IMC.
4. Why might a marketing manager choose to promote his or her product using persuasion? Give some current examples of persuasive promotion.
5. Discuss the roles that personal selling and advertising play in promoting industrial products. How are these used differently when it is consumer products that are being promoted?
6. What are the key differences between relationship selling and traditional methods of selling? What types of products or services do you think would be better served by relationship selling?
7. You are a new salesperson for a well-known business computer system, and one of your customers is a large group of physicians. You have just arranged an initial meeting with the office manager. Develop a list of questions you will ask at this meeting to uncover the group's specific needs.
8. What does sales follow-up involve? Why is it an essential step in the selling process, especially from the perspective of relationship selling?
9. Choose a partner from class, and together interview the owners or managers of several small businesses in your area. Ask them what their promotional objectives are, and why. Are they trying to inform, persuade, or remind customers to do business with them? Also, determine whether they believe they have an awareness problem and whether they need to persuade customers to come to them instead of to competitors. Ask them to list the characteristics of their primary market, the strengths and weaknesses of their direct competitors, and how they are positioning their store to compete. Prepare a report for your class summarizing your findings.
10. Visit **www.teamxrx.com**. In what ways does this Website generate a sense of personal selling?

Application for Small Business

Morgan's is a retail clothing store offering high-quality, reasonably priced merchandise. Its target markets include students at the local university and working individuals, mainly in the age range eighteen to thirty-five. The store is around three miles from the campus in a small mall. For several years the owner has been hiring students as part-time salespeople and assistant managers. He has been able to find good workers, but turnover is high and training new employees takes a lot of time. Sales staff leave partly because they have problems answering customers' questions about products, services, and special offers.

Questions

1. How can the owner decrease sales staff turnover?
2. Should he hire a university graduate as a full-time employee instead of hiring part-time students? Explain.

Do You Know These Terms?

advertising 431
AIDA concept 437
channel 434
cold calling 448
communication 432
decoding 434
differential advantage 429
encoding 434
feedback 434
follow-up 450
informative promotion 436
integrated marketing communications (IMC) 435
interpersonal communication 432
lead generation (prospecting 447
lead qualification 448
mass communication 432
needs assessment 449
negotiation 450
networking 447
noise 434
personal selling 429
persuasive promotion 437
preapproach 448
promotion 429
promotional mix (IMC plan) 429
public relations 431
publicity 431
pull strategy 442
push strategy 442
quota 452
receiver 434
referral 447
relationship selling (consultative selling) 445
reminder promotion 437
sales presentation 449
sales process (sales cycle) 446
sales promotion 431
sales proposal 449
sender 432
straight commission 453
straight salary 453

Boyne USA Resorts *Lifestyles* Magazine: Promoting the Ultimate Playground

Boyne USA Resorts' *Lifestyles* magazine has a circulation of 500,000. Through direct mail, newsstand distribution, and trade show exposure, the magazine reaches an audience from Montana to Michigan and from Washington to Utah. Boyne USA Resorts is the largest privately owned resort corporation in the country and has a very diverse audience. In many ways, *Lifestyles* epitomizes Boyne's integrated approach to communication about available services. All promotional activities—media advertising, sales promotion, personal selling, and public relations, as well as direct marketing—have a consistent, unified message. This integrated approach to promotion can be seen in every issue of *Lifestyles*, which informs the target audience of skiers and golfers, persuades them to come to a Boyne resort, and reminds them of special events and sales promotions.

Lifestyles articles advertise all the amenities of the resorts: the inns, condominiums, and vacation homes; the superb quality of the slopes, cross-country skiing trails, and manicured golf courses; other activities such as hiking, biking, and fishing; and the gourmet restaurants. The section entitled "Distinctive Resort Properties for Sale" lists available real estate for sale and invites readers to contact a Boyne real estate professional who will work one-to-one with prospective buyers. Also highlighted in *Lifestyles* is the Boyne team of convention planners, who offer companies a wide choice of tastefully decorated facilities and conference rooms for 6 to 600 people.

Lifestyles also describes Boyne's special events, which are carefully orchestrated to build good public relations nationwide. By identifying areas of public interest and offering programs to generate public awareness, Boyne USA maintains a positive image and educates the public about its goal to be a premier ski and golf resort. The company's special events calendar at the Michigan resorts is full. Ski with the Greats is a popular event, with celebrities on hand to hold clinics and a challenge race, and to award prizes at the après-ski party. At the Hawaiian Tropic, contestants from around the state come to Boyne Mountain to compete in an evening gown and swimsuit competition, a fashion show, a limbo dance, and a Mr. Boyne contest, all of which culminate in a party with live entertainment. Dannon Winterfest, put on in conjunction with the Dannon Company, has tents and inflatables set up around Boyne Mountain with product sampling, a dance contest, an après-ski party, and merchandise giveaways. And the World Pro Snowboard Tour features international racers, who compete for $250,000 in prize money. These events give the resorts lots of publicity. Regardless of how much advertising is done, nothing generates more excitement about Boyne USA than extensive media coverage.

Besides informing readers about the resorts, *Lifestyles* persuades them to visit. "Want your ten-year-olds to spend more time outside? Get them a FREE Gold Season Pass to Boyne USA Resorts!" This promotion offers a complimentary pass that entitles ten-year-olds to unlimited skiing and snowboarding at Boyne Mountain and Boyne Highlands. Another powerful way to draw skiers to the resorts is to make skiing affordable. As the *Lifestyles* article explains, "No longer will non-skiers be able to use the expense of skiing or snowboarding as an excuse to remain couch potatoes this winter. For just $29, beginners will get a 90-minute lesson, equipment, and a beginner area lift ticket." The promotions information in *Lifestyles* is regularly updated on the Boyne Website to remind vacationers about special events, skiing and golfing packages, and clothing or equipment.

A key element in the promotional mix for Boyne USA resorts is *Lifestyles* magazine's pull strategy to stimulate consumer demand. The photos of the slopes and golf courses, the lovely inns, and the sumptuous restaurants entice readers to learn more about the resorts, and deep discounts on weekday packages encourage readers to call travel agencies, use the toll-free number, or e-mail for information. Once visitors arrive at the resorts, this pull strategy is supported by a push strategy through the personal selling of real estate, clothing and equipment, and conventions. At Boyne, the push strategy is more about relationships and trust; salespeople are viewed as consultants who help the resort connect with its guests. For example, meeting planners work diligently with key accounts to develop long-term relationships, and carefully planned family events, such as Take Your Daughter to the Slopes Day and Ski Free with Lodging, make skiing affordable and so build customer loyalty.

Lifestyles is just the beginning of Boyne USA's well-coordinated promotion strategy, a strategy that is customer focused to bring vacationers back to the ultimate playground year after year.

Bibliography

Boyne USA Resorts, *Lifestyles* magazine: Winter 1997–98; Spring/Summer 1998.

www.boyneusa.com

Questions

1. Using Exhibit 16.1, what is the role of promotion in Boyne USA's marketing mix?
2. How does *Lifestyles* magazine encompass all of Boyne's promotional activities?
3. Using Exhibit 16.4, explain the three tasks of promotion at Boyne USA resorts.
4. How do push and pull strategies affect Boyne's promotional mix?

CHAPTER

17

LEARNING OBJECTIVES

After studying this chapter, you should be able to

1 Discuss the role of advertising in the IMC program

2 Identify the major types of advertising

3 Describe the creative planning process for advertising

4 Describe the media planning process for advertising

5 Discuss the role of sales promotion in the IMC program

6 Describe the most common forms of consumer sales promotion

7 Identify the most common forms of trade sales promotion

8 Discuss the role of public relations in the IMC program

9 Describe the major types of public relations activity

ADVERTISING, SALES PROMOTION, AND PUBLIC RELATIONS

Watch out Labatt. Molson Canadian beer is touching a cord with Canadians and sending the brand's sales up. Ever since Molson developed its successful "I Am Canadian" campaign in 1994, it has been courting Canadians of all ages and lifestyles in an attempt to acquire customer loyalty. This highly integrated communications program, with its consistent message that has changed with the times without radical shifts in positioning, has contributed to Molson's strong hold on the domestic beer market.

With this IMC program, Molson is also attracting young adults who have recently come of legal drinking age. The idea is to develop lifelong loyalty by gaining young drinkers' patronage at the beginning of their beer-drinking careers. As Andrew Bennett, vice-president of Molson brands, says: "A heartfelt pride for Canada exists in a strong majority of young adults. And they are looking for opportunities to identify with and rally around uniquely Canadian icons and moments. Over the last several years 'I AM Canadian' has become much more than a slogan; it has grown into a phrase that celebrates Canadians' dignity, success, and pride" (Molson Website, Investor Relations, Press Release, "Molson Canadian gives proud Canadians something to sing about with latest ad").

Molson's Website (**www.Molson.ca**) shows why the beer is the popular brand among young adults. The "I AM Canadian" theme is the keystone of a highly integrated program of advertising, promotions, sponsorships, events, and public relations. There is an exclusive link, **MolsonInsider.com,** that provides information on the latest promotions, contests, offers, and events, and more. There is also a Molson Brewery virtual tour; on top of this, there is a link that surfers can follow to make their own Canadian movie ("Moviemaker").

Molson's Website is also used to communicate the brewery's innovative sponsored events. One example is the Molson Canadian Big Birthday, which involves bringing music to major Canadian cities on July 1. A TV commercial, "Big Birthday," can be viewed through a hyperlink on the Big Birthday Web page. Public relations is done through

Molson Breweries
Labatt Breweries Limited

See the latest promotional efforts from Molson at its Website. Compare these activities to those used by Labatt. Based on what you see, which beer are you motivated to buy? Explain.

on line

the Investors Relations Web page, which provides community relations messages (e.g., against driving and driving) as well as information on the company and on sponsored events such as the Molson Indy. At Molson Canadian's Big Birthday event, there is a chance to win one of four birthday presents inside specially marked cases.

Molson enjoys prominence in the domestic beer market, and faces the enviable challenge of maintaining its momentum in the face of constant competition from Labatt Blue. Labatt has recently rolled out a very intriguing and attention-grabbing ad campaign of its own.[1]

How does an advertiser like Molson decide which messages it should convey to its target audience? How does Molson decide which media to use to reach its target consumers? What are the benefits of sales promotion, public relations, and the Internet to advertisers like Molson? Answers to these questions and many more will be found as you read this chapter.

The Role of Advertising

1

Discuss the role of advertising in the IMC program

Advertising was defined in Chapter 16 as any form of nonpersonal, paid communication in which the company is identified. It is a popular form of IMC because it reaches such large audiences and can powerfully communicate messages to the consumer. When the economy is strong, advertising expenditures are high—they reached an estimated $5.3 billion in 2000. In a weaker economy, many companies switch funds from advertising to other forms of IMC such as sales promotions and direct marketing.

Total advertising expenditures are high, yet the advertising industry itself is small. There are only ninety-one members of the Council of Canadian Advertising. Depending on the marketplace, advertising spending varies. Car makers such as General Motors spend over $2 billion annually; retail stores such as Sears spend $ 1 billion annually.

Spending on advertising also depends on the stage in the life cycle of the company, product, or service being advertised. When a product is first introduced to the marketplace, a high advertising budget is necessary to get the word out that the new product is available and to explain the product's benefits. In the growth stage, when many competitors are conveying their own messages, a high advertising budget is necessary to communicate the product's superiority. By the mature stage, sales have levelled off and advertising spending is reduced, since its purpose by then is to remind loyal customers of the product's features. Advertising dollars are cut during the decline stage, when sales begin to drop.

How many times can a customer be exposed to an advertisement before he or she begins to be turned off? No one knows for sure, because the answer depends on several factors, such as the nature of the product or service and how the message is communicated. It *is* known that if an advertisement is not shown often enough, it has little or no audience effect, and if it is shown too often, it can have a negative effect. Can you think of a TV ad that drives you mad because you have seen it too often?

Unlike other forms of IMC such as sales promotions and personal selling, there is no way to directly measure the effect of advertising on sales. This is partly because it is very difficult for consumers to know what effect advertising has on their purchasing behaviour.

Major Types of Advertising

A company's IMC objectives determine the type of advertising it uses. If the goal of the IMC plan is to enhance the image of the company, **institutional advertising** is used. If the goal is to build sales of a specific good or service, **product advertising** is used. Often both types are used simultaneously. However, most advertising in Canada is product advertising.

2

Identify the major types of advertising

institutional advertising
A form of advertising that enhances a company's image instead of promoting a particular product.

product advertising
A form of advertising that promotes the benefits of a specific good or service.

Institutional Advertising

Institutional advertising, or corporate advertising, promotes the company as a whole. It is designed to establish, change, or maintain the company's image. Shoppers Drug Mart recently embarked on a corporate campaign to remind customers that the store is still here. The TV ads deal with the store as a whole rather than with any specific goods. The campaign, which featured several life-challenging vignettes such as "until there was life without colds," was designed to attract a new, younger target audience and to remind people that Shopper's Drug Mart still exists. The ultimate goal of institutional advertising is to build a relationship with consumers based on trust.[2]

A form of institutional advertising called **advocacy advertising** is typically used to guard against negative attitudes and to enhance the company's credibility among consumers who already favour it.[3] Often, companies use advocacy advertising to express their views on controversial issues, such as tighter regulations or the outcome of a lawsuit. Advocacy advertising is also used in reaction to criticism or blame.

advocacy advertising
A form of advertising where an organization expresses its views on controversial issues or responds to media attacks.

Product Advertising

Unlike institutional advertising, product advertising promotes the benefits of a specific good or service. The product's stage in its life cycle often determines which type of product advertising is used: pioneering advertising, competitive advertising, or comparative advertising.

The General Electric slogan "We bring good things to life" is a good example of institutional advertising. Notice how its home page focuses on the corporation as a whole rather than on any specific products marketed by the corporation.

Pfizer—Zyrtec
Roche

Pzifer is a pharmaceutical company that manufactures the anti-allergy drug Zyrtec. Even though a doctor's prescription is needed for this drug, the company still advertises to patients. How does its Website reflect this consumer orientation? Compare Pfizer's site with that of Roche, another pharmaceutical company that has also directed advertising at patients. Which company's site demonstrates an attempt to connect with the end users of its products? Why do you think it has followed this strategy?

www.pfizer.com; www.roche.com

pioneering advertising
A form of advertising designed to stimulate primary demand for a new product or product category.

Pioneering Advertising **Pioneering advertising** stimulates primary demand for a new product. Heavily used during the introductory stage of the product life cycle, pioneering advertising offers consumers in-depth information about the benefits of the product while also creating interest. Procter & Gamble used pioneering advertising to introduce the Swiffer Sweeper. The company embarked on an ad campaign to introduce the benefits of the new product and to capitalize on the efficiency of the product. The pioneering ad's goal was to attract people who currently use other house-cleaning tools. P&G also set up demonstration booths at malls and created a Website to introduce and demonstrate product benefits (**www.swiffer.com**).

competitive advertising
A form of advertising designed to influence demand for a specific brand.

Competitive Advertising **Competitive advertising**, also known as brand advertising, is used when a product enters the growth phase of the product life cycle. At this stage, other companies are entering the marketplace with similar products. The goal of competitive advertising is to influence demand for a specific brand over similar brands. Advertisements often stress differences between brands, with strong emphasis on building recall of a brand name and creating a favourable attitude toward the brand. Car advertising has long used very competitive messages, drawing distinctions based on such factors as quality, performance, and image.

comparative advertising
A form of advertising that compares two or more specific competing brands.

Comparative Advertising **Comparative advertising** directly or indirectly compares two or more competing brands on one or more specific attributes. Some advertisers, such as Procter & Gamble, even use comparative advertising against their own brands (e.g., Tide versus Cheer). Products experiencing sluggish growth or entering the marketplace against strong competitors are more likely to use comparative claims in their advertising.

Comparative advertising can be tricky. In May 1999 a U.S. court judge ordered Ralston Purina, the maker of Energizer batteries, to stop running ads comparing the performance of the Advance Formula to that of its main competitor, Duracell Ultra. The comparison was based on an article published in *Popular Science.* Gillette, the makers of Duracell, claimed that the ads were unfair and violated the Competition Act (May 1999, Crain, Communications Inc.).

Steps in Creating Advertising

3
Describe the creative planning process for advertising

Creating an ad involves much more than coming up with a clever idea. It results from the advertising planning process that is set in motion by the IMC program. As outlined in the previous chapter, the IMC program is the promotions "p" of marketing. The IMC planning process identifies the target market, determines the overall promotional objectives, sets the promotion budget, and selects the IMC mix.

advertising objective
The specific communication task to be accomplished for a specified target audience during a specified period.

Advertising is the most creative element of the IMC mix. The first step in developing an advertisement is to determine the advertising objectives. An **advertising objective** identifies the specific communication task an advertisement should accomplish for a specified target audience during a specified period of time. Advertising objectives depend on the firm's overall objectives and on the product being advertised. Some common bases for advertising objectives are:

- To increase awareness of a new product/service
- To motivate the target market to purchase
- To remind the target market of the benefits of a brand
- To alter a company's image.

The DAGMAR approach (**D**efining **A**dvertising **G**oals for **M**easured **A**dvertising **R**esults) is one method of setting objectives. According to this method, all advertising objectives should precisely define the target audience, the desired percentage change in some specified measure of effectiveness, and the time frame in which that change is to occur. An advertising objective for the new Eatons stores might have been to change their image in the minds of 60 percent of the new target market six months before they opened in 2000.

exhibit 17.1

Advertising Campaign Decision Process

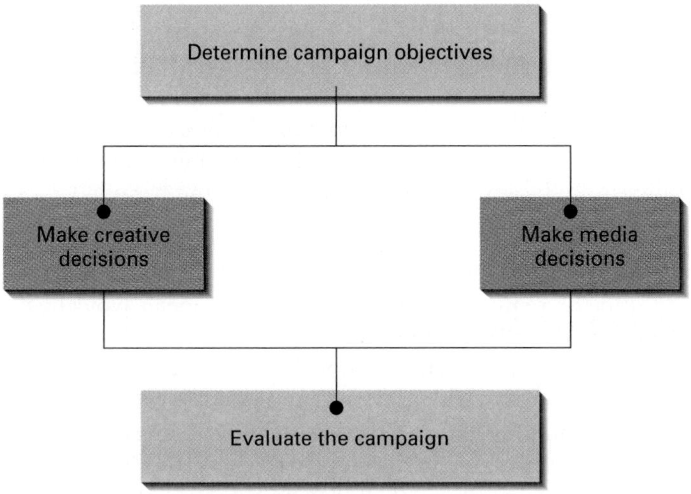

Determine campaign objectives

Make creative decisions

Make media decisions

Evaluate the campaign

Make Creative Decisions

The next step in developing the advertising is to make the necessary creative and media decisions. Note in Exhibit 17.1 that creative and media decisions are made at the same time. Creative work cannot be completed without knowing which **medium,** or communication channel, will be used to convey the message to the target market. Creative planning for a TV ad will likely differ from that for a newspaper or magazine ad. Often the advertising budget dictates the medium and the creative approach to be used. Creative objectives develop from the advertising objectives. Exhibit 17.2 shows some common creative objectives.

medium
The channel used to convey a message to a target market.

One or more creative objectives guide the development of an advertisement.

Identifying Product Benefits A well-known rule of thumb in the advertising industry is "Sell the sizzle, not the steak." That is, in advertising the goal is to sell the benefits of the product, not just its attributes. An attribute is simply a feature of the product such as its easy-open package or special formulation. A benefit is what consumers will receive or achieve by using the product. A benefit should answer the consumer's question, "What's in it for me?" Benefits can be such things as convenience, pleasure, savings, or relief. Consider this example:

> *Attribute*: "The Gillette MACH3 shaving system has three blades aligned progressively nearer to the face, each coated with a microscopic layer of carbon, mounted on a forward-pivoting

shaver to automatically adjust to the curves and contours of a man's face."

Benefit: "So, you'll get a closer, smoother, and safer shave than ever before with fewer strokes and less irritation."[4]

exhibit 17.2

Common Creative Objectives

- To communicate unique product benefits and attributes
- To increase frequency or variety of use
- To attract new targets
- To communicate product improvements
- To communicate promotion incentives
- To communicate a positive corporate image

Marketing research and intuition are usually used to unearth the perceived benefits of a product and to rank consumers' preferences for these benefits. Gillette's rival Schick is advertising its razors on the basis of safety. Schick's research shows that safety is among the top three attributes men look for in a razor. For this reason, its advertising campaign touts the benefits of a safe shave rather than a close shave.[5]

advertising appeal
A strategy for communicating a creative objective.

Creative Strategy—Advertising Appeals An **advertising appeal** is the strategy for communicating a creative objective. Advertising appeals typically play on consumers' emotions and address some need or want the consumer has. An advertisement can use one or more advertising appeals. Several are listed in Exhibit 17.3.

Choosing the best appeal usually requires market research. The appeal first must make a positive impression on the target market. It must also be exclusive or unique; consumers must be able to distinguish the advertiser's message from competitors' messages. Most important of all, the appeal should be believable. An appeal that makes extravagant claims not only wastes promotional dollars but also creates ill will for the advertiser.

exhibit 17.3

Common Advertising Appeals

Positive	Lets consumers know how using the product will result in a positive situation—for example, save them money, or help them reduce weight or get rid of a headache.
Negative	Tells consumers the negative consequences of not using a product. American Express shows a distraught couple who lost their money while on vacation.
Sex	Used often in selling cosmetics, fragrances, clothes, and alcohol.
Fear	MADD (Mothers Against Drunk Drivers) TV ads show the terrible consequences of drinking and driving.
Lifestyle	Shows how well the product will fit in with the consumer's lifestyle. GM's "Like a Rock" TV ads demonstrate the all-terrain usefulness of its FWD truck for rugged lifestyles.
Humorous	Advertisers often use humour in their ads. Visa TV ads feature friendly penguins stealing a Visa card from an innocent family in the water.
Scientific	Uses research or scientific evidence to give a brand superiority over competitors. Pain relievers such as Advil, Bayer, and Excedrin use scientific evidence in their ads.

StarKist Foods

How does StarKist use Charlie to promote its tuna on the company's Website? Do you think he is still an effective advertising tool? Explain.

www.starkist.com

on line

The advertising strategy also guides the development of company slogans. Effective slogans become so ingrained that consumers can immediately conjure up images of the product just by hearing the slogan. Most consumers can easily name the companies or products behind these memorable slogans: "We try harder," "Ring around the collar," and "For everything else, there's ..." Advertisers often revive old slogans or jingles in the hope that nostalgia will create good feelings with consumers. Labatt, in its "Big Song" commercial for Labatt Blue, is using the 1970s Neil Diamond hit song, "Sweet Caroline." After a decade-long absence from national television, Starkist's Charlie the Tuna appeared in television ads with the famous "Sorry Charlie" tag line.

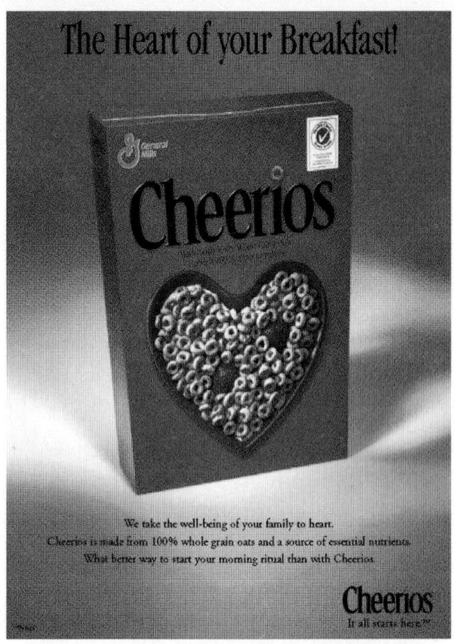

All ad campaigns revolve around an advertising appeal. What do you think is the advertising appeal of this General Mills Cheerios ad? (Consult Exhibits 17.3 and 17.4.)

Executing the Message The style in which the message is executed is one of the most critical elements of an ad. Exhibit 17.4 lists some of the executional styles used by advertisers.

In general, the AIDA (Attention, Interest, Desire, Action) plan is a good blueprint for executing an advertising message. Any ad should immediately draw the consumer's attention. The advertiser must then use the message to hold the consumer's interest, create desire for the good or service, and ultimately motivate the consumer to take action (i.e., purchase the product/service).

Humorous executional styles are more often used in radio and television advertising than in newspapers or magazines, where humour is less easily communicated. Humorous ads are more memorable and can be shown many times before people are turned off.

exhibit 17.4

Ten Common Executional Styles for Advertising

Slice-of-life	Popular for advertising household and personal products; depicts people in normal settings, such as at the dinner table.
Spokesperson/ testimonial	May feature a celebrity, a company official, or a typical consumer making a testimonial or endorsing a product. Basketball star Shaquille O'Neal drinks Pepsi. Wayne Gretsky's father provides a testimonial for the Canadian Arthritis Association and Tylenol.
Fantasy	Creates a fantasy for the viewer built around use of the product. Levi's jean-clad strangers meet on an elevator, eye each other, share the same daydream—fall in love, get married, raise a family—and then silently go their separate ways.
Real/animated	Creates a character that represents the product in advertisements—for example, the Energizer bunny.
Mood or image	Builds a mood or image around the product, such as peace, love, or beauty. The DeBeers ads depicting shadowy silhouettes wearing diamond engagement rings and diamond necklaces are portraying passion and intimacy while communicating that a "diamond is forever."
Product	Shows consumers expected benefits. Laundry detergent ads are famous for demonstrating how their product will clean clothes whiter and brighter.
Musical	Conveys the message through song. The "Khakis Swing" spots by The Gap feature khaki-clad dancers swinging to a Louis Prima tune.

global perspectives

Global Challenges for Advertisers

One of the hottest debates among global advertising professionals today is whether to customize or standardize advertising. According to one argument, an ad's appeal and execution style should be tailored to each individual country or region because cultures perceive and react to advertising differently. According to the opposite argument, there should be a single advertising approach for all countries.

Kodak favours a customized approach to advertising in China because consumer tastes and values vary between mainland China and Taiwan and Hong Kong, which are more progressive. In Taiwan and Hong Kong, Kodak is targeting a young, innovative audience. On mainland China, Kodak's approach is tailored to traditional Chinese lifestyles.

Reebok recently embarked on a $100 million global ad campaign in an attempt to make its message more cohesive around the world. In the past, Reebok sent out confusing messages—it was known as a running shoe in the United Kingdom and as a fashion statement in Canada.

Some advocate a single advertising approach for all countries. Under a standardized approach, the advertiser develops one ad and delivers it, translated into the language of each country, to all target markets. Supporters of this approach insist that consumers everywhere have the same basic needs and desires and can therefore be persuaded by universal advertising appeals. Furthermore, they say, a standardized ad campaign creates a unified brand image worldwide, and the advertiser eliminates the inefficiencies of trying to reinvent the meaning of its brand in every country.

Possibly the best answer to this dilemma is to use a mixture of standardization and customization—that is, to standardize the message while paying attention to local differences in execution. Unilever uses a standardized appeal when promoting its Dove soap, but also uses models from Australia, France, Germany, and Italy to appeal to women in those countries. This mixture of standardization and customization seems to be successful for many global marketers, but it only works as long as the message truly plays to a worldwide audience.

Some of the marketers discussed here have succeeded using a global approach to advertising, but not every product or service is suited for a unified advertising message. What types of products do you think would benefit from a standardized approach to advertising? What types would fare better using a tailored approach?

Executional styles for foreign ads are different from those we are accustomed to. Nike is known for its "in your face" advertising and slogans like "Just Do It." But its brash advertising does not appeal to Europeans. A television commercial of Satan and his demons playing soccer against a team of Nike endorsers was a hit in America. Yet many European stations refused to run it, saying it was too scary and offensive to show in prime time, when kids would be watching.[6]

Global advertising managers are growing more and more concerned about whether they should be standardizing or customizing their advertising appeals and executional styles when delivering advertising messages around the world. Read about this dilemma in the "Global Perspectives" box.

Make Media Decisions

4 Describe the media planning process for advertising

Exhibit 17.5 shows the money spent on advertising by media type in Canada. As you can see, television and newspapers get the lion's share of advertising dollars.

Media Types

The most important media for advertising are newspapers, magazines, radio, television, outdoor media, and the Internet. Exhibit 17.6 summarizes the advantages and disadvantages of each. In recent years, alternative media have emerged that provide advertisers with innovative ways to reach their target audiences and avoid advertising clutter.

exhibit 17.5

National Ad Spending in Measured Media for 2000 (estimates)

Medium	Percentage of total ad spending
Magazines	7.3
Newspapers	38.1
Outdoor media	3.2
Television	38.5
Radio	12.7
Cinema	0.1

Source: "National Ad Spending by Media," **www.adageglobal.com**.

services spotlight

Vancouver's Branded Parking Lots

When the Parking Corporation of Vancouver began to research its market, it wasn't really surprised that most people, if they thought about parking at all, did so only if they had a problem. In fact, share of mind and awareness for the Parking Corp., a public and private partnership with the City of Vancouver since 1948, was a mere 1 percent. "We have done a very poor job of communicating to the marketplace," says Dave Walker, the Corp.'s chairman. So Walker followed an example set in Portland, Oregon, over ten years ago by a similar company, which rebranded itself as SmartPark and saw revenues shoot from $5 million to $6.1 million in the first year alone.

On 23 May 2001 the Parking Corp. launched a $1 million marketing campaign and its new EasyPark brand name. A series of radio and prints ads, created by Vancouver's Hamazaki Wong, are built around the tag line, "Parking may not be the most important thing in your life. Happily, it's the most important thing in ours." The ads talk about things that make EasyPark different: a jerry can of gas, jumper cables, and help to retrieve locked car keys.

EasyPark's thirty-nine downtown parking lots have a 15 percent market share of total inventory in Vancouver, says Walker, and about half of all transient parking—which makes up about 80 percent of its business.

EasyPark is now a trademarked city/municipal brand, and Walker sees its future as a brand identity operating throughout Canada. Again following the example of others, EasyPark has also begun introducing sponsored "theme" parking spots as a way of helping customers find their cars. Eatons has been the first to jump in, painting a section in aubergine and including its corporate logo.

Why are many services, such as parking lots, so difficult to promote when compared to products? What consumer insights does the EasyPark launch campaign tap into? Do you think the campaign does a good job of creating a brand? What other ways can you think of that EasyPark could promote its new brand? In terms of message? In terms of advertising media? In terms of sales promotion? In terms of PR?

Source: Adapted from Eve Lazarus, "Vancouver's Branded Parking Lots," *Marketing Magazine News,* 11 June 2001. DOC # 20010611MM00006.

Newspapers The advantages of newspaper advertising include geographic flexibility and timeliness. Because copywriters can usually prepare newspaper ads quickly and at a reasonable cost, local merchants can reach their target market almost daily. However, newspapers may not be the best vehicle for marketers trying to reach a very narrow market. For example, daily newspapers are not the best media for reaching serious mountain bikers. Newspaper advertising is surrounded by a lot of distractions from competing ads and news stories, so one ad may not be especially visible.

Most newspaper ad revenue comes from local retailers, classified ads, and cooperative advertising. In **cooperative advertising**, the manufacturer and the retailer split the costs of advertising the manufacturer's brand. One reason manufacturers use cooperative advertising is to encourage retailers to devote more effort to the manufacturer's product lines.

cooperative advertising
An arrangement in which the manufacturer and the retailer split the costs of advertising the manufacturer's brand.

on line

Shaw Cable
CBLT
What kind of advertising is done on Shaw Cable's Website? Compare this with the site for CBLT. What differences do you notice? Why do you think a television network would choose not to sell ad space on its Website?
www.shaw.ca; www.cbc.ca/local; www.cbc.ca/sites/cblt

Magazines Relative to other media, the cost per contact in magazine advertising is usually high. However, the cost per target audience may be much lower because magazines are often targeted to specialized audiences and thus reach more potential customers.

One of the main advantages of magazine advertising is its market selectivity. Magazines are published for virtually every market segment. For instance, *Maclean's* is a Canadian national newsmagazine, *Sports Illustrated* is a successful all-around sporting publication, and *Maxim* and *Flare* have a high young adult readership.

Radio Radio has a number of strengths as an advertising medium: target audience selectivity, low unit and production costs, timeliness, and geographic flexibility. Local advertisers are the most frequent users of radio advertising, contributing over three-quarters of all radio ad revenues. Like newspapers, radio also lends itself well to cooperative advertising.

Radio advertising is becoming popular again. As Canadians become more mobile and pressed for time, other media such as television and newspapers are struggling to retain viewers and readers. Also, radio is able to target specific demographic groups; this attracts advertisers who are pursuing narrowly defined audiences. Moreover, radio listeners tend to listen habitually at predictable times, with the most popular radio listening hours during "drive time"[7]

Television Because television is an audiovisual medium, it provides advertisers with many creative opportunities. Television broadcasters include network television, independent stations, cable television, and direct broadcast satellite television. American networks such as ABC, CBS, NBC, and the Fox Network dominate network television, which reaches a broad and diverse market. In Canada, CBC and CTV dominate network TV. Cable television and direct broadcast satellite systems such as Shaw, Roger, Bell ExpressVu, and Star Choice offer consumers a multitude of channels devoted exclusively to particular audiences—for example, women, children, cooks, gardeners, golfers, and lovers of history. Because its channels are targeted, cable television is often characterized as "narrowcasting" by media buyers.

Advertising time on television can be very expensive. One thirty-second spot during 1999's Super Bowl telecast cost advertisers around US$1.6 million. Advertisers forked over a record US$1.7 to $1.8 million for one thirty-second spot during the last episode of *Seinfeld*.[8]

infomercial
A thirty-minute or longer advertisement that looks more like a TV talk show than a sales pitch.

The **infomercial**, a thirty-minute or longer advertisement, is an attractive advertising vehicle because of the inexpensive air time and the relatively small production cost. Advertisers say the infomercial is an ideal way to present complicated information to potential customers. Manufacturers of exercise equipment, diet plans, and household aids are very fond of using infomercials to advertise their products.

Outdoor Media This form of advertising is flexible and low-cost and can take a variety of forms. Examples include billboards, four-sided pillar ads in indoor malls and outdoor strip malls, "painted" buses, transit shelters, giant inflatables, banners in sports arenas, lighted moving signs in bus terminals and airports, and ads painted on the sides of cars, trucks, or even water towers. Outdoor ads reach a broad and diverse market.

The main advantage of outdoor advertising is that it is relatively inexpensive per contact. Also, it can be customized to local marketing needs.

exhibit 17.6

Advantages and Disadvantages of Major Advertising Media

Medium	Advantages	Disadvantages
Newspapers	Geographic selectivity and flexibility; short-term advertiser commitments; news value and immediacy; year-round readership; high individual market coverage; co-op and local tie-in availability; short lead time	Little demographic selectivity; limited colour capabilities; low pass-along rate; may be expensive
Magazines	Good reproduction, especially for colour; demographic selectivity; regional selectivity; local market selectivity; relatively long advertising life; high pass-along rate	Long-term advertiser commitments, slow audience buildup; limited demonstration capabilities; lack of urgency; long lead time
Radio	Low cost; immediacy of message; can be scheduled on short notice; relatively no seasonal change in audience; highly portable; short-term advertiser commitments; entertainment carryover	No visual treatment; short advertising life of message; high frequency required to generate comprehension and retention; distractions from background sound; commercial clutter
Television	Ability to reach a wide, diverse audience; low cost per thousand; creative opportunities for demonstration; immediacy of messages; entertainment carryover; demographic selectivity with cable stations	Short life of message; some consumer scepticism about claims; high campaign cost; little demographic selectivity with network stations; long-term advertiser commitments; long lead times required for production; commercial clutter
Outdoor media	Repetition; moderate cost; flexibility; geographic selectivity	Short message; lack of demographic selectivity; high "noise" level distracting audience
Internet	Fastest-growing medium; ability to reach a narrow target audience; relatively short lead time required for creating Web-based advertising; moderate cost	Difficult to measure ad effectiveness and return on investment; ad exposure relies on "click-through" from banner ads; not all consumers have access to the Internet

Outdoor advertising has been growing in recent years, mainly due to the fragmentation of other media, people spending more time commuting, and improved reproduction quality. Outdoor advertising is also becoming more innovative. At the 2000 Billi Awards, held by the Outdoor Advertising Association of Canada, DaimlerChrysler Canada won gold for its Gas Pump/Parking Meter/Stop Sign billboard campaign (**www.oaac.com**).

The Internet

With ad revenues in Canada at $38.5 million, the Internet has established itself as a solid advertising medium.[9] From 1997 to 1998, traditional marketers nearly tripled their Internet advertising spending, to an average of $750,000. In 1997, only 38 percent of companies were advertising on the Internet; in 1998, 68 percent were doing so. On-line advertising has made significant gains since the early 1990s, but it still makes up only a small portion of companies' total advertising budgets. According to a survey conducted by the Association of National Advertisers, the two biggest barriers to Internet advertising are the difficulty of tracking return on investment and the lack of reliable and accurate measurement information.[10]

Popular Internet sites and on-line service providers such as Netscape and Yahoo! are selling advertising space, called "banners," to companies. Internet surfers click on these banners to link themselves to the advertiser's site. New forms of Web advertising are starting to transcend the static company logo and message in a banner ad. Using new technologies such as Shockwave and Java, advertisers are developing Web ads that incorporate interactivity, e-commerce, sound, and animation. A banner ad from John Hancock Mutual Life Insurance Company lets users input their children's ages to find out how much money they need to invest each month for a university education.[11] On the MuchMusic Website (**www.muchmusic.com/surfrhut**) a user can do the "Rock'em, Sock'em" personality test to win great prizes by hitting the appropriate banner.

A survey on the effectiveness of on-line banner ads found that they actually work as well as their TV or magazine counterparts for brand and advertising awareness. Also, that on-line ads are even more memorable than commercials on TV. After one exposure, people were more likely to recall banner ads than TV ads.[12]

However, Internet surfers generally have to find the marketer rather than vice versa. One Website actually pays consumers to view ads that have been targeted to fit their interests. Users must peruse each Web ad to its last page, then click on a special symbol to receive credit. [13]

Another challenge for Internet advertisers is how to measure the effectiveness of their electronic advertisements or sites. There are ways to count the number of visitors to a Website, but advertisers have no way of knowing how a site ranks against the competition. Also lacking are the kinds of in-depth demographic and psychographic data about Web page users that television, magazines, radio, and newspapers are able to provide about their viewers and subscribers.[14]

internet connections

Marketing by Permission

New York (CNNfn) – Most people are bombarded by advertising every day. They are hit by it when they open the newspaper, turn on the television, open the mailbox, and check their e-mail, and sometimes when they answer the telephone.

Seth Godin, entrepreneur and author, is one who thinks traditional marketing won't work for most companies, particularly new companies, because the advertising is, for the most part, unwanted.

"Finding new ways, more clever ways to interrupt people doesn't work," Goding said at a gathering if e-business executives in New York on Tuesday. Traditional forms of marketing amount to "spamming" people, and spamming has not proved an effective method of getting word out about your company.

A completely passive approach, on the other hand, such as putting up a Web site and hoping someone will notice while out surfing is not a marketing strategy that is likely to draw a ton of customers either.

The keys to successful marketing, according to Godin, are getting people's permission to sell to them and perfecting the art of creating a "viral" marketing campaign. Neither approach is as easy as tacking up a billboard somewhere along Highway 101, but if they work, they will be much more successful than any traditional method.

The difference between traditional marketing and permission marketing is in the relationship the business has to its customers. Traditional advertising tries to court strangers. Permission marketing means you have to turn strangers into friends before selling them a product.

Visit: **cnnfn.cnn.com/2000/10/11/cashflow/g_seth/index.htm#TOP** for the full-text version of this article. It contains a detailed discussion of permission marketing and examples of companies that have used it successfully.

Is permission marketing a viable strategy for all companies or is it more suitable for industries catering to specific "types" of consumers? What is viral marketing, and how does it work? How does permission marketing differ from spam?

The Internet provides countless opportunities for entrepreneurs and small business startups. One entrepreneurial endeavour seeks to sell on-line advertising space targeted to the university crowd. Internet advertising is discussed in more depth in Chapter 19.

Alternative Media Advertisers are looking for new ways to cut through the clutter of traditional advertising media. Alternative vehicles include fax machines, computer screen savers, CD-ROMs, interactive kiosks in department stores, and advertisements at the cinema. In fact, just about anything can become a vehicle for advertising. The Remax air balloon is a common site in city skies across the country.

Media Selection Considerations

The advertising budget strongly affects which media are selected. An important element in any ad campaign is the **media mix**—that is, the combination of media to be used. Media mix decisions are typically based on cost per contact, reach, frequency, and target audience.

media mix
The combination of media to be used for a promotional campaign.

Cost per contact is the cost of reaching one member of the target market. As the size of the audience increases, so does the total cost. Cost per contact enables an advertiser to compare media vehicles such as television versus radio, or magazine versus newspaper, or, more specifically, *Maclean's* versus *Time.* Usually a company chooses the vehicle with the lowest cost per contact to maximize advertising punch for the money spent.

cost per contact
The cost of reaching one member of the target market.

Reach is the number of different target customers who are exposed to an ad at least once during a specific period, usually four weeks. In the introductory and growth phases of a product life cycle, during which brand awareness is critical, media plans emphasize reach. An advertiser might try to reach 70 percent of the target audience during the first three months of advertising.

reach
The number of target consumers exposed to a commercial at least once during a specific period, usually four weeks.

Advertisers repeat their ads so that consumers will remember the message. **Frequency** is the number of times an individual is exposed to a message. Average frequency is used to measure the intensity of a specific medium's coverage.

frequency
The number of times an individual is exposed to a given message during a specific period.

Media selection is also a matter of matching the advertising medium with the product's target market. If marketers are trying to reach teenage girls, they might

entrepreneurial insights

Auto Wrapping Gives Advertisers Another Option

Advertisers that want to hit a specific demographic but are too late for the prime locations of billboards, or can't come up with a car manufacturer for a vehicle, now have the option of using personal vehicles for advertising. Advertising on the sides of vehicles isn't new. What is new is who is driving the vehicle.

Ads on Wheels and Autowraps are two companies that can match up a vehicle owner with an advertiser. Essentially, these companies take the concept of the painted bus or the painted company vehicle to the personal vehicle. Compensation is offered to qualifying drivers registered in the program. Often this compensation is more than monthly car payments.

Here's how it works. Car owners give detailed demographic information about their lifestyle, driving, and parking habits. A global positioning system is then installed in their vehicle for a test period. This information is used to sell the driver and his or her personal vehicle to an advertiser.

The advertisement is placed on the vehicle using high-quality vinyl adhesive with graphic images, and must be maintained by the owner during the life of the contract.

If you are interested in applying, check out these companies' Websites: **www.adsonwheels.com** and **www.autowraps.com.**

Women's Wire

Visit the Women's Wire Website. Are there any ad placements on the site that you have seen recently on television or heard on the radio? Why have advertisers chosen this site over or in conjunction with traditional advertising venues?

www.womenswire.com

on line

select *Seventeen* magazine. If they are trying to reach consumers interested in running, they might choose *Running* magazine. A medium's ability to reach a precisely defined market is its **audience selectivity.** Some media vehicles, such as general newspapers and network TV, appeal to a broad cross-section of the population. Others, such as *Bride's*, *Popular Mechanics*, and the Golf Channel, appeal to very specific groups. A sampling of popular Canadian specialty networks is provided in Exhibit 17.7.

audience selectivity
The ability of an advertising medium to reach a precisely defined market.

Media Scheduling

After choosing the media for the advertising campaign, advertisers must schedule the ads. A **media schedule** designates the media to be used (such as magazines, television, or radio), and the specific vehicles (such as *People* magazine, *Friends* TV show, or the "Don, Joanne and the Coach" morning drive radio program), as well as the dates of the advertising. There are three basic types of media schedules:

- With a **continuous media schedule**, the advertising runs steadily throughout the advertising period. Examples include Ivory soap and Coca-Cola.
- With a **flighted media schedule**, the advertiser may schedule the ads heavily during a condensed time period, and follow this with a period of no advertising. A variation is the **pulsing media schedule**, which combines continuous scheduling with flighting; continuous advertising is simply heavier during the best sale periods. A retail department store may advertise on a year-round basis but place more advertising during special sale periods such as Christmas and back-to-school.
- Certain times of the year call for a **seasonal media schedule**. Products like Contac cold tablets and Coppertone suntan lotion, which are used more during certain times of the year, tend to follow a seasonal strategy. Advertising for champagne is concentrated during the weeks of Christmas and New Year's. Health clubs concentrate their advertising in January to take advantage of New Year's resolutions.

media schedule
Designation of the media, the specific publications or programs, and the insertion dates of advertising.

continuous media schedule
A media scheduling strategy whereby advertising is run steadily throughout the advertising period.

flighted media schedule
A media scheduling strategy whereby ads are run heavily every other month or every two weeks, so as to achieve greater impact through increased frequency and reach.

pulsing media schedule
A media scheduling strategy that uses continuous scheduling throughout the year coupled with a flighted schedule during the best sales periods.

seasonal media schedule
A media scheduling strategy that runs advertising only during times of the year when the product is most likely to be used.

Evaluate the Ad Campaign

How do advertisers know whether the campaign caused an increase in sales or market share, or elevated awareness of the product? Advertisers try to determine whether their money has been well spent by conducting advertising research.

Ad effectiveness can be tested either before or after the advertising has been shown. Before an advertisement is released, advertisers use pretests to determine the best advertising appeal, layout, and media vehicle. After advertisements are placed in the media, post-tests can be done to measure awareness of the ads as well as their effectiveness. Companies do a post-campaign analysis to assess how the advertising could have been more efficient and what factors contributed to its success or failure.

Sales Promotion

5
Discuss the role of sales promotion in the IMC program

Besides using advertising, public relations, and personal selling, marketing managers can use sales promotion to increase the effectiveness of their IMC efforts. Sales promotion is a marketing communication activity that uses short-term incentives to motivate consumers or distribution channel members to purchase a good or service immediately, either by lowering the price or by adding value.

exhibit 17.7

Selected Canadian Specialty TV Networks

APTN	Aboriginal People's TV Network	**www.aptn.ca**
Bravo!	National arts and music	**www.bravo.ca**
CLT	Canadian Learning Television	**www.clt.ca**
CMT	Country Music Television	**www.cmt.ca**
The Comedy Network	Comedy	**www.thecomedynetwork.ca**
Discovery Channel	Educational programs	**www.discovery.ca**
MuchMusic	Music and entertainment programs	**www.muchmusic.com**
YTV Canada Inc.	Youth and family programming	**www.ytv.com**

Advertising offers consumers a *reason* to buy; sales promotion offers an *incentive* to buy. Both are important, but sales promotion is usually cheaper than advertising and easier to measure. A major national TV advertising campaign can cost over $2.5 million to create, produce, and place in the media. A newspaper coupon campaign or promotional contest can cost half as much. It is hard to figure exactly how many people buy a product as a result of seeing a TV ad. With sales promotion, marketers know the precise number of coupons redeemed or the number of contest entrants.

Sales promotion is targeted toward two distinctly different markets. **Consumer sales promotion** is targeted to the ultimate consumer market. **Trade sales promotion** is directed to members of marketing channels, such as wholesalers and retailers. Sales promotion has become an important element in marketers' integrated marketing communications programs (see Chapter 14).

consumer sales promotion Sales promotion activities to the ultimate consumer.

trade sales promotion Sales promotion activities targeted to a channel member, such as a wholesaler or retailer.

Sales promotion expenditures have been increasing steadily in the past several years as a result of increased competition, the ever-expanding number of media choices, consumers and retailers demanding more deals from manufacturers, and the continued reliance on measurable IMC strategies. Also, marketers who have long ignored sales promotion activities, such as residential gas companies, are discovering its marketing power.

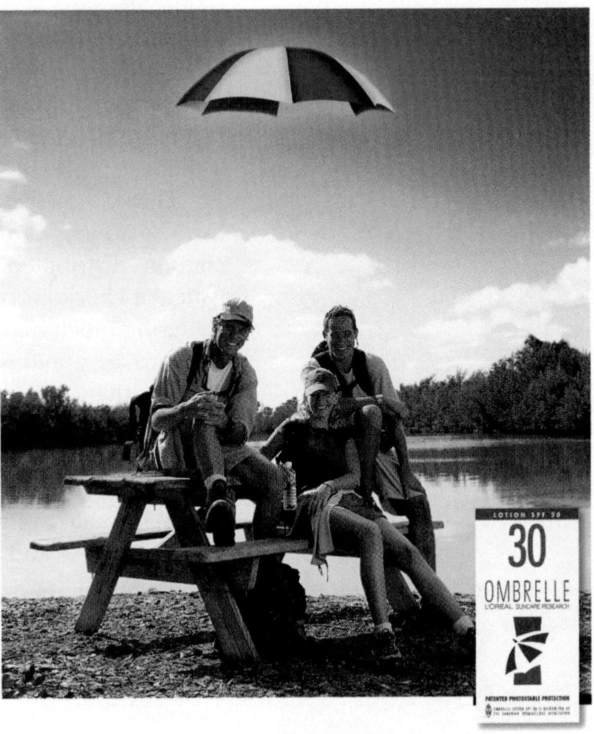

This ad is an example of a seasonal advertising strategy. Besides summertime, what other times of year do you think L'Oreal would benefit from concentrated advertising? How could these be a part of an IMC?

The Objectives of Sales Promotion

Sales promotion usually works best when it aims to change behaviour as opposed to attitudes. The objectives of a promotion depend on the buying behaviour of the target consumers (see Exhibit 17.8). Marketers who are targeting loyal users of their product set out to reinforce existing behaviour or increase product use. Frequent buyer programs that reward consumers for repeat purchases are an effective tool for strengthening brand loyalty. Other types of promotions are more effective with customers who are prone to brand switching or who are loyal to a competitor's product. Money-off coupons, free samples, and eye-catching store displays often entice shoppers to try a different brand. Consumers who do not use the product may be enticed to try it through the distribution of free samples.

Sales promotion activities absolutely must send the same message as other IMC activities. It is also critical that the activities be coordinated. Chapters, in an effort to increase the number of Chapter 1 card holders, sent free-renewal promotion letters to current and lapsed card holders. But too often, when a consumer presented such a letter to the sales staff at a regional store, the staff hesitated to honour the promotion because they didn't know it existed.

6

Describe the most common forms of consumer sales promotion

Tools for Consumer Sales Promotion

Marketing managers must decide which consumer sales promotion devices to use in a specific IMC program. Popular tools for consumer sales promotion are coupons and rebates, premiums, loyalty marketing programs, contests and sweepstakes, sampling, and point-of-purchase promotion.

coupon
A certificate that entitles consumers to an immediate price reduction when they buy the product.

Coupons and Rebates A **coupon** is a certificate that entitles consumers to an immediate price reduction when they buy the product. Coupons are a good way to encourage product trial and repurchase. They are also likely to increase the amount of a product bought.

In Canada, coupon distribution has been steadily increasing as packaged goods marketers increase the face value of coupons. Although the number of coupons distributed directly to consumers has increased by 1 percent to 2.52 billion since 2000, the number of coupons redeemed has dropped to 112 million, down 26 percent from a year ago. (see **www.wattsgroup.com/nch/sr0101.htm**). Part of the problem is that coupons are often wasted on consumers who have no interest in the product—for example, dog food coupons that reach households without pets. Another problem is that most coupons expire before the consumer has the opportunity to use them. Also, coupons are more likely to encourage repeat purchases by regular users of a product than to encourage nonusers to try the brand.[15]

Because of their high cost and disappointing redemption rates, many marketers are re-evaluating their use of coupons. Procter & Gamble has cut coupon distribution in half and shifted to a lower-price strategy. Kraft has distributed a single, all-purpose coupon good on any of its cereal brands. Other marketers are experimenting with on-line coupons over the Internet. Some marketers, such as Toys 'R' Us, are distributing coupons through CoolSavings.com, Inc. (**www.coolsavings.com**), and achieving redemption rates of 10 percent or more. Here marketers are provided with detailed anonymous information about how, where, and when consumers are downloading and using the coupons.

There is a trend toward distributing coupons in stores, where they are most likely to affect customer buying decisions. Instant coupons on product packages, coupons distributed on-shelf in front of the product, and electronic coupons issued at checkout counters (such as the Safeway Membership card) have been achieving much higher redemption rates. The redemption rates for instant coupons are about seventeen times those for traditional newspaper coupons; this suggests that consumers are making more in-store purchase decisions.[16]

rebate
A cash refund given for purchasing a product during a specific period.

Rebates are similar to coupons in that they offer the purchaser a price reduction; however, the reward is not immediate because the purchaser must mail in a rebate form. Traditionally, rebates have been used by food and cigarette manufacturers, but they are now appearing on all types of products, from computers and software to film and undergarments.

Rebates allow companies to offer price cuts to consumers directly. Companies have more control over rebate promotions since they can be rolled out and discontinued quickly. Because buyers must fill out forms with their names, addresses, and other information, companies can use rebate programs to build customer databases. Perhaps the best reason to offer rebates is that even though they are especially good at enticing purchase, most consumers never bother to redeem them. Redemption rates for rebates run between 5 and 10 percent.[17]

premium
An extra item offered to the consumer, usually in exchange for some proof of purchase of the promoted product.

Premiums A **premium** is an extra item offered to the consumer, usually in exchange for proof that the promoted product has been purchased. Premiums reinforce consumers' purchase decisions, increase consumption, and persuade

exhibit 17.8

Types of Consumers and Sales Promotion Goals

Type of buyer	Desired results	Sales promotion examples
Loyal customers People who buy your product most or all of the time	Reinforce behaviour, increase consumption, change purchase timing	• Loyalty marketing programs, such as frequent buyer cards or frequent shopper clubs • Bonus packs that give loyal consumers an incentive to stock up or offer a premium in return for proof of purchase.
Competitor's customers People who buy a competitor's product most or all of the time	Break loyalty, persuade to switch to your brand	• Sampling to introduce your product's superior qualities compared to their brand • Sweepstakes, contests, or premiums that create interest in the product
Brand switchers People who buy a variety of products in the category	Persuade to buy your brand more often	• Any promotion that lowers the price of the product, such as coupons, price-off packages, and bonus packs • Trade deals that help make the product more readily available than competing products
Price buyers People who consistently buy the least expensive brand	Appeal with low prices, or supply added value that makes price less important	• Coupons, price-off packages, refunds, or trade deals that reduce the price of the brand to match that of the brand that would have been purchased

Source: From Don E. Schultz, William A. Robinson, and Lisa A. Petrison, *Sales Promotion Essentials,* 2nd ed. Reprinted by permission of NTC Publishing Group, 4255 Touhy Ave. Lincolnwood, IL 60048.

loyalty marketing program
A promotional program designed to build long-term, mutually beneficial relationships between a company and its key customers.

frequent buyer program
A loyalty program that rewards loyal consumers for making multiple purchases of a particular good or service.

nonusers to switch brands. Premiums like tote bags and umbrellas are available when consumers rent cars, buy cosmetics, and so on. A premium can also involve more product for the regular price, as with two-for-the-price-of-one bonus packs. Kellogg's was hugely successful with its promotion of Pop Tarts that added two more pastries to the current six in a package without increasing the price. Kellogg's used the promotion to boost the market share it had lost to private-label brands of pastries and new competitors.[18]

Probably the best example of the use of premiums is the "gift with purchase" offered by major cosmetic manufacturers. With a minimum purchase of a Clinique product, the customer receives a gift pack of product.

Loyalty Marketing Programs **Loyalty marketing programs**, and **frequent buyer programs** reward consumers for making multiple purchases. Loyalty marketing, which was popularized by the airline industry in the mid-1980s through frequent flyer programs, is designed to capture greater profits from customers already loyal to the product or company.[19] One study found that a company that retains an additional 5 percent of

Faced with declining redemption rates for coupons, marketers are experimenting with new kinds of discounts. Save.ca allows consumers to print their own coupons and gives companies using this service information on coupon users.

on line

Save.ca

Describe the special deals you can find advertised on Save.ca. Are there any coupons that you would print and use? What seems to be the target market for this site? Are any premiums currently being offered?

www.save.ca

its customers each year will increase its profits by at least 25 percent. Furthermore, improving customer retention by a mere 2 percent can decrease costs by as much as 10 percent.[20]

The purpose of loyalty marketing programs is to build long-term, mutually beneficial relationships between a company and its customers. The coffee card at Second Cup coffee outlets rewards coffee lovers with one free regular coffee after the purchase of six cups of coffee. The Bay, in conjunction with Zellers, recently implemented the HBC point card. With every purchase made at the retailer, a loyal customer is awarded points that can be redeemed for products.

Contests and Sweepstakes Contests and sweepstakes are designed to create interest in the good or service, and often to encourage brand switching. Contests are promotions in which participants use some skill to compete for prizes. A consumer contest requires entrants to answer questions, complete sentences, or write a paragraph about the product and submit proof of purchase. In contrast, winning a sweepstakes depends on chance or luck, and participation is free. Sweepstakes usually draw about ten times more entries than contests.

When setting up contests and sweepstakes, sales promotion managers must be sure the award will appeal to the target market.

Mac's Convenience Stores Inc., which operates under the Mac's, Becker's, Mike's Mart, and Winks banners, is part of Canada's largest convenience store chain. Mac's developed an on-line and in-store contest for Froster, its proprietary frozen carbonated beverage. Its cool new Froster.ca contest is part of a multimillion-dollar chain-wide upgrade to create a whole new convenience store experience.

sampling
A promotional program that allows the consumer the opportunity to try the product or service for free.

point-of-purchase display
Promotional display set up at the retailer's location to build traffic, advertise the product, or induce impulse buying.

Sampling Many consumers are afraid of trying something they won't like (such as a new food item), or spending too much money and getting too little reward (such as fragrances). **Sampling** allows the customer to try a product risk-free. According to recent research on sampling effectiveness, 71 percent of consumers who had never before purchased a given product indicated that a free sample would encourage them to try it. Also, 67 percent said that they had switched brands in the past because they were satisfied with a free sample.[21]

Sampling can be accomplished by directly mailing the sample to the customer, by delivering the sample door to door, by packaging the sample with another, or by offering a sample at a retail store. In October 1999, Tim Hortons gave away free cake and coffee to mark the reopening of its first store in Hamilton, Ontario. The special event was attended by guests such as Sheila Copps, Canada's culture minister, and was heavily covered by the press. This gala event, in conjunction with its publicity and free sampling, attracted new and previous customers to the coffee company.

Contests are a longstanding way to attract attention to a product. Do you think this Froster contest, which provides weekly giveaways of products such as Sony Playstations and music CDs, will appeal to the target youth market and help promote Mac's new image?

Distributing samples where consumers go for a specific purpose, such as a health club or a doctors' office, is one of the most efficient methods of sampling. Health club members are good prospects for health food products or vitamin supplements. Likewise, patients of doctors who specialize in diabetes management are excellent candidates for trial samples of sugar-free snacks, diagnostic kits, and other diabetes-related products. Also, the health club or the doctor's office amounts to a powerful third-party endorsement of the distributed product.[22]

Point-of-Purchase Promotion A **point-of-purchase display** is any promotional display set up at the retailer's location to build traffic, advertise the product, or induce impulse buying. Point-of-purchase promotions include shelf "talkers" (signs attached to

Tim Hortons

How does Tim Hortons use its Website as a loyalty marketing program? Visit and see.

www.timhortons.com

on line

store shelves), shelf extenders (attachments that extend shelves so that products stand out), ads on grocery carts and bags, end-aisle and floor-stand displays, television monitors at cosmetic counters, in-store audio messages, and audiovisual displays. One advantage of point-of-purchase promotion is that it offers manufacturers a captive audience in retail stores. As much as 70 percent of all purchase decisions are made in-store, according to research conducted by the Point-of-Purchase Advertising Institute; also, 88 percent of food purchase decisions are made in-store.[23] It follows that point-of-purchase promotions work better for products bought without prior decision than for planned purchases. Fifty-two percent of soft drink sales and 31 percent of chip and snack sales are attributable to in-store point-of-purchase promotions.[24]

7
Identify the most common forms of trade sales promotion

Tools for Trade Sales Promotion

Consumer promotions pull a product through the channel by creating demand; in contrast, trade promotions push a product through the distribution channel (see Chapter 12). Trade promotions use the same tools as consumer promotions—sales contests, premiums, point-of-purchase displays, and so on. However, several tools are unique to manufacturers and intermediaries:

- *Trade allowances*: A **trade allowance** is a price reduction offered by manufacturers to intermediaries such as wholesalers and retailers. The price reduction or rebate is given in exchange for doing something specific, such as allocating space for a new product or buying something during special periods. A local dealer could receive a special discount for running its own promotion on GE telephones.

trade allowance
A price reduction offered by manufacturers to intermediaries, such as wholesalers and retailers.

- *Push money:* Intermediaries receive **push money** as a bonus for pushing the manufacturer's brand through the distribution channel. Often the push money is directed toward a retailer's salespeople. Through its Retail Masters incentive program, Sony retailers earn extra money by restricting displays of competing electronics.

push money
Money offered to channel intermediaries to encourage them to "push" products—that is, to encourage other members of the channel to sell the products.

- *Training:* Sometimes a manufacturer will train an intermediary's personnel if the product is rather complex, as computer and telecommunications equipment often is. If a large department store purchases an NCR computerized cash register system, NCR may provide salespeople with free training in how to use it.
- *Free merchandise*: Often a manufacturer offers retailers free merchandise in lieu of quantity discounts. A breakfast cereal manufacturer may throw in one case of free cereal for every twenty cases ordered by the retailer. Sometimes free merchandise is used as payment for trade allowances normally provided through other sales promotions. Instead of giving a retailer a price reduction for buying a certain quantity of merchandise, the manufacturer may throw in extra merchandise "free" (i.e., at a cost that would equal the price reduction).
- *Store demonstrations*: Manufacturers can arrange with retailers to perform in-store demonstrations. Food manufacturers often send representatives to supermarkets to let customers sample products while shopping. Cosmetics companies send their representatives to department stores to promote their beauty aids by performing facials and makeovers.
- *Business meetings, conventions, and trade shows:* Trade association meetings, conferences, and conventions are an important aspect of sales promotion and a growing, multibillion-dollar market. At these shows, manufacturers, distribu-

tors, and other vendors have the chance to display their goods or services. The cost per customer contacted at a show is estimated to be only 25 to 35 percent that of a personal sales call. Trade shows have been uniquely effective in introducing new products. They can establish products in the marketplace more quickly than can advertising, direct marketing, or sales calls. Companies participate in trade shows to attract and identify new prospects, serve current customers, introduce new products, enhance their corporate image, test the market response to new products, and gather competitive product information.

Trade promotions are popular for many reasons. Trade sales promotion tools help manufacturers gain new distributors for their products, obtain wholesaler and retailer support for consumer sales promotions, build or reduce dealer inventories, and improve trade relations. Every year, car makers sponsor dozens of auto shows for consumers. These shows attract millions of consumers and provide dealers with increased store traffic as well as good leads.

Public Relations

8

Discuss the role of public relations in the IMC Program

Public relations is the element of IMC that evaluates public attitudes, identifies issues of public concern, and executes programs to gain public acceptance. Like advertising and sales promotion, public relations is a vital link in a progressive company's marketing communication mix. Marketing managers plan solid public relations campaigns that fit into the firm's overall marketing plans and focus on targeted audiences. These campaigns strive to maintain a positive image for the corporation in the eyes of the public.

Many people associate public relations with publicity. Publicity is the effort to capture media attention through human interest stories. Corporations usually initiate publicity through press releases. A company about to introduce a new product or open a new store may send press releases to the media in the hope that the story will be published or broadcast. Savvy publicity can often create overnight product sensations. Books picked to be in Oprah's Book Club become instant bestsellers, flying off the shelves of bookstores nationwide.

Donating products or services to worthy causes also creates favourable publicity. Corporate funds are often used to raise capital for public buildings. A plaque recognizing the donation is then placed in the building as a permanent reminder to building users.

Public relations departments may perform any or all of the following functions:

9

Describe the major types of public relations activity

- *Press relations:* placing positive, newsworthy information in the media to attract attention to the company or its products/services.
- *Product publicity*: publicizing specific products or services.
- *Corporate communication:* creating internal and external messages to promote a positive image for the organization.
- *Public affairs:* building and maintaining community relations.
- *Lobbying*: influencing legislators and government officials to promote or defeat legislation and regulation.
- *Employee and investor relations:* maintaining positive relationships with employees, shareholders, and financiers.
- *Crisis management:* responding to unfavourable publicity or a negative event.

Major Public Relations Tools

Public relations professionals typically have several tools at their disposal, including new product publicity, product placement, consumer education, event sponsorship, and company Websites.

New Product Publicity Publicity is instrumental in introducing new products and services. Public relations professionals write press releases or develop videos in an effort to generate news about their new products. They also jockey for exposure of their product or service at major events, on popular television and news shows, or in the hands of influential people. Fragrance manufacturers often display videos of their new products at counters in the Bay or Sears. Usually a fragrance depends heavily on the image associated with it, so its video must provide a powerful message of what it is all about.

id Software, the maker of the popular computer games Doom and Quake, distributes early versions of its games free over the Internet, creating word-of-mouth excitement among the company's followers. The test version for Quake II was downloaded more than a million times. id further enticed followers by releasing manuals, game photos, and commentary from the game's programmers. As a result, Websites dedicated to Quake play were abuzz with discussion of the new, soon-to-be-released version.[25]

Product Placement Companies reap invaluable product exposure through product placement, usually at a fraction of the cost of paid-for advertising. Often, the fee for exposure is in merchandise. Roots outfitted the Canadian Olympic Team at the 1998 and 2002 Winter Olympics. This provided exclusive exposure for Roots during those games; it also helped associate Roots with Canadian national pride.

Consumer Education Some firms believe that educated consumers are more loyal. Financial planning firms often sponsor free seminars on money management, retirement planning, and investing in the hope that those attending will choose them for their future financial needs. Computer firms sponsor seminars and free in-store demonstrations. BMW Canada holds driver training courses in major cities across Canada. The courses focus on better driving habits and techniques for all drivers, including current and prospective BMW owners near the end of their leases.

Event Sponsorship To achieve press coverage, public relations managers can sponsor events that are newsworthy. These events reinforce brand identification. Sporting, music, and arts events remain the most popular choices of event sponsors. These are often tied in with schools, charities, and other community service organizations. Telus was the main sponsor for the World Championships in Athletics, which were held in Edmonton in 2001. The games were televised worldwide, providing Telus with exposure everywhere. Tobacco manufacturers have sponsored major art events to gain exposure, especially since television advertising is not an option for them. The Annual Du Maurier Jazz Festival in Toronto is an example. Whether this is good public image making is controversial.

Marketers can create their own events tied around their products. The publicity surrounding the Molson Indy is strong both before and during the high-profile international car race.

Consumer education can influence buying decisions; it can also result in better, more loyal customers. BMW's instructional driving program is a way to show its vehicle capabilities to prospective purchasers and current owners without mounting expensive advertising campaigns. Check out www.BMW.ca.

If you have a question, please don't raise your hand.
BMW Driver Training
BMW

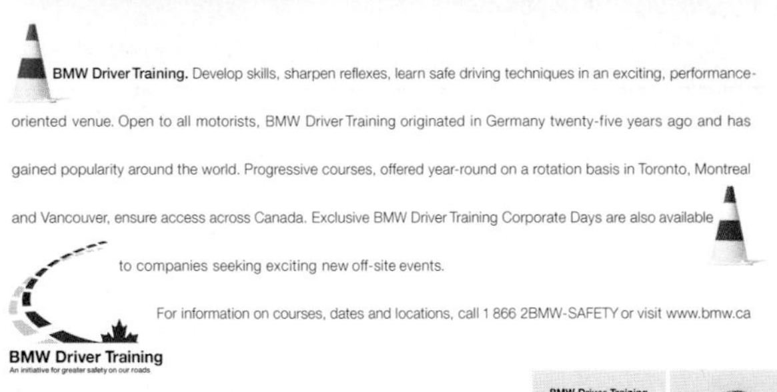

BMW Driver Training. Develop skills, sharpen reflexes, learn safe driving techniques in an exciting, performance-oriented venue. Open to all motorists, BMW Driver Training originated in Germany twenty-five years ago and has gained popularity around the world. Progressive courses, offered year-round on a rotation basis in Toronto, Montreal and Vancouver, ensure access across Canada. Exclusive BMW Driver Training Corporate Days are also available to companies seeking exciting new off-site events.
For information on courses, dates and locations, call 1 866 2BMW-SAFETY or visit www.bmw.ca
BMW Driver Training
An initiative for greater safety on our roads
BMW Driver Training
www.bmw.ca
1-866-2BMW-SAFETY
The Ultimate Driving Experience.
© BMW Canada Inc "BMW," the BMW logo and "The Ultimate Driving Experience" are trademarks of BMW AG, used under licence by BMW Canada Inc.

Issue Sponsorship Corporations can build public awareness and loyalty by supporting their customers' favourite issues. The CIBC supports national breast cancer organizations, and the Body Shop does not test its products on animals.

"Green marketing" is an important way for companies to build awareness and loyalty. Older, highly educated women prefer and are willing to pay more for products made by environmentally friendly companies.[26] By positioning their brands as ecologically sound, marketers can convey concern for the environment and society as a whole. In an effort to decrease waste in landfills, Burger King and McDonald's no longer use styrofoam cartons to package their burgers. Tim Hortons has smoke-free locations.

Company Websites Many marketers used their Websites originally to advertise their products or services; public relations professionals now use these sites to post news releases on products, strategic relationships, and financial earnings. The company Website can also be an open forum for product ideas, as well as a channel for user feedback.

Managing Unfavourable Publicity

Although most marketers try to avoid unpleasant situations, crises do happen. Ford faced this reality after the Bridgestone/Firestone tires it was using on its sport utility vehicles were found responsible for fatal accidents. **Crisis management** involves a coordinated effort to handle the effects of unfavourable publicity and ensure fast and accurate communication in times of emergency.

crisis management
A coordinated effort to handle the effects of unfavourable publicity or of another unexpected, unfavourable event.

A good public relations staff is perhaps more important in bad times than in good. Critics chastised Trans World Airlines after one of its planes crashed off Long Island. It was widely perceived that the airline was slow and uncooperative with family members wanting information about survivors, and that it was also too slow answering calls from the media. Also, it was felt that TWA's CEO was slow to reassure families and the public that his airline was doing all it could. All public relations professionals learned a valuable lesson from this blunder: companies must have a communication policy firmly in hand before a disaster occurs, because timing is uncontrollable.

LOOKING BACK

Now that you have finished reading this chapter, think back to the opening story about Molson Canadian. The staff of Molson's communication team go through the same creative steps as other marketers, from determining which appeal to use to choosing the appropriate style of execution. They expend enormous effort deciding which medium will do the best job of reaching the desired target markets, taking into account such things as reach, frequency, cost per contact, and audience selectivity. Molson complements its TV advertising with effective public relations—for example, events and sponsorships that target young adults. The brewery also has a very informative and interactive Website.

Summary

1 Discuss the role of advertising in the IMC program. First, advertising helps marketers increase or maintain brand awareness and, it follows, market share. Typically, new brands (i.e., at the introduction stage) are allotted bigger advertising budgets than older brands (i.e., at the mature stage). Second, advertising affects consumers' daily lives as well as their purchases. Advertising rarely changes strongly held consumer values, but it may transform a consumer's negative attitude toward a product into a positive one. Third, when consumers are very loyal to a brand, they may buy more of it when it is advertised more. Fourth, advertising can change a brand's appeal to consumers, or consumers' perceptions of the brand's benefits.

2 Identify the major types of advertising. Advertising is any form of nonpersonal, paid communication in which the company is identified. The two main types of advertising are institutional advertising and product advertising. Institutional advertising fosters a positive company image among the general public, the investment community, customers, and employees. Product advertising promotes goods and services. There are in turn three categories of product advertising: pioneering, competitive, and comparative. A product's place in the product life cycle is a major determinant of the type of advertising used to promote it.

3 Describe the creative planning process for advertising. Developing advertisements is a stepwise process. Promotion managers first set specific advertising objectives. These objectives flow from the company's IMC plan. They then make creative decisions, often with the aid of an advertising agency, centred on developing advertising appeals. Once creative decisions have been made, media are evaluated and selected. Finally, the advertisement is assessed through various forms of testing.

4 Describe the media planning process for advertising. Media evaluation and selection are critical steps in the communications process. Major types of media include newspapers, magazines, radio, television, outdoor advertising, and the Internet. Recent trends in advertising media include fax, video shopping carts, computer screen savers, and movie advertising. Promotion managers choose the advertising media mix on the basis of the following: cost per contact, reach, frequency, and the characteristics of the target market. After choosing the media mix, a media schedule designates when the advertisement will appear and which specific media vehicles it will appear in.

5 Discuss the role of sales promotion in the IMC program. Sales promotions are marketing communication activities in which a short-term incentive motivates consumers or members of the distribution channel to purchase a good or service immediately. The main objectives of sales promotion are to increase trial purchases, repeat purchases, and product inventory. Sales promotion is also used to encourage brand switching and to build brand loyalty. Sales promotion supports advertising and personal selling activities.

6 Describe the most common forms of consumer sales promotion. Consumer forms of sales promotion include coupons and rebates, premiums, loyalty marketing programs, contests and sweepstakes, sampling, and point-of-purchase displays. Coupons are certificates entitling consumers to an immediate price reduction when they purchase a product or service. Coupons are an especially good way to encourage product trial and brand switching. Rebates also provide purchasers with a price reduction, although it is not immediate. Premiums offer an extra item or incentive to the consumer for buying a product or service. They also reinforce the consumer's purchase decision, increase consumption, and persuade nonusers to switch brands. Loyalty marketing programs involve rewarding

Do You Know These Terms?

advertising appeal 466
advertising objective 464
advocacy advertising 463
audience selectivity 474
comparative advertising 464
competitive advertising 464
consumer sales promotion 475
continuous media schedule 474
cooperative advertising 469
cost per contact 473
coupon 476
crisis management 482
flighted media schedule 474
frequency 473
frequent buyer program 477
infomercial 470
institutional advertising 463
loyalty marketing program 477
media mix 473
media schedule 474
medium 465
pioneering advertising 464
point-of-purchase display 478
premium 476
product advertising 463
pulsing media schedule 474
push money 479
reach 473
rebate 476
sampling 478
seasonal media schedule 474
trade allowance 479
trade sales promotion 475

loyal customers. They are extremely effective at building long-term, mutually beneficial relationships between a company and its key customers. Most contests and sweepstakes are designed to create interest and encourage brand switching. Because consumers perceive risk in trying new products, sampling is an effective method for gaining new customers. Finally, point-of-purchase displays at the retailer's location build traffic, advertise the product, and induce impulse buying.

7 Identify the most common forms of trade sales promotion. Manufacturers' promotions and consumer promotions use many of the same tools, such as contests, premiums, and point-of-purchase displays. Manufacturers and channel intermediaries also use several unique-to-trade promotional strategies: trade allowances, push money, training programs, free merchandise, store demonstrations, and meetings, conventions, and trade shows.

8 Discuss the role of public relations in the IMC program. Public relations is a vital part of a firm's IMC program. A company fosters good publicity to enhance its image and promote its products. Popular public relations tools include new product publicity, product placement, consumer education, event sponsorship, issue sponsorship, and company Websites. An equally important aspect of public relations is managing unfavourable publicity in such a way that a firm's image is damaged as little as possible.

9 Describe the major types of public relations activity. Public relations firms typically perform the following functions for a company: press relations, product publicity, corporate communication, public affairs, lobbying, employee and investor relations, and crisis management.

Discussion and Writing Questions

1. How can advertising, sales promotion, and publicity work together? Give an example.
2. Discuss why a new brand with a smaller market share might spend proportionately more on advertising and sales promotion than a brand with a larger market share. Use a specific example.
3. At what stage in a product's life cycle are pioneering, competitive, and comparative advertising most likely to occur? Give a current example of each type of advertising.
4. What is an advertising appeal? Give examples of five different advertising appeals you have observed recently in the media.
5. What are the advantages of radio advertising? Why is radio becoming more popular as an advertising medium?
6. You are the advertising manager of a sailing magazine, and a large potential advertiser has questioned your rates. Write the firm a letter explaining why you believe your audience selectivity is worth the extra expense.
7. Discuss how different forms of sales promotion can erode or build brand loyalty. Give examples.
8. As the new public relations director for a sportswear company, you have been asked to set public relations objectives for a new line of athletic shoes to be introduced to the teen market. Draft a memo outlining the objectives you propose for the shoe's introduction, as well as strategies for reaching these objectives.
9. Reports have just surfaced that your company, a fast food chain, sold contaminated food products that have made several people seriously ill. As your company's public relations manager, devise a plan to handle the crisis.
10. Identify an appropriate media mix for the following products, giving reasons for your choices:
    a. chewing tobacco

b. *People* magazine
c. Weed-Eaters
d. foot odour killers
e. "drink responsibly" campaigns by beer brewers

11. Design a full-page magazine advertisement for a new brand of soft drink. The name of the new drink, as well as package design, is at the discretion of the student. On a separate sheet, specify the creative objectives, strategies, and tactics used to develop the advertisement.

Application for Small Business

Service quality is increasingly the basis for deciding where to do business. Customers are five times more likely to return to a particular business they see providing higher-quality service.

The Student Copy Centre is a local business competing with Kinko's and a couple of other national franchise copy centres. Its owner, Mack Bayles, just attended a small business administration workshop on customer service. He learned that when people say they expect good customer service, they most often mean they want prompt and accurate service from friendly, knowledgeable, and courteous employees. The presenter also emphasized that all market segments, even the most price conscious, expect good customer service. Mack wants to use this knowledge to develop an effective advertising campaign.

Mack has no idea what his customers think about either his copy business or that of his competitors. So he decides to ask his customers to complete a brief survey while in his store. From his survey he learns that Student Copy Centre is considered friendlier and more courteous than the major competitors but is rated lower on speed of service.

Questions

1. What should Mack do before developing his advertising campaign?
2. Should Mack use comparative ads?
3. What advertising appeal would be most effective for Mack? Explain.

Government Ads

Should government ads be paid for by the taxpayer? The answer seems clear—yes! What's not so clear is, when is a government ad no longer an ad for and by the people but a political party promotion?

The idea that the government needs to have airtime to give the public information is innocent enough. For example, a TV advertisement for *Help Line for Kids* gives information on the organization and a contact telephone number. The ad is paid for by the taxpayer.

But a Canadian government ad put out by the Chrétien government just before the last federal election was more like a Liberal Party ad. The ad, which was touted as a "message from the Canadian government" on health care issues, cost the Canadian taxpayer $5.2 million. Health care was a controversial issue by which the last election was influenced.

Another government ad, this time with Ontario Premier Harris stating his position on the Ontario teachers' strike several years ago, was seen as a platform for the premier to talk about his party's education reform. This cost the Ontario taxpayer $1.3 million.

Jonathon Rose, professor of political science at Queen's University, believes these two commercials are actually political ads posing as government ads, and as such should be paid for by the political party. He adds that it is "a thin form of democracy" because the taxpayer has no way of directly communicating back to the government about the messages in the commercials.

He cites the 1990 series of four Mulroney government ads on the GST as a turning point in government ads. The ads cost the taxpayer $10.6 million. Instead of helping the taxpayer understand the GST or help file the GST form, it tried to persuade people to accept the new and unpopular tax.

Rose also sees the more recent Harris government commercials on making the Ontario government more efficient as the worst misuse of taxpayer dollars for a clearly partisan commercial. First of all, the leader of the party was doing the talking, and second, the issue was highly contentious.

So, what *are* the rules on government ads? In Canada, there doesn't appear to be any federal communication policy beyond the vague statement that "government ads are not partisan ads"! Neither Premier Harris nor Chris Hodgson, minister for government advertising policy, says there is a need for enforceable standards to clearly identify what is and what isn't a government ad.

In the United Kingdom, the Broadcast Clearing Centre must give the go-ahead for advertising paid for by the taxpayer. If the ad is deemed political, it won't be aired. There are clear rules for defining an ad as political: for example, when a government is blowing its own horn on how wonderful a piece of legislation is. The Mulroney GST ad, the Harris efficiency ad, and the Chrétien health care ad were shown to Eustian MacLean, the head of the Advertising Clearing Centre. None of these ads would pass the British criteria. The Mulroney ad was described as trying to persuade people to feel good about the GST—a then-controversial government issue. The Harris efficiency ad was seen as a political party thumping its own chest on how great it is. The Chrétien ad was shown prior to an election and was about proposals that the government would put into effect if re-elected.

Neither the Treasury Board, nor the Privy Council, nor the minister responsible for government communications was available for comment on whether political bias is an issue in Canadian government advertising.

Source:
CBC, *Undercurrents,* "Government Ads," January 14, 2001.

Questions

1. What is the main objective of a political party advertisement?
2. What is the main objective of a government advertisement?
3. Who should decide whether a specific ad is a government ad or a political party ad and why do you say that?
4. What rules should there be for government advertising?

CHAPTER

18

LEARNING OBJECTIVES

After studying this chapter, you should be able to

1 Define one-to-one marketing, and discuss its relationship to database technology

2 Discuss the forces that have influenced the emergence of one-to-one marketing

3 Describe the one-to-one marketing communications process

4 List the advantages and disadvantages of one-to-one marketing

5 List eight common one-to-one marketing applications

6 Discuss the basics of one-to-one marketing database technology

7 Discuss privacy issues related to one-to-one marketing

ONE-TO-ONE MARKETING

"You can't buy cool." So says Peter van Stolk, the marketing maverick behind North America's hottest—or coolest—beverage: Jones Soda. When you're a young entrepreneur from Vancouver who is looking to take on the big guys like Coke and Pepsi in the $10 billion, new-age beverage industry, "cool" is a very good brand position to take. The trick, of course, is to become known as cool.

Jones Soda was launched in 1996. The success the company has enjoyed so far is founded on the premise that it shares common beliefs and attitudes—a common vision—with its target audience. Better than its competitors, Jones delivers the "alternative" to the "mainstream." Its one-to-one marketing strategy, coupled with its capacity to use the Internet and database technology, lets it focus on the customer as the key unit of analysis. The customer defines everything that *is* Jones. Marketing has always used overall market share as a key indicator of growth. Increasingly, however, technology is enabling companies to focus on share of *customer.* For a product like Jones Soda, whose target customer is any one of the 50 million twelve-to-twenty-four-year-old Net-savvy and individualistic consumers (a group with over $300 billion to spend annually), the individual customer is where it's at.

This is reflected in the company's unique approach to marketing and packaging. The typical Jones customer is encouraged to take more control over the marketing process, and happily does so. Taking an innovative step outside the traditional packaging box, van Stolk has established an "emotional connection" between the customer and his product with a strikingly direct one-to-one marketing approach.

Visitors to **www.Jonessoda.com** are immersed immediately in a virtual consumer community. They can interact directly with the company and deal directly with Jones product development. They can watch videos, enter contests, and purchase merchandise at the main site. They can even choose images for their bottle labels (or submit their own). All of this is about creating a connection between the company, the brand, and the customer.

Von Stolk understands that in today's youth market every brand is an accessory and every purchase is a statement. So he has

Jones Soda Co.

Visit the Jones Website and build your own custom bottle of pop. How does the "experience" of the Jones Website differ from some of the other advertising and marketing sites you have been exposed to? What does this tell you about the company's market and strategy?

www.jonessoda.com

on line

created a product that is unique—Jones Soda comes in flavours such as Fufu Berry, Crushed Melon, and Happy—and that can be individualized. The focus at Jones is on direct interaction with customers. Through its Website and through its mobile marketing (a big orange RV that criss-crosses the country for promotional events), the company works hard to track the moving target that is the youth market. It also supports alternative and amateur athletes; this further enhances the grass-roots feel of the brand while maintaining credibility with its market, which is mainly urban.

Von Stolk refers to this marketing approach as grounding. It involves "realizing that a brand has to grow from the ground up to the consumers ... as opposed to putting the brand in front of somebody and letting them walk into it."

The company and its culture have received unprecedented attention in all major media. The *New York Times,* magazines like *People, Entrepreneurial Edge,* and *Inc.*, and all the major television networks have profiled Jones Soda. In an industry in which it often takes multimillion-dollar ad campaigns to gain product recognition, Jones has shown that a customer-focused approach works. Just like its customers, Jones has its own ways of getting noticed.[1]

What Is "One-to-One Marketing" and Why Is It Important?

1

Define one-to-one marketing, and discuss its relationship to database technology

One-to-one marketing is a revolutionary means of approaching what has long been the essence of marketing: communicating with customers on a one-to-one basis. Contemporary marketers, from retailers to consumer goods manufacturers to business-to-business resellers, are being urged to look at their customers as individual entities rather than as mass markets. There are a number of reasons why. The ability to connect with customers on an individual basis often provides a huge competitive advantage. It also allows smaller players to enter markets.

Most businesses today follow the time-honoured *mass marketing* rule: advertise and sell products to the greatest possible number of people. The point is to increase market share by selling more goods to more people. Selling more goods to *fewer* people through one-to-one marketing is more efficient and more profitable, and in today's competitive business world, efficiency and profitability are central to any growth strategy. One-to-one marketing focuses on "share of customer" rather than "share of market." Mass marketers develop a product and then try to find customers for that product; in contrast, one-to-one marketers develop a customer and then try to find products for that customer. This distinction is fundamental.

This approach is beginning to change—sometimes inconspicuously, sometimes dramatically—how almost every facet of marketing is carried out. In the present literature on marketing, there are many definitions and applications of one-to-one marketing. For our purposes, one-to-one marketing is any marketing activity that focuses on the interactions of individual customers with the business's product or service in order to increase sales or enhance customer loyalty. In other words, it is *customer-based,* meaning that the customer is the focal point of the strategy; it is *information-intensive,* meaning that the marketer must know a great deal about the customer or potential customer; it is *long-term oriented,* meaning that the goal is to strengthen and enhance interaction with the customer; and it is *individualized,* which simply acknowledges that every customer is different. Once we can agree that the customer is at the core of marketing activity, this approach makes sense.

The Evolution of One-to-One Marketing

One-to-one marketing is not at all new. In fact, it is essentially a very old-fashioned idea. Before the Industrial Revolution there was no mass advertising. Small businesses thrived and supported the community. Care of the customer flourished. Early small-town merchants remembered the products each customer purchased and made recommendations based on past purchases and lifestyles. Products could even be custom-produced or modified to fit the particular needs of the customer.[2]

one-to-one marketing
A customer-based, information-intensive, long-term-oriented, and individualized marketing method that focuses on share of customer rather than share of market.

Mass production led to volume buying and mass media advertising. Businesses grew and prospered on the principle of "make and sell"—that is, companies manufactured large quantities of the same product, advertised it to the masses, and let the sheer numbers generate profitable sales.[3] As a result, marketers developed a different view of the customer. All customers were perceived not as unique but rather as having the same needs and as reachable through the same channels with the same message. As Henry Ford said it, "We'll give you any color you want, as long as it's black."[4]

Today's customers are demanding more choice. They want to buy what meets their needs and wants precisely, and they expect individualized attention. More and more, they are dictating who they will do business with. With today's technology, companies can interact with their customers in new ways through Websites and databases. In the same way, technology (in the form of the Internet) lets customers to research, compare, and buy products and services much more easily than ever before. Companies are now using various technologies to tailor products, services, and communications[5]; and customers are using the same technologies to control how they interact with companies.

As a result of one-to-one marketing and the benefits of technology, companies are moving away from a product-driven orientation toward a customer-driven emphasis. Two early proponents of this change were Stan Rapp and Tom Collins, who co-wrote the 1987 book *Maxi-Marketing,* in which they summarized this new direction:[6]

> Every established norm in advertising and promotion is being transformed ... We are living through a shift from selling virtually everyone the same thing a generation ago to fulfilling the individual needs and tastes of better-educated consumers by supplying them with customized products and services. The shift [is] from a "get a sale now at any cost" to building and managing customer databases to track the lifetime value of your relationship with each customer. As the cost of accumulating and accessing data drops, the ability to talk directly with prospects and customers, building one-to-one relationships with them, will grow.

As one-to-one marketing takes hold, it is no longer enough to understand customers and prospects by group profiles. The one-to-one future requires that marketers understand their customers and collaborate with them, rather than use them as targets. The battle for customers will be won by marketers who understand how and why their customers individually buy their products, and who learn how to win them over, and keep them, one customer at a time.[7]

One company that has embraced one-to-one marketing with great success is Federal Express. The world's largest shipper recently transformed itself from a product-oriented marketer into a customer-oriented one-to-one marketer. FedEx gathered information on its customers and then segmented them based on each individual customer's service needs and value to the company. FedEx can now target different customers with different messages based on what the company knows about them. Say, for instance, that FedEx learns that ACME Industries uses FedEx only for overnight letters and uses UPS to ship domestic boxes. It will target messages to this company to educate its managers about FedEx's domestic services. Similarly, if FedEx learns that ACME uses another carrier to ship packages internationally, it can then make sure ACME receives information about FedEx's international shipments. So far, FedEx's one-to-one approach has been successful. In its small-shipper segment, the company has realized an 8 to 1 return on its one-to-one marketing costs.[8]

One-to-One Marketing and Database Technology

How can marketers communicate with their customers one at a time? How can huge corporations such as Federal Express and Hewlett-Packard communicate with each and every one of their thousands or millions of customers on a personal level? How can a customer indicate his or her needs directly to a retailer or service provider?

Fundamentally, one-to-one marketing is about the relationship a salesperson cultivates with a customer. A successful salesperson builds a relationship over time, constantly thinks about what the customer needs and wants, and pays heed to the trends and patterns in the customer's purchase history. A good salesperson often knows what the customer needs even before the customer does. The salesperson can inform, educate, and instruct the customer about new products, technologies, and applications in anticipation of future requirements. A good salesperson also listens closely to the customer.

This kind of thoughtful attention is the basis of one-to-one marketing—with one major difference. With successful salespeople, the process of building one-to-one relationships is intuitive, and learned over time through experience. In contrast, one-to-one marketing uses technology to facilitate the process; it is deliberately planned and consciously implemented. Also, customer information is available quickly and inexpensively to anyone in the company. Databases are central to all this. Ideally, a database stores pertinent information about all of the company's customers and contacts and makes it readily available to the sales and marketing staff, who use it to assess, analyze, and anticipate customers' needs.[9] One-to-one marketing is thus a form of strategic initiative, one that the company takes to "connect" with individual customers. In this effort, technology is used for capturing customer information and organizing it so that marketers can use it. This key strategic foundation of one-to-one marketing is broadly defined as **customer relationship management (CRM).**

customer relationship management (CRM)
A key component of a top-down, one-to-one strategic initiative taken by a company to "connect" with each individual customer, that uses technology to enable the capture of customer information.

Today's computer technology allows marketers to do what the old-fashioned storekeepers of the 1900s did—get to know their customers on a personal, one-to-one basis. However, early merchants may have had only 50 or 200 customers to keep track of; in contrast, today's one-to-one marketers can track their customers as individuals through database technology, even if they number in the millions. In this age of increasing amounts of information, database technology allows marketers to sift through millions of pieces of data to target the right customers, to develop the right communication based on these customers' needs, and to monitor ongoing relationships, making adjustments in message strategy as needed.

youtopia.com

How does youtopia.com use its Website to collect information about its consumers? Can you see where the line between market research and selling might become blurred? Is this a good thing or a bad thing for consumers?

www.youtopia.com

on line

one-to-one marketing

Peppers and Rogers Group: Taking a Dose of Their Own CRM Medicine

As a leading management consulting and media firm specializing in customer relationship management (CRM) and e-business solutions, Peppers and Rogers Group is recognized globally for its ability to understand and communicate how technology is changing the way companies build relationships with their customers. However, the Peppers and Rogers Group Website, **www.1to1.com**, a basic brochureware site, did not capitalize on the Internet's potential to expand the company's brand and market leadership.

The company decided in early 2000 to "practise what it preached" and develop a content-rich, highly personalized Website that would enhance the company's position in the marketplace. Visitors to the company's site go one-on-one with some of the most recognized voices in the industry. Other CRM sites focus on technology or implementation issues; in contrast, 1 to1 provides the strategies and foundation on which technology tools can be utilized and implementation game plans formulated.

Besides focusing on one-to-one/CRM strategies, the site constitutes a working example of what personalization can do for attracting and keeping potential customers. On their first visit to the site, visitors share their preferences with the 1to1 team. With each subsequent visit, they are directed to new content on the site that meets their stated needs.

This is a direct reflection of how Peppers and Rogers defines "one to one"—you are engaged in a one-to-one customer relationship whenever a customer tells you something about how he or she wants to be served, and you change your behaviour with respect to this individual customer based on that interaction. It is an interactive, adaptive, ongoing process. The more the customer tells you, the more tailored your behaviour can be toward that customer. In essence, the relationship with the customer gets "smarter and smarter" with every interaction.

What competitive advantage does a company practising true one-to-one marketing develop over time? Explain. Who in the company should be involved in developing and maintaining a one-to-one marketing approach? Who does Peppers and Rogers view as having great one-to-one Websites?

Sources: Buzzbytes.com, 04/27/2001; Business Week Online, 06/15/2001.

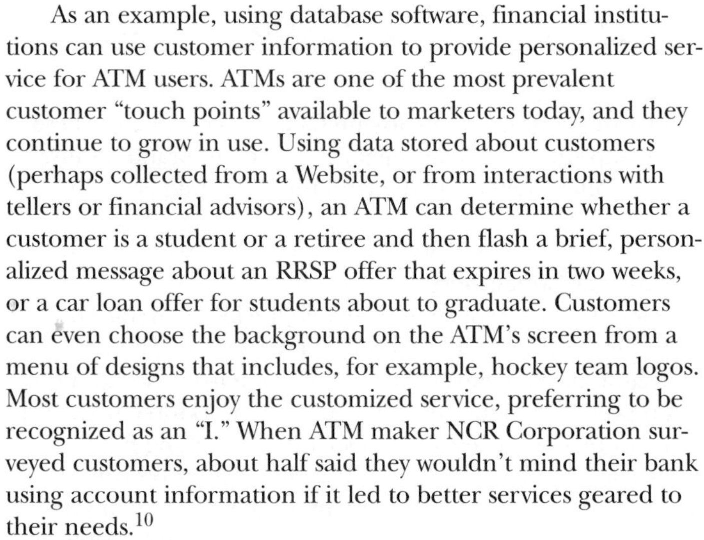

As an example, using database software, financial institutions can use customer information to provide personalized service for ATM users. ATMs are one of the most prevalent customer "touch points" available to marketers today, and they continue to grow in use. Using data stored about customers (perhaps collected from a Website, or from interactions with tellers or financial advisors), an ATM can determine whether a customer is a student or a retiree and then flash a brief, personalized message about an RRSP offer that expires in two weeks, or a car loan offer for students about to graduate. Customers can even choose the background on the ATM's screen from a menu of designs that includes, for example, hockey team logos. Most customers enjoy the customized service, preferring to be recognized as an "I." When ATM maker NCR Corporation surveyed customers, about half said they wouldn't mind their bank using account information if it led to better services geared to their needs.[10]

Even smaller businesses are investing in database technology to practise one-to-one marketing. Any business, whatever its size, can create a system that utilizes databases and the Internet to better understand its customer relationships. For an example, read this chapter's "Entrepreneurial Insights" box.

The VP of Sales and Marketing at Moosehead is leading the brewer's charge into direct marketing.

Netflix.com

Netflix.com uses database technology to attract customers and secure repeat business. Identify some of the customer and product information that netflix.com captures and how it uses those data to provide customers with a better way of renting movies. Would you say that consumers can "customize" the site to themselves? If the service was available in Canada, would you use it?

www.netflix.com

on line

entrepreneurial insights

Loyalty at Moosehead

Moosehead Breweries may be the third-largest beer company in Canada, but Steven Poirier, vice-president of marketing for the Saint John, N.B.–based brewer, admits it's very small compared to Molson and Labatt.

"So," he says frankly, "we can't go head-to-head with them in the areas where the people with the most money win." ACNielson reports that Labatt parent Interbrew spent $60.4 million and Molson roughly $47 million on Canadian measured media advertising in 1999. Compared with that, Moosehead's $1.5 million looks downright puny.

The larger beer companies have the ability to create huge customer databases that allow them to engage in traditional direct marketing (DM). With its own DM activities, Moosehead will concentrate on reaching only what it calls its "most valuable customers" (MVCs). "We're working with the 20–80 rule," says Poirier. "Twenty percent of your customers drink 80 percent of your product. So we're focusing with this initiative on the 20 percent."

Moosehead used a direct response agency to help create its core database of MVCs. Then it launched the first of its major direct-marketing initiatives. It pulled the names of all MVCs who ranked fishing high on their list of favourite pastimes. Then it sent a specially designed Moosehead fishing fly to each of them.

This type of careful segmentation helps set Moosehead apart. Instead of using customer information to fuel a direct marketing campaign aimed at getting more converts, the company is employing it to reward existing customers and build brand loyalty. "We want to make our consumers feel special," says Poirier, "so they know that this beer company really cares what they think and wants to know what they like. By being smaller, we have the opportunity to get closer to our consumers because we don't have to go after that broad consumer base."

If consumers respond to a survey indicating a love for fishing and then receive something in the mail that caters to that love, it's natural that they will be interested in telling the company even more about themselves.

Can you explain how Moosehead uses database technology to enable its one-to-one marketing strategy?

Source: Reprinted with permission of *Marketing Magazine.*

Forces Influencing One-to-One Marketing

2
Discuss the forces that have influenced the emergence of one-to-one marketing

Several forces have helped shape the new one-to-one focus on customers. These include more demanding and time-poor consumers, a decline in brand loyalty, the explosion of new media alternatives, and demand for marketing accountability.[11]

More Demanding, Time-Poor Consumers

Today's consumers are more strapped for time than any previous generation. More women are joining the workforce, more mothers are working, and the number of single-parent households—mostly headed by women—is rising. All of this means that women represent a higher percentage of the workforce than ever before. On the whole, consumers have less time to spend on anything but the most pressing details of their lives. This has had a profound impact on consumers' buying behaviour. Consumers are becoming more demanding, more impatient, and much less likely to spend time agonizing over small purchases or driving across town to the mall.

Decreasing Brand Loyalty

In a 1975 survey of male and female heads of households, over three-quarters agreed with this statement: "I try to stick to well-known brand names." Ten years later, only a little over half agreed with this statement. This trend has continued into the new century. Consumers are now more likely to experiment with generic (nonlabelled) brands and to switch back and forth between major brands in a category. They are also more likely to shop for discounts. Also, if presented with two comparable brands, they are likely to choose based on price.

This decline in brand loyalty can be attributed in part to excessive couponing, trade deals, and deep price promotions by manufacturers and retailers that have encouraged consumers to look for the best deal. In addition, brand loyalty has wavered because of the proliferation of brands—thousands are introduced each year. With so many product choices, consumers often find it hard to differentiate products. Also, they lack the time to learn about each new brand. As a result, consumers often end up basing their purchase decisions on price.

The decrease in brand loyalty can also be attributed to the increasing power of many retailers. Retailers—another key "customer" for many businesses—are taking more and more control of their relationships with brand marketers, dictating price, product placement, and the level and type of in-store promotions. These retailers are also becoming more sophisticated when it comes to developing their own customer communications programs, including multicoupon direct mail and relationship-oriented marketing programs. As a result, consumers are building more relationships with particular retailers than they are with particular brands. Consumers may drive 20 kilometres or more to a Zellers store to shop even though they can get the same brands at relatively the same prices in their own neighbourhood.

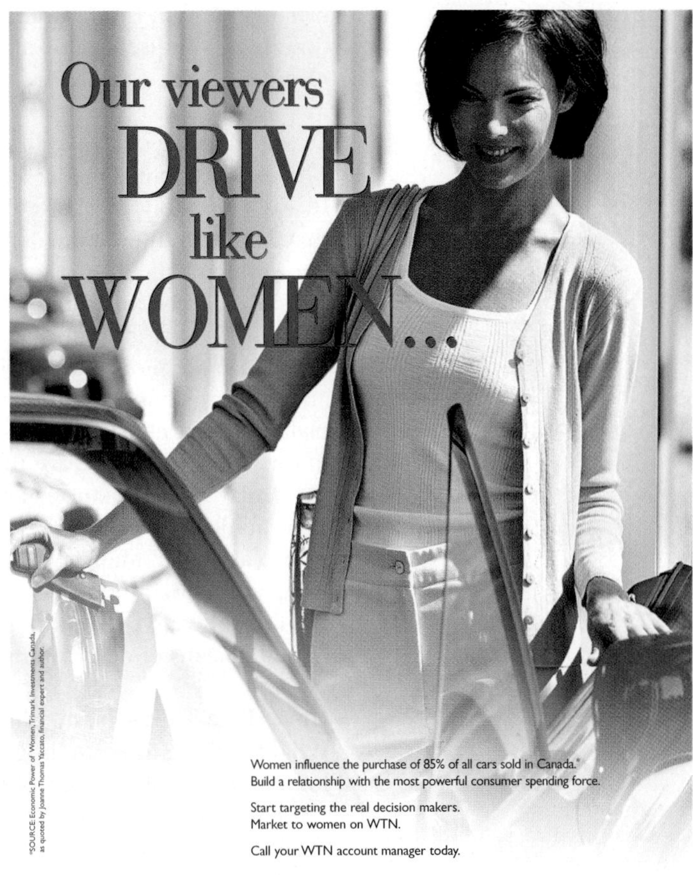

The purchasing power of women, regardless of their age or marital status, has increased greatly in the past twenty years. One-to-one marketing has been a highly successful response to this particular demographic shift.

Emergence of New Media Alternatives

Three decades ago most Canadians spent their evenings in front of their TV sets, watching network programming on CBC, CTV, NBC, CBS, or ABC. They were also more likely to read newspapers and to subscribe to general newsmagazines such as *Maclean's* and *Time*. Marketers reached consumers by blanketing the mass media (television, radio, and newspapers) with image advertising.

Today's busy consumers are far less likely to spend their evenings watching the latest sitcoms on network TV. Instead, they may well be surfing the hundreds of channels available through their direct satellite systems, watching rented movies, or visiting their favourite game sites or news sites on the Internet. At the same time, newspapers and general-interest magazines have given way to an abundance of specialty publications that cater to a wide range of interests.

With the emergence of new and varied media alternatives, mass media advertising will never be the same, simply because potential markets can now be reached in so many different ways. Marketers are finding that they must divvy up their marketing dollars among the various media available, concentrating on the ones that will bring them the most bang for their buck. Mass media advertising on network television or in general-interest magazines will always play an important role in communicating brand messages; that being said, it will never again be as dominant as it used to be, and it will increasingly be part of *integrated* marketing campaigns that utilize more than one medium to reach customers.

Demand for Accountability

The impact of mass media advertising on sales has always been difficult to measure. Generations of marketers have quoted John Wanamaker, the turn-of-the-century American merchant: "I know half of my advertising is wasted—I just don't know which half." In the past, the results of newspaper and TV advertising expenditures could be measured only through future sales of the advertised offering, increases in market share, or increases in store traffic. Even sales promotional tactics, which are more measurable than mass media efforts, have come under attack. For example, coupons distributed through the inserts found in the Saturday paper are just as much a form of mass media advertising as full-page images in the same paper, and are therefore largely unaccountable.

Today's manufacturers are under pressure to maintain growth and profits for shareholders. It is no longer acceptable to say that sales increased after an advertising campaign. Management now wants proof that the money spent on advertising and marketing will deliver results. The measurement tools available through the Internet and other data recording techniques offer a much simpler and more reliable means of determining the success of various marketing initiatives.

How Have These Trends Influenced One-to-One Marketing?

What are these forces telling marketers? How are they pushing forward the customer-focused philosophy of one-to-one marketing?

First, society has become more diverse, which means that the one-size-fits-all marketing of earlier days no longer works. Consumers do not want to be treated like the masses. Instead they want to be treated like individuals with their own unique sets of needs and wants. Because it is personalized by nature, one-to-one marketing works better with today's consumers.

Second, consumers no longer have as much time as they would like to shop. One-to-one marketing is personal and targeted, and allows consumers to spend less time making purchase decisions and more time doing the things that are more important to them.

Third, today's consumers are loyal only to those companies and brands that have earned their loyalty and reinforced it with every purchase. With one-to-one marketing, companies locate their best customers, reward those customers for their loyalty, and thank them for their business.

Fourth, mass media approaches are declining in importance. Market research techniques and database technology are evolving to enable marketers to collect detailed information on their specific customers—their names, addresses, and so on. Companies no longer have to rely on demographics, which are much fuzzier. One-to-one marketing is growing in importance because it provides more cost-effective means for reaching customers.

Fifth and finally, the demand for accountability will drive the growth of one-to-one marketing and justify its continued existence.

One-to-one marketing requires a huge commitment, as well as a complete reversal in thinking for those marketers who have spent the past five decades focusing exclusively on mass marketing. Probably, mass marketing will always be part of the promotional mix, especially to create brand awareness or to remind consumers of products; that being said, marketers cannot ignore the advantages of one-to-one marketing. In the coming decades, the new commandment of marketing's future will ring loudly in every marketer's ears: "Know thy customer and communicate with him or her based on what you know."[12]

At the Core: A Revised Marketing Communications Process

3 Describe the one-to-one marketing communications process

With traditional mass marketing, everyone receives essentially the same message through the same channel. Using some type of mass marketing channel, such as a television ad or an outdoor billboard, the advertiser or marketer sends a promotional message to the target audience. "Noise" from competing advertisements affects how clearly the consumer receives these messages. Feedback on the effectiveness of the communication comes through market research and through the tracking of changes in sales levels or market share. Mass marketing is still a fundamental part of marketing, but one-to-one practices are beginning to have a major impact.

The **one-to-one marketing communications process** flows as follows:

one-to-one marketing communications process
A revised marketing process characterized by the use of personalized communication, a lack of "noise," and the ability to capture customers' responses.

1. The one-to-one marketer (i.e., the sender) creates individualized messages for customers and prospects, who have been identified from one or more databases.
2. The message is sent through a direct communication channel, such as direct mail, a salesperson, or a telemarketer, or it is sent over the Internet.
3. The customer or prospect (i.e., the receiver) interprets the personalized message.
4. The customer or prospect responds to the communication—for example, by making a purchase.
5. The one-to-one marketer captures this response and feeds it back into the marketing database, where it will help shape the next marketing communication.

The flow of the one-to-one marketing communications process is basically the same as with traditional processes, with a few significant differences that have been enabled by technology. To begin with, the message is personalized. With mass communication, the same message is sent to a large group of potential respondents, who may or may not be interested; with one-to-one marketing, the communication is personalized and is sent to relatively few individuals, who are already known to be interested.

Nike Canada provides an example of this. Fitness instructors are a key segment of Nike's market, so they are offered a discount on the merchandise they

exhibit 18.1

The One-to-One Marketing Communications Process

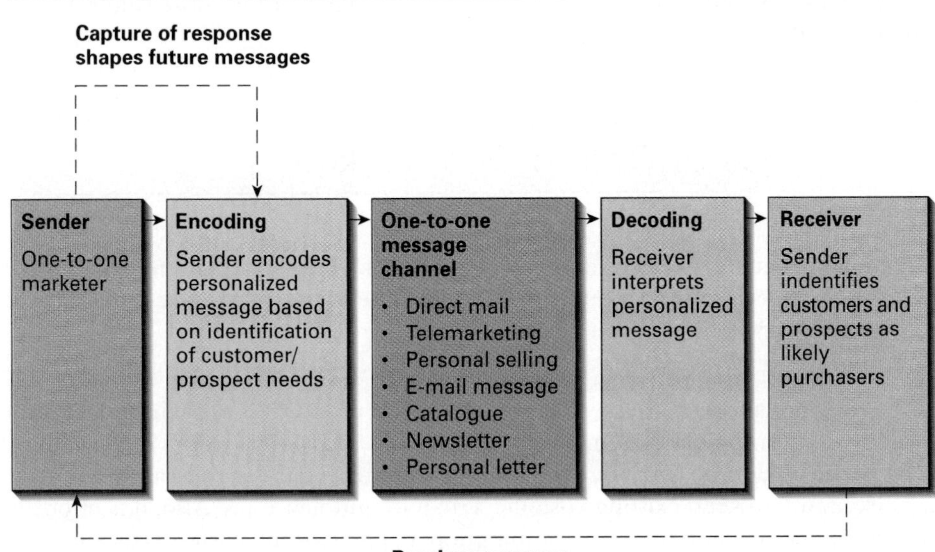

order through a Nike catalogue that is aimed specifically at them. The expectation is that students will see their instructors wearing Nike gear and be encouraged purchase it as well. To reduce costs, Nike has created an on-line version (**www.nikeinp.ca**) of its catalogue exclusively for its Instructor Network Program. In effect, this has established a one-to-one relationship between Nike and the instructors. The ordering process is simple, and products and services are updated annually and tailored to instructors' needs. Nike saves money on printed catalogues and mailing and can now track the preferences of individual instructors, as well as their changes of address.

Second, the channel used to send the message is direct rather than "mass." With mass media channels such as television and newspapers, marketers do not personally know the people with whom they are trying to communicate. With direct, one-to-one channels, marketers have some information about their individual customers and are positioned to gather more. Also, a company that uses mass media channels cannot respond immediately to customers' reactions to its message. Instead, it must wait to see whether people are reacting positively or negatively by conducting research or by monitoring sales and market share. With a one-to-one channel, marketers can capture individual customer responses and use this information to shape future communications. Indeed, the trend is toward customers telling companies what information they want to receive.

Third, "noise" from news articles, competitors' advertisements, and other store displays is not present in one-to-one marketing. This is because the communication travels directly from the marketer to the customer or prospect. Although no communication environment is completely free of interference—the dog may be barking, the stereo blaring, or the telephone ringing—one-to-one communication comes as close as as any process can to being noise-free. As a result, the receiver is more likely to receive and interpret the communication in the desired way.

Finally, with one-to-one communications, individuals' responses can be captured. Marketers can use the responses gathered to update customer records, tailor later marketing efforts, and judge the cost efficiency of marketing efforts.

Chris Zane, president of Zane's Cycles of Branford, Connecticut, uses past responses from customers to tailor future marketing communications. Every March, Zane searches his database for customers who bought baby seats three years earlier. Knowing that they may wish to buy a child's bike soon, Zane sends these customers a postcard showcasing his inventory of children's bikes and offering a small discount on the purchase. About 60 percent of those who receive the postcard return to buy a bike.[13]

The Advantages of One-to-One Marketing

4

List the advantages and disadvantages of one-to-one marketing

A company that knows its customers on a one-to-one basis enjoys boundless advantages. Specifically, marketers that practise one-to-one marketing using database technology benefit from the following:[14]

1. *The ability to identify the most profitable customers:* Marketers waste fewer marketing dollars because they can spend a larger proportion of their budgets on the most profitable customers.
2. *The ability to create long-term relationships with customers:* It is significantly less expensive to keep existing customers than to find new ones. Also, it is often more profitable to increase consumption among existing customers, or to cross-sell to them, or to get them to trade up, than it is to gain new customers. Remember here that satisfied customers are more likely to respond to

chapters.indigo.ca

How does chapters.indigo.ca track its customers? What kind of information can chapters.indigo.ca provide you once it has developed a customer profile on you?

www.chapters.indigo.ca

on line

other promotions if they already trust the marketer. A customer's "lifetime value" can be significant to a business.

3. *The ability to target marketing efforts only to those people most likely to be interested:* Companies that adopt one-to-one marketing find it easier to predict responses to their marketing offers. Instead of sending out thousands of pieces of direct mail or e-mail, marketers can target offers only to the few hundred—or possibly even the handful—of customers who are really interested. This increases response rates and decreases costs. The dollars once wasted reaching customers who aren't interested can now be directed to influence the purchase decisions of likely purchasers (see this chapter's Entrepreneurial Insights box).
4. *The ability to offer varied messages to different consumers:* Instead of blindly advertising to the masses, marketers can tailor marketing communications according to each customer's needs or buying history. Marketers can treat customers as individuals and create a deeper, more mutually beneficial relationships.
5. *Increased knowledge about customers and prospects:* Mass marketers know very little about their customers. Using well-developed databases, one-to-one marketers can easily develop in-depth, censuslike information about their customers and hold on to it as long as it is relevant. This allows them to make more informed marketing decisions.

Database marketing can increase a company's revenues and profitability; on the other hand, marketing databases can be quite expensive to create. For this reason a company may decide to contract with an outside provider that offers customer relationship management services and/or software. Use your Internet search engine to find a company that provides database services for businesses. Compare the company you locate with SAP (www.sap.com/crm).

One-to-one marketing does have some disadvantages. First of all, marketing databases can be quite costly and time consuming to create. It can take only a few thousand dollars and a few months to create a basic customer list. At the other end of the scale, a company can spend millions of dollars over several years to create a large customer database that will be used in every business decision it makes. Many companies find themselves unable to simply reinvent internal processes. Or they cannot afford to invest heavily in initiatives that may not pay off for some time.

Furthermore, unless the database is carefully planned and unless the company knows exactly why it is developing one, it can easily fail to do any good. Some companies have spent years building a customer marketing database only to scrap it after realizing it didn't meet their needs and expectations. The marketing database must be carefully tooled to the strategy of the business, and must serve all employees as well as all customers. As well, all levels of management must actively support the strategy; if they don't, the database is going to be a shaky investment indeed.

Yet another disadvantage of one-to-one marketing relates to the privacy concerns of consumers. Companies are collecting a great deal of sensitive information about customers. Although many customers enjoy being treated as individuals through one-to-one marketing techniques, just as many feel that marketers already know too much about them already. Privacy issues related to one-to-one marketing and database technology will be discussed later in this chapter.

One-to-One Marketing Applications

5
List eight common one-to-one marketing applications

As noted earlier, a marketing database is not an end in itself; rather, it is a tool for helping one-to-one marketers interact with customers and prospects. The information in marketing databases is helpful only after it has been carefully analyzed. Only then can marketers identify sales opportunities and tailor their communications to address those opportunities. Various one-to-one applications for marketing databases are listed in Exhibit 18.2.[15]

exhibit 18.2

Eight Common One-to-One Database Marketing Applications

1. Identify the best customers
2. Retain loyal customers
3. Cross-sell other products or services
4. Design targeted marketing communications
5. Reinforce consumer purchase decisions
6. Induce product trial by new customers
7. Increase the effectiveness of distribution channel marketing
8. Maintain control over brand equity

Identify the Best Customers

Smart marketers have found that not all customers are created equal—that most sales are to a minority of customers. When companies examine closely where their sales are coming from, most find that the 80/20 rule applies: 20 percent of customers account for 80 percent of sales. If a company can identify that 20 percent of customers and develop a relationship with them, chances are it will enjoy high profitability. A one-to-one marketing database can be invaluable for tracking the 10 or 20 percent of customers who provide the majority of sales. Pitney Bowes, the mail system specialist, analyzed its database of 1.2 million customers and found that fewer than 10 percent provided more than two-thirds of its customer base value. The company also found that it had a major retention and profitability problem with its low-volume, low-cost accounts, among whom cancellation rates ran as high as 40 percent.[16]

Retain Loyal Customers

Once a company knows who its best customers are, it should make every effort to maintain and increase their loyalty. One study concluded that with every 5 percent of customers a company retains each year, profits increase by at least 25 percent. What's more, improving customer retention by only 2 percent can decrease costs by as much as 10 percent.[17]

Loyalty programs, such as those used by Canadian Tire, Zellers Club Z, and Aerogold Visa, reward loyal consumers for making multiple purchases. The goal of a loyalty program is to build long-term, mutually beneficial relationships between the company and its key customers. These programs use database technology to identify those customers.

Cross-Sell Other Products or Services

One-to-one marketing provides tremendous opportunities for cross-selling related products. This is what is meant by "share of customer." Using a database, marketers can match product profiles to consumer profiles with the goal of cross-selling customers other products that match their demographics, lifestyles, and

HMV.com

Can you build a customer profile at HMV.com without purchasing anything? Go to its Website to find out. Explain what you discover.

www.HMV.com

on line

behaviours. The Internet music retailer HMV.com develops profiles of music buyers on the basis of past purchases. After a buyer searches for or purchases music titles that match a profile, he or she is presented with titles that others in the profile have bought.

Product and customer profiling can also be applied in business-to-business situations. Pitney Bowes, which is known for its highly independent product divisions, is using database technology to break down its internal barriers and identify cross-selling opportunities. Too often, one division's existing customers were another division's prime prospects. Nowadays, Pitney Bowes's salespeople are using the company's database to cross-sell to—say—users of the company's mailing systems who are not currently using its fax or copier equipment and services.[18]

Design Targeted Marketing Communications

Databases of transactions, purchases, and even Web-surfing patterns allow marketers to track customers' relationships to their products and services and modify their marketing messages accordingly. For example, a company may divide its customers into infrequent users, moderate users, and heavy users. It may then devise different communication strategies according which group the customer falls into. So, for example, marketing communications to infrequent users might encourage repeat purchases through direct incentives such as limited-time price discounts. Communications to moderate users might use fewer incentives and more reinforcement of past purchase decisions. Targeted communications to heavy users might focus on loyalty and on reinforcing purchase decisions, rather than on price promotions.

When marketers know other personal or demographic information besides past transaction data, they can tailor their messages accordingly. Shoppers Drug Mart used information it had collected through its Healthwatch program to develop different messages and promotions based on specific concerns users had about their prescriptions, or about factors in their lives that could affect their health.

Reinforce Consumer Purchase Decisions

As you have already learned, cognitive dissonance is the feeling consumers get when they notice an inconsistency between their values and opinions and their behaviour—that is, when they begin to doubt the soundness of a purchase decision. A database helps marketers reach out to customers to reinforce their purchase decisions. By thanking customers for their purchases and by letting them know they are important to the business, marketers can strengthen profitable, long-term relationships. They can even take it a step farther and solicit product feedback and input.

Induce Product Trial by New Customers

A lot of one-to-one marketing focuses on encouraging repeat purchases by the firm's best customers. That being said, a marketing database can also be used to identify new customers. A firm using a marketing database already has a profile of its best customers; it can use the same database to help it find new customers that fit that profile.

Typically, one-to-one marketers match up demographic and behavioural data with existing customer data to generate a detailed customer profile. This profile can be a powerful tool for evaluating lists of prospects. If a firm's best customers are between nineteen to twenty-five, live in the suburbs, do not own a car, like to eat at Thai restaurants, and enjoy mountain biking, the company should be able to find prospects already in its database of customers who use competitor's products and who match or almost match this profile.

Increase the Effectiveness of Distribution Channels

In Chapter 12 you learned that a *marketing channel* is a business structure consisting of the interdependent organizations (e.g., wholesalers and retailers) that move a product from producer to consumer. Most marketers rely on a number of layered, indirect channels to move their products to the end user. This means that they often lose touch with customers as individuals because the relationship is really between the retailer and the consumer. Marketers in this situation tend to view their customers merely as statistics, because specific customer information is hard to gather.

One-to-one marketing databases provide manufacturers with a tool for understanding who is buying their products. Samsonite, the world's largest luggage manufacturer, uses customer purchase information gathered through product registration cards and its 800 number to determine what its customers' needs are and how to design products to meet those needs. It then passes on this information to retailers so that they can understand their customers better and tailor their luggage departments to meet customer needs. Samsonite's database now includes demographic, lifestyle, and purchase data on over 1.5 million customers.[19]

Maintain Control over Brand Equity

Brand equity is the image or feeling that consumers have when they see, hear about, or remember a product. In effect, a brand is a promise made to consumers. Marketers of consumer products—Disney, Tide, and Roots, for example—spend a great deal of time and money developing and maintaining brand equity. In multiple-distribution environments, maintaining brand equity control is a growing problem for marketers. Procter & Gamble may go to great lengths to make sure an advertisement for Tide is not overshadowed by that of a competitor. On the other hand, retailers that sell Tide are loyal to their consumers rather than to specific products. In sales flyers they may advertise two competing brands on the same page, in the hope of attracting users of both products. With one-to-one marketing, the marketer assumes complete control over the message being communicated to customers. The marketer controls what it says, who is says it to, and how it says it.

The Basics of Marketing Database Technology

6 Discuss the basics of one-to-one marketing database technology

One-to-one marketing is almost always characterized by the creation of a large, computerized file of customers' and potential customers' profiles and purchase patterns. This file is then used to direct marketing communications, product development, and research. One-to-one marketing using technology is often referred to as *data-driven marketing*, or *customer relationship marketing*. By gathering, enhancing, and analyzing information about customers and prospects, marketers can implement more effective initiatives and carry out precise marketing. Marketers communicate to individuals, not to mass market segments, and they do so one-to-one, using data, technology, and statistical techniques.[20]

database
A collection of data, especially one that can be accessed and manipulated by computer software.

At the very core of one-to-one marketing is, of course, the company database. According to the *Random House Webster's Dictionary*, a **database** is "a collection of data, especially one that can be accessed and manipulated by computer software."[21] More specifically, a **marketing database** is a list of names, addresses, and other pieces of pertinent information about individual customers and prospects that affects what and how marketers sell to them.

"A database is sort of a collective memory," says Richard Barlow, president of Frequency Marketing Inc., a Cincinnati-based consulting firm. "It deals with you in the same personalized way as a mom-and-pop grocery store, where they knew customers by name and stocked what they wanted."[22]

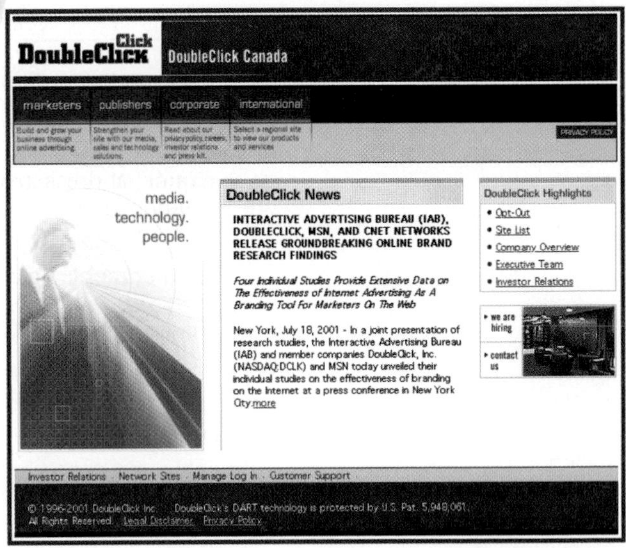

When one-to-one marketing efforts succeed, it is almost always because they have involved constructing a comprehensive database to store and sort valuable customer information. DoubleClick helps its clients build Websites and monitor their effectiveness. To see who DoubleClick works with and what it does, visit its site, click on the Corporate link, and then head to the Press Release. www.doubleclick.com

A database can store almost any kind of information about consumers. In its most basic form, database marketing relies on transactional processing systems that record the details of individual purchase transactions. For example, when a consumer makes a purchase by credit card, a database records the store name, the store location, the date of the purchase, and the purchase price, among other things. Over time this produces a transaction history for every customer. This basic system provides critical information about purchasing patterns and preferences—information that can be valuable for creating new products or sales offers. Transaction data can be enhanced with additional information about individual customers: age, income level, interests, and so on. Exhibit 18.3 lists various categories of basic information that marketers can collect on their customers and prospects, be they individuals or businesses.

A database often provides marketers with access to vast amounts of customer information—information that traditionally was stored in various computer systems throughout the company. Data kept for other purposes, such as financial data (kept by the billing department) and customer service data (kept by the service area), are merged to provide a complete picture of each customer.

marketing database
The compilation of names, addresses, and other pieces of pertinent information about individual customers and prospects that affects what and how marketers sell to them.

It used to take days, weeks, or even months to pull reports showing differences in sales by region, item, or salesperson from data stored in various computer systems. Programmers used to have to write a program and run it overnight before they could answer a question that couldn't be answered with a standard report. For this reason, managers tended not to ask many questions back then. Today's marketing managers are equipped with database programs that make it possible to get answers far more quickly. Marketing decision makers can now ask "what if" questions—for example, "What if we sent the last offer only to the top 20 percent of our customers instead of the top 50 percent?" When marketers can go from one question to the next in minutes rather than in days or weeks, they ask not only more questions, but better ones—and, it is hoped, the right ones.[23]

Marketers should remember that a marketing database is not an end in itself. A database is a tool for making the most of one-to-one marketing. Any marketer can develop a database of customer information. However, if the right data are not collected, or if the data gathered are not manipulated carefully to provide answers and insights, or if the data are not properly maintained to ensure their integrity, the marketer will have enormous difficulty making the best use of the information—and justifying the expense of collecting it.

Building a Marketing Database

Database marketing experts Rob Jackson and Paul Wang state in their book *Strategic Database Marketing,* "A database is only as powerful as the information it houses."[24] Data are the cornerstones of data-driven, one-to-one marketing. A company can buy the most elaborate and expensive database system available and hire all the statistical professionals and marketing experts it wants, but if the right data are not collected, the other building blocks will never be used to their potential.

exhibit 18.3

Basic Consumer and Business-to-Business Data

Consumer data	Business-to-business data
• Name, address, telephone number, e-mail address	• Name, genderization (e.g., Mr./Mrs./Ms.), title of buyer, direct telephone number, e-mail address
• Demographic data: age, income, gender, ethnicity, household size, etc.	• Company name, address, and telephone number
• Lifestyle and leisure interests	• Company demographics: SIC code, number of employees, sales volume, number of branches, key contacts
• Financial characteristics such as credit history and rating	• Recency, frequency, and monetary transaction history by date, dollar amount of purchase, and products purchased
• Recency, frequency, and monetary transaction history by date, dollar amount of purchase, and products purchased	• Financial characteristics such as credit history and rating
• Source of order, inquiry, or referral	• Predictive complementary product information (purchase behaviour that indicates a propensity to purchase a complementary product)
• Promotional response data	• Industry surveys
	• Assigned salesperson

Many firms make it a point to gather customer information at the time of purchase, while they are gathering transaction data. Disney includes a postage-paid postcard in every video it sells asking for customer information. Black & Decker includes product registration cards that can be returned with the purchase of every appliance. Marketers often provide incentives in exchange for customer information. To build its database, which now contains information on over 4 million customers, FedEx asks for detailed customer information in return for a coupon or a FedEx premium.

Data gathering can be obvious to the consumer or not so obvious. Members of frequent shopper clubs generally understand that the retailer is collecting information about purchases in exchange for discounts or gifts. Shoppers Drug Mart collects transactional data through its Optimum program. Customers swipe a membership card at checkout time. The data collected this way include the store location, the items purchased (including quantity, brand, and size), the method of payment, and whether coupons were used.[25]

In contrast, the data gathering conducted by the Inter-Continental Hotel is generally invisible to consumers. The hotel keeps track of guests' preferences and provides them with individualized service, right down to the question of whether they will want soft or firm pillows. The data gathering is very subtle—most guests don't even realize their choices are being recorded.[26]

Enhancing Customer Data

A customer database becomes even more useful to one-to-one marketers when it is enhanced to include more than simply customers' or prospects' names,

Do you have a loyalty card? Perhaps you have more than one—say, AirMiles, ClubZ, and perhaps an Aerogold Visa. What growing loyalty-card problem does Acarta hope to help retailers solve? Do you think this is a good idea? Visit Acarta's site to find out.

www.acarta.com

on line

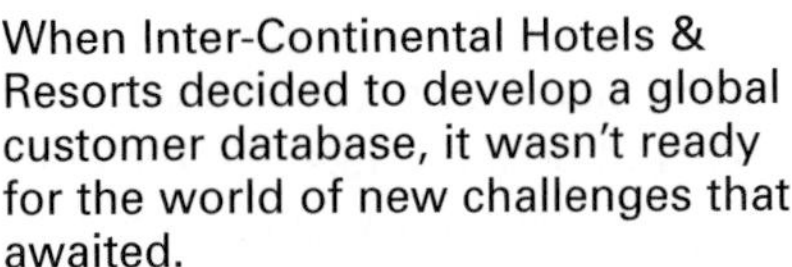

global perspectives

Inter-Continental Hotel Creates a Global Customer Database

When Inter-Continental Hotels & Resorts decided to develop a global customer database, it wasn't ready for the world of new challenges that awaited.

Hospitality service providers have a huge advantage over most other industries when it comes to building a marketing database: free data! Every time a customer reserves a room or checks into a property, an abundance of valuable data is provided during the transaction. Unfortunately for Inter-Continental, the systems that stored these transactions had not been designed with marketing in mind. What seemed like a gold mine of customer data proved difficult to access and utilize.

Inter-Continental's marketing database, Global 2000, grew out of a need to know its customers on a worldwide basis. Before its database went on-line, marketers and decision makers at the hotel could not answer even simple, basic questions about customers. They could calculate how many total stays had occurred at its hotels and how many room nights were produced, but they could not determine how many guests they had altogether.

Furthermore, with the exception of guests who were members of its frequent stay program, marketers and decision makers had no way of totalling multiple stays at different properties into one comprehensive guest history. For example, if Janine Davis stayed at one of Inter-Continental's hotels in London, New York, Sydney, and Montreal, they could not measure her value as a repeat customer.

Building an international database such as Global 2000 posed a number of challenges for the database development team at Inter-Continental Hotels & Resorts. Developing standards for tracking customer information from nearly one hundred hotels located in more than sixty countries proved to be a formidable task. Once the standards were established, an even more monumental feat was training all the hotel employees to use the system according to those standards.

Due to the international nature of the data, the team encountered numerous difficulties in summarizing revenue information into broad categories—room, telephone, room service, and so on. The team was also faced with the job of converting more than forty currencies into U.S. dollars and keeping the conversion tables up to date. Conversion rates alone created some interesting results. Just when the team thought revenue figures were valid, a country would devalue its currency, resulting in the discovery of hotels with $10,000 room rates!

Data integrity continues to be a challenge. When a guest from London stays at an Inter-Continental Hotel in Abidjan, Ivory Coast, his home address is often entered in French as Londres, Angleterre. His stays in Europe and the United States, however, yield an English-language home address of London, England. This inconsistency may prevent guests from being properly matched in the database. As a result, the team spent over three months adapting its match logic to encompass cultural and language influences to match guests correctly.

Address changes are also not easy to obtain internationally, so the Inter-Continental development team must rely heavily on the accuracy of data collection at the hotels. Prior direct marketing efforts revealed that only 66 percent of hotel guest records had mail addresses that were correct. This percentage has improved over time, but even so, a recent mailing resulted in nearly 15 percent of the pieces being returned for insufficient or incorrect address.

Although there have definitely been challenges in creating Global 2000, marketers and decision makers at Inter-Continental Hotels & Resorts feel it has all been worthwhile. Customer information is now collected from over eighty hotels all over the world at the time of checkout and is sent on a weekly basis to the central database via an internal e-mail system. Since 1994, the database has processed data from over 5.9 million stays; it now holds customer profiles and stay histories for 2.9 million guests. Today, management can determine the travel patterns and revenue contributions of each guest, as well as make projections of lifetime value.

Source: Reprinted from Annette Kissinger, "You Say London, I Say Londres," *Marketing Tools*, May 1997. Copyright 1997. PRIMEDIA Intertec.

addresses, telephone numbers, and transaction histories. **Database enhancement** involves overlaying more information onto customer or prospect records for the purpose of better describing or better determining the responsiveness of customers or prospects.[27] Enhancement data typically include demographic, lifestyle,

database enhancement
Overlaying more information onto customer or prospect records for the purpose of better describing or better determining the responsiveness of customers or prospects.

and behavioural data about customers. Data enhancement enables marketers to maximize the benefits of one-to-one strategies.

There are three main reasons to enhance a database with outside sources of information.[28] First, marketers can use database enhancement to learn more about customers and prospects. By overlaying demographic, lifestyle, and behavioural data onto customer records, they can gain a valuable picture of the relative value of customers. Say, for example, that a marketer of athletic equipment finds it useful to identify its best customers using past transaction data. If that same marketer also learns that these customers have incomes over $60,000, enjoy outdoor recreation activities—especially biking and kayaking—and have recently purchased of in-line skates, it will have a better understanding of who its customers really are.

Having arrived at profiles of their best customers, marketers can seek out prospects that match those profiles; these prospects will be more likely to respond positively to marketing communications.

Note well here that database marketing is not the same as market research. Though databases are an important part of marketing research, there are many questions that cannot be answered by a database alone. Ken Mison, senior vice-president of The Commitments Management Group at Marketing Facts in Toronto, notes: "It is highly unlikely that I'd be able to predict Coke or Pepsi drinkers in a database because there would be nothing to distinguish the two in any consistent manner." Foster Parents Plan of Canada is now considering matching survey research with in-house databases to determine levels of commitment among its foster parents. The two types of information combined work much more effectively to help FPP determine its "best customers."

Finding Answers by Looking Closely at Customer Data

A very important part of one to-one marketing involves manipulating the information in the database to profile the best customers or customer segments, analyze their lifetime value, and, ultimately, predict their purchasing behaviour. James R. Rosenfield's recent comments on database marketing sum it up: "Marketers confuse a marketing database, which can simply be stored information about customers, with database marketing, which is a dynamic approach to managing customers. You can't do database marketing without modeling and profiling—that's what it's all about."[29]

As noted earlier, the real value of one-to-one marketing is not found in the data itself. In fact, large quantities of data can remove value from one-to-one marketing by making the process confusing and complex. Though data are necessary, for them to be valuable they must be transformed into marketing information in the form of customer profiles, scores, and predictions. They must be transformed from operational bits and bytes into the information marketers require to succeed in their initiatives.[30]

Customer Segmentation In essence, *customer segmentation* involves breaking large groups of customers into smaller, more distinct groups. One-to-one marketers use this type of analysis to paint a picture of their customers—especially their best customers. They identify segments of customers in the database by any number of means, such as surveys, purchase data, responses, Web "click-stream" activity, and word of mouth; they then find ways to compare these customer segments with the rest of their customers. These segmentations can be based on characteristics such as demographics, geographic location, previous purchase behaviour, and psychographic variables.

Vancouver-based Intrawest Corporation operates seven ski resorts in the United States and Canada. It also develops high-end resort properties near its ski areas ($187,000 to $675,000-plus per unit). To find buyers for its properties,

Intrawest segments its database of over 700,000 skiers who have visited its resorts by geographic location and income and then sends presale invitations to preferred lists of potential buyers. Since it began segmenting its customer database, the company has been selling out properties during presale shows. One recent presale event sold out in less than two hours. There were more than three backup offers for each property.

In the same vein, Kellogg Canada and Special K have been encouraging women to take better care of their health and to push back against negative stereotypes about body image, weight, and dieting. Recently, these two entities have partnered with *Chatelaine* magazine to reach women in new ways. Specifically, they have created the Take Care Challenge quiz to test and expand women's knowledge of health and nutrition. The Challenge reaches women through traditional venues, such as print ads on Special K boxes and full-page ads in the magazine. It is also being conveyed through one-on-one contacts in more than 400 chain supermarkets, where nutrition reps provide health information and distribute copies of the quiz. Alternatively, women can take the challenge on-line at two Websites, **www.chatelaine.com** and **www.specialk.ca**. The information collected helps bring women—in particular, a specific segment of women—full circle with Special K. It also offers useful insights into the wants and needs of this market.

recency–frequency–monetary analysis (RFM)
A data manipulation technique that determines the firm's best customers by identifying those customers who have purchased most recently, bought most frequently, and spent the most money.

Recency–Frequency–Monetary Analysis (RFM) **Recency–frequency–monetary analysis (RFM)** identifies the customers most likely to purchase from the firm again because they have bought most recently, bought most frequently, or spent a specified amount of money on the firm's goods and services. Using this information, a firm can easily identify its "best customers." Scores are assigned to database records based on the above factors. Customers are then ranked, and this ranking enables the firm to identify the customers who have been good sources of revenue.

lifetime value analysis (LTV)
A data manipulation technique that projects the future value of the customer over a period of years using the assumption that marketing to repeat customers is more profitable than marketing to first-time buyers.

Many marketers take RFM analysis one step beyond this by folding profitability into the equation. A customer may be at the top of the RFM list when just the monetary value of purchases is considered. However, if this customer only buys items when they are on sale, he or she isn't as profitable a customer as one who spends the same amount on items that aren't on sale.

Lifetime Value Analysis (LTV) Recency, frequency, and monetary data can also be used to create lifetime value models for customers in the database. RFM looks at how valuable a customer is to the firm in the present time; in contrast, **lifetime value analysis (LTV)** projects the future value of the customer over a period of years. A basic assumption in any lifetime value calculation is that marketing to repeat customers is more profitable than marketing to first-time buyers.[31] In terms of promotion and gaining trust, it costs more to find a new customer than it does to sell more to a customer who is already loyal.

Steven Poirier, vice-president of sales and marketing at Moosehead in Saint John, New Brunswick, uses customer data to identify and then direct-market to its most valuable customers (MVCs).

Customer lifetime value has a number of uses:

- It indicates to marketers how much they can afford to spend to acquire new customers.
- It indicates how much they ought to spend to retain old customers.
- It provides a basis for targeting new customers who look like a company's most profitable customers.[32]

Lifetime value analysis enables marketers to identify their most valuable customers and profit from them over the long term by building relationships. Cadillac has calculated that the lifetime value of its top customers is $332,000. Pizza Hut figures that its customers are worth $8,000 in bottom-line lifetime value.[33]

L.L. Bean

Does L.L. Bean's Website aid in the company's efforts at data analysis? If so, how? If not, what changes in the site would you recommend that would make it a more effective one-to-one marketing tool?

www.llbean.com

data mining
The process of using statistical analysis to detect relevant patterns in purchasing behaviour in a database.

Data Mining A sophisticated data analysis technique is data mining. **Data mining** involves the automated discovery of "interesting," nonobvious patterns hidden in a database that have a high potential for contributing to the overall efficiency and effectiveness of a company's operations. The discovery process often involves sifting through massive quantities of data such as electronic point-of-sale transactions, inventory records, and on-line customer orders matched with demographics.[34] Data mining can create customer profiles, help determine reasons for customer loyalty, analyze the potential return for pricing, promotion, and direct mail strategies, and even help forecast sales. Without data mining, customer databases have limited utility.[35]

One-to-One Marketing to Businesses

At the start of the chapter we pointed out that one-to-one marketing is not new; also, as a concept or theory it will never go away. It's important to remember that one-to-one marketing can also be used to gain business customers as well as individual ones. As an example, companies of all sizes need to purchase supplies and contract out such things as shipping, warehousing, hiring, and production. Likewise, they need facilities that allow employees to work to their full potential, and they need systems that function well on a day-to-day basis so that they run smoothly. These *business processes* must be sought out and paid for, often as separate transactions but also as part of broader service agreements. Invariably there are easier, more efficient, or less expensive means available for a business to acquire the products or services it needs. (At least there should be.) One-to-one marketing in this context involves looking at the process or product from the customer's perspective and simplifying the aquisition of the process or product for it. Here, one-to-one strategies require marketers to understand the needs of the business they are selling to and providing that business with an individualized solution. These solutions may vary greatly from one business customer to the next.

Toronto-based Real Facilities Inc. took a common business process—finding, leasing, and outfitting office space—and turned what would ordinarily be a complex and time-consuming process involving many different outside vendors into a simple, one-stop experience. Customers from anywhere in North America that need to move to the Toronto area can log on to the Real Facilities Website and start narrowing their search by entering very specific requirements.

Database Technology Investments Increase

More and more companies are investing in database technology to support one-to-one marketing. According to a recent survey, eight in ten companies have some sort of database. Investment in database technology is increasing in all industries but especially in health care, utilities, and finance. Financial institutions are trying to solve their customer retention and satisfaction problems. Utility companies, faced with an unregulated future, are for the first time trying to understand their customers. Insurance companies are looking for means to store "life events," such as marriage or childbirth, to serve as sales triggers.[36] Donnelley Marketing recently found that 85 percent of manufacturers and retailers believe they will need a marketing database to be competitive beyond the year 2001.[37]

Many databases are astonishingly big. Ford Motor Co. has 50 million names on its database, Kraft General Foods 25 million, and Citicorp 30 million. Kimberly Clark (maker of Huggies diapers) has 10 million new parents' names in its database. GM has a database of 12 million GM credit card holders; this gives the company access to a vast amounts of data on buying habits. GM also surveys these customers to gather information on driving habits and needs. Every size and type

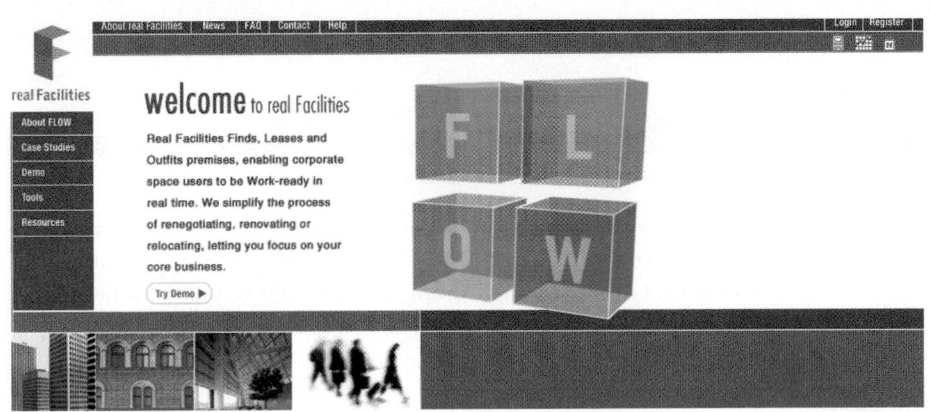

How does Real Facilities provide businesses with customized solutions to their office space needs? Could this function be done without the benefit of the Internet or databases?

of company is looking to database technology to improve its business success and competitiveness.

It can be expensive to develop a database for one-to-one marketing, but the corresponding returns can be huge. Land Rover used its database to identify 4,000 Range Rover owners and invited them to a special marketing event, where it sold 1,000 new vehicles at $52,000 each. The cost of database management and the subsequent mailing was only $150,000, so this represented a 346 percent return on investment.[38]

One-to-One Marketing and the Internet

One of the most important trends in one-to-one marketing relates to the Internet. Many marketers have adopted the Internet as a new channel for promotions and sales (e.g., through on-line catalogues), but only recently have marketers capitalized fully on the Web's marketing capabilities. These marketers have integrated electronic commerce with traditional marketing channels to create a true multimedia marketing initiative.

On-line marketers use customer transaction histories to identify buying patterns; they can then deliver personalized promotions. They can also generate personalized catalogues based on information they have gathered about the customers visiting their site—for example, information about colour and brand preferences, geographic location, and past transactions.[39]

Garden Escape, an on-line nursery, creates a personal store for each and every one of its on-line customers. When customers visit they are greeted by name and can tinker with garden plans using the site's interactive design program. They can even take notes on a private, on-line notepad. Dell Computer has created some 1,500 customized home pages for its best business customers; this provides those customers with direct access to company-specific personal computers, negotiated discounts, and records of orders and payments.[40] Marketers can send personalized e-mail messages based on previous on-line transactions or on other information they have gathered about their customers. Gap.com, The Gap's on-line store, sends periodic e-mail messages highlighting new clothing lines or special prices to customers who have registered at their site.

Because of the Web's interactive, real-time nature, on-line one-to-one marketers can react immediately if their promotions are not generating the responses projected. Messages can be reviewed for simplicity and for weaknesses in pricing, copy, or image; or the target audience can be redefined "on the fly" to maximize responses. An entire one-to-one marketing campaign can be launched, refined based on its degree of success, and relaunched within hours, as opposed to the months typically required for print, catalogue, direct mail, and broadcast media.[41]

on line

The Gap

Experience the results of on-line, one-to-one marketing at the Website of The Gap. Join and visit the site, then return later in the week to see how well the company has built your profile.

www.gap.com

Privacy Concerns with One-to-One Marketing

7

Discuss privacy issues related to one-to-one marketing

Before rushing out to invest in computer hardware and software to build a database, marketers should consider how consumers are reacting to the growing prevalence of databases. One-to-one marketing is a concern to many Canadians because it has the potential to invade their privacy. This concern revolves around the sheer volume of information that is being collected in databases and the vulnerability of this information to unauthorized access and use.

Most consumers don't know how personal information is collected, used, and distributed; they also don't realize the extent to which technology is helping collect personal data. So when they are developing on-line initiatives, marketers must consider the ethics involved. Vast amounts of data are being collected through various means—credit card transactions, surveys, contests, Web traffic records, and so on—and much of this information is being made available to businesses for their own purposes. Services such as AdForce and DoubleClick are developing data-gathering technologies to help companies build immense databases for managing multiple-site campaigns, for compiling statistics, and for targeting consumers in ever more specific demographics. Again, technology—specifically the Internet and databases—is making it much easier to collect, sort, store, and share data.

The laws governing the proper gathering and use of personal information via the Internet or other digitally assisted means are still evolving. Governments and marketers themselves now recognize the need for tighter controls; that being said, the laws are still quite lax and there are not yet any international standards. The Internet being such a borderless entity, this poses problems for both consumers and lawmakers.

Care for a Cookie Anyone?

As a marketing tool, the Web offers some wonderful advantages for advertisers. Web ads can be posted instantaneously, so marketers can start, stop, and change their campaigns in mere minutes. And with Web ads, direct responses are possible; this isn't the case with print ads, billboards, and TV spots. Furthermore, the effectiveness of Web campaigns can easily be measured by tracking responses—or the lack of them—from individual surfers. Also, the Web can be used to convert ad viewers into participants in the marketing process—whether they want to be or not. This is one of the emerging points of contention in the world of on-line one-to-one marketing. Many consumers feel that personalization enhances their on-line experience but also wonder whether the information they divulge on Websites is being distributed without their permission or knowledge. The essential technology behind all this is fostered by the use of "cookies."

Cookies—small text files placed by Websites on Internet users' computers—are a powerful tool for profiling users' activities, behaviour patterns, and on-line preferences. Typically, a cookie stores a unique customer number. The data associated with that number can then be read and updated by the Website's server whenever a user visits that site. Clearly, this is a boon for on-line advertisers, since in a competitive environment where marketing dollars are scarce, they benefit greatly from seeing proof that the money they are spending is paying off (i.e., providing return on investment). Many one-to-one Internet initiatives we've looked at in this chapter rely on cookies to "remember" and respond to surfers' preferences.

New technologies that perform the same function as cookies are quickly being developed. Meanwhile, consumer advocates are campaigning to restrict the extant to which data can be captured, linked, and distributed without the permission or knowledge of the consumer. Consumers often don't understand existing privacy laws and regulations. Microsoft plans to release a version of its Explorer browser that will give users the option of rejecting cookies altogether. Faced with this, Web marketers are rushing to find more sophisticated ways to target ads, track visitors, and analyze data, while staying within the bounds of ever more focused privacy policies.

On-line privacy concerns were understandably heightened when statistics were released showing that fewer than 50 percent of Websites in the United States were in compliance with the Fair Information Practice Principles set by the Federal Trade Commission.

Although individual industry associations, including the Canadian Direct Marketing Association, have created their own privacy standards, many consumers are questioning how much of the information collected and stored in databases is really necessary to making a sale. Read about the ethical implications of one-to-one database marketing by drug companies in this chapter's "Ethics in Marketing" box.

ethics in marketing

Smells Like Teen Research

The Net has become a vital tool for marketers gathering information about teenagers, who are among the heaviest users of the Internet. On-line data collection software has reduced the waiting period on surveys to a mere seventy-two hours. In addition, real-time on-line chat rooms are borderless, as well as more affordable than "live" focus groups. Web-based research is both more affordable and more efficient, and this is promising to change the entire face of market research. On-line research companies such as NRG Group in Toronto are developing communities of teens, whose likes and dislikes will be at the disposal of corporate clients. This increased focus on the whims of young people is causing concern among some market research experts: the line between selling and researching is becoming blurred.

At Youtopia.com, the first on-line loyalty site for teens across North America, teens log on to the site (thereby creating a personalized profile) to e-mail friends, chat with spokes-star Britney Spears, and play interactive games, for which they receive "Youdollars." These can be redeemed for gift certificates at retailers such as HMV, La Senza Girl, and Suzy Shier. The games are in fact surveys designed to build profiles of the players. "What we have done is made the unsurveyable surveyable via Youtopia," says president Randi Shinder. "So whereas you can't really call up a household and ask to speak to the thirteen-year-old, sponsors can actually survey, through an interactive and fun way, the demographic and extract information from them, en masse." Because teens don't have credit cards, an on-line currency like Youdollars is a strong incentive, motivating them to return to the games again and again.

This whole approach raises the ethical issue of how marketers should conduct themselves when polling minors for information. The Professional Market Research Society has recently introduced guidelines for researchers dealing with children under twelve—guidelines that restrict questions about family income and other sensitive issues such as sex. Though the on-line teen market remains fair game, the popularity of consumer profiling on-line may blur the lines between pure market research and research for the purposes of "indirect" sales.

Says Doug Snetsinger, president of Grey Data: "When you register info on a Website, does the individual, whether they be a parent, or an adult or a child, understand the purpose for which it's being extracted? Some do, some don't." Marketers get around this issue by offering participants payment, in some shape or form, in return for providing personal information. But with this sensitive target market, is that providing real value in exchange for the information taken?

Source: Carey Toane, "Smells Like Teen Research," *Marketing*, 24 July 2000.

LOOKING BACK

Jones Soda has embraced one-to-one marketing as an alternative to mass media marketing. One-to-one marketers learn about customers on an individual basis through the Internet and database technology; this is an efficient and effective approach to offering them the individualized attention they demand. Jones uses its Web-managed community of customers to develop personalized products and further establish its brand. Jones, like many other marketers, is using one-to-one marketing to establish itself. Other companies are using it to stay competitive in ever more competitive markets.

Summary

1 Define one-to-one marketing, and discuss its relationship to database technology. One-to-one marketing is a customer-based, information-intensive, long-term-oriented, individualized marketing method that focuses on share of customer rather than on share of market. It is radically changing virtually every facet of marketing. Database technology and the Internet are making it possible for companies to interact with customers on a personal, one-to-one basis. A database stores pertinent information about a company's customers and contacts and makes it readily available to the sales and marketing staff for assessing, analyzing, and anticipating customers' needs. Database technology is allowing marketers to sift through the millions of pieces of data to target the right customers, to develop the right communication based on these customers' needs, and to monitor ongoing relationships, making adjustments in message strategy as needed.

2 Discuss the forces that have influenced the emergence of one-to-one marketing. The forces that have helped shape one-to-one marketing include more demanding and time-poor consumers, a decline in brand loyalty, the explosion of new media alternatives, changing channels of distribution, and the demand for marketing accountability. Consumers no longer want to be treated like the masses. One-to-one marketing allows consumers to be treated as individuals with their own unique sets of needs and wants. Also, consumers today have less time to spend shopping for the products they need. Because it is targeted, one-to-one marketing can decrease the time consumers need to make purchase decisions. Furthermore, consumers are less brand loyal than they used to be. One-to-one marketing techniques increase brand loyalty by focusing on finding the firm's best customers, rewarding them for their loyalty, and thanking them for their business. As mass media approaches become less important, one-to-one marketing will increase in importance and offer marketers more cost-effective avenues for reaching customers. Finally, the demand for marketing accountability will drive the growth of one-to-one marketing and justify its continued existence.

3 Describe the one-to-one marketing communications process. In mass media marketing, the advertiser or marketer "flows" a promotional message through a mass marketing channel to its target audience. Noise from competing advertisements affects the encoding and decoding of the message. Feedback on the effectiveness of the communication comes through market research and changes in sales levels or market share. In one-to-one marketing, the flow is similar; however, the message encoded by the marketer is personalized and the marketer can capture the response from the consumer and feed this information back into the marketing database for future use.

4 List the advantages and disadvantages of one-to-one marketing. Businesses that know their customers on a one-to-one basis enjoy many advantages: They can identify their most profitable and least profitable customers. They can create long-term relationships with their customers. They can target their marketing efforts only to those consumers most likely to be interested. They can vary their messages to different consumers. And they know more about customers and prospects. Disadvantages include the cost and time involved in creating a one-to-one marketing database and the consumers' growing concerns about privacy.

5 **List eight common one-to-one marketing applications.** Common marketing applications of customer databases include (1) identifying the best customers, (2) retaining loyal customers, (3) cross-selling other products or services, (4) designing targeted marketing communications, (5) reinforcing consumer purchase decisions, (6) inducing product trial by new customers, (7) increasing the effectiveness of distribution channel marketing, and (8) maintaining control over brand equity.

6 **Discuss the basics of one-to-one marketing database technology.** One-to-one marketing is characterized by the creation of a large computerized database of customers' and potential customers' profiles and purchase patterns and then using it to direct marketing communications. A marketing database is a compilation of names, addresses, and other pieces of pertinent information about individual customers and prospects. Database marketing relies on transactional processing systems that record the details of individual purchase transactions. These data can then be enhanced using external sources. Marketers can manipulate customer data using segmentation, recency–frequency–monetary analysis, or lifetime value analysis. Marketers have only recently been capitalizing on the Internet's interactive capabilities for one-to-one marketing. E-commerce provides on-line one-to-one marketers with the ability to deliver personalized promotional messages using past customer transaction histories. Marketers can also send personalized e-mail messages based on previous on-line transactions or other information they have gathered about customers. The Internet's real-time interactive nature makes it possible for on-line one-to-one marketers to react immediately if promotions are not generating the results projected. Messages can be reviewed and changed "on the fly" to maximize responses.

7 **Discuss privacy issues related to one-to-one marketing.** One-to-one marketing concerns many Canadians because of the potential for invasion of privacy—specifically, the sheer volume of information that is collected in databases and the vulnerability of this information to unauthorized access and use. Most consumers are unaware of how personal information is collected, used, and distributed, and also unaware of how technology facilitates the collection of personal data. Also, there is widespread misunderstanding among consumers about existing privacy laws and regulations. Frustrated by their lack of control, consumers want more opportunities to determine how their personal information will be used. The popularity of the Internet for direct marketing and consumer data collection, and as a repository of sensitive consumer data, has also alarmed privacy-minded consumers.

Discussion and Writing Questions

1. Explain why one-to-one marketing today would not be possible without database technology.
2. Explain the one-to-one marketing process. Why is it becoming a more widespread strategy among marketers?
3. List several local businesses that you feel would benefit from one-to-one marketing. Choose one business and develop a one-to-one database development plan. Consider marketing applications, data requirements, likely existing data and enhancement data, data manipulation, and data maintenance.
4. Explain this statement: "A database is only as powerful as the information it houses."

Do You Know These Terms?

customer relationship management (CRM) 492
data mining 508
database 502
database enhancement 505
lifetime value analysis (LTV) 407
marketing database 503
one-to-one marketing 491
one-to-one marketing communications process 497
recency–frequency–monetary analysis (RFM) 507

5. Assume that you are the manager of a local dry cleaning business. What types of information do you currently collect about your customers that you could use to develop one-to-one relationships? What factors would determine your best customers?
6. Explain the concept of lifetime value. Why is this type of data manipulation so important to one-to-one marketers?
7. What problems might a larger company face in implementing a one-to-one marketing strategy?
8. Is there a difference between one-to-one marketing and customer relationship management (CRM)?

Application for Small Business

The Stalk Exchange is a small flower shop in Winnipeg, Manitoba. The proprietor, Molly Edwards, has always measured the success of her business based on market share, which she estimates at roughly 10 percent. This is based on a report published by the Winnipeg Chamber of Commerce that provides total flower sales from area flower shops in her city. This does not include flowers purchased at grocery stores.

Molly has used traditional mass-marketing approaches in an attempt to increase her market share, such as advertising heavily in the *Winnipeg Free Press* during holidays such as Valentine's Day and Mother's Day and offering discounts during the low periods in between. These measures have increased sales, she believes, but she is not sure by how much. Also, the ads cost money and the discounts eat into her profits. She knows that grocery stores cut into her business by offering lower prices on lower-quality flowers and arrangements, but she is not sure how to counter this because lowering her prices across the board would be devastating to her profits.

Molly has a number of customers who order from her time and again, but she has never thought much about how to take advantage of this loyal customer base. Shuffling through a stack of flower orders on her desk from the past year, she begins to look closely at the information she actually does collect about her customers. On each order form are the following: the customer's name, address, telephone number, and date of order; the date that flowers are to be delivered; the type of flower arrangement requested; the total price; to whom the flowers were sent; and what was to be printed on the card. Also, seven in ten orders were purchased over the phone with a credit card.

Questions

1. Suggest a one-to-one marketing plan whereby Molly will be able to use the customer information she collects to (a) identify her best customers, (b) increase sales from her best customers, and (c) reinforce their purchase decisions.
2. Through credit card records, Molly can overlay data onto her customer database to provide more information about her customers. What additional enhancement data would you suggest she overlay?
3. What can Molly do to determine how much business her customers give to floral departments in grocery stores? With this information, what one-to-one marketing techniques could influence her customers to choose The Stalk Exchange more often?

Toronto Blue Jays: One Fan at a Time

The Toronto Blue Jays score high marks with local baseball fans through their one-to-one marketing program, a customer-based, information-intensive method that focuses on one baseball lover at a time. By using database technology, the Jays can make a pitch to each fan and cultivate long-term relationships. The team's database is carefully planned to gather pertinent information about customers and contacts so that the sales and marketing staff can analyze it and use it to provide better customer service.

The need for one-to-one marketing results from today's more demanding and very busy sports enthusiasts. Baseball fans are more strapped for time now than in any previous generation. They demand better, faster service, are more impatient, and don't want to get stuck in line waiting to buy tickets. In today's ballgame, people prefer to order tickets and merchandise by phone, mail, or e-mail.

How do the Blue Jays create their database? A compilation of bits of key information about customers, the database stems from several sources: season ticket subscribers; group season ticket subscribers; single ticket holders who purchase by telephone or mail; and community programs such as "K for Kids," a fundraiser that relies on phone-in pledges. Tickets are sold at the SkyDome, at the Bullpen Souvenir Store, over the "Sport-Line," or toll free at 1-888-OKGOJAYS. Tickets are also available on-line at the Jays' Website.

The Blue Jays's season ticket form asks for the subscriber's name, address, phone number, zip or postal code, and e-mail address. This information, which is stored in a database along with seating options (which fall into several price ranges from preferred to general), is used regularly by the sales staff to design all sorts of marketing initiatives. The zip or postal code indicates a subscriber's neighbourhood, which often pinpoints subculture, social class, income level, and lifestyle. This kind of geographic information can help direct further marketing efforts. For example, if enough subscribers live in a postal code that has a large Asian community, the Blue Jays may consider advertising in Asian-language neighbourhood publications. The database also helps identify fans who purchase high-end seats; they can then be rewarded with special perks.

A space for questions and comments on the ticket form provides additional information to help staff hone in on the right mix of products and services to offer. If a fan indicates that she or he is hard of hearing, the Jays can provide free of charge a hearing aid, called Phonic Ear, that amplifies sound levels and makes the game far more enjoyable. Amateur coaches, players, and parents of little leaguers seeking assistance in fundamental baseball skills can receive information about an inexpensive instructional video titled "A Coaching Clinic."

The e-mail address on the subscription form allows the Jays to communicate easily with individual subscribers. By contacting subscribers one at a time rather than hitting the entire community with direct mail, the Jays reach those who live and breathe baseball, rather than waste valuable marketing dollars on those who don't. E-mail is also a fast way to provide season ticket holders with particulars about ordering postseason tickets over the Internet.

The season ticket form is not the only method the Jays use to collect crucial information. On group ticket sales forms, the staff ask for detailed information. This information enables them to offer group benefits to businesses and other organizations. Through preferred group seating, promotional posters, and announcements of group names on the Jumbotron, the group sales staff really step up to the plate to help businesses and organizations promote themselves.

Database technology enables the Jays to cross-sell their many products and services. Staff marketers match products to consumer profiles to cross-sell products that match demographic, lifestyle, or behavioural characteristics. At the Blue Jays Baseball Camp, an intense, skill-oriented program for boys and girls between eleven and nineteen, registration information (including age) is stored in the database. This gives the Jays the opportunity to mail the campers merchandise information about youth jackets, jerseys, and caps, or Blue Jays Kids Stuff—a youth batting glove, school kit, helmet bank, or MVP bear. These items may be available at retail outlets around Toronto; however, the Jays's database has made it possible to explore selling through direct mail.

Database marketing also helps the Jays retain loyal fans. By tracking season ticket holders, they can offer them special benefits. Loyalty is strengthened by identifying long-standing fans who have generated the most revenue, by creating different messages for new and long-term subscribers, and by finding out exactly what the fans want.

A database this extensive takes time to build, but the investment has paid off for the Toronto Blue Jays. With one-to-one marketing, the Jays hit a home run with the fans every time.

Bibliography

www.bluejays.ca

Questions

1. Why do the Toronto Blue Jays use one-to-one marketing?
2. Why is one-to-one marketing timely?
3. What are the sources of the Toronto Blue Jays' database?
4. Describe some of the ways the Toronto Blue Jays use database technology.

CHAPTER

19

INTERNET MARKETING

Find this chapter on the Student CD-ROM to accompany *The Subject Is Marketing*, Second Canadian Edition, and on the Website (www.lamb.nelson.com).

LEARNING OBJECTIVES

After studying this chapter, you should be able to

1. Have a basic understanding of the origins of the Internet, the birth of e-commerce/e-business, and the evolution of business practices, in particular the marketing function, to meet the needs of the new, dynamic e-nvironment
2. Be familiar with the demographic composition of the global population of Internet users and the characteristics that define e-consumers
3. Appreciate the need for timely, accurate information in the new economy and the new methodologies available to collect market research information
4. Understand the impact of Internet technologies on the market planning process
5. Be able to ask the questions necessary to develop a comprehensive marketing strategy that mixes traditional and new economy methods

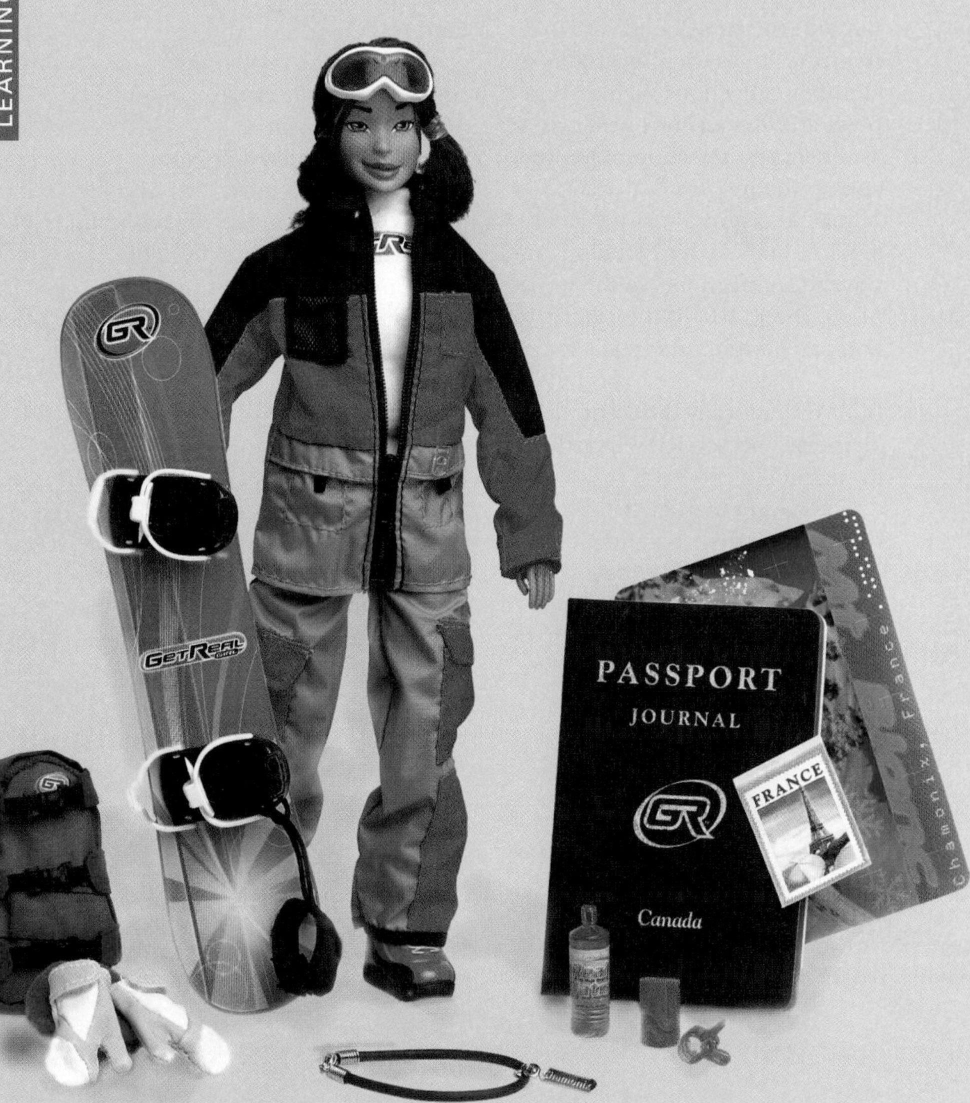

4

marketing miscues

Eatons

Consider this. It's Fall, 2000. There is a flagship department store in a downtown mall that is ready to open. The store is positioned as an "upscale" retailer, with merchandise like the "higher end" of the Bay and the "lower end" of Holt Renfrew. It has exclusive rights to clothing collections such as Tempesta and Apriori by Escada, as well as the largest selection of junior and contemporary Canadian brands and several private label apparel lines such as Studio E and Casual Connection.[1] In the words of the then CEO of the parent company owning the retail store, "the new stores…are expected to offer dramatically different merchandise and service selected to attract new customers."[2]

The target market of this new department store is young, bold achievers with discretionary income and taste to match!

Now consider this. The department store is named Eatons. The T. Eaton Company was purchased by Sears Canada Inc. Sears acquired 18 Eatons department stores and opened 5 stores in key downtown locations under the Eatons brand name. The rest were turned into Sears stores. Sears Canada Inc. also bought the Eatons brand name and trademark.

Promotions for the new store included TV and radio commercials, as well as print ads. TV commercials included 4–5 minute 1940s-style mini-music ads with elements of MGM movie musicals and an Esther Williams finale. The main message was that the store was hip to the younger generation. So why choose music that the "older" customer would relate to? Why take the risk of turning off the core Eatons's customer with confusing messages?

The new Eatons was to look like the retailer described in the opening paragraph. So why name the "new" store with an "old" name?

Pricing is another issue. Given that merchandise is now upscale, so are the prices. However, why are expensive items being sold at the suggested retail price even after other retailers in the same mall are selling the exact same item (including colour) for 25% and 50% off the original price? It appears that Eatons is not to be part of the sales frenzy that major competitor retailers use in their fight to gain customers.

Revenues included in Sears Canada second quarter, 2000 was a gain of $8.9 million related to the acquisition of Eatons. "No gain was recorded in the quarter this year (2001) from the Eatons acquisition"[3]. Are we surprised?

Questions

1. What is the original name communicating to the customer?
2. What are the errors Sears Canada Inc. made in marketing the new retail brand? Consider the 4 "P's".
3. Develop an improved marketing plan.

1. Fawzia Sheikh, "Retail Renaissance," *Marketing Magazine,* December 11, 2000.
2. "Sears Readies Eaton's Brand for Fall 2000 Relaunch," http://pubzone.com/pubzone/stories/sears-eatons.html.
3. "2nd Quarter Results—2001," www.sears.ca.

Critical Thinking

Nike, Inc.

The year 1998 will be remembered in the athletic footwear industry as the end of one marketing era and the beginning of another. In that year, consumers caught the world's leading sport-shoe maker Nike off-guard with a sudden fashion shift away from the flashy basketball shoes the company made famous, as well as a cultural rejection of the brash athletes that wore them and promoted them. As a result, Nike was faced with a difficult dilemma: how to reinvent the meaning of Nike.

The Nike Story

In 1957, the future cofounders of Nike, track coach Mike Bowerman and student Phil Knight, met for the first time at the University of Oregon in Eugene and began what would become a lifelong relationship. Five years later, after completing his MBA, Knight speculated that low-priced, high-tech, well-merchandised athletic shoes from Japan could end Germany's domination of the U.S. athletic shoe industry. Contracting with a Japanese company, Onitsuka Tiger, to supply the shoes, Bowerman and Knight formed a partnership with $500 each and started Blue Ribbon Sports, the progenitor to Nike.

By 1971, Bowerman and Knight decided to end their relationship with Tiger to manufacture their own line of athletic shoes that would push the boundaries of comfort and lightness. What emerged was a brash, young, entrepreneurial company named after Nike, the greek goddess of victory. Less than a decade later, Nike claimed 50 percent of the U.S. running shoe market.

The introduction in 1979 of Nike-Air cushioning, a patented gas pressurized inside a tough, flexible urethane shell to cushion impact, represented a major revolution in athletic footwear design. Sales shot upward as Nike continued to improve on the air-cushioned shoe, introducing the Air Max in 1987 that provided a see-through window in the sidewall of the outsole and ending in 1990 with more than $2 billion in revenue. No longer a small company, Nike now sold shoes in more than forty countries across the globe.

Nike's Marketing Machine

Nike's marketing and advertising evolved along with its innovations in more comfortable and lighter sport shoes. Pairing with Portland, Oregon, advertising agency Wieden & Kennedy in 1982, the two companies generated the kind of creative fireworks that made Nike's swoosh a cultural icon and its irreverent "Just Do It" theme synonymous with the sporting experience and athletic competition all around the world. The campaign, which debuted in 1987, is considered one of the best ad campaigns in history, taking Nike from an 18 percent share of the domestic, sport-shoe business to 43 percent.

A large part of Nike's marketing strength lies in its lucrative athletic superstar endorsements with the likes of Michael Jordan, Charles Barkley, Bo Jackson, and John McEnroe over the last two decades. In exchange for endorsement money, star players sport the company's trademark swoosh on the game floor and in television commercials, increasing Nike's "coolness" factor among its many fans.

Nike's fiscal 1997 global marketing budget, which included athlete endorsements and media advertising, was an estimated $891 million. Measured media advertising, such as print and television, commanded $159 million of this figure. Nike produces some one hundred fifty to two hundred television commercials every year.

The Sport-Shoe Market Cools

From 1994 to 1997, Nike experienced phenomenal growth and soaring revenues. Sales grew almost two and a half times from $3.8 billion in 1994 to an astonishing $9.2 billion in 1997. At the end of 1997, Nike's market share of the athletic shoe market was 47 percent, three times that of its nearest competitor, Reebok International, with 15 percent. The ranks of Nike employees also ballooned from 9,500 employees to 21,800 employees worldwide.

Then, the bottom fell out in 1998. Although the entire athletic shoe industry took a hit as casual and "athleisure" footwear gained in popularity, Nike was hit especially hard. The industry leader posted fiscal 1998 sales of $9.6 billion, up 4 percent, but its fourth-quarter footwear sales plunged 11 percent in the United States. Sales in the United States plunged another 13 percent in its first quarter of the 1999 fiscal year. Nike was left reeling, with millions of boxes of unsold athletic shoes and apparel. Nike CEO Knight blamed an over-saturation of signature products (those products endorsed by star athletes) combined with consumer dismay about athletes' antics for sluggish sales industry-wide of basketball and cross-training shoes, the biggest segments.

Consumer aggravation with the bad-boy behaviour of professional athletes, those stars who provided the backbone to Nike's cool image, certainly contributed to the company's sales decline. Sports professionals' antics, like Denis Rodman's insolent behaviour on and off the court, Charles Barkley's legal troubles, Allen Iverson's drug problems, Latrell Sprewell's alleged assault of his coach, and sportscaster Marv Albert's sex scandal, eroded the effectiveness of sports star endorsements. Sports star misbehaviour even invaded the college level with the gambling scandals at Arizona State University.

Top Ten Athletic Footwear Brands

exhibit A

Rank	Brand	Share of Market 1997 (%)	Share of Market 1996 (%)	Measured Advertising 1997 ($ million)	Measured Advertising 1996 ($ million)
1	Nike	47.0	45.2	159.0	149.0
2.	Reebok	15.2	16.5	55.0	84.0
3.	Adidas	6.1	5.4	21.0	14.0
4.	Fila	6.0	7.7	15.0	13.0
5.	Converse	3.5	2.7	8.0	5.0
6.	New Balance	3.3	2.8	4.0	3.0
7.	Keds	2.2	2.2	3.0	3.0
8.	Airwalk	2.2	2.8	2.0	9.0
9.	Asics	1.6	1.8	2.0	2.0
10	Foot-Joy	1.5	1.5	2.0	2.0
	Total top 10	88.8	88.6	271.0	284.0
	Total market sales	$8,100.0	$7,200.0	$309.7	$320.0

Note: Dollars are in millions. Measured media from CMR. Market share from *Sportitng Goods Intelligence.*

Source: Jeff Jensen, "Athletic-Shoe Markets Look for New Formulas," *Advertising Age,* 28 September 1998, p. S-20.

Further, experts believe Nike's brand ubiquity contributed to the hit. Consumers, saturated with Nike products and Nike-endorsed sports stars, were burned out on the swoosh. The company, which for so long had reveled in its underdog status, was now the top dog and could be found everywhere.

Nike's stumble can also be blamed partly on its misjudgment of America's youth, who traditionally drive the footwear market. College students railed against Nike for its alleged exploitation of child labour in Asia and for its overcommercialization of sports. Teens into extreme sports resented Nike's intrusion into their sports. Kids knew Nike not as the rebel it once was but as the establishment. Nike had lost its "coolness" with America's youth market, who were turning to brown shoes—hiking boots and walking shoes—over Nike's flashy sneakers. Brown shoes now make up about 10 percent of the athletic footwear market and this segment continues to grow.

Nike's Response

The marketing formula that worked for Nike in the past—athlete endorsers, flashy shoes, and brash advertising—was crumbling. The company quickly launched the kinder and gentler "I can" advertising campaign, which broke away from the deified-athletic-endorser model that elevates star athletes to the status of the gods. Instead, the "I can" campaign encompassed messages about products, new technology, community involvement, and athletes—professional and everyday—on a more human scale. The swoosh was noticeably absent from the ads. After a few months, though, the softer "I can" ads faded away, with Knight calling the effort "ineffective." The campaign was followed with the "What are you getting ready for?" campaign that positioned sports training as integral to the average person's lifestyle, focusing on running instead of basketball.

As a result of the downturn, Nike slashed its global marketing budget by $100 million, including athlete endorsement money. Although Nike has let some athlete endorsement contracts expire, it insists that it is not abandoning its athletes, but instead is rethinking how athletes are depicted in ads, moving away from the rhetoric that characterized past marketing campaigns in favour of lower-key approaches. In the latest "What are you getting ready for?" campaign, celebrity athletes were used sparingly, almost anonymously, fulfilling the function of making a product point or a joke that superseded their star personalities.

The Competitive Scene

Nike's competitors did not miss the chance to gain from Nike's slump. Ads from Reebok, the number two sport-shoe marketer, focused on technology and performance, rather than cocky sports superstars, as centre stage in their athletic footwear branding campaigns. In a gutsy move, Reebok dropped Shaquille O'Neal as an athlete spokesperson. Reebok commercials introducing its Icon DMX 10 running shoe featuring new cushioning technology even took a definitive anti-Nike stance. The first spot featured six thousand runners, all clones labelled with the same number—97005, the ZIP code for archrival Nike. The ads were designed to make a statement about the current athletic shoe industry in which all brands look alike and talk alike in an attempt to catch up with Nike.

New Balance, long known for its product focused and "endorsed by no one" advertising stance, tripled its ad budget to launch its ordinary-person-centered "Achieve New Balance' campaign. The ads focused on the theme that sports are important but they're not all that people do. New Balance's campaigns relied on running themes instead of basketball, a sport that demographic research suggests turns off teens and young adults.

The backlash against traditional sports like basketball by teens and young adults has created a market for alternative brands, such as Airwalk and Vans, to dominate. Airwalk, which straddles fashion and performance with products grounded in alternative pop culture and extreme sports, tripled its U.S. television ad budget in 1998. Airwalk and Vans have also initiated major efforts to sell and promote their shoes through their Websites.

Future Marketing and Advertising Efforts

As Nike struggles with the vision of what its future identity should be, several marketing and advertising efforts may possibly push it further along in its quest. New advertising campaigns will focus on Nike's latest technological advance in running shoe design—Visible Zoom Air, or VisiZoom. The innovation consists of thousands of small fibres surrounded by compressed gas that provide enhanced spring action. Because the technology occupies a thinner space, it allows for ultimate responsiveness while maintaining a low profile close to the ground.

Whereas shoe innovations have been harder to come up with in recent years, Nike is revving up its marketing machine with the introduction of the Alpha program. Under the program, Nike will market its most expensive apparel, sporting goods, and sneaker products as a unit—or under the same "halo." For example, an ad might feature an athlete wearing a Nike watch, Nike sunglasses, a Nike jacket, and Nike sneakers. Certain "Alpha Athletes" such as Tiger Woods will be seen wearing Nike from head to toe and even have a say in the products' design.

Nike is also charging head-on into sports it does not currently dominate, most notably soccer. The company poured $40 million in advertising into World Cup '98 telecasts to increase its visibility in the sport, Six World Cup '98 teams—Brazil, Holland, Italy, Nigeria, South Korea, and the United States—competed in uniforms designed by Nike.

Source:

Nike Website at **http://www.nikebiz.com.** *Nike Inc. 1998 Annual Report.* Bob Garfield, "Nike's New 'I Can' Just Doesn't Do It as Well," *Advertising Age,* 19 January 1998, p. 47. Jeff Jensen, "Athletic-Shoe Marketers Look for New Formulas," *Advertising Age,* 28 September 1998, pp. S-20, S-24. Jeff Jensen, "Reebok Blocks New Shoe with Anti-Nike Stance," *Advertising Age,* 25 May 1998, p. 4. Jeff Jensen, "Nike to Slice Marketing by $100 Mil," *Advertising Age,* 23 March 1998, pp. 1, 46. Jeff Jensen, "Performance, Shoe Tech Take Ad Stage for '98," *Advertising Age,* 12 January 1998, pp. 3, 36. Bill Richards, "Tripped Up by Too Many Shoes, Nike Regroups," *Wall Street Journal,* 3 March 1998, p. B1. Joan Voight and Eleftheria Parpis, "Where Did the Magic Go?" *ADWEEK,* 22 June 1998, p. 23.

Questions

1. Since the success of its long-running "Just Do It" advertising campaign, Nike has been struggling with a new identity. What advertising strategies and themes would you suggest Nike undertake to reconnect with its customers?

2. In the past, professional athletes were not always chosen to endorse a company's product because of their role model behaviour on and off the court. In light of consumer's current attitudes toward the transgressions of pro athletes, what role

do you feel they should play in a sport-shoe marketer's promotional campaign?

3. With more, younger consumers turning to brown shoes and alternative sports, what promotional actions can Nike take to become "cool" to the youth market?

4. Nike's Alpha project plans to group the company's best products together in joint promotions. Group together several Nike products with a Nike athlete endorser and write a brief advertising creative and executional plan.

5. Nike has been criticized in global markets for pushing its "bad-boy" image, as it did in its U.S. advertising. Should Nike take a standardized or a customized approach to its global advertising?

Additional Readings

Alice Z. Cuneo and Jeff Jensen, "Fashion Trend-Setters Push to Stay 'Hip' with Youth Niche," *Advertising Age,* 5 October 1998, pp. S-22, S-24.

Pat Sloan, "Keeping It Cool Harder Than Thought, Even on a Budget," *Advertising Age,* 20 October 1997, pp. S-8, S-24.

5

RESULTS

CHAPTER

20

LEARNING OBJECTIVES

After studying this chapter, you should be able to

1. Undertake the strategic market planning that leads to the formal, written marketing plan
2. Develop the marketing objectives that will guide the marketing plan
3. Undertake a thorough situation analysis
4. Select strategic alternatives that match the market situation
5. Build a marketing strategy based on customer value
6. Develop a coordinated marketing mix
7. Implement, evaluate, and control the marketing plan
8. Apply several techniques that help make strategic planning effective

MARKETING STRATEGY: HOW IT ALL FITS TOGETHER

The soft drink giant Cola-Cola Ltd. is moving into the coffee business with a new product directed at the current market craze for sweet, milky-tasting coffee. The product being introduced by Coca-Cola is similar to the very popular frappuccino and mochaccino drinks that have become very trendy among young adults.

The product, named Planet Java, represents "an opportunity to tap into a rapidly growing market," says Christopher Johnston, a group brand manager for Toronto-based Coca-Cola Ltd. "We've had an excellent response to it."[1] The product, launched in September 2001, comes in a multicoloured bottle that looks nothing like typical Coca-Cola soft drink bottles. The bottle is shrink-wrapped in plastic with "psychedelic-type graphics."

Planet Java contains milk, sugar, and coffee and according to the company has a taste similar to a latte. Lattes are very popular with the eighteen-to-thirty-six age group. The product will be available in convenience stores, restaurants, and anywhere else young adults gather, but it won't be cheap. Planet Java will be priced at $1.99 for a 281 mL bottle.

Coca-Cola is launching Planet Java in Canada. One reason for this is the high level of coffee drinking in this country. Nearly three-quarters of adult Canadians are regular coffee drinkers, and Canadians drink 30 percent more coffee per capita than Americans.[2] If Planet Java sells as well as expected, the product will be quickly moved into the American market and distribution will be expanded to supermarkets and vending machines.

Planet Java is similar to the line of frappuccino and mochaccino drinks already being marketed by rival Pepsi-Cola. The Pepsi line is manufactured by Starbucks and then sold through the Pepsi distribution system to grocery stores, convenience stores, and restaurants.

According to Mr. Johnston, Planet Java did so well in pilot tests with coffee drinkers that Coca-Cola decided to launch the product nationally in Canada without further market tests. After testing a variety of flavours, Coca-Cola decided to go with two initially. Javadelik is described as "a rich-chilled coffee flavour"; Caramocha has a decidedly "chocolate and caramel flavour."[3]

Coca-Cola

What can you learn about Coca-Cola's mission and marketing activities from its Website? How well do you feel Planet Java fits into Coca-Cola's marketing plan?

www.cocacola.com

on line

Industry publications have given somewhat mixed but generally favourable reviews to the new Coca-Cola product. Becky McKinnon, president of Timothy's Coffees of the World, a Toronto-based chain of gourmet coffee outlets, wasn't sure that Planet Java really qualified as a coffee product. But she feels that the product will appeal to young, transitional twenty-something consumers who are experimenting with coffee.

Does Coca-Cola have good reason to introduce Planet Java into Canada with no market testing? With a number of competitors already on the market, is Coca-Cola coming into the market too late? What sort of marketing plan is needed to successfully launch Planet Java? If you were the brand manager for Planet Java, what sort of marketing plan would you put together? These issues will be addressed in this final chapter.

Strategic Market Planning in Practice

1
Undertake the strategic market planning that leads to the formal, written marketing plan.

As you know from the previous nineteen chapters, every business requires a strategic marketing plan in order to succeed. **Strategic market planning** is the process of creating and maintaining a fit between the organization's objectives and resources and evolving market opportunities. Every organization, from a small, local tool-and-die shop to the Ford Motor Company, from local governments to the federal government and even to charities, is involved in strategic market planning.

strategic market planning
Creating and maintaining a fit between the organization's objectives and resources and evolving market opportunities.

The marketing plan is part of an overall corporate strategy. The corporate strategy is the central business scheme for utilizing the company's financial, production, R&D, personnel, and marketing resources. Corporate strategy also focuses on the businesses in which the company will participate. When Magna, Canada's largest auto parts company, decided it would assemble complete new vehicles for some of its customers (e.g., DaimlerChrysler and Renault) in Austria, this represented a major commitment of resources; it also raised the possibility that Magna would annoy some of its other automotive customers.

In the strategic planning process, companies try to match their resources and strengths with the opportunities and threats in their business environment. An important consideration in selecting a **corporate strategy** is the firm's capabilities. Firms may have superior capabilities in production technology, R&D, human resources, marketing, or any of a number of different business functions. When a firm has superior capabilities relative to its competitors, it is said to possess a **competitive advantage**. In strategic market planning, it is important to identify competitive advantages and utilize them. Magna has superior hydroforming technology and utilizes this production advantage to win many automotive parts contracts.

corporate strategy
The central business scheme for utilizing the company's financial, production, R&D, personnel, and marketing resources.

competitive advantage
A capability, superior to that of your competitors, that can be utilized as a central part of the company's stategic plan.

Developing the Formal Marketing Plan

Successful marketing planning must anticipate future events and determine appropriate strategies for achieving the organization's objectives. Marketing planning is the basis for all marketing strategies and decisions. Issues such as which products the company will sell, which distribution channels will be used, which

Rollerblade

Typically, some insight into a company's strategies can be found on its Website. Rollerblade has chosen to pursue multiple markets with multiple products. Visit Rollerblade's Website to learn more about its strategies.

www.rollerblade.com

Saturn Logic : If you can return a toaster,
you can return a car.

THE 2002 SATURN S-SERIES Sometimes people change their minds. At Saturn, we think people have a right to. That's why every Saturn comes with a 30-day or 2,500 km money back guarantee. It's our way of showing confidence in what we sell.

2.9% finance rate up to 60 months

$178 mo/48 mos. 3.9% lease rate $1,700 downpayment $14,995 MSRP

The Saturn Difference: 30-Day or 2,500 km Money Back Guarantee • No Hassle No Haggle Buying Experience • Dent-Resistant Polymer Panels • 3 year or 60,000 km Warranty • 5 year or 100,000 km Powertrain Warranty • Our MSRP includes freight, PDI and excise tax, if applicable

SATURN.
A DIFFERENT KIND *of* COMPANY. A DIFFERENT KIND *of* CAR.
Buy online at saturncanada.com • 1-888-4SATURN

License, taxes and a refundable security deposit are extra. Lease payment is based on a lease of 80,000 km over 4 years with an extra charge of 12 cents per kilometre over that distance. Rates apply only to customers with approved credit. Example: $10,000 at 2.9% APR, the monthly payment is $180 for 60 months. Cost of borrowing $755. If you'd like to buy your 2002 Saturn vehicle at lease end, it's $6298 for the 2002 SL 1SA plus taxes. Retailers are free to set individual selling and lease prices.

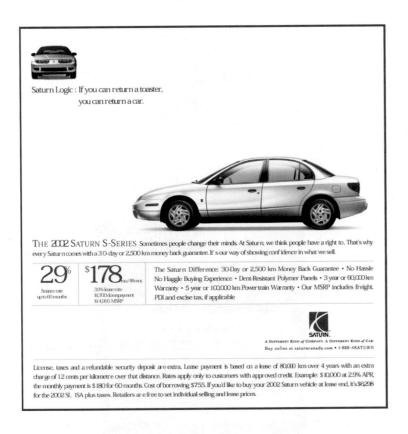

Extensive long-term marketing planning was needed before General Motors committed well in excess of $2 billion to develop Saturn Motors.

marketing communications will be undertaken, and what prices will be charged are all outlined in the marketing plan. The **formal marketing plan** serves as a guidebook of marketing activities for the marketing manager. *The formal marketing plan is the end result of the marketing planning process.*

formal marketing plan
A written document that acts as a guidebook of marketing activities for the marketing manager.

A formal marketing plan has a number of benefits for a firm:

- It serves as a road map to tell everyone in the organization how it is going to get from where it is today to where it wants to be at some point in the future.
- It identifies the role each individual is to play in accomplishing the company's objectives.
- It identifies the resources that will be needed to achieve corporate objectives.
- It helps stimulate thinking to make better use of limited resources.
- It pinpoints a company's strengths and weaknesses.
- It helps the company better understand its competitors.
- It helps the marketing manager become aware of problems, opportunities, and threats.
- It helps set proper priorities.

exhibit 20.1

The Marketing Planning Process

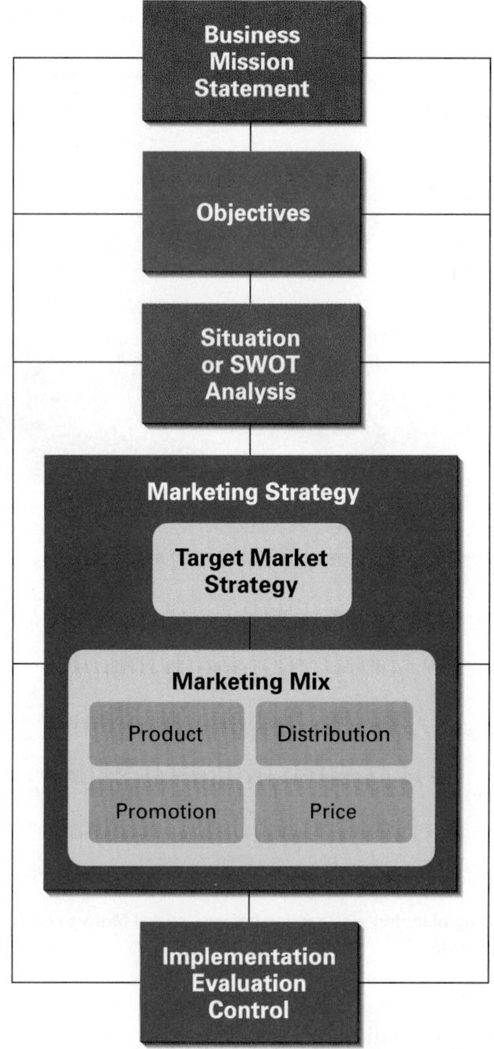

- It helps coordinate all marketing activities.
- It establishes dates and deadlines and allows for meaningful review.

The formal marketing plan must always be committed to writing. If it isn't, well thought out strategies will be forgotten, deadlines will be overlooked, and details will be lost. After the marketing plan is written down, it can serve as a reference point for future strategic marketing activities.

There are many different ways to present a formal marketing plan. Regardless of how it is presented, some elements are always present. The business mission and objectives are defined; a situation analysis is performed; a target market is delineated; and the components of the marketing mix are established. Exhibit 20.1, which was also presented in Chapter 2, shows these elements. A marketing plan may also include budgets, implementation timetables, plans for marketing research, and elements of advanced strategic planning.

A complete marketing plan allows the organization to achieve its marketing objectives, succeed in the marketplace, and grow. However, the marketing plan is only as good as the information it contains and the effort, creativity, and thought that went into it. A good marketing information system and a wealth of competitive intelligence (see chapters 7 and 8) are critical to a successful marketing plan.

Perhaps the greatest value of a well-conceived marketing plan is that it provides management with a working document aimed at achieving specific results. It is important, however, not to confuse the marketing plan with marketing planning. Marketing planning is the activity that goes into developing each part of the marketing plan. The marketing plan is the written document that is the outcome of planning.

Define the Business Mission

The starting point in developing a marketing plan is the company's mission statement. Understanding the organization's mission helps ensure that marketing goals and objectives are compatible with how top management views the organization. A firm's **mission statement** is a clear and concise statement—generally one or two paragraphs—that explains the organization's reason for existing. It is based on a careful analysis of the benefits sought by present and potential customers and on an analysis of existing and anticipated environmental conditions. The firm's long-term vision, embodied in the mission statement, establishes boundaries for all later decisions, objectives, and strategies. Examples of mission statements are provided in Exhibit 20.2.

mission statement
A clear and concise statement that explains the organization's reason for existing.

A mission statement should focus on the market or markets the organization is attempting to serve rather than on the good or service offered or the company's desire to earn a profit. FedEx's mission statement (**www.fedex.com**) puts

exhibit 20.2

Mission Statement Examples

Gerber's Mission Statement

The people and resources of the Gerber Products Company are dedicated to assuring that the company is the world leader in, and advocate for, infant nutrition, care, and development.
www.gerber.com/contact us

Reader's Digest Mission Statement

The Reader's Digest Association, Inc., is built on a heritage of service. Today our company is a global publisher and world leader in direct mail marketing. Our magazines, books and home entertainment products provide customers with hours of reading, listening and viewing pleasure. The legacy of service and quality live on—timeless ideals guiding us in our mission: to profitably develop, produce and market high quality products that enrich, inform and entertain people all over the world.
www.readersdigest.com

UPS Mission Statement

Customers—Serve the ongoing package distribution needs of our customers worldwide and provide other services that enhance customer relationships and complement our position as the foremost provider of package distribution services, offering high quality and excellent value in every service.
People—Be a well-regarded employer that is mindful of the well-being of our people, allowing them to develop their individual capabilities in an impartial, challenging, rewarding, and cooperative environment and offering them the opportunity for career advancement.
Shareowners—Maintain a financially strong, manager-owned company earning a reasonable profit, providing long-term competitive returns to our shareholders.
Communities—Build on the legacy of our company's reputation as a responsible corporate citizen whose well-being is in the public interest and whose people are respected for their performance and integrity.
www.ups.com

The Body Shop

Some companies combine company mission statements with societal or ethical values. What do you think this does for a company?

www.bodyshop.com

on line

people first, service second, and profit third. A well-devised mission statement for any organization should answer five basic questions:

1. Who are we?
2. Who are our customers, and how will we serve them?
3. What does our organization stand for?
4. What differentiates our organization from others?
5. What impressions does this organization want key publics (e.g., customers, employees, the public, government agencies) to have of us?

A mission statement that answers each of these questions provides a sound starting point for the marketing plan. The mission statement should tell everyone within the organization what the organization stands for and why it exists.

In devising the mission statement, management must remember that if the statement is too broad, it will be meaningless. A statement of "satisfying the transportation needs of all people in the world" is probably too broad even for the giant General Motors Corporation. A mission statement that is too broad can lead a company into developing plans and strategies in areas where it has limited strengths. The performance of Starbucks slipped recently when it expanded into areas such as tea, full-service restaurants, compact discs, and product licensing. Starbucks Chairman Howard Schultz now acknowledges that some of these strategic decisions were a mistake. Possibly Starbucks expanded too widely because its mission statement—"to establish Starbucks as the most recognized and respected brand in the world"—was too broad (**www.starbucks.com**).

On the other hand, an overly narrow mission statement may constrain a firm from moving into potentially profitable areas of business. In an earlier chapter we used the term *marketing myopia* to describe the problem of viewing a firm or its markets too narrowly. It would be myopic for Blockbuster Entertainment to view itself as being only in the video rental business instead of being in the home entertainment business.

strategic business unit (SBU)
A subgroup of a single business or collection of related businesses within the larger organization.

Large organizations may have to develop a mission statement and marketing plan for each **strategic business unit (SBU)** within the organization. A properly defined SBU will have a distinct mission and specific target market, control over its own resources, its own unique competitors, and plans independent of the other SBUs in the organization. Sony has a number of SBUs, including the following: Sony Music (music CDs and videos), Sony Electronics (consumer electronics, business electronics, and computer products), Sony Movies (films and videos from Sony subsidiary companies such as TriStar and Columbia), Sony Television (Sony produces *Jeopardy* and *Days of Our Lives* and also produced *Seinfeld*), Sony Games (video games and video game players), Sony Theatres (Sony movie theatres), Sony Gear (apparel products), and Sony Worldwide (music and radio programming).

Guiding the Marketing Plan Through the Marketing Objectives

2
Develop the marketing objectives that will guide the marketing plan

Marketing objectives establish the path that the marketing plan will take. As Casey Stengel, former major league baseball player and manager of the New York Yankees, once said, "If you don't know where you're going, you might end up somewhere else." If you don't have solid marketing objectives to set the course for your plan, your marketing plan is liable to take you in a direction you don't want to go.

The objectives of the marketing plan will develop naturally from the mission statement and will anticipate the problems and opportunities facing the company. An objective can be viewed as a problem to be solved or as an opportunity to be exploited. Essentially, marketing objectives are the core of the marketing plan: all parts of the plan involve either establishing objectives or setting out to achieve them.

A company's marketing objective is a clear, measurable statement of what is to be accomplished through the company's marketing activities by a specific point in time. The point in time is the end of the period covered by the marketing plan. Marketing objectives should meet a number of criteria if they are to be of any use in developing the rest of the marketing plan. These criteria are outlined in Exhibit 20.3.

exhibit 20.3

Criteria for Well-Stated Marketing Objectives

- Suitable—Marketing objectives must support the company's mission and move the company in the direction of accomplishing its mission.
- Measurable—The objectives should be specific so that at the end of the marketing plan period you can measure accurately whether the objectives have been accomplished.
- Feasible—The objectives must be feasible. If the stated objectives are impossible to accomplish, they will motivate no one.
- Acceptable—The objectives must be acceptable to the people in your organization responsible for accomplishing them. If people are to "buy in" to the objectives, they must agree with them.
- Motivating—The objectives should challenge people to work hard. If objectives are too easy to reach, they will not motivate.
- Understandable—The objectives should be stated in clear, simple language.

Sound marketing objectives provide direction for lower-level marketing managers. They serve as motivators by creating something for employees to strive toward. They force all marketing executives to clarify their thinking. They form a basis for controlling marketing activities.

Understand Your Company's Market Situation

3

Undertake a thorough situation analysis

Before an appropriate strategy can be developed, marketing managers must understand the current and likely future environment in which the company's product or service will be marketed. A situation analysis, or SWOT analysis, involves reviewing the firm's strengths (S) and weaknesses (W) along with the external opportunities (O) and threats (T) facing it.

A SWOT analysis is a simple procedure that provides important information for developing the marketing strategy. It involves assessing the fit between the organization's strengths and the opportunities that exist in the marketplace. At the same time, it identifies what the organization cannot do (because of its weaknesses) and what the marketing strategy must guard against (the threats). Much of the information for the SWOT analysis will come from the company's decision support system and its ongoing marketing research activities (review Chapter 7 for a complete discussion).

In an earlier chapter the term *environmental scanning* was used to describe the process of analyzing the firm's marketplace situation. Exhibit 20.4 identifies what might be included in a thorough situation analysis.

Dofasco

Examine the number of different product/market segments served by Dofasco, one of Canada's largest steel companies. Each of these product/market segments would represent an SBU.

www.dofasco.ca

on line

A SWOT analysis must be thorough to be useful, and the more thorough, the more useful. In most companies a number of SWOT analyses must be conducted, as the environment will be different from product to product and service to service. A major stamping operation (e.g., the Canadian company FABCO) may be selling its products to automotive customers, airlines, construction companies, and others. Each of these customer groups constitutes a different environment. A SWOT analysis undertaken for the automotive sector would not likely be sufficient to develop a marketing strategy for the company's airline customers.

brand competitor
A competitor that is very much like you in terms of products offered for sale, price, promotion, distribution, and the market(s) targeted.

A SWOT analysis must examine all current and potential competitors. Some competitors will be much like the firm; these are often referred to as **brand competitors**. But competition extends beyond this. For example, Pepsi is an obvious brand competitor for Coca-Cola. However, Coca-Cola also competes with products in other categories (e.g., coffee, tea, juice, beer, powdered drinks) and even with

exhibit 20.4

Elements of a Thorough SWOT Analysis

External analysis	Internal analysis
• Customer analysis: Segments, motivations, unmet needs. • Competitor analysis: Identity, strategic units, performance, image, objectives, strategies, culture, cost structure, strengths, weaknesses. • Market analysis: Size, projected growth, profitability, entry barriers, cost structure, distribution systems, trends, key success factors. • Environmental analysis: Technological, governmental, economic, cultural, demographic scenarios, information-need areas.	• Performance analysis: Profitability, sales, shareholder value analysis, customer satisfaction, product quality, brand associations, relative cost, new products, employee capability and performance, product portfolio analysis. • Determinants of strategic options: Past and current strategies, strategic problems, organizational capabilities and constraints, financial resources and constraints, strengths, and weaknesses.
↓ Opportunities, threats, trends, and strategic uncertainties	↓ Strategic strengths, weaknesses, problems, constraints, and uncertainties

↓ Strategy Identification and Selection

Source: Adapted from David A. Aaker, *Strategic Market Management*, John Wiley & Sons, 1998, p. 19.

generic items such as water. Kodak had always viewed Fuji, Konica, and Polaroid as its main competitors, but with the appearance of digital cameras in the market, Sony and Canon have become major new competitors. Major new brand competitors can show up in the market at any time, as the "Global Perspectives" box discusses. Gathering information on competitors was discussed in Chapter 8.

Finally, it is important for a SWOT analysis to examine issues from the perspective of consumers. It doesn't matter what a company thinks of its reputation, product quality, and service. What matters is what the customers think of its reputation, product quality, and service.

The matrix in Exhibit 20.5 illustrates that a marketing manager should try to match the company's strengths with marketplace opportunities, and that over time the company must try to convert weaknesses into strengths and threats into opportunities.

Dofasco is divided into five major product groups and seven major customer groups. Each of these would be treated as a separate SBU in Dofasco's marketing planning.

Strategic Opportunities

Once the situation analysis has been completed, the marketing manager should be able to begin identifying strategic opportunities. These opportunities are sometimes referred to as *strategic windows.* As discussed in an earlier chapter, a strategic window is a situation in which a marketplace opportunity is especially well suited to a strength of the firm and the firm is able to respond quickly to the opportunity.

The name is appropriate in the sense that most opportunities, or windows, don't remain open for long. Companies must respond quickly, before they close. In 2001, Heinz recognized a marketplace opportunity among kids—the biggest consumers of ketchup—for a line of coloured ketchups to make eating more fun. Heinz, already the market leader in traditional red ketchup, introduced Blastin' Green ketchup, which became a major new product success. Blastin' Green ketchup increased Heinz's market share in the ketchup category from 54 percent to 59 percent.[4]

exhibit 20.5

A SWOT Matrix

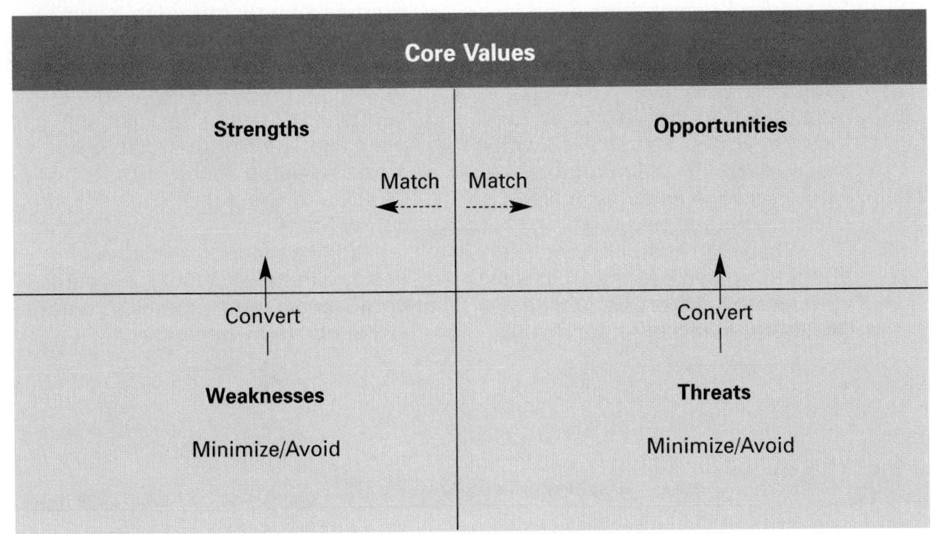

Source: Adapted from O.C. Ferrell, M.D. Hartline, G.H. Lucas and David Luck, *Marketing Strategy*, The Dryden Press, 1998, p. 66.

global perspectives

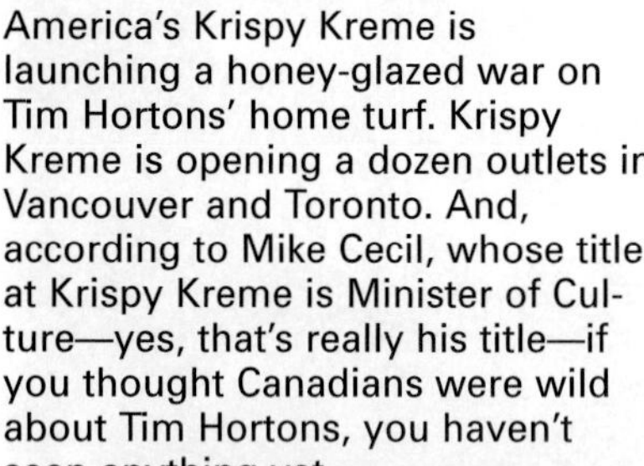

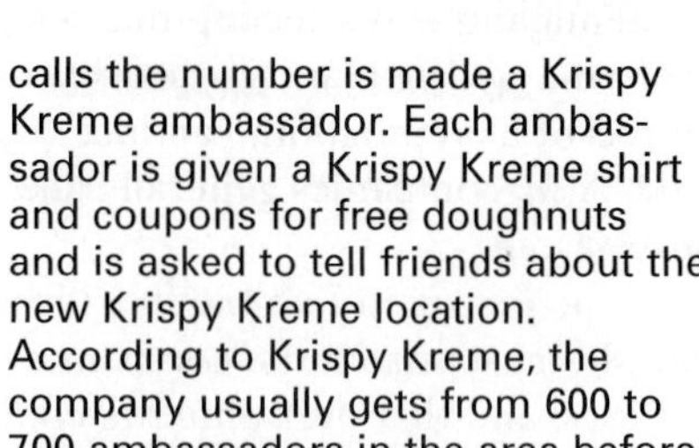

A Holey War on Canadian Soil

America's Krispy Kreme is launching a honey-glazed war on Tim Hortons' home turf. Krispy Kreme is opening a dozen outlets in Vancouver and Toronto. And, according to Mike Cecil, whose title at Krispy Kreme is Minister of Culture—yes, that's really his title—if you thought Canadians were wild about Tim Hortons, you haven't seen anything yet.

For every Tim Hortons story we have seen in its "True Stories" ad campaign, Mike Cecil has a reply. Mike talks about the guy whose car was broken into. The thief ignored all the expensive camera equipment in the car, but stole a box of Krispy Kreme doughnuts. Cecil also claims that 350 cases of Krispy Kreme honey-glazed doughnuts are loaded onto a U.S. Army C-130 Hercules every Wednesday, are flown to a NATO base in Keflavik, Iceland, are put up for sale in the commissary at nine the next morning, and are gone by noon.[5] Now Krispy Kreme is coming after Tim Hortons, the undisputed leader in the Canadian coffee and doughnut market.

In the United States, its home market, Krispy Kreme sales grew 33 percent in 2000. Average sales per outlet for Krispy Kreme are US$2.8 million, compared to US$650,000 per outlet for its major American competitor, Dunkin' Donuts. Investors like Krispy Kreme as much as doughnut lovers do. When Krispy Kreme went public in April 2000, share prices jumped from $21 to $71.[6]

Compared to Tim Hortons, Krispy Kreme is really quite small. Currently, Krispy Kreme operates fewer than 200 outlets in twenty-seven American states and has total sales revenue of slightly under US$500 million. In comparison, Tim Hortons operates nearly 2,000 outlets and has sales of nearly C$2 billion. But when we compare doughnuts, Krispy Kreme will make and sell 1.4 billion in 2001, just about the same number as Tim Hortons. Tim Hortons' higher revenues are the result of selling many items (e.g., soups, sandwiches, bagels, soft drinks, pies, cakes). Krispy Kreme sells pretty much only coffee and doughnuts.

Krispy Kreme has a very good reason for coming to Canada to take on Tim Hortons: Canada is the promised land of doughnuts. Canadians eat far more doughnuts than Americans. This year, the average Canadian—men, women, and children—will consume over fifty doughnuts.[7] Most of those doughnuts are, of course, made by Tim Hortons.

A big part of Krispy Kreme, besides the taste of its honey-glazed doughnuts, is the novelty of its outlets. Each Krispy Kreme store is equipped with an industrial-grade doughnut-making machine that is capable of punching out between 3,000 and 12,000 doughnuts an hour. Part of the Krispy Kreme experience is watching the cartoonish machines pumping out doughnuts right before your eyes. Whenever a fresh batch is ready, a neon sign in front of the Krispy Kreme store lights up with the message: "Hot Doughnuts Now." As soon as the sign lights up, customers come running.

Whenever Krispy Kreme is about to open a new store, it puts up a sign on the property with a telephone number. Anyone who calls the number is made a Krispy Kreme ambassador. Each ambassador is given a Krispy Kreme shirt and coupons for free doughnuts and is asked to tell friends about the new Krispy Kreme location. According to Krispy Kreme, the company usually gets from 600 to 700 ambassadors in the area before the store is even opened!

Toronto is a logical market for Krispy Kreme to enter, as it is the largest in Canada. Vancouver represents a good opportunity, as Tim Hortons isn't as strong in the West as it is in the East. However, both Vancouver and Toronto are very expensive markets in which to do business.

Many American companies have come into Canada and made a big impression. Wal-Mart and Home Depot are just two of many examples in the retail sector. Keep your eyes open—the doughnut war may be coming to a location right around the corner.

What do you think of some of Krispy Kreme's promotional activities? Do you think they will work as well in Canada as they have in the United States? Do you think Krispy Kreme can be a formidable competitor to Tim Hortons? What sort of marketing plan would you develop for Krispy Kreme, being a smaller competitor coming up against a giant like Tim Hortons? What sort of marketing plan should Tim Hortons develop to counter this new brand competitor?

You can learn more about Krispy Kreme—its activities, company history, and expansion plans—at **www.krispykreme.com.**

Strategy Design

4
Select strategic alternatives that match the market situation

Once a strategic window has been identified, a marketing strategy for responding to the opportunity is needed. Exhibit 20.6 illustrates broad marketing strategies (discussed in an earlier chapter), which begin with a consideration of the company's current products and markets. Simple strategic alternatives that a firm can explore include the following: (1) *market penetration*—increasing market share among existing customers; (2) *market development*—attracting new customers to existing products; (3) *product development*—creating new products for present markets; and (4) *diversification*—introducing new products to new markets.

Identifying and Selecting Strategic Alternatives

In identifying and selecting marketing strategies, all of the information gathered in the marketing planning process to this point must be used. Different companies use different tools to analyze and categorize the information they have gathered. Also, companies generally take one of two approaches to the timing of profits: some pursue profits right away, while others begin by increasing market share, and later pursue profits. In the long run, market share and profitability are compatible goals. Many companies have long followed this credo: build market share, and profits will surely follow. Toyota and Honda were willing to lose money in North America for a number of years to build market share. Now that sales of these Japanese car makers have grown, North America is a highly profitable market for them. On the other hand, Lou Gerstner, CEO of IBM (**www.ibm.com**), has stressed profitability and stock valuation over market share.

Krispy Kreme is using a market development strategy to move into Canada and take on market leader Tim Hortons.

A number of tools exist for helping marketing managers select strategic alternatives. Two of these tools, the *portfolio matrix* and the *market attractiveness/company strength matrix*, will be discussed next.

Portfolio Matrix Recall that large organizations engaged in strategic planning may create strategic business units. Each SBU may have its own growth potential, associated risk, and ROI objective. Management must strike a balance among the SBUs that yields the desired growth and profits for the organization overall, with an acceptable level of risk. Some SBUs generate large amounts of cash over and above what is required for operating expenses or for additional marketing, production, R&D, or inventory. Other SBUs need cash to grow. The challenge is to balance the organization's "portfolio" of SBUs for the best long-term performance.

3M

How would you characterize 3M's overall strategy based on the splash page of its Website? Create a portfolio matrix for 3M based on the information on its Website.

www.3m.com

on line

At General Electric, sales, profitability, and share value grew enormously over the twenty years that Jack Welch was CEO.

To determine the future cash contributions and cash requirements that can be expected for each SBU, managers can use the Boston Consulting Group's **portfolio matrix**. The portfolio matrix classifies each SBU according to its present or forecasted growth and market share. The underlying assumption is that market share and profitability are strongly linked. The measure of market share used in the portfolio approach is relative market share—that is, the ratio between the company's share and the share of the largest competitor. Thus, if firm A has a 50 percent share and its largest competitor has 5 percent, the ratio is 10 to 1. If firm A has a 10 percent market share and its largest competitor has 20 percent, the ratio is 0.5 to 1.

Exhibit 20.7 is a hypothetical portfolio matrix for a large computer manufacturer. The size of the circle in each cell of the matrix represents dollar sales of the SBU relative to dollar sales of the company's other SBUs. The following categories are used in the matrix:

- *Stars:* A **star** is a market leader and is growing fast. Computer manufacturers have identified notebook computers as stars. Star SBUs usually enjoy big profits but need a lot of cash to grow rapidly. The best marketing tactic is to protect existing market share by reinvesting earnings in product improvement, better distribution, more promotion, and production efficiency. Management must strive to capture new users as they enter the market.
- *Cash cows:* A **cash cow** is an SBU that generates more cash than it needs to maintain its market share. It is in a low-growth market, but the product has a dominant market share. In Exhibit 20.7, personal computers are categorized as cash cows. The basic strategy for a cash cow is to maintain market dominance by being the price leader and by making technological improvements in the product. Managers should avoid extending the basic line unless they can dramatically increase demand by doing so. Instead, they should allocate excess cash to product categories where the growth prospects are greatest. Clorox Corporation owns Kingsford Charcoal, Match Charcoal Lighter, Prime Choice steak sauce, and a restaurant chain. Its cash cow is Clorox bleach, which has a 60 percent market share in a low-growth market. Clorox Corporation has been highly successful in stretching the Clorox line to include a liquid formula in addition to the original dry bleach.
- *Problem children:* A **problem child**, also called a **question mark,** shows rapid growth but poor profit margins. It has a low market share in a high-growth industry. Problem children need a great deal of cash. Without cash support, they eventually become dogs. For problem children there are three basic strategy options: invest heavily to gain better market share, acquire competitors to get the necessary market share, or drop the SBU. Sometimes a firm can reposition the SBU's products, thereby moving them into the star category.
- *Dogs:* A **dog** has low growth potential and a small market share. Most dogs eventually leave the marketplace. In the computer manufacturing industry, mainframe computers have become dogs. Two other dogs are Warner-Lam-

portfolio matrix
Classifies each SBU by its present or forecasted growth and market share.

star
In the portfolio matrix, a business unit that is a fast-growing market leader.

cash cow
In the portfolio matrix, a business unit that usually generates more cash than it needs to maintain its market share.

problem child (question mark)
In the portfolio matrix, a business unit that shows rapid growth but poor profit margins.

dog
In the portfolio matrix, a business unit that has low growth potential and a small market share.

exhibit 20.6

Marketing Strategy Matrix of Heinz

	Present product	New product
Present market	Market penetration: Heinz sells more traditional red ketchup.	Product development: H.J. Heinz increases ketchup market share by adding coloured ketchups.
New market	Market development: Heinz expands ketchup sales to China, a new market for the company.	Diversification: Heinz adds seaweed ketchup (a new product) to be sold in Japan (a new market).

bert's Reef mouthwash and Campbell's Red Kettle soups. Frito-Lay has produced several dogs, including Stuffers cheese-filled snacks, Rumbles granola nuggets, and Toppels cheese-topped crackers—a trio irreverently known as Stumbles, Tumbles, and Twofers. The strategy options for dogs are to harvest or divest.

After classifying the company's SBUs in the matrix, the next step is to allocate future resources for each. With regard to this, there are four basic strategies:

exhibit 20.7

Portfolio Matrix for a Large Computer Manufacturer

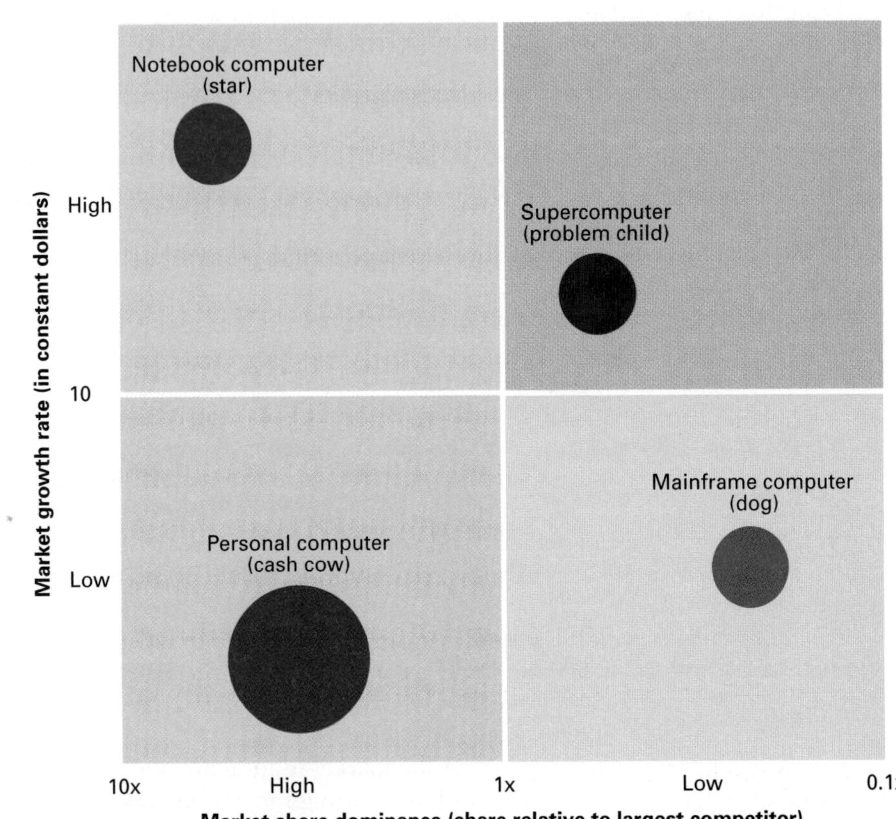

General Electric

General Electric developed the market attractiveness/company strength matrix for marketing planning and marketing strategy development purposes. What can you learn about GE's markets and marketing strategies at its Website?

www.ge.com

on line

- *Build:* If the SBU has the potential to become a star—it is probably a problem child at present—building is an appropriate goal. The organization may decide to sacrifice short-term profits and use its financial resources to make it a star. In the 1990s, Procter & Gamble built Pringles from a money loser into a record profit maker.
- *Hold:* When the SBU is a successful cash cow, a key goal will certainly be to maintain it as one—that is, to preserve market share so that the organization can benefit from the strong positive cash flow. Bisquick has been a cash cow for General Mills for over two decades.
- *Harvest:* This strategy is appropriate for all SBUs except those classified as stars. The basic goal is to increase the short-term cash return without too much concern for the long-run impact. It is especially appropriate when more cash is needed from a cash cow whose long-run prospects are unfavourable because of a low market growth rate. Lever Brothers has been harvesting Lifebuoy soap for a number of years with little promotional backing.
- *Divest:* It is often appropriate to dump SBUs with low shares of low-growth markets. This strategy is most suitable for problem children and dogs. Procter & Gamble dropped Cincaprin, a coated pain reliever, because of its low growth potential. General Motors has decided to divest itself of Oldsmobile by the end of the 2004 model year.

Smaller companies that are not divided into SBUs can also use the portfolio matrix. Strategy alternatives for each *brand* in the firm's product mix can be identified exactly as described above. The portfolio approach to strategy determination was "invented" by the Boston Consulting Group (**www.bcg.com**).

Market Attractiveness/Company Strength Matrix A second model for selecting strategic alternatives, originally developed by General Electric, is known as the **market attractiveness/company strength matrix**. The dimensions used in this matrix—market attractiveness and company strength—are richer and more complete than those used in the portfolio matrix, but are also harder to quantify.

market attractiveness/company strength matrix
A tool for allocating resources among SBUs on the basis of how attractive a market is and how well the firm is positioned to take advantage of that market's opportunities.

Exhibit 20.8 presents a market attractiveness/company strength matrix. The horizontal axis, *business position*, refers to how well positioned the organization is to take advantage of market opportunities. Does the firm have the technology it needs to penetrate the market effectively? Are its financial resources adequate? Can manufacturing costs be held below those of the competition? Will the firm have bargaining power over suppliers? Can the firm cope with change?

The vertical axis measures *market attractiveness*, which is expressed both quantitatively and qualitatively. Some attributes of an attractive market are high profitability, rapid growth, a lack of government regulation, consumer insensitivity to price increases, a lack of competition, and availability of technology. The grid is divided into three overall zones of attractiveness for each dimension: high, medium, and low.

SBUs (or markets) with low overall attractiveness should not be entered. If the firm is already in them, it should either harvest or divest the SBUs. It should selectively maintain markets with medium attractiveness. When attractiveness begins to slip, it should withdraw from the market.

Investment is most appropriate when the market is attractive and the company is well positioned to enter it successfully. Through marketing research, Black & Decker uncovered the "serious do-it-yourself" market. These consumers were willing to pay a premium price for quality home tools. For example, research

exhibit 20.8

Market Attractiveness/ Company Strength Matrix

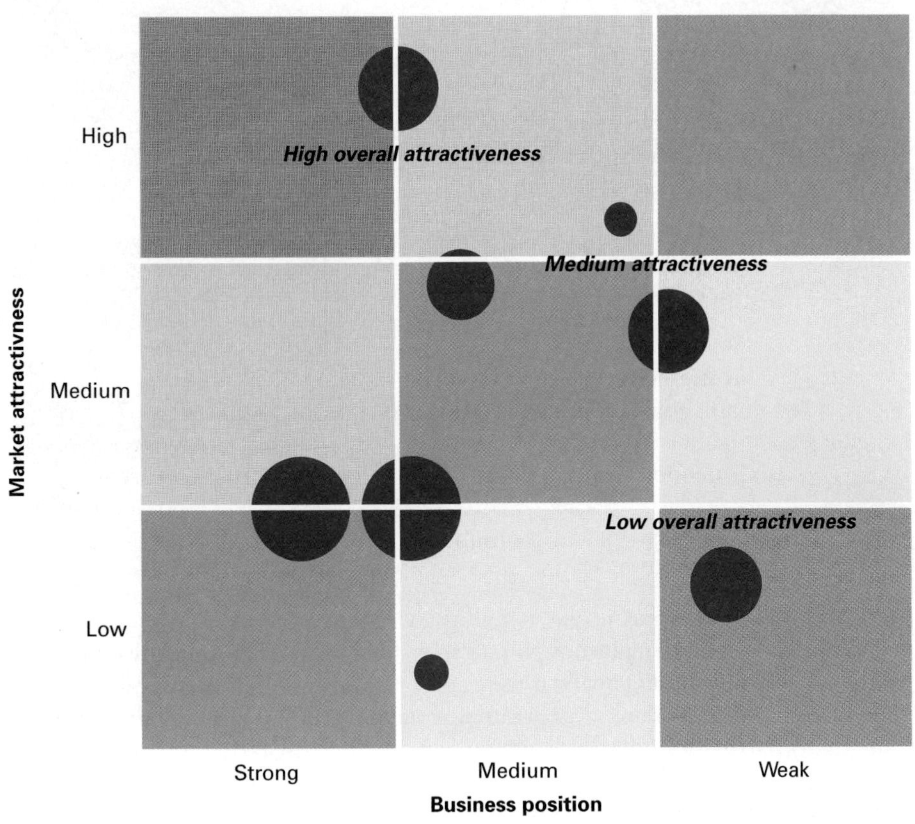

found that these people wanted a cordless drill that didn't run out of power before the job was complete. Black & Decker responded with a new line called Quantum.

Sustainable Advantage

To ensure a successful marketing plan, marketing managers must find a sustainable advantage. A firm is said to enjoy a sustainable advantage when it possesses capabilities that allow it to serve customers' needs better than the competition. A **sustainable advantage** is one or more unique aspects of an organization that cause target consumers to patronize that firm rather than competitors. A sustainable advantage may exist in the firm's image. IBM has advantages in its reputation and in its ability to provide solutions for entire systems. Sustainable advantages can arise from any element in the marketing mix. Superior product quality gives a firm such as Hewlett-Packard a competitive advantage over other makers of laser printers. Wal-Mart's very low-cost distribution system gives it an advantage over other discount department stores. Intel's superior advertisements have made the Intel Pentium computer chip a household term. Firms can possess advantages in functions other than marketing—in human resources, R&D, or production technology.

sustainable advantage
One or more unique aspects of an organization that cause target consumers to patronize that firm rather than competitors.

Two basic sources of sustainable advantage are superior skills and superior resources. *Superior skills* are unique capabilities that distinguish a firm's managers and workers from those of competing firms. Because of Steve Jobs and the many skilled people he attracts to the company, Apple possesses superior computer design capabilities. *Superior resources* are more tangible. Popular brand names such as Coke, Nike, and Gucci have immeasurable value. Sony has large, high-tech manufacturing facilities that cannot be easily copied. Magna International offers the world's most advanced hydroforming capabilities.

Magna possesses many technical advantages that have helped it become the largest auto parts company in Canada and one of the ten largest in the world.

A company must be able to maintain its sustainable advantage. Any company can make golf balls, but Nike is the only company that can make golf balls with Tiger Woods' name on them. Magna's hydroforming advantage is secure because of the many patents it holds on its technology. A company trying to compete solely on the basis of price may find that type of advantage quickly copied by a competitor. Many economy airlines collapsed after their low fares were matched by the major airlines.

To be sustainable, the identified competitive advantage must be based on the competencies the firm possesses. Also, it must be desired by the target market and must be an advantage relative to direct competitors.[8] Thus, there is no point to a firm pursuing a quality strategy unless it has the R&D and manufacturing technology to deliver a quality product. Furthermore, a company cannot maintain a service advantage over its competitors unless it has the delivery system, sales network, and corporate culture that will maintain high levels of service.

For an advantage to be sustainable, it must be valued by the target customers. A well-conceived strategy supported by company competencies will still fail if those competencies aren't important to customers. Procter & Gamble failed with Pringles potato chips for many years because it concentrated on offering a consistent product, a long shelf life, and a crush-proof container. These were qualities based on Procter & Gamble's competencies, but they didn't interest customers: the market was concerned only with taste. Only after Procter & Gamble improved the taste of Pringles did its sales pick up.

In developing a marketing strategy, it is important to identify sustainable advantages in relation to the competition. The key issue is the firm's ability to convince customers that what it is offering is superior to what the competition is offering.

Creating a Marketing Strategy Based on Customer Value

5
Build a marketing strategy based on customer value

A marketing strategy involves selecting one or more target markets and developing and maintaining a marketing mix that will produce mutually satisfying exchanges with those target markets. This is illustrated in Exhibit 20.9.

Starting with the Target Market

In examining Exhibit 20.9, several things need to be remembered. First and most important is that all marketing strategy planning begins with a consideration of the firm's target market. This should be clear from the previous nineteen chapters, but it is important to point out this fact once again.

Second, a marketing strategy represents a blending of the firm's product strategy, price strategy, promotion strategy, and place strategy. All parts of the marketing mix must fit together, like the pieces of a puzzle, if the marketing strategy is to work.

Any market segment that is targeted must be fully described. Demographics, psychographics, and buyer behaviour must be assessed. Buyer behaviour was covered in Chapters 4 and 5. If segments are differentiated by ethnicity, multicultural aspects of the marketing mix should be examined. If the target market is international, it is especially important to consider differences in culture, economic and technological development, and political structure that may affect the marketing plan.

The Importance of a Coordinated Marketing Mix

6 Develop a coordinated marketing mix

Among many other things, the marketing manager must ensure that all the pieces of the marketing mix puzzle fit together properly to create a well-coordinated marketing strategy. Any marketing mix is only as good as its weakest component. The first pump toothpastes were distributed over cosmetic counters, and failed. Not until pump toothpastes were distributed the same way as tube toothpastes did the products succeed. The best promotion and the lowest price cannot save a poor product. Similarly, an excellent product with poor distribution, pricing, or promotion will probably fail. Tender Care, a disposable diaper that kept babies drier and that had the endorsement of pediatricians as superior in preventing diaper rash, failed because the small company that produced Tender Care diapers could not match the pricing, promotion, or distribution efforts of larger competitors such as Procter & Gamble and Kimberly-Clark.

exhibit 20.9

A Marketing Strategy Starts with the Target Market

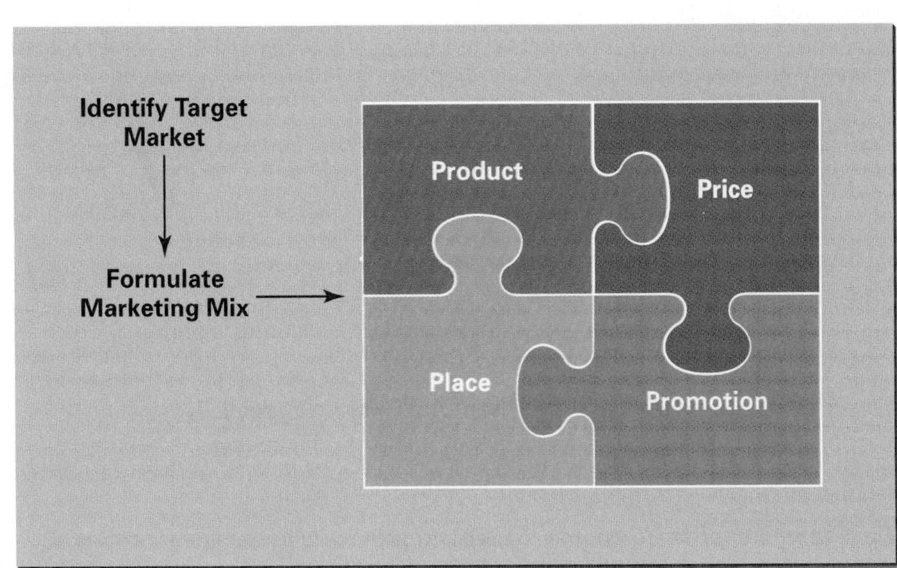

ethics in marketing

Undercover Marketing: Does It Work?

You are at a bar with some friends. A group of people next to you is raving about a new organic energy drink. They're young, professional looking, and having a good time. "You've really got to try this stuff," one of them says to you.

Intrigued, you order a bottle of the new energy drink. What you don't know is that the young people next to you are being paid to create interest in it. This is called undercover marketing, and it's being heralded by some as a powerful tool for creating interest in new products. Critics call it deceptive and unethical.

Does undercover marketing work? One of the promotion firms that uses this tactic for its clients says that some of his groups have been able to get nearly everyone in a bar to try the product they are pushing.

There are other undercover marketing approaches. Doormen at upscale apartment buildings are paid to leave boxes with the name of a retail store in the lobby. The purpose is to make residents think their neighbours are shopping at the store. Another tactic is to plant people in Internet chat rooms to promote a new movie, recording, or anything else.

In defence of this form of undercover marketing, is it really much different from companies paying Steven Spielberg to place their products in his movies, or paying star athletes to claim they use a particular product? "I'm fascinated by the whole thing," says Chris Legein, president of Mosaic Marketing Services Canada, a Toronto firm. "I think it's a great idea."[9] What do you think of this form of promotional strategy?

Variations in marketing mixes do not occur by chance. Astute marketing managers devise marketing strategies to gain advantages over their competitors and to best serve the needs and wants of a particular target market. By manipulating elements of the marketing mix, marketing managers can fine-tune the customer offering and achieve competitive success.

Let's look at one example of a hugely successful marketing strategy: the one devised for the Sony Walkman. The *product*'s design was consistent with the *promotion* theme: "quality sound for people on the go." The *product* itself was pocket-sized and had lightweight headphones. The entire unit weighed only 280 grams. The name Walkman was consistent with the main product advantage being offered. The *promotion* featured people "on the go" wearing Walkman sets. The product was mass distributed (*place*), so it was easy to buy. The *price* was affordable to young people, the target market. Each element of the Walkman marketing mix was consistent with the rest, and this contributed to making the marketing program a huge success.

In their efforts to assemble successful marketing plans, companies can sometimes cross ethical boundaries, as this chapter's "Ethics in Marketing" box indicates.

Building the Marketing Plan Around Customer Value

Marketing managers have organized marketing plans in various ways. One approach—which should be central to all marketing programs—involves creating value for the target market.

Value is a difficult issue to get a precise handle on, because it means different things to different people. To some, value means high quality; to others, it means low price. The most common view of value relates customer benefits to costs. A simple formula for customer value might be this one:

CV = cb + cc

Customer value = Customer benefits/Customer costs

It is important to remember that value is relative: it can be judged only in comparison to what is being offered by other firms.

customer benefits
Everything that a customer receives when dealing with a firm.

Customer Benefits **Customer benefits** represent everything a customer receives when dealing with a firm. Benefits include the quality of the product

Caterpillar

Caterpillar has long been recognized as a leader in creating customer value. Caterpillar has created customer value by providing high-quality products, ensuring that parts and servicing are widely available, and developing a strong sales force.

www.caterpillar.com

on line

received, the product's features, the image associated with the brand name, the service provided with the product, and everything else of importance the customer acquires when buying the product. For service firms, benefits are represented by the quality and reliability of the service offering and by the atmosphere provided with the service offering.

customer costs
Everything that the customer gives up to obtain the benefits provided by the product or service that is being purchased.

Customer Costs **Customer costs** include everything the customer must give up to obtain the benefits provided by the product or service. The most obvious cost is the money the customer must pay for the product or service. However, there are other costs besides this. Examples: the time and effort it takes to make the purchase, and the risks involved in making the purchase.

Customer costs can be reduced by making the product or service more widely available; this reduces the time it takes to make the purchase. When a product or service is widely available—for example, when it can be purchased over the telephone, by mail order, or through the Internet—less effort is involved in making the purchase. Guarantees and warranties reduce the risks associated with the purchase.

Caterpillar creates a high level of customer satisfaction and customer value through its high-quality products and services.

Creating Customer Value Once marketing managers understand the benefits the target market is looking for and the costs their target customers incur in a purchase, they can design marketing programs that are geared to maximizing customer value. Value can be enhanced by adjusting each element of the marketing mix to increase customer benefits or reduce costs. 7-Eleven stores enhance customer value by making products available in more convenient settings relative to supermarkets. Godiva offers a strong image and a guarantee of high-quality chocolate. McDonald's reduces customer costs (risks) by providing a known product at a known level of quality at its restaurants in any country in the world.

Different target market customers will have different perceptions of value. So marketing managers must understand their target markets—in particular, their customers' perceptions as to what value *means*—and set their marketing mixes accordingly.

Putting the Marketing Plan into Action

7
Implement, evaluate, and control the marketing plan

After the pieces of the marketing mix have been assembled, the marketing plan must be launched.

Implementation

intended strategy
What the organization intended—the formal marketing strategy as found in the marketing plan.

realized strategy
What actually occurs—the marketing strategy put into play in the marketplace.

Implementation is the *how* of marketing planning. Implementation involves arriving at detailed job assignments, activity descriptions, timelines, budgets, and communication. Many organizations fail when it comes to implementing strategy because their *intended strategy* and their *realized strategy* turn out not to be the same. The **intended strategy** is what the organization *wants* to happen; the **realized strategy** is what actually does happen.[10] Marketing plans are doomed if they aren't properly implemented.

Implementation is part of the final stage of the marketing planning process. If each element of the marketing plan is to be implemented successfully, the marketing manager must do the following:

- Take complete responsibility for implementing the plan. This includes taking responsibility for seeing that each strategy element is initiated and that each strategy element is undertaken as described in the plan.
- Track all activities, tactics, and strategies, and compare what is taking place with what is outlined in the plan.
- Track the environment as the plan is being implemented to see what activities may have to be altered to conform to the changing marketplace.

Evaluation and Control

Once implementation of the marketing plan is underway, the plan must be periodically evaluated. Evaluation involves gauging the extent to which marketing objectives, as outlined in the plan, are being achieved. A second issue is financial. Unit sales, market shares, revenues, and costs must all be monitored against what was budgeted or forecasted in the plan.

As the marketing plan unfolds, its effectiveness must be monitored. The plan must be controlled to ensure that the *realized strategy* is the same as the *intended strategy*. Corrective actions must be taken when necessary to bring the strategy back in line with the plan's goals. Then the results must be evaluated in light of those goals.

Control is often achieved through a marketing audit. As described in an earlier chapter, a marketing audit is a thorough, systematic evaluation of the goals, strategies, structure, and performance of the marketing organization. A marketing audit has four characteristics:

- *Comprehensive*: It covers all the major marketing issues facing the organization, not just trouble spots.
- *Systematic*: It takes place in an orderly sequence and covers the organization's marketing environment, internal marketing system, and specific marketing activities. The diagnosis is followed by an action plan that contains both short-run and long-run proposals for improving overall marketing effectiveness.
- *Independent:* It is usually conducted by an inside or outside party that is independent enough to be objective and to have top management's confidence.
- *Periodic*: It is carried out on a regular schedule instead of only during a crisis. Any organization can benefit greatly from a marketing audit.

A marketing audit develops a full profile of the organization's marketing efforts and provides a basis for developing and revising the marketing plan. It should isolate weaknesses in the marketing plan and recommend corrective actions. The elements of a complete marketing audit are shown in Exhibit 20.10.

The support of upper management is a critical element of any strategic marketing plan. Brookstone's CEO, Michael Anthony, has actively helped remodel all regular and seasonal stores.

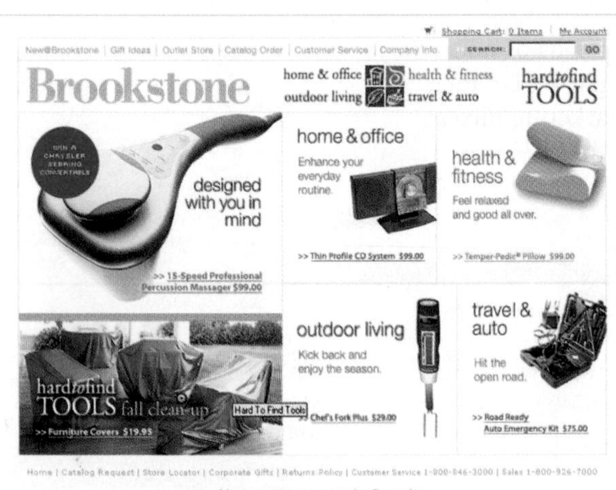

exhibit 20.10

Guide to Conducting a Marketing Audit

I. Mission and Goals

A. Does the corporate mission statement offer a clear guide to the company's product-markets? If not, how should the mission statement be altered to provide such a guide?

B. Have objectives been established for the company as a whole and for marketing in particular? What are they, and do they provide clear direction?

C. Is information available for the review of company progress toward objectives, and are the reviews conducted on a regular basis? When was the last review?

D. Has past marketing strategy been successful in meeting corporate/marketing objectives?

E. Are opportunities or problems pending that may require altering current marketing strategies? What are these opportunities and/or problems?

II. Marketing Strategy

A. Situation analysis

1. Is marketing's role and responsibility in the overall corporate strategy clearly specified?
2. Are responsibility and authority for marketing strategy assigned to one executive?
3. How well is the marketing strategy working? Do problems exist? What are they?
4. Are changes likely to occur in the marketing environment that may affect the current marketing strategy? What are these changes?

B. Marketing plan and organization

1. Are annual and longer-range marketing plans being developed? Are they being used?
2. Are the responsibilities of the various members in the marketing department clearly specified? Is each member's input to the marketing plan clear? Is each member's responsibility for the marketing plan clear?
3. What are the strengths and limitations of the key members of the marketing staff? What is being done to develop people to their full potential?
4. Is the organizational structure for marketing appropriate for devising and implementing marketing plans?

C. Target markets

1. Has each target market been clearly defined, and has its importance to the firm been established?
2. Have demand, industry, and competition in each target market been analyzed, and have key trends, opportunities, and threats been identified?
3. Has the proper target market strategy for each market segment been identified and adopted?
4. Should repositioning or exit from any product-market be considered?

D. Objectives

1. Have objectives been established for each target market, and are these consistent with overall company objectives and available resources? Are the objectives realistic? Is achievement of objectives being monitored?
2. Are sales, cost, and other information available for monitoring the progress of planned performance against actual results?

3. Are regular appraisals made of marketing performance? If not, why not?
4. Where do gaps exist between planned and actual results? What are the probable causes of the performance gaps?

E. Marketing program

1. Are all elements of the marketing program fully integrated and coordinated?
   Is the role selected for each mix element consistent with the overall corporate/marketing objectives, and does it properly complement other mix elements?
2. Are adequate resources available to carry out the marketing program? Are resources committed to target markets according to the importance of each?
3. Are allocations to the various marketing mix areas too low, too high, or about right in terms of what each is expected to accomplish?
4. Is the effectiveness of the marketing program appraised on a regular basis?

III. Marketing Program Activities

A. Product

1. Is the product mix geared to the needs that the firm wants to meet in each product-market?
2. Does the firm have a sound approach to product planning, and is marketing involved in product decisions?
3. Are additions to, modifications of, or deletions from the product mix needed to make the firm more competitive in the marketplace?
4. Is the performance of each product evaluated on a regular basis?

B. Channels of distribution

1. Has the firm selected the type and intensity of distribution appropriate for each of its product-markets?
2. How well does each channel reach and penetrate important target markets?
3. Are channel intermediaries carrying out their assigned functions properly?
4. Is the physical distribution function being managed as an integrated set of activities?
5. Are desired customer service levels being reached, and are the costs of doing this acceptable?

C. Pricing

1. How sensitive are target markets to price variations?
2. What role and objectives does price have in the marketing mix?
3. How do our pricing strategy and tactics compare to those of our major competitors?
4. Is a systematic approach used to establish prices?
5. Are there indications that changes may be needed in pricing strategies or tactics?

D. Advertising and sales promotion

1. Have a role and objectives been established for advertising and sales promotion in the marketing mix?
2. Is the budget adequate to carry out the objectives assigned to advertising and sales promotion?
3. Do the promotional channels used represent the most cost-effective means of communicating with target markets?
4. Do advertising copy and content effectively communicate intended messages?
5. How well does the advertising program measure up in meeting its objectives?

E. Sales force

1. Are the role and objectives of personal selling in the marketing mix clearly specified and understood by the sales organization?
2. Do the qualifications of salespeople correspond to their assigned role?
3. Is the sales force of the proper size to carry out its function, and is it efficiently deployed?
4. Are sales force results in line with management's expectations?
5. Is each salesperson assigned performance targets, and are incentives offered to reward performance?
6. Are sales force compensation levels and ranges competitive? Are good salespeople being lost?

IV. Implementation and Control

A. Have the causes of all performance gaps been identified?

B. Is implementation of planned actions taking place as intended? Is implementation being hampered by other functional areas of the firm (e.g., manufacturing, finance)?

C. Does the marketing plan require modification because of changing conditions, competition, or other factors?

D. Has the audit revealed areas requiring additional study before action is taken?

Effective Strategic Planning

Apply several techniques that help make strategic planning effective

Effective strategic planning requires continual attention, creativity, and management commitment:

- Strategic planning should *not* be an annual exercise; marketing managers should *not* go through the motions and then forget about strategic planning until next year. It *should* be an ongoing process, because the environment is always changing and the firm's resources and capabilities are always evolving.
- Sound planning is based on creativity. Managers should challenge assumptions about the firm and the environment and establish new strategies. The major oil companies developed the concept of the gasoline service station in an age when cars needed frequent and rather elaborate servicing. They held on to the full-service approach; meanwhile, independents responded quickly

to new realities and moved to lower-cost self-service and convenience store operations. The majors took several decades to catch up.

- Perhaps the most critical element in successful strategic planning is top management's support and participation. Michael Anthony, CEO of Brookstone, racks up hundreds of thousands of frequent flyer miles searching the world for manufacturers and inventors of unique products that can be carried by Brookstone in both retail outlets and catalogues. Anthony has co-developed some of these products and has also been active in the remodelling efforts of Brookstone's 200 permanent and seasonal stores. Anthony's participation is paying off in higher revenues and earnings per share.[11]

LOOKING BACK

Look back at the story about the introduction of Planet Java by Coca-Cola. Coca-Cola had to conduct a great deal of strategic marketing planning before introducing this new product. You should now understand that planning is a continuous process. The strategies for Planet Java, like those for any new product, may need to be modified as market tastes change and competition looms.

You should now be able to identify the marketing plan elements for Coca-Cola's introduction of Planet Java, including a measurable marketing objective, the components of a situation analysis, and an initial marketing mix program. You should also be able to identify the target market for Planet Java and describe the basic elements of its marketing mix. Finally, you should be able to visualize certain aspects of Coca-Cola's implementation, evaluation, and control procedures.

Summary

1 Undertake the strategic market planning that leads to the formal, written marketing plan. To be successful, every organization needs to undertake strategic market planning. The marketing plan is a written document that acts as a guidebook of marketing activities for the marketing manager. By specifying objectives and defining the actions required to attain them, a marketing plan provides the basis on which actual and expected performance can be compared.

There is no set outline for a marketing plan to follow; however, there are some basic similarities across marketing plans. Because the marketing plan serves as the road map to guide marketing strategy, it must be written down. Otherwise, important issues may be forgotten or overlooked.

2 Develop the marketing objectives that will guide the marketing plan. Before the details of a marketing plan can be developed, goals and objectives for the plan must be delineated. Without objectives, there can be no basis for evaluating the effectiveness of the plan. Marketing objectives are the core of the marketing plan, in the sense that everything in the plan aims at achieving them. Sound marketing objectives will be suitable, measureable, feasible, acceptable, motivating, and understandable.

3 Undertake a thorough situation analysis. The situation analysis, or SWOT analysis, is geared to identifying the firm's strengths (S) and weaknesses (W) and marketplace opportunities (O) and threats (T). Environmental scanning is used to conduct the SWOT analysis. The six macroenvironmental forces most often studied are social, demographic, economic, technological, political and legal, and competitive. The SWOT analysis should lead to the identification of a sustainable competitive advantage. The marketing manager must work to match

strengths with opportunities, and to convert weaknesses to strengths and threats to opportunities.

4 Select strategic alternatives that match the market situation. Four major strategic marketing alternatives are market penetration, product development, market development, and diversification. The portfolio matrix is a method of determining the profit potential and investment requirements of a firm's SBUs by classifying them as stars, cash cows, problem children, or dogs, and then determining appropriate resource allocations for each. A more detailed alternative to the portfolio matrix is the market attractiveness/company strength matrix, which measures company and market viability. Following the matrix analysis, strategy options of build, hold, harvest, and divest can be considered.

5 Build a marketing strategy based on customer value. All marketing strategy must begin with a consideration of the firm's target market. Companies must give target customers a reason to purchase from them rather than from competitors. To this end, the firm must offer superior customer value relative to its competitors. Customer value can be thought of as the relationship between the level of customer benefits provided and customer costs incurred.

6 Develop a coordinated marketing mix. The marketing mix is a blend of product, place/distribution, promotion, and pricing strategies. For a marketing mix to result in a successful marketing strategy, all elements of the marketing mix must be coordinated. If any element of the marketing mix is out of place, the entire marketing mix program is likely to fail.

7 Implement, evaluate, and control the marketing plan. Implementation involves putting the marketing plan into action. Poor implementation can result in the failure of an otherwise well-conceived plan. It is important to ensure that the realized plan is the same as the intended plan. Evaluation involves comparing the outcome of the marketing plan against what was forecasted in the plan. Control provides the mechanisms for taking corrective action. Control is often exercised through the a complete marketing audit.

8 Apply several techniques that help make strategic planning effective. Management must realize that strategic planning is an ongoing process and not a once-a-year exercise. Also, good strategic planning involves a high level of creativity. Finally, successful strategic planning relies on top management's support and cooperation.

Do You Know These Terms?

brand competitor 532
cash cow 536
competitive advantage 526
corporate strategy 526
customer benefits 542
customer costs 543
dog 536
formal marketing plan 527
intended strategy 543
market attractiveness/company strength matrix 538
mission statement 529
portfolio matrix 536
problem child (question mark) 536
realized strategy 543
star 536
strategic business unit (SBU) 530
strategic market planning 526
sustainable advantage 539

Discussion and Writing Questions

1. You are the owner of a small business. Your business has grown over the past several years without the benefit of any formal planning. You now have reached the size where you feel that a marketing plan is necessary. However, you are not sure whether it is necessary to commit the plan to writing. Could you simply communicate it orally to your employees? Argue in favour of a written plan.
2. Identify any well-known company. What would be a good mission statement for that company? Check out the company's Website to see if you can find its actual mission statement. Compare the company's actual mission statement with what you felt was an appropriate mission statement for the company.
3. Krispy Kreme Doughnuts is just moving into Canada to compete with the undisputed leader in the Canadian market, Tim Hortons. What would be a reasonable marketing objective for Krispy Kreme in its first year in Canada? What would be a reasonable five-year objective?
4. Break into groups of four. Have each member of the group identify one product for which he or she can describe a clear, sustainable competitive

advantage. Have each person identify one product for which he or she cannot think of a sustainable competitive advantage. As a group, come to a consensus about which product has the clearest sustainable competitive advantage, and which most clearly offers no advantage.

5. Pick out a well-known company. Gather as much information about its products as you can from its Website. From the information you are able to gather and from what you know about the company, put together a portfolio matrix for the company.
6. Using the portfolio matrix you developed in question 5, determine an appropriate marketing strategy for each of the company's SBUs or products.
7. In 1980, Eatons was one of the most successful retailers in Canada. That same year, Wal-Mart had no stores in Canada. Today, Wal-Mart is one of the most successful retailers in Canada, while Eatons has gone through bankruptcy and has been purchased by Sears Canada. What basic marketing strategy issues can you identify that have made Wal-Mart's marketing plan so successful while Eatons' has failed?

Application for Small Business

Karen Taylor is ready to retire, and she's only thirty-three. The owner of Karen's Chocolates began making chocolate novelty candies when she was sixteen and still in high school. Karen's road to early retirement began when she took a chocolate-making course. "I found it fun and then I had all these chocolates, so I had to sell them," Karen recalls.[12]

Karen began showing samples of her chocolates to shops in her neighbourhood and was soon selling chocolates to forty stores. By the time she graduated from high school and moved on to Algonquin College, she was ready to expand. Karen set up kiosks at four shopping malls and hired part-time help to staff them.

After finishing at Algonquin College in 1991, Karen spent $70,000 outfitting a small retail store in Ottawa's Westgate Shopping Centre. The entire $70,000 came from Karen's savings on the sales from the four kiosks.

Sales at the retail store, Karen's Chocolates, grew so rapidly that Karen opened a small chocolate manufacturing plant. Karen's Chocolates now sells not only her own creations but other chocolates purchased from forty other suppliers.

After ten years of running Karen's Chocolates, Karen is now ready to retire. At thirty-three, she wants to start raising a family.[13]

Questions

1. Assume that you have decided to purchase Karen's Chocolates. You are preparing a marketing plan. What is an appropriate mission statement for Karen's Chocolates (or whatever new name you would give to the business)?
2. State one clear marketing objective that you would set.
3. What strengths, weaknesses, opportunities, and threats might you face as you take over the business?
4. What strategic alternatives are open to you?
5. On a portfolio matrix, how might you classify Karen's Chocolates?
6. Briefly describe the elements of the marketing mix that you would put together for your new business.

Eureka! Ranch: Big Time Marketing Planning Comes to PEI

Since founding Richard Saunders International in 1986, Doug Hall's client list has read like the *Fortune* 500. Companies that have paid $150,000 for three-day sessions at the Eureka! Ranch include Coca-Cola, Procter & Gamble, Frito-Lay, PepsiCo, Disney, Kellogg, Compaq Computer, Nike, Ford, DaimlerChrysler, Johnson & Johnson, American Express, NASCAR, and just about every other big-name company you can think of.

After graduating with a degree in chemical engineering, Doug Hall spent ten years in marketing at Procter & Gamble. Even with all of the world-class marketing talent at P&G, Doug Hall still stood out as one of the best at the company. In one year, Doug helped bring nine new products to market. With this valuable experience behind him, Doug was ready to try it on his own.

Richard Saunders International (**www.eurekaranch.com**) was formed in Doug's basement in 1986. Richard Saunders was the pen name used by Benjamin Franklin when he wrote *Poor Richard's Almanac*. Initially, Richard Saunders International was divided into two businesses: (1) a new product idea division, and (2) a market research division.

Doug Hall, a very inventive/creative type, was more interested in the new product work he was doing and soon sold the market research business. Richard Saunders International achieved early success and the business quickly moved from Doug's basement to an estate which Doug named Eureka Mansion. In 1997, Doug built a much larger complex alongside Eureka Mansion and gave it the name Eureka! Ranch. The seminars and training sessions conducted by Doug's company are undertaken at the Eureka! Ranch. Doug and his wife and three children now live in Eureka Mansion.

Doug's company, which is now divided into three SBUs, undertakes a full range of marketing planning and marketing strategy activities for its clients. The client sessions might take place at the Eureka! Ranch, or Doug can send a team of his "Trained Brains," as he calls them, to your company. Sessions at the Eureka! Ranch take place in large "play" rooms filled with video games, jukeboxes and toys. It's not unusual for a Eureka! Ranch session to begin with a Nerf gun fight. Doug feels that fun leads to more creative output.

Richard Saunders International is currently divided into three businesses: Eureka Inventing, TrailBlazer Training, and Merwyn. Eureka Inventing is the original business of Richard Saunders International. Eureka Inventing sessions generally run for three days at the Eureka! Ranch and include the client's top marketing people and a team from Doug's company. The unorthodox and highly creative sessions might be geared toward generating new product ideas, new line extensions, new advertising campaigns, new advertising positioning for products, promotion and PR programs, or turnaround strategies for failing products, or full marketing planning. In one recent session with Gardetto, a snack food company, well over 200 new product ideas were generated the first morning. By evening, this number was whittled down to 31 very good ideas, which would be discussed further the next morning.

FACTORY TOURS
CAVENDISH FIGURINES LTD.

TrailBlazer Training is the on–client site portion of the business. Sessions ranging from one day to a week or more (at $50,000 per day) can cover any of the topics covered in Eureka Inventing programs as well as sessions on how to make your corporation more creative.

Merwyn is the newest of Doug Hall's businesses. Merwyn is a computer simulation test marketing and expert coaching software program. Based on the experiences Richard Saunders International has had with new product successes with its clients and further data from a number of major research organizations, Merwyn will assist clients in forecasting the probability for success for new product concepts and make recommendations for improving the success chances for the concept.

The success of Richard Saunders International has brought fame and wealth to Doug Hall. He has been featured on the cover of many business magazines and has a net worth well into seven figures. For his one-hour lectures, Doug Hall commands fees of $20,000 and more. With all this, Doug is still restless. One recent avenue for Doug's energy was an expedition to the North Pole.

At forty-two, Doug still searches for more to do. He recently decided to change his corporate and life mission. One new direction he has taken is to extend his expertise and knowledge to small businesses that generally wouldn't be able to afford the services of his company. Doug now devotes several days a month, along with his staff, to assisting small entrepreneurs. If things work out, Doug would like to put together a number of travelling "Trained Brain Teams" that would take a mini-version of the Eureka! Ranch program on the road to small businesses at affordable prices.

Doug decided to test market his small business program on Prince Edward Island. Why there? Doug's

mother is from New Brunswick, and Doug has a vacation home on PEI. Furthermore, PEI has many small businesses that would never otherwise have a chance to meet for several days with a world-famous marketing guru.

Doug Hall organized a one-day creativity seminar for four small PEI businesses: Cavendish Figurines, Wooly Wares, Island Windchimes, and Mic Mac Productions. Cavendish Figurines Ltd. (**www.cavendishfigurines.com**) creates and sells heirloom-quality figurines based on characters from great literary classics (Anne of Green Gables is a leading seller). The company has been in business since 1989 and has seven full-time employees. Wooly Wares (**www3.pei.sympatico.ca/ cjmacleod/**) is a retail store operated on John and Carol MacLeod's sheep farm. Wooly Wares sells hand-made wool felt products. Island Windchimes (**www.islandwindcraft.com**) is essentially a one-man business. Peter Baker makes and sells approximately 1,000 hand-tuned wind chimes a year. Mic Mac Productions (**www.peisland.com/micmac/crafts.htm**) sells handmade native crafts such as beadwork, carvings, drums, pipes, masks, pottery, rattles, headdresses and moccasins.

After the one-day creativity seminar with the owners of Cavendish Figurines, Wooly Wares, Island Windchimes, and Mic Mac Productions, Doug arranged to meet with each of the business owners for a two-hour one-on-one session.

Doug Hall approached the two days he would spend with the PEI entrepreneurs with two goals. First, he wanted to help them think smarter and more creatively. Second, he wanted to make sure that each business approached marketing planning logically by clearly identifying target markets, identifying its business mission, and identifying a clear competitive advantage it had to offer. Each began to develop a marketing plan that would focus on its competitive advantage.

How did things go? Inside of two hours at Cavendish Farms, Doug and his crew had developed a new promotional brochure for the business, recommended a new display for its leading figurines, developed a new promotional message, and recommended a new product assortment. Wooly Wares was persuaded to concentrate on several product offerings that were clearly superior to others the company crafted, and Doug and his group came up with some catchy brand names for the products. Peter Baker at Island Windchimes was advised to stay with top-of-the-line chimes, where he had an advantage over the competition, and not get into low-priced products. As well, new product descriptions were developed, along with new brand names, for a new promotional campaign. Mic Mac Productions was advised to change its name to Mic Mac Legends, build a promotional campaign around the legends associated with its products, expand its product line, develop a new pricing strategy, and organize product combination packages.

Source

CBC, *Venture*, "PEI Meets Doug Hall," March 13, 2001.

Questions

1. What do you think Doug Hall's corporate mission statement might have been in 1986 when he founded Richard Saunders International? What do you think it might be today?
2. What would you describe as the sustainable competitive advantage of Richard Saunders International?
3. Into which cell of the portfolio matrix do you feel each SBU of Richard Saunders International falls?
4. Can the marketing strategies used for the large clients of Doug Hall work for small entrepreneurial businesses?
5. Do you feel that Doug Hall might learn something from his work with small businesses that he can successfully incorporate into his marketing strategies for large clients?
6. Visit the Websites of Eureka! Ranch and the four small PEI businesses assisted by Doug Hall. What can you learn about marketing strategy planning from these sites?
7. (Optional) Have you ever had an innovative new product idea? If so, visit the Merwyn Website of Eureka! Ranch (**www.merwyn.com**). You can describe the new product concept to the Merwyn simulation model and it will give you a forecast of the product's likelihood of success.

marketing miscues

DoubleClick is a global Internet advertising company that delivers more than 5 billion on-line ads per month via its fourteen country networks. Through these sophisticated country networks, advertisers can reach computer users in over eighty countries with one ad purchase. These ads, which include sponsorships, pop-ups, and banners, can target users in any country in their native language. The company's yearly sales revenue was almost $200 million in 1999. However, this was only a small portion of industry on-line ad revenue of $3 billion in 1999—a market that is growing and expected to reach $12 billion by 2003.

DoubleClick, a 1995 entrepreneurial start-up, does not perform the creative aspects of advertising. Rather, the company sells and manages ads that appear on a network of around 1,500 Websites that represent nearly 50 percent of all Web traffic. The company also provides the technology for tracking and customizing on-line ads, thereby allowing companies to tailor advertising for specific audiences (a service for which advertisers willingly pay a premium). Through the 1999 purchase of Abacus, a direct marketing company, DoubleClick garnered the power to cross-reference consumers' on-line habits with their names and addresses in databases at Abacus. This ability to link on-line habits with a person's identity ignited consumer outrage in early 2000.

Observing the buying habits of consumers is not a new phenomenon. Surveillance cameras view consumers as they shop, and credit card purchases make it easy for companies to understand consumers' buying practices. These buying practices can be linked easily to individual consumer identities, yet credit card companies do not sell this information to other companies to use in their advertising. Never before had an external organization been able to track computer activity on the Web and cross-reference (or associate) that activity with a person's name and address. The closest companies had come to being able to do this was if the computer user provided an e-mail address. Additionally, most retailers on the Web provided privacy information guaranteeing that personal information would not be sold to other companies. While tracking by software files called "cookies" allow for the monitoring of user movements on the Internet, user habits are not linked to a person's name and address. The potential for DoubleClick and Abacus to link specific individuals and their Internet habits (site visits, purchases) is enormous and could lead to DoubleClick having the most comprehensive consumer database in the world.

Consumers as well as consumer protection groups were outraged that DoubleClick would even think about invading the privacy of Internet users in this manner. The onslaught of lawsuits and accompanying negative publicity led to a decline in DoubleClick's stock value. Additionally, two business partners, Altavista and Kozmo, announced that they would either withdraw ads linked to DoubleClick or limit user information made available to the company.

Faced with such problems, DoubleClick halted its plan to link the capabilities of DoubleClick and Abacus. The company's CEO admitted the company had made a mistake and announced that it would not use its data mining capabilities until the Internet industry and the federal government had established guidelines to protect user privacy. Additionally, in an attempt to regain trust, the company created the DoubleClick Privacy Advisory Board and a new position of chief privacy officer. The company also began a national campaign to educate consumers about on-line privacy.

Bibliography

Mark Anstead, "Taking a Tough Line on Privacy," *Marketing,* 13 April 2000, p. 31.

Steven Cherry, "DoubleClick Recants on Privacy Issue," *IEEE Spectrum,* April 2000, pp. 63–4.

Mark Fitgerald et al., "Triple Trouble for DoubleClick," *Editor & Publisher,* 21 February 2000, p. 3.

Loren Fox, "DoubleClick Climbs to the Top of the Ad World," *Upside,* February 2000, pp. 58ff.

Anita Hamilton, "Data Mining: DoubleClick's Double Take," *Time,* 13 March 2000, p. 95.

David E. Kalish, "Internet Ad Firm Yields to Critics Privacy," *The Orange Country Register,* 3 March 2000, p. C4.

www.doubleclick.com.

Critical Thinking

Questions for Discussion

1. Should companies be allowed to monitor consumer habits on the computer?
2. When buying behaviour is tracked, should companies be allowed to sell the information to other companies, who can then bombard consumers with on-line advertising and product offers?
3. How do you feel about your computer habits being tracked and, in essence, made public? How is this different from selling individual purchase information that is accumulated at traditional bricks-and-mortar outlets?
4. Do companies need to know who you are in order to provide you with a relevant on-line experience?

Staples.com: Reaping the Benefits of a Clicks-and-Bricks Strategy

Staples Inc., a $9 billion retailer of office supplies, furniture, and technology, is out to conquer the business-to-business market with its on-line business, Staples.com. At the core of Staples' e-business strategy is the technical interface that allows large corporate buyers to easily buy both products and services from various vendors. Such marketing alliances and partnerships could allow Staples.com to sell virtually everything to small business owners—from notepads to insurance—as part of the company's Business Solutions Center.

In late 1999, Staples Inc. named Kelly Mahoney as chief marketing officer at Staples.com, a new position within Staples. While the company is both a bricks-and-mortar business and an on-line retailer, it is sending the signal that it recognizes that the two businesses are distinct by dividing the company into two core businesses—retail and delivery, and the Staples.com Internet business. Mahoney must develop the marketing program that will allow the company to maintain its current customer base, while establishing itself as a premier dot.com company.

Staples is credited with inventing the office superstore concept. The largest operator of office superstores in the world, the company employs over 46,000 people in its more than 1,100 bricks-and-mortar stores, its mail order direct marketing business, and its e-commerce business. Founded in the mid-1980s, the company has grown quickly from its single store in Brighton, Massachusetts. Headquartered in Framingham, Massachusetts, the company now has retail stores throughout the United States, Canada, the United Kingdom, and Germany.

Major Competitors

Until around the mid-1980s, the office product industry was dominated by independent specialty stores. However, three retailers—Staples, Office Depot, and OfficeMax—entered the market and revolutionized the industry. These retailers combined low overhead costs with high volume buying, bringing warehouse retailing to office products. Today they remain the top three office supply retailers.

Worldwide, the office supply retail market is expected to grow at 6 to 8 percent annually. The North American market, alone, is valued at about $200 billion. With annual sales of around $10 billion, Office Depot operates around 900 stores in the United States, Canada, France, and Japan. The number three office supply superstore, OfficeMax, has annual sales of around $5 billion.

Clicks and Bricks

The office supply superstores have entered the clicks-and-bricks domain with vigour. Websites for the three major competitors are among the most heavily visited retail sites on the Net. The on-line market for office supplies is estimated to be around $100 million in 2000 and expected to reach $1.2 billion by 2003. Staples, Office Depot, and OfficeMax are building on their existing brand names/brand recognition to create a synergy between their bricks-and-mortar stores and their on-line sites.

Other e-tailers in the office supply market include Works.com, Onvia.com, BizBuyer.com, and Officesupplies.com. Offerings of e-tail office suppliers vary from providing products on-line (e.g., Onvia) to linking buyers of products with sellers of products via bid solicitation from a database of vendors (e.g., BizBuyer).

E-commerce at Staples

Staples estimates that 70 percent of its on-line business is incremental sales, with its revenue estimated in late 1999 to be around $24 million. The dot.com business has become so successful that Staples Inc. now recognizes it as a distinctive core business. In late 1999, the company issued a tracking stock that reflected the value it places in its e-commerce efforts. By 2003, Staples hopes to achieve revenues of $1 billion on its dot.com endeavours.

Success in e-commerce has allowed Staples to expand beyond its office products in meeting the needs of its business-to-business customers. It is becoming an invaluable component of its customers' businesses by providing all aspects of services like high-speed Internet access, payroll management, financial services, and health insurance. Revenue-wise, Staples would receive commissions on services bought and sold. Staples expects to drive its dot.com business by establishing small business portals in which the company would not partner with existing service providers. Rather, Staples would serve as the technical interface between buyers and sellers.

Thus, the company will sell its current physical products both in the stores and on-line. It will then enhance its offerings and build on its brand recognition by becoming an on-line service provider. Mahoney and her team must formulate a business-to-business marketing strategy that allows Staples to build on a brand that is known for convenience.

Bibliography

John E. Frook, "Staples.com Takes on Office Depot," *Crain Communications, Inc.*, 10 April 2000, pp. 1ff.

Robert D. Hof, "Clicks Don't Need Mortar," *Business Week E.BIZ,* 5 June 2000, p. EB 126.

Chris Reidy, "B2B, That Is Staples' Quest," *Boston Globe,* 18 February 2000, p. C3.

Ara C. Trembly and Susanne Sclafane, "Staples.com to Offer Insurance Online," *National Underwriter,* 31 January 2000, p. 27.

Mike Troy, "Office Supplies: Clicks-and-Mortar Dominates—For Now," *Discount Store News,* 13 December 1999, pp. 57ff.

———. "Staples Maintains Its Momentum," *Discount Store News,* 8 November 1999, pp. 33ff.

Lauren Wiley, "Staples.com Names Mahoney Marketing Chief," *Adweek,* 22 November 1999, p. 2.

www.officedepot.com.

www.OfficeMax.com.

www.staples.com.

Questions for Discussion

1. What is the difference between Staples' bricks-and-mortar stores and its dot.com business?
2. How will Staples.com allow the company to further penetrate the small business marketplace?
3. How do clicks-and-bricks companies differ from pure e-tailers?
4. What is Staples Inc. doing to establish a competitive edge in the office supplies industry?

GLOSSARY

A

accessory equipment
Goods, such as portable tools and office equipment, that are less expensive and shorter-lived than major equipment.
adaptive channel
An alternative channel initiated when a firm identifies critical but rare customer requirements that they do not have the capability to fulfil.
adopter
A consumer who was happy enough with his or her trial experience with a product to use it again.
advertising
Impersonal mass communication about a product or organization that is paid for by a marketer.
advertising appeal
A strategy for communicating a creative objective.
advertising campaign
Series of related advertisements focusing on a common theme, slogan, and set of advertising appeals.
advertising objective
The specific communication task to be accomplished for a specified target audience during a specified period.
advertising response function
Phenomenon in which spending for advertising and sales promotion increases sales or market share up to a certain level but then produces diminishing returns.
advocacy advertising
A form of advertising where an organization expresses its views on controversial issues or responds to media attacks.
agents and brokers
Wholesaling intermediaries that facilitate the sale of a product from producer to end user by representing retailers, wholesalers, or manufacturers; they do not take title to the product.
AIDA concept
Model outlining the process for achieving IMC goals in terms of stages of consumer involvement with the message; stands for Attention, Interest, Desire, and Action.
applied research
Attempts to develop new or improved products.
ARAPNET
The original Internet, part of a military networking project.
aspirational reference group
Groups that an individual wants to join.
assurance
The knowledge and courtesy of employees and their ability to convey trust.
ATC
See **average total cost**
atmosphere
The overall impression conveyed by a store's physical layout, decor, and surroundings.
attitude
A learned tendency to respond consistently toward a given object.
auctions
Potential buyers bid on-line for an item; typically, the highest bid wins. Sellers have the option of setting a reverse bid.
audience selectivity
The ability of an advertising medium to reach a precisely defined market.
audit
A form of observation research that features people examining and verifying the sale of a product.
augmented product
A product or service developed when a company adds features not expected by the customer.
automatic vending
The use of machines to offer goods for sale.
AVC
See **average variable cost**
average total cost (ATC)
Total costs divided by quantity of output.
average variable cost (AVC)
Total variable costs divided by quantity of output.

B

baby boomers
People born between 1946 and 1964.
bait pricing
A price tactic that tries to get consumers into a store through false or misleading price advertising and then uses high-pressure selling to persuade then to buy more expensive merchandise.
base price
The general price level at which the company expects to sell the good or service.
basic research
Pure research that aims to confirm an existing theory or to learn more about a concept or phenomenon.
basing point pricing
A price tactic that charges freight from a given (basing) point, regardless of the city from which the goods are shipped.

BehaviorScan
A scanner-based research program that tracks the purchases of 3,000 households through store scanners.
belief
An organized pattern of knowledge that an individual holds as true about his or her world.
benefit segmentation
The process of grouping customers into market segments according to the benefits they seek from the product.
brainstorming
Getting a group to think of unlimited ways to vary a product or solve a problem.
brand
A name, term, symbol, design, or combination thereof that identifies a seller's products and differentiates them from competitors' products.
brand competitor
A competitor that is very much like you in terms of products offered for sale, price, promotion, distribution, and the market(s) targeted.
brand equity
The value of company and brand names.
brand loyalty
A consistent preference for one brand over all others.
brand mark
The elements of a brand that cannot be spoken.
brand name
That part of a brand that can be spoken, including letters, words, and numbers.
break-even analysis
A method of determining what sales volume must be reached before total revenue equals total costs.
bricks and clicks
An enterprise that integrates both a physical and a Web presence.
business analysis
The second stage of the screening process, when preliminary figures for demand, cost, sales, and profitability are calculated.
business marketing
The marketing of goods and services to individuals and organizations for purposes other than personal consumption.
business product (industrial product)
A product used to manufacture other goods or services, to facilitate an organization's operations, or to resell to other customers.
business services
Expense items that do not become part of a final product.
buyer
A department head who selects the merchandise for his or her department and may also be responsible for promotion and personnel.
buying centre
All the people who become involved in the purchase decision.

C

cannibalization
The situation that occurs when sales of a new product cut into sales of a firm's existing products.
cash cow
In the portfolio matrix, a business unit that usually generates more cash than it needs to maintain its market share.
cash discount
A price reduction offered to a buyer in return for prompt payment of a bill.
category killers
The term often used to describe specialty discount stores because they dominate so heavily their narrow merchandise segment.
central-location telephone (CLT) facility
A specially designed phone room used to conduct telephone interviewing.
chain stores
Stores owned and operated as a group by a single organization.
channel
A medium of communication—such as TV, radio, a newspaper, a magazine, or a salesperson's facial expressions and gestures—for transmitting a message.
channel conflict
A clash of goals and methods between distribution channel members.
channel control
A situation that occurs when one marketing channel member intentionally affects another member's behaviour.
channel leader (channel captain)
The member of a marketing channel that exercises authority and power over the activities of other channel members.
channel members
All parties in the marketing channel that negotiate with one another, buy and sell products, and facilitate the change of ownership between buyer and seller in the course of moving the product from the manufacturer into the hands of the final consumer.
channel partnering (channel cooperation)
The joint effort of all channel members to create a supply chain that serves customers and creates a competitive advantage.
channel power
The capacity of a particular marketing channel member to control or influence the behaviour of other channel members.

CI audit
A competitive intelligence audit of (a) employees by their type of expertise, (b) independent in-house databases, and (c) marketing research studies available internally.
CI directory
CI audit data entered into a database management file.
closed-ended question
Interview question that asks the respondent to make a selection from a limited set of responses.
CLT
See **central-location telephone facility**
co-branding
Placing two or more brand names on a product or its package.
cognitive dissonance
The inner tension that a consumer experiences after recognizing an inconsistency between behaviour and values or opinions.
cold calling
Form of lead generation in which the salesperson approaches potential buyers without any prior knowledge of the prospects' needs or financial status.
commercialization
The decision to market a product.
communication
The process by which we exchange or share meanings through a common set of symbols.
comparative advertising
A form of advertising that compares two or more specific competing brands.
Competition Bureau
The federal department charged with administering most marketplace laws.
competitive advantage
The unique features of a company and its products that are perceived by the target market as significant and superior to the competition; *or*, a capability, superior to that of your competitors, that can be utilized as a central part of the company's strategic plan.
competitive advertising
A form of advertising designed to influence demand for a specific brand.
competitive intelligence
An intelligence system that helps managers assess their competition and their vendors in order to become more efficient and effective competitors.
component lifestyles
When individuals choose goods and services that do not conform to traditional lifestyles but rather meet their own diverse needs and interests.
component parts
Either finished items ready for assembly, or products that need very little processing before becoming part of some other product.
computer-assisted personal interviewing
Interviewing method whereby the interviewer reads the questions from a computer screen and enters the respondent's data directly into the computer.
computer-assisted self-interviewing
Interviewing method whereby a mall interviewer intercepts and directs willing respondents to nearby computer terminals; respondents then read questions off the terminal screens and key their answers directly into the computer.
concentrated targeting strategy
A strategy used to select one segment of a market for target marketing efforts.
concept test
Test to evaluate a new product idea, usually before any prototype has been created.
consumer behaviour
The processes a consumer uses in making purchase decisions or in using or disposing of purchased goods or services; also includes factors that influence purchase decisions and how products are used.
consumer decision-making process
The step-by-step process used by consumers when buying goods or services.
consumer sales promotion
Sales promotion activities to the ultimate consumer.
continuous media schedule
A media scheduling strategy whereby advertising is run steadily throughout the advertising period.
control
Provides the mechanisms for evaluating marketing results in light of the plan's goals and for correcting actions that do not help the organization reach those goals within budget guidelines.
convenience product
A relatively inexpensive item that merits little shopping effort.
convenience sample
A form of nonprobability sample using respondents who are convenient or readily accessible to the researcher—for example, employees, friends, relatives.
convenience store
A miniature supermarket that carries only a limited line of high-turnover convenience goods.
cookies
Computer codes that enter users' hard drives and act as identifiers so that organizations can present repeat visitors with customized sites.

cooperative advertising
An arrangement in which the manufacturer and the retailer split the costs of advertising the manufacturer's brand.
core service
The most basic benefit the consumer is buying.
corporate social responsibility
See **pyramid of corporate social responsibility**
corporate strategy
The central business scheme for utilizing the company's financial, production, R&D, personnel, and marketing resources.
cost competitive advantage
Being the low-cost competitor in an industry while maintaining satisfactory profit margins.
cost per contact
The cost of reaching one member of the target market.
coupon
A certificate that entitles consumers to an immediate price reduction when they buy the product.
credence quality
A characteristic that consumers may have difficulty assessing even after purchase because they do not have the necessary knowledge or experience.
crisis management
A coordinated effort to handle the effects of unfavourable publicity or of another unexpected, unfavourable event.
CRM
See **customer relationship management**
cross-tabulation
A method of analyzing data that lets the analyst look at the responses to one question in relation to the responses to one or more other questions.
culture
A set of values, norms, attitudes, and other meaningful symbols that shape human behaviour; *also,* the artifacts—or products—of that behaviour as they are transmitted from one generation to the next.
cumulative quantity discount
A deduction from list price that applies to the buyer's total purchases made during a specific period.
customer benefits
Everything that a customer receives when dealing with a firm.
customer costs
Everything that the customer gives up to obtain the benefits provided by the product or service that is being purchased.
customer relationship management (CRM)
A key component of a top-down, one-to-one, strategic initiative taken by a company to "connect" with each individual customer, that uses technology to enable the capture of customer information.
customer satisfaction
The feeling that a product has met or exceeded the customer's expectations.
customer value
The ratio of benefits to the sacrifice necessary to obtain those benefits.
cyber-intermediaries
A new type of intermediary formed to handle functions unique to an electronic business environment.

D

database
A collection of data, especially one that can be accessed and manipulated by computer software.
database enhancement
Overlaying more information onto customer or prospect records for the purpose of better describing or better determining the responsiveness of customers or prospects.
database marketing
The creation of a large, computerized file of customers' and potential customers' profiles and purchase patterns.
data mining
A technique used by researchers to search for patterns in data sets that will provide insight into consumer behaviour.
decision support system (DSS)
An interactive, flexible computerized information system that enables managers to obtain and manipulate information as they are making decisions.
decline stage
A long-run drop in sales.
decoding
Interpretation of the message the source has sent through a channel.
demand
The quantity of a product that will be sold in the market at various prices for a specified period.
demographic segmentation
Segmenting markets by age, gender, income, ethnic background, and family life cycle.
demography
The study of people's vital statistics, such as their age, race and ethnicity, and location.
department store
A store housing several departments under one roof.
derived demand
The demand for business products.

development
The stage in the product development process when a prototype is developed and a marketing strategy is outlined.
differential advantage
One or more unique aspects of an organization that influence target consumers to purchase its products or services.
differential competitive advantage
The advantage achieved when a firm provides something that is unique and valuable to buyers beyond simply offering a lower price than the competition.
diffusion
The process by which the adoption of an innovation spreads.
direct channel
A distribution channel in which producers sell directly to consumers.
direct marketing (direct-response marketing)
Techniques used to get consumers to make purchases from their home or office, or some other nonretail setting.
direct retailing
Representatives sell products door to door, office to office, or at home parties.
discount store
A retailer that competes on the basis of low prices, high turnover, and high volume.
discrepancy of assortment
Lack of all the items a customer needs to receive full satisfaction from a product or products.
discrepancy of quantity
The difference between the amount of product produced and the amount a customer wants to buy.
disintermediation
The shortening of the distribution channel as the result of technologically enhanced links between buyers and sellers.
distribution resource planning (DRP)
An inventory control system that manages the replenishment of goods from the manufacturer to the final consumer.
diversification
A strategy of increasing sales by introducing new products into new markets.
dog
In the portfolio matrix, a business unit that has low growth potential and a small market share.
DRP
See **distribution resource planning**
DSS
See **decision support system**
dual distribution (multiple distribution)
The use of two or more channels to distribute the same product to target markets.

E

EDI
See **electronic data interchange**
EDLP
See **everyday low prices**
80/20 principle
The principle that 20 percent of all customers generate 80 percent of the demand.
elastic demand
The situation in which consumer demand is sensitive to changes in price.
elasticity of demand
Consumers' responsiveness or sensitivity to changes in price.
electronic data interchange (EDI)
Information technology that replaces paper documents with electronic transmission.
electronic distribution
A distribution technique that involves any kind of product or service that can be distributed electronically, for example, through fiber-optic cable or satellite transmission.
empathy
Caring, individualized attention to customers.
empowerment
Delegation of authority to solve customers' problems quickly—usually by the first person the customer notifies regarding a problem.
encoding
Conversion of the sender's ideas and thoughts into a message, usually in the form of words or signs.
environmental management
When a company implements strategies that attempt to shape the external environment within which it operates.
environmental scanning
The collection and interpretation of information about forces, events, and relationships in the external environment that may affect the future of the organization or the implementation of the marketing plan.
evaluation
Gauging the extent to which the marketing objectives have been achieved during the specified time period.
everyday low prices (EDLP)
The price tactic of permanently reducing prices 10 to 25 percent below traditional levels while eliminating trade discounts that create trade loading.

evoked set (consideration set)
A group of brands, resulting from an information search, from which a buyer can choose.
exchange
The idea that people give up something to receive something they would rather have.
exclusive distribution
The form of distribution that establishes one or a few dealers within a given area.
experience curves
Curves that show costs declining at a predictable rate as experience with a product increases.
experience quality
A characteristic that can be assessed only after use.
experiment
Method a researcher uses to gather primary data.
expert
Someone with in-depth knowledge of a subject or activity.
express warranty
A written guarantee.
extensive decision making
The most complex type of consumer decision making, used when buying an unfamiliar, expensive product or an infrequently bought item; requires the use of several criteria for evaluating options and much time for seeking information.
external information search
The process of seeking information in the outside environment.
extranet
A private electronic network that links a company with its suppliers and customers.

F

factory outlet
An off-price retailer owned and operated by a manufacturer.
family brand
Marketing several different products under the same brand name.
family life cycle (FLC)
A series of stages determined by a combination of age, marital status, and the presence or absence of children.
feedback
The receiver's response to a message.
field service firm
A firm that specializes in interviewing respondents on a subcontracted basis.
fixed costs
Costs that do not change as output is increased or decreased.
FLC
See **family life cycle**
flexible pricing (variable pricing)
A price tactic in which different customers pay different prices for essentially the same merchandise bought in equal quantities.
flighted media schedule
A media scheduling strategy whereby ads are run heavily every other month or every two weeks, so as to achieve a greater impact through increased frequency and reach.
FOB origin pricing
A price tactic that requires the buyer to absorb the freight costs from the shipping point ("free on board").
focus group
Seven to ten people who participate in a group discussion led by a moderator.
follow-up
The final step of the selling process, in which the salesperson ensures that delivery schedules are met, that the goods or services perform as promised, and that the buyers' employees are properly trained to use the products.
formal marketing plan
A written document that acts as a guidebook of marketing activities for the marketing manager.
four Ps
Product, place, promotion, and price, which together make up the marketing mix.
frame error
Error that occurs when a sample drawn from a population differs from the target population.
franchise
A licensed agreement between a parent company and an independent merchant that gives the merchant the right to operate under the trademark of the parent company in exchange for financial returns.
franchisee
Individual or business that is granted the right to sell another party's product.
franchiser
Originator of a trade name, product, methods of operation, and so on, that grants operating rights to another party to sell its product.
freight absorption pricing
A price tactic in which the seller pays all or part of the actual freight charges and does not pass them on to the buyer.
frequency
The number of times an individual is exposed to a given message during a specific period.
frequent buyer program
A loyalty program that rewards loyal consumers for making multiple purchases of a particular good or service.

fulfilment
The capability to fill orders in accordance with customer expectations.
full-line discount stores
A retailer that offers consumers very limited service and carries a broad assortment of well-known, nationally branded "hard goods."
functional discount (trade discount)
A discount to wholesalers and retailers for performing channel functions.

G

gap model
A model identifying five gaps that can cause problems in service delivery and influence customer evaluations of service quality.
Generation X
People currently between the ages of nineteen and twenty-nine.
generic product
A no-frills, no-brand-name, low-cost product that is identified simply by its product category.
generic product name
Identifies a product by class or type, and cannot be trademarked.
geodemographic segmentation
Segmenting potential customers into neighbourhood lifestyle categories.
geographic segmentation
Segmenting markets by region of the country or world, market size, market density, or climate.
gross margin
The amount of money the retailer makes as a percentage of sales after the cost of goods sold is subtracted.
group dynamics
Group interaction essential to the success of focus group research.
growth stage
The second stage of the product life cycle, when sales typically grow more quickly, many competitors enter the market, and companies are healthy; also, large companies may start acquiring small pioneering firms.

H

heterogeneity
A characteristic of services that makes them less standardized and uniform than goods.
horizontal conflict
Channel conflict among members on the same level.
hypermarket
A retail store that combines a supermarket and full-line discount store in a space ranging from 200,000 to 300,000 square feet.

I

ideal self-image
The way an individual would like to be.
IMC
See **integrated marketing communications.**
IMC plan
Plan for the integrated use of the elements of promotion: advertising, public relations, personal selling, and sales promotion.
IMC program
See **promotional mix**
implementation
The process that turns marketing plans into action assignments and ensures that these assignments are executed in a way that accomplishes the plans' objectives.
independent retailers
Retailers owned by a single person or partnership and not operated as part of a larger retail institution.
individual branding
Using different brand names for different products.
industrial espionage
An attempt to learn competitors' trade secrets by illegal or unethical means, or both.
inelastic demand
A situation in which an increase or a decrease in price will not significantly affect demand for the product.
inflation
A general rise in prices without a corresponding increase in wages, which results in decreased purchasing power.
infomercial
A thirty-minute or longer advertisement that looks more like a TV talk show than a sales pitch.
informational labelling
Labelling designed to help consumers make proper product selections and lower their cognitive dissonance after the purchase.
informative promotion
Increasing the awareness of a new brand, product class, or product attribute; explaining how the product works; suggesting new uses for a product; building a company image.
InfoScan
A scanner-based sales-tracking service for the consumer packaged-goods industry.
innovation
A product perceived as new by a potential adopter.
inseparability
A characteristic of services that allows them to be produced and consumed simultaneously.
institutional advertising
A form of advertising that enhances a company's image instead of promoting a particular product.

intangibility
Means that services cannot be sensed—that is, touched, seen, tasted, heard, or felt—in the same manner that goods can be sensed.
integrated interviewing
A new interviewing method in which a respondent is interviewed on the Internet.
integrated marketing communications (IMC)
The method of carefully coordinating all promotional activities to produce a consistent, unified message that is customer focused.
intended strategy
What the organization intended—the formal marketing strategy as found in the marketing plan.
intensive distribution
A form of distribution aimed at having a product available in every outlet at which target customers might want to buy it.
internal information search
The process of recalling past information stored in the memory.
internal marketing
Treating employees as customers and developing systems and benefits that satisfy their needs.
Internet
Worldwide telecommunications network allowing access to data, pictures, sound, and files throughout the world.
interpersonal communication
Direct, fact-to-face communication between two or more people.
introductory stage
The full-scale launch of a new product into the marketplace.
inventory control system
A method of developing and maintaining an adequate assortment of products to meet customer demand.
involvement
The amount of time and effort a buyer invests in the search, evaluation, and decision processes of consumer behaviour.

J

JIT
See **just-in-time production**
joint costs
Costs that are shared in the manufacturing and marketing of several products in a product line.
joint demand
The demand for two or more items used together in a final product.
just-in-time production (JIT)
Redefining and simplifying manufacturing by reducing inventory levels and delivering raw materials just when they are needed on the production line.

K

keystoning
The practice of marking up prices by 100 percent, or doubling the cost.

L

lead generation (prospecting)
Identifying those firms and people most likely to buy the seller's offerings.
lead qualification
Determining a sales prospect's authority and ability to buy.
leader pricing (loss leader pricing)
A price tactic in which a product is sold near or even below cost in the hope that shoppers will buy other items once they are in the store.
learning
A process that creates changes in behaviour—immediate or expected—through experience and practice.
lifestyle
A mode of living as identified by a person's activities, interests, and opinions.
lifetime value analysis (LTV)
A data manipulation technique that projects the future value of the customer over a period of years using the assumption that marketing to repeat customers is more profitable than marketing to first-time buyers.
limited decision making
The type of decision making that requires a moderate amount of time for gathering information and deliberating about an unfamiliar brand in a familiar product category.
logistics
The process of strategically managing the efficient flow and storage of raw materials, in-process inventory, and finished goods from point of origin to point of consumption.
logistics information system
Information technology that integrates and links all the logistics functions of the supply chain.
logistics service
Interrelated activities performed by a member of the supply chain to ensure that the right product is in the right place at the right time.

loyalty marketing programs
A promotional program designed to build long-term, mutually beneficial relationships between a company and its key customers.
LTV
See **lifetime value analysis**

M

macrosegmentation
A method of dividing business markets into segments based on general characteristics such as geographic location, customer type, customer size, and product use.
major equipment (installations)
Capital goods such as large or expensive machines, mainframe computers, blast furnaces, generators, airplanes, and buildings.
mall intercept interview
Survey research method that involves interviewing people in the common areas of shopping malls.
management decision problem
A broad-based problem that requires marketing research in order for managers to take proper actions.
manufacturers' brand
The brand name of a manufacturer.
marginal cost (MC)
Change in total costs associated with a one-unit change in output.
marginal revenue (MR)
The extra revenue associated with selling an extra unit of output, or the change in total revenue with a one-unit change in output.
market
People or organizations with needs or wants and the ability and willingness to buy.
market attractiveness/company strength matrix
A tool for allocating resources among SBUs on the basis of how attractive a market is and how well the firm is positioned to take advantage of that market's opportunities.
market development
Attracting new customers to existing products.
marketing
The process of planning and executing the conception, pricing, promotion, and distribution of ideas, goods, and services to create exchanges that satisfy individual and organizational goals.
marketing audit
A thorough, systematic, periodic evaluation of the goals, strategies, structure, and performance of the marketing organization.
marketing channel (channel of distribution)
A set of interdependent organizations that ease the transfer of ownership as products move from producer to business user or consumer.
marketing concept
The idea that organizations have a right to exist to the extent that they satisfy the needs and wants of their customers while meeting their own objectives.
marketing-controlled information source
A product information source that originates with marketers promoting the product.
marketing database
The compilation of names, addresses, and other pieces of pertinent information about individual customers and prospects that affects what and how marketers sell to them.
marketing intelligence
Everyday information about developments in the marketing environment that managers use to prepare and adjust marketing plans.
marketing intelligence system (MIS)
A type of marketing database that builds on the information captured in a customer information system by capturing a greater array of data than basic customer and transaction information.
marketing mix
A unique blend of product, distribution, promotion, and pricing strategies designed to produce mutually satisfying exchanges with a target market.
marketing myopia
When business is defined in terms of goods and services rather than in terms of the benefits that customers seek.
marketing objective
A statement of what is to be accomplished through marketing activities.
marketing plan
A written document that acts as a guidebook of marketing activities for the marketing manager.
marketing planning
Designing activities relating to marketing objectives and the changing marketing environment.
marketing research
The process of planning, collecting, and analyzing data relevant to a marketing decision.
marketing research objective
Specific information needed to solve a marketing research problem; the objective should provide insightful decision-making information.
marketing research problem
Determining what information is needed and how that information can be obtained efficiently and effectively.

marketing strategy
The activities of selecting and describing one or more target markets and developing and maintaining a marketing mix that will produce mutually satisfying exchanges with target markets.

market opportunity analysis
Describing and estimating the size and sales potential of market segments that are of interest to the firm, and assessing key competitors in these market segments.

market orientation
The philosophy that assumes that a sale does not depend on an aggressive sales force but rather on a customer's decision to purchase a product.

market penetration
A marketing strategy that tries to increase market share among existing customers.

market segment
A subgroup of people or organizations sharing one or more characteristics that cause them to have similar product needs.

market share
A company's product sales as a percentage of total sales for that industry.

markup pricing
The cost of buying the product from the producer, plus amounts for profit and for expenses not otherwise accounted for.

Maslow's hierarchy of needs
A method of classifying human needs and motivations into five categories in ascending order of importance: physiological, safety, social, esteem, and self-actualization.

mass communication
Communication to large audiences.

mass customization (build-to-order)
A strategy that uses technology to deliver customized services on a mass basis; *also*, a production method whereby products are not made until an order is placed by the customer and products are made according to customer specifications.

mass merchandising
A retailing strategy using moderate to low prices on large quantities of merchandise and lower service to stimulate high turnover of products.

master brand
A brand so dominant in consumers' minds that they think of it immediately when a product category, use situation, product attribute, or customer benefit is mentioned.

materials handling system
A method of moving inventory into, within, and out of the warehouse.

materials requirement planning (MRP)
An inventory control system that manages the replenishment of raw materials, supplies, and components from the supplier to the manufacturer.

maturity stage
A period during which sales increase less quickly.

MC
See **marginal cost**

measurement error
Error that occurs when there is a difference between the information desired by the researcher and the information provided by the measurement process.

media mix
The combination of media to be used for a promotional campaign.

media schedule
Designation of the media, the specific publications or programs, and the insertion dates of advertising.

medium
The channel used to convey a message to a target market.

merchant wholesaler
An institution that buys goods from manufacturers and resells them to businesses, government agencies, and other wholesalers or retailers; it receives and takes title to goods, stores them in its own warehouses, and later ships them.

microsegmentation
The process of dividing business markets into segments based on the characteristics of decision-making units within a macrosegment.

MIS
See **marketing intelligence system**

mission statement
The firm's long-term vision, based on a careful analysis of benefits sought by present and potential customers and analysis of existing and anticipated environmental conditions; *or*, a clear and concise statement that explains the organization's reason for being.

modified rebuy
A situation where the purchaser wants some change in the original good or service.

motive
A driving force that causes a person to take action to satisfy specific needs.

MR
See **marginal revenue**

MRP
See **materials requirement planning**

multiculturalism
When all major ethnic groups in an area—such as a city, country, or census tract—are roughly equally represented.

multiplier effect (accelerator principle)
A phenomenon whereby a small change in consumer demand can produce a much larger change in demand for the facilities and equipment needed to make the consumer product.
multisegment targeting strategy
A strategy that chooses two or more well-defined market segments and develops a distinct marketing mix for each.

N

NAFTA
See **North American Free Trade Agreement**
NAICS
See **North American Industry Classification System**
need recognition
The result of an imbalance between actual and desired states.
needs assessment
Determining the customer's specific needs and the options that customer has for satisfying them.
negotiation
The process of both the salesperson and the prospect offering special concessions in an attempt to arrive at a sales agreement.
networking
The process of finding out about potential clients from friends, business contacts, co-workers, acquaintances, and fellow members of professional or civic organizations.
new buy
A situation requiring the purchase of a product for the first time.
new product
A product new to the world, the market, the producer, the seller, or some combination of these.
new product committee
An ad hoc group whose members manage the new product development process.
new product department
Performs the same functions as a new product committee but on a full-time basis.
new product strategy
Linking the new product development process with the objectives of the marketing department, the business unit, and the corporation.
newsgroups
On-line discussion forums that typically have periodic e-mail distribution of relevant news items related to a particular topic.
niche
One segment of a market.
niche competitive advantage
The advantage achieved when a firm seeks to target and serve effectively a small segment of the market.
noise
Anything that distorts, interferes with, or slows down the transmission of information.
nonaspirational reference groups
Groups with which an individual does not want to associate.
noncumulative quantity discount
A deduction from list price that applies to a single order rather than to the total volume of orders placed during a certain period.
nonmarketing-controlled information source
A product information source that is not associated with advertising or promotion.
nonprobability sample
Any sample in which little or no attempt is made to get a representative cross-section of the population.
nonprofit organization
An organization that exists to achieve some goal other than the usual business goals of profit, market share, or return on investment.
nonprofit organization marketing
The effort by nonprofit organizations to bring about mutually satisfying exchanges with target markets.
nonstore retailing
Shopping without visiting a store.
norm
A value or attitude deemed acceptable by a group.
North American Free Trade Agreement (NAFTA)
An agreement among Canada, the United States, and Mexico that created the world's largest free trade zone.
North American Industry Classification System (NAICS)
A detailed numbering system developed by Canada, the United States, and Mexico to classify North American business establishments by their main production processes.

O

observation research
A research method that relies on three types of observation: people watching people, people watching activity, and machines watching people.
odd-even pricing (psychological pricing)
A price tactic that uses odd-numbered prices to connote bargains and even-numbered prices to imply quality.

off-price retailer
A retailer that can sell at prices 25 percent or more below traditional department store prices because it pays cash for its stock and usually doesn't ask for return privileges.

one-to-one marketing
A customer-based, information-intensive, long-term-oriented, and individualized marketing method that focuses on share of customer rather than share of market.

one-to-one marketing communications process
A revised marketing process characterized by the use of personalized communication, a lack of "noise," and the ability to capture customers' responses.

open-ended question
An interview question that encourages an answer phrased in the respondent's own words.

opinion leader
An individual who influences the opinions of others.

optimizer
The type of business customer that considers many suppliers, both familiar and unfamiliar, solicits bids, and studies all proposals carefully before selecting one.

order processing system
System whereby orders are entered into the supply chain and filled.

outsourcing (contract logistics)
A manufacturer's or supplier's use of an independent third party to manage an entire function of the logistics system, such as transportation, warehousing, or order processing.

P

penetration pricing
A pricing policy whereby a firm charges a relatively low price for a product initially as a way to reach the mass market.

perception
The process by which people select, organize, and interpret stimuli to form meaningful and coherent pictures.

perceptual mapping
A means of displaying or graphing, in two or more dimensions, the location of products, brands, or groups of products in customers' minds.

perishability
A characteristic of services that prevents them from being stored, warehoused, or inventoried.

personality
A way of organizing and grouping the consistencies of an individual's reactions to situations.

personalized economy
Delivering goods and services at a good value on demand.

personal selling
Planned presentation to one or more prospective buyers for the purpose of making a sale.

persuasive labelling
Labelling that focuses on a promotional theme or logo; consumer information is secondary.

persuasive promotion
Encouraging brand switching; changing customers' perceptions of product attributes; influencing customers to buy now; persuading customers to call.

pioneering advertising
A form of advertising designed to stimulate primary demand for a new product or product category.

planned obsolescence
The practice of modifying products in such a way that those which have already been sold become obsolete before they actually need replacement.

planning
The process of anticipating future events and determining strategies to achieve organizational objectives.

point-of-purchase display
A promotional display set up at the retailer's location to build traffic, advertise the product, or induce impulse buying.

portal
A Website that provides a starting point and home base for Web-based activities.

position
The place a product, brand, or group of products occupies in consumers' minds relative to competing offerings.

positioning
Developing a specific marketing mix to influence potential customers' overall perception of a brand, product line, or organization in general.

preapproach
The "homework" that must be done by the salesperson before he or she contacts the prospect.

predatory pricing
The practice of charging a very low price for a product with the intent of driving competitors out of business or out of a market.

premium
An extra item offered to the consumer, usually in exchange for some proof of purchase of the promoted product.

prestige pricing
Charging a high price to help promote a high-quality image.

price
That which is given up in an exchange to acquire a good or service.
price bundling
Marketing two or more products in a single package for a special price.
price equilibrium
The price at which demand and supply are equal.
price fixing
An agreement between two or more firms on the price they will charge for a product.
price lining
The practice of offering a product line with several items at specific price points.
price skimming
A pricing policy whereby a firm charges a high introductory price, often coupled with heavy promotion.
price strategy
The basic, long-term pricing framework, which establishes the initial price for a product and the intended direction for price movements over the product life cycle.
primary data
Information collected for the first time; can be used for solving the particular problem under investigation.
primary membership groups
Reference groups with which people interact regularly on an informal, face-to-face basis, such as family, friends, and fellow employees.
primary research
Research conducted for a specific purpose at the time it is needed.
private brand
A brand name owned by a wholesaler or a retailer.
private label brands
Brands that are designed and developed using the retailer's name.
probability sample
A sample in which every element in the population has a known statistical likelihood of being selected.
problem child (question mark)
In the portfolio matrix, a business unit that shows rapid growth but poor profit margins.
processed materials
Products used directly in manufacturing other products.
product
Everything, both favourable and unfavourable, that a person receives in an exchange.
product advertising
A form of advertising that promotes the benefits of a specific good or service.
product category
All brands that satisfy a particular type of need.
product development
A marketing strategy that entails creating marketable products and converting new technologies into marketable products.
product differentiation
A positioning strategy that some firms use to distinguish their products from those of competitors.
product item
A specific version of a product that can be designated as a distinct offering among an organization's products.
production orientation
A philosophy that focuses on the internal capabilities of the firm rather than on the desires and needs of the marketplace.
product life cycle
A concept that provides a way to trace the stages of a product's acceptance, from its introduction (birth) to its decline (death).
product line
A group of closely related product items.
product line depth
The number of product items in a product line.
product line extension
Adding additional products to an existing product line in order to compete more broadly in the industry.
product line pricing
Setting prices for an entire line of products.
product mix
All the products an organization sells.
product mix width
The number of product lines an organization offers.
product modification
Changing one or more of a product's characteristics.
product offering
The mix of products offered to the consumer by the retailer, also called the product assortment or merchandise mix.
profit
Revenue minus expenses.
profit maximization
When marginal revenue equals marginal cost.
promotion
Communication by marketers that informs, persuades, and reminds potential buyers of a product in order to influence an opinion or elicit a response.
promotional allowance (trade allowance)
A payment to a dealer for promoting the manufacturer's products.

promotional mix (IMC plan)
Plan for integrating the elements of promotion: advertising, public relations, personal selling, and sales promotion.

PSA
See **public service advertisement**

psychographic segmentation
Market segmentation on the basis of personality, motives, lifestyles, and geodemographics.

publicity
Public information about a good or service for which the company doesn't pay.

public relations
Marketing function that evaluates public attitudes, identifies areas within the organization that the public may be interested in, and executes a program of action to earn public understanding and acceptance.

public service advertisement (PSA)
An announcement that promotes a program of a federal, provincial, or local government or of a nonprofit organization.

pull strategy
A marketing strategy that stimulates consumer demand to obtain product distribution.

pulsing media schedule
A media scheduling strategy that uses continuous scheduling throughout the year coupled with a flighted schedule during the best sales periods.

pureplay
An organization or enterprise operating strictly in an on-line environment.

push money
Money offered to channel intermediaries to encourage them to "push" products—that is, to encourage other members of the channel to sell the products.

push strategy
A marketing strategy that uses aggressive personal selling and trade advertising to convince a wholesaler or a retailer to carry and sell particular merchandise.

pyramid of corporate social responsibility
A model which suggests that a company's social responsibility is composed of its economic, legal, ethical, and philanthropic responsibilities, and that its economic performance supports the entire structure.

Q

qualitative research
Data collection activities where the research results are not subject to quantification or quantitative analysis.

quantitative research
Uses mathematical techniques to analyze data, yielding results that are typically objective and statistically robust.

quantity discount
A price reduction offered to buyers buying in multiple units or above a specified dollar amount.

quota
Statement of the individual salesperson's sales objectives, usually based on sales volume alone but sometimes including key accounts (those with greatest potential), new accounts, and specific products.

R

random error
Error that occurs because the selected sample is an imperfect representation of the overall population.

random sample
A sample arranged so that every element of the population has an equal chance of being selected as part of the sample.

raw materials
Unprocessed extractive or agricultural products, such as mineral ore, lumber, wheat, corn, fruits, vegetables, and fish.

reach
The number of target consumers exposed to a commercial at least once during a specific period, usually four weeks.

realized strategy
What actually occurs—the marketing strategy put into play in the marketplace.

real self-image
The way an individual actually perceives himself or herself.

rebate
A cash refund given for purchasing a product during a specific period.

receiver
The person who decodes a message.

recency–frequency–monetary analysis (RFM)
A data manipulation technique that determines the firm's best customers by identifying those customers who have purchased most recently, bought most frequently, and spent the most money.

reciprocity
A practice where business purchasers choose to buy from their own customers.

recruited Internet sample
Respondents are prerecruited; after qualifying to participate, they are sent a questionnaire by e-mail or directed to a secure Website to fill out a questionnaire.

reference group
A group in society that influences an individual's purchasing behaviour.
referral
A recommendation to a salesperson from a customer or business associate.
relationship marketing
The strategy that involves forging long-term partnerships with customers.
relationship selling (consultative selling)
Sales practice of building, maintaining, and enhancing interactions with customers in order to develop long-term satisfaction to both buyer and seller.
reliability
The ability to perform a service dependably, accurately, and consistently.
reminder promotion
Reminding consumers that the product may be needed in the near future; reminding consumers where to buy the product; maintaining consumer awareness.
repositioning
Changing consumers' perceptions of a brand in relation to competing brands.
research design
Specifies which research questions must be answered, how and when the data will be gathered, and how the data will be analyzed.
response list
A customer list that includes the names and addresses of individuals who have responded to an offer of some kind, such as by mail, telephone, direct response television, product rebates, contests or sweepstakes, or billing inserts.
responsiveness
The ability to provide prompt service.
retailer
A channel intermediary that sells mainly to consumers.
retailing
All the activities directly related to the sale of goods and services to the ultimate consumer for personal, nonbusiness use.
retailing mix
The traditional four Ps of the marketing mix (product, place, promotion, price), and in addition, personnel and presentation.
return on investment (ROI)
Net profit after taxes divided by total assets.
revenue
The price charged to customers multiplied by the number of units sold.
reverse auctions
Sellers bid for consumer purchases; typically, the lowest price wins.
RFM
See **recency–frequency–monetary analysis**
ROI
See **return on investment**
routine response behaviour
The type of decision making exhibited by consumers buying frequently purchased, low-cost goods and services; requires little search and decision time.

S

sales orientation
The idea that people will buy more goods and services if aggressive sales techniques are used and that high sales result in high profits.
sales presentation
A face-to-face explanation of the sales proposal to a prospective buyer.
sales process (sales cycle)
The set of steps a salesperson goes through in a particular organization to sell a particular product or service.
sales promotion
Marketing activities—other than personal selling, advertising, and public relations—that stimulate consumer buying.
sales proposal
A formal written document or professional presentation that outlines how the salesperson's product or service will meet or exceed the prospect's needs.
sample
A subset of a population.
sampling
A promotional program that allows the consumer the opportunity to try the product or service for free.
sampling error
Error that occurs when a sample somehow does not represent the target population.
satisfier
The type of business customer that places an order with the first familiar supplier to satisfy product and delivery requirements.
scaled response question
A closed-ended question designed to measure the intensity of a respondent's answer.
scanner-based research
A system for gathering information from a single group of respondents by continuously monitoring the advertising, promotion, and pricing they are exposed to and the things they buy.

scrambled merchandising
The tendency to offer a wide variety of nontraditional goods and services under one roof.
screened Internet sample
An Internet sample with quotas based on desired sample characteristics.
screening
The first filter in the product development process, which eliminates ideas that are inconsistent with the organization's new product strategy or are obviously inappropriate for some other reason.
search quality
A characteristic that can be easily assessed before purchase.
seasonal discount
A price reduction for buying merchandise out of season.
seasonal media schedule
A media scheduling strategy that runs advertising only during times of the year when the product is most likely to be used.
secondary data
Data previously collected for any purpose other than the one at hand.
secondary membership groups
Reference groups with which people associate less consistently and more formally than with primary membership groups, such as a clubs, professional groups, and religious groups.
secondary research
Research based on existing data or information.
segmentation bases (variables)
The characteristics of individuals, groups, or organizations.
selective distortion
The process whereby a consumer changes or distorts information that conflicts with his or her feelings or beliefs.
selective distribution
The form of distribution achieved by screening dealers to eliminate all but a few in any given area.
selective exposure
The process whereby a consumer notices certain stimuli and ignores other stimuli.
selective retention
Process whereby a consumer remembers only that information which supports his or her personal beliefs.
self-concept
How a consumer perceives himself or herself in terms of attitudes, perceptions, beliefs, and self-evaluations.
selling against the brand
Stocking well-known branded items at high prices in order to sell store brands at discounted prices.
sender
The originator of the message in the communication process.
service
The result of applying human or mechanical efforts to people or objects.
service mark
Trademark for a service.
shopping product
A product that requires comparison shopping, because it is usually more expensive than a convenience product and is found in fewer stores.
simulated (laboratory) market testing
The presentation of advertising and other promotion materials for several products, including a test product, to members of the product's target market.
simultaneous product development
A new, team-oriented approach to new product development.
single-price tactic
Policy of offering all goods and services at the same price.
social class
A group of people in a society who are considered nearly equal in status or community esteem, who regularly socialize among themselves both formally and informally, and who share behavioural norms.
socialization process
How cultural values and norms are passed down to children.
societal orientation
The idea that an organization exists not only to satisfy customer wants and needs and to meet organizational objectives but also to preserve or enhance individuals' and society's long-term best interests.
spam
Unsolicited, mass-distributed commercial e-mail.
spatial discrepancy
Difference between the location of the producer and the location of widely scattered markets.
specialty discount store
A retail store that offers a nearly complete selection of single-line merchandise and uses self-service, discount prices, high volume, and high turnover.
specialty product
A particular item for which consumers search extensively and for which they are very reluctant to accept substitutes.
specialty store
A retail store specializing in a given type of merchandise.
star
In the portfolio matrix, a business unit that is a fast-growing market leader.

status quo pricing
Pricing objective that maintains existing prices or meets the competition's prices.
stimulus
Any unit of input affecting one or more of the five senses: sight, smell, taste, touch, hearing.
stimulus discrimination
The learned ability to differentiate among stimuli.
stimulus generalization
A form of learning that occurs when one response is extended to a second stimulus similar to the first.
stitching niches
A strategy for multicultural marketing that combines ethnic, age, income, and lifestyle markets, on some common basis, to form a large market.
straight commission
A method of compensation in which the salesperson is paid some percentage of sales.
straight rebuy
A buying situation in which the purchaser reorders the same goods or services without looking for new information or investigating other suppliers.
straight salary
A method of compensation in which the salesperson receives a salary regardless of sales productivity.
strategic alliance (strategic partnership)
A cooperative agreement between business firms.
strategic business unit (SBU)
A subgroup of a single business or collection of related businesses within the larger organization.
strategic channel alliance
A cooperative agreement between business firms to use each other's already established distribution channels.
strategic planning
The managerial process of creating and maintaining a fit between the organization's objectives and resources and evolving market opportunities.
strategic window
The limited period during which there is an optimum "fit" between the key requirements of a market and the particular competencies of a firm.
subculture
A homogeneous group of people who share elements of the overall culture as well as unique elements of their own group.
supercentre
A retail store that combines groceries and general merchandise goods with a wide range of services.
supermarket
A large, departmentalized, self-service retailer that specializes in food and some nonfood items.
supplementary services
A group of services that support or enhance the core service.
supplies
Consumable items that do not become part of the final product.
supply
The quantity of a product that will be offered to the market by a supplier at various prices for a specified period.
supply chain
The connected chain of all of the business entities, both internal and external to the company, that perform or support the logistics function.
supply chain management (integrated logistics)
A management system that coordinates and integrates all the activities performed by supply chain members from source to the point of consumption; the result is enhanced customer and economic value.
supply chain team
An entire group of individuals who orchestrate the movement of goods, services, and information from the source to the consumer.
survey research
The most popular technique for gathering primary data, whereby a researcher interacts with people to obtain facts, opinions, and attitudes.
sustainable advantage
One or more unique aspects of an organization that cause target consumers to patronize that firm rather than competitors.
sustainable competitive advantage
A differential advantage that cannot be copied by the competition.
SWOT analysis
Identifying internal strengths (S) and weaknesses (W) and also examining external opportunities (O) and threats (T).

T

tangibles
The physical evidence of a service, including the physical facilities, tools, and equipment used to provide the service.
target market
A defined group most likely to buy a firm's product; *also*, a group of people or organizations for which an organization designs, implements, and maintains a marketing mix intended to meet the needs of that group, resulting in mutually satisfying exchanges.
teamwork
The collaborative efforts of people to accomplish common objectives.
telemarketing
Using the telephone to sell directly to consumers.

temporal discrepancy
The difference between when a product is produced and when a customer is ready to buy it.
test marketing
The limited introduction of a product and a marketing program to determine the reactions of potential customers in a market situation.
trade allowance
A price reduction offered by manufacturers to intermediaries, such as wholesalers and retailers.
trade loading
The practice of temporarily lowering the price to induce wholesalers and retailers to buy more goods than can be sold in a reasonable time.
trademark
The exclusive right to use a brand or part of a brand.
trade sales promotion
Sales promotion activities targeted to a channel member, such as a wholesaler or retailer.
two-part pricing
A price tactic that charges two separate amounts to consume a single good or service.

U

UCC
See **Uniform Commercial Code filings**
unbundling
Reducing the bundle of services that comes with the basic product.
undifferentiated targeting strategy
A marketing approach that views the market as one big market with no individual segments and thus requires a single marketing mix.
Uniform Commercial Code (UCC) filings
Filings by banks with government agencies that identify goods that are leased or pledged as collateral.
uniform delivered pricing
A price tactic in which the seller pays the actual freight charges and bills every purchaser an identical, flat freight charge.
uniform reference locator (URL)
Similar to a street address in that it identifies a unique location on the Web.
unitary elasticity
A situation in which total revenue remains the same when prices change.
universal product codes (UPCs)
Series of thick and thin vertical lines (bar codes), readable by computerized optical scanners, that represent numbers used to track products.
universe
The population from which a sample will be drawn.
unrestricted Internet sample
Anyone with a computer and modem can fill out the questionnaire.
unsought product
A product unknown to the potential buyer, or a known product that the buyer does not actively seek.
UPCs
See **universal product codes**
URL
See **uniform reference locator**
usage rate segmentation
Dividing a market by the amount of product bought or consumed.

V

value
An enduring belief that a specific mode of conduct is personally or socially preferable to another mode of conduct.
value-based pricing
The price is set at a level that seems to the customer to be a good price compared to the prices of other options.
value impressions
The features of a product or service that signal value to the customer.
variable costs
Costs that vary with changes in the level of output.
venture team
A market-oriented group staffed by a small number of representatives from different disciplines.
vertical conflict
Channel conflict that occurs between different levels in a marketing channel, typically between manufacturer and wholesaler or manufacturer and retailer.

W

want
Recognition of an unfulfilled need and a product that will satisfy it.
warehouse membership clubs
Limited service merchant wholesalers that sell a limited selection of brand-name appliances, household items, and groceries on a cash-and-carry basis to members, usually small businesses and groups.
warranty
Confirms the quality or performance of a good or service.
World Wide Web (Web)
Component of the Internet designed to simplify text and images.

Z

zone pricing
A modification of uniform delivered pricing that divides the country (or the total market) into segments or zones and charges a flat freight rate to all customers in a given zone.

ENDNOTES

CHAPTER 1

1. Coca-Cola Website and from "The Power of Reflection" by Michael Hammer and Steven A. Stanton, *Fortune*, November 24, 1997. © 1997 Time Inc. All rights reserved. Reprinted by permission.
2. Peter D. Bennett, *Dictionary of Marketing Terms*, 2d ed. (Chicago: American Marketing Association, 1995), p. 115.
3. Philip Kotler, *Marketing Management*, 9th ed. (Englewood Cliffs, NJ: Prentice-Hall, 1997), p. 11.
4. Stephen Baker, "A New Paint Job at PPG," *Business Week*, 13 November 1995, pp. 74, 78.
5. Graham J. Hooley, John A. Saunders, and Nigel Piercy, *Marketing Strategy & Competitive Positioning* (London: Prentice-Hall Europe, 1998), p. 6.
6. J. W. Marriott, Jr., and Kathi Ann Brown, *The Spirit to Serve: Marriott's Way* (New York: Harper Business, 1997), p. 5.
7. Hammer and Stanton, p. 294.
8. David Cravens, Charles W. Lamb, Jr., and Victoria Crittenden, *Strategic Marketing Management Cases*, New York: McGraw-Hill, 1999), p. 81.
9. Sean Mehegan, "Sun Lotions Go Back into Frying Pan," *Brandweek*, 3 March 1997, p. 2.
10. Cravens, Lamb, and Crittenden, p. 79.
11. "Russia Warms to Canadian Homes". *The Globe and Mail*, 26 September 2000, p. B15.
12. Kevin J. Clancy and Robert S. Shulman, "Marketing—Ten Fatal Flaws," *The Retailing Issues Letter*, November 1995, p. 4.
13. Jonathan B. Levine, "Customer, Sell Thyself," *Fast Company*, June-July 1996, p. 148.
14. Roland T. Rust, Anthony J. Zahorik, and Timothy L. Keiningham, *Service Marketing* (New York: HarperCollins, 1996), p. 375.
15. Leonard L. Berry, "Relationship Marketing of Services," *Journal of the Academy of Marketing Science*, Fall 1995, pp. 236–245.
16. Berry, p. 241.
17. From "Main Street Revisited" by Becky Ebenkamp, *Brandweek*, April 7, 1997. © 1997 ASM Communications Inc. Used with permission from *Brandweek*.
18. Gary Samuels, "CD-ROM's First Big Victim," *Forbes*, 28 February 1994, pp. 42–44.
19. Samuels, p. 42.
20. Hooley, Saunders, and Piercy, pp. 8, 10.
21. Kotler, p. 22.
22. "The Checkoff," *Wall Street Journal*, 26 November 1996, p. A1.

CHAPTER 2

1. Peter Verburg, "Prepare for Takeoff," *Canadian Business*, 25 December 2000, pp. 94–9.
2. Verburg, p. 94.
3. Lily Nguyen, "WestJet Soars with Another Profit," *The Globe and Mail*, 2 August 2001, pp. B1, B2.
4. Ernest Beck, "Soap Makers Aim Laundry Tablets at Europe's Young and Harried," *The Wall Street Journal*, 27 May 1998, p. B8.
5. Greg Burns, "What Price the Snapple Debacle?" *Business Week Online*, 14 April 1997.
6. Gary McWilliams, "Compaq's Power Play," *Business Week Online*, 9 February 1998.
7. Bill Vlasic, "German Carmakers in the Fast Lane," *Business Week Online*, 13 April 1998.
8. Suntanu Dalal, "If you Can't Join'Em, Beat'Em," *Canadian Business*, 25 December 2000, pp. 107–10.
9. Dalal, p. 108.
10. Theodore Levitt, "Marketing Myopia," *Harvard Business Review*, 1 September 1975, pp. 1–14.
11. Saturn Corporation, *Face to Face with the Future* (Detroit: Saturn Corporation, 1994).
12. Anne Fisher, "The World's Most Admired Companies," *Fortune*, 27 October 1997, pp. 220–40.
13. Kathy Rebello, "Inside MicroSoft," *Businesss Week*, 15 July 1996, pp. 56–67.
14. Dave Enber, "P&G Launches Products to Boost Sales," *The Globe and Mail*, 18 May 2000, p. B10.
15. Nikhil Dogun and Jonathan Karp, "For Coke in India, Thums Up Is the Real Thing," *The Wall Street Journal*, 29 April 1988, pp. B1, B2. Reprinted with permission of Dow Jones. Copyright Clearance Center.
16. Carole Sugarman, "Can Eating Get Any Easier?" *The Washington Post*, 20 January 1999, p. 1F.
17. Julian Lichtbau, "Ritz Foods: Upscale Chips from the Lowly Yucca," *Business Week Online*, 6 August 1998.
18. **www.terrachips.com**

CHAPTER 3

1. Oliver Bertin, "Labatt Brews Profit from Premium Suds," *The Globe and Mail*, 13 March 2001, p. B9.
2. Ibid.
3. Ibid.
4. Ibid.
5. "No Place Like Home," *Wall Street Journal*, 16 June 1997, p. R4.
6. "Are Tech Buyers Different?" *Business Week*, 26 January 1998, pp. 64–68.
7. Gerry Myers, "Selling to Women," *American Demographics*, April 1996, pp. 36–42.
8. Jophn Heinzl, "Imperial Tobacco Tries Out Stealth Marketing Weapon," *The Globe and Mail*, 7 May 2001, pp. B1, B5..
9. Statistics Canada, CANSIM, Matrix 6900 (2001), and Melinda Beck, "Next Population Bulge Shows Its Might," *Wall Street Journal*, 3 February 1997, pp. B1, B6.
10. Statistics Canada, Cat. No. 81–229–XIB (2001), and "Marketing to Generation X," *Advertising Age*, 6 February 1995, p. 27.
11. "Understanding Generation X," *Marketing Research*, Spring 1993, pp. 54–55.
12. "Xers Know They're a Target Market, and They Hate That," *Marketing News*, 6 December 1993, pp. 2, 15.
13. "Easy Pickup Line? Try Gen Xers," *Advertising Age*, 3 April 1995, pp. 5–22.
14. "Survey Sheds Light on Typical Boomer," *Marketing News*, 31 January 1994, p. 2.

15. Statistics Canada, CANSIM, Matrix 6900 (2001).
16. "Boomers Come of Old Age," *Marketing News*, 15 January 1996, pp. 1, 6.
17. Ibid.
18. "Mature Market Often Misunderstood," *Marketing News*, 28 August 1995, p. 28.
19. Michael Major, "Promoting to the Mature Market," *Promo*, November 1990, p. 7.
20. "Bond Stronger with Age," *Advertising Age*, 28 March 1994, pp. 5–6.
21. "Baby-Boomers May Seek Age-Friendly Stores," *Wall Street Journal*, 1 July 1992, p. B1.
22. Charles Schewe and Geoffrey Meredith, "Digging Deep to Delight the Mature Adult Customer," *Marketing Management*, Winter 1995, pp. 21–34.
23. Statistics Canada, *Canadian Dynamics*, Cat. No. 96–311 (September 2000).
24. Mark MacKinnon, "A Little Country, A Little High Tech," *The Globe and Mail*, 8 March 1999, pp. B1, B5.
25. Statistics Canada, 1996 Census, *Nation* tables.
26. Statistics Canada, *Canadian Population Dynamics*, Cat. No. 96–309E, (2001).
27. Statistics Canada, *Market Research Handbook*, Cat. No. 63–224 (1999).
28. Elaine Carey, "1 in 10 Canadians a Minority," *Toronto Star*, 18 February 1998, pp. A1, A25.
29. "Grizzlies Capitalize on Asian Fan Interest in the NBA," *Marketing*, 5 August 1997, p. 2.
30. Jon Berry, "An Empire of Niches," Superbrands: A Special Supplement to Adweek's *Marketing Week*, Fall 1991, pp. 17–22.
31. Statistics Canada, *Income Distribution by Size in Canada,*, Cat No. 13-207 (2001).
32. Ibid.
33. Eric Beauchesne, "Ontarians Top Earners," *Windsor Star*, 10 June 2000, pp. C1, C2.
34. www, statcan.ca/current economic indicators
35. Bruce Little, "B.C. Economy Posts Weakest Growth Rate," *The Globe and Mail*, 11 November 2000, p. B6.
36. "The New Business Cycle," *Business Week*, 31 March 1997, pp. 58–60.
37. "Motorola's Prospects Are Linked to New Technologies," *Wall Street Journal*, 11 April 1996, p. B4.
38. "The Internet Unplugged," *Fortune* (Technology Guide), Winter 2001, pp. 160–2.
39. Patrick Brethour, "Canadians, Swedes Used the Net Most in 2000," *The Globe and Mail*, 16 May 2001, p. B6.
40. John Yaukey, "E-Mail Out of Control," *The Globe and Mail*, 7 May 2001, p. B1.
41. "Frito-Lay Devours Snack-Food Business," *Wall Street Journal*, 27 October 1995, pp. B1, B4.
42. Jacquie McNish and Marina Strauss, "Pulp Fiction," *The Globe and Mail,*, 14 May 2001, pp. B1, B7, B8.
43. Ibid.
44. Ibid.
45. From Nikhil Deogun and Amy Barrett, "France Rejects Coca-Cola's Purchase of Orangina," *Wall Street Journal*, September 18, 1998. Reprinted by permission of Dow Jones. Copyright Clearance Center.
46. This section adapted from Archie B. Carroll, "The Pyramid of Corporate Social Responsibility: Toward the Moral Management of Organizational Stakeholders," *Business Horizons*, July–August 1991, pp. 39–48; also see: Kirk Davidson, "Marketers Must Accept Greater Responsibilities," *Marketing News*, 2 February 1998, p. 6.
47. Rashanda Williams, "Burger King to Aid Storm Victims," *Windsor Star*, 20 November 1998, p. B1.
48. Madelaine Drohan, "Corporations Add Values," *The Globe and Mail,*, 24 February, 2000, p. B14.
49. Suzanne Alexander, "Life's Just a Bowl of Cherry Garcia for Ben & Jerry's," *Wall Street Journal*, 15 July 1992, p. B3.
50. Cara Appelbaum, "Jantzen to Pitch in for Clean Waters," *Adweek's Marketing Week*, 6 April 1992, p. 6.

CHAPTER 4

1. Sharon Moore, *We Love Harry Potter! We'll Tell You Why*, New York: St. Martin's Griffin, 1999.
2. "J.K. Rowling Closing on Mao," *National Post*, Thursday May 3, 2001, B7.
3. Anna Kohn, "Under Harry's Spell," *Context*, Holiday 2000, Volume 1, No. 1, 80-82.
4. "J.K. Rowling Closing on Mao," *National Post*, Thursday May 3, 2001, B7.
5. Collector's Quest, *Collector's Value Guide: Harry Potter Collectibles*, Middletown, CT: Checkerbee, 2000.
6. www.fao.ca
7. www.harrypotter.warnerbros.com
8. *Strategy Magazine*, 11 September 2000.
9. Nancy Ten Kate, "The Marketplace for Medicine," *American Demographics*, February 1998, p. 34.
10. Ibid.
11. Ibid.
12. D. S. Sundaram and Michael D. Richard, "Perceived Risk and the Information Acquisition Process of Computer Mail-Order Shoppers," in 1995 *Southern Marketing Association Proceedings*, eds. Brian T. Engelland and Denise T. Smart (Houston: Southern Marketing Association), 1995, pp. 322–326.
13. Eric D. Bruce and Sam Fullerton, "Discount Pricing as a Mediator of the Consumer's Evoked Set," in 1995 *Atlantic Marketing Association Proceedings*, eds. Donald L. Thompson and Cathy Owens Swift (Orlando: Atlantic Marketing Association), pp. 32–36.
14. F. Kelly Shruptrine, "Warranty Coverage: How Important in Purchasing an Automobile?" in 1995 *Southern Marketing Association Proceedings*, eds. Brian T. Engelland and Denise T. Smart (Houston: Southern Marketing Association), 1995, pp. 300–303.
15. Greg Johnson, "Hoping Fixers Will Be Uppers: Big Firms See Profitable Market in Repair Services, *Los Angeles Times*, 2 October 1997, p. D-1.

16. Don Umphrey, "Consumer Costs: A Determinant of Upgrading or Downgrading of Cable Service," *Journalism Quarterly*, Winter 1991, pp. 698–708.
17. Robert L. Simison, "Infiniti Adopts New Sales Strategy to Polish Its Brand," *Wall Street Journal*, 10 June 1996, p. B1, B7.
18. Brandon Mitchener, "Mercedes Dealers Offer New Kind of Test Drive," *Wall Street Journal*, 26 March 1998, p. B8.
19. Michael J. McCarthy, "Kellogg Stirs Health Claims into Cereal Ads," *Wall Street Journal*, 4 June 1997, p. B7.
20. *Toronto Sun*, 6 June 2001.
21. Bill Stoneman, "Beyond Rocking the Ages: An Interview with J. Walker Smith," *American Demographics*, May 1998, pp. 44–49.
22. Data obtained from The New Products Showcase & Learning Center, Ithaca, New York, Web site at www.showlearn.com, 1998.
23. David B. Wolfe, "The Psychological Center of Gravity," *American Demographics*, April 1998, pp. 16–19.
24. Diane Crispell, "Core Values," *American Demographics*, November 1996.
25. Jerry W. Thomas, "Finding Unspoken Reasons for Consumers' Choices," *Marketing News*, 8 June 1998, p. 10.
26. Carl Quintanilla, "Despite Setbacks, Whirlpool Pursues Overseas Markets," *Wall Street Journal*, 9 December 1997, p. B4.
27. Robert Levine, "The Pace of Life in 31 Countries," *American Demographics*, November 1997, pp. 20–29; John Robinson, Bart Landry, and Ronica Rooks, "Time and the Melting Pot," *American Demographics*, June 1998, pp. 18–24; John P. Robinson, Toon Van Der Horn, and Ryichi Kitamura, "Less Work, More Play: Life's Good in Holland," *American Demographics*, September 1993; Robert Levine, "Re-Learning to Tell Time," *American Demographics*, January 1998, pp. 20–25.
28. John W. Schouten and James H. McAlexander, "Subcultures of Consumption: An Ethnography of the New Bikers," *Journal of Consumer Research*, June 1995, pp. 43–61.
29. Rebecca Piirto Heath, "Life on Easy Street," *American Demographics*, April 1997.
30. Elia Kacapyr, "Are You Middle Class?" *American Demographics*, October 1996.
31. Rebecca Piirto Heath, "The New Working Class," *American Demographics*, January 1998, pp. 51–55.
32. Heath, "Life on Easy Street."
33. Grahame R. Dowling and Richard Staelin, "A Model of Perceived Risk and Intended Risk-Handling Activity," *Journal of Consumer Research*, June 1994, pp. 119–134.
34. Chip Walker, "Word of Mouth," *American Demographics*, July 1995, pp. 38–44.
35. Norihiko Shirouzu, "Japan's High-School Girls Excel in Art of Setting Trends," *Wall Street Journal*, 24 April 1998, pp. B1, B6.
36. Matthew Klein, "He Shops, She Shops," *American Demographics*, March 1998, pp. 34–35.
37. Nancy Ten Kate, "Two Careers, One Marriage," *American Demographics*, April 1998, p. 28.
38. Maxine Wilkie, "Names That Smell," *American Demographics*, August 1995, pp. 48–49.
39. Yumiko Ono, "Victoria's Secret Launches Cosmetics Line," *Wall Street Journal*, 14 September 1998, p. B6.
40. Nora J. Rifon and Molly Catherine Ziske, "Using Weight Loss Products: The Roles of Involvement, Self-Efficacy and Body Image," in *1995 AMA Educators' Proceedings*, eds. Barbara B. Stern and George M. Zinkhan (Chicago: American Marketing Association, 1995), pp. 90–98.
41. William D. Wells and David Prensky, *Consumer Behavior* (New York: John Wiley & Sons, Inc., 1996), p. 46.
42. Robert M. McMath, "What's in a Name?" *American Demographics*, December 1996.
43. Elizabeth J. Wilson, "Using the Dollarmetric Scale to Establish the Just Meaningful Difference in Price," in *1987 AMA Educators' Proceedings*, ed. Susan Douglas et al. (Chicago: American Marketing Association, 1987), p. 107.
44. Sunil Gupta and Lee G. Cooper, "The Discounting of Discounts and Promotion Thresholds," *Journal of Consumer Research*, December 1992, pp. 401–411.
45. Mark Stiving and Russell S. Winer, "An Empirical Analysis of Price Endings with Scanner Data," *Journal of Consumer Research*, June 1997, pp. 57–67; also see Robert M. Schindler and Patrick N. Kirby, "Patterns of Rightmost Digits Used in Advertised Price: Implications for Nine-Ending Effects," *Journal of Consumer Research*, September 1997, pp. 192–201.
46. Stacy Kravetz, "Dry Cleaners' New Wrinkle: Going Green," *Wall Street Journal*, 3 June 1998, pp. B1, B2.
47. Maria Mallory and Kevin Whitelaw, "The Power Brands," *U.S. News & World Report*, May 13, 1996, p. 58.
48. "Asian Culture and the Global Consumer," *Financial Times*, 21 September 1998, p. 1.
49. Yumiko Ono, "Tiffany Glitters, Even in Gloomy Japan," *Wall Street Journal*, 21 July 1998, pp. B1, B18.
50. Gene Del Vecchio, "Keeping It Timeless, Trendy: From Barbie to Pez, 'Ever-Cool' Kids Brands Meet Both Needs," *Advertising Age*, 23 March 1998, p. 24.
51. Kate Fitzgerald, "The Marketing 100: Starbucks Ice Cream Shari Fujii," *Advertising Age*, 29 June 1998, p. s39.
52. Gregory L. White, "Jeep's Challenge: Stay Rugged but Add Room for Golf Clubs," *Wall Street Journal*, 26 August 1998, pp. B1, B4.
53. Jean Halliday and Laura Petrecca, "Volvo Effort Extends Image Positioning," *Advertising Age*, 30 March 1998, p. 9; William J. Holstein, "Volvo Can't Play Safe: To Survive, the Swedish Auto Maker Needs to Be Fun, Too," *U.S. News & World Report*, 27 July 1998, pp. 40–41.

CHAPTER 5

1. *Technology Forecast* (Menlo Park, California: Price Waterhouse, 1997), p. 1.

2. Figure supplied by Cisco Systems.
3. "In Search of a Perfect Market," *The Economist*, 19 May 1997, on-line.
4. "In Search of a Perfect Market," on-line.
5. Alan M. Patterson, "Customers Can Be Partners," *Marketing News*, 9 September 1996, p. 10.
6. Adapted from Robert L. Rose, "For Whirlpool, Asia Is the New Frontier," *Wall Street Journal*, 25 April 1996, pp. B1, B4.
7. Michael D. Hutt and Thomas W. Speh, *Business Marketing*, 5th ed. (Fort Worth, TX: Dryden, 1998), p. 121.
8. Frank G. Bingham, Jr., and Barney T. Raffield, III, *Business Marketing Management* (Cincinnati, OH: South-Western College Publishing, 1995), pp. 18–19.
9. Hutt and Speh, pp. 139–141.
10. Jonah Gitlitz, "Direct Marketing in the B-to-B Future," *Business Marketing*, July/August 1996, pp. A2, A5.
11. Ira Sager, "How IBM Became a Growth Company Again," *Business Week*, 9 December 1996, pp. 155–156.
12. Robert W Haas, *Business Marketing*, 6th ed. (Cincinnati, OH: South-Western College Publishing, 1995), p. 190.
13. Amy Cortese, "Here Comes the Intranet," *Business Week*, 26 February 1996, p. 76.

CHAPTER 6

1. Modrobes media kit; Lisa D'Innocenzo, "From Underground to Top of Mind Without Losing Cool," *Strategy*, 15 January 2001; Hilary Davidson, "Out of the Mainstream," *Profit*, November 1999; Astrid Van den Broek, "Targeting Yourself," *Marketing*, 2 August 1999.
2. John Gray, "Gen Y Identifies With Brands," *Strategy Magazine*, 24 May 1999.
3. Statistics Canada Population Projections.
4. Emily Nelson, "Kodak Focuses on Putting Kids Behind Instead of Just in Front of a Camera," *Wall Street Journal*, 6 May 1997, p. B8.
5. The Associated Press, "Little Girls, Big Bucks," *Marketing News* 32 No. 7, 30 March 1998, p. 1.
6. Statistics Canada.
7. David K. Foot and Daniel Stoffman, *Boom, Bust, & Echo*, Stoddart Publishing, 2000.
8. Abbe Edelson, "The Underdog," *Marketing Magazine*, 7 May 2001.
9. Mark Maremont, "Gillette's New Strategy Is to Sharpen Pitch to Women," *Wall Street Journal*, 11 May 1998, p. B1; Tara Parker-Pope, "Minoxidil Tries to Grow Women's Market," *Wall Street Journal*, 27 January 1997, p. B1.
10. Margaret Littman, "Women Fans Have Gridiron Pros Grinning," *Marketing News*, Vol. 32 No. 3, 2 February 1998, p.1.
11. From "Europe Is Deaf to Snap! Crackle! Pop!" by Ernest Beck and Rehka Balu, *Wall Street Journal*, June 22, 1998. Reprinted with permission of Dow Jones. Copyright Clearance Center.
12. Anne Faircloth, "Value Retailers Go Dollar for Dollar," *Fortune*, 6 July 1998, pp. 164–166.
13. Louise Lee, "Discounter Wal-Mart Is Catering to Affluent to Maintain Growth," *Wall Street Journal*, 7 February 1996, pp. 1, 6.
14. Patrick Lejtenyl, "Underlying Differences," *Marketing Magazine*, 5 June 2000.
15. Alex Taylor III, "Porsche Slices Up Its Buyers," *Fortune*, 16 January 1995, p. 24.
16. Karen Benezra, "The Fragging of the American Mind," *Superbrands*, 15 June 1998, pp. S12–S19.
17. Sally Beatty, "Drug Companies Are Minding Your Business: Reader's Digest Targets Patients By Their Ailments," *Wall Street Journal*, pp. B1, B3.
18. Stan Rapp and Thomas Collins, T*he New Maxi Marketing*, excerpted in *Success*, April 1996, pp. 39–45.
19. Nicole Harris, "Home Depot: Beyond Do-It-Yourselfers," *Business Week*, 30 June 1997, pp. 86–88.
20. IDC Canada Ltd. and from John Shoesmith, "Psst...wanna buy a pen?," *Canadian Business Magazine*, 5 March 2001
21. Much of the material in this section is based on Michael D. Hurt and Thomas W. Speh, *Business Marketing Management*, 6th ed. (Hinsdale, IL: Dryden Press, 1998), pp. 176–181.
22. Susan Chandler, "Kids' Wear Is Not Child's Play," *Business Week*, 19 June 1995, p. 118.
23. Jason MacDonald, "Suds Studs," *Canadian Business Magazine*, 18 September 2000.
24. Leon Jaroff, "Fire in the Belly, Money in the Bank," Time, 6 November 1995, pp. 56–58.
25. Sara Smith, "Roots Air Likely Grounded for Good," *Marketing Magazine*, 14 May 2001.
26. Steve Gelsi, "GMC Moves Further into Luxury Tier," *Brandweek*, 15 April 1997, p. 4.
27. These examples were provided by David W. Cravens, Texas Christian University.
28. Steve Gelsi, "Staying True to the Sole," *Brandweek*, 8 April 1996, pp. 24, 26.
29. Elaine Underwood, "Sea Change," *Brandweek*, 22 April 1996, pp. 33–36.
30. D'Arcy Jenish, "Up in the Air," *Macleans*, 2 April 2001.
31. Louise Kramer, "Mountain Dew Stays True to Its Brand Positioning," *Advertising Age*, 18 May 1998, p. 26.
32. Ellen Rooney Martin, "Midas Breaks $25M Makeover Effort," *Brandweek*, 11 March 1996, p. 8.

CHAPTER 7

1. Experiment designed and undertaken for Waltec Industries by one of the authors.
2. "Keebler Learns to Pay Attention to Research Right from the Start," *Marketing News*, 11 March 1996, p. 10.
3. "Why Some Customers Are More Equal Than Others," *Fortune*, 19 September 1994, pp. 215–224.
4. Ibid.
5. "Major U.S. Companies Expand Efforts to Sell to Consumers Abroad," *Wall Street Journal*, 13 June 1996, pp. A1, A6.
6. "Hey Kid, Buy This," *Business Week*, 30 June 1997, pp. 63–66.
7. Andrew Bean and Michael Roszkowski, "The Long and Short of It," *Marketing Research*, Winter 1995, pp. 21–26.
8. John Vidmar, "Just Another Metamorphosis," *Marketing*

Research, Spring 1996, pp. 16–18; Sharon Munger, "Premium Medium," *Marketing Research*, Spring 1996, pp. 10–12; and William Nicholls, "Highest Response," *Marketing Research*, Spring 1996, pp. 5–8.
9. James Watt, "Using the Internet for Quantitative Survey Research," Quirk's *Marketing Research* Review, June/July 1997, pp. 18–19, 67–71.
10. Quote from Cyber Dialogue Web site, http://www.cyberdialogue.com/NewPages/PS/PSFrame.html, April 16, 1997.
11. Sharon Weissbach, "Internet Research: Still a Few Hurdles to Clear," *Quirk's Marketing Research Review,* June/July 1997, pp. 22–26.
12. Ibid.
13. James Watt, "Using the Internet for Quantitative Survey Research," *Quirk's Marketing Research* Review, June/July 1997, p. 67.
14. Bill Eaton, "Internet Surveys: Does WWW Stand for 'Why Waste the Work?'" *Quirk's Marketing Research* Review, June/July 1997, pp. 28–30; also see: Robert Peterson, Sridhar Balasubramanian, and Bart Bronnenberg, "Exploring the Implications of the Internet for Consumer Marketing," *Journal of the Academy of Marketing Science*, Fall 1977, pp. 329–346.
15. This section is adapted from James Watt, "Using the Internet for Quantitative Survey Research," *Quirk's Marketing Research* Review, June/July 1997, pp. 67–71.
16. See Donna Guido, "Constructing an Effective Mystery Shopping Program," *Quirk's Marketing Research* Review, January 1985, pp. 12–13, 48–49.
17. From "Familiar Refrain: Consultant's Advice on Diversity Was Anything But Diverse" by Douglas A. Blackmon, *Wall Street Journal*, March 11, 1997. Reprinted by permission of The Wall Street Journal, © 1997 Dow Jones & Company, Inc. All Rights Reserved Worldwide.

CHAPTER 8

1. From "Selling the Sizzle" by Robert Lieber, *Fortune,* June 23, 1997. © 1997 Time Inc. All rights reserved.
2. Heather Scoffield, "Bombardier Looks Certain to Win Loan," *The Globe and Mail*, 26 May 2001, pp. B1, B4.
3. "Competitor Intelligence Considered More Vital Now," *Marketing News*, 9 October 1995, p. 3.
4. Sheena Sharp, "New Techniques for Corporate Foresight," *Research Conference Report,* May 1998, pp. 7–8.
5. "Hugh McBride, "They Snoop to Conquer," *Canadian Business*, July 1999, pp. 45–7.
6. David Kirkpatrick, "Houston, We Have Some Problems," *Fortune*, 23 June 1997, pp. 102–105.
7. Edward Parker, "Learn from the Masters of Competitive Intelligence: The Spy Fighters," *Success*, April 1994, pp. 33–39.
8. McBride, p. 46.
9. McBride, p. 47.
10. From "Toward Strategic Intelligence Systems" by David Montgomery and Charles Weinberg, *Marketing Management,* Winter 1998, pp. 44–52. Reprinted by permission of the American Marketing Association.
11. McBride, p. 47.
12. From *The New Competitor Intelligence* by Leonard M. Fuld. Copyright © 1995 by Leonard M. Fuld. Reprinted by permission of John Wiley & Sons, Inc.
13. Fuld, p. 236.
14. Nathalie Borris Carlyle, "Expert Advice: A New Look at Advisory Boards," *Canadian Business Review*, Autumn 1996, pp. 27–8.
15. Fuld, p. 236.
16. Fuld, p. 236.
17. From "Browsers Get Peak at Rivals' Secrets" by B. G. Yovovich, *Marketing News*, November 10, 1997, pp. 1, 6. Reprinted by permission of the American Marketing Association.
18. David Vine, "I Spy—Gathering Business Intelligence," *Internet World,* March 1997, pp. 48–51.
19. Edward Robinson, "China's Spies Target Corporate America," *Fortune*, 30 March 1998, pp. 118–22.
20. Ibid.
21. "Corporate Spies Feel a Sting," *Business Week*, 14 July 1997, pp. 76–77.
22. Robinson, p. 119.
23. Bernard Marotte, "T-Shirt Maker Alleges Espionage," *The Globe and Mail*, 7 April 2001, pp. B1, B2.
24. From "The Ethics of Business Intelligence" by Norman O. Schultz, Allison B. Collins, and Michael McCulloch, *Journal of Business Ethics*, Vol 13, Issue 4, April 1994, pp. 305–314. Copyright Kluwer Academic Publishers Group Apr 1994. Reprinted with kind permission from Kluwer Academic Publishers and the author.
25. "That VROOM! You Hear May Not Be a Harley," *Business Week*, 20 October 1997, pp. 159–160.

CHAPTER 9

1. From "Taking Off the McWraps" by Karen Benezra and Stephanie Thompson, Brandweek, May 21, 1998. © 1998 ASM Communications, Inc. Used with permission from BRANDWEEK.
2. Yumiko Ono, "Limited Tips Hand in Lauder Raid," *Wall Street Journal*, 23 June 1998, pp. B1, B6.
3. Chris Roush, "At Times, They're Positively Glowing," *Business Week*, 12 July 1993, p. 141.
4. Matt Murray, "Kodak Considers Selling Discount Film to Compete with Private-Label Brands," *Wall Street Journal*, 4 June 1997, p. B3.
5. Stephanie Thompson, "Hostess Promises Great Taste Plus Nutrition with New Cereal Bar Line," *Brandweek*, 9 March 1998, p. 44.
6. Stephanie Thompson, "No-Mess Packs Aimed at Steak Sauce," *Brandweek*, 24 August 1998, p. 6.
7. Stephanie Thompson, "Choice Soup Intros Gloss Up Brand," *Brandweek*, 30 June 1997, p. 3.
8. Noreen O'Leary, "The Old Bunny Trick," *Brandweek*, 18 March 1996, pp. 26–30.
9. Brandon Mitchener, "Mercedes Adds Down-Market Niche Cars," *Wall Street Journal*, 21 February 1996, p. A10.
10. Sean Mehegan, "Would She Buy Dandruff Shampoo?" *Brandweek*, 26 January 1998, p. 6.
11. "Make it Simple," *Business Week*, 9 September 1996, p. 96.
12. Ibid.
13. Jonathan Welsh, "Black & Decker to Shed Some Lines and

Focus on Tools," *Wall Street Journal*, 28 January 1998, p. B7.
14. "Teens Name Coolest Brands," *Marketing News*, 12 February 1996, p. 6.
15. Diane Crispell and Kathleen Brandenburg, "What's in a Brand?" *American Demographics*, May 1993, pp. 26–32.
16. Bernhard Warner, "Digitizing Dinner," *Brandweek*, 16 February 1998, p. 38.
17. From "The Name Game Heats Up" by Steve Rivkin, *Marketing News*, April 22, 1996, p. 8. Reprinted by permission of the American Marketing Association.
18. Susan Bourette, "Private Label Share Has Peaked," *The Globe and Mail*, 30 November 1998, pp. B1, B3.
19. "Kmart Accelerates Private Label Push," *Brandweek*, 29 January 1996, p. 6.
20. Ellen Neuborne and Stephanie Anderson Forest, "Look Who's Picking Levi's Pocket," *Business Week*, 8 September 1997, pp. 68, 72.
21. Janet McFarland, "Hotels Forge Chain Links," *The Globe and Mail*, 1 July 1997, p. B5.
22. Bruce Orwall, "Multiplying Hotel Brands Puzzle Travelers," *Wall Street Journal*, 17 April 1996, p. B1.
23. Marina Strauss, "Loblaw Looks to Expand President's Choice Brand," *The Globe and Mail*, 25 January 2000, pp. B1, B11.
24. Karen Benezra, "New Tabasco Product a Chip Shot for Frito," *Brandweek*, 22 April 1996, p. 8.
25. Stephanie Thompson, "The O's Have It," *Brandweek*, 30 March 1998, p. 1.
26. Steven C. Bahls and Jane Easter Bahls, "Fighting Fakes," *Entrepreneur*, February 1996, pp. 73–76.
27. Michael Rapoport, "Clash of Symbols: DKNY Sues DNKY Over Trademark," *Wall Street Journal*, 26 August 1996, p. A7B.
28. From "'Ti-Gear': Owning Up to a Name" by Michelle Wirth Fellman, *Marketing News*, October 26, 1998, p. 2. Reprinted by permission of the American Marketing Association.
29. Lisa Brownlee, "Polo Magazine Angers Polo Ralph Lauren," *Wall Street Journal*, 21 October 1997, p. B 10.
30. Michael J. McCarthy, "Fake King Cobras Tee Off the Makers of High-End Clubs," *Wall Street Journal*, 11 February 1997, p. A1, A17.
31. Maxine Lans Retsky, "Who Needs the New Community Trademark?" *Marketing News*, 3 June 1996, p. 11.
32. Betsy Spethmann, "Getting Fresh," *Brandweek*, 20 May 1996, pp. 44–47.
33. Stephanie Thompson, "Welch's Redesigns Entire Line for More Unified Shelf Presence," *Brandweek*, 28 April 1997, p. 6.
34. Tammy Reiss, "Hey, It's Green—It Must Be Healthy," *Business Week*, 13 July 1998, p. 6.
35. Raju Narisetti, "Plotting to Get Tissues into Living Rooms, *Wall Street Journal*, 3 May 1996, pp. B1, B12.
36. Stephanie Thompson. "C&H Pours Forth Innovation in Sugar," *Brandweek*, 23 March 1998, p. 14. Reprinted with permission.
37. "Just Enough Packaging," *Wall Street Journal*, 7 September 1995, p. A1.
38. "A Biodegradable Plastic Gains Notice," *Wall Street Journal*, 4 February 1993, p. A1; Robert McMath, "It's All in the Trigger," Adweek's Marketing Week, 6 January 1992, pp. 25–28.
39. Pam Weisz, "Price Tools for Pfixer-Uppers," *Brandweek*, 18 April 1994, p. 8.
40. Hugh Pope, "Plying Ex-Soviet Asia with Pepsi, Barbie and Barf," *Wall Street Journal*, 6 May 1998, pp. B1, B6.
41. Hugh Filman, "A Brand New World: Packaged Goods Companies Go Global with Their Wares," *Marketing Executive Report*, June 1992, pp. 22–23.
42. "Make it Simple," p. 102.
43. Howard Alport, "Global, Interactive Marketing Call for Innovative Packaging," *Marketing News*, 6 January 1997, p. 30.

CHAPTER 10

1. John Heinzl, "Heinz Squeezes Out Purple Ketchup," The Globe and Mail, 7 August 2001, p. B8.
2. Ibid.
3. Ted Whipp, "Taste of Things to Come," Windsor Star, 23 July 1999, p. B3.
4. Brian O'Reilly, "The Secrets of America's Most Admired Corporations: New Ideas, New Products," *Fortune*, 3 March 1997, p. 60.
5. Howard Rudnitsky, "One Hundred Sixty Companies for the Price of One," *Forbes*, 26 February 1996, p. 57; William C. Symonds, "Gillette's Edge," *Business Week*, 19 January 1998, p. 71.
6. Richard Gibson, "A Cereal Maker's Quest for the Next Grape Nuts," *Wall Street Journal*, 23 January 1997, p. B1.
7. Sam Bradley, "Hallmark Enters $20B Pet Category," *Brandweek*, 1 January 1996, p. 4.
8. "Never Say 'Old and Lousy'," *Fortune*, 13 October 1997, p. 40.
9. "New But Not Necessarily Improved," *Wall Street Journal*, 15 January 1997, p. A1.
10. Stephanie Thompson, "Quaker Puts $15M into Indulgence-Oriented Rice Cake Makeover," *Brandweek*, 2 March 1998, p. 6.
11. Philip Demont, "Canada Drier," *Windsor Star*, 1 March 2000, pp. B3, B5.
12. Ibid., p. B3.
13. *New Product Management in the 1980s* (New York: Booz, Allen and Hamilton, 1982), p. 3.
14. "Search and Employ," *Forbes*, 3 June 1996, p. 88.
15. "New Products," *Fort Worth Star-Telegram*, 11 May 1997, p. E1.
16. Norhiko Shirouzu, "For Coca-Cola in Japan, Things Go Better with Milk," *Wall Street Journal*, 20 January 1997, p. B1.
17. Shirouzu, p. B1.
18. Mark Marmount, "How Gillette Brought Its MACH3 to Market," *The Wall Street Journal*, 15 April 1998, p. B1.
19. Maremont, p. B1.
20. Tom Lynch, "Internet: A Strategic Product Introduction Tool," *Marketing News*, 22 April 1996, p. 15.
21. Linda Grant, "Gillette Knows Shaving—and How to Turn Out," *Fortune*, 14 October 1996, on-line.
22. "Procter & Gamble Co. to Test a New Spray for Removing Odors," *Wall Street Journal*, 8 May 1996, p. A5.
23. Karen Benezra, "Contour Can Sales Drop," *Brandweek*, 19 May 1997, p. 2.
24. Maremont, p. B1.
25. Lynch, p. 15.

26. Dennis D. Jorgensen, "Now, We Have a Brief Word from Our Sponsors," *Marketing News*, 30 March 1998, p. E4.
27. Robert M. McMath, "Copycat Cupcakes Don't Cut It," *American Demographics*, January 1997, p. 60.
28. Rolf Kiermaier and Stephan A. Butscher, "Develop Only What Customers Want, at Their Price," *Marketing News*, 17 March 1997, p. 10.
29. Joel Baumwall, "Why Didn't You Think of That?" *Marketing News*, 22 April 1996, p. 6.
30. David W. Cravens, *Strategic Marketing*, 5th ed. (New York: McGraw-Hill, 1997), pp. 244–245.
31. Ibid., p. 437.
32. Timothy D. Schellhardt, "David in Goliath," *Wall Street Journal*, 23 May 1996, p. R14.
33. Michael D. Hutt and Thomas W. Speh, *Business Marketing Management*, 5th ed. (Fort Worth, TX: Dryden Press, 1998), p. 334.
34. "Is the Cassette Doomed?," *Fortune*, 27 October 1997, p. 74.

CHAPTER 11

1. Adapted from Kim Hanson, "Perks Help Keep Four Seasons Staff Pampering Guests," *The National Post*, 13 January 2001, p. D8. © 2001 National Post. All Rights Reserved. 20010113NP1300302
2. Don Little, Statistics Canada Services Division, "Employment and Remuneration in the Services Industries Since 1984," (3rd Quarter, 1998); Statistics Canada Services Division, "How Resilient Is the Services Sector to Recession?" (3rd Quarter, 1997).
3. "The Manufacturing Myth," *The Economist*, 19 March 1994.
4. Greig Dymond, "Aussie Rules," *Report on Business*, April 2001.
5. Lynn Beresford, "Visual Aid," *Entrepreneur*, March 1996, p. 38.
6. Greg Wilson, "Domestic Automakers Offer Better Guarantees," *The National Post*, 23 February 2001, p. F4.
7. Valarie A. Zeithaml and Mary Jo Bitner, *Services Marketing*, (New York: McGraw-Hill, 1996).
8. Zeithaml and Bitner.
9. Chad Rubel, "Managers Buy Into Quality When They See It Works," *Marketing News*, 25 March 1996, p. 14.
10. Much of the material in this section is based on Christopher H. Lovelock, *Services Marketing* (Englewood Cliffs, NJ: Prentice-Hall, 1996), pp. 39–40.
11. Douglas McArthur, "Can Virgin Deliver?" *The Globe and Mail*, 6 June 2001.
12. Leslie Young, "The Battle on the Home Front," *Marketing*, 11 June 2001, p. 25.
13. www.citizensbank.ca/personal-banking/chequingsavings.html
14. www.amazon.com
15. Cliff Edwards, "McDonald's Switching to Made-to-Order Service," *Fort Worth Star-Telegram*, 27 March 1998, p. D1.
16. Astrid Van Den Broek, "Branding the Passion," *Marketing*, 14 May 2001, p. 8; Derek Decloet, "CIBC Looks Good When It's in Disguise," *The National Post*, 20 December 2000, p. C2.
17. Greig Dymond, "Aussie Rules."
18. Much of the material in this section is based on *Lovelock*, pp. 238–40.
19. Much of the material in this section is based on Leonard L. Berry and A. Parasuraman, *Marketing Services* (New York: Free Press, 1991), pp. 132–50.
20. Carolyn Green, "Room Perk a Bit Hard to Swallow," *The National Post Special Report: Passport*, 27 November 2000, p E2.
21. Berry and Parasuraman, pp. 151–2.
22. Stephanie Whittaker, "Charities Make On-Line Pitch," *Marketing: Digital Marketing Report*, 20 November, 2000.
23. Silvia Sansoni, "Gucci, Armani and . . . John Paul II?" *Business Week*, 15 April 1996, p. 108.

CHAPTER 12

1. Daniel Lyons, "Games Dealers Play," *Forbes*, 19 October 1998, pp. 132–134; Andrew Serwer, "Michael Dell Rocks," *Fortune*, 11 May 1998, p. 58; David E. Kalish, "Dell Computer Outsmarts IBM, Compaq," *AP Online*, 19 August 1998; Raju Narisetti, "IBM Plans to Sell Some Gear Directly to Fight Its Rivals," *Wall Street Journal*, 5 June 1998, p. B6; Evan Ramstad, "PC Playing Field Tilts in Favor of Dell," *Wall Street Journal*, 21 May 1998, p. B8; "Dell Selling PCs in China Through Its Internet Store," *The New Straits Times*, 25 August 1998, p. 22.
2. Evan Ramstad, "Gateway Unit to Bolster Ties to PC Dealers," *Wall Street Journal*, 20 April 1998, p. B2.
3. Louise Lee, "School's Back, and So Are the Marketers," *Wall Street Journal*, 15 September 1997, pp. B1, B6.
4. John Heinzl, "Internet Becomes World's Biggest Car Lot," *The Globe and Mail*, 23 September 1998, p. B25; Phil Scott, "Modem Up, Move 'Em Out," *Sydney Morning Herald*, 1 August 1997, p. 6; Gina Fann, "Consumers Hop on the Internet to Price and Research Vehicles," *Knight-Ridder Tribune Business News*, 2 February 1998; Rebecca Blumenstein, "Haggling in Cyberspace Transforms Car Sales," *Wall Street Journal*, 30 December 1997, p. B1; "Change Is Fast, But Most Dealers Are Adapting," *Automotive News*, 9 February 1998, p. 12; Gregory L. White, "General Motors to Take Nationwide Test Drive on Web," *Wall Street Journal*, 28 September 1998, p. B4; Auto-By-Tel Web site at www.autobytel.com.
5. Vanessa O'Connell, "Starbucks, Kraft to Announce Pact for Selling Coffee," *Wall Street Journal*, 28 September 1998, p. B4.
6. "Fujitsu, Oracle Form Strategic Alliance in Asia," *Reuters*, 21 August 1997.
7. William M. Bulkeley and Joseph Pereira, "Toy Stores Spur Buying Frenzies with Exclusives," *Wall Street Journal*, 2 December 1997, pp. B1, B10.
8. G. Bruce Knecht, "Rack or Ruin: How Magazines Arrive on Shelves, and Why Some Soon May Not," *Wall Street Journal*, 26 February 1998, pp. A1, A6.
9. William M. Bulkeley and John R. Wilke, "Toys Loses a Warehouse-Club Ruling with Broad Marketing Implications," *Wall Street Journal*, 1 October 1997, p. B10.
10. Laura Bird and Wendy Bounds, "Stores' Demands Squeeze Apparel Companies," *Wall Street Journal*, 15 July 1997, pp. B1, B3.

11. Stephanie N. Mehta, "Cellular Carriers Bypass Dealers, Creating Static," *Wall Street Journal*, 9 March 1998, pp. B1, B10.
12. Mary J. Cronin, "The Travel Agents' Dilemma," *Fortune*, 11 May 1998, pp. 163–164.
13. David Frederick Ross, *Competing Through Supply Chain Management: Creating Market-Winning Strategies Through Supply Chain Partnerships* (New York: Chapman & Hall, 1998), pp. 60–61.
14. "Retailing: General," *Standard & Poor's Industry Surveys*, Volume 166, Number 6, Section 1, 5 February 1998, p. 21.
15. Richard Gibson, "Merchants Mull the Long and the Short of Lines," *Wall Street Journal*, 3 September 1998, pp. B1, B4.
16. Matt Murray, "On the Road with a Rolling Bank Branch," *Wall Street Journal*, 6 November 1997, pp. B1, B13.
17. Tyler Hamilton, "Internet Travel Market Expected to Grow Sixfold," *The Globe and Mail*, 7 January 2000. p. B2.
18. Janet McFarland, "Gillette Tries to Nick Schick in Japan," *The Globe and Mail*, 4 February 1998, p. B8
19. Cindy Kano and Alex Taylor III, "The Cult of the Astro Van," *Fortune*, 18 August 1997.

CHAPTER 13

1. Matthew McKenna, "He Delivers," *Report on Business Magazine,"* December 2000; Terry Poulton, "Grocery Gateway Builds Total Brand Personality," *Strategy*, January 2000; **www.grogate.com**.
2. Francis J. Quinn, "Supply-Chain Management Report: What's the Buzz?" *Logistics Management*, February 1997.
3. Ross, *Competing Through Supply Chain Management*, pp. 9–12.
4. Quinn, "Supply-Chain Management Report: What's the Buzz?"
5. Ross, *Competing Through Supply Chain Management*, pp. 9–12.
6. Ibid.
7. This section based on John L. Kent, Jr. and Daniel J. Flint, "Perspectives on the Evolution of Logistics Thought," *Journal of Business Logistics*, Volume 18, Number 2 (1997), p. 15 and Francis J. Quinn, "What's the Buzz?" *Logistics Management & Distribution Report*, 1 February 1997.
8. Benefits based on Francis J. Quinn, "The Payoff! Benefits of Improving Supply Chain Management," *Logistics Management*, December 1997, p. 37.
9. Theodore P. Stank, Patricia J. Daugherty and Alexander E. Ellinger, "Pulling Customers Closer Through Logistics Service," *Business Horizons*, September 1998, p. 74.
10. Ibid. p. 74.
11. James Aaron Cooke, "Warehousing: Great Expectations," 1998 Annual Report, *Logistics Management & Distribution Report*, July 1998.
12. "KPMG: Customer Service Increasingly Important in Supply Chain Management," M2 PRESSWIRE, 28 September 1998.
13. Adapted from Report on Business Magazine, April 2001: pp. 88–90, 92.
14. Quinn, "Supply-Chain Management Report: What's the Buzz?"
15. Francis Quinn, "Team Up for Supply-Chain Success," *Logistics Management*, October 1997, p. 39.
16. Toby B. Gooley, "On the Front Lines," Logistics Management, June 1997, p. 39.
17. Gooley, "On the Front Lines," p. 39.
18. Susan Avery, "Purchasing Forges New Supplier Relationships," *Purchasing*, 5 June 1998.
19. Canada Newswire, Celestica Press Release, 15 June 2001 and Celestic corporate materials.
20. Erick Schonfeld, "The Customized, Digitized, Have-It-Your-Way Economy," *Fortune*, 28 September 1998, pp. 114–124.
21. Evan Ramstad, "PC Playing Field Tilts in Favor of Dell," *Wall Street Journal*, 21 May 1998, p. B8; Andrew Serwer, "Michael Dell Turns the PC World Inside Out," *Fortune*, 8 September 1997; Evan Ramstad, "Dell Takes Another Shot at Booming Home-PC Market," *Wall Street Journal*, 16 December 1997, p. B4.
22. Craig Saunders, "Hudson's Bay Plan Massive CRM Push, " *Strategy Magazine*, 17 July 2000.
23. Robert Keehn, "Transforming the Grocery Industry," *Meeting the Challenge of Global Logistics*, Report Number 1207-98-CR (New York: The Conference Board, Inc., 1998), pp. 25– 27.
24. Ross, *Competing Through Supply Chain Management*, p. 232.
25. Ken Cottrill, "Reforging the Supply Chain," *Journal of Business Strategy*, 19 November 1997.
26. William Pesek, Jr., "Inventory Control Stabilizes Economy: Better Management Helps Companies Avoid Missteps," *Wall Street Journal*, 29 August 1997, p. B8B.
27. Scott Woolley, "Replacing Inventory with Information," *Forbes*, 24 March 1997, p. 54.
28. Anna Wilde Mathews, "Cargo in Ships Offers Clues to What Will Go Under Tree," *Wall Street Journal*, 6 August 1997, p. B1.
29. Evan Ramstad, "Dell Takes Another Shot at Booming Home-PC Market," *Wall Street Journal*, 16 December 1996, p. B4.
30. Anna Wilde Mathews, "New Gadgets Trace Truckers' Every Move," *Wall Street Journal*, 14 July 1997, pp. B1, B10.
31. Douglas A. Blackmon, "Shippers Pitch Power of Gizmos, Gadgets," *Wall Street Journal*, 2 June 1997, pp. B1, B4.
32. Paul Gettings, "Top Three Trends in Logistics Today," *Industrial Distribution*, November 1997, p. S17.
33. Helen Atkinson, "Use of 3rd-Party Logistics Rising," *Journal of Commerce*, 13 October 1998, p. 16A.
34. Eryn Brown, "Costs Too High? Bring In the Logistics Experts," *Fortune*, 10 November 1997.
35. Ibid.
36. Raju Narisetti, "How IBM Turned Around Its Ailing PC Division," *Wall Street Journal*, 12 March 1998, pp. B1, B6.
37. Anna Wilde Mathews, "Logistics Firms Flourish amid Trend in Outsourcing," *Wall Street Journal*, 2 June 1998, p. B4.

CHAPTER 14

1. Brian Hutchinson, "Merchants of Doom," *Canadian Business*, May 1997, p. 38.

2. "Roots: Our Story," retrieved 29 May 2001 from www.Roots.com/about_roots/our_story/our_story.htm.
3. "Roots to Outfit 2002 U.S. Olympic Team," Roots press release, retrieved 29 May 2001 from www.roots.com/about_roots/press_releases/isoc_feb_09_01.html.
4. Ibid.
5. Ibid.
6. "The Top 1000," *Report on Business Magazine*, June 2001.
7. Paul M. Jacobson, "1998 State of the Industry Report," prepared for the Retail Council of Canada.
8. "Wal-Mart—About Wal-Mart," retrieved 29 May 2001 from www.walmart.com/cservice/aw_samsway.gsp.
9. Derek DeCloet, "Blink and You've Missed It," *Canadian Business*, December 1999.
10. Sean Silcoff, "2nd Time Ready," *Canadian Business*, December 1999.
11. Hilary Stout, "Tiny Toy Stores Scramble for Ways to Lure Customers," *Wall Street Journal*, 9 December 1997, p. B2.
12. Laura Bird, "Woolworth Is Hoping to Score in Sportswear," *Wall Street Journal*, 12 March 1997, pp. B1, B6.
13. Government of Ontario, "Food Service Industry Sales, Ontario and Canada 1999," retrieved 24 July 2001 from www.gov.on.ca/OMAFRA/english/stats/food/indsales.html.
14. Karen J. Sack, "Restaurants," *Standard & Poor's Industry Surveys*, Volume 166, Number 23, Section 1, 4 June 1998, p. 11.
15. Ann Carrns, "Fill It Up and a Cheeseburger, Please: Gas Stations, Fast-Food Outlets Sharing Prime Space," *Wall Street Journal*, 15 October 1997, p. B18.
16. Retrieved 19 June 2001 from www.mmmeatshops.com.
17. Jacobson Consulting, 1999, "The Retail Sector in Canada," prepared for the Retail Council of Canada.
18. Statistics Canada, "Average Weekly Food Expenditure per Household," retrieved on 19 June 2001 from www.statcan.ca/english/Pgdb/People/Families/ famil27a.htm.
19. Citizenship and Immigration Canada, 1996, "Citizen ship and Immigration Canada Statistics Report," retrieved 19 June 2001 from www.cic.gc.ca/english/pdf-files/pub/1993stats.pdf.
20. Wal-Mart Data Sheet, 28 August 1998, www.wal-mart.com; "Wal-Mart Enters Korea, Continues Asia Expansion," Wal-Mart press release, 10 July 1998, www.wal-mart.com; Robert O'Connor, "Target Europe: Wal-Mart Set Up a Beachhead in Germany," *Chain Store Age*, March 1998, pp. 55–60.
21. Jeffrey Arlen, 1999, "Zellers: Carving Out a New Niche," *Discount Store News* 38(4), p. 8, retrieved from Web on 28 May 2001.
22. Maureen C. Carini, "Retailing: Supermarkets and Drugstores," *Standard & Poor's Industry Surveys*, Volume 166, Number 14, Section 1, 2 April 1998, p. 15.
23. Anne Faircloth, "Value Retailers Go Dollar for Dollar," *Fortune*, 6 July 1998, pp. 164–6.
24. Robert J. Izmirlian, "Retailing: Specialty," *Standard & Poor's Industry Surveys*, Volume 166, Number 4, Section 2, 22 January 1998, pp. 14–15.
25. Carini, "Retailing: Supermarkets and Drugstores," p. 15.
26. Mary Bellis, "The History of Vending Machines," retrieved on 21 June 2001 from inventors.about.com/sceince/inventors/library/inventors/blvendingmachine.htm.
27. Lorrie Grant, "Vending Machines Offer Movie T-Shirts," *USA Today*, 3 April 1998, p. 6B.
28. Profitguide.com—The Business Resource for Canadin Entrepreneurs, *Profit 100—Canada's Fastest Growing Companies 2001*. Retrieved 9 August 2001 from www.profitguide.com/profit 100/2001/p100_detail.asp?Rank=66.
29. My Favourite Doll Inc. Website, www.mfd.net.
30. Calmetta Y. Coleman, "Mail Order Is Turning into Male Order," *Wall Street Journal*, 25 March 1996, p. B9A.
31. IKEA—About Us Web page, retrieved 21 June 2001 from www.ikea.ca/about_ikea/about.asp.
32. Government of Canada: Telemarketing under the Competition Act, retrieved on 21 June 2001 from strategis.ic.gc.ca/SSG/ct01067e.html.
33. Phonebusters Website, retrieved on 21 June 2001 from www.phonebusters.com/Eng/Statistics/canada_stats1_2000.html.
34. Judann Pollack, "Food Marketers Develop Taste for Selling on QVC," *Advertising Age*, 2 June 1997, p. 20.
35. Statistics Canada:Connectedness Series—Internet Shopping in Canada, retrieved on 21 June 2001 from www.statcan.ca/english/research/56F0004MIE/56F0004MIE01003.pdf.
36. IBM/RCC 1998 CEO Survey: The Future of Canadian Retailing and the 1998 State of the Industry Report, retrieved on 13 March 2001 from www.retailcouncil.org/ceoreport/section1/ibmrcc_lead_page.html.
37. Ibid.
38. Industry Canada: Electronic Commerce in Canada, retrived on 22 June 2001 from e-com.ic.gc.ca/english/index.html.
39. Stephen Bonisteel, "Toys 'R' Use Sued over Christmas Fulfillment," Biz Report Website, 01/12/2000, retrived on 22 June 2001 from www.bizreport.com/news/2000/01/20000112-5.htm.
40. Tip Top Tailor Website, retrived on 20 June 2001 from www.tiptop.ca.
41. "Sears to Carry Line of Clothing Designed by Benetton Group," *Wall Street Journal*, 6 October 1998, p. B4.
42. Corporate Infro—Marks Work Wearhouse, retrieved on 20 June 2001 from www.marksworkwearhouse.ca.
43. David Todd, 1999, "Zellers Goes Truly Private Label," *Strategy—The Canadian Marketing Report*, retrieved on 24 June 2001 from www.strategymag,com/articles/magazine/19991025/27061.html.
44. William M. Bulkeley, "Office-Supply Superstores Find Bounty in the Boonies," *Wall Street Journal*, 1 September 1998, pp. B1, B4.

45. "Updated Site-Selection Guide Covers All Bases," *Chain Store Age*, October 1998.
46. Bill Levine, "The Store Stands Alone: For Some Retailers, Free-standing Sites Look Good from All Angles," *Chain Store Age*, April 1998, pp. 107–108.
47. Faircloth, "Value Retailers Go Dollar for Dollar," p. 166.
48. Industry Canada, 2001: "Rent-to-Own," *Canadian Consumer Hankbook*, retrieved on 26 July 2001 from strategics.gc.ca/SSG/ca01505e.html
49. Emily Nelson, "Why Wal-Mart Sings, 'Yes, We Have Bananas!'," *Wall Street Journal*, 6 October 1998, pp. B1, B4.
50. "Data Mining Is More Than Beer and Diapers," *Chain Store Age*, June 1998, pp. 64–8.
51. Diane Welland, "Rhythm and Chews," *Cooking Light*, January/February 1997, p. 22.
52. "Repeat Business," *Chain Store Age*, October 1998.
53. About.com—The Retail Industry (2000): New Study—A Snapshot of Canadian Online Retailers.
54. Karen J. Sack, "Mergers, Rivalry, and Price Sensitivity Will Continue," *Standard & Poor's Industry Surveys*, 9 May 1996, pp. R75–R78.
55. "Global Retailing '97," Ernst & Young special report for *Chain Store Age*, December 1997, p. 4.
56. "Global Retailing '97," pp. 14–18.
57. "Global Retailing '97," p. 18.
58. Norihiko Shirouzu, "Japan's Staid Coffee Bars Wake Up and Smell Starbucks," *Wall Street Journal*, 25 July 1996, pp. B1, B8; Martin Wolk, "Starbucks to Enter S. Korea in Pacific Plan," Reuters News Service, 1 October 1997; Seth Sutel, "Japan Wakes Up and Smells the Latte—Starbucks Is Here," *The San Diego Daily Transcript*, Internet address: /96wireheadlines/08_96/DN96_08_02/DN96_08_02_fa.html, 2 August 1996.
59. Sack, "Retailing: General," p. 1.
60. Izmirlian, "Retailing: Specialty," p. 3.
61. Ibid.
62. Calmetta Y. Coleman, "Grocery List: Peas, Veal, Throat Culture," *Wall Street Journal*, 20 May 1998, pp. B1, B26.
63. Ahmed Taher, Thomas W. Leigh, and Warren A. French, "The Retail Patronage Experience and Customer Affection," The Cutting Edge IV, Proceedings of the 1995 Symposium on Patronage Behavior and Retail Strategy, Ed. William R. Darden, American Marketing Association, May 1995, pp. 35–51.
64. Alice Z. Cuneo, "Gap Puts Delivery on Menu for Summer," *Advertising Age*, 15 June 1998, p. 8.
65. This section based on "Customer Management," State of the Industry special report, *Chain Store Age*, August 1998, pp. 20A–23A.

CHAPTER 15

1. From Stephen Whitlock, "Going, Going, ... Not Going," *Conde Nast Traveler*, July 1998. Courtesy Conde Nast Traveler. Copyright 1998 by Conde Nast Publications, Inc.
2. From Brandon Michener, "Ethnic Pricing Means Unfair Airfares," *The Wall Street Journal*, 5 December 1997. Reprinted by permission of The Wall Street Journal, **c** 1997 Dow Jones & Company, Inc. All Rights Reserved Worldwide.
3. Adapted from Anne Swardson, "In France, It's on Sale When the State Says So," *International Herald Tribune*, 6 January 1997, p. 2.
4. "Good-Bye to Fixed Pricing?" *Business Week*, 4 May 1998, pp. 71–84.
5. "Fixed Prices: Thing of the Past?" *Internet World*, 1 June 1998, p. 54.
6. "Web Offers Biggest Prize in Product Pricing Game," *Marketing News*, 6 July 1998, p. 8.
7. "Stores' Demands Squeeze Apparel Companies," *The Wall Street Journal*, 15 July 1997, pp. B1, B2.
8. William Dodds, Kent Monroe, and Dhruv Grewal, "Effects of Price, Brand, and Store Information on Buyers' Product Evaluations," *Journal of Marketing Research*, August 1991, pp. 307–19; see also Akshay Rao and Wanda Sieben, "The Effect of Prior Knowledge on Price Acceptability and the Type of Information Examined," *Journal of Consumer Research*, September 1992, pp. 256–70; Ajay Kalra and Ronald Goldman, "The Impact of Advertising Positioning Strategies on Consumer Price Sensitivity," *Journal of Marketing Research*, May 1998, pp. 210–24.
9. Donald Lichtenstein and Scott Burton, "The Relationship between Perceived and Objective Price–Quality," *Journal of Marketing Research*, November 1989, pp. 429–43.
10. Edward Desmond, "What's Ailing Kodak? FUJI," *Fortune*, 27 October 1997, pp. 185–92.
11. Joseph P. Guiltinan and Gregory T. Gundlack, "Aggressive and Predatory Pricing: A Framework for Analysis," *Journal of Marketing*, July 1966, pp. 87-102.
12. "Eliminated Discounts on P&G Goods Annoy Many Who Sell Them," *The Wall Street Journal*, 11 August 1992, pp. A1, A6.
13. "Ed Artzt's Elbow Grease Has P&G Shining," *Business Week*, 10 October 1994, pp. 84–6. For an excellent study of EDLP and its impact on retailers and manufacturers, see Stephen J. Hoch, Xavier Dreze, and Mary E. Purk, "EDLP, Hi-Lo, and Margin Arithmetic," *Journal of Marketing*, October 1994, pp. 16–27.
14. Charles Quigley and Elaine Notarantonio, "An Exploratory Investigation of Perceptions of Odd and Even Pricing," in *Developments in Marketing Science*, ed. Victoria Crittenden (Miami: Academy of Marketing Science, 1992,), pp. 306–9.
15. "Nine Cents of Separation," *American Demographics*, May 1998, p. 41.
16. "Three for $3 and Other Numerical Pitches Work Magic in Stores," *The Wall Street Journal*, 12 March 1998, p. A1.

CHAPTER 16

1. PepsiCo 1997 Annual Report; "Top 200 Brands: January–June 1997," *Advertising Age*, 3 November 1997, p 48; "Pepsi's Supermarket Squeeze," *Brandweek*, 1 June 1998, p. 1; "A-B Buddies Up with Frito for Fall Promo," *Brandweek*, 6 July 1998, p. 12; Kirk Laughlin, "Bowled Away," Food & Beverage Mar-

keting, January 1998, p. 6; Greg Johnson, "Chips Are Down in Marketing Olestra Food: Critics Say the Fat-Free Additive Poses Health Risks," Los Angeles Times, 10 March 1998, p. A-1; Judann Pollack, "Frito Claims Success, but Sales Slow for Wow! Chips," *Advertising Age*, 20 July 1998, pp. 1, 30; Sarah Lorge, "Top of the Charts: No. 3 Frito-Lay," *Sales & Marketing Management*, July 1998, p. 38; Frito-Lay press releases, www.fritolay.com.

2. Frank G Bingham, Jr., Charles J. Quigley, Jr., and Elaine M. Notarantonio, "The Use of Communication Style in a Buyer–Seller Dyad: Improving Buyer–Seller Relationships," *Proceedings: Association of Marketing Theory and Practice*, 1996 Annual Meeting, Hilton Head, South Carolina, March 1996, pp. 188–195.

3. Rekha Balu, "Ingredients for Holiday Sales: Red Dye, Green Sprinkles," *Wall Street Journal*, 15 December 1997, pp. B1, B10.

4. Jeanne Whalen, "Pizza Hut Uses Events to Help Give Away 1 Mil New Pies," *Advertising Age*, 9 June 1997

5. Philip J Kitchen, "Marketing Communications Renaissance," *International Journal of Advertising*, 12 (1993), pp. 367–386.

6. Kitchen, p 372.

7. AIDA concept based on the classic research of E. K. Strong, Jr., as theorized in *The Psychology of Selling and Advertising* (New York: McGraw-Hill, 1925) and "Theories of Selling," *Journal of Applied Psychology*, 9 (1925), pp. 75–86.

8. Thomas E Barry and Daniel J. Howard, "A Review and Critique of the Hierarchy of Effects in Advertising," *International Journal of Advertising*, 9 (1990), pp. 121–135.

9. Elyse Tanouye, "Drug Ads Spur Patients to Demand More Prescriptions," *Wall Street Journal*, 22 December 1997, p B1; Patricia Braus, "Selling Drugs," *American Demographics*, January 1998, pp. 26–29; Michael Wilke, "Prescription for Profit," *Advertising Age*, 16 March 1998, pp. s1, s-26; Robert Langreth and Andrea Petersen, "A Stampede Is on for Impotence Pill," *Wall Street Journal*, 20 April 1998, pp. B1, B6; Ira Teinowitz, "New TV Guidelines Bring Wishes for Further Changes," *Advertising Age*, 16 March 1998, p. s10; also see David Stipp and Robert Whitaker, "The Selling of Impotence," *Fortune*, 16 March 1998, pp. 115–124.

10. Bingham, Quigley, and Notarantonio, pp. 188–195.

11. Marvin A. Jolson, "Broadening the Scope of Relationship Selling," *Journal of Personal Selling & Sales Management*, Fall 1997, p. 75; also see Donald W. Jackson, Jr., "Relationship Selling: The Personalization of Relationship Marketing," *Asia-Australia Marketing Journal*, August 1994, pp. 45–54.

12. Bingham, Quigley, and Notarantonio, pp. 188–195.

13. Geoffrey Brewer, "The Customer Stops Here," *Sales & Marketing Management*, March 1998, pp. 30–36.

14. Erika Rasmusson, "How to Manage Long-Term Leads," *Sales & Marketing Management*, January 1998, p. 77.

15. Sarah Lorge, "Online Bidding Keeps Suppliers in Line," *Sales & Marketing Management*, August 1998, p. 16; Gregory Dalton, "Web Services Help Buyers Get Right Price—Online Bidding Being Used for Mortgages and Airline Tickets," Information Week, 27 April 1998, p. 26; "UTC Uses Net-Based Auction to Help Craft Optimal Supply Base," *Purchasing*, 18 June 1998, p. s4; Claudia Coates, "Online Auction: Ding! The Price of Widgets Just Went Down," *The Associated Press*, 11 March 1998; Clinton Wilder, "What's Your Bid?—FreeMarkets' Real-Time Online Bidding Technology Lets Clients Drive Down Costs and Improve Product Value," *Information Week*, 10 November 1997, p. 54.

16. "By the Numbers: How Web Sites Are Used," *Sales & Marketing Management*, February 1998, p. 20; Direct Marketing Association.

17. Sarah Lorge, "The Best Way to Prospect," *Sales & Marketing Management*, January 1998, p. 80; Tricia Campbell, "What's a Referral Worth to You?" *Sales & Marketing Management*, September 1997, p. 103.

18. Lorge, "The Best Way to Prospect," p. 80.

19. Michele Marchetti, "Is Cold Calling Worth It?" *Sales & Marketing Management*, August 1997, p. 103.

20. "Leads Are a Terrible Thing to Waste," *Sales & Marketing Management*, August 1997, p. 108; Center for Strategic Communication.

21. Marvin A. Jolson and Thomas R. Wotruba, "Selling and Sales Management in Action: Prospecting: A New Look at This Old Challenge," *Journal of Personal Selling & Sales Management*, Fall 1992, pp. 59–66.

22. Jolson, "Broadening the Scope of Relationship Selling," p. 75.

23. Adapted from Bob Kimball, *Successful Selling*, Chicago: American Marketing Association, 1994.

24. Geoffrey Brewer, "Dell's 'Expert' Advice for Customers," *Sales & Marketing Management*, April 1997, p. 77.

25. Colleen Cooper, "Overcoming Last-Minute Objections," *Sales & Marketing Management*, March 1997, p. 32; Sarah Lorge, "How to Close the Deal," Sales & *Marketing Management*, April 1998, p. 84.

26. Cooper, "Overcoming Last-Minute Objections," p. 32.

27. Sarah Lorge, "The Best Way to Negotiate," *Sales & Marketing Management*, March 1998, p. 92.

28. "Can Your Reps Sell Overseas?" *Sales & Marketing Management*, February 1998, p. 110.

29. Andy Cohen, "Global Dos and Don'ts," *Sales & Marketing Management*, June 1996, p. 72; Esmond D. Smith, Jr., and Cuong Pham, "Doing Business in Vietnam: A Cultural Guide," *Business Horizons*, May–June 1996, pp. 47–51; "Five Tips for International Handshaking," *Sales & Marketing Management*, July 1997, p. 90, from Dorothea Johnson, director of The Protocol School of Washington; Tricia Campbell, "What to Give Overseas," *Sales & Marketing Management*, September 1997, p. 85; "Negotiating: Getting to Yes, Chinese-Style," *Sales & Marketing Management*, July 1996, pp. 44–45; Michelle Marchetti, "Selling in China? Go Slowly," *Sales & Marketing Management*, January 1997, pp. 35–36; Sergey Frank, "Global Negotiating: Vive Les Différences!"

Sales & Marketing Management, May 1992, pp. 64–69.
30. Geoffrey Brewer, "America's Best Sales Forces: No. 5 Hewlett-Packard," *Sales & Marketing Management,* October 1997, p. 58.
31. Vincent Alonzo, "Getting the Best Out of 'Em," *Sales & Marketing Management,* October 1997, pp. 34–38; "More Incentives on the Way," *Sales & Marketing Management,* December 1997, p. 96.

CHAPTER 17

1. www.labatt.com
2. Jean Halliday, "Ford Corporate Ads Push 'A Relationship of Trust'," *Advertising Age,* 4 May 1998, p. 3.
3. Michael Burgoon, Michael Pfau, and Thomas S. Birk, "An Inoculation Theory Explanation for the Effects of Corporate Issue/Advocacy Advertising Campaigns, Communication Research, August 1995, p. 485(21).
4. Maremont, "How Gillette Brought Its MACH3 to Market," pp. B1, B10; Klahr, "Gillette Puts $300 Mil Behind Its Mach3 Shaver," p. 6.
5. Mark Maremont, "Close vs Safe: Rivals Prepare to Market New Razors," *Wall Street Journal,* 29 September 1997, pp. B1, B6.
6. Roger Thurow, "Shtick Ball: In Global Drive, Nike Finds Its Brash Ways Don't Always Pay Off," *Wall Street Journal,* 5 May 1997, pp. A1, A10.
7. "Radio: No Longer an Advertising Afterthought," *Standard & Poor's Industry Surveys,* 20 July 1995, p. M36; Rebecca Piirto, "Why Radio Thrives," *American Demographics,* May 1994, pp. 40–46.
8. Rekha Balu, "Heinz Ketchup Readies Super Bowl Blitz," *Wall Street Journal,* 5 January 1998, p. B6; Chuck Ross, "Super Sein-off," *Advertising Age,* 11 May 1998, pp. 1, 62.
9. Kate Maddox, "ANA Study Finds Marketers Triple 'Net Ad Budgets," *Advertising Age,* 11 May 1998, p. 63.
10. "Year in Review: Interactive/Web Becomes a Viable Channel," *Advertising Age,* 22 December 1997, pp. 21–22.
11. Sally Goll Beatty, "Internet Ad Proponents Try a New Tack," *Wall Street Journal,* 25 September 1997, p. B8.
12. www.cybergold.com.
13. Laurie Freeman, "Internet Visitors' Traffic Jam Makes Buyers Web Wary," *Advertising Age,* 22 July 1996, pp. S14–15.
14. Laura Reina, " Manufacturers Still Believe in Coupons," *Editor & Publisher,* 28 October 1995, p. 24; Betsy Spethmann, "Coupons Shed Low-Tech Image; Sophisticated Tracking Yields Valuable Consumer Profile," *Brandweek,* 24 October 1994, p. 30(2); and Scott Hume, "Coupons: Are They Too Popular?" *Advertising Age,* 15 February 1993, p. 32.
15. Kate Fitzgerald, "Instant-Reward Coupons Show Rebound," *Advertising Age,* 12 May 1997, p. 20.
16. William M Bulkeley, "Rebates' Secret Appeal to Manufacturers: Few Consumers Actually Redeem Them," *Wall Street Journal,* 10 February 1998, pp. B1, B2.
17. Judann Pollack, "Pop Tarts Packs More Pastry for Same Price," *Advertising Age,* 5 August 1996, p. 6.
18. Mark Lacek, "Loyalty Marketing No Ad Budget Threat," *Advertising Age,* 23 October 1995, p. 20.
19. Ginger Conlon, "True Romance," Sales & *Marketing Management,* May 1996, pp. 85–90.
20. "Samples Have Ample Impact," *Sales & Marketing Management,* September 1997, p. 108.
21. Kate Fitzgerald, "Venue Sampling Hot," *Advertising Age,* 12 August 1996, p. 19.
22. Matthew Martinez and Mercedes M. Cardona, "Study Shows POP Gaining Ground as Medium," *Advertising Age,* 24 November 1997, p. 43.
23. Rebecca Piirto Heath, "Pop Art," *Marketing Tools,* April 1997.
24. Dean Takahashi and Evan Ramstad, "Quake Sequel Beefs Up Blood and Guts," *Wall Street Journal,* 9 December 1997, pp. B1, B16.
25. James A. Roberts, "Green Consumers in the 1990s: Profile and Implications for Advertising," *Journal of Business Research* 36 (1996), pp. 217–231.

CHAPTER 18

1. www.jonessoda.com
2. Rob Jackson and Paul Wang, *Strategic Database Marketing* (Lincolnwood, IL: NTC Business Books, 1997), p. 10.
3. Ernan Roman, *Integrated Direct Marketing* (Lincolnwood, IL: NTC Business Books, 1996), p. 1.
4. Jackson and Wang, *Strategic Database Marketing,* p. 3.
5. Roman, *Integrated Direct Marketing,* p. 1.
6. Gerri Knilans, "Database Marketing: Fad, Fantasy or Reality?" *Direct Marketing,* May 1997, p. 48.
7. Jackson and Wang, *Strategic Database Marketing,* p. 3.
8. Laura Loro, "Case Study: FedEx Mines Its Database to Drive New Sales," *Business Marketing,* March 1997, p. 4.
9. Paula Kephart, "Knowledge Is Power: One-to-One Database Marketing," *Marketing Tools,* October 1997, p. 32.
10. Matt Murray and Raju Narisetti, "Bank Mergers Hidden Engine: Technology," *Wall Street Journal,* 23 April 1998, pp. B1, B9.
11. This section based on Jackson and Wang, *Strategic Database Marketing,* pp. 4–11; and Frederick Newell, *The New Rules of Marketing: How to Use One-to-One Relationship Marketing to Be the Leader in Your Industry* (New York: McGraw-Hill, 1997), pp. 10–32.
12. Jackson and Wang, *Strategic Database Marketing,* p. 11.
13. Chad Kaydo, "Planting the Seeds of Marketing Success," *Sales & Marketing Management,* August 1998, p. 73.
14. Jackson and Wang, *Strategic Database Marketing,* pp. 13–15.
15. This section based in part on Jackson and Wang, *Strategic Database Marketing,* pp. 39–53.
16. "Success Stories: Pitney Bowes," Peppers and Rogers Group, Marketing 1 to 1 Web site, http://www.1to1now.com/tools/ success-stories/index.html.
17. Ginger Conlon, "True Romance," *Sales & Marketing Management,* May 1996, pp. 85–90.

18. Melanie Berger, "It's Your Move," *Sales & Marketing Management,* March 1998, pp. 45–56.
19. Shelly M. Reese, "Suitcase Savvy," *Marketing Tools,* June 1995.
20. Jackson and Wang, *Strategic Database Marketing,* p. 21.
21. *Random House Webster's Dictionary* (New York: Random House/Ballantine Books, 1993), p. 165.
22. Jonathan Berry, "A Potent New Tool for Selling: Database Marketing," *Business Week,* 5 September 1994, pp. 56–62.
23. Jack Schmid and Alan Weber, *Desktop Database Marketing* (Lincolnwood, IL: NTC Business Books, 1998), pp. 33–34.
24. Jackson and Wang, *Strategic Database Marketing,* p. 83.
25. Knilans, "Database Marketing: Fad, Fantasy or Reality?" p. 48.
26. Heath, "Loyalty for Sale" p. 40.
27. Jackson and Wang, Strategic *Database Marketing,* p. 86.
28. Jackson and Wang, Strategic *Database Marketing,* pp. 86–87.
29. James R. Rosenfield, "The Myth of Database Marketing," *Direct Marketing,* February 1998, p. 28.
30. David Cameron, "Do You Really Need a Data Warehouse?" *Direct Marketing,* June 1998, p. 43.
31. Schmid and Weber, *Desktop Database Marketing,* p. 132.
32. Newell, *The New Rules of Marketing,* p. 82.
33. Heath, "Loyalty for Sale," p. 40.
34. Peter R. Peacock, "Data Mining in Marketing: Part 1: The Revolution Is upon Us, So Choose Your Weapons Carefully," *Marketing Management,* Winter 1998, pp. 9–18.
35. Skip Press, "Fool's Gold?" *Sales & Marketing Management,* June 1998, pp. 58–62.
36. Richard H. Levey, "What's Your Database IQ?" *Direct,* February 1998, p. 1.
37. Jagdish Sheth and Rajendra Sisodia, "Feeling the Heat—Part 2," *Marketing Management,* Winter 1995, pp. 19–33.
38. Knilans, "Database Marketing: Fad, Fantasy or Reality?" p. 48.
39. Michael Rowsom, "Bridging the Gap from Traditional Marketing to Electronic Commerce," *Direct Marketing,* January 1998, p. 23.
40. Robert D. Hof, Heather Green, and Linda Himelstein, "Now It's Your Web: The Net Is Moving Toward One-to-One Marketing—and That Will Change How All Companies Do Business," *Business Week,* 5 October 1998, p. 164.
41. Rowsom, "Bridging the Gap from Traditional Marketing to Electronic Commerce," p. 23.

CHAPTER 19

1. www.ideafinder.com/history/inventions/story081.htm
2. "Get Real Girl Takes on Barbie," Summit News Service, *Saint John Times Globe,* 30 August 2001, p. A2.
3. www.redherring.com/story_redirect.asp?layout=story_generic&doc_id=RH410014041&channel=70000007
4. www.pbs.org/internet/timeline/timeline-txt.html
5. www.nua.ie/surveys/how_many_online/index.html
6. www.nua.ie/surveys/how_many_online/index.html
7. www.ipsosreid.com/media/content/displaypr.cfm?id_to_view=1229
8. www.newsbytes.com/news/01/165542.html
9. www.nua.ie/surveys/index.cgi?f=VS&art_id=905356776&rel=true
10. www.nua.ie/surveys/index.cgi?f=VS&art_id=905356775&rel=true
11. www.nua.ie/surveys/index.cgi?f=VS&art_id=905356501&rel+true
12. www.acneilsen.ca/sect_fastfacts/index_ff_inter.htm
13. www.scarborough.com/scarb2000/press/pr_internetstudy1.htm
14. *Marketing News,* 3 July 2000, p. 15.
15. *FastForward* 2.0, p. 6.
16. www.centris.com/subannounce.htm
17. "Facts, Figures, and Forecasts," *CommerceNet Newsletter* 1(6), June 1999.
18. *Marketing News,* 3 July 2000, p. 16.
19. Amy Yoffe, "Bad Data." www.thestandard.com/article/0,1902,7477,00.html
20. Carl McDaniel, Jr. and Roger Gates. 1998. *Marketing Research Essentials,* Cincinatti, OH: South-Western.
21. Gilbert A. Churchill. 1995. *Marketing Research: Methodological Foundations,* 6th ed. Fort Worth, TX: The Dryden Press.
22. Tom Greenbaum, "Internet Focus Groups: An Oxymoron," *Marketing News,* 3 March 1997.
23. Gerry McGovern, "Branding For Dummies." www.nua.com/nkb/index.cgi?f+VA&art_type+NT&art_id=619
24. www.gvu.gatech.edu/user_surveys/survey-1998-10/graphs/graphs.html#general
25. Dr. Ralph Wilson, "Differentiating Your Companies Products and Services," *Web Marketing Today,* 11 April 2000. www.wilsonweb.com/wmt5/product-difference.htm
26. K. Dane Brooksher, "E-commerce and Logistics," *Traffic World,* 15 November 1999.
27. Steve Alexander, "E-commerce Distribution," *Computerworld,* 20 March 2000. www.computerworld.com/cwi/story/0,1199,nav47_sto41939,00.html
28. "Napster Users Still Trading Merrily," *Wired,* 6 April 2001. www.nua.ie/surveys/index.cgi?f=VS&art_id=905356638&rel=true
29. *The Economic and Social Impact of Electronic Commerce: Preliminary Findings and Research Agenda,* OECD, 1999.

CHAPTER 20

1. Oliver Bertin, "New Coca-Cola Drink Takes Aim at Cool Coffee Set," *The Globe and Mail,* 29 August 2001, p. B2.
2. Ibid.
3. Ibid.
4. Kevin Libin, "Holey War," *Canadian Business,* 21 August 2000, pp. 34-40.
5. Ibid., p. 36.
6. Ibid., p. 37.
7. John Heinzl, "Heinz Squeezes Out Purple Ketchup," *The Globe and Mail,* 7 August 2001, p. B8.
8. David A. Aaker, *Strategic Market Management,* John Wiley & Sons, Inc., 1998, p. 142.

9. John Heinzl, "Advertising Slinks Undercover," *The Globe and Mail,* 20 July 2001, p. M1.
10. Ibid.
11. O.C. Ferrell, M. D. Hartline, G. H. Lucas and David Luck, *Marketing Strategy,* The Dryden Press, 1998, p. 130.
12. Carrie Shook, "The Art of Conspicuous Consumption," *Forbes,* June 1998, pp. 73-76.
13. Iris Winston, "She's Covered in Chocolate," *The Windsor Star,* 18 June 2001, p. B3.
14. Ibid.

COMPANY AND ORGANIZATION INDEX

A

B

C

D

E

F

G

H

I

J

K

L

M

N

O

T

U

V

W

X

Y

Z

SUBJECT INDEX

C

D

E

M

Q

R

S

T

U

V

W

Z

INTERNET INDEX

ABC Canada Literacy Foundation	http://www.abc-canada.org
Aboriginal Peoples Television Network	http://www.aptn.ca
Acarta	http://www.acarta.com
Ad Age	http://www.adage.com
Ads On Wheels	http://www.adsonwheels.com
Air Canada	http://www.aircanada.ca
Airmiles	http://www.airmiles.ca
Altavista Digital	http://www.altavista.digital.com
AMA	http://www.ama.org
Amazon Books	http://amazon.com
American Demographics	http://www.demographics.com
Apple Computers	http://apple.com
Arts and Entertainment Television Network	http://aande.com http://biography.com http://mysteries.com http://historychannel.com http://historytravel.com
AT&T	http://www.att.com
Auchan	http://www.auchan.com
Auto Connection	http://www.autoconnection.com
Auto Trader	http://www.autotrader.ca
Autobytel.ca	http://www.autobytel.ca
Autowraps	http://www.autowraps.com
Bally Fitness	http://www.ballyfitness.com
Barbie.com	http://www.barbie.com
Ben & Jerry's	http://www.benjerry.com
Bizrate.com	http://www.bizrate.com
Blue Jays	http://www.bluejays.ca
BMW	http://www.BMW.ca
Bodyshop	http://www.bodyshop.com
Borderfree Inc.	http://www.borderfree.com
Boston Consulting Group	http://www.bcg.com
Boyne USA Resorts	http://www.boyneusa.com
Bravo	http://www.bravo.ca
Burger King	http://www.burgerking.com
Burke Inc.	http://www.burke.com
Burton Snowboards	http://www.burton.com
Business 2.0	http://www.business20.com
Business to Business	http://www.business2business.on.ca
Business Week	http://www.businessweek.com/1998/17/b3575155.htm
Business Wire	http://www.businesswire.com
Canada's Business and Consumer Site Industry Canada	http://www.strategis.ic.gc.ca
Canadian Egg Marketing Agency	http://www.canadaegg.ca
Canadian Institute of International Affairs	http://www.ciia.org
Canadian Learning Television	http://www.clt.ca
Canadian Marketing Association	http://www.cdma.org
Caterpillar	http://www.caterpillar.com
CBC	http://www.cbc.ca/onair/
Chapters Indigo	http://www.chapters.indigo.ca
Charity.ca	http://www.charity.ca
Chatelaine	http://www.chatelaine.com
Christmas Depot	http://www.christmasdepot.com
Citizens Bank of Canada	http://www.citizensbank.ca
Clearly Canadian	http://www.clearly.ca
CNN	http://www.cnn.com
Coca Cola	http://www.cocacola.com
Columbia House	http://www.columbiahouse.com
Comedy Network	http://www.thecomedynetwork.ca
Commerce Times	http://www.ecommercetimes.com
Companyname.com	http://www.companyname.com
Contracts Canada	http://contractscanada.gc.ca/

Cool Savings	http://www.coolsavings.com
Country Music Television	http://www.cmt.ca
Cyber Mall	http://www.cybermall.com
DaimlerChrysler	http://www.daimlerchrysler.ca
Dell	http://www.dell.ca
Department of Foreign Affairs and International Trade	http://www.dfait-maeci.gc.ca
DineAid	http://www.dineaid.com
Disney	http://disney.go.com
Dofasco	http://www.dofasco.com
Dominion Bond Rating Service	http://www.dbrs.com
DoubleClick Canada	http://www2.doubleclick.net/ca
Dow Jones Interactive	http://www.djnr.com
EBay	http://www.ebay.com
Embassy Web	http://www.embpage.org
Encyclopaedia Britannica	http://www.britannica.com
epublic eye - Web Watch Dog	http://www.webwatchdog.com
EXE Technologies	http://www.exe.com
Export-Import Bank of the United States	http://www.exim.gov
Express Style	http://www.express.style.com
Federation of International Trade Associations	http://www.fita.org
Federal Express	http://www.fedex.com
Foot Locker	http://www.footlocker.com
Ford	http://www.ford.com
Four Seasons Hotel and Resorts	http://www.fourseasons.com
Fragrance Net	http://www.fragrance.com
Frito-Lay	http://www.fritolay.com
From Here to Maternity	http://www.fromheretomaternity.com
Fuji Film	http://www.fujifilm.net
Fulcrum Analytics	http://www.cyberdialogue.com
Gap	http://www.gap.com
Gartner Research	http://www.gartner.com
Gatorade	http://www.gatorade.com
GE	http://www.ge.com
Genentech Inc.	http://www.gene.com
General Electric Information Services	http://www.geis.com
General Mills	http://www.generalmills.com
Gerber	http://www.gerber.com/contactus
Get Real Girl	http://getrealgirl.com
Gillette	http://www.gillette.com
Globe & Mail	http://www.globeandmail.ca
Godiva Chocolates	http://www.godiva.com
Grand & Toy	http://www.grandandtoy.com
Grand Circle Travel	http://www.gct.com
Greenfield Online	http://www.greenfieldonline.com
Grocery Gateway	http://www.grocerygateway.com
Harley-Davidson	http://www.harley-davidson.com
Healthy Choice	http://www.healthychoice.com
Heinz	http://www.heinz.com
Hewlett-Packard	http://www.hp.com
HMV	http://www.HMV.com
IBM	http://www.ibm.com
Info Tobacco	http://www.infotobacco.com
Intellectual Property Owners Association	http://www.ipo.org
Internet Shopping Network	http://www.isn.com
Ipsos Reid	http://www.angusreid.com
Jones Soda	http://www.jonessoda.com
Keebler	http://www.keebler.com
Kraft Foods	http://www.kraftfoods.com
Krispy Kreme	http://www.krispykreme.com

L.L. Bean	http://www.llbean.com
Labatt	http://www.labatt.com
Land Rover	http://www.best4x4.landrover.com
Lands' End	http://www.landsend.com
Lansbridge University	http://www.learnsoft.ca/lansbridge.html
La-z-boy	http://www.lazboy.com
Lee Valley	http://www.leevalley.ca
Levi Strauss & Co.	http://www.levi.com
Loblaws	http://www.loblaw.com
Loctite	http://www.loctite.com
M&M/Mars	http://www.m-ms.com
Macy's	http://www.macys.com
Mark Lundholm Enterprises	http://www.marklundholm.com
Marriot International	http://www.marriott.com
Mary Kay	http://www.marykay.com
Maupintour	http://maupintour.com
Maytag	http://www.maytag.com
Mazda	http://www.mazda.com
McDonald's	http://www.mcdonalds.com
MCI	http://www.mci.com
Modrobes	http://www.modrobes.com
Molson	http://www.molson.ca
Monster.ca	http://www.monster.ca
Mountain Equipment Co-Op	http://www.mec.ca
MSN Carpoint	http://carpoint.msn.com
Much Music	http://www.muchmusic.com
My Favourite Doll	http://www.mfd.net
Mystery Shopper, USA	http://www.bmiltd.com
MyVirtualModel.com	http://www.myvirtualmodel.com/
Nabisco	http://www.nabisco.com
Napster	http://www.napster.com
National Post	http://www.nationalpost.com
Nestle	http://www.nestle.com
NetCasino	http://www.netcasino.com
New Balance	http://www.newbalance.com
Nike	http://www.nike.ca
Nutrasweet	http://www.nutrasweet.com
Oneida	http://www.oneida.com
Oprah Winfrey	http://www.oprah.com
Outdoor Advertising Association of Canada	http://www.oaac.com
Palm	http://www.palm.com
Peppers & Rogers Group	http://www.1to1.com
Pepsico	http://www.pepsico.com
Pfizer	http://www.pfizer.com
Pharmacia	http://www.upjohn.com
Pizza Hut	http://www.pizzahut.com
Priceline	http://www.priceline.com
Procter & Gamble	http://www.pg.com
Quaker Oatmeal	http://www.quakeroatmeal.com
Ragu	http://www.ragu.com
Reader's Digest	http://www.readersdigest.com
Real Facilities	http://www.realfacilities.com
Reflect	http://www.reflect.com
ResearchInfo.com	http://www.researchinfo.com
Retail Canada	http://www.retailcanada.com
Roche	http://www.roche.com
Rollerblade	http://www.rollerblade.com
Roots	http://www.roots.ca
Royal Bank	http://www.royalbank.com/trade/
Rubbermaid	http://www.rubbermaid.com

Sabian	http://www.sabian.com
SAP	http://www.sap.com/crm
Sears	http://www.sears.com
Senco	http://www.senco.com
Shaw	http://www.shaw.ca
Smith & Hawken	http://www.smithhawken.com
Society of Competitive Intelligence Professionals (SCIP)	http://www.scip.org
Southwest Airlines	http://www.iflyswa.com
Special K	http://www.specialk.ca
Sprint	http://www.sprint.com
Spy Company	http://www.spycompany.com
Staples	http://www.staples.com
Star Alliance Network	http://www.star-alliance.com
Starbucks	http://www.starbucks.com
StarKist	http://www.starkist.com
Statistics Canada	http://www.statcan.ca
Stevia.net	http://www.stevia.net
TD Waterhouse	http://www.Tdwaterhouse.ca
The Canadian Trade Commissioner Service	http://www.infoexport.gc.ca
The Gift	http://www.thegift.ca
The Shopping Channel	http://www.tsc.ca
3M	http://www.3m.com
Tide	http://www.tide.com
Tim Hortons	http://www.timhortons.com
Time	http://www.time.com
Too Faced	http://www.toofaced.com
Toys R Us	http://www.toysrus.com
Trade Compass	http://www.tradecompass.com
TurnPike	http://emporium.turnpike.net
Tylenol	http://www.tylenol.com
U.S. Census Bureau	http://www.census.gov
UPS	http://www.ups.com
Vancouver Aquarium	http://www.vanaqua.org
Verisign	http://www.verisign.com
Verizon	http://www22.verizon.com
Via Rail	http://www.viarail.ca
Volvo	http://www.volvocars.com
Wall Street Journal	http://www.wsj.com
Wal-Mart	http://www.wal-mart.com
Waltec Faucets (Delta Faucet Company)	http://www.deltafaucet.com
WebCom	http://www.webcom.com
Wendy's	http://www.wendys.com/the_ads/ads_frame.html
WestJet	http://www.westjet.ca
Wickaninnish Inn	http://www.wickinn.com
Wrigley's	http://www.wrigley.com
WWW Search Engines	http://www.alta-vista.com
	http://www.askjeeves.com
	http://www.directhit.com
	http://www.excite.com
	http://www.hotbot.com
	http://www.go.com
	http://www.ipl.org
	http://www.lycos.com
	http://www.northernlight.com
	http://www.w3.org/vl
	http://www.yahoo.com
	http://www.google.com

WWW Search Engines (cont'd)	http://www.inktomi.com http://www.looksmart.com http://www.search.msn.com http://search.netscape.com
Xerox	http://www.xerox.com
Youtopia	http://www.youtopia.com
YTV	http://www.ytv.com

PHOTOGRAPH CREDITS

Part 1 Opener: Corbis/Magma; Chapter 1 Opener: © Reuters NewMedia Inc./Corbis/Magma; Page 5: PT Cruiser and PT Cruiser Vehicle Design are trademarks of Daimler Chrysler Corporation. Image used by permission; Page 6: Courtesy of Toyota Motor Corporation; Page 9: Reprinted by permission of BHP Diamonds. Image Janet Foster/Masterfile. Model provided by Montizambert Photography; Page 10: Reprinted by permission of Diners International and Air Canada Aeroplan; Page 11: Courtesy of FedEx; Page 14: © Richard Hull; Page 16: Courtesy of Ontario Society of the Prevention of Cruelty to Animals; Page 20: © Karl Weatherly/Corbis/ Magma; Chapter 2 Opener: CP Picture Archive (Ted Brellisford); Page 25: Photo by C. Behr; Page 30: Courtesy of The Gillette Company; Page 32: Reprinted by permission of Krispy Kreme Doughnut Corporation; Page 33: Associated Press (Aynsley Floyd); Page 35: © Duomo/Corbis/Magma; Page 36: Courtesy Godiva Chocolatier, Inc.; Page 43: © Ed Bock/The Stock Market; Chapter 3 Opener: Reprinted with permission of Labatt Brewing Company Limited; Page 51: Reprinted with permission of Saturn Corporation; Page 53: © Tom and DeAnn McCarthy/The Stock Market; Page 54: © Susan Werner/Tony Stone Images; Page 58: Reprinted with permission of CIBC Aboriginal Banking; Page 60: © 2001 Amazon.com, Inc. All Rights Reserved. Page 70: © W.Marc Bernsau/The Image Works; Part 2 Opener: Russell Illiq/PhotoDisc; Chapter 4 Opener: © Richard Hull; Page 82: Copyright 2000 by Consumers Union of U.S., Inc. Yonkers, NY 10703-1057, a nonprofit organization. Reprinted with permission from CONSUMER REPORTS® for educational purposes only. No commerical use or photocopying permitted. To subscribe, call 1-800-234-1645 or visit us at www.ConsumerReports.org; Page 87: © 2001, Universal Music, a division of Universal Studios Canada Ltd.; Page 92: Courtesy of Marketing Media Group; page 94: Reprinted with permission of Reader's Digest; Page 98: Courtesy of Modrobes; Page 107: Courtesy of Ann Bradley/Nelson Thomson Learning; Page 108: © Richard Hull; Chapter 5 Opener: © AFP/Corbis/Magma; Page 119: These materials have been reproduced by Nelson Thomson Learning with the permission of Cisco Systems Inc. COPYRIGHT © 2001 CISCO SYSTEMS, INC. ALL RIGHTS RESERVED; Page 122: © Andy Sacks/Tony Stone Images; Page 126: Photo: Alcan; Page 129: © Richard Hull; Page 132: © Bob Daemmrich/The Image Works; Page 134: Reprinted with permission of Sears Canada, Inc.; Chapter 6 Opener: Courtesy of Modrobes; Page 141: © Steven L. Lewis; Page 148: Courtesy of Dairy Farmers of Ontario; Page 158: © Elke Price; Page 161: Reprinted with permission of Pepsi-Cola Company; Chapter 7 Opener: Courtesy of Delta Faucet; Page 174: TM and © Warner Bros. (s01); Page 182: Ryan McVay/PhotoDisc; Page 183: Courtesy of cyber dialogue: Page 186: © Michael Greenlar/The Image Works; Page 191: © Stone; Chapter 9 Opener: © Richard Hull; Page 202: © Tom Wagner/SABA; Page 203: Reprinted with permission of Maytag Canada; Page 204: John Ulan/Ulan Photography; Page 206: Courtesy of Nutrasweet; Page 207: Courtesy of TELUS Mobility; Page 209: Courtesy of Society of Competitive Intelligence Professionals (www.scip.org); Page 212: © 1998 Nations Business/T. Michael Keza; Page 213: John A. Rizzo/PhotoDisc; Page 216: Courtesy of SpyCompany.Com; Part 3 Opener: Neil Beer/PhotoDisc; Chapter 9 Opener: © Richard Hull; Page 231: Patrick Olear/Photo Edit; Page 232: Courtesy of Waterford Wedgwood Canada Inc.; Page 233: Courtesy of Campbell Soup Company Ltd; Page 234: Courtesy of Loblaws Company Limited; Page 235: © Louise Gubb/The Image Works; Page 242: © The Procter and Gamble Company. Used by permission; Page 244: Permission granted by Nabisco; Page 245: © Richard Hull; Page 249: © Steve Hanson/Picture Quest; Chapter 10 Opener: © Richard Hull; Page 257: © James Schneph/Liaison International; Page 261: © 1994 Jose Azel/AURORA/Picture Quest; Page 263: © The Procter and Gamble Company. Used by permission; Page 264: © Paulo Fridman/Sygma/ Corbis; Page 268: Screen capture supplied courtesy of Pfizer Canada Inc., Pfizer Consumer Group, Schick Division; Page 269: CP Picture Archive (Tom Hanson); Page 270: © Joel W. Rogers/Corbis/ Magma; Page 275: © Kevin Horan/Stone; Chapter 11 Opener: Courtesy of Four Seasons Hotels and Resorts; Page 283: © Fujifotos/The Image Works; Page 284: © AFP/Corbis/Magma; Page 289: Reprinted with permission of PetCare Insurance Brokers Ltd.; Page 291: Courtesy of Grocery Gateway Inc.; Page 293: Patrick Clark/PhotoDisc; Page 296: Reprinted with permission, ABC CANADA Literacy Foundation, 2001; Page 298: © Massimo Listri/Corbis/Magma; Page 302: Reprinted with permission of Terra Com Communications Group; Chapter 12 Opener: Reprinted with permission of Dell Computer Corporation; Page 310: © Layne Kennedy/Corbis/Magma; Page 314: This web page is the property of autobytel.ca inc., a subsidiary of Autobytel Inc. and is reproduced herein

with its express permission; Page 319: © Richard Hull; Page 320: © Richard Hull; Page 324: © Richard Hull; Page 328: © Stone; Chapter 13 Opener: Courtesy of Grocery Gateway, Inc.; Page 333: Reprinted by permission of i2 Technologies; Page 341: CP Picture Archive (Kevin Frayer); Page 348: Reproduced with permission of UPS; Page 349: Associated Press (Katsumi Kasahara); Part 4 Opener: Steve Cole/PhotoDisc; Chapter 14 Opener: CP Picture Archive (Tom Hanson); Page 363: © Richard Hull; Page 365: Reprinted by permission of Borderfree Inc.; Page 366: © Richard Hull; Page 371: © Richard Hull; Page 375: Reprinted with permission of Retail Canada; Page 382: © Richard Cummins/Corbis/ Magma; Page 388: © Richard Hull; Chapter 15 Opener: Courtesy of priceline.com; Page 398: © AP/Wide World Photos/Jay Malonson; Page 399: PhotoDisc; Page 403: © Adam Woolfitt/Corbis /Magma; Page 408: © Catherine Karnow/Corbis/ Magma; Page 410: These materials have been reproduced with permission of eBay Inc. COPYRIGHT © EBAY INC. ALL RIGHTS RESERVED; Page 414: © Tom Wagner/SABA; Page 418: © Cindy Karp/Black Star; Page 420: © 2001 Marriott International, Inc. All rights reserved. Reprinted with permission of Marriott International, Inc.; Page 424: © Jose Azel/AURORA/Picture Quest; Chapter 16 Opener: Reprinted by permission of Frito-Lay, Inc.; Page 430: Reprinted by permission of Procter and Gamble Inc.; Page 431: Reprinted by permission of Ontario Lottery and Gaming Corporation; Page 433: Reproduced by permission of Chanel; Page 439: CP Picture Archive (Aaron Harris); Page 441: Skip Nall/PhotoDisc; Page 445: Reprinted by permission of Acclivus Corporation; Page 450: Jacobs Stock Photography/PhotoDisc; Page 458: © Karl Weatherly/Corbis/Magma; Chapter 17 Opener: CP Picture Archive (Greg Agnew); Page 463: Reprinted with permission of GE Canada; Page 467: Courtesy of General Mills Canada Inc.; Page 473: Courtesy of Autowraps, Inc.; Page 475: Courtesy of L'oreal Canada Inc.; Page 477: Courtesy of Save.ca Inc.; Page 478: Reprinted by permission of Mac's Convenience Stores Inc.; Page 481: © 2001 BMW Canada Inc. All rights reserved. The BMW trademark and logo are registered trademarks. This Work is reproduced with the permission of BMW Canada Inc. for educational purposes only, and is not intended to apply to the purchase, sale or use of the products depicted; Chapter 18 Opener: Courtesy of Jones Soda; Page 493: Courtesy of Moosehead Breweries Limited; Page 495: Reprinted with permission of WTN — Women's Television Network; Page 499: SAP, the SAP logo, and any other SAP products and services are trademarks or registered trademarks of SAP AG in Germany and several other countries. This graphic is reproduced with the permission of SAP AG; Page 503: Reprinted with permission of Doubleclick Canada Inc.; Page 507: Reprinted with permission of Photography Flewwelling; Page 509: Permission to reprint granted by Real Facilities Inc.; Page 515: © Jose Azel/AURORA/Picture Quest; Chapter 19 Opener: Reprinted by permission of Get Real Girl, Inc.; Part 5 Opener: Steve Cole/PhotoDisc; Chapter 20 Opener: © Spencer Grant/Photo Edit; Page: 527: Reprinted with permission of Saturn Saab Isuzu Canada, General Motors of Canada Limited; Page 533: CP Picture Archive; Page 535: Reprinted by permission of Krispy Kreme Doughnut Corporation; Page 536: CP Picture Archive (Beth A. Keiser); Page 540: CP Picture Archive (Phill Snel); Page 543: © Michael Newman/Photo Edit; Page 544: Reprinted by permission of Brookstone, Inc.